Civil Liberties and Human Rights in England and Wales

DAVID FELDMAN

CLARENDON PRESS · OXFORD
1993

Oxford University Press, Walton Street, Oxford OX2 6DP
Oxford New York Toronto
Delhi Bombay Calcutta Madras Karachi
Kuala Lumpur Singapore Hong Kong Tokyo
Nairobi Dar es Salaam Cape Town
Melbourne Auckland Madrid
and associated companies in
Berlin Ibadan

Oxford is a trade mark of Oxford University Press

Published in the United States
by Oxford University Press Inc., New York

British Library Cataloguing in Publication Data
Data available

Library of Congress Cataloging in Publication Data
Feldman, David.
Civil liberties and human rights in England and Wales / David
Feldman.
p. cm.
1. Civil rights—England. 2. Civil rights—Wales. 3. Human
rights—England. 4. Human rights—Wales. I. Title.
JC599.G72G74 1993
323'.0942—dc20 93-17530
ISBN 0-19-876232-1
ISBN 0-19-876229-1 (Pbk)

Set by Hope Services (Abingdon) Ltd.
Printed in Great Britain
on acid-free paper by
Biddles Ltd
Guildford & King's Lynn

In memory of Alec Feldman, FRIBA

1910–1976

PREFACE

This book is the result of an attempt to give a picture of the law of civil liberties in England and Wales as it stands at 1st January 1993 (although, thanks to the kindness of the editorial staff of the Oxford University Press, it has been possible to incorporate some later material), and to evaluate it in the light of the obligations accepted by the United Kingdom under various international human rights treaties. Of these treaties, the most significant is the European Convention on Human Rights, both because of its highly developed system of enforcement and because it is the regional instrument specially designed to protect rights in European democracies. Reference is also made, where appropriate, to other instruments, including the International Covenant on Civil and Political Rights, and the International Convention on the Rights of the Child, and to the law in other jurisdictions when it seemed that this would clarify the issues faced by English lawyers or provide an instructive alternative perspective. I have grouped issues by reference to the liberties affected rather than by conventional legal classifications. Civil liberties and human rights in England and Wales do not form a discrete topic, and attempting to regard them as if they were inevitably distorts the picture. To begin with, treating England and Wales as a unit fails to respect other influences, notably from the separate legal systems of Scotland and Northern Ireland. Secondly, civil liberties do not form a category known to English law, although interestingly, and encouragingly, they are now allocated a title to themselves in *Halsbury's Statutes*, containing a small number of significant Acts including the habeas corpus legislation, the Equal Pay Act 1970, the Sex Discrimination Acts 1975 and 1986, and the Race Relations Act 1976. Any selection of liberties which might be examined is bound to reflect the personal interests of the author, and this is true of this book. I hope that the themes which emerge from the liberties and rights examined here are not entirely unrepresentative of more general concerns, but some people will undoubtedly believe that my choice of rights and themes is over-personal and too subjectively determined. However, those are problems which afflict any book which sets out to review a varied and complex area, particularly when it is written by a single author with a correspondingly limited viewpoint. I have tried, as far as possible, to provide a fair and balanced overview of a changing field, and at the same time to make a small contribution to a developing debate.

The main purpose of a Preface is to acknowledge—one can never

properly repay—the debts which one incurs in the course of writing a
book. Many of these are recognized in the Notes, but I am indebted to a
number of people in ways which are not reflected there. My erstwhile
colleagues at the University of Bristol provided the most friendly, sup-
portive working atmosphere for which anyone could wish. They are living proof of the value of a spirit of co-operation in the community of
scholars. I am particularly grateful to Mr David Clarke, with whom I
taught a postgraduate course on Civil Liberties and Human Rights for a
number of years, and who has commented most helpfully on several
chapters in draft. Professor Stephen Cretney first introduced me to the
field of civil liberties twenty years ago, and more recently has given
me information on family law matters. Dr Malcolm Evans guided me
through the thickets of international law. Mr Roger Kerridge gave me
the benefit of his expertise on the European Convention on Human
Rights. Professor Rod Morgan has been a mine of information in relation
to prisons. Mr John Parkinson suggested improvements in my discussion
of legal and political theory. Elizabeth Roberts advised on medico-legal
matters, and Ms Chris Willmore provided information about local government, and advice about sex and race discrimination. Outside Bristol, I
am much indebted to Dr Clive Walker of the University of Leeds, who
read and commented on nearly half the manuscript in draft, saving me
from a number of errors and making valuable suggestions for improvement; and to Mr Peter Bailey OBE, of the Australian National
University, who generously shared his thoughts on the subject of human
rights and much else. My new colleagues at the University of
Birmingham, by the kind way in which they have welcomed me, have
eased the final stages of the book's production. At the Oxford University
Press, Mr Richard Hart has been a tower of strength. He has encouraged
when encouragement was needed, provided advice when asked, and
been tolerant but firm in the face of delays and difficulties. The people
who have suffered most from the book are my immediate family: Jill,
Rebecca, and Jonathan. They supported me at times when it seemed that
the task was never-ending, and tolerated my prolonged absences in the
garden shed where most of the book was written.

They have earned deep respect and gratitude for the way in which
they have withstood the pressures which the writing of any book imposes
indiscriminately on people who were innocent of its conception. I am
grateful to all these colleagues, friends, and relations for the many kind-
nesses which they have shown, and which are responsible for any merits
which the book may have. Shortcomings are, of course, entirely my
responsibility.

The book is dedicated to the memory of my father. He believed that
freedom, to be worthwhile, had to be combined with social responsibil-

ity, and that it is possible to prevent liberalism from sliding into relativism. I hope that he would have approved of what follows.

D.F.

Faculty of Law, University of Birmingham
14 February 1993

CONTENTS

PART III. PRIVACY

PART IV. EXPRESSION

CONTENTS XV

TABLE OF UNITED KINGDOM CASES

TABLE OF CASES FROM OTHER JURISDICTIONS

Australia

xxxiv   TABLE OF CASES FROM OTHER JURISDICTIONS

Canada

Agnes Securities and R, Re (1976) 70 DLR (3d) 504 421
Alder and R, Re (1977) 37 CCC (2nd) 234 411

Borowski, Re (1971) 19 DLR (3d) 537 .... 744, 746
Borowski v. Attorney-General of Canada (1987) 39 DLR (4th) 731, Sask. CA 112
Boucher v. R [1951] 2 DLR 369, S Ct 676, 678

Capotinsky v. Olsen (1981) 27 BCLR 97 455
Chiarelli v. Minister of Employment and Immigration [1990] 2 FC 299 341

Gowling & Henderson and R, Re (1982) 136 DLR (3d) 292 450

Hunter v. Southam Inc (1984) 11 DLR (4th) 641 .... 401, 422

Imperial Tobacco Sales Co. v. Attorney General for Alberta [1941] 2 DLR 673 411

Kokesh v. R. (1990) 1 CR (4th) 62 .... 401, 422, 427

Laporte and R, Re (1972) 29 DLR (3d) 651 453

McCann v. R. (1975) 68 DLR (3d) 661 287
Morentaler, Smoling and Scott v. R (1988) 44 DLR (4th) 385, SC 112

Operation Dismantle v. R. (1985) 18 DLR (4th) 481, SC 97

Pacific Press Ltd and R, Re (1977) 37 CCC (2d) 487 627

R v. Baptiste (1981) 66 CCC (2d) 438 (Ontario Prov. Ct.) 138
R v. Colvin, ex parte Merrick [1970] 3 OR 612 411
R v. Dupperon [1985] 2 WWR 369 (CA of Sask) 136
R v. Dyment (1988) 55 DLR (4th) 503, SC 455
R v. Geraldes (1965) 46 CR 365 (Quebec CA) 138
R v. Kopyto (1987) 47 DLR (4th) 213, Ontario, CA 748
R v. Lundry (1981) 128 DLR (3rd) 726 Ontario CA 407
R v. Miller and Cockriell (1975) 70 DLR (3d) 324 287
R v. Wray (1970) 11 DLR (3d) 673, Sup.Ct 246
Royal American Shows Inc. v. R; Hahn, ex parte [1975] 6 WWR 571 411

Solosky v. R (1979) 105 DLR (3d) 745, S Ct 277, 278, 402, 450
Superintendent of Family and Child Services and Dawson, Re (1983) 145 DLR (3d) 610 119

Tremblay v. Daigle (1990) 62 DLR (4th) 634 112

European Commission and Court of Human Rights

Abdulaziz, Cabales and Balkandali v. UK Series A, No. 94; Judgment of 28 May 1985;
    7 EHRR 471 .... 371, 528–9
Acmanne v. Belgium (10453/83) 40 DR 251 (1984) 144
Airey v. Ireland Series A, No. 32; Judgment of 9 Oct. 1979; 2 EHRR 305 369
Amekrane v. UK Application No. 5961/72 329
Andersson v. Sweden Series A, No. 226; Judgment of 25 February 1992; 14 EHRR 615 537
Arrowsmith v. UK (7050/72) DR 19, 5 132
Ashingdane v. UK Series A, No. 93; Judgment of 28 May 1985; 7 EHRR 528 .... 299, 313
Association X v. UK Application No. 7154/75; 14 DR 31 372
Autronic AG v. Switzerland Series A, No. 178; Judgment of 22 May 1990 593

European Court of Justice

France

Germany

International Court of Justice

India

Ireland

New Zealand

United Nations

United States

Zimbabwe

TABLE OF UNITED KINGDOM LEGISLATION

TABLE OF LEGISLATION FROM
OTHER JURISDICTIONS

TABLE OF INTERNATIONAL INSTRUMENTS

PART I
FROM THEORY TO PRACTICE

THE NATURE OF CIVIL LIBERTIES AND
HUMAN RIGHTS

1

THE POLITICAL PHILOSOPHY OF CIVIL LIBERTIES

The drive to protect civil liberties presupposes that freedom is worth fostering. Yet the seemingly simple notion that those who live in a free society are more fortunate than those who live under less liberal conditions is problematic. This study of civil liberties therefore begins by examining the various meanings of freedom, the ways in which people can be free or unfree, and the kinds of reasons which may justify treating liberty as a good which individuals and society should pursue. Is the exercise of free choice and action a good in itself, as some liberal individualists would argue? If so, it requires us to limit the power of the state to interfere with individual autonomy, even to the extent of restricting the state's capacity to advance collective goals. Does the exercise of individual freedoms tend to produce the greatest good, as utilitarian liberals suggest? If so, does this mean that a freedom can legitimately be abridged in order to secure advantages for some which outweigh the benefits, in the aggregate, which flow from the exercise of the freedom in question? These are issues which have a practical importance for lawyers and politicians, as they affect both the range of rights which societies are prepared to acknowledge that their members have, and the principles determining the limits of the rights when they collide either with other rights or with important social interests, such as the relief of hunger or the maintenance of democracy. For some assertions of rights, and some methods of protecting them, may not always be compatible with other ideals. In order to clarify some basic issues, this chapter examines the philosophical foundations of civil liberties and rights, and the relationship between models of rights, models of democracy, and constitutional structures.

1.1 THE NOTION OF LIBERTY AS A GOOD

Since the entire structure of civil liberties presupposes that freedom is worth fostering, it is useful to start by briefly examining two questions. First, why and under what conditions is freedom a good? Secondly, what types of rights are needed in order to protect whatever sort of freedom is thought to merit protection?

(1) Why is freedom a good?

We can distinguish between two broad approaches to this question. They may be called respectively the *deontological* and the *teleological*. The *deontological* approach seeks to explain freedom generally (or a particular freedom) as a good in itself, something to be sought whether or not it advances any ulterior purpose. The *teleological* approach associates the value of freedom with some further good which the exercise of freedom advances, an advantage either for society as a whole (as in the case of John Stuart Mill's utilitarian defence of liberty,[1] or the critical social theory of Roberto Unger which has been called 'super-liberalism')[2] or for an individual or group, such as the right of minorities to follow their particular religious practices. Teleological reasoning limits access to goods. They will be available only where making them available, to particular people and in particular circumstances, advances the desired ulterior object. Teleological theories therefore require principles controlling the distribution of goods, and objectives by reference to which any pattern of distribution may be evaluated. Deontological theories, on the other hand, are non–distributive. Once something has been identified as a good, it must *prima facie* be made available to all, without differentiating by reference to preferred outcomes.

However, at a certain point the distinction between deontological and teleological theories of rights collapses, since any idea of rights must necessarily depend ultimately on an evaluation of the proper ends of human beings in the light of a vision of the human condition.[3] This may be based in part on experience; indeed, it would be a poor theory of rights which left experience of human aspirations out of account. Yet experience takes us only so far. If anthropologists tour the world and find that there is a virtually universal taboo on the taking of life, this may suggest that life is important and is universally valued. However, it does not require us to hold that people have a right to live, still less that all people always have a right to live. Ultimately, a commitment to any right must be based on a belief about the range of aspirations which it is proper or desirable for people to pursue. This requires an evaluative assessment which is additional to, and may even supplant, observation of existing

---

[1] J. S. Mill, *On Liberty*, in Mary Warnock (ed.), *Utilitarianism* (London: Fontana, 1962), 126–250. Mill's views are discussed below.

[2] Roberto Mangebeira Unger, *Law and Modern Society: Toward a Criticism of Social Theory* (New York: Free Press, 1976), 192–223, 238–42; Roberto Mangebeira Unger, 'The Critical Legal Studies Movement' 96 *Harv. LR* 563–675 (1983); W. Ewald, 'Unger's Philosophy: A Critical Legal Study', 97 *Yale LJ* 665–756 (1988) at pp. 733 ff; Richard F. Devlin, 'On the Road to Radical Reform: A Critical View of Unger's Politics' (1990) 28 *Osgoode Hall LJ* 641–721.

[3] This point is explained later in this section, and in s. 1.2(2) below.

practices. For this reason, the anthropological school of natural rights writing, typified by Margaret Mead, is wanting.[4]

The guiding principle for many liberal rights theorists may be seen as respect for individuals' own aspirations, as a means of giving the fullest expression to each individual's moral autonomy. A fundamental principle entailed by respect for moral autonomy is that individuals should *prima facie* be free to select their own ideas of the Good, and develop a plan for life, or day-to-day strategy, accordingly. Their choice of goods should be constrained only to the extent necessary to protect society and the similar liberties of other people. The law should protect at least the basic liberties, that is, those necessary to the pursuit of any socially acceptable conception of the good life. This is the approach which John Rawls adopts in *A Theory of Justice*.[5] It requires that basic liberties be given considerable respect, and that they should have priority over the pursuit of social goods (such as economic development) perhaps even to the extent of giving them the status of entrenched, constitutional rights, in order to shield them from challenge in the day-to-day rough and tumble of political contention.[6] This gives liberty a priority over other values, which, whether viewed as a description of liberal society or as a prescription for its improvement, is very controversial. Philosophers have doubted whether there are adequate grounds for the priority of liberty. Professor H. L. A. Hart has argued that (at least in a society where there is limited abundance of wealth and resources) it is rational to prefer basic freedoms to an improvement in material conditions only if one harbours the ideal of 'a public-spirited citizen who prizes political activity and service to others as among the chief goods of life and could not contemplate as tolerable an exchange of the opportunities for such activity for mere material goods or contentment'.[7]

A rather different thesis runs through Professor Joseph Raz's book, *The*

---

[4] Margaret Mead, 'Some Anthropological Considerations Concerning Natural Law', 6 *Natural Law Forum* 51–64 (1961).

[5] John Rawls, *A Theory of Justice* (Oxford: Clarendon Press, 1972), 90–5, 130–6, 407–16. Associated with this notion may be an idea that the driving force behind a person's choice of goods is, or should be, the search for self-improvement and self-fulfilment, which gives a distinctive moral justification for nurturing individual freedom of choice. Rawls made this the basis of the psychology which underpins his theory. He called it the 'Aristotelian principle': *ibid.*, 424–33. As will be seen, however, this is not a necessary part of liberal theory.

[6] This underlies the idea of rights as 'trumps' which in case of conflict will defeat other interests which do not amount to rights: Ronald Dworkin, *Taking Rights Seriously* (London: Duckworth, 1976), especially ch. 7.

[7] H. L. A. Hart, 'Rawls on Liberty and its Priority', in Norman Daniels (ed.), *Reading Rawls: Critical Studies of* A Theory of Justice (Oxford: Basil Blackwell, 1975), 230–52 at p. 252. (Repr. in H. L. A. Hart, *Essays in Jurisprudence and Philosophy* (Oxford: Clarendon Press, 1983), 223–47).

Morality of Freedom:[8] people are autonomous moral actors, and autonomy is given expression primarily through making one's own decisions, but such freedom is valuable partly because it advances social ends. Raz points out that the identification of basic liberties therefore depends, in part at least, on governmental notions of the public good. In respect of rights to freedom of expression, privacy, freedom of religion, and freedom from discrimination, for example, 'one reason for affording special protection to individual interests is that thereby one also protects a collective good, an aspect of a public culture'.[9] At the same time, certain social goods are needed if freedom is to have value. Freedom is useful only if the social and economic structure of society provides a sufficient range of choices to allow people's capacity for choice to be exercised. Accordingly, freedom is seen as a collective rather than an individual good.[10] This may constrain the range of freedoms and the purposes to which they may morally be put: a decision to make a freedom into a constitutional right is an expression of the collective political culture of a community. This thesis does not make the morality of freedom depend on people striving for perfection: individuals may not always, or ever, think about the moral consequences of their decisions, or may consciously make decisions which do not make for self-improvement. Instead, it looks only for a social commitment to the idea of the moral significance of individual choice. Raz marries the idea of the individual to that of society by recognizing that individual freedom of choice is contingent on social arrangements.

The belief in human beings as social individuals, beings for whom both sociability and individuality are essential parts of their make-up, is ultimately a deontological belief. This is liable to leave one open to charges of subjectiveness, and one's theory to the accusation that it represents no more than a personal preference. However, beliefs of this sort may be objectively assessed as being more or less rational, according to how well they fit people's observable behaviour and psychologies. One of the most interesting applications of this approach is that of Professor Finnis, who grounds his view of humanity in two principles: the idea that certain objects of desire are self-evidently good, and so are not chosen merely through subjective preference; and the claim that one of these self-evident goods is practical reasonableness, which helps one to identify the other self-evident goods.[11] Although Finnis argues that the self-evident desirability of certain goods means their selection is not subjective, his claim is just as fully grounded in an idea of the human condition as any other. The importance of the idea of self-evidence is that it combines, on

[8] Oxford: Clarendon Press, 1986.   [9] Ibid. 256.   [10] Ibid. 255–60.
[11] John Finnis, *Natural Law and Natural Rights* (Oxford: Clarendon Press, 1980), chs. 3, 4, and 5.

the one hand, a recognition of the deontological nature of ideas about the values which make life worth living with, on the other hand, an assertion that deontological beliefs (despite not being logically verifiable or falsifiable) need be no less rational than teleological ones.

This is a convincing position (even if one does not accept that Finnis's self-evident goods are as self-evident as Finnis believes them to be), because any teleological position which is morally valuable ultimately rests on a deontological claim. For example, utilitarianism at first sight appears to avoid deontology by adopting an apparently scientific principle for maximizing happiness (or minimizing pain). John Stuart Mill, in justifying liberty, assumed that liberty would make available new ways of looking at the world, and that this would be more likely than censorship to lead to a better-understood and better-ordered world. The benefits of allowing freedom of thought and expression, therefore, would tend to outweigh any short-term disadvantages, as long as certain limits are imposed to prevent freedoms from being used so as to precipitate actual harm to other people.[12] This way of measuring advantages and disadvantages, however, depends on certain assumptions. One is that everyone is sufficiently alike, feeling pleasure and pain in the same way and to the same extent, for their responses to be commensurable. This idea, expressed by Bentham in the maxim that each person is to count for one, and nobody is to count for more than one,[13] is fundamental to democratic as well as utilitarian theory, but it reflects a value judgment which cannot be scientifically tested and which rests on metaphysical assumptions. Another of Mill's presuppositions is that the pains of being subjected to offence are less weighty, but the pain of physical harm is weightier, than the benefits which flow from advancing knowledge. This again rests on an act of faith rather than logical derivation from some other value, and so is properly regarded as deontological. Behind every teleological justification lurks a deontological belief.

The deontological belief, or set of beliefs, which best serves to justify rights and liberties seems to me to be that which forms the foundation for Raz's thesis: a belief that freedom of will and a capacity for self-directed action are the most characteristic features of human beings. This is, in essence, the notion of the moral autonomy of individuals: the capacity for independent decision making and action, where one's will is not overborne by coercion. In order to respect each other's autonomy in this sense, we must be given room to experiment with different ideas and aims, to select our favoured goals, to decide on the best way of achieving

---

[12] J. S. Mill, *On Liberty*, ch. 4.

[13] Jeremy Bentham, Introduction to *Constitutional Code*, in John Bowring (ed.), *Works of Jeremy Bentham* (Edinburgh: William Tait, 1843), ix. 5–8; J. S. Mill, *Utilitarianism*, in Warnock, *Utilitarianism*, 319.

them, and to give effect to that decision. If one has such a view of human beings, then freedom is essential; freedom is a good for all.[14] Furthermore, because the idea is based on what is assumed to be human nature, there is an underlying idea that people are equally entitled to any goods that are going, or (where the goods are in limited supply) to an equal opportunity to compete for them. This leads both to a presumption in favour of sharing out goods on a *per capita* basis, and to a presumption that the *per capita* share should be equal unless there are reasonable grounds, related to the nature of the good in question, for distinguishing between people.[15]

(2) What sort of freedoms does moral autonomy demand?

It might seem that the idea of autonomy implies merely that people should be free from interference by others. It does not appear at first sight to give any right to the assistance of others in giving effect to one's autonomous choices. It seems to be satisfied by rights to non-interference (liberties) rather than rights to assistance, or compliance with some other form of positive duty, by others (what one might call, following Hohfeld, claim–rights).[16] But this merits a brief examination. A liberty is a kind of right, in the sense that when one person has a liberty to do something others have at least a duty not to interfere. A liberty, then, implies a freedom from interference or coercion. A claim–right implies that other people owe a positive duty to the right-holder which goes beyond a mere duty not to interfere. The claim–right correlates with a duty on the part of another person to take care to act, or to abstain from action, in accordance with the interests of the right-holder.

This reflects a difference between the ways in which liberty-holders and claim-right-holders respectively are conceived of. A liberty-holder is treated as an autonomous individual with full responsibility for his own actions who can, if he wishes, make decisions and implement them in the exercise of free will. A claim-right-holder is a person who may or may not be fully autonomous, in the sense of being capable of exercising rational choice, but towards whom others have responsibilities, discharged through the performance of duties. For instance, a legal system

[14] See Rawls, *Theory of Justice*; Raz, *Morality of Freedom*; Robert Nozick, *Anarchy, State and Utopia* (Oxford: Basil Blackwell, 1974); Sir Isaiah Berlin, *Four Essays on Liberty* (Oxford: Clarendon Press, 1969), 121–31.

[15] Peter Westen, *Speaking of Equality: An Analysis of the Rhetorical Force of 'Equality' in Moral and Legal Discourse* (Princeton, NJ: Princeton University Press, 1991), 146–62, offers the most comprehensive analysis in the literature to date of the moral foundations of claims to equal *per capita* distributions.

[16] Wesley Newcomb Hohfeld, *Fundamental Legal Conceptions as Applied in Judicial Reasoning* (New Haven, Conn.: Yale University Press, 1923).

might not recognize children or people with a mental disability as fully autonomous, but despite (or because of) this might regard them as being the beneficiaries of duties owed to them for their benefit by parents, doctors, or governmental bodies.[17] The focus of a claim-right is on what other people can do for the right-holder rather than on what the right-holder can do for himself. In the effort to enumerate rights to which all people, or all citizens of a state, are entitled, the distinction between claim-rights and liberties will be significant. The selection of rights will depend to a large extent on whether the dominant political theory stresses the autonomous nature of people as individuals or the moral responsibilities which fellow members of societies have for each other's welfare. If the stress is laid on autonomy, the guaranteed rights are likely to be predominantly of the liberty type, with only such guaranteed claim-rights as are necessary to give substance to the liberties. If the emphasis is on responsibilities for other people's welfare, a greater range of claim-rights will result, perhaps with a view to ensuring that all guaranteed liberties have at least a certain minimum value to all people, but the range of guaranteed liberties may have to be reduced to allow the interference with autonomy required to enforce the claim-rights of all. This is likely, because claim-rights, once recognised, have by their nature greater moral weight than liberties, allowing or requiring liberties to be restricted to the extent necessary to secure the claim-rights.

The attitude which has long dominated the law in Britain is a *liberal* conception of rights: it demands respect for the freedom of others, but does not appear to place any obligations on people beyond the duty not to interfere improperly with the freedom of others. It therefore seems to make no demands of the state. However, this is an incomplete account of the liberal tradition. Even radical liberals like Friedrich Hayek and Robert Nozick accept that the state has certain responsibilities in respect of freedom, the main one being to create or foster conditions in which freedoms may be protected.[18] There must therefore be a legal system and a police force available to remedy attempts by one person to infringe or prevent the exercise of another's freedoms. The state must provide this. Nozick approvingly describes a state which provides security from internal and external threats, but performs no other functions, as a 'minimal state'.[19] The rights which citizens enjoy in such a state can be described

[17] The idea that those whose interests are served by the performance of duties have rights is known as the 'interest' or 'benefit' theory of rights, and is distinguished from the 'will' theory according to which capacity to hold a right depends on being able to exercise the will to assert or give effect to the right. See Jeremy Waldron, *Theories of Rights* (Oxford: Oxford University Press, 1984), 9–12.

[18] Friedrich Hayek, *The Constitution of Liberty* (London: Routledge Kegan Paul, 1960), ch. 15, especially p. 223; Nozick, *Anarchy, State and Utopia*, chs 5 and 6.

[19] *Anarchy*, 26–8, 333–4.

as negative liberties: freedoms from harm, rather than rights to goods.[20] According to liberals, the state has no responsibility for taking positive steps to ensure that people are able to take advantage of liberties, but only to prevent other people from improperly interfering with the liberties. On this view, the only illegitimate interference with autonomy consists in what other people do to you.[21]

However, not being interfered with by others is only one of the conditions for autonomy. If (like Raz) one sees liberties as being useful only to the extent to which they can be enjoyed, and as being contingent on a fair opportunity to take advantage of such liberties as one wishes to exercise, the value of any liberty will be seriously curtailed if the opportunity to make use of it is not available.[22] Where there are serious inequalities of wealth and opportunity, the negative freedoms which the state guarantees are most valuable to those who can best afford to exploit them, and may have no value at all to people who live at or below subsistence level and have no time or money to spare from the vital task of surviving. To say that such people are free is true (if at all) only in terms of legal theory. Descriptively, in reality, they are to some degree unfree. On this view, freedom of the press is not a valuable liberty unless everyone has a reasonable opportunity to use the press as a medium of communication and to read the resulting publications. Similarly, freedom of movement is valueless unless people have adequate resources of money and leisure to enable them to travel. If this has to be earned, freedom to work is essential; but the latter freedom is worthless unless all people have access to an education system which is sufficient to enable them to do the work which is available, a health-care system adequate to keep them (as far as possible) fit enough to work, and economic conditions which provide sufficient employment opportunities. Transfers of wealth may be needed for socially useful purposes, such as to provide grants for educating those who cannot afford to educate themselves by their own assets. And so on. The negative liberties guaranteed by a minimal state mean less to some citizens than to others, and the differentiation is imposed by the social or economic structure of society without regard to any rational moral criteria. On this view, the state ought to act to create the conditions in which

---

[20] Berlin, *Four Essays on Liberty*, 122–3.

[21] For further discussion, see John Gray, *Hayek on Liberty*, 2nd edn. (Oxford: Basil Blackwell, 1986), pp. 67–71, 125–9; Jeffrey Paul (ed.), *Reading Nozick* (Oxford: Basil Blackwell, 1982).

[22] Thus Raz instances a man in a pit with some food, whose only choice is whether or not to eat, and a lone woman on a desert island whose entire attention is consumed by the need to avoid being caught by a fierce carnivorous animal, and argues that: 'Neither the Man in the Pit nor the Hounded Woman enjoys an autonomous life.' Raz, *Morality of Freedom*, at pp. 373–4. See also Neil McCormick, *Legal Right and Social Democracy: Essays in Legal and Political Philosophy* (Oxford: Clarendon Press, 1982), 42–3.

everyone's autonomy has an opportunity to flourish. This means that people should be guaranteed a basic standard of living, so that all have a real chance to make and exploit additional opportunities for themselves.

This leads to an extended notion of freedom, under which a person is unfree if the range of his or her choices is constrained *either* by human interference *or* by shortage of resources or physical capacity. On this view it becomes possible to argue that liberties are of value only if supported by claim-rights which obligate other members of society to make available the resources which each person needs to give effect to his or her choices. This in turn opens the way to a broadened theory of individual rights and civil liberties in which negative freedom is complemented and at the same time limited by positive social or economic rights. These rights are very different from classical liberties, but are justified on the basis that they are needed in order to make negative liberty equally valuable to all. In other words, they seek to create a bridge between the value of liberty and the different values of equality and social justice.

This model of rights has implications for the content and scope of negative freedoms. For example, all negative freedoms may have to be restricted in order to secure the economic rights which enable all citizens to have access to a similar range of freedoms. It is important to remember, when assessing claims to rights based on this sort of argument, that one right is not being restricted in favour of another of the same logical type; rather, the *availability* of one freedom is restricted in order to enhance the *practical value* to others of a different freedom. There is, therefore, a distinction between: (*a*) rights which maximise the range of freedoms; and (*b*) rights which maximise the utility of those freedoms.

This is the source of the notion of positive rights, mainly social and economic in nature. The rights to a minimum wage, to health care, to housing, to support when unemployed or raising a family, are all designed, first, to ensure that people do not need to starve, and, secondly, to enable them to devote additional earnings to purposes of their choice. (The so-called 'poverty trap', in which people whose income increases lose a corresponding or even greater sum in welfare benefits, is one way in which the second objective may be frustrated.)[23] These rights correlate with duties, not of forbearance, but of active assistance, which society is expected to discharge through the medium of the state. Thus positive economic or social rights envisage that the role of the state is take active steps to improve the lot of the worst-off groups in society. This may require transfer payments through taxation and the distribution of welfare

[23] Frank Field, Molly Meacher, and Chris Pond, *To Him Who Hath: A Study of Poverty and Taxation* (Harmondsworth: Penguin, 1976), 56; Institute for Fiscal Studies, *The Structure and Reform of Direct Taxation: Report of a Committee Chaired by Professor J. E. Meade* (London: George Allen and Unwin, 1978), 82–7.

benefits, or provision of services and facilities, or a degree of regulation of market activities, all of which must be paid for by taxing better-off members of society.

One's reaction to this will depend in part on one's view of the market. If it is seen as a natural forum for allocating resources, regulation looks like an attempt to use a human artefact—the state redistribution system—to interfere with the natural order of the world. On the other hand, if one sees the market itself as a human artefact, there may be no reason to deny ourselves the opportunity to modify its operation by means of another artefact when the uncontrolled functioning of market mechanisms produces results which seem to us to be antisocial or unfair.

The political and legal implications can be illustrated by considering possible legal and governmental responses to discrimination. If it turns out that some groups are systematically disadvantaged in education, for example because prejudice against their colour makes them vulnerable to low pay and this limits the educational opportunities which are available to them or their children, there are two possible responses. One, the liberal freedom-based response, is to ask whether members of such groups have a right to be free from discrimination on the ground of colour. If the answer is 'yes', Parliament makes law to forbid (and provide remedies for) discrimination by individuals on that ground. This is essentially the approach adopted in Britain in the Race Relations Act 1976,[24] which treats discrimination as being as much a matter of individual responsibility as a social evil. On the other hand, the social rights approach would be to make laws which required members of those groups to be given advantages in education and employment (and perhaps other relevant fields) until they no longer stood at a disadvantage as compared with members of other groups. This latter approach (sometimes called 'affirmative action') involves positive action by the state which goes beyond merely policing negative freedoms. Finally, there is an intermediate approach (elements of which are incorporated within the U.K. legislation), making a state agency (here, the Commission for Racial Equality) responsible for fostering awareness of the legal and social obligations on employers, educators, and others, to avoid discriminating, and for assisting victims of unlawful discrimination to enforce their rights.

However, the social rights approach is attacked by liberals precisely because it involves extensive state intervention in private lives and negative freedoms. It is argued that it is improper for the state to make people pay for other people's welfare if, unlike the position in relation to provision of policing and security services, the payers receive no benefit in return for their contribution. To take someone's hard-earned pay in

---

[24] See Ch. 18 below.

order to provide an advantage for someone else is, according to Nozick, tantamount to the state imposing forced labour on the taxpayer.[25] This claim deserves attention, because, if supportable, it defeats all assertions of positive economic and social rights. It depends on the root idea that nobody has a right to interfere with property once the right to that property has vested in the right-holder. Indeed, it is sometimes said that the institution of property arises before society, and it is the primary aim of people in coming together in civil society to protect their property.[26] The Irish State, for instance, in Article 43 of its Constitution, acknowledges that 'man, in virtue of his rational being, has the natural right, antecedent to positive law, to the private ownership of external goods', and 'accordingly guarantees to pass no law attempting to abolish the right of private ownership or the general right to transfer, bequeath, and inherit property'. At the same time, the State recognizes that these rights 'ought, in civil society, to be regulated by the principles of social justice', and accordingly retains the right 'to delimit the exercise of the said rights with a view to reconciling their exercise with the exigencies of the common good'.

Nozick's argument, like Article 43, gives property rights the same status as rights to personal integrity, such as the freedoms from enslavement and attack. However, unlike Article 43, Nozick denies the right of the State to regulate property rights according to principles of social justice. It is not clear what supports Nozick's assertion of such a privileged status for property rights. The main argument is a negative one, denying the justice or effectiveness of interfering with property rights merely to advance a programme of achieving greater fairness in the distribution of social or economic goods. It is said that achieving and maintaining any pattern of distribution which could be called fair requires continuous redistribution by the state; as unfairnesses creep in as soon as uncontrolled competition occurs, a single redistribution will be insufficient to achieve long-term

---

[25] Nozick, *Anarchy*, 169–72.

[26] John Locke, *Two Treatises of Civil Government*, II, s. 1, described people coming together to protect their property, that being therefore one of the fundamental obligations of the civil magistracy, but as Alan Ryan, *Property and Political Theory* (Oxford: Basil Blackwell, 1984), 15, 24, points out, this may have been part of Locke's attempt to show that the jurisdiction of the civil power is entirely secular, in opposition to the divine-right theories of Filmer. Whether or not this is a correct interpretation of Locke, the idea was influential in *Entick* v. *Carrington* (1765) 19 St. Tr. 1029 at col. 1066, where Lord Camden CJ observed, 'The great end for which men entered into civil society, was to secure their property. That right is preserved sacred and incommunicable in all instances, where it has not been taken away or abridged by some public law for the good of the whole.' This curiously anticipates the formulation in the French Declaration of the Rights of Man, 1791.

fairness of what Nozick calls the 'patterned' type. This redistribution will be unproductive or counterproductive for either of two reasons.

First, according to Hayek, no person or government has sufficient knowledge about the complex interactions of causes and effects in the economy to be able to predict what the results of conscious interference with the historical processes of the market will be. It is therefore safest to leave market processes to determine the best distribution of benefits and burdens in society.[27] Secondly, according to Nozick, government redistributions of goods will fail to do justice to people's 'historical' entitlements, that is, to the benefits which they accumulated in the past and expected to be free to enjoy under the rules in force at the time of their acquisition. Redistribution to achieve a just 'patterned distribution' is tantamount to retrospective legislation, because it infringes historical entitlements. As such, it is said to infringe a basic principle of the rule of law forbidding retrospective legislation in most circumstances. On this view, the only achievable form of justice of distribution is that which results from the fair application and enforcement of existing rules on property acquisition and devolution in a market economy: the 'hidden hand' of market forces produces a result, and there are no means of adjudging that to be unjust while respecting historical entitlements.[28]

These arguments presuppose either that the rules of acquisition themselves are fair, or that they are unchallengeable. This, however, would make it illegitimate for the rules ever to be amended. Such a limitation on the legislative authority of the state should not readily be accepted, particularly where the state legislatures are democratically accountable, as the restriction would severely circumscribe the scope of the lawmaking powers of representative legislatures.[29] The basis of the presupposition needs to be examined. On the historical entitlements theory, the result of exchanges, acquisitions, and disposals according to the existing legal rules can be treated as just only if the historically first acquisition was itself just. The rule most often relied on is that a person who expends time and energy in cultivating or improving land, or drawing from the land a naturally occurring substance, thereby becomes entitled to treat the land or resulting produce and profit as his own property. Were this not so, it is said, there would be no reason for anyone to improve the lot of society as a whole by cultivating or producing more than he needs for his own

---

[27] F. A. Hayek, *Law, Legislation and Liberty* (Routledge & Kegan Paul, 1981), i. 8–54; Gray, *Hayek on Liberty*, chs 1 and 2.

[28] *Anarchy*, 180.

[29] For the idea that some such limits are implicit in the notion of the rule of law, see Hayek, *Law, Legislation and Liberty*, iii esp. ch. 18; Geoffrey de Q. Walker, *The Rule of Law: Foundation of Constitutional Democracy* (St. Lucia: Queensland University Press, 1989).

subsistence and making the excess available through the market or charitable donation.[30]

This general right of original acquisition by labour is not absolute,
however. Locke recognised some limits on the extent to which individuals may legitimately annex things for their own benefit. The main one is
that the right to acquire land by applying one's labour to it operates only
so far as enough land remains for others who want or need it, and the
remainder is as of good quality as that which is taken.[31] This has been
developed by Waldron, who has argued that exclusive rights of property
are morally justifiable only if everyone is able to exercise actual dominion
of the same extent over at least some other assets of the same kind.[32] If
this is not possible, the right to property is not genuinely open to all, as
not all enjoy the conditions necessary to exercise it, and so property
rights fail to comply with the liberal justification of being equally available to all.

A further limitation, which Locke imposed on property acquisition, is
that property, once acquired, must not be allowed to go to waste.[33] This
is related to the idea that the needy have a right to the surplus property of
others which the needy require in order to survive. This right is not
dependent on charity: Locke considered that the needy owned the surplus property of others for this purpose.[34] It follows that, for Locke, if the
resource is vital to life and, after acquisition, it becomes scarce (as where
land which has been enclosed by someone includes a waterhole which, in
a drought, becomes the sole source of drinking water in the area, or there
is a shortage of clothing in cold weather), the person who acquired the
property is obligated to make it available to all who need it, rather than
leaving them to die of thirst or profiteering from the natural calamity
which has dried up other sources of water.

Nozick seems to accept that a model for the original acquisition of
property would be morally unacceptable if such conditions are not
included, even though he ultimately balks at admitting them as legal limitations in modern capitalist conditions.[35] Even in the liberal model of
property rights, therefore, original entitlements are justified and restricted

[30] This prudential justification is brought out most clearly in Nozick, *Anarchy,* 265–8;
Locke, *Two Treatises of Civil Government*, II, s. 34.

[31] Locke, *Two Treatises*, II, s. 48.

[32] Jeremy Waldron, *The Right to Private Property* (Oxford: Clarendon Press, 1988), ch.
12.

[33] Locke, *Two Treatises*, II, s. 47. For thorough discussion of the theories by which
Locke and Nozick justified rights to property, see Waldron, *Private Property*, chs 6 and 7.

[34] Ryan, *Property and Political Theory*, 34.

[35] *Anarchy*, 178–82. See the discussions in Paul (ed.), *Reading Nozick*, by Onora
O'Neill, 'Nozick's Entitlements', at 305–22, and Cheyney C. Ryan, 'Yours, Mine, and
Ours: Property Rights and Individual Liberty', at pp. 323–43.

instrumentally in order to advance some social values.[36] That being so, it would be odd to claim that these conditions ceased to bind those who acquire property further along the historical chain of entitlements. To be consistent, liberals such as Nozick should accept that the obligation on individuals to allow enough good quality resources for all when appropriating resources for themselves constitutes a condition on their moral right to hold property at all.

However, this may impose an obligation on the state to regulate markets, limiting some liberties in the process. If, under the influence of the 'hidden hand' in a market economy, private individuals cannot judge how much of a given resource is available to all in society, and lack the instrumentalities for ensuring that all have their share, the job must perforce be done by the state. In redistributing shares in this way through taxation and welfare benefits, the state is not interfering with property rights properly vested in the people who held the property immediately before the redistribution; it is giving effect to the essential conditions for allowing people to enjoy property rights at all. After all, the rules which allow acquisition of property by applying one's labour to a commodity are social rules. Society adopted them in the first place, and it is proper for society through its authorized agency, the state, to enforce the rules if people are unable or unwilling to observe the conditions contained within the rules.[37] Were this not so, it would have been irrational for any society to have adopted rules which allowed the acquisition of more than small amounts of personal property. It would have been more rational to hold, first, that the labourer might acquire a right to no more (but no less) than the profits which flow from his work (rather than complete freedom to deal with the capital asset), and, secondly, that users have a duty to manage the land and other profit-making resources for the benefit of the community as a whole.

The claim that property rights have some special status therefore breaks down, so that interference by the state for the purpose of securing the survival and security of members of the community and enhancing their enjoyment of their liberties may be legitimate. This might, for example, justify taxation to provide some welfare benefits and health care.

---

[36] Rawls, *Theory of Justice*, does exactly this.

[37] This is a form of what is sometimes called a 'concession' theory of property, because it presents property as a concession by the state and accordingly subject to conditions imposed by the state from time to time. Concession theories have been bedevilled by those who seek to distinguish them from 'contract' theories, which treat property as arising naturally from (rather than being a necessary condition for) agreements (express or implied) between free individuals. It should therefore be made clear that the argument advanced in the text does not depend on the idea that property is, or should be, a special privilege of a limited class (quite the reverse), nor on the notion that it consists of a limitation on any general principle of common ownership in law or morality.

Whether taxation may legitimately go beyond this is a matter of political judgement for each society. If the rules which permit the holding of private property are social rules, not eternally valid and unchallengeable divine law, then the conditions for holding property, the permissible extent of holdings, and the acceptable justifications for interfering with holdings, are also social rules, and are legitimately liable to be changed in order to give effect to a democratically approved social plan. Protections for property rights are needed, but they may be no greater (though, perhaps, no less) than the protections given to other liberties, such as freedom of speech or freedom from arbitrary arrest and detention.

It follows that there is nothing in democratic liberal theory which necessarily excludes legal protection for positive social and economic rights. People who deprecate attempts to enforce such rights (for example, those on the political Right who consider that the European Social Charter does not deserve to be considered as conferring rights on anyone or imposing duties on governments) are articulating a personal preference for one type of political or economic programme over others. Their claims, when analyzed, do not turn out to have an irrebuttable philosophical foundation.

If an idea of rights as including a right to enjoy freedoms which are theoretically available to all can be defended against extreme liberals such as Hayek and Nozick, the whole idea of individual rights needs to be defended against a socialist critique. Some radical critics of liberal individualism, such as Marx, have accepted that individual rights are necessarily individualistic and reject them as symptomatic of the alienation and egoism of people under capitalism, which must be replaced by an emancipated and united society. In socialist states, notably in the U.S.S.R. before its break-up, constitutions do not give a high priority to individual rights. The Constitution of the U.S.S.R. actually contained an impressive list of individual rights guaranteed to its citizens, but their exercise was stated to be legitimate only so far as it was consistent with the supreme goal of the state, defined in the Preamble as 'the building of a classless communist society in which there will be public, communist self-government'. Teleology reigned supreme, and the steps needed to achieve the goal, as defined by the executive, took precedence over individual liberties and theories of rights.[38]

In such a system, it is often thought, there is no room for individual democratic or other rights. However, this may be unnecessarily pessimistic. It may be possible to reconcile socialist teleology with individual freedom.[39] The definition of rights and liberties is not wholly selfish. It is

---

[38] Alice Erh-Soon Tay, 'Marxism, Socialism and Human Rights', in Eugene Kamenka and Alice Erh-Soon Tay (eds.), *Natural Rights* (London: Edward Arnold, 1978), 104–12.

[39] For attempts to achieve such a reconciliation, see e.g. Tom Campbell, *The Left and*

part of a process whereby people attempt to fashion the conditions in which co-operation becomes possible, protecting the freedom which we need if we are to fulfil our social responsibilities towards other people as well as to advance our own interests. This reflects the mixed character, what has been called the 'unsocial sociability', of human society, rather than simply generalized alienation.[40] It should, therefore, not surprise anyone that the Constitution of the U.S.S.R. acknowledged rights, but that they were socialist rather than individual rights, required to serve social goals. In the event of conflict between the goals and the socialist rights as formally expressed in the Constitution, the goals had to prevail.

(3) Political rights

Another type of right now needs to be introduced, which is not designed to increase either the availability or utility of moral autonomy to individuals, but which enables individuals to participate in political decisions. We can call these *political rights*. They presuppose both the need for coercive state action and the legitimacy of coercive limits on liberties. However, political rights stipulate the methods of selecting the people who are to settle the limits of liberties and the terms on which they are to act. For example, in a representative democracy citizens will have rights in the selection of representative members of a legislature; coercive limits to liberties may be said to be legitimate if (perhaps only if) imposed by a given number of the elected representatives. In a direct democracy citizens will have rights to vote in, and even initiate, referenda on particular issues; coercion is then justified if approved by a given majority of voters. In either case, the legislative authority may be required by constitutional arrangements to act within limits to its coercive powers, to refrain from infringing certain rights, or to advance specified interests; these conditions may or may not be legally enforceable.

Political rights must not be confused with negative liberties. Political rights may, if exercised in certain ways, result in the scope for individual self-determination being maintained or increased, but (as Sir Isaiah Berlin has observed) are primarily concerned to control the types of body to which, and the conditions under which, citizens surrender their individual autonomy, rather than protecting the freedom of each citizen to give effect to his or her plan for life.[41] Political rights are essentially procedural: they define an individual's power to influence the coercive

---

Rights (London: Routledge & Kegan Paul, 1983); Christine Sypnowich, *The Concept of Socialist Law* (Oxford: Clarendon Press, 1990).

[40] A. I. Melden, *Rights and Persons* (Oxford: Oxford University Press, 1977), 234–5.

[41] Sir Isaiah Berlin, 'Two Concepts of Liberty', in *Four Essays on Liberty*, pp. 118–72 at 129–31; see also the Introduction at p. xliii *et seq.*

processes of the state; they do not guarantee that the combined effect of all exercises of individuals' political rights will be to maintain liberties. Even some forms of democracy may produce illiberal results, and any state organization requires citizens to recognize that they may sometimes legitimately be coerced and their liberties restricted against their wills.

Some theorists argue that if one has agreed (expressly or by implication) to abide by a form of political organization, or even if one should rationally have agreed to it (whether or not one has done so in fact), the restrictions on one's liberty which that organization imposes should properly be regarded as emanations of one's own will and not coercive at all. Locke, Kant, Hegel, Rousseau, Bentham, and Marx, amongst many others, have argued that 'true' freedom comes only through subjecting one's desires to the common good, to rationality, or to some other ideal which effectively withdraws the individual's capacity for self-direction. This idea is evident in theories of democracy according to which citizens submit to the will of the community expressed through the ballot-box in exchange for a right to participate, to have one's voice counted, in the ballot. Here the right to self-determination is treated as an aspect of liberty.

This is not liberty as we have understood it so far, however. It replaces the will of the individual with an external assessor's view of what is good for the individual, a form of paternalism, or (even less individualistically) it substitutes the good of the community for the good of the individual. This does not lead to individual self-fulfilment unless the individual is trained (or brainwashed) always and only to want what is considered by the external decision-maker to be good for the community. Only then will the 'true' (or rational) desires of the individual be identical with the result of the collective decision-making process.

Even then, the resulting deemed satisfaction of individual wants will not advance individual autonomy, as liberties do. While collective self-determination may require certain political rights for individuals, it is the autonomy of the group, rather than that of individual members of it, which self-determination advances. Although the desire for self-fulfilment may perhaps sometimes be satisfied by identifying myself with the interests of the community, this is as likely to lead to self-abnegation as to the realization of actual (as contrasted with hypothetical, idealized, or metaphysical) desires.

The power of a group to determine how its members shall act does not entail any necessary protection for the liberties of individuals within it. As Sir Isaiah Berlin and others have observed, individual members may prefer to be subject to autocratic government by other members of the group rather than benefit from the paternalism of a well-meaning colonial power, but this form of *positive* liberty is a claim to be recognised and respected as a member of a particular group, rather than a freedom to pursue one's individual goals. Democracy, self-determination, and liberty, are different values which may conflict;[42] they are not necessarily capable of being contained within a coherent moral framework. We will return to this point in § 1.3.

1.2 NATURAL AND POSITIVE RIGHTS

So far we have introduced the relationship between autonomy, freedom, and a number of kinds of liberties and rights, and have seen some of the implications of each. We now turn to look at the systems of reasoning and justification which support those values. Are normative, or ought-based, structures needed to make it possible to assert particular rights or liberties, and to assess claims to particular liberties in specified circumstances? This section examines two broad traditions of thought which have influenced the ways in which rights and liberties are formulated in western societies. These are the *natural rights* tradition and the *positive rights* tradition. As will be seen, they do not always lead to the same results. Each is powerful, but any practically useful theory of liberties is likely to attempt a degree of synthesis between them. To complicate the matter further, the traditions are not atomic; each is comprised of a number of different elements. The brief discussion of them which follows is intended to do no more than indicate some of the elements, illustrate their relationship, and suggest some of their consequences.

(1) The natural rights tradition

The natural rights tradition arises out of classical natural-law theories, although it was not originally a major part of them: most early natural lawyers were more concerned with duties owed by citizens to God, the state, or society, than with any citizens' rights which might correlate with duties on God, the state, or society.[43] Nevertheless, a number of societies have displayed a strong tradition of respect for and pride in freedom which forms part of their fundamental social values. The idea that it is important for people to be able to say that they are free of arbitrary government, and that the state has a fundamental responsibility (either social

---

[42] Berlin, *Four Essays on Liberty*, at 167 *et seq.*; Richard Rorty, *Contingency, Irony and Solidarity* (Cambridge: Cambridge University Press, 1989), chs 1–3.

[43] See generally A. P. d'Entrèves, *Natural Law: An Introduction to Legal Philosophy*, 2nd edn. (London: Hutchinson, 1970), ch. 4; Richard Tuck, *Natural Rights Theories: Their Origin and Development* (Cambridge: Cambridge University Press, 1979), *passim*; Jerome J. Shestack, 'The Jurisprudence of Human Rights', in Theodor Meron (ed.), *Human Rights in International Law: Legal and Policy Issues* (Oxford: Clarendon Press, 1984), ch. 3.

or legal) to maintain that freedom against internal or external threats, is sometimes derived from divine law as interpreted by the major religions. It was significant in shaping the social characteristics of ancient Israel, Athens, and Rome, and of the Netherlands in the seventeenth century.[44] Appeals to divine law could, however, have the effect of merely legitimating a regime which was absolutist rather than liberal. The use made of the doctrine of the 'Divine Right of Kings' asserted by the early Stuart monarchs in seventeenth-century England exemplifies the absolutist tendencies of divine law, particularly in a state with an established church.

This led some liberals to turn away from reliance on divine revelation and attempt instead to discover natural laws from the observable state of the world and human behaviour. The idea that people could profitably employ their rationality for such important matters, instead of relying on divine revelation, was not entirely new. The thirteenth-century conception of natural law embraced by St Thomas Aquinas and Duns Scotus had recognised an interpretative role for human rationality in elucidating the divine will.[45] However, the eighteenth century saw the emergence of a particularly optimistic view of human nature and potential. Jean-Jacques Rousseau's influential view of man as innately noble and free, but corrupted by conventional civilisation,[46] contrasted starkly with the traditional Christian view of man as innately corrupt and needing to be saved by religion. By putting the individual in the centre of the moral universe, Rousseau created an individualistic philosophy which concentrated on the importance of man's moral and intellectual independence. Self-discipline was the foundation of moral improvement.[47]

In such a theory, rights, and particularly individual freedoms, needed to be protected against interference by society and the state in the name of social morality or propriety. In Rousseau's vision, this was to be done by laws to which all citizens were to contribute—the laws would reflect the 'general will'—and to which all would be required to maintain

[44] See Simon Schama, *The Embarrassment of Riches* (London: Collins, 1987), ch. 2 on the significance of Old Testament parallels in Dutch culture.

[45] Thomas Aquinas, *Summa Theologica*, Qu. XCIII, Art. 3, and Qu. XCIV, Arts. 2–4. Duns Scotus used rationality principles to argue that ownership of property (*dominium*) was incompatible with natural law, because in a state of innocence the optimal arrangement is common use of assets: *Questiones in Librum Sententiarum* 15.2, in *Opera Omnia* (Paris, 1894), xviii. 256–7. For discussion, see Tuck, *Natural Rights Theories*, 21; d'Entrèves, *Natural Law*, ch. 3.

[46] Jean-Jacques Rousseau, *Du contrat social* (1762), Book I, translated in Sir Ernest Barker (ed.), *Social Contract: Essays by Locke, Hume, Rousseau* (London: Oxford University Press, 1971), 167–307.

[47] For analysis, see John Plamenatz, *Man and Society: A Critical Examination of Some Important Social and Political Theories from Machiavelli to Marx*, 2nd edn., rev. M. E. Plamenatz and Robert Wokler (London: Longman, 1992), ii, ch. 4.

allegiance on pain of banishment or death.[48] This distinctly illiberal conclusion of the theory disappoints many liberals, but it provides the basis
for the legal protection of liberties: the laws which will help to hold elements of society in a slightly uneasy equilibrium are themselves required
to respect the liberties which underpin the legitimacy of society.

The trust which Rousseau had in human nature and self-discipline was
not rational. It was an act of faith. However, any starting point for rational speculation about the good society or the good life must begin with a
set of beliefs about the ends of human life and the objects of societies.
The eighteenth-century rationalists were often prepared to allow considerable scope for enlightened despotism on the part of rulers, without limiting it by reference to the general will. On a less optimistic view than
Rousseau's of human nature, this is not an irrational course: one needs to
have means to control the effects of people's baser instincts in order to
secure co-operation. Thomas Hobbes's advocacy of Leviathan, the state
to which all owe obedience, is an example of the way in which a form of
secular natural law can have a tendency towards absolutism.[49] Natural law
on its own, therefore, does not guarantee rights, because the use to
which it is put will depend on the political aspirations of those who
invoke it.

In France and the United States of America, the meritorious objective
of limiting governmental power was institutionalized through secular,
rather than religious, political theory in the eighteenth and nineteenth
centuries, and natural law was driven by revolutionary objectives.[50]
When it became clear after the French Revolution, in the wake of the
Terror which Robespierre unleashed, that populist governments could
disregard human freedom and rationalism as much as aristocratic ones,
the pressure for human rights grew. Activists like Tom Paine used the
notion of human rights as a way of translating the ideal of individual freedom into action. Human rights formed both a reason for action and a
blueprint for the post-revolutionary regulation of government. It is in
this role that natural rights appear in the United States' Declaration of
Independence and the French Declaration of the Rights of Man, specify-

[48] *Du contrat social*, Book I, s. 7; Book II, s. 3–6; Book IV, *passim*.
[49] Thomas Hobbes, *Leviathan* (1651; ed. John Plamenatz, London: Fontana, 1962), chs
13, 14, 15, 18, 20, 21; Gregory S. Kavka, *Hobbesian Moral and Political Theory* (Princeton,
NJ: Princeton University Press, 1986), 245.
[50] The link between secular philosophy and rights theories is noted by E. J.
Hobsbawm, *The Age of Revolution 1789–1848* (London: Sphere Books, 1973), who notes
at p. 270 that Thomas Paine 'is as famous for having written the first book to demonstrate
in popular language that the Bible is not the word of God (*The Age of Reason*, 1794), as
for his *Rights of Man* (1791)'. He goes on (at p. 288) to note the link between free enterprise and a natural right to liberty.

ing the basic beliefs of the founding fathers as to the values which were to guide the politics of the new states.[51]

Across much of the world since then, the idea of liberties, derived from secular natural-law reasoning, has exercised a compellingly powerful hold on popular imaginations. In England, by contrast, we will see that the law has developed by throwing off the conservative aspects of natural law without replacing it with anything which rests explicitly on natural-law foundations; yet it will be argued that natural law presuppositions of a rationalist type underlie much of English positivism.

In what rational, secular sense is a commitment to freedom 'natural'? There are several ways in which it has been argued that law, freedom, or rights, or some particular laws or freedoms, are ordained by nature. Law may be natural because human nature makes it essential for people to be constrained by rules in order to survive or achieve some purpose which is thought to constitute a natural goal of humanity. To this, it has been objected that rules, duties and rights are not natural facts but 'ought statements', or, as philosophers say, are normative. As a matter of logic, one cannot derive an 'ought' from an 'is' statement, but only from another 'ought'. As a matter of formal logic, this is no doubt correct. It does not follow directly from the fact that being killed makes it impossible to exercise one's democratic freedoms that one has a democratic right to life. The factual consequences of death do not logically entail a right not to be killed. However, it misrepresents natural rights arguments to present them as attempts to derive values directly from facts.[52] The arguments aim instead to derive rights indirectly, by way of layers of normative argument or assumptions which are sometimes explicit but are often tacit.

A relatively sophisticated natural rights argument can be represented in the following propositions.[53]

1. One of the features typical of human nature is that people commonly consider that it is worth their while to try to construct a picture of their relationship with things outside themselves. This is thought to be worthwhile for its own sake, irrespective of any practical advantage which might accrue: it is a natural facet of human curiosity and a certain cast of mind which seeks order in apparent chaos.

2. If such activities are thought to be independently valuable, they are

---

[51] On France, see George Rudé, *The French Revolution* (London: Weidenfeld & Nicolson, 1988), 59–60; Simon Schama, *Citizens* (London: Viking Penguin, 1989), 746–847. On the USA, see Leonard Levy, *Constitutional Opinions: Aspects of the Bill of Rights* (New York: Oxford University Press, 1986), 124–5.

[52] Finnis, *Natural Law and Natural Rights*, 33–48.

[53] This paragraph and the one following are heavily influenced by Finnis, *Natural Law and Natural Rights*, chs 3, 4, 5, and 6, although they do not purport to be an account of Finnis's theory.

likely to be important to people's assessments of the quality of their lives.

3. One of the proper functions of society is to enable people to optimize the quality of their lives as far as possible.

4. People have a right to intellectual freedom.

These propositions are linked, but they do not follow logically from one another. The fundamental proposition is (3), a statement of values, not fact. Proposition (4), in form a statement of social fact (the recognition in a society of a right) but one which involves the acceptance of certain values, follows from (3) only under the conditions specified in (1) and (2), which are wholly factual hypotheses. In other words, natural rights are logically derived from values, not facts. The factual propositions supporting the rights merely specify the conditions which make a freedom particularly valuable and under which it will be possible to say that in a given society, with a particular view of the human condition, at a specified time, people are entitled to that freedom. Like the conditions, the techniques for establishing propositions (1) to (3) are culturally specific. In societies where the prevailing intellectual ethos is rationalist, people are likely to adopt a mix of empirical and reflective methods which make up what Finnis calls 'practical reasonableness'.[54] The test of last resort for particular rights or freedoms may be the political process or a judicial process or a combination of the two. In other societies, such questions may not be open to speculation, being finally disposed of by statements of absolute and final authority. The authoritative statements may emanate from a human autarch, from express agreement of individuals or states party to international conventions, or may stem from a deity and be manifested through oracular techniques or techniques of textual interpretation which may include elements of practical reasonableness.

This theory of natural rights will surprise some readers because of the modesty of the claims made for the rights under it. They are not seen as eternal, unchanging, or universal, nor is it necessary to see any rights as absolute, although it is not necessary to argue that there are *no* absolute rights.[55] They derive their authority from present conditions and beliefs. It is a mistake to see natural rights or natural law as any more uniform and unchanging than nature (human or other) is. To say that a right is natural is to assert only that it springs from a given society's view of human nature and the aspirations and responsibilities of members of that

---

[54] *Natural Law and Natural Rights*, 88 ('being able to bring one's own intelligence to bear effectively . . . on the problems of choosing one's actions and lifestyle and shaping one's own character').

[55] For argument supporting the view that there are absolute rights, see Alan Gewirth, 'Are there any Absolute Rights?' in Jeremy Waldron (ed.), *Theories of Rights* (Oxford: Oxford University Press, 1984), 91–109.

society. Societies change, and the nature of the changes is controlled by a multiplicity of factors. It may be that the rights which seem to flow naturally from capitalist forms of social organisation will not be seen as natural in a post-capitalist society (whatever form that may take), and that is to take account of only one of the possible variables (economic structure). Other factors which affect the perceived naturalness of kinds of rights include differing understandings of what count as justifying arguments for rights, differing epistemologies which determine how one can seek to establish the existence of the conditions for particular rights, and differing political arrangements for settling disputes about rights.

Practical natural rights theories are thus founded on a mixture of moral and political analysis, social psychology, and practical reason. Natural rights do not float in a Platonic heaven of ideal, eternal concepts, despite the assumptions of many of their critics.[56] They are as tough, real, variable, and elusive as nature itself. 'Natural' rights should be understood not in contradistinction to 'human' or 'social' rights—society is after all a natural aspect of most human conditions—but as advancing values which are good in themselves, rather than being justified by reference to consequentialist arguments.

(2) Positive rights, utilitarianism, and legal positivism

The positive rights tradition is closely linked to legal positivism, just as the natural rights tradition is linked to natural-law theories. Historically, legal positivism in Britain is rooted in rationalist, reforming thought of the late eighteenth and early nineteenth centuries. In particular, it is a child of utilitarianism,[57] and developed as a reaction against what Jeremy Bentham saw as the conservative tendencies of the common lawyers who called in aid natural law to discourage the use of legislation for social reform, while perpetuating an inhuman, inconsistent, and inefficient system of positive law.[58] As part of the process of making reforming legislation respectable, Bentham attacked the idea of natural rights, which (as he saw it) acted sometimes as illegitimate constraints on reform, and at other

---

[56] For the most famous critique, see Jeremy Bentham, *Anarchical Fallacies*, in John Bowring (ed.), *The Works of Jeremy Bentham*, ii. 491 ff. For a balanced, rationalist approach from a natural lawyer, see d'Entrèves, *Natural Law*, ch. 4. A thorough discussion of the historical foundations of natural rights theories is provided by Tuck, *Natural Rights Theories, passim*. For a shorter account, see Eugene Kamenka, 'The Anatomy of an Idea', in Eugene Kamenka and Alice Erh-Soon Tay (eds.), *Human Rights* (London: Edward Arnold, 1978), 1–12.

[57] H. L. A. Hart, *Essays on Bentham* (Oxford: Clarendon Press, 1982), ch. 4; Elie Halévy, *The Growth of Philosophical Radicalism* (London: Faber & Faber, 1972), 155–81.

[58] See Gerald Postema, *Bentham and the Common Law Tradition* (Oxford: Clarendon Press, 1986), ch. 8.

times precipitated a breakdown of the lawful authority on which systematic reform depended, as when the Declaration of the Rights of Man and
the Citizen helped to cement the French Revolution of 1789.[59] For
Bentham, legitimate, enforceable rights came not from nature but from
laws duly passed by the supreme political authority of the state, the sovereign legislature. The scope of freedoms is always to be established first by
way of the political and then through the legal process, and justified by
consequentialist arguments of utility.

Bentham's positivism had a liberating political influence, in that it
enabled law, as a system of rules posited and so open to amendment by a
politically sovereign body, to become a tool in the hands of social
reformers. At the same time the felicific calculus, the system advocated by
Bentham as the most rational way of assessing the desirability of laws, is
capable of taking into account many of the factors which would lead a
natural rights theorist to assert an entitlement to a freedom. The evaluation of pleasure according to its intensity, duration, and so on is as applicable to pleasure derived from an activity which is a good in itself as it is
to one which brings pleasure indirectly and consequentially.

However, scientific utilitarians face two problems. The first is to show
that units of measurement for pleasure and pain can be applied equally to
different types of pleasure and pain. One way of resolving this problem is
to find a way of assigning an economic value to all pleasures and pains,
based on the sums which a rational person would think it worth paying
to obtain or avoid them. This attempt lies at the heart of the discipline of
welfare economics. But it leads on to the second problem: the felicific
calculus and welfare economics, in their crude forms, can each be
accused of failing to take liberties (or rights) sufficiently seriously. This is
because it is essential to the method of the felicific calculus that the pleasure derived from exercising a freedom, and thus the justification for
allowing that freedom, can at any time be outweighed by a countervailing pain to others from allowing the exercise of the freedom. Whilst the
pleasure which I derive from freedom to write this chapter is to be taken
into account in deciding whether or not I should continue to be allowed
to write it, classical utilitarianism does not give that pleasure any greater
weight or importance than the pleasure which might flow to others from
denying me that freedom, nor does it attempt to distinguish between
good and bad *reasons* for wanting to deny me that freedom. In quantify-
ing pleasure and pain it takes no account of the moral significance of
freedoms and of interference with them. It provides no framework for
the moral evaluation of freedoms unless one considers that the maximisa-
tion of pleasure and the minimisation of pain together form an exhaustive

[59] H. L. A. Hart, *Essays in Jurisprudence and Legal Philosophy* (Oxford: Clarendon Press,
1983), chs 8 and 9.

catalogue of important moral values. Few people would be prepared to accept that.

The risk of losing rights which even utilitarians regard as having fundamental importance has led some people to qualify classical utilitarianism to give added protection to such rights against a simple balance of pain or preference. As no right can sensibly be allowed absolute protection, in order to establish a shield for liberties it was necessary to define both the scope of the protected interests and the grounds on which interference with liberty was to be permitted. Only in assessing whether those grounds had been sufficiently made out in a particular case were the balance of pleasures and pains to be taken into account. The most notable attempt to amend utilitarianism in this way was made by John Stuart Mill in his essay *On Liberty*, published in 1859. He asserted the primacy of freedom, and argued that individuals or society could legitimately exercise coercion and control over other individuals only for the purpose of self-protection. In defending this thesis he relied on consequentialist arguments, while allowing that rights had a 'special utility'. Freedom of thought and discussion were to be protected because when suppressing views one could never know whether they were true or false. The risk of losing a truth is too serious to be justifiable on utilitarian grounds; even if the suppressed opinion is false, it is valuable because, by demonstrating its falsity, the truth can be reinforced. Individuality is valuable because variety maximises the chances of valuable inventions and innovations being made; intellectual and market freedoms expand the range of options available to everyone. As a correlative of this libertarian individualism, the role of the state is to be reduced; sometimes activities should be left to the private sector even if it is likely that they would be done better by government agencies, because trying to do the job will broaden people's experience and stimulate them to new efforts, with a consequential benefit for them and (perhaps) for society as a whole.[60]

This is a paternalist form of liberalism. It makes it clear that utility is not about what people want but about what is (or is thought to be) good for them. They must take responsibility even if they would rather not have it, because, even if they suffer extreme pain as a result of their failure, they will be better people, and deemed to have enjoyed extra pleasure, for having made the attempt. Underlying the individualism is a deep distrust of popular democracy as a process for settling where the balance of utility lies. In itself, that would be neither suprising nor unusual: similar expressions of distrust are to be found in earlier writers from Plato to John Austin and later writers from Lenin to Schumpeter and Dahl. It is more perturbing, however, to note that Mill's defence of liberty succeeds

[60] J. S. Mill, *On Liberty*, chs 2 and 4.

if and only if one accepts that the social dis-benefits of interfering with freedom of expression are as compellingly serious as he supposed. Such dis-benefits are speculative rather than immediate, and the argument based on them invites a response which simply gives greater weight to the protection of society against equally speculative harm, supposedly flowing from abuse of the liberty. Sir Patrick (later Lord) Devlin gave just such a response in arguing that it is proper, and sometimes even necessary, to impose coercive limits on freedom of the person in order to defend society against the 'harm' inflicted by homosexuality. In his exchange with Professor H. L. A. Hart, Devlin was playing the utilitarians at their own game, demonstrating that utilitarianism offers no reliable defence for liberties against the operation of the felicific calculus.[61]

The positivist conception of liberties and rights was developed at a time when democratic processes were relatively undeveloped. There was no approach to universal suffrage in Britain until nearly 130 years after the first publication of Bentham's *Introduction to the Principles of Morals and Legislation* in 1789. Bentham himself died in the year of the 1832 Reform Act. At such a time, the felicific calculus was in the relatively safe hands of scientific philosophers (as they regarded themselves). Burgeoning democracy threatened to substitute real preferences for the scientific balance of pleasure and pain; latter-day utilitarians viewed the prospect without enthusiasm, and like Mill moved to entrench certain liberties, or at least provide for a presumption in favour of maintaining liberty, putting a heavy burden on those who advocated restrictions. This, however, could not be justified from within utilitarian theory itself, unless (like Mill, but unlike Bentham) one were to stipulate a special utilitarian value in protecting rights.

Legal positivism, then, is not necessarily incompatible with guaranteeing protection of specified liberties and rights. If the constitutional law of a particular jurisdiction permits it, legislation can be passed protecting specified liberties, and can be entrenched. English positivists, however, have faced particular problems in relation to the entrenchment of rights. There are two reasons for this. First, the constitutional law of England, and perhaps also of Scotland and Northern Ireland, until recently recognised no limitations on the legislative competence of the UK Parliament. One of the paradoxical consequences of this extreme version of parliamentary sovereignty was that Parliament could not in theory limit its own power, even by restricting the conditions under which it would forthwith be capable of interfering with fundamental liberties or rights.

---

[61] See H. L. A. Hart, *Law, Liberty, and Morality* (Oxford: Oxford University Press, 1963); Patrick Devlin, *The Enforcement of Morals* (Oxford: Oxford University Press, 1965). For a more recent liberal approach to the problem, see Joel Feinberg, *Harmless Wrongdoing: The Moral Limits of the Criminal Law* (Oxford: Clarendon Press, 1988).

This doctrine has recently become less significant in the light of the sub-jection of UK law to the supra-national legal order of the EEC, but it retains some significance in fields which are not yet covered by Community law.[62]

Secondly, British democratic theory has been dominated, as has its legal complement in positivist theory, by the idea of the importance of political judgments of the electorate through the ballot-box as the ulti-mate source of legislative legitimacy.[63] Entrenching rights is seen as anti-democratic, in that it restricts the power of the citizens at the ballot-box and the legislative power of their elected representatives in the House of Commons, the dominant part of Parliament, often increasing the power of judges. These judges are, in the U.K., not electorally accountable, and are unlikely to have available either the information needed to decide the social questions which arise in adjudication about fundamental rights, or the procedures for obtaining that information.[64] These considerations bring us face to face with the political aspect of civil liberties and human rights claims.

(3) The relationship between natural and positive rights

This section concludes the examination of natural rights and positive rights theories as the basis for human rights and civil liberties law, by drawing attention to the relationship between the theories and some of the implications. Both natural and positive theories of rights have strengths, but neither can operate effectively on its own. If rights can be identified only by reference to moral values, a natural-law element (within the meaning ascribed to natural law above) is a necessary back-ground to provide substance for the scheme of human rights law. On the other hand, identifying specially important moral values will do little good unless people respect them. The rights produced by a natural law approach will be of little practical use unless society is unusually commit-ted to the morality which produced the rights or can be coerced into respecting them. A system of politics is needed to give social recognition and authority to the scheme of rights and translate them into positive law.

---

[62] See Joseph Jaconelli, *Enacting a Bill of Rights* (Oxford: Clarendon Press, 1980). This matter is discussed further in Ch. 2 below.

[63] P. P. Craig, 'Bentham, Public Law and Democracy' [1987] *PL* 407–27; id., *Public Law and Democracy in the United Kingdom and the United States of America* (Oxford: Clarendon Press, 1991), ch. 2.

[64] J. A. G. Griffith, 'The Political Constitution' (1979) 42 *MLR* 1–21, especially at p. 16; Craig, *Public Law and Democracy*, ch. 7. Courts in the U.K. have a restrictive atti-tude to class actions and representative plaintiffs, and no equivalent of the American Brandeis brief. For discussion of the implications, see David Feldman, 'Public Interest Litigation and Constitutional Theory in Comparative Perspective' (1992) 55 *MLR* 44–73.

Legal positivism alone cannot suffice to identify the interests which should be protected by rights, because positivism, aiming to be neutral between different sets of non-legal values, serves merely to show how such values may be converted into legal rules; but the paraphernalia of positive law and legal institutions are important aids to securing respect for rights, performing educational, coercive, and symbolic roles according to circumstances.

It seems, then, that certain natural law and positivist approaches to rights are complementary rather than in conflict. Indeed, those parts of positive law which consist of statements of proper or desired behaviour, backed by a reward or sanction, presuppose the rightness of those forms of behaviour. Such ideas of rightness can be derived only from a system of social or moral values operating independently of law.[65] Despite Bentham's imprecations against natural law,[66] every law reformer must start with a supra-legal objective or standard and move to implement it in positive law through the medium of politics. Bentham's attack, properly understood, was on the petrification of natural law by Blackstone, who regarded natural law as a definitive and unchanging set of rules embodied in the common law, rather than on the natural-law approach described in this chapter.[67] Natural law, seen as a method of argument and justification rather than as a collection of immutable truths, is always necessary.

On the other hand, the loss of the cosmic dimension to natural law and natural rights means that they require careful analysis, and may (probably will) be influenced by attitudes and needs which are specific to particular cultures, societies, and economic systems. It will be impossible to identify values which are regarded as equally fundamental in every society, although if people in different societies produced a list of their 'top ten' rights or freedoms some rights would probably appear on most lists. What sort of rights would these be?

H. L. A. Hart suggested that, if there are such things as natural rights at all, they must encompass a right to liberty, as other rights are valuable only to the extent that one has a right to the freedom necessary to exercise them.[68] This attractive view is fundamental to much liberal thinking,

---

[65] The importance of this intimate connection between legal rule-making and moral standards is developed in Ronald Dworkin, *Taking Rights Seriously* (London: Duckworth, 1977), and the same author's *Law's Empire* (London: Fontana, 1986). See also Claire Palley, *The United Kingdom and Human Rights* (London: Sweet & Maxwell, 1991), ch. 1.

[66] The best-known example is in his *Anarchical Fallacies*, above, n. 56.

[67] See Postema, *Bentham and the Common Law Tradition*, 328–36.

[68] H. L. A. Hart, 'Are there any Natural Rights?' (1955) 64 *Philosophical Rev.* 175–91. Reprinted in Anthony Quinton (ed.), *Political Philosophy* (Oxford: Oxford University Press, 1967), 53–66.

but it depends on a number of variable factors. This section concludes its examination of natural and positive rights by raising four such factors.

(i) *The sort of rights being discussed.* The idea of a right to liberty helps to explain negative rights, such as freedom of speech and freedom from arbitrary arrest. Unless there is a claim right to support such freedoms, they become unenforceable in law. However, it is not clear that the right to liberty is either a necessary or a sufficient condition for the recognition of positive rights, such as a right to be freedom from hunger. A right to liberty is not a precondition to accepting such positive social rights, because positive rights do not depend on any freedom to exercise them. Indeed, some positive rights, notably social and economic rights, cannot be exercised. Instead, they impose duties on others to act to benefit those who hold the rights. The social and economic rights themselves are seen as preconditions to the proper enjoyment of those negative rights which are the stuff of classical liberal theory. Thus a right to liberty may be seen as a condition, together with economic or social rights, for the universal opportunity to exercise negative (freedom of choice) rights.

(ii) *Assumptions about the content of other natural rights.* Hart's idea of a right to liberty seems to assume that the negative rights which a right to liberty would underpin make up the central, if not the only, kind of right which would be produced by applying natural rights reasoning. Despite its apparent value-neutrality and generalizability, Hart's right to liberty is itself a product of liberal theory. If one's view of natural rights stems from a socialist tradition, allowing for economic and social rights as 'natural', the right to liberty would provide an inadequate foundation, and one would have to find a different fundamental natural right.

(iii) *Rights and the contingent nature of social organization.* This in turn suggests that one's conception of natural rights is conditional on a particular set of political values. Indeed, rights-talk may be seen as a way of expressing a vision of the world in such a way as to give extra rhetorical force to such political values. An idea of this sort has been powerfully developed by Richard Rorty, through ideas which he calls 'contingency' and 'irony'.[69]

The ironic approach to freedom portrays the human condition and human values as contingent, rather than inevitable, developments. People see things as they do because of an accidental confluence of contingencies, which they seek to explain in language which makes sense of it for their purposes at that particular time. The ironist, however, maintains

[69] Richard Rorty, *Contingency, Irony and Solidarity.*

radical and continuing doubts about the vocabulary currently in use to describe values and the world, and does not look to this vocabulary to resolve these doubts, but instead tries out other ways of describing things and values ('languages') to see whether they seem to do the job better.[70] This approach eschews the language of self-evident goods and the essential nature of humanity or society. On this view, which Rorty derives from Freud, Wittgenstein, Heidegger, and Nietzche among others,[71] it is unhelpful to ask, or to try to answer, questions about the essential nature of beings, about the nature of truth, or the nature of morality. People can mould the world by redescribing it in new language, and the advantage of a liberal community over an illiberal one is that it allows more freedom to develop new languages, and more opportunity for people to choose the form of language which best advances their purposes.[72] The idea of openness to new visions differs from the arguments advanced by Mill, in that whereas Mill assumed that the availability of new ways of looking at the world would necessarily lead to a better-understood and better-ordered world, Rorty suggests only that it may perhaps lead to a differently understood and differently organized world which may for some purposes be better (but may equally be worse for others).

According to Rorty, the advantage of his view of liberty and liberal society lies in its capacity to accommodate an account of liberty which suits the prevailing ethic of moral pluralism better than other available candidates. It frees one to decide (within the limits imposed by language) how to formulate freedoms so as to reflect one's understanding of the best resolution of competing moral imperatives. This is undoubtedly an advantage in that it frees us to construct a system of liberties from scratch. Of course, irony itself does not help us to choose a system, and so to choose the purposes for which we want to restate our visions of the world. However, it usefully emphasizes the importance of social or institutional acceptance to any conception of rights. The rhetorical usefulness of rights-talk will be very limited unless everyone who matters accepts the language of rights in the same way.

(iv) *Constitutional and political culture.* This latter aspect of Rorty's ideas highlights another characteristic of ideas of rights already noted in relation to Hart's notion of a right to liberty. Both the rights people have and the ways in which they can be protected and enforced arise out of a constitutional and political culture which dictates the language in which rights-talk is conducted. It thereby tends to reinforce the existing arrangements, and limits the range of alternatives which are likely to be taken seriously by people—or by those who matter—in that society. Nevertheless, in a

---

[70] *Contingency, Irony and Solidarity*, 73.   [71] Ibid., chs 2 and 3.
[72] Ibid., ch. 1.

pluralist society such as that which obtains in Britain, the political system has to accommodate many different cultures, each with a distinctive attitude to rights. We live in a society characterized by disagreement about the proper use of rights-talk. Conceptions of rights are controversial, as this chapter has shown.

However, at present the dominant conception of rights in municipal English legal culture is based on liberal theory. Liberties predominate over claim-rights. At the same time, Britain is part of an international legal community which is increasingly committed to a view of rights expressed in the language of claim-rights against the state. There is a tension between the language and tradition of English and Scots law and the language and culture of international human rights law to which the nation and the government subscribe, albeit sometimes reluctantly.[73]

1.3 RIGHTS, DEMOCRACY, AND THE RULE OF LAW

The final issue which this chapter addresses briefly is the relationship between rights, democracy, and the rule of law. By recognizing freedoms on the ground of moral autonomy, however one defines it, the state is committed to accepting that certain matters are, for the time being, properly to be regarded as lying in the private rather than the public sphere of decision-making. This distinction between the public and private spheres of life is thought by many to be a fundamental dichotomy in liberal society and legal systems.[74] It does not imply that the state or society has no legitimate interest in the matters in question. Rather, it suggests that the individual's choice should normally outrank social preferences in relation to matters lying within the private sphere. Once the boundaries have been set, and appropriate legal rules have been made and promulgated, the doctrine of the rule of law means that it is the job of the courts to ensure that people are able to exercise their freedoms and that the boundaries between the public and private spheres are not overstepped (particularly by the state).

This might be thought to introduce a tension between freedom and democracy, in that the creation of a sphere of private autonomy, and the work of the courts in policing it, prevents normal democratic decision-making processes from operating in that area. This is especially worrying to democrats in countries which have constitutionally entrenched and

---

[73] For governmental disapproval of the terminology employed in the European Convention on Human Rights and Fundamental Freedoms in 1950, see Anthony Lester, 'Fundamental Rights: The United Kingdom Isolated' [1984] PL 46–72.

[74] See the discussion by Ed Sparer, 'Fundamental Human Rights, Legal Entitlements, and the Social Struggle: A Friendly Critique of the Critical Legal Studies Movement', 36 Stanford LR 509–74 at 515–52 (1984).

judicially enforceable Bills of Rights. For example, the First Amendment to the U.S. Constitution prevents Congress from legislating to abridge press freedom. This places a restriction on the power of the democratically accountable representatives of the people. Furthermore, because the rule of law imposes a duty on politically independent judges to determine issues of constitutional law, the scope of the restriction falls to be determined by judges who are not generally democratically accountable. However, the clash between freedoms or rights on the one hand and democracy on the other is not as stark as it might appear, for two reasons. First, the delimitation of the private and public spheres remains a matter for public debate and, ultimately, decision. This is the case even where individual rights are constitutionally defined and protected against amendment by ordinary legislation, since every constitution has procedures whereby it may be amended. The need for constitutional amendment to change the scope of a freedom gives some freedoms a privileged place in political discussion, but does not remove them from the political stage. They may remain highly controversial. Even the judges who have to determine the scope of constitutional protections for the rights are likely to be influenced by public debate on the issues. This is the reason why methods of appointing new Justices to the U.S. Supreme Court, taking account of their known political views, becomes so important in a democratic state. It provoked the extended political debates in the Senate Judiciary Committee which resulted in the Senate's rejection of Judge Bork, nominated by President Reagan,[75] and the eventual (somewhat grudging) confirmation of Judge Clarence Thomas, nominated by President Bush to replace the recently retired Justice Thurgood Marshall in 1991.

Secondly, citizens must have certain guaranteed rights if an effective democratic structure is to be put in place and maintained. It is impossible to imagine a properly functioning democracy in a country where people by and large are not guaranteed freedom of expression, a free press, a right to vote, a right to petition Parliament, freedom of protest, and freedom from arbitrary arrest and detention by government agencies. Such rights are fundamental to the notion of democracy, and could not be abrogated by democratic decision-makers in the public sphere without undermining the very democracy which is said to legitimize public decision-making. However these rights are formulated, and whatever means (constitutional law or political convention) may be used to protect them, it would be perverse to argue that there is anything undemocratic about a restriction on the capacity of decision-makers to interfere with the rights which are fundamental to democracy itself.

[75] For discussion, see Philip Bobbitt, *Constitutional Interpretation* (Oxford: Basil Blackwell, 1991), 83–108.

2

WAYS OF IDENTIFYING AND PROTECTING
RIGHTS AND LIBERTIES

Chapter 1 examined a variety of philosophical theories which may
ground an attachment to liberties or rights. This chapter first looks at
the protection of human rights in international law generally, under the
International Covenant on Civil and Political Rights, and under the
European Convention on Human Rights. It then looks at a variety of
ways in which rights may be protected in domestic law, depending on
the constitutional structure and social values of different societies and
legal systems. Next, the general approach adopted in the United
Kingdom, and England and Wales in particular, is examined, and the
chapter concludes with a discussion of the debate about the possibility of
introducing a Bill of Rights for the UK. For convenience, the word
'right' will be used to include liberty, unless the context otherwise
requires.

2.1 INTERNATIONAL HUMAN RIGHTS LAW

This section examines the general nature of human rights and the rights
of peoples in international law.[1]

(1) International human rights law as the synthesis of natural and positive rights

Throughout the world, in international relations and international law,
debates about the protection of rights are being conducted in the language of human rights. This is an increasing trend, and represents the
significant inroads which are being made by the international community
of nations on the notion of state sovereignty. Until relatively recently,
attempts by one nation to tell another how to treat the latter's citizens on

---

[1] Good general introductions are provided by Paul Sieghart, *The Lawful Rights of Mankind* (Oxford: Clarendon Press, 1986), and A. H. Robertson and J. G. Merrills, *Human Rights in the World: An Introduction to the Study of the International Protection of Human Rights*, 3rd edn. (Manchester: Manchester University Press, 1989). On the theory of international human rights law, see Claire Palley, *The United Kingdom and Human Rights* (London: Sweet & Maxwell, 1991).

its territory would have been dismissed as a blatant attempt to interfere in the internal affairs of a sovereign state. Now, however, particularly in the aftermath of the Second World War, it has been recognized that states cannot be trusted to treat their citizens properly, and that humanity has a common interest in the treatment of people by governments, wherever they may be.

As explained in Chapter 1, the idea at the root of human rights thinking is that there are certain rights which are so fundamental to people's well-being and to their chance of leading a fulfilling life that their governments are obligated to respect them, and the international order has to protect them. The identification of the human rights which are to be protected is, generally, the result of discussion between states' representatives in the course of negotiating multilateral treaties. Each state must decide what it wants from others, and what it is prepared to concede itself while safeguarding its most significant interests. The actual drafting of the treaties is in the hands of lawyers, and the final drafts are the result of attempts to encapsulate those rights on which agreement can be reached in language which is acceptable to all the States Parties. The final form of rights enshrined in international human rights instruments is, therefore, likely to be a compromise between the objectives of the various states, influenced by various methods of thinking about human rights, and channelled through different legal, moral, political, and economic cultures, and then reduced to legal language with as much precision as can be achieved given the pressure to find a form of words which will be acceptable to all.

For a state to accept international obligations in relation to the treatment of its own citizens always involves the state in accepting a certain limitation of its national sovereignty in its internal affairs. Governments will not normally do this unless either (a) there are compelling reasons for doing so, in the shape of balancing advantages to be gained, or (b) they are cynical or complacent enough to believe that they will not need to take any steps to bring their law and practice into line with their new obligations. The main spur to accepting human rights obligations has always been widespread public horror at some shocking revelation. Calls for the protection of human rights in international law have been most persuasive and effective as a response to serious episodes of disregard for humanitarian values, such as nineteenth-century concern over the slave-trade, which seems to have originated international human rights agreements. These treaties made the slave-trade illegal, and required states to take action against it. Humanitarian law, particularly to protect combatants and non-combatants in wartime, followed. Next came treaties to protect minority population groups in the newly created or reformed countries which arose after the First World War, by virtue of the Treaty of Versailles.[2] In the U.K., these have been given legal effect by a series of statutes and executive actions. For example, slavery had been held to be incompatible with English common law in *Somersett's case*,[3] but stamping out the slave-trade required governments to co-operate in stopping and searching slaving ships as they crossed the Atlantic. In international law, any of the powers would have been justified in regarding as illegal the search of a vessel flying its flag by a ship of another power. Treaties were accordingly entered into between the U.K. and France (1831 and 1833) and Spain (1835), allowing each country's navy to search ships flying the others' flags, which led to British cruisers capturing more than one hundred vessels, flying the Spanish flag but equipped to carry slaves, between 1835 and 1840.[4] The searches were a source of conflict with the U.S.A., with whom there was no treaty, until after the American civil war, and action had to be taken against American slaving vessels. This was held by the English courts to be protected as an act of state.[5] Other treaties, requiring domestic legislation to introduce criminal penalties and extend the jurisdiction of the U.K. courts over acts committed elsewhere, include genocide, torture, and crimes against the laws of war.[6]

But it was the public revelation, with the defeat of Hitler's Germany in 1945, of the inhumanity which people acting in the name of their states could inflict on others, which sparked a huge explosion in the range and number of human rights instruments. In the aftermath of the nationalist-inspired racial slaughter in Germany under the Third Reich, the General Assembly of the United Nations on 10 December 1948 adopted a Universal Declaration of Human Rights, noting in its Preamble that 'disregard and contempt for human rights have resulted in barbarous acts which have outraged the conscience of mankind, and the advent of a world in which human beings shall enjoy freedom of speech and belief and freedom from fear and want has been proclaimed as the highest aspiration of the common people'.[7] The Universal Declaration was not

---

[2] On this background, see Robertson and Merrills, *Human Rights*, 14–21.

[3] *Somersett* v. *Stewart* (1772) 20 St. Tr. 1, where Lord Mansfield held that a slave brought to England was legally free, even though slavery was lawful in the country from which he had been brought.

[4] Sir Llewellyn Woodward, *The Age of Reform 1815–1870*, 2nd edn. (Oxford: Clarendon Press, 1962), 240–1, 370.   [5] *Buron* v. *Denman* (1848) 2 Ex. 167.

[6] See Genocide Act 1969, incorporating Art. II of the Convention on the Prevention and Punishment of the Crime of Genocide (approved by UN General Assembly, 1948) in the Schedule; Criminal Justice Act 1988, s. 134, creating a crime of torture, defined in accordance with the UN Convention against Torture and Other Cruel, Inhuman or Degrading Treatment or Punishment (1984); and the War Crimes Act 1991, controversially passed by the use of the Parliament Acts 1911 and 1949 after twice being rejected by the House of Lords.

[7] UN Doc. A/811, reproduced in Ian Brownlie (ed.), *Basic Documents on Human Rights*, 3rd edn. (Oxford: Clarendon Press, 1992), 21–7.

intended to impose binding obligations, as a matter of law, on the member states of the United Nations, but has formed the basis for a large number of binding international human rights instruments, and is incorporated by reference in others.[8] These other instruments, including regional ones open to states in the Americas, Africa, and Europe, are expressed in different terms, protecting rights defined in different ways, with a variety of monitoring and adjudication procedures. Nevertheless, there are common threads linking them, and it has been suggested that there is a gradual convergence of standards.[9]

The United Kingdom is party to, *inter alia*, the International Covenant on Civil and Political Rights, and the European Convention on the Protection of Human Rights and Fundamental Freedoms. Both these instruments are legally binding in international law, and have implementation procedures which will be examined later in this chapter. The rights guaranteed by the states which ratified these instruments are a mixture of individual rights (as in the European Convention on Human Rights) and social and economic rights (as for example under the International Covenant on Economic, Social and Cultural Rights, 1966, the various Conventions drafted by the International Labour Organisation,[10] and the European Social Charter, 1961). International law thus seeks to protect rights of many different types.

All these various rights are turned from what, in Chapter 1, were described as natural rights claims into positive legal rights by their adoption or recognition as legally binding on states in international law. The range of these rights is still increasing, and now takes in the collective right of peoples to self-determination, unknown in times of imperial expansion, during which western ideas of rights and individualism estab-

---

[8] See e.g. the International Covenant on Civil and Political Rights (1966); various regional instruments, including the European Convention for the Protection of Human Rights and Fundamental Freedoms (1950), the American Convention on Human Rights (1969, which also derives from the American Declaration of the Rights and Duties of Man, 1948), and the African Charter on Human and Peoples' Rights (1981); and the agreement to abide by the provisions of the UN Charter and Universal Declaration in s. VII of the Final Act of the Helsinki Conference (1975: see Brownlie (ed.), *Basic Documents*, at p. 396).

[9] Craig Scott, 'The Independence and Permeability of Human Rights Norms: Towards a Partial Fusion of the International Covenants on Human Rights' (1989) 27 *Osgoode Hall LJ* 769–878.

[10] The ILO is one of the specialized agencies which were brought into a special relationship with the United Nations under Arts. 57 and 63 of the UN Charter. See Ian Brownlie, *Principles of Public International Law*, 4th edn. (Oxford: Clarendon Press, 1990), 568–9; Francis Wolf, 'Human Rights and the International Labour Organisation', in Theodor Meron (ed.), *Human Rights in International Law: Legal and Policy Issues* (Oxford: Clarendon Press, 1984), ch.r 7. For the texts of the Conventions, see Brownlie (ed.), *Basic Documents* 243–316.

lished an hegemony. Interestingly, this right is included, as Article 1, in both the International Covenant on Civil and Political Rights and the International Covenant on Economic, Social and Cultural Rights, yet the nature of self-determination is controversial, particularly in relation to groups which form a minority population within a sovereign state.[11] Cultural groups which, though temporarily submerged, survived, now seek to reassert their group identities. Peoples which have deployed arguments based on these rights include the Jews in relation to the establishment of the state of Israel in 1948, the claims of Palestinians to a national homeland at present, and the claims of indigenous peoples in the USA, Australia, New Zealand, Canada, and elsewhere.[12] Pressure for aboriginal rights and concern for the plight of aboriginals developed in Australia parallel to similar concerns in other parts of the world, helped by the influence of international conventions outlawing genocide and guaranteeing the rights of peoples.[13] The combination of international law with domestic and international political pressure has finally forced the governments of the Australian Commonwealth and states to address the problem of accommodating the legal rights of the aboriginal people to the commercial interests of the Australian economy.[14]

Such rights, although encapsulated in positive international law, remain controversial, both because the scope and implications of (for example) the rights of a people to self-determination are uncertain,[15] and because the effects which a state will be willing to attribute to such rights will depend largely on their background political and philosophical attitude

[11] See Ian Brownlie, 'The Rights of Peoples in Modern International Law', in James Crawford (ed.), *The Rights of Peoples* (Oxford: Clarendon Press, 1988); Russel L. Barsh, 'Indigenous Peoples and the Right to Self-Determination in International Law', in Barbara Hocking (ed.), *International Law and Aboriginal Human Rights* (Sydney: Law Book Co., 1988), 68–82.

[12] There is a massive literature on these subjects. For a good introduction, see Rosalie Schaffer, 'International Law and Sovereign Rights of Indigenous Peoples', in Hocking (ed.), *Aboriginal Rights*, 19–42. For a discussion of the rights of Australian aborigines, see Peter Bailey, *Human Rights: Australia in an International Context* (Sydney: Butterworths, 1990), 192–206.

[13] For summary, see Brownlie, *Public International Law*, 579–80.

[14] The way in which this is being done is outside the scope of this book. See Bailey, *Human Rights: Australia*, 192–213; *Mabo* v. *Queensland* (1992) 66 ALJR 408, HC of Australia. As part of the process of preparing to celebrate the centenary of the Commonwealth Constitution in 2000, the Australian federal government has declared its intention of introducing a major initiative to satisfy the legitimate claims of aborigines to self-determination before the end of the century. However, it is not clear what form this is likely to take, or how the legal and constitutional hurdles might be overcome.

[15] For consideration of these questions by the ICJ, see *The South West Africa Case* (Preliminary Objections), [1962] ICJ Reports 319; see also *The South West Africa C* (Second Phase), [1966] ICJ.Reports 6.

towards rights.[16] Nevertheless, the idea that human rights are uncertain or vague, and for that reason are otiose or unenforceable, is a misconception. Once embodied in a legally binding international instrument, they are no less certain or more vague than most domestic law statutes. They can be construed like the legal texts which they are. 'Accordingly, the need for standards founded on systems of divine or natural law has disappeared, and with it the need for the legal positivist to object to them.'[17] English lawyers, therefore, need not fear that they will be incapable of interpreting international human rights instruments; they have the necessary techniques and experience readily to hand.

The charge of vagueness or uncertainty is more fairly levelled at rights under customary international law,[18] which, being a reflection of the practice of states, is subject to change and difficulties of definition. Nevertheless, there is growing acceptance that certain rights, originally protected only by treaty, have, by reason of acceptance in the practice of states, become part of customary international law, and so are capable of binding even those states which have been reluctant to sign human rights conventions. The International Court of Justice has recognized several such rights in the course of its decisions, influenced by the fact that they form fundamental principles enunciated in the UN Charter and the Universal Declaration of Human Rights.[19] The rights include freedom from wrongful deprivation of freedom in conditions of hardship, and (it has been suggested) 'the right not to be subjected to torture or cruel, inhuman or degrading treatment or punishment and the right to liberty and security of the person',[20] and may well go much further, including rights of peoples to self-determination. However, following the ICJ's judgment in *Military Activities in Nicaragua*[21] concerning the military support given by the United States to the Contra rebels in Nicaragua, it seems that all the human rights recognized in customary international law can be traced to some international instrument, such as the UN Charter or the Universal Declaration of Human Rights. It also seems that, where the rights are contained in an instrument such as the International

---

[16] See Brownlie, *Public International Law*, 595–8.

[17] Paul Sieghart, *The International Law of Human Rights* (Oxford: Clarendon Press, 1983), 15. See also id., *Lawful Rights of Mankind*, 40–41.

[18] Full discussion is provided by Theodor Meron, *Human Rights and Humanitarian Norms as Customary Law* (Oxford: Clarendon Press, 1989).

[19] *The Tehran Hostages Case*, [1980] ICJ Reports 3; Nigel S. Rodley, 'Human Rights and Humanitarian Intervention: The Case Law of the World Court' (1989) 38 *ICLQ* 321–33; Meron, *Human Rights and Humanitarian Norms*, 106–14.

[20] Rodley, 'Human Rights and Humanitarian Intervention', at p. 327; id., *The Treatment of Prisoners in International Law* (Oxford: Clarendon Press, 1987), 63–9.

[21] 1989, discussed in Rodley, 'Human Rights and Humanitarian Intervention', at 327 ff.

Covenant on Civil and Political Rights or the European Convention on Human Rights, and the parties to a dispute are also parties to that instrument, the appropriate means of settling the matter is that laid down under the instrument in question. It appears to follow that the acceptance of human rights as part of customary law extends the range of parties bound to respect the rights beyond those states which are parties to the relevant international instruments, but does not alter the substance of the obligations on those states which, like the UK, are parties. If the range of recognized rights were to increase, to take in some which are in instruments to which the UK is not currently a party, it is possible that the scope of the UK's international law obligations would be increased. However, it is likely that the UK would have become a party to any such instrument before the rights in it had received sufficient acceptance by states to be regarded as part of customary international law.

2.2 INTERNATIONAL LAW: THE UNITED NATIONS, AND THE INTERNATIONAL COVENANT ON CIVIL AND POLITICAL RIGHTS

(a) The United Nations and human rights

A number of instruments operating under the umbrella of the United Nations in the realm of international law affect individuals' human rights and offer a route to redress.[22] The Charter of the United Nations (1945) contains references to human rights,[23] and Article 1 specifies, as one of the purposes of the organisation, promoting respect for human rights and fundamental freedoms. The Economic and Social Council (ECOSOC), established under Article 7 of the UN Charter, was permitted to make recommendations for that purpose, and to prepare draft conventions.[24] Under Article 68, ECOSOC established a Commission on Human Rights, which was to have, as one of its first tasks, the drafting of an international Bill of Rights. The first step was to draft a declaration, which was considered by ECOSOC and adopted (as the Universal Declaration of Human Rights) by the UN General Assembly in 1948. The next step was for the Commission to draft what turned out to be two Covenants which were to be open to signature by states which were members of the UN or of one of its specialized agencies, any state party to the Statute of the International Court of Justice, and any other state

---

[22] For a general survey, see Robertson and Merrills, *Human Rights in the World*, chs 2, 3, and 7.

[23] Preamble; Arts. 1, 13, 55, 62, 68, 76.   [24] Art. 62.

invited by the General Assembly to become a party to the Covenants.[25] This gave the Covenants a potentially wider reach than the UN Declaration, which had been in the form of a proclamation by members of the UN General Assembly. As treaties, the Covenants were binding on those who ratified them. The drafting of the Covenants proved a longer and more contentious task than that of the Declaration. Political and ideological differences came to the fore. It was 1966 before the International Covenant on Civil and Political Rights (ICCPR) and the International Covenant on Economic, Social and Cultural Rights (ICESCR) were adopted by the General Assembly and opened for signature, and 1976 before they were in force.

The decision to embody the two sets of rights in separate instruments was a way of allowing states to accept obligations in respect of one type of rights if they were not prepared to accept both. This was a pragmatic response to the deep philosophical and political differences of opinion as to the 'true' meaning of freedom, noted in Chapter 1. It also enabled different enforcement and monitoring procedures to be adopted in respect of each. The rights contained in ICESCR are heavily dependent on the economic conditions prevailing in different parts of the world, and on the state of the economies of each state party to the Covenant. The rights in ICCPR are less dependent, and generally speaking protect individuals' freedoms rather than positive rights to state assistance or intervention.[26] It was therefore possible for the UN Commission on Human Rights to include, and the General Assembly to adopt, a procedure for implementing ICCPR which included some element of evaluation of the performance of states parties in giving effect to the Convention, as well as the usual role of maintaining communication with states.

Between 1945 and 1966, however, the Secretary-General of the UN received very large numbers of communications alleging human rights infringements. Where these came from individuals or non-governmental organisations,[27] the UN Commission on Human Rights took the view that these could not be considered in an international forum, as entertaining communications from people or bodies other than states would amount to unjustified 'intervention in matters which are essentially

[25] International Covenant on Civil and Political Rights, Art. 48; International Covenant on Economic, Social and Cultural Rights, Art. 26.

[26] The major exception is that Art. 1, identical in ICCPR and ICESCR, provides for the right of all peoples to self-determination. For reasons considered in Ch. 1, this is outside the scope of a book on civil liberties. See Dominic McGoldrick, *The Human Rights Committee: Its Role in the Development of the International Covenant on Civil and Political Rights* (Oxford: Clarendon Press, 1991), 14–16 and ch. 5.

[27] On the latter, see David Weissbrodt, 'The Contribution of International Non-Governmental Organisations to the Protection of Human Rights', in Meron (ed.), *Human Rights in International Law*, ch. 11.

within the domestic jurisdiction of States', contrary to Article 2(7) of the UN Charter. However, as the number of members of the UN grew, a different view developed. In 1966, the General Assembly passed Resolution 2144(xx), encouraging ECOSOC to find ways of improving the capacity of the UN to stop human rights violations wherever they occurred. In 1970, ECOSOC responded by authorizing the UN Commission on Human Rights, by ECOSOC Resolution 1503, to consider 'communications, together with replies of governments, if any, which appear to reveal a consistent pattern of gross and reliably attested violations of human rights and fundamental freedoms within the terms of reference of the Sub-Commission'.[28]

The Resolution 1503 procedure, as it is known, is conducted by a five-member Working Group of the Sub-Commission on the Prevention of Discrimination and Protection of Minorities. The Working Group considers communications and the governments' replies to them. It identifies cases which disclose a 'consistent pattern of gross and reliably attested violations' involving many people over an extended period. It refers these to the Sub-Commission. The proceedings are confidential, but summaries of communications and developments in relation to them are supplied to representatives of all states on the UN Commission on Human Rights. In rare cases, where a country's responses to a communication are unsatisfactory, the communication is passed by the Sub-Commission, via the Commission, to ECOSOC, at which point ECOSOC may make it public. The system works through pressure rather than adjudication, and allows the UN to examine matters which are not otherwise open to review by any authority outside the country which is the subject of the communication.[29]

Alongside the Resolution 1503 procedure, the UN Commission on Human Rights and the Sub-Commission from time to time undertake comprehensive investigations of the human rights position in particular countries, and thematic investigations of the status of particular rights in all member States. In the case of the thematic investigations, they work through specially appointed working groups or individual rapporteurs.[30] Apart from this, there are also specialist expert committees, which are set up under treaties and are independent of the UN, charged with the implementation of particular human rights treaties, including the Convention on the Elimination of All Forms of Racial Discrimination (1965), the Convention on the Elimination of All Forms of Discrimination against Women (1979), and the Convention against Torture and Other Cruel, Inhuman or Degrading Treatment (1984).[31]

---

[28] Resolution 1503, s. 1; Brownlie, *Basic Documents*, 16.
[29] Robertson and Merrills, *Human Rights in the World*, 74–8.
[30] Ibid., 78–89.   [31] Ibid., 89–96.

(b) The operation of the ICCPR

The body set up under Article 28 of ICCPR to implement the Covenant is the Human Rights Committee (HRC).[32] This is made up of eighteen people, 'of high moral character and recognized competence in the field of human rights',[33] elected by representatives of the states parties, from a list of people nominated by the states parties,[34] for a period of four years.[35]The Committee may not include more than one national of the same state.[36] Those elected serve in their personal capacity, not as representatives of their states.[37] The HRC makes an annual report on its activities to the UN General Assembly,[38] and although it is not formally accountable to it, being established under a separate Covenant, the HRC is dependent on the UN for its secretariat and resources.[39] It has three main functions.

(i) *Studying reports from states parties.* The HRC studies reports received from states parties, under Article 40(1), on the measures which the states parties have taken to give effect to the rights recognized in ICCPR and the progress made in the enjoyment of those rights. These reports are to be submitted by a state party within one year of the time when the Covenant enters into force for that state party, and thereafter when the HRC requests. In practice, the reports are often late and sometimes not very informative; states parties tend to paint a bland, rosy picture, rather than highlighting difficulties which they may be facing. The HRC therefore interviews the representative of the State Party concerned, and sometimes requests a supplementary report in order to illuminate matters of concern. The HRC then has to transmit its reports, and such comments as it considers appropriate, to the State Parties, and may also transmit them to ECOSOC.[40] The HRC has taken a robust view of its functions, using evidence derived from sources other than the often anodyne reports received from states parties, and making searching evaluations and suggestions. This monitoring function is intended to be constructive, and to assist the states parties in what is assumed to be their endeavour to improve respect for human rights in their jurisdictions.

It has certainly proved possible to exert some moral pressure through this reporting procedure, establishing dialogue with states and conducting it in a probing and not uncritical manner, without allowing meetings to become unduly confrontational. However, the success of this process

---

[32] McGoldrick, *Human Rights Committee*, provides a comprehensive account of HRC and its work, to which the following brief sketch is deeply indebted.
[33] ICCPR, Art. 28(1), (2).   [34] Ibid., Art. 29(1).   [35] Ibid., Art. 32.
[36] Ibid, Art. 31(1).   [37] Ibid., Art. 28(3).   [38] Ibid., Art. 45.
[39] McGoldrick, *Human Rights Committee*, 52–3, 97–8.   [40] ICCPR, Art. 40(4).

depends heavily on the willingness of states to participate in it. In practice, there is generally a reasonable level of co-operation. This makes it possible for Dr McGoldrick to conclude that, despite some deficiencies, 'the reporting procedure has been developed into a much more useful procedure of international implementation (in the broad sense) than might confidently have been predicted when the Covenant was adopted in 1966'.[41]

(ii) *Receiving communications from states parties.* The second function of the HRC is to receive communications under Article 41 to the effect that a state party is not fulfilling its obligations under ICCPR. Such communications can be considered only if both the tate party making the allegation, and the state party against whom it is made, have made declarations recognizing the competence of the HRC to receive and consider them. In addition, the HRC must normally have ascertained that all available domestic remedies have been exhausted, unless the application of the remedies is unreasonably prolonged. The HRC may then make available its good offices to try to achieve a friendly solution. If this fails, the HRC will prepare a report on the facts and submissions of the states parties, and may, with the prior consent of the states parties concerned, appoint an *ad hoc* Conciliation Commission, which attempts to achieve a friendly solution in accordance with respect for human rights. If this proves impossible, the Conciliation Commission will report to HRC, setting out its findings on relevant facts and its views on the possibility of an amicable solution,[42] and the HRC will include its account of the matter in its next annual report, which is considered by the Third Committee of the General Assembly. At that point, the available procedures run out. It is a long drawn out, cumbersome procedure, and holds out little prospect of success. It seems, therefore, unsurprising that this procedure has not, so far, been invoked.[43]

(iii) *Receiving communications from individuals.* The third function of the HRC arises under the Optional Protocol to ICCPR. Any State Party which signs the Optional Protocol recognizes the competence of the HRC to receive and consider communications from any individual who is subject to the jurisdiction of the state party and who claims to be a victim of violation by that state party of any of the rights set forth in ICCPR.[44] Communications which are anonymous, or which the HRC

---

[41] McGoldrick, *Human Rights Committee*, 102.   [42] ICCPR, Art. 42.

[43] McGoldrick, *Human Rights Committee*, 50.

[44] Optional Protocol, Art. 1. Communications may be submitted by an individual on behalf of another who is prevented by the state in question from communicating directly, and the HRC may then require the state to permit the victim to communicate directly

considers to be an abuse of the right to submit communications or to be incompatible with the Covenant, are inadmissible.[45] Before considering an admissible communication, the HRC must ascertain that the matter is not being considered under any other procedure of international investigation or settlement, and that the individual has exhausted available domestic remedies (unless the application of those remedies is unreasonably prolonged).[46] The state party concerned has six months to submit written explanations or statements clarifying the matter and setting out any remedial action which the state may have taken.[47] The HRC considers the matter at closed meetings, and then forwards its views to the individual and the state concerned.[48]

The HRC has developed a substantial case-load under the Optional Protocol, and has taken a robust approach to states which try to avoid co-operating with its deliberations.[49] For example, if a state merely offers a blanket denial of the individual's claim, without any detailed rebuttal of the facts alleged in the communication, the HRC has treated the unsupported denial as insufficient to counter the allegations, and has taken the view that the individual's claim is made out.[50] When that view is reached, and is notified to the individual and state concerned, the HRC has more or less exhausted its powers. Its effectiveness depends on the willingness of the state to comply, or on the publicity (at present very weak) which it can muster for its view in order to bring pressure to bear on the state. While the state concerned sometimes takes action to rectify any deficiency which the HRC identifies, the record on co-operation and compliance with HRC's considerations is patchy, and a majority of states parties to the Covenant (including the U.K.) have not signed the Optional Protocol. The summary which is included in the HRC's annual report to the General Assembly,[51] and consideration by the Third Committee of the General Assembly, does not unduly worry states unless they have unusually thin skins in relation to their international reputations. In Dr McGoldrick's balanced assessment of the Optional Protocol, its significance lies, first, in the effect which it may have over a period of

with the HRC. On this, and the refusal to extend *locus standi* to organizations, see McGoldrick, *Human Rights Committee*, 132–4, 169–77.

[45] Optional Protocol, Art. 3.   [46] Ibid., Art. 5.   [47] Ibid., Art. 4.
[48] Ibid., Art. 5(3), (4).
[49] Two excellent selections of decisions are published as: Human Rights Committee, *Selected Decisions Under the Optional Protocol (Second to Sixteenth Sessions* (New York: UN, 1985); *Selected Decisions of the Human Rights Committee Under the Optional Protocol*, ii. *Seventeenth to Thirty-second Sessions* (New York: UN, 1990).
[50] See e.g. *J. L. Massera and Others* v. *Uruguay* Annual Report of the HRC, 1979, UN Doc. A/34/40, p. 124; Human Rights Committee, *Selected Decisions under the Optional Protocol*, i. p. 40; McGoldrick, *Human Rights Committee*, 147–9.
[51] Optional Protocol, Art. 6.

decades in encouraging progress in the international protection of human rights, and, secondly, in the enhanced status which it (like Article 25 of the European Convention on Human Rights) gives to individuals in international law; but 'it is of little comfort to victims of human rights violations'.[52]

2.3 INTERNATIONAL LAW: THE EUROPEAN CONVENTION ON HUMAN RIGHTS

(1) Background

In the United Kingdom we are fortunate to be the beneficiaries of the dedicated work of those who drafted the European Convention on Human Rights in the late 1940s under the aegis of the Council of Europe.[53] The Convention was signed by the states parties in 1950, and entered into force in 1953. It was the first international human rights instrument to provide means for its own interpretation and enforcement: it established a Commission to receive and examine complaints about infringements of rights by the states parties, and a Court to adjudicate finally on complaints in the light of its authoritative interpretation of the Convention, and it also gave the Committee of Ministers of the Council of Europe both an adjudicative role and a monitoring role in relation to compliance by states. Still more importantly, Article 25 of the Convention enabled any state party to recognise the jurisdiction of the Commission to examine petitions from victims (including individuals or organizations) of breaches of the Convention by that state. This was unusual, in that only sovereign states normally have standing in international law, but it is an important provision for those people who do not have another state taking an interest in their rights, and has been copied in other instruments (such as the International Covenant on Civil and Political Rights, as explained above).

On 14 January 1966, the UK made a declaration under Article 25 recognising the right of individual petition in respect of events occurring after that time. The declaration was originally made for a period of only five years, but has so far been renewed every five years, save that petitions relating to the Isle of Man have been excluded since 1976 (following Manx concerns at the petition in *Tyrer*, a case concerning judicial

---

[52] McGoldrick, *Human Rights Committee*, 204.

[53] For general background, see Robertson and Merrills, *Human Rights in the World*, 102–5. For a more detailed account, see A. H. Robertson, *Human Rights in Europe*, 2nd edn. (Manchester: Manchester University Press, 1977), 1–21.

birching in the Isle of Man).[54] In 1981, the declaration gave the Commission jurisdiction to receive individual petitions concerning violations in the UK's remaining overseas territories, other than Hong Kong.

(2) Procedure

The procedure is as follows.[55] Any High Contracting Party, or (where the right of individual petition is operative) a person who claims to be a victim of an infringement of the Convention, may address a petition to the Secretary-General of the Council of Europe, who forwards it to the Commission. Before the Commission can examine a petition, several requirements must be satisfied. First, the petitioner must have exhausted his domestic remedies. Secondly, the petition must be presented within six months of the date of the final decision in the domestic forum.[56] Thirdly, the petition must not be anonymous. Fourthly, it must raise a matter which is not substantially the same as one which has already been examined by the Commission or submitted to another procedure of international investigation or settlement, unless the new petition contains relevant new information.[57] Finally, the Commission must reject any petition which it considers incompatible with the provisions of the Convention, an abuse of the right of petition, or manifestly ill-founded.[58]

If the Commission decides a petition is admissible, it ascertains the facts. The states concerned exchange their views on the petition with the Commission, and are bound to furnish all necessary facilities for the purpose of establishing the facts. The Commission then makes itself available to the parties with a view to securing a friendly settlement 'on the basis of respect for human rights as defined in this Convention'.[59] If this is successful, the Commission reports to the states concerned, the Committee

[54] The case reached the European Court of Human Rights: *Tyrer* v. *UK* Eur. Ct. HR, Series A, No. 26, Judgment of 25 Apr. 1978. This case is discussed further in Ch. 4 below. Because individual petitions concerning the Isle of Man are now excluded, it will not be possible (for example) for any individual to challenge the continued criminalization there of homosexual acts between consenting adults. *Cp. Dudgeon* v. *UK* Eur. Ct. HR, Series A, No. 45, Judgment of 22 October 1981.

[55] Robertson and Merrills, *Human Rights in the World*, ch. 4; P. Van Dijk and G. J. H. Van Hoof, *Theory and Practice of the European Convention on Human Rights*, 2nd edn. (Deventer: Kluwer, 1990) chs. 2, 3, and 4; J. E. S. Fawcett, *The Application of the European Convention on Human Rights*, 2nd edn. (Oxford: Clarendon Press, 1987), 340–95.

[56] European Convention on Human Rights, Articles 26, 27(3).

[57] ECHR, Arts. 27(1), 29.

[58] ECHR, Arts. 27(2), 29. An initial decision that a petition is inadmissible may be made by a bare majority of the Commission (Art. 34); but any subsequent decision to reject the petition on the basis of one of the grounds in Art. 27 must be unanimous (Art. 29). On the principles applied, see Fawcett, *Application of ECHR*, 367–73.

[59] ECHR, Art. 28.

of Ministers, and the Secretary-General of the Council of Europe, giving a brief statement of facts and of the solution agreed. This report is published. It is then for the States concerned to take any steps agreed in the friendly settlement. For example,[60] Ms Harriet Harman applied to the Commission after being held liable in the English courts to penalties for contempt of court, because she had revealed to a journalist confidential material supplied by the Home Office on discovery, despite the fact that the material had virtually all been read or referred to in open court. The Commission's good offices resulted in a friendly settlement under which the UK Government agreed (*inter alia*) to pay Ms Harman's costs and to introduce a new rule into the Rules of the Supreme Court to make it clear that revealing material in such circumstances is not necessarily a contempt.[61] This is considered further in Chapter 16, section 2(2) below.

If, however, it proves impossible to reach a friendly settlement, the Commission sends a private report to the Committee of Ministers (consisting of the Foreign Ministers of the High Contracting Parties) and the states concerned. This report deals with the facts, expresses an opinion (which is not legally binding) as to whether the facts found disclose a breach by the state concerned of its obligations under the Convention, and may make proposals for the disposition of the matter.[62] The matter can, within a period of three months, then[63] be referred to the Court by the Commission, or by the High Contracting Party which referred the matter to the Commission, the one whose national is alleged to be a victim, or that against which the complaint is made, so long as the High Contracting Parties concerned are either subject to the compulsory jurisdiction of the Court or accept the jurisdiction of the Court for the purpose of the particular proceedings. The victim of the alleged violation has no power to refer the matter to the Court, nor has he *locus standi* before the Court, although the Court usually permits applicants to express views through the Commission or to assist the Commission, or to be separately represented as *amici curiae*.[64] However, when Article 5 of the Ninth Protocol comes into force, it will amend the Convention to give com-

---

[60] This application followed the decision in *Home Office* v. *Harman* [1983] 1 AC 280, [1982] 1 All ER 532, HL.

[61] RSC Ord. 24, r. 14A. On the effect of the rule as interpreted by the English courts, see *Bibby Bulk Carriers Ltd*. v. *Cansulex Ltd., The Cambridgeshire* [1989] QB 155, [1988] 2 All ER 820.

[62] ECHR, Art. 31.   [63] ECHR, Art. 47.

[64] ECHR, Art. 48. The Court's Rules give applicants a right to present argument or to be represented: see van Dijk and van Hoof, *Theory and Practice*, p. 170; Alastair R. Mowbray, 'Procedural Developments and the European Convention on Human Rights' [1991] *PL* 353–61. Neither the Court nor the Commission has power to order interim measures to protect the position of applicants pending a final decision: *Cruz Varas* v. *Sweden* Eur. Ct. HR, Series A, No. 201, Judgment of 20 Mar. 1991, 14 EHRR 1.

plainants the right to refer a case to court. If the Court decides that there has been an infringement of the applicant's rights, it has power to order the state concerned to make 'just satisfaction',[65] which may include an equitable sum in relation to the applicant's costs.

If the question is not referred to the Court within three months, the Committee of Ministers decides, by a majority of two-thirds of the members entitled to sit on the Committee, whether there has been a violation of the Convention. If they decide that there has, the Committee decides what measures the state concerned must take, and sets a time-limit for the implementation of the measures. If the state does not take satisfactory measures within the stipulated period, the Committee decides (again by a two-thirds majority) what effect shall be given to its original decision, and publishes the report from the Commission. (A projected Tenth Protocol would, if and when it comes into force, substitute simple majorities for the two-thirds majority requirements.) These decisions of the Committee of Ministers bind the High Contracting Parties concerned.[66]

The effect of a decision of the Court or the Committee of Ministers holding that a High Contracting Party has violated the Convention is to impose an obligation on the Party in international law to amend its domestic law to bring it into line with the Convention, to compensate the victim if ordered to do so, and to take such other steps as may be required of it by the Court or Committee. The process is therefore doubly valuable: it may well secure 'just satisfaction' for a victim where domestic law has failed to provide an adequate remedy, and lead to a change in that law so that other people do not in future have their rights under the Convention violated.

2.4 APPROACHES TO PROTECTING RIGHTS IN DOMESTIC LAW

(1) Background: ordinary and fundamental rights

In many legal and constitutional systems, although not in the UK, it is possible to distinguish between two kinds of rights. *Ordinary* rights are those which are believed in a particular society at a particular time to embody an appropriate normative balance between citizens and the state, but are considered to be properly subject to the political processes, liable

---

[65] ECHR, Art. 50. On the principles governing the award, see van Dijk and van Hoof, *Theory and Practice*, 171–85; Jeremy McBride, 'Redress for Human Rights Violations', in Geoffrey Hand and Jeremy McBride (eds.), *Droit sans Frontières: Essays in Honour of L. Neville Brown* (Birmingham: Holdsworth Club, 1991), 161–74.

[66] ECHR, Art. 32.

at any time to change or extinction. *Fundamental rights are those which are thought to be particularly important, for instrumental or symbolic reasons*, and which are therefore properly given some measure of protection against the operation of the political process.

The methods of protecting fundamental rights will be different from the methods used to protect ordinary rights. This is largely because of the different people or bodies against which ordinary and fundamental rights have to be protected. An ordinary right will require protection against citizens, and against unauthorized state interference, but by definition will not attract any coercive protection against legislative amendment or abrogation. A fundamental right, by contrast, may or may not be protected against infringement by citizens (some constitutional rights can often be asserted only against state agencies, reflecting the Lockean social-contract theory on which such constitutions are frequently based), but will enjoy a measure of protection against any state interference, including restriction or repeal of the right by the legislature through normal political processes. The methods of protecting a right must therefore reflect the understanding of the community, or of the dominant grouping within it, as to the status of the right. As noted above, some states do not distinguish in their constitutions between fundamental and ordinary rights, and the UK is one of this dwindling number. In the UK, the basic methods used to safeguard people against infringements of all rights are essentially the same. But in states where a distinction is made between different types of rights, fundamental rights are likely to be safeguarded against legislative infringement.

The first necessary step will always be to encapsulate the right in an authoritative rule, or norm. Without such a rule, considered to be in some way binding, the right will be at best an expectation and at worst merely an aspiration. The norm may be part of the law of the state, perhaps contained within the Constitution, or may be part of public international law. The next step will be to decide on the appropriate method of applying the rule, which may depend on whom it is thought to bind, and how. This is largely determined by the constitutional law and practice of the state. In countries such as the United States or Germany, where the constitutions provide that a duly ratified treaty can have effects in municipal law without the need for further legislation, the courts can grant remedies for breaches of an individual's rights under international law. By contrast, the UK constitution does not automatically incorporate treaty obligations into municipal law,[67] unlike customary international law, which is incorporated in the absence of inconsistent statutory provisions.

However, it would be misleading to suppose that the legal adjudication

---

[67] *Rustomjee* v. *R.* (1876) 2 QBD 69.

on and enforcement of rights is the only, or even the most valuable, system for advancing respect for rights and preventing infringements.
Judicial techniques are at their most effective when providing a remedy
for infringements which have already occurred, although by clarifying the
law and proclaiming the impropriety of certain conduct the courts may
well incidentally reinforce respect for rights and prevent future infringements. We must remember that other methods are available for protecting rights.

International diplomacy and *law* are the only courses available where the
aggrieved individual lacks standing to enforce a right conferred by international law. The right must then be taken up by another state on behalf
of the individuals affected, as occurred when the Republic of Ireland took
action against the United Kingdom under the European Convention on
Human Rights in respect of the treatment meted out to suspected terrorists by the British army in Ulster.[68] In that case, a legal procedure was
available because both states were parties to the Convention; this remains
the only inter-state case so far to have been decided by the European
Court of Human Rights. Where the states are not party to an international instrument, the resolution will depend on pure diplomacy and
international pressure. In Europe, a non-judicial forum for such diplomacy and pressure was established under the Helsinki Final Act (1975), in
the shape of the Conference on Security and Co-operation in Europe
(CSCE).[69]

Municipal judicial protection may provide a remedy where the right is
enshrined in municipal law and is regarded as being justiciable or remedi-
able by courts. In relation to ordinary rights, the judicial enforcement
will not be available to restrain legislative enactments or constitutional
amendments which threaten the rights. However, where there are constitutionally protected rights, these may be judicially enforceable in a way
which leads to substantive legal restrictions on the power of the legislature, with judicial review of the constitutionality of legislation. This is
commonplace in many countries.

Where there are express constitutional limitations on the powers of a

[68] *Ireland* v. *UK* Eur. Ct. HR Series A, No. 25, Judgment of 18 Jan. 1978.

[69] For the text of part VII of the Final Act, which is a declaration of intent on the part
of the participating states to respect 'human rights and fundamental freedoms, including
the freedom of thought, conscience, religion or belief, for all without distinction as to
race, sex, language or religion', see Brownlie (ed.), *Basic Documents*, 395–6. For brief
commentary, see Robertson and Merrills, *Human Rights in the World,* 148–56. See also s.
II.2 above. A very good selection of materials on subsequent developments in the
Helsinki process, with a valuable introduction, is provided by Arie Bloed (ed.), *From
Helsinki to Vienna: Basic Documents of the Helsinki Process* (Dordrecht: Martinus Nijhoff,
1990).

legislature, courts in the USA,[70] Australia,[71] and elsewhere, have concluded that the doctrines of the separation of powers and the rule of law require them to act as the final arbiters of the constitutionality of legislation. It is not normally considered necessary for the constitution to have made express provision for judicial remedies in such cases, although sometimes (as for Canada under the Constitution Act 1982, section 24) a constitution will do so. In the United Kingdom, a power of judicial review of primary parliamentary legislation has been thrust on our judges by the demands of European Community law, which, when directly effective and (in the case of regulations) directly applicable, has primacy over inconsistent municipal law, including Acts of Parliament.[72]

This review role is controversial under constitutions like those of the UK, the USA, and Australia, which (unlike that of Canada) do not expressly provide for judicial review of legislation, or lay down limits to it, because it gives courts the capacity to frustrate even a democratically approved legislative programme. But in countries where judicial review is a well-entrenched part of the constitutional heritage, such as the USA, most of the controversy concerns the principles of constitutional interpretation which should guide the exercise of the review power, rather than the existence of the power.[73]

Even when acting within any formal limits on legislative power, the legislature may find that the law offers a measure of special protection to some rights. Under classical Westminster constitutions, with legislatures which, within their limits, are said to be sovereign (in the Diceyan sense of all-powerful), the common law may impose some restrictions on what Parliament can do, or on the methods which must be adopted to produce particular results. There are two ways of achieving this. One is to develop presumptions which will apply when interpreting statutes, allowing judges to resolve any ambiguities in statutes in such a way as to minimise the impact of the statute on any principles or rights which they regard as particularly important elements of the common law. This is a relatively weak protection for special rights, as it can be overridden by express words or necessary implication.

The other approach is more direct, and represents an explicit common-law limitation on legislative power. Here, judges identify certain

[70] *Marbury* v. *Madison* 1 Cranch. 137 (1803).

[71] Geoffrey Lindell, 'Duty to Exercise Review', in Leslie Zines (ed.), *Commentaries on the Australian Constitution* (Sydney: Butterworths, 1977), 150–90; Brian Galligan, *The Politics of the High Court* (St. Lucia, Qld: Univ. of Queensland Press, 1987), ch. 2.

[72] Case C-213/89, *Factortame Ltd.* v. *Secretary of State for Transport (No. 2)* [1991] 1 All ER 70, CJEC and HL.

[73] See the discussion of methods of interpretation on review in Philip Bobbitt, *Constitutional Fate: Theory of the Constitution* (New York: Oxford University Press, 1982); Philip Bobbitt, *Constitutional Interpretation* (Oxford: Basil Blackwell, 1991).

standards as fundamental to the historical common law, and deny that Parliament has the power to abrogate them. This is an approach which has been suggested by Sir Robin Cooke, the President of the Court of Appeal in New Zealand, as a possible corrective to a constitution which appears on its face to place vast legislative power in a Parliament dominated by an executive over which there are few, if any, effective checks between elections.[74]

This is not as radical as it sounds. As Mr. T. R. S. Allan has pointed out, in the UK the judges exercise some control over what Parliament can legislate for effectively, through the way in which they interpret legislation. A number of presumptions operate in the absence of evidence of a contrary legislative intent. These include the presumption that legislation is not intended to be retroactive, is not intended to interfere with vested property rights, and (most significantly for administrative law) is not intended to oust the jurisdiction of the courts.[75] These presumptions protect some of the rights of which Sir Robin Cooke was speaking, although he also included the right to a fair hearing before an unbiased tribunal and the right to be free of torture (very much the sorts of rights protected under the main human rights instruments in international law, and which, if part of customary international law, would be automatically incorporated into domestic law in the absence of inconsistent domestic provisions).

But these presumptions are not always sufficiently weighty to protect rights, as recent UK decisions allowing a retrospective operation to certain social security legislation show.[76] The presumptions are not in themselves common-law rights. Rather, they give limited protection to people's legitimate expectations. If the courts are to be active in creating a set of common-law fundamental rights, capable of restricting the effect of legislation, they will have to do it directly, by finding guarantees of rights embedded immovably in the common-law system.[77] It would not

---

[74] *New Zealand Drivers' Association* v. *New Zealand Road Carriers* [1982] 1 NZLR 374 at p. 390; *Fraser* v. *State Services Commission* [1984] 1 NZLR 116 at p. 121; *Taylor* v. *New Zealand Poultry Board* [1984] 1 NZLR 394 at p. 398. See J. Caldwell, 'Judicial Sovereignty: A New View' [1984] *NZULJ* 357–9; Philip A. Joseph, 'Beyond Parliamentary sovereignty' (1989) 18 *Anglo-Amer. LR.* 91–123.

[75] *Anisminic Ltd.* v. *Foreign Compensation Commission* [1969] 2 AC 147, HL. See T. R. S. Allan, 'Legislative Supremacy and the Rule of Law: Democracy and Constitutionalism' [1985] *CLJ* 111–43; T. R. S. Allan, 'Constitutional Rights and Common Law' (1991) 11 *Oxf. J. Legal Studies* 453–80.

[76] *R.* v. *Secretary of State for Social Security, ex parte Britnell* [1991] 1 WLR 198, HL; *Secretary of State for Social Security v. Tunnicliffe* [1991] 2 All ER 712, CA.

[77] This is, in effect, what Coke CJ did, *obiter*, in *Dr. Bonham's case* (1610) 8 Co. Rep. 114 at p. 118, suggesting that a statute making someone a judge in his own cause would be void. However, as Stanley de Smith and Rodney Brazier, *Constitutional and Administrative Law*, 6th edn. (Harmondsworth: Penguin, 1989) observe at p. 71 n. 34, in

be easy to justify such a move in a democracy, but it might be done, and the scope of the rights might be usefully delimited, if the judges concentrated on enforcing only those rights which are essential to a democratic society. Such a limited set of common law fundamental rights has recently been embraced by the High Court of Australia in *Australian Capital Television Pty Ltd. v. The Commonwealth*, enabling the Court to strike down parliamentary legislation which had attempted to restrict political advertising before elections and referendums.[78] It would derive support from those theories of judicial review which see review as legitimate if directed to securing and enforcing the conditions for democratic politics as carried on in the society in question, although these theories are not uncontroversial and may not be easily transplanted from the context of the U.S. Constitution in which they were grown.[79]

The idea of the special constitutional status of the common law was central to the permeating influence of English common law abroad. In the days of the British Empire, the English common law was carried round the world on shipboard, and colonial legislatures, which were in this respect (and in others) legally inferior to the Westminster Parliament, were initially unable to amend it save in so far as it was inappropriate to local conditions. Even when freed from that fetter, the colonial judges often presumed, as a principle of statutory interpretation, that their local legislatures did not intend to change the common law as received into the colony. This made it necessary, ultimately, for the Westminster Parliament to make it clear that the local legislatures had power to modify the common law, by passing the Colonial Laws Validity Act 1865. In more recent times, the Privy Council, on appeal from common-law jurisdictions, has treated some common-law rights as fundamental, and still sometimes seems to apply what has been called an 'Imperial common law' which limits the scope for common-law variations between jurisdictions and partially protects certain fundamental common-law rights (i.e.

his *Institutes*, book 4, p. 32, Coke seems to accept the absolute sovereignty of Parliament. See further J. W. Gough, *Fundamental Law in English Constitutional History* (Oxford: Clarendon Press, 1955), ch. 3.

[78] (1992) 66 ALJR 695, HC of Australia.

[79] See John Hart Ely, *Democracy and Distrust: A Theory of Judicial Review* (Cambridge, Mass.: Harvard University Press, 1980); David Feldman, 'Democracy, the Rule of Law and Judicial Review' (1990) 19 *Federal LR* 1–30. For critiques of the approach, see e.g. D. J. Galligan, 'Judicial Review and Democratic Principles: Two Theories' (1983) 57 *ALJ* 69–79; Ronald Dworkin, *A Matter of Principle* (Oxford: Clarendon Press, 1986), 57–69; Laurence H. Tribe, *Constitutional Choices* (Cambridge, Mass.: Harvard University Press, 1985), 3–20; Mark Tushnet, *Red, White, and Blue: A Critical Analysis of Constitutional Law* (Cambridge, Mass.: Harvard University Press, 1988); P. P. Craig, *Public Law and Democracy in the United Kingdom and the United States of America* (Oxford: Clarendon Press, 1990), 106–13.

those rights which are fundamental to the common law, rather than fundamental to the people subject to it).[80] The need for courts to adopt this sort of approach in the UK may increase if resistance to a domestic Bill of Rights is not overcome.

Regulatory or *administrative protection* may be offered to some rights. Special bodies may be set up to monitor compliance with right-conferring rules, with powers to make recommendations and reports to Parliament (e.g. the Parliamentary Commissioner for Administration, who investigates a range of complaints of injustice caused by maladministration forwarded by MPs),[81] or to make efforts to secure settlement of disputes or initiate or support legal action in support of rights (e.g. the Commission for Racial Equality and the Equal Opportunities Commission in the UK, or the Human Rights and Equal Opportunities Commission in Australia).[82] This is particularly likely to be applied to service provision, most typically the subject of economic and social rights, and is often a convenient and effective way of encouraging compliance. However, as a way of enforcing rights it suffers from potential weaknesses. The emphasis placed by some (though not all) regulators on accommodation and friendly settlement may lead to rights being compromised rather than just satisfaction being secured for breaches.[83] Indeed, the fact that the rights have been put in the care of a regulator rather than a court may lead courts to regard those rights as less important than others, and treat the regulator as if it was an emanation of the state interfering with rights rather than as a protector. Some commentators feel that this has been the fate of the Commission for Racial Equality in the UK.[84]

Regulators face a further difficulty in that they are required to play a dual role: they must try to change attitudes in the long term, as well as provide short-term remedies for individual victims of unlawfulness. In such an enterprise, adopting a confrontational attitude may be counterproductive. Regulators have to continue to work with offenders, and there are well-documented tendencies to identify with their problems to the point where the agency ceases to be effective as a regulator.

[80] J. W. Harris, 'Privy Council and Common Law' (1990) 106 *LQR* 574–600.

[81] On the work of the PCA, see Richard Rawlings, 'The MP's Complaints Service' (1990) 53 *MLR* 22–42, 249–69; Gavin Drewry and Carol Harlow, 'A "Cutting Edge"? The Parliamentary Commissioner and MPs' (1990) 53 *MLR* 745–69. The PCA deals with complaints against central government departments. A parallel body, the Commission for Local Administration, deals with local government, but has no direct access to Parliament.

[82] On the latter, see Bailey, *Human Rights: Australia*106–246.

[83] Bridget M. Hutter, *The Reasonable Arm of the Law: The Law Enforcement Procedures of Environmental Health Officers* (Oxford: Clarendon Press, 1988).

[84] Robert Baldwin and Christopher McCrudden, *Regulation and Public Law* (London: Weidenfeld & Nicolson, 1987), chs. 4 and 11.

Nevertheless, in the UK at the time of writing (1993) the government of Mr John Major is relying increasingly heavily on finding ways to protect rights to public provision which do not depend on law, and which rely only peripherally on regulation. This is clear in the flagship of the government's programme for protection of inhabitants of the UK, the *Citizen's Charter*.[85] The emphasis is on securing standards of performance by monitoring and regulation, and wherever possible relieving people of the need to depend on the state. This is to be done by encouraging them to seek private landlords, privatizing public services such as refuse collection and delivery of elctricity and other main services, and relying on the market and commercial pressures to keep providers up to scratch. This has been described as a move from allowing people a voice in public services to facilitating their exit from reliance on public services; accordingly, it denies people legal rights in the services in question. Instead, it offers choice between potential service providers: doctors, schools, landlords. This right to choose is intended to keep providers responsive, because their incomes will depend on their performance; dissatisfied customers will move elsewhere.

It remains to be seen how effectively this approach will protect rights. The market will not operate properly unless people have enforceable rights and know how to enforce them. It does not provide rights. This is implicitly recognized in the *Charter*, which accepts that regulation is needed where the providers of services enjoy a substantial monopoly, as is the case in relation to gas, electricity, and water services within a region. Here the right to choose is an inadequate protection for service quality, because there is no competing provider for a person to turn to if dissatisfied with the current one. If, as seems possible, the range of competitors is reduced in a recession, market forces will tend to produce monopolies or oligopolies in a range of services. Rights which are entirely dependent on market forces are, at best, very weak rights. The *Citizen's Charter* approach to rights is a long way from conferring rights in economic and social programmes, or creating what Charles Reich called 'the new property'[86] from rights to public assets and public support.

Informal government action may be successful in persuading people or bodies in a client relationship to government to observe rights. For example, government agencies can make it a condition of placing orders for goods or services with particular firms that they should meet criteria, set by government, for the proportion of employees who are to be women or members of ethnic minorities. This method of advancing the rights of under-privileged citizens, known as 'contract compliance', has

---

[85] Cm. 1599 (London: HMSO, 1991).
[86] Charles Reich, 'The New Property' 73 *Yale LJ* 733–87 (1964).

been more widely used in the USA than in the UK, although it was less favoured by George Bush's Republican administration than by those of some former Democratic presidents, notably President Jimmy Carter.[87] It depends heavily on the commitment of government to particular rights, and is sensitive to changes of political direction, as it involves a conscious exercise of the economic muscle of government (that which Daintith has called the *dominium* as opposed to the *imperium* power of the state).[88]

Legislative techniques place the responsibility for protecting rights squarely on the legislature itself. There are various self-policing steps which a parliament can take to try to ensure that it does not infringe rights, or does not do so without due consideration. One is to have a standing committee which scrutinises all legislation to check for human rights or civil liberties implications. In the Australian Commonwealth Parliament, the Senate Scrutiny of bills Committee performs this function in relation to Bills, and the Senate Regulations and Ordinances Committee deals with subordinate legislation which has to be laid before Parliament. Both committees are advised by independent legal advisers of acknowledged independence and expertise (so far they have been academic lawyers of high repute), and have small dedicated secretariats staffed by parliamentary public servants. They seek explanations for any apparent breaches of rights from the department responsible for the legislation, and if an explanation is not forthcoming or is unsatisfactory the committees report to that effect to the Senate. The Regulations and Ordinances Committee can also move for disallowance of subordinate legislation. The committees are heavily dependent on the goodwill and respect of both the Senate and the government. The Regulations and Ordinances Committee has succeeded in achieving a remarkable success rate in inducing drafting changes, helped by operating in a multi-party Senate in which the government often does not command a majority. The Scrutiny of Bills Committee is still relatively inexperienced, having been set up only in 1981. Both committees work on a cross-party basis, avoiding controversy by reviewing only on grounds on which there is consensus and avoiding any discussion of the policy objectives of the legislation.

Another model is the New Zealand Parliament's Select Committee on Legislation. This subjects each Bill to a public hearing at which objections on human rights grounds can be voiced, and reports back to the Parliament. The effectiveness of this committee depends even more than the Australian Senate committees on the goodwill of the government,

---

[87] For an excellent review, see P. E. Morris, 'Legal Regulation of Contract Compliance: An Anglo-American Comparison' (1990) 19 *Anglo-Amer. LR* 87–144.

[88] Terence Daintith, 'The Executive Power Today: Bargaining and Economic Control', in Jeffrey Jowell and Dawn Oliver, *The Changing Constitution*, 2nd edn. (Oxford: Clarendon Press, 1989), 193–218.

which normally has a clear majority in New Zealand's unicameral assembly and exercises tight party control. The role of all these committees is deliberative rather than adjudicative; that is to say, they have no power to disallow legislation, but can only report to the full legislative body which may decide to allow legislation to proceed despite a committee's reservations.

A third approach merges legislative and adjudicative techniques. It allows a special tribunal to adjudicate authoritatively on the constitutionality of legislation during its parliamentary passage. In France, for instance, Article 61 of the Constitution of the Fifth Republic makes provision for a special body to do this. The ordinary courts in France, including the *tribunaux administratives* headed by the *Conseil d'État*, do not have authority to declare primary legislation in the form of *lois* to be unconstitutional.[89] However, if in the course of the deliberations on a proposed measure in the National Assembly sixty deputies or sixty senators insist on it, the measure is referred to the *Conseil Constitutionnel*, a court of nine members who are appointed, three each, by the President of the Republic, the President of the Senate, and the President of the National Assembly, for a period of nine years. This body examines the proposed legislation, and decides whether it is constitutional and what restrictions are to be imposed on its scope to bring it into line with the written constitution and with certain general principles of law and constitional principles derived from (*inter alia*) the 1789 Declaration of the Rights of Man.[90] The judgment of the *Conseil Constitutionnel* is binding. This is not a judicial review process, because it operates on the proposed *loi* at a formative stage; the members of the *Conseil* need not be lawyers, although their approach to constitutional questions has been influenced by that of the lawyers of the *Conseil d'État* to the constitutionality of subordinate legislation in the form of *ordonnances*. In fact, the process is seen as a stage in the political contest over the legislation; it has been used increasingly by opposition parties to delay or restrict government proposals, and it can offer a useful bargaining counter to the opposition. Nevertheless, the *Conseil* has shown itself to be an independent voice in the legislative process, taking its adjudicative and constitutional role seriously, and has restricted legislative programmes on a number of occa-

---

[89] However, the *Conseil d'État* will disapply under Art. 55 of the Constitution a *loi* which conflicts with treaty obligations, including rights or obligations having direct effect under EC law: see e.g. *Nicolo*, decision of 20 Oct. 1989, noted by Roger Errera [1990] *PL* 134–6, who points out the possible impact on French law of international human rights instruments as a result of the decision; *Palazzi*, decision of 8 July 1991, and the commentary by Roger Errera [1991] *PL* 614–16.

[90] See Alec Stone, 'In the Shadow of the Constitutional Council: The "Juridicisation" of the Legislative Process in France' (1989) 12(2) *West European Politics* 12–34; John Bell, *French Constitutional Law* (Oxford: Clarendon Press, 1992), 29–56.

sions to protect rights.[91]

Finally, *managerial* techniques may be a valuable way of advancing rights within an organization. They allow the organisation to police its own performance, formulating guidance and promulgating it to staff, and setting up mechanisms for monitoring the behaviour of staff through peer review, supervision, and appraisal systems. Sometimes a special office will be set up within an organisation to oversee the process. For example, in the USA, it has been realized that the anti-discrimination provisions of the Civil Rights Act 1964 have not yet resulted in equalizing the opportunities for members of ethnic minorities and women to rise to senior positions in organizations in numbers proportional to their representation in the population as a whole. Some organizations, such as universities, have responded by appointing 'affirmative action officers' to attempt to improve the position. The holders of these imaginative appointments have a necessarily limited scope for action, usually needing to act in an accommodating rather than an authoritarian way, and may be subject to conflicting loyalties where their affirmative action objectives go against the wider business interests of the organization.[92]

2.5 THE UK APPROACH

(1) The political ethos

The approach to protecting rights in the UK traditionally involved a minimum of state activity. The nation has pursued a predominantly liberal political theory, and its constitution is the product of hundreds of years of evolution and tinkering, rather than the result of a turbulent period of revolution which might, as in France and the USA, have concentrated people's minds on thorough and principled constitutional reform. There has been an assumption that this is a free country. In Britain, there was thought to be a minimum of state intervention in people's lives, and any intervention was allowed only after rigorous

[91] Barry Nicholas, 'Fundamental Rights and Judicial Review in France' [1978] *PL* 82–101, 155–77; Burt Neuborne, 'Judicial Review and Separation of Powers in France and the United States', 57 *New York University LR* 363–442, esp. at 377–410; Michael H. Davis, 'The Law/Politics Distinction, the French Conseil Constitutionnel, and the US Supreme Court', 34 *Amer. J. Comparative Law* 45–92 (1986); John Bell, 'Equality in the Caselaw of the *Conseil Constitutionnel*' [1987] PL 426–46; Cynthia Vroom, 'Constitutional Protection of Individual Liberties in France: The *Conseil Constitutionnel* since 1971', 63 *Tulane LR* 265–334 (1988); Tony Prosser, 'Constitutions and Political Economy: The Privatisation of Public Enterprises in France and Great Britain' (1990) 53 *MLR* 304–20.

[92] See R. J. Townshend-Smith, 'The Role of Affirmative Action Officers in North American Universities' (1990) 19 *Anglo-Amer. LR* 325–44.

scrutiny by Parliament, dominated by the representative House of Commons. The remaining freedom was protected by the judges. So far as Parliament and the common law had not taken away our freedom, typically in the interests of protecting either other people's freedoms or the state as a whole, the people remained free to do whatever they wanted to do.

The result is that the British have typically thought in terms, not of liberties or freedoms, but liberty or freedom. That is, the dominant idea has been of an undifferentiated mass of liberty, encroached on only in clearly particularized ways and for specified and democratically justifiable purposes. The people have relied on their electorally accountable MPs to protect their freedom. This has even affected the thinking of British philosophers.[93] By comparison, continental systems for protecting rights are seen as restricting them: some rights are defined and protected, but others are lost in the process. Where is the need for specific rights to be identified and protected, as in the French Declaration of the Rights of Man and the Citizen (1789) or the Declaration of the Rights of Man (1791), or the first ten amendments to the US Constitution (1789–91), when we enjoy a *prima facie* presumption in favour of liberty in all circumstances? Enumerating our freedoms could, on this view, only have the effect of narrowing them.

There are, of course, examples of pieces of legislation which give the appearance of protecting important rights. Magna Carta, the first version of which was agreed between King John and his barons in 1215, and the Bill of Rights 1689, imposed on the monarchy when William, Prince of Orange and his wife Mary were offered the English throne in 1688, have attracted a degree of respect beyond anything which their practical importance merits. Even at the time when they were promulgated, those instruments had little impact on the well-being of the average English subject. They did nothing to turn most subjects into active citizens. All they did was to protect the interests of some subjects (generally the more powerful ones) against a recurrence of former abuse of power by a monarch (in the case of Magna Carta, King John; in the case of the Bill of Rights, King James II) who had ill-advisedly acted in a way which threatened the interests of powerful subjects. The rights were, in reality, limited assertions of the interests of powerful groups.

Over time, others have benefited from the ethos of government produced by Magna Carta and the Bill of Rights. However, to say that they offer effective protection to rights ignores the reality of modern, and perhaps pre-modern, legislation and administration. The doctrine of par-

---

[93] e.g. Professor H. L. A. Hart argued that, if there are any natural rights, the first must be a right to (general and undifferentiated) liberty. See 1.2(3), above.

liamentary supremacy, which Dicey advanced as a way of ensuring coninuing democratic accountability for legislation, left Parliament with the more or less untrammelled power to restrict or abrogate rights and freedoms, as well protect them. Magna Carta and the 1689 Bill of Rights can be repealed or amended by implication by statutes, without even the need for express words. Except in relation to the protection of property against unauthorized taxation,[94] the Bill of Rights has been restrictively interpreted, for example denying a remedy to prisoners under the clause forbidding cruel and unusual punishment unless the punishment could be shown to be both cruel and unusual.[95] Furthermore, the gradual extension of the state in the nineteenth century, through the Factory Acts and other social legislation, and the increasing role of inspectorates and local boards of works, meant that some of the old negative liberties were chipped away in order to secure improved quality of life (economic and social rights) for the worst off groups in society.[96] As the process continued in the twentieth century, the protective function of the courts for negative freedoms was increasingly displaced by new tribunals, which were established to implement new social rights rather than to protect liberties.

This was noted during the 1930s. Some writers, such as Sir Ivor Jennings and W. A. Robson, approved. Others, such as Lord Hewart, then Lord Chief Justice, did not. Once the traditional liberal certainties were called into question, and the assumption that negative freedoms were more important and deserving of respect than social engineering was contested, the nature of the rights which people should have could more easily be debated.[97] In that situation, attention would naturally turn from respect for liberty, protected principally by the good sense of the legislature, to controversy over particular liberties and rights, especially when they were seen to conflict. This new concentration on the nature and scope of individual rights and freedoms, and debate over the best means of protecting them, was undoubtedly further stimulated by the international human rights instruments to which the UK had become a party. However, the movement to agree on and give legal embodiment to some rights for all faced difficulties in the UK. There were three reasons for this.

(i) *The political constitution.* The Constitution has always been predomi-

---

[94] *Congreve* v. *Home Office* [1976] QB 629.

[95] *Williams* v. *Home Office (No. 2)* [1981] 1 All ER 1211, below, ch. 6, s. 3(4).

[96] Derek Fraser, *The Evolution of the British Welfare State*, 2nd edn. (London: Macmillan, 1984), 1–145.

[97] For an account of this process, see Carol Harlow and Richard Rawlings, *Law and Administration* (London: Weidenfeld & Nicolson, 1984), chs. 1 and 2.

nantly political rather than legal. To restrain parliamentary legislation which might interfere unduly with people's rights, the UK has generally been content to rely on the good sense of politicians and the conventions and social proprieties which they are expected to observe. Since the time when Parliament and the common-law courts challenged the Crown's powers of uncontrolled legislation and taxation, Parliament has been seen as a buttress of liberty rather than a threat to it. There seemed little need for limits to be placed on the power of Parliament. Once the process for selecting members of the House of Commons began to be democratized in the nineteenth century, with more or less regular elections allowing members to be held accountable to a substantial proportion of those whom they represented, it seemed reasonable to rely on political rather than legal processes for containing any threat to liberties which might flow from Parliament's vast (according to Dicey, towards the end of the nineteenth century, unlimited) legislative power.

There was, therefore, no call for judicial review of legislation until relatively recently. Now pressure is growing for constitutional change which might restrict the power of Parliament to interfere with rights. This has happened partly because decisions of the European Court of Human Rights have cast doubt on the ability of political controls to protect domestic rights, and partly because of doubts about the capacity of Parliament to restrain the growing power of the executive. These doubts have gone hand in hand with criticisms of the UK's political system, which many people consider to be far less democratic than many others, having developed little since the UK took the first steps towards democracy during the nineteenth century.

(ii) *Public complacency.* The British have displayed a degree of complacency about the extent of their liberties. If there is a presumption in favour of individual liberty, it makes sense to think of citizens as free except to the extent that the freedom has been lawfully abridged by the sensible and politically accountable legislature. In such circumstances little would be gained, and much might be lost, by trying to codify the rights of citizens. The notion of residual liberties is then likely to offer reasonable protection for individual freedoms. However, the presumption in favour of freedom has ceased to restrain governments and Parliament as much as it once did, yet many people have not noticed that their residual liberties may be decreasing.[98] Once this happens, there is an incremental threat to freedom, and more to gain than lose (from the perspective of protecting rights) from codifying those rights which it is thought ought to be protected.

[98] For different views on this, see K. D. Ewing and C. A. Gearty, *Freedom under Thatcher: Civil Liberties in Modern Britain* (Oxford: Clarendon Press, 1990), ch. 1; Michael Zander, *A Bill of Rights?* 3rd edn. (London: Sweet & Maxwell, 1985), 45.

(iii) *Concern about state and judicial intervention.* When the emphasis is on residual individual freedom, there is little scope for state intervention to protect rights. Any intervention is likely to be perceived as a threat to freedom rather than an aid to it. The prevailing ethos then resembles classic economic liberalism: people are to be left as free as possible to pursue the widest possible range of activities as well or badly as they can, and are entitled to take the rewards of their activity. This has tended to exclude certain types of claim from the status of rights. For example, people unable to support themselves were long seen as the concern of charity; only after the Second World War did the state begin to treat such people as having a *right* to support, enabling us to speak of 'welfare rights' and the other rights to commercial and domestic assistance from the state which Charles Reich dubbed 'the new property'. Even now, people are conscious that these rights are not quite as well-rooted in the system as classic liberties. Liberalism also places the burden of enforcing their rights on individuals rather than the state; the courts are at their disposal, but usually only where a person can establish breach of a right in tort (or, occasionally, contract) giving rise to a right to damages.

Slowly, however, the state has begun to recognise new rights as the political ethos has changed to reflect growing concern about the plight of the worst-off groups in society. The structure of the welfare state reflected a belief that problems of poverty, homelessness, ignorance, and sickness were too pervasive and intractable to be left to charity. It was also thought to be wrong that the *value* of freedom to individuals should vary wildly because of their hugely different resources: to paraphrase Anatole France, the freedom to contract for a night's board and lodging at a comfortable hotel is worth nothing to a homeless person without the means to pay for it. Once the idea of an obligation on society to care for its casualties through state assistance gained ground, the state began to create agencies to monitor and enforce the new rights which it was recognising. The right to be free from discrimination on morally irrelevant grounds such as race and sex has been recognised in legislation after English common law proved inadequate to provide a remedy. The right is protected by the Equal Opportunities Commission (sex) and the Commission for Racial Equality (race). A right to housing was recognised, and its provision was made the responsibility of local authorities, as were rights to education (local education authorities, based on county councils) and health care (regional and area health authorities). Some of these matters are discussed in Chapter 18 below.

(2) The impact of Europe

This gradual development of rights-consciousness, as distinct from liberty-consciousness, has been influenced by the UK's closer association with European institutions. Those European nations which came under the influence of the French Declarations of the Rights of Man, etc., during the Napoleonic period have tended to have a closer attachment to human rights than has previously been observable in the UK. The UK's accession to the European Convention on Human Rights was an important step towards increasing the influence of human rights thinking in the UK, although, as Mr. Anthony Lester has shown, the British Government took the step only reluctantly and suspiciously (despite having been closely concerned in the drafting of the Convention),[99] and probably signed the Convention (as Mr. Roger Kerridge has suggested)[100] only because they expected never to be challengeable under it. As it turned out, the UK was to be regularly placed in the position of having to defend itself against charges of infringing rights protected by the Convention, and has often changed domestic law to give effect to decisions of the European Commission and Court of Human Rights.

However, the Convention has no direct effect on English law, because as an international treaty it does not form part of English law unless and to the extent[101] that legislation is passed transforming it from an international convention to English domestic law. Accordingly, a UK citizen aggrieved by an alleged infringement of her human rights will be unable to obtain a remedy from an English or Scottish court for breach of the right unless the wrong also constitutes a tort or breach of contract in municipal private law. If, for example, she alleges an infringement of her right to respect for her private or family life under Article 8 of the

[99] Anthony Lester, 'Fundamental Rights: The United Kingdom Isolated' [1984] PL 46–72.

[100] Roger Kerridge, 'Incorporation of the European Convention on Human Rights into United Kingdom Domestic Law', in M. P. Furmston, R. Kerridge, and B. E. Sufrin (eds.), The Effect on English Domestic Law of Membership of the European Communities and Ratification of the European Convention on Human Rights (The Hague: Martinus Nijhoff, 1983), 247–82.

[101] There may be problems in establishing how far a convention has been adopted by legislation. For example, the Geneva Conventions Act 1957 gave the British courts criminal jurisdiction in respect of 'grave' breaches of the Geneva Conventions of 12 Aug. 1949 on humanitarian protection of people in times of armed conflict. This was all that was required by the Convention. However, the Act included in its Schedules the full texts of all four conventions. It has been suggested that this amounts to recognition in domestic law having the effect of giving the UK courts jurisdiction in respect of all breaches of the Conventions, not only in respect of grave breaches of them: see Françoise Hampson, 'The Geneva Conventions and the Detention of Civilians and Alleged Prisoners of War' [1991] PL 507–22 at pp. 517–19.

European Convention on Human Rights, she will not be able to make use of the domestic courts to seek a remedy unless she can fit the case within an established head of claim under domestic law, even though the Convention has been ratified by the United Kingdom, as a state, and so binds it in international law. The aggrieved citizen must turn to the European Commission of Human Rights to get satisfaction.[102]

This does not mean, however, that the Convention is incapable of playing any part in English law. It may have an impact in three ways. First, when interpreting statutes, the courts are entitled to make use of a presumption that Parliament does not intend to legislate in a way inconsistent with the UK's obligations under international law. The Convention would be admissible only in order to resolve a genuine ambiguity in the statute. Secondly, the courts will have regard to the Convention when developing common law in areas which impinge on freedoms guaranteed by the Convention. This happened in the course of the *Spycatcher* litigation, discussed in Chapter 14 below.

Thirdly, the UK is a member state of the European Communities. In member states, rights having direct effect under Community law can be relied on in domestic courts, which have an obligation to provide adequate remedies for breach. This may include disapplying an otherwise valid statute.[103] Here, the courts' obligation arises by virtue of a supranational, rather than international, legal order, and one which is recognized (in the UK) in the European Communities Act 1972, section 2. In interpreting Community legislation, the European Court of Justice has recognized the European Convention on Human Rights, and the case-law developed by the European Court of Human Rights, as providing the basis for general principles of Community law to which the ECJ, and, presumably, national courts interpreting Community law, must have regard when relevant to a question of Community law. This provides a means whereby the European Convention may have a substantial, though indirect, impact on UK domestic law, in cases concerning Community law having direct effect, without the need for implementing domestic legislation.[104]

---

[102] See e.g. *Malone* v. *Metropolitan Police Commissioner* [1979] Ch. 344, [1979] 2 All ER 620; *Malone* v. *UK* Eur. Ct. HR, Series A, No. 82, Judgment of 2 Aug. 1984, 5 EHRR 385. On the status of the Convention in the states, see A. Z. Drzemczewski, *The European Human Rights Convention in Domestic Law* (Oxford: Clarendon Press, 1982).

[103] See e.g. Case C–213/89, *Factortame Ltd.* v. *Secretary of State for Transport (No. 2)* [1991] 1 All ER 70, CJEC and HL.

[104] C.-D. Ehlermann, 'Accession of the European Community to the European Convention on Human Rights', in Colin Campbell (ed.), *Do We Need a Bill of Rights?* (London: Maurice Temple Smith, 1980), 114–32; Nicholas Grief, 'The Domestic Impact of the European Convention on Human Rights as Mediated Through Community Law' [1991] PL 555–67.

However, the courts have refused to give remedies for breaches of the Convention which are not related to directly effective Community rights and which do not give rise to a cause of action in English law. They will not grant a declaration that there has or has not been an infringement of the Convention.[105] Nor will English courts usually entertain applications for judicial review of administrative actions merely on the ground that they are said to breach the Convention. It does not amount to illegality or unreasonableness for a minister to refuse to consider himself bound by a provision in the Convention.

However, there may be scope for Convention-based reasoning. In *Brind v. Secretary of State for the Home Department*[106] the Secretary of State had issued directives to the IBA and the BBC prohibiting them from broadcasting the sound of statements by representatives of proscribed organisations in Northern Ireland. Journalists challenged the directives, arguing that the directives were *ultra vires*, and that the Home Secretary had acted perversely and disproportionately and had violated the right to freedom of expression under Article 10 of the European Convention on Human Rights. The Court of Appeal held that Parliament, in rejecting several proposals to incorporate the European Convention, had shown that it intended that the Convention should not be used by British judges. (Scottish judges have taken the same view.)[107]

On appeal to the House of Lords, only Lords Ackner and Lowry took the same line as the Court of Appeal, going so far as to hold that it would not be unreasonable for a Home Secretary to refuse even to consider the Convention's requirements. Lord Ackner concluded that requiring the Home Secretary to have proper regard to the Convention 'inevitably would result in incorporating the convention into English law by the back door'.[108] The other Law Lords gave more weight to rights. Lord Bridge, while rejecting the argument that courts should assume that Parliament intended an apparently unfettered discretion to be exercised only in accordance with the Convention, accepted that the Convention might be relevant in reviewing the exercise of such powers so as to prevent infringements of fundamental rights. He concluded that Article 10 required a balancing of interests. The primary duty to strike a balance lay on the Home Secretary, but the courts had a secondary, reviewing, duty to decide whether the balance struck was reasonable. On the facts, it could not be said that the directives had struck a balance unreasonably

---

[105] *Malone v. Metropolitan Police Commissioner* [1979] Ch. 344, [1979] 2 All ER 620.
[106] 1991] 1 All ER 720, HL.
[107] *Kaur v. Lord Advocate* 1981 SLT 322; *Moore v. Secretary of State for Scotland* 1985 SLT 38; J. L. Murdoch, 'The European Convention on Human Rights in Scots Law' [1991] PL 40–51.
[108] [1991] 1 All ER at 734–35 (Lord Ackner), 736 (Lord Lowry).

unfavourable to the right to freedom of expression.[109] Lord Templeman, whose speech was not entirely unambiguous, nevertheless applied the Convention's principles, allowed the Home Secretary the 'margin of appreciation' prescribed under the case-law of the European Court of Human Rights, and concluded that the Home Secretary had not abused his powers.[110] Lord Templeman said:[111]

The subject matter and date of the *Wednesbury* principles cannot in my opinion make it either necessary or appropriate for the courts to judge the validity of an interference with human rights by asking themselves whether the Home Secretary has acted irrationally or perversely. It seems to me that the courts cannot escape from asking themselves only whether a reasonable Secretary of State, on the material before him, could reasonably conclude the the interference with freedom of expression which he determined to impose was justifiable. In terms of the convention, as construed by the European Court of Human Rights, the interference with freedom of expression must be necessary and proportionate to the damage which the restriction is designed to prevent. My Lords, applying these principles I do not consider that the court can conclude that the Home Secretary has abused or exceeded his powers.

The approach of the majority therefore allows scope for rights–based reasoning in setting standards for a carefully limited review of executive action and secondary legislation.

Furthermore, it might be possible to argue that the Convention engenders a legitimate expectation that decision-makers will at least consider rights guaranteed under it when making decisions which affect people's rights. This does not seem to be an excessively intrusive approach. It does not accord an overriding effect to the Convention, but might give *locus standi* to a person whose Convention rights are infringed to challenge the decision on other, more conventional, substantive grounds. Alternatively, as Lord Bridge seems to have thought in *Brind*, it might be thought reasonable to treat the Convention as a relevant requirement, albeit one which might be overridden by others which have greater weight in particular circumstances. The potential scope for international human rights law to influence administrative law remains.[112]

The protection of rights in the UK is now, therefore, very much more complicated than at any time in the past, because the range of rights is more varied and the institutions which give effect to them are more numerous. At the same time, reluctance to protect rights unequivocally is evident from the ambivalent attitude of judges to the Convention. It may be that the judges are simply feeling their way slowly towards recogniz-

---

[109] [1991] 1 All ER at 723–24 (Lord Bridge), 724 (Lord Roskill).
[110] [1991] 1 All ER at 725–26.   [111] [1991] 1 All ER at 726.
[112] See Peter Bayne, 'Administrative Law, Human Rights and International Humanitarian Law' (1990) 64 *ALJ* 203–8.

ing Convention rights, in rather the same way that they moved slowly towards unequivocal acceptance of the primacy of Community law. If so, we can expect a gradual relaxation of the judges' attitudes to the Convention as time goes on.

2.6 INSTITUTIONS PROTECTING RIGHTS IN THE UK

Parliament has the primary responsibility for protecting rights, both positively by legislating for new rights, and negatively by refraining from legislating in a way which abridges existing rights. Legislative creation or abridgement of a right is usually instigated by the government, which introduces a bill to give effect to it, although there have been some notable private members' bills. (One example was the controversial Abortion Act 1967, which was a private member's bill introduced by David Steel MP.) It is the responsibility of individual members to bring to the attention of Parliament any threat to rights in proposed legislation. There is no committee which has responsibility for monitoring and reporting on the impact of bills on rights. It would be possible to introduce such a committee, on the model of the Select Committee on European Legislation which scrutinizes law emanating from the Community to consider whether it raises questions of legal or political importance.[113] The House of Commons and the House of Lords also have Select Committees and a Joint Committee on Delegated Legislation, which examine delegated legislation to check that it does not infringe constitutional proprieties and that standards of drafting are maintained.[114] Additional protection for rights could be given if the committees took active steps to monitor delegated legislation for infringements of rights guaranteed under the European Convention on Human Rights, as the Australian Senate's Regulations and Ordinances Committee does. There might also be scope for extending this approach by creating a Scrutiny of Bills Committee, on the model of that operating in the Australian Commonwealth Senate since 1981. However, the success of such scrutiny appears to depend heavily on cross–party co-operation, and that might be harder to achieve in relation to the substance of policy programmes which are embodied in bills than in relation to the (supposedly more technical) matters contained in delegated legislation.

Enforcement and protection agencies include the Commission for Racial Equality and the Equal Opportunities Commission, policing the Race Relations Act 1976, and the Sex Discrimination Act 1975 and equal pay

---

[113] See J. A. G. Griffith and Michael Ryle, *Parliament: Functions, Practice and Procedures* (London: Sweet & Maxwell, 1989), 436–8.

[114] Griffith and Ryle, *Parliament*, 444–5.

legislation, respectively. Each has power to attempt to conciliate between parties to disputes and to support legal action against those who are alleged to have breached rights, but the main system for enforcing the rights under the legislation is for aggrieved citizens to bring actions claiming compensation in an appropriate tribunal or court. The main role of the Commissions is to monitor developments and to educate the public, seeking to encourage good race or sex relations rather than enforce rights aggressively. Where a right is new, and social attitudes have to change to accommodate it, a coercive attitude on the part of the Commissions could be counter-productive. The present approach is to try to improve public awareness by drawing up and promulgating codes of practice and offering advice. Yet these steps are not always effective, and the Commissions have been accused of being oversensitive to the dangers of coercion. When dealing with discrimination in employment, for example, it is always difficult to judge when best to change from a strategy of co-operation to one of coercion.

Courts defend rights primarily through the law of tort, providing a route to compensation for infringements. This has in the past meant that the law of remedies in relation to civil liberties has been tied closely to private law causes of action: freedom from restraint was guaranteed by the action for false imprisonment or trespass to the person; freedom from unauthorized searches and seizures was secured by actions for trespass to property, or, where search warrants had been unlawfully obtained, by the tort of abuse of process.[115] This left certain rights unprotected. For example, there is no tort remedy for interference with freedom of speech or of association. Nor is there a remedy for infringement of any right to privacy as such, unless the means of interference constitutes a trespass to person or property.[116] To some extent the courts have been able to circumvent these problems. Where statutes have imposed duties on public bodies to provide services, it is sometimes possible to bring actions for breach of statutory duty as a way of securing compensation for failure to comply with the duty, effectively coupling the statutory duty with a private right.[117] The existence of a statutory duty may also create a sufficiently proximate relationship between the provider of services and the client to enable the courts to impose a duty of care, breach of which will sound in damages for negligence, although the scope for developing

[115] David Feldman, *The Law Relating to Entry, Search and Seizure*, (London: Butterworths, 1986), 394–401.

[116] *Malone* v. *Metropolitan Police Commissioner* (see n. 105); *Kaye* v. *Robertson* [1991] FSR 62, CA, where the court regretted the absence of a remedy for invasion of privacy by journalists (the case did not concern actions of officials).

[117] K. M. Stanton, *Breach of Statutory Duty* (London: Sweet & Maxwell, 1986).

tort rights for citizens from statutory duties on public bodies, which was expanding after 1977, has been much reduced recently.[118]

The judges have sometimes deployed new or previously underdeveloped torts. The tort of abuse of process has already been mentioned. Another tort, misfeasance in a public office, has come to prominence, and offers a way of obtaining compensation where a public official knowingly acts in disregard of a legal duty, knowing that it was likely to cause damage to the victim.[119] However, in English common law there is no tort of causing loss or injury by the unlawful administrative action of a public authority. To obtain compensation, a plaintiff must show not merely that the authority acted unlawfully, but also that the act breached a duty owed to the plaintiff as a matter of private law. If the breach of a legal duty does not amount to a tort or breach of contract, compensation will not be available through the courts. Legal remedies will then be limited to judicial review of the impugned act, leading to an order quashing it or a declaration of invalidity, together perhaps with a mandatory order requiring the authority to comply with its legal obligations. Judicial review has become a more valuable protection against unlawful executive action since the procedures were streamlined in 1978, and it is now an important forum for protecting (for example) the rights of parents and children against local authorities' child-care decision-making processes, the rights of prisoners, and those of immigrants. Nevertheless, there are procedural disadvantages which an applicant for judicial review must overcome, as compared with the position of a plaintiff in a tort action. An applicant for judicial review requires the leave of the court to proceed; does not get discovery as of right, but must show a strongly arguable case of unlawfulness and show that discovery is likely to be necessary to the fair disposal of the proceedings; and is not normally entitled to cross-examine witnesses, as the hearings are usually conducted on the basis of written affidavits.

One of the most worrying factors limiting the effectiveness of judicial review to provide remedies for breaches of civil liberties is that the courts have hitherto been unwilling to grant coercive relief against the Crown.[120] This has meant that a litigant in proceedings against a representative of the Crown is unable to claim a mandatory injunction or mandamus. This is not too serious a problem in relation to the final judgment, because the court will make a declaration of the duties of the Crown and this declaration is, by convention, honoured. There is,

---

[118] *Anns* v. *Merton LBC* [1978] AC 728, HL, overruled in *Murphy* v. *Brentwood DC* [1990] 2 All ER 908, HL.

[119] *Bourgoin S.A.* v. *Ministry of Agriculture, Fisheries and Food* [1986] QB 716, [1985] 3 All ER 585, CA.

[120] *Factortame Ltd.* v. *Secretary of State for Transport* [1990] 2 AC 85, HL.

however, a serious problem over pre-trial relief: the Crown cannot be enjoined to refrain, pending trial, from further action which might infringe the citizen's rights. The courts have no power to grant an interim declaration, and interim injunctions are not generally available against the Crown any more than final ones are. These problems may be easing somewhat, however. It may be possible to grant a stay, which has many of the same effects as an injunction.[121] Where plaintiff or applicant is asserting an individual right under European Community law, it has been held that under Community law an interim order can and some-times must be made against the Crown in order to ensure that an effec-tive remedy will be available for breach of directly effective Community law.[122] Domestic law should be amended by statute so that British citi-zens asserting rights under domestic law enjoy the same advantages as anyone suing the Crown in reliance on individual rights under Community law.

Tribunals are the source of remedies for many breaches of rights. In particular, the industrial tribunals and employment appeal tribunal pro-vide remedies for race and sex discrimination in employment; social secu-rity appeal tribunals deal with disputes in relation to some welfare rights; immigration appeal tribunals consider appeals against administrative deci-sions in immigration matters; mental health review tribunals provide pro-tection for the rights of those compulsorily detained under the Mental Health Act 1983; and prison boards of visitors provide both the main (supposedly independent) system for ventilating prisoners' grievances and try the more serious allegations of breaches by prisoners of the prison rules (although their disciplinary functions would be removed from them, and divided between prison governors and the criminal courts, under proposals made by the Woolf Inquiry and currently being prepared for a bill to be put before Parliament).

Complaints procedures, self-regulation, and *internal review* by *official bodies* provide other checks on infringements of rights.[123] Efficient procedures for handling complaints, and rectifying problems which they disclose, should be accompanied by systems of management and monitoring which allow problems to be identified or foreseen and dealt with. In order to provide a safeguard for the public, it is also important to publi-cize the rights which people have and the standards which are being used to judge performance, review the standards regularly, and publish infor-

---

[121] R. v. *Secretary of State for Education and Science, ex parte Avon County Council* [1991] 1 All ER 282, CA.

[122] *Factortame Ltd.* v. *Secretary of State for Transport (No. 2)* [1991] 1 All ER 70 at p. 106, HL.

[123] Patrick Birkinshaw, *Grievances, Remedies and the State* (London: Sweet & Maxwell, 1985), ch. 1.

mation regularly to show the extent to which the standards are being met. These types of measures are central to the attempts by Mr. John Major's government to improve the responsiveness and accountability of public services. The *Citizen's Charter*[124] insists on this, as do the specialist Charters dealing with individual public services. For example, the *Patient's Charter* encourages people to provide feedback to the health providers about the quality of service received, waiting times, and so on. It exhorts people not to be put off by the notion that they will be victimized by doctors for making complaints.[125] At the same time, the Charters make clear the responsibilities of the recipients of services to contribute to the efficiency of the service: the *Patient's Charter* points to the inefficiency which results from people failing to turn up to appointments without warning staff, and the *Parent's Charter*[126] emphasizes the responsibility which parents share with teachers for their children's education.

There is no doubt that such procedures are important in improving the quality of the service delivered, and that there is room for them to supply remedies for service users which are not otherwise available, so long as the procedures are administered properly and are advertised.[127] However, it is not clear that, without more, this is an adequate way of protecting, or enhancing the value of, rights. A level of independence is needed. The dangers of lack of rigour in reviewing the work of colleagues, failure to adopt adequate procedures or to publicize them properly, and public reluctance to take complaints to the departments which are the subject of the complaints, all emphasize the importance of having outside scrutiny, and ideally control, over the complaints process, particularly when the complainants are likely to belong to a vulnerable group, such as prisoners, sick patients, or children in care.[128] An externally operated ombudsman scheme forms a useful backup to internal procedures, but, as ombudsmen are typically concerned with maladministration rather than rights, they may not always be able to remedy injustices which flow from infringements of rights.

---

[124] Cm. 1599 (1991).

[125] Dept. of Health, *The Patient's Charter* (London: HMSO, 1991), 18.

[126] Dept. of Education, *The Parent's Charter* (London: HMSO, 1991).

[127] N. Lewis, S. Cracknell, and M. Seneviratne, *Complaints Procedures in Local Government* (Sheffield: Univ. of Sheffield, 1987), provides a valuable study of attitudes to complaints process in one area of the public service. For comments, see Colin Crawford, 'Complaints, Codes and Ombudsmen in Local Government' [1988] *PL* 246–67. Support for internal review and appeal procedures comes from a US study, which is not blind to the potential drawbacks (although arguably underestimates their importance): Jerry L. Mashaw, *Bureaucratic Justice: Managing Social Security Disability Claims* (New Haven, Conn.: Yale University Press, 1983).

[128] Michael J. Lindsay, 'Complaints Procedures and Their Limitations in the Light of the "Pindown" Inquiry' [1991] *JSWFL* 432–41.

The combination of internal and external checks can be illustrated by reference to the police. They act as self-regulators under the Police and Criminal Evidence Act 1984, which (together with its associated Codes of Practice) lays down rules designed to secure the rights of those who come into contact with the police.[129] Rights which are safeguarded under the Act and Codes include the rights to know why one is being arrested or searched, to have access to legal advice when being questioned, to have an accurate record kept of interviews and to inspect the record, and to be free of torture, oppression, and inhuman or degrading treatment while in custody. The principal methods of restraining breaches are bureaucratic: records must be kept and monitored by a senior officer, and important decisions relating to custody must be taken by an officer who is independent of the investigation. There is evidence which raises doubts about the efficacy of this process.

Outside control over the police exists, but is limited. Applications to magistrates are needed for search warrants and warrants for detention of suspects without charge for over 36 hours. There is a system of lay visitors to police stations, to make inspections without warning. The Police Complaints Authority, a body independent of the police, oversees complaints investigations, and takes control of the more serious investigations.[130] Nevertheless, the main responsibility for safeguarding the rights of citizens who are in contact with the police lies with the police themselves, and particularly with custody officers. The courts have begun to show signs that they are not happy with the quality of self-regulation, and are now using their discretion to exclude evidence as a way of expressing their disapproval of the more flagrant infringements of people's rights by the police.[131] The courts have also been prepared to award exemplary damages where civil actions are brought successfully against the police. This is a recognition that internal review is not sufficient without public scrutiny, publication of standards, and (perhaps most important of all, but most difficult to measure) the growth of a public service mentality among service providers.[132]

Another example of a remedy by way of internal review is the admin-

[129] These are considered in detail in the chapters which follow.

[130] For a comparative survey of police complaints processes, see the papers in Andrew J. Goldsmith (ed.), *Complaints against the Police: The Trend to External Review* (Oxford: Clarendon Press, 1991). On the British experience, see Mike Maguire, in Goldsmith (ed.), *Complaints*, ch. 5; M. Maguire and C. Corbett, *A Study of the Police Complaints System* (London: HMSO, 1991).

[131] This is a controversial development: see Mark Gelowitz, 'Section 78 of the Police and Criminal Evidence Act 1984: Middle Ground or No Man's Land?' (1990) 106 *LQR* 327–42.

[132] David Feldman, 'The Developing Debate on Policing Law and Management' (1991) 20 *Anglo-Amer. LR* 1–14 at 9–11.

istration of the system of welfare benefits under the Social Fund. This is not strictly speaking a protection for rights. The discretionary system of supplementary benefits for those in urgent need was replaced by a rule-based system under the Social Security Act 1980, under which claimants who fell within the criteria for benefit had an enforceable right to the benefit. However, the Social Security Act 1986 returned to a discretionary system, subject to tight budgetary limits. Here there are few rights. The eligibility for a grant or loan from a local office of the Department of Social Security depends, first, on any directions issued by the Secretary of State; secondly, on the state of the budget of the local office; and, thirdly, on whether the applicant's need has been allocated a high priority by the management of the local office. An applicant whose need is not excluded absolutely by a direction from the Secretary of State has at least a right to be considered, but there is no independent body to whom to appeal against the refusal of a grant or a loan by a social fund officer. Instead, there is a right to have the decision reviewed by another social fund officer or a social fund inspector, with the possibility of judicial review of the decision if it can be shown to be wrong in law. The main responsibility for policing the social fund system lies inside the local offices of the Department of Social Security.

What happens when rights are not protected, or legal remedies run out? At this stage individuals must turn to the political arena or to international law, considered above. As yet, we have no constitutional and legally enforceable protection for rights against legislative intervention. Whether or not we should have such protection forms the subject of the final section of this chapter.

2.7 THE BILL OF RIGHTS DEBATE

(1) The debate[133]

Concern about the encroachment by government and Parliament on rights has heightened interest in the possibility of enacting a Bill of

---

[133] Of the voluminous literature, the following is particularly useful: Sir Leslie Scarman, *English Law. The New Dimension* (London: Stevens, 1974); P. Wallington and J. McBride, *Civil Liberties and a Bill of Rights* (London: Cobden Trust, 1976); Lord Lloyd of Hampstead, 'Do We Need a Bill of Rights?' (1976) 39 *MLR* 121–9; A. J. M. Milne, 'Should We Have a Bill of Rights?' (1977) 40 *MLR* 389–96; *Report of the Select Committee on a Bill of Rights*, HL Paper No. 176 of 1976–7 (London: HMSO, 1977); Joseph Jaconelli, *Enacting a Bill of Rights* (Oxford: Clarendon Press, 1980); Colin Campbell (ed.), *Do We Need a Bill of Rights?* (London: Temple Smith, 1980); Michael Zander, *A Bill of Rights?* 3rd edn. (London: Sweet and Maxwell, 1985); Advisory Committee to the Constitutional Commission, *Report: Individual and Democratic Rights* (Canberra:

Rights. Various models have been suggested, but all are controversial. The European Convention on Human Rights is an obvious model, but others have been used, such as Canada's Bill of Rights Act 1960. Bills to enact a Bill of Rights into English law have been introduced into the House of Lords a number of times, and in 1987 Sir Edward Gardner introduced a private member's bill into the House of Commons, but none has reached the statute book. Demands for such a bill have grown since Sir Leslie (now Lord) Scarman published his trend-setting analysis in *English Law—the New Dimension* in 1974. The idea of enacting a Bill of Rights received the support of a narrow majority of the House of Lords Select Committee in 1977,[134] and most recently, in 1991, detailed proposals for Bills of Rights have been drawn up and published by Liberty (the National Council for Civil Liberties) and the Institute for Public Policy Research.[135]

It is usually accepted that, if a Bill of Rights were to be enacted, the easiest and best approach would be to adopt the text of the European Convention on Human Rights, or those parts of it which the UK has ratified, as this would save much argument.[136] However, this idea attracts opposition, particularly from those on the political Left, because the rights protected are predominantly individual rights. The Convention does not protect social rights, such as a right to a decent standard of living, and some of those which it does protect (such as property rights, under Article 1 of the First Protocol) could, if interpreted broadly, be used to place important limits on the ability of a future Labour government to introduce programmes for redistributing wealth or restricting land use for environmental reasons. The Left would like to see some of the rights under the European Social Charter, or the International Covenant on Economic, Social and Cultural Rights, or the ILO Conventions, included, but this would be vigorously opposed by the political Right.

Commonwealth of Australia, 1987); K. D. Ewing and C. A. Gearty, *Freedom Under Thatcher: Civil Liberties in Modern Britain* (Oxford: Clarendon Press, 1990), ch. 9; P. P. Craig, *Public Law and Democracy in the United Kingdom and the United States of America* (Oxford: Clarendon Press, 1990), ch. 7.

[134] *Report of the Select Committee on a Bill of Rights*, HL 176 of 1977–8.

[135] See Zander, *Bill of Rights?* 1–26; S. H. Bailey, D. J. Harris, and B. L. Jones, *Civil Liberties Cases and Materials*, 3rd edn. (London: Butterworths, 1991), 18–23; Liberty, *A People's Charter: Liberty's Bill of Rights* (London: Liberty, 1991); Institute for Public Policy Research, *The Constitution of the United Kingdom* (London: IPPR, 1991).

[136] This was unanimously accepted by the House of Lords Select Committee (above, n. 134) in 1977. For full and illuminating analysis of the arguments, concluding that incorporation would be sensible, see Kerridge, 'Incorporation' (n. 100 above).

(2) The issues

The choice of rights is therefore highly controversial. There are also three further controversies surrounding the debate which is continuing about a Bill of Rights. Do we need one? Should it, and could it, be entrenched? Who should be responsible for enforcing it? In the discussion which follows, the issues are addressed in the following order: (i) Do we need a Bill of Rights? (ii) How should we decide what rights any such Bill should contain? (iii) Should it be entrenched? (iv) Who should enforce it?

(i) *Do we need a Bill of Rights?* This question is often posed by opponents of a Bill of Rights, who feel that the rights and liberties which we need are already adequately protected, and who do not see the need for further protective measures which might engender difficulties which we should avoid unless it becomes essential to risk them. On this view, which is well in line with nineteenth-century political assumptions, the electoral system, responsible government, and a representative Parliament are the best guarantees of moderation and common sense, which in turn are the best security for civil liberties against legislative or executive infringement. Moderation might be best ensured by increasing the role of the people in legislation, for example by instituting a requirement for a referendum as part of the legislative process for certain types of controversial legislation.[137] A Bill of Rights would only be needed if this system of political checks and balances failed, and a tyrannical government were to take power. While this might happen, with or without popular support (and the Hitler government in Germany was an elected government), any such government would be unlikely to allow a Bill of Rights to stand in its way. As Sir Harry Gibbs, a former Chief Justice of Australia, put it, in the context of a debate about whether Australia should amend its Constitution to include a Bill of Rights:

One may hope that the danger of a conflict between races, classes or sections of society so bitter as to endanger fundamental civil liberties remains remote. If such a danger were perceived—and some have apprehended a threat of that kind in the United Kingdom and Canada—it would be a question whether a bill of rights would avert it.[138]

This is an important point, but it addresses only one aspect of the issue. It is unsafe to assume that a Bill of Rights is going to be needed only *in*

[137] Geoffrey de Q. Walker, *Initiative and Referendum: The People's Law* (Sydney: Centre for Independent Studies, 1987).
[138] Sir Harry Gibbs, 'Eleventh Wilfred Fullagar Memorial Lecture: The Constitutional Protection of Human Rights' (1982) 9 *Monash Univ. LR* 1–13 at p. 11.

extremis, indeed in circumstances so desperate that the bill is almost bound to be useless. While it is undoubtedly true that a spirit of tolerance and a popular commitment to liberty are the best guarantees that freedom will flourish, two points suggest that there may still be a place for a Bill of Rights in circumstances which do not fall into the category of tyranny.

First, one may ask how the spirit of tolerance and the popular commitment to liberty are to be nurtured. By and large, the UK seems to be an unusually tolerant society (although immigrants, members of ethnic minorities, and journalists might not always agree). However, it is unsafe to assume that the spirit of tolerance will survive unscathed, particularly in times of economic recession. The upsurge of attacks on minority groups in the late 1980s bears witness to this; it is not necessary to look back as far as Germany in the 1930s. Clear leadership is needed to ensure that reasonable people do not begin to feel that intolerance is socially acceptable. This leadership may be expressed in many ways, but for the country's political leaders to enact a code of tolerance and respect for liberty, in the form of a Bill of Rights, would be an impressive start. This bill could be more than a piece of political rhetoric. If it were used in schools and colleges, as the basis for courses in civics, current affairs, and general studies, it would have an educational role, helping to shape the awareness of the next generation of its responsibilities and rights. This would foster a sense of being a citizen, rather than a mere subject, which might in turn encourage people to make the best possible use of the democratic system on which the politics of liberty rests. In short, a Bill of Rights could be a useful element (at least as useful as the *Citizen's Charter*) in the education of citizens, and in defining the responsibilities of legislators, a matter on which at present they receive virtually no education or guidance.

Secondly, following from the previous point, a Bill of Rights could be useful where legislators or executives ignore, or temporarily lose sight of, the value of liberty and tolerance, and the judges at present have no power to remind them of it. This can easily happen under the pressure of circumstances. The detention and deportation of numerous Arabs in the UK during the lead up to, and course of, hostilities in the UN–Iraq campaign in 1990 and 1991 is recent dramatic evidence of this.[139] It has been suggested that the enactment of successive Prevention of Terrorism (Temporary Provisions) Acts, and particularly that of 1974, pushed through Parliament in two days and almost without amendment in the atmosphere of outrage which followed the Birmingham pub bombings,

---

[139] See Ian Leigh, 'The Gulf War Deportations and the Courts' [1991] PL 331–9; Françoise Hampson, 'The Geneva Conventions and the Detention of Civilians and Alleged Prisoners of War' [1991] PL 507–22.

provide a further example.[140] In such circumstances, infringements of liberty may occur which seem not to affect most voters directly, and so do not engender a massive public reaction or put the government at risk of losing crucial votes in the House of Commons, but which nevertheless chip away at one of the foundations of belief in the idea of liberty, namely that liberty is important for all, and compelling reasons are needed to justify limiting it. This may lead in time to civil liberties regarded as being not *that* important, an optional preference which may be overridden for reasons of political or social convenience, rather than being fundamental to our way of life and political system. This devalues civil liberties, and facilitates their infringement.

Even in a society which remains predominantly tolerant and liberal, therefore, a Bill of Rights may have value in fostering those virtues, educating people to value them, and helping to correct certain inadequacies in the political system of checks and balances. In a sense, 'do we need a Bill of Rights?' is the wrong question to ask, and it is surprising to find that even some supporters of Bills of Rights persist in asking it.[141] Instead, we should ask, first, 'would one be useful?' (to which, it is suggested, the answer is in the affirmative), and, secondly, 'could one be put in place without incurring inconvenience which would outweigh the advantages?' The remainder of this section relates to the latter question.

(ii) *How should we decide what rights might be included?* This is a controversial matter, as noted earlier. One way out of what might become an impasse would be to adopt the rights, or at least some of them, guaranteed in those parts of those international instruments to which the UK is a party. This would avoid a number of difficulties. In particular, it would avoid the appearance of hypocrisy which results from agreeing at the international level to guarantee rights, and exhorting other countries to do the same, but failing to incorporate systematic guarantees for those rights in English law and so denying access to them on the part of our citizens. The merit in enacting the European Convention on Human Rights, or those parts of it which the UK has ratified and subject to any reservations which the UK has entered, would be that it would be the logical culmination of the reasoning of those who first ratified the Convention and then granted the right of individual petition to UK citizens.[142]

If the English text of those parts of the Convention were enacted as they stand, it would also avoid a further question about the drafting. Should the rights be drafted with a high degree of specificity, or would it

---

[140] See e.g. Ewing and Gearty, *Freedom Under Thatcher*, ch. 7.

[141] *Vide* the title of an otherwise valuable collection of essays, Colin Campbell (ed.), *Do We Need a Bill of Rights?* (London: Maurice Temple Smith, 1980).

[142] See Kerridge, 'Incorporation' (n. 100, above).

be better to draft them more loosely and leave it to the enforcing bodies to interpret them as seems best in the light of the hard facts of litigated cases? Does the answer depend on who is to do the interpreting? If we leave the language fairly open-textured, it will make it easier for inter- preters in a hundred years' time to adjust the effect of the Bill of Rights to accord more closely with their dominant ideology of rights. This may produce results which seem sensible to them but which we, from our twentieth-century perspective, would find surprising if not actually dis- tasteful. On the one hand, that might make the idea of a Bill of Rights more attractive, making it potentially less of a millstone round the necks of our successors and more of an aid to constructive thinking in accor- dance with changing ideas.

However, as discussed below, this might put considerable power into the hands of those entrusted with the task of interpreting and re- interpreting the Bill of Rights. It also raises a possibly intractable problem of the relationship between the British judges' interpretation of the text of the Bill of Rights and the interpretation of the Convention by the European Court of Human Rights. Would the European Court become a court of appeal from our courts in human rights matters, as it would if the Bill were to provide that decisions of the European Court should be followed by our courts? If the Bill were entrenched against amendment by the UK Parliament, this would abrogate Parliament's ultimate legisla- tive power in respect of an unlimited range of matters, in favour of the Strasbourg court. Such a result is unlikely to command wide support. It would be preferable to use the Convention as a basis, but to change the text of each article, so that it would be open to the domestic courts to interpret it, compatibility with the Convention being separately assessed afterwards by the Strasbourg court without in any way threatening the legislative competence of the UK Parliament.

Perhaps, then, the ideal form of an expression of human rights depends on whether it is to be legally enforceable, and if so by whom. The idea that the best form for rules to take depends (amongst other considera- tions) on what they aim to achieve and to whom they are primarily directed is not new,[143] but its significance for the debate over the desir- ability of Bills of Rights and the proper role of the judges in enforcing them has not been generally noticed.

(iii) *Should a Bill of Rights be entrenched?*[144] This depends on a number of factors. First, it should only be entrenched to the extent that entrench-

---

[143] For an example of a discussion in the context of regulatory rules, see Robert Baldwin, 'Why Rules Don't Work' (1990) 52 *MLR* 321–37.

[144] For full discussion of this subject, much of which lies outside the scope of this book (being more related to constitutional law than to civil liberties), see Joseph Jaconelli, *Enacting a Bill of Rights* (Oxford: Clarendon Press, 1980).

ment is possible as a matter of constitutional law. It would be futile to pretend to entrench something which would later be held by the judges to be no more than an ordinary statute. The availability of entrenchment is compromised in the UK by the doctrine of parliamentary sovereignty, which some experts, most notably Professor Sir William Wade, consider excludes entrenchment of legislation by means of (for example) imposing conditions as to the manner and form in which any future legislation impinging on the Bill of Rights is to be passed. This is said to follow from the fact that, unlike other legislatures which have been held to be capable of being bound by manner and form provisions, the UK Parliament derives its authority not from a higher law in the form of a constitutional document, but from judicial acceptance.[145]

However, all is not necessarily lost to those who might want to entrench a Bill of Rights. At least three possible courses of action may be open. First, the Wade view, though highly influential, is not universally accepted, and it might be possible in the future to argue that properly enacted manner and form requirements should be effective, as a matter of statutory interpretation and common law doctrine, to limit the legislative competence of Parliament.[146] Next, Professor Wade has suggested that, as parliamentary sovereignty depends on the judges, it might be possible to entrench constitutional provisions such as a Bill of Rights simply by changing the judicial oath to require judges to be loyal to the provisions in question over other legislation.[147] This is an interesting idea, but, as the oath is itself a creature of statute, it is hard to see what would prevent Parliament from changing it back again should it seem desirable to do so. Finally, it is possible that the courts would take a different line if faced by a provision which declared itself to be a fundamental constitutional pro-vision from that which they adopt in relation to ordinary statutes. It is possible, for example, that a Bill of Rights would have a greater chance of being treated as immune to overruling if it were part of a fully fledged Constitution Act, which declared itself to be the fundamental basis for the allocation and limitation of constitutional power amongst public

[145] H. W. R. Wade, 'The Basis of Legal Sovereignty' [1955] CLJ 172–97; E. C. S. Wade, 'Introduction' to A. V. Dicey, Introduction to the Study of the Law of the Constitution, 10th edn. (London: Macmillan, 1959), pp. xxxiv ff.

[146] For evaluation of the Wade view, see R. F. V. Heuston, Essays in Constitutional Law, 2nd edn. (London: Stevens, 1964), ch. 1; A. W. Bradley, 'The Sovereignty of Parliament—in Perpetuity?' in Jeffrey Jowell and Dawn Oliver (eds.), The Changing Constitution, 2nd edn. (Oxford: Clarendon Press, 1989), 25–52. On the rather special Scottish approach, which gives some binding significance to the Treaty of Union and the Acts of Union, see J. D. B. Mitchell, Constitutional Law, 2nd edn. (Edinburgh: W. Green & Son, 1968) 63–91; T. B. Smith, in The Stair Memorial Encyclopaedia, Constitutional Law, para. 350.

[147] H. W. R. Wade, Constitutional Fundamentals (London: Stevens, 1980), 37–9.

bodies. This is one reason why it might be sensible to regard a Bill of Rights as part of a more extensive piece of constitutional reform and codification, rather than as something which could usefully stand on its own.[148]

Secondly, the desirability of entrenchment depends on the form which the Bill takes. If it purports to be a collection of enforceable individual rights, designed to limit the legislative and executive competence of Parliament and government agencies, it might make sense to attempt to entrench it (subject to one's view on the further arguments considered below). On the other hand, if it is intended to provide a set of less precise, and arguably non-justiciable, social and economic aspirations, perhaps derived (in part at least) from the European Social Charter, there could be something to be said for making part of the bill a set of policy directives for government. This is done, for example, in the Irish and Indian Constitutions, where social goals are set out in parts of the Constitution entitled 'Directive Principles of State Policy'. Being policy-oriented, it would be counter-democratic to attempt to entrench them, so reasonably straightforward amendment processes are provided under the Indian Constitution. At the same time, and despite a constitutional injunction against judicial enforcement of the directive principles, the Indian courts have used them as a basis for conducting judicial review of governmental acts and decisions, requiring the directive principles to be taken into account as relevant considerations when making decisions which affect interests which the directive principles protect.[149] It would at least be possible to do something similar in any British Bill of Rights, and this might incidentally ease the fears of those who oppose the notion of according constitutional status to social and economic policy goals.[150]

Thirdly, there is a danger that entrenching a Bill of Rights would be counter-democratic, in that it would remove the control of the people, or the representatives of the people, over the rights which were to be enjoyed, and give excessive power to an unaccountable group of judges. These arguments deserve careful attention. There would be powerful arguments against entrenching some types of Bill of Rights, but not others. For example, a Bill of Rights limited to protecting democratic rights would not be seriously open to a charge of being counter-democratic so far as the standards to be enforced are concerned. If the

---

[148] For an example of such an approach, see Institute of Public Policy Research, *The Constitution of the United Kingdom* (London: IPPR, 1991).

[149] I have discussed this further in 'Public Interest Litigation and Constitutional Theory in Comparative Perspective' (1992) 55 *MLR* 44 at p. 64 *et seq*.

[150] This has been suggested by the late Professor Sir James Fawcett, among others: J. E. S. Fawcett, 'Bills of Rights: Some Alternatives', in Campbell (ed.), *Do We Need a Bill of Rights?* 133–9 at 133–4.

method of entrenchment included a requirement for a referendum before the bill could be amended, it would actually give more power to the people than they presently enjoy in relation to legislation in the UK. As for the idea that a Bill of Rights would increase the power of the judiciary, there are various ways of dealing with that. One possibility would be to appoint a special tribunal to decide questions concerning the compatibility of legislation with the Bill of Rights. This might be a parliamentary body, which would report to Parliament during the progress of legislation, rather than reviewing it subsequently, on the model of the French *Conseil Constitutionnel*. Another possibility would be to leave the policing of legislation to a specialist non-judicial and non-parliamentary human rights commission. A further possibility would be to create a specialist supreme constitutional court, which might have judges appointed by the executive and ratified by the legislature for life (as on the US model) or for a fixed period. Finally, the power of the judiciary could be limited by including in the Bill of Rights an override clause, on the model of section 33 of the Canadian Charter of Fundamental Rights and Freedoms. This enables some rights to be overridden by federal and provincial legislatures. The precise effect of this provision in the Canadian Constitution Act 1982 is controversial. Not all rights can be overridden. Those judged to be fundamental to the balance of power between provinces and federal government, and those which guarantee the position of minorities, are excluded from the operation of section 33. In addition, some commentators argue that, because section 33 does not state that section 1 may be overridden, a legislature may invoke section 33 only when the conditions laid down in section 1 of the Charter are satisfied. Section 1 provides that interferences with rights under the Charter are permitted only so far as they come within 'such reasonable limits as can be demonstrably justified in a free and democratic society'. Other commentators argue that, once a particular Charter provision is overridden by a subsequent statute, there is no operative right for section 1 to protect, so it is implicitly overridden.[151] Section 33 was included to enable all the provinces except Quebec (which was never happy about the Constitution Act 1982 or its Charter provisions) to accept the Charter, having previously regarded it as an unjustifiable restriction on the democratic power of their legislatures. A similar provision might relieve the fears of democrats in the UK.

Fourthly, it should be remembered that entrenchment is always a matter of degree. Nobody would advocate making a Bill of Rights absolutely

---

[151] For argument that s. 33 is subject to s. 1, see Brian Slattery, 'Override clauses under section 33' (1983) 61 *Canadian Bar Rev.* 391–7; Brian Slattery, 'A Theory of the Charter' (1987) 25 *Osgoode Hall LJ* 701–47. For the contrary view, see P. W. Hogg, *Constitutional Law of Canada*, 2nd edn. (Toronto: Carswell, 1988), 691.

impossible to alter. The questions concern the nature of the restraints which are to operate. One might have different amendment procedures for different provisions, depending on their perceived importance to (for instance) democratic politics or the structure of the state. Under the Canadian Constitution Act 1982, for example, there are several different amendment procedures catering for different types of amendment. The choice, therefore, is not a simple one between entrenchment and total flexibility. It is a more complex one between levels of constraint on amendment.

(iv) *Who would enforce it?* It is often assumed that a Bill of Rights, if entrenched and (perhaps) even if not entrenched, would have to be enforced by judges. This, if correct, raises questions concerning the legitimacy of different types of bodies doing particular jobs. There are concerns about the representativeness of judges, and their ability to interpret a Bill of Rights in a politically neutral way. Some commentators have drawn attention to the fact that judges, at least in the United Kingdom, do not at present represent a cross-section of the community. In particular, women and some minority ethnic groups are seriously under-represented.[152] It is suggested that this would undermine the legitimacy of judicial enforcement of a Bill of Rights, as it removes any basis (in the absence of any democratic accountability for judicial action) for the claim that politically independent judges should be entitled review the policy-making and policy-implementation activities of democratically accountable legislatures or executives.

This raises two questions, one theoretical, the other empirical. The empirical question arises if the objection is to the effect of class, gender, and ethnic background on the substance of decision-making: to what extent does the judges' ethnic background, gender, and class affiliation affect their decision-making? It has been argued that the courts have a 'historic mission to safeguard capital from working class challenges'.[153] Yet if one major influence on judges is the constitutional structure under which they are working, and the values which underpin that constitution, appointing judges with different upbringings and ethnic backgrounds should make little difference to the type of decisions which they then make. If that hypothesis, after testing, proves to be correct, it would

---

[152] J. A. G. Griffith, *The Politics of the Judiciary*, 4th edn. (London: Fontana Press, 1991), 35; Louis Blom-Cooper and Gavin Drewry, *Final Appeal* (Oxford: Oxford University Press, 1972); Robert Stevens, *Law and Politics: The House of Lords as a Judicial Body 1800–1976* (London: Weidenfeld & Nicolson, 1979).

[153] H. J. Glasbeek, 'Contempt for Workers' (1990) 28 *Osgoode Hall LJ* 1–52, at p. 1, in the context of contempt of court decisions under the Canadian Charter of Fundamental Rights and Freedoms.

mean that any arrangements for enforcing a Bill of Rights would have to take account of, or fundamentally change (by means of an entirely new constitutional structure) the legal and constitutional principles which fetter judicial decision-making.

The theoretical question is independent of any issue as to the causal connection between personal backgrounds and legal results. To what extent is it democratically important for a body of judges to reflect the ethnic make-up of the community? A predominantly white, Anglo-Saxon, Protestant, male judiciary reflects badly on the educational, cultural, and professional standards and organization of a plural society. However, it is not clear why that should constitute an objection to the legitimacy of judicial action to enforce a Bill of Rights, particularly if the standards set out in the bill are democratically acceptable. In the UK, the legislature is as unrepresentative (in the sense of comprising a cross-section of the community) as the judiciary. That is a situation which calls for improvement, but (to put it at its lowest) such considerations undermine the legitimacy of judicial enforcement of a Bill of Rights no more than that of legislation emerging from Parliament.

In any case, this type of objection to Bills of Rights makes questionable assumptions. In particular, it assumes that the Bill of Rights is to be strongly entrenched, and justiciable by the ordinary judiciary. As noted above, these assumptions need not be correct. Like the Canadian Bill of Rights Act 1960, or the New Zealand Bill of Rights Act 1990, it would be possible to enact a Bill of Rights which would be no more than guidance to legislators on how they ought to approach the task of legislating, and to judges on how they should approach the task of interpreting legislation. Of course, this would (on one view) unreasonably limit the likely effectiveness of the Bill of Rights in protecting rights, but it would preserve the forms and substance of legislative supremacy.

(3) Conclusion

The desirability of a Bill of Rights, and the form which it should take, depends on how seriously one takes rights, and how one weighs the value of different rights in relation to the maintenance of democratic controls. If we take rights seriously, which rights should be protected against becoming political footballs, subject to the fashions and fancies of majorities and governments? Such debates can never be concluded, since dominant ideologies of rights can change. However, it is worth drawing attention to a number of matters, some already canvassed in Chapter 1, and others which the reader will have to consider as the book progresses. How seriously do we take our own current conception of rights? Is it based on the idea of individual freedom and personal autonomy, or on a desire to achieve social goals? If it is based on autonomy, is it the sort of autonomy advocated by Raz, requiring some guarantees of the social conditions suitable to its exercise? If so, it might justify protecting some welfare rights, as well as the classic liberal freedoms from interference which alone are espoused by Berlin, Hayek, and Nozick. Are the constitutional principles which operate at the moment capable, without serious alteration, of taking rights seriously? If not, does it matter?

My own view is briefly as follows. The British approach to rights and freedoms is substantially in tune with the idea of moral autonomy, but the attachment to rights is at present less strong than the attachment to an idealized model of representative democracy in which government is expected to formulate and implement social and economic policy. Parliament scrutinizes government, and is in turn watched closely by the electorate. Parliament can broadly be trusted to ensure that the government does not overstep the mark; the electorate is trusted to ensure that Parliament does not trespass unduly on liberty. Commitment to this political method of working out the tension between liberty and social programmes can be said to form the dominant ethos of the society and the state.

Any constitutional arrangement regarding rights must be reasonably well in tune with the prevailing dominant ethos as it defines the legitimate expectations of citizens, since it will depend on that ethos to sustain it and will, in turn, be expected to make it possible for those who wish to organize their lives according to that ethos to do so. Advocates of constitutional changes must be sensitive to this, and also to certain limitations, imposed by the prevailing constitutional ethos, on the direction and distance in which, and the speed at which, a constitution can be made to change the way in which citizens are treated. The British constitution is slow moving (for all its flexibility), and citizens are (rightly or wrongly) particularly concerned to maintain national self-determination; popular and political attachment to parliamentary supremacy may be seen as a symptom of this. These factors make it unlikely that the domestic entrenchment of the European Convention on Human Rights would be accepted easily, implying as it probably would the subjection of the UK Parliament and judiciary to a form of international control over a far wider range of matters than is currently exercised by the European Community.

At the same time, rights are inadequately protected at present in this country, because people attach more significance to democracy than to rights as a means of controlling abuse of power by government or Parliament. This failure to protect even those rights which make democracy possible puts at risk democracy itself, and with it the fragile protection for rights which we currently have. Attitudes need to be changed, as only then will it be possible to put in place a structure for the domestic protection of rights which has a reasonable chance of enduring. As a way of changing attitudes and making people think more in terms of rights and less in terms of politics, a non-entrenched Bill of Rights statute would provide a useful starting-point. It would probably take a generation before enough people had been brought up under the statute, and educated to take it seriously, to make it possible to persuade them that an entrenched Bill of Rights is a practical and desirable possibility. In Canada, a Bill of Rights was in place for thirty years, as an ordinary statute, having relatively little legal effect but gradually impinging on the consciousness of citizens. When the Constitution Act 1982 gave a new Charter of Rights and Freedoms constitutional status and protection but with democratic safeguards, senior lawyers and judges had had time to acclimatize themselves to the ideas of rights (helped but not dominated by their knowledge of the U.S. Constitution). They set to work with a will. Many have been upset by what has been done with the Charter, but it would have been impossible thirty years earlier. In time, New Zealand's Bill of Rights Act 1990 may prove to have a similar effect there on the constitutional ethos.

This is likely to be the best way to proceed in a country, such as ours, with a deep commitment to Parliamentary democracy, with all its advantages and drawbacks. Lay the foundations for the change now, without doing anything dramatic. In twenty or thirty years, the time will be ripe for the next step in constitutional development; citizens, judges, and politicians will be ready. An entrenched Bill of Rights, drawing inspiration from all available models and adapting them to our own needs, with judicial review of legislation on the basis of it by a special constitutional court (rather as judicial review of administrative action is already conducted by specialist judges in the Divisional Court hearing the Crown Office List), would give well-qualified judges a chance to test their capacities for rights-based reasoning. Because the bill would not simply incorporate the European Convention, the judges' work would not bring them directly into conflict with, or under the thumb of, the European Court of Human Rights in Strasbourg, although it would be the responsibility of government to ensure that our law is ultimately consistent with the Convention. The judges have shown that they are capable giving a broad and purposive interpretation to Bills of Rights in appeals to the Privy Council.[154] There is reason to think that they could do the same domestically.

The need for our law on rights to be consistent with our international obligations will be a powerful reason for not entrenching the Bill too

---

[154] A.-G. of Trinidad and Tobago v. Whiteman [1992] 2 All ER 924, PC.

inflexibly, as it might be necessary to change it to satisfy international obligations. This would have a further advantage: as the constitutional ethos changes, it might be thought desirable to change or extend the nature of rights which are guaranteed. Initially these would be likely to be related directly to advancing individual autonomy and social democracy; later, constitutional recognition for social or economic rights might be wanted. It must be possible to add or subtract rights as the ethos develops, preferably without depending entirely on judges' willingness to reinterpret existing rights.

This is a relatively long-term solution to the immediate problem of protecting rights. Patience is needed, but might ultimately be rewarded. Impatience, rushing into a Bill of Rights before we are ready, could simply discredit the bill and the judges who administer it. By taking things slowly, and thinking ahead, we might end up with a bill which is both functional and popular.

PART II
LIFE, LIBERTY, AND PHYSICAL INTEGRITY

THE RIGHT TO LIFE

3.1 THE BASIS OF THE RIGHT TO LIFE

The International Covenant on Civil and Political Rights, Article 6(1), recognizes that 'Every human being has the inherent right to life', and provides that, 'This right shall be protected by law. No one shall be arbitrarily deprived of his life.' The European Convention on Human Rights, too, requires action from national legislatures to provide legal protection for the right to life, which is impliedly recognized rather than conferred. Article 2(1) of the European Convention begins, 'Everyone's right to life shall be protected by law.' In England, this is achieved in two ways: by threatening penal sanctions against those who commit, attempt, or incite murder or manslaughter, or other acts likely to lead to death, including aiding and abetting suicide; and by giving the estate of deceased persons the right to sue for damages by way of compensation where death is caused intentionally or negligently.

A useful area for exploring theories grounding the right to life is the responsibility of doctors to keep alive those who, like handicapped babies or cardiac arrest victims, would be likely to die if not treated. Here, we are dealing with a mixture of liberty-based values and social rights to state aid. It is clear, on individual freedom and autonomy principles, that an adult who is conscious and understands the implications of the decision may decline medical treatment, since any treatment without the patient's consent is prima facie a battery and an unlawful interference with his bodily integrity. However, where the patient is incapable of making that decision, or is consciously demanding treatment, is there a positive obligation on health-service providers to make assistance available? The problems here are twofold: shortage of material resources may make it impossible for a clinician to make treatment available to all who need it, necessitating rationing; and there may be cases in which, even if necessary resources are available, clinicians or others decide that it is not in the patient's best interests to attempt to preserve life. These issues overlap, since (for example) if it becomes necessary to exclude a certain number of people from treatment because resources are scarce, views about the extent to which a particular patient is likely to benefit from treatment (in terms of improvement in the quality as well as length of life) will inevitably affect the way in which the resources are allocated. Nevertheless, to some extent, they can be considered separately. Those issues relating to the autonomy and best interests of the patient are considered in this chapter. Those concerned with rationing and rights to health-service provision are dealt with in Chapter 18, below.

If the right to life as a positive claim on government is interpreted as being a right to a certain quality of life, it raises contentious issues, for instance in relation to health care that of the survival of handicapped and sick babies. Is there a duty to exercise medical resources in order to save the life of a child whose quality of life is likely to be very low on any criteria with which we are familiar? What is the nature of such a person's right to life? This question is especially agonizing in that it opens up fears of life and death decisions being made for the purpose of eugenics.

The foundations for extending the right to life so that it confers both a right not to be killed and a right that other people take positive steps to keep me alive are controversial. It goes beyond the negative freedom from interference, which can be justified by any liberal individualist theory. Can liberal individualism impose a duty to act to keep people alive? The most convincing attempt to construct such a theory is that of Professor Raz.[1] He uses the notion of autonomy as the basis for his morality of freedom. Autonomy is the ultimate goal, and a course of action which increases a person's range of possible choices is that most favoured by his version of liberalism. As people have infinitely more choices open to them when they are alive than after they have died, the maintenance of life is a fundamental duty towards autonomous individuals. The duty to advance autonomy is imposed, in Raz's political philosophy, on the state, not merely on individuals, so that Raz can claim to have produced a liberal theory (i.e. one based on individual freedom) which nevertheless authorizes, and in many cases will demand, action by the state to improve the lives of individuals. Contrary to the arguments advanced by libertarians who see the market as the most efficient mechanism for maximizing individual freedom and who accordingly deprecate any state interference save in so far as it is absolutely necessary to protect a core of negative freedoms for participants in markets, Raz argues that the notion of autonomy (which is at the centre of his idea of freedom) must be backed up by state action in support of a relatively wide range of individual interests.[2]

Raz's approach is the most convincing attempt so far to develop a justification for an interventionist state within liberal theory. However, it is important to be aware of a feature of his theory which affects the rights

[1] Joseph Raz, *The Morality of Freedom* (Oxford: Clarendon Press, 1986), discussed in Ch. 1, above.
[2] See Ch. 1, above.

which form the subject of this chapter. As mentioned above, the notion of autonomy is not the same as the idea of negative freedom. It allows for the use of state power in the citizen's life. However, it is not a paternalistic use of power. In the case of people who are capable of making decisions for themselves, but are temporarily incapable of doing so or lack the skills or resources to give effect to their preferred choice, the Razian state would act to give effect to the actual or presumed preference of the individual, rather than (as in a paternalist state) the state's own view of what a right-thinking person *ought* to prefer. Thus a state which allows a person to die, regardless of that person's wishes, because death is thought to be in the person's own best interests or those of society as a whole, breaches that individual's right to autonomy.

There are marginal cases, however. Suppose I decide to kill myself, but the state steps in and saves my life, or legally requires a doctor to do so. On one view, this maximizes my future autonomy, but on the other hand it fails to take seriously my decision to exercise that autonomy in such a way as to end my life. If freedom of choice is the essence of autonomy, are we not required to respect people's earlier choices, even when this limits the scope for protecting their future freedom of choice? If we do not respect past choices, there is a form of disguised paternalism in Raz's idea of autonomy: people must be free to choose, as long as they choose in such a way as not to restrict (unreasonably) their freedom to choose; and as any choice restricts future freedom by changing the circumstances in which future choices will be made, the state decides whether any particular choice results in an unreasonable restriction of the chooser's future freedom. Raz can partially avoid this problem by treating the value of life as lying in its position as a uniquely important precondition for the exercise of free choice. If life is a necessary precondition for autonomy, the need to protect it might not depend on the individual's choice to continue it. Instead, autonomy remains the fundamental human value, but life (being so central a condition for autonomy) has to be protected against being curtailed even by an exercise of autonomous choice.[3] On this approach, life is not a right but a liberal duty, or (in Hohfeld's terms) a disability, since the individual is unable to alter his own legal position in respect of it.

If the value of life lies in its contribution to autonomy, and the value of choice depends on making the right choices, it raises the possibility that life is not of equal value to all living creatures. The value of life to any

[3] For a similar argument, see Michael R. Flick, 'The Due Process of Dying', 79 *Calif. LR* 1121–67 (1991). Flick argues that patients' desires not to be treated should be overridden if there is a reasonable chance of successful treatment; doctors should act paternalistically, overriding autonomy to force patients to accept those 'choices' which preserve the capacity to make choices in the future.

individual might depend on that individual's capacity for autonomy, i.e. to make choices. Individuals who are incapable of making choices, or choices which society regards as rational, will not be treated as autonomous or free except within narrow limits, and their lives may be considered to be less valuable than those of fully rational individuals. Once a choice is made, rights to autonomy may require that the state provides resources to help to give effect to it, but does the value of autonomy in itself justify preserving the lives of those who are not capable of choice? This may depend on the future prospects. Children are not ordinarily considered to be fully autonomous individuals, although as they get older the law and society recognize that their capacity for understanding and rational choice increases. The likelihood that any particular child is on the way to becoming an autonomous member of society justifies investing human and economic resources in maintaining the child's life and health. The same applies to people who, through illness or accident, are temporarily incapable of exercising rational choice. But there are individuals who are likely never to be capable of exercising free choice (depending on the preferred definition of free choice): amoebas, insects, perhaps all non-humans fall into this category. These individuals will, on Raz's approach, be unable to assert a right to life.

What is the position of humans who are so severely mentally handicapped that they are unlikely ever to be able to make rational choices? The autonomy argument does not help to support a right to have their lives maintained. The most powerful argument for maintaining them is that the dignity of all humans requires us to be concerned for the lives of fellow humans. This right to equal concern (and, perhaps, as Dworkin[4] argues, to respect) is not, however, a right to life. In the context of life-and-death decisions, it requires decision-makers to keep the interests of the subject in the forefront of their minds, and to safeguard those interests so far as possible within available resources and without failing to give equal consideration to the competing interests of others. The remainder of this chapter examines how these and related questions are affected by the European Convention on Human Rights and domestic law.

3.2 WHAT CONSTITUTES AN INFRINGEMENT OF THE RIGHT TO LIFE?

(1) What form should legal protection for the right to life take?

A state might provide protection either directly or by imposing duties on others. For example, French law imposes a duty on passers-by to rescue

---

[4] Ronald Dworkin, *Taking Rights Seriously* (London: Duckworth, 1977), ch. 7.

those who are in danger of death, while, by contrast, English law normally does not.[5] Again, it might be thought necessary to criminalize only intentional taking of life, since it is on intentional deprivation that the European Convention on Human Rights concentrates, and the existence of a criminal sanction is unlikely to deter unintentional killing. Article 2(1) of the Convention therefore leaves it to the national authorities to define the scope of the right to life, but insists on the minimal requirement that 'No one shall be deprived of his life intentionally . . .'. In other words, a legal system which failed to criminalize intentional murder would be failing in its obligations under the Convention unless some other form of legal protection were offered. On the other hand, it is for the legislatures of each state to decide whether and in what form to criminalize intentional acts such as drunken driving and medical negligence which, though not intended to cause death, may lead to death.

(2) Is it sufficient if what is done significantly interferes with a person's ability to survive or to fulfil a plan for life?

In the USA, as Paul Sieghart pointed out,[6] there are dicta suggesting that the protection offered to 'life' in the Fourteenth Amendment to the Constitution:

extends to all those limbs and faculties by which life is enjoyed. The prohibition equally prohibits the mutilation of the body by the amputation of an arm or leg, or the putting out of an eye, or the destruction of any other organ of the body through which the soul communicates with the outer world. The deprivation not only of life, but of whatever God has given to every one with life, for its growth and enjoyment, is prohibited by the provision in question, if its efficacy be not frittered away by judicial decision.[7]

In so far as an occurrence is life-threatening in the victim's own circumstances, this receives support from the decisions of the European Commission of Human Rights in X v. *Federal Republic of Germany*[8] and *Simon-Herold* v. *Austria*,[9] discussed below. However, it seems inappropriate to extend it to matters which do not affect the victim's capacity to survive but rather the ability to develop a life plan or to procreate and have a family. Such matters are best dealt with under Articles 3 (inhuman or degrading treatment) or 8 of the Convention (respect for private and family life). Attempting to smuggle them within Article 2 risks devaluing

[5] See Geoffrey Mead, 'Contracting into Crime: A Theory of Criminal Omissions' (1991) 11 *Oxf. J. of Legal Studies* 147–73.

[6] Paul Sieghart, *The International Law of Human Rights* (Oxford: Clarendon Press, 1983), 134

[7] *Munn* v. *Illinois*, 94 US 113 (1876) at p. 142 *per* Field J., dissenting.

[8] (5207/71) CD 39, 99.   [9] (4340/69) CD 38, 18.

the latter. It is significant that English cases concerned with non-consensual sterilization of mentally handicapped people have been discussed in terms of the 'victim's' right to procreate or right to bodily integrity, or the right to life of the 'victim's' potential future children, rather than the 'victim's' own right to life.[10]

(3) Do state agencies have a positive duty to act so as to preserve life?

The Convention does not demand that states or citizens be placed under any positive obligation to save life, or to allocate resources to secure its prolongation. This is a significant issue when it becomes necessary for courts, doctors, or others to decide whether, for example, handicapped babies should be allowed to die, or treatments to relieve pain which incidentally hasten death should be allowed; the domestic implications for England are considered in sections 3(3) and (4) below.

A further, related, issue concerns the extent of a state's obligation to take positive action in order to preserve life in response to the right to have one's life protected by law. The Commission has decided that states have no duty to provide bodyguards indefinitely to protect the lives of people who fear that they are likely to be attacked.[11] It is not clear whether there is a short-term obligation, at least until a person can make alternative arrangements for his own protection. It has also been said that the state, when setting up an immunization programme which was designed to prevent disease but which created an incidental threat to life, was required to impose a supervision and control system in order to reduce as far as possible the number of fatalities which would result.[12]

Does a law or government programme which permits the existence of a state of affairs which indirectly makes a person's life more vulnerable breach the requirement of Article 2 of the Convention and Article 6 of the Covenant that the right to life be protected by law? There are indications that Article 2 might be interpreted so as to require the law to take account of, and protect against, such indirect threats. The Commission has held in *X v. Federal Republic of Germany*[13] that to allow a person to be evicted from his home when, because of his state of health, eviction may endanger his life, may infringe Article 2. The Commission also declared admissible a complaint by a prisoner in *Simon-Herold v. Austria*[14] that the

---

[10] See *Re B. (A Minor) (wardship: sterilisation)* [1987] AC 199, [1987] 2 All ER 206, especially *per* Lord Hailsham LC; Jane E. S. Fortin, 'Legal Protection for the Unborn Child' (1988) 51 *MLR* 54–83.

[11] *X v. Ireland* (6040/73) CD 44, 121 Eur. Comm. HR (fear of attack by the IRA).

[12] *Association X v. UK* (7154/75) DR 14, 31, Eur. Comm. HR (measles).

[13] (5207/71) CD 39, 99.

[14] (4340/69) CD 38, 18; a friendly settlement was later achieved: Eur. Comm. HR, Report of 19 Dec. 1972.

conditions and treatment which he suffered in prison had led to serious illness and breached Article 2. This approach is consistent with, though not identical to, Raz's claim that individual autonomy requires society to provide the conditions necessary for the worthwhile exercise of choice, as discussed in Chapter 1. This is particularly true of prisoners, who are unable to control their surroundings, and are entirely reliant on the state for opportunities to maintain health. If the decisions of the Commission are followed, it seems that there might be a duty on national authorities under Article 2 to frame all law so as to require courts to have regard in all cases (including applications for recovery of property) to the risk to health and life which might result from depriving a person of means of support or housing.

This derives interesting support from a decision of the Supreme Court of Canada concerning the impact of the Charter of Rights and Freedoms, section 7 ('Everyone has the right to life, liberty and security of the person and the right not to be deprived thereof except in accordance with the principles of fundamental justice') and section 1 (Charter rights guaranteed 'subject only to such reasonable limits prescribed by law as can be demonstrably justified in a free and democratic society') on the testing of nuclear weapons. In *Operation Dismantle* v. *R.*,[15] a group challenged the Canadian government's policy of allowing American cruise missiles, capable of carrying nuclear warheads, to overfly Canada. The plaintiffs argued that the policy created a threat to life which infringed the right guaranteed under section 7 of the Charter. The Supreme Court accepted that the policy was justiciable under the Charter, even though it concerned international relations. Nevertheless, the challenge was struck out, because it was inevitable that the plaintiffs would fail at trial to prove that the policy represented a sufficiently direct and substantial threat to the plaintiffs' interests to justify granting them a remedy. Despite this, the recognition that rights to life and personal security may be infringed by government programmes suggests that Article 2 of the European Convention on Human Rights might prove to have interesting implications for government policy.

(4) Genocide

Special provision is made in the Convention on the Prevention and Punishment of the Crime of Genocide for (among other things) killing 'with intent to destroy, in whole or in part, a national, ethnical, racial or religious group, as such'.[16] States parties are bound to implement

---

[15] (1985) 18 DLR (4th) 481, SC Canada.
[16] Article II. See generally Sieghart, *Internatiional Law*, 134–5.

legislation allowing for the prosecution of all persons guilty of these crimes before a competent tribunal of the state where the act was committed, or by an international penal tribunal. States parties are also to provide for effective remedies, and must ensure that for extradition purposes genocide offences are not treated as political (as normally extradition would not be permitted for political offences). In the UK, these matters are dealt with by the Genocide Act 1969, which incorporates the Genocide Convention in its Schedule.

(5) Restrictions on the right to life

The right to life is not absolute. There are circumstances, recognized by Article 2, in which the right must give way to other interests. Sometimes these are private interests, as when a person is attacked and defends himself. If reasonable self-defence were to be criminal, it might be thought to undervalue the victim's life for the sake of that of an aggressor. Sometimes they are or purport to be public interests, as where the state authorizes capital punishment, or where the death results from a necessary use of force to apprehend a suspected offender. The balance between different interests, or between the rights of different people to live, is likely to depend on cultural values which can differ widely. For example, even if we all accept that a person who is attacked should be able to defend himself, what do we say of the amount of force which the victim is entitled to use? How do we cope with the problem of a climber, roped to a colleague, who slips, and is likely to pull the colleague to her death unless she cuts the rope and lets him fall to his? Again, the approach adopted by the European Convention on Human Rights is to recognize the difficulties, to lay down certain minimum standards which are to be observed by all, but to leave decisions in the controversial areas to the national law-making authorities.

The Convention specifies two sets of circumstances in which states are authorized to abridge the right to life without it being a violation of Article 2. The first follows a judicial hearing; the second covers situations in which the right to life can be limited without a judicial hearing.

(1) Intentional deprivation of life in the execution of a sentence of a court following conviction of a crime for which the death penalty is provided by law

This is of some significance in the UK, where civilians face death for treason or arson in Her Majesty's Dockyards, and members of the armed forces remain subject to the death penalty for certain offences committed in time of war. The Sixth Protocol to the Convention requires the abolition of the death penalty, save in respect of acts committed in time of war or imminent threat of war. However, the UK has not yet ratified the

Sixth Protocol. Under Article 2 and the Protocol, the penalty must be 'provided by law'. There is no caselaw on the meaning of this term in the context of the death-penalty provisions. However, in other contexts it has been held that the expression means that the circumstances in which a consequence is to follow must be specified with reasonable certainty in published, valid legal norms, and that the due process requirements of the rule of law must be complied with.[17] It is to be expected that this would apply to Article 2: given the requirement that the sentence must have been imposed by a court, the requirement for a trial observing due process standards can be implied, and is in any case expressly required by Article 6.

While judicial execution is not ruled out under those parts of the Convention to which the UK is a party, the manner of,and circumstances surrounding its execution may contravene the prohibition under Article 3 of the Convention, forbidding torture and inhuman and degrading treatment or punishment. Thus in *Soering* v. *United Kingdom*[18] the applicant was held in the UK with a view to extradition to the United States for trial in Virginia on a charge of capital murder, an offence which made him liable to the death penalty there. Because of the circumstances attending imposition of the death penalty in the USA, with long periods of confinement and the threat of imminent execution hanging over the defendant (the so-called 'death row phenomenon'), the European Court of Human Rights unanimously held that extraditing the applicant to the USA would put him at risk of inhuman and degrading treatment, and would infringe his rights under Article 3 of the Convention. As a result, the UK government refused to extradite the applicant to the USA on any charge for which the penalty might include the death penalty. The USA, in a diplomatic note, confirmed that in the circumstances US law would prohibit the prosecution of the applicant in Virginia for the offence of capital murder, and the UK was prepared to extradite him on that understanding.[19]

The International Covenant on Civil and Political Rights imposes further substantive and procedural restrictions on the death penalty. Under Article 6(2), it may be imposed only for the most serious crimes in accordance with the law in force at the time of the commission of the crime, pursuant to a final judgement rendered by a competent court. By Article

[17] For a comparative survey of the importance of due process in relation to capital punishment, see David Pannick, *Judicial Review of the Death Penalty* (London: Duckworth, 1982), chs. 2 and 8; and, generally, Nigel Rodley, *The Treatment of Prisoners under International Law* (Oxford: Clarendon Press, 1987), ch. 7.

[18] Eur. Ct. HR, Series A, No. 161, Judgment of 7 July 1989, 11 EHRR 439.

[19] Resolution DH(90)8 of the Committee of Ministers, adopted 12 Mar. 1990, appendix.

6(5), it shall not be imposed for crimes committed by persons under 18 years of age, and shall not be carried out on pregnant women.[20] (This last is a curious concession to revulsion against an idea: either the idea of killing a woman in a state of incipient motherhood, a condition accorded special reverence in most societies, or the idea of causing the death of an innocent foetus, despite the doubt as to whether the foetus can be regarded as having any right to life.) Under Article 6(4), anyone sentenced to death shall have the right to seek pardon or commutation of the sentence, which (together with an amnesty) is to be available in all cases. There is no requirement that decisions concerning amnesty, pardon, or commutation of sentence are to be governed by legal procedures; they are matters for executive discretion. This reflects the position in English law, which has not in the past permitted judicial review of a decision by the Home Secretary to refuse a pardon or a commutation of sentence.[21] However, that case was decided at a time when it was usually thought that no exercise of a prerogative power was reviewable. This is no longer the case,[22] so it is possible that this matter might be open to argument in the future.[23]

(ii) Deprivation of life which results from the use of force which is no more than is absolutely necessary:

(a) in defence of any person from unlawful violence;
(b) in order to effect a lawful arrest or to prevent the escape of a person lawfully detained;
(c) in action lawfully taken for the purpose of quelling a riot or insurrection.

This group of abridgements of the right to life allows the state to permit anyone to take another's life in the circumstances set out. It appears to presuppose that the killer does not intend to kill, in the sense that the objective is to achieve one of the specified aims and the killing is merely a consequence of using an absolutely necessary amount of force in doing so. Under (a), the state may take account not only of self-defence but also of the need to rescue others from unlawful violence, although not from lawful violence or threats of natural or accidental disaster. Under (b) and

---

[20] See Rodley, *Treatment of Prisoners*, 186–7.

[21] *Hanratty* v. *Lord Butler of Saffron Waldon* (1971) 115 Sol. Jo. 386; *The Times*, 13 May 1971. Also New Zealand: see *Burt* v. *Governor-General* [1989] 3 NZLR 64, discussed by B. V. Harris, 'Judicial Review of the Prerogative of Mercy?' [1991] *PL* 386–407.

[22] *Council of Civil Service Unions* v. *Minister for the Civil Service* [1985] AC 374; *R.* v. *Secretary of State for Foreign and Commonwealth Affairs, ex parte Everett* [1989] QB 811, [1989] 1 All E.R. 655; and see also *R.* v. *Secretary of State for the Home Dept., ex parte Handscomb* (1987) 86 Cr. AR. 59.

[23] See A. T. H. Smith, 'The Prerogative of Mercy: The Power of Pardon and Criminal Justice' [1983] *PL* 398–439, on the circumstances in which the power to pardon is used; and see Harris, 'Judicial Review'.

(c), the action (taken usually, but not necessarily, by law enforcement agencies) must be 'lawful'. This requires that the power to act, and to use force of the type and amount actually employed, must be conferred by law, and that that law must be available to the public and make it reasonably clear what sorts of activity will make a person liable to be lawfully killed. Nothing in ECHR Article 2 permits a state to legalize the deliberate taking of life as an act of kindness with a view to relieving suffering. The status of laws which allow people to help those who wish to kill themselves, but are incapable of doing so by reason of disability, is uncertain: see section 3(4) below.

The second group of exceptions is apt to cover any death resulting from the use of force for an authorized purpose. If an innocent bystander is killed by accident, that death is not to be required to be treated as in breach of Article 2. While national law may go further than Article 2 and provide sanctions or duties to compensate for taking life in such circumstances, it is not required to do so by the Convention.

(6) Policing crime and public order

So far as the negative protections for the right to life are concerned, English and Scottish law is in line with the Convention in most, but not all, respects. The circumstances in which the death penalty may be imposed are clearly set out in statutes as interpreted by the courts. The position is sufficiently clear to enable lawyers to give advice reasonably confidently. The sentence can only be imposed by a court, which (even in wartime) will follow the procedural requirements laid down under the Convention.

English law on the use of force to protect people from violence also meets the Convention requirements. The degree of force used must not only be necessary, but must also be reasonably related to the threat. This is clearly true of the law of self-defence, under which a person who uses excessive force to defend himself against attack, or fails to retreat if a line of retreat is reasonably available, will not be entitled to an acquittal (although he may be guilty of the lesser crime of manslaughter rather than murder). There is a special problem where someone kills or helps to kill under duress, which has particular repercussions where terrorists try to use innocent people as instruments of violence. English law does not recognize duress as a defence to murder either as a principal or as an accessory.[24] For example, a person whose car is hijacked by gunmen and filled with explosives, and who is told to drive it to an army checkpoint

---

[24] *Abbott* v. *R.* [1977] AC 755, [1976] 3 All ER 140, PC; *R.* v. *Howe* [1987] AC 417, [1987] 1 All ER 771, HL, overruling *Lynch* v. *D.P.P. for Northern Ireland* [1975] AC 653, [1975] 1 All ER 913, HL

where it will be detonated, faces a serious problem if the hijackers threaten to kill him or members of his family if he does not comply. Should someone be killed in the explosion, the driver will not be able to use duress as a defence to a murder charge. It appears that the Convention offers no guidance on the appropriateness or otherwise of recognizing such a defence. The likelihood is that someone will die whatever the driver does. Prudentially, it makes sense for him to adopt the course which seems least likely to cause death. But from the point of view of human rights, it seems more plausible to say that the right to life of the deceased has been infringed by the driver if deaths result from the explosion than if the driver refuses to drive the car and he or his family are killed. In human rights terms, then, the refusal to recognize the defence of duress to a murder charge is justified, even though little is to be gained in terms of deterrence (since a person in that position is unlikely to know the law or to regard it as a major factor influencing his decision).

The use of force allowable in order to make a lawful arrest or to prevent the escape of a person lawfully detained is governed by the rules set out in the Criminal Law Act 1967, section 3, and the Police and Criminal Evidence Act 1984, section 117. Under the 1967 Act, force may be used only if it is necessary, and the amount of force must be reasonable. The cases show that courts take an indulgent view of these requirements, particularly where security forces face a perceived threat from supposedly dangerous criminals, allowing some leeway in deciding whether it is necessary to use force.[25] This is, in principle, acceptable under the Convention. The requirement of absolute necessity under Article 2 relates to the amount of force to be used; it does not impose an objective standard of necessity on law enforcers or others when deciding whether or not any force should be used. Thus it is permissible for the law to take account of the reasonable apprehensions of victims or law enforcers in deciding whether to use force. English law therefore seems to go further than required by the Convention in requiring that force may be used only if necessary.

However, this may be deceptive, for two reasons. First, the House of Lords, in another context, has held that 'necessary' means less than 'absolutely indispensable', though more than merely 'convenient'.[26] Nevertheless, there is little doubt that in this respect our law meets the minimal European requirements, and is well within the margin of appreciation which the European Court of Human Rights allows to states to set their own standards within the limits laid down by the Convention.

[25] See e.g. *Farrell* v. *Secretary of State for Defence* [1980] 1 All ER 1667, HL.
[26] *Re an Inquiry under the Company Securities (Insider Dealing) Act 1985* [1988] AC 660, [1988] 1 All ER 203, HL

Secondly, it is important that the courts, in each case, carefully consider whether, on the facts, the amount of force used was necessary. This is difficult, as it demands a careful analysis of the operational implications of different sorts of weaponry and tactics,[27] but it must be done if the security and police forces are to be made accountable to law for interferences with the right to life. By appearing to apply a reasonableness test, English law falls short of Convention requirements. For this reason, the European Commission of Human Rights held admissible a complaint concerning use of deadly force by the security forces in Northern Ireland after the British courts had dismissed a claim for damages, and the applicant and the government achieved a friendly settlement.[28] Nevertheless, it has to be recognized that combating terrorism presents special problems, because it may be necessary to use or threaten a high level of force in order to protect the community against people who are themselves using or threatening extreme and arbitrary violence. Measures become necessary which would not otherwise be considered justifiable, including the availability of deadly force and the readiness to use it.[29]

There is room for further doubt about the legality, under the Convention, of the Police and Criminal Evidence Act 1984, section 117, allowing 'reasonable' force to be used, which applies to all powers conferred on constables under the Act which do not specifically require the consent of another person. As Article 2(2) of the Convention speaks of force 'which is no more than absolutely necessary', it is arguable that Parliament, in employing the standard of 'reasonable force', allowed greater force to be used than is permissible under the Convention. On the other hand, it could be argued that when a person is put in peril of his life in order to secure his, or someone else's, arrest (rather than to save the life of another), it is unreasonable to use more force than is absolutely necessary. On this view, the standards of reasonableness and absolute necessity converge. However, in English law there is no ruling to this effect, nor could there easily be. The reasonableness of the degree of force used is a question for the finder of fact. It is not regarded as a matter of law for the judge. It is therefore possible that the law fails to measure up to the standards required by the Convention, in that it does not

[27] For a very instructive account of the implementation of tactics involving deadly force, see P. A. J. Waddington, *The Strong Arm of the Law: Armed and Public Order Policing* (Oxford: Clarendon Press, 1991), ch. 4.

[28] *Farrell* v. *UK*, (6861/75) 3 DR 147, 3 EHRR 466; (9013/80) 5 EHRR 466, Eur. Comm. HR. A subsequent application has been held to be inadmissible: *Stewart* v. *UK* (10044/82) 7 EHRR 453.

[29] For balanced accounts and evaluations of the measures taken in relation to Northern Ireland, see R. J. Spjut, 'The "Official" Use of Deadly Force by the Security Forces Against Suspected Terrorists' [1986] PL 38–66; Gerard Hogan and Clive Walker, *Political Violence and the Law in Ireland* (Manchester: Manchester University Press, 1989), 64–9.

specify as a matter of law that only such force as is absolutely necessary may be used.

There is another respect in which English law on this subject may fall short of the Convention standards. The use of force for the control of public disorder is governed largely by common law rather than statute. Apart from the powers of arrest under the Police and Criminal Evidence Act 1984, common-law powers of arrest in connection with breaches of the peace are expressly preserved by the Act, which also leaves untouched the related common-law powers to take any reasonable steps to prevent or defuse a breach of the peace which is in progress or is reasonably apprehended and imminent. These powers are discussed in detail in Chapter 17, below. Here, however, it should be noted that they permit the use of force, and if the force were to lead to someone's death it would be necessary to decide whether it flowed from action in order to effect a lawful arrest (Article 2(2)(b)) or from action lawfully taken for the purpose of quelling a riot or insurrection (Article 2(2)(c)). As observed above, the standard of lawfulness under the Convention involves the power being conferred by a law which is accessible to the public and which makes reasonably clear (with the benefit of legal advice if necessary) the circumstances in which it may be exercised.

There are two respects in which it is arguable that the law on breach of the peace in England fails to match up to these standards. First, by relying on the idea of reasonableness (both in respect of the foreseeability of the breach and the amount of force which may be used) it fails to lay down sufficient legal guidance on the circumstances in which force may be lawfully employed. Secondly, it is possible that the legal criteria for a breach of the peace are insufficiently clear to enable a person to know when one is taking place or is imminent and reasonably apprehended.[30] However, it is submitted that the law is reasonably clear. The standard of reasonableness is one which admittedly defies further analysis, but it is one which should be sufficiently accessible to ordinary people for it to be understood by them, even though there will be room for disagreement as to whether a particular apprehension, or a specified amount of force, is reasonable or not.

3.3 BENEFICIARIES AND VICTIMS

While the Convention requires national authorities to protect the right to life, it does not define the scope of the right. There are cultural differ-

---

[30] R. v. Howell [1982] QB 416, [1981] 3 All ER 383, CA. Compare R. v. Chief Constable of Devon and Cornwall, ex parte Central Electricity Generating Board [1982] Q. 458, [1981] 3 All ER 826, CA.

ences as to the scope of the right. One such difference concerns the meaning of 'everyone'. Does it, for example, protect the life of an unborn foetus? Another problem concerns euthanasia: does the right to life require the state to protect people, in a paternalistic way, against choosing to die?

As already noted, neither the Convention nor, usually, English law imposes obligations to assist strangers to preserve their lives. Where English law does impose such an obligation, it is usually on people who are regarded as having special responsibilities, either because of their pre-existing contractual or family relationship to the endangered person, or because (like life-guards) they have a position which leads society to have higher expectations of them than of the community at large.[31] This may lead to criminal liability, to civil liability, or both. In such cases, liability is imposed in respect of an omission rather than an act.

Particularly difficult problems therefore arise in the context of doctor–patient relationships. The extent of a doctor's duties towards foetuses, to treat severely handicapped neonates, and to keep alive terminally ill patients, are specially sensitive issues. The extent and nature of the regulation which the state exercises over these matters is a significant element in the strength of protection for the right to life. This section considers some aspects of these matters which are particularly relevant to the civil liberties and human rights of the patients concerned.

(1) Do foetuses have a right to life?

So far, the European Court of Human Rights has not had to decide whether foetuses have a right to life, but there are decisions of the European Commission of Human Rights which suggest that they do not. In *X* v. *United Kingdom*[32] the Commission doubted whether 'everyone' in Article 2(1) included a foetus, but thought that even if the right to life began at conception it would be subject to an implied restriction to permit an abortion in order to protect the mother's life or health. The issue arose directly for decision in *Paton* v. *United Kingdom*,[33] in which the father of an unborn child had unsuccessfully sought to persuade the English courts to prevent the mother from having an abortion. The father argued that the failure to prevent the abortion had infringed the foetus's right to life. The Commission decided that Article 2 applies only to people who have been born, because the life of the foetus is intimately connected with that of the mother. If Article 2 applied to a foetus, the Commission reasoned, abortions would have to be prohibited even where

---

[31] Mead, 'Contracting into Crime'.   [32] (8416/78) DR 19, 244.
[33] (1980) 3 EHRR 408.

continuation of the pregnancy would present a serious risk to the mother's life, giving the foetus's life a higher value than the mother's, as there is no provision in Article 2 allowing a person to be deliberately killed in order to save the life of another.[34]

In this respect, English law gives more protection to the life of a foetus than is required under the Convention. A number of statutes create criminal offences in order to protect the life of a foetus. A pregnant woman who, with intent to procure her own miscarriage, unlawfully administers to herself any poison or other noxious thing, or uses an instrument or other means to the same end, is guilty of an offence under section 58 of the Offences Against the Person Act 1861. So is anyone who administers drugs or uses an instrument or other means with intent to procure the miscarriage of any woman, whether or not she is in fact pregnant. A person who supplies any poison, noxious thing, instrument, or anything else, knowing that it is intended to be used to procure a miscarriage, commits an offence under section 59.

However, while English law treats foetuses as having *interests* worthy of protection, and as deserving respect,[35] like the European Commission of Human Rights it does not regard them as having *rights* at all. The foetus is not even within the jurisdiction of the English courts until born. Thus a foetus cannot be made a ward of court until it has been born alive. Indeed, the Commission's decision in *Paton* was influential in persuading the Court of Appeal not to extend the protection of the wardship jurisdiction to an unborn child.[36] Similarly, although a child is entitled to sue for prenatal injuries,[37] causes of action do not vest until birth, so a father cannot sue as the unborn child's next friend to seek an injunction restraining a mother or doctor from procuring an abortion.[38] Nevertheless, the closer a foetus comes to birth, the more likely it becomes that doctors will be permitted to perform a Caesarian section on

[34] See the Commission's decision at p. 413, para 8, and p. 415, para 19.

[35] See Dept. of Health and Social Security, *Report of the Committee of Inquiry into Human Fertilisation and Embryology* (Chairman: Dame Mary Warnock), Cmnd. 9314 (London: HMSO, 1984). This is sometimes based on the potential of the foetus to develop into a human being: see the report of the Polkinghorne Committee, *Review of the Guidance on the Research Use of Fetuses and Fetal Material* (Cm. 762). It is a matter of dispute whether foetuses have the potential to become human beings or are already human beings: see e.g. Judith Jarvis Thompson, 'A Defence of Abortion', in R. M. Dworkin (ed.), *Philosophy of Law* (Oxford: Oxford University Press, 1977), 112–28; John Finnis, 'The Rights and Wrongs of Abortion: A Reply to Judith Thompson', in Dworkin (ed.), *Philosophy of Law*, 129–52.

[36] *Re F. (in utero)* [1988] Fam. 122, [1988] 2 All ER 193, CA. See generally Gillian Douglas, *Law, Fertility and Reproduction* (London: Sweet & Maxwell, 1991), ch. 6.

[37] Congenital Disabilities (Civil Liability) Act 1976; *Burton v. Islington Health Authority* [1992] 3 All ER 833 CA.

[38] *Paton v. British Pregnancy Advisory Service* [1979] QB 276, [1978] 2 All ER 987.

the mother against her will in order to safeguard the life of the child. In such circumstances, Sir Stephen Brown P. recently granted a declaration that it would not be unlawful to perform an emergency Caesarian on a mother who had refused surgery on religious grounds.[39] Some US courts have made similar decisions, although the balance of authority now upholds the mother's autonomy. This raises fundamental moral issues, which should be settled by thorough legislation, not by *ad hoc* judical action under severe time pressure.[40]

(ii) *A woman's right to an abortion?* The European Convention, while not mandating protection for the life of a foetus, does not confer on a pregnant woman any right to an abortion on demand either directly or (probably) as an aspect of the right to respect for private life under Article 8. Pregnancy was held not to be a wholly private matter, because the mother's right to respect for privacy was bound up with the life of the developing foetus.[41] It is left to the parties to the Convention to decide whether, and when, to permit abortions. It has been suggested by one commentator that the Commission, in holding that the foetus has no right to life, must impliedly be recognizing that the pregnant woman has a right to an abortion in at least some circumstances.[42] This does not seem to follow, however. The fact that the Convention might not protect the foetus's interests as rights does not thereby increase the rights of anyone else to be free of the effects of regulation by the state to safeguard the foetus's interests. The relationship between the rights of the woman and those (if any) of the foetus does not affect the relationship between the rights of the woman and the responsibility of the state to protect the interests of those who or which cannot represent themselves.

In Ireland, no abortions are legally available. This was the position under section 58 of the Offences against the Person Act 1861, and is

[39] *Re S. (Adult: Refusal of Treatment)* [1992] 4 All ER 671.

[40] Ian Kennedy, *Treat Me Right: Essays in Medical Law and Ethics* (Oxford: Clarendon Press, 1991), ch. 19. On the early US cases, see Nancy K. Rhoden, 'The Judge in the Delivery Room: The Emergence of Court Ordered Caesarians', 74 *Calif. LR* 1951–2030 (1986).

[41] *Brüggeman and Scheuten* v. *Federal Republic of Germany* (6959/75) DR 10, 100, Eur. Comm. HR, Report of 12 July 1977; *Paton* v. *UK* (8416/78), Eur. Comm. HR, decision of 13 May 1980, 3 EHRR 408. In *Open Door Counselling Ltd.* v. *Ireland* and *Dublin Well Woman Centre Ltd.* v. *Ireland* Eur. Ct. HR, Judgment of 29 Oct. 1992, the Court left open the possibility that some restrictions on abortion might be required by Art. 2 as applied to the foetus. If so, a balance will be needed between the mother's rights under Art. 8 and those of the foetus under Art. 2, and states are likely to be allowed a wide margin of appreciation. See K. D. Ewing and C. A. Gearty, 'Terminating Abortion Rights?' (1992) 142 *NLJ* 1696–8.

[42] Margherita Rendel, 'Abortion and Human Rights' (1991) 141 *NLJ* 1270–1, at p. 1271.

reinforced by the constitutional guarantee of the right to life under Article 40.3.3 of the Constitution, introduced following a referendum in 1983 at the instance of pro-life campaigners. However, in *Attorney-General* v. *X* [43] the Supreme Court was faced with a conflict between the right to life of the mother and that of the foetus. The Attorney-General, relying on the right to life of the unborn child under Article 40.3.3, had obtained an injunction restraining a pregnant 14-and-a-half-year-old victim of rape from travelling to England for an abortion. The girl's right to travel (one of the 'unenumerated rights' of the Constitution) was out-weighed by the child's right to life. However, there was a real and sub-stantial risk that the girl, if denied an abortion, would commit suicide. In these circumstances, a majority of the court held that the threat to the girl's right to life outweighed the unborn infant's right to life, and it was not proper to prevent the girl from obtaining an abortion. An incidental effect of this reasoning appears to be that there is now no constitutional bar to the legalization of abortion in Ireland itself in situations where there is such a real and substantial risk to the mother's life, even if the risk is of self-inflicted death.

The position in the UK was for a long period in effect much the same as in Ireland under sections 58 and 59 of the Offences Against the Person Act 1861, above, which presented a simple but harsh answer to the prob-lem of balancing the interest in the life of the foetus against the woman's rights to life and to control over her own body. It weighted the interest in the foetus's life above that in the mother's life, health, or happiness. It made a woman or doctor potentially liable to life imprisonment for per-forming an abortion even when the mother's life and health were threat-ened by continuing the pregnancy. This liability might be avoided, for example by invoking the doctrine of double effect: it might have been possible in some cases to argue that a drug was administered to save the woman's life, and it had the incidental effect of procuring a miscarriage. Alternatively, it was said that performing an abortion to save the woman's life would have been justifiable on ordinary criminal law principles, and so would not have been unlawful within the meaning of section 58 of the 1861 Act. [44] However, even if this is accepted, it arguably left no scope for abortions to preserve mental health or to avoid risks which were not life-threatening. Back-street abortions by unqualified or dis-qualified practitioners resulted, without the benefit of the appropriate

---

[43] [1992] 1 IR 1, 17, SC of Ireland.

[44] In *R*. v. *Bourne* [1939] 1 KB 687, [1938] 3 All ER 615, the jury was told that, if a doctor was entitled to an acquittal under proviso to s. 1(1) of the Infant Life (Preservation) Act 1929 (below), his action would not have been 'unlawful' within the meaning of ss. 58 and 59 of the 1861 Act.

back-up in case of complications, and many women lost their lives as a result.

The balance moved slightly in favour of the woman when the Infant Life (Preservation) Act 1929 was passed. Section 1(1) created a new offence of child destruction, committed by a person who, with intent to destroy the life of a child capable of being born alive, by a wilful act causes the child to die before it has an existence independent of its mother. This section was actually designed to trap people who procured abortions of foetuses at an advanced stage of gestation, when they can be born alive but cannot then survive. But under the proviso to the sub-section, nobody was to be convicted unless it was proved that the act which caused the death had not been done in good faith for the purpose only of preserving the mother's life. This added nothing substantial to the justification which was available under the 1861 Act, but it placed the burden of proof on the prosecution instead of the defence. This did not, however, help doctors or pregnant women who procure abortions before the child is capable of being born alive; they continued to carry the burden of proof as to the justification under the 1861 Act.

The curious result followed that the criminal law seemed to offer more protection to a less mature foetus than to a more mature one. This is counter-intuitive: as we shall see, in Canada and the USA courts have regarded the state as having a greater interest in protecting more mature than less mature foetuses. The restrictive nature of the proviso, applying only to steps to save the life of the mother, might also seem to have put doctors at continuing risk of prosecution in cases where the mother's life was not under immediate threat. However, in *R. v. Bourne*[45] the judge, Macnaghten J., instructed the jury that preserving the mother's life had to be given an extended meaning. As life depends on physical and mental health, an abortion performed to prevent severe harm to the mother's physical or mental health would be regarded as preserving her life.

This was a recognition of the woman's interests, but it did not go as far as they increasingly wanted in allowing them to control their bodies. It did not allow a way of avoiding the stigma attaching to unmarried mothers, nor of saving many families from the social and economic hardship to which having an unwanted child could lead. Often, those who could not face the prospect of a child still relied on illegal abortions. Deaths continued to occur, and back-street abortionists to flourish. As a result, increasing pressure developed during the 1950s and 1960s for an amendment which would permit lawful abortions in a wider range of cases. Governments felt that the moral issues which bore on abortion made it too hot a subject for them to handle, and it was left to the Liberal, Mr

---

[45] [1939] 1 KB 687, [1938] 3 All ER 615.

(now Sir) David Steel MP, to pilot through Parliament a private member's bill, which received the royal assent as the Abortion Act 1967. This legalized abortions in cases where a pregnancy was terminated by a registered medical practitioner after two registered medical practitioners had formed the opinion, in good faith, either: (a) that continuing the pregnancy would give rise to a risk to the life of the pregnant woman, or of injury to the physical or mental health of the woman or any existing children of her family, greater than the risk if the pregnancy were terminated, taking account of the woman's actual or reasonably foreseeable environment; or (b) that there was a substantial risk that the child, if born, would have suffered from such physical or mental abnormalities as to be seriously handicapped.[46]

The freedom given to doctors to take account of environmental (in this context, social, housing, and economic) matters gave a discretion to allow something close to abortion on demand. Increasingly, interest groups concerned with the life of the foetus (which could not represent itself) claimed that abortions were being performed for the convenience of the mother rather than to prevent a real risk of harm. It was also said that many abortions were performed privately by doctors on women from abroad, who flew in from places where abortion is illegal (such as Ireland) purely to take advantage of the ready availablity of the procedure in this country. Finally, although the Act did not affect the Infant Life (Preservation) Act 1929, so it would still be child destruction to perform an abortion where the foetus was 'viable'[47] (i.e. capable of being born alive, albeit only for one or two minutes[48]), it was asserted that viable foetuses were being aborted and then, instead of being treated, were left lying around to die, and then disposed of without the birth being registered.[49] It was not clear when 'viability' began, but it was generally thought to be somewhere between the twenty-fourth and twenty-eighth weeks of pregnancy. Because of delays in obtaining test results under the National Health Service, a doctor could often not offer an abortion to a woman with a seriously abnormal foetus unless the abnormality was detected by the nineteenth week of pregnancy at latest.[50]

After several attempts to introduce amending legislation, the supporters

[46] Abortion Act 1967, s. 1(1), (2) (now amended by Human Fertilisation and Embrology Act 1990, below).

[47] Abortion Act 1967, s. 5(1).

[48] See *Report of the Select Committee on the Infant Life (Preservation) Bill*, HL No. 50 of 1987–8, para. 18; *Rance v. Mid-Downs Health Authority* [1991] 1 All ER 801 at p. 812 *per* Brooke J.

[49] See J. K. Mason and R. A. McCall Smith, *Law and Medical Ethics*, 3rd edn (London: Butterworths, 1991), 117–18.

[50] *Rance v. Mid-Downs Health Authority* [1991] 1 All ER 801 was one such case.

of the life of the unborn foetus finally forced an amendment to the 1967 Act. As amended by section 37 of the Human Fertilisation and Embryology Act 1990, section 1 of the Abortion Act 1967 now provides that an abortion is legal (i.e. does not constitute an offence under section 58 or 59 of the Offences Against the Person Act 1861) if it is performed by a registered medical practitioner[51] and one of the following four conditions is met:

(a) two registered medical practitioners have formed the opinion, in good faith, that continued pregnancy would involve a risk of injury to the physical or mental health of the pregnant woman or any existing child of her family, greater than that involved in termination, and that the pregnancy has not passed the end of the twenty-fourth week; or

(b) a doctor has formed the view, in good faith, that continuing the pregnancy would involve a risk of *grave and permanent* injury to the physical or mental health of the woman (so that in such cases an emergency abortion is now legal without waiting for a second opinion); or

(c) a doctor has formed the view, in good faith, that continuing the pregnancy would involve a risk to the life of the woman (so that in such cases an emergency abortion is now legal without waiting for a second opinion); or

(d) two registered medical practitioner have formed the view, in good faith, that there is a *substantial* risk that the child, if born, would suffer from such physical or mental abnormalities as to be *severely* handicapped (no guidance being given on what is a severe handicap).

In some respects, this represents a tightening of the law, so that the 'environmental' health abortion under (a) is not available after the twenty-fourth week. This should reduce the number of abortions which lead to live births, and the upset and outrage they cause to nursing staff and pro-life groups. However, in other respects, under (b) and (c), the controls are relaxed. It is too early to say how the new regime will affect the availability of abortions, and the protection of the rights of foetuses as against their mothers.[52] However, it is continuing evidence of the significance of the state's interest in foetal life in this country, an interest

---

[51] Much of the actual procedure is performed by nurses. However, it has been held (in order to avoid practical resource and staffing problems which could have severely limited the availability of abortions) that 'performed' in s. 1 means 'initiated'. Once a registered medical practitioner has initiated the procedure and instructed nursing staff to continue it, it is treated as performed by (because under the authority and control of) the doctor: *Royal College of Nursing of the UK* v. *Dept. of Health and Social Security* [1981] AC 800, [1981] 1 All ER 545, HL

[52] For discussion of the amendments, see Andrew Grubb, 'The New Law of Abortion: Clarification or Ambiguity?' [1991] *Crim. LR* 659–70.

reaffirmed in the provisions, in the Human Fertilisation and Embryology Act 1990, for regulating research on embryos.[53]

(iii) A North American comparison: the reasoning of rights. The law in the USA and Canada provides an interesting contrast to that in the UK. In Canada, where the right to life is constitutionally protected under section 7 of the Charter of Rights and Freedoms, it has been held that the foetus's interest in life does not become a constitutionally protected right until birth.[54] The courts recognize that the state has a legitimate interest in protecting the life of the unborn foetus, partly because of the general social concern to maintain moral standards, which include a proper regard for those potential members of the community who are unable to protect (or even appreciate) their own interests. Accordingly, it is constitutionally proper for the state to regulate abortion by legislation. However, to force a woman to carry a baby to term is an infringement of the mother's right, also under section 7 of the Charter, to security of the person. In assessing the constitutionality of legislation regulating the availability of abortion by reference to the woman's reasons for wanting one, the judges have to weigh the woman's right to security against the state's legitimate interest, according to the criteria set out in section 1 of the Charter: the limits on the woman's right to security of the person must be reasonable, prescribed by law, and demonstrably justified in a free and democratic society. Since the strength of the state's legitimate interest increases as the unborn child matures and comes closer being a member of the community, the state is entitled to inquire more closely into a woman's reason for wanting an abortion in the later stages of pregnancy than the earlier ones.[55]

In the USA, too, there is a balancing act between the interest of the state in the welfare of the foetus and the rights of the mother, rather than between the rights of the mother and any supposed rights of the unborn

[53] Mason and McCall Smith, *Medical Ethics*, 380–4. See further Margaret Brazier, 'Embryo's "Rights": Abortion and Research', in M. D. A. Freeman (ed.), *Medicine, Ethics and the Law* (London: Stevens & Sons, 1988), 9–22; Simon Lee, 'Re-reading Warnock', in Peter Byrne (ed.), *Rights and Wrongs in Medicine* (London: King's Fund, 1986), 37–52; Jonathan Montgomery, 'Rights, Restraints and Pragmatism: The Human Fertilisation and Embryology Act 1990' (1991) 54 *MLR* 524–34.

[54] *Borowski* v. *A.-G. of Canada* (1987) 39 DLR (4th) 731, Saskatchewan CA.

[55] *Morgentaler, Smoling and Scott* v. *R.* (1988) 44 DLR (4th) 385, SC of Canada. The account in this paragraph combines the approaches of Dickson CJ and Wilson J. The case is discussed by M. L. McConnell, 'Abortion and Human Rights: an Important Canadian Decision' (1989) 38 *ICLQ* 905–13; Geoffrey Marshall, 'Liberty, Abortion and Judicial Review in Canada' [1988] *PL* 199–210; Jamie Cameron, 'Cross Cultural Reflections: Teaching the Charter to Americans' (1990) 28 *Osgoode Hall LJ* 613–40. The Supreme Court recently reaffirmed its view in *Tremblay* v. *Daigle* (1990) 62 DLR (4th) 634.

child. The rights of women in the USA in this context are privacy rights, rather than rights to personal security, but privacy rights have constitutionally protected status in the USA and are capable of making it unconstitutional for the state to deprive a woman of the opportunity for an abortion.[56] In *Roe* v. *Wade* the US Supreme Court held, as in Canada, that the state's interest, and so its freedom to interfere, increased as the foetus came closer to full term. The Supreme Court adopted a fairly mechanistic approach to the stages by which the state's interest grows. In the first three months (trimester) of pregnancy, the interest is very weak, and any state interference with a woman's freedom to obtain an abortion will be unconstitutional. In the second trimester, the state was entitled to intervene, but only to secure its interest in the health of the *mother*, not the child. In other words, in the second trimester it is permissible to restrict abortion where (for example) the risk to the mother from the abortion exceeds the risk of carrying the child to term.

Only in the third trimester, according to *Roe* v. *Wade*, was the state entitled to intervene in the interests of the foetus, because by then the foetus is likely to be 'viable', that is, capable of sustaining life independently of its mother if given suitable clinical aid. This is usually thought to happen sometime between the twenty-fourth and twenty-eighth weeks. However, as subsequent cases have made clear, the test for viability depends on the ability of clinicians to save the lives of premature babies. As clinical abilities increase the chances of survival of children born earlier in pregnancy, the moment of viability, and the time when the state is entitled to intervene, will also become earlier. The Supreme Court has therefore subsequently rejected the trimester rule, while maintaining much of the spirit of *Roe* v. *Wade*.[57] Even then, the limitations imposed by the state will be scrutinized to ensure that they comply with due process requirements. Limiting abortions to cases where there is a risk to the life of the mother was said in *Roe* v. *Wade* to be unconstitutionally vague (in European Convention terms, too uncertain to meet the 'according to law' criterion), although 'life and health' is acceptable.

This looks, on the face of it, far more liberal than the UK position under the Abortion Act 1967, which specifies the grounds on which abortions may be performed, in a way which would be unconstitutional in the USA (at least in relation to the first trimester). However, it is actually more complicated than that. In the classic liberal individualist tradition of the US Constitution, the American woman's right, to an abortion before the foetus is viable, is in reality a right that the state refrain from

[56] *Roe* v. *Wade* 93 S. Ct. 705 (1973).
[57] *Akron* v. *Akron Center for Reproductive Health,* 462 US 416 (1983), US Supreme Court, at 455–6 *per* O'Connor J.; *Planned Parenthood of South-Eastern Pennsylvania* v. *Casey,* 112 S.Ct. 2791, 120 L.Ed. 2d 674 (1992).

stopping her from procuring an abortion. This means that a woman who can afford to pay for an abortion cannot be prevented from having one (before viability). A woman who cannot afford to pay for it has no right that the state shall procure an abortion for her on demand. Where public money is put into a health programme, the state is entitled to specify the way in which the money is to be used.[58] It follows that, while the wealthy can more easily obtain a legal abortion in the USA than in the UK, the poor are likely to be at least as well off in the UK. Here, as elsewhere, we find a difference between rights which secure negative liberty—the right to be let alone—and discretions which may be exercised to secure positive benefits which make liberty more valuable to the right-holder (see Chapter 1).

In view of the importance which different legal systems attach to the moments when a foetus 'quickens', or becomes 'viable', or is born, in deciding how far the law should protect the interests of that foetus, it is tempting to suppose that foetuses are entitled to protection when they become people, and that there is some easy, mechanical way of identifying when that moment arrives. However, this is a misconception. The process of development is a continuous one. Each watershed is a perceived, rather than real, one: we attach significance to certain developing characteristics for our own purposes, but they have no greater significance in the development of the child than any other. Accordingly, certain methods of non-barrier, post-coital birth control (such as IUD, or the so-called 'morning after pill') raise legal and ethical questions concerning the sanctity of life as profound as does surgical abortion.[59] Like the choice of their birthdays as a time to give people presents, the choice of moments when foetuses should receive additional protection or consideration is conditioned by social or moral considerations. The question, 'When does a person/child/foetus acquire a right to life?' is, in reality, quite different from the question 'When does an ovum/sperm/foetus become a person?' One might want to say that the answer to each should identify the same moment as crucial, but it is not absurd, and it might help to avoid confusion, to consider it possible that the state may have a responsibility to protect entities before they become people (and some, like animals, which will never become people). Conversely, and more controversially (and, perhaps, dangerously), it might be legitimate to suppose that some people towards whom the state has responsibilities may not acquire rights. It is at least as reasonable to say that a person is a being

---

[58] *Harris* v. *McRae*, 448 US 297 (1980); *Webster* v. *Reproductive Health Services*, 492 US 490 (1989) noted by A. I. L. Campbell, 'The Constitution and Abortion' (1990) 53 *MLR* 238–48.

[59] Ian Kennedy, *Treat Me Right: Essays in Medical Law and Ethics* (Oxford: Clarendon Press, 1991), ch. 3; Mason and McCall Smith, *Medical Ethics*, 99–100.

with a right to life as it is to say that the right to life is inherent in every person.

(2) A right to be aborted?

Is it ever appropriate to hold that a doctor has a duty to a foetus (or the person who the foetus, if born alive, will be) to abort the foetus? Suppose, for example, a foetus is suffering from severe abnormalities which would make an abortion permissible, but the doctor fails to detect this, and the child is born severely disabled. The only circumstances in which loss to the child could be established would be if the child's life could be said to be worse than no life at all. If the child's life, even with its handicaps, is better than non-existence (assuming that such a judge-ment could ever be made), the child is a net beneficiary of the failure to abort it, and could not establish any loss which would sound in damages. Even if it could be shown that the child's life is worse than non-existence, the Law Commission considered that allowing an action in such circumstances would be contrary to public policy, because it would encourage doctors to perform abortions in marginal cases rather than allowing the pregnancy to proceed and risk liability in damages to the infant.[60] The Law Commission's recommendation may have been enacted in the Congenital Disabilities (Civil Liability) Act 1976, section 4(5). However, this provision is not unambiguous, and it has been argued that it does not entirely rule out actions for so-called wrongful life.[61]

At common law, independently of the Act, the answer seems to be that the action is regarded as contrary to public policy. In *McKay* v. *Essex Area Health Authority*,[62] an action for negligence brought on behalf of a severely handicapped child, a health authority had failed to detect the fact that a foetus had been infected with the rubella virus. The mother was therefore not offered an abortion. The child was born severely handi-capped, and sued for negligence resulting in wrongful life. The Court of Appeal rejected the child's claim, holding that it would be contrary to public policy to impose on doctors a duty to abort, in place of the discre-tion under the Abortion Act 1967. Such a duty would place a low value on the life of handicapped children, and would come close to giving a right to be born normal (whatever that may be) or not born at all.

It should be noted, however, that the child's lack of any right not to be born does not prevent the mother from recovering damages for her

---

[60] Law Com. No. 60, *Report on Injuries to Unborn Children*, Cmnd. 5709 (1974).

[61] Jane E. S. Fortin, 'Is the "Wrongful Life" Action Really Dead?' [1987] *JSWL* 306–13.

[62] [1982] QB 1166, [1982] 2 All ER 771, CA. The events giving rise to the action occurred before the Congenital Disabilities (Civil Liability) Act 1976 became law.

distress, pain, and suffering, and the costs of maintenance, resulting from having the child.[63] It has been suggested that it would be reasonable to compensate the child, too, on the basis of a comparison between a handicapped existence and a normal existence.[64] This, however, seems to place responsibility on the doctor for the fact that the child was not born normal. In cases like *McKay*, nothing the doctor could do would result in a normal child being born. The absence of normality cannot, therefore, be laid at the doctor's door, and without doing gross violence to the law of tort the only basis for awarding damages against the doctor would be wrongful life, rather than wrongful deprivation of quality of life. It is therefore submitted that in such cases the handicapped child should be assisted, if at all, by way of the social security system.

(3) 'Treating to die with dignity' and the right to life

Once a child is born alive, it has as much right to life as other living people. What implications does this have for the treatment of children born with multiple handicaps to the point where they are unlikely ever to function as members of the community, and who fall ill? How far is a doctor required to go to preserve life? Are there cases where a child's life is so miserable that it would, in truth, be better off dead? If so, what are the doctor's duties, and what control does the law exert? The criminal law has so far failed to provide answers to these questions.[65]

These matters have been considered by the Court of Appeal on a number of occasions,[66] usually where the parents have wanted doctors to withhold treatment and the local authority has made the child a ward of court. The decisions make it clear that neither the parents nor the doctors have the final say as to whether a handicapped baby should be allowed to die. The court must decide, and the wishes of parents and doctors must be given some weight, but the court is primarily concerned with the interests of the child. On this view, it will be assumed that continued life

---

[63] See the comments of Lord Donaldson MR in *Re J. (a minor) (wardship: medical treatment)* [1990] 3 All ER 930, CA, at p. 935, and the failed sterilization cases: *Emeh* v. *Kensington and Chelsea and Westminster Area Health Authority* [1985] QB 1012, [1984] 3 All ER 1044, CA; *Thake* v. *Maurice* [1986] QB 644, [1986] 1 All ER 497, CA. The cause of action is discussed by Andrew Grubb, 'Conceiving—A New Cause of Action?', in M. D. A. Freeman (ed.), *Medicine, Law and Ethics*, 121–46.

[64] See Mason and McCall Smith, *Medical Ethics*, 144–9, and the works cited there.

[65] See M. J. Gunn and J. C. Smith, '*Arthur's* Case and the Right to Life of a Down's Syndrome Child' [1985] *Crim LR* 705–15, which generated some correspondence in the *Criminal LR*; Kennedy, *Treat Me Right*, ch. 8.

[66] *Re B. (a minor) (wardship: medical treatment)* [1981] 1 WLR 1421, CA; *Re C. (a minor) (wardship: medical treatment)* [1990] Fam. 26, [1989] 2 All ER 782, CA; *Re J. (a minor) (wardship: medical treatment)* [1991] 2 WLR 140, [1990] 3 All ER 930, CA.

is in the child's best interest unless there is compelling evidence to the contrary.

The first case, *Re B. (a minor) (wardship: medical treatment)*,[67] concerned a child born with Down's syndrome and an intestinal blockage which would have been fatal if not operated on. The question was whether the court, exercising the wardship jurisdiction, should authorize the operation, overriding the wishes of the parents that the child should be permitted to die. On the evidence, it was clear that the baby would be severely mentally and physically handicapped if she survived, but that her faculties would not be completely destroyed. Beyond that, it was too early to offer any prognosis. The court contemplated the possibility that there might possibly be cases in which it was certain that the child's life would be bound to be so demonstrably intolerable and full of pain and suffering that the child ought to be allowed to die. However, in the instant case, if the operation succeeded, baby B 'may live the normal span of a mongoloid child with the handicaps and defects and life of a mongol child, and it is not for this court to say that life of that description ought to be extinguished'.[68] That being so, the court had no alternative but to authorize the local authority to direct that the operation take place. It follows that the doctors would have been neglecting their duty had they failed to operate (otherwise than on medical grounds).

This was, on the principle enunciated, a relatively easy case. The next case, *Re C. (a minor) (wardship: medical treatment)*,[69] was somewhat more difficult, because baby C was suffering from exceptionally severe hydrocephalus, and, despite anything that could be done for her, was dying. The local authority in whose care she was and the doctors invoked the wardship jurisdiction, asking the judges to decide the extent to which intrusive and unpleasant procedures should be applied to prolong life in the event that the child contracted infections or became impossible to feed through a syringe. The Court of Appeal accepted that the overriding consideration in such circumstances was that baby C's suffering should be relieved as far as possible, in the judgement of those caring for her, in order to allow her to die, as Ward J. expressed it, 'peacefully and with the greatest dignity and the least of pain, suffering and distress'. However, the Court of Appeal made it clear that no court could authorize a doctor to take active steps to terminate a patient's life.

The approach in this case, recognizing the inevitability of the ward's more or less imminent death, was to set broad objectives for the medical staff, but to leave the method of achieving the objectives to their judgement and discretion. The courts have neither the skill nor the foresight to

[67] [1981] 1 WLR 1421, CA.
[68] (1981) [1990] 3 All ER 927 at p. 929 *per* Templeman LJ.
[69] [1990] Fam. 26, [1989] 2 All ER 782, CA.

give more detailed instructions to doctors. However, when the child patient is not close to death but is chronically ill and severely handicapped, the judges have to decide when it will cease to be worth trying to save him. This was the situation in *Re J. (a minor) (wardship: medical treatment)*.[70] Baby J. had suffered serious, irreversible brain damage at the time of his premature birth, and was epileptic. He had suffered two periods of collapse requiring ventilation, but if no further collapse occurred he was expected to survive for some years. He was likely to develop severe spastic quadriplegia and to be blind and deaf, and was unlikely ever to be able to speak or develop even limited intellectual abilities. However, he was likely to have a normal sensitivity to pain. Baby J. was a ward of court, and the medical team (who in non-wardship cases would have made decisions in consultation with the parents) sought the court's authorisation for a treatment plan. The question was whether J. should be resuscitated and ventilated if he were to suffer another collapse. Scott Baker J. authorized treatment in accordance with a doctor's opinion recommending sucking out his airway to prevent choking, and giving oxygen by face mask, but not to reventilate 'unless to do so seems appropriate to the doctors caring for him given the prevailing clinical situation'. In the event of J. contracting a chest infection, the doctor recommended treatment with antibiotics and administering fluids, but no prolonged ventilation. The Official Solicitor, representing the child, appealed, arguing that the court should never withhold consent to treatment which could enable a child to survive a life-threatening condition, regardless of the general quality of the child's life. Alternatively, he argued that treatment should be withheld only in the circumstances outlined in *Re B.*, above, and that these had not been shown to obtain in J.'s case.

The Court of Appeal did not accept that the dicta in *Re B.* laid down a general test to be satisfied before withholding treatment. The judges distinguished between the absolute duty not to kill, and the much more circumscribed duty to keep alive. In deciding how to treat a patient, it was accepted that the interests of the child are the first and paramount consideration, and that there is a strong presumption in favour of taking all steps capable of preserving life, but the court also accepted that in exceptional circumstances it might be in a child's best interests not to have life prolonged. The court has to balance the benefit of prolonging life against the pain and suffering involved in the treatment, taking account of the likely quality and length of the life which would follow the treatment. Lord

Donaldson MR[71] approved the approach of Asch J. in an American case, *Re Weberlist*:[72]

There is a strident cry in America to terminate the lives of *other* people—deemed physically or mentally defective . . . Assuredly, one test of a civilization is its concern with the survival of the 'unfittest', a reversal of Darwin's formulation . . . In this case, the court must decide what its ward would choose, if he were in a position to make a sound judgment.

This had been applied in a Canadian case, *Re Superintendent of Family and Child Services and Dawson*, where McKenzie J. had said:[73]

The decision can only be made in the context of the disabled person viewing the worthwhileness or otherwise of his life in its own context as a disabled person— and in that context he would not compare his life with that of a person enjoying normal advantages. He would know nothing of a normal person's life having never experienced it.

In *Re J.*, therefore, Lord Donaldson MR said that the decision-maker must

look at it from the assumed point of view of the patient. This gives effect, as it should, to the fact that even very severely handicapped people find a quality of life rewarding which to the unhandicapped may seem manifestly intolerable. . . . But in the end there will be cases in which the answer must be that it is not in the interests of the child to subject it to treatment which will cause increased suffering and produce no commensurate benefit, giving the fullest possible weight to the child's and mankind's, desire to survive.[74]

Invasive medical procedures cause distress and can be hazardous, and Scott Baker J. had been entitled to decide, on the evidence, that the distress was not justified by the unfavourable prognosis and the poor quality of life enjoyed by the patient.

The approach in *Re J.* is consistent with a non–paternalistic approach to the problem of the right to life, but is not entirely congruent with a purely Razian analysis, based on autonomy in the sense of maximizing opportunities to make choices, as there might be cases in which a child with some chance of achieving or recovering sufficient intellectual capacity to enable it to choose how it wanted to live might nevertheless be denied treatment on the ground that it would very probably choose to die.

The reasoning respects human life without treating it as an end in itself, worthy of fighting for in all circumstances. It has been developed by judges in cases concerning young babies, in the exercise of the court's wardship jurisdiction, but it is equally applicable to decisions by doctors

[71] [1990] 3 All ER 930 at p. 938. [72] 360 NYS 2d 782 (1974) at p. 787.
[73] (1983) 145 DLR (3d) 610 at pp. 620–1. [74] [1990] 3 All ER 930 at p. 938.

in consultation with relatives concerning the treatment of adults who for some reason are temporarily or permanently unable to decide whether or not to consent to treatment. The desirability of attempting to resuscitate a heart attack victim, for example, must depend on the distress (if any) which the treatment would be likely to cause to the patient, the likelihood that the treatment would succeed, and the probable quality of life which the patient would enjoy afterwards, judged (so far as possible) from the patient's perspective.

However, one aspect of the reasoning in *Re J.* is questionable. It is impossible for a judge or doctor to get inside the mind of a child who, as in *Re J.*, is unlikely ever to develop any intellectual capacity. It is instructive to note that, in cases where life is not threatened, judges have adopted a very different approach. In *Re F. (mental patient: sterilisation)*[75] the House of Lords held that a court could declare that it would be in the best interests of an adult voluntary in-patient at a mental hospital to undergo a sterilization operation, and that it would not be unlawful for doctors to perform the operation despite the patient's incapacity to consent. The test applied to determine what was in the best interests of the patient was not whether the patient would have chosen to be treated if she had had the necessary capacity, but whether the proposed treatment would be accepted as appropriate by a responsible body of doctors skilled in that form of treatment. Why should this test not apply to decisions about administering potentially life-saving treatment?

The issues in *Re J.* and *Re F.* were essentially similar. The main difference lies in the nature of the wardship jurisdiction which applies to minors only, and takes decision-making responsibilities out of the hands of parents and doctors. In *Re J.* treatment was *prima facie* lawful. Indeed, the doctors had a *prima facie* obligation to treat, because it would on the face of it be negligent for a doctor not to try to save a person who is in imminent danger of dying. The patient's presumptive right to life made it necessary to decide whether consent might be given to allowing death to occur. In *Re F.* the doctors favoured treatment, but the treatment would have been a battery in the absence of consent. The patient was incapable of giving consent, and the question was whether in the circumstances treatment could lawfully be administered. Yet the underlying issue was the same: on what basis should the court decide what is in the patient's best interests? In the former case, the Court of Appeal has said that the court must decide, balancing the interests as they would be seen by a person in the ward's position. In the latter case, the House of Lords left the decision to a responsible body of medical opinion, with the criminal law

[75] [1990] 2 AC 1, *sub nom. F* v. *West Berkshire Health Authority and another (Mental Health Act Commission intervening).* [1989] 2 All ER 545, HL.

and the law of tort providing a review process. (Lord Griffiths would have stipulated that the treatment would always be unlawful unless a court had declared it to be lawful, effectively shifting responsibility back from doctors to courts, but this was rejected by all the other Law Lords.) Perhaps the reason for willingness of the majority of the Law Lords to leave it to the doctors in *Re F.* was that English judges, unlike the European Convention on Human Rights, regard the right to life as more fundamental than, and requiring more extensive judicial oversight than, rights to other aspects of bodily integrity such as the right to procreate.

The problem of a doctor's duties in respect of irretrievably injured patients is not, of course, limited to neonates. Those who suffer traumatic injury may be reduced to a state in which they are not dead (in the sense of brain-stem death now accepted for medical purposes) but are comatose and insensate, have no voluntary bodily functions, and have no hope of recovery. People in what is described as 'persistent vegetative state' (PVS) cannot swallow, and so are dependent on artificial feeding, usually through a nasogastric tube. They may continue to breathe unaided for years after it becomes is clear that there is no hope of recovery, but are prone to infections and other secondary conditions which would end their lives unless treated. What are the duties of doctors towards such patients? In *Airedale NHS Trust* v. *Bland*[76] doctors applied, with the support of the patient's relations, for a declaration that it would not be unlawful to stop feeding a PVS patient and to withhold all treatment save that necessary to enable the patient to end his life with dignity and with the least possible suffering. The House of Lords upheld the decision of Sir Stephen Brown P. and the Court of Appeal to grant the declarations. Their Lordships accepted that judges could grant declarations to guide doctors where the patient was incapable of giving or withholding consent to further care. Searching for criteria to apply, their Lordships rejected the American 'substituted judgement' test (which Lord Donaldson had favoured in respect of minors in *Re J.*) under which the court attempts to decide what the patient would have done if capable of forming a rational view. Instead, the court must decide what is objectively in the patient's best interests. Lord Goff considered that it could sensibly be said to be not in the best interests of the patient to continue life-prolonging care (including feeding) where the patient was wholly unconscious and there was no prospect of any improvement in his condition. Such care served no therapeutic purpose, and could legitimately be stopped. The removal of the nasogastric tube would not constitute murder or manslaughter any more than would turning of a life-support machine when all prospect of recovery had gone.

[76] [1993] 2 WLR 316; [1993] 1 All ER 821, HL.

The courts regarded *Bland* as a fairly clear case. However, in more marginal cases it may be difficult to decide what is in the patient's best interests. Most of their Lordships favoured the *Bolam* test, as applied in *Re F.*: the doctors must reach a view which is supported by a responsible and competent body of relevant medical opinion, preferably with guidance from the British Medical Association. However, Lord Mustill expressed reservations about applying such a test to matters which were ethical rather than medical, and which involved the criminal law of murder and manslaughter rather than civil liability for negligence. Lord Mustill's doubts are compelling. There is little reason to grant a power to the medical professions to authorize the ending of attempts to preserve life on the basis of their own professional standards. Nevertheless, that is what commonly happens, in effect, in accident and emergency rooms at present, and it has largely been sanctioned by courts in the cases discussed in this section. At present, the danger is that decisions will be taken by people who are not publicly accountable for them, while responsibility is passed back and forth between the courts and the medical professions. Their Lordships were surely correct to express the view that the matter should be urgently examined by Parliament. In the mean time, the right to life appears to operate only if the person concerned is capable of benefiting from it.

(4) Does the right to life necessitate the outlawing of euthanasia?

It would seem that a state which, like the Netherlands, permits euthanasia might be offering its citizens insufficient protection to comply with the Convention. It is clear that no state is permitted to legalize mercy-killing to which the 'victim' does not consent, but does the 'victim's' consent have any force? It has been argued by Jacobs[77] that any purported waiver of the right to life should be ignored for legal purposes, because of the right's fundamental nature and on public policy grounds. As already noted, the Convention does not accord the right any more fundamental a status than any other right; indeed, as Sieghart[78] pointed out, the Convention does not grant a right to life but merely recognizes its existence and requires its protection.[79] Nevertheless, it seems clear that euthanasia requires an intentional taking of life, and does not fall within

---

[77] Francis G. Jacobs, *The European Convention on Human Rights* (Oxford: Clarendon Press, 1975), at p. 22.

[78] Sieghart, *International Law*, 130–1.

[79] It was suggested above that the same is true of the International Covenant on Civil and Political Rights, Article 6(1), which provides: 'Every human being has the inherent right to life. . .'. It must be admitted, however, that it is possible to argue that this bestows a right rather than merely recognizing it.

the exceptions in Article 2. The 'victim's' consent is therefore irrelevant, and permitting euthanasia would appear to breach Article 2.

On the other hand, it would not necessarily breach Article 6(1) of the International Covenant on Civil and Political Rights, which provides that the right to life 'shall be protected by law. No one shall be arbitrarily deprived of his life.' As the Covenant speaks of arbitrary rather than intentional deprivation, it is strongly arguable that euthanasia would not breach Article 6(1) if performed with the 'victim's' consent or at his request and after considering the 'victim's' medical circumstances and any other relevant circumstances. The Covenant is therefore less restrictive, and (according to taste) more forward looking and either more or less civilized, than the Convention.

In English law at present, euthanasia would constitute murder. The consent of the 'victim' would be irrelevant to liability, as the law does not recognize consent to serious injury or death. Even suicide, the intentional taking of one's own life, was a criminal offence until 1969, and while the Suicide Act 1969 legalized suicide and attempted suicide, inciting or aiding and abetting suicide remain criminal offences. Now people who are physically capable of doing so may attempt to take their own lives without risk of criminal liability, but those who are not so capable but who wish to die are dependent on the willingness of other people to risk a charge of homicide by helping them. English law on this point is therefore well within the requirements of both the Convenant and the Convention regarding protection against intentional or arbitrary deprivation of life. However, while it is undoubtedly a criminal act to do anything intending to hasten another person's death, there is no absolute duty on a doctor to try to save the life of a patient, for two reasons.

The first is that any treatment is *prima facie* a trespass to the person, and if the patient is adult and competent to consent it will be unlawful without that consent. A doctor therefore acts lawfully—indeed, could not lawfully act otherwise—when he withholds treatment at the request of a terminally ill patient. This has been called passive, as distinct from active, euthanasia.[80] To ensure that medical staff know of their wishes, some people have executed what are sometimes called 'living wills', giving directions to medical staff to withhold treatment in specified circumstances, and making their wishes known to anyone who might be appointed as their representative in the event that they become incapable for any reason.[81] The efficacy of such prior indications was accepted, *obiter*, by Lord Goff in *Airedale NHS Trust* v. *Bland*, above. In such circumstances, the patient voluntarily accepts non-treatment while in a state

---

[80] See generally Mason and McCall Smith, *Medical Ethics*, ch. 15, especially at p. 321.

[81] A form for a living will is printed in Mason and McCall Smith, *Medical Ethics*, at pp. 450–1.

to do so rationally. However, where there is the slightest doubt about the wishes of a patient, that patient should be treated, because the paternalism which decides for someone else when it is best to die is effectively denying them the opportunity to make the most of their lives as autonomous individuals.[82] Furthermore, it would seem to be wrong in principle to put pressure to bear on a patient to elect to die. In those states of the USA where voluntary euthanasia is lawful, the ethical problems for patients, doctors, next of kin, and nursing staff are immense.[83] Where the patient is not mentally competent to confirm the choice to die at the time when the choice is about to be given effect, it will always be impossible to know whether the choice expressed earlier was truly voluntary, whether the consent was informed, and whether or not the patient would want to reconsider were he able to do so. In the Netherlands, where it is lawful to practise voluntary euthanasia, it seems that the procedural safeguards designed to protect people against involuntary euthanasia are very hard to enforce and are regularly flouted.[84]

Secondly, the doctrine of double effect allows the doctor to take steps which carry a substantial risk to life in order to treat, in good faith and with the patient's consent, some disease or symptom. This is essential, because virtually any treatment carries some risk to the patient. It is particularly relevant to the euthanasia issue in cases where the primary object (e.g. pain control in terminal cancer treatment) can only be achieved by administering drugs at a level which is likely to shorten life, but enhances the quality of life while it lasts. A trade-off between length of life and quality of life is permissible.[85] However, there is a risk to the doctor if the steps taken turn out not to command the approval of a body of respectable medical opinion, and the consent of the patient has not been obtained. In such circumstances, a charge of murder (or attempted murder if it not clear whether the patient was actually killed by the disease or the treatment) is possible.[86]

[82] See Michael R. Flick, 'The Due Process of Dying', 79 *Calif. LR* 1121–67 (1991); Mason and McCall Smith, *Medical Ethics*, 319–25; Margaret Brazier, *Medicine, Patients and the Law* (Harmondsworth: Penguin, 1987), ch. 20; *Re T. (Adult: Refusal of Medical Treatment)*. [1992] 4 All ER 649, CA.

[83] For a full and interesting discussion, see Kennedy, *Treat Me Right*, chs. 16 (on doctors' duties), 17 (on patients' requests not to receive further treatment), and 18 (on switching off life-support machines).

[84] See John Keown, 'The Law and Practice of Euthanasia in the Netherlands' (1992) 108 *LQR* 51–78.

[85] Jonathan Glover, *Causing Death and Saving Lives* (Harmondsworth: Penguin, 1977).

[86] The well-known case of Dr Leonard Arthur, acquitted on a charge of attempted murder, was one such. Another is the case of Mr Nigel Cox, convicted in 1992 on a charge of attempted murder in connection with the death of a patient suffering from a non-terminal disease (chronic arthritis) following an injection of a toxic substance of no therapeutic value.

3.4 CONCLUSION

The right to life, which in a way is incontestably the most fundamental right which we can assert, turns out on close examination to be problematic and surprisingly conditional. The law, both domestic and international, provides a substantial measure of protection against arbitrary deprivation of life. However, the point when the right vests in a particular person, the scope of the duties on others which arise from the right, and the scope of people's rights to release other people from those obligations, are all highly controversial. Developments in medical technology and skill, which now make it possible to preserve some spark of life in people who would previously have been incontestably dead, are likely to ensure that the boundaries of this right remain battlegrounds for politicians and human rights advocates for the foreseeable future.

4

OTHER RIGHTS TO BODILY INTEGRITY

Apart from a right to life, citizens generally enjoy a right to be free of physical interference. This chapter considers the scope and incidents of this right, and the manner of its protection. It covers negative liberties: freedom from physical assaults, torture, medical or other experimentation, immunization and compelled eugenic or social sterilization, and cruel or degrading treatment or punishment. Positive rights to minimum standards of health care, physical conditions in prisons and hospitals, and freedom from arbitrary arrest and detention are examined in subsequent chapters.

4.1 THE RIGHT TO BE FREE OF PHYSICAL INTERFERENCE

This right is well established in English law, although (as with other civil liberties) the primary means of protection is by way of the civil law of tort rather than constitutional, public-law provisions. At common law, any physical interference with a person is *prima facie* tortious. If it interferes with freedom of movement, it may constitute a false imprisonment. If it involves physical touching, it may constitute a battery. If it puts a person in fear of violence, it may amount to an assault. For any of these wrongs, the victim may be able to obtain damages. Where the tort is committed by a person holding a public office, exemplary damages may sometimes be awarded. The same acts may also amount to crimes, making the offender liable to penalties. In order to avoid liability, the defendant has to establish that he had legal authority for the act. This authority may derive from statute (for example, the power to use reasonable force if necessary to make an arrest, under sections 24 and 116 of the Police and Criminal Evidence Act 1984), or from common law powers and duties (such as the power of parents and teachers to discipline children, or the duty to prevent breaches of the peace), from the 'victim's' own consent (as where a patient consents to an operation which would otherwise be a battery), from necessity (as where a doctor operates on a patient who is unconscious and unable to consent), or from a court order (as in the case of a court authorizing medical treatment on a ward of court). If the justification is not proved, the act is unlawful.

These principles apply equally to interferences by private citizens and by state agencies, yet the state has more powers than most citizens to interfere legally with people's bodily integrity. The duties on state agencies to safeguard the welfare of the weak, to administer the law, to maintain a tolerable level of order, and to regulate many aspects of life, carry with them a wide range of powers to stop, detain, search, hospitalize, imprison, and take into care. Apart from the state, most of the legal powers to interfere with bodily integrity reside with doctors in relation to patients and with parents and teachers in respect of children. Here we will examine some general considerations stemming from international agreements, and those aspects of the powers which raise considerations specifically relevant to the civil liberties and human rights of children, people subject to medical treatment, and convicted offenders.

(1) Background in international law and English law

In 1688/9, immediately after the accession of King William and Queen Mary, the English Parliament purported to enact a Bill of Rights, which provided (among other things): 'That excessive bail ought not to be required nor excessive fines imposed nor cruell and unusuall punishments inflicted.' The prohibition on cruel and unusual punishments was adopted internationally, being incorporated in the Eighth Amendment to the USA Constitution in 1789-91, and in many other similar instruments since.

In the series of international human rights instruments agreed since the Second World War, similar provisions appear. Article 5 of the Universal Declaration of Human Rights and Article 7 of the International Covenant on Civil and Political Rights both provide: 'No one shall be subjected to torture or to cruel, inhuman or degrading treatment or punishment.' This is wider in three respects than the 1689 Bill of Rights: first, in covering torture; secondly, in dealing with treatment generally in addition to punishment; and, thirdly, in covering inhuman or degrading treatment and punishment rather than only cruel and unusual punishment. The European Convention, Article 3, drops the reference to cruelty, contenting itself with forbidding torture or inhuman or degrading treatment or punishment.[1]

Torture has been defined in the Convention against Torture and Other Cruel, Inhuman or Degrading Treatment or Punishment, a subsidiary

---

[1] See generally P. J. Duffy, 'Article 3 of the European Convention on Human Rights' (1983) 32 *ICLQ* 316–46. For a brief account of the disagreements which led to the adoption of the present form of Art. 3, see J. E. S. Fawcett. *The Application of the European Convention on Human Rights*, 2nd edn. (Oxford: Clarendon Press, 1987), 41–3.

instrument under the aegis of the United Nations.[2] Article 1, paragraph 1, states that for the purposes of the Convention 'torture' means:

any act by which severe pain or suffering, whether physical or mental, is intentionally inflicted on a person for such purposes as obtaining from him or a third person information or a confession, punishing him for an act he or a third person has committed or is suspected of having committed, or intimidating him or coercing him or a third person, or for any reason based on discrimination of any kind, when such pain or suffering is inflicted by or at the instigation of or with the consent or acquiescence of a public official or other person acting in an official capacity. It does not include pain or suffering arising only from, inherent in or incidental to lawful sanctions.

This ties the idea of torture to the purpose for which the suffering is inflicted.

There are similarities in the approach taken to the idea of torture in the context of the European Convention, Article 3. Torture has been discussed by the European Commission and Court in two seminal cases: *Denmark, Norway, Sweden and the Netherlands* v. *Greece*,[3] and *Ireland* v. *UK*.[4] The Commission in those cases took the view that torture is an aggravated form of inhuman treatment which has a purpose such as obtaining information or confessions or inflicting punishment. This approach was adopted by the Court of Appeal of Northern Ireland, for the purpose of deciding whether to exclude confession evidence obtained through torture, in *R.* v. *McCormick*.[5] However, in *Ireland* v. *UK* thirteen judges of the European Court of Human Rights, forming a majority, adopted a more stringent test for torture based on the special intensity of the suffering caused, saying that torture was 'deliberate inhuman treatment causing very serious and cruel suffering'. There is a distinction to be made between techniques which amount to inhuman and degrading treatment and those which cause specially intense suffering which amount to torture. Thus the so-called 'five techniques' in the *Ireland* case, used by members of the UK security forces against suspected terrorists, were said to constitute torture by the Commission, but not by the majority of the Court: 'wall standing', being spreadeagled for hours against a wall in a physically stressed position; 'hooding', keeping a dark bag over detainees' heads; subjecting the detainees to continuous loud noise; depriving them of sleep before interrogating them; and giving detainees reduced amounts of food and drink. On the other hand, there seems little

---

[2] Adopted by UN General Assembly Resolution 39/46 of 10 Dec. 1984.

[3] (3321–3/67; 3344/67) Report (1969) 12 *Yearbook of the European Convention on Human Rights: The Greek Case* .

[4] (5310/71) Eur. Comm. HR, Report: 25 Jan. 1976 (1976) 19 *Yearbook* 512; Eur. Ct. HR, Series A, No. 25, 2 EHRR 25.

[5] [1977] 4 NIJB 105.

doubt that the direct application of physical pain by beating on the soles of the feet, electric shocks, kicking people in the genitals, extracting hair, burning with cigarettes, placing a large stick in a person's rectum, and other traditional medieval tortures, would amount to torture under the Convention, even on the Court's view.[6]

Only four judges in *Ireland* v. *UK* thought this definition too restricted, but it has been criticized by commentators who suggest that it reflects the idea that there is a common understanding that people should be stigmatized as torturers only if their acts can be characterized as extreme barbarity, thus excluding more subtle psychological and technological methods of overriding the human will which are more readily available to advanced industrial countries than to developing ones.[7] Furthermore, in the same case Judge Fitzmaurice, dissenting, doubted the relevance of the purpose for which the inhuman treatment was meted out, arguing in view of the unconditional wording of Article 3 that torture is constituted by sufficiently inhuman treatment inflicted on a person by compulsion, an objective criterion which did not depend on the subjective purpose of those responsible.

The UK legislation on torture, the Criminal Justice Act 1988, section 134, broadly follows the UN Convention on the quantum of suffering involved, but not on the purposes for which it is inflicted. The offence is committed by somebody who inflicts severe pain or suffering (thus including psychological torture) on another, where the offender is a public official or person acting in an official capacity, in the performance or purported performance of his official duties, or is acting at the instigation, or with the consent or acquiescence, of such a person performing or purporting to perform his official duties.[8] This definition is wide enough to encompass, for example, mistreatment of patients by nurses and medics in the prison medical service, a matter to which we will return in section 4(3) below, as the purpose of the torturer is irrelevant: only the status of the offender as a public official (or someone under his instigation, etc.), acting in purported performance of his official duties, is significant. The maximum penalty is life imprisonment, and the offence is always a serious arrestable offence for the purposes of police investigative powers.[9]

There is a defence where the defendant had lawful authority, justification, or excuse under the law of the part of the UK which was

---

[6] These types of assault were held to amount to torture in *Denmark* et al. v. *Greece*, above.

[7] See R. J. Spjut, 'Torture under the European Convention on Human Rights', 73 *AJIL* 267 (1979) at p. 271; Nigel Rodley, *The Treatment of Prisoners under International Law* (Oxford: Clarendon Press, 1987), 83–86.

[8] Criminal Justice Act 1988, s. 134(1), (2).

[9] Ibid., ss. 134(6), 170(2), and Sched. 15, para. 20.

the situs of the torture, or (where it was inflicted abroad by a UK official) the law of the part of the UK under which the official was purporting to act, or (where it was inflicted abroad by an official of a foreign state) under the law of the country in which it was inflicted.[10] This is rather wider than the relatively narrow exception provided under Article 1, paragraph 1 of the UN Convention relating to lawful sanctions: the defence under the 1988 Act would encompass, for example, duress and mistake of fact as defences. There is some doubt about the idea that the intentional infliction of severe suffering can ever be justified. On one view, it opens the way to justifying torture on utilitarian principles, by reference to domestic legislation (such as, perhaps, some future amended version of the Northern Ireland (Emergency Powers) Act 1991) designed to cater for some exigent circumstances or pressing military or social need. However, under Article 3 of the European Convention on Human Rights the obligation of the state is absolute and non-derogable, and the same applies to the obligations under the UN Convention.[11] The Attorney-General's consent is required for a prosecution in England and Wales.[12]

There can be little doubt that the definition of torture under the 1988 Act is wider than that adopted by the majority of the European Court of Human Rights in the *Ireland* case. On the other hand, unlike Article 3 of the European Convention, the 1988 Act imposes no special liability in respect of inhuman or degrading treatment short of torture, so the extended meaning given to torture is understandable.

The international instruments also outlaw inhuman or degrading treatment or punishment. The term 'punishment' imports the idea of a disagreeable experience inflicted as a consequence of conviction for a crime. As such, it is narrower than 'treatment', which is apt to cover anything done to a person in any circumstances. The International Covenant on Civil and Political Rights, Article 7, singles out one form of treatment for special mention: 'In particular, no one shall be subjected without his free consent to medical or scientific experimentation.' This is not particularized in the European Convention, but was held to be a crime against international law by the Nuremberg War Crimes Tribunal.[13] It is very likely that experimentation which presented a serious threat to life or health would be cognizable by the European Court or Commission of Human Rights, as an infringement of the right to life under Article 2 or a special form of torture or inhuman treatment under Article 3. While an experiment which inflicted severe suffering or loss of dignity on a subject would be, respectively, inhuman or degrading treatment, people can be

[10] Ibid., s. 134(5).   [11] For full discussion, see Rodley, *Treatment of Prisoners*, 74–8.
[12] Criminal Justice Act 1988, s. 135.
[13] See further Rodley, *Treatment of Prisoners*, 232–5.

used for experimentation—for example, as part of a sample in a clinical trial of a drug, or in tests for the effects of radioactivity—without knowing it, and without it inflicting any serious injury on them. While it might be argued that experimentation without consent disregards a subject's moral autonomy and dignity, and therefore degrades him, the caselaw to date under the Convention demands that the subject knows at the time that his dignity is threatened in a fairly severe way before treatment will be regarded as degrading. Accordingly much undisclosed experimentation may fall outside Article 3 of the Convention. Attempts in the Council of Europe to draft a special convention on medical treatment have so far come to nothing. In England, administering a drug without a person's consent would be a battery, but if the patient consents to its administration it ceases to be a battery. English cases have held that consent need not be fully informed in order to provide a defence to an action for battery, although a doctor who had failed to give the patient such information as would be thought reasonable by a reputable body of medical opinion practising in the field might be liable in an action for negligence if harm resulted.[14]

It is clear from the instruments, and has been expressly decided by the European Court and Commission of Human Rights, that the obligations of states under these provisions are absolute, non-derogable, and unqualified.[15] As Sieghart observed, 'All that is therefore required to establish a violation of the relevant Article is a finding that the State concerned has failed to comply with its obligation in respect of any one of these modes of conduct: no question of justification can ever arise.'[16]

In addition, states parties have obligations under the European Convention on the Elimination of Torture, to criminalize torture, provide severe penalties for it, and secure the prosecution of anyone who has committed torture who is present within their jurisdictions. There is a monitoring body, the Committee for the Prevention of Torture (CPT), which will be referred to further below.

Rights to security of the person, which initially look as if they might be relevant, turn out to be unpromising sources of guidance in this context. Article 3 of the Universal Declaration of Human Rights stated: 'Everyone has the right to . . . liberty and security of the person', words echoed in Article 9(1) of the International Covenant on Civil and

---

[14] *Chatterton* v. *Gerson* [1981] QB 432, [1981] 1 All ER 257; *Sidaway* v. *Board of Governors of the Bethlem Royal Hospital and the Maudsley Hospital* [1985] AC 871, [1985] 1 All ER 643, HL.

[15] *Ireland* v. *UK* (5310/71) Report: 25 Jan. 1976; Judgment: 2 EHRR 25; *Tyrer* v. *UK*, Eur. Ct. HR, Series A, No. 26, (1978) 2 EHRR 1.

[16] Paul Sieghart, *The International Law of Human Rights* (Oxford: Clarendon Press, 1983), 161.

Political Rights and Article 5(1) of the European Convention. In the European context, 'liberty and security of the person' has been relatively narrowly interpreted: although the Commission has said that liberty and security are two separate rights,[17] it has been held that both refer only to physical liberty and security, and are in effect restricted to freedom from arbitrary arrest and detention.[18]

4.2 JUDICIAL PUNISHMENT

Any judicial punishment which involves detaining a person against his or her will and imposing undesired restrictions or pain on him or her is potentially degrading. One of the objects of punishment is to make the offender and others regard the offender's conduct as unacceptable, and this may incidentally lower the offender in his or her own, and other people's, estimation. However, particular problems emerge in relation to corporal punishment and prison conditions for those detained by court order.

(1) Judicial corporal punishment

Whipping as a judicially imposed penalty was abolished in England and Wales by the Criminal Justice Act 1948, but remains a possibility in the Isle of Man.

In *Tyrer* v. *UK*[19] the European Court of Human Rights held by a majority that a judicially imposed birching, conducted in the Isle of Man on a 15-year-old boy, which caused pain but no serious injury, constituted a degrading punishment. The majority held that the institutionalized infliction of violence on a person by the state, authorized and carried out according to law by state authorities, is intrinsically degrading:

. . . although the applicant did not suffer any severe or long-lasting physical effects, his punishment—whereby he was treated as an object in the power of the authorities—constituted an assault on precisely that which it is one of the main purposes of Article 3 to protect, namely a person's dignity and physical integrity. . . The institutionalised character of this violence is further compounded by the whole aura of official procedure attending the punishment and by the fact that those inflicting it were total strangers to the offender. . . . [I]n

---

[17] *Kamma* v. *Netherlands* (4771/71) DR 1, 4; *Engel* et al. v. *Netherlands* (5100–2/71; 5354/72; 5370/72) Report of 19 July 1974.

[18] *Guzzardi* v. *Italy* 3 EHRR 333; *Arrowsmith* v. *UK* (7050/72) DR 19, 5; *X* v. *UK* (5877/72) CD 45, 90. See Sieghart, *International Law*, at p. 142 n. 7.

[19] Eur. Ct. HR, Series A, No. 26, (1978) 2 EHRR 1.

addition to the physical pain he experienced, Mr Tyrer was subjected to the mental anguish of anticipating the violence he was to have inflicted on him.[20]

This reasoning is not entirely convincing. It was strongly criticized by Judge Fitzmaurice, dissenting. He argued that it is necessary to take account of social standards and expectations when deciding whether something is degrading, because the degrading nature of treatment or punishment had been held in earlier cases to depend on whether it constituted an assault on the victim's personality and lowered the victim in his own eyes and in the estimation of others. Beating is a common, if often controversial, part of child-rearing practice in many cultures, where it does not degrade the victim (although the victim and others may consider it to be cruel). By contrast, beating an adult is an assault on the adult's social and cultural expectations, and is likely to be degrading, although there are circumstances in which violence may legitimately be used against adults (for example, in order to prevent crime) without it being regarded as degrading. The majority decision in *Tyrer* fails to take account of the importance of context.

Furthermore, it seems odd for the majority to concentrate so heavily on the institutional aspects of the punishment. If the fact that it was authorized by law, after a judicial hearing, and inflicted by agents of the state (subject to strict rules about the size of the birch and the manner of infliction), makes the punishment intrinsically degrading, it seems to imply that it would have been preferable had it been administered unofficially and without any safeguards being provided by law. This strange suggestion has implications for other judicial punishments which humiliate people in their own eyes (it was said to be unnecessary for the person to be humiliated in other people's eyes). It can be argued that any punishment, including imprisonment or community-service orders, necessarily involves at least a threat of violence, because the state reserves the right to use force to ensure that the sentence is carried out. It is intended to make it clear that the offender has behaved unacceptably, in order to mark society's disapproval of the offence, and this may necessitate an assault on an offender's self-respect. If the intentional infliction by the state of an assault on a person's physical integrity is degrading treatment or punishment, it is hard to see how any punishment which impinges on a person's physical integrity or liberty would not be capable of contravening Article 3. It would have been more convincing had the majority in *Tyrer* concentrated exclusively on the features incidental to the infliction of the punishment as making it degrading.

Despite its argumentational deficiencies, *Tyrer* reflects an international trend towards the abolition of judicial corporal punishment, and the

---

[20] Para. 33 of the judgment.

decision has been instrumental in encouraging the effective abolition by judicial decision of corporal punishment in Zimbabwe, on the ground that it constitutes inhuman and degrading punishment contrary to the Constitution of Zimbabwe.[21]

(2) Prison conditions

In a recent report,[22] the European Committee for the Prevention of Torture and Inhuman or Degrading Treatment or Punishment expressed the view that 'the cumulative effect of overcrowding, lack of integral sanitation and inadequate regimes [at Brixton, Leeds and Wandsworth Prisons] amounts to inhuman and degrading treatment'. This echoes the conclusion expressed repeatedly by Judge Stephen Tumim, HM's Chief Inspector of Prisons. If this is correct (and the UK Government rejected the assertion in its Response to the Report), it means that the UK could be at risk of having to pay compensation to very large numbers of prisoners and former prisoners by virtue of its obligations in international law under the European Convention on Human Rights, since the regime under which prisoners in these (and no doubt many other) prisons are held contravenes Article 3.[23] This is bound to precipitate a substantial number of claims under Article 3, and it remains to be seen whether the European Commission of Human Rights will agree with the view of the Committee. In an earlier case, the Commission and the Committee of Ministers decided that alleged overcrowding in mental hospital dormitories, combined with failure to explain medical treatments administered to inmates, did not amount to degrading treatment under Article 3 of the Convention.[24] In the mean time, the domestic legal remedies for such an alleged breach are very limited. This matter is discussed in Chapter 6, below.

4.3 DISCIPLINING CHILDREN

The rights of children to personal liberty and dignity are necessarily curtailed by reason of the dependent nature of children. As people, children

[21] State v. Ncube [1988] LRC (Const.) 442, and A Juvenile v. State [1989] LRC (Const.) 774, SC Zimbabwe, noted by A. W. Bradley, 'Inhuman or Degrading Punishment? Judicial Whipping in Zimbabwe' [1991] PL 481–4.

[22] Report to the UK Government on the Visit to the UK Carried Out by the European Committee for the Prevention of Torture and Inhuman or Degrading Treatment or Punishment, adopted by the Committee, 21 Mar. 1991. On the work of the Committee, see Malcolm Evans and Rod Morgan, 'The European Convention for the Prevention of Torture: Operational Practice' (1992) 41 ICLQ 590–614.

[23] This point is well made by Malcolm Evans and Rod Morgan, 'Inhuman and Degrading?', The Times, 7 Jan.1992.

[24] B. v. UK Eur. Comm. HR, Report of 7 Oct. 1981, 32 DR 5, 6 EHR 204.

are *prima facie* entitled to enjoy all the rights which attach to people. On the other hand, as people with special needs they attract special treatment: other (adult) people have responsibilities for their welfare and development, over and above the ordinary responsibilities which we all have for each other's welfare and development; and in order to discharge those developmental responsibilities, and also to protect young people against the worst dangers which threaten as a result of their relative inexperience and incompletely developed understanding, it is necessary to permit interferences with the rights of children which would not be permitted in the case of normal adults. There is therefore a tension, in relation to children's rights, between the desire to protect them against harm and exercise control in order to make possible a more perfect autonomy in their adulthood, and a need to respect them as people in their own right, with their own claims to dignity and self-respect. The way in which these objectives are accommodated in law and child-rearing practices varies between societies and times.

The main constraints on children's civil liberties which do not apply to adults relate to the needs of education and development, and (as an element therein) socialization and discipline. These are held in the UK to justify a certain amount of restriction of freedom of movement, a subjection to the opinions of parents or guardians and teachers, and a limited liability to treatment which might be regarded as degrading if applied to adults.

English law allows a certain latitude to parents, guardians, and teachers in bringing up and disciplining the children in their charge. Parental views on upbringing generally are required to be respected by Article 8 of the European Convention (respect for private and family life) and Article 2 of the First Protocol (education in accordance with parents' religious and philosophical convictions). English law permits parents to apply reasonable force to their children for the purpose of punishing them. As long as the force used is not excessive, and the manner of applying it is reasonable, the parent has a justification which will prevent the infliction making the parent liable for assault or battery.[25] A similar freedom was allowed to teachers at common law, although (as explained below) its use been considerably limited by statute. To that extent the child's right to physical integrity is restricted. However, if the manner of infliction is unreasonable or the degree of force threatened or used is excessive, having regard to the age and character of the child, the nature of the offence, and the circumstances of the infliction, the punishment becomes an assault or battery.[26]

[25] J. L. Caldwell, 'Parental Physical Punishment and the Law' (1989) 13 *New Zealand Universities LJ* 370–88.
[26] *R. v. Hopley* (1860) 2 F. & F. 202; *Cleary v. Booth* [1893] 1 QB 465, DC; *R. v. Mackie* (1973) 57 Cr. A R. 453, CA; *R. v. Dupperon* [1985] 2 WWR 369, CA of Saskatchewan.

The subject of physical punishment of children is a contentious one. The prevailing view among doctors and educational psychologists in this country is that physical punishment has negative results, and is ineffective in the long term in instilling self-discipline or improving the behaviour of a child. It has been argued that the intentional infliction of physical harm on a person degrades both the victim and the inflicter, and perhaps observers as well. Professor Michael Freeman has suggested that corporal punishment is akin to child abuse, and the Scottish Law Commission has recommended that in Scotland a parent should be both civilly and criminally liable for striking a child with any implement, whether or not it causes pain or injury, or acting in a way which causes, or risks causing, injury or more than transient pain to a child.[27] In mainland Britain, the last vestiges of corporal punishment of adults disappeared with the abolition of flogging in prisons by the Criminal Justice Act 1967. When it comes to physical punishment in the home and the school, the element of state coercion is missing, so the question is whether the state, by allowing 'reasonable' physical punishment, is failing to protect children against degrading treatment. In many other European countries, including Sweden, Finland, Denmark, Norway, and Austria, corporal punishment at home has been restricted by law, but an attempt in the House of Lords to introduce criminal sanctions in the Children Act 1989 was unsuccessful.

(i) *Punishment at home.* The right to beat children is apparently confined to parents or guardians, and other people having lawful control or charge of children.[28] It has been held that it does not extend to other people who have temporary *de facto*, but not *de iure*, responsibility for the care of the children, such as the child's elder brother.[29] This stems from an understandable desire to limit the range of people who are free to decide whether to inflict violence on the child. There is more opposition now than formerly to any beating of children, and there are many who would like to see the parent's or guardian's right withdrawn by law. In community homes accommodating children in local authority care, corporal punishment has been abolished. However, there is a grey area surrounding the core meaning of corporal punishment, where it fades into

---

[27] M. D. A. Freeman, *The Rights and Wrongs of Children* (London: Francis Pinter, 1983), 111–14; Scottish Law Commission, *Report on Family Law* (SLC No. 135, 1992), para. 2.105; Chris Barton, 'It's OK to Belt your Kids' (1992) 142 *NLJ* 1262–3.

[28] This was recognized by Parliament in the Children and Young Persons Act 1933, s. 1(7). It may now be restricted to people who have parental responsibility for the child under Children Act 1989, and those to whom the responsibility is delegated.

[29] *R. v. Woods* (1921) 85 JP 272.

restraint and accepted physical contact with a view to reinforcing an injunction. If all else fails, is it an unjustified assault to strike a child who is intent on sticking his fingers into an electrical socket? Is it an assault, or an unlawful detention, to confine a child to her bedroom after requiring her to surrender her outer garments, as in the 'pin-down' regime operated for a time in childrens' homes in Staffordshire and elsewhere? The latter is certainly a more extensive assault on the dignity and self-esteem of the 'victim' than is the former. The issues are different in each case. In the former case, the question is whether the beating is punishment or education. In the latter, the issue is whether the manner of the punishment is or is not unjustified. In terms of the Convention, it is fairly clear that the latter is more degrading than the former. But in terms of English domestic law, the question in every case is whether the punishment is of a justifiable type and administered for a justifiable purpose.

For some parents, an attempt to ban corporal punishment in the name of the rights of the child would, apart from being unenforceable, itself amount to an assault on the family and privacy rights of the parents. In Sweden, the Parliament had attempted to discourage parental beating of children by making the application of corporal punishment contrary to the Code of Parenthood. Members of a Free Protestant sect had petitioned the European Commission, alleging breaches of Article 8 of the Convention. It was said that this infringed their right to respect for family life under Article 8 of the Convention. It interfered with their freedom to organize their families and rear their children in accordance with their religious precepts, they claimed, because, although there were no penal sanctions for breach of the Code, it was taken into account in making decisions about when the State should interfere in child care. It was therefore possible that their children might be more likely to be taken into care by the authorities than the children of parents who had different religious beliefs. The Commission held that the application was inadmissible, but only because the Code had no direct legal effects and the applicants had not shown that they had suffered or were at substantial risk of having their family lives interfered with on this account.[30]

In the domestic law of England and Wales, and other common-law countries where such issues have arisen, it is settled law that, in the nature and extent of corporal punishment, parents must be guided by accepted norms in the society in which they live. Special sets of beliefs, or norms

---

[30] *X and Y v. Sweden* (8819/79), 29 DR 104 (Commission); see also *G. Hendriks* v. *Netherlands* (8429/78), 18 DR 225 (Commission); CM Resolution 82/4 of 10 Dec. 1982 (Committee of Ministers).

derived from other societies, do not justify punishment which is excessive according the norms of this society. Thus the criminal liability of immigrants and members of religious sects for assaulting their children in the name of discipline will be settled according to standards current in the wider society. The reasonableness of a punishment, like the intention of the defendant to use an unlawful degree of force,[31] is therefore always a question of fact for the jury to decide (where there is a jury),[32] although the fact that one is a recent immigrant unfamiliar with local child-rearing practices may be a mitigating factor at the sentencing stage.[33] But this approach does not require a British court or legislature to outlaw all corporal punishment in the home when there is no evidence that the current consensus regards such punishment as unacceptable. As Judge Fitzmaurice observed, dissenting in *Tyrer*, most people in most societies have been subjected to beating or the threat of it as part of growing up, and continue to use it on their own children.

(ii) *Punishment at school.* The Court has held that physical punishment at school in Scotland does not amount to degrading treatment in *Campbell and Cosans* v. *UK*.[34] Whereas in *Tyrer* the Court had discounted the fact that a large proportion of the Manx population approved of judicial birching, in *Campbell and Cosans* the judges accepted that widespread public approval in Scotland of the long-standing tradition of corporal punishment in schools, while not conclusive, was relevant in deciding that: 'it is not established that pupils at a school, where such a punishment is used, are, solely by reason of the risk of being subjected thereto, humiliated and debased in the eyes of others to the requisite degree at all'. Nor was there any evidence that victims suffered adverse psychological effects which might make them feel humiliated or debased.[35] This was the very argument that Judge Fitzmaurice had criticised the majority of the Court for ignoring in *Tyrer*.

In the United States, the Supreme Court has reached a similar conclusion by a very different route. Under the Eighth Amendment to the US Constitution, there is a right to be free of cruel and unusual punishments.

---

[31] This is a part of the *mens rea* of assault: *R.* v. *Gladstone Williams* (1983) 78 Cr. App. R. 276, CA, although in one case it has been held that, in cases concerning punishment, where the defendant is attempting to justify an application of force which is *prima facie* unlawful, an intention to use any force suffices if the degree of force is objectively unreasonable: *R.* v. *Smith* [1985] Crim. L. R. 42, CA, and Commentary by Professor J. C. Smith.

[32] *R.* v. *Derriviere* (1969) 53 Cr. App. R. 637, CA; in Canada, *R.* v. *Baptiste* (1981) 66 CCC (2d) 438 (Ontario Provincial Ct.).

[33] *R.* v. *Geraldes* (1965) 46 CR 365 (CA of Quebec).

[34] Eur. Ct. HR, Series A, No. 48, (1982) 2 EHRR 293.

[35] Judgment at paras. 29–30.

In *Ingraham* v. *Wright*[36] a school pupil had been severely beaten with a wooden paddle, a form of school punishment permitted by state law. It was held by a majority of five to four that this did not infringe the Eighth Amendment, because, even if the punishment in that case was cruel and unusual, the constitutional prohibition on cruel and unusual punishments applied only to judicial punishments. The Constitution, unlike the European Convention, contains no prohibition against types of treatment, as distinct from punishment, so the pupil had no constitutional remedy, although (as in England and Wales) he would have had a tort remedy had unreasonable force been used.

Under Article 7 of the International Covenant on Civil and Political Rights, by contrast, the Human Rights Committee has apparently (though not unambiguously) taken the view either that all corporal punishment breached children's right to be free of inhuman and degrading treatment, or that excessive corporal punishment did so, although one of the delegates suggested that applying Article 7 to educational discipline might trivialize the article, in which case school punishments might be excepted from Article 7 by a *de minimis* principle.[37] Article 28(2) of the UN Convention on the Rights of the Child, to which the UK is a party, goes further, requiring states to 'take all appropriate measures to ensure that school discipline is administered in a manner consistent with the child's human dignity', which might be violated by treatment which would not be regarded as inhuman or degrading.

Subsequently, in *Warwick* v. *UK*,[38] the European Commission of Human Rights, apparently preferring the approach of the Human Rights Committee to that of the European Court of Human Rights in *Campbell and Cosans*, ruled by twelve votes to five that corporal punishment as a disciplinary measure at school constituted degrading treatment. The Committee of Ministers, however, was unable to achieve the two-thirds majority necessary to decide whether or not Article 3 had been violated, so the matter dropped.[39] Nevertheless, in two subsequent cases, the Commission has decided that applications relating to corporal punishment in British schools were admissible.[40] The British Government has paid substantial amounts in compensation for school punishments.[41]

[36] 430 US 651 (1977).

[37] See Dominic McGoldrick, *The Human Rights Committee: Its Role in the Development of the International Covenant on Civil and Political Rights* (Oxford: Clarendon Press, 1991), 365, especially nn. 43 and 44, referring to M. Tarnopolski.

[38] Eur. Comm. HR, Report of 18 June 1986. See also Application No. 9303/81, *B. and D.* v. *UK*, Eur. Comm. HR, 49 DR 44.

[39] Committee of Ministers, Resolution DH(89)5, 2 Mar. 1989.

[40] *Costello-Roberts* v. *UK* (13134/87) and *X and Y* v. *UK* (14229/88); 1 HRCD 228.

[41] On 28 Sept. 1988, Ngaio Crequer in *Independent*, p. 4, reported that the government had paid £51,000 to 16 families who had complained to the Commission about

The cumulative effect of the cases has been to produce a change in domestic law. The result of *Campbell and Cosans* was that the United Kingdom was held to be in breach not of Article 3 of the Convention but of Article 2 of the First Protocol, because the parents of the children concerned were said to have had a genuine philosophical conviction that corporal punishment was the wrong way to educate their children, and that conviction was overridden by a legal system (in that case, the Scottish legal system, but there is no relevant difference in this field between Scots and English law) which permitted a teacher to beat children regardless of the parents' wishes. In other words, rights in relation to beating of children by teachers are, under the European Convention, rights of the parents to have their children educated in accordance with their philosphical convictions. They are not part of the child's own right to be free of degrading treatment, because where general social norms regard moderate beating as an acceptable, even desirable, part of child-rearing practice, it will not normally be degrading. A child whose parents' philosophical convictions were not opposed to beating might, however, be able to claim that she had suffered degrading treatment if the punishment were administered in a particularly humiliating way. For example, *Campbell and Cosans* dealt with the case where a moderate beating was administered in private, without offending principles of modesty. It might be different if the beating were carried out in public, or if the beating were administered by a person of the opposite sex or accompanied by any sort of indecency. It is also possible that a beating which would not be considered degrading if administered to a young child would humiliate and degrade an older child or adolescent, or that the manner in which a punishment is delivered might humiliate and degrade a girl but not a boy.

The English and Scottish law on beating in schools was changed in the Education (No. 2) Act 1986 to take account of the decision in *Campbell and Cosans*. Ignoring the Commission's view, not supported by the Court, that corporal punishment at school constitutes degrading treatment, it would have been open to Parliament to do no more than allow parents to opt their children out of corporal punishment on the ground of philosophical convictions. However, teaching unions and others objected that this might lead to two children who had committed the same offence together being punished in very different ways on account

school beatings. Two families, in each of which two children had been victims, received £4,500 each; the others received £3,000 each. In *Y* v. *UK* Eur. Ct. HR, Judgment of 29 Oct. 1992, the Court ordered a case brought under Arts. 3 and 13 of the Convention to be struck out of the list after noting a friendly settlement under which the UK government agreed to pay £8,000 and costs to the complainant in respect of injuries suffered from four strokes of the cane at an independent school.

of their parents' beliefs rather than their own merits. This was regarded as unsatisfactory. Many people advocated the total abolition of corporal punishment in schools of any kind. This, however, would have interfered with the freedom of all educators to provide a style of education desired by those whose religious or philosophical beliefs included a belief (based perhaps on fundamentalist biblical interpretation) that corporal punishment might be necessary and desirable. The government accordingly introduced section 47, which (as extended by the Education Reform Act 1988, Schedule 12, the Children Act 1989, s. 63, and the Children's Homes Regulations 1991) removes a teacher's defence of lawful authority in legal proceedings relating to corporal punishment administered to any pupil at a grant aided, armed forces, or maintained school, or at any children's home (including any independent boarding school with fewer than fifty boarders). It is also unlawful to administer corporal punishment to any child whose attendance at an independent school is being funded wholly or partly by public funds (such as the assisted places scheme established under the Education Act 1981). Parents who regard beating as a necessary or desirable part of education are still at liberty to send their children to those independent schools where the practice continues.[42]

4.4 MEDICAL TREATMENT AND EXPERIMENTATION

The general principle is that any medical treatment constitutes a trespass to the person which must be justified, by reference either to the patient's consent or to the necessity of saving life in circumstances where the patient is unable to decide whether or not to consent.

Rights with regard to medical treatment fall essentially into two categories: first, rights to receive or be free of treatment as needed or desired, and not to be subjected involuntarily to experimentation which, irrespective of any benefit which the subjects may derive, are intended to advance scientific knowledge and benefit people other than the subject in the long term; secondly, rights connected incidentally with the provision of medical services, such as rights to be told the truth by one's doctor. The right to have access to one's medical records is considered in Chapter 8, section 4, below.

(1) The adult's right to refuse treatment

As any medical treatment is *prima facie* an assault, it is unlawful without the patient's consent. A corollary of this unlawfulness is that the patients

---

[42] For discussion, see A. F. Phillips, 'Teachers, Corporal Punishment and the Criminal Law: A Retrospect and Prospect' 1992 *Juridical Review* 3–17.

normally have a right not to accept treatment, or (to put it slightly differently) a right to choose whether to avail themselves of a form of treatment which is available. However, this right cannot be exercised by people who are incapable, or deemed by law to be incapable, of making the choice. Some categories of patients are therefore liable to have the choice made for them by others. Parents normally make choices on behalf of their children; doctors do so on behalf of patients to whom the Mental Health Act 1983 applies, or who are unconscious; the courts do so on behalf of wards of court and, in certain circumstances, on behalf of others, although in such cases the courts are guided by medical opinion to such an extent that it is the doctors, rather than the courts, who are effectively making the decision.

The position of children is considered in section 4.2(2), and that of prisoners in section 4.2(3), below. This section concentrates on consent by adults. The particular issues are considered. First, what is meant by consent? Secondly, what steps are available when an adult is incapable of giving a valid consent? Thirdly, when can a capable adult's decision to refuse treatment be overridden?

(i) *Meaning of consent.*[43] English law demands consent in order to protect the doctor, generally assumed to be acting in good faith for the benefit of patients, against actions for battery, and the law is therefore doctor-oriented. If the issue were, 'What must be done in order to safeguard, to the fullest extent possible, the right of the patient as an autonomous person to choose between courses of action affecting him or her?', it would probably produce rules requiring doctors to give to patients full information, in comprehensible language, about their conditions, the treatment options which are available, and the likely effects of each, with (when appropriate) an opinion as to the course of action which is clinically indicated. Consent given in such circumstances would be fully informed, and the right to be free of non-consensual treatment would effectively give the patient an entitlement to participate in the process of making decisions about treatment.

However, the law, being doctor-oriented, has been developed in the context of the question, 'What is a doctor reasonably required to tell and ask a patient in order to protect himself or herself against liability in damages?' The resulting rules have been framed as an aspect of the law of professional negligence rather than patients' rights. Instead of demanding fully informed consent, the law protects doctors against liability where (*a*) the patient is capable of understanding the implications of the consent,

[43] For a valuable selection of authorities on consent, with commentary, see Ian Kennedy and Andrew Grubb, *Medical Law: Text and Materials* (London: Butterworths, 1989), 171–367.

and (b) the doctor has given as much information as a body of respectable medical opinion would consider reasonable, given the scale of the risks, the options available, and the patient's emotional and intellectual state.[44] This is some way short of giving patients a right to be fully informed about their condition and treatment, and so cannot ground a right to give fully informed consent or to participate actively in decision-making (although in practice in many cases medical staff encourage patients to do so). The question is whether there is real consent, rather than whether there is informed consent.

The practice of obtaining a patient's signature on a consent form before (or, especially in the case of dental treatment, after) treatment is of questionable legal effect. A typical clause consenting to surgery is drafted so as to allow a surgeon to do whatever the surgeon considers necessary in the light of circumstances discovered during the operation. As the patient will usually be unconscious at that stage, it might be a useful protection. However, it is not clear that it has any legal effect. If the procedure which is carried out is radically different from that which the patient envisaged, the signing of the consent form could not be said to be real consent to *that* procedure, much less informed consent. If the procedure is urgently needed, although the need was unforeseen, the surgeon would be protected by the doctrine of necessity, regardless of actual consent. If it is not urgent, in England (unlike, perhaps, Scotland) it seems that the consent form will not protect a surgeon who performs a procedure where there is no urgency, so that it would have been reasonable to wait and discuss it with the patient later.[45]

There are further difficulties surrounding the nature of consent to tests and to experimental procedures. Does the patient have to consent only to a physical intrusion, or must the consent cover the purpose to which the intrusion is directed as well? Take, for example, a patient is suffering from a combination of opportunistic infections. There might be various possible explanations, including the possibility that he is suffering from AIDS. Suppose the doctor decides to take a blood sample, intending to have it tested for (*inter alia*) HIV antibodies. Does the doctor require consent only to the taking of the sample, or must the consent also cover the nature of the intended tests on the sample? It might be difficult to tell the patient that the doctor suspects AIDS, and could cause unnecessary suffering—if the test proves negative, the patient will have been needlessly upset, while, if it proves positive, there is at present no cure for the

---

[44] *Sidaway* v. *Board of Governors of the Bethlem Royal Hospital and the Maudsley Hospital* [1985] AC 871, [1985] 1 All ER 643, HL.

[45] *Devi* v. *West Midlands Regional Health Authority* [1981] CA Transcript 491. See generally J. K. Mason and R. A. McCall Smith, *Law and Medical Ethics*, 3rd edn. (London: Butterworths, 1991), 228–52.

disease (although treatment may increase life expectancy). Because of this, it might be regarded as an infringement of the patient's rights to take a sample without telling the patient what it is to be tested for. However, one must consider exactly which rights are infringed. If the patient consents to having a needle inserted, knowing that the purpose is to take a blood sample for testing, the right to physical integrity is not infringed merely because the doctor intends to have the sample tested for a condition or conditions which he has not mentioned to the patient. There is no unlawful battery. If any right is infringed, it is either a right to be free of mental suffering (more likely to be infringed if the object of the sampling is disclosed than otherwise) or a right to privacy or confidentiality (which is of uncertain scope in English law, and has never been used to prevent a test but only to prevent disclosure to third parties of the results of the test).[46] A doctor might, perhaps, be liable in negligence for failing to warn the patient of what the test was for, but until it is generally accepted medical practice to tell patients what they are being tested for, it will not be part of the doctor's duty of care as laid down in *Sidaway* to tell patients the specific tests which it is planned to run on each sample taken.[47]

A related difficulty concerns the need to inform people of the effects of immunizations when carrying out a state-sponsored programme designed to eradicate or reduce the incidence of particular diseases. These programmes have been successful in the UK in virtually eradicating polio and tuberculosis, for instance. Epidemiological evidence shows that programmes of mass immunization can enormously benefit the health of the community as a whole. Yet, on an individual level, they entail a small but appreciable risk of damage to particular recipients from the immediate effects of vaccines. Usually there will be no more than a degree of discomfort and perhaps a mild fever, but occasionally there are more serious side effects. The communal benefit of programmes may be put at risk if individual recipients (or their parents) give so much weight to the risk to themselves that substantial numbers refuse the immunization. Is it permissible for doctors or the state to encourage people to be immunized by not mentioning or playing down the significance of possible damage? If there is no opportunity to obtain real consent in individual cases, does it breach

---

[46] *X* v. *Y* [1988] 2 All ER 648. The European Commission of Human Rights has held that certain mandatory medical tests infringe the right to respect for private life under Art. 8 of the European Convention: *X* v. *Austria* (8278/78), (1979) 18 DR 154 (blood test); *Acmanne* v. *Belgium* (10453/83), (1984) 40 DR 251 (chest X-ray and tuberculin test). See Paul Sieghart, *AIDS and Human Rights: A UK Perspective* (London: BMA Foundation for Aids, 1989), 30–3.

[47] See John Keown, 'The Ashes of AIDS and the Phoenix of Informed Consent' (1989) 52 *MLR* 790–800, discussing the conflicting opinions given by leading counsel to various bodies on these points.

the common–law rights of people who suffer injury? In the UK, this issue
has been defused by providing a statutory compensation scheme under
the Vaccine Damage Act 1979 for people who suffer damage from vaccine. It is recognized that the people who suffer damage are injured in
the interests of the wider community's fight against disease as a social evil,
and should be compensated for the special loss which they have sustained
in the common cause. A flat-rate payment of £20,000 is made to victims.
However, there remains the difficulty (which is hard for most claimants
to overcome, particularly in relation to whooping-cough immunization)
that claimants must show that the vaccine caused their symptoms.

If parents are deprived of the chance to make informed decisions on
behalf of their children, does it breach the right to respect for family life
under Article 8 of the Convention? The protection of the community's
health is a permitted ground for interfering with the right, under Article
8(2). So long as the state properly weighs the risks, and permits interference only to the extent required for the permitted purpose, it does not
breach Article 8 rights; any breach of the right to respect for family life is
justifiable, particularly where those who suffer injury have a statutory
right to compensation.[48]

Experimentation on patients is a further difficult area.[49] Where experiments are performed for the good of the patient, as where the patient's
life is threatened by a condition which has resisted treatment by established methods, and it seems that only innovative methods can succeed,
there usually is little difficulty in seeking and obtaining the patient's consent. Nor is that consent vitiated by the mere fact that studying the results
of the treatment might ultimately prove to be of more benefit to others
than to the patient. However, when the experiment is likely to do little
or no good to the individual patient, a dilemma arises. The clinical testing of techniques and drugs may be desirable on general utilitarian terms,
but harm those who are guinea pigs.[50] In the aftermath of the Second
World War, the Nuremberg war crimes tribunal had to decide how to
approach the cases of doctors in concentration camps who had performed
experiments on inmates. The result was a ten–point code,[51] which was
later taken up by the medical profession, refined, and is now encapsulated
in the Declaration of Helsinki, drawn up by the World Medical

[48] *Wain* v. *UK* (10787/84) Eur. Comm. HR, 9 EHRR 122, in relation to the administration of the triple vaccine against diphtheria, whooping cough, and tetanus.

[49] Erwin Deutsch, 'Medical Experimentation: International Rules and Practice' (1989)
19 *Victoria Univ. of Wellington LR* 1–10, provides an introduction to this complex field.

[50] See Ian Kennedy, *Treat Me Right: Essays in Medical Law and Ethics* (Oxford:
Clarendon Press, 1991), ch. 10.

[51] *US* v. *Rose* 'The Medical Case' (1949), *Trial of War Criminals before the Nuremberg
Military Tribunals*, i, ii. See also *Re Brandt and others* (1947) 14 ILR 296 at p. 298, US
Military Tribunal, Nuremberg.

Association in 1964, as revised in 1975.[52] This approach, allowing the medical profession to set its own standards subject to the demands of international humanitarian law and, where the state takes an interest, domestic law, is acceptable only so long as the profession polices the standards rigorously, taking account of public moralities and public interests. Under Article 7 of the International Covenant on Civil and Political Rights, as noted earlier, states have an obligation to guarantee that 'no one shall be subjected without his consent to medical or scientific experimentation', which is treated as a special form of torture or inhuman or degrading treatment. In the UK, this is one of the responsibilities of hospital ethical committees, widely established in accordance with the recommendations of the Warnock Committee report.[53]

The distinction between therapeutic treatment and clinical research is blurred in the area of heroic efforts to save life. The category into which a procedure falls would seem to depend both on the balance of risks to the patient and the ethical acceptability of the procedure to the profession. Transplanting a baboon's heart into a young infant who would otherwise have faced certain death from heart disease, and in the event died equally inevitably from the effects of rejection of the heart, was close to the borderline.[54] The patient (or those representing him) must in principle have the ultimate right to say yes or no in each case. However, it may be extremely difficult to obtain consent to random sample testing. Seeking consent may not always be possible without undermining the purpose of the experiment. For example, double blind testing (where patients are allocated to groups receiving different types of treatments without either the patients or their physicians knowing which groups are which) presents serious problems, especially where the condition from which people suffer is life-threatening. In such areas, the importance of active monitoring and licensing of experiments is paramount in order to prevent, so far as humanly possible, foreseeable harm (or loss of therapeutic benefit) to a patient. The benefits to society from experiments may be considerable, but it is doubtful whether we should seek those benefits where the cost to innocent members of society, who derive no benefit, is substantial.

A final problem concerns consent to clinical or research non-treatment. As consent is required to protect the doctor against an action

[52] One further subparagraph was added in 1983. The Declaration is printed in Mason and McCall Smith, *Medical Ethics*, 446–9.

[53] Dept. of Health and Social Security, *Report of the Committee of Inquiry into Human Fertilisation and Embryology* (Chairman: Dame Mary Warnock), Cmnd. 9314 (London: HMSO, 1984).

[54] L. L. Hubbard, 'The Baby Face Case' (1987) 6 *Medical Law* 385; Mason and McCall Smith, *Medical Ethics*, 362–4.

for battery only when treatment is to take place, it seems to follow that no consent is needed where the doctor decides not to treat. The decision may render the doctor liable to an action for negligence, but the consent of the patient is not usually relevant to a negligence claim, which does not normally aim to safeguard the patient's autonomy. The failure of English law to give a *right* to patients to participate in decisions concerning their treatment is a dangerous threat to their autonomy and, where the doctor has odd ideas, to their lives. This was made clear by the Cartwright report[55] on the disastrous consequences of a New Zealand doctor's eccentric view that women with cervical cancer did not require any treatment, which has led one commentator to conclude that the Declaration of Helsinki should be incorporated into New Zealand domestic law.[56] If that is right for New Zealand, it would also be good for the UK.

(ii) *Adults who are unable to consent.* Where a patient is seriously incapacitated, so as to be incapable of giving consent, the doctrine of necessity or that of implied consent will protect a doctor who embarks on treatment in an emergency.[57] More difficult problems arise where the cause of inability to give a valid consent is the otherwise fit patient's lack of mental capacity. Here, two situations need to be distinguished.

(a) Where a patient is detained compulsorily under the Mental Health Act 1983, there is statutory provision for doctors to make decisions on behalf of the patient as to treatment for the mental condition in respect of which the patient has been detained.[58] This is subject to two limitations. First, so-called irreversible treatments cannot be administered without the patient's consent, which must be verified by a specially appointed doctor and two specially appointed non-medical witnesses.[59] These include procedures which result in the destruction of brain tissue or brain function, and the surgical implantation of hormones to control the male sex drive. Such treatment, even if apparently appropriate, can be administered without the patient's properly witnessed consent only if it is necessary to save the patient's life, in which case there is a defence for doctors both under statute and at common law.[60] Secondly,

---

[55] Judge Cartwright, *Report of the Cervical Cancer Inquiry* (Auckland: NZ Government Printer, 1988).

[56] Sandra Coney, *The Unfortunate Experiment* (Wellington, NZ: Penguin, 1988), p. 258.

[57] It is possible that a patient might want treatment to be withheld. On the right to be left to die, and living wills, see ch. 3 above.

[58] Mental Health Act 1983, s. 63.   [59] Ibid., s. 57.

[60] Ibid., s. 62(1); *In re F. (mental patient: sterilisation)* [1990] 2 AC 1, [1989] 2 All ER 545, HL, below.

treatments defined as hazardous may be administered only with the patient's consent, verified by the medical officer responsible for treatment or by a specially appointed medical practitioner, unless an appointed medical practitioner certifies that the patient is incapable of giving consent but that the treatment would benefit him.[61] Consent or certification can be bypassed only to save the patient's life or prevent a serious deterioration in his condition, again providing justifications for doctors under either statute or common law.[62]

Treatment for other conditions, unrelated to the mental condition, can be given only with the patient's consent, subject to the powers of the court under *In re F.*, below.

(b) Where a patient is not compulsorily detained, there is no provision under the Mental Health Act 1983 for treatment to be given without the consent of the patient, but the patient may be incapable of understanding what treatment is proposed, and so be unable to consent. The doctor would be protected by the doctrine of implied consent or necessity when treating the patient for a life-threatening disorder, but has no such protection where the treatment is for a less serious, though perhaps debilitating and unpleasant, condition. Here, the House of Lords in *Re F. (mental patient: sterilisation)*[63] has recently held that the courts, while lacking power to consent on behalf of the patient, may still grant a declaration that the doctor would not be acting unlawfully in administering treatment, if the court is convinced that the treatment is in the patient's best interests.

The history of this development provides an interesting example of the effect of developing ideas about individual rights and liberties.[64] The Court of Protection used to have a jurisdiction in respect of the affairs of lunatics. This derived from the responsibility of the Crown as *parens patriae* to care for those who were incapable of looking after their own interests. It included a power to make decisions about medical treatment. When the compulsory treatment of mental disorder was put on a statutory footing, the statutory powers gradually eroded the common-law jurisdiction of the Court of Protection. They placed great freedom in the

---

[61] Mental Health Act 1983, s. 58.

[62] Ibid., s. 62(1)(*b*); *In re F.*, above. A patient can withdraw consent at any time: s. 60. For further details, see Mental Health (Hospital, Guardianship and Consent to Treatment) Regulations 1983, SI 1983/893; Mason and McCall Smith, *Medical Ethics*, 402–3.

[63] [1990] 2 AC 1, [1989] 2 All ER 545 *sub nom. F.* v. *West Berkshire Health Authority (Mental Health Act Commission intervening)*, HL.

[64] This is reviewed by the Law Commission Consultation Paper No. 119, *Mentally Incapacitated Adults and Decision-Making: An Overview* (London: HMSO, 1991), 55–60.

hands of the doctors concerned. When the legislation was revised in the light of the standards laid down in the European Convention on Human Rights and the developing caselaw under it, it was decided to omit powers to take decisions on behalf of voluntary patients. However, some of these patients were too severely affected by their conditions to be able to understand the nature of the treatment which was recommended for them, or to consent to it. This placed the doctors treating these patients in a dilemma where treatment became, in their view, desirable, but did not relate directly to either the mental condition for which the patient had consented to treatment or to life-threatening disorders for which the principle of necessity (or that of implied consent) might have offered protection.

The House of Lords in Re F. decided that the Crown's prerogative powers had been abrogated by statute, and had not sprung up again when the Mental Health Act 1983 omitted to give authority to make decisions on behalf of voluntary patients.[65] However, even without a power to consent on behalf of the patient (which Lord Ackner, alone among the Law Lords, would have been prepared to create under common law), the House decided that the courts had a responsibility to declare prospective treatment to be lawful if in the patient's best interests.

The main difficulty with the decision in Re F. is that it replaces autonomy with judicial paternalism, without unambiguous and clear guidelines as to the basis on which the power is to be exercised. It is unfortunate that the main area in which the power is used appears to relate to the sterilization of women who are sexually active but are unable to comprehend the consequences of sexual intercourse, and would be unable to care adequately for any children who might be born as a result. The House of Lords in Re F. was inevitably content to be guided by doctors and social workers as to the patient's best interests. The test applied to determine what was in the best interests of the patient was not whether the patient would have chosen to be treated if she had had the necessary capacity, but whether the proposed treatment would be accepted as appropriate by a responsible body of doctors skilled in that form of treatment. This opens the way to major surgery on a patient carried out for any purpose which would be regarded as appropriate by a responsible body of doctors, a negation of the rights of patients.[66] Furthermore,

[65] This was similar to the conclusion of Brenda Hoggett, 'The Royal Prerogative in Relation to the Mentally Disordered: Resurrection, Resuscitation, or Rejection?', in M. D. A. Freeman (ed.), Medicine, Ethics and the Law (London: Stevens & Sons, 1988), 85–102 at 96–7.

[66] M. D. A. Freeman, 'Sterilising the Mentally Handicapped', in Freeman (ed.), Medicine, Ethics and the Law, 55–84; Kenneth McK. Norrie, 'Sterilisation of the Mentally Disabled in English and Canadian Law' (1989) 38 ICLQ 387–95; D. Ogbourne and

although Lord Griffiths would have favoured making sterilization unlawful without a court order, the other members of the House in Re F. disagreed, so major surgery can be performed with neither consent nor the
leave of the court if doctors and health authorities are prepared to take
the risk of subsequent court action.

A further, though less serious, difficulty with Re F. is that it does not
remove uncertainty and risk from doctors. While a declaration such as
was granted there will protect doctors from subsequent civil action, it
could not give guaranteed protection against criminal liability, because
neither the doctrine of issue estoppel nor the rules on abuse of process
will provide an absolute bar to a prosecution in respect of surgery carried
out in accordance with a declaration granted by a civil court.[67]
Legislation is required to resolve the issue of responsibility, and the
grounds on which consents are to be given; almost any resolution would
be preferable to the present situation. The matter is currently under consideration by the Law Commission, and it is to be hoped that its recommendations, when they emerge, will be speedily adopted in legislation.

(iii) *Adults who refuse to consent*. The general rule is that a capable adult
who refuses consent to treatment may not lawfully be treated. As noted
in Chapter 3, some patients make 'living wills', directing that they are not
to be treated if their condition deteriorates to a point where they are
incapable of giving or refusing consent. However, there are two recent
decisions which suggest that the refusal of consent by an apparently competent adult may sometimes be overridden. In the first case, *Re T. (Adult:
Refusal of Medical Treatment)*,[68] the patient, T., who was pregnant, had
been injured in a car accident. Her mother was a Jehovah's witness, and
although T. was no longer a member of the sect she gave written instructions to medical staff, after discussing the matter with her mother, that
she did not want a blood transfusion as it would be a sin and bar to eternal salvation. She was given an emergency Caesarian, and her condition
deteriorated to a point where the doctor would normally have considered
a transfusion advisable but was inhibited by the written refusal of consent.
On an application by her father and boyfriend, Ward J. and the Court of

R. Ward, 'Sterilization, the Mentally Incompetent and the Courts' (1989) 18 *Anglo-Amer.
LR* 230–40; Josephine Shaw, 'Sterilisation of Mentally Handicapped People: Judges Rule
OK?' (1990) 53 *MLR* 91–106. For a slightly different analysis of *Re F.* and options for
reform, see The Law Commission, *Mentally Incapacitated Adults and Decision-Making*,
101–10. On sterilization generally, see Gillian Douglas, *Law, Fertility and Reproduction*
(London: Sweet & Maxwell, 1991), 53–61.

[67] *Imperial Tobacco Ltd.* v. *A.G.* [1981] AC 718, [1980] 1 All ER 866, HL; David
Feldman, 'Declarations and the Control of Prosecutions' [1981] *Crim. LR* 25–37;
Hoggett, 'Royal Prerogative', at p. 87.
[68] [1992] 4 All ER 649, CA.

Appeal held that the refusal of consent was vitiated because the doctors had wrongly minimized to T. the risks of refusal; she had also been subjected to undue influence, her will being overborne by the persuasion of her mother when T. had been very tired. Later T. had been under the influence of pethidine and in no condition to exercise independent judgement. Where the refusal is vitiated by factors such as these, and subsequently the patient is incapable of making a decision, the doctors have to treat the patient according to their clinical judgement.

In the second case, *Re S. (Adult: Refusal of Medical Treatment)*,[69] Sir Stephen Brown P. overrode a pregnant mother's refusal, on religious grounds, to submit to an emergency Caesarian in an attempt to save the life both of the baby and the mother. The value of the life of a viable foetus was allowed to override the value of the mother's autonomy.

These decisions indicate the tendency of the courts to prefer consent to medical treatment to refusal of consent, where life is at risk. Although the judges insisted that a decision by a competent adult to refuse treatment, properly reached, should be respected (however irrational it might seem), they raise the possibility of a person being treated as incapable by reason of the irrationality (from the court's or doctor's point of view) of the decision to risk death by refusing treatment. The court balanced the value of life against the value of autonomy, but there is a risk that life will be preserved even when its value is, to the patient, outweighed by other values. That might be justified if one accepts that doctors and judges have a responsibility to protect the interests of an unborn child, in *Re S.*, but it cannot be justified in the circumstances of *Re T.*, where the Caesarian had been performed (the child, sadly, died), unless one either imports a high degree of paternalism, which is inconsistent with the notion of the right to refuse consent, or allows the court to take account of the distress of friends and relations as a countervailing interest to that of personal autonomy. These considerations arise again in the next section.

(2) Consent by and on behalf of children

Three special questions arising in relation to the giving of consent to medical procedures for children concern the relationship between the rights of children to give or withhold consent and the rights of adults or the courts to do it for them. The questions are: (i) whether children are capable of giving consent without consulting, or contrary to the wishes of, their parents or guardians; (ii) whether parents, guardians, or courts, can override a child's consent or refusal of consent; and (iii) whether children can veto a consent given on their behalf by a parent or guardian.

[69] [1992] 4 All ER 671.

(i) *Consent by children and young persons.* The legal capacity of children to decide for themselves whether or not to obtain medical treatment has only recently been directly addressed in English law. Certain principles are clear.

First, under the Family Law Reform Act 1969, section 8, a person aged 16 but under 18 is entitled to consent to treatment to the same extent as an adult. This recognizes the validity of a consent of a 16-year-old to therapy or experimentation, as long as she is capable of understanding the implications of what is to be done. This does not, however, say anything about whether the young patient's *refusal* of consent is to exclude consent given on her behalf by parent or guardian. This matter falls to be dealt with on general principles applying to minors.

Secondly, parental rights do not extend to vetoing a minor's consent to treatment, whether over or under the age of 16, as long as the minor is of sufficient understanding to comprehend the advice which is given to her and the implications of it. This was established in *Gillick* v. *West Norfolk and Wisbech Area Health Authority*,[70] where a mother sought to prevent a health authority from allowing doctors under its control to give contraceptive advice to underage children. The rights of parents to control their children's access to contraceptive advice were considered in depth, and it was clear that the same principles applied to obtaining treatment as to obtaining advice. The majority of the House of Lords held that the parent's rights were waning, and children's rights increasing. Parents have responsibilities for their children, and their rights extend only as far as necessary in order to allow them to discharge their responsibilities. As children grow in maturity and understanding, they are to be allowed to exercise for themselves those choices of which they are capable of understanding the implications and consequences. The majority held that the decision whether a child should receive advice on contraception without the parents' consent must be based on the doctor's judgement of the patient's maturity and understanding. Wherever possible, the parents should be consulted, but if the child refuses to agree to the parents being informed the doctor, whose first responsibility is to the patient, must probably accept that, if he considers that the child is mature enough to be given the advice sought.

This is simply another way of saying that, as with adult patients, the doctor is protected by the patient's consent if the consent is 'real', but that the doctor's view of the patient's level of understanding and the significance of the treatment is relevant to the reality of the patient's consent. A 13-year-old might therefore be '*Gillick*-competent' and able to

---

[70] [1986] AC 112, [1985] 3 All ER 402, HL. See discussion by Brenda Hoggett, 'Parents, Children and Medical Treatment: The Legal Issues', in Peter Byrne (ed.), *Rights and Wrongs in Medicine* (London: King's Fund, 1986), 158–76.

consent to major surgery necessary to treat a life-threatening disorder, or to minor treatment with no long-term implications for an ingrowing toe-nail, but not to major surgery to reconstruct his face for purely cosmetic reasons. A 4-year-old would in all probability not be competent to con-sent to anything. The child's rights therefore grow with the child's capac-ity to understand the consequences of exercising them in particular ways, and a child's consent will be more readily acceptable in respect of urgent treatment or advice than other treatment. Such an approach is consistent with the theory that autonomy is the value at the root of the moral justification of freedom: the greater one's capacity to exercise a choice in an informed way, the stronger is one's claim to be free to exercise it.[71]

(ii) *When can a parent or court decide to give consent to treatment?* A parent's power to decide whether to allow a child to undergo medical treatment is not unlimited even when the child is an infant. If parents refuse con-sent to a life-saving procedure, the state can and probably will step in, and appropriate the responsibility for making the decisions. The social services department of the local authority is likely to take the child into care and authorize treatment, or make the child a ward of court and ask the court to do so. Under the Children Act 1989, a court can make a child assessment order in respect of a child's health, development, or the way he has been treated, and this will normally protect the professional who carries out the assessment. However, the Act expressly states that the child, if of sufficient understanding to make an informed decision (a level of understanding apparently intended to be equivalent to *Gillick*-competence), may refuse to submit to the assessment, and in such cir-cumstances any examination is likely to be an assault or battery, and give rise to criminal liability and liability in damages.[72] Similarly, a court mak-ing an interim care order or interim supervision order may give direc-tions concerning a medical or psychiatric examination for the child, and this will normally protect the doctor, but the child, if competent, may refuse to submit to the examination or assessment.[73] The same applies to an order given in an emergency protection order.[74] In relation to a supervision order, the court may include in the order a provision requiring the supervised child to submit to medical or psychiatric examinations, but, where the child has sufficient understanding to make an informed decision, the court is not permitted to include such a requirement unless it is satisfied that he consents to its inclusion.[75] This shows a clear legisla-tive policy of giving the fullest possible rein to a competent child's autonomous decision-making capacity, even to the extent of allowing

[71] See Ch. I, above.   [72] Children Act 1989, s. 43(1), (8).
[73] Ibid., s. 38(6).   [74] Ibid., s. 44(6), (7).   [75] Ibid., Sched. 3, Pt. I, para. 4(4).

such a child to override the judgment of a court as to the child's best interests in medical and psychiatric matters.

In extreme cases, a parent who fails to obtain adequate medical treatment for a child may be liable to criminal penalties for offences such as child neglect.[76] If it proves to be too late, and the child dies, the parent may even be guilty of manslaughter.[77] This state intervention in the parent–child relationship is justifiable because the parent's power to decide on behalf of the child is there to be used in fulfilment of the parent's duty to look after the child, as pointed out in *Gillick*, not to prevent the child receiving care. In addition, if there is any hierarchical ordering of rights, most people would place the child's right to receive appropriate medical treatment (in extreme cases, to have its life saved) above the parent's right to decide what is best for the child.

Sometimes, however, the parents are refusing consent to treatment for conscientious reasons rather than through mere neglect. For example, they may genuinely believe that it is the best interests of a severely handicapped child to be allowed to die, as the parents did in *In re B. (A Minor) (Wardship: Medical Treatment).*[78] The position of English law, reflected in that case, is that the parent's wishes will be only one factor for a court to take into account, and will be relatively insignificant if they conflict with the court's view of the child's best interests. Again, certain religious denominations (such as the Jehovah's Witnesses) refuse to permit blood transfusions, so that the intervention of state agencies to allow a blood transfusion to a sick child may violate the parent's right to exercise his or her religion and to bring up children according to his or her philosophical convictions. Nevertheless, the law will treat failure to permit *necessary* treatment as a crime, thereby protecting the autonomy of the child against infringement by adult relations.[79] Where the child is very young, the parent's freedom of religion should not be used to allow a serious detriment to be imposed on a child who is incapable of consent. The parent's religious conviction should no more be allowed to dispose of the issue of the child's treatment if death threatens than should the religious convictions of one whose religion requires child sacrifice.

Where the child is older, and is both *Gillick*-competent and capable of understanding the dictates of the religion and its implications, the posi-

---

[76] Children and Young Persons Act 1933, s. 1, as amended by Children and Young Persons Act 1963 and Children Act 1975, Scheds. 3 and 4; *R. v. Sheppard* [1981] AC 394, [1980] 3 All ER 889, HL.

[77] However, the statutory offence will usually be more appropriate: *R. v. Lowe* [1973] QB 702, CA.

[78] [1981] 1 WLR 1421, CA.

[79] *R. v. Senior* [1899] 1 QB 283, CCR. For the position if the child, as well as the parent, wants to refuse treatment, see (iii) below.

tion is more difficult. Here, the relevant principles are those which are considered under (iii).

(iii) *Can the child withhold consent to necessary treatment, or override the consent given by parents or guardians?* If the child wants to refuse treatment which the doctors consider to be necessary, intervention may disregard the child's right to autonomy. Where the child is refusing treatment on religious grounds, intervention disregards the child's right to religious freedom. In such cases, the law has two options open to it. It could require the court to apply the *Gillick* test, and treat the child's wishes as authoritative if the court (or the doctor) is satisfied that the child understands what it is doing and the consequences of its choice.[80] This would respect that child's autonomy and capacity to make decisions, while allowing the court to act to protect children who are, in its opinion, incapable of making such decisions.

Alternatively, the court could say that, while minors sometimes have the right to *seek* advice or treatment without their parents' consent (as in *Gillick*), they have no right to decide to *refuse* treatment where that will threaten their lives. The principle of autonomy, on this view, compels the court to insist that life is maintained, at any rate where a tolerable quality of life will be possible,[81] until the minor comes of age. Only when the law recognizes a person as having full capacity in all matters should it recognize his right to refuse consent to a life-saving treatment. In the meantime, the court would have to balance the wishes of the child against the court's or parent's view of the child's long-term best interests or other relevant objectives. Where there is a risk of death, it will normally outweigh the harm done to a child's autonomy by ignoring the child's wish to be let alone. In relation to treatment for conditions which are not life-threatening, a substantial benefit from the treatment will tend to outweigh the child's short-term objection, but the smaller the benefit is, the more easily it will be outweighed by the child's aversion (always assuming that the child is capable of understanding the issues and their implications). *Gillick*-competence is therefore a relative matter.[82]

The most thorough English judicial examination of these issues was conducted in *Re R. (A Minor) (Wardship: Medical Treatment).*[83] The case

---

[80] In cases of religious refusal, it would be necessary to consider the stage at which a child can be said to have a religion, and whether the child needs to understand the reasons for the religious injunction, as well as the implications of refusing or accepting treatment.

[81] See *In re C. (a minor) (wardship: medical treatment)* [1990] Fam. 26, CA, discussed by S. E. Roberts, 'When Not to Prolong Life' (1990) 106 *LQR* 218–22.

[82] See *Re R. (a minor) (wardship: medical treatment)* [1991] 4 All ER 177 at p. 187 *per* Lord Donaldson MR.

[83] [1991] 4 All ER 177, CA.

arose under the court's wardship jurisdiction. A 15-year-old girl with a history of violent relationships with her parents was received into voluntary care after a fight with her father. While in care she asked not to see her father. Concern about her mental state developed. She had bouts of being flat, expressionless, and resistant to being touched, and sometimes seemed to be experiencing visual and auditory hallucinations and suicidal thoughts. After returning home briefly, she ran off and was found on a bridge threatening suicide. That night she absconded from a children's home, and was found the next day at her parents' home. An interim care order was made, and she was persuaded to return to a children's home, but her behaviour was increasingly disturbed. She was admitted to a psychiatric unit. In her lucid periods, she denied hallucinating, and ultimately refused consent to medication. Doctors sought the local authority's permission to administer anti-psychotic medication. This was at first granted, but, after the patient had telephoned the psychiatric social worker and had a long conversation in which she seemed lucid and rational, the local authority decided that it would not give permission for drugs to be administered against the patient's will. She continued to refuse her consent. At this point, the doctors decided that they were not willing to keep the patient in their care unless she consented to treatment. The local authority thereupon commenced wardship proceedings. Waite J., exercising the wardship jurisdiction, gave consent to treatment. The Official Solicitor, representing the child patient, appealed.

The three members of the Court of Appeal (Lord Donaldson MR, Staughton LJ, and Farquharson LJ) agreed that Waite J. had acted correctly, on the basis that the girl was not *Gillick*-competent: her decision to refuse treatment had been affected by her immaturity and, perhaps, her medical condition. They held that *Gillick* could have no application to a case where the patient was suffering from mental illness, even with periods of lucidity. In such cases, the court in wardship proceedings had to exercise its discretion in the objective best interests of the child. That would have disposed of the case, but the judges went on to give, *obiter*, two rather different accounts of what the position would have been in relation to a child who could be regarded as *Gillick*-competent. As a result, the principles on which the powers of parents, guardians, and courts to consent to treatment on behalf of children are based remain uncertain.

Staughton LJ, with whom it seems that Farquharson LJ agreed, distinguished between the powers of a parent to override the wishes of a child (exercisable only when the child is not *Gillick*-competent), and the powers of the court in wardship proceedings, where the best interests of the child are paramount and may require the court to override the wishes even of a *Gillick*-competent child. Accordingly, on this view, parents or guardians cannot override the grant or refusal of consent by a *Gillick*-competent child, but a court exercising wardship jurisdiction can.

Lord Donaldson MR took a rather different approach. Starting from the position that the court was protecting the *interests* of the child but the *rights* (specifically, the right not to be sued for battery) of the doctor treating her, he asked whether only the child was capable of offering the doctor protection. He imagined a door which had to be opened in order to give access to treatment, and suggested that there were several keyholders for the door. One is the child, if *Gillick*-competent; another was the parent or guardian, whether or not the child was *Gillick*-competent; a third was the court, exercising its wardship jurisdiction. Although *Gillick* allowed the competent child to give consent which could not be overridden by the parent, *Gillick* did not, he considered, allow the child to refuse treatment where those responsible for her welfare thought it desirable in her interests that treatment should be administered.

On Lord Donaldson's view, then, even a *Gillick*-competent child has no *right* to refuse treatment, but only a right to accept it. It is submitted that this deprives the decision in *Gillick* of much of its force, and runs counter to the approach of the majority in the House of Lords. Lord Scarman, in particular, had spoken of parental rights terminating once the young patient was competent.[84] In addition, it was unnecessary to go that far once it had been decided that, in any case, a mentally ill child could not be regarded as *Gillick*-competent. The effect is to give the medical profession the widest possible discretion, including a discretion in all cases to search round to find someone in authority who can countermand the patient's refusal of consent. It is understandable that this might be thought desirable, as in the other English case where the question has arisen the child was a 15-year-old Jehovah's Witness who was endangering his life by refusing a blood transfusion, with his parents' support.[85] In such a case, it is understandable that the court should want to preserve the patient's life until the child is of full age and free from the influence of his parents. However, the best way of dealing with such cases is to invoke the wardship jurisdiction, on the model set out in the judgment of Staughton LJ.

In view of the decision in *Re R.* that the patient was not *Gillick*-competent, it is strongly arguable that the whole of the discussion of the principles governing refusal of consent by *Gillick*-competent children was *obiter*. Nevertheless, when Lord Donaldson reconsidered his approach, in the light of critical commentary on the earlier decision, in *Re W. (A Minor) (Medical Rreatment)*,[86] he essentially reaffirmed it in a case where

---

[84] *Gillick's* case, [1985] 3 All ER 402 at 421, 423–4.
[85] *Re E. (a minor)*, 21 Sept. 1990, unreported, Ward J.
[86] [1992] 4 All ER 627, CA.

the patient was a *Gillick*-competent girl aged 16 who was suffering from anorexia nervosa, and wished to continue to receive treatment of one type when her doctor wanted to change to another type. Lord Donaldson replaced the 'keyholder' analogy with another: consent acts as a 'flak jacket' for doctors, protecting them against criminal or civil liability. The doctor needs only one flak jacket, and it may be provided either by the consent of a *Gillick*-competent minor, or by another person having parental responsibilities, or by the court acting in the best interest of the minor. There is to be what Balcombe LJ called 'a predilection to give effect to the child's wishes on the basis that prima facie that will be in his or her best interests', but that predilection can be overborne in appropriate cases. The child's protection against ill-advised consent by a parent lies in the medical ethics of the doctor, or the good sense of the court.

In evaluating these decisions, two points should be borne in mind. First, the judgments relate only to the wardship jurisdiction, which has been narrowed in scope since the Children Act 1989 came into force in November 1991. Secondly, as noted above, the statutory scheme for assessment and examination of children under orders made pursuant to the 1989 Act expressly permits a *Gillick*-competent child to override a consent to assessment or examination given by a court. This suggests that the legislative policy lying behind the 1989 Act may be inconsistent with the suggestions in *Re R.* that a *Gillick*-competent child can never effectively veto a consent given by a parent (*per* Lord Donaldson) or a court (*per* Staughton and Farquharson LJJ). Although the statutory provisions are concerned with interim and supervision orders rather than specific issues orders, as Lord Donaldson pointed out in *Re W.*, the House of Lords in *Gillick* treated examinations and advice on the same footing as treatment. It is, therefore, possible that in the future, even in the wardship jurisdiction, judges will assimilate the principles which apply in wardship to those operating under the Children Act 1989.

In any case, the question is likely to be academic in most cases. If the child is refusing treatment which doctors regard as desirable to treat a serious condition (*a fortiori* where the condition is life-threatening), courts are very likely in all cases to regard that decision itself as sufficient to indicate that the child is not *Gillick*-competent. This is an area where, even after *Gillick*, children have few rights.

When the procedures are not being administered for their therapeutic properties (if any), but for some other reason, there must always be a presumption against allowing them, whether the child wants them or not. This applies, for example, to blood tests to establish paternity,[87] examina-

---

[87] Cf. *S.* v. *S.* [1972] AC 24, HL.

tion in relation to child-abuse inquiries,[88] non-therapeutic experimentation,[89] and tattooing.[90] It also applies to various forms of mutilation carried out for religious or social reasons: ear piercing, circumcision, and
clitorectomy (sometimes called female circumcision).[91] Arguments that
these practices should be permitted in order to give effect to the right to
practice religious beliefs founder, because the beliefs in question are those
of the parents, and one person's religious freedom should not be used in
order to justify an interference with another person's right to bodily
integrity.[92] This is a classic example of a case where the parent's freedom
ends where the child's nose (or other anatomical protuberance) begins. A
stronger argument presents mutilation as necessary in order to protect the
child's future as a member of the social or religious group. An uncircum-
cised Jewish boy is at a social disadvantage in the Jewish community;
similar considerations (*mutatis mutandis*) may apply to Muslims and other
communities. But whatever may be the position under Muslim, Jewish,
or other law, Article 3 of the European Convention guarantees the
absolute right to be free from inhuman treatment, which cannot be
qualified to give effect to any other right (let alone a social benefit). It is
arguable that circumcision and other forms of mutilation, conducted
without the victim's 'real' consent and for non-therapeutic purposes,
constitute inhuman treatment, particularly if they are irreversible. If so,
the UK is failing in its international obligations if its law permits such
procedures to be carried out.

Two questions fall to be answered in relation to this. First, can treatment
be inhuman without being degrading, or is inhuman treatment an aggravated form of degrading treatment? If the latter is the case, and if (as in
Campbell and Cosans, above) one takes the view that treatment is not
degrading if it is in tune with social morality, and so does not lower the
recipient in his own eyes or those of ordinary people in that society, it may
be that circumcising male children is on a par with ear piercing: a relatively
trivial and commonplace form of mutilation; while female circumcision is

[88] The Children Act 1989 provides that the court, when deciding whether to authorize a medical examination of a child, is not to do so if the child does not wish to co-
operate and is *Gillick*-competent.
[89] See Mason and McCall Smith, *Medical Ethics*, 368–74.
[90] Tattooing of minors, otherwise than by or under the direction of a registered medical practitioner for medical reasons, is an offence: Tattooing of Minors Act 1969, s. 1.
[91] Clitorectomy and related practices, but not circumcision of males, are criminal
offences unless performed for reasons of medical necessity for the physical or mental
health of the patient by a registered medical practitioner or, in certain cases, a registered
midwife: Prohibition of Female Circumcision Act 1985, ss. 1, 2.
[92] The Prohibition of Female Circumcision Act 1985, s. 2(2), expressly excludes matters of custom and ritual from consideration when deciding whether an operation is necessary for the mental health of the woman.

definitely not acceptable. On the other hand, if treatment can be inhuman without degrading the sufferer, the inhumanity of the treatment is depends not on local social morality but on internationally accepted standards. In principle, this is a preferable approach: it should not be internationally acceptable for any society to inflict severe suffering on people. This leads to the second question: is the degree of suffering caused to the child sufficient to amount to inhuman treatment? This must be decided in the light of the long-term and short-term consequences of the procedure, but it is perhaps unlikely that the degree of severity would normally match that level of intentional harm which has been held to amount to inhuman treatment in the cases considered earlier in this chapter.

(3) Medical treatment in prisons

To what extent do rights in respect of medical treatment—the right to be free from treatment without consent, and the right to a normal quality of medical treatment—form part of the residual rights of prisoners? There is no reason in principle why prisoners, as distinct from people with mental disabilities, should lose any of their medical rights. However, the medical treatment of prisoners is in several respects different from treatment of free people.

First, prisoners are not free to change their medical practitioners. They can normally only make use of those staff employed in the prison service, or practitioners who are prepared to visit the prison, or to whom the prison authorities are prepared to escort the prisoner.

Secondly, the quality of medical facilities in prison is, generally speaking, inferior to that outside. The prison health service is separate from the National Health Service, and is funded from the prisons budget by the Home Office rather than the Department of Health. This fuels concerns that prisoners are less well treated than other people. As a recent inquiry report put it, 'Prisoners (and their families) must feel confident that the medical treatment prisoners receive in prison is of comparable standard to that which they would receive in normal life from the National Health Service. The Inquiry has seen a considerable body of evidence which indicates that there is a failure to fulfil this principle'.[93]

Thirdly, it has been held that the standard of care which the prison health service owes to prisoners is lower than that normally owed by medical staff to patients. Nursing and other staff tend to be less well qualified in prison hospitals than in the NHS, so the courts have so far simply accepted the inevitability that the quality of care will be lower. There seems to be some confusion: recognizing the special security needs

---

[93] The Rt. Hon. Lord Justice Woolf and His Honour Judge Stephen Tumim, *Prison Disturbances April 1990*, Cm. 1456 (London: HMSO, 1991), paras. 12.131–12.132.

of prison authorities, the Home Office has refused to allow normal health provision for prisoners even if there is no reason to believe that it would threaten security. As a result, prisoners are treated differently from other people in respect of their health, a context in which neither their needs nor their desert justifies such a distinction. This appears to breach the European Social Charter, which the United Kingdom ratified in 1961. Part I, para. (11) of the Charter provides: 'Everyone has the right to benefit from any measures enabling him to enjoy the highest possible standard of health obtainable.' This provision means that discriminating between citizens in the standard of health care available to them is contrary to the Charter, and breaches the United Kingdom's obligations in international law. The UN Standard Minimum Rules for the Treatment of Prisoners suggest that:

Sick prisoners who require specialist treatment shall be transferred to specialist institutions or civil hospitals. Where hospital facilities are provided in an institution, their equipment, furnishings and pharmaceutical supplies shall be proper for the medical care and treatment of sick prisoners, and there shall be a staff of suitably trained officers.

Successive reports from the House of Commons Home Affairs and Health Select Committees have felt that these standards are not being reached consistently within the prison medical service, and have recommended that the prison health service should be taken over by the NHS, but so far no progress has been made.

Certain specific matters demand more detailed attention, and have been the subject of litigation in England and before the European Commission and Court of Human Rights.

(i) *Right to consent to treatment*: There is no doubt that prisoners who are not mentally incapable retain the right to consent, or withhold consent, to medical treatment. Any medical procedure carried out without the prisoner's consent is therefore *prima facie* tortious, but treatment to which the prisoner has consented is not.

This presents a particular problem in relation to the treatment of disruptive prisoners. It has been regularly suggested that such people are having drugs administered to them, particularly when put into punishment cells, in order to sedate them and make them easier to manage, even if they have no diagnosed psychiatric condition. This overadministration of drugs for non-therapeutic reasons is a procedure known as the 'chemical cosh', which the Home Office has consistently denied permitting (though it may go on without official sanction).[94] The report by

[94] See S. H. Bailey, D. J. Harris and B. L. Jones, *Civil Liberties Cases and Materials*, 3rd edn. (London: Butterworths, 1991), p. 686.

Lord Justice Woolf and Judge Tumim, *Prison Disturbances April 1990*, had this to say in relation to Strangeways Prison in Manchester:

It was suggested that one prisoner in the punishment cells had been forcibly injected with drugs, but our investigation failed to establish the truth, or otherwise, of what had been alleged. However, . . . [a] full-time medical officer of the prison, . . . when giving evidence, quite inappropriately suggested that drugs could be used for controlling prisoners when they were no more than a nuisance. It is possible therefore that the control of the administration of drugs was not as strict as it could have been. . . .[95]

Later, the report noted:

. . . there existed among prisoners a suspicion that largactyl was being used too frequently 'down the block' for control reasons rather than for medical reasons. We obtained reports from the Director of Prison Medical Services on the allegation. It was categorically denied by those responsible for administering medical treatment at Manchester. However . . . [a]ny rumour or accusation that any particular prisoner is being over-medicated should be taken with the greatest seriousness by prison management. Every effort should be made to communicate to relatives, friends and other prisoners the medical reasons and the necessity for any treatment given, subject only to the need to preserve medical confidentiality. In carrying out these tasks, it may well be necessary to involve medical professionals not connected with the prison service.[96]

In other words, even if all is being done according to the book, there is sufficient concern to justify putting some treatment, at least, in the hands of independent professionals, if only as a public-relations measure to boost confidence in the treatment given.

This would be less of a problem if one could be sure that drugs were administered only where prisoners have consented. But there is some ambiguity over the nature of consent to medical treatment in hospital, because the prison hospital officers and prison doctors are prison officers with the same powers under the Prison Rules 1964 as other officers to coerce prisoners. There may be a fine line between advice to a prisoner, perhaps forcefully expressed, and an order, and the prisoner might not be alive to the distinction. The prisoner's freedom of choice may be overborne if the prisoner does not realize that he has that freedom. For this reason, it was argued in *Freeman* v. *Home Office (No. 2)*[97] that a prisoner had been incapable in law of validly consenting to injections of drugs by prison hospital officers, so that the administration had been a battery. Mr Freeman was serving a life sentence, and alleged that he had been forcibly injected with drugs for non-therapeutic reasons, in order to control his disruptive behaviour. He argued that valid consent could be given by a

---

[95] Cm. 1456, para. 3.87 (Lord Justice Woolf).   [96] Ibid., paras. 12.132–12.133.
[97] [1984] QB 524, [1984] 1 All ER 1036, CA.

prisoner only if the medical staff were not prison officers; only then would the prisoner be able to make a choice without worrying about the effect the choice might have on his treatment in and date of release from prison. Had this been upheld, any treatment by a prison hospital officer or prison doctor would have been a battery. It would have compelled the Home Office to integrate the system of prison medical treatment into the N.H.S. so that prisoners could lawfully receive treatment without their consent following compulsory admission under section 2 or 3 of the Mental Health Act 1983. However, the trial judge found as a fact that Freeman had consented to treatment, and he and the Court of Appeal held that the consent was valid and effective in law. Prisoners do not lose the capacity to consent to treatment merely because they are in prison. The question is whether their consent is real, not why it was given (although they could sue for negligence if the information on which they were asked to consent did not meet the standards expected by a responsible body of appropriately qualified medical opinion).[98]

The use of drugs to alter a prisoner's state of mind or pattern of behaviour is a particularly sensitive matter, because there will inevitably often be a suspicion on the part of objective observers that the reason for prescribing is in the interests of order and discipline in prison as much as, or more than, the patient's own therapeutic requirements.[99] From this viewpoint, the argument that a prisoner is simply incapable of giving effective consent to medical treatment by a member of the prison medical staff is comprehensible as an attempt to protect prisoners against suffering invasive procedures for the convenience of the prison authorities under the colour of a consent which can only ever be questionable. However, the argument goes too far, because, instead of inviting the court to examine whether a prisoner's consent is real, in view of the pressures under which it is given, it would, if successful, remove the prisoner's right to consent to bona fide medical treatment even where he genuinely wants to do so. This would narrow, rather than widen, the scope of prisoners' residual liberties.

Integrating the prison medical service into the mainstream National Health Service would have two main benefits in terms of treatment for prisoners with suspected mental disorders. First, it would make it easier for medication to be administered, regardless of lack of consent, to those patients who really needed it. At present, prisoners in a prison service acute psychiatric unit, such as Grendon Underwood, are not compulsorily detained for treatment within the meaning of the Mental Health Act

---

[98] *Sidaway* v. *Board of Governors of the Bethlem Royal Hospital and the Maudsley Hospital* [1984] 1 All ER 1018, CA, affirmed HL [1985] AC 871, [1985] 1 All ER 643.

[99] See Margaret Brazier, 'Prison Doctors and their Involuntary Patients' [1982] *PL* 282–300.

1983. If they do not take their medication voluntarily, they cannot have it forced on them. Some prisoners become caught up in a cycle of illness, refusing treatment until they become ill enough to be compulsorily detained in a National Health Service secure mental hospital, such as Broadmoor, and compulsorily treated. When the treatment has returned them to a more rational state, they are transferred back to the prison unit, where they refuse the medication which stabilized their condition and become ill again. An NHS mental hospital regime for all psychiatrically ill prisoners, if such an arrangement could be achieved, would vastly improve the treatment offered to such prisoners.

Secondly, integration into the National Health Service would offer all prisoners the protection against unjustified compulsory treatment which is provided under the system of reviews and checks instituted by the Mental Health Act 1983 (see Ch. 6, s. 5, below), bolstered by independent monitoring of the actions of prison nursing staff. This would be a very desirable development, and would serve to defuse much of the suspicion which prisoners and their families currently express, whether or not it is justified, about the treatment which prisoners receive from prison health officers.

(ii) *Forced feeding*. Hunger striking is one non–violent means of protest by which prisoners can air their grievances lawfully. It is a powerful form of protest. The slow process of wasting, leading eventually in the absence of intervention to death, allows pressure on the authorities to build up gradually over a considerable period. Short of surrendering to prisoners' demands, the only course open to prison authorities is to employ forced feeding. This is an unpleasant and dangerous procedure, which must be performed by a doctor. The prisoner is physically restrained, while a tube is inserted into a nostril and down the throat into the oesophagus. Liquid is then passed through the tube and into the prisoner's stomach. In the UK, the procedure was used against suffragettes who went on hunger strike when imprisoned for offences committed in connection with their campaign to win the right to vote, during the early years of this century.

The legal and ethical considerations relating to forced feeding are complex. First, it can be said that the state has a responsibility to prevent people from taking their own lives and health, if they can be saved without flouting the law. This was the view of Lord Alverstone CJ in *Leigh* v. *Gladstone*,[100] an action brought by a suffragette who had been forcibly fed in prison. He held that prison officials had a legal duty, under the Prison Rules and (although this was *obiter*) at common law, to protect the life and health of any prisoner, and that this duty justified what would

[100] (1909) 26 TLR 139.

otherwise have been a serious assault. This paternalistic argument is less convincing now, since suicide has ceased to be a crime by virtue of the Suicide Act 1961, than it was at the time. Today, the right of an adult of sound mind to refuse consent to medical treatment and other forms of battery would normally extend to refusing life-saving treatment. This would lead to any attempt at force-feeding a mentally competent, non-consenting prisoner being regarded as unlawful. It would be thought to be an infringement of the person's autonomy and physical integrity, and might well amount to degrading treatment under Article 3 of the European Convention on Human Rights. Nevertheless, even today the issue is not clear cut in the prison setting. So far as the prison authorities are concerned, they owe a duty of care to the prisoners under their control, a special duty above and beyond that which other people would owe. How extensive is that duty? It seems unlikely that it is more extensive than a doctor's to care for ordinary patients, and this does not require the doctor to take steps which the patient has forbidden. Indeed, it would be a tort for a doctor to take such steps.

In practice, forced feeding is no longer employed in British prisons, so the problem is dormant if not dead. As a matter of professional ethics, the British Medical Association decided in 1974 to leave forced feeding to the conscience of individual doctors, following professional and public concern at the forced feeding of the Price sisters, convicted female IRA bombers who were in prison in England and were campaigning by means of a hunger strike for a transfer to a prison in Northern Ireland. In the same year, the Home Secretary announced that prison doctors would not be required to feed a prisoner against his will.[101] The following year, the doctor's ethical dilemma was eased by guidance from the World Medical Association in the Declaration of Tokyo, 1975.[102] Paragraph 5 provides that a prisoner who is refusing nourishment is not to be artificially fed, if the doctor has explained the consequences of refusing nourishment and, together with an independent doctor, has formed the view that the prisoner is capable of forming an unimpaired and rational judgement concerning the consequences of refusal. This declaration would be a powerful indication, in any action for negligence, that a doctor who refused to force nourishment into a prisoner on hunger strike was not acting negligently. That being so, it is inconceivable that the prison authorities, which would rely on doctors to perform the feeding procedure, could have a duty more extensive than that owed by the doctors. One can be fairly confident that *Leigh* v. *Gladstone* would not be followed today.

[101] 877 HC Deb., col. 451, 17 July 1974.
[102] *Statement on Torture and Other Cruel, Inhuman or Degrading Treatment or Punishment*, repr. in Mason and McCall Smith, *Medical Ethics*, 3rd edn., 442–3.

(iii) *Quality of treatment.* No statute deals with the legal duty on prison authorities to provide any particular standard of medical care for prisoners. In a number of cases the courts have had to deal with the problem of quality of treatment. There has been some indirect support for the view that the standard of care required of health workers in prisons is the same as that which applies to health carers generally, namely that their conduct and advice should be such as would be reasonable in the view of a body of respectable medical opinion.[103] There were *obiter dicta* to this effect in *Freeman* v. *Home Office (No. 2)*, where Stephen Brown LJ said that prisoners can give valid and effective consent which provides a defence to an action for trespass to the person, and would be entitled to sue for negligence on *Sidaway* principles if the information on which a decision has to be made was inadequate.[104] The existence of the normal private law duty of care was also the basis on which McNeill J., hearing the Crown Office List in *R.* v. *Secretary of State for the Home Office*,[105] held that an application for judicial review of the failure by the prison medical officer, the governor, and the Secretary of State, to take steps to arrange for a prisoner to have a bone graft as advised by a consultant orthopaedic surgeon (treatment for a bullet wound to the arm sustained while being arrested) was misconceived. It was said to be entirely a private-law matter, governed by normal principles of tort law.

On the other hand, it might seem that a differential standard of care has been accepted in *Knight* v. *Home Office*.[106] A court had ordered a man who had pleaded guilty to an offence of violence to be admitted within 28 days to a secure mental hospital. While awaiting admission to hospital he was being held in the hospital wing at Brixton prison. Being known as a suicide risk, he was on 'Special Watch B', being observed every 15 minutes, but he managed to commit suicide by hanging. His administratrices and son sued the Home Office for negligence, claiming that in view of his history he should have been held in conditions offering less opportunity for suicide. In particular it was said that he did not receive appropriate treatment (contact with people on an open ward and opportunity for counselling, therapy, support, and advice). Such treatment would have been given at a psychiatric hospital with between 0.8 and 2 staff per patient, but could not be provided in a prison hospital. Instead, he was held in an ordinary cell or, on some occasions, a special cell stripped of nearly all amenities and furniture (a strip cell). Pill J. held that the failure to provide in a prison hospital the facilities which would have been available in a specialist psychiatric hospital did not breach a duty of

---

[103] *Bolam* v. *Friern Hospital Management Committee* [1957] 1 WLR 582, [1957] 2 All ER 118; *Sidaway*, above.
[104] [1984] 1 All ER at p. 1043; see also Sir John Donaldson MR at p. 1044.
[105] [1987] 2 All ER 1049, [1987] 1 WLR 881.   [106] [1990] 3 All ER 237.

care to the prisoner. It was not reasonable to expect prison hospitals to provide ideal psychiatric care, given their level of resources. While the standard of reasonable care is that which is reasonably demanded in the circumstances, so that the proper basis for comparison is not the standard currently available in other prisons but the standard applicable to people under a duty to provide health care, the court had to bear in mind the limited resources allocated by Parliament to the prison health service, and the fact that the prison's central function is not to provide health care but to detain people deprived of their liberty. The duty of the prison health service is to provide treatment for mentally ill prisoners, and if necessary to protect them against themselves, but the standard of care to be met in prison was not the same as that in a psychiatric hospital outside prison. In view of the central function of a prison, the level of care provided in the hospital wing at Brixton was held not to breach the duty of care owed to the prisoner.

In resource terms this looks a sensible decision. One can reasonably expect different levels of resource in different situations. As Pill J. pointed out, one would not expect a general practitioner's surgery to provide the same level of facilities for treating emergencies as the accident and emergency department at a large hospital. To that extent, the decision is unexceptional. However, when examined in the perspective of civil liberties and human rights it is more than a little worrying that the court was not prepared to consider whether the Home Office was negligent in its provision of resources to the Brixton prison hospital wing, if (and there was no evidence as to this) the prisoner was being denied access to a psychiatric hospital which would have been accorded him earlier had he not been a prisoner. The real ground for serious complaint in terms of the civil liberties and human rights of prisoners is not that different standards of care are expected of different types of medical centre, but rather that (*a*) prisoners' opportunities for obtaining timely and appropriate treatment are more circumscribed than those of others purely on account of their status as prisoners, and (*b*) the prison medical service, being part of the prison administration, has to treat its patients as prisoners first and patients second.[107] This matter was not addressed in *Knight*, but it needs to be addressed as a matter of urgency by the government, before the denial of appropriate prison care is held to breach Article 3 of the European Convention.

[107] See Richard Smith, 'Prison Doctors: Ethics, Invisibility, and Quality' (1984) 288 *Brit. Med. J.* 781–3.

4.5 CONCLUSIONS

The discussion in this chapter has highlighted a number of spheres in which there is a tension between the law in England and Wales and ordinary expectations of human rights. In part, these are the result of a misfit between the terms in which human rights are customarily expressed and the form of English legal rules. For example, English law is not used to thinking about concepts such as torture or inhuman and degrading treatment and punishment (a matter to which we will return, in the context of prison conditions, in Chapter 6), and finds it hard to adapt the legal categories of the common law to such concerns. Much therefore depends on legislation, and the reports and inquiries which may act as a stimulus to legislative reform. For example, there can be no doubt that the Law Commission's consideration of the problems relating to decision-making for and by mentally incapacitated adults will include proposals which, if enacted, will clarify the law in the area and do so from a rights-based perspective. The problem which may then arise is lack of political commitment to giving effect to worthwhile recommendations, especially where the recommendations would benefit a group which is generally accorded a low priority in political decision-making. For example, prisoners are not, on the whole, seen as a deserving group, and are politically disfranchised, so proposals to improve their lot in line with human rights entitlements are slow to gain ground.

A further problem is that values in these areas are in the process of substantial change and development. The rights of parents over their children are giving way to the rights of children, and the legislature is increasingly recognizing children as having a degree of moral autonomy which deserves respect. At the same time, it is not yet clear how the rights of children as ordinary people can be accommodated to the special responsibilities which adults have towards them. The lines separating adult paternalism (in the strict sense) from juvenile free choice have not yet been drawn firmly, and are still shifting. This is bound to affect perceptions about, for example, the proper extent of parents' and teachers' disciplinary powers.

Finally, the fields discussed in this chapter and the previous one illustrate another major hurdle which advocates of rights face: the paternalism of professional groups, such as doctors, whose codes of ethics operate largely independently of the state but which may fundamentally affect people's rights, particularly where the law displays substantial regard for the judgement of the professionals on their own territory. This is less a human rights problem than one of social power.

5

FREEDOM FROM ARBITRARY STOP, SEARCH, ARREST, AND DETENTION

This chapter concerns the extent of powers under English law to interfere with a person's freedom of movement for the purposes of criminal investigations. We start from the proposition that any interference with freedom of movement is *prima facie* a tort. Interferences can, however, be justified under certain circumstances. Historically, the legal justifications included arrest and detention of people in order to bring them before a court, or to restrain a breach of the peace. Arrest powers in respect of breaches of the peace are governed by common law, and are considered in Chapter 17 below. Police powers of arrest in respect of criminal offences are now codified in statute. Arrest and imprisonment in civil proceedings are now regarded as anomalous, but still occur, and are governed by a mixture of statute and common law. Here, we will concentrate on police powers in respect of criminal investigations.

Three main issues form the background for the legal analysis in this chapter. First, for what purposes and in what circumstances may powers of arrest and detention be exercised? Secondly, what legal safeguards are provided against abuse of arrest powers? Thirdly, to what extent do the powers of arrest and the safeguards under English law comply with the UK's obligations under the protective scheme of the European Convention on Human Rights? These questions will not be examined separately, since they inevitably overlap at many points, but they provide the main themes around which the discussion is organized.

5.1 ARREST, DETENTION, AND VOLUNTARY ATTENDANCE DISTINGUISHED

Any deprivation of liberty is a detention. Although *prima facie* unlawful, it may be justified according to law. A detention may be lawful for a number of different reasons. For example, a person may be imprisoned pursuant to a lawful sentence of a properly constituted court; or restrained for his or her own good by a parent, guardian, or teacher; or detained in hospital according to procedures laid down in the Mental Health Act 1983. Again, legislation may provide for people to be detained for specified purposes in connection with investigations of crimes. Detention need not be preceded by an arrest; it is lawful if it is carried out for a lawful purpose and in compliance with required procedures.

An arrest is in principle different from a detention. It is one of a number of procedures for initiating a lawful detention, and it is distinctive in that it initiates or forms part of a legal process which was traditionally (but is not necessarily today) intended to lead to judicial proceedings. This feature distinguishes arrests and the detentions which follow them from other lawful detentions. It applies both to arrests of people and to arrests of ships in admiralty actions which are said to be conducted *in rem* (that is, a ship is arrested, and proceedings commenced against it, for wrongs notionally committed by it). In criminal matters, the law on arrest underlines the connection between arrests and criminal proceedings in a number of ways. Under the European Convention on Human Rights, Article 5(1)(*c*) provides that an unconvicted person may be arrested in connection with an offence only in accordance with a procedure prescribed by law 'effected for the purpose of bringing him before the competent legal authority on reasonable suspicion of having committed an offence or when it is reasonably considered necessary to prevent his committing an offence or fleeing after having done so'. In other words, arrests must be for the purpose of preventing, or instituting proceedings for, an offence. In the same way, English law usually insists on reasonable grounds to suspect that the person arrested has committed one of certain kinds of offences before an arrest is justifiable, and requires that the arrested person be taken to a police station so that a custody officer can decide whether detention should be authorized. (However, in practice the power of arrest is often used for other purposes: see section 5.3(4)(ii), below.)

An arrest, then, is a special way of initiating a lawful detention for particular purposes. An arrest changes the legal rights of the person arrested: he will not be entitled to use reasonable force to resist the arrest or to escape the subsequent detention; he will not be entitled to go on his way unhindered; he will be subject to the lawful application of coercion. Arrest produces a temporary change in the person's status, from free to unfree. Because of this, it has been hedged about with restrictions and formalities. These are designed to ensure that the person arrested is aware of his change of status, and that his liberty is not interfered with for improper purposes or on insufficient grounds. The law places limits on the grounds for arrest, the formalities of arrest, and the procedures which must be observed in relation to detention following an arrest.

People who voluntarily assist the police with their inquiries (as the hoary old expression has it) are, in theory, neither detained nor under arrest. They are free to go at any time. Even when they are being questioned at a police station and suspected of an offence, they must be allowed to leave unless the police decide to make an arrest, must be given information about the availability of legal advice if they ask about it, and, if it becomes appropriate to caution them, they must be told that they are not under arrest, are free to leave, and are entitled to free legal advice.[1] However, the distinction between detainees and volunteers has been gradually eroded in practice, and is now less significant than the theory would indicate. Before the police had power to arrest a person reasonably suspected of an offence in order to question him, the suspect might be induced to go to a police station by a form of words (such as 'I think we had better sort this out down at the station') which did not constitute an arrest, and so left the suspect as a volunteer, but which gave him a clear impression that he had no option but to go with the officers and do as he was told. This produced the fiction of the person helping the police with their inquiries.[2] It was clear that in many cases these volunteers were not acting of their own free will. Law reform bodies in various parts of the world have had to consider the appropriate response. One approach would have been to create a power to detain people for questioning short of arrest, as adopted to a limited extent in Scotland in the Criminal Justice (Scotland) Act 1980. Another approach would have been to regulate voluntary co-operation, to try to ensure that it was genuinely voluntary. This was the recommendation of a majority of the Australian Law Reform Commission in 1975, arguing that the unregulated concept of voluntary co-operation, without controls or time constraints, was 'very much stretched in Australian police practice'.[3] In England and Wales, the approach was to leave voluntary co-operation more or less untouched, but to recognize arrest as a legitimate part of an interrogation process, and impose safeguards on detention after arrest for the benefit of suspects.[4]

After PACE, the necessity principle imposed on detention following arrest (discussed below) meant that there were potential advantages for

[1] Police and Criminal Evidence Act 1984 (PACE), s. 29; *Code of Practice for the Detention, Treatment and Questioning of Persons by Police Officers* (Code C), paras. 3.15, 3.16. However, failure to comply will not lead to the exclusion from evidence of any statement made by the interviewee if it is clear that the person must have understood the position: *R. v. Rajakuruna* [1991] Crim. LR 458, CA.

[2] David Dixon, 'Detention for Questioning in Australia and England: A Comparative Perspective on the Legal Regulation of Policing', 7–24 (unpubl. paper for the Joint Meeting of the Law and Society Association and the Research Committee on the Sociology of Law of the International Sociological Association, Amsterdam, 26–9 June 1991).

[3] The Law Reform Commission, Report No. 2, *Criminal Investigation* (Commonwealth of Australia: AGPS, 1975), 28–9.

[4] A broadly similar solution was adopted in Canada, where, however, the Charter is a powerful constitutional influence on treatment of suspects: Law Reform Commission of Canada, Report No. 29, *Arrest* (1986), ch. 2.

investigating officers in avoiding an arrest: it helped to evade many of the restrictions and bureaucratic controls imposed by PACE. Although Note for Guidance 1A to Code C stresses that people voluntarily assisting investigations should be treated with no less consideration than detainees, and have absolute rights to communicate with people and to obtain legal advice, some police forces continued to make extensive use of the idea that people were providing voluntary assistance when, in reality, they had no choice.[5] Some forces have introduced a special form of record-keeping in relation to people who are at police stations voluntarily, to limit the threat to people's rights which flows (paradoxically) from their not having been arrested. However, this emphasizes the blurring of the distinction between suspects being arrested and offering voluntary assistance.

Searches of the person, though falling short of arrests, entail a detention, albeit usually for only a short period. They infringe people's liberty, privacy, and bodily integrity, and statutory constraints have been introduced to protect these rights. These are considered in the following section. Thereafter, the chapter examines various aspects of arrest, and the rights which suspects have while in police detention.

5.2 STOP AND SEARCH POWERS

(1) Background

Until the passing of the Police and Criminal Evidence Act 1984, there was a patchwork quilt of police powers to stop and search people and vehicles, varying across the country. There were some applicable powers which could be used by constables of any police force in the country, such as the power to stop people and search them on reasonable suspicion of possession of controlled drugs under the Misuse of Drugs Act 1971, section 23(2). Some police forces had local powers to stop people and vehicles and search them for stolen goods, such as that under the Metropolitan Police Act 1839, section 66. Others had no such power. There were no standard conditions for the exercise of the powers.[6] The Royal Commission on Criminal Procedure accepted that the powers

---

[5] Ian McKenzie, Rod Morgan, and Robert Reiner, 'Helping the Police with Their Inquiries: The Necessity Principle and Voluntary Attendance at the Police Station' [1990] *Crim. LR* 22–33; David Dixon, Clive Coleman and Keith Bottomley, 'Consent and the Legal Regulation of Policing' (1990) 17 *J. Law and Soc.* 345–62 at 354–6.

[6] The position before PACE was set out by the Royal Commission on Criminal Procedure, *The Investigation and Prosecution of Criminal Offences in England and Wales: The Law and Procedure* Cmnd. 8092–1 (London: HMSO, 1981), hereafter 'RCCP, *Law and Procedure*', 8–10 and app. 1.

were useful and should be retained, and recommended their rationalization.[7] The majority of the Commission recommended that stops and searches for stolen goods and offensive weapons should be available across the country, subject to a requirement of reasonable suspicion and other controls to limit the risk of arbitrary or discriminatory exercise of the search power. The main constraints concerned giving the reasons for the search to the people who were being searched, keeping records of the search, and publishing stop and search statistics for each force showing how often the powers were used and how accurate the constables' suspicions were.

(2) Stop and search under the Police and Criminal Evidence Act 1984 (PACE)

PACE broadly adopted the Royal Commission's recommendations. It repealed all other stop and search powers, except so far as they were expressly saved by the Act or created subsequently. It changed the scope of remaining stop and search powers in three main ways. First, it provided for the first time that all statutory stop and search powers have to be exercised in accordance with procedures laid down in the Act and in its associated *Code of Practice for the Exercise by Police Officers of Statutory Powers of Stop and Search* ('Code A'). Secondly, it created a new, uniform stop and search power, applicable on a country-wide basis, for dealing with people reasonably suspected of being in possession of stolen articles, offensive weapons, and certain other items. Thirdly, it provided a codified statutory scheme for road checks (or blocks). This section and section (4) below examine each of these in turn. Section (3) below looks at criticisms of the powers.

(i) *Uniform procedures for searches.* Before PACE, there were decisions which suggested that many of the formalities which are required on an arrest, such as informing the detainee of the reason for the detention, applied also, by analogy, when people were detained for a search.[8] Under sections 2 and 3 of PACE, the procedures to be followed before, during, and after a search are spelt out.

These provisions apply only to searches, not to stops. Accordingly, a stop which does not lead to a search under a legal power does not entail compliance with the procedures in PACE, sections 2 and 3. Indeed, PACE makes no provision for authorizing a constable to stop a person or vehicle; this power is either to be inferred from section 1(2)(*b*), which

---

[7] Royal Commission on Criminal Procedure, *Report*, Cmnd. 8092 (London: HMSO, 1981), hereafter 'RCCP, *Report*', 25–32.

[8] See e.g. *Pedro* v. *Diss* [1981] 2 All ER 59, DC; *Lodwick* v. *Sanders* [1985] 1 W.LR 382, [1985] 1 All ER 577, DC.

permits a constable to detain a person or vehicle for the purpose of such a search (which would be impossible if the person or vehicle were not stationary), and section 2(9)(b), providing that a power of search does not in itself confer a power on a constable *not in uniform* to stop a vehicle, or alternatively may be derived from another statute. In relation to vehicles on the road, the Road Traffic Act 1988, section 163, makes it an offence for a person driving a vehicle or riding a bicycle to fail to stop when required to do so by a constable in uniform. This allows a stop for any purpose connected with a constable's duties, without the need for reasonable suspicion that the driver has committed an offence. A vehicle may therefore be stopped in order to discover whether there are grounds to suspect a person; this effectively permits random stops which may lead to suspicion which could ground a search of the vehicle or person, or (to some people, more controversially) a suspicion that the person in charge has been drinking, making possible a breath test.[9] This power does not apply to pedestrians, and is not available to constables in plain clothes, so it does not on its own provide all the powers needed to make search powers work.

The procedures under sections 2 and 3 of PACE apply to searches of people and vehicles (a term which includes vessels, aircraft, and hovercraft) without making an arrest, under any power which has not been specifically excepted from the need to follow the statutory procedures. The only powers which are excluded are those of constables employed by statutory undertakers, such as the British Transport Police and the British Nuclear Fuels Police (PACE, section 6), and the power to search people at airports under the Aviation Security Act 1982, section 27(2). The procedures are of four kinds: giving information to the person searched; making a record of the search; providing a copy of the record on request; and collating records in each police area so that information about searches can be included, as it must, in the annual reports of the chief officer of police for that area.

Before a search is commenced, the constable must take reasonable steps to bring five matters to the attention of the person to be searched. These are: (a) the constable's name, and the police station to which he is attached;[10] (b) the object of the search, i.e. whether he is searching for stolen goods, weapons, etc., in the light of which the reasonableness of the constable's grounds for suspicion will be judged;[11] (c) the grounds for proposing to make the search,[12] which will facilitate review of the reas-

---

[9] *Chief Constable of Gwent* v. *Dash* [1986] R.T.R. 41, DC; *DPP* v. *Wilson* [1991] Crim. LR 441, DC.

[10] PACE, s. 2(2)(ii) and (3)(a). Where the constable is making inquiries linked to terrorism, he need only give his warrant number: see Code A, para. 2.4(i).

[11] PACE, s. 2(3)(b).   [12] PACE, s. 2(3)(c).

onableness of the grounds in the event of a challenge to the legality of the search; (*d*) the right of the person to request a copy of the record of the search, unless it appears to the constable that it will not be practicable to make a record (for example, where large numbers of people are being searched together: see below);[13] and (e) finally, if the constable is not in uniform, documentary proof that he is a constable, in the form of his warrant card,[14] in order to defuse fears that he might be a mugger or thief pretending to be a policeman, perhaps precipitating a violent reaction from the person in self-defence.[15] Where a constable searches an unattended vehicle, he must leave on or in the car a notice stating that the vehicle has been searched, and giving the name of the police station to which the officer is attached, and to which a request for a copy of the search record and any claim for compensation should be addressed.[16]

The written record of the search mentioned in (*d*) above is to be made on the national search record form as soon as practicable after every search, unless it is not practicable to do so for operational reasons such as public disorder or the numbers being searched.[17] This must be done on the spot, unless circumstances such as very bad weather or other immediate duties make it impracticable.[18] The record must contain the matters mentioned under (*a*), (*b*), and (*c*) above. In relation to (*c*), the grounds for making the search, it 'must, briefly but informatively, explain the reason for suspecting the person concerned, whether by reference to his behaviour or other circumstances'.[19] This might be embarrassing, but is essential in making the reasons reviewable. The record must also contain the name (or a description, where the person refuses to give his name) of the person, and a description of any vehicle searched (including the vehicle's registration number); the date and time when the search was made; the place where it was made; the results of the search; and a note of any injury or damage to property which resulted from it.[20] The record must also include a note of the person's ethnic origin,[21] a provision which was initially greeted with suspicion by ethnic minority communities but which is intended to allow records to be monitored for differential treatment of ethnic groups which, it has been shown, was common before PACE.

The record has three purposes. The first is to enable the person searched, or the owner or person in charge of a vehicle which was

---

[13] PACE, s. 2(3)(d), (4).

[14] PACE, s. 2(2)(i); Code A, para. 2.5. Where the investigation is related to terrorism, the constable need not reveal his name.

[15] This occurred, before PACE, in *R. v. Geen* [1982] *Crim. LR* 604, CA.

[16] Code A, paras. 4.8, 4.9.   [17] PACE, s. 3(1); Code A, paras. 4.1, 4.3.

[18] PACE, s. 3(2); Code A, para. 4.2.   [19] Code A, para. 4.7.

[20] PACE, s. 3(3), (4), (5), (6); Code A, paras. 4.4, 4.5.   [21] Code A, para. 4.5(ii).

searched, to obtain a copy, either to satisfy himself of the lawfulness of the search or to use it in connection with any complaint or legal proceedings. He must request a copy of the record within a period of twelve months beginning with the date of the search.[22] The second purpose of the record is to enable the behaviour of police officers to be monitored continuously by their senior officers. The recording requirements sometimes perform these functions, but often they are ineffective: most supervising officers do not use the records as a way of supervising the exercise of search powers, and officers seem often not to record the searches which take place.[23] This is a point to which we will return below. The third purpose is to allow for publication of statistical information relating to searches and road checks, since this must be included in the chief officer's annual report.[24] This allows trends in recorded searches to be tracked, a potentially useful procedure although it must be borne in mind that many searches are not recorded (see below), and changes in the statistics do not make it clear whether they result from changes in search practices or variations in recording practice.

The Act is largely silent on the manner in which searches are to be conducted, but there was clear evidence that insensitivity on the part of constables carrying out searches was damaging the reputation of the police, particularly with young people and members of ethnic minorities who were disproportionately likely to be subjected to searches. Before PACE, the manner in which the powers were used was often objectionable. Officers routinely displayed a lack of sensitivity, used excessive force, and failed to try to obtain people's co-operation or maintain good police–public relations. The anger which built up over racism and so-called 'hard policing' in relation to the use of the powers in London was a major contributing factor leading to the anti-police riots in Brixton in 1981, and also contributed to the riots in the St Pauls area of Bristol.[25]

However, it would be wrong to regard the PACE provisions as aimed solely at improving the quality of policing in areas with substantial ethnic minority populations.[26] A personal search in public is a particularly embarrassing and upsetting experience. It is also a major interference with people's right to privacy, and a relatively minor interference with the

---

[22] PACE, s. 3(7), (8), (9).

[23] David Dixon, Clive Coleman, and Keith Bottomley, 'PACE in Practice' (1991) 141 *NLJ* at 1586–7.

[24] PACE, s. 5.

[25] Lord Scarman, *The Brixton Disorders*, Cmnd. 8427 (London: HMSO, 1981), 64–5; David J. Smith and Jeremy Gray, *Police and People in London: The PSI Report* (Aldershot: Gower, 1985), ch. 15; Michael McConville, 'Search of Persons and Premises: New Data from London' [1983] *Crim. LR* 604–14.

[26] For the suggestion that this is a common view amongst police in some areas, see Dixon, Coleman, and Bottomley, 'PACE in practice', at 1586–7.

right to freedom from physical interference. Five kinds of limits on the extent and manner of the search are accordingly imposed by PACE and Code A.

First, Code A attempts to limit the discretion which might appear to be given to the police by the rather indeterminate standard of 'reasonable grounds for suspicion' which is used in one form or another as the basis for nearly all statutory search powers.[27] The means employed to achieve this limitation are a series of provisions in the Code which give examples of certain types of factors which may or may not give rise to reasonable suspicion. This approach follows the recommendations of the Royal Commission on Criminal Procedure and earlier official bodies, which had concluded that it would not be practicable to give an exhaustive definition of the matters which would be sufficient to provide reasonable suspicion.[28] Noting that there must be some objective basis for the suspicion before it becomes reasonable, taking account of all the surrounding circumstances, the Code points out that officers must consider:

the nature of the article suspected of being carried in the context of other factors such as the time and the place, and the behaviour of the person concerned or those with him. Reasonable suspicion may exist, for example, where information has been received such as a description of an article being carried or of a suspected offender; a person is seen acting covertly or warily or attempting to hide something; or a person is carrying a certain type of article at an unusual time or in a place where a number of burglaries or thefts are known to have taken place recently.[29]

Furthermore, in order to foster good community relations and avoid mistrust of the police,[30] personal factors may never be used as the sole basis on which to search a person (although the Code does not prevent a constable from considering them in combination with non-personal factors). The examples which the Code gives of personal factors are: a person's colour, age, hairstyle or manner of dress, or the fact that he is known to have a previous conviction for possession of an unlawful article'.[31] This is clearly intended to make it more difficult for constables to indulge their

[27] The power of search under the Prevention of Terrorism (Temporary Provisions) Act 1989, Sched. 5, para. 4(2) is not dependent on reasonable grounds for suspicion. It is therefore said by Code A, Note for Guidance 1C, that, unlike the other search powers in the 1989 Act, it is not a stop and search power affected by Code A. It is not clear why this should be so, but at least the Note recommends that the procedures laid down in the Code should be followed as far as practicable.

[28] RCCP, *Report*, 9, para. 3.25, expressing agreement with the conclusions of the Advisory Committee on Drug Dependence, *Powers of Arrest and Search in Relation to Drug Offences* (London: HMSO, 1970) and the (Thomson) Committee report, *Criminal Procedure in Scotland (Second Report)* Cmnd. 6218 (Edinburgh: HMSO, 1975).

[29] Code A, para. 1.6.   [30] Code A, Note for Guidance 1A.

[31] Code A, para. 1.7.

preconceptions or prejudices about particular groups, such as young Afro-Caribbean men, whom previous research has shown to be particularly vulnerable to stops and searches and among whom systemic anti-police feelings have resulted.

Secondly, people should be treated courteously and considerately.[32] Efforts should be made to secure consent to any search, even if the person initially objects, and the voluntary production of item such as suspected stolen goods, particularly where the person in possession of them may be innocent of the offence.[33] While there is power to use reasonable force if necessary under most search powers, including that under section 1 of PACE,[34] this should be done only once it has been established that the person is not prepared to co-operate or is actively resisting.[35] These provisions are of questionable value, however. The evidence suggests that attitudes towards searches which the law would classify as consent encompass a range of mental states including acquiescence resulting from ignorance of the right to refuse, fear (sometimes justified) of what the officers might do if the person makes trouble, and reluctant submission to the imbalance of the social power relationship which exists between police officers and ordinary citizens, regardless of the extent of legal powers.[36] This has implications which will be explored further below.

Thirdly, search powers do not confer any power to detain people against their wills merely to ask them questions[37] or seek grounds for justifying a search, nor can refusal to answer a question give rise to reasonable grounds for suspicion to justify a search.[38] However, some preliminary conversation will inevitably be necessary to see whether suspicions can be set at rest,[39] to try to obtain the person's consent to a search, and to try to impart the information which is demanded by the provisions mentioned above.

Fourthly, no power to search without an arrest is to be construed as conferring a power to authorize a constable to require a person to remove any clothing in public other than an outer coat, jacket, or gloves,[40] although the constable may ask a person to remove other articles of clothing in the hope that he will comply voluntarily.[41] These searches in the street or other public places should be limited to a superficial examination of outer clothing and, if necessary, hand baggage.

---

[32] Code A, Note for Guidance 1A.   [33] Code A, paras. 1.5, 3.2
[34] PACE, s. 117.   [35] Code A, para. 3.2.
[36] David Dixon, Clive Coleman, and Keith Bottomley, 'Consent and the Legal Regulation of Policing' (1990) 17 *J. L. and Soc.* 345–62 at 347 ff.
[37] This contrasts with the position in Scotland, where constables have such a power under the Criminal Justice (Scotland) Act 1980, s. 1(2) in relation to people who are at the
[38] Code A, paras. 2.1, 2.3.   [39] Code A, para. 2.2.
[40] PACE, s. 2(9)(a).   [41] Code A, Note for Guidance 3A.

Where a more thorough search, involving removal of other clothing or headgear,[42] is required, it should be conducted nearby but out of the public view, for example in a police station or police van, and if it goes beyond removal of headgear or footwear it must be carried out by an officer of the same sex as the person being searched. Nobody of the opposite sex may be present unless the person being searched requests it (for example, a young boy wanting to be accompanied by his mother or elder sister).[43]

Finally, the permissible extent of a search will depend on the type of item which the person is reasonably suspected of possessing. Small and easily concealed items, such as drugs in a search under the Misuse of Drugs Act 1971, section 23(2), may justify a more extensive search than bulkier articles like weapons (where the search is under the Firearms Act 1968, sections 47(3) and 49, or section 1 of PACE). If the suspected item was seen to be slipped into a particular pocket the search must not go beyond that pocket unless there are reasonable grounds to suspect that other stolen or prohibited items are concealed in other places, as will usually be the case where (for instance) stolen goods are found in the first pocket searched.[44] A search must be concluded within a reasonable time, and once it is completed the person may no longer be detained, but must be allowed to go or, if there is sufficient cause, arrested.[45]

(ii) *The new country-wide search power under PACE, and its relationship with other powers.* To tidy up the mess of local search powers, the 1984 Act abolished them, leaving only a few powers extant.[46] In their place, a new power was enacted, applying to the whole of England and Wales, to search people, vehicles, and anything in or on a vehicle, for stolen articles, prohibited articles, and articles in relation to which a person has committed, is committing, or is going to commit an offence under section 139 of the Criminal Justice Act 1988.[47] The constable must have reasonable grounds for suspecting that he will find the articles in question before embarking on the search.[48] The power may be exercised only in places to which the public have access, on payment or otherwise, as of

---

[42] This is a matter of particular sensitivity to Sikhs and members of other religious groups, such as orthodox Jews, who are required to keep their heads covered.

[43] Code A, paras. 3.4, 3.5.   [44] Code A, para. 3.3.

[45] See Code A, para. 3.3, and (in relation to searches under s. 1 of PACE) PACE, s. 1(2)(b).

[46] PACE, ss. 6, 7; David Feldman, *The Law Relating to Entry, Search and Seizure* (London: Butterworths, 1986), 284–97; Vaughan Bevan and Ken Lidstone, *The Investigation of Crime: a Guide to Police Powers* (London: Butterworths, 1991), 86–9. The Annex to Code A provides a list of the main remaining stop and search powers.

[47] PACE, s. 1(2) and (8A), added by Criminal Justice Act 1988, s. 140.

[48] PACE, s. 1(3).

right (e.g. public footpaths) or by virtue of express or implied permission, and in places other than dwellings to which at the time people have ready access (such as an field adjoining a public highway which are not securely fenced, or with an open gate).[49] People and vehicles may be searched in a garden, yard, or other land occupied with and used for the purposes of a dwelling, but not if the person searched, or the person in charge of the vehicle, resides in the dwelling, nor if the person or vehicle is there with the a resident's permission. This preserves the legal privilege of a person's messuage.[50]

If the constable finds any article which he has reasonable cause for suspecting is an article for which search under section 1 is permitted, he may seize it,[51] after which the retention powers and associated duties under section 22(2) of the 1984 Act apply in relation to the article. As regards the three categories of articles for which constables may search, the first, stolen goods, requires no explanation. Prohibited articles fall in two groups. First there are offensive weapons. These are articles made or adapted for causing injury to persons, and any article intended, by the person having it with him, for use for causing injury to persons, whether he intends to use it for that purpose himself or intends that someone else shall do the injuring. Secondly, there are articles made or adapted for use in the course of, or in connection with, burglary, theft, taking motor vehicles or other vehicles without authority, or obtaining property by deception; together with other articles which are intended, by the person having them with him, to be used for one of those purposes, whether by him or by someone else.[52] The third category of articles, those relating to an offence under section 139 of the Criminal Justice Act 1988, are articles which have a blade or are sharply pointed, whatever use they are intended for, which are in a person's possession in a public place. The only exception is a folding pocket knife which has a blade less than three inches long. If such an article is found on a person, he is guilty of an offence under section 139 of the 1988 Act unless he can establish one of the defences in section 139(5).

(3) Criticisms of the search powers

The Act was a considerable step forward in terms of the clarity and consistency of the law and of the rights of suspects, who for the first time were entitled by statute to an account of the purposes of the search and the reasons for it. Nevertheless, the provisions relating to stop and search powers were among the most controversial of those proposed in the bills.

[49] PACE, s. 1(1).
[50] PACE, s. 1(4), (5). See Feldman, *Entry, Search and Seizure*, 8–11, 282–3.
[51] PACE, s. 1(6).   [52] PACE, s. 1(7), (8), (9).

There was a strong body of opinion favouring the outright repeal of all or most stop and search powers. The main objections to the powers are easily summarized.

(i) *The uncertainty of the reasonable suspicion standard.* The first objection concerns the difficulty of defining the concept of reasonable suspicion, which was and is used as the threshold requirement for most stops and searches. It has been argued that the test is too flexible to act as any real constraint on an officer. The provisions of Code A, noted above, give too little guidance as to the meaning of 'reasonable'. For example, once the courts have to review the grounds for a constable's suspicion, it is not clear whether the notion implies that there are matters which an officer *must* always consider, or merely requires some reason which is not actually improper for acting in a particular way. Nor is it obvious whether the standard of reasonableness is that of tort, asking whether a reasonable person would reasonably have acted on the the strength of the grounds possessed by the officer, or is that of administrative law, which tends to accept as reasonable any decision which is not so unreasonable that no reasonable person could properly have arrived at it. Before PACE, there were signs in cases on stop and search powers that the standard being applied was closer to that of negligence than to that of administrative law. This gives the best possible protection to people's rights, by judging the police by the standards of a reasonable person rather than asking only whether the constable's view was so unreasonable that no reasonable person could have taken it. However, in relation to reasonable suspicion for arrests there are signs, discussed below, that the courts have abandoned the 'reasonable person' standard, upholding instead any decision which was not wholly unreasonable.[53] This could easily slip across into the field of stop and search powers.

(ii) *The reluctance of the police to be bound by the reasonable suspicion standard.* There is a risk that the standard of reasonableness cannot or will not be used by the police in practice. There are indications from research into police activities that officers regarded the rules as being, in the typology of David Smith and Jeremy Gray, merely 'presentational' rather than 'inhibitory' or 'working' rules.[54] That is to say, the police had not generally internalized the legal rules, or made them part of the working morality on which they based their decisions about the proper action to take ('working rules'). Often, because the standard of reasonable suspicion is so malleable, and the facts so easily adjusted to make it seem that it was

[53] *Mohammed-Holgate* v. *Duke* [1984] AC 437, [1984] 1 All ER 1054, HL, discussed below, s. 5.3(4)(iii) and (v).

[54] Smith and Gray, *Police and People in London*, 440–3.

satisfied, the police did not even regard them as significant inhibitory rules (i.e. rules which would discourage them from behaving in certain ways, limiting the range of available action). More recent research has tended to confirm this picture. The idea of reasonable suspicion is out of tune with the way in which the police form suspicions when on the street. The legal rules requiring reasonable suspicion thus form little or no part of police decision-making processes in relation to searches, but officers recognize their presentational importance, i.e. after the event any explanations for stops and searches which might be required in legal proceedings will have to be presented in terms of the reasonableness of their suspicions at the time. The reasons will then tend to be ex post facto rationalizations rather than real reasons, and the need for them will not unduly inhibit police searches.[55]

If officers tend to act on the spur of the moment, on hunches, without articulating their grounds of suspicion, the grounds might often be present, so that officers' experience enabled them to identify grounds for suspicion without the need for conscious thought. However, in many cases, researchers before and since PACE have found little sign that this was happening; many stops appear to be conducted without any suspicion. Some police officers are unhappy at what they feel is the unreasonably high standard imposed by the reasonable suspicion requirement, and believe that the powers are being used less as a result.[56] The figures and observational studies do not bear this out, but rather suggest that more stops are being carried out (or more recorded stops, which is a rather different matter),[57] and that the recorded stops are tending to be more productive (at least in terms of arrests for burglary).[58]

(iii) *Differential use of powers.* If decisions to stop people were often made unreasoningly, the evidence suggested that they were not made randomly. Men were more likely to be stopped than women, young people were likelier targets than old people, black people more vulnerable to unreasoning searches than whites. There seemed to be clear evidence, exploited by opponents of these powers, that police officers regarded these factors as important determinants of suspicion. In short, young black males were several times as likely as young white males to be

---

[55] David Dixon et al., Reality and Rules in the Construction and Regulation of Police Suspicion' (1989) 17 *Int. J. Soc. Law* 185–206.

[56] David Brown, *Investigating Burglary: The Effects of PACE*, Home Office Research Study 123 (London: HMSO, 1991), 76.

[57] W. Skogan, *The Police and Public in England and Wales: A British Crime Survey Report*, Home Office Research Study No. 117 (London: HMSO, 1990); compare Dixon, Coleman and Bottomley, 'PACE in practice' , 1586.

[58] Brown, *Investigating Burglary*, 76.

stopped and searched on the streets of London, and young white males were several times as likely to be stopped as middle-aged white females. As a matter of principle, many felt that powers which were habitually used in such a differential way against different groups were objectionable.[59]

(iv) *Effectiveness*. There is considerable doubt about the effectiveness of the powers. Huge numbers of stops were recorded; these were probably only a small proportion of those which took place. Relatively few stops led to arrests, and there was no evidence of the reason for those arrests which took place or the ultimate result of the cases. Many of the arrests which followed searches for stolen goods or drugs were made not for possession of the articles sought but for assaulting officers in the execution of their duties in resisting a search. (This was how many of the cases on reasonable suspicion came to be decided: for if the officer lacks reasonable grounds for the suspicion which legitimated the search, the search is an unlawful trespass to the person, and the victim is entitled to use reasonable force to resist; on the other hand, if the search is justified, resisting by force is not.) This made the success rate reported for the exercise of the powers (a mere 13 per cent or so, based on crude numbers of arrests following searches, although the proportion of successful finds of drugs following searches under the Misuse of Drugs Act 1971 is higher, but falling from around 30 per cent in 1972 to around 20 per cent) even less impressive as evidence of the usefulness of the powers. In short, it may be argued, the stop and search powers represent a serious interference with people's freedom and dignity in public places, and produce no benefit commensurate with it.

(v) *Consensual searches*. A final doubt concerns the consensual searches. There is evidence[60] that the consent given to searches is not what one would, in medical contexts, call real or informed consent, but is more in the nature of passive acquiescence. Nevertheless, the police in some forces have used the fact that people do not object to a search to avoid the requirements of section 2 of PACE. In particular, it is certain that there is a substantial under-recording of searches, and the unrecorded searches are likely to be predominantly unsuccessful ones. This makes it very difficult for supervising officers to use the reports as a means of controlling search practices among their subordinates, even when they are

[59] See Carole F. Willis, 'The Use, Effectiveness and Impact of Police Stop and Search Powers', in Kevin Heal, Roger Tarling and John Burrows (eds.), *Policing Today* (London: HMSO, 1985), pp. 94–106; RCCP, *Law and Procedure*, app. 2; Smith and Gray, *Police and People in London*.
[60] e.g. Dixon, Coleman and Bottomley, 'Consent and Legal Regulation', 345–62.

inclined to do so. It also deprives many people who are searched of the most important of the protections for their rights which it was the purpose of section 2 to provide, namely that the grounds for and purpose of the search should be recorded and should be made available to the person searched. Some force orders, and a Crown Court decision under the original version of Code A, have insisted that, where a legal power to insist on searching exists, the police must comply with section 2 procedures.[61] However, the 1991 revised version of Code A does not unambiguously provide that consensual searches, where there is a power to search, must comply with the recording provisions of PACE and Code A. Many officers are still not recording searches which, to protect suspects' rights and give a proper picture of the frequency with which searches are taking place and their success rates, ought to be recorded.

(4) Road checks

These are sometimes useful tools in investigating crime, but interfere (usually only briefly) with the freedom of movement of people who are not suspected of any offence. PACE, section 5, contains a watered-down version of the regime recommended by the Royal Commission on Criminal Procedure[62] for controlling road checks (or road blocks, as they are sometimes called). An officer of at least the rank of superintendent may authorize, in writing, a road check, i.e. an exercise of the power to stop vehicles under section 163 of the Road Traffic Act 1988 (as amended) in such a way as to stop all vehicles, or vehicles selected by any criterion, in a particular locality, continuously or at specified times, for a specified period not exceeding seven days.[63] The permitted purpose of the road check is to ascertain whether any vehicle is carrying a person who has committed or is intending to commit an offence (other than a road traffic or vehicle excise licence offence), or a witness to such an offence, or a person who is unlawfully at large.[64] An officer of lower rank may authorize a road check in case of urgency, but must as soon as practicable report it to a person of the rank of superintendent or above, who may authorize it to continue or order that it be ended.[65]

Before an authorization is given, certain conditions must be met. Where the check is for a person who is unlawfully at large, the officer must have reasonable grounds for suspecting that the person is, or is about to be, in the locality. Where the check is part of a search for wit-

---

[61] Ibid., at 349–52; R. v. Fennelley [1989] Crim. LR 142.

[62] RCCP, Report, 30–2.

[63] PACE, s. 4(1), (3), (11). The authorization is renewable for periods not exceeding 7 days: s. 4(12).

[64] PACE, s. 4(2).   [65] PACE, s. 4(5)–(9).

nesses, the officer must have reasonable grounds for believing that the offence was a serious arrestable offence within the meaning of section 116 and Schedule 5 to PACE, explained in section 5.6(1)(iii) below. Where the check is for an offender or potential offender, the officer must have reasonable grounds for believing that the offence concerned is a serious arrestable offence, and reasonable grounds for suspecting (the lower standard, which justifies searches of the person and of vehicles, and arrests) that the person is, or is about to be, in the locality of the proposed road check.[66]

The safeguards against improper use of road checks under section 4, apart from the need for a written authorization, are threefold. First, the authorisation must specify the name of the authorizing officer, the locality of the check, and (most importantly) the purpose of the check, including any serious arrestable offence in respect of which the authorization is granted.[67] This helps to concentrate the mind of the authorizing officer on the relevant matters. Secondly, any person in charge of a vehicle which is stopped is entitled to a written statement of the purpose of the check if he applies for it within twelve months.[68] This facilitates review of the propriety of the check, in an action for damages, in an application for judicial review, in a defence to a prosecution (for example, for obstructing a constable in the execution of his duty by failing to stop when required to do so), or in disciplinary proceedings following a complaint. Thirdly, the statistics concerning checks in each police area must be collated and included in the chief police officer's annual report.[69] This enables the number of checks and their success rate to be monitored. It is likely to be more effective than the comparable reports of the use of stop and search powers, because the number of checks will be far smaller than the number of searches, and the requirement for authorization by a superintendent is likely to mean that all checks are properly recorded, unlike the position in relation to searches.

Although the restrictions on road checks under section 4 are substantial, there are other powers which permit the police to stop vehicles. These powers are not affected by section 4, which is additional to them, rather than in place of them.[70] Apart from the powers under the Road Traffic Act 1988, already mentioned, there is the important common-law power to control traffic in order to prevent or stop a breach of the peace. This was the legal basis on which the extensive police road blocks were set up around areas containing coalfields during the miners' strike of 1984-5, and (as noted in Chapter 17 below) has the capacity to interfere substantially with people's freedom of movement without the safeguards imposed on road checks set up under section 4 of the 1984 Act.

[66] PACE, s. 4(4).   [67] PACE, s. 4(13), (14).   [68] PACE, s. 4(15).
[69] PACE, s. 5(1)(b)(ii).   [70] PACE, s. 4(16).

5.3 GROUNDS FOR ARREST

This section examines the grounds for arresting people in connection with criminal offences. Arrests to prevent or stop a breach of the peace (which in England and Wales, unlike Scotland, is not a substantive offence) are considered in Chapter 17 below.

(1) Arrest under warrant

A justice of the peace is empowered to issue a warrant to arrest a person and bring him before a magistrates' court if an information is laid that the person has committed, or is suspected of having committed, an offence.[71] Where the person to be arrested is over 17 years of age, a warrant may issue only where the offence is an indictable offence punishable with imprisonment, or where the person's address is not known with enough precision to allow a summons to be served.[72] Where an arrest is made under warrant for an offence, it is not necessary for the constable who executes it (or a warrant for commitment or distress, unless the warrant concerns non-payment of rates) to have the warrant in his possession at the time he makes the arrest, but the warrant must be shown to the arrestee as soon as practicable.[73] This provision allows a person to be arrested without them being able immediately to check the authority for the arrest, and is a small but significant incursion on rights to be free of arbitrary or unjustified deprivation of liberty. As there is also a power to enter premises, if need be by force, to execute an arrest warrant 'issued in connection with or arising out of criminal proceedings' if the person to be arrested is reasonably believed to be in the premises,[74] this also indirectly allows entry under warrant when the warrant which justifies the entry is not in the constable's possession. This is an infringement of the right to privacy and freedom from interference with property. It is particularly unsatisfactory in view of the fact that, if the entry were under a search warrant, the warrant would have to be in the constable's possession, and shown to the occupier before the search began.[75]

(2) Criminal offences to which powers of arrest without warrant apply

The law on arrest without warrant used to depend on the technical and largely illogical distinction between felonies, for which one could be arrested at any time, and misdemeanours. When felonies were abolished

---

[71] Magistrates' Courts Act 1980, s. 1(1).   [72] Ibid., s. 1(4).
[73] Ibid., s. 125(3), as amended by PACE, s. 33.   [74] PACE, s. 17(1)(a)(i), (2).
[75] PACE, s. 16(5).

by the Criminal Law Act 1967, arrest without warrant was placed on a statutory footing. Section 2 created a class of 'arrestable offences', in respect of which a suspect was liable to be arrested without a warrant. These were the more serious crimes, for which there was thought to be a specially strong public interest in bringing offenders to justice. The fairly crude criterion of seriousness was the maximum sentence which could be imposed for the offence on a person convicted of it for the first time. If the maximum sentence was five years or more, or if the sentence was fixed by law (for example, the mandatory sentence of life imprisonment for murder), it was an arrestable offence. The details of the actual offence were unimportant for this purpose; the significant matter was the legal classification of it and the sentence which a court could impose. This did not mean that the details of the offence, and the characteristics of the suspect, were to be unimportant in the decision whether or not to make an arrest. The *power* to arrest summarily existed in respect of any arrestable offence, but there was no *duty* to arrest. A constable or other person considering whether to arrest a suspect had a discretion to take into account the special features of the case.

This remains broadly the position, although the law has been recodified by the Police and Criminal Evidence Act 1984, and changed somewhat in the process. The main points to note are the following.

(1) The concept of the arrestable offence is retained in section 24(1). The main test for arrestability remains the availability of a sentence fixed by law of five years or more on first conviction for the offence after trial on indictment.[76] This covers most of the types of offence which we would normally consider to be inherently serious. However, a number of other offences, which were thought to be of a kind justifying arrest without warrant but which do not meet those criteria, were added to the list of arrestable offences.[77] They include: offences for which there is a power of arrest under the Customs and Excise Management Acts; offences under the Official Secrets Act 1920 and (with limited exceptions)[78] the Official Secrets Act 1989; causing the prostitution of women or procuring a girl under the age of 21 for the purposes of prostitution, contrary to sections 22 and 23 of the Sexual Offences Act 1956; and taking a motor vehicle or other conveyance without authority, or going equipped for stealing, etc., contrary to sections 12(1) and 25(1) respectively of the Theft Act 1968. It is also an arrestable offence to conspire,

---

[76] PACE, s. 24(1)(a), (b).

[77] PACE, s. 24(1)(c), 24(2) as amended.

[78] Offences under s. 8(1), (4), and (5) are not arrestable (unauthorized retention by a Crown servant or contractor of, or lack of care in failing to safeguard or in disclosing, certain documents): PACE, s. 24(2)(bb), inserted by Official Secrets Act 1989, s. 11(1).

attempt, incite, aid, abet, counsel, or procure the commission of an arrestable offence.[79]

(2) Various offences exist for which a power of arrest without warrant has been granted by other legislation but which do not fall within the definition of an arrestable offence in section 24 of PACE. These offences are, therefore, not 'arrestable offences' despite the fact that a suspect can be arrested for them without a warrant. The only significance of their not being arrestable offences lies in the fact that they can never be 'serious arrestable offences', a sub-group of arrestable offences in respect of which special police powers are sometimes available.

(3) A special power was granted in PACE, section 25, to arrest without warrant for offences in respect of which there would not normally be a power to arrest. This special power arises when (i) an officer has reasonable grounds for suspecting that any offence has been or is being committed or attempted, *and* (ii) the officer has reasonable grounds for suspecting that a particular person has committed or attempted, or is committing or attempting, the offence, *and* (iii) it appears to the officer that the service of a summons on that person for that offence is impracticable or inappropriate because any one of what are called the 'general arrest conditions' are satisfied.[80] These conditions are:

(*a*) that the officer does not know, and cannot readily find out, the person's name (for example, where the suspect is running away);

(*b*) that the officer has reasonable grounds for doubting whether a name given by the person is his real name (as where the person has no means of identification available);

(*c*) that the person has failed to give a satisfactory address for serving the summons, or the officer has reasonable grounds for doubting whether an address given by the person is satisfactory for service (for example, where the address is that of a hotel or hostel at which the person has no established roots);

(*d*) that the officer has reasonable grounds for *believing* (a higher degree of confidence than mere suspicion) that arrest is necessary to prevent the person
   (i) causing physical harm to himself or another,
   (ii) suffering physical injury,
   (iii) causing loss of or damage to property,
   (iv) committing an offence against public decency, or
   (v) causing an unlawful obstruction of the highway;

(*e*) that the constable has reasonable grounds for *believing* that arrest is necessary to protect a child or other vulnerable person from the person arrested.

[79] PACE, s. 24 (3).   [80] PACE, s. 25(1), (2).

The object is to allow a person to be arrested where it seems that it would otherwise be impossible to proceed against him by way of summons. The power is open to criticism as extending the wide discretion of the constable to interfere with the liberty of citizens in cases which are, by definition, not terribly serious. It would be less objectionable were the exercise of the constable's discretion to be subject to more closely controlled criteria. As it is, the general arrest conditions give the appearance of a rag-bag without coherent principle.

Conditions (a), (b), and (c) are related to the integrity of the legal process. They treat the arrest as replacing the summons, the commencement of criminal process, in cases where there are reasonable grounds to doubt whether criminal proceedings could be effectively initiated in any other way. This is in line with the justification for making an arrest under Article 5(1)(c) of the European Convention on Human Rights. On the other hand, there are elements of paternalism—protecting the person against himself—in condition (d)(i), while the suspect is to be protected against others in (d)(ii), and other people are protected from the suspect by (d)(i), (d)(iii), and (e). Condition (d)(iv) seems designed to protect general public decency against what Feinberg calls 'harmless wrongdoing', but it is limited to cases where members of the public, going about their ordinary business, cannot reasonably be expected to avoid the person concerned,[81] and so is actually directed more towards Feinberg's category of 'offense to others'. The power to arrest under (d)(v) replaced a similar power in relation to a person causing an unlawful obstruction of the highway under the Highways Act 1980, section 137(2), presumably in order to provide, so far as possible, a comprehensive code of arrest powers in sections 24 and 25 of the 1984 Act.

There is a risk, particularly in relation to the preventive powers of the constable under conditions (d)(iv) and (v), that the power under section 25 might be used to deprive people of the opportunity to protest in public about matters of public concern. However, the actual impact of section 25 is minimal in this context, first because (as will be seen in Chapter 17 below) the police have numerous powers, at common law and under statute, to take action to control or stop public protest apart from this section, and secondly because a person must already be reasonably suspected of committing or having committed an offence before the section 25 power may be used (although the offence need not be of a type which itself gives rise to the risk under condition (d) justifying arrest rather than summons).

---

[81] PACE, s. 25(5).

(3) Who may make arrests, and when?

(i) *Offences in progress.* Anyone may arrest a person who is, or whom he has reasonable grounds for suspecting to be, in the act of committing an arrestable offence. This covers the case where a suspect is caught in the act, in the process of performing the act or omission which the person making the arrest has reasonable grounds for suspecting is an arrestable offence. The person making the arrest is protected against liability if it subsequently turns out that the person arrested was not committing an offence. For example, if somebody sees a person breaking a shop window, this will normally give reasonable grounds for suspecting that person of criminal damage or burglary, both arrestable offences. If it turns out that the suspect was the owner of the shop who had locked himself out without his keys, and was breaking the window in order to gain access to his own premises, he will not be guilty of any offence, but neither will the arrestor be liable to him in damages for false arrest, false imprisonment, or trespass to the person (so long as no unreasonable force was used to make the arrest).

However, the power of arrest without warrant arises only if the offence which is suspected is, in law, an arrestable offence. If the arrestor wrongly but in good faith believes that an offence is arrestable when it is not, the honesty or reasonableness of his belief will not provide a defence to an action for damages. There is a difference between a reasonable but mistaken exercise of a power which exists in law, and the purported exercise (whether reasonable or not) of a power which does not exist in law. For example, in *Wershof* v. *Metropolitan Police Commissioner*[82] police officers purported to arrest a solicitor for obstructing them in the execution of their duties, contrary to section 51(3) of the Police Act 1953. There is no power of arrest under that section: the offence is not an arrestable offence, and, despite the fact that one of the leading authorities on police law made a categorical assertion to the contrary,[83] it was held to be unlawful to arrest for it unless the obstruction gives rise to a breach of the peace or a reasonable apprehension of an imminent breach of the peace, or impedes a lawful arrest.[84] This might seem harsh on a constable following the advice in an authoritative text, and even harder on an ordinary citizen, particularly in the light of the misunderstanding which

[82] [1978] 3 All ER 540. See to the same effect *Gelberg* v. *Miller* [1961] 1 All ER 291, DC, where the court regarded the matter as being of high constitutional significance, and the absence of a power of arrest was ultimately conceded by the Attorney-General; *Riley* v. *DPP* (1989) 91 Cr. App. R. 14, DC, at p. 22 *per* Watkins LJ.

[83] *Moriarty's Police Law*, 23rd edn. (1976), 18.

[84] It might now also be possible to arrest under PACE, s. 25, if one of the general arrest conditions is fulfilled.

seems to reign amongst police officers and some judges.[85] However, people are entitled to expect that their liberty will be protected against interference which is not authorized by law. Since ignorance of the law does not excuse a wrongdoer, ordinary citizens (including people such as store detectives and security operatives, who are not constables but who make their livings wholly or partly from combating crime) who make arrests, without knowing whether the offence which they suspect is an arrestable offence in law, do so at their peril.

(ii) *Completed and future offences.* With regard to arrests for offences for past or apprehended offences, the powers of police officers are in some respects wider than those of ordinary citizens. In respect of completed offences, a constable may make a lawful arrest if he reasonably suspects that an arrestable offence has been committed by the arrestee. The constable will be protected against liability if it turns out that no offence had in fact been committed, so long as he had reasonable grounds to suspect that something which was in law an arrestable offence had been committed.[86] In this regard constables are in a better position than other members of the public who make an arrest (including store detectives), since people who are not constables are permitted to arrest for an arrestable offence only if an arrestable offence has, in fact, been committed.[87] Ordinary members of the public, unlike constables, are not protected against liability to an action for false arrest or false imprisonment if it turns out that no arrestable offence had in fact been committed, however reasonable their suspicions may have been.

In relation to arrests for apprehended offences, constables have a preventive power to arrest someone who is, or whom they have reasonable grounds for suspecting to be, about to commit an arrestable offence.[88] Ordinary citizens have no such anticipatory power, and must usually wait until the offence is in progress before they can lawfully effect an arrest. There is an exception where a citizen reasonably apprehends an imminent breach of the peace, and makes the arrest to prevent it: all citizens, not only constables, have a duty to preserve the peace and are entitled to take reasonably necessary steps to that end.[89]

[85] The law reports are full of arrests which purport to be for obstructing constables in the execution of their duty: see e.g. *Stunt* v. *Bolton* [1972] RTR 435, DC. In some cases where the matter was not central to the case, the judges have not had the law explained by counsel, and so have appeared wrongly to accept, or not to deny, that such arrests are lawful: e.g. *Ledger* v. *DPP* [1991] Crim. LR 429, DC; *Green* v. *DPP* [1991] Crim. LR 782. These lapses on the part of counsel are unfortunate: the police must be left in no doubt of the limits to their powers. See the comments of Professor J. C. Smith in his commentary on *Ledger*, [1991] Crim. LR at p. 441.

[86] PACE, s. 24(6).   [87] PACE, s. 24(5); *R.* v. *Self* [1992] 3 All ER 476, CA.
[88] PACE, s. 24(7).   [89] *Albert* v. *Lavin* [1982] AC 546, [1981] 3 All ER 878, HL.

(4) Structuring the discretion to arrest

There is nothing objectionable on civil liberties grounds about the power to make an arrest in itself. Arrests are permitted under the European Convention on Human Rights, Article 5(1), so long as the deprivation of liberty is 'in accordance with a procedure prescribed by law' and is: '(*c*) the lawful arrest or detention of a person effected for the purpose of bringing him before the competent legal authority on reasonable suspicion of having committed an offence or when it is reasonably considered necessary to prevent his committing an offence or fleeing after having done so'. The competent legal authority is said by one eminent authority to be similar to the 'judge or other officer authorised by law to exercise judicial power' by whom the lawfulness of the detention must be reviewable under Article 5(3).[90] The extent to which English law complies with these conditions will be considered below.

There are circumstances in which the prosecution process might be frustrated if an arrest were impossible. If there are problems, they concern the width of the discretion which an arresting officer has, and the relative weakness of the principles by which the law structures the discretion and guards against its abuse by police officers.

(i) *The arresting officer's wide discretion.* Normally, when a public official is given a discretionary power by law, there are limits placed on it. These include the circumstances in which it can lawfully be exercised (in connection with arrestable offences, as described above); the purposes for which it can be exercised; and the matters which are to be taken into consideration when deciding how it should be exercised. Together, these constraints provide a legal framework within which the official must work if his exercise of power is to be lawful; they are sometimes said to 'structure' discretions. The constraints may be explicitly set out in the statute which grants the power, or they may be implied from the statute by reference to the purposes for which it was supposedly granted.

In relation to arrests without warrant in English law, the principal legal constraints on the exercise of an officer's discretion are the requirement, contained in PACE, for reasonable grounds to suspect the person of an arrestable offence, and the further requirement (derived from general principles of administrative law) that the power to arrest should be exercised reasonably and for a proper purpose. This only partially meets the demands of Article 5(1) of the European Convention: the necessity element is not part of English law, and it is open to Parliament to legislate

[90] J. E. S. Fawcett, *The Application of the European Convention on Human Rights* 2nd edn. (Oxford: Clarendon Press, 1987), 88.

allowing an arrest to be made without suspicion based on reasonable grounds.

For example, before its repeal in 1987 section 11 of the Northern Ireland (Emergency Provisions) Act 1978 permitted arrest of anyone whom the officer suspected of being a terrorist. This was held in *Fox, Campbell and Hartley* v. *United Kingdom*[91] to contravene the requirement of reasonable suspicion to ground an arrest under Article 5(1) of the European Convention on Human Rights. While recognizing the special problems facing those who have to police against terrorist crime, the European Court of Human Rights held by four votes to three that the requirement of reasonable grounds constituted an essential safeguard against arbitrary arrest and detention. While the state was not required to reveal its sources of information in order to show that reasonable grounds existed, particularly in relation to terrorism, it must offer some evidence suggesting that the suspicion of the arresting officers, as well as being genuine, was reasonable. As the evidence did not support the government's assertion that the bona fide suspicion in that case had been reasonable, the majority of the Court upheld the complaint under under Article 5(1).[92]

The provision which has replaced section 11 of the 1978 Act is the Prevention of Terrorism (Temporary Provisions) Act 1989, section 14, which allows arrest on (*inter alia*) reasonable grounds for suspicion that the arrestee is or has been concerned in the commission, preparation, or instigation of acts of terrorism connected with the affairs of Northern Ireland or foreign countries.[93] It remains to be seen whether this suspicion is equivalent to 'reasonable suspicion of *having committed* an offence' for the purposes of Article 5(1). It is arguable that, if the person need not be suspected of having actually committed an offence, the power of arrest can be used merely for information gathering, which is outside Article 5(1). As we shall see, even powers which appear to be tied to the commission of offences are in practice regularly used merely to facilitate information gathering, and this seems to breach Article 5.

(ii) *Reasonable grounds for suspicion.* Under section 24 of PACE, there must be reasonable grounds for suspecting (*a*) that an arrestable offence has been, is being, or is about to be committed, and (*b*) that the person being

---

[91] Eur. Ct. HR, Series A, No. 182, Judgment of 30 Aug. 1990, 13 EHRR 157.

[92] The case is illuminatingly discussed by Wilson Finnie, 'Anti-Terrorist Legislation and the European Convention on Human Rights' (1991) 54 *MLR* 288–93.

[93] Prevention of Terrorism (Temporary Provisions) Act 1989, s. 14(1)(*b*), (2). For comparison of these provisions with s. 11 of the Northern Ireland (Emergency Provisions) Act 1978, see Gerard Hogan and Clive Walker, *Political Violence and the Law in Ireland* (Manchester: Manchester University Press, 1989), 47–50.

arrested has committed, is committing, or is about to commit it. These are two distinct suspicions, which will be considered separately.

The first matter in relation to which there must, under certain parts of section 24, be reasonable grounds for suspicion is that an arrestable offence has been, is being or is about to be committed. This means that the arresting officer must have reasonable grounds for suspecting that a state of affairs exists which, if it did exist, would constitute an arrestable offence. As noted above, it is not sufficient for him to believe, wrongly, that an offence is arrestable; he must get the legal classification of the offence correct. Were the law otherwise, it would authorize arrests for non-arrestable offences, giving greater arrest powers to ignorant or negligent officers than to those who correctly understand the limits of their lawful authority. The fact that the constable wrongly thought that he had a power of arrest in the circumstances could not confer a power where none existed as a matter of law.

The second necessary suspicion for which there must be reasonable grounds is that a particular person is a guilty party. At this point it is clearly important that the suspicion should be reasonable, as the suspect will suffer an infringement of his liberty. However, the term 'reasonable grounds to suspect' provides only an indeterminate standard for assessing the adequacy of evidence to justify an arrest. The caselaw on the meaning of the term in the context of arrests (it also appears elsewhere in the law on police powers as a justifying standard, and as we shall see is subject to similar uncertainty whenever it is applied) shows that it does not impose a very rigorous standard on arresting officers, who need only have as much material as a reasonable person would need in the circumstances to hold the relevant suspicion. Since suspicion is a less assured state of mind than belief, less material is needed to produce it in a reasonable person. As Lord Devlin made clear when delivering the advice of the Privy Council in *Shaaban Bin Hussien* v. *Chong Fook Kam*,[94] reasonable cause does not need to be based on anything which would be admissible in evidence in court; still less need there be what a court would regard as a *prima-facie* case:

'Reasonable cause' is a lower standard than information sufficient to prove a prima facie case. Reasonable cause may take into account matters that could not be put into evidence at all or matters which, although admissible, would not on their own prove the case. The circumstances of the case should be such that a reasonable man acting without passion or prejudice would fairly have suspected the person of having committed the offence.

The looseness of the standard is a recognition of the difficulties facing operational police officers who often have to make difficult judgements

_____
[94] [1970] AC 942, PC, at p. 948.

in haste. It would be unreasonable to apply too exacting a standard when evaluating their actions with the benefit of hindsight. On the other hand, in the sensitive field of interference with civil liberties, adopting too loose a standard risks removing any realistic chance of obtaining remedies for careless police action. Although the police are called upon to justify their actions after the event by reference to the standard of reasonable suspicion, there is evidence that much investigation proceeds on the basis of hunches.[95] An investigator forms a view of where the truth is likely to lie, and sets out to test (or sometimes simply to confirm) that hypothesis. This is inevitable, and it would probably be impossible to conduct investigations effectively on the basis of the statutory standards. Those standards therefore become *ex post facto* 'presentational' rules rather than inhibitory rules (which are not fully accepted by the police but hold out threats of sanctions which tend to discourage officers from acting in certain ways) or fully internalized working rules,[96] and lose their power to structure police discretion. The power to arrest, like that to stop and search, may then be used in a way which discriminates against certain groups in society according to the experiences (or prejudices) which dictate an officer's hunches.

This is particularly likely to happen when the courts exercise only a very lax scrutiny over the reasonableness of police action. In earlier decades, the courts were quite demanding: for example, it was said that reasonable suspicion arose only if a reasonable constable, not merely an ordinary person in the constable's position, would have thought that the suspect probably committed the offence.[97] However, this can apply in its full rigour only if the arrest is seen as the commencement of criminal proceedings, leading normally to a charge. As we shall see, the House of Lords in *Mohammed-Holgate* v. *Duke*[98] accepted that in many cases it was reasonable for the police to arrest in order to facilitate the collection of information, and that is now the normal reason for arresting. That being so, it might well be far too early, at the time of arrest, to decide whether the suspect *probably* committed the offence. There ought to be reasonable grounds to suspect that she did, and that seems to demand a lower level of likelihood of guilt than is implied in 'probably'. In practice, however, it is not unusual for the police to arrest people simply to make it easier to

---

[95] David Dixon, Keith Bottomley, and Clive Coleman, 'Reality and Rules', 185–206, offers an acute and perceptive discussion of the practical effects of the reasonable suspicion requirement, based on an observational study of a North of England police force.

[96] For this classification, see Smith and Gray, *Police and People in London*, 440–3.

[97] See e.g. *Dallison* v. *Caffery* [1965] 1 QB 348 at p. 371, *per* Diplock LJ; *Wiltshire* v. *Barrett* [1966] 1 QB 312 at p. 322, *per* Lord Denning MR. See also Michael Zander, *The Police and Criminal Evidence Act 1984*, 2nd edn. (London: Sweet & Maxwell, 1990), 61.

[98] [1984] AC 437, [1984] 1 All ER 1054, HL.

obtain information, without any real suspicion that the person being arrested was personally involved in an offence.[99] This breaches Article 5(1)(c) of the European Convention on Human Rights, since an arrest or detention is lawful under Article 5(1) only if it aims to achieve one of the purposes which are permitted under that paragraph.[100] The gathering of information is not a permitted purpose.

Nevertheless, it is implicit in the Police and Criminal Evidence Act 1984 that it is permissible to arrest and hold a suspect for a period in order to question him, to seek information about the offence. Arrest cannot properly be regarded as the initiation of a legal process any more; it is part of the investigative process, and must be regulated as such. This may have the effect of extending police powers, but (as the Australian Law Reform Commission noted in 1975) it is not clear whether the appropriate response is to accept the practical reality of police investigative practice, legalize it, and legislate to give the suspect protection against abuse of police powers, or is rather to reassert the old common-law orthodoxy, outlaw police practices, and risk creating a situation in which the police feel forced to bend the law and take liberties (usually other people's) in order to do their jobs, while suspects have no institutional protection.[101]

The courts seem to have become too permissive in dealing with police powers of arrest. In a number of cases, it has come to appear that the courts (and particularly the Court of Appeal and House of Lords) are loath to subject to any searching analysis the basis of police claims that they had reasonable suspicion. In three cases, the Court of Appeal has held that, so long as the police can point to some grounds which might conceivably have led a reasonable person to conclude that a person might have committed an arrestable offence, the courts should be prepared to accept even thin grounds for suspicion as adequate.[102] With respect, this is unsatisfactory, despite the fact that the cases concerned actions for damages against the police rather than the suspects' alleged criminal liability. The job of the courts in actions against anyone, but particularly against public officials, is to ensure that *prima facie* unlawful action can be prop-

---

[99] Smith and Gray, *Police and People in London*, 462–71, found several examples of this happening in their pre-PACE research on the Metropolitan Police, even where the person arrested was not really suspected of involvement in the offence. This led the authors to express the 'informed opinion' (at p. 578) that 'people who are known not to have committed an offence but do have information about it would *normally* be arrested in order to bring pressure to bear on them to divulge the information'. (Italics in original.)

[100] *Bouamar* v. *Belgium* Eur. Ct. HR, Series A, No. 129, Judgment of 29 Feb. 1987, 11 EHRR 1 (on detaining a minor for educational purposes).

[101] The Law Reform Commission, Report No. 2, *Criminal Investigation* (1975), 38–9.

[102] *Ward* v. *Chief Constable of Avon and Somerset Constabulary*, *The Times*, 26 June 1986, CA; *Holtham* v. *Metropolitan Police Commissioner*, *The Times*, 28 Nov. 1987, CA; *Castorina* v. *Chief Constable of Surrey* [1988] NLJ Rep. 180, CA.

erly justified, and to award compensation if it cannot be. To adopt a gentler standard in dealing with defendants who are public servants than with others makes inroads on rule-of-law principles, sends messages to the police which they are likely to perceive as giving them a licence to stretch the law.[103] It may, in addition, mean that the reasonable suspicion requirement is not applied in accordance with a procedure 'prescribed by law' within the meaning of Article 5 of the European Convention of Human Rights.

Because of this, it has sometimes been suggested that the discretion to arrest should be cabined by statutory rules as to the matters which can and cannot give rise to reasonable cause or grounds, in the hope of excluding sexual and racial prejudices and stereotypes from the decision-making process. However, reasonable cause for suspicion is ultimately a matter of fact and judgement rather than law. The matters which can give rise to it are infinitely various, and successive official reports have rejected as impracticable a catalogue of permissible considerations.[104] A compromise solution has been found in the context of searches of the person, as noted above: Code A specifies certain matters which may *never* be treated as giving rise to reasonable cause for the purpose of conducting a search. A similar approach might be possible in relation to arrests, but there is as yet no code of practice on arrests, and no statutory authority for the Home Secretary to introduce one.

Despite the generally permissive attitude which judges have taken to police actions, there are certain guide-lines in the caselaw, especially on the torts of false imprisonment and malicious prosecution, as to what types of considerations constitute reasonable grounds for suspicion. For example, the fact that a suspect has previous convictions for an offence of the same or another type will not on its own normally give reasonable grounds for suspicion, although it may reinforce the strength of other information implicating the suspect.[105] The police are entitled to take account of information from an informant, despite the fact that it may be hearsay or the informant may not be known to the officers, although it may often be unreasonable to attach very much importance to it.[106] The officers should consider whether the informant is known to be reliable, whether witnesses seem sure of their stories, and whether the information appears credible in the light of other known facts.[107] It may be unreasonable to rely on a long

---

[103] For further discussion, see R. Clayton and H. Tomlinson, 'Arrest and Reasonable Grounds for Suspicion', *Law Society Gazette*, 7 Sept. 1988, p. 22, especially at p. 26.

[104] Advisory Committee on Drug Dependence, *Powers of Arrest and Search in Relation to Drugs Offences*; RCCP, *Report*, para. 3.25.

[105] *McArdle* v. *Egan* (1933) 150 LT 412, CA.

[106] *Lister* v. *Perryman* (1870) LR 4 HL 521, HL.

[107] Ibid.; *Dallison* v. *Caffery* [1965] 1 QB 348, [1964] 2 All ER 610, CA.

delayed complaint, in the absence of other evidence, and where the information concerns the whereabouts of a suspect or of articles which could have been moved, it is particularly important not to rely on it unless it is reasonably up to date.[108] It is not reasonable, when contemplating an arrest under section 25 of PACE, to doubt a suspect's account of his name and address, in the absence of other factors, merely because experience suggests that people who commit offences tend to lie about their names and addresses.[109] Something is needed to suggest that the person in question is lying.

While the constable need not search round in order to negative any answer which a suspect might possibly give to the allegation,[110] there will be circumstances (such as where there is no great urgency, the information is uncorroborated, etc.) in which it will be unreasonable to act on information which is not itself obviously reliable. The constable must, in short, take reasonable care to inform himself of the facts so far as they can be ascertained, and if he fails to do so the reasonableness of his suspicion should be judged on the basis of the information which he would have had if he had taken reasonable steps, rather than asking merely whether the information which he actually had gave rise to reasonable suspicion.[111]

It would therefore be misleading to accept, without qualification, the assertion made by Purchas LJ in *Castorina* v. *Chief Constable of Surrey*[112] that the possible need for further inquiries to confirm suspicion was irrelevant to the presence or lack of reasonable grounds for suspicion. The true position is more complicated. An officer may have a suspicion at any time, based on reasonable grounds or otherwise. The power to arrest under section 24 of PACE arises only when there are grounds to support a suspicion, and the grounds are reasonable. The fact that there is a suspicion and that there are grounds for it take the officer only two-thirds of the way towards establishing that he has a power to arrest. The grounds will not be reasonable if a reasonable person would not have regarded them as giving reasonable grounds for an arrest. If a reasonable person, looking at the grounds, would have said that, in the light of all that is known about the suspect, more investigation would be needed to support the indications of guilt before the grounds for suspecting her could

[108] *Hogg* v. *Ward* (1858) 3 H. & N. 417, 27 LJ Ex. 443.

[109] *G.* v. *DPP* [1989] Crim. LR 150, DC.

[110] *Glinski* v. *McIver* [1962] AC 726 at p. 745, [1962] 1 All ER 696 at p. 701 *per* Viscount Simonds.

[111] *Glinski* v. *McIver* [1962] AC at p. 768, [1961] 1 All ER at p. 715 *per* Lord Devlin; *Abrath* v. *North Eastern Railway Co.* (1883) 11 QBD 440, CA, at 450–1 *per* Brett MR, 459–60 *per* Bowen LJ.

[112] [1988] NLJ Rep. 180, CA; see also ambiguous dicta in *Ward* v. *Chief Constable of Avon and Somerset Constabulary, The Times*, 26 June 1986, CA.

be considered reasonable, then more investigation is needed, and failure to check the information will remove the justification for an arrest.

(iii) *Whose reasonable suspicion?* Is it necessary for the officer himself either to hold the suspicion or to be in possession of the grounds on which suspicion might reasonably be based? The section does not always require either.[113] Where an arrestable offence *actually has been or is being* committed, the section provides that anyone may arrest without warrant a person who *is* committing an arrestable offence[114] or who *has* committed one,[115] whether or not there are reasonable grounds to suspect them. Similarly, a constable is permitted to arrest without warrant anyone who *is about to* commit an arrestable offence.[116] In none of these cases are reasonable grounds required, and the arrest (presumably on the strength of a hunch, or of information received which would not be strong enough to ground a reasonable suspicion) is justified by the achievement of the desired end, namely the apprehension of the offender.

Where reasonable grounds for suspicion are required in order to justify the arrest of someone who turns out to be innocent, the Act requires that the constable personally has reasonable grounds for the suspicion, and it would seem to follow that he is not protected if, knowing nothing of the case, he acts on orders from another officer who, perhaps, does have such grounds. On the other hand, under statutes which require only the objective existence of reasonable grounds for suspicion, it is possible that the officer need neither have the reasonable grounds nor himself suspect anything; he can simply follow orders. There are some decisions which seem to suggest the contrary, but this appearance is deceptive. In *Siddiqui* v. *Swain*,[117] it was held that a requirement in the Road Traffic Act 1972 (since repealed and replaced by the Road Traffic Act 1988) that the constable 'has reasonable grounds to suspect' imported the requirement that the constable actually did suspect the matter in question. However, in relation to those parts of section 24 of the 1984 Act which do not require that a constable *has* reasonable grounds, but only that there *are* reasonable grounds, the reasoning in *Siddiqui* v. *Swain* is inapplicable. One cannot interpret differently worded statutes as if they were the same. For the same reason, decisions on section 2 of the Criminal Law Act 1967, in which the words were 'anyone whom he with reasonable cause suspects', are an unsafe guide to the interpretation of section 24 of the 1984 Act.[118] As long as there are grounds which are objectively reasonable, it does not matter whether or not the officer is aware of them. On the other hand,

---

[113] Unlike the Criminal Law Act 1967, s. 2, which was replaced by s. 24 of PACE.
[114] PACE, s. 24(4)(*a*).   [115] PACE, s. 24(5)(*a*).   [116] PACE, s. 14(7)(*a*).
[117] [1979] RTR 454, DC.
[118] e.g. *Holtham* v. *Metropolitan Police Commissioner*, *The Times*, 28 Nov. 1987, CA.

where the officer is doing something (such as making an entry or arrest) which is *prima facie* tortious, there is no room for the application of the maxim *omnia praesumuntur rite esse acta* (everything is presumed to have been done properly). The action is unlawful unless the officer can justify it according the standards laid down by the statutory provisions in question. Where a provision, like section 17 of the 1984 Act (entry to make an arrest), requires the officer making the entry to have reasonable grounds for believing that the person sought is on the premises,[119] the officer must be able to show that he was, in fact, in possession of information giving him reasonable grounds.[120] For this reason, the decision of the Divisional Court in *Kynaston* v. *DPP*[121] is erroneous so far as it suggests that courts are entitled to assume that a constable was acting lawfully when his acts are *prima facie* unlawful, and that the burden is on the suspect to negative the reasonableness of the grounds for suspicion.

In relation to arrests based on reasonable suspicion, then, section 24 of PACE appears to require that the officer who actually makes the arrest should be in possession of the reasonable grounds. This might seem to be a highly technical point of little practical importance, but it actually has practical significance because of the organization and hierarchical structure of police forces. Police officers in many investigations operate in teams. The same officer will not always undertake all parts of an investigation; some officers will be given instructions by more senior officers which they will be expected, on pain of disciplinary sanctions, to carry out, whether or not they are told the reasons for them. Under pressure, the amount of information which can be passed between them, by radio or otherwise, may be limited. In major inquiries, information is collated and analysed centrally from a large number of sources, sometimes with the aid of a computer program such as the HOLMES and HOLMES 2 systems. The officers in charge of the investigation who decide that somebody should be arrested might not pass all the information on which the decision was based to the officers who are to make the arrest. Where the arresting officer is required to hold a reasonable suspicion, or to be in possession of reasonable grounds for it,[122] is one officer entitled to rely on the judgement of others, and assume that the orders or requests from other officers are based on reasonable grounds, or will the arrest be

---

[119] PACE, s. 17(2)(*a*).

[120] *Chapman* v. *DPP* (1988) 89 Cr. App. R. 190, DC. However, it was probably wrong for the court to suggest that the officer must also have reasonable grounds for believing that it was an arrestable offence: s. 17(1)(*b*) requires that the entry should be for the purpose of arresting someone for an arrestable offence, but not that the constable's belief that the offence is arrestable should be based on reasonable grounds.

[121] (1987) 84 Cr. App. R. 200, DC.

[122] As under PACE, s. 24(4)(*b*), (5)(*b*), (6), and (7)(*b*).

unlawful unless the arresting officer makes whatever checks, and asks whatever questions, are needed in order to satisfy the required standard? Two cases suggest that they may be permitted to rely on each other's judgement as giving reasonable grounds for their own suspicion.

In *R. v. Francis*[123] the Court of Appeal accepted that an officer was entitled to rely on the word of another officer to the point where, in effect, one constable's reasonable cause to suspect somebody became the common property of all constables involved in an attempt to apprehend an escaped suspect. This is an unacceptably wide principle, and is open to criticism as undermining the individual responibility of an arresting officer on which legal accountability for arrest decisions in English law depends.[124] Nevertheless, on the facts of *Francis* it would have been fair to say that one constable, who was told by another what the latter had seen, thereby acquired reasonable grounds for suspicion of his own (as long as the constable giving the information was not a known liar). Furthermore, on the wording of those parts of section 24 of PACE which (unlike section 2 of the Criminal Law Act 1967, which was the governing provision in *Francis*) require only that there be reasonable grounds for suspicion, without specifying who is to be in possession of those grounds, the reasoning of the Court of Appeal in *Francis* appears unexceptionable.

In *McKee v. Chief Constable of Northern Ireland,*[125] a constable in Northern Ireland had been instructed by his sergeant to arrest the plaintiff because he was a suspected terrorist. The constable duly arrested the plaintiff under section 11(1) of the Northern Ireland (Emergency Provisions) Act 1978 (now repealed), which provided: 'Any constable may arrest without warrant any person whom he suspects of being a terrorist.' The evidence showed that the constable did honestly believe his sergeant when told that the plaintiff was a terrorist. In those circumstances, the House of Lords held that the arrest was lawful, notwithstanding the fact that the constable did not know the grounds on which the sergeant had based his opinion and instruction. On the wording of the Act, the suspicion needed to be genuinely held by the constable making the arrest, but suspicion implies an absence of belief,[126] and can exist without reasonable grounds. There was no requirement in the Act that the constable's suspicion should be reasonable or that, if the suspicion was based on an instruction from a superior, the constable should know the background which gave rise to the instruction. This case underlines the importance of the wording of the arrest power in the statute. The focus is

---

[123] (1972) 116 Sol. Jo. 632, [1972] Crim. LR 549, CA.
[124] Feldman, *Entry, Search and Seizure,* 205–6.
[125] [1984] 1 WLR 1358, [1985] 1 All ER 1, HL
[126] See *Hussien v. Chong Fook Kam,* above.

always on the arresting officer, not on those instructing him, but the state of mind demanded of that officer will depend entirely on the statute in question.[127]

However, the limits of this must be noted. While statutes might not demand that officers who are sent to arrest someone know the grounds giving rise to the suspicion, they will at least need to know the type of offence for which they are making the arrest. If they did not, they would be unable to tell the arrestee of the offence for which he is being arrested, and (as we shall see) this failure would make the arrest unlawful. If a constable sees other constables engaged in a fight, or attempting to detain somebody, but has not been told why, he is not entitled to assume that they are acting lawfully and that there are reasonable grounds to suspect that the person on the receiving end has committed an arrestable offence. If he goes to their assistance, and it turns out that they were acting unlawfully, he will be held not to have acted in the execution of his duty.[128] Professor Sir John Smith has described this as questionable: 'When [the officer] saw his colleagues struggling with a man whom they had arrested, did he not have reasonable grounds for suspecting that an arrestable offence had been committed?' The answer, however, is that, knowing nothing about the offence, his suspicion could only be based on blind faith in his colleagues. This is no ground for depriving somebody of his liberty; the police too often get it wrong (as they did in that case—the purported arrest was for a non-arrestable offence). The correct policy is to encourage officers to take a questioning attitude to colleagues, in order to limit the scope for officers to connive at each other's improprieties. This is sensible in terms of civil liberties, although in the light of the complex, co-operative nature of some police work, it might be regarded as imposing an unrealistic burden on the police, and as perpetuating a myth which portrays every constable as independently accountable to law for the propriety of his or her actions. Such a portrayal is at odds with the organization of modern police forces.

(iv) *Reasonableness, proper purposes, natural justice.* If there are reasonable grounds for suspicion, or whatever the statute requires, to bring into play

---

[127] S. 11, originally intended to provide an arrest power leading to internment without trial, was repealed by the Northern Ireland (Emergency Provisions) Act 1987. Arrests in Northern Ireland must now be made under the Northern Ireland (Emergency Provisions) Act 1991, s. 18 (members of HM armed forces on duty may arrest without warrant, and detain for not more than 4 hours, a person who they have reasonable grounds to suspect is committing, has committed, or is about to commit any offence), or for specific crimes under ordinary criminal procedure legislation. For discussion of these provisions, see Gerard Hogan and Clive Walker, *Political Violence and the Law in Ireland*, (Manchester: Manchester UP, 1989), 47–50.

[128] *Riley* v. *DPP* (1989) 91 Cr. App. R. 14, [1990] Crim. LR 422, DC.

the power to arrest a person, on what basis will the officer's exercise of the power be reviewable? Over and above the requirement that there should be reasonable suspicion that a particular person has committed an arrestable offence, the House of Lords made it clear, in *Mohammed-Holgate* v. *Duke*[129] that, irrespective of the statutory grounds for arrest which apply in particular cases, once the constable is within the four corners of a power to arrest without warrant, the lawfulness of a decision to arrest can be challenged only on general principles of public law governing the exercise of discretions. These principles fall into three main categories.[130]

Natural justice, or procedural due process, and particularly the idea that a person should be given the chance to respond to allegations which affect his legal position, could play a part in structuring investigative processes. However, English law has generally turned its back on the idea that investigators should comply with the rules of natural justice. The requirement for checking information before using it as the grounds for an arrest is derived from the notion of reasonableness, as noted above, rather than that of fairness to the suspect. If there are other ways of checking suspicions, it will not be necessary to put them to the suspect. Indeed, in criminal investigations it may well be counter-productive to allow a suspect a chance to make representations before arrest. It could alert him, allowing him and associates to escape, destroy or conceal evidence, and salt away proceeds of crime.

Illegality, or *ultra vires,* simply requires the official to be acting within the four corners of a power which the official actually has. This criterion, in relation to arrests, is exhausted by the matters discussed above under the heading of reasonable cause to suspect. However, it should be noted that, in *Wills* v. *Bowley*,[131] the House of Lords by a majority of three to two (Lords Wilberforce, Bridge, and Russell, with Lords Elwyn-Jones and Lowry dissenting) were prepared to give an expansive reading to a statute which required a constable to 'take into custody, without warrant, and forthwith convey before a justice, any person who within his view commits' one of the offences described in the section.[132] This should not be interpreted literally, the majority said, because it is in the public interest that a constable acting in good faith should be protected as long as he

---

[129] [1984] AC 437, *sub nom. Holgate-Mohammed* v. *Duke* [1984] 1 All ER 1054, HL.

[130] *Council of Civil Service Unions* v. *Minister for the Civil Service* [1985] AC 374, HL, at 410–11 *per* Lord Diplock. See generally D. J. Galligan, *Discretionary Powers* (Oxford: Clarendon Press, 1986).

[131] [1983] 1 AC 57, [1982] 2 All ER 654, HL.

[132] Town Police Clauses Act 1847, s. 28. The words conferring the arrest power have now been repealed by PACE, s. 119, and Sched. 7, Part I.

acted on reasonable grounds. The courts had to balance the interest of society in preserving liberty against that in upholding the law and apprehending criminals. The section was therefore to be interpreted as permitting an arrest where the constable honestly believed, on reasonable grounds, that the person to be arrested was committing an offence.[133] However, as Robilliard and McEwan have pointed out,[134] where Parliament has provided protection by statute, under PACE, for the constable acting on reasonable grounds, the protection given by the statute should be regarded as adequate and should not be further extended by judicial interpretation.

Irrationality as a ground of review of a discretion to arrest goes beyond the idea of reasonable cause for suspicion. The idea that the suspicion which grounds the legality of the arrest should be reasonable is fundamental to the existence of the power in the first place. But in addition, once the power has arisen, the decision to make the arrest (in which the presence of reasonable grounds for suspicion is but one component) should be reasonable. A number of elements are involved here, clustered round what is sometimes called '*Wednesbury* unreasonableness' after the case in which it received its classic formulation.[135] First, the decision should not be so unreasonable that no reasonable officer could properly have made it; secondly, it must be based on relevant considerations; thirdly, it must be made in good faith for a proper purpose.[136]

The notion of unreasonableness is elastic, but, as *Mohammed-Holgate* v. *Duke* shows, the courts are generally unwilling to question the opinion of experts in the field as to what is reasonable in the light of operational requirements. This deference to perceived expertise is not confined to policing matters,[137] but is particularly marked there. In *Mohammed-Holgate*, a detective constable had reasonable cause to suspect the plaintiff of burglary of jewellery. The detective went to the plaintiff's house, and arrested her without a warrant, because it was likely that a confession would be needed to establish her guilt to the satisfaction of a jury, and the detective believed that the plaintiff would be more likely to confess if taken to a police station and questioned there than if questioned in her own house. At the police station the officers who had originally investigated the burglary, which had occurred four months earlier, would have been available to question the plaintiff; this was regarded as a relevant factor in deciding to arrest her. In the event, no charges were laid against

---

[133] [1982] 2 All ER at p. 680 *per* Lord Bridge.

[134] St. John Robilliard and Jenny McEwan, *Police Powers and the Individual* (Oxford: Basil Blackwell, 1986), 105.

[135] *Associated Provincial Picture Houses Ltd.* v. *Wednesbury Corporation* [1948] 1 KB 223, CA.

her, and she sued the police for false imprisonment. The county court judge found that the detective's purpose in arresting the plaintiff had been to subject her to the greater stress and pressure involved in an arrest and deprivation of liberty, in the belief that she would then be more likely to confess, but that the police had conducted themselves entirely properly once she was at the police station. The judge held that the arrest had been unreasonable and unlawful, and awarded the plaintiff £1,000 damages.

This decision was reversed by the Court of Appeal, whose decision was upheld by the House of Lords. Lord Diplock, with whom Lords Keith, Bridge, Brandon, and Brightman agreed, noted that the practice of arresting people in order to question them, rather than to initiate charges immediately, was of long standing and had been recognized in the Report of the Royal Commission on Criminal Procedure[138] and in the statutory power given to the police to grant bail to an arrested person where the inquiry cannot be completed forthwith[139] It was not *Wednesbury* unreasonable to use the period of detention 'to dispel or confirm the reasonable suspicion [which had given rise to the power to arrest] by questioning the suspect or seeking further evidence with his assistance'.[140] In deciding to do so, the detective constable had not taken account of an irrelevant consideration, acted for an improper purpose, or behaved in a way in which no reasonable officer in the circumstances could have behaved. The arrest was therefore within his discretion, and lawful. The reviewability of arrest decisions on *Wednesbury* principles is in accordance with general public-law rules. It supplements the examination of the reasonableness of grounds for suspicion, rather than replacing it. If a decision is *Wednesbury* unreasonable, it will be unlawful in the public-law sense, and will take a constable outside the protection against civil liability offered to him when lawfully exercising a public-law power.

A fourth ground for judicial review of official action was tentatively advanced by Lord Diplock in the *GCHQ* case. This was *proportionality*, a

---

[136] The latter two points are treated here as aspects of irrationality, although for reasons which are not relevant here the House of Lords has suggested that they are, in fact, aspects of illegality rather than irrationality: *R. v. Secretary of State for Trade and Industry, ex parte Lonrho plc* [1989] 1 WLR 525, [1989] 2 All ER 609, HL.

[137] David Feldman, 'Public Law Values in the House of Lords' (1990) 106 LQR 246–76 at 256–7, 263–4.

[138] RCCP, *Report*, para. 3.66. Previously there had been a gap between the rhetoric of the courts, which tended to assume that suspects would be charged and brought before a court immediately on arrest, and the practice of the police, who relied on an informal norm of 24 hours' leeway before bringing an arrested person before a magistrate and had made liberal use of the fiction that people in police stations being questioned had agreed, or been persuaded, to help the police volutarily with their inquiries. Dixon, 'Detention for Questioning', 7–24.

doctrine developed in the public law of a number of European civil-law systems, and adopted by the European Court of Justice and the European Court of Human Rights to form a general principle of the law of the European Communities and of the European Convention of Human Rights. The doctrine requires that the methods adopted to achieve any purpose which threatens a person's rights must be proportionate to the good to be achieved, subject to the state's 'margin of appreciation'. The doctrine operates on three levels. At the general level of formulating policies, legislation, and institutional systems for achieving goals, it demands that powers granted to officials should be reasonably related to the purposes to be achieved. It will not be permissible to take a sledgehammer to crack a nut. This is related to the *Wednesbury* unreasonableness principle in English administrative law, outlined above. But adopting a reasonable policy will not in itself satisfy the proportionality doctrine. At the level of implementation, the institutional system adopted must provide adequate protection for the interests of people affected. In particular, where the system requires an individual's interests to be weighed against those of other people or the community as a whole, the weighting process must be conducted by an independent person or body.[141] Finally, each exercise of the power must be directed to a proper purpose.

Despite Lord Diplock's suggestion that English law might embrace the proportionality doctrine, it has so far made little headway. In *R.* v. *Secretary of State for the Home Department, ex parte Brind,*[142] the House of Lords was not satisfied that the doctrine yet formed part of English law (although on the facts they held that the action taken had not been disproportionate in any event).

(v) *Conclusion.* The flexibility of the 'reasonable grounds' standard leaves police officers a very wide discretion which may be exercised for undisclosed and improper reasons. Regardless of the legal limits on the power, it seems the power to arrest, like that to search people in the street, is used differentially. Police officers use it differently in different areas,[143]

---

[139] Magistrates' Courts Act 1980, s. 43(3) as amended. It has now been clearly accepted in the detention and interrogation provisions of PACE and the associated Codes of Practice.

[140] [1984] 1 All ER at p. 1059 *per* Lord Diplock. However, if it can be proved that the arresting officer knew that there was no possibility of the person being charged, it is open to a jury to decide that the arrest was unreasonable: *Plange* v. *Chief Constable of South Humberside Police, Independent,* 17 Apr. 1992, CA.

[141] *Gaskin* v. *UK* Eur. Ct. HR, Series A, No. 160, Judgment of 23 June 1989, at para. 49.

[142] [1991] 1 All ER 720, HL.

[143] Royal Commission on Criminal Procedure, Research Study No. 9, *Arrest, Charge and Summons* (London: HMSO, 1980).

and seem to differentiate between racial groups.[144] They also differentiate between people who are polite and submissive and those who are rude, uncooperative, or abusive. The latter are seen as threatening the fragile authority of the police, which must be reasserted by using legal powers so as to put the challengers in their place.[145] There is, in short, far more going on when a constable decides whether or not to arrest a suspect than might be suggested by the need for formal compliance with the legal rules. Because of the nature of police work and the forms of legal control, this is unlikely to be satisfactorily monitored or contained by law. It is too easy for a constable to work out reasonable grounds for suspicion after the event, and judges are (perhaps rightly) wary of substituting their view of reasonable police behaviour for that of the officers on the spot under the *Wednesbury* principles. If the practice of arrest is to match the standards laid down in the European Convention much will depend on the attitudes and training of police officers, and their willingness to take such standards seriously as part of their decision making and monitoring processes.

5.4 ARREST FORMALITIES

This section examines the formal legal requirements for an arrest. There are certain steps which must be taken to make a lawful arrest out of what would otherwise be a false imprisonment, and further steps which must be taken after the arrest in order to make the subsequent detention lawful.

(1) What constitutes an arrest?

An arrest is not defined in PACE, which merely lays down the conditions for one and steps to be taken when making one. The definition of arrest is therefore a matter for common law, and may be crucial to the civil and criminal liabilities of police and suspects for two reasons. First, a person is entitled to use reasonable force to resist a battery or a false

[144] P. Stevens and C. F. Willis, *Race, Crime and Arrests*, Home Office Research Study No. 58 (London: HMSO, 1979); Robert Reiner, 'Police and Race Relations', in John Baxter and Laurence Koffman (eds.), *Police: The Constitution and the Community* (Abingdon: Professional Books, 1985), 149–87 at 166–9; Robert Reiner, *The Politics of the Police* (Brighton: Wheatsheaf, 1985), 124–35.

[145] See Smith and Gray, *Police and People in London*, 351–4, on the importance in police culture of maintaining control and not losing face. For a good example of a case where this seems to have affected events, see *G. v. Director of Public Prosecutions* [1989] Crim. LR 150, DC (abusive behaviour in police station).

imprisonment, but not to resist an arrest. Secondly, a constable is entitled to use reasonable force if necessary for certain purposes, one of which is making an arrest, but force will be unlawful (and the constable acting outside the execution of his duty) if directed to an unauthorized purpose, such as holding someone for questioning without arresting him.[146] However, the meaning of arrest, and particularly the distinction between an arrest and a detention, is fraught with problems.

Because of the effect of an arrest on the rights of the person arrested, and particularly the freedom to use reasonable force to resist an unlawful assault or imprisonment, the formalities of arrest stress the need to make it clear to the arrestee that the arrestor requires the arrestee to submit to him and has authority to do so. There must also be a definable moment at which the arrestee's status changes from free to (partially) unfree, and some basis on which the arrestee, and, if necessary, a court or disciplinary tribunal, may decide whether the constable is acting within a legal power. In order to achieve this, there are three essential elements to an arrest.

First, either the arrestee must submit to the arrest, or there must be an act of physical restraint enforcing the arrestee's detention. There may often be a purely formal or symbolic touching of the arrestee, signifying the change in his legal position, followed by submission. At other times, the suspect may submit without any physical touching. Where an arrest takes place in a police station, the suspect having gone there voluntarily, the necessary physical restraint is provided by the surroundings.[147]

Secondly, the arrestor must signify by clear words that he is arresting the arrestee.[148] As this need not happen immediately where it is not reasonably practicable, for instance because the arrestee has escaped before it could be done[149] or is fighting, there is an implication that one may have a lawful arrest when the arrestor attempts physically to take the arrestee into custody, and that this arrest subsequently becomes an unlawful detention only if the arrestee is not made aware of the legal basis for the action as soon as practicable thereafter.[150] The act of physical restraint

[146] *Rice* v. *Connolly* [1966] 2 QB 414, [1966] 2 All ER 649, DC; *Kenlin* v. *Gardiner* [1967] 2 QB 510, [1966] 3 All ER 931, DC.

[147] This is implicit in PACE, s. 29, which provides that: 'Where . . . a person attends voluntarily at a police station or at any other place where a constable is present or accompanies a constable to a police station or any such other place without having been arrested—. . . (b) he shall be informed at once that he is under arrest if a decision is taken by a constable to prevent him from leaving at will.'

[148] PACE, s. 28(1). Where the arrest is made by a constable (but, by implication, not when made by anyone else) this information must be given even if it is obvious.

[149] PACE, s. 28(5).

[150] *R.* v. *Brosch* [1988] Crim. LR 743, CA. Note, however, that (as Di Birch pointed out in her commentary on the case at p. 744) the Court of Appeal was wrong in supposing (*obiter*) that a constable must inform the arrestee that he is under arrest immediately, whether or not it is practicable to do so.

(such as rugby-tackling a fleeing suspect) must be intended by the arrestor to be in pursuance of a power of arrest. Whether or not it was so intended will be a matter for the trier of fact, to be decided on the basis of the evidence available.[151]

Thirdly, the arrestor must make clear to the arrestee the ground for his arrest.[152] This must be done on, or as soon as is practicable after, the arrest; if it is longer delayed, the arrest becomes an unlawful detention. The delay permitted under the Act is very limited. It is clear that the arrestor is not permitted to delay once it becomes practicable to give a reason for the arrest, even if there might be good reasons for delaying, although the test for practicability may take account of the surrounding circumstances and the effect that giving the information would have on the police operation. In an appeal from Northern Ireland, *Murray* v. *Ministry of Defence*,[153] the House of Lords decided that giving reasons for arrests and (where a person is *not* resisting restraint) informing a person that she is under arrest might be delayed where necessary in order to prevent a risk that the alarm might be given to others, giving rise to danger. It is clear from the leading speech of Lord Griffiths that this exception was crafted in the light of the exigencies of military policing in Northern Ireland,[154] and it is unlikely that a similar delays would be acceptable on the mainland.[155]

Under section 28 of PACE, the danger of an alarm being given will excuse a delay only if it makes it impracticable, rather than merely inconvenient, to give the information. It is, however, significant that the European Court of Human Rights, in *Fox, Campbell and Hartley* v. *United Kingdom*, accepted that the standard laid down in Article 5(2) of the European Convention that a person who is arrested 'shall be informed promptly, in a language which he understands, of the reason for his arrest and of any charge against him' permitted a person (again in the context of

---

[151] *R.* v. *Brosch*, above.

[152] PACE, s. 28(3). Where the arrestor is a constable (and, by implication, not otherwise), this must be done even if the ground is obvious: s. 28(4).

[153] [1988] 2 All ER 521, HL.

[154] See Lord Griffiths's discussion of 'soldiers . . . employed on the difficult and potentially dangerous task of carrying out a house arrest of a person suspected of an offence in connection with the IRA', circumstances which were held to justify a soldier in following set search and arrest procedures (apparently, whatever they might be): [1988] 2 All ER at p. 527. This certainly does not reflect the law on the mainland, where the responsibility for adopting appropriate procedures, as laid down by law rather than superior officers, lies on the arresting officer: see above.

[155] The absence of any authority for the exception in *Murray*, and the appearance given by the House of Lords of reasoning back from a desired conclusion rather than forward from principle, laid the decision open to convincing and destructive criticism by Professor Glanville Williams, 'When is an Arrest?' (1991) 54 *MLR* 408–17 and Clive Walker, 'Army Special Powers on Parade' (1989) 40 *NILQ* 1–33 at 6–10.

Northern Ireland anti-terrorism policing) to be taken to a police station before being given the information.[156] If this happens before the suspect is questioned, it still allows him to know the suspicion against which he has to defend himself, but it does not allow him or, subsequently, a court to check the grounds for the arrest actually operating in the mind of the arresting officer at the time, so it may restrict the opportunity for review of the lawfulness of detention under Article 5(4).[157]

In the event of delay in giving the information, the arrest will still initially be lawful until such time as it becomes practicable to give the information but the arrestor fails to do so. In the intervening period (if any), the constable will be acting in the execution of his duty, so that an assault on him will be an assault on him in the execution of his duty,[158] despite the fact that it subsequently becomes an unlawful detention. The information may be given in general terms, as long as it makes clear, in the circumstances, the offence (or one of the offences) of which the arrestee is suspected; precision is desirable, but not usually essential.[159] The grounds for the suspicion need not be given. Similarly, when the arrest is made under section 25 (the general arrest conditions), it is sufficient to tell the arrestee the offence for which he is being arrested. It is desirable, but not strictly necessary, to tell the suspect that he will be arrested unless he gives the constable his name and address, and it is probably not necessary, after making the arrest, to tell him that he has been arrested because he has not supplied a name or address, or to tell him that the name and address are required in order to allow a summons to be served.[160] What is important is that the arrestee should know as soon as possible on what grounds his liberty is being restrained.

(2) Can failures be rectified later?

If a person is detained unlawfully because the arrestor has failed to inform him of the fact that he has been arrested or of the grounds for arrest, can the detention later be turned into a lawful arrest by giving the arrestee the necessary information? Alternatively, is it necessary for the police to release, then re-arrest, the arrestee? This is a significant issue, as it affects the availability and quantum of damages for false imprisonment. It may

[156] Eur. Ct. HR, Series A, No. 182, Judgment of 30 Aug. 1990, 13 EHRR 157.
[157] For a slightly different view, see Finnie, 'Anti-Terrorism Legislation', 292–3.
[158] *DPP* v. *Hawkins* [1988] 1 *WLR* 1166, [1988] 3 All ER 673, DC.
[159] This was the position under the common-law rules before PACE: *Abbassy* v. *Metropolitan Police Commissioner* [1990] 1 WLR 385, [1990] 1 All ER 193, CA. As the object of s. 29 of PACE seems to be to codify the common-law rules, deriving from *Christie* v. *Leachinsky* [1947] AC 573, [1947] 1 All ER 567, HL, there is no reason to suppose that greater particularity is required under the statute.
[160] *Nicholas* v. *Parsonage* [1987] RTR 199, DC.

also be necessary to decide at what point an unlawful detention becomes an arrest in order to decide whether a detainee who tries to free himself is committing an offence such as assaulting or wilfully obstructing a constable in the execution of his duty. If the detention is unlawful, the constable will not be in the execution of his duty, and any obstruction will have a lawful justification and so will not be wilful.

Before the 1984 Act, the Court of Appeal (Criminal Division) had held in R. v. Kulynycz[161] that an unlawful detention may become a lawful arrest when the necessary information is given, and the Court of Appeal (Civil Division) decided in Lewis v. Chief Constable of the South Wales Constabulary[162] that the position is the same after the 1984 Act. In that case, the two plaintiffs were sisters who had been travelling in a car when they were stopped, arrested without being told the reason for the arrest, and taken to a police station. There they saw the custody officer, and were separately told, ten and twenty-three minutes respectively after their arrests, that they had been arrested on suspicion of burglary. Five hours later they were both released. They sued the Chief Constable for false arrest and wrongful imprisonment. The trial judge ruled that the arrest, although initially unlawful, had become lawful when the plaintiffs were told the reason for it, and awarded damages of £200 in respect of periods of unlawful detention of ten and twenty-three minutes respectively. The plaintiffs appealed, but the Court of Appeal upheld the decision. Balcombe LJ, with whom Taylor LJ agreed, started from the position that PACE had not changed the law on the constituents of a valid arrest. He then referred to two dicta in earlier House of Lords decisions. The first was from Viscount Dilhorne in Spicer v. Holt,[163] a breathalyser case: '"Arrest" is an ordinary English word . . . Whether or not a person has been arrested depends not on the legality of the arrest but on whether he has been deprived of his liberty to go where he pleases.' The other citation was from Lord Diplock in Mohammed-Holgate v. Duke:[164]

arrest is a continuing act: it starts with the arrestor taking a person into his custody (sc. by action or words restraining him from moving anywhere beyond the arrester's control), and it continues until the person so restrained is either released from custody or, having been brought before a magistrate, is remanded in custody by the magistrate's judicial act.

Balcombe LJ held that it followed from treating arrest as a fact rather than a legal concept that a failure to comply with a necessary formality cannot

---

[161] [1971] 1 Q.B. 367, [1970] 3 All ER 881, CA.
[162] [1991] 1 All ER 206, CA.
[163] [1977] AC 987 at p. 1000, [1976] 3 All ER 71 at p. 79.
[164] [1984] AC 437 at p. 441, [1984] 1 All ER 1054 at p. 1056.

make the act of initiating an arrest a nullity: 'Arrest is a situation. . . .
Whether a person has been arrested depends not on the legality of his
arrest but on whether he has been deprived of his liberty to go where he
pleases.'[165] It followed that the arrest, being a *continuing* situation, could
be made lawful for the future, though not the past, by complying with
the necessary formality and supplying the information.[166]

This end result has common sense to recommend it. There would be
little point in requiring a person to be released and then immediately
rearrested. However, the means by which the court reached the conclusion is, with respect, unconvincing. If an arrest means no more than factual detention or restraint, why use the word 'arrest' at all? It would make
better sense to use the word 'restrain', a nice, factual term without legal
overtones. What is required is more careful attention to the legal implications of the terms used, rather than pretending that the terms have no
legal significance. It is worth distinguishing between detentions generally,
most of which (like those used by schools for disciplinary purposes) have
no connection with the legal process, and arrests for the purposes of the
criminal process. The word arrest should be used only in relation to
detention in reliance on a power conferred for the purpose of upholding
the law, as under sections 24 and 25 of PACE. Where a person is
detained in purported exercise of a power of arrest which actually exists,
but the legal conditions for the exercise of that power are not fulfilled, it
makes sense to speak of a purported (but unlawful) arrest, although it
would be preferable to limit the use of the word 'arrest' to those detentions which are both objectively capable of being an arrest and are legally
justified. On the other hand, if a detention does not purport to be an
arrest, or is not made pursuant to a lawful power of arrest, or (having
been made lawfully) is not followed by the giving of the required information, it is not an arrest but a detention, and is *prima facie* unlawful and
resistable. Where the arrest criteria are objectively not met, it invites ana-
lytical confusion to speak of an arrest. Despite the unfortunate tendency
to speak of an 'unlawful arrest' in the latter situation, the word 'arrest'
should be confined to circumstances where there is something which
could objectively be viewed as an arrest, and the question is whether that
arrest is justified. Other interferences with people's liberty are detentions,
which may or may not be legally justified.[167]

One might go further, and suggest that an arrest is, in truth, a legal term
of art, and is used in that sense in PACE. On this view, one either has a
lawful arrest or no arrest at all; a purported arrest which fails one of the
legal conditions for its validity would be void. This would have the merit

[165] [1991] 1 All ER at p. 210. See also *Murray* v. *Ministry of Defence* [1988] 2 All ER
521, HL.
[166] Following *R.* v. *Kulynycz* [1971] 1 QB 367, [1970] 3 All ER 881, CA.

of simplicity, but would be impossible to reconcile with the dicta from the House of Lords quoted above. But whichever usage one adopts, the police in *Lewis* could have effected a lawful arrest of the plaintiffs at the police station merely by making it clear that the plaintiffs were under arrest and that the reason was that they were suspected of burglary. In effect, it seems that this was what the custody officer did, so it would have been unnecessary to hold that the entire five hours of the plaintiffs' detention had been unlawful. It would certainly not have been necessary for the police to release and then rearrest the plaintiffs, since, if they were not under arrest, they could hardly be required to be released before being arrested.

(3) How detailed and accurate need the information be?

The arresting officer need not tell the suspect the precise legal nature of the offence for which the arrest was made. If it is obvious, as where a burglar is caught climbing out of a window of a house with stolen goods in his hands, very little precision in the indication of the offence is needed, although it is desirable to be as precise as possible; all that is required is a clear notification of the fact that the suspect is under arrest. In other cases, however, a general indication of the type of offence is needed, without using technical language which might, in any case, only confuse the arrestee. Of course, the offence for which a person is arrested might be quite different from any charge which is subsequently laid against him. This does not affect the legality of the arrest, which is judged according to the reasonableness of the officer's suspicions on the basis of material available at the time of the arrest.

5.5 TREATMENT FOLLOWING THE ARREST

Under the European Convention on Human Rights, Article 5(3):

Everyone arrested or detained in accordance with the provisions of paragraph (1)(*c*) of this Article shall be brought promptly before a judge or other officer authorised by law to exercise judicial power and shall be entitled to trial within a reasonable time or to release pending trial. Release may be conditioned by guarantees to appear for trial.

How far does English law meet these demands?

Once a lawful arrest has been made, the arresting officer has a number of consequential powers and duties. The object is to provide sufficient protection for the suspect's rights and liberty against abuse of power by the police, while allowing the investigation to continue expeditiously. This calls for a nice sense of balance. The solution adopted in PACE was to place relatively few substantive limits on the powers of the police following arrest, but to introduce administrative and bureaucratic safeguards, requiring records to be kept and copies to be provided to the suspect, with reviews and monitoring of the process being provided by more senior police officers. In the event, the rules, particularly those governing interrogation of suspects, have been given some teeth by the exclusionary rules of evidence contained in sections 76 and 78 of PACE and robustly interpreted by the courts. Section 76 requires the trial court to exclude any confession which has been obtained by oppression or in consequence of anything said or done which was likely in the circumstances to make the confession unreliable. Section 78 as interpreted gives the court an exclusionary discretion where, in the circumstances, it would compromise the proceedings in some way to admit evidence. The details of the operation of these provisions is a matter for the law of evidence, and is outside the scope of this book. However, we should note that one effect of the ways in which the courts have interpreted them has been to make exclusion of statements a way of protecting the rights given by PACE to suspects in police detention, and arguably to provide a means by which the courts can express their disapproval of police malpractice.[168] It also brings the English position closer to the American exclusionary rule in relation to confessions than was previously the case, partly because the American courts have been moving away from the strict *Miranda* position as the English courts have edged towards it.[169]

(1) Taking the arrestee to a police station

The main duty, which arises when the suspect is arrested in a place other than a police station, is to take the arrestee to a police station as soon as

[167] RCCP, *Law and Procedure*, 15. For further discussion, see David Telling, 'Arrest and Detention: The Conceptual Maze' [1978] *Crim. LR* 320–31; K. W. Lidstone, 'A Maze in Law!' [1978] *Crim. LR* 332–42 at p. 332; David N. Clarke and David Feldman, 'Arrest by Any Other Name' [1979] *Crim. LR* 702–7; Williams, 'When is an Arrest?', 408–17. For different views, see M. Zander, 'When is an Arrest not an Arrest?' (1977) 127 *NLJ* 352–4, 379–82; J. C. Smith, [1977] *Crim. LR* 293, commenting on *Spicer* v. *Holt* [1977] AC 987.

[168] There is a voluminous literature on this subject. See e.g. Andrew Ashworth, 'Excluding Evidence as Protecting Rights' [1977] *Crim. LR* 723–35; A. A. S. Zuckerman, 'Illegally Obtained Evidence: Discretion as a Guardian of Legitimacy' [1987] *CLP* 55–70; Di Birch, 'The Pace Hots Up: Confessions and Confusions under the 1984 Act' [1989] *Crim. LR* 95–116; Andrew Choo, 'Improperly Obtained Evidence: A Reconsideration' (1989) 9 *Legal Studies* 261–83; David Feldman, 'Regulating Treatment of Suspects in Police Custody: Judicial Interpretation of Detention Provisions in the Police and Criminal Evidence Act 1984' [1990] *Crim. LR* 452–71; Mark Gelowitz, 'Section 78 of the Police and Criminal Evidence Act 1984: Middle Ground or No Man's Land?' (1990) 106 *LQR* 327–42.

[169] Mark Berger, 'The Exclusionary Rule and Confession Evidence: Some Perspectives on Evolving Practices and Policies in the United States and England and Wales' (1991) 20 *Anglo-Amer. LR* 63–79.

practicable after the arrest.[170] However, there is power to search the suspect and certain premises before taking the suspect to a police station,
and to delay taking the suspect to the police station in order to carry out
investigations elsewhere, in specified circumstances. These cases are
examined below.

The police station to which an arrestee is taken is normally to be a *designated police station*.[171] Designated police stations are those which are for
the time being designated by the chief constable in each police area for
use for the purpose of detaining arrestees.[172] In each designated police
station there must be at least one custody officer, who is meant to be a
sergeant who is independent of the investigation[173]and is generally
responsible for ensuring that arrestees are treated in accordance with the
requirements of PACE and the Codes of Practice, and that all records are
made and kept as required by PACE and the Codes.[174] The role of the
custody officer is therefore central to the protection of suspects' rights
under PACE, and arrestees taken to non-designated police stations would
be at a significant disadvantage in relation to the monitoring of their
treatment and safeguarding of their rights.

Nevertheless, sometimes it is permissible to take an arrestee to a non-
designated police station. The only circumstances where this is allowed
are: (*a*) where the constable *either* belongs to a body of constables maintained by an authority which is not a police authority, such as the
Transport Police, *or* is working in a locality covered by a non-designated
police station,[175] *and* it appears to the constable that it will not be necessary to keep the arrestee in detention for more than six hours;[176] (*b*)
where the arrest was made by a single constable, or the arrestee was
arrested by someone who was not a constable and handed into the custody of a single constable, and, no other constable being available to assist
that constable, it appears to him that he will be unable to take the arrestee
to a designated police station without the arrestee injuring himself, the
constable, or some other person.[177] If the arrestee is taken to a non-
designated police station, he must be transferred to a designated police
station within six hours of his arrival, if he has not been released
earlier.[178]

The choice of a six-hour period is significant, since the Royal
Commission on Criminal Procedure, on whose report much of PACE

---

[170] PACE, s. 30(1).   [171] PACE, s. 30(2).

[172] PACE, s. 35(1), (4). The chief officer of police in the area has responsibility for des-
ignating police stations which seem to provide sufficient accommodation for that purpose:
s. 35(2).

[173] PACE, s. 36, which also specifies the steps to be taken when this is impracticable.

[174] PACE, s. 39(1).   [175] PACE, s. 30(4).   [176] PACE, s. 30(3).

[177] PACE, s. 30(5).   [178] PACE, s. 30(6).

was based, found that the vast majority of arrestees are released, with or without charge, within six hours. It remains true that it is only in cases which present difficulties that people are usually detained without charge for more than six hours.[179]

As the main independent protection for arrestees' rights is the custody officer, located at the designated police station, it is important that the arrestee should be taken to the police station as quickly as possible. It is too easy for improper pressure to be brought to bear on a suspect if police officers are allowed to drive him round for long periods, carrying on informal discussions, which may or may not be accurately remembered and recorded later. In some cases, where confessions were allegedly made in the backs of cars on the way to police stations, and the evidence of what was said was not reliable, the police having sacrificed reliability by breaking the rules on making records and showing them to the arrestee for comments, it has been held that the evidence should have been excluded as unfair.[180]

Nevertheless, there are circumstances in which the police are entitled to delay taking the arrestee to any police station.[181] These arise in two situations: first, where the police are conducting a search following arrest (considered below); secondly, where the presence of the arrestee is necessary in order to carry out such investigations as it is reasonable to carry out immediately.[182] The latter provision is open to abuse, and the necessity principle should be strictly applied, with regard (for example) to the urgency of the investigation, and the importance of having the arrestee at the spot (for example, to identify a place or person). It might be necessary and reasonable to take the suspect somewhere else before going to a police station, regardless of any urgency, if the suspect has offered an explanation or alibi and he wishes to be taken to a place or a person to try to supply evidence in support of his account. On the other hand, after a person has been arrested at a hotel as part of an investigation into a suspected drugs conspiracy, it is not proper to hold him in his hotel room to prevent him being seen by accomplices leaving the hotel with investigators.[183] Nor is it reasonable to take the suspect to see if a witness to the offence can identify him. All identifications are to be conducted in accordance with the *Code of Practice for the Identification of Persons by Police*

---

[179] Barry Irving and Ian McKenzie, *Regulating Custodial Interviews* (London: Police Foundation, 1988).

[180] *R. v. Hassan Khan, Independent*, 2 Mar. 1990, CA; *R. v. Edwards* [1991] 2 All ER 266, CA.

[181] Whenever there is a delay in taking an arrestee to a police station, the reasons must be recorded when he first arrives at a police station: PACE, s. 30(11).

[182] PACE, s. 30(10).   [183] *R. v. Kerawalla* [1991] Crim. LR 451, CA.

Officers (Code D). Again, it is important to restrict the amount of time during which an arrestee is in the hands of investigating officers without any procedural safeguards.

(2) Search of the person and premises following arrest otherwise than at a police station

The operation of the search power varies according to whether the suspect is arrested at a police station, after attending there volutarily, or elsewhere. This section deals with arrests which do not take place in police stations. Those occurring in police stations are dealt with in section (3), below.

(i) *Search of the person.*[184] If the suspect is arrested anywhere other than in a police station, there is a power for a constable to search him if the constable has reasonable grounds for *believing* that the arrestee may present a danger to himself or others.[185] The constable may seize and retain anything he finds which he has reasonable grounds for believing the arrestee might use to cause physical injury to himself or another.[186] This power does not extend to a person who is not a constable, but who makes citizen's arrest. It is possible that citizens may be able to use their common-law power to take reasonable steps in order to prevent a breach of the peace, if one is reasonably apprehended and appears imminent, as any physical attack on a person would amount to a breach of the peace.[187] In addition, a constable with reasonable grounds to believe that an arrestee may have concealed on him anything which he might use to escape from lawful custody[188] is entitled to search the arrestee,[189] to the extent reasonably required for the purpose of discovering any such item.[190] In each case, when a search is carried out in public, the arrestee is not to be required to remove clothing other than an outer coat, jacket, or gloves.[191]

All those can be described as non-evidential searches, since they seek to safeguard people and secure the arrestee rather than find evidence. There is an additional power to search an arrestee for evidence relating to any offence (not necessarily the offence for which he has been arrested), if the constable has reasonable grounds for believing that the arrestee may have concealed on him any such evidence.[192] The search must be no more extensive than is necessary for the purpose of discovering any such

---

[184] Feldman, *Entry, Search and Seizure*, 227–8, 233–4.   [185] PACE, s. 32(1).
[186] PACE, s. 32(8).   [187] See Ch. 17 below.   [188] PACE, s. 32(5).
[189] PACE, s. 32(2)(a)(i).   [190] PACE, s. 32(3).   [191] PACE, s. 32(4),
[192] PACE, s. 32(2)(a)(ii), (5).

item,[193] and when it is carried out in public the arrestee is not to be required to remove clothing other than an outer coat, jacket, or gloves.[194] The reasonable grounds for belief may be based on what the constable sees or on other information. In drugs cases, it will usually be reasonable to search for controlled drugs. In other cases, the reasonableness of a belief may be harder to establish.

(ii) *Search of premises after arrest other than at a police station.* A constable who has reasonable grounds for believing that there is evidence of the offence for which the arrestee was arrested[195] (but not other offences, for which a search would normally require a warrant) is empowered to enter and search any premises[196] in which the arrestee was when arrested, or immediately before he was arrested, for such evidence.[197] Whether the officer has reasonable grounds will depend on the facts of each case. Where the suspect has been arrested on his own premises, there may well be reasonable grounds to believe that there is evidence on the premises, although it will depend to some extent on what crime is suspected and where it is alleged to have taken place. When the suspect is arrested having just left premises, it may still be reasonable to search the premises, even if he was only a visitor there. For example, where officers are watching premises which they believe are being used for drug dealing, and a person is arrested outside the premises and found to be in possession of heroin, it would be reasonable to search the premises for evidence of heroin dealing by him.[198]

The search must be no more extensive than is reasonably required for the purpose of discovering such evidence.[199] In a Crown Court decision, it was held that the power under section 32 is intended to be used immediately following the arrest, and not to give a constable power to return to the scene later—in that case, four hours later—at his convenience and as often as he wants.[200] This has been criticized, as the section does not provide for any time limit, and the existence of another power to enter premises, under section 18, which is clearly not limited as to time, shows that there was no legislative policy opposed to open-ended entry powers.[201] Nevertheless, the decision seems correct, since (a) section 32 was designed to give statutory effect to a common-law power which was

---

[193] PACE, s. 32(3).   [194] PACE, s. 32(4).   [195] PACE, s. 32(6).

[196] For the meaning of 'premises' see below, Ch. 9. When premises are divided into separate dwellings, the power to search is limited to the dwelling in which the arrestee had been immediately before his arrest, together with the common parts of the premises: PACE, s. 32(7).

[197] PACE, s. 32(2)(b).   [198] Cf. *R. v. Beckford* [1991] Crim. LR 918, CA.

[199] PACE, s. 32(3).   [200] *R. v. Badham* [1987] Crim. LR 202.

[201] Bevan and Lidstone, *Investigation of Crime*, 116.

limited to the time and immediate environs of the arrest,[202] and (b) the relationship between section 32 and section 18 is complex, and section 18 contains procedural and substantive limitation which are not present in section 32.

Under section 18 of PACE, a constable has power to enter and search any premises occupied or controlled by a person who is under arrest for an arrestable offence, if he has reasonable grounds for suspecting that there is evidence on the premises, other than items subject to legal privilege, which relates to the offence for which the person was arrested or some other arrestable offence which is connected with or similar to that offence.[203] Normally, this power may be exercised only if authorized in writing by an officer of the rank of inspector or above,[204] and the search will take place after the arrestee has been taken to the police station and authority in writing has been applied for and given. However, there is an exception: the constable may conduct the search without authorisation, and before taking the arrestee to a police station, if the presence of the arrestee at 'a place other than a police station' is 'necessary for the effective investigation of the offence'.[205] The curious feature of this formulation is that it appears to allow an unauthorized search of the arrestee's premises, even if the place where the arrestee is needed is not his premises. However, it is submitted that the provision must be interpreted purposively as meaning that the power to search without written authorization is to come into operation only where the arrestee's presence is needed, for example, to permit access to the premises.

The relationship between sections 18 and 32 is relatively straightforward. No written authorization is ever required under section 32 to search the place where the person is arrested or was immediately beforehand. If the arrest is not for an arrestable offence, or those premises are not occupied or controlled by the arrestee, they cannot be searched under section 18, but only under section 32. To search other premises, a warrant will normally be needed (if available), unless the premises are occupied or controlled by the arrestee and he has been arrested for an arrestable offence (section 18). Even then, some authority is usually

---

[202] *Dillon* v. *O'Brien and Davis* (1887) 20 LR Ir. 300, 16 Cox CC 245; *Chimel* v. *California* 395 US 753 (1969); *Vale* v. *Louisiana* 399 US 30 (1970); Feldman, *Entry, Search and Seizure*, 241–8.

[203] PACE, s. 18(1).

[204] PACE, s. 18(4). The authorization must be written on the Notice of Powers and Rights, which under the *Code of Practice for the Searching of Premises by Police Officers and the Seizure of Property found by Police Officers on Persons or Premises* (Code B), para. 5.7, must be given to the occupier of the premises if practicable: see Code B, para. 3.3.

[205] PACE, s. 18(5). If the constable searches under this subsection, he must, as soon as practicable, inform an officer of the rank of inspector or above that he has done so: s. 18(6).

required (the inspector's written authorization) unless there is a need to have the arrestee himself present, providing both a reason for acting as quickly as possible and a witness independent of the police. When it comes to the grounds for the entry and search, section 18 is in two respects less demanding than section 32: instead of reasonable grounds to *believe*, section 18 requires only reasonable grounds for *suspecting*; and instead of the search being for evidence of the offence for which the person was arrested, section 18 allows search on the basis of reasonable grounds for suspecting that evidence will be found which relates to that offence or related arrestable offences.

Section 18 is, therefore, a good way of obtaining access to the premises of someone arrested for an arrestable offence, whether or not the person was arrested there. Considering that many arrests are made on or near premises controlled by the arrestee, it is not surprising that the police use section 18 far more often than section 32.[206]

(iii) *What may be seized during, and retained after, searches?* A constable searching premises under any of these powers is given certain seizure powers under the sections themselves. After a search of the person under section 32(2)(*a*), the constable may seize and retain anything he finds, other than items subject to legal privilege, if he has reasonable grounds for *believing* that 'he' (grammatically meaning the constable, but presumably intended to refer to the arrestee) might use it to escape from lawful custody, or that it is evidence of any offence or has been obtained in consequence of the commission of any offence.[207]

Seizures after searches of premises are more complicated. Nothing in section 32 specifies what may be seized after a search of premises under section 32(2)(*b*). The powers must therefore be those given by section 19 to a constable who is 'lawfully on premises'. This section gives power to seize anything on the premises, other than items which the officer has reasonable grounds for believing are subject to legal privilege,[208] which the constable has reasonable grounds for *believing* is evidence of, or has been obtained in consequence of the commission of, any offence, whether that which he is investigating or any other. The seizure may, however, be made only if the constable has reasonable grounds for

---

[206] Bevan and Lidstone, *Investigation of Crime*, pp. 110, 112, report the use of s. 18 to ground 54.2% of searches without warrant, compared to the use of s. 32 in 2.1% of entries. Dixon, Coleman, and Bottomley report s. 18 being used as the basis of 62% of searches in their study: 'PACE in practice', 1587. For an extensive study of the use of these powers, see Ken Lidstone and Vaughan Bevan, *Search and Seizure under the Police and Criminal Evidence Act 1984* (Sheffield: Univ. of Sheffield Faculty of Law, 1992), ch. 3.

[207] PACE, s. 32(9).

[208] PACE, s. 19(6).

believing that it is necessary to do so in order to prevent it being concealed, lost, tampered with, or destroyed.[209]

Section 18 permits the constable to seize and retain anything, other than items subject to legal privilege, which he has reasonable grounds for suspecting is evidence relating to the arrestable offence for which the arrestee was arrested or to another arrestable offence which is connected with or similar to that offence (such as evidence of other burglaries where the person is arrested for burglary).[210] It is not necessary for the necessity condition under section 19 to be satisfied if the seizure is made under section 18, as the powers in section 19 are additional to, rather than a qualification of, other seizure powers.[211] On the other hand, any seizure which relates to an offence unconnected with that for which the arrest was made will have to be justified by reference to section 19, including the necessity condition.

(3) Search of the person and premises after arrest at a police station.

If a person is arrested at a police station, he must immediately be told that he is under arrest,[212] and he becomes the responsibility of the custody officer or person performing the functions of custody officer, who must decide whether or not a charge or detention should be authorized. (The role of the custody officer and the rights of the suspect are described below.) If detention is authorized, the custody officer opens a custody record. He must then record everything which the arrestee has with him.[213] This gives rise to powers of search which are the same as those which a custody has where the person is brought to the police station having been arrested elsewhere. These are discussed below, in the context of treatment of arrested suspects. All searches are controlled by the custody officer.

Searches of the premises controlled or occupied by a person arrested at the police station are controlled by section 18, above, where the arrest was for an arrestable offence. In other cases, access to premises depends either on the consent of the occupier or on obtaining a warrant to enter (if one is available).

---

[209] PACE, s. 19(2), (3). There is also power to require information contained in a computer accessible from the premises to be produced so it can be taken away, on similar grounds: s. 19(4).

[210] PACE, s. 18(2).   [211] PACE, s. 19(5).   [212] PACE, s. 29.

[213] PACE, s. 54(1).

5.6 RIGHTS OF DETAINED SUSPECTS BEFORE CHARGE

The Royal Commission on Criminal Procedure recommended that the common-law powers in relation to detention without charge, which were uncertain and hard to enforce, should be replaced with a code which would give the powers to the police which were needed in the fight against crime, but would balance them with protections for the rights of suspects. This principle was carried into the Police and Criminal Evidence Act 1984 so successfully that, while civil liberties groups complained that the police were being given sweeping new powers which infringed people's liberties, the police complained that they were being hamstrung by the new rights given to suspects and the complicated procedures put in place to safeguard them. Neither party's assessment was fair, and it is arguable that the Act's capacity to engender disapproving rhetoric from all sides is the best indication that the right balance was found.

The Act gave suspects a number of enforceable rights for the first time. The suspect's right to inform a person that he had been arrested, first given (but in a more limited form and without any enforcement procedure) by section 62 of the Criminal Law Act 1977, was extended: section 56. A right to legal advice was given for the first time by section 58. The Act extended the period for which people could be held without charge, but only in respect of a new class of 'serious arrestable offences', and a system of reviews was established to authorize detention, including (after a maximum of 36 hours) a hearing by a magistrates' court. Elaborate reporting and recording provisions were established to make it as difficult as possible for the police to abuse their powers. The *Code of Practice for the Detention, Treatment and Questioning of Persons by Police Officers* (Code C) laid down standards to be met in the treatment of those in custody. The custody officer was made responsible for ensuring compliance with the Act and Codes, breach of which became a disciplinary offence. This section deals with these matters from the viewpoint of the protection of suspects' rights.[214]

(1) The right not to be held unnecessarily

(i) *General.* The custody officer is responsible for ensuring that suspects are not held at all if there is no necessity for doing so, and are not held

---

[214] For detailed treatment of the provisions as they affect police powers and procedures generally, see Michael Zander, *The Police and Criminal Evidence Act 1984*, 2nd edn. (1990); Bevan and Lidstone, *Investigation of Crime*; Keith Bottomley *et al.*, *The Impact of Pace: Policing in a Northern Force* (Hull: Centre for Criminology and Criminal Justice, 1991).

for longer than necessary. The necessity principle was recommended by the Royal Commission on Criminal Procedure as the proper basis for police powers of detention, in order to minimize the ambiguity and uncertainty of the detention powers as they operated before PACE.[215] As soon as practicable after a person has been arrested at a police station, has been brought to a station after arrest elsewhere (either without warrant or under a warrant which is not endorsed for bail), or has gone to a police station to surrender to police bail, the Act provides that the custody officer must first decide whether there is sufficient evidence to charge him with the offence for which he was arrested. The custody officer may detain the suspect for such period as is necessary to enable him to make this decision.[216] If there is enough evidence, the suspect must be either released without charge or charged forthwith,[217] and either released (on bail or without bail) or detained to appear before a magistrates' court. If there is insufficient evidence to charge the suspect, he has a right to be released immediately, on bail or without bail, unless the custody officer has reasonable grounds for believing (not merely suspecting) that detention without charge is 'necessary to secure or preserve evidence relating to the offence for which [the suspect] is under arrest or to obtain such evidence by questioning him'.[218] This gives statutory recognition to the propriety of arresting a person for the purpose of questioning him, making arrest and detention a step in the investigation process rather than the commencement of the prosecution process. Where the custody officer has such grounds, he (and he alone) may authorize detention.[219]

Although the decision to charge or release is the custody officer's, he is not sufficiently independent of his police colleagues to be regarded as a 'judge or other officer authorised by law to exercise judicial powers' within the meaning of Article 5(3) of the European Convention. His review of the grounds for detention therefore does not provide the prompt judicial or quasi-judicial review required by the Article. Nor does review by an executive rather than judicial officer, the Secretary of State, after 48 hours under the terrorism legislation. This seems to have been accepted by the government in *Brogan* v. *United Kingdom*.[220] That this is correct is borne out by the fact that, in practice, the custody officer

[215] RCCP, *Report*, paras. 3.94–3.110.   [216] PACE, s. 37(1), (10).
[217] PACE, s. 37(7).   [218] PACE, s. 37(2).   [219] PACE, s. 37(3).
[220] Eur. Ct. HR, Series A, No. 145, Judgment of 29 Nov.1988. If a sufficiently independent legal professional had to make the decision, it would apparently satisfy the demands of Article 5(3) even if the person was connected with the prosecution process. A District Attorney was held to be acceptable in *Schiesser* v. *Switzerland*, Eur. Ct. HR Series A, No. 34, (1979) 2 EHRR 417, so a solicitor in the Crown Prosecution Service would probably be equally acceptable. Cp. *De Jong, Baljet and Van Den Brink* v. *Netherlands* Eur. Ct. HR Series A, No. 77, (1984) 8 EHRR 20 on military arrests. *A fortiori*, a magistrates' court would be adequately judicial.

inevitably relies so heavily on the account given by the arresting officer (both because of the lack of independent sources of information and because of a desire not to compromise the perceived authority of the arresting officer in the presence of outsiders) that it is almost unknown for him to refuse to authorize detention, at least initially, if the arresting officer requests it.[221] Indeed, the evidence is that the process of authorizing detention quickly became formalized so that the grounds for arrest or detention are rarely checked at all, making the necessity principle entirely ineffective as a protection for suspects' rights. David Dixon *et al.* write of their observational study of a North of England force:

> in almost all observed cases, custody officers did not inquire into the circumstances of arrest: they simply asked a question such as 'What has she been arrested for?', expecting and getting only the briefest of answers (for example, 'shop theft' or 'breach of the peace') needed to complete the custody record section for 'reasons for arrest'. . . . We observed no instances of a custody officer refusing to accept a suspect into detention.[222]

As soon as detention is authorized, the custody officer must open a custody record for the detainee, and in it must record the reasons for detention.[223] In practice these usually simply parrot the statutory terms (for example, 'detained to obtain evidence by questioning him'). This is less a protection for the suspect's right to be free of arbitrary detention than a bureaucratic protection for the police officers against disciplinary proceedings for procedural wrongdoing.[224] The suspect must be told the reason for his detention unless he is incapable of understanding what is said, is violent or likely to become violent, or is in urgent need of medical attention.[225]

Once detention has been authorized, the right to be free of unnecessary detention becomes a right to be free of unnecessarily prolonged detention. If the detainee is not promptly released, Article 5(3) of the European Convention guarantees a prompt appearance before a judge or other judicial officer. In *Brogan v. United Kingdom*,[226] the European Court of Human Rights accepted that the length of time which may be allowed to elapse without infringing the 'promptness' requirement had to be

---

[221] Ian McKenzie, Rod Morgan and Robert Reiner, 'Helping the Police with Their Inquiries: The Necessity Principle and Voluntary Attendance at the Police Station' [1990] Crim. LR 22–33 at 23–24; David Dixon, Keith Bottomley, Clive Coleman, Martin Gill, and David Wall, 'Safeguarding the Rights of Suspects in Police Custody' (1990) 1 *Policing and Society* 115–40 at 129–30.

[222] Dixon *et al.*, 'Safeguarding', 129–30.

[223] Code C, para. 2.1; PACE, s. 37(4), s. 39(1)(*b*).

[224] See McKenzie, Morgan and Reiner, 'Helping the Police', 24–6.

[225] PACE, s. 37(5), (6).

[226] Eur. Ct. HR, Series A, No. 145, (1988) 11 EHRR 117.

judged in the light of the object of the Article, which is to protect an individual's fundamental right to liberty against arbitrary state interference. Under the Prevention of Terrorism (Temporary Provisions) Act 1984, detention without charge for 48 hours was permitted, after which time there would be a review by the Secretary of State who could authorize a further period of five days, making a week in all. The majority of the Court held that 'promptly', or *aussitôt* as in the French text of the Convention, demands less delay than words like 'speedily'. Even allowing for the special problems of terrorist investigations, only limited flexibility was permitted. Accordingly the Court held by twelve votes to seven that there had been a breach of Article 5(3) when people were held without judicial control for periods of which the shortest was four days and six hours. Despite this, for security reasons the government felt unable to introduce independent judicial controls on the period of detention without charge in terrorist cases when it replaced the 1984 Act with the Prevention of Terrorism (Temporary Provisions) Act 1989, and has entered a derogation from Article 5(3) to cover such cases. The validity of this derogation is the subject of cases declared admissible by the European Commission of Human Rights, where applicants are arguing that the derogation goes further than is necessitated by the exigencies of the situation in Northern Ireland.[227]

In relation to the period for which people can lawfully be detained in non-terrorist cases in England and Wales, PACE imposes an upper limit on detention without charge of 24 hours from the time of arrival at the police station following arrest elsewhere, and, where the arrest took place at the station, 24 hours from the time of the arrest, in most cases.[228] The overall effect of the detention provisions seems to have been that people in more serious cases are being detained without charge for less time than before PACE came into force. On the other hand, in straightforward or less serious cases people are being detained for slightly longer periods, perhaps because of the additional procedural and record-keeping demands made of the police by the Act.[229]

The Act specifies that reviews of detention must be carried out within prescribed periods, to ensure that the criteria for detention are still met. Where the suspect has not yet been charged, the criteria for continuing to detain him are the same as those for initial authorization of detention,[230] save that the review must be carried out by a review officer of at

[227] The derogation applies only to Northern Ireland. See Art. 15; *Brannigan and McBride* v. *UK*, Applications Nos. 14553/89 and 14554/89, declared admissible by the Commission on 28 Feb. 1991.

[228] PACE, s. 41(1), (2).

[229] Irving and McKenzie, *Regulating Custodial Interviews*; Dixon *et al.*, 'Safeguarding', 128–9, 132.   [230] PACE, s. 40(8).

least the rank of inspector, rather than the custody officer.[231] Where the suspect has been charged before the review, the review officer is the custody officer, who must order his release (either on bail or without bail) unless: (i) there is reasonable doubt about his name or address; or (ii) the custody officer has reasonable grounds for believing that the person's detention is necessary for his own good or to prevent him causing physical injury to another or loss of or damage to property; or (iii) the custody officer has reasonable grounds for believing that the accused will fail to appear in court, or that detention is necessary to prevent him from interfering with the administration of justice or with the investigation of any offence; or (iv) the person is an arrested juvenile, and the custody officer has reasonable grounds for believing that he ought to be detained in his own interests.[232]

The evidence is that these reviews tend to be as formalized as the initial detention decision. Even the right to make written or oral representations, given by the Act to the detainee (unless he is asleep at the time of the review) and to his solicitor if available at the time of the review,[233] seems to be rarely exercised, largely because solicitors have found that representations rarely make any difference to the outcome of the review.[234] Despite this, the opportunity to make representations has been treated as mandatory in at least one case before a stipendiary magistrate, so that an authorization of detention after a review where the right to make representations has been improperly denied is invalid. This makes the subsequent detention unlawful, and any magistrates' court to which the police apply for a warrant of further detention after 36 hours lacks jurisdiction to grant the warrant.[235]

The time limits within which reviews must be carried out (the first within six hours of the initial authorization of detention, later ones within nine hours of the one before)[236] and the right to make representations on reviews are, therefore, not a strong protection to the rights of suspects to be free of unnecessary detention.

---

[231] PACE, s. 40(1)(b).   [232] PACE, ss. 38(1), 40(1)(a).

[233] PACE, s. 40(12), (13). The review officer need not hear oral representations from the detainee if he considers that the detainee is unfit to make them by reason of his condition or behaviour: s. 40(14).

[234] See Dixon et al., 'Safeguarding', 130–1.

[235] *In the matter of an application for a warrant of further detention* [1988] Crim. LR 296.

[236] PACE, s. 40(3). There is provision for postponing a review to the first practicable time if it is not practicable to carry it out before the set time, for example because the suspect is being interviewed and the review officer is satisfied that interrupting the questioning would prejudice the investigation, or if no review officer is available at that time: s. 40(4), (5). In any case, time limits are to be treated as approximate only: s. 45(2).

(ii) *Detention beyond twenty-four hours.* After twenty-four hours from the time when detention was first authorized (not counting time spent being treated in hospital without being questioned by the police),[237] the suspect must be released (either on bail or without bail) if he has not been charged.[238] However, in certain cases there are procedures for continuing detention without charge. This can be authorized by a superintendent or above, at any time after the second review by the review officer but before twenty-four hours have elapsed from the time when detention was first authorized.[239] It can be authorized for a period of up to twelve hours following the time 24 hours after detention was first authorized.[240] Before authorizing this continued detention, the superintendent who is responsible for the station must have reasonable grounds for believing: (*a*) that continued detention without charge is necessary to secure or preserve evidence relating to an offence for which the suspect is under arrest or to obtain such evidence by questioning him, thus maintaining the form of the necessity principle; *and* (*b*) that the suspect is under arrest for a serious arrestable offence, as distinct from any offence for which an arrest may be made which may justify detention for up to twenty-four hours; *and* (*c*) that the investigation is being conducted diligently and expeditiously (indicating, again, that the suspect is not being kept waiting in detention for an unnecessarily long time).[241]

The review should be carried out in person, not over the telephone.[242] The superintendent, besides being more senior than an inspector, is likely to be more remote from the investigating officers, and inspire a good deal of respect. It is not surprising, therefore, that Dixon *et al.* observed in their North of England research force that 'such reviews were more rigorous than inspectors' reviews; investigating officers did not assume that such an extension would be granted (as they did with earlier reviews)'.[243] This offers greater security for the right not to be unnecessarily detained than do the earlier procedures, both because the officers concerned are unlikely to seek a continuation of detention without good reason and because the conditions to be met are likely to form rules which genuinely govern police behaviour at all levels, rather than merely presentational rules which are used to justify behaviour after the event but exercise little real influence over the decision-making process.[244]

---

[237] PACE, s. 41(6).   [238] PACE, s. 41(7).   [239] PACE, s. 42(4).

[240] PACE, ss. 41(8), 42(1) and (2).   [241] PACE, s. 42(1).

[242] Code C, Note for Guidance 15C, which nevertheless allows earlier reviews to be conducted by telephone if that is the only practicable way of proceeding, so long as the procedural requirements of PACE and of the Prevention of Terrorism (Temporary Provisions) Act 1989, Sched. 3, are complied with.

[243] 'Safeguarding', 131.

[244] For the classification of rules, and discussion of presentational rules in particular, see Smith and Gray, *Police and People in London*, 440–3.

(iii) *Serious arrestable offences*. This is a convenient point at which to explain the nature of serious arrestable offences. A serious arrestable offence, as the name suggests, is an offence which (*a*) is arrestable within the meaning of section 24 of PACE, discussed earlier, and (*b*) satisfies one of the statutory criteria for seriousness. These statutory criteria are of two kinds. There are some listed offences which are always serious. It is always a serious arrestable offence to do anything which constitutes offences involving treason, murder, manslaughter, rape, kidnapping, incest with a girl under the age of 13, buggery with a boy under the age of 16 (with or without consent) or with anyone who has not consented, or indecent assault which constitutes an act of gross indecency.[245] Offences under section 2 of the Explosive Substances Act 1883 (causing an explosion likely to endanger life), section 5 of the Sexual Offences Act 1956 (intercourse with a girl under the age of 13), the Firearms Act 1968, sections 16 (possessing a firearm with intent to injure), 17(1) (using a firearm or imitation firearm to resist arrest), and 18 (carrying a firearm with criminal intent), hostage–taking under the Taking of Hostages Act 1982, section 1, hijacking under the Aviation Security Act 1982, section 1, torture under section 134 of the Criminal Justice Act 1988, causing death by reckless driving under section 1 of the Road Traffic Act 1988, and sections 1 (endangering safety at aerodromes), 9 (hijacking ships), and 10 (seizing control of fixed drilling platforms) of the Aviation and Maritime Security Act 1990, are always serious arrestable offences.[246] So are those offences listed in paragraphs (*a*) to (*d*) of the definition of drug-trafficking offences in section 38(1) of the Drug Trafficking Offences Act 1986.[247]

Next, there is a category of offences which, though not intrinsically necessarily serious enough to justify the application of extended police powers to their investigation, may become serious enough if the facts of particular cases display certain characteristics. These are offences which have led or are intended to lead, or involve a threat which if carried out would be likely to lead, to any of the following consequences:[248]

(*a*)   serious harm to the security of the state or to public order, which brings in, for example, numerous offences under the Official Secrets Act 1911–1989 and the Public Order Act 1986;

(*b*)   serious interference with the administration of justice or with the investigation of offences or of a particular offence, which potentially brings in contempt of court, conspiring to pervert the course

---

[245] PACE, s. 116(2)(*a*) and Sched. 5, Part I.

[246] PACE, s. 116(2)(*b*) and Sched. 5, Part II.

[247] PACE, s. 116(2)(*aa*), inserted by Drug Trafficking Offences Act 1986, s. 36. These offences include assisting another person to retain the proceeds of drug trafficking.

[248] PACE, s. 116(3), (4), (6).

of justice, and making a disclosure which prejudices a drug-trafficking investigation;[249]

(c) the death of any person;

(d) serious injury[250] to any person, thus encompassing a threat to infect a person with HIV or to adulterate food with a noxious substance as part of a blackmail plot;

(e) substantial financial gain to any person, so that the amount stolen may make a serious arrestable offence out of a simple theft; and

(f) serious financial loss to any person, judged according to its seriousness for the person who suffers it,[251] so that stealing a small amount from a poor pensioner might be a serious arrestable offence while stealing goods to a larger value from a large store,[252] or from a group of joint owners none of whom has a particularly valuable share,[253] might not be one.

Finally, there are some offences under the Prevention of Terrorism (Temporary Provisions) Act 1989 which are always serious arrestable offences for the purpose of deciding whether to delay allowing an arrested suspect to inform someone that he has been arrested or obtain legal advice, but which are not necessarily serious for other purposes, including deciding whether to authorize continued detention. These offences are those under section 2 (membership of, and soliciting or inviting support for, a proscribed organization, etc.), section 8 (failing to comply with an exclusion order, or facilitating breach of one), and sections 9, 10, and 11 (soliciting, inviting, or receiving, giving or lending, or assisting in the retention or control of, funds for contributing to acts of terrorism or proscribed organizations), together with attempts and conspiracies to commit those offences. When making decisions about these offences for purposes for which they are not necessarily regarded as serious arrestable offences, or in relation to other offences under the Act, the police must either rely on the special provisions of the 1989 Act where they are applicable or show that one of the special considerations under section 116(6) of PACE, above, applies to the case.

(iv) *Detention beyond thirty-six hours after the first authorization of detention.* If the investigating officers feel the need to detain a suspect without charge for more than thirty-six hours, they must apply to the magistrates' court for a warrant of further detention.[254] There must be a full hearing of the

---

[249] See Drug Trafficking Offences Act 1986, s. 31.

[250] 'Injury' includes any disease, and any impairment of a person's physical or mental condition: PACE, s. 116(8).

[251] PACE, s. 116(7).   [252] *R.* v. *Smith (Eric)* [1987] Crim. LR 579.

[253] *R.* v. *McIvor* [1987] Crim. LR 409.

[254] If the application is made after the 36 hour period expires, and the magistrates

application, at which the suspect will be entitled to be present and represented by a solicitor or barrister.[255] The application for a warrant of further detention must be made on oath by a constable and supported by an information, which must state the nature of the offence for which the arrest was made, the general nature of the evidence supporting the arrest, the inquiries which have been made and the further inquiries which the police propose to make, and the reasons for believing that the continued detention of the arrestee is necessary for the purposes of the further inquiries, and must satisfy the magistrates that there are reasonable grounds for believing that the application is justified.[256] Detention is justified only if the offence is a serious arrestable offence, the investigation is being conducted diligently and expeditiously, and detention without charge is necessary to secure or preserve evidence relating to an offence for which the detainee is under arrest or to obtain such evidence by questioning him.[257] If the magistrates are satisfied, they may issue a warrant which authorizes further detention for such a specified period, not exceeding thirty-six hours, as the magistrates think, fit having regard to the evidence before them,[258] particularly considering the importance of the necessity principle. If, at the end of the further period, the police still consider that it necessary to detain the person without charge, they may make a new application to the magistrates' court for an extension to the warrant of further detention. The criteria and procedures for applying for and granting the extension are the same as those for granting the warrant in the first place,[259] although it is to be expected that magistrates will view the reasons which are said to justify detention without charge with increasing scepticism as time passes. The extension, if granted, will be for a specified period not exceeding thirty-six hours, and the total time spent in detention without charge after the relevant time, within the meaning of section 41(2) of the 1984 Act, must not exceed ninety-six hours.

Strict observance of time limits is not of the essence in relation to the detention provisions: section 45(2) provides, 'Any reference in this Part of this Act to a period or time of day is to be treated as approximate

consider that it would have been reasonable to make it before the time limit expired, the court must dismiss the application: PACE, s. 43(7). The detainee must then be immediately charged or released, on bail or without bail, and cannot be rearrested or subjected to a renewed application for that offence without fresh evidence which has come to light since the application was dismissed: PACE, s. 43(17), (18), (19).

[255] PACE, s. 43(2), (3). This means, incidentally, that the power to delay a suspect's exercise of the right to inform a person of his whereabouts and the right to receive legal advice cannot be delayed beyond the 36-hour period.

[256] PACE, s. 43(1), (14). The detainee must have been provided with a copy of the information: s. 43(2).

[257] PACE, s. 43(4).   [258] PACE, s. 43(11), (12).

[259] PACE, s. 44(1) and s. 43(4).

only.' This flexibility makes allowance for problems which may arise in practice. However, the limits are important protections for the fundamental rights of detainees, and going beyond a limit will always require a compelling explanation of the exigencies which made it unavoidable. The onus on the police is very substantial. For example, it has been held that they must contact the magistrates' clerk in good time to allow a bench to be assembled before the time limit expires. If the police fail to do so, bearing in mind such factors as the times of the magistrates' luncheon recess and when the time limits expire, the magistrates will have to reject the application, and the suspect will have to be either charged or released.[260]

(2) Rights to have someone informed of arrest and to consult solicitor

The evidence so far suggests that, at least until detention is reviewed by a superintendent after twenty-four hours, the necessity principle is of little help in limiting the period of detention. Of more significance to the suspect are the rights which he has while in detention, and the right to be told of his rights at the time of his arrival at the police station after arrest elsewhere, or the time of his arrest at a police station.

The custody officer must tell the suspect clearly about his rights to have someone informed of his arrest, to consult privately with a solicitor, available free of charge, and to consult the Codes of Practice.[261] It must be made clear that these are continuing rights, and, if not exercised at once, may be exercised at any time unless delayed in accordance with the Act. The custody officer is responsible for asking the suspect to sign the appropriate place in the custody record to signify whether or not he wants legal advice at that point, and, if it is requested, the custody officer must act to secure advice without delay.[262] Evidence from the USA, concerning the constitutional requirement, under the Fifth Amendment, that a person be informed of his right of silence and his right to counsel, suggested that the right to be informed can be thwarted by the manner in which the information is given. There is some evidence that the police in England and Wales too were giving the information, deliberately or not, in ways which either discouraged suspects from exercising their rights or

---

[260] R. v. Slough Justices, ex parte Stirling [1987] Crim. LR 576, DC.

[261] Code C, para. 3.1. The right to consult the Codes does not entitle a person arrested on suspicion of drunken driving to delay the taking of any specimen which is authorized under the Road Traffic Act 1988: DPP v. Billington [1988] RTR 231, DC; DPP v. Cornell, The Times, 13 July 1989, DC; Code C, Note for Guidance 3E. For criticism, see David Tucker, 'Drink-Drivers' PACE Rights: A Cause of Concern' [1990] Crim. LR 177–80.

[262] Code C, para. 3.5.

interfered with their understanding of the rights.[263] To some extent, this should be alleviated under the revised Code C, paragraph 3.2 of which provides for suspects to be provided with two written notices, one setting out the above three rights and explaining the arrangements for obtaining legal advice, the other setting out his other entitlements while in custody. The suspect can then read the notices at his leisure, if able to do so. Citizens of independent Commonwealth countries, and foreign nationals, must be informed as soon as practicable of their right to communicate with their countries' High Commissions, Embassies, or Consulates.[264]

There is some difficulty about the idea that a person who declines to exercise his rights does so voluntarily. People in custody are likely to be intimidated by the situation in which they find themselves, and amenable to any suggestion that they should not immediately exercise their rights. For example, suggestions that waiting for a solicitor will slow down the process and delay release might make the suspect feel that it is inappropriate to insist on rights. Consent to delay or waive exercise of rights is therefore questionable, even when it is apparently freely given.[265] For those who regard civil liberties principally as protecting people's autonomy, it goes against the grain to try to protect people against their own weakness. One can, however, justify imposing protection and regulation in situations which are inherently likely to overwhelm people's normal capacity for self-determination and free choice. Being detained in a police station is such a situation.

It is therefore proper to seek to control the extent to which a person who wishes to exercise rights can have his request for a solicitor, or to have someone informed of his arrest, overridden by the police. This is the approach which the Act takes. In particular, there must be a poster prominently displayed in every police station advertising the right to have legal advice.[266] The revised Codes of Practice further provide that no attempt should be made to dissuade the suspect from obtaining legal

---

[263] Andrew Sanders and Lee Bridges, 'Access to Legal Advice and Police Malpractice' [1990] *Crim. LR* 494–509, suggest that the police are using rule-bending 'ploys' when giving information, which result in suspects deciding not to exercise their rights in a significant proportion of cases (498–501). See also Michael McConville, Andrew Sanders, and Roger Leng, *The Case for the Prosecution* (London: Routledge, 1991). Other researchers disagree. For example, Dixon *et al.*, 'Safeguarding', 117, write: 'In general, rather than being a deliberate attempt to block access to rights, such practices are the product of a belief that suspects do not benefit from reading the Codes. (Problems increase when such assumptions are taken further, such as assuming that a suspect would not benefit from seeing a legal adviser.)' See also David Dixon, 'Legal Regulation and Police Malpractice' (1992) 1 *Soc. and Legal Studies* 515–41.

[264] Code C, para. 3.3.

[265] Dixon, Coleman, and Bottomley, 'Consent and the Legal Regulation', 356.

[266] Code C, para. 6.3.

advice, and reminders of the right must be given to the suspect every time an interview begins or recommences after a break, before every review of detention, before identification procedures are initiated, and before an intimate sample is requested.[267]

Before the 1984 Act, there was no right to legal advice. While there was a right to make a telephone call to a person, there was no sanction for interference with the right. The 1984 Act introduced rights to have someone informed that the suspect has been arrested, and to have legal advice in private, subject to a power to delay, designed to protect the administration of justice. A considerable caselaw has developed round these rights and the power to delay their exercise, but the right to legal advice in particular has been held on a number of occasions to be fundamental to the scheme of the detention provisions under the 1984 Act: this was one of the safeguards which was intended to balance the extension of police detention powers, and any infringement of the right is likely to lead to a challenge to the admission at trial of evidence obtained as a result.[268] Here, we consider the scope of the rights, and the circumstances which may be held to justify delaying their exercise.

(i) *The scope of the right to have someone informed.* This right comes into operation whenever an person has been arrested and is being detained in a police station or other premises. Such a person is entitled to have somebody informed, by the police, of the fact that he has been arrested and of where he is being detained. The classes of person whom a detainee is entitled to have contacted are widely drawn. The detainee may request to have a friend or relative contacted, or any other person who is known to him or who is likely to take an interest in his welfare. Once the request has been made, the police must comply with it as soon as practicable, unless delay is authorized.[269] This right applies every time a detainee is moved to new premises or another police station.[270] There may be some difficulty in complying: the person might not be contactable by telephone, and there may be a delay before a constable can be sent to the house to make contact in person. In addition, there may be reasons for an officer to make the call in person rather than by telephone. For example, when the police want to search the detainee's premises and do not want to alert other occupiers beforehand, it is easiest (and avoids the necessity for a formal authorization of delay) simply to deliver the message at the same time as searching the house.[271] If the first person named by the suspect cannot be contacted, the suspect must be invited to

---

[267] Code C, paras. 6.3, 6.4, 6.5, 11.2 and 15.3; Code D, paras. 2.15(ii) and 5.2.
[268] *R. v. Samuel* [1988] QB 615, [1988] 2 All ER 135, CA.
[269] PACE, s. 56(1).   [270] Code C, para. 5.3.
[271] Dixon *et al.*, 'Safeguarding', 118.

name up to two others; if they cannot be contacted either, the custody officer or the officer in charge of the investigation has a discretion to go on trying other people, but need not do so.[272]

Apart from the general right under section 56, the custody officer has special responsibilities under section 57 where the detainee is a child or young person (hereafter 'child') within the meaning of the Children and Young Persons Act 1933. First, such steps as are reasonably practicable must be taken to find out who is responsible for the child's welfare (i.e. his parent or guardian,[273] or other person who has for the time being assumed responsibility for his welfare).[274] That person must then be informed, as soon as practicable, of the arrest and the reason for it, and where the child is being held.[275] These 'rights' are in addition to those in section 56, and are not subject to the provisions authorizing delay, discussed below, which apply in relation to the rights under sections 56 and 58.

Code C, paragraph 5.4, provides that, at the custody officer's discretion, any detainee may receive visits. Under paragraph 5.6 a suspect is entitled to be supplied with writing materials on request, and is to be allowed to speak on the telephone for a reasonable time to one person. These, by contrast with the right under section 56 of PACE, are expressed to be privileges, not rights. They may be at the public expense, at the custody officer's discretion.[276] They do not figure in the 1984 Act itself, and under the Code can be delayed or denied by an officer of at least the rank of inspector who considers that the conditions which would justify delaying the right to have someone informed of the suspect's whereabouts under section 56 apply.[277] Furthermore, the suspect must be told that anything he says or writes (other than a communication to a solicitor, which is likely to attract legal professional privilege) may be read or listened to, and given in evidence, and a telephone call may be terminated if it is being abused (a nicely vague term).[278] Under paragraph 5.8, a record must be made of all letters, messages, telephone calls, or visits made or received.

---

[272] Code C, para. 5.1. Where a friend, relative, or person with an interest in the suspect's welfare contacts the police to inquire about the suspect, the police must give the information if the suspect agrees, unless delay has been authorized: Code C, para. 5.5.

[273] This includes the authority having care of a child who is in the care of a local authority, or a voluntary organization in which parental rights and duties have been vested. On the role of parents as appropriate adults, see s. (3) below.

[274] Where the child is subject to a supervision order, the person responsible for his supervision must also be informed as soon as practicable.

[275] Children and Young Persons Act 1933, s. 34, as amended by PACE, s. 57.

[276] Code C, para. 5.7.   [277] Code C., para. 5.6.   [278] Code C, para. 5.7.

(ii) *The scope of the right to legal advice.* Section 58(1) of PACE provides that the detainee is entitled, if he so requests, to consult a solicitor privately at any time. When a request is made, it must be complied with as soon as practicable, and the custody officer must act on it without delay except so far as a delay is authorized in accordance with the section.[279] Where the person detained was a juvenile, or a mentally disordered or mentally handicapped person, who might not have understood the significance of what was being said, some custody officers used to take the view that they ought not to act on a request for legal advice unless and until an 'appropriate adult' arrived and ratified the request. However, this was always rather odd, as people in those vulnerable groups particularly need advice and representation. Accordingly, the revised Code C makes it clear that requests from such people for legal advice should be acted on immediately, without waiting for an appropriate adult.[280]

If a legal adviser arrives uninvited at the police station to see the detainee, the detainee must be told that the adviser is there, and asked whether he wants to see him, even if the detainee has previously declined legal advice.[281] If there is a delay before a solicitor can be contacted or can reach the police station, the suspect must normally not be interviewed (or interviewed further) until he has received the legal advice. There are four exceptions permitted to this rule.

First, delay in exercising the right may in appropriate cases be authorized in accordance with the procedure prescribed in Annex B to Code C. Secondly, an officer of the rank of superintendent or above may authorize an interview to continue or begin if he has reasonable grounds for believing that delay will involve an immediate risk of harm to persons or serious loss of or damage to property, or that awaiting the solicitor's arrival would cause unreasonable delay to the process of investigation. Once sufficient information has been obtained to avert the danger, the interview must cease until the adviser arrives.[282] Thirdly, an officer of the rank of inspector or above may authorize an interview without further delay if the suspect's selected solicitor cannot be contacted, or has indicated that he does not wish to be contacted, or has declined to attend, and the suspect has declined the offer of advice from a duty solicitor or the duty solicitor is unavailable.

The second and third grounds are rather too open-ended for comfort. In such cases there are good public-interest grounds for proceeding as quickly as possible, but it might better balance the rights of the suspect against the public interest in expeditious investigation to advise the

---

[279] PACE, s. 58(4); Code C, para. 6.2.

[280] Unfortunately, despite the importance of this provision, it is only in Note for Guidance 3G, rather than being an authoritative provision of the Code.

[281] Code C, para. 6.15.   [282] Code C, para. 6.7.

suspect of the difficulty and ask if he wants to contact another solicitor who might be able to get to the police station more quickly. Finally, where a suspect who initially asked for advice has changed his mind, and has given agreement in writing or on tape to be interviewed without receiving legal advice, an officer of the rank of inspector or above may permit the interview to start.[283]

Suspects are only statutorily entitled to be advised by solicitors.[284] 'Solicitor' is defined as 'a solicitor qualified to practise in accordance with the Solicitors Act 1974'.[285] This excludes articled or other clerks, legal executives, and private detectives or 'runners', presumably because such people are not subject to the code of professional ethics or the disciplinary controls enforced by the Law Society and the High Court. Nevertheless, such people are employed by some solicitors for the purpose of providing an advice service in police stations. Legal aid funding being limited, it would be uneconomic for many firms to provide a service to detainees in police stations if a qualified solicitor always had to attend. The viability of the service therefore depends heavily on some, if not most, attendances at police stations being conducted by unqualified personnel. Accordingly, the Code permits a solicitor to send a clerk or legal executive to give advice on his behalf, and provides that such people shall be admitted to police stations, subject to the discretion of an officer of the rank of inspector or above to exclude them if he 'considers that such a visit will hinder the investigation of crime'. The officer should exercise this discretion in the light of several considerations, including whether the identity and status of the person have been satisfactorily established, and whether he is of suitable character to provide legal advice (this would justify checking whether the person has a criminal record, and excluding him if he has one, unless the conviction was for a minor offence some while ago). In addition, any other matters in a letter of authorization from the solicitor should be considered.[286] If an inspector decides to exclude the clerk or legal executive, he should immediately inform the detainee and the solicitor, who may make alternative arrangements.[287]

This provision was introduced in response to concerns expressed by some senior police officers that wholly inappropriate people were being sent to advise suspects. This culminated in an application by a Bristol firm of solicitors for judicial review of instructions to exclude people whom they were sending as clerks to advise clients. The Divisional Court held that the police had a discretion to exclude people on various grounds, including the suitability of the person on the grounds (*inter alia*) of age,

---

[283] Code C, para. 6.6.   [284] PACE, s. 58(1).   [285] Code C, para. 6.12.
[286] Code C, paras. 6.12, 6.13.
[287] A record must be made in the custody record. Code C, para. 6.14.

mental capacity, appearance, and supposed criminal orientation.[288] This gave an immensely wide discretion to the inspector, and the revised Code C narrows the range of relevant considerations somewhat, while recommending in Note of Guidance 6F that inspectors who consider that a particular solicitor or firm is consistently sending unsuitable people should inform a superintendent, who may wish to complain to the Law Society. In practice, many of the clerks sent to police stations are former police officers, who may have close ties with the investigating officers, giving rise to a risk (or at least the appearance of one) that they will be more in sympathy with the police than with their clients. This could reduce the value of the advice and support which they give, and should be borne in mind by courts when considering whether people's rights have been adequately protected by having a clerk in attendance at an interview.[289]

Legal advice is often given on the telephone rather than in person.[290] In 1991 the legal aid rules were altered so as to allow payment to solicitors in certain classes of cases only if they attended in person at the police station. In view of the economic pressures, it seems more likely to have the effect of encouraging solicitors to give advice by telephone and not charge for it, than to cause them to attend more often at police stations. When an adviser does attend at the police station, the detainee must be permitted to have the adviser present during any interview which takes place while the adviser is available.[291] Once a legal adviser is present in an interview, the police may require him to leave only if his conduct is such that the investigating officer is unable properly to put questions to the suspect. If that occurs, the matter should be referred to an officer not below the rank of superintendent or (if no such officer is readily available) inspector, who will speak to the solicitor and then decide whether the interview should continue in the presence of the solicitor. If he decides that it should not, the suspect will be given an opportunity to consult another solicitor, and the interview will be delayed to allow the replacement to arrive. Removing a solicitor in this way should not occur unless the solicitor's conduct makes it appropriate to consider reporting him to the Law Society and, if he is a duty solicitor, to the Legal Aid Board.[292]

The adviser's role is to advise and support the detainee, not merely to be an independent witness. Not all advisers are conscious of this, and

---

[288] R. v. Chief Constable of Avon and Somerset, ex parte Robinson [1989] 1 WLR 793, [1989] 2 All ER 15, DC.

[289] Dixon et al., 'Safeguarding', 123–5; cp. R. v. Dunn [1990] Crim. LR 572, CA.

[290] A. Sanders, L. Bridges, A. Mulvaney, and G. Crozier, Advice and Assistance at Police Stations and the 24 Hour Duty Solicitor Scheme (London: Lord Chancellor's Dept., 1990).

[291] Code C, paras. 6.8, 6.12.   [292] Code, C, paras. 6.10 and 6.11.

there are good reasons for solicitors or clerks who regularly visit a police station to avoid acting in such a way as to sour their relations with the police. In practice, legal advisers rarely interfere with the conduct of an interview, and tend to assist investigations by encouraging clients to tell their stories more often than they interfere with it by advising silence.[293] The passive adviser is no danger to the police; if anything, there is reason to doubt the usefulness of legal advice to the suspect. It is, perhaps, not surprising that only around 25 per cent of detainees request legal advice, nor particularly worrying that not all of those actually receive it.

(iii) *Grounds for delaying exercise of the rights*. The criteria for delaying exercise of the right to have someone informed that one has been arrested, and the right to legal advice, are the same, although the application of the criteria varies slightly between the two rights because of the difference between giving information to someone who may be a concerned in the crime and obtaining advice from a professional. In each case, delay may be authorized only by an officer of the rank of superintendent or above, in relation to a person who has been arrested for a serious arrestable offence or under the terrorism provisions.[294] Before the superintendent may authorize delay, he must have reasonable grounds for believing that the exercise of the right in question at the time when the detainee wants to exercise it would have one of three effects in relation to most serious arrestable offences, with other grounds in respect of arrests under the terrorism provisions and offences for which confiscation orders can be made:

(*a*) it will lead to interference with or harm to evidence connected with a serious arrestable offence (not necessarily that for which the suspect was arrested), or to interference with or physical injury to other people; or

(*b*) it will lead to the alerting of other people suspected of having committed such an offence but not yet arrested for it; or

(*c*) it will hinder the recovery of any property obtained as a result of such an offence.[295]

Where the offence is a drug-trafficking offence or one which falls within the provisions of the Criminal Justice Act 1988, Part VI (i.e.

---

[293] Dixon *et al.*, 'Safeguarding', 124; David Dixon, 'Politics, Research and Symbolism in Criminal Justice: The Right of Silence and the Police and Criminal Evidence Act' (1991) 20 *Anglo-Amer. LR* 27–50 at 43–46.

[294] PACE, ss. 56(2), (10), (11); 58(6), (12), (13). The terrorism provisions are those which allow for arrest and detention without warrant in relation to terrorist offences, proscribed organisations and exclusion orders: Prevention of Terrorism (Temporary Provisions) Act 1989, s. 14 and Scheds. 2 and 5; PACE, s. 65.

[295] PACE, ss. 56(5), 58(8).

offences for which orders can be made to confiscate the proceeds of crime), the exercise of the rights can also be delayed where the superintendent has reasonable grounds to believe that:

(d) the person detained has benefited from the offence, and that the recovery of the benefits in respect of which a confiscation order might be made following conviction will be hindered by the exercise of the right.[296]

Where the person is detained under the terrorism provisions, the exercise of the right may be delayed where the superintendent has reasonable grounds to believe that:

(e) it will lead to interference with the gathering of information about the commission, preparation or instigation of acts of terrorism (bringing to mind the fact that the arrest and detention powers under the Prevention of Terrorism (Temporary Provisions) Act 1989 are intended to be used principally for detention for intelligence gathering rather than purely for detaining suspects before charge); or

(f) by alerting any person, it will make it more difficult to prevent an act of terrorism, or to secure the apprehension, prosecution, or conviction of anyone in connection with the commission, preparation, or instigation of such an act.[297]

It is important to bear in mind the other side of the coin: there are numerous considerations which will *not* justify delaying the exercise of rights. The grounds relied on to justify a delay in the exercise of the rights must be reasonably supportable by reference to the facts as known at the time. For example, in *R. v. Samuel*[298] the police claimed that they had delayed the detained suspect's access to legal advice because they feared that an accomplice still at large might be alerted, yet the suspect's mother had been told of the suspect's arrest hours before the superintendent took the decision to delay access to a solicitor. The Court of Appeal held that an alleged confession made without the benefit of legal advice should have been excluded as a result, and quashed the conviction. In *R. v. Alladice*[299] a suspect had been openly arrested in court, amongst people known to him, and his house had been searched in his mother's presence, so the police claim to have believed that a solicitor might have tipped off other suspects was hard to believe.

Where other suspects remain at large, it may well be reasonable to delay informing a detainee's friends or family that he has been arrested under section 56 of PACE, if they are likely to be in contact with the

---

[296] PACE, ss. 56(5A), 58(8A).
[298] [1988] QB 615, [1988] 2 All ER 135, CA.
[297] PACE, ss. 56(11) and 58(13).
[299] (1988) 87 Cr. AR. 380, CA.

other suspects. On the other hand, it will not often be reasonable to delay access to legal advice on this ground, unless there are reasonable grounds for believing that the particular legal adviser whom the detainee wants to see is likely to give away to other suspects the fact that the police are on to them. The superintendent must therefore examine separately the grounds for delaying each of the rights.[300] It is not usually argued that the solicitors are likely intentionally to aid or abet a suspect's escape. However, it is sometimes suggested that solicitors are gullible, and can be manipulated by criminals into passing on coded messages without realizing their significance. Some judges are ready to accept that this is a real danger,[301] while others are more sceptical,[302] but all accept two principles: first, that the police are entitled to be suspicious of legal advisers until they know who the adviser is to be (particularly as so many advisers are clerks or 'runners' rather than qualified solicitors); secondly, that they are not entitled to deny access to a reputable and experienced person with no known criminal connections.[303] The second principle is supported by Note for Guidance B4 in Annex B to Code C, advising that the superintendent may authorize delay 'only if he has reasonable grounds to believe that the specific solicitor will, inadvertently or otherwise, pass on a message from the detained person or act in some other way which will lead' to any of the grounds justifying delay coming about.

A special problem arises where several suspects are in custody waiting to be interviewed and they ask for the same solicitor. In such cases the risk of accidental contamination of evidence, prejudicing the investigation, is marked, and solicitors, recognizing a risk that they will appear to be helping suspects to co-ordinate their stories, will usually co-operate with police by arranging for the suspects to be advised by different people. Any question of a conflict of interest is for the solicitor to resolve in the light of the relevant code of professional ethics; it is not a matter for the police. On the other hand, where unreasonable delay will be caused to the investigation if the same solicitor has to advise several suspects, the police may be justified in proceeding to interview a suspect before the solicitor has seen him.[304]

As Code C, Annex B, paragraph 3, makes clear, the police are not justified in delaying access to legal advice merely because they fear that a solicitor will advise the suspect to remain silent. Where access has been improperly denied on this ground, a subsequent admission made without the benefit of advice is likely to be excluded from evidence on the ground of unfairness under section 78 of PACE.[305] The right to receive

---

[300] R. v. Parris [1989] Crim. LR 214, CA; Code C, Annex B, Note for Guidance B5.
[301] e.g. Lord Lane CJ in Alladice, above; Re Walters [1987] Crim. LR 577, DC.
[302] e.g. Hodgson J. in Samuel, above.   [303] Samuel, above.
[304] Code C, para. 6.6(b)(ii); Note for Guidance 6G.   [305] R. v. Samuel, above.

advice must not become a right to receive only such advice as suits the police. In England and Wales (unlike Northern Ireland) the common-law right to refuse to answer questions has not been removed from suspects.

(iv) *Ending the delay.* Exercise of the rights may only be delayed for as long as the grounds justifying delay continue to obtain,[306] and in any case must end after 36 hours (or, in the case of people detained under the terrorism provisions, 48 hours) when detained suspects have to be either charged, released, or brought before a magistrates' court.[307] When the authorization of delay no longer applies, the suspect must be told, asked as soon as practicable whether he wants legal advice, and, if he does, it must be obtained in the normal way.[308] If this is not done, and an interview takes place without legal advice for the suspect, the breach of the Code is quite likely to be regarded as making unfair the admission of any statement made as a result.[309]

(3) Special protection for the rights of vulnerable groups

Suspects who are, or who appear to be,[310] juveniles, mentally handicapped, mentally disordered, blind, visually handicapped, or unable to read are in specially vulnerable positions, and the Act and Code C give them special protection in the form of the attendance of an 'appropriate adult'. The appropriate adult's job is not merely to act as a witness, but is to support and advise the suspect in accordance with his best interests, and to facilitate communication. The custody officer should explain this to the detainee,[311] and (at least where he is present at an interview) it should also be explained to the appropriate adult.[312] The appropriate adult may request legal advice on behalf of the detainee, even if the detainee has declined acess to legal advice.[313]

(i) *Juveniles.*[314] The Act provides that the custody officer must arrange for an 'appropriate adult' to attend when a juvenile is detained. The appropriate adult for a juvenile is the parent or guardian (or, if he is in care, the local authority of voluntary organisation in whose care he is), or a social worker, or, failing either of those, another responsible adult who is not a police officer or police employee.[315] Normally, the preference is to use

---

[306] PACE, ss. 56(9), 58(11).   [307] PACE, ss. 56(3) and (11)(*b*), 58(5) and (13)(*a*).
[308] Code C, Annex B, paras. 4, 9.
[309] See *R.* v. *Walsh* [1989] Crim. LR 822, CA.   [310] Code C, para. 1.6.
[311] Code C, para. 3.12.   [312] Code C, para. 11.16.   [313] Code C, para. 3.13.
[314] David Dixon, 'Juvenile Suspects and the Police and Criminal Evidence Act', in David Freestone (ed.), *Children and the Law: Essays in Honour of Professor H. K. Bevan* (Hull: Hull University Press, 1990), 107–29.
[315] Code C, para. 1.7(*a*).

the parent or guardian, as being the person most likely to feel responsible for and have a sympathetic relationship with the juvenile. However, there are circumstances in which this may not be the case. For example, as the appropriate adult has an advisory role, it is important that the juvenile should be able to veto the selection of a parent who is estranged from the juvenile and in whom he puts no trust.[316] The police are therefore advised not to ask an estranged parent to act as appropriate adult if the juvenile expressly and specifically objects to his presence.[317]

Even parents who are not estranged might not always be the best people to advise their children in police stations. Some research has shown that parents tend to be anything but sympathetic towards children who have been arrested, reporting one case in which 'a police officer intervened to stop a mother assaulting her 12 year old daughter with a slipper for having "brought shame on the family". It was evident that some young suspects were afraid of their parents and of being punished when they got home.'[318] Such a parent might be thought to be an inappropriate adult to be giving advice. Another class of parent who would make an inappropriate adult are people of such low intelligence that they are unable to understand the significance of what is happening, let alone advise the juvenile. Where such a person acts as the appropriate adult, it is likely to be regarded as unfair to admit in evidence any statement made by the juvenile during the interview.[319]

All information required to be given to a detainee must be repeated in the presence of the appropriate adult.[320] If the appropriate adult is available at the time of a review of detention, he must be given the opportunity to make representations to the review officer.[321] A juvenile must not be interviewed in the absence of an appropriate adult, even if the juvenile requests it, unless an officer of the rank of superintendent or above considers that delay will involve an immediate risk of harm to persons or serious loss of or serious damage to property.[322] If this is ignored, any admission made by the juvenile during the interview is likely to be excluded from evidence at a subsequent trial, either as being unreliable (on the view that juveniles are particularly suggestible or weak-willed) and so inadmissible under section 76(2)(b) of PACE,[323] or on the basis of unfairness under section 78.[324]

---

[316] *DPP* v. *Blake* [1989] 1 WLR 432, DC.   [317] Code C, Note for Guidance 1c.

[318] Paul Softley (with the assistance of David Brown, Bob Forde, George Mair, and David Moxon), 'Police Interrogation: An Observational Study in Four Police Stations', in Kevin Heal, Roger Tarling, and John Burrows (eds.), *Policing Today* (London: HMSO, 1985), 115–30 at 119.

[319] *R.* v. *Morse* [1991] Crim. LR 195, CA.   [320] Code C, para. 3.11.

[321] Code C, paras. 15.1, 15.2.   [322] Code C, para. 11.14, and Annex C, para. 1.

[323] e.g. *DPP* v. *Blake* (see n. 316).

[324] *R.* v. *Grier* [1989] (Apr.) *Legal Action* 14, Wood Green Crown Court.

Special rules apply where the juvenile is a ward of court. Although leave of the court is not needed before an arrested juvenile can be questioned, leave is needed to interview a ward as a potential witness, whether for the prosecution or the defence, without arresting him.[325] If it is proposed to caution the juvenile as an alternative to prosecution, it would first require the court's leave, as there is an issue as to whether admitting the offence rather than going for trial is in the ward's best interests.[326]

Whether or not the juvenile is a ward of court, if an interview is desired it should be conducted away from school if at all possible, to protect the child against embarrassment.[327]

(ii) *Mentally handicapped or disordered detainees.* Where a person arrested for an offence appears to be suffering from a mental handicap or a mental disorder, the custody officer must contact the police surgeon (or in urgent cases arrange for the person to be taken to hospital),[328] and contact an appropriate adult, inform him of the person's detention and whereabouts, and ask him to come to the police station. The provisions relating to appropriate adults then apply as they do in respect of juveniles. The appropriate adult for a mentally disordered or handicapped suspect is to be a relative, guardian, or other person responsible for his welfare, or someone with experience of dealing with such people who is not a police officer or employed by the police (such as a psychiatric social worker). Failing those, it may be any responsible adult aged 18 or over who is not a police officer or employed by the police.[329] Generally, a person with experience or training in the care of mentally handicapped or disordered people is preferable to an untrained relative, unless the detainee insists on the relative.[330] As numerous cases like the Maxwell Confait investigation[331] have shown, people with a mental disorder or a mental handicap may be very suggestible, so no interview is to take place in the absence of an appropriate adult unless an officer of the rank of superintendent or above considers that delay will involve an immediate risk of harm to persons or serious loss of, or serious damage to, property.[332] If an interview is carried out without the appropriate adult, the evidence of any statement made by the detainee is likely to be inadmissible by reason

[325] In re K. and others (minors) (wardship: criminal proceedings) [1988] Fam. 1, [1988] 1 All ER 214; Practice Direction [1988] 1 All ER 223; *Practice Direction* [1988] 2 All ER 1015; *Re R. and others (minors) (wardship: criminal proceedings)* [1991] 2 All ER 193, CA.
[326] *Re R., Re G. (minors)* [1990] 2 All ER 633.   [327] Code C, para. 11.15.
[328] Code C, para. 9.2.   [329] Code C, para. 1.7(b).   [330] Note for Guidance 1E.
[331] *Report of the Inquiry by the Hon. Sir Henry Fisher into the Circumstances Leading to the Trial of Three Persons on Charges Arising out of the Death of Maxwell Confait and the Fire at 27 Doggett Road, London SE6*, HC 90 of 1977–8.
[332] Code C, para. 11.14 and Annex C, para. 1.

of unreliability under section 76(2)(*b*) of PACE, or excluded for unfairness under section 78.[333] Even if the evidence is admitted, the judge must warn the jury that there is a special need for caution before convicting substantially on the evidence of any admission.[334]

(iii) *Blind or visually handicapped detainees*. Where a detainee is blind, visually handicapped, or unable to read, the custody officer should ensure that his solicitor, a relative, an appropriate adult, or some other independent person likely to take an interest in him is available to help him to check any documentation and sign anything necessary on his behalf.[335] This is particularly important, as so many of the controls and monitoring systems under PACE rely on records of consents, interviews and requests being checked and signed by the detainee.

(iv) *Deaf and speech-handicapped detainees or appropriate adults, or detainees who do not appear to speak English*. Interviews must not be conducted where detainees or appropriate adults appear to be deaf or speech-handicapped, or where detainees appear not to understand English or to be unable to communicate with their solicitors, except in the presence of an interpreter, who must be given an opportunity to check records of interviews and certify their accuracy. The only exception is where a superintendent considers that the usual conditions of urgency obtain under Annex C of Code C.[336] Copies of the various notices which are to be given to detainees are made available, as encouraged by Note for Guidance 3B to Code C, in Welsh, the main ethnic minority languages, and the main EC languages, when they are likely to be helpful.

(v) *Detainees who are ill*. The custody officer must immediately call the police surgeon, or arrange for hospital treatment, for a detainee who appears to be ill, mentally disordered, or injured, or who is not responding normally to questions or conversation (unless he is merely drunk), or otherwise appears to need medical attention.[337] The police surgeon must also be called if the detainee requests a medical examination.[338] Generally, the provisions of section 9 of Code C require the custody officer to be very cautious when dealing with anyone who seems ill.

---

[333] *R. v. Everett* [1988] Crim. LR 826, CA; *R. v. Moss, The Times*, 1 Mar. 1989, CA.
[334] PACE, s. 77; *R. v. Lamont* [1989] Crim. LR 813, CA.
[335] Code C, para. 3.14.
[336] Code C, paras. 3.6, 13.5–13.7, 13.9. Interpreters are provided at public expense, and this should be made clear to the detainee: para. 13.8.
[337] Code C, para. 9.2.   [338] Code C, para. 9.4.

(4) Conclusion

The protective rights given by PACE and the Codes of Practice are dependent on the work, initially, of the custody officer. The primary means of monitoring the performance of the custody officer is by way of entries in the custody record, and monitoring of complaints about treatment, which must be reported immediately to an officer of the rank of inspector or above who is not connected with the investigation. The roles of the custody officer and the review officer are crucial. These roles call for considerable personal authority and independence and the officers may be in a difficult situation. First, they are torn between commitment to the usual police role—a desire to get results by detecting crime—and their statutory responsibilities to remain apart from the investigation and act independently to ensure the the the detainee is treated properly and given his entitlements. Secondly, they are inevitably subject to pressures imposed by the bureaucratic burden of the recording requirements. Thirdly, there is the pressure from investigating officers, some of whom may be of higher rank than the custody officer.[339] The Act contemplates that the last point will be catered for by referring any conflict of decisions or directions relating to the treatment or detention of a detainee to an officer of the rank of superintendent or above who is responsible for the police station.[340] This appears to happen rarely in practice. On the other hand, investigating officers have expressed concerns about the loss of their control, for example over detention times. They perceive their concerns as being different from those of custody and review officers.[341] Perhaps the most surprising feature of the scheme, therefore, is that it seems, on the whole, to have worked reasonably well so far.

Where the suspect has rights, including access to legal advice, the rights are not easy to enforce by law. The main remedy for breach is the inadmissibility of evidence which fails to satisfy the requirements of section 76(2) of PACE, and the discretion of the court to exclude evidence if it would be unfair to admit it under section 78. The Royal Commission in 1981, in rejecting a proposal for mandatory exclusion of illegally obtained evidence on the United States model, relied heavily on studies which did not show any conclusive evidence that the mandatory exclusionary rule actually improved the lot of most suspects.[342] It could only directly affect those suspects who are charged, tried, and plead not guilty, challenging the evidence against them. Others might benefit indirectly, but the preponderance of the research suggested that American police practices were

---

[339] For discussion of some of the main pressures on custody officers, see John Rodie, 'The Undervalued Custody Officer' (1988) 4 *Policing* 4–27.

[340] PACE, s. 39(6) (custody officer); s. 40(11) (review officer).

[341] Brown, *Investigating Burglary*, 77–8.   [342] RCCP, *Report*, paras. 4.123–4.134.

not changed by the rule in a way which safeguarded rights. Instead, the police complied with the letter, but not the spirit, of the rules requiring suspects to be informed of their rights to remain silent and to have counsel: the information would be given in a way which minimized its impact on the suspect.[343] However, there is now some evidence that the exclusionary rule has a real deterrent effect on officers.[344] Even if it had none, it might be a useful, though not a comprehensive, protection for the rights of an accused.[345]

The Royal Commission also rejected a reverse onus exclusionary rule, under which there is a presumption that unlawfully obtained evidence is not to be admitted unless the prosecution is able to justify the unlawfulness by reference to considerations such as the urgency of the situation, the good faith of the officers, and the seriousness of the illegality. The reverse onus rule is broadly the one which operates in Scotland,[346] and was recommended by the Australian Law Reform Commission in 1975.[347] However, the practice in most common law jurisdictions has been to adopt a presumption of admissibility, subject to a discretion to exclude. In Canada, before the enactment of the Charter of Rights and Freedoms gave judges an instrument by which to exclude more unconstitutionally obtained evidence, the exclusionary discretion was very narrow: it arose only where the evidence was of little or no probative value.[348] In England, there was a discretion to exclude evidence where its admittance would be unfair, but this was rarely exercised, and had been narrowed down by the House of Lords to cases where the prejudicial weight of evidence excluded its probative value.[349] In Australia, a balancing-of-interests test prevailed, with the court deciding whether the illegality was so serious that it would be improper to allow the evidence to be used.[350]

The measured but active use which the English courts have made of sections 76 and 78 of PACE since 1976 has shown a surprising but wel-

---

[343] See, on the exclusionary rule, Dallin C. Oaks, 'Studying the Exclusionary Rule in Search and Seizure' 37 *Univ. of Chicago LR* 665 (1970). On *Miranda* v. *Arizona* 384 US 436 (1966), see Liva Baker, *Miranda: Crime, Law and Politics* (New York: Atheneum, 1983).

[344] Myron W. Oldfield, Jun., 'The Exclusionary Rule and Deterrence: An Empirical Study of Chicago Narcotics Officers' 54 *Univ. of Chicago LR* 1016–69 (1987).

[345] A. J. Ashworth, 'Excluding Evidence as Protecting Rights' [1977] Crim. LR 723–35.

[346] See e.g. *Lawrie* v. *Muir* 1950 J.C. 19; *McGovern* v. *HM Advocate* 1950 JC 33; *Bell* v. *Hogg* 1967 JC 49; *Hay* v. *HM Advocate* 1968 JC 40.

[347] Report No. 2, *Criminal Investigation*, ch. 11.

[348] *R.* v. *Wray* (1970) 11 DLR (3d) 673, SC of Canada.

[349] *R.* v. *Sang* [1980] AC 402, [1979] 2 All ER 1222, HL.

[350] *R.* v. *Ireland* (1970) 126 CLR 321, HC of Australia; *Bunning* v. *Cross* (1978) 141 CLR 54, H.C. of Australia.

come commitment to the idea of using evidential rules to protect rights. However, other remedies are needed for cases which never reach the stage of a contested trial. Disciplinary proceedings against officers do not give people any right to compensation. Legal proceedings are difficult and often unlikely to succeed: refusal of access to legal advice does not make the detention unlawful, so habeas corpus is not an appropriate remedy, and the only tort which aggrieved suspects could use to obtain redress is misfeasance in a public office. We can expect to see this tort being deployed more often by plaintiffs as its importance as a bastion of statutory rights is more widely recognized.

5.7 INTERVIEWS AND THE RIGHT OF SILENCE

The right to refuse to answer questions, without suffering prejudice as a result, is fundamental to the principle that, in a criminal prosecution, the Crown must prove the guilt of the accused, and should not be in a position to force the accused to condemn himself.[351] The report of the Royal Commission on Criminal Procedure in 1981 led to various changes·in the provisions governing the conduct of interviews by the police. To some extent the position of the suspect was weakened by the provisions for detention without charge for more than 24 hours in relation to serious arrestable offences. As explained above, this was balanced by rights given to suspects, particularly in relation to legal advice. Crucially, and contrary to the earlier controversial decision of the Criminal Law Revision Committee,[352] the Commission recommended that suspects should not be compelled to answer questions, and that it should not generally be permissible at trial to draw inferences from silence adverse to an accused. The only exception which the Commission was prepared to contemplate was if the suspect had full information at all times about his rights, and about the evidence against him. Only then would it be proper to draw inferences from a refusal to answer questions. The government was not prepared to give suspects the right to know all the evidence against them, and accordingly PACE retained the suspect's common-law right to refuse to answer questions without suffering any disadvantage.

The Act and Codes give certain rights to suspects being held at police stations in relation to the circumstances in which interviews may take place. First, if an officer has reasonable grounds for suspecting that a person has committed any offence, he must caution him before any

[351] The Australian Law Reform Commission, Report No. 2, *Criminal Investigation*, ch. 5, provides a clear account of the argument surrounding this principle.

[352] Criminal Law Revision Committee, 11th Report, *Evidence (General)*, Cmnd. 4991 (London: HMSO, 1972).

questions are put to him for the purpose of obtaining evidence for possible court proceedings, though not before questions are put for other purposes such as establishing his ownership of a vehicle, or in searching him under stop and search powers.[353] If the suspect is not under arrest at the time, he must be so informed and told that he is not obliged to remain with the officer.[354] If the arrest takes place at a police station, the suspect must also be told of his right to legal advice.[355] A caution must be given on arrest, unless the suspect's condition or behaviour makes this impracticable or he been cautioned immediately before, when reasonable grounds for suspicion first came to light.[356] A caution must also be given each time questioning resumes after a break, unless there is no doubt that the suspect is aware that the caution still applies.[357] The caution should be in the form, 'You do not have to say anything unless you wish to do so, but what you say may be given in evidence'. Minor deviations are permitted, but the sense must be preserved. The officer may go on to explain the meaning of the caution and its implications if required.[358] Where a juvenile or mentally disordered or mentally handicapped person is cautioned in the absence of an appropriate adult, the caution must be repeated in the presence of the appropriate adult.

The duty to caution reflects the orthodox position that people are under no obligation to answer questions from investigators.[359] This is related to the common-law principle that nobody should be obliged to incriminate themselves, although it goes further, applying to answers to all questions, whether incriminating or not. However, the principle is not sacrosanct. Statute has whittled it away by imposing duties to provide information to investigators in relation to certain complex or particularly serious investigations.

For example, under the Official Secrets Act 1920, section 6, an inspector or superintendent, on the authorization of the chief constable and usually with the permission of the Secretary of State, may require a person believed, on reasonable grounds, to have information about an espi-

---

[353] Code C, para. 10.1.   [354] Code C, para. 10.2.   [355] Code C, para. 3.15.
[356] Code C, para. 10.3.
[357] Code C, para. 10.5. See *R. v. Manji* [1990] Crim. LR 512, CA; *R. v. Sparks* [1991] Crim. LR 128, CA.
[358] Code C, para. 10.4 and Notes for Guidance 10C, 10D.
[359] *Rice v. Connolly* [1966] 2 QB 414, [1966] 2 All ER 649, DC. Although it has been held that abuse may amount to obstruction (*Ricketts v. Cox* (1981) 74 Cr. App. R. 298), the abuse must be such as to make it more difficult for the officers to do that which they are entitled to do. If it merely makes it more difficult for them to obtain answers to questions, as where a person abusively advises another of his right to refuse to answer questions, there is no wilful obstruction, because the police are merely denied something to which they had no right, namely answers to their questions: *Green v. DPP* [1991] Crim. LR 782, DC.

onage offence, to give any information in his power. Failure to comply with the requirement, or giving false information, is itself an offence under the section. The Prevention of Terrorism (Temporary Provisions) Act 1989, section 18, goes a step further, obliging people to volunteer to the police, without waiting to be asked, any information which might be of material assistance in preventing an act of terrorism or in apprehending, prosecuting, or convicting someone suspected of terrorism in connection with the affairs of Northern Ireland.

Those provisions do not normally infringe the privilege against self-incrimination. Some provisions aimed at complex frauds go further. The Director of the Serious Fraud Office has power to insist on anyone whom he has reason to believe has relevant information providing it, answering questions, and producing specified documents unless they are subject to legal professional privilege, on pain of imprisonment.[360] Department of Trade inspectors, and liquidators, also have powers to demand information, and these powers have been held to override the privilege against self-incrimination,[361] and, *a fortiori*, the right to refuse to answer other, non-incriminating, questions. The House of Lords has treated the powers of the Serious Fraud Office as defeating the privilege even after the suspect has been charged, and has also limited the scope of the privilege in civil proceedings so that it is not available where the prosecuting authorities state unequivocally that information revealed in the civil proceedings will not be used in criminal proceedings against the person providing it.[362]

These investigations usually concern matters which are peculiarly within the personal knowledge of the suspects. However, the government launched a wider, sustained assault on the right of silence in 1988, based on the view (advanced by the police) that innocent people have nothing to fear from telling the truth, so it should be permissible to draw adverse inferences from a refusal to answer questions. The law in Northern Ireland was changed to allow a trial court to draw such inferences as seem proper from a suspect's failure to mention a fact which he could reasonably have been expected to mention and on which he seeks to rely at trial, and further to treat the failure to mention the facts as being capable of amounting to corroboration of any evidence given

---

[360] Criminal Justice Act 1987, s. 2.

[361] *Ex parte Nadir, The Times,* 5 Nov. 1990, DC (powers of SFO under the Criminal Justice Act 1987, s. 2); *Re London United Investments plc,* [1992] 2 All ER 842, CA (powers of DTI inspectors appointed under Companies Act 1985, s. 432); *Bishopsgate Investment Management Ltd. (in provisional liquidation)* v. *Maxwell;* [1992] 2 All ER 856, CA (powers of provisional liquidators under Insolvency Act 1986, ss. 235 and 236).

[362] *Smith* v. *Director of Serious Fraud Office* [1992] 3 All ER 456, HL; *AT&T Istel Ltd.* v. *Tully* [1992] 3 All ER 523, HL. It is not clear how a suspect is to be protected against the use of the information in a private prosecution.

against the suspect to which the fact is material.[363] The government announced its intention of introducing comparable legislation for England and Wales, and set up a working group to consider the matter. This group reported in 1989, recommending (unsurprisingly) the course for which the government had already expressed a preference.[364]

The report accepted police assertions that the right to silence, taken together with the statutory rights which suspects were given under PACE, tipped the balance too far in the suspect's favour. The working party was impressed by police evidence that the right of silence is widely invoked, particularly by experienced professional criminals, that those who exercise their right to legal advice are particularly likely to be advised to remain silent, and that this represents a major obstacle to the police in obtaining evidence and securing convictions. The report sparked a storm of protest from critics who attacked its wholesale acceptance of police assertions without adequate research. The critics argued that very few people actually refuse to answer questions,[365] that solicitors do not, in practice, adopt a blanket policy of advising clients not to answer questions, and that there is no evidence that silence often interferes with the ability of the prosecution to secure convictions.[366]

---

[363] Criminal Evidence (Northern Ireland) Order 1988.

[364] *Report of the Home Office Working Group on the Right of Silence* (London: Home Office, 1989). For a general critique of the report, see A. A. S. Zuckerman, 'Trial by Unfair Means: The Report of the Working Party on the Right to Silence' [1989] *Crim. LR* 855–65.

[365] For analysis of the figures found in various studies, see Roger Leng, *The Right to Silence in Police Interrogation: A Study of Some of the Issues Underlying the Debate*, Royal Commission on Criminal Justice Research Study No. 10 (London: HMSO, 1993); Steven Greer, 'Background to the Debate', in Steven Greer and Rod Morgan (eds.), *The Right to Silence Debate* (Bristol: Bristol Centre for Criminal Justice, 1990), 6–17; Steven Greer, 'The Right to Silence: A Review of the Current Debate' (1990) 53 *MLR* 709–30; David Dixon, 'Politics, Research and Symbolism in Criminal Justice: The Right of Silence and the Police and Criminal Evidence Act' (1991) 20 *Anglo-Amer. LR* 27–50; David Dixon, 'Common Sense, Legal Advice and the Right of Silence' [1991] PL 233–54.

[366] See, in addition to the works cited in the previous note, John Coldrey, 'The Right to Silence: Should it be Curtailed or Abolished?' (1991) 20 *Anglo-Amer. LR* 51–62. The figures produced by studies conducted by the police tend to suggest that a substantial proportion of people refuse to answer at least some questions for some period. However, the other studies suggest that very few detainees remain silent throughout an interview, and many solicitors and runners are mindful of their need to foster good relations with the police, with whom they come regularly in contact, and may encourage clients to talk: Dixon [1991] PL at 235–51. The evidence is that the increase in the proportion of people receiving legal advice is not equalled by the increased use of the right of silence: Brown, *Investigating Burglary*, 80–3. People who have legal advice are charged more often than others, suggesting that the police use other sources of information and do not rely on confessions in most cases: David Brown, *Detention at the Police Station under the Police and Criminal Evidence Act 1984*, Home Office Research Study No. 104 (London: HMSO, 1989); Andrew Sanders *et al.*, *Advice and Assistance at Police Stations and the 24 Hour Duty*

Furthermore, the reasons for silence deserve careful analysis, as they are relevant to the circumstances in which it might be appropriate to draw inferences from silence, and the nature of those inferences. In particular, the critics pointed out that people in police stations are under stress, they probably do not know the full details of the case against them, have not had time to give careful thought to what happened, and are likely to be disorientated. Under such circumstances, it is often sensible to say nothing, as there is a real risk that anything which the suspect said in the heat of the moment might turn out to be innocently mistaken, with unjustifiably prejudicial consequences. In assessing what adverse inferences, if any, it is proper to draw from a suspect's silence, it is important to look at the context in which the refusal to answer questions arose. Did the suspect know what case he was being required to answer? Were there factors, such as lack of access to legal advice or to an appropriate adult, which made it hard for the suspect to understand what was being alleged against him? Were the police exerting unfair pressure? All these matters affect the meaning which can properly be attributed to silence. Yet the Working Party advocated looking only at the explanation offered by the defendant for refusing to answer, rather than at the context as a whole.[367]

The government has so far taken no action on the working party's report. However, the police seem likely to maintain pressure for change, on the ground that the reliability of evidence about confessions is now more readily guaranteed by, for example, tape recording of statements than it was when the miscarriages of justice occurred which resulted in the convictions of the Birmingham Six and the Guildford Four. It is true that the 1984 Act improved the lot of many detainees. In particular, Code C provides for regular meals for detainees, drinks with meals and on reasonable request between mealtimes, at least eight hours rest from questioning and travel in each twenty-four-hour period, the right to an individual cell so far as practicable, and brief outdoor exercise if practicable.[368] The Code also provides that there must be adequate lighting in cells, a reasonable standard of bedding, and access to toilet and washing facilities. It further specifies that nobody may be interviewed unless adequate clothing has been offered to him, and that interview rooms must, as far as practicable, be adequately heated, lit, and ventilated.[369]

Solicitor Scheme (London: Lord Chancellor's Dept., 1989). Only where evidence is weak is the right to silence potentially decisive of the results of cases: S. Moston, G. Stephenson, and T. Williamson, 'Police Interrogation Styles and Suspect Behaviour' (unpubl., cited in Brown, *Investigating Burglary*, at p. 83).

[367] Zuckerman, 'Trial by Unfair Means' [1989] Crim. LR 855–65.

[368] Code C, s. 8, especially paras. 8.1, 8.6, 8.7, and 12.2.

[369] Code C, paras. 8.2–8.5, 12.4. However, nothing in the Code gives rise to a private-law cause of action (PACE, s. 67(10)), so it may be difficult to obtain remedies for failure to provide appropriate conditions of detention. This matter is discussed in Ch. 6, below.

Nevertheless, a suspect in a police station is under severe stress. The balance of power is always in favour of the police, on whose territory the suspect and his legal adviser or appropriate adult are.[370] What safeguards are provided to ensure that the interview process itself is fair to him, and is likely to produce reliable results? The first point to note is that, once an interview begins, the custody officer drops out of the picture. When the custody officer allows an investigating officer to take the suspect into an interview room for questioning, or out of the police station (for example, to conduct a search of the suspect's premises),[371] the investigating officer becomes responsible for ensuring that the provisions of PACE and the Codes are complied with. The investigating officer must account for the treatment of the suspect when he delivers him back to the custody officer at the end of the interview, but during it the custody officer has no power to protect the suspect's rights. The review officer can intervene, but only if a review becomes due.[372] Where no appropriate adult or legal adviser is present, there is ample room for different accounts of what happened to be given by the officer and the detainee, particularly as the detainee's perception of events is likely to be affected by the pressures of his position. Tape recording of interviews is not normally possible outside police station interview rooms, and in any case is not required in relation to terrorist offences.[373]

Protecting the integrity and reliability of the interview therefore depends heavily on the good sense and honesty of the interviewer. To minimize the opportunities for the record of an interview to be intentionally or unintentionally corrupted, there are extensive provisions in the Codes concerning methods of recording of interviews. If the interview is tape-recorded, there should be no problem (unless it is later alleged that some impropriety occurred before the tape was turned on or after it was turned off). Tape recording has worked well, and the police have on the whole become supporters of it. It has several benefits for them. It frees them from the need to make laborious, manual, verbatim records, which slowed down the pace of questioning and could destroy the effect of a line of questions.[374] It tends to improve rapport with interviewees, and tends to discourage challenges to confessions. It also restricts allegations of 'verballing' (crediting suspects with statements which were

---

[370] Dixon, [1991] PL at p. 239.

[371] This must be authorized by the custody officer: Code C, para. 12.1.

[372] PACE, s. 39(2), (3).

[373] Code E (The Code of Practice on Tape Recording), made by the Secretary of State for the Home Dept. under PACE, s. 60(1).

[374] Carole F. Willis, John Macleod, and Peter Naish, The Tape-Recording of Police Interviews with Suspects: A Second Interim Report, Home Office Research Study No. 97 (London: HMSO 1988), ch. 3.

never made), as verballing can now only take place outside formal interviews, and such statements are unlikely to be considered fairly admissible unless the suspect voluntarily repeats them on tape.

In order to control the practice of conducting interviews outside police stations, evading the tape-recording requirements, Code C provides that, after arrest for an offence, a suspect must not be interviewed about that offence except at a police station or other authorized place of detention, unless the delay would be likely to lead to one of the consequences which would justify a superintendent in authorizing delay in exercising the rights to have someone notified of the arrest and to have access to legal advice: interference with or harm to evidence, interference with or physical harm to other people, alerting suspects not yet under arrest, or hindering recovery of the proceeds of an offence.[375]

One possible source of corruption to the record remains, however. The tape is rarely fully transcribed unless there is a dispute about the record. In other cases, a summary of the interview is made, which often becomes more important than the tape for practical purposes. A survey of these summaries found that they are of uneven quality, being misleading, distorted, of poor quality, or omitting much relevant detail in nearly half of the summaries examined, although the police are said to be paying more attention now to training officers in techniques of accurate summarizing.[376]

Where tape recording is not available, the officer must make an accurate record of the interview, wherever it occurs. The record must be made during the course of the interview, unless in the officer's view this would not be practicable or would interfere with the conduct of the interview, and must be either a verbatim record or an adequate and accurate summary.[377] Where the record is not made during the interview, it must be made as soon as practicable afterwards, and the reason for the delay recorded in the officer's pocket book (where the order of pages can be checked, and ESDA tests most easily applied to establish whether there have been later insertions or deletions).[378] Unless it is impracticable, the interviewee and, if present, an appropriate adult or solicitor, must be given the opportunity to read the record (or, if he cannot read, have it read to him), and to sign it as correct, or to indicate the respects in which he considers it to be inaccurate.[379] The police have sometimes taken liberties with these requirements. In R. v. Canale[380] the officers failed to make a contemporaneous record. They recorded their reasons with the

---

[375] Code C, para. 11.1.

[376] John Baldwin and Julie Bedward, 'Summarising Tape Recordings of Police Interviews' [1991] Crim. LR 671–9.

[377] Code C, para. 11.5.

[378] Code C, paras. 11.7, 11.9.

[379] Code C, paras. 11.10, 11.11.

[380] [1990] 2 All ER 187, CA.

cryptic note 'BW', which (they later explained) stood for 'best way'. Lord Lane CJ commented, 'In the officers' view the reason for failing to record the interview contemporaneously was that the best way was not to record the interview contemporaneously, which of course is not a reason at all.'[381] The judicial criticism which followed led the Metropolitan Police to tighten the controls exercised over interrogation techniques. It is to be hoped that the police will treat these provisions with the respect which they deserve, as they are important protections for suspects, and the courts have shown an increasing willingness to exclude evidence which is obtained in breach of these provisions.[382]

The next issue is the meaning of 'interview'. Before the revision to the Codes of Practice, there was some disagreement on this point between different judges. The new Code C clarifies the matter in Note for Guidance 11A, which (although it does not have the force of a provision of the Code) is likely to be treated by the police as an operating rule. An interview is described, broadly following the formulation in *R.* v. *Maguire*,[383] as

the questioning of a person regarding his involvement or suspected involvement in a criminal offence or offences. Questioning a person only to obtain information or his explanation of the facts or in the ordinary course of the officer's duties does not constitute an interview for the purposes of this code. Neither does questioning which is confined to the proper and effective conduct of a search.

The early part of this definition is unexceptionable, but the final sentence may underestimate the extent to which the police ask questions in the course of searches which are designed to confirm suspicions, rather than merely seek information. It was held in *R.* v. *Christou*[384] that the protections for interviewees outside police stations come into play only if the suspect knows that the interviewer is a police officer, and is therefore likely to feel the psychological effects of being subject to the legal power of the officer. If the officer is working under cover, masquerading as a criminal, there is no such perceived inequality of power. The result is sensible: to require the interview procedures to be followed in such circumstances would defeat the purpose of much undercover work; but the reasoning offers a potentially easy way for the police to evade the requirements of the Code of Practice. This was noted in *R.* v. *Bryce*,[385] where the Court of Appeal discouraged it pragmatically by excluding the

---

[381] [1990] 2 All ER 187, at p. 190.
[382] *R.* v. *Doolan* [1988] Crim. LR 747, CA; *R.* v. *Delaney* (1988) 88 Cr. AR. 339, CA; *R.* v. *Canale*, [1990] 2 All ER 187, CA.
[383] (1989) 90 Cr. AR. 115, CA.   [384] [1992] 4 All ER 559, CA.
[385] [1992] 4 All ER 567, CA.

statements so obtained. This produces satisfying effects which are, however, hard to reconcile on principled grounds.

The Codes give no guidance on the conduct of interviews. Under PACE, section 76(2), a confession, if challenged by the defence, is inadmissible unless the prosecution can prove beyond reasonable doubt that it was not obtained (*a*) by oppression, or (*b*) in consequence of anything said or done which was likely, in the circumstances, to render unrealiable any confession which might be made in consequence thereof. Furthermore, if the circumstances surrounding the confession (or alleged confession) are such that it would taint the proceedings with unfairness to admit the evidence, it may be excluded (and usually should be excluded) under section 78. A considerable body of caselaw has built up round these provisions, but their value in protecting the rights of suspects is limited, because the admissibility or exclusion of evidence is a valuable sanction against police malpractice only if the case comes to court (i.e. is not dropped beforehand) and is contested (i.e. the accused does not plead guilty). However, the caselaw has had the effect of establishing some ground rules for police interviews, breach of which may make confessions inadmissible or liable to exclusion.

(i) *The meaning of oppression.* ' "Oppression" includes torture, inhuman or degrading treatment and the use or threat of violence.'[386] This statutory exegesis of the term is not exhaustive, and the Court of Appeal has treated oppressive conduct as extending beyond those types of treatment to take in potentially any burdensome, harsh, or wrongful exercise of authority, or unjust or cruel treatment of subjects and inferiors. There are conditions, however: oppression will probably not be found in the absence of improper behaviour by the investigator.[387]

This has two implications. First, it means that the conduct must produce a situation which oppresses the suspect more severely than is inevitable when in detention. Secondly, it imports a subjective element to the evaluation of police conduct: the investigators must probably be aware that what they are doing is improper, and intend it to produce an effect on the suspect, before conduct falling short of inhuman or degrading treatment will be held to amount to oppression. In *R. v. Fulling,*[388] the defence argued that a confession had been or may have been obtained by oppression. The defendant, a woman, had been arrested on suspicion of having been one of a number of people who had allegedly made fraudulent claims from insurance companies in respect of bogus burglaries. She refused to say anything under repeated questioning over a period

[386] PACE, s. 76(8). On the meaning of torture and inhuman and degrading treatment under international law, see chs. 4 and 6.
[387] [1987] QB 426, [1987] 2 All ER 65, CA.   [388] Ibid.

of more than twenty-four hours. Eventually, one of the investigators told her that her cohabitant had been having an affair for three years with one of the other suspects, a woman who had been arrested and was in a cell next to the defendant's. At this stage, it was said, she could no longer face being in the cell, and confessed. On these facts, the trial judge not surprisingly rejected the suggestion of oppression, and the Court of Appeal dismissed the defendant's appeal.

However, where conscious and serious impropriety by the police is alleged and is not disproved beyond reasonable doubt by the prosecution, the evidence of any confession resulting from it is to be excluded on the ground of oppression. For example, in *R. v. Ismail*[389] the prosecution conceded, and the Court of Appeal accepted, that the trial judge had rightly excluded evidence of a confession on the ground of oppression. The defendant had been arrested in relation to an indecent assault, and was detained at a police station. The investigating officer had misled the custody officer as to the purpose of an interview, making it impossible for the custody officer to perform his duty when deciding whether or not to permit the interview. The defendant was not offered the chance to obtain legal advice, and the recording requirements were breached during the interview. Although the suspect continued to deny the allegations at that interview, there were three later interviews, culminating in a signed confession. The Court of Appeal held that the effects of the oppression at the earlier interview, together with other breaches of PACE and Code C, might well have lingered on, affecting the suspect's will to a point where it was unfair to admit the evidence.[390]

Heavy-handed or bullying interview techniques may amount to oppression. In *R. v. Beales*[391] the suspect had been arrested for assaulting a 2-year-old boy. The interviewing officer had misrepresented the evidence against the suspect, inventing some evidence which did not in fact exist, had misrepresented the effect of the suspect's own answers, and had adopted a hectoring a bullying demeanour throughout the interview to the point where, after 35 minutes, the suspect had accepted that he must have assaulted the child although he claimed to have no recollection of having done so. The trial judge accepted that this strayed into the realms of oppression, and held that the admission was inadmissible.

---

[389] [1990] Crim. LR 109, CA.

[390] It is not clear whether the evidence of the final interview was excluded under s. 76(2)(a) or s. 78. See the commentary by D. J. Birch, [1990] Crim. LR at 110–11. On the potentially lingering effects of oppression on the mind of the suspect and (a different matter) the fairness of proceedings for the purposes of s. 78, see also *R. v. Davison* [1988] Crim. LR 442, a first instance decision.

[391] [1991] Crim. LR 118, a Crown Court decision.

(ii) *Hectoring, bullying, and strategems*. Generally, it will not be necessary to stigmatize hectoring and bullying behaviour as oppressive in order to have resulting confessions excluded. It will often be possible to rule the evidence inadmissible on the ground that the manner of the interview made the confession unreliable, under section 76(2)(*b*), or to exclude the evidence on the basis that it would be unfair to admit it, under section 78, even if there is no breach of PACE or the Codes of Practice. Much will depend on the age and competence of the suspect, and, if there was police impropriety, whether it had the effect of depriving the suspect of his protective rights under PACE. It has been held, for example, that evidence of confessions should be excluded where suspects or their solicitors have been misled about the strength of the evidence against their clients,[392] and where bullying or hectoring approaches have been adopted at interviews, particularly with a young or vulnerable suspect.[393] Nevertheless, in one respect oppression may have a longer lasting effect than other forms of unfairness or impropriety. Oppression in an earlier interview is likely to be accepted as tainting the quality or fairness of evidence obtained at later interviews with the same person. Where police misbehaviour does not amount to oppression, courts will look for clearer evidence that it continued to put the suspect at a disadvantage or under pressure in later interviews before excluding evidence of those later interviews,[394] although it will sometimes be clear that it has done so.[395] It is particularly likely to have had a continuing effect when it reduces the effectiveness of the protective provisions of PACE, such as the protective role of the custody officer or (most powerfully) the usefulness of the right to legal advice.[396] This reflects the increasingly protective attitude of the courts towards interviewees, which is developing in the light of growing realization of the pressures (sometimes subtle, at other times less so) which can lead a person, especially if young, mentally handicapped or disordered, or confused, to confess to crimes which they could not possibly have committed.

[392] *R. v. Mason* [1987] 3 All ER 481, CA; *R. v. Blake* [1991] Crim. LR 119; *R. v. McGovern* [1991] Crim. LR 124, CA.

[393] *R. v. Everett* [1988] Crim. LR 826, CA; *R. v. Beales* [1991] Crim. LR 118.

[394] *Y v. DPP* [1991] Crim. LR 917, DC.

[395] *R. v. Canale* [1990] 2 All ER 187, CA; *R. v. Gillard and Barrett* [1991] Crim. LR 280; *R. v. Ismail*, above.

[396] *R. v. McGovern* [1991] Crim. LR 124, CA; see also *Matto v. Wolverhampton Crown Court* [1987] RTR 337, DC.

5.8 INTERFERENCE WITH BODILY SECURITY: SEARCHES AND FINGERPRINTS

(1) Search by custody officer

The Police and Criminal Evidence Act 1984 makes provision for a number of different types of invasion of people's personal security and integrity. The first is a power for the custody officer to search the detainee on arrest at the police station or arrival at the police station after arrest or committal elsewhere, in order to make a record of the items which the person has on him.[397] This power is not a duty: it is to be exercised only when it seems possible that the custody officer will have continuing duties in respect of the person over an extended period.[398] The custody officer is entitled to seize and retain anything the detainee has on him, except for clothes and personal effects,[399] which are defined in Code C, paragraph 4.3 as 'those items which a person may lawfully need or[400]use or refer to while in detention but do not include cash or other items of value'. They ought, therefore, to include a watch (essential in order to check the time limits around which the detention provisions revolve), spectacles, and the notices given out by the custody officer. Clothes and personal effects may be retained by the custody officer only if (a) he believes (not necessarily on reasonable grounds) that the detainee may use them to cause physical injury to himself or anyone else, to damage property, interfere with evidence, or to assist an escape; or (b) he has reasonable grounds for believing that they may be evidence in relation to any offence (not necessarily the one for which the detainee was arrested).[401]

Any constable may search a detainee anywhere and at any time for anything in (a) above, and may seize anything he finds, other than clothes and personal effects, which are liable to seizure only if they fall under either (a) or (b) above.[402]

The power to search does not extend to an intimate search, which must be separately authorized (see below). It may, however, extend to a strip search in the police station (i.e. one which involves removing more than outer clothing), so long as the custody officer considers it to be necessary in order to remove an article which the detainee would not be

---

[397] PACE, s. 54(1), (2).   [398] Code C, Note for Guidance 4A.
[399] PACE, s. 54(3), (4).
[400] This appears to have been introduced in error for 'to'.
[401] PACE, s. 54(4). The person must be told the reason for the seizure unless he is violent or likely to become so, or is incapable of understanding what is said: s. 54(5).
[402] PACE, s. 54(6A), (6B), (6C), added by Criminal Justice Act 1988, s. 147(b).

entitled to keep while in custody.[403] A strip search is an embarrassing and upsetting procedure, representing a major invasion of privacy. It ought not, therefore, to be routine. Any search must be carried out by a constable of the same sex as the detainee.[404]

(2) Fingerprinting

(i) *During the investigation.* Normally, an 'appropriate consent' is needed before a person's fingerprints can be taken.[405] The appropriate consent for a person of 17 years of age or over is that of the person himself. If the person is under 17 years old but over 14, the person and his parent or guardian must both consent; if he is under 14, the parent or guardian's consent alone is sufficient,[406] and reasonable force can then be used against the child if necessary in order to take the fingerprints.[407] Because of concern over the reality of consent when a person is in custody, the consent of the person to be fingerprinted must be in writing if he gives it at a police station.[408] However, where a person is charged with, or told that he will be charged with, a recordable offence and has not had his fingerprints taken in the course of the investigation, the appropriate consent may be dispensed with. In its place, the Act provides for an authorization (normally in writing, but confirmed in writing if given orally) by an officer of at least the rank of superintendent, who must have reasonable grounds (*a*) for suspecting that the person has been involved in a criminal offence, and (*b*) for believing that fingerprints will tend to confirm or disprove his involvement[409] (for example, where fingerprints were found at the scene of the crime which cannot otherwise be accounted for).

This has given rise to concern that it might enable the police to build up a computerized fingerprint database covering many people, giving rise to fears of a threat to privacy and to people's freedom from police interference. The statutory safeguards against abuse of this power, as so many others under PACE, are based on the giving of reasons and keeping records. If a person's fingerprints are taken without the appropriate con-

---

[403] PACE, s. 54(7); Code C, para. 4.1 and Annex A, para. 5.
[404] PACE, s. 54(8), (9). [405] PACE, s. 61(1).
[406] PACE, s. 65, on the meaning of 'appropriate consent'.
[407] PACE, s. 117; Code D, para. 3.2. [408] PACE, s. 61(2).
[409] PACE, s. 61(3), (4), (5). Under the Prevention of Terrorism (Temporary Provisions) Act 1989, s. 15(10) and Sched. 5, para. 7(6), an authorization may also be given if the superintendent is satisfied that it is necessary to do so in order to assist in determining whether a person has been concerned in the commission, preparation or instigation of acts of terrorism, or is subject to an exclusion order, or has been involved in a terrorism offence. There are also powers to take fingerprints of suspected illegal immigrants under the Immigration Act 1971, Sched. 2, para. 18(2).

sent, he must be told the reason beforehand, and the reasons must be recorded (in the custody record if he is in police detention at the time) as soon as practicable after taking the fingerprints.[410] In addition, if given by a suspect who is later cleared of the offence, the police are required to destroy the fingerprints as soon as possible; and if given by someone else for the purposes of an investigation, they must be destroyed as soon as they have fulfilled the purpose for which they were taken. Copies and computer records must also be destroyed. People may, if they wish, witness the destruction of their own fingerprints, and in the case of computerized records, are entitled to a certificate stating that access to the data has been made impossible.[411] They must be told of this right.[412] Nevertheless, there are suspicions that the provisions are being breached, mainly because they depend so heavily on trusting the police; it would be easy for the police to breach them if so inclined.

(ii) *After conviction.* There is special provision under section 27 of PACE for fingerprinting people who have been convicted of a recordable offence, have not been in police detention at any time in relation to the offence (because they were proceeded against by way of summons rather than arrest), and have not had their fingerprints taken at any time in relation to the offence. Within a month of the conviction, a constable may require the person to attend a police station within seven days to be fingerprinted. After conviction for a recordable offence, the appropriate consent to fingerprinting is not required.[413] If the person fails to attend, a constable may arrest him without warrant. Detention in such a case will be limited to the time necessary to take the fingerprints.

---

[410] PACE, s. 61(7), (8).

[411] PACE, s. 64, as amended by Criminal Justice Act 1988, s. 148. Code D, para. 3.4, attempts to limit the right to witness destruction to cases where the person applies to witness it within 5 days of being cleared or informed that he will not be prosecuted. This limitation of the right appears to conflict with the absolute right given under s. 64(6), and to that extent is *ultra vires*. The explanation probably is that it is envisaged that the fingerprints would normally be destroyed within 5 or 6 days, and a person who does not ask to witness their destruction within that time will inevitably be disappointed if the police have complied with their duty to destroy them as soon as practicable.

[412] Code D, para. 3.1.

[413] PACE, s. 61(6). A recordable offence is one which potentially punishable with imprisonment, and certain other specified non-imprisonable crimes such as loitering or soliciting for the purposes of prostitution, possessing a weapon with a blade or point in a public place, tampering with a motor vehicle, and improper use of a public telephone communications system: National Police Records (Recordable Offences) Regulations 1985, SI 1985/1941, as amended.

(3) Intimate searches

A search of a person's body orifices ('an intimate search')[414] is highly intrusive, and is *prima facie* a serious battery, invasion of privacy, and interference with bodily integrity. It has the capacity to cause serious injury to the person being searched, besides being degrading and humiliating. If carried out insensitively (for example, there have been anecdotal reports of women being required to stand naked on a table with their legs apart, and to jump up and down, in the presence of male officers) it comes close to the kind of degrading treatment which would fall foul of Article 3 of the European Convention on Human Rights. One would normally expect that no such search would be permitted without the consent of the person searched. However, Parliament decided that there are circumstances in which these fundamental individual rights may properly be overridden to advance some other interest. These interests lie in the safety of the person concerned or other people, preventing escape, and detecting drugs offences. (Drugs are often hidden in body orifices, sometimes even being swallowed in bags to avoid detection.)

An intimate search must be specially authorized by an officer of at least the rank of superintendent. He must have reasonable grounds for believeing (not merely for suspecting) that a person who has been arrested, and is in police detention at the time,[415] may have concealed on him either: (*a*) something which he could use to cause physical injury to himself or others (the usual example is a razorblade), and which he might use for that purpose while in the custody of the police or a court; or (*b*) a Class A drug (within the meaning of section 2(1) of the Misuse of Drugs Act 1971), which he had in his possession, with intent to supply it or to smuggle it, before his arrest (thus excluding possession for his own use, or drugs received from fellow prisoner after his arrest), and that the article cannot be found without an intimate search.[416] There is no power to authorize a search for evidence of offences, however serious, unless that evidence is reasonably believed to consist of a Class A drug. However, once the search has been carried out, anything found can be seized if the custody officer (*a*) believes (reasonable grounds being unnecessary) that the person may use it to cause physical injury to himself or another, to damage property, to interfere with evidence, or to assist him to escape, or (*b*) has reasonable grounds for believing that the article may be evidence of any offence.[417]

The grounds which would be needed for such a search would

---

[414] PACE, s. 118(1).

[415] There is no power to arrest someone purely in order to carry out an intimate search.

[416] PACE, s. 55(1), (2).   [417] PACE, s. 55(12).

therefore be substantial. There would need to be evidence (and more evidence than is needed to justify the arrest) that the person is in possession of the article, and that (in the case of a search for an injurious article) the person is liable to use it, or (in the case of a drugs search) the person is a dealer in or courier of drugs, and Class A drugs in particular. But no independent authority reviews the evidence on which the authorization is given before the search is made.[418]

The safeguards for the detainee are therefore somewhat limited. The Code of Practice requires that the reasons for the search be explained to the person concerned before the search takes place,[419] so the person presumably has a chance to persuade the officers that no search is justified or himself to remove the articles in question, making a search unnecessary. Once it is decided that the search should go ahead, there are safeguards of two sorts.

First, there are safeguards against arbitrary behaviour and abuse of power. Like other such safeguards under the PACE detention provisions, these consist of requirements as to the giving of information (for example, about the reasons for the search and the reasons for seizing anything found)[420] and record-keeping.[421] These records are to be collated for each police area, and the chief constable's annual report must give information about the number and purpose of searches, the manner in which they were conducted, and the results, allowing for some monitoring of the global use of the powers.[422]

Secondly, there are some safeguards for the dignity and physical safety of the detainee. A Class A drugs search may be conducted only at a hospital, a doctor's surgery, or other place used for medical purposes, and must be conducted by a suitably qualified person: a registered medical practitioner or registered nurse.[423] Other intimate searches are normally to be carried out by a suitably qualified person, but may be conducted at a police station as well as the other places in which a drugs search would be permitted, and may be carried out by a police officer as long as the officer is of the same sex as the person searched although the search may be conducted by an officer of the opposite sex if the superintendent considers that it would be impracticable to find an officer of the same sex to carry it out.[424] Juveniles may be searched only in the presence of an

---

[418] In this respect, a person detained under PACE is in a worse position than one being searched by a customs officer at the port of entry, who can insist on the grounds for a search being reviewed by a justice of the peace: Customs and Excise Management Act 1979, s. 164(2).

[419] Code C, Annex A, para. 1.

[420] PACE, s. 55(3), (13); Code C, Annex A, para. 1.   [421] PACE, s. 55(10), (11).

[422] PACE, s. 55(14), (15), (16).   [423] PACE, s. 55(4).

[424] PACE, s. 55(5), (6), (7).

appropriate adult (which has the same meaning as under the detention provisions), unless the juvenile signifies, in the presence of the adult, that he does not wish the adult to be present and the adult agrees. When an appropriate adult is in attendance on a juvenile or a mentally disordered or mentally handicapped person, the adult may be present for the search, but must be of the same sex as the person searched, unless the detainee specifically requests the presence of a particular adult of the opposite sex.[425]

Intimate searches raise problems of two sorts, apart from the inevitable degradation and risk of physical injury from an intrusive procedure, which may sometimes be conducted by an unqualified person. The first problem is a general one, concerning the relationship between the power to conduct an intimate search and the general purposes and values of a legal system. The idea of a person being held down while her vagina or anus is physically searched against her will is repulsive to civilized feelings. If a film or video were to portray such a scene, it would be generally regarded as worthy of condemnation and, perhaps, prosecution. It is hard to imagine how a legal system could be justified in authorizing police officers to commit such acts, without even the check of a prior review by an independent person of the grounds for a search. This is a case where the law has conferred a power which contravenes the civilized values which it is the main job of law to foster.

The other problem is more specific, and relates to the position of doctors and nurses who are asked by the police to conduct an intimate search against the will of the person to be searched. The doctor is not protected by any statutory authority against an action for trespass to the person. As there is no medical necessity for the procedure, the doctor or nurse is, on normal principles (for which see Chapter 4 above), not entitled to ignore or override the absence of consent from the detainee unless there is statutory authority or a court order. There is no judicial determination of the best interests of the detainee. The only statutory authority justifying the use of force against a non-consenting person to exercise a power under PACE is in section 117 of PACE, and that protects only a police officer, not a doctor or nurse. The doctor is therefore apparently not protected against an action for trespass. Furthermore, if the detainee suffers injury as a result of the procedure, the doctor or nurse may be liable in damages for negligence. If the injury results from the detainee's struggles, it is hard to see how a doctor could defend a negligence action: there could hardly be a more clear-cut case of medical negligence than that of a doctor performing a non-therapeutic, intrusive procedure on a person who is actively resisting, in circumstances where that is obviously likely to make

---

[425] Code C, Annex A, para. 4.

the procedure particularly risky. Unless the courts produce some previously unknown public-policy defence for doctors carrying out searches at the request of the police, the only case in which the doctor is likely to succeed is if it can be shown that, on the balance of probabilities, the risk to the detainee from the concealed article is greater than the risk from performing the procedure, so that the doctor was acting in the detainee's best interests.

Even in cases where the doctor or nurse acts lawfully, it is far from clear that he or she would be acting ethically. The British Medical Association has recommended to its members that they should not conduct intimate body searches for evidence of drugs offences without the free and informed consent of the detainee, and stigmatized the power to conduct intimate body searches as oppressive and objectionable.[426] This is surely correct. Article 1 of the Declaration of Tokyo (1975) provides: 'The doctor shall not countenance, condone or participate in the practice of torture or other forms of cruel, inhuman or degrading procedures, whatever the offence of which the victim of such procedures is suspected, accused or guilty, and whatever the victim's beliefs or motives, and in all situations, including armed conflict and civil strife.' The power to conduct intimate searches may be very useful to the police, but its benefits are achieved at too high a price in human dignity and standards of civilized behaviour to be compatible with the responsibilities of the medical profession and the principles of a civilized legal system.

(4) Intimate and non-intimate samples

Intimate samples (defined in section 65 as a sample of blood, semen or other tissue fluid, urine, saliva, or pubic hair, or a swab taken from a person's body orifice) may be taken only with the appropriate consent (which has the same meaning as in relation to fingerprinting) and then only if an officer of the rank of superintendent or above authorizes it in writing (or, if authorized orally, with confirmation in writing as soon as practicable). The sample may be authorized only if the superintendent has reasonable grounds (a) for suspecting that the person concerned has been involved in a serious arrestable offence, and (b) for believing that the sample will tend to prove or disprove his involvement.[427] The person must be informed of the grounds for the authorization, which must also be recorded (in the custody record if the person is in custody at the time). The sample must be taken by a medical practitioner unless it is of saliva or urine.

---

[426] See W. Russell, 'Intimate Body Searches: For Stilettos, Explosive Devices, et al.' (1983) 286 *Brit. Med. J.* 733.

[427] PACE, s. 62(1), (2), (3), (4).

This power raises fewer problems than the power to conduct intimate searches. The appropriate consent cannot be dispensed with, although there are serious doubts as to the propriety of allowing a parent or guardian to give consent on behalf of a child who is *Gillick*-competent and is refusing his consent: the Act seems to be premised on the same assumptions as those which informed the *obiter* discussion of Lord Donaldson MR in *Re R. (a minor) (wardship: medical treatment),*[428] and which, as noted in Chapter 4 above, are incompatible with the approach taken to consent to medical examinations in the Children Act 1989. In most cases, therefore, the interests of doctors and detainees are protected. The interests of justice are also protected, by section 62(10), which permits a court or jury to draw such conclusions from refusal of consent as appear proper. In particular, the refusal may be treated as capable of corroborating any evidence against the defendant to which his refusal is relevant.

A non–intimate sample is a sample of hair (other than pubic hair), a sample taken from a nail or under a nail, a swab taken from part of a person's body other than a body orifice, and a footprint or similar impression of part of a person's body, other than a hand (which would constitute a fingerprint).[429] Non-intimate samples normally require the person's written consent, but this may be dispensed with if an officer of the rank of at least superintendent authorizes the taking of the sample. This may be done on the same grounds as justify giving authority for an intimate sample.[430] However, after a non-intimate sample has been authorized, reasonable force may be used if necessary to take it.[431] This may be traumatic for the person from whom it is taken, but it is far less degrading and dangerous, and so less objectionable, than the power to conduct intimate searches.

5.9 TREATMENT AFTER CHARGE

Once a detainee has been charged, he must be either released (on bail or without bail) or brought before a magistrates' court, where he will either be released on bail, remanded in custody to await committal proceedings or trial, or remanded into police custody to enable the police to investigate other offences.

Once charged, and if they are not being investigated in relation to other offences, defendants generally have a right to be released on bail, which may be withheld only in accordance with the conditions specified

---

[428] [1991] 4 All ER 177, CA.   [429] PACE, s. 65.
[430] PACE, s. 63.   [431] PACE, s. 117.

in the Bail Act 1976. If a juvenile is to be detained, the custody officer has a duty to ensure that he is held in secure local authority accommodation if possible, but if the custody officer is not satisfied that there is appropriately secure local authority accommodation available he may detain him at the police station.[432]

The court has power to impose conditions on the grant of bail, such as curfews, or requirements that the defendant should live at a specified address, surrender his passport, or report regularly to the police station. These conditions must be for the purpose of ensuring that the defendant appears for trial and does not commit offences in the mean time. The conditions may affect other rights, such as the right to freedom of movement. Furthermore, as noted in Chapter 17 below, a court can (but ought not to) use bail conditions to limit the freedom of a defendant to exercise rights to protest and express political views pending trial. Such potential abuses of bail procedures need careful monitoring.

If remanded in custody, the accused is entitled to have a summary trial or committal hearing within a set time (in most places now 70 days, although there are some regional variations), and there is a limit to the time which may elapse between committal and trial on indictment (now 112 days). The period may be extended by the court, but if the procedures are not complied with the defendant must be given bail.[433]

5.10 CONCLUSION

At the end of this huge chapter, it is worth taking a paragraph to identify some of the threads which run through it. First, it would be wrong to claim that PACE and the Codes of Practice represented major infringements of people's rights in this area. The principal new powers are the country-wide power to search the person for stolen or prohibited articles, and the power to hold people without charge for over twenty-four hours in respect of serious arrestable offences. The search power is open to criticism, but no more than other search powers which existed before and, like that under the Misuse of Drugs Act 1971, section 23(2), remain in force. The power to detain without charge is an extension of the previous law, and is considerably greater than that which applies in Scotland, where detention without charge following arrest is limited to a maximum period of six hours. However, both the search and the detention powers

---

[432] PACE, s. 38(6); *R.* v. *Chief Constable of Cambridgeshire, ex parte M.* [1991] 2 All ER 777, DC.

[433] Prosecution of Offences Act 1975, s. 22(3); Prosecution of Offences (Custody Time Limits) Regulations 1987, SI 1987/299, as amended; *R.* v. *Sheffield Justices, ex parte Turner* [1991] 2 WLR 987, [1991] 1 All ER 858, DC.

are hedged about with provisions which are intended to protect people's rights. The threat to restrict the right of silence has been repelled, temporarily at least, in mainland Britain, and it is to be hoped that a careful research programme will lead to its reinstatement in Northern Ireland. Perhaps the only new power which is both objectionable in principle and subject to safeguards which are patently inadequate is the power to conduct intimate searches.

Secondly, counterbalancing the new powers are new (or newly stated in statutory form) rights for detainees. The right to legal advice, the right of members of vulnerable groups to have an appropriate adult present, and the right to communicate with people outside the police station are all important. The efficacy of the first of these rights depends crucially on the operation of an effective 24-hour duty solicitor scheme. This is a case, therefore, where civil liberties depend crucially on the expenditure of public money to make the detainee's freedom to obtain legal advice a real one. This illustrates the point made by Raz (Chapter 1 above) about the way in which many individual freedoms depend on social and governmental action to make them realizable.

Thirdly, there are questions about the adequacy of the safeguards. Many of these depend on the requirement for reasonable grounds for belief or suspicion. There is some scepticism, supported by the observational studies, about the ability of such statutory standards to control police behaviour. Others turn on record-keeping, an exercise of questionable value unless senior officers and defence solicitors are routinely prepared to spend time checking the records. In these areas, police attitudes are more important than legal rules. As an aid to changing those attitudes, the approach of the courts to the detention and questioning provisions, excluding substantial numbers of alleged confessions under section 78 of PACE for breaches of the rules, or holding them to be inadmissible under section 76, is potentially powerful, as well as being, in my view (although some others disagree), a welcome and belated reassertion of the values of the rule of law in relation to the law governing policing.

Finally, the comparison of English law with the requirements of the European Convention on Human Rights has disclosed a number of areas in which the law of arrest and detention, worked out mainly with a view to investigative efficiency rather than individual rights, falls short of the Convention standards. In particular, the purposes for which arrests may be made and (in terrorist cases) the procedures for reviewing detention have been singled out. This failure of concern for rights is unfortunate, but not surprising in view of the lack of a developed concern for individual rights in English public law. It mirrors the findings of a number of other chapters of this book.

6

RIGHTS UNDER RESTRAINT: DETENTION OF PRISONERS AND PATIENTS

This chapter considers the detention of people for reasons which have nothing to do with criminal investigation. The conditions in which people are imprisoned after conviction, and the detention of people for medical reasons, form the subjects of the chapter, both in respect of the justifiability of the detention and in relation to the rights of those who are detained.

The provisions of English law governing the punishment and treatment of convicted offenders are highly complex. While some forms of punishment have been abolished (such as flogging), and others have been heavily attenuated (such as hanging),[1] other types of punishment available to sentencers have proliferated. The main form of sentence which has implications for the right to liberty is imprisonment, and the first part of this chapter considers the conditions under which imprisonment is lawful. The later part of the chapter examines the compulsory treatment of patients under the Mental Health Act 1983.

6.1 IMPRISONMENT IN INTERNATIONAL HUMAN RIGHTS LAW AND UK LAW

Deprivation of liberty as a punishment is within the contemplation of the European Convention on Human Rights, Article 5(1)(a), so long as it follows conviction by a competent court and is 'in accordance with a procedure prescribed by law'. Where these conditions are not complied with, Article 5(5) requires that victims 'shall have an enforceable right to compensation'. As noted in Chapter 4, Article 10(3) of the International Covenant on Civil and Political Rights insists that the essential aim of the treatment of prisoners is to be 'their reformation and social rehabilitation'. Article 10(1) further requires that people deprived of their liberty are to be treated with humanity and with 'respect for the inherent dignity of the human person'. Article 7 of the International Covenant on Civil and Political Rights (ICCPR), and Article 3 of the European Convention on Human Rights, each outlaws torture and inhuman or degrading treat-

---

[1] See Chs. 3 and 4 above.

ment or punishment. The implications of these provisions for conditions of imprisonment and medical detention form one of the themes of this chapter.[2]

Under the ICCPR, the Human Rights Committee has held that conditions of detention amount to inhumanity and fail to respect the dignity of the person where people were held in isolation, yet subjected to continuous surveillance, were malnourished, kept without natural light or exercise, and denied family visits, over a long period.[3] Another example was where a prisoner was kept for a long period in isolation in a dirty cell which was excessively hot in summer and cold in winter, without light.[4] These are very serious conditions, which could easily threaten physical or mental health. Under Article 3 of the European Convention, the Commission found a breach of the prohibition on inhuman or degrading treatment in *Denmark* et al. v. *Greece*,[5] where prisoners were subjected to severe overcrowding in cells and corridors used as sleeping and living accommodation with little natural light, were given no beds or mattresses, and experienced refusal to provide, or delays in providing, medical treatment for significant illnesses, and these conditions continued for long periods. However, under Article 3 it seems that the Commission regards the duration of the treatment, its strictness, and the object pursued, as being crucial.[6] For example, in *Kröcher and Möller* v. *Switzerland*[7] it decided that being kept for two months in solitary confinement, under constant artificial light, subject to surveillance, did not violate Article 3. Applications relating solely to solitary confinement have accordingly had no success.[8]

There are certain international instruments which go further in laying down detailed standards for prison authorities to observe. The United Nations Standard Minimum Rules for the Treatment of Prisoners set out principles of good practice in the treatment of prisoners and the management of prisons, to be applied in the light of local conditions. These are

[2] See generally Nigel Rodley, *The Treatment of Prisoners in International Law* (Oxford: Clarendon Press, 1987), ch. 9.

[3] *Estrella* v. *Uruguay*, Application No. 79/1980, and *Cámpora* v. *Uruguay*, Application No. 66/1980.

[4] *Manera* v. *Uruguay*, Application No. 123/1982.

[5] (3321–3/67, 3344/67) (1969) 12 *Yearbook of the European Convention on Human Rights The Greek Case*; (1968) 11 *Yearbook* 690, 730.

[6] Paul Sieghart, *The International Law of Human Rights* (Oxford: Clarendon Press, 1983), 168.

[7] (8463/78) Eur. Comm. HR (1983).

[8] See e.g. *Brady* v. *UK* (8575/79) 3 EHRR 297, Eur. Comm. HR; P. J. Duffy, 'Article 3 of the European Convention on Human Rights' (1983) *ICLQ* 316 at pp. 329–35; Graham Zellick, 'Human Rights and the Treatment of Offenders', in J. A. Andrews (ed.), *Human Rights in Criminal Procedure* (The Hague: Martinus Nijhoff, 1981), 375–416.

aspirational principles. They include a requirement for prisoners normally to be accommodated at night in single cells (rule 9(1)), and to be allowed natural light, fresh air, and artificial light when desired (rule 11). Sanitation should be such as to permit prisoners to comply with the needs of nature when necessary, and in a clean and decent manner (rule 12). There are provisions relating to medical services (rules 22-6), and requiring communication with family and reputable friends, including visits, at regular intervals (rule 37).

The European Prison Rules, adopted in 1987,[9] attempt to outline the proper objectives of prison authorities in setting standards for treatment and accommodation of prisoners. European Prison Rule 71(3), for example, requires authorities to provide useful work or other purposeful activities to keep prisoners actively employed for a normal working day; rule 14(1) provides that prisoners shall normally be lodged at night in individual cells unless it is considered that there are advantages in sharing with other prisoners; rule 17 requires that sanitary arrangements 'enable every prisoner to comply with the needs of nature when necessary and in clean and decent conditions'. However, neither the UN Standard Minimum Rules nor the European Prison Rules are binding in international law or in the domestic law of the UK. They are intended as guidelines for national authorities, and also for the Human Rights Committee and the European Commission and Court of Human Rights when relevant to human rights complaints which they are considering.

There is increasing evidence that the conditions in British prisons fall far below the standard envisaged by the UN Standard Minimum Rules and the European Prison Rules. At present, many prisons in the UK fall far short of desirable standards of sanitation, and the normal allowance of visits is 15 minutes per weekday for remand prisoners and one monthly 30-minute visit for convicted prisoners. As the Woolf/Tumim inquiry report pointed out, this is woefully inadequate for maintaining family contact, and should be substantially liberalized.[10] That inquiry also identified overcrowded and insanitary conditions in prisons as one of the underlying factors creating the conditions for the prison riots of 1990.[11] As the report notes, 'Successive Chief Inspectors [of Prisons] have made it clear that they regard the practice of slopping out as uncivilised, unhygienic and degrading'.[12] The government is committed to improving conditions, but progress so far has been slow.

---

[9] Recommendation No. R(87)3 of the Committee of Ministers of the Council of Europe, adopted 12 Feb. 1987.

[10] Rt. Hon. Lord Justice Woolf and His Honour Judge Stephen Tumim, *Prison Disturbances April 1990*, Cm. 1456 (London: HMSO, 1991), paras. 14.225 f.

[11] Ibid., paras. 11.81–11.112.

[12] Ibid., para. 11.101.

The UK is a party to the European Convention for the Prevention of Torture and Inhuman or Degrading Treatment or Punishment.[13] The European Committee for the Prevention of Torture and Inhuman or Degrading Treatment (CPT) is the monitoring agency under the Convention.[14] The CPT visited a number of prisons and police stations in the UK in 1990. Its Report[15] found some things to praise, but made a number of damning criticisms. These included:[16]

(a) overcrowding, with several people to a cell designed for one;

(b) the need to defecate in buckets in the presence of other people in a confined space used as a living area is degrading;

(c) slopping out the buckets when cells are unlocked in the morning is debasing for the prisoners and supervising officers;

(d) lack of decency even where toilet facilities are available, especially within shared cells;

(e) inadequate exercise and work facilities, leading to many prisoners being locked in cells for 22 or more hours a day, while work which was available tended to be dull and repetitive and did not involve skills which might be useful to the prisoner on release.

The CPT's conclusion was that 'the cumulative effect of overcrowding, lack of integral sanitation and inadequate regimes amounts to inhuman and degrading treatment'.[17] This is in line with criticisms levelled at prison conditions by Judge Stephen Tumim, HM Chief Inspector of Prisons, in a series of reports, the most recent of which, in 1991, almost coincided with the publication of the CPT's report. In looking at the cumulative effect of conditions and treatment, the CPT's approach is in line with that of the Human Rights Committee to establishing breaches of Article 7 of the International Covenant on Civil and Political Rights. On the other hand, the conditions described perhaps do not fall quite as far below normal humanitarian standards as the conditions found in cases where the Human Rights Committee and the European Commission of Human Rights have so far upheld allegations of inhuman or degrading treatment. The implication is that the UK may be in breach of the European Convention for the Prevention of Torture, and of the International Covenant on Civil and Political Rights and Article 3 of the European Convention on Human Rights, but it is by no means

---

[13] Discussed by Antonio Cassese, 'A New Approach to Human Rights: the European Convention for the Prevention of Torture' (1989) 83 *Amer. J. Int. L.* 128–53.

[14] On the work of the CPT, see Malcolm Evans and Rod Morgan, 'The European Convention for the Prevention of Torture: Operational Practice' (1992) 41 *ICLQ* 590–614.

[15] Adopted by the CPT on 21 Mar. 1991 and published as CPT/Inf (91) 15 on 26 Nov. 1991.

[16] Report, paras. 40, 45, 47, 50, 53–6.   [17] Report, para. 57.

certain that the Human Rights Committee or the European Commission of Human Rights would so find. There is little doubt that the European Commission will soon have to consider the matter, since prisoners in the UK have a right of individual petition under it to the European Commission of Human Rights,[18] and the CPT report is likely to encourage them to lodge petitions. Under the European Convention, the government could be required to compensate prisoners for any breaches of their rights under the Convention.

It is, therefore, not surprising that the UK Government's response to the report,[19] while accepting that conditions in many prisons are unsatisfactory and setting out the steps which are in train to improve them, disagreed with the CPT's conclusion that conditions amounted to inhuman and degrading treatment. While a number of improvements are being planned, phasing out the more degrading aspects of cell-sharing and slopping out over a period, the full response to this report and those of Judge Tumim is likely to take a long time to have effect. Some programmes are under way, but most await the result of the debate which is continuing about the future of prison reform in the wake of the Woolf report.[20] In the mean time, redress for aggrieved prisoners is difficult to obtain under English law. We return to this matter in section 3 below.

The UK's current legal regime for prisons is governed by statute—the Prison Act 1952—and subordinate legislation (the Prison Rules 1964). A breach of the rules by prisoners can lead to disciplinary action, with sanctions including loss of remission (the period, not exceeding one-third of the nominal length of the sentence, by which the term of imprisonment is reduced if the prisoner behaves well). The status of the Rules is not entirely free from doubt. It has been held that they are justiciable to the extent that the court, on an application for judicial review of a disciplinary 'award' (as penalties in prison are quaintly called), can determine whether the governor or Board of Visitors which decided the case interpreted the rule correctly, and whether it is *intra vires* in the sense of being consistent with the Prison Act and other primary legislation.

On the other hand, it has also been decided that a breach of the rules by the governor or prison officers will not in itself give rise to an action for breach of statutory duty at the suit of an aggrieved prisoner.[21] Instead, they typically impose obligations on prisoners. As Stephen Shaw points

---

[18] See Ch. 2 above.

[19] The response was published by the Council of Europe on 26 Nov. 1991, as CPT/Inf (91) 16.

[20] The government has issued a White Paper, *Custody, Care and Justice* (London: HMSO, 1991), setting out its plans.

[21] R. v. *Deputy Governor of Parkhurst Prison, ex parte Hague; Weldon* v. *Home Office* [1991] 3 All ER 733, HL.

out,[22] our Prison Rule 28(1), dealing with work, provides that prisoners 'shall be required to do useful work', making it in effect one of the pains of imprisonment rather than a dignity-enhancing right, and placing no obligation on the authorities to provide useful work for the prisoners to do. One of the recommendations in the report of the inquiry by Lord Justice Woolf and Judge Tumim, *Prison Disturbances April 1990*, was that a new regime should be instituted, by amending the Prison Rules 1964, including contracts between prison authorities and inmates.[23] These would set out the kind of regime which each establishment would undertake to provide for its inmates, while each inmate would agree to comply with the responsibilities placed on him by the contract. In some cases, contracts could be specific to a particular prisoner, and would be regularly reviewed, giving progressively more preparation for release as the end of the sentence approached. This would facilitate effective planning of what was to be achieved during a sentence.[24] The accommodation and regime agreed under the contract would become a legitimate expectation for the inmate. The contracts would not ground private rights, or actions for damages for breach of contract, so it is not clear how the terms of the contract could be enforced against the prison authorities. One possibility would be to have monitoring by area managers and Boards of Visitors, with a grievance procedure in case of disagreements. Another option, though unlikely to be very effective, would be that contracts giving rise to a legitimate expectation might be enforceable in an application for judicial review. All this lies in the future.

6.2 THE INITIATION OF IMPRISONMENT IN UK

In general, the requirements of Article 5(1)(*a*) of the European Convention on Human Rights—that imprisonment must only follow conviction by a competent court, and must be in accordance with a procedure prescribed by law—are met by English law, which lays down in detail the circumstances in which detention or imprisonment can be imposed as a punishment for offences, and the maximum terms which can be imposed. In Northern Ireland, however, the possibility of detention without charge by administrative order (internment), utilized from 1971 to 1975 in Northern Ireland, remains open under the Northern Ireland (Emergency Provisions) Act 1991, despite successive reports recommending repeal.[25] In the light of a concerted bombing and terrorism

---

[22] Stephen Shaw, 'Prisoners' Rights', in Paul Sieghart (ed.), *Human Rights in the UK* (London: Human Rights Network, 1988), 40–9 at p. 42.

[23] Cm. 1456, paras. 12.120–12.129.   [24] Ibid., paras. 14.57–14.83.

[25] e.g. Lord Colville, *Review of the Northern Ireland (Emergency Provisions) Act*, Cm. 1115, ch. 11.

campaign by the IRA in late 1991 and early 1992, the Secretary of State for Northern Ireland, Mr Peter Brooke, repeatedly refused to say what circumstances might make him consider that the reactivation of internment would be justified. In *Ireland* v. *United Kingdom*,[26] the European Court of Human Rights held that internment breached Article 5 of the Convention. However, the UK had entered a derogation from Article 5 in respect of the situation in Northern Ireland. The Court unanimously held that the derogation was permissible, as there was (under Article 15) a 'public emergency threatening the life of the nation', and accepted that the UK had not overstepped the bounds of the margin of appreciation left to states in deciding what steps were strictly required to deal with the emergency (the proportionality requirement).

There is a lacuna, however, in relation to the enforceable right to compensation under Article 5(5). Where a court sentences a person to be detained in circumstances in which there was no legal power to do so, there is sometimes a right to compensation, but this will depend on the type of judicial officer who imposed the sentence. Justices who (for example) sentence a person to be detained, without complying with a statutory precondition requiring that he is entitled to legal aid, act beyond their jurisdiction. The detention is tortious, and the justices who authorized it are liable in damages for false imprisonment without the need to prove malice or lack of reasonable and probable cause.[27] However, a circuit judge who made the same mistake is not liable, being protected by a common-law immunity designed to allow judges to act fearlessly as they think right, so long as they are acting in good faith in purported performance of his or her duties. This difference according to the nature of the judge was criticized by Lord Denning MR, who attempted to extend the common law immunity to cover justices as well as judges in *Sirros* v. *Moore*.[28] However, the continued vulnerability of justices to liability for wrongful imprisonment was reaffirmed, together with the immunity of judges sitting in superior courts of record, by the House of Lords in *In re McC. (a minor)*.[29] The effect of these rules is to allow some chance of obtaining compensation as of right to those wrongly imprisoned by justices, who in England and Wales here by far the highest proportion of criminal cases, but at the same time to deny a legal remedy to those sentenced by judges in the Crown Court, High Court, and Court of Appeal.

Even when wrongly sentenced by justices to detention, the victim may be denied substantial compensation by the Justices of the Peace Act 1979, section 52(1), which limits to one penny the damages payable by justices who 'in the execution of [their] office' (a term which encompasses acts

---

[26] Eur. Ct. HR, Series A, No. 25, Judgment of 18 Jan. 1978.
[27] Justices of the Peace Act 1979, s. 45.
[28] [1975] QB 118, CA.   [29] [1985] AC 528, HL.

done as a justice, even if technically outside jurisdiction)[30] wrongly commit a person to prison, where it is shown (*a*) that the accused actually committed the offence, and (*b*) that he underwent no greater punishment than that assigned by law for the offence. If a person is imprisoned for an offence for which he is not liable to imprisonment as a matter of law, or is imprisoned for longer than the law allows, he will always have suffered a punishment greater than that assigned by law, and so will be able to recover damages at large for the imprisonment.[31] However, if the person could lawfully have been committed to the term of imprisonment but the order was vitiated by a procedural error, his damages will be limited to one penny.[32]

As a result, there are cases in which a person sentenced to imprisonment otherwise than in accordance with a procedure prescribed by law is unable to obtain compensation at large. The right to compensation under Article 5(5) of the European Convention on Human Rights requires more than nominal damages of one penny; this might compensate for material damage where the defendant could have been properly imprisoned anyway, but there must be an enforceable right to real compensation for the moral as well as material damage.[33] English law provides no compensation at all where the imprisonment is wrongfully authorized by a superior court judge acting in execution of his office, and no real compensation for moral injury when it is authorized by a justice who is protected by section 52 of the Justices of the Peace Act 1979. The real anomaly in the compensation provisions from a human rights law perspective, then, would not be remedied by Lord Denning's proposed move to extend the protection of judges to justices of the peace, but would require a right to substantial compensation, against the state if not against the individual judge or justice, to be extended to all cases where a person is wrongfully imprisoned.

At present, the only limited statutory right to compensation is that for those whose convictions are quashed, under the Criminal Justice Act 1988. The person must show beyond reasonable doubt that there has been a miscarriage of justice, either by proving that the conviction resulted from non-disclosure of evidence which was not wholly or partly due to him, or by producing new evidence. It is for the Home Secretary to decide whether or not a person is entitled to compensation, subject to judicial review on the usual public-law grounds. If he decides that

---

[30] *R. v. Waltham Forest Justices, ex parte Solanke* [1986] 2 All ER 981, CA.
[31] *R. v. Manchester City Magistrates' Court, ex parte Davies* [1989] QB 631, [1989] 1 All ER 90, CA.
[32] *R. v. Waltham Forest Justices, ex parte Solanke* [1986] 2 All ER 981, CA.
[33] *Huber* v. *Austria* (6821/74) 6 DR 65, Eur. Comm. HR.

compensation is due, he appoints an assessor, who must be legally qualified, to determine the amount which is to be paid.[34]

This does not help those whose sentence of detention was wrongfully imposed, but whose convictions are not quashed. Until an enforceable right to compensation is extended to such cases, our law fails to comply with the requirements of Article 5(5) of the European Convention.

6.3 REMEDYING POOR CONDITIONS OF DETENTION IN UK LAW

Generally, three questions arise in relation to prisoners. First, what rights do prisoners retain when they enter captivity? Secondly, what special rights (if any) accrue to them? Thirdly, how are their rights enforceable?

(1) Retained rights

At common law, it used to be the case that prisoners, at any rate if convicted of felonies, lost all their civil rights and liberties. They even lost the right to bring legal proceedings, so that they became, in legal terms, non-people. In Australia, this view, derived from early nineteenth-century English law, prevailed long after it had altered in the United Kingdom, until changed by statute.[35]

However, this view is inconsistent with modern attitudes to rights. In the USA it has long been held that a prisoner's right to apply to federal courts for a writ of habeas corpus cannot be inhibited by states,[36] and habeas corpus has therefore become an important weapon in the armoury of convicted murderers seeking to delay or avoid execution of the death penalty. The right of access to courts also demands a right to legal advice from advisers with legal training, and adequate library facilities.[37] In England, too, a convicted prisoner does not now become a non-person. Rule 1 of the Prison Rules 1964 provides that the purpose of imprisonment is to enable the prisoners on their release to lead good and useful lives. This reflects the insistence in Article 10(3) of the International Covenant on Civil and Political Rights that the essential aim of the treatment of prisoners is their reformation and social rehabilitation, as noted in section 1.

---

[34] Criminal Justice Act 1988, s. 133 and Sched. 12.

[35] *Dugan* v. *Mirror Newspapers Ltd*. (1978) 142 CLR 583, HC of Australia; Felons (Civil Proceedings) Act 1981 (NSW).

[36] *Ex parte Hull* 312 US 546 (1941); *Johnson* v. *Avery* 393 US 483 (1969).

[37] *Procunier* v. *Martinez* 416 US 421 (1974): ban on interviews with law students or paralegals unconstitutional; *Bounds* v. *Smith* 430 US 817 (1977).

Consistently with the UK's obligations under international law, courts have held that prisoners retain all their rights except so far as they are taken away expressly by legislation or by necessary implication, having regard to the nature of imprisonment.[38] The right which is most obviously lost on incarceration is that to liberty, and there are other rights which are inevitably restricted, either in order to maintain security and order in prison or because a person's freedom of choice is automatically attenuated under conditions of imprisonment. Restrictions here, as in the United States, include limitations on privacy rights and freedom of communications.[39] The nature of the rights which are lost and those which are retained has been the subject of attention both in the English courts and, under various Articles of the European Convention on Human Rights, in the European Commission and Court of Human Rights.[40]

Thus prisoners retain the right under Article 6 of the European Convention on Human Rights to have access to the courts to have their civil rights and obligations determined, and it is a contempt of court for anyone, including the prison authorities, to attempt to interfere with the exercise of the right (for example, by intercepting or censoring letters which are attempting to initiate court proceedings).[41] However, this does not encompass a right to be transported to court at public expense for a hearing. The Home Secretary retains a discretion to require a prisoner to pay for transport and escort services, subject to judicial review on ordinary public-law principles. In *R.* v. *Secretary of State for the Home Department, ex parte Wynne*,[42] the court accepted that this might breach the prisoner's right of access to the court under Article 6 of the European Convention on Human Rights but thought that the Home Secretary was under no obligation in English law to exercise his discretion according to the requirements of the Convention. This is very likely to lead to an application to the European Commission of Human Rights.

Prisoners also retain the right to respect for their correspondence under

---

[38] *R.* v. *Hull Prison Board of Visitors, ex parte St. Germain* [1979] 1 QB 425 at 455; *Raymond* v. *Honey* [1983] 1 AC 1, [1982] 1 All ER 756 at 759 per Lord Wilberforce. The same is true in Canada: Solosky v. R. (1979) 105 DLR (3rd) 745 at 760 *per* Dickson J. in the Supreme Court of Canada.

[39] *Turner* v. *Safley*, 482 US 78 (1981).

[40] See Gillian Douglas and Stephen Jones, 'Prisoners and the European Convention on Human Rights', in M. P. Furmston, R. Kerridge, and B. E. Sufrin (eds.), *The Effect on English Domestic Law of Membership of the European Communities and of Ratification of the European Convention on Human Rights* (The Hague: Martinus Nijhoff, 1983); Genevra Richardson, 'Time to Take Prisoners' Rights Seriously' (1984) 11 *J. L. and Soc.* 1–23. For a comparative survey of prisoners' rights in the UK, Australia, the USA, and Canada, see Gordon Hawkins, *Prisoners' Rights: A Study of Human Rights and Commonwealth Prisoners*, Human Rights Commission Occasional Paper No. 12 (Canberra: AGPS, 1986).

[41] *Raymond* v. *Honey* [1983] 1 AC 1, [1982] 1 All ER 756, HL.

[42] [1992] 2 All ER 301, CA.

Article 8 of the Convention. The Prison Rules and Standing Orders, which previously made provision for extensive examination, reading, and stopping of correspondence, have been substantially liberalized following decisions of the European Court of Human Rights holding that the restrictions violated the right to respect for correspondence under Article 8(1) were not in accordance with a procedure prescribed by law, and went further than was justified by reference to any of the permissible justifying purposes for interference under Article 8(2).[43] Revisions to the Prison Rules allowing mail to be sent unread in connection with legal proceedings to which the inmate is a party (Rule 37A(1)) were held not to apply to letters in connection with an application to the European Commission of Human Rights, because the Commission was regarded (probably wrongly) as not exercising any judicial functions.[44] The European Court of Human Rights, however, has held the opening of such mail to be an unjustifiable interference with the inmate's right to respect for privacy of correspondence under Article 8 of the Convention.[45] But the problem is more general. In *Prison Disturbances April 1990*,[46] Lord Justice Woolf and Judge Tumim, after identifying that petty restrictions on correspondence were a source of considerable frustration among prisoners and that censorship imposes a substantial burden on staff, recommended that routine censorship should be removed from most prisoners' correspondence, being retained mainly where there was reason to suspect that a person's letters represented a threat to security,[47] and this proposal is being implemented.

Generally, prisoners retain the right to be free of torture and inhuman or degrading treatment or punishment. The prison regime must respect these rights, both because it is a requirement of the European Convention and because it helps to maintain order. In addition, there is a possibility that prisoners who suffer from inhuman or degrading treatment have a cause of action in damages under English law. This is examined in this section.

As noted above, neither the Prison Act 1952 nor the Prison Rules 1964 lay down standards of accommodation for prisoners or standards of

[43] See *Golder* v. *UK* Eur. Ct. HR, Series A, No. 18, Judgment of 21 Feb. 1975; *Silver* v. *UK* Eur. Ct. HR, Series A, No. 61, Judgment of 25 Mar. 1983; *Boyle and Rice* v. *UK* Eur. Ct. HR, Series A, No. 131, Judgment of 27 Apr. 1988; and *McCallum* v. *UK* Eur. Ct. HR, Series A, No. 183, Judgment of 30 Aug. 1990, where the government conceded that there had been a breach of Art. 8.

[44] *Guilfoyle* v. *Home Office* [1981] QB 309, [1981] 1 All ER 943, CA.

[45] *Campbell* v. *UK* Eur. Ct. HR, Series A, No. 233, Judgment of 25 Mar. 1992.

[46] Cm. 1456 (1991), pp. 407–9.

[47] The need for prison authorities to check letters where there is a reasonable suspicion that this is required in the interests of security was recognized by the Supreme Court of Canada in *Solosky* v. *R.* (1979) 105 DLR (3rd) 745.

treatment. Certain rules provide for detailed matters: for example, Rule 43 provides that a prisoner may be segregated from other prisoners for the maintenance of good order and discipline or in his own interests, a provision much used to keep sex offenders apart from other prisoners who might be likely to attack them. But there is no comprehensive set of standards for prison authorities to meet. Successive reports have made recommendations for improving minimum standards of prison conditions. The May Committee of Inquiry into the UK Prison Service in 1979 recommended that conditions should be improved to remove the need for prisoners to share cells (something which Jeremy Bentham's panopticon prison designs in the early years of the nineteenth century were intended to eliminate) and slop out their excreta from buckets, and (following calls from HM Chief Inspector of Prisons and the House of Commons Select Committee on Education, Science, and the Arts, both in 1983) that a code of standards should be introduced legislatively. As Stephen Shaw comments,[48] 'Establishing a code of more specific, enforceable standards—a role neither the Convention on Human Rights nor the European Prison Rules were designed to fulfil—has become a unifying demand of all the parties to the penal debate, with the critical exception of the British government'. It remains to be seen whether the government's response to the Woolf Inquiry recommendations is more vigorous than that to previous calls for improvement. The main problem is the cost of the necessary building works and administrative reorganization.

In the mean time, prisoners have attempted to press their claims to improved conditions through the courts, by bringing applications for judicial review and actions for damages for false imprisonment or trespass to the person, claiming that the conditions in which they have been confined breach the Prison Rules, the Bill of Rights 1689, or common-law standards. While judicial review applications have had some impact on prison disciplinary procedures, they have failed to make any impact in the field of prison conditions. In this, our courts are doing no better, but probably no less well, than the US federal courts, which generally defer to the expertise of prison administrators on the conditions which prison authorities can reasonably be expected to provide and the rules by which they are governed, which, unlike many other types of administrative rules, are not subjected to strict scrutiny analysis.[49] However, the US Supreme Court has used the prohibition on cruel and unusual punishment, under the Eighth Amendment to the US Constitution, to impose a

[48] Shaw, 'Prisoners' Rights', 42.
[49] *Turner* v. *Safley* 482 US 78 (1981), especially at pp. 84–5; Louis Fisher, *American Constitutional Law* (New York: McGraw-Hill, 1990), 1065; Geoffrey P. Alpert (ed.), *Legal Rights of Prisoners* (Beverley Hills, Calif.: Sage, 1980).

30-day limit on the period for which prisoners may be held in isolation cells in Arkansas prisons. The Court acknowledged, and was influenced by, the fact that prisoners in Arkansas suffered bad nutrition, violence, and overcrowding, and described conditions as 'a dark and evil world completely alien to the free world'.[50] This, however, is a small step on a long road.

Moreover, all the means so far used in England and Wales to seek damages to compensate for bad conditions have been unsuccessful, but there is a possibility that a new approach, based on a common-law duty of care (i.e. a simple negligence action) might enjoy more success. In the text which follows, the various heads of recovery which have been tried so far will be examined, finishing with a look at the possibilities offered by negligence.

(2) False imprisonment

It has been established for nearly 400 years that a public officer who imprisons a person pursuant to a statutory power, but detains him for a longer period than is authorized by statute or in an unauthorized place, is liable for false imprisonment.[51] It is also well established that a prisoner whose liberty within the prison is restricted in an allegedly unauthorized way can maintain an action for false imprisonment, as where an imprisoned debtor (normally permitted a good deal of freedom within the prison walls) was confined to a secure part of the prison known as the 'strongroom'.[52]

Section 12(1) of the Prison Act 1952 now provides that a prisoner may be lawfully confined in any prison, and there is provision for remand prisoners to be held in police cells under the Imprisonment (Temporary Provisions) Act 1980. In a number of first-instance decisions, it was held that these provisions provide a defence for the Secretary of State or prison authorities against an action for false imprisonment where the imprisonment has been authorized according to law and occurs in a place prescribed by law: the prisoner was said to have a cause of action for false imprisonment in respect of the nature of the imprisonment, as Goddard LJ said in *Arbon* v. *Anderson*,[53] but he could sue in relation to the conditions of imprisonment only if his treatment or other attendant circum-

---

[50] *Hutto* v. *Finney* 437 US 678 at p. 680 (1978).
[51] *Scavage* v. *Tateham* (1601) Cro. Eliz. 829, 78 ER 1056 (justice of the peace detaining suspected robber at justice's house for 18 days; statute authorized detention for only 3 days at a gaol).
[52] *Yorke* v. *Chapman* (1839) 10 Ad. & El. 207, 113 ER 80.
[53] [1943] KB 252 at pp. 254–5, [1943] 1 All ER 154 at p. 156.

stances amounted to a breach of statutory duty or some other tort.[54] This was followed in *R. v. Gartree Prison Board of Visitors, ex parte Sears*,[55] an application for judicial review of a decision of the Board of Visitors finding the applicant guilty of a disciplinary offence in prison and awarding him eight days confinement in his cell and loss of privileges. The relief sought included damages for false imprisonment. Mann J. held that, where a person is lawfully imprisoned, a variation in the conditions of confinement cannot constitute the tort of false imprisonment.

However, this attitude was based on a policy of protecting prison discipline: as Goddard LJ said in *Arbon* v. *Anderson*:[56] 'It would be fatal to all discipline in prisons if governors and warders had to perform their duty always with the fear of an action before their eyes if they in any way deviated from the rules.' Lord Denning MR echoed that in *Becker* v. *Home Office*:[57] 'If the courts were to entertain actions by disgruntled prisoners, the governor's life would be made intolerable. The discipline of the prison would be undermined.'

The importance of this consideration has tended to be downgraded in legal argument in more recent times. Prison governors' disciplinary decisions have been opened up to judicial review,[58] and the right of prisoners to have access to the courts has been upheld in a series of cases including *Raymond* v. *Honey*.[59] As a result, more recent decisions have moved away from the earlier first-instance decisions, although some uncertainty still exists as to the present rule.

The first decision was *R. v. Commissioner of Police of the Metropolis, ex parte Nahar*,[60] where defendants had been remanded in custody to Brixton Prison. Because they could not be admitted to Brixton, the prisoners were detained in a police cell under the Imprisonment (Temporary Provisions) Act 1980, section 6(2). This was lawful, but the defendants argued that the conditions in the police cells were so poor that their conditions should be considered unlawful. Stephen Brown J. in the Divisional Court thought that there must be some minimum lawful conditions for holding prisoners implied into the Act, and held that conditions falling below those standards would make the detention unlawful. On the facts, he decided that the conditions were not bad enough to amount to false imprisonment, but his general approach to the law was

---

[54] *Arbon* v. *Anderson* [1943] KB 252, [1943] 1 All ER 154; *Williams* v. *Home Office (No. 2)* [1981] 1 All ER 1211, affirmed on procedural grounds [1982] 2 All ER 564, CA.

[55] *The Times*, 20 Mar. 1985.

[56] [1943] KB 252 at p. 255, [1943] 1 All ER 154 at pp. 156 7.

[57] [1972] 2 QB 407 at p. 418, [1972] 2 All ER 676 at p. 682.

[58] *Leech* v. *Deputy Governor of Parkhurst Prison* [1988] AC 533, [1988] 1 All ER 485, HL.

[59] [1983] 1 AC 1, [1982] 1 All ER 756, HL.   [60] *The Times*, 28 May 1983.

subsequently accepted by the Court of Appeal in *Middleweek* v. *Chief Constable of the Merseyside Police*, where Ackner LJ said:[61]

. . . it must be possible to conceive of hypothetical cases in which the conditions of detention are so intolerable as to render the detention unlawful and thereby to provide a remedy to the prisoner in damages for false imprisonment. A person lawfully detained in a police cell would, in our judgment, cease to be so lawfully detained if the conditions in that cell were such as to be seriously prejudicial to his health if he continued to occupy it, e.g. because it became and remained seriously flooded, or contained a fractured gas pipe allowing gas to escape into the cell. We do not therefore accept as an absolute proposition that, if detention is initially lawful, it can never become unlawful by reason of changes in the conditions of imprisonment.

However, once again the conditions did not fall to those excessively low standards in that case.

A difference of opinion was already emerging between those who thought that conditions would constitute false imprisonment if sufficiently intolerable (such as Stephen Brown J. in *ex parte Nahar*) and others who would require conditions to be seriously prejudicial to the prisoner's health (such as the Court of Appeal in *Middleweek*). The matter finally received the attention of the House of Lords in two cases which fell for decision in 1991: *R.* v. *Deputy Governor of Parkhurst Prison, ex parte Hague*[62] and *Weldon* v. *Home Office*.[63] Unlike *ex parte Nahar* and *Middleweek*, both cases concerned conditions for convicted offenders serving terms in prison, but in *Weldon* v. *Home Office* the Court of Appeal decided that the same principles would apply.[64] Following the decision of the House of Lords, it seems that the same principles apply whenever people are subject to the regime of the Prison Act 1952, because of the statutory defence which the Act offers to prison authorities, but different principles apply to imprisonments which fall outside the scope of the 1952 Act.

In *Weldon*, the Home Office sought to have a claim by a prisoner for false imprisonment struck out. The plaintiff alleged that he had been taken to a cell in the punishment block of Leeds Prison, then to a strip cell where he had been left without clothes overnight, and claimed that this amounted to false imprisonment. The Court of Appeal declined to strike out the claim, holding that interference with a prisoner's residual liberty within a prison could amount to false imprisonment, and that section 12 of the Prisons Act 1952 did not protect the Home Office against

[61] (1985) [1990] 3 All ER 662 at p. 668.
[62] [1990] 3 All ER 687, CA, affirmed *sub nom. Hague* v. *Deputy Governor of Parkhurst Prison* [1991] 3 All ER 733, HL.
[63] [1990] 3 All ER 672, CA, reversed HL [1991] 3 All ER 733.
[64] [1990] 3 All ER 672, CA.

vicarious liability for acts of a prison officer which restricted a prisoner's residual liberty. Ralph Gibson L.J. thought that, were this not so, a prisoner would be unable to maintain an action against a fellow prisoner who deprived him of his residual liberty. However, this is wrong. As Taylor LJ pointed out in the Court of Appeal in *R. v. Deputy Governor of Parkhurst Prison, ex parte Hague*,[65] and the House of Lords confirmed, a fellow prisoner, or indeed a prison officer acting contrary to the directions of the prison governor, who restricted the residual freedom of a prisoner would be unable to make use of the defence under section 12 of the 1952 Act. On the other hand, as Parker LJ said in *Weldon*,[66] if the Home Office submissions were correct, the prisoner would have no right to damages if the detention in the strip cell had continued for weeks or if he were locked in a remote shed, so long as it was within the perimeter of the prison. Such a result would, said Parker LJ, offend against common sense.

In *ex parte Hague*, as in *Weldon*, the relevant test was said to be whether conditions were intolerable. Nicholls LJ said that physical conditions must not be intolerable, and treated references in *Middleweek* to substantial threats to health as being mere examples of intolerable physical conditions.[67] Although the court in *ex parte Hague* speaks of physical conditions, there should be no doubt that intolerable psychological conditions, such as extensive sensory deprivation or denial of sleep, would also be actionable. As Taylor LJ pointed out, an action based on intolerable conditions cannot be for false imprisonment *sinpliciter*, as the essence of false imprisonment is a deprivation of physical liberty, not intolerable conditions. But where a lawful imprisonment is conducted in an unauthorized manner, it deprives the imprisoner of the defence to an action based on justification.[68] Intolerable psychological conditions, which are capable of amounting to inhuman or degrading treatment under Article 3 of the European Convention on Human Rights, should be no less liable to nullify the prison officers' justification than intolerable physical conditions.

Ralph Gibson LJ in *Weldon* would have restricted actionability to cases where residual liberty was interfered with by prison officers intentionally, without reasonable cause, and knowing that they had no reasonable cause: in other words, in bad faith. If no protection were given against liability for unauthorized acts done in good faith, Ralph Gibson LJ thought that it would not be conducive to the maintenance of the proper working of the prison and well-ordered community life within the prison.[69] This special protection for prison officers acting in excess of

---

[65] [1990] 3 All ER 687, CA, at p. 707. [66] [1990] 3 All ER at p. 686.
[67] [1990] 3 All ER 687 at p. 709. [68] Ibid. at p. 706.
[69] [1990] 3 All ER at pp. 681, 684–5; Parker and Fox LJJ concurred: p. 686.

authority but in good faith was not fully argued in *Weldon*,[70] so the comments are strictly *obiter*. Ralph Gibson LJ was influenced by the supposed threat to good order which would flow from making acts by prison officers actionable.[71] That risk has been treated by judges in other cases (notably by Lord Bridge in *Leech* v. *Deputy Governor of Parkhurst Prison*[72]) as overstated. There is much to be said, as Lord Bridge pointed out, for developing the common law in a principled way, and avoiding creating special exceptions for special circumstances. If exceptions cannot be justified on principle, courts should not create what Ronald Dworkin calls 'checkerboard solutions'[73] in which people get treated unequally without any morally acceptable justification. Because of this, the Court of Appeal in *R.* v. *Deputy Governor of Parkhurst Prison, ex parte Hague* held that bad faith was not a necessary element in an action for false imprisonment by a prisoner. As Taylor LJ said, where bad faith is present it grounds an action for misfeasance in public office[74] rather than false imprisonment. 'To require proof of bad faith would be to alter the tort of false imprisonment and in effect to create a new tort special to prisons and prisoners.'[75]

This was a more principled and satisfactory approach than that of Ralph Gibson LJ in *Weldon*, and it was the one which the House of Lords adopted when the two cases came before them to be argued and decided together. The House unanimously rejected the idea of introducing special ingredients to the tort of false imprisonment in relation to people who are in prison pursuant to a court order. In all such cases, the order of the court justifies the imprisonment, and the prison governor and those officers who act in accordance with his directions are protected against liability for false imprisonment by section 12 of the Prisons Act 1952. However, this means that the tort of false imprisonment now offers no protection at all to prisoners against being detained in intolerable conditions. As Lord Bridge said:[76]

the proposition that the conditions of detention may render the detention itself unlawful raises formidable difficulties. If the proposition be sound, the corollary must be that when the conditions of detention deteriorate to the point of intolerability, the detainee is entitled immediately to go free. It is impossible, I think, to define with any precision what would amount to intolerable conditions for this purpose. . . . The law is certainly left in a very unsatisfactory state if the legality or otherwise of detaining a person who in law is and remains liable to

---

[70] [1990] 3 All ER at p. 681. [71] [1990] 3 All ER at p. 681.

[72] [1988] AC 533, [1988] 1 All ER 485, HL.

[73] Ronald Dworkin, *Law's Empire* (London: Fontana, 1986).

[74] *Bourgoin SA* v. *Ministry of Agriculture Fisheries and Food* [1986] QB 716, [1985] 3 All ER 585, CA.

[75] [1990] 3 All ER at p. 707. [76] [1991] 3 All ER at p. 746.

detention depends on such an imprecise criterion and may vary from time to time as the conditions of his detention change.

Lord Jauncey delivered a judgment to the same effect, and Lords Ackner, Goff, and Lowry agreed with both Lord Bridge and Lord Jauncey. A prisoner suffering such conditions would be entitled to a public-law remedy by way of judicial review, but the private law of false imprisonment is not to be twisted into service to combat defective conditions.

(3) Breach of statutory duty

The tort of breach of statutory duty has been explored as an alternative way to provide remedies for poor conditions or special regimes in prison. A breach of the Prison Act 1952 may give rise to an action for damages if the provision breached is one which is capable of giving rise to a right in an individual prisoner. For instance, section 14(2) of the Act provides: 'No cell shall be used for the confinement of a prisoner unless it is certified by an inspector that its size, lighting, heating, ventilation and fittings are adequate for health . . .'. As this is clearly intended to benefit the prisoner, a breach of the provision should ground an action for breach of statutory duty. If this is so, those in prison are better off than people detained in police stations. The conditions of the latter are governed by the Code of Practice (Code C), section 8 of which lays down standards for the conditions which should be provided for detainees in police stations. However, section 67(10) of PACE provides that failure to comply with the Code does not in itself give rise to civil or criminal liability, although the Code is admissible in evidence and may be relevant to the scope of any duty of care in a negligence action,[77] and breach of the Code may also make an officer liable to disciplinary proceedings.[78]

A breach of merely regulatory or administrative provisions of the Prison Act 1952, or of the Prison Rules 1964, for example by denying a prisoner association under rule 43 in circumstances where segregation is not justified under the rule, would not to be actionable as a breach of statutory duty. The Prison Rules are said to be regulatory only, intended to provide a framework for the running of the prison system rather than to confer rights on individual prisoners. As noted above, this is consistent with the language in which the rules are framed, and is one of the main differences between the Prison Rules 1964 and the European Prison Rules promulgated by the Council of Europe.

As the Prison Rules 1964 are merely regulatory, breach of the Rules does not give rise to an action for breach of statutory duty, as they are generally not intended to give rights to prisoners or to operate for their

[77] PACE, s. 67(11).   [78] PACE, s. 67(8).

benefit. This was established in *R. v. Deputy Governor of Parkhurst Prison, ex parte Hague*.[79] Not only can a breach of the rules not ground an action in itself, but the House of Lords accepted that it cannot deprive the prison authorities of the benefit of any defence to an action for false imprisonment based on section 12(1) of the Prison Act 1952. This makes it impossible to use a breach of statutory duty action as a means of obtaining compensation for intolerable prison conditions at present, although if the nature of the Prison Rules were to change in the future breach of statutory duty might become useful. In the mean time, a breach of the Prison Rules 1964, or the Prison Act 1952, is likely to provide no more than a basis for an application for judicial review of the act, omission, or decision in question. This may be a useful remedy, but will be more effective in relation to disciplinary matters, where the court's discretion is likely to be exercised in favour of the prisoner once illegality, irrationality, or procedural impropriety is shown, than in respect of general prison conditions, where the discretion is likely to be used to avoid dictating to the Home Office on matters of policy and resource allocation and management.

(4) The Bill of Rights 1689

It was accepted in *Williams v. Home Office (No. 2)*[80] that the prohibition on cruel and unusual punishment in the Bill of Rights 1689 is capable of giving rise to an action in damages, since breach of the prohibition makes the punishment unlawful unless the particular punishment is authorized by the Prison Act 1952. (The Prison Rules, being merely secondary legislation, cannot override the prohibition in the Bill of Rights.) It may also be possible to apply for judicial review of a decision to place a prisoner in a particular type of accommodation on the ground that the conditions amount to cruel or unusual punishment.[81] It is not clear whether breach of the Bill of Rights 1689 is a special tort, or whether it is a type of breach of statutory duty.

This resulted, in *ex parte Herbage (No. 2)*, in the majority of the Court of Appeal holding that leave to apply for judicial review had been properly granted where the applicant, who was seriously overweight and as a result was immobile and could not climb stairs, had on that account been accommodated on the ground floor of the hospital wing at Pentonville Prison, which was the prison psychiatric hospital. There he was sur-

---

[79] [1991] 3 All ER 733, HL, approving *dicta* of Tudor Evans J. in *Williams v. Home Office (No. 2)* [1981] 1 All ER at pp. 1240–2.

[80] [1981] 1 All ER 1211.

[81] *R. v. Secretary of State for the Home Dept., ex parte Herbage (No. 2)* [1987] QB 1077, [1987] 1 All ER 324 (CA majority decision, May LJ dissenting).

rounded by schizophrenics, psychopaths, and others in conditions which made it impossible for him to sleep. This, he argued, amounted to cruel and unusual punishment. In the same way it was argued in *Williams* that the plaintiff's detention in the special control unit at Wakefield Prison was actionable as a cruel and unusual punishment. He had been denied association and, for a time, exercise, kept without visual or auditory relief, had insufficient light, had dull and repetitious work sewing mail-bags, was subject to constant surveillance and searches, denied the opportunity to gain remission for good behaviour, and was subject to indefinite prolongation of his term in the unit. This raises a number of issues.

First, as the Bill of Rights speaks only of punishments, and not (unlike the European Convention) of treatment generally, what is a punishment? In *Williams*, Tudor Evans J. accepted that confinement in the unit, being part of the sentence which the plaintiff was serving, was a punishment.[82] However, in *ex parte Herbage* the applicant had not been convicted of any offence, but was remanded in prison awaiting extradition to the United States for trial on fraud offences. It is hard to see how a person who is awaiting trial or extradition can be said to be undergoing punishment. If, as seems likely, remand prisoners are not protected by the Bill of Rights prohibition on cruel and unusual punishments, their rights are paradoxically protected less well than those of convicted prisoners.

Next, when is punishment cruel and unusual? The judge in *Williams* decided that the Bill of Rights prohibits punishments only if they are both cruel and unusual: the words are to be read conjunctively, not disjunctively. In reaching this decision he followed a decision of the Supreme Court of Canada in *R. v. Miller and Cockriell*[83] that the words were to be read conjunctively in the context of the Canadian Bill of Rights 1960, in preference to a contrary opinion of Heald J. in *McCann v. R.*[84] There had been no previous suggestion, particularly in the judicial and academic literature on the Eighth Amendment to the US Constitution, that it was proper to read the words conjunctively. Nevertheless, Tudor Evans J. adopted the conjunctive interpretation. A regime might therefore be cruel, judged according to prevailing standards of morality, yet not be unusual (and hence not be actionable) if prison practice here and abroad lags behind public morality. He went on to hold that the special control unit had not been unusual, because the conditions in it were not notably different from those under certain other regimes in English prisons—notably those applied to prisoners segregated at their own request under rule 43 of the Prison Rules 1964—or from control units abroad, notably in the USA and British Columbia.

[82] [1981] 1 All ER at p. 1242.   [83] (1975) 70 DLR (3d) 324.
[84] (1975) 68 DLR (3d) 661.

Tudor Evans J. then turned to the question whether the regime was cruel. He adopted a two-standard test for cruelty. First, there are minimal standards accepted by public standards of morality, and any regime which falls below those standards will automatically be cruel. Secondly, a regime may be at or above that standard, but still be cruel if the suffering it imposes is disproportionate to any legitimate penological objective. These matters are to be judged objectively, by reference to the standards current in the society in question at the present time.[85] This approach is consistent with some of the caselaw of the US Supreme Court in relation to the death penalty, which was held to be cruel in *Furman* v. *Georgia*[86] because it was not shown to serve any penological objective which could not be achieved otherwise. Tudor Evans J. decided that the standards did not fall below the irreducible minimum required of prisons by public morality. He then decided that the need to maintain order and contain inveterate trouble-makers in prison justified the use of segregation and control units, having regard to the fact that the long-term segregation of prisoners in poor conditions for the purpose of maintaining order had been accepted as necessary in 1968 by a subcommittee of the Advisory Council on the Penal System, chaired by Professor Radzinowicz[87] and in 1973 by the Home Office working party established to consider ways of controlling disruptive maximum security prisoners in the light of widespread prison disturbances in 1972.

This approach to the issue of cruelty is unsatisfactory, and is in reality inconsistent with the professed aim of judging these matters objectively according to prevailing standards of public morality. The judge, instead of assessing whether the regime was necessary in the light of a publicly accepted penal objective, was content to be guided by the opinion of a Home Office working party, having no claim to be independent of the executive, and which had not been required by its terms of reference or otherwise to direct its attention to the demands of public morality. Like so many other Home Office working parties, this one had been given a limited and functional brief, with no scope to review penal policy. This made the judge's approach a mere rubber stamp for the executive decision to implement the regime of its working party: hardly a satisfactory way of protecting prisoners against cruel and unusual punishments. Special control units were abolished in 1975, and the main reason for their abolition was the public outcry generated by publicity about the treatment of prisoners in the units.

---

[85] [1981] 1 All ER at p. 1245.   [86] 408 US 238 (1972).
[87] *The Regime for Long Term Prisoners in Conditions of Maximum Security* (London: Home Office, 1968).

(5) Misfeasance in a public office

As noted above, any prison officer who, in the performance of his duties as a prison officer, intentionally commits an unlawful act or omission, realizing that it is likely to cause loss or injury to a prisoner, is liable in damages for misfeasance in a public office to the prisoner if loss or injury results.[88] However, this tort is unlikely to come often into play; even when the elements of the tort are present, it will usually also constitute a battery or some other tort which will be easier to establish, depending on a less demanding mental element on the part of the tortfeasor.

(6) Negligence

As has already been observed, in *Weldon* and *Hague* the House of Lords rejected attempts to build a remedy for intolerable prison conditions on the twin bases of false imprisonment and breach of statutory duty. However, their Lordships accepted that there ought to be a remedy, and expressed the view (*obiter*) that it lay in the field of negligence rather than intentional torts. As Lord Bridge put it:[89]

Whenever one person is lawfully in the custody of another, the custodian owes a duty of care to the detainee. If the custodian negligently allows, or, a fortiori, if he deliberately causes, the detainee to suffer in any way in his health he will be in breach of that duty. But short of anything that could properly be descibed as a physical injury or an impairment of health, if a person lawfully detained is kept in conditions which cause him for the time being physical pain or a degree of discomfort which can properly be described as intolerable, I believe that could and should be treated as a breach of the custodian's duty of care for which the law should award damages.

This has the advantage of allowing compensation to be obtained without making the detention itself unlawful, but immediately raises the difficult issue of the extent of the duty of the prison authorities. In any such action, the court would have to consider whether a prison governor has discharged the duty of care which he owes to a prisoner. It would not be necessary to decide what the threshold of tolerability is; the questions would be: (*a*) was it reasonably foreseeable that the conditions would cause physical injury, impairment of health, or intolerable pain or discomfort? and, if the answer to that is yes, (*b*) would it have been reasonable for the governor to alleviate the conditions? The difficulty for plaintiffs is likely to come under part (*b*), since the governor's ability to

---

[88] *Bourgoin* (as in n. 74); *R.* v. *Deputy Governor of Parkhurst Prison, ex parte Hague* [1990] 3 All ER at 707, CA, *per* Taylor LJ; [1991] 3 All ER 733, HL, at p. 745 *per* Lord Bridge.

[89] [1991] 3 All ER at p. 746.

improve conditions is likely to be heavily dependent on matters outside his control. Much may depend on the level of resources provided by the prison department of the Home Office, on the state of and amount of space in the buildings, and on the number of prisoners whom the governor is required to accommodate. If an action is brought against the governor, these contingencies are likely to restrict the scope of his duty of care. If an action is brought against the Home Office, the court is unlikely to be prepared to hold that government has a common-law duty to provide a particular level of resource for prisons, as so to hold would impose on the judges the task of setting public expenditure targets, a job for which they are ill suited under the doctrine of the separation of powers.

It seems to follow that liability in negligence is likely to be most readily incurred where prisoners are subjected to special regimes which are dictated by disciplinary or other special considerations rather than by staff shortages or inadequacy of resources. It might have offered a way in which Messrs. Williams, Weldon, and Hague could have improved their lot, but does not offer a way of securing compensation for the general run of poor conditions in British prisons. However, the scope of negligence liability is limited. In *H. v. Home Office*,[90] where through the negligence of the prison authorities a prisoner's conviction for sexual offences was discovered by fellow inmates, making it necessary to keep the prisoner in protective solitary confinement under rule 43 of the Prison Rules, the Court of Appeal held that the severe restriction of educational and recreational facilities and loss of quality of life could not give rise to damages for negligence. In the light of *Hague*, the court decided that negligence damages were available for intolerable conditions, but that a regime of solitary confinement authorized under the Prison Rules could not, as a matter of law, be regarded as so intolerable as to give rise to an action for breach of a duty owed to a prisoner.

This is important. Although Lord Bridge suggested in *Hague* that, in practice, the problem will not often arise, the mounting evidence in official reports, such as that from Sir Harry Woolf on the Strangeways riots, the regular reports of Judge Stephen Tumim, HM Chief Inspector of Prisons, and the recent report of the Council of Europe Committee on Torture, that conditions in Britain's prisons are inhuman and degrading, has already been referred to. It is hard to imagine how one could live in such conditions without suffering impaired mental health or intolerable mental discomfort. At the same time, the remedies depend so heavily on the supply of resources from government that it is hard to imagine that a duty of care in tort would ever adequate to provide a remedy for

[90] *Independent*, 6 May 1992, CA.

those who are condemned to live in those conditions. If it is ultimately decided that the conditions amount to inhuman or degrading treatment, the result is likely to be that there is no satisfactory domestic remedy for the breach of detainees' rights under Article 3 of the European Convention on Human Rights. This would lead to a flood of petitions to the European Commission of Human Rights from prisoners in an attempt to obtain a settlement of their claims, or compensation under the just satisfaction provisions of Article 50 of the Convention. This would damage the UK's standing in the eyes of the world community. It would be preferable to provide a domestic compensation programme to operate during the transitional period until improvements can be introduced to conditions across the whole prison sytem.

6.4 DETERMINACY OF SENTENCE AND THE RIGHT TO RELEASE

The normal rule is that a prisoner is entitled to know the term, or the maximum term, which he will have to serve. However, there are a number of circumstances in which the prison term may be more or less indeterminate. The main ones relate to release on licence, or 'parole' as it is known. Release on licence is an option in relation to most prisoners, and is discretionary, so that it is governed by ordinary public-law principles in judicial review proceedings. It is particularly important in relation to prisoners who have been sentenced to life imprisonment, for whom release on licence is their one hope of release.

The prisoner has no right to release, and there are established procedures for deciding whether or not to release prisoners on licence. Once released, the prisoner remains liable to be recalled to prison until the period of his sentence has been served. Prisoners serving life sentences are therefore permanently liable to recall. This raises civil liberties issues. The procedures are affected by changes introduced by the Criminal Justice Act 1991, designed in part to improve the procedures in response to criticisms by the European Court of Human Rights. The relevant provisions have not at the time of writing been brought into force. This section therefore examines the rights of prisoners in relation to decision-making about release, and their liability to be recalled after release, both under the pre-existing law and under the 1991 Act.

(1) The operation of the parole scheme

The operation of the parole system has until now been under the control of the Home Secretary, who decides whether or not to grant parole after consultation with the Parole Board (which, in the majority of cases, is the effective decision-maker), the Lord Chief Justice, and the trial judge where he is still available.[91] The process has been highly discretionary. Prisoners have normally been eligible to be considered for release on licence when they have served one-third of their sentence. Prisoners' cases are considered by the Parole Board, which makes a recommendation to the Home Secretary. No reasons are given for Parole Board recommendations, so a prisoner is not entitled to know why his application was successful or unsuccessful.[92] All cases are considered on the basis of documentary reports; although the Parole Board is under a duty to act fairly, it is performing an administrative rather than a quasi-judicial function, so the doctrine of natural justice has been held not to apply. Therefore neither statute not common law requires the Parole Board to give the prisoner an oral hearing.[93] Nor, until recently, was the Board required to disclose the material on which it is reaching a decision so as to allow the prisoner to know the case which he has to answer.

Being a discretionary matter, the Home Secretary is entitled, on general administrative-law principles, to have policy in relation to the date at which people who commit different sorts of offences may first be considered for release on licence, so long as the policy does not prevent him from considering cases on their merits and allowing for special circumstances,[94] amd so long as the policy adopted is not, in the circumstances, irrational or perverse (as it was held to be, unusually, in *R. v. Secretary of State for the Home Department, ex parte Handscomb).*[95]

This preference for a more or less unfettered administrative discretion is understandable in the context of prisoners who are serving fixed-term sentences. For them, early release is indeed a privilege, although a very important one directly related to the right to liberty, and where a court has formally sentenced a person to imprisonment for a set period it is right for the executive to exercise great circumspection in interfering with that sentence. This argument is, however, somewhat weakened by what is in effect a right to remission of up to one-third of a fixed term of imprisonment subject to the prisoner's good behaviour. Moreover, there are particular problems in relation to prisoners who are serving life sentences. There are two classes of life prisoners: those serving mandatory life sentences, usually for murder, and those serving discretionary life sentences for serious offences such as rape, where the court which sentenced the prisoner considered that he represented such a danger to society that

---

[91] Criminal Justice Act 1967, s. 61.

[92] *Payne v. Lord Harris of Greenwich* [1981] 1 WLR 754, CA; *R. v. Parole Board, ex parte Bradley* [1990] 3 All ER 828, DC.

[93] *R. v. Secretary of State for the Home Dept., ex parte Gunnell* [1985] Crim. LR 105, CA.

[94] *In re Findlay* [1985] AC 318, [1984] 3 All ER 801, HL.

[95] (1988) 86 Cr. App. R. 59, DC.

there ought to be a discretion to imprison him even after he has served the period which would normally have been imposed as the 'tariff' for that offence. In the case of discretionary life prisoners, the tariff (or the period of imprisonment which an offence displaying those characteristics would normally be thought to merit on purely retributive and deterrent principles) has been settled behind closed doors by the Lord Chief Justice in consultation with the trial judge, and only when that period has been served will parole normally be considered. But even thereafter, such people will never acquire an entitlement to be released. Their only hope of release depends on executive discretion, and the operation of the parole scheme. For such people, to dismiss their claim to be entitled to know why they are continuing to be imprisoned is to condemn them to never having any say over their destiny. This is a dehumanizing experience, and, it is submitted, fails to treat these prisoners with the humanity and the respect for the dignity of the human person which is demanded by Article 10(1) of the ICCPR.

It is therefore a welcome development in administrative law whereby the judges have held that a prisoner serving a life sentence has a right, arising out of the rules of natural justice, to know the 'tariff' period of imprisonment recommended by the trial judge and any facts which might affect the Home Secretary's or Parole Board's decision, and to make representations in writing.[96] Furthermore, where the Home Secretary has a discretion as to the 'tariff' period to be served, it is likely, as regards discretionary life prisoners, that the policy of successive Home Secretaries of accepting the judge's recommendation has created a legitimate expectation that the judge's recommendation will be accepted. As regards mandatory life prisoners, if there is a considerable discrepancy between the judge's recommendation and the Home Secretary's decision, and no reasons are given for departing from the recommendation, the decision might be open to review on the ground of irrationality.[97]

In relation to the liability to recall, the European Court of Human Rights held by eighteen votes to one, in *Thynne, Wilson and Gunnell v. United Kingdom*,[98] that the arrangements for considering the release of discretionary life prisoners breaches Article 5(4) of the European Convention on Human Rights. This provides: 'Everyone who is deprived of his liberty by arrest or detention shall be entitled to take proceedings by which the lawfulness of his detention shall be decided speedily by a court and his release ordered if the detention is not lawful.' The Court pointed out that the requirement of lawfulness required the

[96] *R. v. Parole Board, ex parte Wilson* [1992] 2 All ER 576, CA; *R. v. Secretary of State for the Home Dept. ex parte Doody* [1993] 1 All ER 151, CA.

[97] *R. v. Secretary of State for the Home Dept., ex parte Doody*, [1993] 1 All ER 151, CA.

[98] Eur. Ct. HR, Series A, No. 190, Judgment of 25 Oct. 1990, 13 EHRR 666.

detention to be in conformity with the law of the Convention and the purpose of the detentions permitted by Article 5(1), as well as in conformity with domestic law. The process by which release decisions were made was defective under the Convention, because, even after the period of retributive imprisonment (the tariff) had ended, when the prisoner was being detained because of his dangerousness rather than for the offence for which he was convicted, he is only entitled to have his detention reviewed by an executive body, not by a court. The Court rejected the suggestion that an application for judicial review of the Secretary of State's decision could be adequate for the purpose, because the court in judicial review proceedings does not review the merits of the case, but only examines the Home Secretary's decision for signs of manifest illegality, irrationality, or procedural impropriety. There was therefore insufficient judicial control to satisfy the demands of Article 5(4).

Under the Criminal Justice Act 1991, some changes are introduced to subject the Home Secretary's discretion to legal rules, and to give prisoners some rights in relation to the parole process. For the first time, the Home Secretary has a positive duty to release short-term prisoners (defined as those serving terms of up to four years) after half their sentence, and long-term prisoners (serving terms of four years or over) after two-thirds of their sentences.[99] Prisoners sentenced to less than twelve months are to be released unconditionally; those serving more are to be released on licence.[100] In respect of other long-term prisoners, the Home Secretary has a power, but no duty, to release them after half their sentence.

Prisoners serving discretionary life sentences will have the 'tariff' period fixed openly as part of the sentence. After serving that period, the prisoner can require the Home Secretary to refer the case to the Parole Board. If the Board is satisfied that the prisoner's confinement is no longer necessary for the protection of the public, it can direct that the prisoner be released, and the Home Secretary is obliged to comply with that direction.[101] This reduces the Home Secretary's discretion, and places the decision to release in the hands of a non-political body. However, it does not give the prisoner the right to have his detention reviewed by a court.

In relation to the recall of prisoners who have been released on licence, the 1991 Act provides some new procedural safeguards. Under the new regime, instead of being subject to the whims of the Home Secretary, a prisoner may normally be recalled only if the Parole Board considers it to be expedient in the public interest. The Home Secretary is permitted to act without a recommendation from the Board only if it appears to him that it is expedient in the public interest to recall the per-

---

[99] Criminal Justice Act 1991, s. 33.   [100] Ibid., s. 33(1).   [101] Ibid., s. 34.

son to prison before it would be practicable to seek a recommendation from the Board.[102] In such a case, the matter must then be considered by the Board. The Act imposes a duty to disclose to the prisoner the reasons for the recall, and gives him a right (of which he must be informed on his return to prison) to make representations in writing.[103]

Even before coming into force, the Act had an effect. The Court of Appeal decided in *R. v. Parole Board, ex parte Wilson*[104] that it would be unfair to deny discretionary life prisoners the right to see what evidence is advanced to support the view that it would be unacceptably dangerous to the public to release them. Departing from its previous decisions[105] on the ground that the liberty of the subject was at stake, the court held that fairness required disclosure of reports. Moreover, although the Act leaves the decision-making power to a non-judicial body and does not give a right to prisoners to have their detention reviewed by a court, the judges have shown signs of acting where Parliament will not. In *R. v. Secretary of State for the Home Department, ex parte Walsh*,[106] the Divisional Court (Nolan LJ and Potts J.) reviewed the refusal of the Home Secretary to allow the applicant to be considered for parole by the local review committee until 1990. He had been sentenced, with seven others, to a discretionary life term for causing explosions likely to endanger life and conspiracy in 1973, following four car bombings in London. Five of the others had already been released. The Home Secretary had apparently taken the view that he had to accept the view of the trial judge and the Lord Chief Justice as to the appropriate tariff term, following *ex parte Handscomb* where the court had held that to depart from the judicially advised tariff would be *prima facie* irrational. However, in *ex parte Walsh* the court pointed out that the Home Secretary was not there merely to rubber-stamp the judicial view on the tariff. If there were circumstances which made the judicial view of the tariff, expressed at the time the sentence was imposed, seem wildly out of line with subsequent determinate sentences imposed for similar offences, the Home Secretary had a duty to consult the judges afresh. The judges would decide what the factors relevant to retribution and deterrence were, and the Home Secretary would then have to consider as a matter of policy what weight should be attached to them. As the Home Secretary had not realized this, he was required to reconsider his decision. Furthermore, the court held that he had a duty to tell the prisoner what the recommended length of the tariff element of the sentence was, and thereafter to deal fairly with all matters arising in relation to the sentence and this was upheld by the Court of

---

[102] Ibid., s. 39(1), (2).   [103] Ibid., s. 39(3).   [104] [1992] 2 All ER 576, CA.
[105] *Payne v. Lord Harris of Greenwich* [1981] 1 WLR 754, CA; *R. v. Secretary of State for the Home Dept., ex parte Gunnell* [1985] Crim. LR 105, CA.
[106] *Independent*, 17 Dec. 1991, DC; *Independent*, 8 May 1992, CA.

Appeal. Where the prisoner did not know the length of the tariff element
in his sentence, it substantially diminished the value of his right to petition the Home Secretary on the subject of his tariff period. This innovative decision does much to inject some reality and respect for human
dignity into the process, limiting the baneful effects of the earlier cases
and of the government's refusal to legislate in accordance with the decision of the European Court of Human Rights in *Thynne, Wilson, and
Gunnell.*

(2) Recalling prisoners released on parole

The prisoners who are released on licence remain liable to be recalled
until the term of their sentence is served. For those sentenced to life
imprisonment that means that they are liable to recall until the day they
die. This executive discretion is normally exercised only where the prisoner is convicted of a further offence which makes it appear that he poses
a threat to the public, making it desirable to contain him again. However,
in a number of cases people have been recalled to prison following relatively minor offences—certainly offences which would not in themselves
normally be thought to merit a life sentence, or even the reactivation of
an earlier life sentence. The recall decision has traditionally been, and
largely remains under section 39 of the Criminal Justice Act 1991, wholly
executive, without independent judicial control. Because of this, the
European Court of Human Rights held in *Weeks* v. *United Kingdom*[107]
that the procedure breached Article 5(4) of the European Convention on
Human Rights, as there was no opportunity for a court to consider the
merits of the decision to detain the prisoner again. Because, in English
legal theory, a person released on licence remains a prisoner, the government did not act to change the law in the light of *Weeks*. It is possible
that the government regarded *Weeks* as a case on its own rather peculiar
facts: the prisoner had been imprisoned for life in 1966, at the age of 17,
for armed robbery after stealing 7s. (35p) from a pet shop, armed with a
starting pistol loaded with blanks. The trial judge and the Court of
Appeal had regarded the life sentence as being more merciful and allowing for earlier release than would have been possible had he been given a
long but determinate prison term. It is, indeed, true that many lifers are
released earlier than they would be if they had been given fixed terms.
However, unlike people who have served fixed terms, they remain liable
to be called on to resume their indefinite detention.

In *Thynne, Wilson, and Gunnell*, above, the European Court of Human
Rights made it clear that *Weeks* had not depended on its own special facts,

---

[107] Eur. Ct. HR, Series A, No. 145, Judgment of 5 Oct. 1988, 10 EHRR 293.

but rather identified a structural weakness in the English penal system and a systemic infringement of the European Convention. The Court insisted that there must be an opportunity for judicial control over the recall decision, as over the release decision. Indeed, it seems intuitively that the case for judicial control is even stronger in the case of a recall than it is in the case of a decision to refuse to release on licence, as, once the prisoner has been released, the recall deprives him of a status and a liberty which he has, rather than merely denying him an opportunity for which he was hoping. Nevertheless, the government has not acted on either *Weeks* or *Thynne, Wilson, and Gunnell*. Even under the Criminal Justice Act 1991, the decision to recall remains wholly administrative or executive,[108] despite a recommendation from a House of Lords Select Committee that an independent tribunal should be set up to deal with these decisions,[109] and the UK remains in breach of the European Convention.[110]

Perhaps because the government and Parliament have been slow to recognize the human rights of life prisoners or to bring law in the UK into line with the UK's international legal obligations, the courts have shown signs of a rather more interventionist approach to judicial review of the Home Secretary's decisions in relation to recall decisions than heretofore. In *R. v. Parole Board, ex parte Georghiades*,[111] the applicant had left the country while on parole in 1976 without telling the probation service, and his licence was revoked. On his return, in 1990, he was arrested. In 1992 he made representations to the Parole Board, but the Board did not recommend his immediate release. He applied for judicial review of the Board's decision, claiming that he should have been told what material would be put before the Board. The Divisional Court held that, although the decision to recall a prisoner is discretionary, in the special circumstances of the case the applicant was entitled, under the principles of natural justice, to be told the material which would be put before the Parole Board, when it reviewed the case, to justify the recall. Although he knew the factors justifying revocation of the licence in 1976, it was not clear that these were still operative as reasons for imprisoning the applicant in 1992. This marks a welcome extension of judicial control over administrative control of imprisonment.

[108] Criminal Justice Act 1991, s. 28.
[109] House of Lords Select Committee on Murder and Life Imprisonment, *Report of the Committee 1988–89*, i, HL 78–1 of 1988–9, paras. 182–8. The report is discussed in a Symposium, (1990) 29 *Howard J. of Crim. Justice* 291–305, by Lord Windlesham, 'From Tariff to Penal Sanction' (291–5), Rod Morgan, 'Less Life and More Justice' (296–300), and Genevra Richardson, 'The Select Committee and the Sentencing Structure for Murder' (300–5).
[110] See Genevra Richardson, 'Discretionary Life Sentences and the European Convention on Human Rights' [1991] *PL* 34–40.
[111] *Independent*, 27 May 1992, DC.

Similarly, in R. v. *Secretary of State for the Home Department, ex parte Cox*[112] Popplewell J. was prepared unhesitatingly to characterize as perverse the Home Secretary's decision to cancel the provisional release date given to a life sentence prisoner, who in 1990 had been transferred from prison to a pre-release employment scheme hostel with a view to release subject to continued good behaviour. While there, he had pleaded guilty to fraudulent use of a tax disc and possession of a small quantity of cannabis, and fined. He was returned to a closed Category C prison, and in January 1991 the Home Secretary ordered that there should be a further review in January 1992. This would lead, if all went well, to the prisoner being released again, but not for several more years, during most of which time he would be in a closed prison. On an application for judicial review of the decision, Popplewell J. decided that the matters relied on by the Home Secretary as demonstrating bad behaviour could not reasonably be said to show that the prisoner merited, or public safety demanded, that he should spend several more years in a closed prison. Any risk which he presented appeared to be minimal compared with the draconian effects of the recall to a closed prison.

This was a case where, by using the ground of irrationality or perversity, the judge came very close to reviewing the merits of the Home Secretary's decision, asserting something approaching the judicial role which the European Court of Human Rights had demanded but for which the government had refused to legislate. This, together with the decision in R. v. *Secretary of State for the Home Department, ex parte Walsh*,[113] suggests that the courts are losing patience with a system of executive detention which pays no respect to the rights of prisoners or normal rule-of-law principles, and is at best arbitrary in the consideration which it gives to public safety and the wider public interest. However, the ability of judicial review to plug a human rights gap is limited. The proper course is for the government to legislate for decisions of this sort to be made by an appropriate independent tribunal or court, properly established, in accordance with the requirements of the European Convention.

6.5 DETENTION UNDER HEALTH LEGISLATION

(1) Medical detention in European human rights law and English law

(i) *The European Convention on Human Rights.* Some interferences with detainees' rights were held to contravene the European Convention on Human Rights in a series of cases before the Commission and Court in the

---

[112] *Independent*, 8 Oct. 1991, DC.   [113] *Independent*, 8 May 1992, CA.

late 1970s. Article 5(1) of the Convention provides: 'No one shall be deprived of his liberty save in the following cases and in accordance with a procedure prescribed by law: . . . (e) the lawful detention of persons for the prevention of the spread of infectious diseases, of persons of unsound mind, alcoholics or drug addicts, or vagrants . . .'. This lays down obligations of three types: first, to ensure that the detention powers are limited to the kinds of people and purposes specified in the Article; secondly, to ensure that the detention is in accordance with a procedure prescribed by law; thirdly, to ensure that it is lawful (and, under Article 5(4), to provide access to proceedings in which the lawfulness of the detention can be determined and in which release can be ordered if the detention is unlawful).

The potentially excessively indeterminate notion of 'unsound mind' has been somewhat tied down by the Commission and the Court, which have imposed three limitations.[114] First, there must be objective criteria on the basis of which an expert medical opinion is reached that the patient is suffering from a recognized psychiatric disorder. Secondly, the degree of the disorder must be such as to justify deprivation of liberty. Thirdly, the lawfulness of continuing to detain a person must depend on the continuance of the condition which initially justified detention. Once the patient's condition has been stabilized, it ought to be possible to release him.

(ii) *Preventing the spread of infectious diseases.* The Secretary of State has power to order the hospitalization and, if considered necessary, exceptionally, to prevent or control an epidemic, detention in quarantine of people who have infectious diseases, in order to prevent the spread of the disease.[115] This could, if necessary, be invoked in relation to a disease such as AIDS. However, the evidence is that, as it is relatively difficult to transmit the HIV virus under normal circumstances, the compulsory detention of sufferers would be unreasonable and unnecessary. It would therefore breach the necessity principle, which the European Commission and Court of Human Rights have imposed in respect of the other grounds for depriving people of their liberty under Article 5 of the European Convention.[116] As Sieghart argued,[117] there is no reason for

---

[114] *Winterwerp* v. *Netherlands*, Eur. Ct. HR, Series A, No. 33, Judgment of 24 Oct. 1979, 2 EHRR 387; *Luberti* v. *Italy*, Eur. Ct. HR, Series A, No. 75, Judgment of 23 Feb. 1984, 6 EHRR 440; *Ashingdane* v. *UK*, Eur. Ct. HR, Series A, No. 93, Judgment of 28 May 1985, 7 EHRR 528.

[115] Public Health (Infectious Diseases) Regulations 1985, SI 1985/434. See in particular regulation 3.

[116] *Lawless* v. *Ireland*, Eur. Ct. HR, Series A, No. 3, (1961) 1 EHRR 15, *Bouamar* v. *Belgium* Eur. Ct. HR, Series A, No. 129, Judgment of 29 Nov. 1987, 11 EHRR 1; *Caprino* v. *UK*, Eur. Comm. HR, Report: (1980) DR 12, 14 at p. 20.

[117] Paul Sieghart, *AIDS and Human Rights: A UK Perspective* (London: BMA Foundation for AIDS, 1989), 41–6.

failing to impose the same standard of necessity in relation to medical detention under Article 5(1)(e). Indeed, there are signs that the necessity principle does apply: in relation to detention of people of unsound mind, the Court has held (as noted above) that the continued detention of a patient after the condition has been relieved is usually a breach of Article 5, suggesting that the necessity principle applies at least to that limb of Article 5(1)(e). In addition, detention of HIV-positive or AIDS patients in an emergency would have to be reviewed by a court, and the absence of such a procedural protection would breach Article 5.

At the moment, AIDS is not a notifiable disease in the UK (i.e. a disease all cases of which must be reported to the Department of Health), although health authorities are required by the AIDS (Control) Act 1987 to provide regular reports on the number of cases in their areas (but without identifying the sufferers) to the Minister, so that the progress of the disease may be monitored. The identification and control of people who are HIV-positive or suffering from pre-AIDS or AIDS raises serious civil rights and civil liberties issues, some of which are examined in the section on privacy, below. The matter has attracted considerable controversy abroad. Sweden has a programme of compulsorily detaining and isolating sufferers in hostels away from centres of population, and in Sydney, New South Wales, in 1989 a prostitute who was found to be HIV-positive was imprisoned for some days before being released when it was found that there was no legal power to detain her. Compulsory detention of all sufferers, on the Swedish model, seems to go further than necessary to protect other people, and would almost certainly be held to breach Article 5 of the European Convention.

On the other hand, it is arguable that some action may be necessary if the sufferers are in jobs which raise particular risks of passing on the disease. Those who deal regularly with bleeding patients, such as ambulance officers, surgeons, and dentists, or who have sexual intercourse with others, such as prostitutes, may well put their patients or clients at risk. Nevertheless, it does not seem necessary to detain such people. Counselling on methods of controlling the risks, and if need be regular monitoring of procedures, is often all that is required. Detention may be required where, for example, sufferer is found bleeding heavily in public, but arguably only for as long as it takes to control the bleeding and ensure that it is unlikely to begin again. At the moment, there is no legal procedure for securing such a detention lawfully in the UK.

(iii) *Mental patients.* Historically, the care of people of unsound mind in England and Wales was ultimately the responsibility of the Crown, which had prerogative powers in respect of their welfare and the management of their affairs. These powers were exercised by the Court of Protection.

The legal framework for the treatment and detention of mental patients was progressively put on a statutory footing, and the prerogative powers were finally superseded in 1960 when the Mental Health Act 1959 entered into force.[118] Following various challenges to the regime under the Mental Health Act 1959, before the European Commission and Court of Human Rights, a series of statutes put the law on a new footing, and were consolidated in the Mental Health Act 1983.

Under the 1983 Act, there are two classes of patients: those admitted voluntarily, or informally, to hospital, and those admitted compulsorily, or using the formal statutory procedures. These will be considered in sections 2 and 3 below.

(2) Informal or voluntary patients

These may be treated in the usual way by their general practitioner or others. If it becomes desirable for them to enter hospital for psychiatric treatment, and they do so voluntarily, they are free to leave at will.[119] The Law Commission noted in 1991 that:

well over 90% of admissions to mental hospitals are now on an informal basis. This is probably because, in practice, compulsion is only needed when a patient actively refuses to cooperate with the treatment or care which his doctors or other professionals consider that he needs for his own sake or for the protection of others.[120]

However, there is a difficulty relating to such patients. Though admitted informally, their condition may make them incapable of understanding the nature and implications of treatment or care sufficiently to give real consent. Their admission is therefore not necessarily truly voluntary, and there is often concern about treating patients while they are apparently co-operating but perhaps not genuinely consenting.[121] The understandable desire on the part of relatives and professionals to avoid having to stigmatize people leads to the compulsory procedures being rather rarely used, but has the consequence that the safeguards which the Mental Health Act 1983 offers for the interests of compulsory patients are denied them. 'For what may be very good, practical and humane reasons,

[118] For a good, brief account of the history, see Law Commission Consultation Paper No. 119, *Mentally Incapacitated Adults and Decision-Making: an overview* (London: HMSO, 1991), pp. 55–60.

[119] Mental Health Act 1983, s. 131.

[120] Law Commission, *Mentally Incapacitated*, 73 (footnote omitted), citing DHSS figures for 1982–6.

[121] Concerns have been expressed by the Mental Health Act Commission: *First Biennial Report 1983–85*, 11; *Second Biennial Report 1985–87*, 50; *Third Biennial Report 1987–89*, 35, cited in Law Commission, *Mentally Incapacitated*, 74.

important decisions may be taken on behalf of mentally incapable people with none of the safeguards which would be available if they or their families were actively opposed'.[122] Furthermore, if a patient attempts to leave, the doctor in charge of the patient may change his status to that of a compulsory patient if it appears to the doctor that an application ought to be made to have the patient compulsorily admitted. This permits detention for up to 72 hours, in order that an application may be made to the court.[123] If the doctor in charge or his delegate is not available when the patient tries to discharge himself, and it is immediately necessary to restrain the patient, a nurse can restrain the patient from leaving the hospital for up to six hours or (if sooner) until it is practicable to secure the doctor's attendance.[124] However, if the patient's status is changed from informal to formal patient, he must be notified and given an opportunity to seek review (by the manager or the Mental Health Review Tribunal). Failure to do this will infringe his right under Article 5(3) of the European Convention on Human Rights to have the legality of the detention promptly decided by a court.[125]

An area of concern which remains concerns children who are detained for treatment. Normally they will have been admitted with their parents' consent, so that they are formally voluntarily rather than involuntarily detained patients. However, they will not themselves necessarily have consented either to detention or to treatment. The safeguards which apply to adults who are detained compulsorily do not apply to these 'voluntary' child patients. Where a local-authority social services department is responsible for the care of the child, some external and interdisciplinary monitoring of the child's treatment can take place. In cases where there is a difference of opinion between the parents and the local authority, the authority can apply to have the child made a ward of court, whereupon the Family Division of the High Court takes responsibility for all decisions relating to the welfare of the child, and must give its consent before 'voluntary' detention or treatment is allowed. Yet there remain cases in which children are detained without their consent, though with the agreement of their parents on their behalf, and where no external monitoring is available. This would, on the face of it, seem to be contrary to the European Convention's guarantees under Article 5. Nevertheless, the European Court of Human Rights has taken a different view. In *Nielsen* v. *Denmark*,[126] it had to consider a claim by a 12-year old illegitimate child who had been admitted to a mental hospital at his mother's request.

---

[122] Law Commission, *Mentally Incapacitated*, 95.
[123] Mental Health Act 1983, s. 5(1), (2).   [124] Ibid., s. 5(4).
[125] See *Van der Leer* v. *Netherlands*, Eur. Ct. HR, Series A, No. 170, (1989) 12 EHRR 567.
[126] Eur. Ct. HR, Series A, No. 144, Judgment of 28 Nov. 1988, 11 EHRR 175.

There was no procedure under Danish law for an independent judicial body to determine the lawfulness of his detention, and he claimed that this breached Article 5(1). For the Danish Government, it was first argued that for the state to intervene in a matter of this sort, overriding the parent's wishes, would be incompatible with respect for family life under Article 8. This argument was unanimously rejected. The Court accepted that the state had obligations under Article 5 to protect children against infringements of their right to liberty, and that this justified some degree of interference with parental decisions. However, by a narrow nine to seven majority the Court held that there had been no breach of Article 5. According to the majority, the parent's decision to have her son committed was within the constraints on children's rights necessarily connected with their upbringing. At that age, it was normal for some decisions to be taken for children by parents. The responsibility of the state to safeguard the child's liberty did not go beyond ensuring that expert medical advice was provided for the child.

With respect, this seems to narrow the responsibilities of the state, and the rights of children, almost to vanishing point. Allowing the state to evade its responsibility to protect children, or to provide procedures whereby children can protect themselves, against ill-conceived and potentially harmful parental action makes children liable to be committed to mental institutions by their parents without any right to have the rationality or legality of the committal tested by anyone except medical professionals, who have neither training nor legitimacy as protectors of rights. It makes the child liable to arbitrary interference with his privacy and family life without any legal remedy, and represents a failure to take appropriate action to provide special protection for the child who is temporarily or permanently deprived of his family environment, thereby contravening Articles 16 and 20 of the UN Covenant on the Rights of the Child, which the UK ratified in 1991. The decision in *Nielsen* is therefore an unsafe basis on which to seek to justify or develop the current state of English law.

(3) Formal, or compulsory, patients

Compulsory admissions to hospital, as noted above, are the exception rather than the rule. Patients are admitted to hospital by hospital managers, and thereafter detained, on the authority of sections 2, 3, or 4 of the 1983 Act. There are three types of admission.

(i) *Admission for assessment.* Under section 2 of the Mental Health Act 1983, two requirements for admission to hospital must be satisfied. They are: (*a*) that the patient is suffering from a mental disorder of a nature or degree which warrants detention in hospital, at least for a limited period; and (b) that it is necessary that the patient be detained, in the interests of his own health or safety or with a view to the protection of other persons. The effect of an admission is that the patient, once admitted, may be detained for up to twenty-eight days for assessment, after which he must be released unless an admission is justified under section 3.

The process is subject to various safeguards. First, the application must be made by the patient's nearest relative, or someone authorized to act on the patient's behalf, or by an approved social worker. Whoever the applicant is, he must have seen the patient within the previous fourteen days. Secondly, the application must be supported by two registered medical practitioners, one of whom must be a psychiatrist. Thirdly, the patient must be informed of the legal effects of admission, and his rights must be explained to him. Fourthly, the patient is immediately entitled to have the admission reviewed by the hospital manager, and, at any time during the first fourteen days following admission, is entitled to apply to a Mental Health Review Tribunal to have his case reviewed. The manager or the tribunal can order his release if they disagree with the doctors' assessment.

(ii) *Admission for treatment*. Under section 3 of the 1983 Act, the patient can be admitted for treatment. The patient can be detained for up to six months, and detention can be renewed (initially for a further six months, and thereafter for periods of up to a year at a time) if the conditions for detention are still satisfied.[127] During the period of detention, the medical officer responsible for treating the patient may give the patient leave of absence, subject to any conditions which the medical officer considers necessary in the interests of the patient or for the protection of others.[128] If, while the patient is on leave but before the end of the authorized period of detention, it appears to the responsible medical officer that it is necessary to recall the patient to hospital in the interests of his health or safety or for the protection of others, he may be recalled.[129] This is likely to be the case, for example, if the patient stops taking prescribed drugs so that his condition, which had been stabilized, deteriorates. It has the effect of making possible a period of compulsory treatment in the community. However, neither an initial admission under section 3 nor a recall under section 17 can be used to force a patient to attend for short-term treatment as an out-patient: admission and recall must lead to him becoming a detained patient again. This leads to some inconvenience

---

[127] Mental Health Act 1983, s. 20(1), (2).   [128] Ibid., s. 17(1).
[129] Ibid., s. 17(4). Where the patient has been on leave for over 6 months, he may be recalled only if he has either returned to hospital or been transferred to another hospital, or he is absent without leave at the end of the period of leave: s. 17(5).

where all that is needed is to administer drugs regularly to a patient who can then be left to his own devices, but McCullough J. held, in *R. v. Hallstrom, ex parte W. (No. 2), R. v. Gardner, ex parte L.,*[130] that the power to recall for compulsory out-patient treatment is not available, and that attempts by two doctors to use the power in that way was not justified by the Act. The learned judge also expressed the view that it would be an abuse of power to recall a patient from leave for one night purely in order to prevent the period of six months leave, after which he would not be liable to recall under section 17, from expiring.

The conditions for admission under section 3(2), all of which must be satisfied, are that (*a*) the patient is suffering from a mental illness, psycho-pathic disorder, or mental impairment, of a nature or degree which makes it appropriate for him to receive in-patient treatment; (*b*) where the patient is suffering from psychopathic disorder or mental impairment, the treatment is likely to alleviate or prevent deterioration of his condition; (*c*) it is necessary for the health or safety of the patient, or the protection of other persons, that he should receive such treatment; and (*d*) the treatment cannot be provided unless the patient is detained under section 3. The section therefore cannot be used in order to protect other people; it must enable treatment to be given which will benefit the patient. Nor can section 3 be used initially purely for providing care and nursing, or treatment which is not likely to benefit the patient, unless the patient is suffering from mental illness. However, if the period of detention is being extended, there is an alternative ground to (*b*) if the patient is suffering from mental illness or *severe* mental impairment and is unlikely, if discharged, to be able to care for himself, to obtain the necessary care, or to guard himself against serious exploitation.[131]

The safeguards under section 3 are, first, that the application for admission must be made by the closest relative or person authorized to act on the patient's behalf or an approved social worker (who must have consulted the relative); secondly, that it must be founded on the written recommendations of two registered medical practitioners, each stating that the conditions for admission under section 3 are complied with, and including particulars of the grounds for their opinions in relation to conditions (*a*) and (*b*) above, and the reasons for thinking that (*c*) and (*d*) are met, specifying whether other methods of dealing with the patient are available and, if they are, why they are inappropriate.[132] Finally, the patient has the right to apply to have his case reviewed by a Mental Health Review Tribunal.

---

[130] [1986] QB 1090, [1986] 2 All ER 306, DC.
[131] Mental Health Act 1983, s. 20(4).   [132] Ibid., s. 3(3).

(iii) *Emergency admission*. This procedure, under section 4 of the 1983 Act, is available where the applicant has seen the patient within the previous 24 hours, and requires a recommendation from just one doctor, who need not be a psychiatrist but should, if practicable, have previous acquaintance with the patient.[133] The admission is for a period of 72 hours, after which time the patient must be released unless it is converted into an admission for 28 days for treatment, obtaining an additional supporting opinion from a psychiatrist. If this is done, the patient must be told of the legal position and has the right, within 14 days, to apply for review by a Mental Health Review Tribunal, as under section 2.

(4) Rationales for detention, and patients' liberties

The compulsory detention of mental health patients is justified either on the basis of a paternalistic test, acting in the patient's own best interests, or a protective test, safeguarding other people against the patient. This raises problems for a civil liberties theory based on personal autonomy. Is paternalism compatible with idea of autonomy? As we have seen above, in relation to consent to medical treatment in Chapters 3 and 4, enforced treatment of someone who is incapable of consenting or unwilling to consent is not necessarily incompatible with the patient's autonomy. Treatment may be necessary in order to restore the patient's rationality to a point where he is capable of evaluating options and making rational choices. In other words, it may restore a sick person's capacity for autonomy; he might even be said to have a right to be compulsorily treated (at any rate on an interest, or benefit, theory of rights).

This, however, depends on adopting a model of autonomy which makes it inseparable from rationality, and so denies people the option of choosing to be systematically irrational. This has the capacity to empower professionals to impose their ideas of right bases for choice on the patient. That is acceptable if the patient has been convicted of an offence: there is no *prima facie* compelling reason to respect the freedom of a person to choose criminality. On the other hand, most compulsory patients have not been convicted of any offence. The risk is that the line which separates personal or political eccentricity from illness will become obscured, as it did, notoriously, in the Soviet Union. This risk is particularly acute under section 3 of the 1983 Act, as mental illness is not defined in the Act and depends on professional judgement. The Act does limit the extent to which a doctor can use the category of mental illness to enforce his own view of right behaviour on an unwilling person. It specifies in section 1(3) that 'promiscuity or other immoral conduct, sexual deviancy

---

[133] Mental Health Act 1983, s. 4(3).

or dependence on alcohol or drugs' are not on their own to be regarded as constituting a mental disorder. Mann J. has accordingly decided that, despite the contrary opinion of the doctors in the case, a sexual appetite involving an attraction to young girls cannot on its own ground a diagnosis of psychopathic disorder.[134]

Although in that case there was an avenue for correcting the error of the doctors and the mental health review tribunal, the case shows fears that doctors will make the test of mental disorder overinclusive, labelling a wide range of conduct as psychopathic merely because it is antisocial and perhaps leading to what has been called 'an undue medicalisation of deviant behaviour'.[135] All the tests essentially rely on the medical expertise of the examining doctors, in consultation with social workers and the patient's family. We depend heavily on the objectivity and professional judgement of doctors, with the independent Mental Health Review Tribunals as an important safeguard against medical misjudgement. Perhaps the extensive powers under the 1983 Act mean that we have to trust them more than is ideal.

Even if one is satisfied that paternalism is justifiable on civil liberties grounds, there is at first sight a curious anomaly in that mental patients appear to be subjected to this sort of paternalism in cases where patients with purely physical disorders are not. This is explicable only on the basis that the disorder suffered by a mentally disordered patient interferes with the capacity to make decisions in a way which purely physical disorders do not; this explains and, perhaps, justifies a more interventionist line in relation to decision-making for mental patients than would be thought admissible in relation to other patients. As Professor Tom Campbell has pointed out in an acute discussion of the problem, it may reflect an assumption that humanity is, in some way, linked to rationality, and that the capacity to exercise rights is a feature of humanity which is, in turn, diminished if mental disorder reduces one's capacity for rationality.[136]

There is a further threat to civil liberties in the power to detain mentally ill patients on the basis that they pose a threat to others, without the need for any criminal offence to have been proved against them. This protective detention is not available in respect of people who suffer no mental disorder (although the latter may be required to be bound over to keep the peace or be of good behaviour). It is justifiable only if the

---

[134] R. v. Mental Health Review Tribunal, ex parte Clatworthy [1985] 3 All ER 699, DC.

[135] J. K. Mason and R. A. McCall Smith, Law and Medical Ethics, 3rd edn. (London: Butterworths, 1991), 401. See also Joseph Jacob, 'The Right of a Mental Patient to his Psychosis' (1976) 39 MLR 17–42.

[136] Tom Campbell, 'The Rights of the Mentally Ill', in Tom Campbell, David Goldberg, Sheila McLean, and Tom Mullen (eds.), Human Rights: From Rhetoric to Reality (Oxford: Basil Blackwell, 1986), 123–47 at pp. 125–32.

prediction of dangerousness is reliable. In many cases, it will be based on assaults which the patient has already carried out, whether or not he has been charged with them. In other cases, it will be based purely on prognistication. There is no general correlation between mental illness and criminality, and predictions of future dangerousness are unreliable. Very great care is therefore needed when admitting a patient compulsorily on protective grounds. This risk can be exaggerated. As noted above, admission under section 3 is permitted only in order to receive treatment, not simply to keep the patient out of circulation for a period. However, if the treatment is unsuccessful and the patient is thought to be dangerous, a renewed admission under section 17 can be permitted, even if there is unlikely to be any improvement in the patient's condition from further treatment, merely as a measure of containment. This should be done only if there is clear evidence that the patient is violent, and the matter should be decided by a court, rather than being left to doctors and managers subject to review by a Mental Health Review Tribunal.

(5) Review of detention

After detention has been authorized, the patient has the right to apply for release first to the hospital manager, and secondly (within fourteen days, in the case of admissions under section 2) to a Mental Health Review Tribunal. The European Convention on Human Rights, Article 5(4), gives those who lose their liberty a right to have the legality of their detention reviewed regularly by a court, and the European Court of Human Rights has held that this right applies to those compulsorily detained for treatment for mental disorders following convictions for criminal offences as it does to other patients. Patients who are detained for treatment for mental disorders may recover or have their conditions stabilized, and once that has happened there may be no further medical (as opposed to retributive, deterrent, or political) reason for detaining them in mental hospitals. It was therefore an infringement of a patient's right under Article 5 for the decision to release him, recommended on medical grounds by doctors or a Mental Health Review Tribunal, to be subject to the approval on non-medical grounds by the Secretary of State. This was the position in English law, in relation to those detained after conviction or being found unfit to plead, under the regime of the Mental Health Act 1959. Decision-making processes of this sort were disapproved by the European Court in several cases, including *X* v. *United Kingdom*.[137] The law was accordingly changed, and under the Mental

---

[137] Eur. Ct. HR, Judgment of 5 Nov. 1981, Series A, No. 46. See also *van Droogenbroeck*, *Winterwerp* Eur. Ct. HR, Series A, No. 33, (1979) 2 EHRR 387, and *Van der Leer* v. *Netherlands*, Eur. Ct. HR, Series A, No. 170, (1989) 12 EHRR 567.

Health Act 1983 the Mental Health Review Tribunal has authority to order the discharge of any patient without the Secretary of State being able to override the order.[138] To protect applicants for release who are notorious criminals against media campaigns designed to prejudice the tribunal against them, and to satisfy the requirement of the European Convention that the review of detention should be carried out by a court, it has been held that the Mental Health Review Tribunal is a court of law for the purposes of the law of contempt of court, and attempts to prejudice its proceedings are punishable as such.[139]

The tribunal must give reasons for its decisions.[140] The reasons must be sufficiently clear to show that the conditions for detention remain satisfied, and must be based on an adequate evaluation of the evidence.[141] It is subject to the supervisory jurisdiction of the courts, either by way of case stated or by way of the application for judicial-review procedure. The supervisory jurisdiction has been used both by aggrieved patients and by the Department of Health to ensure that the tribunal observes the rules and to clarify the principles on which the tribunal acts.[142] When it was first invoked by a patient against a doctor who had admitted her, the judicial review application was met with the argument that it constituted 'civil proceedings', which are not available in respect of anything purporting to be done in pursuance of the 1983 Act unless the act was done in bad faith or without reasonable care.[143] This would have excluded judicial review on the basis of most of the classic heads of review (*ultra vires*, natural justice, and irrationality). This argument succeeded at first instance, but was rejected by the Court of Appeal. As it appeared that the 1983 Act was intended to protect doctors against actions for damages or criminal liability rather than to take away a patient's access to a forum for testing the legality of the detention, the Court of Appeal applied the principle that judicial review cannot be excluded except by the most clear and explicit statutory language, and restricted the scope of the term 'civil proceedings' to the type of damages action for false imprisonment or trespass to the person at which it was aimed.[144]

[138] Mental Health Act 1983, ss. 72, 73.

[139] *Pickering* v. *Liverpool Daily Post and Echo Newspapers plc* [1991] 2 WLR 513, [1991] 1 All ER 622, HL.

[140] Mental Health Review Tribunal Rules 1983, SI 1983/942, rule 23(2).

[141] *Bone* v. *Mental Health Review Tribunal* [1985] 3 All ER 330; *R.* v. *Mental Health Review Tribunal, ex parte Clatworthy* [1985] 3 All ER 690, DC; *R.* v. *Mental Health Review Tribunal, ex parte Pickering* [1986] 1 All ER 99, DC.

[142] *R.* v. *Oxford Regional Mental Health Review Tribunal, ex parte Secretary of State for the Home Dept.* [1988] AC 120, [1987] 3 All ER 8, HL; *Secretary of State for the Home Dept.* v. *Mental Health Review Tribunal for Mersey Regional Health Authority* [1986] 1 WLR 1170.

[143] Mental Health Act 1983, s. 139(1).

[144] *Ex parte Waldron* [1986] QB 824, *sub nom. R.* v. *Hallstrom, ex parte W.* [1985] 3 All ER 775, CA.

(6) Arresting mental patients

In certain cases, there are powers to arrest or forcibly remove mentally disordered people from wherever they happen to be. The first of these powers, rarely used, is exercisable only for the benefit of the person to be detained. Under section 135 of the Mental Health Act 1983, an approved social worker can lay an information on oath before a justice of the peace showing that there is reasonable cause to suspect that a person, who is believed to be suffering from a mental disorder, has been or is being ill-treated, neglected, or not kept under proper control, or is living alone but is unable to care for himself. The social worker need not name the patient.[145] If it appears to the justice that the facts are as described by the social worker, and that the person is within his geographical jurisdiction, he may issue a warrant authorizing any constable, who must be accompanied by an approved social worker and a medical practitioner, to enter, if need be by force, the premises specified in the warrant where the person in believed to be, and, if they think fit, to remove him to a place of safety, which may be a police station (although this is not encouraged).[146]

The second power requires no warrant and is given only to constables in public places. Under section 136(1) of the 1983 Act, a constable may remove to a place of safety anyone whom he finds in a place to which the public have access and who appears to be suffering from a mental disorder. This power may be exercised either in the person's own interests or for the protection of other persons. This power is, unfortunately, being used increasingly frequently as people are returned to the community after the closure of long-stay mental hospitals without adequate housing and hostel provision being made. It presents constables with a problem: it requires them first to decide whether the person is suffering from a mental disorder or from a mental handicap (to which the section does not apply), and then to make an assessment of the person's dangerousness to others and to himself. These matters are not easy for someone who lacks experience in the care or treatment of people with mental disorders or mental handicaps. It will be much simpler for the constable if the person is reasonably suspected of having committed an offence, which will give rise to a power of arrest either under section 24 of PACE (if it is arrestable) or under section 25(*d*)(i) or (ii) (in order to protect that person or another from causing or suffering physical injury). If an arrest is made under one of those provisions, the person is a suspect who must be taken to a police station and there dealt with in accordance with the regime outlined in Chapter 5, above.

Where a person is at a police station after being detained under section

[145] Mental Health Act 1983, s. 135(1), (5).   [146] Ibid., s. 135(1), (4).

136 of the Mental Health Act 1983, the Code of Practice under PACE stresses the importance of having him assessed as soon as possible by an approved social worker and a doctor.[147] The person can be detained for up to 72 hours under section 135 or section 136, but must not be held in a police station for longer than necessary to interview and examine him and make suitable arrangements for his treatment or care.[148] A police cell is self-evidently inappropriate as a place of safety for a mentally disordered person.

A final, somewhat draconian, power arises where a person who has been admitted to a hospital as a compulsory patient under the Mental Health Act 1983 absents himself without leave, or overstays a leave of absence given under section 17 of the 1983 Act. Such a person is unlawfully at large, within the meaning of PACE, section 17(1)(d), which permits a constable to enter and search any premises, without a warrant, for the purpose of recapturing a person who is unlawfully at large and whom he is pursuing. In *R. v. D'Souza*,[149] the Divisional Court held that 'pursuit' might be delayed, allowing for those handling the situation to proceed with 'patience, sensitivity, calmness and tact'. In that case, however, constables and nurses broke into the house of the patient's parents to recapture her, and were attacked by her and her father. Both were convicted of assaulting constables in the execution of their duty. The Divisional Court upheld the conviction, and the patient appealed to the House of Lords. Their Lordships unanimously allowed the appeal, holding that the word 'pursuing' could not be widened to encompass mere seeking. A pursuit necessarily involved chasing the patient, and an entry to premises under section 17(1)(d) of PACE must follow more or less immediately on arrival at the premises.

The interpretation of 'pursuing', which will apply to all cases where the police seek to enter premises under section 17(1)(d) of PACE, may indicate a shift away from the view that the police should unquestioningly be given the powers which they claim to need, although it remains to be seen whether this will be extended from cases in which criminal procedure overlaps with mental health law to straightforward criminal investigations. In any case, the decision is a welcome reassertion of the principle that the courts should respect statutory limitations on officials' powers to interfere with the rights and liberties of citizens, preventing the police from evading the minimal safeguards demanded where a warrant is issued under section 135 of the 1983 Act.

[147] Code C, para. 3.10.
[148] Mental Health Act 1983, ss. 135(3) and 136(2); Code C, para. 3.10. See further Vaughan Bevan and Ken Lidstone, *The Investigation of Crime: A Guide to Police Powers* (London: Butterworths, 1991), 416–18.
[149] [1992] Crim. LR 119, DC; [1992] 1 WLR 1073, [1992] 4 All ER 434, HL.

(7) Legal redress for aggrieved patients

Under Article 5(5) of the European Convention on Human Rights, a person who has been arrested or detained in contravention of Article 5 shall have an enforceable right to compensation. This is provided in English law by civil actions for damages. In the context of the detention of patients in mental hospitals, the scope for such proceedings is somewhat restricted, in that section 139 of the Mental Health Act 1983 provides, so far as material:

(1) No person shall be liable, whether on the ground of want of jurisdiction or any other ground, to any civil or criminal proceedings to which he would have been liable apart from this section in respect of any act purporting to be done in pursuance of this Act or any regulations or rules made under this Act, or in, or in pursuance of anything done in, the discharge of functions conferred by any other enactment on the authority having jurisdiction under Part VII of this Act, unless the act was done in bad faith or without reasonable care.

(2) No civil proceedings shall be brought against any person in any court in respect of any such act without the leave of the High Court; . . .

As noted above, it was held in *Ex parte Waldron*[150] that subsection (1) did not exclude applications for judicial review. It does, however, exclude actions for damages for false imprisonment or trespass to the person against anyone in respect of acts purporting to be done in pursuance of the legislation. It will always be necessary to prove negligence or bad faith. This leaves open the possibility of an ordinary action for negligence on the basis of the duty of care which all doctors owe to their patients and which, it was held in the context of prisons, everyone who detains anyone owes to the detainee.[151] It also leaves open the possibilities of actions for misfeasance in a public office, or malicious abuse of legal process.

The statutory limitation of liability is worrying in civil liberties terms. It is probably a recognition of the particular risks which those caring for mental patients run, especially when treating patients compulsorily, of being subjected to unfounded allegations of abuse and to vexatious litigation. However, small-scale and large-scale abuses do sometimes occur in mental hospitals. The requirement in subsection (2) that plaintiffs should not begin an action without obtaining leave from the High Court, akin to the restriction imposed on habitually vexatious litigants, is a powerful protection. Although the plaintiff need not convince the court that he has a *prima facie* case or even that there is a serious issue to be tried, he must show that the case is not clearly hopeless, and that it deserves the

---

[150] [1986] QB 824, *sub nom. R.* v. *Hallstrom, ex parte W.* [1985] 3 All ER 775, CA.
[151] *Hague* v. *Deputy Governor of Parkhurst Prison* [1991] 3 All ER 733, HL; above, s. 6. 3.

fuller consideration which it will receive if the action is allowed to proceed. This balances the rights of patients to access to the courts against
the need to protect doctors against harassment by clearly hopeless litigation.[152] Together with the inherent credibility problem facing a mental
patient who sets his word against that of a doctor or nurse, this ought to
be sufficient protection for carers against harassment. The further protection offered in subsection (1) is a sign of the special tenderness of the law
for professionals, and, perhaps, for doctors most of all, and seems arguably
to be excessive. It is curious that this shield is given in the mental health
legislation when no such protection is given by statute to prison governors and their staff, who are at least as likely to be subjected to problems
and harassment as mental health carers. The protection given to carers
under the Mental Health Act 1983 is more extensive than that which is
available to doctors in Scotland under the Mental Health (Scotland) Act
1984 or Scots common law.[153] The Scottish approach should, in principle, also apply in England and Wales.

The availability of a negligence remedy still keeps the door open to
some legal scrutiny of hospital regimes. It is consistent with the position
in relation to negligence liability for prison conditions, established in
Hague v. *Deputy Governor of Parkhurst Prison*, above, s. 6.3(2), that Henry
J. in *Furber* v. *Kratter*[154] was prepared to give leave under section 139(2)
of the Mental Health Act 1983 for a mental patient to bring an action for
damages for negligence in respect of an allegedly unnecessarily harsh hospital regime. It was alleged that the patient, after an attack on a ward sister, had been put naked and alone in a cell, containing only a mattress,
and left there for 16 days without care, clothing, or reading and writing
materials, for punitive rather than therapeutic reasons. Henry J. held that
there might be a cause of action in negligence in respect of the discomfort, suffering, and loss of amenity which the patient allegedly suffered. In
this respect, at least, English law provides a remedy in relation to a matter
which does not fall within Article 5 of the European Convention, which
was held in *Ashingdane* v. *United Kingdom*[155] not to be concerned with
conditions of detention for mental patients. Any claim under the
Convention in respect of conditions would have to be brought under
Article 3. Nevertheless, the lead which English law has over the
Convention in this regard may be more imaginary than real. In relation

---

[152] *Winch* v. *Jones*; *Winch* v. *Hayward* [1986] QB 296, [1985] 3 All ER 97, CA. This
case is part of a long-drawn-out attempt by Miss Winch to obtain redress for her treatment by doctors, the courts, and the Public Trustee following a dispute over her mother's
estate: it began in 1977, and is still continuing.

[153] See *Black* v. *Forsey*, *The Times*, 31 May 1988, HL (Sc.).

[154] *The Times*, 21 July 1988; *Independent*, 9 Aug. 1988; full text available on Lexis.

[155] Eur. Ct. HR, Series A, No. 93, (1985) 7 EHRR 528.

to prisons, the duty of the authorities with regard to conditions seems to be limited to avoiding intolerable conditions, such as would be likely always to contravene the right to be free of inhuman or degrading treatment under Article 3. It remains to be seen whether a more extensive duty applies to conditions in mental hospitals. In principle, it should: patients, unlike prisoners, are not detained for punishment, and are entitled to expect a higher standard of accommodation and a more liberal regime than would be normal in some prisons. If it turns out that the English law of negligence can be used to give remedies for hospital conditions which are better, even marginally, than those which would constitute degrading treatment under Article 3, we will for once be ahead of our obligations under the Convention.

7

FREEDOM OF MOVEMENT INTO AND OUT OF BRITAIN

7.1 BACKGROUND

From the earliest times, commercial necessity has combined with diplomatic propriety to dictate that in normal circumstances people should be free to enter and leave the country with a minimum of restriction and formality. In Magna Carta of 1215, subsequently confirmed repeatedly without material alteration in this regard, chapter 41 recognized the right of merchants to be safe and secure in leaving, entering, staying, and travelling in England to buy and sell, unless they came from enemy countries in time of war. In that event, they were to be held safely until it was known how English merchants were treated in their country; if our merchants were safe there, theirs were to be safe here. By chapter 42, there was a more general provision, covering people who were not merchants, that (apart from short periods in time of war for the common good of the realm) anyone was to be permitted to leave and re-enter the realm safely and securely, subject to his allegiance to the king, excepting only those who had been imprisoned or outlawed according to law, and enemy aliens. In the USA, the Supreme Court has recognized the right to travel abroad as an aspect of personal liberty, and thus constitutionally protected under the Fifth and Fourteenth Amendments to the Constitution, with their due process requirements.[1] These rights are necessarily restricted by any form of immigration or emigration law, and it is one of the purposes of sections 1 to 3 of this chapter to examine the extent of the restriction in England and Wales, and its relationship with principles enshrined in human rights treaties.

There is also, under some constitutions, a right for citizens and others to move freely within the country. As already noted, chapter 41 of Magna Carta recognized that merchants had this right in England. The right of citizens to move freely without penalty is guaranteed under the Indian Constitution of 1949, and by the US Constitution.[2] It is also

---

[1] *Kent* v. *Dulles* 357 US 116 (1958).

[2] *Aptheker* v. *Secretary of State* 378 US 500 (1964); *US* v. *Guest* 383 US 745 (1966); *Shapiro* v. *Thompson* 394 US 618 (1969); *Griffin* v. *Breckenridge* 403 US 88 (1971); *Dunn* v. *Blumstein* 405 US 1, 23 (1972). Cp. *Marston* v. *Lewis* 410 US 679 (1973); *Burns* v. *Fortson*

guaranteed under certain international human rights instruments. In section 4 of this chapter, a limitation on this right as it applies to movement between parts of the United Kingdom is examined, once again in the context of international human rights law.

The principal provisions in international law are: Article 13 of the UN Declaration on Human Rights (1948); the Fourth Protocol (1968) to the European Convention on Human Rights, to which the UK is not a party; and Article 12 of the International Covenant on Civil and Political Rights (1976), to which the UK entered various significant reservations at the time of signature and on ratification.[3] These will be considered as they become relevant, concentrating on the ICCPR, as the main obligation-imposing instrument to which the UK is party.

(1) Emigration

Article 12(2) of the ICCPR provides: 'Everyone shall be free to leave any country, including his own.'[4] The UK has made no reservation to this paragraph. Indeed, the United Kingdom, and, earlier, England, can be said to have shown a high level of respect for the right to leave the country. Unlike the regime under the now defunct Soviet Union, which severely restricted emigration of people wanting to go to the West by allowing people to leave only if they had an exit visa and making it very difficult to obtain one (giving the word 'refusenik' to the English language, via Yiddish), governments in this country have not tried to stop those who wanted to leave from doing so, unless they were trying to evade the process of law. Indeed, English governments from medieval times gave moral, and sometimes material, support to those going abroad on commercial ventures, knowing that success as a trading nation, and the acquisition and development of the colonies, largely depended on the freedom given to British explorers, traders, and adventurers to go where they wanted.

There has been a presumption that Britons would be free to travel abroad. Far from needing a passport or visa to permit egress, a special writ (*ne exeat regno*) was required in order to prevent a person leaving the country. When the British passport was developed, it was a guarantee of protection from the Crown for British travellers abroad, and a demand for protection from the authorities in the countries through which the

410 US 686 (1973), on residency requirements as a precondition to voting rights in a state.

[3] See Paul Sieghart, *The International Law of Human Rights* (Oxford: Clarendon Press, 1983), pp. 174–5, 464–5.

[4] This provision reflects Art. 13(2) of the Universal Declaration, and is identical with Art. 2(2) of the Fourth Protocol to the ECHR.

traveller would pass. Although issuing a passport was and is a discretionary exercise of a prerogative power, it started as an expression of official support for freedom of movement, an express extension of royal protection and the king's peace to the person of the holder, not as a condition for its exercise.

Today, the British passport, issued by the Passport Office (a department of the Home Office, has become bureaucratized and Europeanized, and is a condition for entry to most other countries which needs to be supplemented by visas permitting entry to certain countries. Because it has become a practical necessity for anyone travelling abroad to have a passport, refusing a person's passport application substantially limits his freedom of movement.[5] The courts have therefore extended judicial review to the decisions by which passports are denied: they are no longer seen as privileges, but as *prima facie* rights attracting judicial protection against arbitrary executive infringement.[6] This is in some ways a more rights-conscious approach than that which operates in the United States. In *Kent* v. *Dulles*[7] the US Supreme Court held that the Secretary of State had exceeded his statutory authority in withholding passports, during the McCarthy anti-communist witchhunts, from people who had associations with the Communist Party. Perhaps wary of becoming too embroiled in political controversy, the court did not rule on the further question of the constitutionality of withholding passports from US citizens, and so restricting their ability to travel abroad. When the constitutional issue was squarely raised later in *Haig* v. *Agee*,[8] the court decided that there was no constitutional protection for the right to travel abroad. Accordingly it upheld the power of the executive to revoke the passport of Philip Agee, a former CIA agent, who was planning to make revelations which would identify American agents still operating abroad.[9] Our law is, at least, no less liberal, and may be more liberal, than that of the USA in this regard.

(2) Immigration[10]

International law recognizes the right of sovereign states to control entry to their territories by nationals of other states. It does, however, impose

---

[5] On the principles on which passports are granted or refused, see Stanley de Smith and Rodney Brazier, *Constitutional and Administrative Law* 6th edn. (Harmondsworth: Penguin, 1989), 454–5.

[6] *R.* v. *Secretary of State for Foreign and Commonwealth Affairs, ex parte Everett* [1989] QB 811, [1989] 1 All ER 655, CA.

[7] 357 US 116 (1958).   [8] 453 US 280 (1981).

[9] The court also held that the ban on travel abroad did not infringe Mr Agee's First Amendment rights to freedom of speech.

[10] See generally Ian A. MacDonald and Nicholas Blake, *Immigration Law and Practice*, 3rd edn. (London: Butterworths, 1991). On the historical and political background, see

responsibilities on states in respect of their own nationals, and also imposes duties in respect of those foreign nationals who have been lawfully admitted to a state's territories. Under Article 12(4) of ICCPR, 'No one shall be arbitrarily deprived of the right to enter his own country.' This is a relatively narrow formulation of the right. It assumes that the right exists, rather than requiring that such a right be created where it does not exist. Article 12(4) also implies that a non-arbitrary deprivation of this right is permissible. Accordingly, the UK Government, on ratifying the ICCPR on 20 May 1976, entered a reservation in the following terms:

The government of the United Kingdom reserve the right to continue to apply such immigration legislation governing entry into, stay in and departure from the United Kingdom as they may deem necessary from time to time and, accordingly, their acceptance of article 12(4) and of the other provisions of the Covenant is subject to the provisions of any such legislation as regards persons not at the time having the right under the law of the United Kingdom to enter and remain in the United Kingdom. The United Kingdom also reserves a similar right in regard to each of its dependent territories.

Article 12(4) therefore offers less protection to individuals than is envisaged under Article 13(2) of the Universal Declaration ('Everyone has the right to leave any country, including his own, and to return to his country'), or Article 3(2) of the Fourth Protocol to the ECHR ('No one shall be deprived of the right to enter the territory of the State of which he is a national').

The UK's reservation set out above, while representing successive governments' attitudes to immigration control since the mid-1960s, does not reflect the earlier history of British immigration law and practice. On the whole, it is fair to say that British officials have over the centuries displayed a respectable level of tolerance towards those who came to settle here, and discharged their responsibilities towards refugees fleeing from oppression elsewhere. For a long time, until well into the twentieth century, it was officially accepted that racially discriminatory entry requirements were undesirable, although, under our constitution, there was nothing to stop Parliament from introducing such requirements.[11] At times immigrants have been welcomed and even encouraged, making up for shortages of labour, skills, or capital in the domestic economy. Yet British attitudes to foreigners have never been unconditionally friendly. Officials have always been slightly patronizing, and usually severely utilitarian, and even official approval has not always protected settlers from a

Vaughan Bevan, *The Development of British Immigration Law* (London: Croom Helm, 1986), ch. 2; Ann Dummett and Andrew Nicol, *Subjects, Citizens, Aliens and Others: Nationality and Immigration Law* (London: Weidenfeld & Nicolson, 1990).

[11] See Dummett and Nicol, *Subjects, Citizens, Aliens*, 136–41, for discussion of the parliamentary debates on the British Nationality Act 1948.

certain level of discrimination, abuse, and occasional outbursts of violence. The massacre of the Jews in 1189, following the accession of King Richard I, in all major English cities except Winchester, remains perhaps the most notorious of the outpourings of popular hatred on an alien community over the succeeding centuries. So long as people from foreign parts have contributed positively to a thriving economy, amused the British public, and supported the English cricket team, they have generally been tolerated and even welcomed. But if they have wanted to retain their cultural or religious identities, it has usually had to be done quietly and away from the public eye, and if the economy has lapsed into recession, or public services and resources were strained, the immigrant communities, which are usually distinctive and highly visible, have borne the brunt of unhappiness. Jews, Afro-Caribbeans, and East African Asians are only some of those who, accepted into the country as refugees or economic migrants, or actively encouraged to come in times of labour or skill shortage, have become the butt of those who lose most heavily when economies turn down in their eternal cycles. When times are hard, there are regular calls to exclude people from the country, sometimes on blatantly racial criteria.

The first systematic attempt to forge an immigration policy and to give it statutory form was the Aliens Act 1905, which required immigration officers to refuse entry to people who were deemed undesirable. These included people who, if admitted, would be liable to extradition; those who could not show that they would be able to support themselves and their dependants; and those who, because of their physical condition, were likely to become a charge on the rates or a detriment to the public. The general principle was that all who were not undesirable would continue to be allowed to enter. Large numbers of immigrants, initially those from Central and Eastern Europe (particularly Jews) and later, after the Second World War, increasingly from the New Commonwealth, entered under these provisions. However, more recently there has been increasing anti-immigration feeling, often mixed with racism based largely on colour, to which the politicians have been sensitive. Since the enactment of the Commonwealth Immigrants Act 1962, as Professor J. M. Evans has written, immigration policy has aimed primarily at limiting immigration from the (predominantly black) New Commonwealth, while allowing descendants of the (mainly white) emigrants who had settled the lands of the Old Commonwealth to return to the mother country. To be respectable, it was necessary to find 'appropriate legal means for implementing this objective without resorting to laws that expressly discriminate on grounds of race or ethnic origin'.[12]

[12] J. M. Evans, *Immigration Law*, 2nd edn. (London: Sweet & Maxwell, 1983), 3.

The form which immigration law takes has tended, therefore, to swing between two approaches. When times are good and immigrant labour or skills are needed to boost the economy, the law imposes only those controls which are needed to ensure that undesirable individuals are excluded. When times are harder, immigration is restricted to those who are strictly within groups which have been given rights to enter by reason of their pre-existing connection with the UK. At present, the dominant approach is restrictive of immigration.

Any sort of immigration control is bound to make entry from abroad more difficult for foreigners than for Britons (however defined). Under the European Convention on Human Rights, the Commission and the Court have accepted that international law recognizes the right of states to control entry to their territories.[13] However, it has been held that the controls, in their effects, must either treat alike all those who are not British nationals, or at any rate not differentiate between people on the basis of arbitrary racial categories. In the *East African Asians*[14] case, the European Commission of Human Rights under the European Convention on Human Rights decided that immigration-control legislation which discriminated against people by singling them out for differential treatment purely on the ground of their race might constitute a special form of affront which would amount to degrading treatment, lowering them in rank, position, reputation, or character in their own and other people's eyes. In such a case, it will constitute degrading treatment, breaching Article 3 of the Convention. In the *East African Asians* case, the UK's immigration control legislation imposed tighter controls on entry from the New Commonwealth than from the predominantly white Old Commonwealth. The Commission decided that this was a form of discrimination on racial grounds which tended substantially to lower Asian and African immigrants in their own eyes and in the estimation of others. Unfavourable treatment for Asians expelled from African states (notably Uganda) was therefore held to have violated the Convention. However, as the Asians were then admitted in accordance with the decision of the Commission, and the law was reviewed to apply the same standards without reference to race, the Committee of Ministers took no further action on the violation.[15] To the extent that the substance of immigration controls in any country is likely to reflect social and cultural prejudices, compliance with the Commission's standards may be hard to achieve.[16]

---

[13] *Patel and others (The East African Asians)* v. *UK* Applications Nos. 4403–19/70, CD 36, 92; Report: (1981) 3 EHRR. 76, Eur. Comm. HR; *Vilvarajah and others* v. *UK*, Eur. Ct. HR, Judgment of 30 Oct. 1991.   [14] *Patel* (see n. 13); Report (see n. 13).
[15] Resolution DH(77)2, Committee of Ministers.
[16] See Dummett and Nicol, *Subjects, Citizens, Aliens*, ch. 14.

Furthermore, the operation of any controls on entry may be more or less in tune with the requirements of the Convention. In the case of the UK, the steps taken to determine whether people are entitled to enter— whether they are indeed who they say they are, and are related to those who claim to be their parents or other relatives—can be demeaning and unreliable. X-ray tests for determining age were used until 1981, when the experts changed their minds about their reliability; vaginal tests, to determine whether women, claiming to be the fiancées of men settled here, were virgins, were discontinued in 1979 after an outcry over the discriminatory nature of such tests on Asian women. Widespread executive discretion within the system to relax the rules, or to apply them in a racially discriminatory way, results in a system which appears to be rule-based but which, because of the strange status of the Immigration Rules, can operate in an unpredictable and unprincipled way.[17] Rights, and remedies for unfairness, are worthy of examination in this field.

The next three sections of this chapter are therefore concerned with people from abroad: their entry by right, as having a right of abode or EC citizenship, as refugees, or by executive discretion; their removal (by way of deportation); and their remedies.

7.2 RIGHTS OF ENTRY

The Immigration Act 1971, as amended (principally by the British Nationality Act 1981), provides the structure governing immigration to the UK. Its provisions are fleshed out by the Immigration Rules, which have an uncertain status but which are, probably, akin to the PACE Codes of Practice, governing official action and decision-making and so having legal effect, subject to judicial review of the rules for illegality, procedural impropriety, and irrationality, and subject also to the overriding discretion of the Secretary of State.

(1) Citizenship, nationality, and rights of entry

The right to enter and leave the UK without any let or hindrance, except such as is required or permitted under statute, is given to people by section 1(1) of the Immigration Act 1971, on the basis of their citizenship status under the British Nationality Act 1981. There are several groups of people who have British citizenship. Irish citizens, under section 50(1) of the British Nationality Act 1981, are not aliens. A Common Travel Area free of most immigration restrictions operates between the UK and

[17] Carol Harlow and Richard Rawlings, *Law and Administration* (London: Weidenfeld & Nicolson, 1984), chs. 16 and 17.

Ireland, although the Home Secretary's power to deport Irish citizens if this is conducive to the public good, or to restrict travel under the Prevention of Terrorism (Temporary Provisions) Act 1989 (below, section 7.5) may be invoked. This section provides a very brief outline of the main substantive rules.[18]

(i) *Those with rights of abode before the British Nationality Act 1981 came into force (1 January 1983).*[19] This category includes all who had citizenship of the UK and Colonies by virtue of having been born, adopted, naturalized, or (save in the case of women married to a citizen before the passing of the 1971 Act) registered, in some part of the UK or Islands; those whose parent was a citizen of the UK and Colonies with a right of abode at the time when the child was born or adopted, or whose grandparent had citizenship of the UK and Colonies at the time when the parent was born or adopted; citizens of the UK and Colonies who have at any time been settled in the UK, and had at that time been ordinarily resident there as a citizen for the previous five years or more; and Commonwealth citizens born to or legally adopted by a parent who at the time of birth or adoption had citizenship of the UK and Colonies by reason of having been born in the UK. In addition, certain women had a right of abode by virtue of being a Commonwealth citizen and either being or having been the wife of a citizen of the UK and Colonies or a Commonwealth citizen who, during the marriage, had a right of abode under the above rules, or would have had but for dying before the British Nationality Act 1948 commenced. All these people were 'patrials' who became British citizens under the 1981 Act. They had a close connection with the UK, and were predominantly white. Other Commonwealth citizens, who might have no other citizenship apart from that of a former British colony, were left with no place in which they had an unquestionable right to settle: they were left 'stranded on the beach by the ebbing tide of British imperialism'.[20] They might hold British Dependent Territories Citizenship, British Overseas Citizenship, or have the status of British subjects or British protected persons, but they are not British citi-

---

[18] On the substantive law, see MacDonald and Blake, *Immigration Law and Practice*. A concise account is provided in de Smith and Brazier, *Constitutional and Administrative Law*, ch. 23; Ann Dummett with Ian Martin, *British Nationality: the AGIN Guide to the New Law* (London: AGIN/NCCL, 1982).

[19] Immigration Act 1971, s. 2, as saved by the British Nationality Act 1981, s. 11, in respect of people with a right of abode before the commencement of the 1981 Act. See Evans, *Immigration Law*, 2nd edn., 70–2.

[20] Evans, *Immigration Law*, 68. See Ian Martin, 'Racism in Immigration Law and Practice', in Peter Wallington (ed.), *Civil Liberties 1984* (Oxford: Martin Robertson, 1984), 245–57.

zens and have no right of abode, unless they fall within one of the other categories below.

(ii) *People who are, or have been born to or adopted by, or are descended from, British citizens, or have become naturalized or have registered as British citizens, on or after 1 January 1983.*[21] These complex classes of people also have a right to enter without let or hindrance, and to settle. The familial connection can now be tested fairly accurately by using DNA-profiling methods, which have shown that most people are honest when claiming to be related to people who have a right to enter. The stringent tests for familial connection which are employed by entry clearance officers and immigration officers do not breach the right to respect for family life under Article 8 of the European Convention on Human Rights; indeed, by stressing the significance of the family relationship, they are, in a sense, expressions of this respect.[22]

(iii) *EC nationals.* Under Community law, the nationals of a member state have rights of entry to other member states, pursuant to paragraph (*c*) of Article 3 of the Treaty of Rome, which includes among the 'activities of the Community' the 'abolition, as between member states, of obstacles to freedom of movement for persons, services and capital'. This is not a right which can be exercised for all purposes: the purposes of the Community are economic, and the European Court of Justice has held in *Levin* v. *Secretary of State for Justice*[23] that the right of free movement applies only where people are moving in order to perform activities of an economic nature. Article 7 prohibits discrimination on the grounds of nationality within the field of application of the Treaty. There are specific rights for workers to accept offers of employment in other member states, and to move for that purpose, subject to any limitations justified on the grounds of public policy, public security, or public health.[24] There is a right of establishment for self-employed people and undertakings, for the purposes of business.[25] Finally, there is a right to supply services in other member states.[26] The explanation of these rights lies outside the scope of this book.[27] However, it is noteworthy that these primarily economic

---

[21] British Nationality Act 1981, ss. 1–11. See Evans, *Immigration Law*, pp. 72–90; S. H. Bailey, D. J. Harris and B. L. Jones, *Civil Liberties Cases and Materials*, 3rd edn. (London: Butterworths, 1991), 632–6.

[22] *Kamal* v. *UK* Application No. 8378/78, 20 DR 168; (1982) 4 EHRR. 244, Eur. Commn. HR.

[23] [1982] 2 CMLR 454 at p. 470.

[24] EEC Treaty, Arts. 48 and 49; Regulation 1612/68.

[25] EEC Treaty, Arts. 52–8.   [26] EEC Treaty, Arts. 59–66.

[27] Authoritative and up-to-date accounts are provided by Derrick Wyatt and Alan Dashwood, *The Substantive Law of the EEC*, 2nd edn. (London: Sweet & Maxwell, 1987),

rights may have a significant, albeit indirect, impact on other freedoms for nationals of member states. For example, most of the rules on free-dom of movement have direct effect, and so confer rights which may be enforced by nationals against organs of the states.[28]

(2) Refugees

People who are seeking asylum as political refugees from another country form a relatively small[29] but, from a human rights standpoint, very important group of entrants.

(i) *The basis of refugee status.* The UK has obligations under the Conven-tion Relating to the Status of Refugees,[30] adopted by the UN Conference on the Status of Refugees and Stateless Persons at Geneva in 1951. It entered into force in 1954. While the original Convention applied only to those who became refugees as a result of events occurring before 1 January 1951, that restriction was removed by the Protocol Relating to the Status of Refugees[31] which was adopted by the UN General Assembly in 1966 and entered into force in 1967. In 1951, the UN established the Office of High Commissioner for Refugees. The High Commissioner has on occasion intervened in litigation concerning the treatment of refugees.[32] The Executive Committee to the Office, and the High Commissioner, have the task of providing advice and guidance respectively as to the interpretation and implementation of the Convention and Protocol.[33] Under the Convention, a person is a refugee if he:

chs. 8 and 9; N. Green, T. C. Hartley, and J. A. Usher, *The Legal Foundations of the Single European Market* (Oxford: Oxford University Press, 1991), 91–193.

[28] On direct effect, see T. C. Hartley, *The Foundations of European Community Law*, 2nd edn. (Oxford: Clarendon Press, 1989), ch. 7.

[29] This is a relative assessment. The numbers of applications are in the tens of thou-sands annually, and are thought to have increased substantially in recent years. In 1991, the government's concern that the country was being flooded by asylum requests, many of which were said to be bogus (although this claim was hotly denied), led the Home Secretary to introduce an Asylum Bill into Parliament. This attempted to speed up the repatriation of those who make unfounded claims to refugee status, by streamlining the processing of claims, reducing appeal time limits, and restricting the availability of legal assistance. The measure aroused intense controversy, and was dropped in Mar. 1992 in order to leave parliamentary time for other legislative business to be completed before Parliament was dissolved for the Apr. 1992 general election.

[30] For the text, see *UK Treaty Series*, No. 39, Cmd. 9171 (1954).

[31] *UK Treaty Series*, No. 15, Cmnd. 3906 (1969).

[32] See e.g. *R. v. Secretary of State for the Home Dept., ex parte Sivukamaran (UN High Commissioner for Refugees intervening)* [1988] AC 958, [1988] 1 All ER 193, HL.

[33] The High Commissioner publishes (*inter alia*) the *Handbook on Procedures and Criteria for Determining Refugee Status*, which however is not binding on any domestic court or

(a) is outside the country of his nationality;

(b) has a well-founded fear of being persecuted for reasons of race, religion, nationality, membership of a particular social group, or political opinion; and

(c) is unable or, because of that fear, unwilling to avail himself of the protection of that country.[34]

The grounds which justify a person in seeking asylum clearly exclude people who are emigrating in order to escape famine or to seek improved economic or social conditions. States may provide sanctuary for such people as an humanitarian gesture, but have no obligation to do so under the Convention. Thus the Hong Kong authorities have felt justified in returning to Vietnam large numbers of illegal Vietnamese immigrants who are considered to be economic migrants, without a well-founded fear of persecution from the Vietnamese authorities on their return.

The notion of a well-founded fear of persecution has been the subject of judicial attention in the course of reviewing asylum decisions. The UN High Commissioner for Refugees has argued that the test for a well-founded fear is basically subjective. On this view, the immigration authorities should ask, first, whether the asylum-seeker has a real fear of persecution, and, if so, should accept that he is a refugee unless that fear is objectively unreasonable. This gives strong protection not only against likely persecution but against reasonable fears of persecution. The Home Secretary, on the other hand, has accepted that fear is subjective, but has argued that the test of well-foundedness is objective, to be assessed by the immigration authorities in the light of their evaluation of the information available to them, rather than purely in the light of what the asylum-seeker knows or believes. In *R. v. Secretary of State for the Home Department, ex parte Sivakumaran (UN High Commissioner for Refugees intervening)*[35] the House of Lords, reversing the Court of Appeal, opted for the Home Secretary's contention in preference to that of the High Commissioner. The applicants, Tamils from Sri Lanka, were fleeing from brutal treatment meted out by the Sinhalese and Indian armies in quelling the Tamil insurrection in Sri Lanka, and claimed that they feared persecution if they were returned to Sri Lanka. The House decided that it was for the Secretary of State to decide whether that fear was well-founded, in the light of all the available evidence. Agreeing with the US Supreme Court, the House accepted that the asylum-seeker did not need to show that he was more likely than not to be persecuted.[36] The test was

decision-maker: *R. v. Secretary of State for the Home Dept., ex parte Sivakumaran (UN High Commissioner for Refugees intervening)* [1988] AC 958, [1988] 1 All ER 193, HL.

[34] Art. 1A(2) of the Convention.   [35] [1988] AC 958, [1988] 1 All ER 193, HL.

[36] *Immigration and Naturalization Service v. Cardoza-Fonseca* 94 L. Ed. 2d 434 (1987), US Supreme Court. For comparison of the US and UK positions, see Sajid Qureshi,

whether there was, objectively, a 'reasonable chance', a 'serious possibility', or 'substantial grounds for thinking', that the fugitive will be persecuted if returned. As it seemed to the Home Office that military efforts to root out Tamil extremists did not amount to persecution of Tamils as such, the Home Secretary was entitled to conclude that the Tamils' fear of persecution was not well-founded (although a subsequent appeal by the Tamils on the facts was upheld, and the Secretary of State's decision reversed, by the immigration adjudicator).

The diplomatic sensitivity of cases where people claim to be refugees, and the gravity of the threat to life and liberty which refugee status implies, has resulted in all asylum decisions in England being taken by the Home Office, in the light of the Convention and Protocol.[37] As the obligations of the UK towards refugees operate in international law by virtue of treaties, they do not directly form part of English law. However, they are in effect incorporated into the Immigration Rules by rule 75 of the Immigration Rules 1990. The English courts can therefore strike down a decision to reject a claim for asylum on the basis that the Secretary of State has misconstrued the Convention or Protocol when interpreting the rules, in the same way that they can treat any misinterpretation of the rules as an error of law.[38] While the advice or guidance offered by the Executive Committee and High Commissioner are not part of the rules, it is open to the courts to review the Secretary of State's decision for unreasonableness or failure to take account of relevant considerations, for example if he does not give adequate consideration to a matter which, under the Convention and Protocol, he is required to consider.[39]

On the other hand, the decision of the House of Lords in *R. v. Secretary of State for the Home Department, ex parte Sivakumaran (UN High Commissioner for Refugees intervening)*[40] (the Tamil refugee case, mentioned above) reflects a general principle that the courts will not treat factual decisions made by the immigration authorities under the legislation and Immigration Rules as reviewable unless they are procedurally flawed, although they will subject to particularly close scrutiny decisions which, if flawed, may imperil life or liberty.[41] The proper remedy for people

'Opening the Floodgates? Eligibility for Asylum in the USA. and the U.K.' (1988) 17 *Anglo-Amer. LR* 83–107.

[37] Immigration Rules 1990, r. 75.

[38] *R. v. Chief Immigration Officer, Gatwick Airport, ex parte Kharrazi* [1980] 1 WLR 1396, [1980] 3 All ER 373, CA.

[39] *Bugdaycay v. Secretary of State for the Home Dept.* [1987] AC 514, [1987] 1 All ER 940, HL.

[40] [1988] AC 958, [1988] 1 All ER 193, HL.

[41] *Bugdaycay v. Secretary of State for the Home Dept.* [1987] AC 514 at pp. 535–7, [1987] 1 All ER 940 at pp. 955–6 *per* Lord Templeman.

affected by factual decisions which are merely wrong is to appeal, rather than to apply for judicial review.[42] Unfortunately, however, they may well already have been deported before they are permitted to appeal, and the reversal of the decision may come too late to benefit them. In the case of the Tamils, several of them had been ill treated after being repatriated to Sri Lanka and before being allowed to return to the UK in compliance with the Immigration Adjudicator's decision.

(ii) *The rights of refugees*. A refugee within the meaning of the Convention is entitled not to be expelled or returned to the frontiers of any territory where where his life or freedom would be threatened on account of his race, religion, nationality, member of a particular social group, or political opinion.[43] This does not necessarily confer a right to settle in the UK. If the applicant has come to the UK from his country of nationality via a third country, the UK Government considers that it is entitled to return him to that third country without considering the merits of the claim to refugee status if the third country was one where the applicant could have remained, safe from persecution.

Many refugees have to enter the country in ways which would normally be illegal. For example, they might have been compelled to travel on false passports, without obtaining a valid entry clearance before leaving. They might have lied (or been economical with the truth) on first confronting an immigration officer at the port of entry, because of trauma, language difficulties, or suspicion of officials. They are also likely to have been stowaways on the ship or aircraft on which they arrived, having bribed an employee to let them board: carriers have been discouraged from taking people on board officially without valid travel documents by section 1 of the Immigration (Carriers' Liability) Act 1987, which makes the owners or agents of a ship or aircraft liable to a fine of £1,000 if they bring someone to the UK who is then unable to produce appropriate documentation when required to do so by an immigration officer.

Where the applicant entered in one of these ways, or clandestinely, directly from his country of nationality, it is obviously inconsistent with the Convention to remove an immigrant who is claiming refugee status to the country from which he fled, pending a decision on the merits of the claim. In such cases, the person must be allowed to remain in the UK pending a determination of his claim to asylum, and the courts will either

---

[42] Judicial review is a remedy of last resort, normally to be used only when other avenues have been tried, unless there is no other equally convenient procedure for challenging the decision: R. v. *Secretary of State for the Home Dept., ex parte Swati* [1986] 1 WLR 477, [1986] 1 All ER 717, CA.

[43] Art. 33(1) of the Convention (the so-called 'non-refoulment' provision).

accept an undertaking from the Home Secretary that he will not be removed, or impose a stay of proceedings in a judicial review application to prevent the applicant being removed. Furthermore, merely disembarking without proper papers does not make the refugee an illegal entrant for the purpose of a prosecution under section 25(1) of the Immigration Act 1971, as this would have the effect of making virtually all refugees illegal entrants.[44] Where the applicant came via a safe third country, the courts have accepted the government's view that he can be sent back to the third country, despite this being contrary to the advice on procedure given by the UN High Commissioner for Refugees. This is subject to the proviso that the Secretary of State must, before having the applicant removed, give appropriate consideration to the possibility that the third country might, in breach of the Convention, return the applicant to the country in which there is a risk of persecution. Thus where a person fleeing Uganda, because of a well-founded fear of persecution there, came to this country via Kenya, where there was no risk of persecution, the Home Secretary was not entitled to return him to Kenya without giving serious consideration to the risk that the Kenyans would return him to the Ugandan authorities.[45]

Once it has been accepted that a person is a refugee and has not come from a safe third country, he is entitled to settle in the UK. He has certain obligations, particularly to conform to laws and regulations and measures taken to maintain public order.[46] He may, therefore, be removed from the country if, but only if, this is necessary on grounds of national security and public order, following a decision reached in accordance with due process of law. The refugee must be given time to find a third country prepared to accept him.[47] He will not be removed if the only country to which he could go is one to which he is unwilling to go because of a well-founded fear of persecution.[48]

(iii) *Refugees and human rights.* The Universal Declaration on Human Rights, Article 14, specifies everyone's right to seek and enjoy in other countries asylum from persecution, but neither the International Covenant on Civil and Political Rights nor the European Convention on Human Rights includes this right. However, there are certain rights under the European Convention which may support a right not to be

---

[44] R. v. *Secretary of State for the Home Dept., ex parte Muboyayi* [1991] 4 All ER 72, CA. If the Home Secretary breaches an undertaking given on his behalf, the Court of Appeal has held that he commits a contempt of court: *M.* v. *Home Office* [1992] 4 All ER 97, CA. An appeal to the House of Lords against the finding of contempt is pending. On prosecutions for illegal entry, see R. v. *Naillie and Kanesarajah*, [1992] 1 WLR 1099; [1992] 1 All ER 75, CA.

[45] *Bugdaycay* (see n. 41).

[46] Convention, Art. 2.

[47] Ibid., Arts. 32, 33(2).

[48] Immigration Rules 1990, r. 173.

returned to a country where one is likely to suffer persecution. Such a return may well breach the right to be free of inhuman and degrading treatment, under Article 3 of the European Convention. Other rights under the European Convention may be in issue in refugee cases. If a person claiming refugee status is returned to his country of origin without a right to a judicial hearing, it may breach the right to have the legality of detention tested judicially under Article 5(4), and if it has the effect of splitting up a family it may breach the right to respect for private and family life under Article 8.

In 1972, an unsuccessful attempt was made on the life of the King of Morocco. The same day, a helicopter with two Moroccan Air Force officers on board arrived in Gibraltar, and the officers sought political asylum. This was refused, and the following day they were returned to Morocco, where they were executed. The widow of one of them, Lt. Col. Amekrane, lodged an application under the European Convention, alleging breaches of Articles 3, 5(4), and 8, and the European Commission of Human Rights declared it to be admissible. The UK Government subsequently paid her £37,500 in a friendly settlement, without admitting any violation.[49]

Paul Sieghart suggested that, by operating Article 3 extra–territorially in that case, the European Commission could have effectively created a right under the Convention, if not to asylum, at least to non–return to the place of persecution.[50] Subsequent caselaw has shown that this is possible, although in a narrow range of circumstances. In order to establish an infringement of Article 3, it is necessary to show that the refugee was returned notwithstanding evidence establishing a real risk of injury serious enough to constitute torture, or inhuman or degrading treatment or punishment, within the meaning of Article 3 (discussed in Chapter 4, above). In *Vilvarajah* v. *United Kingdom*,[51] the Tamils who had failed to establish refugee status in *R.* v. *Secretary of State for the Home Department, ex parte Sivakumaran (UN High Commissioner for Refugees intervening)*[52] lodged petitions under the European Convention on Human Rights, alleging (*inter alia*) a breach of Article 3 on the ground that their repatriation to face ill-treatment amounted to inhuman or degrading treatment. The Commission rejected this claim on the casting vote of the President. The case was referred to the European Court of Human Rights.

The Court accepted that a decision to expel a person seeking asylum might give rise to an issue under Article 3, but only where substantial grounds have been shown, at the time of the expulsion, for believing that

[49] *Amekrane* v. *UK* Application No. 5961/72; Report of 19 July 1974, Eur. Comm. HR.
[50] Sieghart, *International Law*, 190.   [51] Eur. Ct. HR, Judgment of 30 Oct. 1991.
[52] [1988] AC 958, [1988] 1 All ER 193, HL.

there is a real risk that he will be subjected to torture or inhuman or degrading treatment or punishment on his return. The Court would rigorously examine the evidence, but would consider it primarily with reference to the material available to the state at the time when expulsion was ordered. On the facts, by a majority of eight votes to one, the Court decided that there were no substantial grounds for believing that the applicants, if expelled, would be subjected to a real risk (rather than a mere possibility) of treatment of a severity sufficient to give rise to a breach of Article 3. While applying their own minds to the issue, the Court took account of the knowledge and experience of the UK authorities in dealing with cases of this sort, and of the careful consideration given to each case by the Secretary of State. Accordingly there was no breach of Article 3.

A further issue which arises under Article 13 of the European Convention concerns the adequacy of the administrative-law remedies available in England and Wales to protect the Article 3 rights of people who have claimed and been refused refugee status. In *Vilvarajah's case,* above, in addition to alleging a breach of Article 3, the Tamil refugees alleged a breach of Article 13, on the ground that proceedings before the English courts had failed to provide an adequate remedy to enforce the rights of the refugees under the Convention. The Commission took the view, by thirteen votes to one, that the domestic remedies available to the applicants were not effective, breaching Article 13. The Court, emphatically differing from the clear opinion of the Commission, decided by seven votes to two that judicial review proceedings were an effective remedy in cases of this sort. In an earlier decision, *Soering* v. *United Kingdom,*[53] the Court had held that judicial review was adequate protection for a person's Article 3 rights, because the English courts could review the reasonableness of a decision (in that case, an extradition decision) on *Wednesbury* principles, and would have jurisdiction to quash a decision where a serious risk of inhuman or degrading treatment was established. The majority felt that extradition could not be distinguished from repatriating asylum-seekers. The English courts had shown themselves able to quash asylum decisions, and had stressed their special responsibility in such cases to subject decisions to the most anxious scrutiny. As Lord Templeman had said in relation to an earlier case,[54] and repeated when Vilvarajah's case[55] was before the House of Lords, 'where the result of a flawed decision may imperil life or liberty a special respon-

---

[53] Eur. Ct. HR, Series A, No. 161, Judgment of 7 July 1989.

[54] *Bugdaycay* v. *Secretary of State for the Home Dept.*[1987] AC 514 at p. 537, [1987] 1 All ER 940 at p. 956, HL.

[55] R. v. *Secretary of State for the Home Dept., ex parte Sivakumaran and conjoined appeals (UN High Commissioner for Refugees intervening)* [1988] AC 958, [1987] 1 All ER 940, HL.

sibility lies on the court in the examination of the decision-making process'. Such a remedy was thought to be adequate to protect Article 3 rights, given the fact that the Convention leaves a margin of discretion to states as to the type of remedy which should be provided.

The decision of the majority of the European Court of Human Rights in *Vilvarajah's case* seems to give more weight to the English judges' expressions of concern than they can reasonably bear. As noted above, the English courts have asserted the power to review decisions for illegality, but European Court of Human Rights may have overestimated the scope of review for irrationality. The majority of the Court chose to disregard the clear decisions of the House of Lords to the effect that the role of the English courts in judicial review proceedings is limited to examining the decision-making process, rather than the merits of the decision. It is now clearly established, following the decision of the House of Lords in *R. v. Secretary of State for the Home Department, ex parte Brind*,[56] that it is not irrational, in the *Wednesbury* sense, for the Home Secretary to make a decision which is not compatible with the Convention. While it is not incorrect to say that a court would have jurisdiction to use the standards of Article 3 of the Convention in assessing the lawfulness and rationality of the Home Secretary's decision, the courts will not force the Home Secretary to use those standards. In such circumstances, it is hard to accept that the majority of the European Court of Human Rights was correct in holding that judicial review provides an effective remedy for breach of Article 13 rights.

(3) Other groups: discretionary admittance

Those people who wish to enter but do not have a right of abode under the above rules are admitted under the Immigration Rules 1990,[57] which permit the imposition of limits on the circumstances in which people may be admitted, and the period and purposes for which they are allowed to stay. Those who may be admitted as temporary entrants include visitors for short periods as tourists or for private medical treatment, and students (other than Iraqis, whose entry was severely curtailed during the run-up to the Gulf War in 1990-1) who have been accepted for full-time courses at educational institutions. Other categories may be admitted for limited periods in the first instance, but with the possibility of being

---

[56] [1991] 1 AC 696, [1991] 1 All ER 720, HL (a decision on the power of the Home Secretary to give directions to broadcasters concerning the use of recordings of statements by members of proscribed organizations in Northern Ireland, and its compatibility with Art. 10 of the ECHR). Cf. *R. v. Secretary of State for the Home Department, ex parte Chahal, Times*, 12 March 1993, DC.

[57] *Statement of Changes in Immigration Rules*, HC 251 of 1989–90, amended by HC 454 of 1989–90, Cm. 1220 (1991), and HC 160 of 1990–1.

allowed to remain for longer, or indefinite, periods subsequently. These include people with work permits, including permits for training and work experience who have jobs which have been made open to them before arrival; people seeking to establish themselves in business or in self-employment, with the means to do so and to support themselves; people with the means to support themselves without taking employment; dependents of such people; and fiancés and fiancées, with an entry clearance, entering for the primary purpose of marrying people settled in the UK and intending to live with them permanently as man and wife. This, and particularly the independent-means head of admittance, has been characterized as replacing a test based on colour of skin with one based on the colour of money.[58]

7.3 DEPORTATION

The power of the Secretary of State for the Home Department to deport people who are not British citizens is given by section 3 of the Immigration Act 1971. There is no power to deport British citizens; Commonwealth and Irish citizens who were settled here on 1 January 1973 become exempt from deportation after five years' residence.[59]

The power to deport applies in four groups of cases.[60] The first is where people who have entered with limited leave to remain overstay their leave, or break one of the conditions attached to their leave to enter (as where a person who enters as a visitor is found to have taken employment). The second is where the Secretary of State deems a person's deportation to be conducive to the public good. The third is where another person to whose family the deportee belongs has been, or has been ordered to be, deported. The fourth is where a person over the age of 17 years has been convicted of an offence for which he is punishable with imprisonment, and the court on his conviction made a recommendation for his deportation. In all these cases, the Home Secretary has a discretion which is exercised in accordance with the Immigration Rules 1990. The first and fourth cases present no special civil liberties problems in principle, but the other two are highly sensitive.

(1) Person's deportation deemed conducive to the public good

There are no rules laid down for deciding when this is the case. In deciding the matter, the Home Secretary considers personal factors relating to

---

[58] Geoffrey Robertson, *Freedom, the Individual and the Law*, 6th edn. (Harmondsworth: Penguin, 1989), 318–19.

[59] Immigration Act 1971, s. 7. On the meaning of these categories see s. 7.2(1), above.

[60] Ibid., s. 3(5), (6), as amended by the British Nationality Act 1981.

the deportee, and in particular his age, length of residence, strength of local connections, personal history, including conduct and employment record, domestic circumstances, compassionate circumstances, and any representations made on the person's behalf (by friends, relatives, MPs, etc.).[61] It can be used where a person has been convicted of offences but the court has made no recommendation for deportation, and this is the most usual type of case in which it is used.[62] However, there are a few cases where it seems that people have been deported in order to achieve some ulterior purpose which infringes civil liberties.

The power has several times been invoked to remove people with political views which the government finds uncongenial. Rudi Dutschke, a student activist, was removed in 1971; successive Home Secretaries have apparently regarded it as an appropriate use of the power to remove or exclude people whose public utterances would be likely to offend sections of the community, or whose very presence might be offensive.[63] In some cases, the power has been used to remove people who are thought to be threatening particular harm to national security, but occasionally the use of the power has gone too far. Mark Hosenball and Philip Agee, Americans who had published information which was said to have prejudiced national security and put the lives of British agents in the field at risk in the course of an account of the activities of the CIA, were removed in 1977, despite the facts that the damage was no less likely to be caused with them abroad than with them here, and that it was unclear what further damage could be done to make their presence here unconducive to the public good in the future.[64] Large numbers of Iraqi or Kuwaiti residents were deported during the Gulf crisis in 1990-1, on information (often highly dubious) from the security services that the people represented a security threat.

In another group of cases, members of the Church of Scientology have been excluded on the basis that the teachings and practices of that church are damaging to its adherents. Even where the people concerned have been EC nationals exercising their prima-facie right to free movement of workers and freedom of establishment, their exclusion has been held to be justified as coming within the exception for public policy.[65] This interferes with freedom of expression and, in the latter case, freedom of

---

[61] Immigration Rules 1990, rr. 164, 167.   [62] Evans, *Immigration Law*, 272.

[63] Ibid., 272–3.

[64] *R. v. Secretary of State for the Home Dept., ex parte Hosenball* [1977] 1 WLR 766, [1977] 3 All ER 452, CA.

[65] *Schmidt v. Secretary of State for Home Affairs* [1969] 2 Ch. 149 (a case of refusal to renew leave to remain, rather than a deportation during the term of a right to remain); *Van Duyn v. Home Office* [1974] 1 WLR 1107; *Van Duyn v. Home Office* [1974] ECR 1337, ECJ.

religion (if, unlike the English courts, one regards scientology as a religion), and as we shall see it occurs without any judicial hearing and usually without the safeguards of the rules of natural justice being observed.

Finally, and squarely within the group of cases which concern political freedom, it has sometimes been suggested that the deportation power has been used to get round restrictions on extradition. There are various formalities which must be complied with before a person can be extradited to face trial in another country, including the conclusion of an extradition treaty between the two countries concerned, and a judicial hearing to establish cause for extradition. There are also substantive limitations, of which the most important is that the offence for which the person is to be extradited must not be one regarded by the courts as a political offence. It is often easier, and more conducive to good international relations, to deport a person as someone whose presence is not conducive to the public good rather than to go through the tortuous and often unsuccessful process of extradition. However, to use deportation in this way evades a person's due-process protections against being returned to face political charges in another jurisdiction. The use of extradition in this way is an abuse of power. The argument was first raised in *R. v. Governor of Brixton Prison, ex parte Soblen*,[66] where Soblen was wanted for trial in the USA, and the US Government had asked the British Government to return him to them. The offence for which Soblen was wanted in the USA was espionage, an offence for which extradition is not available. Soblen wanted to go instead to Czechoslovakia, which was prepared to accept him, but the Home Secretary ordered his deportation to the USA. This order was upheld by the Court of Appeal in habeas corpus proceedings, as it had not been shown that the Home Secretary would not have removed Soblen to the USA even had the request for his delivery not been made. It is therefore open to the court to review a deportation decision for an abuse of power if it is an attempt at disguised extradition, although it seems that the deportation order will be regarded as an abuse of power in such cases only if the desire to achieve extradition by the back door was the sole reason for making the order.[67]

(2) Family of person deported

One of the difficulties which may flow from a deportation is that the deportee's family will be split up, breaching the right to respect for family life under Article 8 of the European Convention on Human Rights. This is, to some extent, taken into account by the Secretary of State when

[66] [1963] 2 QB 243, CA.

[67] *R. v. Bow Street Magistrates, ex parte Mackeson* (1982) 75 Cr. App. R. 24, CA; *R. v. Guildford Magistrates' Court, ex parte Healy* [1983] 1 WLR 108, DC.

exercising his discretion under the Immigration Rules 1990, rules 164 and 169. As regards the deportee, the family connection may be a factor (in relation to domestic or compassionate circumstances) influencing the Home Secretary to allow him to remain. Following one case, *Uppal* v. *United Kingdom (No. 2)*,[68] the Home Secretary revoked a deportation order after the Euorpean Commission of Human Rights held that it might breach the applicant's Article 8 rights by dividing the family. If it has been decided to deport him, or not to revoke a deportation order, on the other hand, the family ties will militate in favour of deporting the rest of the family as well. At this stage, therefore, if the family wants to remain, it will do well to stress its independence of the deportee, its connection with other relatives in the UK, other ties with the UK, the spouse's independent employment record, the family's ability to support itself here, and the disruptive effect on the children and their education if they were to be forcibly removed.[69] There can be no doubt that decisions of this sort are very demanding and require the most sensitive consideration. One of the difficulties, however, is the general inadequacy of appeal mechanisms, to which we now turn.

7.4 RIGHTS OF APPEAL AND DUE PROCESS

International-law obligations accepted by the UK impose two kinds of procedural constraints on the expulsion of aliens. First, under the ICCPR, Article 13, an alien lawfully within the territory of a state may be expelled

only in pursuance of a decision reached in accordance with law and shall, except where compelling reasons of national security otherwise require, be allowed to submit the reasons against his expulsion and to have his case reviewed by, and be represented for the purpose before, the competent authority or a person or persons especially designated by the competent authority.

While the UK Government, on ratification, made reservations in respect of the application of this provision to Hong Kong, no reservation was entered in respect of its application in the UK itself. As we shall see, the executive review and appeal system is broadly in accord with this provision, the Home Secretary being the competent authority for this purpose, although there is provision for expulsion where the Home Secretary deems it to be conducive to the public good, a term which seems broader than the exception permitted under Article 13 in relation to compelling reasons of national security.

---

[68] (1981) 3 EHRR 399.   [69] Immigration Rules 1990, rr. 169, 170, 171.

Secondly, people who are detained in order to be removed as illegal immigrants, or deported for any reason, have their liberty interfered with. Article 5(4) of the European Convention on Human Rights, providing for an entitlement to take proceedings speedily to test the lawfulness of detention, and Article 6(1), providing (*inter alia*) that in the determination of civil rights and obligations everyone is entitled to a fair and public hearing within a reasonable time by an independent and impartial tribunal established by law, between them lay down a framework against which to assess the procedures for challenging the legality of detentions pending removal.

The review and appeal processes in these cases are of four types: review by an official, appeals to an adjudicator or tribunal,[70] review by an advisory body, and review by a court. Those who are to be deported following a recommendation by a court on conviction for an offence will already have had a judicial hearing. The Secretary of State's obligations to them are merely to consider fairly, in the light of the factors set out in the Immigration Rules, whether to give effect to the recommendation for deportation. The factors include age, length of residence, strength of local connections, personal circumstances, the nature of the offence and any previous convictions, any compassionate circumstances, and any representations received from the convict. It is not necessary to put to the convict the case against him unless there is some new factor, of which the person does not know, which may tip the scales against him, or if arguments against deportation have been advanced by the convict which might alter the earlier picture, suggesting that the recommendation requires reconsideration.[71]

In other deportation cases, a judicial hearing is likely to be a last, rather than a first, resort.

(1) Official review of the decision

There is a procedure for administrative review of a deportation order. The deportee can apply to have the deportation order revoked.[72] This matter is normally decided by officials of the department, acting in the name of the Home Secretary,[73] but may be decided by the Home

---

[70] The appeal structure is based on recommendation in the Report of the Wilson Committee on Immigration Appeals, Cmnd. 3387 (London: HMSO, 1967).

[71] *R.* v. *Secretary of State for the Home Dept., ex parte Santillo* [1981] QB 778, [1981] 2 All ER 897, CJEC, DC, and CA.

[72] See Immigration Rules 1990, r. 180.

[73] It is normal for the decision on deportation to be taken by immigration inspectors authorized by the Home Secretary to act on his behalf, and this practice was upheld by the House of Lords in *Oladehinde* v. *Secretary of State for the Home Dept.* [1991] 1 AC 254,

Secretary in person (with advice from his officials) if the deportation involves particularly sensitive political, legal, or diplomatic issues.

(2) Appeals to an adjudicator or the Immigration Appeal Tribunal

Following, or instead of, the administrative review, there is an appeal process. A person aggrieved by refusal of entry or by a deportation order normally has a right of appeal to an Immigration Adjudicator or, where the deportation order is made on the ground that the person's removal is conducive to the public good or the person is part of the family of a deported person, to the Immigration Appeal Tribunal.[74] Where the Home Secretary in person makes the deportation order or refuses to revoke it, rather than leaving the matter to be dealt with by officials in the Home Office, there is no right of appeal to either the tribunal or an adjudicator.[75] Instead, the matter becomes subject to a review by an advisory panel, the so-called Three Wise Men, considered below.

The adjudicators are normally officials who have been immigration officers, members of the Immigration Department of the Home Office. The Immigration Appeal Tribunal consists of members independent of the Home Office, but until 1987 selected by the Home Office. This gave the impression that the appeals against Home Office decisions were being determined by members of the same body which made them, making the Home Office effectively judges in their own cause. Since 1987 the appeal process has been administered by the Lord Chancellor's Department. This seems to have been intended to give the impression that the appellate process is truly independent, although the adjudicators are still selected from among the ranks of immigration officers and the tribunal is still heavily dependent on the way in which cases are put before it by those representing the immigration authorities.[76] There must remain a suspicion, however, that the arrangements violate Article 6(1) of the European Convention.

There are two further problems relating to the appeal process. First, there is a technical matter relating to the powers of appellate bodies. When a person appeals to an adjudicator or to the Immigration Appeal Tribunal against a deportation order made on the ground that he, or the

[1990] 3 All ER 393, as falling within the principle that duties placed on a minister might lawfully be discharged by any member of the dept.: *Carltona Ltd.* v. *Commissioners of Works* [1943] 2 All ER 560, CA.

[74] Immigration Act 1971, ss. 13, 15.   [75] Ibid., s. 15(4).

[76] See Carol Harlow and Richard Rawlings, *Law and Administration* (London: Weidenfeld & Nicolson, 1984), chs. 16 and 17. An empirical study and analysis of the immigration appeals system is provided by Charles Blake and Jim Gillespie, 'The Immigration Appeal Process: A Study in Legal Ritual', an unpubl. 1979 paper.

person to whose family he belongs, has breached a condition of his leave to remain, the appellate power is limited to considering whether 'on the facts of the case there is in law no power to make the deportation order for the reasons stated in the notice of the decision'.[77] The House of Lords has interpreted this as excluding appeals on the ground of procedural impropriety or *vires*, as where it is said that a decision is made by some- one who lacks power to make it.[78] Any challenge to the capacity of the decision-maker, rather than the lawfulness of the reasons for the decision, must be by way of an application for judicial review. Secondly, people refused entry or, having entered, being removed as illegal entrants must normally leave the country before they can exercise their right of appeal.[79]

The position of illegal entrants is a matter of particular concern, given the wide meaning given to illegal entry by the courts (including people with apparently valid leave to enter which was obtained by a decep- tion).[80] There are powers to arrest people whom a constable reasonably believes to be committing an offence under the 1971 Act (e.g. illegal entry or overstaying leave), and a search warrant may be obtained to search premises where it is reasonably suspected that an illegal entrant may be found.[81] Once detained, the person is subject to executive discre- tion of a largely uncontrolled kind. Not being lawfully in the territory of the UK, illegal entrants are not entitled to the protections usually avail- able to those lawfully in the territory under Article 13 of the ICCPR. The Home Office has a wide discretion in deciding how to proceed against people who are thought to be illegal entrants, and who cannot show that they are entitled to be treated as refugees. The officials can choose whether remove them without a prosecution or deportation order under section 4 and Schedule 2 of the Immigration Act 1971; to prosecute them for illegal entry contrary to section 24, leading to the likelihood of a recommendation for deportation on conviction; or to make a deportation order under section 3 on the ground that deportation is conducive to the public good. Those immigrants in the first category will have no prior hearing in a court or tribunal; those in the second cat- egory will have the benefit of a court hearing before their deportation is recommended, but will then have to leave the country before they can appeal against the making of the deportation order itself. Those in the

---

[77] Immigration Act 1988, s. 5(1).
[78] *R.* v. *Secretary of State for the Home Dept., ex parte Oladehinde* [1991] 1 AC 254, [1990] 3 All ER 393, HL.
[79] Immigration Act 1971, ss. 13(3), 15(4).
[80] *R.* v. *Secretary of State for the Home Dept., ex parte Khera; R.* v. *Secretary of State for the Home Dept., ex parte Khawaja* [1984] AC 74, [1983] 1 All ER 765, HL.
[81] Immigration Act 1971, ss. 24(2), 25(3), and Sched. 2, para. 17.

third category will have the right to appeal to the Immigration Appeal Tribunal before being deported, but only if their deportation was ordered by an official of the Home Office rather than by the Home Secretary in person.[82] The decision to proceed by one route rather than the other is effectively unreviewable by the courts, and has a direct effect on the scope of appeal rights and the way in which they can be exercised.[83]

Yet, despite the restrictions of appeal rights in the Immigration Act 1971 by the Immigration Act 1988, the number of immigrants in the country awaiting a decision by the Home Office or appellate authorities on an application for asylum has grown, and the government has used the pressure on the appeal system to justify introducing legislation which, if passed, will further restrict rights of appeal. The Asylum and Immigration Appeals Bill, which at the time of writing is receiving its second reading in the House of Lords, would impose tight time limits on the period within which appeals must be lodged, make it more difficult for immigrants to obtain legal advice, and generally make it more likely that larger numbers of immigrants would be more quickly repatriated without enjoying an appeal. The desire to streamline the administrative process appears to be accompanied by a less well acknowledged policy of restricting numbers of immigrants, with a consequential threat to standards of due process and fairness in dealing with applicants.

(3) Deportation without appeal: the hearing by the extra-statutory advisers

The third process relates to those people against whom deportation orders have been made by the Secretary of State personally on the ground that their deportation would be conducive to the public good. These people are normally deported on national security grounds, or as part of tit-for-tat expulsions of foreign diplomats. A statutory right of appeal to a tribunal in such cases, granted by the Immigration Appeals Act 1969 and used only once, in the Rudi Dutschke case, was repealed by the Immigration Act 1971 on the ground that such cases are not well suited to determination by independent tribunals and raise issues on which it is likely to be contrary to public policy to reveal information and sources. Instead, there is a non-statutory procedure.[84] When the Home Secretary has made a decision to deport, he gives the deportee such details of the allegations and information against him as do not reveal their sources. The statement of reasons served on the deportee[85]

---

[82] Ibid., s. 15(4).

[83] See Evans, *Immigration Law*, chs. 6 and 7, and especially p. 342.

[84] Immigration Rules 1990, r. 157.

[85] As required by the Immigration Appeals (Notices) Regulations 1984 (SI No. 2040 of 1984), regs. 3 and 4.

has been held to be sufficient if it states that he is being deported for reasons of national security, because of the possible prejudicial effect on national security were the Secretary of State to be required to give the supporting reasons in more detail.[86]

The deportee is then allowed to make representations in writing or in person to three advisers (the Three Wise Men, of whom the chairman is at present Lord Justice Lloyd). This non-statutory procedure replaced a right to a statutory appeal for all deportees under earlier legislation. It was a concession to MPs who wanted to retain the statutory appeal procedure, during the passage of the bill (which became the Immigration Act 1971) which sought to abolish the statutory procedure. Under the non-statutory, advisory procedure, legal representation is not granted, but the detainee may be assisted by a friend.[87] The advisers then offer their advice confidentially to the Home Secretary, who reconsiders his decision.[88] Grounds for deportation need not be revealed to the deportees, in order to protect sources and security. Individual rights and principles of fairness give way to national security considerations.[89] The deportees will therefore not necessarily know the case which they have to answer. Although it will be difficult for a detainee before the advisers to rebut reasons for deportation which cannot be fully revealed, in *R. v. Secretary of State for the Home Department, ex parte Cheblak*,[90] Lord Donaldson MR held that the advisers must act as fairly as possible within their terms of reference. This involves making available an outline of the allegations against the deportee so far as this can be done without endangering security or revealing sources. This calls for considerable care and tact on the part of the advisers, but in *Cheblak*'s case, concerning the deportation orders issued against a number of people who were suspected of representing a security risk during the Iraq–Kuwait crisis in 1990–91, the Court of Appeal expressed its confidence in the ability of the advisers to perform this delicate function fairly and efficiently. They were to some degree vindicated by the

---

[86] *R. v. Secretary of State for the Home Dept., ex parte Cheblak* [1991] 2 All ER 319, CA.

[87] The procedure is as described by Mr Reginald Maudling, then Home Secretary: 819 HC Debs. (5th Ser.) col. 376, 15 June 1971.

[88] In the cases arising out of the Gulf War, a substantial number of deportation orders were revoked following the advice of the advisers, which was thought to have shown that allegations that those detained had connections with organizations sympathetic to Iraq were based on inadequate, misleading, or out-of-date information from the security services.

[89] *R. v. Secretary of State for the Home Dept., ex parte Hosenball* [1977] 1 WLR 766, [1977] 3 All ER 452, CA.

[90] [1991] 2 All ER 319, CA. In an earlier case, Lord Denning M.R. had been prepared to contemplate review on unfairness grounds, but only if the advisers were to refuse to hear any representations: *R. v. Secretary of State for the Home Dept., ex parte Hosenball* [1977] 1 WLR 766, [1977] 3 All ER 452 at p. 459.

results of the reviews of those orders: of 33 cases considered by the advisers up to 1 March 1991, 19 detainees, including Mr Cheblak, had been released.[91] However, a process which had a basis in law might command more confidence as a buttress for rights than one which depends on an executive concession and a willingness to listen to advisers.

Attempts to challenge the Three-Wise-Men procedure, or the decisions of the Home Secretary, in judicial review proceedings have so far been unsuccessful: although the procedure does not comply with normal principles of natural justice, and may well fail to meet the standards laid down in Articles 5 and 6 of the European Convention on Human Rights, the courts have held that the principles of natural justice are liable to be curtailed where national security is at stake. Furthermore, since the Home Secretary is in a better position than the courts to decide what national security demands, and to balance its demands against those of individual rights and civil liberties, the courts will assume that his decision is not irrational.[92]

Nevertheless, this sort of executive prerogative, reviewable only for bad faith on the part of the Home Secretary, devalues the notion of judicial protection for rights. The refusal of the English courts to review the procedures adopted in decisions about national security deportations contrasts markedly with the approach of Canadian courts, which have held that for a review committee to take evidence in the absence of the deportee was an unjustified breach of section 7 of the Canadian Charter of Rights and Freedoms.[93] Furthermore, the lack of any procedure laid down by law for reviewing the decision to deport makes it questionable whether the deportation of aliens, who were in the territory lawfully, on grounds of public good is 'in pursuance of a decision reached in accordance with law' as required by Article 13 of the ICCPR. This is an area of law and procedure which should be urgently reviewed.

(4) Review by a court

Finally, there are two processes whereby the legality of detention may be tested in the courts. These are, first, an application for habeas corpus, and, secondly, an application for judicial review.

[91] Ian Leigh, 'The Gulf War Deportations and the Courts' [1991] *PL* 331–9 at p. 333.

[92] *R.* v. *Secretary of State for the Home Dept., ex parte Hosenball* [1977] 1 WLR 766, [1977] 3 All ER 452, CA; *R.* v. *Secretary of State for the Home Dept., ex parte Cheblak* [1991] 2 All ER 319, CA.

[93] *Chiarelli* v. *Minister of Employment and Immigration* [1990] 2 FC 299; s. 7 provides: 'Everyone has the right to life, liberty and security of the person and the right not to be deprived thereof except in accordance with the principles of fundamental justice.' For comparison of the Canadian and English cases, and a critique of the English procedures, see Leigh, Gulf War Deportations', 331–9.

(i) *Habeas corpus*.[94] Habeas corpus is a writ which requires a person to justify the detention of another. The initial evidential burden lies on the applicant to show some reason to think that the validity of the order authorizing detention might be doubtful. This is a substantial burden, particularly where the power to detain is expressed in a way which makes it dependent on the Home Secretary's subjective state of mind or belief.[95] Only if that burden is discharged is there a legal obligation on the detainer to justify the detention, rather than on the detainee to show that it is unlawful.[96]

There are limits to the usefulness of habeas corpus. The power of the court in habeas corpus proceedings is limited to considering whether the detention is within the legal powers of the person authorizing it. It does not extend to reviewing the procedure adopted in the course of making a decision which the decision-maker had power to make.[97] It will therefore be possible to challenge factual determinations made by the immigration authorities only if they are jurisdictional facts, which must be correctly decided in order to ground the power to make the order for detention, deportation, or removal. A finding that a person is an illegal entrant is of this sort, and so is reviewable by a court on a habeas corpus application.[98] On the other hand, an allegation of breach of natural justice or fairness, or an argument that the decision was unreasonable or the decision-maker was influenced by improper motives or irrelevant considerations, will not be entertained in a habeas corpus application; the only course in such cases is to apply for judicial review.[99]

If the order for detention is quashed on one of these other grounds, the detention will be without valid authorization, and habeas corpus will then be available to secure the detainee's release. The use of *certiorari* in aid of habeas corpus in this way is well established in Canada, and it would seem to be equally possible and convenient to bring a habeas corpus application alongside an application for judicial review in England and Wales.[100]

The immigration authorities must normally show that the jurisdictional requirements are satisfied on the balance of probabilities, that being the

[94] See R. J. Sharpe, *The Law of Habeas Corpus*, 2nd edn. (Oxford: Clarendon Press, 1989).

[95] *R. v. Governor of Brixton Prison, ex parte Ahsan* [1969] 2 QB 222, DC; Sharpe, Habeas Corpus, 86–7.

[96] *Khawaja v. Secretary of State for the Home Dept.* [1983] AC 74, [1983] 1 All ER 765, HL.

[97] *R. v. Secretary of State for the Home Dept., ex parte Muboyayi* [1991] 4 All ER 72, CA.

[98] *Khawaja* (see n. 96).

[99] *Cheblak* (see n. 86); Muboyayi (see n. 97).

[100] Sharpe, *Habeas Corpus*, pp. 51–3; *Khawaja v. Secretary of State for the Home Dept.* [1984] AC 74 at p. 99, [1983] 1 All ER 765 at p. 774 *per* Lord Wilberforce.

civil rather than criminal standard of proof. This standard is flexible, however, and a higher standard of probability is needed to tip the balance where the issue affects individual liberty.[101] Nevertheless, where the Home Secretary claims that deportation is conducive to the public good by reason of national security, the court will not test the accuracy of the statement, which is based on an evaluation which lies within the exclusive competence of the Home Secretary.[102] There is therefore little room to test a deportation order made on these grounds: the leading commentator on habeas corpus refers[103] to 'the contrast between a stated willingness to intervene on the one hand, and a queasiness about actually giving relief on the other' in cases where 'the terms of the statute are broad, and the element of public interest to be considered influences the court to shy away from intervention'.

(ii) *Application for judicial review.* This is a procedure which permits the adequacy of the procedure leading up to the making or confirmation of an order for removal or deportation to be tested by the court on the usual administrative-law principles: illegality, irrationality, and procedural impropriety. It therefore has a wider reach than habeas corpus. Nevertheless, there is one general limitation: an applicant will not be given leave to apply for judicial review if there are other, more appropriate, channels open to him in seeking a remedy. Thus applicants will normally be expected to have made use of the appeal procedures, if they are available, before resorting to the courts.[104] The courts are a second line of defence.[105]

When judicial review is sought in relation to a decision to deport for the public good on national-security grounds, there is a special problem: the courts regard national-security judgments as the exclusive preserve of the executive, and will not quash an executive decision on such matters unless it is manifestly unsupported by proper reasons or evidence.[106] When an applicant is someone who would be an illegal entrant but is claiming asylum as a refugee, the judgment of the Secretary of State as to the reasonableness of the applicant's fear of persecution, and as to whether the applicant could be returned safely to a third country without well-founded fear of being returned from there to the country where the

---

[101] *Khawaja* (see n. 96); *R. v. Secretary of State for the Home Dept., ex parte Momin Ali* [1984] 1 WLR 663, [1984] 1 All ER 1009, CA.

[102] *Cheblak* (see n. 86). [103] Sharpe, *Habeas Corpus*, 122–3.

[104] *R. v. Secretary of State for the Home Dept., ex parte Swati* [1986] 1 WLR 477, [1986] 1 All ER 717, CA.

[105] *Cheblak* (see n. 86).

[106] *Council of Civil Service Unions v. Minister for the Civil Service* [1985] AC 374, [1984] 3 All ER 935, HL; *Hosenball* (see n. 92); *Cheblak* (see n. 86).

risk of persecution exists, are political judgments given by Parliament exclusively to the Secretary of State, and these judgments likewise will not be questioned by the courts unless manifestly without foundation.[107]

(5) Conclusion

The appeal system and the courts are only imperfect protectors of the rights of people to be secure against executive interference with their liberties.[108] It is true, as Lord Donaldson MR pointed out in *ex parte Cheblak*, that the Three Wise Men advising the Home Secretary in some deportation matters are experienced, reputable, and appear trustworthy, but their advice can never amount to a determination safeguarding individual rights. Not only is it merely advisory (although the experience of the Gulf War deportations suggests that it is careful, as fair as possible, and often acted on), but it is given secretly, following a procedure in which fairness to the potential deportee is severely restricted.[109] The rights of immigrants are thus dependent on executive discretion and fairness in a way which puts them on an entirely different footing from the rights of British citizens.

7.5 EXCLUSION ORDERS

So far, this chapter has been chiefly concerned with the rights of immigrants from outside the UK. This section deals with certain anomalous powers to restrict the freedom of British citizens to travel or settle at will within the UK, said by successive governments to be necessary in order to combat terrorism. The provisions conferring these powers were introduced as a measure to control terrorism related to the affairs of Northern Ireland, and are of two sorts.

First, examining officers are empowered by the Prevention of Terrorism (Temporary Provisions) Act 1989, section 16 and Schedule 5,

---

[107] *Bugdaycay* (see n. 41), distinguishing *Khawaja* on the ground that the power of review in the latter case related to objective factual judgments as to the legality of entry, not to impressionistic judgments about conditions in other countries; *Muboyayi* (see n. 97). Home Secretary's decision to return to France a Zairean claiming asylum not reviewable.

[108] See Evans, *Immigration Law*, chs. 7 and 8.

[109] Although it has been asserted that, even in national security cases, the advisers could be subject to judicial review for breach of their truncated duty of fairness, it is hard to imagine a case where a court could ever know enough about the background to form a view as to the extent to which the demands of national security left room for procedural fairness. See, however, dicta in *ex parte Hosenball* and *ex parte Cheblak*, above.

to detain people entering or leaving Britain or Northern Ireland by ship or aircraft, or travelling by land between Northern Ireland and Eire, for up to twelve hours. The purpose of the detention is to allow for them to be investigated and questioned to see whether they are or appear to be concerned in the commission, preparation, or instigation of acts of terrorism; whether they are subject to an exclusion order (explained below); or whether there are grounds to suspect that they have committed any offence in relation to exclusion orders contrary to section 8 of the 1989 Act. No suspicion is required in order to justify this initial detention. If reasonable grounds emerge for suspecting that a person is involved in terrorism, the detention may last for up to twenty-four hours. Further detention may be authorized for specific purposes, including to allow a time to decide whether or not to make an exclusion order or commence criminal proceedings.

Secondly, an order (an 'exclusion order') can be made excluding a person either from Northern Ireland or from mainland Britain. Orders under section 5 of the 1989 Act prevent a person from entering, or being in, Britain; orders under section 6 prevent the person from entering, or being in, Northern Ireland. Section 7 allows orders to be made excluding people who are not British citizens from either Great Britain or Northern Ireland or both. The orders are made by the Secretary of State, and may be used in such a way as appears to him to be expedient to prevent acts of terrorism connected with the affairs of Northern Ireland.[110] An order may be made if the Secretary of State is satisfied that the person in question is or has been concerned in the commission, preparation, or instigation of acts of terrorism connected with the affairs of Northern Ireland, wherever they occurred in the UK, or is attempting or may attempt to enter Great Britain (or, as the case may be, Northern Ireland) with a view to being so concerned.[111] Where the person is ordinarily resident in the place from which he is to be excluded, the Secretary of State must consider whether he has sufficient connection with anywhere else to make it appropriate to exclude him from the country of his residence. No order may be made against a British citizen who has for three years been ordinarily resident in the area from which the order would, if made, exclude him.[112] Once made, notice of the order is served on the person, who may make representations to the Secretary of State and (normally) have an interview with an advisor chosen by the Secretary of State, who will advise whether the order should be revoked.[113] If not revoked, an order stays in force for three years, after which time the matter must be

---

[110] Prevention of Terrorism (Temporary Provisions) Act 1989, s. 4(1), (2).
[111] Ibid., ss. 5(1), 6(1), 7(1).   [112] Ibid., ss. 5(3), (4), 6(3), (4).
[113] Ibid., Sched. 2, para. 3.

reviewed and, if still considered appropriate, another exclusion order made.[114]

In 1983, Lord Jellicoe in his *Report on the Operation of the Prevention of Terrorism (Temporary Provisions) Act 1978* expressed the view that exclusion orders made a useful contribution to public safety, and had been used against people whom there was good reason to believe were part of, or associated with, active service units of the Provisional IRA. The power is selectively used: Lord Colville reported that at the end of 1990 only 97 orders remained in force.[115] Nevertheless, Lord Colville himself is no supporter of the orders. He recommended, in his 1987 report, that the exclusion order provisions should be repealed, although the government did not act on that recommendation, regarding the orders as a useful weapon in the fight to control terrorism, even if it is hard to justify the existence of the power on the basis of legal or political principle.

The orders do not appear to breach the UK's obligations in international law. In international law, the UK has accepted obligations under the ICCPR which include, under Article 12(1), recognizing the right of everyone lawfully within the territory of the state 'to liberty of movement and freedom to choose his residence' within that territory. This reflects the terms of Article 13(2) of the Universal Declaration on Human Rights ('Everyone has the right to freedom of movement and residence within the borders of each state'), and Article 2(1) of the Fourth Protocol to the ECHR, to which the UK is not a party. The right under Article 12(1) is not absolute: under Article 12(3), it may be subject to restrictions, but only those 'which are provided by law, are necessary to protect national security, public order (*ordre public*), public health or morals or the rights and freedoms of others, and are consistent with the other rights recognized in the present Convenant'. Furthermore, on ratifying the Covenant, the UK government reserved the right 'to interpret the provisions of article 12(1) relating to the territory of a State as applying separately to each of the territories comprising the United Kingdom and its dependencies'. It appears that the restrictions on travel between Northern Ireland and the mainland of Britain may be consistent with the provisions of Article 12(3), if they are regarded as being provided by law and necessary to protect national security. Even if one does not accept the government's view on the latter point, the restrictions are within the reservation which the UK entered to Article 12.

Nevertheless, the orders are objectionable for two reasons. First, the idea of people being effectively condemned to a form of internal exile in the UK, although it does not contravene international human rights law,

---

[114] Prevention of Terrorism (Temporary Provisions) Act 1989, Sched. 2, para. 1.

[115] Lord Colville, *Report on the Operation in 1990 of the Prevention of Terrorism (Temporary Provisions) Act 1989.*

is bad for this country's international reputation, particularly as the restriction on liberty is imposed without the need for proof before a judicial tribunal that the subject has committed any terrorism offence.[116] Secondly, there is no right to an independent, judicial determination of the appropriateness of making an exclusion order, although recommendations of the adviser are followed. The evidence which would have to be given might put sources of information, and perhaps even lives, at risk. Nevertheless, there must be a suspicion that the information on the basis of which orders are made will not always be subjected to rigorous scrutiny.

Objections to the orders might be less persuasive if the lack of any prior review by a judicial officer of the grounds for making the order was balanced by the availability of a rigorous review, by an independent tribunal, of the orders when made. But there is no appeal procedure, and there is no independent review of the merits of individual decisions. Unlike patients detained compulsorily under the Mental Health Act 1983, people subject to exclusion orders have no independent tribunal, with power to order the quashing of the order, to which they can take their cases. Instead, the person subject to the order may seek a review by the Secretary of State, and every three years, when the orders lapse, there is an automatic review. In the course of the review, the person concerned is asked to fill in a questionnaire giving information about life-style and nominating referees who may be approached, and may request (but will not necessarily be granted) an interview with the officers (in England, they are from the Metropolitan Police) who inquire into the case and report to the Secretary of State.

However, the value of this opportunity to make representations is somewhat limited by the refusal of the Secretary of State to divulge information about the grounds on which the order was made. In other words, the person does not know the case which he has to answer. In *R. v. Secretary of State for Home Affairs, ex parte Stitt*,[117] the applicant, a social-work student in Northern Ireland who wanted to pursue his studies at postgraduate level in England but had been made the subject of an exclusion order, applied to quash the Secretary of State's refusal to revoke the order following an administrative review. The applicant argued that the denial of reasons for the exclusion order, at least in broad outline and with any restictions necessary to protect the anonymity and confidentiality of intelligence sources, was a breach of natural justice.

The Divisional Court roundly rejected this argument. For Watkins LJ, the necessity for curtailing freedom to travel between Britain and

---

[116] For a thorough critique, see K. D. Ewing and C. A. Gearty, *Freedom under Thatcher: Civil Liberties in Modern Britain*, (Oxford: Clarendon Press, 1990), 217–21.

[117] *The Times*, 3 Feb. 1987, DC; text available on Lexis.

Northern Ireland, in order to prevent injury to life, limb, and property, formed an unquestionable basis for judgment. In view of the fact that the making of exclusion orders was concerned with national security, the court accepted that courts could not require the Secretary of State to provide reasons for his decisions, following the decision of the House of Lords in *Council of Civil Service Unions* v. *Minister for the Civil Service*.[118] Giving any reasons at all, the judges thought, might give an indication of the security forces' sources of information, and leave informants or service personnel at risk. The position was not distinguishable from that in the deportation cases, despite the fact that the applicant was a citizen, not a foreigner. The procedure to be adopted in the matter was governed by the legislation (at that time, the Act in question was the Prevention of Terrorism (Temporary Provisions) Act 1976), the provisions of which formed a comprehensive code, striking the balance between the public interest and fairness to individuals as Parliament deemed appropriate. It was not for the courts to augment the safeguards for individuals, or to alter the balance which Parliament had struck. In the field of national security the common-law rules of fairness and natural justice have no place where there are indications that Parliament has considered, and provided for, that level of protection for individuals rights which is appropriate in the public interest.

This truncated role for judicial review, while consistent with other authorities relating to procedures for making national security decisions, is somewhat disappointing. It leaves people's freedom of movement within the UK subject to an executive discretion which is free of any effective public scrutiny whatever, either by Parliament or the courts. As the government's own adviser, Lord Colville, recommends the repeal of the power on the ground that, in his view, its limited effectiveness is outweighed by the damage which it causes to civil liberties and the UK's reputation, a more extensive judicial review of the way in which the powers are exercised might be a beneficial, although on the authorities as they stand it is unlikely to be achievable without legislation.

7.6 CONCLUSION

The risks to civil liberties which arise in the field of freedom of movement are not, on the whole, the result of a failure of English law to recognize a *prima facie* right to move freely. Generally speaking, people enjoy freedom of movement within the UK, and freedom to leave the UK. So far as immigration law is concerned, the right of states to control entry to

---

[118] [1985] AC 374, [1984] 3 All ER 935, HL.

their territories is well established in international law as an incident of sovereignty, and the terms on which entry is granted are part of the internal affairs of the state with which other states are not generally regarded as having a legitimate concern. Where freedom of movement is threatened in English law, it is partly the result of a lack of political will to insist on having legislation framed in such a way as to extend independent control or review to executive decisions which purport to have been taken for the public good, and partly flows from the judges' conviction that they are not well placed to review the opinions of the government on matters of national security.

The political will is, in practice, more significant than the judges' self-restraint in determining the scope of freedom to enter and leave the territory. No political party depending on public support will happily relax immigration controls at a time when the general public mood opposes easier immigration, as is the case in much of the UK at present. Nor will any party be keen to support improved procedures for reviewing deportation and exclusion decisions in relation to people whose presence is said to be a threat to national security or who are alleged to be concerned in terrorism, if such support is likely to be seen by voters as a sign of lack of resolution in the protection of the country and its people. This is a field in which the rights which are infringed tend to belong to people who, rightly or wrongly, enjoy little public sympathy, and their claims are unlikely to prevail over what politicians see as the political imperative of maintaining their public image of firmness and resolution in countering external or internal security threats. Rights lead in one direction, and democracy in another. In relation to foreigners and suspected terrorists, there are few incentives, and no legal compulsion, for the government to follow the road of rights. Although the law is by no means ideal, for successive governments to have kept alive as much freedom of movement into and out of the various territories of the UK as has survived successive recessions and two decades of terrorism is not an inconsiderable achievement. It has been made possible by a level of restraint and caution in responding to crises which on the whole reflects credit on the judgement of the civil service and senior politicians.

PART III
PRIVACY

8

THE SCOPE OF LEGAL PRIVACY

Part III as a whole examines aspects of privacy rights. This chapter surveys the geography of the subject. Starting with an introduction to the idea of privacy, it will then look at the way in which aspects of privacy developed, and the difficulties which flow from them. This will be illustrated, first, by reference to the development of privacy law in the United States, then by examining its substantial impact on international human rights law, and thirdly by sketching its far more limited effect on English law. The chapter will conclude with a brief reflection on the importance of privacy in legal analysis.

The three chapters which follow examine certain aspects of privacy law in England and Wales in more detail. Chapter 9 explains the legal protections against unreasonable entries, searches, and seizures. Chapter 10 looks at the special position of confidential information, in relation to both the civil and the criminal justice systems. Chapter 11 deals with sexuality and the family, which are particularly sensitive aspects of personality and autonomy protected by privacy interests.

8.1 WHAT IS PRIVACY?[1]

(1) Privacy, individualism, and community

The desire for a private area in life is deeply rooted, and derives its justification from two sources. The first is the notion of personal autonomy, which (as we saw in Chapter 1) is a powerful element in the ideology of freedom. Although not strictly necessary to freedom of choice, privacy, in the sense of a protected field of decision making within which the individual is free from the meddling of others, is valuable in helping to produce the conditions in which freedom of choice can be exercised without interference. This is linked to the desire for defensible space, a physical area marked off in some way from other areas, to which a person

---

[1] For the philosophical background, which is outside the scope of this book, see Alan F. Westin, *Privacy and Freedom* (London: Bodley Head, 1967), and the excellent essays in J. R. Pennock and J. W. Chapman (eds), *Privacy: Nomos XIII* (New York: Atherton Press, 1971).

may withdraw and wherein he may protect himself against all comers, unless entry is clearly justified by some supervening public interest. The second element is the idea of utility: it is arguable that people operate most effectively and happily when they are allowed to make their own arrangements about domestic and business matters without interference from the state. This utilitarian argument also justifies extending privacy rights beyond the home and family, as many business relationships depend on maintaining privacy in the forms of confidentiality and free-dom of contract. In short, then, some rights to privacy are aspects of per-sonal autonomy, a necessary condition for human flourishing.

Such privacy rights are broadly individualistic.[2] They protect a sphere of action and decision making for individuals against the power of the state, wielded in the public interest. Indeed, the notion of privacy arose, historically, before the emergence of the modern nation state, and so may constrain people's conception of the legitimate sphere of the state in social life.[3] Because they tend to restrict the activity of the state, privacy rights are politically controversial. Socialist, Marxist, and communitarian critics have characterized the public–private distinction as an ideology of classical liberalism, and have argued that the notion of the private sphere tends to place the individual outside society, minimizing the scope for the notion of social responsibility.[4] Claims to privacy can be used by to pre-vent the state from taking action to force people to take responsibility for others, or organizing society for the benefit of the weakest groups. More recently, feminist legal theorists have suggested that, by regarding the family as pre-eminently a part of the private rather than the public sphere of social life, the state is discouraged from interfering to change the power structures within the family which systematically disadvantage women. They also argue that similar considerations are relevant to rela-tions within the workplace, and in other social settings which are tradi-tionally regarded as governed by the private arrangements of participants rather than public interests.

On the other hand, it would overstate the case to assert that the notion of privacy allows individuals to displace the community interest. While historically prior to the public role of the state, privacy is neither histori-cally nor logically prior to the constitution of society. A private sphere makes sense only in contradistinction to a public sphere, and nothing in the idea of privacy itself dictates the extent of each sphere relative to the

[2] S. Lukes, *Individualism* (Oxford: Basil Blackwell, 1973).

[3] Morton J. Horwitz, 'The History of the Public/Private Distinction' 130 *Univ. of Pennsylvania LR* 1423–28 (1982).

[4] Eugene Kamenka, 'Public/Private in Marxist Theory and Marxist Practice', in Stanley I. Benn and Gerald Gaus (eds.), *Public and Private in Social Life* (London: Croom Helm and St. Martin's Press, 1983), 267 at 273–4.

other. That is a matter for social decision making according to political principles, and a willingness to join in argument about it forms an essential part of of the practical politics of liberalism.[5] The argument is reflected in economics in the context of debates about the proper extent (if any) of state ownership or state regulation in the management of an economy. In morality, it is reflected in debates about the extent to which people should be free to pursue their sexual preferences, considered in Chapter 11 below, or to control their bodies, a matter examined in the context of abortion and medical procedures in Chapters 3 and 4 above. In law, it shows up in debates within private law, for example on the scope of freedom of contract,[6] and in public law in disagreements over whether or not a separate and exclusive procedure is needed for public-law matters.

The public and private spheres necessarily interact. Understanding the separateness of individuals, to which the idea of privacy is central, is an important reason for choosing a method for making social decisions which gives weight to the preferences or interests of each person, whether on the basis of a democratic system giving equal weight to the vote of each adult citizen or through the mediation of some form of utilitarian calculation.[7]

Individual privacy and social action are, therefore, constantly interacting, and the tension between them is a dynamic one which each society in each period resolves by producing a balance, albeit one which is temporary and unstable. Three factors tend to limit the extent of the protected sphere of privacy. The first is the responsibility which the state adopts for the welfare of its citizens. This responsibility has both a public interest aspect and an individual rights aspect. Public service provision is an example of the public interest aspect. The people responsible for planning public services, such as health, housing, and education, require information, often personal and sensitive information, about everyone in the community, to enable them to forecast how many people will be needing their services over a period, and what kind of services are likely to be most in demand. This information has to be obtained by means which, to a greater or lesser extent, interfere with people's privacy: censuses, access to records held by other parts of the government machine, questionnaires, health records, and other means. The other side of the state's responsibilities is the role which it has in upholding individual rights, and protecting the welfare of those who are in too weak a position to look after their own interests. In the privacy field, child-care law

[5] Lukes, *Individualism*, 62.

[6] For a stimulating discussion, see Hugh Collins, 'The Decline of Privacy in Private Law' (1987) 14 *J. of Law and Soc.* 91–103.

[7] Westin, *Privacy and Freedom*, p. 33; Lukes, *Individualism*, ch. 9.

provides a good example of this: it may be necessary to interfere with a parent's privacy rights in order to protect the rights of children to be free from abuse.

The second factor is the need (if such is accepted) for regulation. Bodies such as Oftel (regulating the telecommunications industry), the Securities and Investments Board (with responsibility for the financial services industries), and the governing bodies of professions, such as the Law Society, need information in order to be able to regulate the members of their professions and protect the interests of consumers of services. Investigative and regulatory agencies, set up for the welfare of the public, need to obtain information about the people and business undertakings which are being investigated and regulated, and this can sometimes justify considerable inroads into the principle of privacy. Invoking the legal process, to remedy an injury or contest a claim, itself involves a loss of privacy.

Thirdly, the public interest in freedom of information may impose limits on the right to privacy. For example, people who wish to carry out construction work on their private land may well need consent for the development from their planning authority. For this, they will need to submit a proposal and plans which will be available for inspection by anyone interested enough to visit the local town hall to see what is being proposed. This entails a restriction of the right to privacy, which is justified by the public interest in making planning decisions on an informed basis in the light of consultation with concerned members of the community. Again, we will see in Chapter 10 below that the legal remedies available to restrain a breach of confidence will not be granted if the defendant can show that publication of the information would be in the public interest, for example by disclosing a possible miscarriage of justice. In these areas, the privacy interest falls to be balanced against the achievement of social objectives in the wider public interest.

This might seem to leave privacy rights in a relatively weak position. They are protected only so far as they are compatible with public interests. Indeed, to the extent that privacy rights are supported by a public interest, and are valued on utilitarian grounds, the private aspects of privacy are hard to distinguish from public interests which can be weighed against each other. The feature of privacy which makes some people willing to give it special status as a fundamental human right, capable of trumping other non-rights-based interests, rather than merely one among many competing public interests, is its close connection with the idea of autonomy.

(2) Positive and negative aspects of privacy rights

Autonomy-related rights have both a negative and a positive aspect, as described in Chapter 1. The negative aspect is the right to be let alone, identified by Dean Prosser as the core sense of privacy.[8] The positive aspects are more elusive and controversial. First, there is a duty on the state and other individuals to foster the conditions in which privacy can be enjoyed. There are, for example, limits to the extent to which a person can realistically expect to enjoy privacy if the only accommodation available to her is a box in a shop doorway on the streets of London or Bristol. Secondly, alongside a right to protect oneself against intrusion in one's private affairs, there may be a right to have access to information held about one, by government or private bodies, which is sensitive and may affect one's ability to give effect to an autonomous decision. For instance, my privacy interests may be infringed if my doctor decides not to reveal the nature of my medical condition, as this may prevent me from exercising my freedom of choice as regards career, treatment, or marriage, in a properly informed way. Where a choice is fully informed, a person's ability to give effect to it may be affected without their knowledge if somebody else makes available to potential employers, banks, or insurers, personal information which is misleading or wrong, without giving them an opportunity to correct the record. Thirdly, where there are circumstances in which it is justifiable to interfere with a person's privacy, the strength of the interest in privacy may demand the imposition of special procedures before an interference can take place in any individual case.

The way in which these aspects of privacy develop, and the difficulties which flow from them, can be illustrated by an examination, first, of the development of privacy law in the United States, and then by examining its substantial impact on international law.

8.2 THE DEVELOPMENT OF PRIVACY AS A LEGAL VALUE: UNITED STATES CASE-STUDY

The process by which privacy came to articulated as a central legal value in common law systems took its first great leap forward in the USA. In 1890, there appeared an article by Warren and Brandeis[9] which has a better claim than most to be described as 'seminal'. The authors pulled together a number of the common-law property protections and the

---

[8] Samuel D. Warren and Louis D. Brandeis, 'The Right to Privacy', 4 Harv. LR 193–220 (1890); Prosser, n. 10 below.

[9] Warren and Brandeis, 'The Right to Privacy', 4 Harv. LR 193–220 (1890).

equitable rules on confidentiality, and argued that underpinning them was a deeper unifying principle, namely the protection of privacy against modern technological and commercial developments.[10] After a slow start, the privacy principle, which, Warren and Brandeis argued, was immanent in the common law, came to exercise a powerful influence in the USA.

The early development was directed to protecting privacy interests against unauthorized commercial exploitation. After the New York Court of Appeals, by a majority, had rejected a claim by a woman whose picture had been used, without her consent, in a flour advertisement, a public outcry led to a New York statute which gave protection against having one's name or image appropriated without written consent for the purposes of advertising or trade.[11] Subsequently, courts outside New York recognized a tort of interference with privacy at common law. In fact, American tort lawyers regarded privacy as a group of four torts, protecting different sorts of interests: (i) intrusion on seclusion, solitude, or private affairs, the classical 'right to be left alone', particularly by the press, which had particularly exercised Warren and Brandeis and which violates interests in property, reputation and feelings; (ii) publication of embarrassing private facts about the plaintiff, violating reputation and feelings; (iii) publicity which places the plaintiff in a false light in the public eye, which is a form of injury to feelings, reputation, honour, and dignity, and may also cause economic loss, combining elements of defamation and injurious falsehood but going further than either; (iv) appropriating the plaintiff's name or likeness for the defendant's advantage, which covers the commercial exploitation cases in which the tort

[10] Warren and Brandeis relied heavily on *Prince Albert* v. *Strange* (1848) 2 De G. & Sm. 652, where Knight Bruce VC had granted an injunction restraining the defendant from publishing etchings made by Queen Victoria and the Prince Consort of their family life. The Vice-Chancellor regarded the proposed publication, without consent, as an invasion of the plaintiff's rights of property and his privacy and home life. For evaluation and criticism of the reasoning of Warren and Brandeis, on which there is a huge literature, see e.g. William L. Prosser, 'Privacy' (1960) 48 Calif. LR 383–423, a hugely influential article in its own right; Leon Brittan, 'The Right of Privacy in England and the United States' (1963) 37 *Tulane LR* 235–68, which examines the patchy response of English law to the challenge of privacy, and discusses Lord Mancroft's Right of Privacy Bill, introduced to the House of Lords in Mar. 1961 but later dropped in the face of government opposition; Edward J. Bloustein, 'Privacy as an Aspect of Human Dignity: An Answer to Dean Prosser' (1964) 39 *New York Univ. LR* 962–1007; Harry Kalven, 'Privacy in Tort Law: Were Warren and Brandeis Wrong?' (1966) 31 *Law and Contemp. Problems* 326; Walter F. Pratt, 'The Warren and Brandeis Argument for a Right to Privacy' [1975] *PL* 161–79; Raymond Wacks, *Personal Information: Privacy and the Law* (Oxford: Clarendon Press, 1989), 31–9.

[11] *Robertson* v. *Rochester Folding Box Co.*, 171 NY 538, 64 NE 442 (1902); New York Sess. Laws, 1903, c. 132, s. 1–2.

was first applied.[12] This four part categorization was adopted in the
Restatement of the Law of Torts, paragraph 867.

Subsequently privacy came to be regarded as a constitutional right.
The process by which this came about is somewhat complex. Privacy is
nowhere mentioned in the text of the US Constitution. Nevertheless,
the courts have been able to find an implied right of privacy. The Fourth
Amendment provides: 'The right of the people to be secure in their persons, houses, papers, and effects, against unreasonable searches and
seizures, shall not be violated . . .'. The First Amendment, preventing
Congress from making any law respecting an establishment of religion, or
prohibiting the free exercise thereof, or abridging the right of the people
peaceably to assemble, has been interpreted as protecting autonomy rights
(including, by implication, freedom of association) which are central to
individual autonomy aspects of privacy. Privacy has been treated as one of
the liberties protected by due process requirements, despite not being
enumerated in the Constitution. The Ninth Amendment provides: 'The
enumeration in the Constitution, of certain rights, shall not be construed
to deny or disparage others retained by the people.' These retained rights
are held to include privacy rights, which are then within Fifth and
Fourteenth Amendment due process guarantees. The Fifth Amendment
provides that no person shall 'be deprived of life, liberty, or property,
without due-process of law', and Section 1 of the Fourteenth Amendment extends the due-process protection so that it operates against the
States as well as the Federal authorities. Out of all this, judges have constructed a constitutional right to privacy. In *Griswold* v. *Connecticut*[13]
Douglas J., writing for the US Supreme Court, argued that the core cases
of privacy under the First, Third, Fourth, Fifth, and Ninth Amendments
were surrounded by 'penumbras' and 'emanations', fading gradually away
from the core cases, in which privacy rights could be shown to be consistent with the core values. The potential scope of the emanations of privacy are uncertain, and the reasoning is controversial. In particular,
judges and scholars who hold that judges should not create new rights by
embellishing the constitutional text disapprove of reasoning which leaves
judges free to give the due process clause in the Fourteenth Amendment
a controversial substantive content in line with their personal opinions;
while those who believe that the proper way of interpreting the
Constitution is to ask what its framers thought they meant by particular
provisions, rather than to develop its concepts in line with changing
social conditions, argue that the framers would not have recognized many
of the interests which fall within the modern reach of privacy. In

[12] This is based on Prosser, 'Privacy' 48 *Calif. LR* at p. 389.
[13] 381 US 479 (1965).

Griswold, therefore, Goldberg J., joined by Warren CJ and Brennan J., relied squarely on the Ninth Amendment, but this reasoning is little more helpful, as it is hard to identify with any certainty the content of the unenumerated, retained rights which it protects.[14]

Despite these doubts, the constitutional right to privacy has been remarkably durable, albeit of uncertain extent. Unlike the right to privacy in tort, the constitutional right is soundly based in the right to make decisions about the conduct of one's own life, within the sphere of personal autonomy. The right of parents to decide what their children should study and where they should be educated was vindicated in two early cases.[15] The Supreme Court called up echoes of the assertion in the Declaration of Independence of the rights to life, liberty, and the pursuit of happiness, arguing that the Constitution protected the rights

to contract, to engage in any of the common occupations of life, to acquire useful knowledge, to marry, to establish a home and bring up children, to worship God according to the dictates of his own conscience, and generally to enjoy those privileges long recognized at common law as essential to the orderly pursuit of happiness to free men.[16]

The interest at the root of the constitutional protection for privacy, therefore, is personal autonomy. In the constitutional sphere, the issue is the extent to which the individual should be protected against interference from public authorities, and the core meaning of privacy is 'the right to be let alone—the most comprehensive of rights and the right most valued by civilized men.'[17] The focus is different from, and in some ways narrower than, that of the private right which developed in tort, yet it has proved to be remarkably extensive in its own sphere.

Privacy rights have been held to underlie the Fourth Amendment,[18] so that one of the tests for an unreasonable search and seizure is whether the public authority has violated the victim's legitimate interest in privacy. This has been used to justify more restricted Fourth Amendment rights in

---

[14] For discussion of such reasoning, see extracts from 'Nomination of Robert H. Bork to be Associate Justice of the Supreme Court of the United States', hearings before the Senate Committee of the Judiciary, 100th Cong., 1st sess. 114–21, 149–51, 240–42 (1st of 5 parts), 1987, as reproduced in Louis Fisher, *American Constitutional Law* (New York: McGraw-Hill, 1990), 1226–32.

[15] *Meyer* v. *Nebraska*, 262 US 390 (1923); *Pierce* v. *Society of Sisters*, 268 US 510 (1925).

[16] *Meyer* v. *Nebraska*, 262 US at p. 399.

[17] *Olmstead* v. *US*, 277 US 438 at p. 478, *per* Brandeis J., one of the authors of the seminal article, and by this time a Justice of the Supreme Court. In this case, he was dissenting from a majority decision that telephone tapping did not violate the Fourth Amendment to the Constitution, because the tap involved no trespass. *Olmstead* was later overruled in *Katz* v. *US*, 389 US 347 (1967).

[18] *Boyd* v. *US*, 116 US 616 (1886) at p. 630; *Mapp* v. *Ohio*, 367 US 643 (1961) at p. 656.

respect of automobiles and mobile homes than in respect of homes and offices.[19] Privacy in one's associations with others was the basis for holding that the First Amendment right of peaceable assembly has a penumbra which extends constitutional protection to the freedom of political, social, and economic association more generally. This freedom was unconstitutionally interfered with when the state attempted to compel organizations to disclose their membership lists.[20] The right to privacy, this time in respect of marital relationships, justified holding unconstitutional a state statute which made it an offence for a married couple to employ contraceptives.[21]

Most famously, and most controversially, in *Roe* v. *Wade*[22] the right to privacy was recognized as creating a realm of protection for the autonomy of women in respect of their bodies. This restricted the grounds on which the state was entitled to intervene in the progress or termination of pregnancy. Yet if *Roe* v. *Wade* and its progeny made a powerful demonstration of the power of privacy, they also illustrated its limitations. The majority in the Supreme Court accepted that the woman's privacy rights were not absolute. They had to be set against the state's legitimate interest in preserving the life and health of both the woman and the child. To that end, the state might legitimately legislate to regulate abortions, but the interests served would change as the pregnancy progressed. Regulation to protect the interests of the unborn child was legitimate from the time of viability, i.e. the moment when the child became capable of an existence independent of the mother, around the beginning of the third trimester of pregnancy. Before that, the state may intervene only to protect the life and health of the mother. Statistical evidence suggested that the risks to the mother of termination in the first trimester were no greater than the risks of childbirth, so the decision on abortion there was to be left to the mother and her medical advisers. In the intervening period (i.e. roughly in the second trimester) the state could regulate abortions only to minimize the risk to the mother, in effect acting paternalistically to avoid her privacy rights being exercised in a way which unnecessarily endangered her.

But this was not uncontroversial. From the standpoint of legal theory, the dissenters in *Roe* v. *Wade* noted that the Fourteenth Amendment protected privacy rights not absolutely, but only against infringement without due process of law. This implies a rationality test for constitutionality:

---

[19] *California* v. *Carney*, 471 US 386 (1985); *New York* v. *Class*, 475 US 106 (1986). This has replaced an earlier rationale for allowing warrantless searches of automobiles, based on the risk that they might be driven away and be out of the state before a warrant could be obtained: *Carroll* v. *US*, 267 US 132 (1925).

[20] *NAACP* v. *Alabama*, 357 US 449 (1958); *NAACP* v. *Button*, 371 US 415 (1963).

[21] *Griswold* v. *Connecticut*, 381 US 479 (1965).   [22] 410 US 113 (1973).

does the impugned law have a rational relationship to a legitimate state objective? They argued that allowing a legislature to weigh the respective interests of women and unborn children was within such a relationship. It was, they argued, improper for the Court, under the colour of the due-process clause, to impose its own weighting of the competing priorities on the people and legislatures of the states without any clear constitutional foundation.

These arguments are gaining ground. The signs are that the scope of privacy rights has been steadily reduced over the last ten years, as the Supreme Court has become more conservative. The Court has held that the positive obligations on the state, arising out of the privacy-based abortion rights of the mother, are restricted. In particular, the Supreme Court has held that states are under no obligation to make public funds or services available to people for non-therapeutic abortions. It has also held that the trimester-by-trimester growth in the state's legitimate interest in protecting first the mother, and later the fetus, is overrigid. States have an interest in life at all stages of pregnancy, and are in principle entitled to make a value judgement that favours childbirth over abortion, so long as they do not interfere with the mother's liberty without due process of law.[23] The majority of the Court in *Webster* v. *Reproductive Health Services* refused to review *Roe* v. *Wade*, but relegated the mother's right from a fundamental constitutional right to an abortion (at least in the first trimester) to a liberty protected by due-process requirements. Accordingly, they did not find it necessary to provide any criteria for determining the extent of this state interest at different times, so it is up to the states to provide legislative frameworks which take adequate account of the various interests involved.

It was widely expected that conservative forces would triumph and the decision in *Roe* v. *Wade* would be overruled when the Supreme Court was forced to address the central issue of the woman's constitutional right to an abortion. The moment of truth came in *Planned Parenthood of South-Eastern Pennsylvania and others* v. *Casey and others*.[24] The Court had to rule on the constitutionality of the Pennsylvania Abortion Control Act of 1982. The petitioners challenged requirements that the woman should give informed consent, and be provided with information at least 24 hours before the procedure, that she should give notice to her husband if she is married, and if a minor should normally have parental consent. There were exceptions for medical emergencies. In a decision with which few people on either side were entirely happy, the central holding in *Roe* survived, but not unscathed. Remarkably, three Republican

[23] *Webster* v. *Reproductive Health Services*, 109 S. Ct. 3040 (1989).
[24] 112 S.Ct. 2791, 120 L.Ed. 2d 674 (1992).

appointees, O'Connor, Kennedy, and Souter JJ, decided that they could not reconcile the overruling of *Roe* with their respect for the doctrine of precedent. They decided that the constitutional guarantee of liberty defined in *Roe* had not proved unworkable, and that neither social facts, legal principles, nor scientific knowledge had altered since 1973 in ways which compelled them to reverse the earlier decision. The undue burden test, as developed by Justice O'Connor in *Webster*, was to provide the criterion of due process against which restrictions on pre-viability terminations would be judged.

The three central judges were supported by Stevens J., in holding that the only requirement of the Pennsylvania statute which constituted an undue burden was the requirement of spousal notice, and by Stevens and Blackmun JJ in refusing to overrule *Roe* v. *Wade*. However, Justice Blackmun, while praising the three for 'an act of personal courage and constitutional principle', criticized them for qualifying the right of women to decide on an abortion without state interference by permitting burdens on the exercise of the right as long as they are not undue burdens. He clearly feared that this left the door open to further restrictions on privacy rights by the court. Rehnquist CJ, and White, Scalia, and Thomas JJ, dissented, arguing that neither the right to an abortion nor the undue burden test had any foundation in the language of the Constitution. In any case, they argued, the right to an abortion could not be described as fundamental, since its regulation had long been acceptable to society. State legislation restricting abortion should be regarded as unconstitutional only if not rationally related to a legitimate state objective.

This represents a draw in the fight over abortion rights. Although the provisions of the Pennsylvania statute were upheld, save that requiring that notice be given to the husband, it will in future be very difficult for the Court to depart from the view that there is a constitutional right to privacy which protects against undue interference a woman's decision to terminate her pregnancy. Nevertheless, for the moment it seems that constitutional privacy protection, if not actually on the retreat, is unlikely to be extended dynamically into new fields, and its basis and implications remain highly controversial.

This concern about the derivation and scope of constitutional privacy rights has grown into a major political, as well as legal, dispute in the United States since 1973. A gradual restriction of the privacy right, and extension of the powers of legislatures, in recent Supreme Court decisions has moved alongside changes in support for political factions. During the 1980s, American conservatives gained the ascendancy over liberals; pro-life groups made headway at the expense of pro-choice groups; evangelical religious fundamentalism advanced against 1960s humanism; and judicial activism retreated in the face of the changes. One aspect of the growth of religious and constitutional fundamentalism—both characterized by a largely uncritical commitment to a sacred text—was that the focus of constitutional inquiries changed. Instead of asking questions about the legitimate range of underlying rights, such as privacy, in a constitution committed to individual freedom, the new conservative judges asked questions about surface rights, such as whether the Constitution entrenches a fundamental right to carry on the particular activity under consideration. Any right which is not apparent in the Constitution became, at best, a liberty to be protected only by the partial shield of due process.

This change of emphasis can be observed in *Bowers* v. *Hardwick*.[25] Hardwick, a practising homosexual adult, challenged the constitutionality of a Georgia statute under which he had been charged with sodomy with another adult male in the bedroom of his house. The majority of the Supreme Court held that the statute did not infringe his constitutional rights. They declined to extend the right to privacy so as to give constitutional due-process protection to a right to commit sodomy. Freedom to commit sodomy was not of the same character as other freedoms traditionally protected by the constitutional right to privacy (marriage, contraception, abortion, procreation, family relationships, child-rearing, and education). Nor was it within the range of those fundamental liberties which had been implied into the Constitution because they were deeply rooted in the nation's history and traditions, or necessary for ordered liberty and justice.[26] The liberty fell within the protection of the rationality requirement, under the due-process clause, but the rationality test was satisfied, as there is nothing irrational about making laws which are based on moral judgments. The Court would be slow to give too substantial a content to the due-process clause, in the absence of clear constitutional justification.

In other words, the majority saw the case as raising the spectre of a fundamental right to engage in homosexual activity, and retreated from it, taking refuge behind the legislative authority of the state and its people. Dissenting, Blackmun J., joined by Brennan, Marshall, and Stevens, JJ., argued that the case was in reality about a deeper issue, the right to be let alone. The level of generality at which an issue is conceptualized fundamentally affects the nature and scope of the resulting right, particularly where the rights in question are not expressly stated in the Constitution.

It remains to be seen whether the inauguration of President Clinton in

---

[25] 478 US 186 (1986).
[26] See *Moore* v. *East Cleveland*, 431 US 494 (1977) at p. 503 (Powell J.).

January 1993 heralds a resurgence of liberalism. The new President is unlikely to appoint committed conservatives to the Supreme Court when the next vacancy arises, but his views on abortion and the rights of homosexuals as revealed during his election campaign are not unequivocally liberal. It would be unsafe to regard his election as a harbinger of a resurgence of 1960s-style constitutional interpretation. In US constitutional law, the scope and derivation of the right to privacy remain a fragile product of controversial judicial glosses on the constitutional text.

This introduction to privacy theory, and its emanation in US constitutional law, suggests three questions with which the remainder of this chapter, and Chapters 9 to 11 below, are concerned. First, how is the right to privacy to be formulated, and what is its scope in international human rights law and in English law? Secondly, what is the scope of protection for the negative aspects of rights? Thirdly, what is the scope of the positive rights implied by a right to privacy?

8.3 PRIVACY IN INTERNATIONAL LAW

(1) The formulation of the right: positive and negative obligations

Most international human rights instruments today recognize a right to privacy in one form or another. There is, however, an interesting contrast between the formulation of this right under the various instruments to which the UK is a party. The International Covenant on Civil and Political Rights (ICCPR) provides in Article 17:

(1) No one shall be subjected to arbitrary or unlawful interference with his privacy, family, home or correspondence, nor to unlawful attacks on his honour and reputation.
(2) Everyone has the right to the protection of the law against such interference or attacks.

This is identical to Article 12 of the Universal Declaration of Human Rights, save that the latter does not divide the article into two paragraphs. Children are given rights in similar terms under the UN Convention on the Rights of the Child, which the UK ratified in 1991.

Several points about the formulation merit attention. It starts with a negative right to freedom from *arbitrary or unlawful* interference with the interests enumerated. The right to be free of interference with privacy, family, home, and correspondence is not absolute. It can be justified if not arbitrary or unlawful. This limited negative right is coupled with a positive right: the state must ensure that that the law protects people against arbitrary and unlawful interference with those interests. The interests themselves are not defined, and privacy in particular is a difficult interest to delimit, particularly as a non-arbitrary interference is justifiable. Does a right to privacy encompass a right to perform in private acts which outrage prevailing ideas of decency? Would criminalizing such acts in order to reinforce popular views on morality or decency be regarded as arbitrary, or would it be justifiable? There is no answer to these questions within the ICCPR. It is clear, however, from the inclusion of the right to be free of unlawful attacks on honour and reputation in Article 17 of ICCPR that the Article is intended to protect human dignity, and that this is the foundation for the rights under the Article rather than serving democracy or any of the other basic values which have been postulated as grounding privacy rights. This limits the scope and value of the rights guaranteed: dignity and self-respect are psychologically important to the enjoyment of autonomy, but relate more to the maintenance of status and one's public and private personality than to the ability to do anything or to influence events which affect one.

The position under the European Convention on Human Rights (ECHR) is somewhat different. Article 8 provides:

(1) Everyone has the right to respect for his private and family life, his home and his correspondence.

(2) There shall be no interference by a public authority with the exercise of this right except such as is in accordance with the law and is necessary in a democratic society in the interests of national security, public safety or the economic well-being of the country, for the prevention of disorder or crime, for the protection of health or morals, or for the protection of the rights and freedoms of others.

The rights conferred by this provision are both more extensive and more clearly drawn than those under Article 17 of ICCPR. The formulation of Article 8(1) does not speak of privacy, but of private and family life, although this difference may be insubstantial. More significantly, it does not link the rights which it confers to honour or reputation. Article 8 is about doing and living, not about maintaining dignity for its own sake. The rights conferred by Article 8(1) are absolute, subject only to the tightly drawn exceptions authorized by Article 8(2) which specify the grounds on which public authorities may justify interference in pursuance of a defined set of public-interest objectives.

Most important of all, the ECHR is unique among international human rights instruments in the way in which rights are conceived in relation to private life. Instead of giving a right to be free of arbitrary or unlawful interference[27] with privacy, Article 8 provides for a right to

---

[27] Thus the Universal Declaration, Art. 12, the ICCPR, Art. 17, and the U.N. Convention on the Rights of the Child, Art. 16. The American Convention on Human Rights, Art. 11(2), forbids 'arbitrary or abusive interference' with anyone's 'private life, his

respect for everyone's private and family life, home, and correspondence. This movement from a right to freedom from interference with privacy to a right to respect for it might seem to weaken the right, as there may be circumstances in which it could be argued that interfering with a person's privacy would not indicate any lack of respect. Examples would be interfering with privacy paternalistically, to protect the individual against further loss of autonomy resulting from untreated illness, deficient family management, or poor child-rearing practices. Sir James Fawcett, speaking of the *travaux préparatoires*, noted that:

> What began in the Teitgen proposals as 'inviolability', and became 'immunity from arbitrary interference', then protection from governmental interference (*immixtions gouvernementales*), ended tamely as 'respect'. These changes may in part reflect various opinions, expressed in the Consultative Assembly but overruled, that 'in these cases [under Article 8] no rights regarded as essential for the function of the democratic institutions were at stake'.[28]

This potential limitation on the negative (freedom from interference) aspects of the right to privacy should not blind us to the considerable extension of the right which the notion of respect may entail, and which has been influential in the caselaw of the Court on Article 8. A right to respect is capable of imposing positive duties on public authorities, because it can be interpreted as requiring them to take active measures to enable people to have a private and family life, going beyond providing remedies for interference.

In a number of recent cases, the European Court of Human Rights has regularly affirmed that positive obligations on the state arise from Article 8. These include framing the law in such a way that people are not inhibited in choosing a mode of private life; ensuring that appropriate de facto, as well as de iure, family relationships are possible and protected; making available suitable remedies for people whose private or family life is interfered with; and allowing people access to information about their early lives and about decisions taken concerning them. The nature of these positive obligations has been worked out from case to case in a way

---

family, his home, or his correspondence . . .'. The American Declaration of the Rights and Duties of Man confers on every person the rights (*inter alia*) to protection of the law against abusive attacks upon his private and family life (Art. V), to the inviolability of his home (Art. IX), and to the inviolability and transmission of his correspondence (Art. X). The African Charter on Human and Peoples' Rights does not confer a right to private or family life, although Art. 29 imposes duties on every individual to 'preserve the harmonious development of the family and to work for the cohesion and respect of the family; to respect his parents at all times, to maintain them in case of need'.

[28] J. E. S. Fawcett, *The Application of the European Convention on Human Rights*, 2nd edn. (Oxford: Clarendon Press, 1987), 211 (footnotes omitted). The significance of a protected sphere of privacy for democracy was mentioned in s. 8.1 above.

which is sensitive to the contexts in which cases arise and which many common lawyers will find attractive. The guiding principle was first expounded in *Marckx* v. *Belgium*,[29] concerning the treatment of children born out of wedlock under Belgian law, where the Court stated that Article 8 does not merely compel the state to abstain from arbitrary interference with family life:

. . . in addition to this primarily negative undertaking, there may be positive obligations inherent in an effective 'respect' for family life. This means amongst other things, that when the State determines in its domestic legal system the régime applicable to certain family ties such as those between an unmarried mother and her child, it must act in a manner calculated to allow those concerned to lead a normal family life. As envisaged by Article 8, respect for family life implies in particular, in the Court's view, the existence in domestic law of legal safeguards that render possible as from the moment of birth the child's integration into his family.

The Court there unanimously accepted that Article 8 imposed positive as well as negative obligations, although some judges dissented as to the nature and scope of those obligations in the context of the legal regime affecting family relationships and their concomitant rights, powers, obligations, and responsibilities. In subsequent cases, the positive obligations have been developed in the context of child care decisions which affect the family. In a series of cases concerning the procedures for removing children from their parents under the English law which existed before the Children Act 1989 came into force, the Court held that the state has a positive obligation to ensure that parents are involved in the process of decision making at least to the extent necessary to provide the requisite protection for their interests under Article 8(1). English law failed to provide for such involvement.[30] This was one of the factors which led to the enactment of a revised set of child-care procedures in the 1989 Act, discussed in Chapter 11 below.

There may also be an obligation on the state to provide legal protection for people by imposing criminal liability on those who gravely interfere with their private lives. In *X and Y* v. *Netherlands*[31] the Court held that the Netherlands had failed to respect the private life of a mentally handicapped teenager who had been forced to have sexual intercourse by the son–in–law of the governor of the home in which she was a resident. The man's behaviour did not constitute rape under Dutch law, and the offence of abusing a dominant position so as to cause a minor to commit an indecent act could be prosecuted only on a complaint laid by the vic-

[29] Eur. Ct. HR, Series A, No. 31, Judgment of 13 June 1979; 2 EHRR 330, at para. 31.
[30] *W.* v. *UK* Eur. Ct. HR, Series A, No. 121, Judgment of 8 July 1987; 10 EHRR 29.
[31] Eur. Ct. HR, Series A, No. 91, Judgment of 26 Mar. 1985, 8 EHRR 235.

tim. Because of her mental condition, the girl was not competent to lay a complaint. This lacuna in the criminal law was held to be a failure to respect the girl's private life, because in such situations only the criminal law could provide deterrent effect adequate to protect her.

Finally, the right to respect for private and family life has been held to impose an obligation in some circumstances to make available to a person information about himself, relating to his private affairs, held by a public authority.[32] It has also been held to breach Article 8(1) for a telephone undertaker to release to a public authority information about numbers dialled by a subscriber, without the subscriber's knowledge or consent.[33]

The idea that rights under the Convention may carry with them positive obligations on the state beyond anything expressly stated in the text of the Convention has also been applied to other Articles of ECHR, where the obligations are necessarily incidental to the rights in question and are required in order to permit effective access to procedures for giving effect to the right. For example, the right to have civil rights and obligations determined by an independent and impartial tribunal after a fair and public hearing, under Article 6, has been held to impose on the State an obligation to make available effective access to a court or tribunal, and provide legal aid to the person who alleges an infringement of civil rights. In *Golder* v. *United Kingdom*,[34] the Court held by a majority that Article 6(1) implied a right of access to a tribunal, and that interfering with correspondence between a prisoner and his solicitor in connection with contemplated legal proceedings breached that right. In *Airey* v. *Ireland*,[35] a majority of the Court held that the right to have access to a hearing when applying for a judicial separation could be made effective only if appropriate legal assistance was provided by the state, and that refusal of legal aid therefore breached a positive obligation arising out of Article 6(1).

(2) The scope of the protected interests under Article 8 ECHR

What, then, are the interests protected, expressly or by implication, under Article 8(1)? In his dissenting opinion in *Marckx* v. *Belgium*[36] Judge Sir

---

[32] *Gaskin* v. *UK* Eur. Ct. HR, Series A, No. 160, Judgment of 7 July 1989, 12 EHRR 36. This does not apply where the material is held for the purposes of national security, e.g. for vetting the person for a sensitive post, provided that there are adequate means (such as review by an independent ombudsman and a board) by which the decision not to release the information can be reviewed: *Leander* v. *Sweden* Eur. Ct. HR, Series A, No. 116, Judgment of 26 March 1987, 9 EHRR 443.

[33] *Malone* v. *UK* Eur. Ct. HR, Series A, No. 82, Judgment of 2 Aug. 1984, 7 EHRR 14.

[34] Eur. Ct. HR, Series A, No. 18, Judgment of 21 Apr. 1975.

[35] Eur. Ct. HR, Series A, No. 32, Judgment of 9 Oct. 1979; 2 EHRR 305.

[36] Eur. Ct. HR, Series A, No. 31, Judgment of 13 June 1979; 2 EHRR 330.

Gerald Fitzmaurice identified the core evil at which the Article was aimed as being subjection to 'the whole gamut of fascist and communist inquisitorial practices such as had scarcely been known, at least in Western Europe, since the eras of religious intolerance and oppression, until (ideology replacing religion) they became prevalent again in many countries between the two world wars and subsequently'. But Sir James Fawcett pointed out that, although Article 8(1) was 'designed, primarily at least, to protect the physical framework of personal life: the family from separation, the home from intrusion, and correspondence from being searched or stopped . . . it goes to inner life as well'.[37]

Accordingly 'private and family life'[38] has been interpreted widely. Unwritten communications, not falling within the category of 'correspondence', are part of private life (unless, presumably, they are intended to be made public). Wire-tapping and the use of electronic devices to intercept verbal or radio communications have been held to interfere with respect for private life, and this places the onus on the state to justify them under Article 8(2).[39]

Respect is demanded for de facto family relationships, where unmarried people and their children are living together, and for rights of access between parents and children after divorce and separation.[40] The Article engenders a positive obligation on the state to provide people who, as children, were taken into care of the local authority, with access to information about their childhood sufficient to enable them to know and to understand their childhood and early development.[41] It also covers sexual life, so that a prohibition on sexual acts in private between consenting partners is an interference with Article 8(1) rights.[42] A disposition to homosexual activity is regarded as an aspect of human personality, and like other manifestations of personality traits in private is entitled to

[37] Fawcett, *Application*, 211.

[38] 'These words are doubtless to be read disjunctively, but they are closely linked.' Fawcett, *Application*, 211.

[39] *Klass* v. *Federal Republic of Germany* Eur. Ct. HR, Series A, No. 23, Judgment of 6 Sept. 1974, 2 EHRR 214; *Malone* v. *UK* Eur. Ct. HR, Series A, No. 82, Judgment of 2 Aug. 1984, 7 EHRR 14; *Huvig* v. *France* Eur. Ct. HR, Series A, No. 176B, Judgment of 24 Apr. 1990, 12 EHRR 528; *Kruslin* v. *France* Eur. Ct. HR, Series A, No. 176A, Judgment of 24 Apr. 1990, 12 EHRR 547.

[40] *Marckx* v. *Belgium* Eur. Ct. HR, Series A, No. 31, Judgment of 13 June 1979, 2 EHRR 330; *Johnston* v. *Ireland* Eur. Ct. HR, Series A, No. 112, Judgment of 18 Dec. 1986, 9 EHRR 203; *Berrehab* v. *Netherlands* Eur. Ct. HR, Series A, No. 138, Judgment of 21 June 1988, 11 EHRR 322.

[41] *Gaskin* v. *UK* Eur. Ct. HR, Series A, No. 160, Judgment of 7 July 1989; 12 EHRR 36.

[42] *Dudgeon* v. *UK* Eur. Ct. HR, Series A, No. 45, Judgment of 22 Oct. 1981; 4 EHRR 149; *Norris* v. *Ireland* Eur. Ct. HR, Series A, No. 142, Judgment of 26 Oct. 1988, 13 EHRR 186.

respect. On the other hand, allocation of gender to a person is seen as essentially a matter for the state, so that transsexuals do not have a right under Article 8 to be reallocated a new status following so-called 'sex change therapy', or to be permitted to marry on the basis of their new gender.[43]

The Article also demands safeguards on breaking up the family. As noted above, a child–care framework which permits a public authority to take children into care without involving the parents in the decision making process will breach the right to respect for family life under Article 8(1). Furthermore, once the children are in care, respect for family life demands that contact between siblings, and between parents and children, be maintained as far as is consistent with the reasons for taking the children into care. Separating the children, placing them far away from the parents' home, and restricting parental visits, may run counter to the object of care, which is normally to achieve to achieve reunification of the family. Where there is no adequate reason to justify these steps, it is liable to make the manner of pursuing the aim disproportionate, and so take it outside the justifications for interfering with family life under Article 8(2), as was held to have occurred in *Olsson* v. *Sweden*.[44]

Breaking up a family by expelling one member in conformity with immigration law may represent a failure of respect for family life.[45] A law which demanded the breaking up of a family for educational purposes, for example by providing that all children were to be educated at boarding schools, would also breach Article 8(1), as would placing a child of the family in a foster home with an indefinite restriction on removal and access.[46] However, if parents want their children to be educated in a particular language, and that is not available in local schools, Article 8(1) does not impose a duty on the state to provide education in that language locally. If the parents send their children away to school to be educated in that way, it is their choice, and the state has not failed to respect private or family life.[47]

[43] *Rees* v. *UK* Eur. Ct. HR, Series A, No. 106, Judgment of 17 Oct. 1987, 9 EHRR 56; *Cossey* v. *UK* Eur. Ct. HR, Series A, No. 184, Judgment of 27 Sept. 1990.

[44] Eur. Ct. HR, Series A, No. 130, Judgment of 24 Mar. 1988, 11 EHRR 259.

[45] See Fawcett, *Application*, 223–26; *Abdulaziz, Cabales and Balkandali* v. *UK*, Eur. Ct. HR, Series A, No. 94, Judgment of 28 May 1985, 7 EHRR 471. See also *Berrehab* v. *Netherlands* Eur. Ct. HR, Series A, No. 138, Judgment of 21 June 1988, 11 EHRR 322 (disproportionate to deport father after divorce from mother: not justifiable under Art. 8(2)); and *Moustaquim* v. *Belgium* Eur. Ct. HR, Series A, No. 193, Judgment of 18 Feb. 1991, 13 EHRR 802.

[46] *Eriksson* v. *Sweden* Eur. Ct. HR, Series A, No. 156, Judgment of 22 June 1989, 12 EHRR 183.

[47] *Belgian Linguistic Cases* Eur. Ct. HR, Series A, No. 6, Judgment of 24 June 1968; 1 EHRR 252.

On the other hand, while respect for private life is linked to the value of personal autonomy, not all personal decisions which an autonomous individual may feel moved to make fall within the scope of the protection for private life. In marked contrast to the position in the USA since 1973, the Commission has rejected claims that respect for private life requires the state to refrain from constraining or regulating the pregnant woman's discretion to seek and obtain a termination of pregnancy. The Commission argued that termination of pregnancy cannot be regarded as solely a matter of the mother's private life,[48] but it is not clear whether the decisive element in the equation was the rights or interests of the child or the responsibility of the State to exercise control over the taking of life.[49] As Article 8 is about an individual's relationships with other members of human society, the Commission has held that the State may also intervene without infringing Article 8(1) in choices which do not affect such relationships. These choices include the freedom to refuse to wear seatbelts in cars,[50] and freedom to keep a dog.[51] Implementing a voluntary vaccination system, with proper medical safeguards, does not infringe Article 8(1), even if the state fails to provide people with detailed information about the risks involved and contra-indications to vaccination.[52] A compulsory vaccination, or other compulsory medical procedure such as a blood test to establish paternity,[53] will be an interference with respect for private life, but may be justifiable under Article 8(2) as a measure in the interests of the protection of health or the protection of the rights and freedoms of others.

Respect for the individual's 'home'—besides ensuring that '[h]e and his family were no longer to be subjected to the four o'clock in the morning rat-a-tat on the door; to domestic intrusions, searches and questionings'[54] —extends to ensuring that a scheme requiring that people who want to live in a particular area, but lack residence qualifications, obtain licences to do so is administered with proper attention to the particular circumstances of an individual's situation. In particular, it breached Article 8 when the Guernsey Housing Authority refused a licence to a couple who had built a residence for themselves and their family at a time when they possessed residence qualifications but who had since lost them by absence. During their absence, the couple had let the property to people

---

[48] *Brüggemann and Scheuten* v. *Federal Republic of Germany* Application No. 6959/75; Report: 10 DR 100, at para. 61.
[49] See Ch. 3, above.   [50] *X* v. *Belgium* Application No. 8707/79, 18 DR 255.
[51] *X* v. *Iceland* Application No. 6825/74, 5 DR 86, Eur. Comm. HR.
[52] *Association X* v. *UK* Application No. 7154/75, 14 DR 31.
[53] *X* v. *Austria* Application No. 8278/78, 18 DR 154.
[54] Sir Gerald Fitzmaurice, dissenting, in *Marckx* v. *Belgium* Eur. Ct. HR, Series A, No. 31.

approved by the Housing Authority, contributing to the housing stock in the island. On their return, they had no other home in the UK or elsewhere. The property was vacant. The licensing scheme was an interference with Article 8(1), and, while in principle justifiable under Article 8(2), its application on the facts of the case was disproportionate.[55]

'Correspondence' refers to written communication. Interference with it is a breach of Article 8(1). In a number of cases it has been held that the UK Prison Rules, allowing for inspection or interception of prisoners' correspondence, breached Article 8, and these led to amendments to the rules.[56] Other communications are protected under the heading of 'private life', as noted above.

(3) Grounds on which interferences may be justified under Article 8(2) ECHR

In order to justify an interference with the right to respect for private and family life, home, and correspondence, the state must show that the interference, of which the applicant is a victim, complies with the criteria laid down in Article 8(2). This paragraph lays down three separate tests which must be satisfied. These can be loosely described as the tests according to rule-of-law criteria, purpose, and necessity/proportionality.

(i) *Rule-of-law criteria*. Any interference must be 'in accordance with the law'. This term, on the face of it, appears to require only that the interference be compatible with domestic law.[57] However, this would make it difficult for any pan-European standards to be applied to the legislation and procedures of States in Convention litigation. Accordingly the Court has given, through its caselaw, a more extensive content to the term. Both here and in Article 10, it is represented in the French text by the term 'prévue par la loi', suggesting that the public authority's interference must be grounded in some positive provision of the domestic law, rather than merely being not inconsistent with any such provision. The Court has treated the requirement similarly, applying to Article 8(2) the interpretation developed for the purposes of Article 10(2), in the context of the law of contempt of court, in the *Sunday Times case*.[58] In each place, it has treated 'in accordance with law' as importing general principles based

---

[55] *Gillow* v. *UK* Eur. Ct. HR, Series A, No. 109, Judgment of 24 Nov. 1984; 11 EHRR 335. See also *Wiggins* v. *UK* Application No. 7456/76, Report: 13 DR 40, Eur. Comm. HR

[56] See Ch. 6, above.

[57] cp. *De Wilde, Ooms and Versyp* v. *Belgium (No. 1)* Eur. Ct. HR, Series A, No. 12, Judgment of 18 June 1971; 1 EHRR 373, at p. 412, para. 93.

[58] Eur. Ct. HR, Series A, No. 30, Judgment of 26 Apr. 1979, 2 EHRR 245. See further Ch. 16, below.

on the ideal of the rule of law, providing a critical standard, external to the vagaries of any particular domestic legal system, by which to evaluate the provisions of the legal systems of all the parties to the Convention. As the Court held in *Malone* v. *United Kingdom*:[59] 'the phrase "in accordance with the law" does not merely refer back to domestic law but also relates to the quality of the law, requiring it to be compatible with the rule of law, which is expressly mentioned in the preamble to the Convention'.

There are two rule of law principles which have been developed in the caselaw of the Court. First, the law must be accessible enough for the citizen to be able to have an adequate indication of the legal rules which will be applicable to any case. This means that the interference must be governed by law, not by administrative practice. Secondly, the law must be formulated with sufficient precision to enable a person to regulate his conduct, foreseeing the consequences of his actions.

These two tests are not absolute, for a number of reasons. It may be permissible to have regard to administrative rules, even if they lack legal status, when deciding whether the way in which the law would be applied is sufficiently clear to enable people to anticipate their rights and liabilities. All laws are to some extent uncertain, and their interpretation and application will often rely on developing practices in connection with them. For this reason, in *Silver's case*[60] the Court accepted that the published Standing Orders issued by the Prison Department of the Home Office in relation to monitoring and intercepting prisoners' correspondence could be taken into account in deciding whether the application of the law to particular prisoners' situations was sufficiently certain. By contrast, it would not be permissible to have regard to unpublished guidelines to officers, such as the Prison Department's Circular Instructions, as these would not assist the person subject to interference to anticipate the way in which the application of the law would affect him. In the same way, in *Malone's case* in 1984 it was not clear that statements of executive practice on interception of communications, contained in a report in 1957 by Birkett L.J.,[61] a discussion paper and a White Paper on interception of communications,[62] and various statements in Parliament by Home Office ministers, were either a full or an up-to-date account of the rele-

---

[59] Eur. Ct. HR, Series A, No. 82, Judgment of 2 Aug. 1984, 7 EHRR 14, at para. 67. See also, in the context of interception of prisoners' letters, *Silver* v. *UK* Eur. Ct. HR, Series A, No. 61, Judgment of 25 Mar. 1983, 5 EHRR 347.

[60] Eur. Ct. HR, Series A, No. 61, Judgment of 25 Mar. 1983, 5 EHRR 347.

[61] *Report of the Committee of Privy Councillors Appointed to Inquire into the Interception of Communications* (Chairman: Birkett L.J.) Cmnd. 283 (London: HMSO, 1957).

[62] Home Office, *The Interception of Communications in Great Britain*, Cmnd. 7873 (London: HMSO, 1980); id., *The Interception of Communications in Great Britain*, Cmnd 9438 (London: HMSO, 1985).

vant practices. They were therefore insufficient to satisfy the second limb of the 'according to law' test.

In relation to laws regulating citizens' behaviour, there should be no justification for failing to make clear the circumstances in which rights or liabilities are to arise. There are special problems, however, in relation to laws conferring discretionary powers on public authorities, especially when the powers relate to the investigation of crime or the maintenance of national security. In these cases, the purpose of granting the power might be frustrated were it possible for the subjects of investigation to anticipate where and when they were likely to be the objects of surveillance or interception of communications. Nevertheless, even in these cases the law should lay down the conditions under which, and purposes for which, the power may lawfully be exercised, with at least sufficient clarity to provide some control over the behaviour of the authorities. If this is not done, there is inadequate legal protection in domestic law against arbitrary interferences with the rights under Article 8(1), particularly where the interferences necessarily take place in secret.

In *Malone*, where an English judge had decided that telephone tapping was lawful because nothing in the law made it unlawful, and its use by public authorities was regulated by administrative rules of practice, the Court held that the UK system for authorizing interceptions failed the 'according to law' test, because at the time it could not be said with certainty what elements in the arrangements were incorporated in legal rules and which ones depended entirely on the discretion of the executive. The same applied to 'metering' of calls, whereby the telephone undertaker, having collected the telephone numbers called from a particular instrument for the purposes of its business, released this information to the investigating authorities without the caller's knowledge or permission. Metering was held to raise an issue under Article 8 because the numbers dialled formed an integral element in the communication by telephone, and so concerned the private life of the caller.

It is not necessary for the legal grounding for the practice to be provided by statute. As the Court recognized in the *Sunday Times case*, a common-law system may give rise to legal norms which are sufficiently certain to satisfy the 'in accordance with the law' requirement. Nevertheless, where principles are developed by judicial decision, those decisions must have the effect of creating legal norms. In common-law systems, such as those operating in the UK, the authority of judges to make law in this way is recognized and institutionalized by the doctrine of *stare decisis*. In systems which do not recognize judicial decisions as creating binding—or sufficiently binding—legal norms, some other form of legislation will be required. For example, under French law, judges are considered to have authority to interpret legislation but not normally to make binding law; there is no formal doctrine of judicial precedent. Perhaps because of this, the Court held in *Huvig* v. *France* and *Kruslin* v. *France*[63] that principles regulating telephone tapping, developed in France by way of administrative guidance and judicial decisions, were evidence of a practice with regard to tapping, but did not provide sufficient foundation in law to satisfy the requirement that interferences with private life should be 'in accordance with the law'.

(ii) *The purpose test.* If the interference has sufficient grounding in law, and is sufficiently certain, to satisfy the rule-of-law part of the test, it must next be shown that the interference was adopted for one of the purposes specified in Article 8(2). Interferences are permitted only if 'in the interests of national security, public safety or the economic well-being of the country, for the prevention of disorder or crime, for the protection of health or morals, or for the protection of the rights and freedoms of others'. Besides the obvious matters which this list covers, it has been held by the Commission to deny prisoners their conjugal rights while in prison,[64] and to justify surveillance of visits to prisoners by members of their families,[65] and requirements that the prisoners wear prison uniforms and be subjected to searches by staff and restrictions on association with other prisoners.[66]

Interferences with Article 8(1) rights in the investigation of crime may be difficult to justify under the criteria in Article 8(2). Sir James Fawcett suggested that on a literal interpretation Article 8(2) would allow the state to justify interferences which are intended to prevent crimes, but not interferences designed to contribute purely to the investigation of past crimes.[67] However, there will often be an appreciable risk that crimes will be repeated if the offender is not caught, so the detection of crime often makes a worthwhile contribution to public safety, the prevention of disorder, and the protection of the rights of others. It is important to note that, in relation to all the legitimate interests which may justify interference under Article 8(2), the Court recognizes that the state has a certain amount of leeway: if a state decides that a measure serves one of the legitimate purposes, the Court will be fairly slow to override its judgment. This is considered further in relation to the next requirement.

(iii) *Necessity and the proportionality requirement.* If an interference is securely grounded on rule of law principles, and serves a legitimate pur-

---

[63] Eur. Ct. HR, Series A, No. 176B, Judgments of 24 Apr. 1990, 12 EHRR 528, 547.
[64] *X and Y* v. *Switzerland* Application No. 8166/78, 13 DR 241, Eur. Comm. HR.
[65] *X* v. *UK* Application No. 8065/77, 14 DR 246.
[66] *McFeeley and others* v. *UK* Application No. 8317/78, 3 EHRR 161, Eur. Comm. HR.
[67] Fawcett, Application, p. 235.

pose under Article 8(2), it still must be shown to be 'necessary in a democratic society' in the interests of that purpose. On the face of it, this is a difficult phrase to which to give substantive content. There are many notions of democracy, and it is not obviously appropriate for the Court to lay down standards for states as to the type of democracy which is to be preferred. 'Necessary' is also susceptible of different interpretations. It might be taken to mean that an interference will be justified only if the Court is satisfied that the legitimate objective could not have been achieved without it, carrying the meaning 'indispensable'. This would give the Court immense power over a state's domestic policy-making, and might be thought to be unacceptable. Alternatively, at the other extreme, it might mean that any measure is acceptable which is not obviously unnecessary.

In practice, the Court has found an elegant way of avoiding many of the pitfalls. It has accepted that states must be allowed a substantial discretion (the 'margin of appreciation') in making policy choices. On the other hand, the freedom is not unconstrained.[68] States must recognize that securing social interests may involve costs both to society and to individuals. The measures adopted must be shown to satisfy two principles. First, they must be a response to a 'pressing social need'. Secondly, they must not exact a higher price than is necessary and acceptable in a democratic society, 'two hallmarks of which are tolerance and broadmindedness';[69] in the terms used by the Court, the interference must be proportionate to the legitimate objective pursued.

When deciding whether these two principles are met, the Court has regard to the margin of appreciation allowed to state legislatures, judiciaries, and executives in identifying situations as problems and framing measures which are appropriate to the local conditions. However, the scope of the margin of appreciation has been held to vary according to the type of interest which the interference is designed to further. Where a right is interfered with in order to protect morals, the margin of appreciation is wide, because moral standards vary greatly from time to time and from place to place, and national authorities must have the freedom to respond to local views on morality. For this reason, the Court in the *Handyside case* was prepared to accept, in the context of Article 10 (freedom of expression), that it could be considered necessary to impose criminal sanctions on the publishers of *The Little Red Schoolbook*, a publication

[68] *The Handyside case* Eur. Ct. HR, Series A, No. 24, Judgment of 7 Dec. 1976, 1 EHRR 737; *Sunday Times case* Eur. Ct. HR, Series A, No. 30, Judgment of 26 Apr. 1979, 2 EHRR 245; applied to Article 8(2) in *Klass case* Eur. Ct. HR, Series A, No. 28, Judgment of 6 Sept. 1978, 2 EHRR 214.
[69] *Dudgeon* v. *UK* Eur. Ct. HR, Series A, No. 45, Judgment of 22 Oct. 1981, 4 EHRR 149, at para. 53.

which was aimed at children and contained accurate, but explicit, advice on matters such as masturbation, homosexuality, and abortion. Where the Court considers that the purpose is less subject to local or national variations, it allows a narrower margin. Accordingly the majority of the Court in the *Sunday Times case* decided that the prejudgment rule in English contempt of court law could not be justified on the basis of being necessary to maintain the authority and impartiality of the judiciary under Article 10(2).

Under Article 8(2), the margin of appreciation in relation to the protection of morals appears to be more limited than under Article 10, perhaps because the rights protected under Article 8 are essentially private while freedom of expression under Article 10 implies a right to publicize one's moral view, imposing it on others rather than merely indulging it in private. In *Dudgeon* v. *United Kingdom*, a majority of the Court accepted that the prevailing moral view in Northern Ireland was opposed to homosexuality, but considered that this could not be decisive as to the necessity for imposing restrictions on the private manifestation of an aspect of human personality. The judgment of the majority noted that the law had not in recent years been enforced, and that there was no evidence that this had harmed moral standards or vulnerable social groups in the province. It concluded that there was no pressing social need to criminalize homosexuality. In any case, the Court decided that criminalizing private consensual homosexual acts between adults was disproportionate to any social need:

On the issue of proportionality, the Court considers that such justifications as there are for retaining the law in force unamended are outweighed by the detrimental effects which the very existence of the legislative provisions in question can have on the life of a person of homosexual orientation like the applicant. Although members of the public who regard homosexuality as immoral may be shocked, offended or disturbed by the commission by others of private homosexual acts, this cannot on its own warrant the application of penal sanctions when it is consenting adults alone who are involved.[70]

The Court felt unable to overlook the changes which had occurred in the moral attitudes of other member states of the Council of Europe, which no longer regarded homosexual behaviour in itself as deserving criminal punishment. This shows that the margin of appreciation, even in relation to a matter as variable as morality, is restricted both by general European thought and by the need for tolerance in a democratic society. This approach will be welcome to some people who live in countries which are less tolerant than others in Europe. However, the juxtaposition

[70] Eur. Ct. HR, Series A, No. 45, Judgment of 22 Oct. 1981, 4 EHRR 149, at para. 60.

of tolerance and democracy in the Court's jurisprudence is not entirely unproblematic. Toleration of opinion and expression is necessary in order to maintain the democratic order. In relation to such toleration, the rights guaranteed, particularly under Articles 9 and 10 of the Convention, buttress democracy, and interference is hard to justify within a democratic society, particularly where it aims merely to avoid offence to other people.[71] When one considers the right to respect for private life, this too has an important democratic role, as noted above. Yet we said in s. 8.1 that the proper sphere of private as distinct from public life is always a subject for debate within a liberal democracy, and Article 8(2) acknowledges that respect for private life may be restricted to preserve health and morals. That being so, it gives an appearance of inconsistency to accept, on the one hand, that morality and the scope of private life fall within the sphere of state sovereignty, as mediated through democratic decision making processes, and yet to assert, on the other hand, that the scope of private life may be restricted by a democratic state only so far as is consistent with the Court's view of the proper balance between competing interests.

This, however, is inevitable when democratic states agree to subscribe to international standards for protecting individual rights within the states. There is a tension between (a) the demands of sovereignty and democratic self-determination within states, and (b) the standard of protection for individual rights which is demanded by the Convention. Having once agreed to an international process for adjudicating on breaches of rights under the Convention, it does not lie in the mouths of states to claim the freedom to restrict those rights in pursuance of democracy and self-determination without any limitation according to the principles of the Convention. Private life, being pre-eminently necessary for self-fulfilment and the enjoyment of other rights guaranteed under the Convention, is particularly in need of protection from the Court against too wide a margin of appreciation being allowed to states.

For this reason, it is proper for the Court to impose procedural requirements on states which interfere with the right to respect for Article 8(1) interests. A state will be unable to show that the risk to society which the interference is designed to avert outweighs the harm to individuals from the measures adopted, unless there are procedures which ensure that those interests are taken into account and that, so far as is compatible with the object of the interference, abuses of power may be remedied. For example, where the interference is necessarily not known to the individual concerned (as where his telephone is secretly tapped), there must be an independent authority to authorize the interference. In

---

[71] *Lingens* v. *Austria* Eur. Ct. HR, Series A, No. 103, Judgment of 8 July 1986, 8 EHRR 103, at para. 41.

Klass v. *Federal Republic of Germany*[72] the Court decided that the provisions of Germany's Law G10 on telephone tapping to protect national security complied with the requirements of Article 8 of ECHR. Under Law G10, authority to intercept communications was granted by a minister of the government, applying criteria laid down in the statute. The decision was reviewable and reversible by a Commission, headed by a person qualified for judicial office and independent of government. The Commission must also decide whether the person subject to surveillance should be notified. At the end of the surveillance, the minister must decide whether the person should be notified, so that he can enforce his legal rights, or whether this would be incompatible with national security. If he decides not to notify, the decision must be ratified by the Commission, and reconsidered at regular intervals to see whether the conditions for withholding notification are still satisfied. During the surveillance, the Commission acting *ex proprio motu*, or at the instance of the person under surveillance if he suspects what is happening, may consider the legality of the surveillance and, if appropriate, order its termination. Finally, the person believing himself to be under surveillance may challenge the order before the *Bundesverfassungsgericht* (constitutional court). Responsibility to Parliament for the overall use of the power is also maintained: the minister has to report half-yearly to a board consisting of five members of the Parliament, which had a monitoring role.

The Court in *Klass* accepted that this set of measures was adequate, at least in the context of national-security investigations. It is not clear whether it would provide sufficient protection against interference with private life in the course of investigations which concerned ordinacy crime rather than national security. The Court was prepared to accept, where national security was concerned, that it was not essential to have the surveillance authorized by a judicial officer independent of the executive, but it regarded judicial authorization as desirable. It may be that allowing non-judicial authorization by a member of the executive would be regarded as disproportionate to the legitimate object pursued in ordinary criminal cases.

If so, it will cause problems for the UK, as the Interception of Communications Act 1985 allows the Home Secretary (or, sometimes, a civil servant) to issue warrants authorizing interceptions of communications in a range of cases going beyond those involving national security. The 1985 Act was a response to *Malone's case*. The Act put the rules on a statutory basis, although in other respects the Act is less than satisfactory and may not have made our law fully compatible with the Convention. This is considered further in Chapter 10, below.

[72] Eur. Ct. HR, Series A, No. 28, Judgment of 6 Sept. 1978, 2 EHRR 214.

8.4 THE LEGAL SCOPE OF PRIVACY IN DOMESTIC LAW

The form in which privacy rights are recognized in any legal system is a matter for that system, and will be affected by cultural and political factors which are peculiar to particular societies. As noted above, some societies, like the USA and Canada, offer constitutional protection to certain privacy interests. Other societies, such as the United Kingdom, do not give legal protection to privacy as such, but protect some of the interests which are normally classified as privacy interests by way of rights of property or confidentiality. The extent, as well as the form, of the rights will also be a matter for political decision and will vary between societies.

(1) Directions in the English development of negative rights to privacy

(i) *English history.* English law has never had much room for the protection of privacy as such. Compared with the interests in property and personal integrity, privacy has had only limited importance in English culture. It need not have been so. Early in English legal history, the idea of the 'peace' acquired an importance which affected a number of subsequent developments.[73] The idea that a person's home and family life were to be free from violent intrusions was powerful. The king's peace eventually developed to cover the whole country, but its roots were in the idea of personal, rather than national, security. The peace of the king was, originally, the peace of the householder writ large. It entitled the monarch to levy compensation for violent acts in the vicinity of the court, which followed the monarch's person travelling round the country. This peace offered the protection of the royal courts and of the king's military force to those in the vicinity of the court. It could be extended in two ways: by granting the protection of the king's peace to individuals who were travelling on royal business or who were performing tasks which benefited the realm; and, more artificially, by announcing that the whole country would come within the king's peace on certain days when there were special reasons (usually religious) for preserving peace, or by asserting that particular parts of the country, usually those of special economic significance such as the main roads, were within the king's peace. The extension of the king's peace from a personal and localized form of protection to a general one took place by stages over several centuries.

---

[73] On the early history, see Sir Frederick Pollock, *Oxford Lectures and Other Discourses* (London: Macmillan, 1890), 65–90; Sir Carleton Kemp Allen, *The Queen's Peace* (London: Stevens & Son, 1953), 23–66; Jack K. Weber, 'The King's Peace: A Comparative Study' (1989) 10 *J. of Legal Hist.* 135–60.

The peace of the commoner's homestead mirrored the original, local-ized, peace of the king. It gave a right of compensation for those brawl-ing within the homestead. It was not simply related to property rights, and could have developed into a legally protected sphere of personal free-dom from interference and oversight, which is the essence of a right to privacy. However, it took another turn, no doubt influenced by prevail-ing economic forms and structures. It became associated at common law with the idea of real property. It spawned the law of nuisance—interference with quiet enjoyment of property rights—rather than a law of privacy. The common law proved resistant to the introduction of new protected interests, so that when other interests acquired economic importance it fell to equity rather than the common law to protect them. For example, equitable relief—particularly in the form of injunctions—was employed to restrain breaches of confidence unrelated to property interests. A famous example was the action brought successfully by the Prince Consort to restrain unauthorized publication of certain etchings made by Queen Victoria and himself, which, apart from considerations of copyright, would have opened to the public eye the home life of the royal family. It was on cases like this that the Warren and Brandeis argu-ment, that the common law protected (*inter alia*) the interest in the pri-vacy of the family in the form of a right to be let alone, was based.

(ii) *England in the twentieth century.* In England, despite the procedural fusion of law and equity late in the nineteenth century, neither Parliament nor the judges took the opportunity to develop a coherent law of privacy. The result is that we do not have one, either to protect us against abuse of power by public authorities or to prevent invasive behav-iour by journalists and peeping toms. So far as privacy is legally protected, it depends on other, independent causes of action: breach of confidence, trespass to land or personal property, copyright, nuisance. Where those are inapplicable for any reason, privacy is not legally recognised. Three official committees have reported on the subject in the last twenty years, all recommending against the creation of a tort of interference with pri-vacy. The main reason for this has been the difficulty of defining privacy with any certainty,[74] although concern about intrusions by journalists led the Calcutt Committee to suggest that there might be a need for legisla-tion to give rights of privacy against the press, if the press is unable to ensure that its agents observe an appropriately high standard of responsi-bility in pursuing news stories. Calls for such legislation have been echoed by the courts.[75]

[74] *Report of the Committee on Privacy* (Chairman: George Younger), Cmnd. 5012 (London: HMSO, 1972), p. 17.
[75] *Report of the Committee on Privacy and Related Matters* (Chairman: David Calcutt)

At the moment, the main focus of legislative intervention has been in relation to confidential information. The protection of personal information has, indeed, sometimes been regarded as the central case of privacy.[76] A regulatory scheme has been established to control the use which may be made of confidential information, and in some situations to give people access to information held by others about them. It has proved easier to define the specific classes of information to which protection is to apply than to define the amorphous nature of privacy.[77] In other areas, protection for privacy is weak.

The lack of a right to privacy as against the state was established, disappointingly but unsurprisingly, in the leading twentieth-century English decision on the subject, *Malone v. Metropolitan Police Commissioner (No. 2)*,[78] which concerned telephone tapping by the police. In the course of a criminal trial, the defendant, Mr Malone, alleged that the police had been intercepting some of his telephone calls, and metering (i.e. obtaining a print-out of the numbers called) all of them. After being acquitted of the criminal charges, Mr. Malone brought a civil action against the police, claiming a declaration that the interception had been unlawful on the grounds that it constituted a breach of confidence, a trespass, and an unlawful interference with his privacy. In accordance with standing policy, the police refused to confirm or deny that they had intercepted the telephone calls, and the litigation was conducted on the assumption that they had done so.

The action was tried by Sir Robert Megarry V.-C., who delivered a judgment which illustrates all the difficulties facing those who seek to develop a common law of privacy. He was quickly able to deal with the claim in trespass. The facilities which now exist to intercept or monitor communications from a distance, electronically, meant that people could intercept communications without trespassing physically on premises or personal property of the target. If conversations can be overheard by using powerful microphones from a distance, or by attaching a listening device to a telephone line outside the target's property, no trespass is committed against the target, although if the device is placed on another person's property without that person's permission it may be actionable at the suit of that person, unless there is a lawful justification. Only if it becomes necessary to make an unauthorized entry to the property of the

Cmnd. 1102 (London: HMSO, 1990); *Kaye v. Robertson* [1991] FSR 62, CA. See further below.

[76] Westin, *Privacy and Freedom*, p. 322; Wacks, *Personal Information*, passim. See s. 8.5, below.

[77] See the Data Protection Act 1984, the Access to Personal Files Act 1987, and the Access to Medical Records Act 1990, considered below.

[78] [1979] Ch. 344, [1979] 2 All ER 620.

target will the target have an action in trespass. As the report of the Younger Committee on Privacy made clear, the power of modern electronic surveillance and interception gadgets is such that it will rarely be necessary to commit trespass in order to find out what is being said inside a house or over a telephone line.[79] The claim in breach of confidence failed, because, although the subject-matters of telephone conversations were capable of being confidential in nature, there was no express or implied undertaking of confidentiality imposed on those who were party to the conversations, by reason either of the circumstances in which the communication took place or of the relationship between the parties. Indeed, Megarry V.-C. appears to have taken the view that communicating by telephone, notorious for its crossed lines and lack of security, indicated a willingness that the conversation should not be regarded as confidential. (This is even more true of mobile telephones, which can easily be intercepted by radio, than of the old-fashioned line-based telephones.)

This reasoning has been much criticized, on both principled and technical grounds.[80] In principle, the idea that a law-abiding citizen in a civilized society should have to anticipate that the telephone may be tapped has been characterized as 'unpalatable'.[81] Technically, it is hard, if not impossible, to reconcile the decision with later decisions, of both Sir Robert Megarry himself[82] and the Court of Appeal. In *Francome v. Mirror Group Newspapers Ltd.*[83] the Court of Appeal distinguished *Malone* on the facts, in holding that a jockey was entitled to an injunction restraining publication of tapes which purported to be recordings, obtained by a journalist by means of tapping, of incriminating telephone conversations between a leading jockey and an associate. It therefore seems that it will not always be true that a person who conducts a telephone conversation will be held to have accepted the risk of tapping. One possible point of distinction between the cases is that a private person who taps a telephone without authority is in a different position from someone who taps a telephone in performance of duties as a servant of the state. This, however, is not consistent with the principle underlying Sir Robert Megarry's judgment in *Malone*, namely that the agents of the state are, for

[79] *Report on Privacy* (1972), 154.
[80] See Vaughan Bevan, 'Is There Anybody There?' [1980] *PL* 431–53.
[81] Law Commission, Report No. 110, *Breach of Confidence*, Cmnd. 8288 (London: HMSO, 1981), para. 6.35; Raymond Wacks, *Personal Information*, 258.
[82] S. H. Bailey, D. J. Harris, and B. L. Jones, *Civil Liberties Cases and Materials*, 3rd edn. (London: Butterworths, 1991), 518, note that in 1981 Sir Robert Megarry granted an injunction restraining publication of tapes which were said to contain recordings of telephone conversations between Prince Charles and Lady Diana Spencer, his fiancée, obtained by telephone tapping.
[83] [1984] 1 WLR 892, [1984] 2 All ER 408, CA.

this purpose, in the same position as ordinary citizens, and that anything which is not forbidden by law is lawful for each. The status of the inter-cepter of a communication cannot logically affect the confidentiality (or otherwise) of the communication; at best, with appropriate legal author-ity, it may enable the state agent to justify the interception. One cannot altogether acquit the judges of a degree of muddled thinking in this admittedly confused area of law.

Even if the communication were regarded as confidential, it would not always avail a plaintiff in Mr. Malone's position. The breach of confidence action will serve to restrain a publication of the confidential material, or to obtain damages if publication has already occurred and loss is sustained as a result. It will also enable the plaintiff to recover any profits made by the defendant from unauthorized use of the material. (This happened in the *Spycatcher* saga: although the injunctions restraining publication by the newspapers of extracts from Mr. Peter Wright's book were eventually discharged by the House of Lords, their Lordships held that the government was entitled to an account of profits earned by the newspapers from publishing extracts in breach of confidence.)[84] However, it will not prevent the defendant from making non-profitable use of any information gained. In *Malone*, the police wanted the informa-tion gained from the tap in order to identify suspected accomplices. The information was not exploited commercially, nor was it used as evidence in court against any of the suspects. It was useful solely for investigative purposes. An action for breach of confidence would have been of no help. Nor would a breach of confidence action be helpful when confidentiality is violated by someone for his own personal, non-profit-making purposes, as where a student obtains access to an examination paper in advance of the examination, copies it in order to aid his prepara-tion for the examination, and returns it without broadcasting the con-tents.[85] There may, however, be a remedy for breach of copyright where the person in possession of the document holds the copyright and an unauthorized copy has been made.[86]

Finally, the claim for interference with privacy foundered when Sir Robert Megarry V.-C. held, somewhat disappointingly, that English law did not entertain actions for interference with privacy unless the interference

[84] *Attorney-General* v. *Guardian Newspapers Ltd. (No. 2)* [1990] AC 109, [1988] 3 All ER 545, HL.

[85] These were the facts of *Oxford* v. *Moss* (1978) 68 Cr. App. R. 183, DC, where the defendant was charged with theft of the information. The court held that there was no property in information; the paper had not been stolen, because there had been no inten-tion to deprive the owner of it permanently.

[86] *British Steel Corporation* v. *Granada Television Ltd.* [1981] AC 1096, [1981] 1 All ER 417, HL, provides an example of such a case, although the breach of copyright was not relevant to those proceedings.

amounted to one of the established causes of action in tort or equity. He accepted that this appeared to be inconsistent with the demands of Article 8 of the European Convention on Human Rights, but took note of the fact that the Convention was not capable of creating directly enforceable rights in English law. Invited to develop the common law along the lines of American law, his Lordship felt unable to do so. As English law is devoted to the maintenance of an undifferentiated mass of liberty (subject to any inroads made on it by law), rather than identifying and protecting a range of specific liberties,[87] he took the view that anyone is entitled to do anything which is not prohibited by law, and argued that on ordinary rule of law principles this applied equally to agents of the state and to citizens.

This is unsatisfactory, as it ignores another aspect of rule of law thinking. The rule of law demands that like cases be treated alike, and unlike cases be treated differently. The law should therefore take account of differences between the status and interests of the state and its agents, on the one hand, and private citizens on the other. Where the state has asserted a right to restrain a breach of confidence in information obtained by public servants during their service, the courts have accepted that the state is in a special position. The law of breach of confidence was developed to protect private interests. The state has no private interest to protect; its interests are public, and must be justified by reference to public-service objectives. Accordingly, the state is not permitted to assert a right to restrain a breach of confidence unless it can show that it is in the public interest that the confidence in question should be protected.[88] If the special position of the state is recognized for that purpose, it should also be accepted that the state has no private interest in liberty. It should be required to show special legal authority for its actions. State organs have powers, not rights or liberties, and the powers are conferred for the good of the public. Each power must be specially identified and authorized, and every exercise of power must be justified. If this is denied, it makes it hard for the judges to perform one of the functions demanded of them by rule of law thinking: namely, to make government legally accountable for their actions in such a way as to restrict the scope for abuse of powers.

As noted in section 3(3) above, *Malone's case* was the subject of an application under the European Convention on Human Rights. The European Court of Human Rights held that the English practice of interception was insufficiently grounded in law to allow it to be justified under Article 8(2). We saw that the Court also requires adequate procedural measures to prevent abuses of power by the executive which inter-

---

[87] See Ch. 2, above.

[88] *A.G.* v. *Guardian Newspapers Ltd.* *(No. 2)* [1990] AC 109, [1988] 3 All ER 545, HL. See further Ch. 14, below.

fere with rights to respect for private life. To answer this demand, the Interception of Communications Act 1985 was passed. It is considered in detail in Chapter 10, below.

(iii) *Privacy rights against the press?* Even were it possible to create a right to protection against official telephone tapping, it would not suffice to protect privacy. Much of the concern about invasion of privacy in this country has arisen from interferences by the press, or press exploitation of breaches of privacy by others, rather than government interference. It was in this context that the Calcutt Committee reported in 1990. Indeed, the terms of reference of the earlier Younger Committee on Privacy expressly restricted the Committee to considering the private law of privacy, rather than privacy rights against government and public agencies.

The press has never had a good reputation for respecting privacy. Journalists are concerned, in the nature of the job, to dig up stories which will sell their newspapers, as well as serving a public interest in freedom of information. The desire to provide stories which are going to cater for popular entertainment sometimes leads them to go beyond the boundaries of good taste. In *Kaye* v. *Robertson*[89] the Court of Appeal accepted that there was no power to restrain an interference with privacy as such in English law. Journalists had photographed and interviewed an actor from a well-known television series, who was seriously ill in hospital following an accident. The newspaper claimed an 'exclusive' for the story. No permission had been given by or on behalf of the the hospital, and the actor, who was recovering from brain surgery, was in no position to give or withhold real consent when the journalists burst into his hospital room. The actor sought an injunction restraining publication of the interview and photographs. He succeeded at first instance on the ground of defamation, as the implication that the actor had consented to be interviewed by the *Sunday Sport* would inevitably have lowered him in the opinion of right-thinking people.[90] On appeal, the Court of Appeal reversed the decision as regards defamation, as it was not inevitable (although it was thought to be likely) that a jury would have held that the material was defamatory. English courts are wary of interfering with press freedom by granting prior restraint of alleged libels, save in very clear cases.[91] The court also rejected claims based on passing off and trespass to the person. Nevertheless, a narrower injunction was granted to

---

[89] [1991] FSR 62, CA.

[90] Cf. *Tolley* v. *J. S. Fry & Sons Ltd.* [1931] AC 333, HL, where an amateur golfer whose image was used without permission in an advertisement for chocolate was held to have been defamed by the implication that he had compromised his amateur status by selling the right to use his image.

[91] See Ch. 13, below.

restrain malicious falsehood, as the court thought it clear that the journalists knew that the actor had not given informed consent to the interview
as the 'exclusive' label on the story implied, and publication of the story
in the *Sunday Sport* would greatly reduce the value of the actor's potentially valuable commercial right to sell the story of his accident to other
newspapers later.

This case illustrates an attitude characteristic of English civil liberties
law. The judges were clearly of the view that the absence of a right to
privacy in English law was so well established that it could be remedied
only by Parliament. The case concerned a gross invasion of privacy, as
Bingham L.J. said, and was an example of particularly bad taste on the
part of the journalists. It is significant that all three judges in the Court of
Appeal expressed concern that privacy rights needed to be protected
against the press, and were more in need of protection than is press freedom. It is felt that the press, or elements in it, abuse their freedom, and
that the balance between the press and individuals needs to be redressed
by law. Glidewell L.J. regarded the case as 'a graphic illustration of the
desirability of Parliament considering whether and in what circumstances
statutory provision can be made to protect the privacy of individuals'.
Leggatt L.J. went further, hoping 'that the making good of this signal
shortcoming in our law will not be long delayed'. This balance will be
considered further in Chapter 13. However, it would be unfortunate if a
law is introduced to protect people against invasion of privacy by private
individuals and commercial concerns but not against similar invasions by
public authorities. Sir David Calcutt, in his *Review of Press Self-
Regulation*,[92] recommended that new criminal offences and a new tort of
invasion of privacy should be introduced to deal with people who invade
privacy to obtain personal information with a view to its publication.
Such privacy laws, aimed exclusively at those who publish information,
and leaving untouched those who invade privacy for other purposes
(whether private or public), would provide protection which would be
too narrow to satisfy those who are concerned at the powers of the security service and investigative agencies, and too wide to be acceptable to
those who regard the press as a principal guardian against corruption in
public life.

(2) Positive rights protecting private and family life

On the basis of the notion that the most fundamental interests in privacy
relate to personal information, the law has increasingly acted to provide
protection for it. This protection is of two kinds. First, there are provi-

---

[92] Cm. 2135 (London: HMSO, 1992), ch. 7.

sions restricting the use to which people can put personal information about others which they hold. Secondly, there are statutes which permit people to claim access to information banks, in order to discover what information is held about them, and to correct mistaken records.

(i) *Restrictions in the use of personal information.* Officials who hold information, obtained in the course of their official business, may (subject to limited exceptions) use it only for the purpose for which it was obtained. There is a general principle of equity which imposes such a restriction as an element in the obligation of confidentiality.[93] This is reinforced by some statutes, which authorize the collection of information but prohibit disclosure. Examples include information gathered in connection with assessing people's tax liabilities,[94] information gathered by the Parliamentary Commissioner for Administration (ombudsman),[95] and material and information collected from authorized telephone taps.[96] There are also more general prohibitions on disclosure under the Official Secrets Act 1989, considered further in Chapter 13 below.

As Dr. Cripps has pointed out,[97] many of these provisions do not admit a public-interest justification for disclosure. In such cases, as under the Health and Safety at Work Act 1974, section 28, it means that it may be impossible legally to warn the public about a danger being created by a commercial polluter. The interests which are protected by non-disclosure requirements, therefore, may concern individuals' privacy, but the requirements are often designed to protect commercial interests.

(ii) *Access to, and correction of, stored information.* Vast amounts of personal information about people are held by an increasing range of bodies. Employers, bankers, doctors, solicitors, and others, hold records on their employees, customers, clients, and patients. Educational establishments hold records on their students, and sometimes on students' families. Government departments which administer programmes such as social security hold detailed personal information about many people. The police have always relied heavily on collecting and collating reports about people, not all of whom are suspected of offences. Until relatively recently, these gobbets of information were routinely held on paper, and

[93] See *Marcel* v. *Metropolitan Police Commissioner* [1992] 1 All ER 72, CA, and Sir Nicolas Browne-Wilkinson's first-instance judgment at [1991] 2 WLR 1118, [1991] 1 All ER 845.

[94] E.g. Taxes Management Act 1970, s. 6 and Sched. 1.

[95] Parliamentary Commissioner Act 1967, s. 11.

[96] Interception of Communications Act 1985, Sched. 2.

[97] Yvonne Cripps, *The Legal Implications of Disclosure in the Public Interest* (Oxford: ESC Publishing, 1986), 122–3.

their mass and the lack of centralization made it hard, and in normal circumstances too much trouble, to link them. As a result, no one person or body could put together a complete view of the activities of individuals based on records. This was traditionally regarded as an important safeguard for individuals: if the state could not find out all about its citizens, it could not easily control them; liberty and autonomy could be preserved. Full information is a valuable tool of repression.

The early history of income tax provides a good example of this principle. On the introduction of income tax[98] during the Napoleonic Wars, the need for the first time to assess people's income raised a threat to the confidentiality of people's private and business affairs. This was eased by having income from different sources assessed under different schedules to the Act by different surveyors, and so began the schedular system of income tax which survives to the present, although the various schedules are no longer assessed by different people. The computer age has facilitated a vast explosion in the amount of material and information which can be stored, and the ability to retrieve and collate information speedily. Combined with improved telecommunications, it has also made it far easier to transfer information from one user to another over large distances, even internationally, virtually instantaneously.[99] Despite attempts by government to play down the implications,[100] this poses two risks to civil liberties.[101]

First, information which is held can do far more damage than previously if passed on to other people, particularly if it is wrong. Security vetting procedures in relation to job applications may sometimes be needed, but can lead to people being denied jobs without ever knowing the grounds on which they have been rejected, or being able to challenge incorrect information.[102] Security vetting at the B.B.C. no longer takes place except for those concerned in war reporting. Previously, all applicants for jobs were vetted. For example, in 1977 MI5 advised the BBC not to appoint a Ms Hilton, because as a student she had been been secretary of the Scotland–China Association, which MI5 regarded as subversive, despite the fact that its members included eminent churchmen and a former governor of Stirling Castle.[103]

[98] Property and Income Tax Act 1798; see B. E. V. Sabine, *A History of Income Tax* (London: Allen & Unwin, 1966).

[99] See, generally, *Report of the Committee on Data Protection* (Chairman: Sir Norman Lindop), Cmnd. 7341 (London: HMSO, 1978); Duncan Campbell and Steve Connor, *On the Record: Surveillance, Computers and Privacy—The Inside Story* (London: Michael Joseph, 1986); Wacks, *The Protection of Privacy*, ch. 4; *id.*, *Personal Information*, ch. 6.

[100] White Paper on Data Protection, Cmnd. 8539 (1982).

[101] Campbell and Connor, *On the R ecord*, ch. 3.

[102] For discussion, see Sandra Fredman and Gillian S. Morris, *The State as Employer* (London: Mansell, 1989), 232–6.   [103] *Independent*, 21 Oct. 1988, p. 3.

Secondly, it has proved to be at least as easy for people to break into computer databanks and abstract information as it ever was to break into a file registry and acquire information from paper files. Amateur computer hackers do it for fun, but professionals can exploit the security problems which face databank managers. These difficulties can be exaggerated, but there is some cause for concern. At present, information is too diffuse to be easily collated on any very large scale. However, it would be very much easier if people had a single reference number which they were required to use for all purposes, such as an identity card number or a national insurance number. The Lindop Committee noted that linkages between databases are not technically impossible, and the adoption of a 'universal personal identifier' would remove some of the existing obstacles.[104] Already, information collected by credit-rating agencies for the purpose of assessing people's creditworthiness may be passed on, or even sold, for commercial purposes. The ability to pool information from medical records, which are increasingly being computerized, insurance applications, credit applications, etc., could pose a major threat to privacy, even without linking these databanks with those held by government.

Problems concerning the accuracy and security of records are common to paper and computerized records, but are raised in an acute form by computer databanks. Wherever they arise, a number of interests have to be balanced. The state has a legitimate interest in collecting information for its manifold purposes, and these include the vetting of people who hold or apply for jobs which are sensitive in terms of national security. As the late Harry Street pointed out, this is inevitable and essential, but the great task is to ensure that the information on which the process depends is reliable.[105] This interest in securing reliability would seem to indicate that there is a public, as well as a private or individual, interest in allowing the subjects of records to have access to them to check and if necessary correct them, at least where this can be done without threatening security. However, here another interest enters the balance. Third parties may be concerned, either as informants, or as advisers or referees who have expressed opinions about the subject of the record, or as subjects whose affairs are bound up with those of the main subject of the record. They might have spoken or written in confidence, and have a privacy interest of their own in preventing the subject from finding out who they are. It may therefore be necessary to restrict access to records which would allow the subject to identify others, if an overriding privacy or national-security interest would be endangered by allowing full access;

[104] Cmnd. 7341, para. 6.08.
[105] Harry Street, *Freedom, the Individual and the Law*, 5th edn. (Harmondsworth: Penguin, 1982), 245.

but any restriction should go no further than necessary to achieve the purpose. These matters have, to some extent, now been covered by legislation. The main pieces of legislation are considered here.

Pressure from organisations such as the Campaign for Freedom of Information led to the passing of the Data Protection Act 1984, which provides a legal framework for controlling the use of personal data.[106] 'Data' are defined as 'information recorded in a form in which it can be processed by equipment operating automatically in response to instructions given for that purpose'. 'Personal data' are 'data consisting of information which relates to a living individual who can be identified from that information (or from that and other information in the possession of the data user), including any expression of opinion about the individual but not any indication of the intentions of the data user in respect of that individual'.[107] It follows that individuals, but not organizations, are protected; the object is to bolster individual liberty and privacy, not commercial or group rights.

The protective scheme has three elements. First, there is an educational element. For the guidance of data users, Schedule 1 sets out eight data protection principles,[108] which are broadly in line with the OECD *Guidelines on the Protection of Privacy and Transborder Flows of Personal Information* (1980), and the Council of Europe *Convention for the Protection of Individuals with regard to Automatic Processing of Personal Data* (1981). The data protection principles demand: (i) that information shall be obtained, and personal data processed, fairly and lawfully; (ii) that personal data shall be held only for specified and lawful purposes; (iii) that it shall not be used or disclosed in any manner incompatible with those purposes; (iv) that it shall be adequate, relevant, and not excessive in relation to those purposes; (v) that it shall be accurate and kept up to date; (vi) that it shall not be kept for longer than necessary for the specified lawful purposes; (vii) that, at regular intervals and without undue delay or expense, individuals shall be entitled to be informed by any data user whether personal data are held on them, to have access to any such data, and, if appropriate, to have such data corrected or erased; and (viii) that appropriate security measures shall be taken against unauthorized access to, or alteration, disclosure, or destruction of, personal data, and against accidental loss or destruction of personal data.[109]

---

[106] For full discussion, see Colin Tapper, *Computer Law*, 4th edn. (London: Longman, 1989).

[107] Data Protection Act 1984, s. 1(2), (3).

[108] Part I of Sched. 1 sets out the principles; Part II contains interpretation provisions.

[109] The protections offered by the data protection principles can be modified by subordinate legislation made by the Secretary of State under s. 2(3) so as to offer additional protection in relation to the racial origin, political opinions, religious or other beliefs, health,

Secondly, a registration system is provided for data users, operated by the Data Protection Registrar.[110] Besides the name and address of the data user, the registration record contains: a description of the personal data to be held by him, and the purposes for which they are to be held or used; a description of the proposed sources of information or data; a description of any person to whom he intends or may wish to disclose the data; the names or a description of countries or territories outside the UK to which he intends or may wish to transfer the data, directly or indirectly; and an address to which data subjects can apply for access to the data.[111] Section 7 places a heavy onus on the applicant for registration: it provides that the registrar may refuse an application for registration only if he considers that the particulars provided are inadequate, or he is satisfied that the application is likely to contravene any of the data protection principles, or he considers that the information available is insufficient to satisfy him that the applicant is unlikely to contravene the principles. This makes compliance with the data protection principles the major criterion for registration. Although the government rejected the Lindop Committee's recommendation that there should be codes of practice, breach of which would be a criminal offence, the registration provisions have teeth, because section 5 of the Act makes it an offence to be a data user, whether public or private, unless registered with the Data Protection Registrar. It is also an offence under section 5 to use personal data for an unregistered purpose or disclose or transfer it otherwise than according to the details on the register. Furthermore, if the registrar is satisfied that a registered data user is breaching one of the data protection principles, he can serve an enforcement notice, requiring him to take specified steps within a specified period,[112] or a deregistration notice, leading to the removal of a data user's registration,[113] or transfer prohibition notice, preventing transfer of data or information by the data user.[114] This creates a potentially powerful regulatory, monitoring, and reporting body[115] for data collection and processing, covering all public and private computerizable personal records, including those collected for research purposes.

---

sexual life, or criminal convictions, of the data subject. The Computer Misuse Act 1990 creates special offences to deal with 'hackers' who gain unauthorized access to computer systems to obtain or corrupt records or programmes.

[110] The registrar's position is created by s. 3; he is required by s. 4 to maintain the register of data users.

[111] Data Protection Act 1984, s. 4(3).   [112] Ibid., s. 10.   [113] Ibid., s. 11.

[114] Ibid., s. 12. There is an appeal to a Data Protection Tribunal against decisions by the Registrar to refuse registration, or to serve an enforcement notice, deregistration notice, or transfer prohibition notice: s. 13.

[115] The registrar's annual reports are published as House of Commons Papers.

Thirdly, in accordance with the data protection principles, the Act gives a data subject (the individual on whom the data user holds data) the rights to be informed whether the data user holds personal data relating to that data subject, and (subject to certain exceptions) to be supplied with a copy of the information constituting such personal data.[116] Compensation can be obtained for damage and distress suffered by the data subject as a result of inaccurate or misleading data, and the High Court can order that the data be rectified or erased.[117]

Although the Act applies to data held by government departments and the police, it does not amount to anything which would be recognized abroad as a freedom of information Act. There are two reasons for this. First, it relates only to personal data. While most applications under the freedom of information legislation in force in (for example) Canada, the USA, and Australia, come from people who want to inspect the records held on them, that is not the only use to which they can be put. Secondly, the Act is concerned only with computerized or computerizable information. It does not give any right of access to paper files. To some extent, this gap has since been filled by other legislation, but, as we will see below, this covers only a restricted range of matters (mainly medical, social services, housing, and local-government records).

Although the data protection principles apply to all data users, the other provisions of the 1984 Act are subject to a number of exceptions. The registration requirement and the data subject's access right do not apply where a minister, on behalf of the Crown, conclusively certifies that an exemption for data is required for the purpose of safeguarding national security.[118] In terms of Article 8 of the European Convention on Human Rights, this may be justified by the national-security exception in Article 8(2). In order to protect the rights of others, particularly their privacy rights, there is a further exception for payroll and accounting data, while people who maintain membership and mailing lists, and other data, on behalf of clubs and for purely domestic purposes, are exempted by section 33. Those who keep other types of data must register, but there are some exemptions from compliance with data subjects' access entitlements. Data held for the purpose of enforcing tax and criminal law, or otherwise relating to the exercise of statutory functions, have an exemption under section 28, a provision typical of the secretive attitudes of the state, which will resurface in subsequent chapters. With similar concern for secrecy, data concerning judicial appointments are exempt from access

---

[116] Data Protection Act 1984, s. 21(1). The High Court can order the data user to comply with this obligation unless it would be unreasonable to do so: s. 21(8). The access provisions do not apply to credit-agency records if the data subject has access rights under the Consumer Credit Act 1974, s. 158: see s. 34(3) of the 1984 Act.
[117] Data Protection Act 1984, ss. 22, 23, 24.   [118] Ibid. s. 27.

under section 31, as are data which are covered by legal professional privilege. Some material held for the purpose of research and statistical purposes is also exempted by section 33.

Finally, section 34 provides that the Act does not prevent a data user from complying with legal requirements for publishing material or making it available for public inspection.[119] It also provides that the Secretary of State may by order exempt personal data from subject-access provisions, where disclosure is prohibited or restricted by any enactment, but, before making such an order, the Secretary of State must carry out a balancing exercise, deciding whether the prohibtion or restriction ought to prevail over the interests of the data subject or others.

The limitations on the scope of the Data Protection Act 1984 led to various moves to expand the scope of a data subject's access to personal information. These have been largely inspired by the Campaign for Freedom of Information, and effectuated through the introduction of Private Members' Bills without the support of the government. Attempts by a Conservative MP, Mr Richard Shepherd, to limit the element of state secrecy by steering, first, a Protection of Official Information Bill, and, later, a Freedom of Information Bill, through Parliament were defeated when the Conservative government issued a three-line whip to force its supporters to vote against them, in 1988 and 1991 respectively. Other, more limited, measures had more success.

The first was a move to extend access rights to non-computerizable files. This was achieved in the Access to Personal Files Act 1987, which originated as a Private Member's Bill introduced by Mr Archy Kirkwood MP. It has a limited impact, giving a right of access in respect of files containing personal information, if held by a Housing Act local authority[120] or a local social services authority. Personal information is defined in section 2(2) in terms similar to the definition of personal data for the purposes of the Data Protection Act 1984.

The authorities' obligations in respect of access are set out in regulations made by the relevant Secretary of State under section 3. These are similar to those which arise where the Data Protection Act 1984 is applicable: to tell people whether personal information is held on a file

---

[119] The combined effect of this provision, s. 17 of the Local Government Finance Act 1982 and s. 79 of the Local Government Act 1985 (inspection of local authority accounts), with the Local Government (Access to Information) Act 1985, made it necessary to enact s. 11 of the Local Government and Housing Act 1989, which exempts personal information about members of the staff of local authorities from the public inspection requirements.

[120] This includes a residuary body created under the Local Government Act 1985, s. 57, and a housing action trust established under Part III of the Housing Act 1988: see Access to Personal Files Act 1987, Sched. 1, para. 2(1), as amended by Housing Act 1988, s. 140 and Sched. 17, Pt 1.

covered by the Act, and to provide a copy of it on payment of a fee not exceeding £10.[121] Where the record also relates to another individual who is identifiable from the record, that person must be given the opportunity to say whether he consents to disclosure.[122] Varying slightly from the pattern of the 1984 Act, section 1(5) provides that the 1987 Act is in general to override any prohibition or restriction on disclosure, subject to any regulations made by the Secretary of State. This Act to some extent remedies the inability of those in the care of the social service departments of local authorities to find out about their treatment. Previously, people had been unable to gain access, because it was argued that access would breach the confidentiality of evidence and advice given to local authorities by third parties.[123] In the *Gaskin case*[124] the European Court of Human Rights accepted that this interest in confidentiality should be considered, but held that, unless there was an independent body to decide whether the interest in confidentiality was weightier than the person's interests in private and family life, the restriction on availability of information was disproportionate to the aim pursued, and so not 'in accordance with law and necessary in a democratic society' as required by Article 8(2) ECHR. The 1987 Act enabled the UK to claim that it had already put in place legislation capable of giving a right for those who as children had been in the care of the local authority to have access to records held about their early history and treatment while in care, thus meeting the obligations arising under Article 8 of ECHR, which the European Court of Human Rights held had been breached in the *Gaskin case*.[125]

Information supplied to a local authority by a health professional is exempted from disclosure.[126] There is as strong an interest in giving patients the chance to check on what doctors are recording about them as there is in open information in any other relationship. Doctors have very intimate information about people, and wield substantial power with it. Furthermore, although the doctor normally has an obligation of confidentiality in relation to the patient, this has been watered down. First, there is the dilution of this protection by what Professor Gerald Dworkin has called 'extended confidence', in which medical records are routinely open to a whole 'health care team', including nurses, secretaries, administrators, and social workers, as well as doctors.[127] Secondly,

[121] Access to Personal Files (Social Services) Regulations 1989, SI 1989 No. 206, and the Access to Personal Files (Housing) Regulations 1989, SI 1989, No. 503, regs. 2, 3.
[122] Ibid., reg. 5.　　　　[123] *Gaskin* v. *Liverpool City Council* [198] 1 WLR 1549, CA.
[124] *Gaskin* v. *UK*, Eur. Ct. HR, Series A, No. 160, Judgment of 23 June 1989, 12 EHRR 36.
[125] Ibid.　　　　[126] SI 1989, No. 206, reg. 8.
[127] Gerald Dworkin, 'Access to Medical Records: Discovery, Confidentiality and Privacy' (1979) 42 *MLR* 88 at p. 90.

the scope of the duty of confidence may be restricted by the public-interest exception.[128] Thirdly, the General Medical Council recognizes that, in addition to the above relaxations, the obligation does not prevent disclosure where the patient has consented expressly or impliedly (for example, where insurers request information in respect of an insurance policy on the patient's life), where disclosure is in the patient's best interests, and where it is ordered by a court.[129] It is important that the patient should be able to make sure that the information recorded is accurate, and to know what is being said about him, unless there are compelling reasons for keeping the record closed.

For this reason, two pieces of legislation have extended to patients a right to know what is being said about them. The first is the Access to Medical Reports Act 1988, dealing with reports written by doctors for insurance companies and employers. The second, which again closely follows the Data Protection Act 1984 and the Access to Personal Files Act 1987, is the Access to Health Records Act 1990.

The 1990 Act applies to information relating to the physical or mental health of an individual who can be identified from that information, or from other information in the possession of the holder of the record, where the record has been made by or on behalf of a registered medical practitioner, dentist, optician, pharmacist, nurse, midwife, health visitor, chiropodist, dietician, occupational therapist, orthoptist, physiotherapist, clinical psychologist, child psychotherapist, speech therapist, art or music therapist employed by a health-service body, or a scientist employed by a health-service body as a head of a department.[130] The Act does not apply where the Data Protection Act 1984 applies. Access is to be allowed to children only if they are *Gillick*-competent (section 4(1)), and may be excluded where the information, in the opinion of the holder, would be likely to cause serious harm to the physical or mental health of the patient or anyone else, or was provided by or relates to another individual who could be identified from the information, unless the latter has consented to disclosure.[131] Incorrect information is to be rectified.[132]

All these statutory provisions serve to protect the interests of individuals in their dignity and their private lives. They should also help to encourage record holders to ensure that the information which they record is accurate and fair, as advocated by the data protection principles under the 1984 Act. If they succeed in this, they will have been useful. They do not provide a comprehensive package of access entitlements.

---

[128] *W. v. Egdell* [1990] Ch. 359, [1990] 1 All ER 835, CA.

[129] See generally J. K. Mason and R. A. McCall Smith, *Law and Medical Ethics*, 3rd edn. (London: Butterworths, 1991), 173–94.

[130] Access to Health Records Act 1990, ss. 1, 2.   [131] Ibid., s. 5.

[132] Ibid., s. 6.

Too many files and records are not yet covered by any legislation. However, a start has been made. The task is to extend rights of access, while protecting the legitimate interests and rights of other people who are identifiable from records, or whose commercial interests are threatened by too wide an access entitlement. For all its limitations, the legislation to date shows that Parliament is beginning to take seriously the positive obligations on the state which flow from the right to private and family life under Article 8 of the ECHR.

8.5 PRIVACY: THE FOUNDATION

In this chapter we have explored the reaction to privacy-based rights in international, US, and English law. We have noted distinctions between positive and negative aspects of privacy rights, and have observed different conceptions about the foundational values which are said to mandate the protection of privacy, and respect for private and family life. There is the view, advanced by Westin and Wacks, that privacy is fundamentally concerned with the control of information. Against this is the view of many judges, both in the US Supreme Court and in the European Court of Human Rights, that the value of privacy or private life is more far-reaching, and protects personal and political autonomy, self-determination, family relationships, and similar interests which have nothing directly to do with information. So far as the ECHR is concerned, it is plausible to argue that the extensive interpretation given to Article 8 is the result of the rights being framed in terms of respect for private and family life, rather than merely a right to privacy. This cannot, however, explain either American developments or the evolutionary way in which the European Court of Human Rights has felt able to develop the notion of private and family life.

It is important to work out where one stands on the question of the fundamental justification for privacy rights, because it is likely to dictate the use to which one can put them. Treating them as essentially about information has the attraction that it makes them relatively easy to handle, and gives them a clear and easily delimited scope. However, it seems artificial to choose a foundational theory for a right merely because that makes the right easier to handle. It allows the practical tail to wag the theoretical dog. If there are good reasons to extend the notion of privacy beyond information, or even to treat the core meaning of privacy as something unrelated to information, we should brace ourselves to grapple with the conceptual problems in order to make our conception of the private sphere of life generate usable principles.

The latter approach is the one which I find more appealing. Historically and theoretically, the notion of privacy has emerged from a political ideal of the individual, the family, and small groups of people working together consensually for a common object, as the basic elements in society. The rights to respect for private and family life, home, and correspondence, as under ECHR Article 8, or the core constitutional privacy rights under the US Constitution (as interpreted by the judges), are founded on the fundamental importance of these units to people's psychology and self-fulfilment, to their opportunity to participate in democratic political processes, and to the welfare of society. Rights to respect for personal information, far from being core elements in the definition of privacy, are usually parasitic on these foundational privacy rights: respect for individual dignity, self-determination, family relationships, etc. Other rights, such as the commercial right to exploit the potential public (rather than private) value of one's information or personality, are derived from a source entirely unrelated to privacy. All the tort and constitutional rights which are grouped together in American privacy law are valuable aids to autonomy. But it is autonomy itself, the freedom to pursue one's own objectives and life-style and to enjoy personal space, which is the fundamental justification for privacy rights.

If one accepts that privacy rights have an importance which is logically and historically prior to the interest in personal information, it means that a legal right to respect for privacy need not be reduced to a mere manifestation of the legal categories and remedies from which Warren and Brandeis derived its existence. Once the significance of privacy has been acknowledged, its centrality to the development of legal protection for personal autonomy can be exploited. It can take off in new directions, and have effects which are unrelated to personal information. For example, the use of privacy to extend the rights of women in *Roe* v. *Wade*, or the restriction of rights to be free of unreasonable searches and seizures (under the Fourth Amendment to the US Constitution, or section 8 of the Canadian Charter of Rights and Freedoms) to situations in which the litigant has a legitimate privacy interest of his own to protect, are expressions of the basis of privacy jurisprudence in human dignity and personal autonomy.

Such developments as these will not be random or unprincipled, so long as the judges base developments securely in the fundamental values of autonomy. This avoids reducing privacy to a redundant or empty concept. It has life and purpose, without becoming unmanageably vague. Adopting a model of privacy based on liberal values does not exempt privacy from political processes, as the scope of the private sphere of life is ultimately a political matter. It does, however, demand that people (including legislators, judges, and other public officers) respect those expectations of privacy which have been accepted as appropriate for all by means of the democratic process. The three chapters which follow examine the extent to which this ideal is realized in various areas of English law.

9

FREEDOM FROM UNREASONABLE ENTRIES, SEARCHES, AND SEIZURES

9.1 BACKGROUND

In England and Wales we have relied mainly on the common law to protect us against arbitrary exercises of public power. As noted in Chapter 8, English law has not developed a right to privacy as such. In the field of search and seizure, this has meant that the common-law rights concerning property and confidentiality have borne the brunt of the burden. People are protected against interference with property and against infringement of equitable or contractual rights to confidentiality. Much of the law of search and seizure therefore concerns the circumstances in which the law will recognise exceptions to those rights in the public interest. Exceptions have been introduced both by statute and by common law. Some of these rely on a degree of control being exercised by an independent judicial officer, who has to decide whether to grant a search warrant authorising the interference. However, an increasing number rely on the competence and good sense of the officers concerned.

Other countries have based their controls on entries, searches, and seizures squarely on a right to privacy, and have been much less willing to permit searches and seizures without independent judicial safeguards. In the United States, the Fourth Amendment to the federal Constitution guarantees the right to be free of unreasonable search and seizure, and provides that no warrant shall issue save on probable cause. As regards other invasions of privacy interests, they constitute a deprivation of liberty under the Fifth and Fourteenth Amendments, and must observe due process requirements, including (normally) independent authorization. Any interference with privacy, or search and seizure, without a warrant is *prima facie* unreasonable, and so unconstitutional, although there are exigent circumstances in which it will not be regarded as unreasonable.[1] In

---

[1] *Katz* v. *US*, 389 US 347 (1967). Exigent circumstances justifying warrantless search or seizure include cases where the police are in hot pursuit of a suspect (*Warden* v. *Hayden*, 387 US 294 (1967)); situations where evidence is in plain view of officers acting with justification, and might be destroyed if not seized immediately (*Coolidge* v. *New Hampshire*, 403 US 443 (1973); and searches for weapons on arrest (*Chimel* v. *California*, 395 US 752 (1969)). See generally Wayne C. LaFave, *Search and Seizure: A Treatise on the Fourth Amendment*, 3 vols. (St. Paul: West, 1978).

Canada, section 8 of the Canadian Charter of Rights and Freedoms, forming Part I of the Constitution Act 1982, guarantees the right to be free of unreasonable searches and seizures. It has been held that this provision too is grounded in a privacy right, and the courts have decided that a system of independent authorisation prior to a search and seizure is normally required.[2]

Even where a country has no constitutional guarantee of a right to be free of unreasonable search and seizure, the common law can provide some protection. It does so by refusing to accept any new common-law exceptions to property and confidentiality rights, and by restrictively interpreting legislation which infringes such rights. The English courts, however, have shown too great a deference towards police officers' estimations of the powers which they require. Well before Parliament set some boundaries to police powers in the Police and Criminal Evidence Act 1984, the Court of Appeal twice extended powers of seizure under warrant, without any statutory justification.[3] The English courts also failed notably to protect items subject to legal professional privilege from seizure under warrant.[4] It was left to Parliament to attempt to reassert sensible limits on police powers (including the protection of privileged material) in the Police and Criminal Evidence Act 1984. The English common law is failing to do its traditional job in this area.

In many other common law countries, by contrast, the judges seek to protect citizens' rights, and leave it to the legislature to provide additional police powers in the public interest if that is thought appropriate (subject to any overriding constitutional limitations on legislative power). For example, New Zealand courts refused to follow the English judicial extensions to police powers in the 1970s,[5] and the New Zealand judges followed their Canadian brethren, and were in turn ultimately followed by the High Court of Australia, in recognizing that the common-law doctrine of legal professional privilege conferred a right which could be asserted even against a search warrant, unless a statute expressly provided that the warrant was to override claims to privilege.[6] This is an approach which shows greater commitment to rights-based, liberal values than does that of the English judges.

[2] *Hunter* v. *Southam Inc.* (1984) 11 DLR (4th) 641; *Kokesch* v. *R.* (1990) 1 CR (4th) 62.
[3] *Chic Fashions (West Wales) Ltd.* v. *Jones* [1968] 2 QB 299, [1968] 1 All ER 229, CA; *Ghani* v. *Jones* [1970] 1 QB 693, [1969] 3 All ER 1700, CA.
[4] *Frank Truman Export Ltd.* v. *Metropolitan Police Commissioner* [1977] QB 952, [1977] 3 All ER 431; *R.* v. *Justice of the Peace for Peterborough, ex parte Hicks* [1977] 1 WLR 1371, [1978] 1 All ER 225, DC.
[5] *McFarlane* v. *Sharpe* [1972] NZLR 838, CA of NZ.
[6] *Solosky* v. *R.* (1979) 105 DLR (3d) 745, SC Canada; *Rosenburg* v. *Jaine* [1983] NZLR 1, CA of NZ; *Baker* v. *Campbell* (1983) 153 CLR 52, HC of Australia.

Nevertheless, there are signs that a change of attitude may be occurring among the English judiciary.| In *Marcel* v. *Commissioner of Police of the Metropolis*[7] Sir Nicolas Browne-Wilkinson VC said: 'Search and seizure under statutory powers constitute fundamental infringements of the individual's immunity from interference by the state with his property and privacy—fundamental human rights.' |Sir Nicolas (now Lord) Browne-Wilkinson is well known for his concern to protect individual rights against the state, of which his judgment in the first *Spycatcher* case, although later reversed by the Court of Appeal and House of Lords, was a notable example.[8] His is not a lone voice, however: when *Marcel*'s case went to the Court of Appeal, the judges, while reversing the decision on the duties owed by the police to people from whom items are seized, agreed with most of Sir Nicolas's judgment, and the passage quoted above was specifically approved by Sir Christopher Slade.[9]

This chapter therefore addresses the following issues: (1) What is the current scope of search and seizure powers in Britain? (2) Are the protections against unreasonable searches and seizures adequate to maintain the human rights of citizens? (3) Does the law, and do the protections, satisfy the requirements of international law to which Britain is subject?

9.2 THE SCOPE OF SEARCH AND SEIZURE POWERS IN ENGLAND

Search and seizure powers exercisable in public places, and those related to arrests and detention in police custody, have been examined in Chapter 5 above. Here, we look at other search powers: searches of premises under warrant, and searches which can be conducted without either a warrant or an arrest.

The basic principle is summed up in two well-known statements: that 'Everyone has the right to respect for his private and family life, his home and his correspondence',[10] and 'That the house of every one is to him as his castle and fortress, as well for his defence against injury and violence, as for his repose'.[11] That these are not unqualified rights is clear from the contexts of these two statements. The right to respect for privacy under Article 8 of the European Convention on Human Rights is subject to qualifications permitted by that Article. The common-law 'home as castle' doctrine was already, by 1604, subject to numerous limitations: it

[7] [1991] 2 WLR 1118 at 851, [1991] 1 All ER 845 at 851.
[8] *A.-G.* v. *Guardian Newspapers Ltd.* [1987] 1 WLR 1248, [1987] 3 All ER 316.
[9] [1992] 1 All ER 72 at 86.
[10] European Convention on Human Rights, Art. 8(1).
[11] *Semayne's case* (1604) 5 Co. Rep. 91*a* at 91*b*.

applied only to dwellings, not to outbuildings or business premises; it gave way to legal process in the name of the king, whether civil proceedings in the king's name or felonies in which the king was always deemed to have an interest; it prevented breaking in, but entry through an unbolted door was permitted in order to serve legal process or distrain for rent; and it applied only to outer doors, so that once on the premises lawfully an officer could force inner doors, cupboards, etc., if necessary.[12] In the seventeenth century, justices of the peace developed the practice of granting warrants to enter premises to search for stolen goods, and this received grudging judicial acceptance. At the same time, statutes began to provide powers of entry for public officials, with or without warrant, notably in respect of regulatory schemes for press licensing. This practice snowballed over the following 300 years, until now there are many entry and search powers for public officials of all kinds, in relation to health and safety, licensing, child care, the provision of public utilities, and for many other purposes.[13]

These powers have chipped away at the general principle of security for the home to a point where it is fair to say that protection for security and privacy depends on safeguards provided by law against *abuse* of the entry and search powers, rather than on any blanket prohibition on entry and search. This chapter examines these safeguards, and particularly those which operate in the field of criminal investigation, which have been substantially overhauled by the Police and Criminal Evidence Act 1984 (hereafter 'PACE') and the ponderously named *Code of Practice for the Searching of Premises by Police Officers and the Seizure of Property found by Police Officers on Persons or Premises* (Code B), a revised version of which was issued in 1991 under section 66 of PACE.

The safeguards are of three sorts. First, compliance with certain conditions justifies an entry or search, making it lawful. These include consent given by or on behalf of the occupier, the possession of a valid search warrant, or reasonable grounds for suspecting that a person who is to be arrested for an arrestable offence is in the premises. Secondly, there are legal principles governing the way in which entry to premises may be obtained. Thirdly, there are rules governing the way in which searches are to be conducted and the range of articles which may be seized.

These statutory safeguards relate to entries to and searches of premises. 'Premises' is a term of art, defined for the purposes of PACE (rather unhelpfully) by sections 23 and 118(1). It is said to include any place

---

[12] See David Feldman, *The Law Relating to Entry, Search and Seizure* (London: Butterworths, 1986), 7–11, 47–53.

[13] For a survey of the legal powers of entry, search and seizure enjoyed by these bodies, see R. T. H. Stone, *Entry, Search and Seizure: A Guide to Civil and Criminal Powers of Entry* 2nd edn. (London: Sweet & Maxwell, 1989).

(which the Act does not define), and the safeguards seem therefore to cover entry to gardens, farmyards, and the like, rather than merely (as one might have expected) to buildings. The wide meaning of 'place' is a way of extending the protection against abuse of power by the police: the effect of an area being a 'place' is that the police must comply with the rules under PACE and Code B when entering and searching it. In order to avoid any risk that the notion of 'any place' could be narrowed down by judicial interpretation, section 23 specifies that it includes any vehicle, vessel (which in turn includes any ship, boat, raft, or other apparatus constructed or adapted for floating on water),[14] aircraft, hovercraft, and off-shore installation[15] (such as an oil-drilling platform). Perhaps most significantly, it also includes any tent or movable structure. This means that the police must observe the safeguards of the Act, including the need to obtain consent or a warrant or have other statutory authority, before entering caravans. The Act thus protects the privacy interests of travellers, a group who are often on the receiving end of popular and police prejudice. The practical significance of this in ordinary cases is somewhat reduced, however, since we will see that in most cases where a constable enters through a gate he will be taking advantage of an implied permission from the occupier, and will not be relying on any power under PACE or other legislation to which the safeguards of PACE and the Code of Practice are attached. The safeguards for people whose premises are entered and searched are considered in the sections which follow.

9.3 CONDITIONS JUSTIFYING ENTRY AND SEARCH

(1) Consent[16]

Many entries to premises and searches are carried out by consent. Even since 1 January 1986, when the statutory police powers to enter and search premises after arresting someone came into effect,[17] it seems that around one-third of all post–arrest searches are still carried out with the consent of the occupier.[18] In an attempt to make it clear to householders that they are entitled to refuse, as well as to consent to, a search, Code B

[14] PACE, s. 118(1).
[15] As defined in the Mineral Workings (Offshore Installations) Act 1971, s. 1.
[16] Feldman, *Entry, Search and Seizure*, ch. 2; Ken Lidstone and Vaughan Bevan, *Search and Seizure Under the Police and Criminal Evidence Act 1984* (Sheffield: Univ. of Sheffield Faculty of Law, 1992), 44–8.
[17] PACE, ss. 18, 32. See Ch. 5, above.
[18] Vaughan Bevan and Ken Lidstone, *The Investigation of Crime: A Guide to Police Powers* (London: Butterworths, 1991), 112, 117; Lidstone and Bevan, *Search and Seizure*, tables 3.2, 3.3, pp. 45–6.

provides that, before seeking consent, the officer in charge must tell the occupier the purpose of the proposed search and inform him that he is not obliged to consent and that anything seized may be produced in evidence. If the person concerned is not at the time suspected of an offence, he must be told of that fact as well.[19] Where a search is conducted with the occupier's consent, that consent must be given in writing, if possible on the Notice of Powers and Rights which officers carry with them, before the search commences.[20] Finally, if the consent is given under duress, or is withdrawn during a search, the officer is not permitted to continue to search.[21]

That, at least, is the theoretical position. However, the reality may well be somewhat different. The elasticity of the notion of consent, and its unreality where people do not know that they have the right to refuse, was noted in Chapter 5 in relation to stop and search powers. The same applies with respect to consent to entry to premises and to searches of premises. Officers often obtain what passes for consent by bluff, relying on the occupiers' ignorance of their rights, unquestioning belief that the police have power to search if they want to, and an implication of guilt if access is refused. Indeed, if access is refused, less experienced officers may regard it as causing a loss of face, and may try to get round it by means of an unlawful search. Instead of seeking informed consent to a search, the officers try to obtain access civilly but informally, without giving occupiers the idea that they have a right to refuse.[22] This militates against compliance with the provisions of Code B on giving information and recording consents, and probably leads to a substantial under-recording of searches which do not rely on legal authority. Where the occupier is in custody, the consent, recorded on the custody record, is likely to be particularly artificial.

In any case, the information need not be given, nor consent recorded, before entry to the premises. It is the search, not the entry, which requires written consent. Any demand for written consent, or provision of information, before entry would be highly unrealistic. Moreover, the need for express consent to entry applies only in respect of houses. Anyone normally has an implied licence from the occupier to go through a garden gate and up a path to the door of a house in order to conduct legitimate business with the occupier, or to carry on the officer's lawful business on the driveway (for example, by inspecting a car which is suspected of having been involved in an accident).[23] This licence can be

---

[19] Code B, para. 4.2.   [20] Code B, para. 4.1.   [21] Code B, para. 4.2.
[22] David Dixon, Clive Coleman, and Keith Bottomley, 'Consent and the Legal Regulation of Policing' (1990) 17 *J. Law and Soc.* 345–62 at 352–3.
[23] *Robson* v. *Hallett* [1967] 2 QB 939, [1967] 2 All ER 407, D.C.; *Lambert* v. *Roberts* [1981] 2 All ER 15, CA; *Pamplin* v. *Fraser* [1981] RTR 494, DC; *Brunner* v. *Williams*

negated by clear words (for example, a notice on the gate expressly denying entry to hawkers or police officers), but otherwise takes effect. On
the other hand, at the outer door there is no implied consent to entry to
the house or flat, even if the door is open; nor is there any implied consent to entering any place to commit a crime.[24] In business premises during business hours, the implied licence normally goes further, permitting
a visitor with lawful business to enter the building, as one expects that
business visitors will be actively encouraged by the occupiers. (It would
be a poor shop proprietor who insisted on every potential shopper
obtaining individual consent to entry.) This implied licence carries over
to police officers and other authorized officials who have lawful business
on business premises, even if their business is not related to the
occupier's. However, outside business hours there is no implied consent
to people entering business premises, even if they have a legitimate reason for wanting to get in (as, for example, where a police officer sees a
door open at night, and enters in case a burglary is taking place).[25]

Where express consent to entry is needed, it may take a number of
forms. An invitation from the householder will, of course, be adequate,
but it seems that anyone with a right of occupation, including children if
of sufficient age and understanding, can invite people on to the premises,
although in the case of a consent by a child it would appear that the
responsible adult is entitled to withdraw or override the invitation.[26] It
seems, too, that any invitee may have authority to invite a visitor on to
the premises, although the invitation will normally be subject to revocation by the occupier unless the visitor has an independent right to remain
(for example, in order to stop a breach of the peace).[27] In the case of
hotels, hostels, student halls of residence, and lodging houses, where
people occupy rooms as licensees but do not have rights to exclude the
landlord from them, the guests or lodgers can normally invite people to
their rooms, but so can the landlord. People living in such accommoda
tion are therefore peculiarly vulnerable to invasion of their limited

[1975] Crim. LR 250, DC; *Morris* v. *Beardmore* [1981] AC 446, [1980] 2 All ER 753,
HL.

[24] *R.* v. *Lundry* (1981) 128 DLR (3rd) 726, Ontario CA; *R.* v. *Jones and Smith* [1976] 1
WLR 672, [1976] 3 All ER 54, CA. Cp. the position when executing legal process:
Southam v. *Smout* [1964] 1 QB 308, [1963] 3 All ER 104, CA, and Feldman, *Entry, Search
and Seizure*, pp. 49–51.

[25] *Great Central Railway* v. *Bates* [1921] 3 KB 578, DC.

[26] *R.* v. *Thornley* (1980) 72 Cr. App. R. 302; *Riley* v. *DPP* (1989) 91 Cr. App. R. 14,
DC. Other examples include *R.* v. *Collins* [1973] QB 100, [1972] 2 All ER 1105, CA;
Robson v. *Hallett* [1967] 2 QB 939, [1967] 2 All ER 407, DC; *Morris* v. *Beardmore* [1981]
AC 446, [1980] 2 All ER 753, HL.

[27] *McGowan* v. *Chief Constable of Kingston upon Hull* [1968] Crim. LR 34, DC; *Jones and
Jones* v. *Lloyd* [1981] Crim. LR 340, DC.

privacy, for instance by having their rooms searched by the police by virtue of a consent given by the landlord or the landlord's agent (for example, the warden of a hostel). This is recognized by Code B, which includes Note for Guidance 4A, advising that in lodging houses or similar accommodation a search should not be made solely on the basis of the landlord's consent unless the tenant is unavailable and the matter is urgent. Naturally, where the landlord refuses consent and the occupier is not present the police can enter only if they have some other authority, such as a search warrant.

Consent may also be given by conduct. Moving backwards from the door when a constable exaplains who he is and why he is there is likely to be interpreted as acquiescence by the police and the court.[28] However, one should be cautious about accepting that acquiescence implies consent. In many cases, the police avoid asking for consent, merely implying that they have a power to enter: asking for consent implies that people have a right to say no, and that would put the police at risk of a loss of face as well as some inconvenience.[29]

Consent to entry may be withdrawn by the person who gave it, unless the visitors have some independent authority for remaining, such as the need to prevent or stop a breach of the peace. Consent may also be withdrawn by anyone with express or implied authority from the occupier to do so, such as an office or shop manager, or (as in *McArdle* v. *Wallace (No. 2)*)[30] the adult son of a café owner, who asked a constable to leave when the latter was making inquiries about some goods which he thought might have been stolen. Where one cohabitant has issued an invitation, the other is not empowered to revoke it unilaterally while the visitors are engaged on the business for which they were invited in.[31] Clear words are needed in order to revoke a licence, particularly when the person on the premises is there on legitimate public business. It is a question of fact whether the revocation has been made suffiently unequivocally. Accordingly, it was held in *Snook* v. *Mannion*[32] to be legitimate for magistrates to decide that the words 'Fuck off!', which might signify mere abuse, were not a revocation of the licence.

Once the licence to enter or remain on premises has been withdrawn, the visitor must start to leave. He must be allowed a reasonable time in which to do so, but if he attempts to remain on the premises, or fails to leave after a reasonable period, he becomes a trespasser, and may be removed by the occupier, using reasonable force if necessary.[33] Use of

---

[28] *Faulkner* v. *Willetts* [1982] RTR 159, DC.   [29] Dixon *et al.*, 'Consent', 352–53.
[30] (1964) 108 Sol. Jo. 483, DC; see also *McArdle* v. *Wallace* [1964] Crim. LR 467, DC.
[31] *R.* v. *Thornley* (1980) 72 Cr. App. R. 302, CA.
[32] [1982] RTR 321, DC; see also *Gilham* v. *Breidenbach (Note)* [1982] RTR 328, DC.
[33] *Davis* v. *Lisle* [1936] 2 KB 434, [1936] 2 All ER 213, DC.

force against a constable is always dangerous, however. If the force is used too early, it will constitute a breach of the peace, justifying the constable and others in remaining or re-entering in order to quell it. Even if the constable has become a trespasser, developments which produce a reasonable apprehension of a breach of the peace will justify the constable in being there, so that he will once again be in the execution of his duty and will no longer be a trespasser.[34] Despite a suggestion to the contrary in an *obiter dictum* in *Kay* v. *Hibbert*,[35] the better view is that the police have no authority to remain on premises in order to complete inquiries once their licence has been withdrawn,[36] unless they are acting under some specific power independent of the original licence, for example in order to make an arrest for an arrestable offence, or to conduct a search under warrant.

(2) Warrants

Before the 1984 Act came into force, the availability of search warrants was haphazard. Search-warrant provisions, usually stipulating that an information for a warrant was to be laid before a justice of the peace, were often included in statutes creating or codifying criminal offences. Those under section 26 of the Theft Act 1968 and section 23(1) of the Misuse of Drugs Act 1971 were particularly widely used. However, no warrants were available for offences which were unregulated by statute. (The common-law warrant to search for stolen goods had long been superseded by statutory provisions.) It followed that warrants were available to search for evidence of illegal betting,[37] but not for evidence of murder.[38] This could be very frustrating for investigators, tempting them to commit unlawful acts in order to obtain evidence of grave offences.

This has been remedied by PACE. The statutory provisions authorizing the grant of search warrants in relation to specific statutory offences are retained, but section 8 of PACE creates a new power for a justice of the peace to grant a warrant to search for evidence of serious arrestable offences in certain circumstances, whether or not there is another specific statutory power to grant a search warrant for that particular offence.[39] The power is exercisable where the justice of the peace is satisfied that

---

[34] *Robson* v. *Hallett* [1967] 2 QB 939, [1967] 2 All ER 407, DC; *R.* v. *Lamb* [1990] Crim. LR 58, DC.

[35] [1977] Crim. LR 226, DC.

[36] *Davis* v. *Lisle* [1936] 2 K.B. 434, [1936] 2 All ER 213, DC.

[37] Betting, Gaming and Lotteries Act 1963, s. 51.

[38] *Ghani* v. *Jones* [1970] 1 QB 693, [1969] 3 All ER 1700, CA

[39] PACE, s. 8(5).

there are reasonable grounds for believing (not merely for suspecting) that each of five conditions is satisfied.[40] They are:

(a) that a serious arrestable offence has been committed;[41]

(b) that there is material, on specified premises, which is likely to be of substantial value (either alone or together with other material) to the investigation of the offence;

(c) that the material is likely to be relevant evidence;[42]

(d) that it does not consist of items subject to legal privilege, or excluded or special procedure material;[43] and

(e) that any one of four further conditions applies.

These four further conditions are:[44]

(i)   that it is not practicable to communicate with anyone entitled to grant access to the premises; or

(ii)   that it is not practicable to communicate with anyone entitled to grant access to the material; or

(iii) that entry to the premises will not be granted unless a warrant is produced; or

(iv) that the purpose of the search may be frustrated or seriously prejudiced if a constable cannot obtain immediate entry on arrival (for instance, because it is thought that the occupier might destroy the evidence unless taken by surprise).

There was, before PACE, no codified set of requirements to be satisfied before warrants could be granted. The matter was governed by a combination of common-law rules, mainly based on little-known cases of considerable antiquity, and statutory preconditions. It was, perhaps, not surprising that most justices of the peace (and, indeed, circuit judges) displayed little understanding of the responsibilities which they bore by law. One pre-PACE study found that magistrates normally issued warrants more or less automatically on request, without any real attempt to test the strength of the grounds for issuing them.[45]

Yet the role of the issuing justices was, and remains, central to the safeguards against the abuse of search-warrant procedures. They are administering an *ex parte* procedure in which the occupier of premises has no opportunity to be heard, and they bear a heavy responsibility for ensuring that warrants, which authorise a grave interference in people's private and

---

[40] PACE, s. 8(1).

[41] On the meaning of 'serious arrestable offence' see PACE, s. 116 and Sched. 6; s. 5.6(1)(iii), above.

[42] This means anything which might be admissible at trial: s. 8(4).

[43] On these categories, for which special provision is made, see below.

[44] PACE, s. 8(3).

[45] K. W. Lidstone, 'Magistrates, the Police and Search Warrants' [1984] Crim. LR 449.

family lives, are not issued without due cause. They have important legal duties in that regard, which include ensuring that the statutory preconditions to the grant of a warrant are satisfied, and that there are no reasons to exercise their discretion against granting one.[46] If this obligation is ducked in any case, the procedure will have failed to give that respect to the private life of the person whose premises are to be entered and searched which is required under Article 8(1) ECHR. The interference with private life will not be justifiable under Article 8(2), because the search, without any independent check on the grounds for it, is liable to be regarded as disproportionate to the legitimate purposes of the search in a democratic society (except, perhaps, where national security is at stake).[47]

This is not a sign of the oversensitivity of the European Convention to the rights of suspects. It is an indication of the significance of the issuing authority (magistrate or judge) as one of the crucial safeguards justifying a serious interference with people's rights. In non–Convention common-law countries, the courts understand this, and have been resolute in quashing warrants whenever there are indications that the issuing justice has had his or her independence undermined, misunderstood his or her role, or misconstrued the relevant legislation. In the United States, a magistrate may not be paid only when he issues warrants, as this gives a financial incentive to authorize searches.[48] A warrant issued without probable cause appearing from the applicant's affidavit, including the reasons for the applicant's belief in information given by others, is invalid.[49] Where the affidavit is verified by an inappropriate officer, it cannot be used as the foundation for an application, and a warrant granted on the strength of it is invalid.[50] The common-law position in Canada, New Zealand, Australia, and England and Wales, is similar.[51]

It follows that any failure to observe the due process requirements for dealing with applications for a warrant is not the fault of the law. It is,

---

[46] For detailed discussion of these responsibilities, see Feldman, *Entry, Search and Seizure*, pp. 72–91.

[47] See the discussion in s .3, above. [48] *Connally* v. *Georgia*, 429 US 245 (1977).

[49] *Grau* v. *US*, 287 US 124 (1932). [50] *Albrecht* v. *US*, 273 US 1 (1927).

[51] For Canada, see *Imperial Tobacco Sales Co.* v. *A-G for Alberta* [1941] 2 DLR 673; *R.* v. *Colvin, ex parte Merrick* [1970] 3 OR 612 (where, however, there was a statutory requirements for the grounds to be stated in the information); *Royal American Shows Inc.* v. *R., ex parte Hahn* [1975] 6 WWR 571; *Re Alder and R.* (1977) 37 CCC (2nd) 234. For New Zealand: *Mitchell* v. *New Plymouth Club (Inc.)* [1958] NZLR 1070. For Australia: *R.* v. *Tillett, ex parte Newton* (1969) 14 FLR 101; *George* v. *Rockett* (1990) 93 ALR 483, HC of Aust. For England and Wales: *Jones* v. *German* [1897] 1 QB 374, CA; *IRC* v. *Rossminster Ltd.* [1980] AC 952, HL (where, however, the majority did not regard failure on the part of the issuing judge to state in the warrant that he was satisfied as being sufficient evidence that he had misunderstood his role); *R.* v. *Guildhall Magistrates' Court, ex parte Primlaks* [1989] 1 WLR 841, DC.

instead, the result of lack of familiarity with the legal requirements, or failure to comprehend or apply them, on the part of the issuing magistrate or judge. This is exacerbated by an absence of training for judges and magistrates in their responsibilities with regard to warrants, and the difficulty of obtaining reliable evidence of what passed between the applicant and the magistrate or judge when the application was made. Only rarely will a reviewing court have available to it evidence that the issuing magistrate did not bother to look at the written information, calling it 'a load of garbage' which she 'didn't have to read', as in the Australian case of *R. v. Sing, ex parte Harrison*.[52]

Issuing authorities, therefore, need to be educated. There are provisions in PACE which seek to alert justices to their responsibilities, and to impress on police officers their duty of candour when applying for warrants. Section 15(2) requires the constable who applies for a warrant to state the grounds for the application and the enactment under which the warrant is sought, and to specify the premises which it is desired to enter and search and (so far as practicable) the articles or people to be sought. Section 15(3) requires the application to be supported by a written information, which, under Code B, paragraph 2.6, must state the enactment under which the application is made, the premises to be searched and the object of the search as specifically as is reasonably practicable, and the grounds on which the application is made. Where the object of the search is to find evidence of an offence, the written statement of grounds must include an indication of how the evidence relates to the investigation. Section 15(4) requires a constable applying for a warrant to answer on oath any questions which the justice of the peace or judge asks. The object of all this is to ensure that the issuing authority, as protector of the privacy and property of the occupier of premises, can thoroughly test the strength of the grounds for issuing a warrant. Note for Guidance 2A to Code B suggests that, where the application is based on information from an informant, the name of the informant need not be disclosed, but the constable should be ready to tell the justice or judge about the reliability of the source.

However, the observance of these requirements remains patchy, and depends as much on the administrative arrangements made by the clerk to the justices, or by senior police officers themselves, for checking on applications as on the performance of the justices themselves. Too often, justices are asked to grant warrants at night, at home, and without the opportunity for them to take advice. Most justices receive no training in recognising and discharging their responsibilities in relation to search warrants. Evidence suggests that warrants are still too readily granted

---

[52] (1979) 36 FLR 322.

without appropriate questioning of officers. The police often have a free choice as to the magistrate whom they approach, subject to any direction issued by the clerk to the justices. This perhaps makes it unsurprising that researchers from the University of Hull found that no officer whom they interviewed had had a warrant application refused.[53] This might mean that the police always prepare their warrant applications in an unexceptionable way. In a research study by Bevan and Lidstone of applications for warrants to search for stolen goods under the Theft Act 1968, following up a pre-PACE study, it was noted that in 61 per cent of the cases studied the only information given to the magistrate was that the application was made 'as a result of information received from a previously reliable source', or some variant on that formula. Magistrates rarely asked about this, because they believed (without asking) that the informants would have been at risk if their identities were revealed, which was sometimes but by no means always the case.[54]

Of course, it is very hard to test reliability objectively. As Bevan and Lidstone point out, the success of the search is only a crude indication. If nothing is seized, goods which were on the premises could have been removed; if articles are seized, they might not be the items which were originally sought. Dixon *et al.* found that of the searches under warrant for drugs which they examined, only 10 per cent resulted in drugs being seized, but searches very often resulted in the seizure of suspected stolen goods; overall, goods not covered by the warrant were seized in 47 per cent of searches under warrant.[55] There should be concern at the continued unwillingness of magistrates to press constables about the reliability of their information. Contrary to the intention of the legislation, it seems likely that the requirement in Code B, paragraph 2.4, that a senior officer must authorize the application for a warrant, is a more substantial protection for the privacy of an occupier of premises than is the application itself. The officer (usually an inspector) is likely to satisfy himself that the investigating officer complied with the other requirements of Code B: that he has taken reasonable steps to check that his information is accurate, recent, and has not been provided maliciously, that anonymous information is corroborated, and that reasonable inquiries have been made to find out about the nature and location of the articles sought, the nature of the premises, whether they have been searched recently, and what is known about the likely occupier.[56]

---

[53] Dixon *et al.*, 'PACE in practice' (1991) 141 NLJ 1586 at 1587. I know from anecdotal reports of two cases in which a magistrate has refused to issue warrants; the magistrate concerned has never again been approached for one.

[54] Bevan and Lidstone, *Investigation of Crime*, 99–100.

[55] Dixon *et al.*, 'PACE in practice', 1587.　　　　　　[56] Code B, paras. 2.1–2.3.

When the justice of the peace or judge has decided to issue the warrant, it is essential to draw the warrant accurately, so that the officers and occupiers know what they are entitled to do. It must specify the name of the applicant, the date on which it is issued, the enactment under which it is issued, the premises to be searched, and (so far as practicable) the articles or people to be sought.[57] It is the responsibility of the magistrate or judge to ensure that the warrant specifies the names of any people who are authorised to accompany the constable executing it.[58] If the form of the warrant is defective, the warrant may not protect the officers who execute it. If the procedure by which a warrant is obtained or the form of the warrant is defective, it will be liable to be quashed on an application for judicial review.

It is hard to monitor the grounds on which warrants are sought and granted. The written information ought to contain a reasonable amount of information, although not the details concerning reliability of sources, but the informations are not required to be kept or analysed. A search record is made, and the warrants are endorsed with the results of the search and returned to the issuing court,[59] but the warrant will not show the grounds on which it was issued. This makes it difficult to assess the effectiveness of review by the issuing magistrates, and we are heavily reliant on research of the type conducted by Bevan and Lidstone, referred to above. A provision requiring the informations for warrants and the records of searches to be collated, and statistical information included in the annual report of the chief officer of police for each area (such as is required in respect of searches of the person and road checks under Part I of PACE), would go some way towards monitoring the quality of the work of magistrates in this field.

In the mean time, one is left with an impression that justices of the peace do not provide the independent judicial scrutiny of proposed entries and searches under warrant which is needed to ensure that interferences with the right to respect for a person's private life and home are justified, as demanded by Article 8(2) of the European Convention on Human Rights. The formal trappings of scrutiny are there, but the substance is sadly lacking in most cases. The English courts have in the past sometimes been unwilling to exert an appropriate degree of control by way of judicial-review proceedings. For example, in *IRC* v. *Rossminster Ltd*[60] the House of Lords by a majority rejected an application for review of a warrant, issued by a circuit judge, which failed to state that the judge

[57] PACE, s. 15(6).
[58] See PACE, s. 16(2); *R.* v. *Reading Justices and others, ex parte South West Meats Ltd.*, [1992] Crim LR 672, DC.
[59] PACE, s. 16(9), (10), (11); Code B, paras. 7.1–7.3.
[60] [1980] AC 952, [1980] 1 All ER 80, HL.

had satisfied himself of the matters which were conditions precedent to the lawful grant of a warrant, making it seem that the judge had relied unquestioningly on the opinion of the person applying for the warrant. The majority held that this did not make the warrant invalid on its face, or provide convincing evidence that the judge had misunderstood or failed to fulfil his responsibilities. A similar attitude prevailed in *R. v. Billericay Justices and Dobbyn, ex parte Frank Harris (Coaches) Ltd.*,[61] where the court refused to assume that the magistrate had failed to consider relevant matters merely because the affidavits did not affirm that he had considered them. The judges felt that it was permissible to assume that the magistrate had considered the matters in question, because he was very experienced.

With respect, this makes a nonsense of the protective role of magistrates and the courts in relation to privacy and property rights. It means that magistrates or judges are effectively unchecked when issuing warrants, because courts will not take seriously a failure to show that the conditions for issuing the warrant have been complied with. This undermines the protective scheme put in place by Parliament when powers to grant search warrants are issued, and does nothing to force the magistrates or judges to comply with the rules laid down. Lord Salmon dissented in *Rossminster*, arguing that the warrant showed evidence of invalidity on its face, which was not contradicted by other evidence. It is submitted that his view is preferable, in that it upholds rule of law values, and is more in tune with common sense and with common-law developments elsewhere in the world where the draconian nature of the search warrant is recognized and the importance of safeguards is respected.[62]

There are signs that England's defective judicial attitude to warrants may indeed be changing. For example, in *R. v. Reading Justices and others, ex parte South West Meats Ltd.*[63] the Divisional Court granted *certiorari* to quash a search warrant which failed to specify the number of people who might enter premises with the constable who was to execute it, as well as awarding exemplary damages against the police and the Intervention Board for Agricultural Produce in respect of the manner of the search and seizure conducted under it. In another case, *Darbo v. Director of Public Prosecutions*,[64] the Divisional Court quashed the defendant's conviction on a charge of wilfully obstructing a constable in the execution of her duty. The constable was searching premises with a warrant issued under the

---

[61] [1991] Crim. LR 472, DC.

[62] See Feldman, *Entry, Search and Seizure*, pp. 132–6; *R. v. Tillett, ex parte Newton* (1969) 14 FLR 101; *George v. Rockett* (1990) 93 ALR 483, HC of Australia.

[63] [1992] Crim LR 672, DC.

[64] [1992] Crim. LR 56, DC; full text on Lexis *sub nom. Darbo v. Crown Prosecution Service*. See also *Ex parte Bradlaugh* (1878) 3 QBD 509.

Obscene Publications Act 1959. Section 3 of the Act permits a search for obscene articles, meaning things tending to deprave and corrupt people who are likely to come in contact with them. The magistrate had drawn the warrant as permitting search for 'books, magazines, films and video cassettes and photographs, and any other material of a sexually explicit nature'. The final six words were wider than the obscene articles for which search could lawfully be authorized under section 3. The Divisional Court held that this made the warrant *ultra vires*, despite the fact that it had been executed by experienced officers who knew what they were looking for. The presence of the police on the premises was therefore unlawful, and they were not in the execution of their duty when obstructed.

These cases provide a welcome reminder to justices of the peace, and those who seek and execute warrants, of their responsibilities to ensure that the statutory preconditions to the grant of a warrant are met, and that the warrant authorizes no more extensive an interference with rights of privacy and property than is necessary and permitted under the statute. It is to be hoped that the message will get through.

(3) Protecting confidences: exceptions from the search-warrant procedure

A group of further statutory provisions in PACE are designed to give additional protection to privacy interests against unjustified infringement. For the first time in England and Wales, it is provided by section 9 that no warrant may issue to permit search for items subject to legal privilege, a special class of confidential material defined in section 10, arising out of the relationship between lawyer and client. Much other confidential material, and material held for the purposes of journalism, is protected against warrants issued by magistrates, except in respect of certain material relevant to drug-trafficking offences. Access to the protected types of material may be obtained only by way of an application to a circuit judge, which will normally be *inter partes*. These provisions are examined elsewhere.[65] They protect specific privacy interests by insisting on a special procedure with particular access conditions, without making it impossible for investigators to get access to evidence.

(4) Arrests and other powers[66]

The police have power to enter premises to make an arrest under section 17 of PACE. The power applies where a constable has reasonable

---

[65] On confidential material generally, see Ch. 10. On journalistic material, see s. 13.4(3) below.

[66] Feldman, *Entry, Search and Seizure*, ch. 8; see also Ch. 5, above.

grounds for believing that the person whom he is seeking is in the premises. Where premises consist of a number of separate dwellings (such as a block of flats) the constable may enter any one dwelling only if there are reasonable grounds for believing that the person is in that dwelling unit.[67] The purposes for which entry may be made are restricted by section 17(1) to: (*a*) executing a warrant of arrest or commitment issued by a magistrates' court; (*b*) arresting a person for an arrestable offence; (*c*) arresting a person for one of a number of offences which are not arrestable offences under section 24 of PACE but are thought to be sufficiently serious to justify a power of entry;[68] (*d*) recapturing a person who is unlawfully and whom the constable is pursuing;[69] and saving life or limb,[70] or preventing serious damage to property. The search must be limited to the extent reasonably required for the purpose for which the entry was effected.[71]

9.4 ENTRY TO AND SEARCH OF PREMISES

(1) General considerations

Under PACE, there is for the first time a uniform set of procedures to be followed by constables who enter premises under statutory powers. Entries to and searches of premises, especially dwellings, are serious infringements of privacy and property rights, and place occupiers under considerable stress. Searches are therefore to be conducted with due consideration for property and privacy, causing no more disturbance than necessary, and using force only when this is necessitated by the occupier's lack of co-operation.[72] Searches are to be conducted at a reasonable hour from the occupier's point of view, unless this might frustrate the object of

---

[67] PACE, s. 17(2).

[68] Political uniforms (Public Order Act 1936, s. 1); entering and remaining on premises (Criminal Law Act 1977, ss. 6, 7, 8, or 10), restricted by PACE, s. 17(3) to constables in uniform only; engendering fear of, or provoking, violence (Public Order Act 1986, s. 4).

[69] See *D'Souza* v. *DPP* [1992] 1 WLR 1073, [1992] 4 All ER 545, HL.

[70] For a common-law power for any person to do this, see *Handcock* v. *Baker* (1800) 2 Bos. & P. 260. Defendants heard the screams of a woman being murdered by her husband, entered the house, and saved her. The husband sued for trespass. He argued (*inter alia*) that defendants should have left the woman to her legal remedies. Lord Eldon CJ at pp. 262–3 commented: 'a wife is only bound to apply to those remedies, where it is probable that the injury to be apprehended will be prevented by such application'. The common-law power has been abolished as it applies to constables: PACE, s. 17(5); but it survives for other people.

[71] PACE, s. 17(4).

[72] Code B, para. 5.10. For a study of police practice generally in relation to searches, see Lidstone and Bevan, *Search and Seizure*, chs. 4 and 6.

the search.[73] The occupier's consent to entry is to be sought, after explaining the authority under which the officer seeks entry, unless the premises are known to be unoccupied, or everyone entitled to grant access is known to be absent, or there are reasonable grounds for believing that alerting people in the premises would frustrate the objects of the search or endanger people.[74]

Once on the premises, a Notice of Powers and Rights must be given to the occupier, specifying the power under which the search is to be carried out and summarizing the extent of the statutory search power, explaining the rights of occupiers (including the right to compensation in appropriate cases), and stating that a copy of Code B may be consulted at any police station.[75] This notice should be given before the search begins, if practicable, unless the officer in charge believes that doing so would frustrate the objects of the search or endanger people. If the occupier is not present, a copy of the notice is to be left on the premises, endorsed with the name of the officer in charge, the name of his police station, and the date and time of the search.[76] Where the occupier is present, he or she must be allowed to ask a friend, neighbour, or other person (it might, for example, be a solicitor) to witness the search, unless the officer in charge has reasonable grounds for believing that this would seriously hinder the investigation.[77] It might do so, for example, if the third person is a suspect, or if it would frustrate the investigation to have to wait for the person to arrive. In any case, the search need not be delayed for an unreasonable period (judged in the light of the purposes and difficulties facing the searcher, as well as the position of the occupier) in order to give time for the person to arrive, so it will often not be practicable for a solicitor to reach the premises in time to witness the search. It is significant that there is no obligation on the officer to tell the occupier of the right to have a third person present.

No more than reasonable force may be used.[78] Searches may be carried no further than necessary to achieve the object of the search, and once the things specified in the warrant have been found, or the officer is satisfied that they are not on the premises, the search must end.[79] When the officer in charge leaves the premises, he must satisfy himself that they are secure,[80] a very important provision when force has been used against an outer door or window in order to gain entry.

---

[73] PACE, s. 16(4); Code B, para. 5.2 and Note for Guidance 5A.
[74] Code B, para. 5.4.   [75] Code B, para. 5.7.
[76] Code B, para. 5.8. In terrorism investigations, the officer should be identified by warrant number rather than by name.
[77] Code B, para. 5.11.   [78] PACE, s. 117.
[79] PACE, ss. 16(8), 17(4); Code B, para. 5.9.   [80] Code B, para. 5.12.

(2) Entry under warrant[81]

There are some special rules governing the execution of warrants, designed to ensure that an authorization to enter premises, invading property and privacy, is not abused by the searchers. Warrants must be executed within one month of issue, and may be used only once.[82] This sensible provision takes account of the fact that the factors which justified issuing the warrant may cease to apply later. A warrant may be executed by any constable,[83] and may authorize people who are not constables to accompany the constable.[84] This means that not everybody who enters will necessarily be subject to police discipline procedures, and may not know the scope of the powers under statute or even the purpose of the search. It makes a clear briefing by the officer in charge, to all who will be involved, in advance of the entry, particularly important. Allowing other people to enter may be useful: it permits the police to take experts, social workers, or customs officers, as appropriate. However, there is a risk of abuse. In particular, it became a common practice in some cases of suspected fraud to combine execution of search warrants by the police with execution of an *Anton Piller* order (whereby a court orders a defendant in civil proceedings to permit the plaintiff's solicitor to have access to premises and to seize evidence: see s. 9.6), allowing them to pool their powers. This has been disapproved by the courts,[85] even though it has been held by the European Court of Human Rights that it is not incompatible with Article 8 of the European Convention on Human Rights.[86] One of the purposes of requiring the police when executing a search warrant to provide the occupier with a Notice of Powers and Rights and a copy of the warrant is so that the occupier knows what is within the powers of the searching officers. If the search becomes entangled with the execution of an *Anton Piller* order, which confers different powers on searchers and different safeguards for the occupiers, there is likely to be confusion as to the powers of the various people on the premises, who has seized what, and what remedies the occupier has against whom.

Similarly, there are dangers in the police executing warrants in company with other public officials acting in pursuit of their own objects. In *R. v. Reading Justices and others, ex parte South West Meats Ltd.*,[87] the police executing a warrant were accompanied by officials of the Intervention

---

[81] Feldman, *Entry, Search and Seizure*, ch. 6.
[82] PACE, ss. 15(5), 16(3); Code B, paras. 5.1, 5.3. [83] PACE, s. 16(1).
[84] PACE, s. 16(2).
[85] *ITC Film Distributors Ltd.* v. *Video Exchange Ltd.* [1982] Ch. 431, [1982] 2 All ER 241; affirmed CA, *The Times*, 17 June 1982.
[86] *Chappell* v. *UK* Eur. Ct. HR, Series A, No. 152, (1989) 12 EHRR 1.
[87] [1992] Crim LR 672, DC.

Board for Agricultural Produce. The warrant should have been executed
by a constable, assisted by the officials of the Board, but instead the officials of the Board conducted the search, decided what should be seized,
and retained it, despite the fact that the seizure powers belonged to the
police and any items seized should have been retained by the police. This
was held to be a trespass involving an abuse of power sufficiently serious
to merit the award of exemplary damages of £22,000 on top of the compensatory damages of £3,000. It illustrates the risks of confusion and illegality which can arise where different groups of people, or officials, enter
simultaneously without being clear about who is entitled to do what. It
also shows the substantial damages which can result. In each case, the
magistrate issuing the warrant must specify, in the warrant, the number of
extra people who are permitted to enter. It is oppressive to leave the
occupiers open to having their premises invaded by a group of people of
unspecified number and identity, at the discretion of the police officer
concerned.[88]

   Where the occupier is present, the officer seeking to execute the warrant must identify himself, producing documentary evidence of identity if
he is not in uniform. He must also produce the warrant, which must
therefore be in his possession at the time of entry.[89] On the natural reading of section 16(5) of PACE, which speaks of 'the time at which a constable seeks to execute a warrant to enter and search', it might appear that
this ought to be done before entry, but such a requirement would often
frustrate the purpose of the search. It might give time for drugs to be
flushed down a toilet, or for violent suspects to prepare and arm themselves. Accordingly, the Court of Appeal held in R. v. Longman[90] that if
necessary the officer may obtain entry by a trick, complying with the
statutory requirements once in the premises. This might give rise to some
concern on two counts. First, it could appear to do violence to the words
of the statute. This may be overstated. The subsection is providing for
obligations on officers when the occupier is present at the time when the
warrant is executed. It does not actually say when the obligations have to
be discharged, although there is an implication that the subsection must
be complied with sooner rather than later. On this reading, the Court of
Appeal's interpretation was correct. Even if one disagrees about the literal
interpretation, the court was doing its best to adopt a construction of the
subsection which is workable, and the fault—if there is any—would
properly lie with Parliament for approving language which would seem
to impose an obligation on officers which tends to undermine the purpose of the warrant. Secondly, it might seem to be inappropriate in prin-

[88] R. v. Reading Justices and others, ex parte South West Meats Ltd., [1992] Crim LR 672,
DC.
[89] PACE, s. 16(5).   [90] [1988] 1 WLR 619.

ciple for a court to be seen to encourage officers to gain entry to premises by a trick. People should know, when asked to consent to entry, whether they are letting in a constable, a gas official, or a burglar. However, as a matter of law, once the door is open there is authority for the proposition that a constable may enter to execute a warrant without further formalities.[91] At least part of the rationale for the formalities laid down in the statute is to prevent the unnecessary breaking of outer doors and other violence. Where the occupier is thought to be violent or likely to destroy evidence, it would seem to be good police practice to gain access with as little force as possible. While tricks should not be encouraged too widely, neither should they be too readily condemned.

Once officers are on the premises under the authority of a warrant, they have the obligations mentioned above with regard to the Notice of Powers and Rights. In addition, they must give a copy of the warrant to the occupier (if practicable, before the search begins, unless this would frustrate the object of the search or endanger people), or leave a copy on the premises if they are unoccupied. The copy of the warrant should be endorsed in the same way as the Notice of Powers and Rights.[92] The idea is that the occupier should be able to satisfy himself that the people on the premises are acting lawfully, and take advantage of the rights which the Act and Code B offer to ensure that the subsequent search is conducted properly and that the occupiers know what remedies are available to them afterwards.

It was noted above that warrants may never be issued authorizing searches for items subject to legal privilege, and that certain items which are held in confidence or for the purposes of journalism ('special procedure material' or 'excluded material') are also excepted from the normal search-warrant jurisdiction. The treatment of items subject to legal privilege and items held in confidence is considered in Chapter 10, and journalistic material in Chapter 13, below. There are some circumstances in which a circuit judge may issue a search warrant in respect of material which falls into the categories of special procedure material or excluded material, and there are special rules about the execution of those materials which are considered in Chapter 10.

---

[91] *Southam v. Smout* [1964] 1 QB 308, [1963] 3 All ER. 104, a case concerning entry on civil process; *Re Agnes Securities and R.* (1976) 70 DLR (3d) 504.
[92] Code B, para. 5.8.

9.5 SEARCH AND SEIZURE

(1) General principles

One of the curious features of the elaborate structure of protection for rights of property and privacy is the laxity of the controls over seizures by the police. This is unlike the basic principle in the U.S.A. and Canada, where the starting-point is that searches and seizures are infringements of rights to privacy. As such, they must be properly authorized, and any search without prior authorization in the form of a warrant, from a magistrate or judge independent of the investigation, is regarded as *prima facie* unreasonable and unconstitutional.[93] This is subject to exceptions, established by the courts; an American commentator has described these as growing so rapidly that they threaten to become the rule,[94] but one still starts from the position that it is for the police or legislature to justify carrying out or authorizing a warrantless search. In England and Wales, by contrast, there is nothing in law to stop the legislature from launching unchecked incursions on the right to privacy.

In the course of searching premises, the police may seize anything for which they were authorized to search, and certain other items as well.[95] As noted in Chapter 5, when searching premises following an arrest under section 18 or 32 of PACE, the police can seize evidence of certain offences besides that for which the arrest was made. When the police are searching under warrant, they are entitled to seize anything authorized by the statute under which the warrant was issued. In addition, under section 19 any constable lawfully on premises (whether by the consent of an occupier, or under warrant or other statutory authority) may seize anything which he innocently comes across (other than items which the constable has reasonable grounds to believe are subject to legal privilege), in relation to which two conditions are satisfied. These are an *evidential* condition and a *necessity* condition.

(i) *The evidential condition.* There should be reasonable grounds to believe that the item either is evidence in relation to some offence (not necessarily that which the constable entered to investigate), or has been obtained in consequence of the commission of an offence, whether or not the per-

---

[93] *Coolidge* v. *New Hampshire*, 403 US 443 (1971); *Katz* v. *US* 389 US 347 (1967) at 357, US Supreme Court; *Hunter* v. *Southam Inc.* (1984) 11 DLR (4th) 641, SC of Canada; *Kokesch* v. *R.* (1990) 1 CR (4th) 62, SC of Canada.

[94] Louis Fisher, *American Constitutional Law* (New York: McGraw-Hill, 1990), 866.

[95] Feldman, *Entry, Search and Seizure*, pp. 192–7; Bevan and Lidstone, *Investigation of Crime*, pp. 130–4; Zander, *The Police and Criminal Evidence Act 1984*, pp. 44–6.

son in possession of it is suspected of the offence.[96] The only real limitation which structures the officer's discretion under the evidential requirement is the criterion of reasonable grounds for the belief. It is potentially a significant restraint on abuse of power, as it allows the law of tort to step in: an indiscriminate seizure will be tortious, as the police will lose their statutory justification for interfering with goods. To satisfy the reasonable-grounds standard, every item must be examined in order to decide whether it is necessary to seize it. Where large quantities of material are being looked at, this may be inconvenient for all concerned, but it is clear that seizing any document without checking first to see whether it is subject to seizure will be an unlawful interference with goods, and substantial damages (including, if appropriate, exemplary damages for abuse of power by a public authority) will be recoverable. In *Reynolds* v. *Metropolitan Police Commissioner*,[97] police officers investigating a suspected insurance fraud had taken large quantities of documents and had sorted them later, returning some and retaining others. In an action for trespass to goods, the jury found for the defendant police officers. The Court of Appeal allowed an appeal by the plaintiff, because the jury had not been asked to decide whether, in relation to each file, book, bundle, or separate document, the officer had reasonable cause to believe that it, or part of it, was of evidential value. If he had not, the seizure was unjustified and tortious. This important principle remains unaltered by PACE.

Generally, however, the evidential requirement is a relatively weak condition, which serves only to ensure that the seizure serves a public interest in the administration of criminal justice. Where that public interest can be invoked, the evidential requirement does not provide any limit on interference with property and privacy rights. For example, under section 19 the police constable may seize any evidential item which he does not have reasonable grounds for believing to be subject to legal privilege.[98] This means that confidential or journalistic material, falling within the categories of special procedure or journalistic material and thus outside the normal search-warrant jurisdiction, may be seized during a search under warrant, despite the fact that no warrant could have issued to search for it. For any substantial limitation, we rely on the necessity condition.

(ii) *The necessity condition.* There should be reasonable grounds to believe that it is necessary to seize the item in order to prevent its concealment, loss, or destruction.[99] This is meant to limit the power to seize items without a warrant, or outside the scope of a warrant, where seizure is not

---

[96] PACE, s. 19(2)(*a*), (3)(*a*).
[98] See s. 19(2), (3), (6).

[97] [1985] QB 881, [1984] 3 All ER 649, CA.
[99] PACE, s. 19(2)(b), (3)(*b*).

actually necessary. In practice, it means that seizure is likely to be lawful only where the person in possession is suspected of being implicated in the offence, or is connected to a suspect, or where the police need to copy or carry out tests on the item. The limitation is particularly important in view of the fact that special-procedure material and excluded material, for which it might well have been impossible to obtain a search warrant, is not privileged from seizure under section 19. The concern shown to prevent searches for confidential items being authorized by a magistrate, who is, in theory at least, independent of the police investigation, does not extend to preventing their seizure by the police on the spur of the moment without any independent authorization or check. The privacy interest in such material is required to be respected under Article 8 of the European Convention on Human Rights. Interference is justified only if it complies with the conditions in Article 8(2), one of which is that interference is necessary (in a democratic society) for the purpose of the prevention of crime (including the detection of crime). Strict compliance with the necessity condition is therefore essential if privacy interests are to be adequately protected in accordance with the Convention.

The constable may photograph or copy anything which he is empowered to seize.[100] This should make it possible to leave most business records in place, minimizing the risk that a search and seizure will bring a business crashing down. That this can happen when massive seizures take place is shown by the aftermath of the *Rossminster* case: vast amounts of client and business information were seized, with the effect that the company was unable to continue trading. After the House of Lords had refused to quash the warrant or order the Inland Revenue officers to return the material, the company which was being investigated was unable to continue in business, despite the fact that no criminal proceedings were ever brought for the alleged tax fraud in relation to which the warrants had been granted. A seizure of business documents may be a quick and relatively easy way of driving a person or company out of business without the need to establish that he or it is guilty of any criminal offence. Copying of evidence will almost always be preferable.

The police may also demand access to information, including confidential information, which is held in or is accessible from a computer on the premises, if the material is covered by the warrant or other statutory authority or the conditions under section 19 are satisfied.[101] The constable can require the information to be produced in a form in which it is visible and legible and in which it can be taken away, so a print-out may be necessary.

[100] PACE, s. 20(5).   [101] PACE, ss. 19(4), 20(1).

(2) Trespassing constables

The above powers apply where the constable is lawfully on premises. (Constables who have had consent to their presence withdrawn and are in the process of leaving when they see the evidence are still lawfully on the premises, unless they have taken an unreasonable time to depart: see s. 9.3(1), above.) It might be thought that the statutory provision of seizure powers in section 19 for a constable who is lawfully on premises impliedly precludes any seizure powers for a constable who is trespassing. Such a view might draw strength from the maxim *expressio unius, exclusio alterius*: if a power is expressed to be applicable in one situation, it can be implied that it is unavailable in others. Such a conclusion would draw support from other considerations, such as the natural desire not to encourage the police to enter premises without authority.

However, this is not necessarily correct. If an officer is trespassing, but on property in which the complainant has no property or privacy interest, the officer may still be in the execution of his duty. For example, it is arguable that a suspect who hops over a hedge into somebody else's premises in order to evade detection or arrest should not be allowed to protest that the constable who follows is acting outside his duty *vis-à-vis* him, even though an action for trespass might lie at the suit of the owner or occupier of the premises. This view has been adopted by the High Court of Australia,[102] and in the USA it has been held that a person other than the occupier has no standing to assert privacy interests under the Fourth or Fourteenth Amendments against a trespassing constable.[103]

At common law in England and Wales before PACE, there was power to seize evidence of grave offences, and it did not depend on the officer being lawfully on the premises at the time.[104] It is at least possible that, where the constable is not lawfully on premises, the common-law power of seizure survives, by virtue of section 19(5) of PACE: 'The powers conferred by this section are in addition to any power otherwise conferred.' If this reference to a 'power otherwise conferred' is interpreted as including powers conferred by common law, as well as those conferred by statute, we need to look at the scope of the common-law powers of trespassing constables. There may be public-interest grounds for allowing the police to seize evidence of grave crimes even when trespassing, and the seizure might be justified even if the police presence on the premises is unlawful. It has to be accepted, however, that this would make it very difficult to decide whether a person who interferes with a trespassing

[102] *Halliday v. Nevill* (1984) 155 CLR 1, by a majority, Brennan J. dissenting.
[103] *Brown v. US*, 411 US 223 (1973).
[104] *Ghani v. Jones* [1970] 1 QB 693, [1969] 3 All ER 1700, CA; Feldman, *Entry, Search and Seizure*, 260–8.

constable, who is attempting to secure evidence of a grave crime, is obstructing the constable in the execution of his duty, committing an offence under section 51 of the Police Act 1964, as normally a trespassing constable is not in the execution of his duty.[105]

The common-law power, as explained by Lord Denning M.R. in *Ghani* v. *Jones*,[106] was limited to cases where the police have reasonable grounds for believing: (i) that a serious crime has been committed; (ii) that the item to be seized is either the fruits of the crime, or the instrument with which it was committed, or is material evidence; (iii) that the person in possession has committed or is implicated in the crime, or his refusal to surrender the item is quite unreasonable.[107] There had been a suggestion in a previous decision that a search without reasonable grounds might be justified after the event by the finding of evidence of sedition, because of the public interest in obtaining such evidence.[108] This was unsatisfactory, and was disapproved in *Ghani* v. *Jones*. Making the legality of police behaviour depend on events occurring after the search would have prevented occupiers from establishing their legal rights with reasonable certainty, breaching the requirement in the European Convention on Human Rights, Article 8(2), that any interference with the right to respect for privacy, the home, and family life should be in accordance with law.[109]

After seizure under the common-law power, the police were not to keep the item, or prevent its removal by the person in possession, for longer than necessary, using a copy if practicable, and (in keeping with the European Convention) the lawfulness of the conduct is to be judged by the circumstances at the time, not by what happens afterwards.[110] As noted above, nothing in PACE limits or abolishes any common-law power of seizure which may exist when a constable is trespassing; indeed, it appears to preserve it expressly, unless a reference to a 'power conferred' is held to mean only powers conferred by statute.[111]

This was a novel and controversial extension by judges of the seizure powers of trespassing constables. It cannot be regarded as a proper exercise of the judicial power. In a democratic society, judges ought not to

---

[105] For full discussion, see Feldman, *Entry, Search and Seizure*, 409–16.

[106] [1970] 1 QB 693, [1969] 3 All ER 1700, CA.

[107] This was an afterthought, and is of questionable authority. See R. M. Jackson, [1970] CLJ 1; *McLorie* v. *Oxford* [1982] QB 1290, [1982] 3 All ER 480, DC.

[108] *Elias* v. *Pasmore* [1934] 2 KB 164.

[109] For explanation of the implications of this term, see Ch. 8 above.

[110] *Ghani* v. *Jones* [1970] 1 QB 693 at pp. 708–09, [1969] 3 All ER 1700 at pp. 1704–5 *per* Lord Denning MR.

[111] PACE, s. 19(5): 'The powers conferred by this section are in addition to any power otherwise conferred.' It would be tempting, but unconvincing, to interpret 'otherwise conferred' as meaning 'conferred by any other statutory provision'.

legislate in order to extend the power of state officials at the expense of citizens' rights. Despite criticisms such as this, the extended powers have been applied in a number of cases in England and New South Wales.[112] On the other hand, they have been roundly rejected by the New Zealand Court of Appeal, which accepted that the previous, more restricted, common-law powers might need to be reformed, but decided that it was the job of the legislature, not the courts, to restrict individual rights and codify police powers if necessary.[113] In Canada, the courts, assisted by the enactment of the Charter of Rights and Freedoms, have developed an exclusionary rule for unreasonable (including most trespassory) searches.[114] This is a more rights-based approach, treating rights as entitled to protection by the courts. In the same way, the U.S. Supreme Court, interpreting the Fourth Amendment to the Constitution, has developed a mandatory exclusionary rule to prevent the police from using as evidence anything seized in the course of an unconstitutional search,[115] although during the 1970s and 1980s the Court, dominated increasingly by conservatives, has developed exceptions to the exclusionary rule. Even in England, the Royal Commission on Criminal Procedure recommended in 1981 that items seized during a search under warrant, but in excess of the authority conferred by the warrant, should not be admissible in evidence, although they rejected any more extensive exclusionary rule for illegally obtained evidence.[116] It is unfortunate that our Parliament made no provision in PACE to cover the problem of the trespassing constable, throwing us back on unsatisfactory common-law principles.

(3) Retention of items seized

When items have been lawfully seized for the purposes of a criminal investigation, the police may retain them for use as evidence at trial, for forensic examination, for investigation in connection with an offence, or (where there are reasonable grounds for believing that it has been obtained in consequence of an offence) to establish the lawful owner.[117] If seized by an officer lawfully on premises, under section 19 or (in relation to computerized records) section 20 of PACE, the retention powers

---

[112] *R. v. Hinde* (1977) 64 Cr. App. R. 213, CA; *Frank Truman Export Ltd.* v. *Metropolitan Police Commissioner* [1977] QB 952, [1977] 3 All ER 431; *Malone* v. *Metropolitan Police Commissioner* [1980] QB 49, [1979] 1 All ER 256, CA; *GH Photography* v. *McGarrigle* [1974] 2 NSWLR 635.

[113] *McFarlane* v. *Sharpe* [1972] NZLR 838, CA of NZ.

[114] e.g. *Kokesch* v. *R.* (1990) 1 CR (4th) 62, SC of Canada.

[115] *Weeks* v. *US* 232 US 383 (1914); *Mapp* v. *Ohio* 367 US 643 (1961).

[116] RCCP, *Report*, para. 3.49.   [117] PACE, s. 22(2).

are wider: such material may be retained for as long as is necessary in all the circumstances.[118] This has serious implications for the people from whom the material is seized. If they are not implicated in the offence, their control over the items is restricted in the public interest; the seizure may interfere with their lawful business activities and cost them a great deal of money. If the items are seized from a suspect who is subsequently charged, police control of the items may make it difficult to prepare the defence adequately. In either case, there is a risk that the police may make the items available to other people who derive an illegitimate advantage from seeing them, whether business competitors, litigants in civil proceedings against the person from whom the items were seized, or investigators in other jurisdictions who could not otherwise have obtained access to the material.[119] For all these reasons, it is important that there should be safeguards on the use which may be made of the material while in police custody.

The first safeguard for people from whom material is seized is that the police must, on request within a reasonable time, provide a list or description of the material to the person from whom it was seized.[120] This does not go as far as the Royal Commission on Criminal Procedure, which recommended that there should be a duty to give a receipt for all items on seizure.[121] Secondly, the person, or his representative, must be allowed supervised access to it, to examine it or have it photographed or copied, unless the officer in charge of an investigation has reasonable grounds for believing that this would prejudice the investigation of an offence or any criminal proceedings.[122] Refusal to allow access may be challenged by an application for judicial review.[123] Thirdly, the police hold property under section 22 of PACE only for the purposes authorized. There is no power to apply it to any other purpose without either the consent of the owner or person from whom it was seized, whose property it remains, or some other legal authority. They owe a duty to maintain the confidentiality of materials which they have seized, subject only to their power to use them for police purposes; however, this duty may be overridden by a countervailing public interest. The clearest example is where a court orders the police to produce material, which is

[118] PACE, s. 20(1).

[119] The last category is now largely covered by statute, since the Criminal Justice (International Co-operation) Act 1990, s. 7, provides for warrants to be issued to search for and seize evidence of offences committed in other jurisdictions following a direction of the Secretary of State at the request of foreign authorities, and for any evidence found to be transmitted to the foreign authorities.

[120] Code B, para. 6.8.   [121] RCCP, *Report*, para. 3.47.

[122] Code B, para. 6.9.; the position is the same as at common law, on which see *Arias* v. *Metropolitan Police Commissioner*, *The Times*, 1 Aug. 1984, CA.

[123] *Allen* v. *Chief Constable of Cheshire*, *The Times*, 16 July 1988, CA.

admissible in evidence in other proceedings, under a *subpoena duces tecum*, but there are other possible exceptions, such as passing information about suspected child abuse to the social services.[124]

9.6 CIVIL ENTRY AND SEARCH: ANTON PILLER ORDERS

Besides entry and search in criminal matters, there is a special type of order which requires a party to civil proceedings to give access to his premises to another party, in order that the latter can seek evidence. This is known as an *Anton Piller* order, after the first case of its type to reach the Court of Appeal.[125] The order is a form of coerced discovery, originally used only in exceptional and emergency cases where there was a serious risk that a conventional order for discovery would be ineffective, because the party subject to it would destroy or hide evidence and thwart the other party's chances of success in the litigation.[126] The making of an order therefore reflects on the honesty of the party against whom it is made. It is a draconian step, equivalent in many ways to a civil search warrant,[127] to be employed only where absolutely necessary and clearly justified. Moreover, as the essence of such an order is surprise, it is crucial that the person on whom the order is served should have no warning, and so the application is *ex parte*, imposing a heavy responsibility on the party applying to put all relevant information before the court. At the same time, it is important that all rights should be adequately protected in the execution of the order: it is *prima facie* a contempt of court to refuse access to premises or material when access is demanded in reliance on an *Anton Piller* order, so the consequences for the person subject to the order are potentially very serious.

In *Anton Piller KG* v. *Manufacturing Processes Ltd.*[128] Ormrod LJ specified three conditions for the grant of an order, and Lord Denning MR added a fourth. The conditions were: (i) that the applicant must show an extremely strong prima facie case, making it very likely that he will succeed at trial; (ii) that the actual or potential damage to the applicant must be very serious; (iii) that there is clear evidence that the defendants have in their possession incriminating documents or things, and that there is a

[124] *Marcel* v. *Commissioner of Police of the Metropolis* [1992] 1 All ER 72, CA, especially *per* Nolan LJ and Sir Christopher Slade at pp. 85, 89.

[125] *Anton Piller KG* v. *Manufacturing Processes Ltd.* [1976] Ch. 55, [1976] 1 All ER 779, CA.

[126] *EMI* v. *Pandit* [1975] 1 WLR 302, [1975] 1 All ER 418.

[127] Martin Dockray, 'Liberty to Rummage: A Search Warrant in Civil Proceedings?' [1977] *PL* 369–88; Anne Staines, 'Protection of Intellectual Property Rights: *Anton Piller* Orders' (1983) 46 *MLR* 274–88.

[128] [1976] Ch. 55, [1976] 1 All ER 779, CA.

real possibility that they may destroy that material before an inter partes application could be made; and (iv) that the inspection under the order will do no real harm to the defendant or his case.

However, as time went on it became clear that orders were being granted more or less as a matter of course, without adequate supporting information or consideration of the issues, and that orders were being executed by solicitors for the plaintiff without proper regard for the need to safeguard the rights of the defendant. After one case, in which the plaintiffs obtained an order in respect of pirated films, knowing that the police intended to execute a warrant to search for obscene material at the same time but without telling the judge that this was so, the defendant applied to the European Commission of Human Rights, arguing that the grant of the order and the manner of its execution infringed Article 8 of the European Convention on Human Rights. The Commission declared the application to be admissible, but in due course the Court decided that the infringement of the defendant's privacy rights had been justifiable under Article 8(2).[129] This did nothing to allay the deep concern which developments were causing both to some judges[130] and to practitioners and academics.[131]

This concern led to a wide-ranging review of the procedures for executing *Anton Piller* orders in the course of a judgment by Sir Donald Nicholls VC in *Universal Thermosensors Ltd.* v. *Hibben.*[132] First, orders are to be executed during office hours on working days, so that the defendant can quickly obtain legal advice before the plaintiff's representatives begin to search. Secondly, where the order is to be executed at a private house and it is at all likely that a woman will be there alone, the solicitor serving the order must be a woman, or be accompanied by one. Thirdly, unless it is seriously impracticable, a detailed list of items to be seized must be prepared at the premises before any items are removed, and the defendant must be given an opportunity to check it. Fourthly, injunctions restraining people from informing anyone other than a lawyer about the order must not last too long. A week, as in that case, was far too long. Fifthly, orders must provide that they are not to be executed at

---

[129] *ITC Film Distributors* v. *Video Exchange Ltd.* [1982] Ch. 431, [1982] 2 All ER 241, affirmed CA. *The Times*, 17 June 1982; *Chappell* v. *UK* (10461/83), Eur. Ct. HR, Series A, No. 152, 12 EHRR 1.

[130] *Columbia Pictures Ltd.* v. *Robinson* [1987] Ch. 38, [1986] 3 All ER 338 at pp. 365–71, 375–80 *per* Scott J.; *Lock International plc* v. *Beswick* [1989] 1 WLR 1268, [1989] 3 All ER 373 (Hoffmann J.).

[131] Martin Dockray and Hugh Laddie, 'Piller Problems' (1990) 106 *LQR* 601–20. Hugh Laddie QC was counsel who, in effect, invented the orders, representing the plaintiffs in the first cases; Professor Dockray has been one of the foremost academic commentators on them.

[132] [1992] NLJ Rep. 195.

business premises save in the presence of a representative of the company or trader in question, unless there is good reason for doing otherwise. Sixthly, it must not be possible for directors or employees of a plaintiff company to search the files of the defendant company if the two companies are business competitors. Finally, the court must consider ordering the plaintiff to instruct, and pay for, an independent solicitor with experience of *Anton Piller* orders to supervise the execution of the order, and to prepare a written report on what takes place. This is to be served on the defendant. The plaintiff should in any case be required to return to court within a few days for an inter partes hearing. As Sir Donald Nicholls said:

> . . . in suitable and strictly limited cases, Anton Piller orders furnish courts with a valuable aid in their efforts to do justice between two parties. Especially is this so in blatant cases of fraud. It is important therefore that these orders should not be allowed to fall into disrepute. If further steps are necessary to prevent this happening, they should be taken. If plaintiffs wish to take advantage of this truly Draconian type of order, they must be prepared to pay for the safeguards which experience has shown to be necessary if the interests of defendants are fairly to be protected.

9.7 SOME CONCLUDING QUESTIONS

There is a developing and welcome recognition that the public interest in the detection of crime and the administration of the civil justice process does not justify wholesale and uncontrolled interference with individual rights. So far, this has been most obvious in decisions of judges in relation to civil proceedings. It is noticeable that Parliament failed in PACE to provide the safeguards for those whose premises are searched in the course of criminal proceedings which the courts have developed in relation to somewhat analogous *Anton Piller* orders. In other jurisdictions, as noted above, entry to premises without prior judicial authorization is presumptively unreasonable and unlawful. If in civil proceedings it is important for entries to be authorized by a judicial personage, why is the same not true of searches in criminal matters? Why is there no demand for an independent watchdog to be present at searches, and for full lists of items seized to be drawn up on the spot whenever possible, in criminal matters?

Here we allow police officers to enter premises, under sections 18 and 32 of PACE, without judicial authorization. The police can also use the occupier's consent to avoid legal limits on their powers of entry.[133] We have no requirement for a judicial hearing inter partes after the execution

---

[133] See Lidstone and Bevan, *Search and Seizure*, 44–7, 157–60.

of every search warrant, to check the legality of what took place; instead, the aggrieved party is left to pursue remedies by way of judicial review. We make no provision for a person to take legal advice before a warrant is executed. Does the criminal process really involve a balance of interests so different from that in civil cases, where serious fraud of one sort or another is suspected, that it justifies allowing police officers to conduct searches with an almost total absence of the safeguards which would be imposed on civil litigants? It might be argued that a party to civil litigation is likely to be particularly partisan, so that the risk of unfairness and flouting of rights is greater in civil than in criminal matters. Yet it seems improbable that the police are generally non-adversarial in their attitudes, at least when dealing with suspects, however much we might wish that it were otherwise. If civil liberties and human rights deserve protection against overzealous parties and their solicitors, how much more do they need to be protected against overzealous officials of the state.

10

PROTECTING CONFIDENCES

Although it may be misleading to regard the protection of personal information as central to the idea of privacy (see section 8.5 above), protecting such information undoubtedly has an important role to play in maintaining the conditions necessary for private life. This chapter examines the treatment of confidential information in English law, principally in the context of protection for personal information, as an aspect of rights to respect for privacy. 'Personal information' has been defined by Professor Wacks as consisting of 'those facts, communications, or opinions which relate to the individual and which it would be reasonable to expect him to regard as intimate or sensitive and therefore to want to withhold or at least to restrict their collection, use, or circulation'.[1] The advantage of speaking of personal information rather than privacy, according to Wacks, is that it enables one to avoid dependence on the problematic notion of privacy, which, he suggests, is largely parasitic on other legal categories such as property and confidentiality. However, Article 8 of the European Convention on Human Rights, while not expressly mentioning personal information, guarantees respect for much of it as an aspect of a person's private and family life, home, and correspondence. English law falls to be evaluated in the light of these privacy-related standards, which therefore cannot be abandoned.

The present chapter looks at the limits imposed on the confidentiality element in privacy rights in English law by the need to further public interests, and particularly the interest in the prevention and detection of crime. It will often be useful to refer to the standards of the European Convention on Human Rights as a basis for evaluating the balance struck by national law. Article 8(2) of the European Convention on Human Rights provides that the exercise of the right to respect for a person's private and family life, home, and correspondence, may be subjected only to such interference 'as is in accordance with the law and is necessary in a democratic society in the interests of national security, public safety or the economic well-being of the country, for the prevention of disorder or crime, for the protection of health or morals, or for the protection of the rights and freedoms of others'. In the context of protecting confidential

[1] Raymond Wacks, *Personal Information: Privacy and the Law* (Oxford: Clarendon Press, 1989), 26.

information against publication, the right to respect guaranteed under Article 8 of the European Convention on Human Rights comes into conflict with the right to free expression and communication of information and ideas guaranteed under Article 10 of the same Convention. Neither right is unqualified. The circumstances under which it is legitimate to interfere with the right to freedom of expression are examined generally in Chapter 12 and with particular reference to the media in Chapter 13.

The scheme of this chapter is as follows. In section 10.1, the scope of the protection for confidential material is considered. In what circumstances do professional or business relationships give rise to duties of confidentiality, in the sense of duties to keep secrets? When can these be overridden? The two sections which follow examine aspects of the relationship between the interest in maintaining confidences and the public interest in the administration of criminal justice. Where these interests come into conflict, what protections against forced disclosure are offered to holders of confidential material? Section 10.2 opens the examination of procedures for confidential material in criminal investigations, concentrating on items subject to legal privilege. Section 10.3 examines the treatment of other confidential material in criminal investigations, and section 10.4 looks at the control of interception of communications. Some conclusions about the importance of confidentiality interests in the criminal justice system are suggested in section 10.5.

10.1 THE SCOPE OF DUTIES OF CONFIDENCE

The duty of confidence operates in equity and in contract. It protects information of certain limited classes. The protection primarily takes the form of equitable remedies, such as injunctions restraining disclosure, but if the disclosure has already been made other remedies may be granted, such as an account of profits made through improper disclosure, so that the person entitled to the information rather than the wrongdoer may benefit, or damages. In order to enjoy protection, the subject-matter of the information must be such as to justify treating it as confidential, it must not be in the public domain, and, if there has been an authorized disclosure to anyone, the disclosure must have ben subject to a duty imposed on the confidant to hold the information in confidence. Finally, even if the information in question passes these tests for confidentiality, the protection may be lost if the court takes the view that the disclosure in question serves a public interest of such importance that it overrides the interest in maintaining confidentiality. Each of these elements will be separately examined.

(1) The confidential quality of the information

As in other areas, the law does not protect the interest of an individual merely because that individual thinks that the interest is important. To allow a person to stipulate unilaterally for protection in situations which affect the interests of other individuals or of society more generally would prevent the courts from taking account of those wider interests. The judges have given protection to information only where, in their view, a powerful public (as well as private) interest is served by protecting it. In practice, this means that the information must arise from or be significant to a relationship or activity which the law recognizes as particularly worthy of support. Initially, the judges recognized two such fields as worthy of protection: information about commercial or manufacturing processes carried on by people for profit,[2] and information about family relationships, particularly the secrets of the marriage bed.[3] The former merited protection because of the market value of business information in a free or mixed economy, and the latter because of the importance of the family to the organization and stability of society.

However, the doctrine of confidentiality is not limited to those fields. It has been substantially widened, to cover any relationship within which there is a recognized public interest in fostering free exchange of information between the parties, avoiding the fear of disclosure to others which might inhibit frankness. Thus, for example, a duty to hold information in confidence prima facie operates in the relationships between patient and medical adviser, penitent and priest, client and lawyer, and pupil and teacher.

(2) Confidant's obligation to hold information in confidence

Normally, a person who receives information is free to transmit it to others. The assumption is that if A is prepared for B to know something, there is no harm in C and D knowing it as well, so B commits no wrong in repeating it. However, when the information is of a confidential nature and is not in the public domain, B is not free to disclose it if he is subject to an obligation of confidence. Such as obligation may be expressly imposed by A at the time of transmission to B, or may be implied by law from the circumstances of the transmission.[4] Express imposition of a duty is straightforward, but the implication of a duty is more difficult to predict. Once again, the public interest which the courts

---

[2] *Coco* v. *A. N. Clark (Engineers) Ltd.* [1969] RPC 41.

[3] *Prince Albert* v. *Strange* (1849) 2 De Gex & Sm. 652, (on appeal) 1 Mac. & G. 25; *Margaret, Duchess of Argyll* v. *Duke of Argyll* [1967] 1 Ch. 302, [1965] 1 All ER 611.

[4] See generally Francis Gurry, *Breach of Confidence* (Oxford: Clarendon Press, 1984).

see as being served by the activity in question, or the harm to the public interest which might flow from disclosure of information of the type in question, is likely to determine both the existence and the scope of any duty of confidence. Generally, the judges have accepted that a public interest is served by confidentiality in particular relationships, such as those between lawyer and client, doctor and patient, and more recently journalist and source, although that interest will not always override competing public interests favouring disclosure.[5] The more personal or commercially sensitive information is, the more likely it is that it will be subjected to an implied duty of confidence. When disclosure of sensitive material is permitted, because there is a public interest in the object in view, the information must be used only for that purpose. For example, in civil litigation documents disclosed to the other side on discovery may be used only for the purposes of the litigation, and unless read in open court must not be published or used for any other purpose,[6] unless the court gives leave for such use on the ground that it serves an overriding public interest.[7] In the same way, confidential information about a drub which the manufacturer passes to an advertising company for use in connection with a promotion may not be passed on to a television company for use in making a programme critical of the effects of the drug.[8]

(3) Information not in public domain

Normally, information loses its confidential quality when it enters the public domain. This is because equity does not act in vain, and the courts will not grant injunctions to prevent disclosure by one person of information which is readily available and may easily be obtained or communicated by others. It was partly for this reason that the government failed to obtain permanent injunctions restraining publication of allegations about the activities of MI5 after they had been widely distributed following the publication of the book *Spycatcher*.[9]

However, this principle is neither universally applicable nor straightforward to use in those areas where it does apply, for two reasons. First, it is not clear when information comes into the public domain. If it were necessary only that the information should have been disclosed to one

---

[5] *Parry-Jones* v. *The Law Society* [1969] 1 Ch. 1, [1968] 1 All ER 177, CA; *British Steel Corporation* v. *Granada Television Ltd.* [1981] AC 1096, [1091] 1 All ER 417, HL; *X* v. *Y* [1988] 2 All ER 648.

[6] *Home Office* v. *Harman* [1983] 1 AC 280, [1982] 1 All ER 532, HL.

[7] *Customs and Excise Commissioners* v. *A. E. Hamlin & Co.* [1984] 1 WLR 509, [1983] 3 All ER 654; *Marcel* v. *Commissioner of Police of the Metropolis* [1992] 1 All ER 72, CA.

[8] *Schering Chemicals Ltd.* v. *Falkman Ltd.* [1982] QB 1, [1981] 2 All ER 321, CA, concerning the anti-arthritis drug Primodos.

[9] See Ch. 14, below.

unauthorized person, a wrongdoer would evade the protection of the law by the very act of wrongdoing which the law is intended to prevent or discourage. Generally speaking, if X passes confidential information to Y, in breach of a duty owed by X to Z to keep the information secret, the recipient Y will be subject to a duty to Z to keep the information from further disclosure, similar in scope to the duty owed by X to Z. This will, at any rate, be the position if Y knows that X is acting improperly in disclosing the information.[10] There are dicta suggesting that a certain number of people must acquire access to the information before it will be regarded as having come into the public domain: a disclosure to a few people, for example by printing a few hundred copies of a book and distributing them privately as presents, will not suffice, because the people who have immediate access do not constitute the public, or a section of the public.[11] Perhaps the moment when material passes into the public domain is the moment when it passes beyond individuals selected by the person making the disclosure.[12]

Secondly, remedies for breach of confidence operate *in personam*, not *in rem*. The question is, strictly, whether or not the defendant is subject to a duty not to disclose information, so it is theoretically possible that particular people may be subject to duties not to speak out even after the information has been made public by others. This is because public interests may affect a defendant in a different way from other people. For example, it may be that if Mr. Wright, the author of *Spycatcher*, were to come within the jurisdiction of the English courts, he could be retrained from making further disclosures about matters which came within his knowledge during his service with MI5, because of a public interest in maintaining the mutual confidence of members of MI5, past and present, by enforcing a principle that they should never speak on such matters, even if they have already been disclosed by other sources. In *Attorney-General v. Guardian Newspapers Ltd. (No. 2)*,[13] the House of Lords acknowledged that a lifelong duty of confidence was owed by members of the security service, and this duty has since been backed by criminal sanctions in section 1 of the Official Secrets Act 1989.[14] It may be justified under the European Convention on Human Rights, despite interfering with Mr Wright's freedom to impart information under Article 10(1), because it

[10] *Fraser* v. *Evans* [1969] 1 QB 349, [1969] 1 All ER 8, CA. In relation to the newspaper serialization of Peter Wright's book *Spycatcher*, this was the position of the *Sunday Times*, against whom an order for an account of profits was made, in *A.-G.* v. *Guardian Newspapers Ltd. (No. 2)* [1990] 1 AC 109, HL. See further Ch. 14, below.

[11] See e.g. Lord Jauncey in *Lord Advocate* v. *The Scotsman Publications ltd.* [1990] 1 AC 809 at p. 827, [1989] 2 All ER 852 at p. 862.

[12] See for general discussion Gareth Jones, 'Breach of Confidence—after *Spycatcher*' [1989] CLP 49–69.

[13] [1990] 1 AC 109, [1988] 3 All ER 545, HL.   [14] See Ch. 14, below.

serves the legitimate aim of protecting national security and, arguably, information received in confidence, under Article 10(2).

Newspapers, on the other hand, would be in a different position from Mr Wright's, because they are under no prior obligation of secrecy, and indeed have a responsibility to keep the activities of the state under public scrutiny in the public interest. The balance of public interests falls in different places according to the position and obligations of the particular defendant.

It follows that the public domain principle is sufficiently flexible to take account of the need to discourage a person who has lawful access to confidential information[15] from misusing it, while not committing the law to a position where it appears to be attempting, Canute-like, to hold back the inevitable rise of the tide of publicity, or to prevent the press from performing public-interest functions. This connects with the following issue.

(4) Overriding public interests justifying disclosure

Even if the person holding information is otherwise subject to a duty to hold it in confidence, there may be countervailing public interests which are sufficiently weighty to justify, or even compel, disclosure. This was at one time expressed in the maxim that there is no confidence in an iniquity: people who commit acts or omissions which are contrary to law or morals have no legitimate claim to keep them secret. However, the iniquity defence to a claim for breach of confidence is merely an example, albeit a central one, of a wider principle which allows for disclosure in the public interest.[16] It is usually in the public interest to reveal information about wrongdoing, but the public interest may also favour disclosure of other information which is of importance to the public or to certain people, even if it does not show that anyone has done anything legally or morally wrong. For example, it may be in the public interest to disclose confidential information which tends to show that a person who has been accused of a crime is innocent, or to reveal a risk to public health or safety.[17] The importance of these interests is reflected in the weight which they carry as possible justifications under Article 8(2) of the European Convention on Human Rights for interfering with privacy rights.

---

[15] Such a person is sometimes called a confidant, but this wrongly implies that he will always have had the information confided in him by another. Sometimes, as in many of the *Spycatcher* allegations, the person making the disclosure has the information from personal, first-hand knowledge, but is under a legal obligation not to disclose it.

[16] *Lion Laboratories Ltd.* v. *Evans* [1985] QB 526, [1984] 2 All ER 417, CA.

[17] *R.* v. *Ataou* [1988] 2 All ER 321, CA. In the context of AIDS treatment, see *X* v. *Y* [1988] 2 All ER 648, discussed below.

An example of factors which might make it desirable to disclose confidential information is *W. v. Egdell*.[18] The plaintiff, W., while suffering from a condition subsequently diagnosed as paranoid schizophrenia, had shot a number of people. He had been detained under a restriction order made under the Mental Health Act 1959. The psychiatrist treating him formed the view that W.'s condition was being controlled by medication, that W. Understood the need to continue with the medication, and that he could in due course be released. W. applied to have his case reviewed by a Mental Health Review Tribunal with a view to conditional discharge. His solicitors instructed Dr Egdell, another psychiatrist, to examine W. and to provide a report to the solicitors for use at the tribunal hearing. Dr Egdell considered that W.'s condition might have been misdiagnosed, and that W. could have been suffering from a paranoid psychosis, which is more difficult to control through medication than paranoid schizophrenia. Dr. Egdell also thought that W. had an abnormal personality, and might still have an unhealthy interest in guns and explosives. He strongly recommended that no steps towards releasing W. should be taken until these and other matters had been fully investigated. On receiving the report, W.'s solicitors withdrew the application to the tribunal. However, Dr Egdell communicated the report to the doctors treating W., and caused it to be sent to the Home Office. W. brought proceedings for breach of confidence, arguing that Dr Egdell had an obligation of confidence towards his patient, W. Scott J. Rejected the claim. Besides owing a duty to W., Dr Egdell owed a duty to the public. In relation to a patient who was held in a secure hospital under an indefinite restriction order following serious crimes the duty to the public would require the doctor to place his report before the appropriate authorities where it was in the public interest to do so,[19] regardless of the patient's wishes.

This illustrates that the public-interest restriction on duties of confidence is not dependent on iniquity: W.'s medical condition could not be said to be equivalent to legal or moral wrongdoing. A wide variety of public interests may come into play, which may have unfortunate consequences for the individuals concerned. For example, it means that patients like W., who are detained following criminal offences, do not

---

[18] [1990] Ch. 359, [1989] 1 All ER 1089.

[19] Scott J. said ([1989] 1 All ER at p. 1104) that the duty to inform the authorities arose if, in the doctor's opinion, it was in the public inerest to do so. Since the scope of the legal duty of confidence is a matter of law, not medical ethics, it should be made clear that the court, not the doctor, has the last word on the assessment of the public interest, although the doctor must make a personal assessment when deciding how to behave, and that assessment will carry considerable weight in subsequent proceedings, particularly if it is consistent with official standards of medical conduct and ethics and was reached in good faith.

enjoy the benefit of as extensive an assurance of confidentiality in their dealings with doctors as do other people. Nevertheless, where people are detained for the protection of society it is essential that the law of confidence should not make it possible to undermine that protection, although perhaps the courts, rather than individual doctors, ought to be responsible for making the final decision as to where the balance of public interests lies, as they are in other fields.[20]

In order to decide whether a person who holds confidential information is justified in disclosing it, the interests favouring disclosure must be weighed against the interests (both public and private) which support maintaining the confidence. Only if the former outweigh the latter will disclosure be justified. Although the public interest in free, informed debate on matters of social importance may tend to support disclosure of information, sometimes disclosing confidential information would tend to inhibit or prejudice other worthwhile activities which are themselves in the public interest. In X v. Y[21] Rose J. Granted a permanent injunction restraining a newspaper from publishing information from confidential hospital records on two practising doctors who were suffering from AIDS. Freedom to publish the medical details was supported by the public interest in freedom of the press, and by the marginal assistance to informed public debate concerning AIDS which would flow from it. But it would also have been very likely to discourage patients from going to hospital to receive monitoring and counselling. There is a powerful public interest in ensuring that patients are monitored and counselled, so that they can organize their lives as positively as possible while avoiding the risk of infecting other people. On careful consideration, Rose J. Decided that the balance of public interests decisively favoured upholding the confidentiality of the information by granting the injunction.

Even if it is legitimate to disclose the information, the public interest might not support a generalized, public disclosure. It might be suitable only to permit disclosure to particular people, or for specific purposes. For instance, it might be proper to disclose evidence that somebody has committed a crime only to the police, and information about a suspected breach of the rules of a regulatory organization to the regulator, not to splash it across the pages of a newspaper.[22] There are two questions. First, is it legitimate to disclose the confidential material at all? Secondly, how and to whom is it in the public interest to disclose it? In W. v. Egdell, although it was proper in the circumstances for the psychiatrist to arrange

---

[20] Cp. the remarks of Lord Bridge in X Ltd. v. Morgan Grampian (Publishers) Ltd. [1991] 1 AC 1 at p. 48, [1990] 2 All ER 1 at p. 13.

[21] [1988] 2 All ER 648.

[22] Francome v. Mirror Group Newspapers Ltd. [1984] 1 WLR 892, [1984] 2 All ER 408, CA.

for the report to be transmitted to the doctors who were responsible for the day-to-day management of W. (for W.'s own medical benefit), and to the Home Office and the review tribunal (for the benefit of the public), it would not have been appropriate to communicate the report to the press.

The scope of the duty of confidence thus depends on the circumstances of the case. Of the public interests which restrict duties of confidence, one of the most compelling is that in the due administration of justice. It is because of this interest that the courts have held that a duty of confidence does not shield a person, as of right, from having confidential information or communications divulged for the purpose of providing evidence in legal proceedings. Only one type of document and communication enjoys such protection as of right: the category covered by legal professional privilege. This includes many communications between lawyer and client for the purpose of seeking or giving legal advice, and material brought into existence predominantly for the purpose of contemplated litigation, and is considered in section 10.2. In relation to other classes of confidential material and information, although a judge has a discretion to relieve a witness from the obligation to produce documents or answer questions when the answer will entail a breach of an undertaking of confidentiality, the judge will have to weigh the competing interests—the importance of the material to the proceedings, and the harm which would flow from disclosure—and decide where the balance falls.

Although journalists, doctors, and others have no privilege at common law which protects confidences and sources of information, there are several special statutory provision which give some limited protection to journalists and their sources.[23] In addition, in relation to criminal investigations, Parliament has legislated to clarify the balance which is to be struck between the competing public interests when evaluating claims by investigators to have access to confidential material, defining the scope of the duty of confidence in the light of the public interest in the prevention and detection of crime, and offering procedural safeguards against unjustified seizure. The overall effect should be to secure compliance with Article 8 of the European Convention on Human Rights, by specifying the circumstances in which the privacy interests covered by the law of confidence can be interfered with for the prevention of disorder or crime, and by ensuring that any interference is in accordance with the law and goes no further than is necessitated by a pressing social need. However, the legislation may not always achieve these purposes.

---

[23] See Ch. 13 below.

10.2 CONFIDENTIALITY AND CRIMINAL INVESTIGATIONS

(1) Background to the PACE provisions

A number of relationships of trust involve the parties in giving and receiving personal information in circumstances which import an obligation of confidence. Such information may sometimes be very useful to an investigator seeking information about criminal offences or suspects. Although it would often offend the conscience of most people to allow the police to invade the offices of a lawyer, doctor, or priest in search of information, the public interest in preventing or detecting crime or maintaining public order might sometimes be held to outweigh the interest in maintaining the integrity of those relationships. For example, where the information is likely to make it possible to prevent serious harm to innocent victims of a threatened crime, an interference would be for a legitimate objective in terms of Article 8 of the European Convention on Human Rights, and would be justifiable if in accordance with the law and necessary in a democratic society for the achievement of the legitimate objective. The European Court of Human Rights has amplified these terms in a number of judgments. To comply with the requirements for justifying an apparent infringement of Article 8(1), the criteria for interference must be laid down by law, they must be reasonably clear and accessible, there must be adequate legal safeguards against abuse, and the extent of any interference must be proportionate to the object pursued.[24]

Many statutes give powers to officials to demand the production of documents which are relevant to their investigations, regardless of duties of confidence which may subsist in relation to the material. For example, the Director of the Serious Fraud Office has power to require a person, by a written notice, to 'produce at a specified time and place any specified documents which appear to the Director to relate to any matter relevant to the investigation or any documents of a specified class which appear to him so to relate'.[25] Failure to comply with the requirement, without reasonable excuse, is a criminal offence,[26] even if the person who is required to provide information has already been charged with an offence and may be incriminating himself if he complies with the requirement.[27] A search warrant may be issued by a justice of the peace if the person fails to comply with the requirement, or it is not practicable to

---

[24] *Malone* v. *UK*, Eur. Ct. HR, Series A, No. 82, Judgment of 2 Aug. 1984; 7 EHRR 14.

[25] Criminal Justice Act 1987, s. 2(3).   [26] Ibid., s. 2(13).

[27] *Smith* v. *Director of Serious Fraud Office* [1992] 3 All ER 456, HL.

serve a written notice, or serving a notice might seriously prejudice the investigation.[28] Documents in respect of which a person could claim legal professional privilege at common law are not subject to this power,[29] but there is no exception for other categories of confidential material. Parliament has here decided that the importance of combating serious or complex fraud takes absolute priority over the interests which were given some protection under PACE in respect of crimes which pose a less immediate or extensive social problem. The powers of the Director of the Serious Fraud Office were introduced at a time when revelations of improper trading and fraud in the city were threatening to undermine public trust in the markets on which the Conservative government relied to extend share ownership to a wider range of individual members of the public than had previously held shares. Comparable powers have long been available to Inland Revenue and Customs and Excise investigators, in order to protect the public purse.[30]

These provisions rely mainly on the investigators themselves to balance the public interest in the investigation of crime against the interests of suspects and their advisers. By contrast, the provisions of the Police and Criminal Evidence Act 1984 authorizing police access to confidential material provide for an independent check. In the first version of the Police and Criminal Evidence Bill, introduced to Parliament in 1982, there were provisions allowing the police to apply to a circuit judge for an order to the person in possession of such material to produce it. Only if the person failed to comply, or it seemed certain that the order would be ineffective, would a search warrant authorizing the police to enter and search premises for confidential material be granted. This would have substantially improved the protection offered to confidential material. Under the law as it then stood in England and Wales, when under statute a search warrant could be issued (often by a magistrate) to enter premises to search for and seize prohibited items (such as controlled drugs or forgeries), confidential material could be seized, including documents subject to legal professional privilege. The statute was regarded as having overridden the protection offered by the duty of confidence or privilege.[31] The procedure proposed in the Bill would have allowed a person to whom an order for production had been addressed to challenge it by way of an application for judicial review before complying, instead of being

---

[28] Criminal Justice Act 1987, s. 2(4). [29] Ibid., s. 2(9).

[30] e.g. Taxes Management Act 1970, ss. 20, 20A; Customs and Excise Management Act 1979, s. 167.

[31] *Parry-Jones* v. *Law Society* [1969] 1 Ch. 1, [1968] 1 All ER 177, CA; *Frank Truman Export Ltd.* v. *Metropolitan Police Commissioner* [1977] QB 952, [1977] 3 All ER 431; *R.* v. *Justice of the Peace for Peterborough, ex parte Hicks* [1977] 1 WLR 1371, [1978] 1 All ER 225, DC.

subjected to a police raid and a magistrate-authorized rummage through the files.

In the event, even this additional protection was regarded as insufficient by many people, and the final version of the Bill, which became the Police and Criminal Evidence Act 1984 (PACE), incorporated a number of additional concessions. There are now several different categories of confidential material, which are regarded as having different weights in the balance of interests, and so have different levels of protection against coerced disclosure. The PACE provisions apply to powers of search and seizure enacted in legislation passed before PACE,[32] but have been incorporated into most later search powers, including that given in section 8 of PACE itself. The main exceptions are search powers to make it easier to track down proceeds of drug trafficking and properly intended to support terrorism. The protections for confidential information are somewhat truncated in such cases, which are examined below.

(2) Items subject to legal privilege

The material which is most securely protected is that falling within the category of 'items subject to legal privilege'. Legal professional privilege is well established in civil litigation, where it operates as a shield against compelled discovery which might require a party to litigation to reveal the advise received from lawyers or the information on the basis of which that advice was given. It bolsters the adversarial nature of civil litigation, where the core assumption is that each party must establish its own case, and must not be forced to establish the other side's case for it. So far as the privilege prevents the courts from receiving valuable evidence, it may perhaps be regarded as irrational. The adversarial nature of the civil process has been somewhat watered down—discovery itself makes inroads on it,[33] as does compelled pre-trial disclosure of reports of expert witnesses[34]—but the privilege remains important in civil litigation. Yet before 1984 the privilege had never become properly established in English pre-trial criminal procedure. This was partly because there is no general system of advance disclosure of evidence by the defence in criminal proceedings, so there was little room for importing from civil procedure a shield against pre-trial disclosure. Another possible reason was that the privilege is grounded in public policy, particularly the public interest in encouraging candour between client and lawyer. In criminal cases, the importance of encouraging candour might be outweighed, more easily than in civil actions between private individuals, by the public interest in

---

[32] PACE, s. 9(2).   [33] RSC Ord. 24.
[34] Civil Evidence Act 1972, s. 2; RSC Ord. 25, and Ord. 38, rr. 37 and 38.

deciding cases on the basis of the best available evidence. On the other hand, warrants to search for evidence of crimes are somewhat akin to coerced discovery in pre-trial criminal proceedings, and it seemed anomalous to have a privilege which protected parties to civil litigation but not defendants in criminal trials.

(i) *What are items subject to legal privilege?* The drafters of PACE defined 'items subject to legal privilege' so as to extend protection to broadly the same types of material as had until then attracted legal professional privilege in civil litigation. The material is defined in section 10. Subject to a single, but very important, exception, an item is subject to legal privilege if it is in the possession of a person who is entitled to possession of it, and it falls within one of the following categories, as set out in section 10(1):

(*a*) communications between a professional legal adviser and his client or any person representing his client made in connection with the giving of legal advice to the client;

(*b*) communications between a professional legal adviser and his client or any person representing his client or between such an adviser or his client or any such representative of his client and any other person made in connection with or in contemplation of legal proceedings and for the purposes of such proceedings;

(*c*) items enclosed with or referred to in such communication and made—
    (i)   in connection with the giving of legal advice;
    (ii) in connection with or in contemplation of legal proceedings and for the purposes of such proceedings[.]

The categories are not identical with those which apply under common law in civil litigation, although there are substantial similarities. The common-law privilege protects only material prepared for or communicated to or from solicitors and barristers, and protects it only from disclosure in civil litigation. The privilege does not protect documents from disclosure in other kinds of proceedings, such as tax investigations, and does not cover material in the hands of accountants and other tax advisers. However, there is a statutory privilege advisers against enforced production of communications between them and their clients for the purposes of the Taxes Acts.[35] This technicality is avoided under PACE, since the term 'professional legal adviser', which is not defined in the Act, may include people such as accountants and licensed conveyancers who give legal advice as part of their professional duties. There is in civil matters now a special statutory extension of legal professional privilege to certain people licensed to do legal work under the Courts and Legal Services Act 1990, section 63.

---

[35] Taxes Management Act 1970, s. 20B(8), (9).

Apart from this, paragraph (*a*) broadly reflects the common-law position under which a solicitor's records of transactions, most draft and final contracts, and other papers accumulated in connection with conveyancing and commercial transactions, are not privileged, because they are not made in connection with the giving of advice.[36] In civil litigation, however, the scope of protected legal advice has been somewhat extended by recent decisions which aim to take account of the variety of advice which modern solicitors are called on to give. For example, lawyers may advise on all aspects of the purchase of a house or business, including how to negotiate the contract and how to finance the purchase. Where the lawyer gives advice on how it is prudent to proceed in the light of the legal situation, that advice (and material communicated in order to obtain it) is covered by common-law legal professional privilege.[37] It is not yet clear whether it is also covered under PACE by paragraph (*a*) above, but it would be inconvenient if section 10 of PACE were to be so restrictively interpreted as to allow the privilege a wider scope in some proceedings than others.

Paragraphs (*b*) and (*c*) have parallels in, but may be different in scope from, the common-law rules. For example, the privilege at common law applies only to material and communications *made for* the *predominant* purpose of obtaining or giving legal advice or of pending or contemplated litigation.[38] This test has two significant features. The first is also a feature of paragraph (*c*) of section 10 of PACE: an item is not privileged if it existed before the need for advice arose.[39] This prevents a criminal client from depriving the police and courts of relevant evidence by the simple expedient of lodging them with his solicitor with a request for advice. The second feature of the common-law rule is not expressly present in the PACE provisions: the predominant purpose for which the item was made must have been to obtain legal advice or for the purpose of litigation. The absence of such a requirement seems to enable the PACE provisions to avoid the complication, only partially resolved by the common law,[40] which arises where a report or plan is originally prepared because the party's insurer insists on it, or in obedience to a company's standing instructions, rather than because litigation is contemplated at the time, but is later passed to lawyers for the purpose of preparing for litigation.

[36] For the common-law position, see *Balabel* v. *Air India* [1988] Ch. 317, [1988] 2 All ER 246, CA. Under PACE, see *R.* v. *Inner London Sessions Crown Court, ex parte Baines & Baines (a firm)* [1988] 1 QB 579, [1987] 3 All ER 1025, DC.

[37] *Balabel* v. *Air India* [1988] Ch. 317, [1988] 2 All ER 246, CA.

[38] *Waugh* v. *British Railways Board* [1980] AC 521, [1979] 2 All ER 1169, HL.

[39] *R.* v. *Guildhall Magistrates' Cout, ex parte Primlaks Holdings Co. (Panama) Inc.* [1990] 1 QB 261, DC.

[40] *Guinness Peat Properties Ltd.* v. *Fitzroy Robinson Partnership (a firm)* [1987] 1 WLR 1027, [1987] 2 All ER 716.

In other respects the common-law privilege appears to be wider than the PACE protection. Unlike paragraph (c) of section 10, the common-law rules cover items which have not been enclosed with or referred to in communications, as long as the items in question were created for the predominant purpose of contemplated legal proceedings.[41] It is also possible that there are other circumstances in which items which attract privilege at common law, if a solicitor makes a selection of documents which are not themselves privileged for the purpose of contemplated legal proceedings, the collection is privileged at common law.[42] Under paragraph (c) the selection is privileged, if at all, only once the material has been communicated to somebody (for instance to counsel in order to obtain an opinion).

Since the effect of PACE was to create a new privilege in criminal proceedings, rather than to reproduce or restrict an existing one, there is no reason to presume that section 10 was drafted or should be interpreted so as to produce results identical with the common-law rules operating in civil litigation. The government, originally committed to only a very narrow privilege in criminal matters, conceded wider protection during the debates on the first and second Police and Criminal Evidence Bills;[43] the privilege moved closer to that operating in civil litigation, until the drafters seem to have tried to adopt at least some of the civil-law rules. It would have been simpler to have said in section 10 no more than, 'Any item in respect of which legal professional privilege would apply in connection with civil litigation is an item subject to legal privilege for the purposes of this Act.' However, there may be good policy grounds for having narrower privileges in criminal investigations than in civil litigation, because of the strong public interest in the discovery of offenders.

Balanced against this, the privilege serves several interests in relation to criminal investigations. There is a public interest in people being able to obtain the best legal advice in relation to their cases, on the basis of full information, an interest related to the public interest in the fairness of the adversarial system of criminal justice. There is also a private interest in maintaining the confidentiality of lawyer—client and related communications, including those relating to clients other than the suspect, although the privilege is usually thought to be founded on public rather than private interests. The privilege prevents police searches, under warrant, of solicitors' files which contain material relating to the affairs of many clients. While an order for production of documents in the hands of a solicitor permits the solicitor to deliver only those documents which are

[41] *Waugh* v. *British Railways Board* [1980] AC 521, [1979] 2 All ER 1169, HL.

[42] *Lyell* v. *Kennedy (No. 3)*, (1884) 27 Ch. D. 1, CA; *Dubai Bank Ltd.* v. *Galadari (No. 7)* [1992] 1 All ER 658.

[43] See Michael Zander, *The Police and Criminal Evidence Act 1984*, 2nd edn. (1990), 30.

covered by the order, a police officer executing a search warrant may rummage in any files, including those of other clients of the solicitor which are reasonably thought likely to contain evidence. The police try to be as sensitive as possible to problems of confidentiality, but warrants present a potential threat to the confidentiality interests of all the solicitor's clients. PACE protects the privacy interests of all of them, not just those of the suspect.

There is an important limitation on the scope of legal privilege under PACE. Section 10(2) reads: 'Items held with the intention of furthering a criminal purpose are not items subject to legal privilege.' On its face, this seems to mean that an item loses its privileged status if the person holding it intends, by doing so, to further a criminal purpose. The relevant intention appears to be that of the person holding the item. Where a solicitor holds items which fall within section 10(1), the items ought, on a literal reading, to remain privileged as long as the solicitor does not intend by holding them to further a criminal purpose. The fact that the solicitor may, by holding them, unknowingly further the criminal purpose of his client or a third party would not deprive the item of its privilege. That interpretation was accepted in *R. v. Crown Court at Snaresbrook, ex parte DPP*,[44] an early case on section 10. It has the merit of simplicity, but it creates practical difficulties for the police, and may not reflect the intention of the drafters of section 10(2). There are cases in which the police are seeking material which is thought to implicate not the person holding it (the solicitor), but the client, or an associate of the client. If a criminal intention on the part of the client or the client's associate were irrelevant, much useful material might be lost to the police. At common law, the privilege belongs to the client, not to be the solicitor, so the intention of the client should in principle be at least as relevant as that of the solicitor.[45] There is no reason for a more extensive privilege to be permitted in pre-trial criminal than in pre-trial civil matters. This appears to reflect the position at common law as expressed both in England and Wales and in the USA.[46]

Making the client's intention central would mean, on the other hand, that the criminal intention of a third party ought to be irrelevant to the privileged status of items held by either the solicitor or the client, unless they know of that intention. This was, indeed, the conclusion reached by the Court of Appeal in relation to civil matters in 1986 in an interlocu-

---

[44] [1988] QB 532, [1988] 1 All ER 315, DC. A petition for leave to appeal was dismissed: [1987] 1 WLR 1502, HL.

[45] *R. v. Cox and Railton* (1884) 14 QBD 153.

[46] *O'Rourke v. Darbishire* [1920] AC 581 at p. 604, PC; *Clark* v. *US* 289 US 1, 77 L. Ed. 993 (1933), US Supreme Court; *US* v. *Zolin*, 491 US 554, 105 L. Ed. 2d 469 (1989), US Supreme Court.

tory appeal concerning discovery of documents.[47] This view is fortified by practical considerations affecting the position of the solicitor, who may be unable to obtain the information necessary to contest a warrant or an order for production if the relevant alleged intention to further a criminal purpose is that of somebody who may not be known to him or the client. Indeed, where the police or Customs and Excise are seeking obtain information enabling them to trace funds for terrorists or the proceeds of drug trafficking, it may be a criminal offence for the solicitor even to inform the client that an order for production has been sought, let alone seek instructions from the client about the intentions of the client or of people who might be the target of the investigation.[48] In such circumstances, a test for privilege which depends on the intention or purpose of someone who does not hold the material in question, and whose evidence cannot be obtained, imposes grave hardship on the practitioner and the client.

Nevertheless, the House of Lords has upheld just such an interpretation of section 10. In *R. v. Central Criminal Court, ex parte Francis & Francis (a firm)*[49] a circuit judge had granted an order requiring a firm of solicitors to produce to investigators material which, it was thought, would enable them to trace the whereabouts of assets thought to be the proceeds of drug trafficking. The order was obtained *ex parte* under the Drug Trafficking Offences Act 1986, which contains an exception for items subject to legal privilege as defined by section 10 of PACE. The material in question concerned advice about the purchase of a business by the solicitor's client, using funds allegedly given to the client by a third party who was a suspected drug trafficker. The advice was prima facie privileged, but the police argued that the holding of the material by the solicitors was part of a plan by the suspect to launder the ill-gotten gains, and that this criminal purpose of a third party excluded the privilege by virtue of section 10(2) of PACE. The solicitors applied for judicial review of the order, relying the decision of the Divisional Court in *R. v. Crown Court at Snaresbrook, ex parte DPP*,[50] interpreting section 10(2) literally. The Divisional Court decided that, since the privilege was that of the client, not the solicitor, the relevant intention was that of the client or a

---

[47] *Banque Keyser Ullmann SA v. Skandia (UK) Insurance Co. Ltd.* [1986] 1 Lloyd's Rep. 336, CA.

[48] Prevention of Terrorism Act 1989, s. 17; Drug Trafficking Offences Act 1986, s. 31, It has been suggested, *obiter*, that a solicitor is always entitled to take instructions, and that this would be a reasonable excuse giving a defence under those sections: *R. v. Central Criminal Court, ex parte Francis & Francis (a firm)* [1989] AC 364 at p. 386, [1988] 3 All ER 775 at p. 792, *per* Lord Griffiths. This is not beyond doubt: see David Feldman, 'Conveyancers and the Proceeds of Crime' [1989] Conv. 389–402 at p. 398.

[49] [1989] AC 346, [1988] 3 All ER 375, HL.

[50] [1988] QB 352, [1988] 1 All ER 315, DC.

third party, not the solicitor.[51] This decision was upheld on appeal by a bare majority of the House of Lords.[52]

This is an unsatisfactory decision.[53] Not only does it fly in the face of the literal meaning of the words of the statute, as Lord Bridge and Lord Oliver pointed out in dissent, but it is based on dubious reasoning. The legal background to the statute might justify taking account of the intention of the client as well as that of the solicitor, but the justification for giving attention to the client's intention does not automatically justify allowing the intention of a third party to defeat the privileged relationship between lawyer and client. The majority of the House of Lords read extra words into section 10(2), and justified this by referring to the difficulties which the police face in tracing the proceeds of drug trafficking. However, if a statute is to make inroads into the common-law rights of citizens, the intention to do so must be clear from the statute, either expressly or by necessary implication. Legal professional privilege is regarded as such a right in Australia, Canada, New Zealand, and the USA,[54] but not, apparently, in England and Wales. The majority of the House of Lords placed their concern to fight crime ahead of their concern for principles of statutory interpretation and the protection of individual rights.

(ii) *Protection given to items subject to legal privilege.* Such items are, in principle, intended to receive virtually absolute protection from seizure and enforced production. Section 9(2) removes from earlier statutes any power to grant a search warrant for such material, and the exemption has been incorporated in all search powers passed subsequently. The person applying for a warrant or an order for production or access carries the burden of satisfying the issuing authority that the items sought are not subject to legal privilege, and the issuing authority must take seriously the obligation to scrutinize applications and to protect the privilege. Where the people in possession of items are solicitors or barristers, it should normally be difficult to persuade a judge that it is proper to grant a warrant or order under PACE.[55] There is no alternative means of seeking pro-

---

[51] [1989] AC 346, [1988] 1 All ER 677, DC.

[52] [1989] AC 346, [1988] 3 All ER 375, HL (Lords Brandon, Griffiths and Goff, Lords Bridge and Oliver dissenting).

[53] See A. L. E. Newbold, 'The Crime/Fraud Exception to Legal Professional Privilege' (1990) 53 MLR 472–84.

[54] *Baker* v. *Campbell* (1983) 153 CLR 52, HC of Australia; *Solosky* v. *R.* (1979) 105 DLR (3d) 745, SC Canada; *Re Gowling & Henderson and R.* (1982) 136 DLR (3d) 292; *Rosenburg* v. *Jaine* [1983] NZLR 1, CA of NZ; *Clark* v. *US*, 289 US 1 (1932); *US* v. *Upjohn*, 449 US 383, 66 L. Ed. 2d 584 (1981), US Supreme Court; Annotation, 81 Am. Jur. 2d pp. 242–3.

[55] *R.* v. *Guildhall Magistrates' Court, ex parte Primlaks Holdings Co. (Panama) Inc.* [1990] 1 QB 261 DC.

duction of items subject to legal privilege. Furthermore, when conducting a search on premises, a constable may not use powers of seizure to seize any item which the constable has reasonable grounds for believing to be subject to legal privilege.[56]

The privilege applies in all investigations, regardless of the seriousness of the offence under investigation. This extensive protection is explicable by reference to the particularly though pressure which the Law Society and the lawyers in Parliament exerted during the passage of the Bill. It reflects the lawyer's perception of the importance of the legal process to civilized society, and of the centrality of uninhibited communication between lawyer and client in order to make an adversarial legal process work. By contrast, protection or the secrets of the doctor–patient or priest–penitent relationships is less thorough.

(3) Other confidential material

Confidential items, even if they are not subject to legal privilege, may have some protection, whether they are in the hands of solicitors or others. Instead of the absolute protection against coerced disclosure accorded to items subject to legal privilege, there are restrictions on coerced disclosure, and procedural safeguards additional to those which apply to other types of material. Section 9 of PACE provides for special treatment of two types of material: excluded material, which is particularly sensitive and arises in the course of a confidential professional relationship; and special procedure material, which with one exception[57] is imparted in confidence but does not arise out of such a sensitive professional relationship, and is not of such a sensitive nature, as excluded material. These two kinds of material are to be accessible to investigators only in the limited circumstances and subject to the restrictive procedures laid down under Schedule 1 to the Act. The procedure, an application—usually *inter partes*—to a circuit judge for an order for the production of or access to the material, with a search warrant issued only if an order has failed to seems bound to fail, is common to both types of material. However, the substantive grounds on which the material is to be accessible differentiate between the two types of material. The Act makes it in some ways easier to obtain an order in respect of the less sensitive category, special procedure material, than in respect of the more confidential category of excluded material. Yet, as we shall see in section 10.3, this generalization hides a number of curiosities.

---

[56] PACE, s. 19(6).

[57] Journalistic material, efined in s. 13, is special procedure material even if it is not held in confidence. If held in confidence, it is excluded material. The provisions relating to journalistic material are explained in Ch. 13, below.

10.3 EXCLUDED MATERIAL AND SPECIAL PROCEDURE MATERIAL

Three matters require consideration. First, the nature of excluded and special procedure material must be explained; the conditions under which an order may be made in respect of each category must be examined; and the procedure for obtaining access must be considered. At each stage, we will try to assess the impact of the legislation and its implementation on the privacy and confidentiality interests of the people who are most closely affected.

(1) The nature of excluded material and special procedure material

(i) *Excluded material* is defined in section 11 of PACE. Apart from journalistic material held in confidence, which is one of the subjects of Chapter 13 below, there are only two kinds of excluded material.[58]

(*a*) Personal records which a person has acquired or created in the course of any trade, business, profession or other occupation or for the purposes of any paid or unpaid office, and which he holds in confidence.

Personal records need not be in documentary form—for instance, computerized records and X-ray photographs are included—but must concern an identifable individual. The material must relate either: (i) to that individual's physical or mental health; or (ii) to spiritual counselling or assistance given or to be given to him; or (iii) to counselling or assistance, for the purpose of his personal welfare, given or to be given to him by a voluntary organization or individual who has responsibilities for his personal welfare by reason of the adviser's office or occupation, or who has responsibilities for his supervision by reason of a court order.[59] Thus medical records are included under (i), and material relating to advice from one's minister of religion under (ii). Social workers' and teachers' records would be included under (iii) so far as they relate to counselling and assistance for individual clients and pupils, but not where they concern the social workers' or teachers' other duties in respect of the clients or pupils. Citizens' Advice Bureaux, the Samaritans, and similar voluntary organizations, would be covered under (iii), since their advisers have responsibilities for the welfare of those who week their advice.

Those bodies also satisfy the further requirement that the person or organization should hold the material in confidence. The Act provides that a person holds material (other than journalistic material) in confidence if he holds it subject either to an express or implied undertaking to hold it

---

[58] PACE, s. 11(1).   [59] PACE, s. 12.

in confidence, of the sort described in section 10.1 above, or to a statutory restriction on disclosure or obligation of secrecy.[60] The legislation thus protects both privacy interests in personal information and public interests in secrecy where they concern personal records, as under the Data Protection Act 1984 and the Interception of Communications Act 1985.

(b) Human tissue or tissue fluid taken for the purposes of diagnosis or medical treatment and which the person holds in confidence.[61]

It is important to note the limits of this provision. Blood samples taken to establish the blood type of an injured person following a road accident in order to match it for a blood transfusion are excluded material, and cannot be subjected to a search warrant; but blood or urine samples taken from the same injured person for testing under statutory powers to establish whether he has been driving illegally are not excluded material, since they are not taken for the purpose of diagnosis or treatment. This allows privacy to be protected, but not absolutely: it can be overridden when Parliament has decided that there are adequate countervailing public interest grounds for doing so. Parliament attaches great weight to the integrity and security of the person. Thus, although a search of a person's body orifices can be made in certain circumstances for specific types of material (as described in Chapter 5 above), and surgery may be authorized by a court if the patient is incapable of consenting and the surgery is for the best interests of the patient (as described in Chapter 4), there is no legal procedure for authorizing a surgical procedure to be performed on a non-consenting person for a purpose which is not in that person's interests. For example, bullets removed from a person shot during a criminal enterprise are not excluded material, as they are neither tissue nor tissue fluid, but the Act does not authorize the making of an order for the surgical removal of the bullets against the victim's will in order to use them as evidence.[62]

This protection for privacy interests is limited in two ways. First, there are circumstances in which samples which are taken may be accessible to the police. Secondly, although the police may not be able to obtain an order giving them access to the material, they will be able to seize such material if they come on it while lawfully on premises, if they have reasonable grounds for believing that it is relevant evidence in relation to any offence, and that it is necessary to seize it in order to prevent it being concealed, lost, altered, or destroyed.[63] To illustrate these points, take the following scenarios.

A driver, D, has been seriously injured in a road accident in which a pedestrian was killed. D is taken unconscious to hospital with a head

---

[60] PACE, s. 11(2).　　　　　　　　　　　　　　[61] PACE, s. 11(1).

[62] On the Canadian position, see Re Laporte and R. (1972) 29 DLR (3d) 651.

[63] PACE, s. 19(3).

wound which is bleeding profusely. While he is still unconscious, a doctor suturing D's wound collects some of the blood flowing it, and has it stored in case it later becomes necessary to establish whether it contained alcohol. The police learn of the existence of the sample, and ask for it to be handed over. The doctor refuses to hand it over unless the police obtain a court order.

The blood was not taken for the purposes of diagnosis or treatment, and so is not excluded material. It may be special procedure material (see below), but it is likely that an order for production will be granted on an application under Schedule 1 to PACE. This is, however, without prejudice to the discretion of a trial court to exclude evidence derived from the sample under section 78 of PACE, on the ground that the circumstances surrounding the taking of the sample (the blood having been taken without D's consent, and without any procedural safeguards to ensure, for example, that D can have part of the sample independently tested) would make the proceedings unfair were the evidence to be admitted.

A driver, D, is in hospital being treated for injuries following a road accident. Nobody else was injured. A police officer, who has reasonable grounds for believing that D was drunk at the time of the accident, is waiting to interview D when he sees the doctor taking a sample of blood from D in order to match its type to enable D to be given a transfusion. The officer insists on taking away the part of the sample which is left over when the Medical Laboratory Scientific Officer has completed the blood group test.

In this case, the doctor took the blood sample in order to treat D, and there is no doubt that in a search warrant or Schedule 1 application the doctor and other hospital staff should be treated as having an obligation of confidence in respect of the sample. It would, therefore, be excluded material. Nevertheless, the seizure powers of the police officer under section 19 of PACE can be lawfully exercised in respect of excluded or special procedure material which the officer finds while lawfully on the premises, without the need to obtain an order for access or production under the restrictive rules in Schedule 1.

This makes it clear that, whatever may have been the original intention, the effect of the legislation is to protect the professional or voluntary adviser against invasion of privacy by the police, and to prevent the police, when seeking evidence against a suspect, from ransacking the records or premises of third parties with a duty of confidence. It does not always protect the privacy of the suspect as such.[64] Nor does it protect

[64] See A. A. S. Zuckerman, 'The Weakness of the PACE Special Procedure for Protecting Confidential Material' [1990] Crim. LR 472–8.

against confidential material being seized from an adviser when officers come on it without infringing the adviser's privacy or property interests. Compare the position in a system where the decision has to be based on constitutional rights. The Canadian Supreme Court, in *R. v. Dyment*,[65] held that taking a blood sample from an unconscious patient for investigative purposes constitutes a seizure within the meaning of section 8 of the Canadian Charter of Rights and Freedoms, and if made without a warrant the seizure requires to be justified by reference to urgency or some other pressing need if it is not to be regarded as unreasonable and so unconstitutional. According to La Forest J., with whom Dickson CJC concurred, the case involved seizure rather than mere finding, and so fell to be reviewed under section 8 of the Charter, because the taking infringed a privacy interest of the patient. Even before the Charter, Canadian judges had allowed an action for replevin to reclaim a sample taken for non-therapeutic purposes from an unconscious patient and passed to the police, holding that the blood was the patient's property and there was no lawful ground for refusing to deliver it to the patient on demand.[66] Although replevin is not an entirely satisfactory remedy in these circumstances, because it raises difficult and unresolved questions about the extent to which people can have proprietary interests in parts of their bodies, these decisions, unlike PACE, genuinely offer protection to the subject of the confidential information or the person from whom samples are taken, rather than merely protecting that person's advisers. This shows how different political judgements about the proper balance between the interests in effective criminal investigation and those in protecting the various parties to confidential relationships may influence the development of legal rules and their effects, particularly in relation to the protection of rights.

(ii) *Special procedure material* is defined in section 14 of PACE. One type of special procedure material is journalistic material, which is subject to special rules considered in Chapter 13 below. Material other than journalistic material is special procedure material if it does not consist of items subject to legal privilege or excluded material, and is in the possession of a person who

(*a*) acquired or created it in the course of any trade, business, profession or other occupation, or for the purpose of any paid or unpaid office; *and*
(*b*) holds it subject to either an express or implied undertaking to hold it in confidence, or a restriction or obligation of secrecy contained in any enactment.

---

[65] (1988) 55 DLR (4th) 503, SC of Canada.
[66] *Capostinsky* v. *Olsen* (1981) 27 BCLR 97.

It follows from this definition that much of the material held by professional advisers for their business purposes, relating to their clients' affairs,
will be special procedure material, even if it does not meet the stringent
conditions needed to qualify as excluded material.

The emphasis is once again on protecting the adviser rather than the
beneficiary of the duty of confidence. The status of the material depends
on the person in whose possession it is. Even if an adviser created or
acquired the information as set out in paragraph (a), the material is not
special procedure material when it is in the possession of the client, but
only when in the possession of the adviser. If an accountant acquires
material in confidence from a client for the purpose of giving business
advice, and creates a document setting out that advice confidentially, the
material and the document are special procedure material in the hands of
the accountant, but cease to be special procedure material when dis-
patched to the client. The object is to protect confidential advisers and
their other clients against invasions of privacy, not to protect suspects in
ways which might thwart the process of criminal investigation even if
nobody else's interests are affected. This reflects the origin of these provisions in pressure from professional and voluntary organizations.

(2) Conditions for making orders for access or production

Circumstances in which courts may grant orders requiring people to give
investigators access to excluded and special procedure material are as follows. Schedule 1 of PACE provides for two sets of 'access conditions'
under which courts may order a person to produce or give access to the
protected types of material.

(i) *The first set of access conditions.* This applies only to special procedure
material. An order may be granted for production of or access to special
procedure material if three requirements are met. These are that:

- (a) there are reasonable grounds for believing that a serious arrestable
offence (as explained in Chapter 5 above) has been committed, and
that there is, on specified premises, special procedure material
which is likely to be relevant evidence, and which does not contain
excluded material;
- (b) other methods of obtaining the material have been tried unsuccessfully, or have not been tried because they appeared at the time to
be bound to fail; and
- (c) access to or production of the material is in the public interest, having regard to both the likely benefit to the investigation, and the
capacity in which the person in possession of the material holds it.[67]

[67] PACE, Sched. 1, para. 2.

The general requirement that the judge must be satisfied of the matters does not mean that a criminal, or even a civil, standard of proof need be met. In *R. v. Norwich Crown Court, ex parte Chethams*[68] the Divisional Court decided that the question is whether the judge is satisfied, not whether the matter has been proved to a criminal, or even a civil, standard. Similarly, in relation to condition (*a*), Mann LJ doubted, in *ex parte Chethams*, that the word 'likely' meant 'more probable than not', preferring the meaning 'such as might well happen'. This is a sensible approach, given that the application is a stage in an investigative procedure, and is not well suited to making final determinations of questions of fact of a kind to which notions of the standard of proof in legal proceedings are usually directed.

At the same time, it has been pointed out that circuit judges, as the people responsible for ensuring that the statutory scheme operates properly, must be scrupulous in ensuring that the relevant criteria are met.[69] Accordingly, requirement (*b*) is fairly strict. An applicant under Schedule 1 to PACE need not show that every remotely possible means of obtaining material has been tried or seriously considered, but those which are readily available, including alternative legal means, should be tried or seriously considered, but those which are readily available, including alternative legal means, should be tried or seriously considered, and the judge should be told why they failed to seem to be impracticable. In *R. v. Lewes Crown Court, ex pate Hill*,[70] the police wanted material relating to four bank accounts, which they thought were likely to provide evidence in respect of seventeen charges of theft then pending against the applicant. They obtained an order under section 7 of the Bankers' Books Evidence Act 1879, but this was later quashed on the ground that the application had been seriously defective. The applicant then granted access to some material by consent, but refused to produce other material without a court order. Instead of applying for another order under the 1879 Act, the police successfully sought an order for production under Schedule 1 to PACE. However, when applying for the Schedule 1 order, the police did not tell the circuit judge of the circumstances surrounding the quashing of the order under the 1879 Act. Because of this inadequacy in the disclosure to the judge, it was later held on an application for judicial review of the order that there had been no material on which the judge could properly have been satisfied that it appeared that a proper application under the 1879 Act would have been bound to fail, and the order was quashed.

---

[68] Unreported, 13 Feb. 1991, DC; text available from Lexis.

[69] See *R. v. Leeds Crown Court, ex parte Switalski* [1991] Crim. LR 559, DC, *per* Neill LJ (transcript from Lexis).

[70] [1991] Crim. LR 376, DC.

One curious result of the drafting of requirement (*b*) is that the all-important factor was the view of the officers when they applied for the Schedule 1 order as to the likely effectiveness of other means of obtaining the material. The real likelihood of obtaining the material by other means is irrelevant. In *ex parte Hill* the police argued at the judicial review hearing that an application under the 1879 Act had, in reality, been bound to be at most partially successful, because the police wanted access not only to records of the suspect's bank accounts, which would have been covered by the 1879 Act, but also to correspondence, which is not within the meaning of 'bankers' books' under the Act. However, because this problem with the 1879 Act had not been in the minds of the applicants at the time when it was decided to apply for a production order under PACE, it could not be said that other means of obtaining the material had appeared to be bound to fail. Accordingly, condition (*b*) had not been met.

The requirement protects advisers against coerced disclosure. No similar requirement applies to search warrants in respect of material which is not excluded or special procedure material, despite the greater threat which the execution of a warrant poses to privacy and property interests.[71] This is because such warrants are likely to affect only the interests of the suspect, not those of the professional advisers and their other, unimplicated, clients.

Requirement (*c*), as it has been interpreted so far by the courts, is more easily satisfied than (*b*). Once a circuit judge decides under (*a*) that there is material, in specified premises, which is likely to be both relevant evidence and of substantial value to the investigation of a serious arrestable offence, it is always likely to be open to the judge to decide, under (*c*), that it is in the public interest that access or production should be ordered. However, it does not follow automatically that it will be in the public interest to make an order in all cases where requirement (*a*) is satisfied. On the wording of Schedule 1 to PACE, this is a matter of judgment for the circuit judge, and may demand detailed consideration of the countervailing public interests in order to arrive at a balance of interests under (*c*). A judge might in appropriate cases, without committing a reviewable error of law, decide that (*a*) is satisfied, yet refuse an order on the ground that it would not be in the public interest to grant one.

Nevertheless, one decision suggests that the judge has no such freedom. In *R. v. Northampton Crown Court, ex parte Director of Public Prosecutions*,[72] Taylor LJ, delivering the judgment of the Divisional Court, held that it would be *Wednesbury* unreasonable—so unreasonable that no

---

[71]   *R. v. Billericay JJ and Dobbyn, ex parte Frank Harris (Coaches) Ltd.* [1991] Crim. LR 472, DC.

[72]   [1991] 93 Crim. App R 376, DC.

reasonable judge could properly do it—to accept that relevant evidence is on premises, and that it would be of substantial value to an investigation into a serious arrestable offence, but then to hold that it would not be in the public interest to order production or access. A broadly similar approach has been adopted in respect of applications for production of journalistic material, although in these cases the competing public interest factors were at least examined.[73] Any such examination seems to be made otiose by the *Northampton* decision, in which Taylor LJ did not explain what scope, if any was left for considering the public interest under requirement (*c*). An interpretation which narrows a statutory judicial discretion to weigh competing interests to a point where the statutory provision loses all possible effect is highly questionable. It is inconsistent with the usual approach where Parliament gives a power to an administrative official to be exercised in the light of a judgment about the balance of public interests. In such cases, judges normally hold that it is the job of the designated decision-maker to strike that balance, and a considered judgment as to the public interest would be interfered with only if it is exercised perversely or on wrong principles. It is not clear why different considerations should be thought to apply where the discretion is exercised against granting an order. The tendency, here and in cases involving journalistic material, to dismantle the protection given to confidential material by the Act suggests a determination to ensure that the police are not inconvenienced by the new legislation, even to the point of flouting the clear meaning of a statute. This may indicate a view, which would be hard to sustain on constitutional grounds, that the protection for confidential information under the Act where people are suspected of serious arrestable offences is incompatible with the public interest, despite having been enacted by Parliament.

When a court restricts confidentiality rights by refusing to permit the circuit judge to exercise the discretion granted by Parliament, to make a judgment about the balance of public interests, it threatens the justification, which might otherwise be available under Article 8(2) of the European Convention on Human Rights, for any consequent interference with respect for private life and correspondence. The justification available under Article 8(2) depends on the legislature which lays down the rules, and the officer who authorizes a particular interference, ensuring that an interference is in accordance with the law and necessary in a democratic society. The legislature enjoys a margin of appreciation in judging what is necessary in a democratic society, but, once the legislature has spoken, courts and other officials would appear to breach the

---

[73] *Chief Constable of Avon and Somerset* v. *Bristol United Press, Independent*, 4 Nov. 1986; *R.* v. *Bristol Crown Court, ex parte Bristol Press & Picture Agency Ltd.* (1986) 85 Cr. App. R. 190, DC. See further s. 13.4(3), below.

Convention if they dispense with a protection for the right, based on a public interest, which the legislature thought necessary.

(ii) *The second set of access conditions.* These, under paragraph 3 of Schedule 1 to PACE, are applicable to excluded material as well as special procedure material. The conditions are that:

- (*a*) there are reasonable grounds for believing that there is material which consists of or includes excluded material or special material (but does not include items subject to legal privilege) on specified premises;
- (*b*) but for the prohibition in section 9 of PACE on issuing search warrants for such material, a search of the premises for that material could have been authorized by a warrant issued to a constable under an enactment other than Schedule 1 itself; *and*
- (*c*) the issue of a warrant would have been appropriate.

A general point about the relationship between the two sets of access conditions emerges from paragraph 3. Whereas the first set of access conditions extends the powers of the police to obtain access to material which would often not previously have been accessible, the second set imposes limitations on access to material for which they could otherwise have obtained a search warrant. This narrower basis for access is the only one on which the police may obtain access to the particularly sensitive category of excluded material. If, even apart from section 9(2) of PACE, no search warrant would be available in respect of particular material or a particular suspected crime, the police will be unable to obtain access to excluded material. It is in this sense that the material is 'excluded' from investigations. On the other hand, if a power to issue a search warrant would otherwise be available, the police may utilize the second set of access conditions to seek access to excluded material, even if the offence in question is not a serious arrestable offence.

Taking the specific requirements of the second set of access conditions in turn, the first present few problems, as long as the applicant is able to satisfy the circuit judge of reasonable grounds for believing that the material is on the premises, and is not subject to legal privilege. The latter point requires special attention when the premises in question are those of a solicitor. The fact that other material, which does not consist of either items subject to legal privilege or excluded or special material, is present does not prevent material falling within the definition from being special procedure material.[74]

Condition (*b*) is less straightforward. Statutory powers to issue warrants which were enacted before PACE are within the scope of the condition.

---

[74] *R.* v. *Preston Crown Court, ex parte McGrath,* unreported, 13 Oct. 1992, DC.

However, powers enacted in or after PACE will not be within the condition if the legislation in question provides that they may not be used to seek excluded material. For example, the general power in section 8 of PACE to grant search warrants for evidence of serious arrestable offences does not apply to excluded material or special procedure material.[75] it could therefore not be said that a warrant to search for such evidence which consists of excluded or special procedure material would be available but for section 9(2). It follows that the police cannot seek an order under Schedule 1, paragraph 3, for access to excluded material by reference to such a provision. For example, before section 8 of PACE was enacted, there was no procedure whereby a search warrant could be obtained to search for evidence of murder. Murder investigations therefore fall outside the second set of access conditions. It follows that murder investigators cannot seek access to a person's medical records by way of a production or access order under Schedule 1, because such records are excluded material which are available only under the second set of access conditions, which do not apply in murder cases.[76] In such cases only special procedure material may be sought, and that must be sought under the first, rather than the second, set of access conditions.

Condition (c) of the second set of access conditions clearly envisages that wider questions than those which relate to mere jurisdiction to issue a warrant will arise, but the nature of these considerations is not expressed. The grant of a search warrant is a discretionary act, and any judge or magistrate who is considering an application for a warrant is a discretionary act, and any judge or magistrate who is considering an application for a warrant ought to exercise that discretion, taking account of the nature of the offence, the capacity in which the person holding the material does so, and whether it would be feasible to obtain access to the material in a less dramatic way. It is arguable that every issuing authority should take account of these matters.[77] Judges assessing applications under the second set of access conditions should consider whether it would have been appropriate to grant a warrant in respect of excluded material in the light of the balance of public interests, having regard to such matters as ought to be considered by justices issuing warrants. It should be borne in mind that orders to produce or allow access to material, directed to people such as solicitors, bankers, building societies, and investment advisers, impose a considerable administrative and financial burden on them, which they are not in a position to pass on to the customers or

[75] PACE, s. 8(1)(d).
[76] R. v. Central Criminal Court, ex parte Brown, unreported, DC, 30 July 1992 (text available from Lexis).
[77] D. Feldman, The Law Relating to Entry, Search and Seizure (London: Butterworths, 1986), 117–20.

clients concerned. Customers will often not even be informed of the order, let alone asked to authorize expenditure in complying with it: there is no contractual obligation on a banker, for instance, to pass information about receipt of an order for production to a customer whose affairs are affected by it. Access should therefore be by consent whenever possible, allowing the person holding the material to arrange matters so as to cause a minimum of disruption to business.

A professional adviser will frequently be unwilling to allow access to confidential material concerning a client's affairs unless compelled to do so by law. The adviser may reasonably take the view that tamely to hand over material might give rise to liability to the client for breach of confidence or breach of contract, and would also damage business confidence by undermining the adviser's reputation for discretion in relation to client's affairs. Where there is a statutory obligation to provide information on request, as in respect of tax matters and funds for terrorism, there is no such problem. However, in relation to information about proceeds of drug trafficking and of other serious crimes legislation gives only partial protection, providing that a person who discloses to a constable a suspicion or belief that property has been obtained, or derives from property which has been obtained, as a result of a crime covered by the legislation, or discloses any matter on which the suspicion or belief is based, 'does not commit a breach of any restriction upon the disclosure of information imposed by contract'.[78] This does not protect advisers or others against liability for breach of confidence in equity. If the suspicions are well founded, the adviser will be able to rely on the defence that 'there is no confidence in an iniquity', but if the suspicion is mistaken and the client is innocent the adviser might well be liable, unless the courts were willing to construct a wide-ranging public policy defence to encourage advisers to shop their clients.

(3) Procedural protections for confidences under Schedule 1 to PACE

If consensual access cannot be achieved, the procedures laid down for applying for orders are calculated, like much of the law considered in this chapter, to protect the interests of the adviser who holds material rather than the interests of the client, whose interests are principally affected by breaches of confidence. It seems to be assumed, usually correctly, that the client is a suspect, and necessarily suffers some detriment in the public interest. The procedures are straightforward.

The officer applying for an order must obtain the consent of an officer of at least the rank of superintendent. This is normally given as a matter

[78] Drug Trafficking Offences Act1986, s. 24(3)(a); Criminal Justice Act 1988, s. 98.

of course, the investigating officers being in the best position to decide whether and when it is appropriate to apply.[79] Notice is served on the people who appear to hold the material,[80] informing them of the application for an order directed to them and of their right to appear to contest the application. The notice need not be served on a suspect on whose behalf the material is being held.[81] The police have a discretion as to whether to supply, in advance of the hearing, the evidence on which they base their application for the order. If supplying the evidence poses no risk to the success of the investigation, they may supply it, but if there is a risk that it would be used to prejudice the investigation they may withhold it until the hearing.[82]

The police will have to describe the material sought to the person in possession of it when the notice is served, because, once the notice has been served on a person holding the material, that person must not conceal, destroy, alter, or dispose of the material to which the application relates without the leave of a judge or the written permission of a constable, until the application has been dismissed or abandoned or any order made has been complied with.[83] Breach of this rule makes the person liable to be dealt with as if for contempt of court. The notice must therefore make the material to which the application relates as clear as possible, to prevent a situation in which a person is liable to be penalized for destroying material which he had no way of knowing that he ought not to have destroyed. In particular, the notice should contain a description of everything which the police hope to obtain, even if that gives rise to some risk that the suspect will be forewarned and the material tampered with.[84] The requirement has the incidental benefit of making it harder for the police to embark on fishing expeditions. Normally the information should be in documentary form, and will usually be included in the written notice, but it will suffice to give the information orally, so long as the police can prove that it was in fact given.[85]

At the hearing before a circuit judge, the applicant will give evidence,

---

[79] Code B, para. 2.4; Ken Lidstone and Vaughan Bevan, *Search and Seizure under the Police and Criminal Evidence Act 1984* (Sheffield: Univ. of Sheffield Faculty of Law, 1992), 145–6.

[80] PACE, Sched. 1, para. 4.

[81] *R. v. Leicester Crown Court, ex parte DPP* [1987] 1 WLR, 1371, [1987] 3 All ER 654, DC.

[82] *R. v. Central Criminal Court, ex pate Adegbesan* [1986] 1 WLR 1292, [1986] 3 All ER 113, DC; *R. v. Crown Court at Inner London Sessions, ex parte Baines & Baines (a firm)* [1988] 1 QB 579, [1987] 3 All ER 1025, DC.

[83] PACE, Sched. 1, para. 11.

[84] *R. v. Central Criminal Court, ex parte Adegbesan* [1986] 1 WLR 1292, [1986] 3 All ER 113, DC.

[85] *R. v. Crown Court at Manchester, ex parte Taylor* [1988] 2 All ER 769, DC.

and may be cross-examined. The applicant must take care not to make misleading or unsupported allegations concerning the person holding the material sought. Any evidence placed before the judge to support the application must, if not previously supplied to the respondent with the notice, be made available to the respondent, and, if it would be difficult for the respondent to deal with it on the spur of the moment, the judge should allow an adjournment.[86] At the end of the hearing, the circuit judge will decide whether to grant the order, and in what terms. Either party may challenge the decision by way of an application for judicial review to the Divisional Court of Queen's Bench Division.[87] The grounds of review are limited by public-law principles, and an order will not be quashed unless the issuing judge acted without authority or on the wrong principles, or somebody failed to observe the proper procedures, or the decision was one which no reasonable judge could have reached. This means that the Divisional Court has little opportunity to influence decisions on the merits of applications. It has been suggested that an alternative procedure, appeal by case stated to the Divisional Court, may be available.[88] If it is, the court might have more freedom to examine the merits of a decision than in judicial-review proceedings.[89] Although an order could be overturned on appeal only if shown to be wrong in law or in excess of jurisdiction,[90] the Divisional Court has treated a decision reached without evidence as erroneous in law.[91] Nevertheless, the appeal would not by any means be a rehearing on the merits.

Once an order has been made and is not being challenged by way of review or appeal, the person to whom it is addressed must comply with it within seven days, unless the judge is persuaded to allow a longer period,[92] perhaps because of the administrative difficulties which are involved in finding and making available the material. The material must be produced for a constable to take away, or made available for inspection. Where material is contained in a computer, it must be provided in a form in which it is visible and legible, and, if the order is for production rather than merely for access, it must be in a form in which it can be taken away. All material produced pursuant to an order is to be treated as if it were material seized by a constable, so sections 21 and 22 of PACE

[86] R. v. Crown Court at Inner London Sessions, ex parte Baines & Baines (a firm) [1988] 1 QB 579, [1987] 3 All ER 1025, DC.

[87] These applications are regarded as being in a criminal cause or matter, so any appeal from the decision of the Divisional Court lies, with leave, directly to the House of Lords: Carr v. Atkins [1987] 3 All ER 684, CA.

[88] R. v. Central Criminal Court, ex parte Carr, Independent, 5 Mar. 1987, per Glidewel LJ.

[89] See R. T. H. Stone, 'PACE: Special Procedures and Legal Privilege' [1988] Crim LR 498–507 at pp. 506–7.

[90] Magistrates' Courts Act 1980, s. 111(1).

[91] Bracegirdle v. Oxley [1947] 1 KB 349.   [92] PACE, Sched. 1, para. 4.

(allowing material to be copied or retained by the police for certain purposes: see Chapter 9 above) apply to it.[93]

Two features of the procedure for obtaining an order make it clear that
the object is to protect people such as advisers who innocently hold
material about a suspect, rather than protecting the privacy or confidentiality interests of the client. First, the notice of an application for an
order is to be served on the person who appears to be in possession of the
material sought, not on the person who is the subject of the records or
samples. The reason is simple: the investigation might be hampered if the
subject found out about it; he might decamp, or destroy or hide evidence.[94] It has even been regarded as an open question whether the subject has standing to apply for judicial review of an order which has been
addressed to the subject's advisers.[95]

Secondly, although there is normally nothing to stop the person holding the material from telling the client of the notice, the police will often
strongly discourage such a course. This makes it more difficult for the
person holding the material to contest the application. Indeed, applications for orders are rarely contested. While solicitors have sometimes,
with the support of the Law Society, contested applications or challenged
orders which have been made, other professionals, such as bankers, rarely
have any incentive to risk incurring substantial and unrecoverable costs in
protecting the interests of a client who is suspected of a crime. Even were
an adviser minded to contest the application, it would usually be difficult
to do so without contacting the client to obtain information relevant to
the case.[96] Moreover, there are certain statutes which make it an offence
for a person to advise another that an order has been applied for or
obtained, specifically where the case concerns the proceeds of drug trafficking or money for use in terrorism. Although it has been suggested
(obiter) that a solicitor's duty to the client would justify giving the information in order to obtain instructions,[97] it is not clear either that this is
correct, or that it would apply to other professions (as there is no duty on
a banker, for example, to take instructions from customers in these

---

[93] Ibid., paras. 5, 6.

[94] R. v. Crown Court at Leicester, ex parte DPP [1987] 1 WLR 1371, [1987] 3 All ER
654, DC.

[95] R. v. Central Criminal Court, ex parte Carr, Independent, 5 Mar. 1987, DC.

[96] See Christine Graham and Clive Walker, 'The Continued Assault on the Vault:
Bank Accounts and Criminal Investigations' [1989] Crim. LR 185–97; David Feldman,
'Conveyancers and the Proceeds of Crime' [1989] Conveyancer 389–402; A. A. S.
Zuckerman, 'The Weakness of PACE Special Procedure for Protecting Confidential
Materal' [1990] Crim. LR 472–8; Lidstone and Bevan, Search and Seizure, 144–8.

[97] R. v. Central Criminal Court, ex parte Francis & Francis (a firm) [1989] AC 346, [1988]
3 All ER 775, HL, per Lord Griffiths.

circumstances)[98] or to people who voluntarily hold material about subjects under investigation.

The overall effect is that the people who are being protected by the
special procedures under Schedule 1 to PACE are the advisers who campaigned for the introduction of the procedures, not those whose confidentiality interests are most directly and adversely affected by the
procedure.

(4) Search warrants for confidential material

There is a further, more draconian procedure available to the police in
respect of material normally accessible under Schedule 1: the grant of a
search warrant. This power is to cater for three types of case. The first
class comprises cases in which it would be ineffective to go through the
production order procedure, either because it would be impossible to
find anyone with authority to comply with the order or because the purpose is to prevent an unlawful disclosure of material which is likely to be
disclosed before any order could be made or executed. The second class
comprises cases where the process of applying for an order for production, with notice being given, would be seriously counter-productive,
allowing for the disappearance of evidence, proceeds of crime, or suspects. The third class comprises cases where a production order has been
granted but has not been complied with.

There are two separate sets of grounds on which a warrant may be
issued. First, if an order for production has been made on the basis of the
second set of access conditions (in other words, on the ground that it
would have been possible and proper to issue a search warrant but for
section 9(2) of PACE) and has not been complied with, a circuit judge
may grant a warrant authorizing a constable to enter and search the
premises where the material is reasonably believed to be.[99] Secondly, a
circuit judge may issue a warrant without first making an order for production under paragraph 4 of Schedule 1 to PACE, if satisfied that either
set of access conditions is fulfilled and also that one of the following preconditions applies:[100]

    (a) that it is not practicable to communicate with any person entitled
        to grant entry to the premises in question;
    (b) that it is not practicable to communicate with anyone entitled to
        grant access to the material sought;
    (c) that the material in question is the subject of a statutory restriction

---

[98] *Barclays Bank plc (trading as Barclaycard)* v. *Taylor* [1989] 1 WLR 1066, [1989] 3 All
ER 563, CA.
[99] PACE Sched. 1, para. 12(*b*).   [100] Ibid., para. 12(*a*), 14.

on disclosure or obligation of secrecy, and is likely to be improperly disclosed if a warrant is not issued; or

(d) that service of notice of an application for an order, as would normally be required, may seriously prejudice the investigation.

There is some overlap between heads (a) to (b). In particular, 'not practicable' has been regarded as having a wider meaning than 'not feasible' or 'physically impossible', so, when deciding whether it would be practicable to communicate with a person for the purposes of (a) and (b), it is permissible to consider whether communicating with them would lead to the destruction of evidence, or similar consequences, which would be equally relevant to (d).[101]

Granting a warrant to search for excluded and special procedure material is a serious matter. The judges have made it clear that warrants under Schedule 1 to PACE are not to be applied for or granted routinely,[102] as routine applications would distort the statutory scheme of protection provided under section 9 and the remainder of Schedule 1 of PACE. The courts have also been prepared to examine warrant applications rather more critically than applications for production orders. Four principles have been established in the case-law.

First, where a warrant is sought on the basis that it would be impracticable to communicate with a person entitled to grant access to the premises or the material, the police have a heavy duty to discharge if they are seeking material on business premises, particularly if it is in a solicitor's office. Where there are receptionists, partners, assistants, and so forth, readily available on the premises, it will not usually be impracticable to contact them, at least during office hours.[103] There is an exception to this, however, where the occupants of the premises to be searched, who hold the material sought, are themselves under suspicion in the investigation of the offence. In these circumstances, it might not be practicable (giving that word a broad meaning) to communicate with a person with authority, as that person might be implicated in the offence.[104]

Secondly, when granting a warrant, the circuit judge must take care to ensure that it is no wider than is justified by the information supporting the application. In *R. v. Central Criminal Court and British Railways Board, ex parte A. J. D. Holdings Ltd., Royle & Stanley Ltd., and others,*[105] a fraud investigation, where the information supporting the application for a warrant referred to grounds for seizing 'all records of business details relating to the finances of [Royle & Stanley Ltd.] namely: letters, notes . . .', the judge granted a warrant authorizing a search for and seizure of

---

[101] *R. v. Leeds Crown Court, ex parte Switalski* [1991] Crim. LR 559, DC.

[102] *R. v. Maidstone Crown Court, ex parte Waitt* [1988] Crim. LR 384, DC.

[103] Ibid. [104] *R. v. Leeds Crown Court, ex parte Switalski* [1991] Crim. LR 559, DC.

[105] [1992] Crim. LR 669, DC.

'material likely to be relevant evidence of that offence, namely: letters, notes [etc.]', without limiting the seizable items by reference to business records concerning the finances of the company. On an application for judicial review of the warrant,[106] it was therefore held that the warrant as drawn was wider than could be supported by reference to the information, and was invalid.

Thirdly, the police and the circuit judge must comply strictly with the formal requirements for warrants and searches. The warrant which must be produced to the occupier of premises (a copy of which must be provided, under section 16(5) of PACE) must provide all the information required by section 15. If any part of that information is unavailable, for example because it is on separate pages inadequately attached to the cover sheet of the warrant, or contained in a schedule which comes adrift from the main body of the warrant, the search will be unlawful.[107] The warrant must also identify so far as practicable the items to be sought, so as to constrain a general rummage through confidential papers.[108]

Fourthly, if a search is conducted in reliance on a warrant which turns out to be invalid, (a) reliance on the warrant will not make the search lawful, and (b) the police will not be permitted to retain any material seized as against the lawful owner.[109] Furthermore, even if the warrant is valid, it will not be held to authorize the seizure or retention of items which do not fall within the description in the warrant of the materials for which search is authorized.[110]

In addition to these principles, entry to search for excluded and special procedure material is hedged about with procedural safeguards. Like applications for production orders, applications for Schedule 1 warrants must be authorized by an officer of at least the rank of superintendent.[111] Empirical evidence suggests that this requirement does not result in many applications being rejected by the superintendent. The main value of the requirement seems to be that it underlines in the minds of investigating officers the seriousness of invoking the search warrant jurisdiction in

---

[106] This is the proper procedure for challenging a warrant. Having once granted a warrant, the circuit judge is *functus officio*, and has no power to hold an *inter partes* hearing to consider revoking the warrant: *R. v. Liverpool Crown Court, ex parte Wimpey plc* [1991] Crim. LR 635, DC.

[107] *R. v. Chief Constable of Lancashire, ex parte Parker*, [1993] 2 WLR 428; [1993] 1 All ER 56, DC.

[108] PACE, s. 15(6)(b). See *R. v. Central Criminal Court and British Railways Board, ex parte A. J. D. Holdings Ltd., Royle and Stanley Ltd. and others* [1992] Crim. LR 669, DC.

[109] *R. v. Central Criminal Court and British Railways Board, ex parte A. J. D. Holding Ltd., Royle & Stanley Ltd., and others* [1992] Crim. LR 669, DC; *R. v. Chief Constable of Lancashire, ex parte Parker and another, Independent*, 1 Apr. 1992, DC.

[110] *R. v. Central Criminal Court and British Railways Board, ex parte A. J. D. Holding Ltd., Royle & Stanley Ltd., and others* [1992] Crim. LR 669, DC.

[111] Code B, para. 2.4.

these circumstances.[112] Once the superintendent has authorized the application, it goes to a circuit judge, supported by a written information in a similar way to other warrant applications. If it is made on the ground that applying for a production order may seriously prejudice the investigation, the application (or, more correctly, the information in writing supporting the application) must indicate the basis for believing that to be so.[113] This ought to apply also where the application is made on the basis that it is impracticable to communicate with anyone entitled to grant access to the premises or material because communicating with them would let the cat out of the bag and interfere with the investigation.

(5) Proceeds of crime legislation: drug trafficking and terrorism

In two fields, Parliament has enacted variants on the PACE procedure for obtaining access and production orders. As part of the drive to make drug trafficking uneconomic by facilitating the tracing and confiscation of proceeds of crime, the Drug Trafficking Offences Act 1986 introduced a procedure under which orders for access to or production of special procedure material. A circuit judge may make an order if satisfied:

(a) that there are reasonable grounds for suspecting that a specified person has carried on or benefited from drug trafficking; and
(b) that there are reasonable grounds for suspecting that specified material is likely to be of substantial value to the investigation, and does not consist of items subject to legal privilege or excluded material; and
(c) that there are reasonable grounds for believing that it is in the public interest that the material should be produced, having regard to the benefit likely to accrue and the capacity in which the person holding the material does so.[114]

Similar provisions apply under the Prevention of Terrorism (Temporary Provisions) Act 1989, Schedule 7, in relation to information about funds intended for terrorism, but the scope of the 1989 Act is wider than that of the drug-trafficking provisions: the 1989 Act, unlike the 1986 Act, applies to excluded material as well as special procedure and ordinary material.[115] Proposals are under consideration to extend penal sanctions further, requiring anyone who, in the course of any trade, business, or vocation, knows or suspects that another person is laundering the proceeds of any offence to disclose the fact to the police, on pain of criminal penalties.[116] Such provisions, which would extend beyond drug

[112] Lidstone and Bevan, *Search and Seizure*, 145–6.
[113] Code B, para. 2.7.   [114] Drug Trafficking Offences Act 1986, s. 27.
[115] There are limited defences under both Acts: see Feldman, 'Conveyancers and the Proceeds of Crime' 396–401.
[116] Home Office Working Group on Confiscation, *Report on Part VI of the Criminal Justice Act 1988* (London: Home Office, 1992), para. 2.47.

trafficking and terrorism-related crime, have precedents elsewhere (notably in Australia and the USA), but raise serious issues for the confidentiality of professional relationships which need to be carefully thought through.[117]

Unlike a PACE application, the officers apply for an order *ex pate* under the 1986 Act and the Prevention of Terrorism (Temporary Provisions) Act 1989, and no notice of the application need be served on the person believed to be holding the material. The courts must therefore carefully weigh applications for such orders, to protect the interests of unimplicated parties who hold the material sought.[118] Once an order is served, it is a contempt of court to refuse to comply with it or to conceal, destroy, or otherwise deal with the material covered by it without the leave of the court. In addition, it is an offence for a person without a lawful authority or reasonable excuse to make any disclosure which is likely to prejudice the investigation.[119] Where the subject of the investigation is a client or customer of the person who holds the material which is sought, it would therefore appear, on the face of it, to be unlawful for the person to whom the order is addressed to tell the client that the order has ben made, or to seek instructions as to whether to release the material or challenge the order. If the people holding the material are unable or unwilling to test the validity of the order, this may force them to choose either to release it in circumstances where the release may be unjustified, or to inform the client and risk criminal liability. In *R. v. Central Criminal Court, ex parte Francis & Francis*, Lord Griffiths, *obiter*, suggested that a professional's duty to look after the affairs of a client might provide a lawful authority or reasonable excuse for informing the client that the investigation is in progress, where this is necessary in order to take instructions from the client.[120] However, if this justification relies on a contractual obligation owed by professionals to their clients, it is severely limited in scope. It has been held that bankers have no contractual obligation to inform their customers about production orders made or sought in respect of material concerning the client.[121] *A fortiori* social workers and voluntary agencies, with no contractual obligations to their 'clients', would find it hard to base a reasonable excuse or lawful justification on the fiduciary relationship which links them to the 'client'. Informing

---

[117] For a comparative survey, see David Feldman, 'Individual Rights and Legal Values in Proceeds of Crime Legislation: A Comparative Approach' (1989) 18 *Anglo-Amer. LR* 261–88.

[118] Guidance for the exercise of the court's power under the 1989 Act was provided in *R. v. Crown Court at Middlesex Guildhall, ex parte Salinger* [1993] 2 WLR 438; [1993] 2 All ER 310, DC.

[119] Drug Trafficking Offences Act 1986, s. 31.

[120] [1989[AC 346 at p. 386, [1988] 3 All ER 775 at p. 792.

[121] *Barclays Bank plc (trading as Barclaycard)* v. *Taylor* [1989] 1 WLR 1066, [1989] 3 All ER 563, CA.

clients that orders under the 1986 or 1989 Acts have been made in respect of material which relates to them is at best a risky business.[122]

It follows, therefore, that it will often be the responsibility of the person holding the material to decide whether to challenge the order by way of an application or judicial review, or apply for its variation or discharge, and what material should be produced in complying with the order. It is important that sufficient information should be served with the order to make it possible for these decisions to e taken. The information which formed the basis for the making of the order may be highly sensitive in drug-trafficking and terrorism cases, and there may be good reasons for not disclosing it, either to the circuit judge to whom the application for the order is made, or to the people holding the material sought. Everyone may have to work on less extensive information in cases where the source of the information is secret than in ordinary cases arising under Schedule 1 to PACE.

In *R. v. Crown Court at Middlesex Guildhall, ex parte Salinger*,[123] a journalist applied for judicial review to require a judge to order the police to serve him with the grounds on which a production order had been made under the terrorism legislation. The case concerned video recordings and other records of interviews conducted by Mr. Salinger in Libya with two Libyans suspected of having planted the bomb which blew up a Pan American World aircraft over Lockerbie in December 1988. The court held that the overall objective should be to provide as much information, preferably in writing, as early in the proceedings, as is consistent with the security of the operation. The court laid down four guidelines: the judge should be given a written statement of the evidence relied on to support the application for an order, although this need not disclose the nature of source of the information if it is too sensitive to allow disclosure; a judge who makes an order should give directions as to the information which should be served on the recipient, and that information should normally be served in the form of a written statement from the constable, which should be as full as possible without compromising security; if it is inappropriate to serve any information at that stage, the judge should consider whether it would be appropriate to serve any in the event of the recipient of the order applying for its variation or discharge; and application for variation or discharge of an order should be heard by the judge who originally made the order. The judge has the job, at every stage, of being as fair as possible to the recipient of the order without defeating the

---

[122] The dilemma is discussed by Graham and Walker, 'Continued Assault on the Vaults' 185–97; D. Wheatley, 'Guilty . . . said the Red Queen?' (1989) 139 *NLJ* 499–500; and Feldman, 'Conveyancers and the Proceeds of Crime' 389–402.

[123] [1993] 2 All ER 310, DC.

purpose of making it or putting at risk the security of the operation. This is no easy task.

Where confiscation of proceeds of crime is envisaged under those Acts, or under Part VI of the Criminal Justice Act 1988 in relation to other offences where the benefit to the criminal reaches £10,000, it is possible to obtain further information by other procedures. An order for disclosure of information or documents is available in High Court proceedings, including an application for a restraint or charging order under the legislation, freezing the assets of those who are thought to have benefited from crime.[124] In order to discover the extent and whereabouts of a person's assets, an investigator applying for a restraint order can seek discovery and administer interrogatories, as if applications for restraint orders were ordinary High Court litigation in which all the usual interlocutory orders were available.[125] This is particularly useful where the drug-trafficking and terrorism provisions do not apply, as there is no power under the 1988 Act to obtain access or production orders in respect of material which is needed to trace the proceeds of a suspected crime.

Useful as these powers are to those who have to track down the proceeds of crime with a view to having them confiscated, they raise issues of principle which were not properly debated when the 1986 and 1989 Acts were passed. Compelling disclosure of material is a major incursion on the right of silence, although this might be of diminishing significance in view of the recent sustained assault on the right of silence by the judges and politicians. Perhaps more significant is the manner in which the rights of suspects in the criminal justice process have been steadily undermined by employing civil procedures, such as discovery and restraint orders, in criminal investigations, moving from a principle that the prosecution must prove all elements of its case on a playing field which, if not level, is tilted in favour of the subject, to a belief that there are certain matters which are so serious that the protections which the legal process normally offers to subjects can justifiably be relaxed. This is an unattractive feature of the legislation, but it is one shared with proceeds of crime legislation in many parts of the world, including some (notably the USA) in which the existence of constitutional guarantees of due process would have led one to expect a higher regard for principle.[126]

[124] For a general account of restraint orders, see D. Feldman, *Criminal Confiscation Orders: The New Law* (London: Butterworths, 1988), ch. 5.
[125] *In re O. (Disclosure Order)* [1991] 2 WLR 475, [1991] 1 All ER 330, CA; M. S. Dockray, 'Restraint Orders' (1991) 107 *LQR* 376–80; *In re Thomas (Disclosure Order)* [1992] 4 All ER 814, CA.
[126] Feldman, 'Individual Rights and Legal Values' 261–88.

(6) A special case: the Security Service Act 1989[127]

In 1989, in an uncharacteristic burst of unsolicited openness following the *Spycatcher* affair, the government decided to put the security service, MI5, on a statutory footing. Peter Wright, in his book, had recounted stories of bugging and burglary by the service in England, actions for which there was no legal authority or public accountability. One of the objects of the Act was, in the words of the long title, 'to enable certain actions to be taken on the authority of warrants issued by the Secretary of State, with provision for the issue of such warrants to be kept under review by a Commissioner . . .'. The result was the Security Service Act 1989, section 1 of which defines the functions of the security service as being 'the protection of national security and, in particular, its protection against threats from espionage, terrorism and sabotage, from the activities of agents of foreign powers and from actions intended to overthrow or undermine parliamentary democracy by political, industrial or violent means' and 'to safeguard the economic well-being of the United Kingdom against threats posed by the actions or intentions of persons outside the British Islands'.[128]

These functions give the service a very wide brief. The powers of entry which are conferred on the service by section 3 of the Act are framed in terms of those wide functions. No entry on or interference with property is to be unlawful if it is authorized by a warrant issued, not by a judge, but by the Secretary of State. A Secretary of State's warrant may be granted, specifying the action which is authorized, if the Secretary of State

(*a*) thinks that the action is necessary in order to obtain information which is likely to be of substantial value in assisting the Service to perform any of its functions, and which cannot be obtained by other means, and

(*b*) is satisfied that satisfactory arrangements are in force to ensure that no information obtained will be disclosed by the Service except so far as is necessary for the discharge of its functions or for the purpose of preventing or detecting serious crime.[129]

Warrants remain in force for six months, but may be renewed. A Security Service Commissioner, who must hold or have held high judicial office, is appointed.[130] Under section 4(3) the Commissioner has particular responsibility for keeping under review the way in which the

[127] For commentaries on the Security Service Act 1989, see Ian Leigh and laurence Lustgarten, 'The Security Service Act 1989' 52 *MLR* 801–36; K. D. Ewing and C. A. Gearty, *Freedom under Thatcher: Civil Liberties in Modern Britain* (Oxford: Clarendon Press, 1990), 175–88.

[128] Security Act 1989, s. 1(2), (3).   [129] Ibid., s. 3(2); see also s. 2(2)(*a*).

[130] Ibid., s. 4(1).

Secretary of State exercises the power to issue warrants, and reports annually to the Prime Minister, who is to lay a copy of the report before each House of Parliament. Complaints from members of the public about the behaviour of the service go in the first instance to a tribunal, but, where the complaint concerns anything done in relation to property, the tribunal refers the complaint to the Commissioner, who first ascertains whether a warrant was issued, and, if one was issued, determines whether it was properly issued or renewed in accordance with judicial review principles. However, the merits of the decision to issue a warrant are not reviewable.

These provisions give cause for concern on a number of grounds. There is no judicial process involved in the issue of a warrant, unlike the position in Canada.[131] There are no statutory controls on the manner in which it may be executed. There is no independent review of the substantive propriety of the issue of warrant. Most seriously, there is no limitation as to the places which may be entered, the material which may be seized or copied, or the means adopted for doing it. No special protection, either substantive or procedural, is given to privacy or confidentiality interests. Items subject to legal privilege, excluded material, and special procedure material, are open to those executing a warrant. It has been rightly observed of section 3: 'The section amounts to statutory authorisation of ministerial general warrants for reasons of state necessity of the kind which the common law disapproved in the celebrated case of *Entick* v. *Carrington*. That decision must now more than ever be regarded as an anachronism of interest mainly to constitutional historians.'[132] This is a sad state of affairs, indicating that Parliament is either unable or unwilling to act as the guardian of constitutional principle in legislation which is put before it. In the context of confidentiality rights, it is particularly worrying that the statute fails to offer effective safeguards, or even to require the Secretary of State to balance the interests involved where confidentiality is put at risk. very often the concerns outlined in section 3 as conditions for the granting of a warrant will outweigh the competing interests of confidentiality and privacy, but it is not self-evident that this will be so in all cases. The Secretary of State should at least be required by the statute to consider the balance of interests where confidentiality is likely to be endangered.

---

[131] Canadian Security and Intelligence Service Act 1984, discussed by Ian Leigh and Laurence Lustgarten, 'The Security Commission: Constitutional Achievement or Curiosity?' [1991] *PL* 215–32, and Stuart Farson, 'Oversight of Canadian Intelligence: A revisionary Note' [1992] *PL* 377–85.

[132] Leigh and Lustgarten, 'The Security Service Act 1989' (1989) 52 *MLR* at p. 825 (footnote omitted).

10.4 INTERCEPTING COMMUNICATIONS

(1) Background

Until 1985, there was no clear legal regime for regulating the interception of communications in the United Kingdom. No legal procedure was required to be invoked for authorizing an interception, either of mail or of telephone calls, and (as noted in Chapter 9) at common law it seemed that none was needed. Meggary V.-C. held in *Malone v. Commissioner of Police of the Metropolis*[133] that interception of telephone calls did not constitute a civil wrong, because no protected interest was affected, and it was not a crime. Therefore no special authorization as needed to justify them. The method of interception involved no trespass to the plaintiff's property, and confidentiality did not attach to telephone conversations. This applied whether the people intercepting them were public officials acting in the performance of their functions, private investigators, industrial spies, or mere trouble-makers. Nor did metering of calls—the monitoring of telephone numbers dialled from the plaintiff's line—breach any confidentiality right, as metering is an essential part of the process of charging for calls made, and disclosing the results to an official authorized by a warrant from the Secretary of State was neither criminal nor tortious, because section 80 of the Post Office Act 1969 provided that information from interceptions might lawfully be passed to a person holding office under the Crown.

Intercepting mail, by contrast, was a criminal offence,[134] and might also constitute a civil wrong in that it constituted an interference with the proprietary interests of the sender or recipient of the package. It therefore needed special authority, but the authorization was administrative. It was given by senior officials of the Post Office, rather than a judicial officer. The Post Office Act 1953 provided that an interference with a postal packet was not to be criminal if authorized by a warrant issued under the hand of the Secretary of State, but did not lay down criteria for giving an authorization.[135] Warrants issued by the Secretary of State both for mail interceptions and for telecommunication interceptions shielded the officials by virtue of the Post Office Act 1969, section 80. The conditions for issuing warrants for interceptions, whether of mail or telephone conversations, were laid down by the Secretary of State in rules of practice, which had no legal force, and were publicized only in the Report of a Committee of Privy Councillors established under the chairmanship of

---

[133] [1979] Ch. 344, [1979] 2 All ER 620; Vaughan Bevan, 'Is anybody there?' [1980] *Pl* 431–53; Ewing and Gearty, *Freedom under Thatcher*, 56–61.

[134] Post Office Act 1953, s. 58.   [135] Ibid., s. 58(1), proviso.

Lord Justice Birkett in 1957 to examine the matter.[136] Different sets of
conditions applied, depending on whether the interception was designed
to assist a criminal investigation or to protect state security.

In relation to crime, the conditions were stated by the Home Secretary
to be: (a) the crime had to be really serious; (b) normal methods had to
have been tried unsuccessfully; (c) there had to be good reason for believing that a conviction would result from the evidence obtained by the
interception. In relation to security matters, two conditions were applied:
an interception could be authorized only in respect of major subversion,
terrorism, or espionage, which was likely to injure the national interest,
and the material to be obtained had to be of direct use in compiling the
information necessary for the security service (MI5) to carry out its functions in protecting state security. There was no external review of the
working of the system: the Birkett Committee in 1957 took the view
that the best safeguard against abuse lay in the final responsibility of the
Secretary of State.[137]

Following the *Malone* case, when reform was under consideration, a
White Paper was produced detailing the procedures,[138] and Lord Diplock
was appointed to review the operation of the procedures for issuing and
implementing warrants. Lord Diplock's annual reports had some effect in
widening, rather than narrowing, the range of cases in which warrants
might be granted, for example by loosening the definition of 'serious
crime'. Neither he nor Lord Bridge, who succeeded him in 1982, found
irregularities in the issue of warrants in respect of the 500 or more authorized telephone taps conducted each year between 1980 and 1985.
Generally speaking, the government seemed satisfied that administrative
controls were working adequately, although others were concerned at
evidence from former officers to the security service, such as Cathy
Massiter, that either the guidelines were not being adhered to or unauthorized telephone tapping was being carried on by officers of the
service.[139]

Two factors combined to persuade the government to change its position, and put interception on a statutory footing. First, the unsuccessful
plaintiff from *Malone* v. *Commissioner of Police of the Metropolis* lodged a
petition under the European Convention on Human Rights, arguing that
the uncontrolled interception of telephone conversations, and metering

---

[136] *Report of the Committee of Privy Councillors Appointed to Inquire into the Interception of
Communications* Cmnd. 283 (London: HMSO, 1957). For discussion, see Bevan, 'Is anybody there?' 431–53.

[137] *Report of the Committee of Privy Councillors*, Cmnd. 283, para. 139.

[138] *The Interception of Communications in Great Britain*, Cmnd. 7873 (London: HMSO,
1980), paras. 7–14.

[139] See Ewing and Gearty, *Freedom under Thatcher*, 51–65.

of calls, contravened his right to respect for private and family life, home, and correspondence under Article 8. The European Commission of Human Rights, and subsequently the Court, upheld this claim. They decided that both tapping and monitoring (or 'metering') of calls interfered with the respect for correspondence guaranteed by Article 8(1): telephone conversations fell within the scope of 'correspondence', and the knowledge that someone might be intercepting the conversation would inhibit free communication and constitute a lack of respect for the privacy of the participants. The threat of interception (whether or not one was actually taking place) which was ever-present under English law at the time was not justifiable under the terms of Article 8(2), because it was neither in accordance with the law nor necessary in a democratic society for the purpose of preventing crime. In order to be in accordance with the law, an interference must have a basis in reasonably accessible positive law. The fact that the action was not unlawful under domestic law was insufficient to satisfy the 'in accordance with the law' test of Article 8(2), which was held to incorporate rule-of-law standards into the justifying framework for interferences. No positive law expressly authorized the practice or provided criteria for it. There were therefore inadequate legal standards to provide safeguards against abuse; there was no guarantee that the power would not be used in a manner disproportionate to the object in view; and there was no legal remedy in most situations. Similarly it has since been held that the French provisions for regulating telephone tapping are not in accordance with the law, because some essential safeguards had to be deduced from scattered judicial decisions in which the trend of authority was not yet settled at the time when the case had arisen. The law was therefore not adequately clear or accessible.[140]

In an earlier case, *Klass* v. *Federal Republic of Germany*,[141] the Court had approved the safeguards in force in West Germany on telephone tapping for security purposes: Law G10 provided for warrants to be issued by a designated Minister only in relation to suspected criminal activity affecting state security; it imposed reviews of individual warrants by a Commission presided over by a person qualified for judicial office, capable of acting of its own motion. It provided that a person whose communications have been intercepted should normally be informed of the fact at the conclusion of the period of interception, unless there are national-security grounds for continuing to keep the matter secret. Proceedings for compensation could then be brought in ordinary courts if appropriate.

[140] *Kruslin* v. *France*, Eur. Ct. HR, Series A, No. 176-A, Judgment of 24 Apr. 1990, 12 EHRR 547; *Huvig* v. *France*, Eur. Ct. HR Series A, No. 176-B, Judgment of 24 Apr. 1990, 12 EHRR 528.

[141] Eur. C. HR, Series A, No. 28, Judgment of 6 Sept. 1978, 2 EHRR 214.

Law G10 also subjected the entire process of granting warrants to the general oversight of a special Parliamentary Board. These safeguards were regarded as meeting the 'in accordance with the law' and 'necessary in a democratic society' criteria in security cases, although the Court did not lay down any minimum standards which such legislation must meet in order to satisfy the justifying conditions of Article 8(2), or say whether more demanding criteria would be applied to interceptions in ordinary criminal investigations than in national-security cases.

The second factor motivating the government to introduce legislation putting interception on a firm legal footing was the privatization of telecommunications services in the Telecommunications Act 1984, which put control over lines into the hands of British Telecom, a private corporation. This made it important to regulate interceptions by law, and to criminalize unauthorized interceptions.

(2) The Interception of Communications Act 1985[142]

The government sought to provide a statutory framework for the legitimate interception of communications, putting in place safeguards against abuse of the system, while at the same time leaving the power to authorize interceptions in the exclusive power of the Secretary of State. The result was the Interception of Communications Act 1985. Section 1 of the Act makes it a criminal offence intentionally to intercept a communication in the course of its transmission through the post or the public telecommunications system, unless the interception is in accordance with a warrant issued by the Secretary of State, or the person concerned has reasonable grounds for believing that either the sender or the recipient of the communication has consented to the interception, or the interception is made for purposes connected with the provision of the service or the enforcement of legislation concerning the use of the service. It is permissible for a person authorized by the Secretary of State to intercept wireless telegraphy transmissions for purposes connected with the issue of licences under the Wireless Telegraphy Act 1949 or to prevent or detect interference with wireless telegraphy.

The ability of one party to a communication to consent to its interception, without the knowledge of the other party, gives rise to potential inroads on privacy interests. It is sensible to allow a person who is expecting to receive a threatening telephone call, or the victim of a blackmail attempt, to authorize the police to listen in on telephone conversations without the need to obtain a warrant from the Secretary of State. In such

---

[142] Ian Leigh, 'A Tapper's Charter?' [1986] *PL* 8–18; Ian J. Lloyd, 'The Interception of Communications Act 1985' (1986) 49 *MLR* 86–95; Ewing and Gearty, *Freedom under Thatcher*, pp. 65–83.

a case, the privacy interests of the offender making the call do not deserve protection, because such a person has no legitimate expectation of privacy for the call. However, unilateral permission may also allow the privacy of innocent callers to be compromised without their knowledge. More seriously, perhaps, provision for unilateral consent to interceptions allows the party who makes a call, rather than the one who receives it, to consent to interception by an associate, not the police, and without the knowledge of the recipient. For example, if a person (X), having an extra-marital sexual liaison with a prominent public figure (Y), sees an opportunity to make money by selling the story to a newspaper, X might initiate a call to Y and record (or allow an accomplice to record) their intimate conversation. The recording might then be sold to a newspaper, and a transcript published. No tort liability arises, because breach of privacy is not tortious in itself, and a defamation action would be met with a defence of truth. No criminal offence is committed, because one party to the conversation—the rogue X—consented to its interception.

However, such cases are relatively rare. A more common justification for intercepting communications is provided by a warrant issued by the Secretary of State.[143] The decision to leave the power to grant all interceptions warrants in the hands of the Secretary of State, contrary to the recommendation (in respect of criminal investigations) by the Royal Commission on Criminal Procedure,[144] is controversial. It fails to provide for the independent, prior scrutiny by a person or body with judicial experience which is offered in a number of other countries, notably Canada and Australia. However, although the European Court of Human Rights in the *Klass* case thought it desirable that, in principle, interceptions should be under judicial supervision, it was not held to be a requirement of the Convention.[145] This is understandable, since in Australia, where a clear separation of powers doctrine operates under the Constitution, it has been held that issuing a warrant is essentially a ministerial, rather than a judicial, function, and may be performed by a person holding judicial office only if that person has been appointed to issue warrants on account of his or her personal qualities (as *persona designata*), rather than by virtue of his or her judicial office.[146]

---

[143] The Secretary of State for Scotland is the competent authority for interceptions in Scotland, and the Home Secretary for interceptions in England and Wales. On the number of warrants issued, see the annual reports of the Commissioner appointed under the interception of Communications Act 1985, which are published in the Command Papers series.

[144] Royal Commission on Criminal Procedure, *Report*, Cmnd. 8092 (London: HMSO, 1981), para. 3.57, recommending that in criminal matters an application for a warrant should be made to a magistrate.

[145] *Klass v. Federal Republic of Germany*, Eur. Ct. HR, Series A, No. 28, Judgment of 6 Sept. 1978, 2 EHRR 214.

[146] *Hilton v. Wells* (1985) 157 CLR 57, HC of Australia, dealing with warrants under

More problematic is the system of remedies which is provided under the Act. A tribunal is appointed to receive complaints from people who believe that their communications have been intercepted. The tribunal finds out whether a warrant had been issued in respect of the alleged interception, and, if there is a warrant, determines whether it was issued on proper grounds and in the appropriate form, applying the standards which would be applicable in judicial-review proceedings. If the tribunal decides that the requirements of the Act have been breached, it must report its conclusion (but not its reasons) to the applicant, and report the findings in full to the Prime Minister. The tribunal may also make an order, if appropriate, quashing the warrant, directing that copies of the intercepted material be destroyed, or directing the Secretary of State to pay a specified sum in compensation.[147] If there was no authorization for an alleged interception, the tribunal lacks jurisdiction, so it provides no protection against unauthorized telephone taps. Operating alongside the tribunal is a Commissioner, who must hold or have held high judicial office (the first to be appointed was Lloyd LJ), and who is responsible for keeping under review the performance of the Secretary of State's functions under the Act and the adequacy of arrangements to ensure that intercepted material is not improperly disclosed, and to assist the tribunal to carry out its functions. Everyone holding office under the Crown, or working in the Post Office or the telecommunication system, must give to the Commissioner any documents or information which he or she may require for the purpose of carrying out his or her functions.[148]

This is a distinct improvement on the complete absence of systematic oversight of interceptions which was a feature of the system before the Act came into force. However, it is less than satisfactory in that the ordinary courts are entirely excluded from the process of review. Neither questions of illegality nor questions of irrationality and procedural impropriety in relation to an interception can be raised in a court. The decisions of the tribunal, including decisions relating to the tribunal's jurisdictions, are neither appealable nor liable to be questioned in any court,[149] effectively outflanking the blow struck for the rule of law by the House of Lords in *Anisminic Ltd. v. Foreign Compensation Commission*[150] in holding that, in the absence of the clearest words, a clause ousting the jurisdiction of the courts could not be interpreted as giving an inferior tribunal an uncontrolled discretion to determine the scope of its own jurisdiction.

the Telecommunications (Interception) Act 1979 (Cth); *Love* v. *A.-G. (NSW)*; *Peters* v. *A.-G. (NSW)* (1990) 169 CLR 307, HC of Australia, dealing with warrants under the Listening Devices Act 1984 (NSW).

[147] Interception of Communications Act 1985, s. 7.   [148] Ibid., s. 8.
[149] Ibid., s. 7(8).   [150] [1969] 2 AC 147, [1969] 1 All ER 208, HL.

It would, in any case, be very difficult to establish that an interception had occurred, since the Act provides that normally no evidence may be adduced, or question asked, in proceedings before a court or tribunal tending to show that a person holding office under the Crown, the Post Office, or anyone engaged in its business, or anyone engaged in the operation or running of a public telecommunication systems, has committed an offence of unauthorized interception or disclosure contrary to the Act, or that a warrant has been issued to any such person. The only exceptions apply where a person is being prosecuted for an offence involving unauthorized interception or disclosure of information, or perjury or contempt in respect proceedings for such an offence, or where a person is taking action for unfair dismissal following dismissal on suspicion of such an offence.[151]

To some extent this limitation is understandable. Restricting proceedings for unauthorized or improperly authorized interceptions to a tribunal which examines evidence in secret is a good way of protecting sensitive information and ensuring that the decisions are made on the fullest evidence, as relevant material might have to be withheld from a court on the grounds of public-interest immunity. However, the improvements in procedure which stemmed from the *Malone* case would never have occurred had counsel for mr. Malone been unable to ask witnesses, in Mr. Malone's trial for allegedly receiving stolen goods, questions designed to show that Mr. Malone's telephone calls had been intercepted by the police, and to ask whether any such interception had been authorized. While review of such a significant infringement of people's expectations of respect for private life, home, and correspondence takes place behind closed doors, with findings and reasons never being made available to the people affected, there will inevitably be a suspicion that the tribunal is acting as a device to bolster the apparent legitimacy of the system of interference while effectively gagging criticism, rather than providing a safeguard for the rights of citizens.

In a case arising before the 1985 Act came into force, Taylor J. Held that the courts could review an exercise of the Secretary of State's power to issue warrants, and seek evidence that the exercise was consistent with the published guidelines, since people have a legitimate expectation that their communications will not be officially intercepted save in accordance with those guidelines.[152] The Act compares unfavourably with the direction which the common law seemed to be taking, and steps away

---

[151] Interception of Communications Act 1985, s. 9.

[152] *R.* v. *Secretary of State for the Home Dept., ex parte Ruddock* [1987] 1 WLR 1482, [1987] 2 All ER 518. The applicants failed, on the evidence, to establish that it would have been improper to issue a warrant. See Ian Leigh, 'The Security Service, the Press and the Courts' [1987] *PL* 12–21 at pp. 13–17.

from openness in the process of review of governmental interferences with privacy rights.

The failure to offer any remedy in the ordinary courts for a breach of the requirements of the Act may undermine the attempt to bring English law into line with the demands of the Convention as interpreted by the European Court of Human Rights in the *Klass* and *Malone* cases. The Court held that an interference would not be 'necessary in a democratic society' within the meaning of Article 9(2) of the Convention unless adequate guarantees against abuse are provided.[153] It is not clear what safeguards would constitute an adequate guarantee, because it was not necessary for the Court to express a view: in *Malone*, the United Kingdom's justification failed on other grounds, and in *Klass* the safeguards were clearly adequate. In the light of *Klass*, where a special commission dealt with warrants in relation to national security, it seems that a non-judicial tribunal is adequate for such cases, but it is far from clear that remedies in respect of warrants dealing with criminal investigations which do not involve national security can legitimately be relegated to a non-judicial tribunal sitting in private.

In any case, the denial of a judicial remedy after the event may contravene Article 13 of the European Convention on Human Rights, which provides as follows: 'Everyone whose rights and freedoms as set forth in this Convention are violated shall have an effective remedy before a national authority notwithstanding that the violation has been committed by persons acting in an official capacity.' In *Malone's case* the majority of the European Court of Human Rights felt that it was unnecessary to decide whether the pre-1985 remedies (or lack thereof) breached Article 13, but there is room for argument about the true scope of what Judges Matscher and Pinheiro Farinha, in their partially dissenting opinion, called 'one of the most obscure clauses in the Convention', the application of which 'raises extremely difficult and complicated problems of interpretation'.[154] Article 13 does not expressly demand a public hearing by a court or tribunal, but it is arguable that the hearing should be in public because of the opening sentence of Article 6(1): 'In the determination of his civil rights and obligations . . ., everyone is entitled to a fair and public hearing within a reasonable time by an independent and

---

[153] *Malone* v. *UK*, Eur. Ct. HR, Series A, No. 82, Judgment of 2 Aug. 1984, 7 EHRR 14, at para. 81.

[154] See also *Klass* v. *Federal Republic of Germany*, Eur. Ct. HR, Series A, No. 28, Judgment of 6 Sept. 1978; *Campbell and Fell* v. *UK*, Eur. Ct. HR, Series A, No. 80, Judgment of 28 June 1984; *Leander* v. *Sweden* Eur. Ct. HR, Series A, No. 116, Judgment of 26 Mar. 1987; *O.* v. *UK*, Eur. Ct. HR, Series A, No. 120, Judgment of 8 July 1987; P. van Dijk and G. J. H. van Hoof, *Theory and Practice of the European Convention on Human Rights*, 2nd edn. (Deventer: Kluwer, 190), 520–32.

impartial tribunal established by law.' The right to be free of authorized interceptions of one's communications may be considered to be a civil right by virtue of the Interception of Communications Act 1985 itself. On the other hand, it might be thought that such a right could only be derived negatively from the enactment in section 1 of criminal sanctions. One might legitimately take the view that one does not have a civil right merely by reason of being the beneficiary of an obligation imposed by the criminal law on others. That view would take the right to respect for privacy in communications outside the scope of the civil rights protected by Article 6(1).

(3) Conditions for granting interception warrants

Section 2 of the Act lays down the conditions for the grant of a warrant. First, a necessity principle applies: Secretary of State must not issue a warrant unless he considers that it is necessary for one of three purposes, and must cancel it if he consider that it is no longer necessary.[155] When deciding whether it is necessary, the Secretary of State must consider whether the information which is needed could reasonably be obtained by other means.[156] The purposes are: (a) in the interests of national security; (b) for the purpose of preventing or detecting serious crime; and (c) for the purpose of safeguarding the economic well-being of the United Kingdom.[157]

(i) *National security.* The Act does not define national security. Indeed, it would probably be impossible to do so, and the predominant opinion when the Bill was being debated in the House of Commons was that it would not be wise to delimit it too closely, particularly as the term mirrors that which appears in Article 8(2) of the European Convention on Human Rights as a legitimate object of an interference with the right to respect for (*inter alia*) correspondence.[158] The first Commissioner to be appointed under the Act, Lloyd LJ, pointed out in his first annual report that national security is not confined to the 'major subversion, terrorism, or espionage' test which was applied under the pre-1985 interception guidelines, and regarded certain warrants issued on national security grounds unrelated to subversion, terrorism, or espionage, as having been properly granted.[159]

[155] Interception of Communications Act 1985, ss. 2(2), 4(4).
[156] Ibid., s.2(2), (3).
[157] Ibid., s. 2(2).
[158] Ewing and Gearty, *Freedom under Thatcher*, 67–8.
[159] *Interception of Communications Act 1985, chapter 56: Report of the Commissioner for 1986*, Cm. 108 (London: HMSO, 1987).

It has been suggested[160] that national security now needs to be considered in the light of the terms of the Security Service Act 1989, section 1, which, it will be recalled, identifies 'threats from espionage, terrorism and sabotage, from the activities of agents of foreign powers and from actions intended to overthrow or undermine parliamentary democracy by political, industrial or violent means' as being at the core of MI5's national security functions. The 1989 Act makes clear, however, that this is not an exhaustive definition, and it is in any case not self-evidently legitimate to read the partial definition in the 1989 Act back into the 1985 Act.

A wide range of activities may therefore be held to threaten national security. This uncertainty leaves a considerable margin of discretion in the hands of the Secretary of State. While some degree of indeterminacy is inevitable, it would be desirable that the boundaries of a power such as this, which allows interference with the confidentiality of communications in ways which make it difficult if not impossible for the parties to the communication even to discover whether the interference has occurred, be established with rather more certitude than has so far been accomplished. This is particularly important in view of the substantial evidence that, before the 1985 Act, the security service and successive Secretaries of State interpreted their national security function as justifying surveillance on, and interception of the communications of, some people who were concerned in wholly legitimate, democratic, political activity, but who espoused causes with which the established was out of sympathy.

For example, it seems that members of the Campaign for Nuclear Disarmament were targets of telephone interceptions.[161] There is at least some credible basis for suggesting that CND posed a threat to national security, if one accepts that security benefited from, or even depended on, maintaining a nuclear capability. However, that claim is politically contentious, and it seems that the security service was advancing the government's (or its own) political perception of the national interest by checking those who manifested support for opposing views. Concerns on this front are only partially alleviated by the instruction given by Mr Harold Wilson, when Prime Minister in 1966, and reaffirmed by every subsequent Prime Minister, that the telephones of M.P.s are not to be tapped.

Perhaps this is inevitable, in a politically charged field such as national security. However, if seemed that all active opposition to government

---

[160] S. H. Bailey, D. J. Harris, and B. L. Jones, *Civil Liberties Cases and Materials*, 3rd edn. (London: Butterworths, 1991), 516.

[161] For discussion of the evidence, see Ewing and Gearty, *Freedom under Thatcher*, 51–5, 61–5; *R. v. Secretary of State for the Home Dept., ex parte Ruddock* [1987] 1 WLR 1482, [1987] 2 All ER 518; Leigh, 'Security Service, Press and Courts' 13–17.

might attract surveillance. In 1986, Harriet Harman (now a Member of Parliament) and Patricia Hewitt (author of an incisive critique of the English law of civil liberties),[162] both of whom had been officers of the National Council for Civil Liberties, complained to the European Commission of Human Rights that they had been placed under surveillance by MI5 after being labelled as subversives, relying on evidence from the former MI5 officer, Miss Cathy Massiter. They alleged violations of their right to respect for private life under Article 8 of the Convention, and of the lack of an effective domestic remedy contrary to Article 13. The Commission held in 1989 that their rights had been breached, because keeping information about somebody's private life is an interference with the right to respect for private life,[163] and the Commission decided that it followed that collecting such information must equally constitute an interference. It could not be justified, because it was not in accordance with the law, there being no rules in English law conferring or regulating the power of the security service to collect such information. Furthermore, because there was no legal procedure allowing subjects of information-gathering to obtain appropriate remedies, there had been a breach of Article 13 as well. The British Government later concluded a friendly settlement with the applicants, and enacted the Security Service Act 1989. As a result, the Committee of Ministers decided that no further action as required.[164]

(ii) *Preventing or detecting serious crime.* 'Serious crime' is defined by section 10(3) of the Interception of Communications Act 1985. A crime is serious for this purpose if, and only if:

(*a*) it involves the use of violence, results in substantial financial gain, or is conduct by a large number of people in pursuit of a common purpose; or

(*b*) it is an offence for which an adult first offender could reasonably expect to receive a sentence of at least three years' imprisonment.

This is wider than the non-statutory guidelines in operation before the Act came into force, in that it includes offences resulting in substantial financial gain, facilitating the use of interception against white-collar criminals.[165]

(iii) *Safeguarding the economic well-being of the United Kingdom.* An interception for this purpose is to be considered necessary only if the information

---

[162] Patricia Hewitt, *The Abuse of Power* (Oxford: Martin Robertson, 1982).

[163] *Leander* v. *Sweden*, Eur. Ct. HR, Series A, No. 116, Judgment of 26 Mar. 1987.

[164] *Harman and Hewitt* v. *UK*, Eur. Comm. HR, Application No. 12175/86; Report of 9 May 1989, and Resolution of the Committee of Ministers, 14 EHRR 657.

[165] Cp. *Interception of Communications in Great Britain*, Cmnd. 7873, para. 4.

which it is considered necessary to acquire relates to the acts or intentions of people outside the British Isles.[166] This makes it clear that the object is to protect access to markets abroad on which our economy depends, and to prevent foreign powers from destabilizing the economy. This would seem to be wide enough to cover the activities of foreign dealers in buying and selling strategic shares and currencies in the markets. The damage which such transactions can do to the national economy was demonstrated in the attack on sterling on the international currency exchanges which led to its withdrawal from the European Exchange Rate Mechanism in September 1992.

(4) The form of the warrant

A warrant must be issued under the hand of the Secretary of State, except in urgent cases where the Secretary of State has expressly authorized its issue, when it may be signed by a senior official of the Department. In the latter case, the warrant must be endorsed with a statement that the Secretary of State expressly authorized its issue.[167] Once issued, a normal warrant stays in force for two months, and is renewable for a further period of two months. A warrant issued under the hand of an official stays in force for two working days, and is renewable by the Secretary of State for two months. At the end of the first renewal period, the warrant may be renewed for further periods of one month at a time, unless the Secretary of State endorses it with a statement that the renewal is considered necessary for the purposes of national security or for safeguarding the economic well-being of the United Kingdom, in which case the renewal takes effect for six months.[168]

The warrant is addressed to the person or body who will be responsible for carrying out the interception. The Act provides that the warrant may require that person to do two things: first, to intercept such communications as are described in the warrant, in the course of their transmission by post or by means of a public telecommunication system; secondly, to disclose the material intercepted to such people, and in such manner, as are described in the warrant.[169] The warrant must define the communications subject to interception by specifying an address or addresses to or from which communications are to be intercepted. The addresses must be likely to be used for the transmission of communications to or from a particular person or set of premises, and that person or premises must be specified or described in the warrant. Other communi-

---

[166] Interception of Communications Act 1985, s. 2(4).   [167] Ibid., s. 4(1).
[168] Ibid., s. 4(6). The Secretary of State must cancel a warrant if at any time he considers that it is no longer necessary: s. 4(4).
[169] Interception of Communications Act 1985, s. 2(1).

cations may also be intercepted if that is necessary in order to intercept communications falling within the definition in the warrant.[170] This helps to avoid general warrants for interceptions. However, the restrictions do not apply to warrants for the interception of external communications (i.e. those sent or received outside the British Isles) if the Secretary of State signs a certificate at the time of issuing the warrant, certifying the descriptions of intercepted material which he considers it necessary to have examined for one of the purposes permitted under section 2 of the Act.[171] The Secretary of State may modify a warrant at any time by inserting a new address or deleting one previously inserted, and may modify a certificate by limiting the definition of the material certified for interception.[172]

(5) The use made of results of interceptions

As the Birkett report noted in 1957, it would be wrong for material obtained in an authorized interception to be disclosed to private people or private bodies. It should be used only for the public purposes for which the interception was authorized.[173] This is also demanded by Article 8(2) of the European Convention on Human Rights, as interpreted by he European Court of Human Rights: an interference with respect for correspondence cannot be justified as necessary in a democratic society unless the law gives adequate protection against the disclosure of private communications for an improper purpose by providing for the destruction of recordings and records when they have fulfilled their legitimate purpose.[174] Section 6 of the Interception of Communications Act 1985 caters for this by requiring the Secretary of State to make arrangements in respect of each warrant (unless there is already general provision for such arrangements in operation) to secure that the extent of any disclosure of material, the number of people to whom material id disclosed, the extent to which material is copied, and the number of copies made, is limited to the minimum necessary to the purpose for which the warrant is granted.[175] Each copy made must be destroyed as soon as its retention is no longer necessary for that purpose.[176]

The material obtained from interceptions is not normally used in evidence in court. In 1980, the Home Office noted that the practice was for it to be used to assist the investigation, not to be tendered in evidence, although the material may lead investigators to evidence which is used in

---

[170] Ibid., s. 3(1).
[171] Ibid., s. 3(2), (3) and (4), and s. 10(1). [172] Ibid., s. 5.
[173] Report of the Committee of Privy Councillors, Cmnd. 283, para. 152.
[174] Kruslin v. France, Eur. Ct. HR, Series A. No. 176-A, at para, 34 of the judgment.
[175] Interception of Communications Act 1985, s. 6(1), (2). [176] Ibid., s. 6(3).

court.[177] There are, in fact, two important restraints on the use in evidence of material derived directly from an interception. First, since section 9 of the Act effectively prevents evidence being tendered to show where the material came from, it becomes difficult, if not impossible, for the prosecution to establish the credibility of the evidence. Secondly, because section 9 also precludes the defendant from discovering where, when, and how the material was obtained, it would be potentially unfair to an accused to be unable to challenge the credibility of the evidence. There would often be suspicions that investigators had tampered with a recording or letter, or had taken it out of context. This might mean that the evidence would have to be excluded in the trial court's discretion, either under the common-law discretion to exclude evidence if its prejudicial weight exceeds its probative value,[178] or under the court's inherent power to make orders necessary to ensure a fair trial,[179] or under the statutory discretion to exclude evidence if, in the circumstances, admitting it would make the proceedings unfair.[180]

Nevertheless, material gleaned from intercepted communications has been recently admitted in evidence in cases concerning drug dealing.[181] In *R. v. Effik*; *R. v. Mitchell*[182] the Court of Appeal held the section 9 of the 1985 Act did not impose a bar on the admissibility of material derived from a telephone interception (in that case, one which was admitted not to have been authorized by any warrant), and refused to hold that the trial judge should have excluded the evidence either because it had been obtained by an illegal telephone interception by the police or because of the issue of fairness to the accused. This refusal to exclude the evidence does not appear to breach the right to a fair trial under Article 6 of the European Convention on Human Rights. In *Schenk* v. *Switzerland*[183] the European Court of Human Rights held by thirteen votes to four that a trial court could admit evidence obtained through an illegal telephone interception without necessarily violating the accused's right to a fair trial under Article 6. However, a further complaint based on Article 8 was held to be inadmissible for failure to exhaust domestic remedies, leaving open the possibility of a challenge under this Article in a suitable case.

Normally, section 9 of the 1985 Act, even if not a complete bar to the

---

[177] *Interception of Communications in Great Britain*, Cmnd. 7873, para. 16.

[178] *R. v. Sang* [1980] AC 402, [1979] 2 All ER 1222, HL; PACE 1984, s. 82(3).

[179] *R. v. Lambeth Metropolitan Stipendiary Magistrate, ex parte McComb* [1983] QB 551, [1983] 1 All ER 3221, CA.

[180] PACE 1984, s. 78.

[181] The cases are discussed by Ian Leigh, 'Evidence from Phone Tapping' (1992) 142 *NLJ* 944–5, 976–7.

[182] (1992) 95 Cr. App. R. 427, CA.

[183] Eur. Ct. HR, Series A, No. 140, Judgment of 12 July 1988, 13 EHRR 242, at para. 46 of the judgment.

admissibility of intercepted communications, will effectively preclude their use. This is because, as the Court of Appeal (Criminal Division) held in *R. v. Preston*,[184] in order to lay the groundwork for the admissibility of evidence it will normally be necessary to disclose the manner in which the evidence was obtained. Nevertheless, if the decision in *Effik* is correct (and, despite doubts, the Court of Appeal in *Preston* regarded it as binding)[185] it means that far more attention will need to be paid, in telephone interception cases, to the way in which the recordings of the telephone conversations are stored, and the provisions for making them available to the defence for inspection. A trial court should also be obliged to adjourn any case in which the prosecution proposes to rely on recordings of tapped telephone conversations, pending the result of a complaint to the Interception of Communications Tribunal, which has power to require the destruction of all recordings and transcripts if it concludes that an interception was authorized improperly. At present, it seems that courts may be unwilling to grant such adjournments, so people could be tried on the basis of material which might have been ordered to be destroyed had the proper review procedures been allowed to operate.[186]

The legislation ought to be amended to deal with these matters, in view of the judgment of the European Court of Human Rights in two cases concerning telephone tapping in France. In *Kruslin v. France*[187] and *Huvig v. France*,[188] the Court held that safeguards under French law were inadequate to satisfy the requirement of necessity in a democratic society under Article 8(2). Among other reasons, the Court relied on the fact that French law made no provision for securing recordings inviolate for inspection by judge and defence counsel. It is likely that in England, similarly, additional procedural provision must be made for the integrity and reliability of material gleaned from telephone interceptions if its admissibility as evidence in criminal proceedings is to meet the requirements of the Convention. The cases in which the content of an intercepted communication can be used as evidence will, in any event, be exceptional. It remains the policy of the Home Office not to confirm or deny suggestions that particular communications may have been intercepted. As the

---

[184] (1992) 95 Cr. App. R. 355, CA at p. 365.

[185] See the note on *Effik* by Professor J. C. Smith, [1992] Crim. LR 580 at p. 581.

[186] Leigh, 'Evidence' (1992) 142 *NLJ* at p. 977 refers to *R. v. Uxbridge Justices, ex parte Ofomah* (unreported, DC), where the court refused an application for judicial review of a decision of a magistrates' court to refuse to adjourn committal proceedings. A court might be more willing to grant a delay at trial than at the committal stage.

[187] Eur. Ct. HR, Series A, No. 176-A, Judgment of 24 Apr. 1990, 12 EHRR 547.

[188] Eur. Ct. HR, Series A, No. 176-B, Judgment of 24 Apr. 1990, 12 EHRR 528, at para. 34.

Court of Appeal pointed out in *R. v. Preston*,[189] the prosecution's admission in *Effik* was improper, and should not have been permitted in the light of section 9 of the 1985 Act.

(6) Evaluation of the Interception of Communications Act 1985

The Act represents a step towards full implementation of the principle of legality—the idea that all official action should be justifiable according to law and subject to an accountability mechanism which is governed by law—and the provision of remedies for breach of privacy in English law. The work of the tribunal has the capacity to be a significant influence working towards accountability for the secret work of the police and the security service. The Act also marks a potentially important recognition, by Parliament and the government, of the legitimacy of human rights claims and the role of the European Court of Human Rights in offering a right-based critique of English law.

However, the potential has not yet been realized. There are particular weaknesses in the legislation.

(i) The Act does not cover the disclosure of the results of monitoring, or metering, of calls, which, as the European Court of Human Rights held in *Malone's case*, lacked adequate controls to satisfy the 'in accordance with the law' and 'necessary in a democratic society' requirements for justification under Article 8(2) of the European Convention on Human Rights.

(ii) It is possible that the legislation does not cover communications using cordless telephones. The Court of Appeal (Criminal Division) held in *R. v. Effik; R. v. Mitchell*[190] that such systems did not form part of a public telecommunications system, and this was regarded as binding a subsequent Court of Appeal in *R. v. Preston*.[191] It is to be hoped that the House of Lords will have an opportunity to consider this matter, as the prevalence of such instruments means that the decision constitutes a serious limitation on the usefulness of the 1985 Act.

(iii) It is possible that the administrative procedures for issuing warrants, without direct independent control, might still not satisfy the requirements of the European Convention on Human Rights. Although prior judicial control is not essential in national-security cases, as held in *Klass*, for ordinary criminal investigations it is possible that the Court might hold that rule-of-law principles demand prior judicial authorization for interceptions, as under the prohibition on unreasonable search and seizure which applies to all interceptions, including interceptions of

---

[189] (1992) 95 Cr. App. R. at p. 365.   [190] Above, n. 182.
[191] *The Times*, 13 May 1992, CA.

conversations conducted from public telephone boxes, under the Fourth Amendment to the US Constitution.[192]

(iv) Once a warrant has been issued, the absence of a general principle such as that found in Germany's G10 law that the subject of an interception authorization is to be informed of the interception after it has taken place, unless this would threaten national security, makes it very difficult for people to know whether their mail and telephone lines have been intercepted. The restriction on questions in legal proceedings means that one way of finding out—the one employed in *Malone's case*—is blocked. Without the knowledge needed to make a complaint to the tribunal, remedies cannot be sought. Apart from recourse to the tribunal, individuals' rights are protected only indirectly, by the general monitoring of interception warrants by the Commissioner. This is hardly a satisfactory guarantee of our freedom from unjustified failures of the respect due to private lie and correspondence.

To give effect to the spirit of Article 8 of the Convention, a change in political attitudes will be needed. The promise in December 1992 to introduce legislation establishing a committee of Privy Councillors to monitor the work of the security and intelligence services is an encouraging sign that a new outlook is beginning to permeate Whitehall, although the Bill will probably not be introduced to Parliament before the 1993/4 session.

10.5 CONCLUSIONS

The conclusions which can be drawn from this chapter's survey of confidentiality and its protection are somewhat discouraging. Although better protected than other aspects of privacy, confidentiality is regarded in English law as one of a number of competing interests which can be relatively easily overridden. The decision in the *Spycatcher* case that governmental bodies do not have confidentiality interests in the absence of a public interest in restraining disclosure gives a welcome, if small, boost to the ideals of open government and open debate in the context of a democratic political process. One the other hand, the individual privacy interests which are protected by the doctrine of confidentiality are too easily defeated by public interests (which are often relatively slight) in advancing criminal investigations.

The ambivalence of English law towards confidentiality is linked to its

---

[192] *Berger* v. *New York*, 388 US 41 (1967); *Katz* v. *New York*, 389 US 347 (1967). The decisions were followed by federal legislation requiring warrants for taps, except in cases of emergency: 18 USC ss. 2510–20.

attitude to privacy as a whole. English law treats privacy as incidentally protected by the law of tort, by equitable remedies, and by criminal law, but as not meriting direct protection in its own right. Privacy is either an interest or a state of affairs, rather than a right. Yet it is important. Article 8 of the European Convention on Human Rights partially comes to terms with this. Its guarantee of respect for private and family life, home, and correspondence identifies key areas in which privacy is important, but avoids the need to define privacy. It also demands that any attempt by the state to limit that respect should be subject to the standards of the rule of law. This may be particularly valuable as a check on governments' and judges' inclinations to legislate and adjudicate in the field of criminal procedure in ways which run counter to the values of fairness and respect for individual freedom. The Convention has had some beneficial impact on English law already, and may have more in the future.

At present, however, every new piece of legislation and judicial decision, such as those relating to the confiscation of the proceeds of crime, extending the powers of the police and the courts to extract information from people against their wills for the purposes of imposing penalties on them or others, threatens both human rights and values, such as the right of silence, the right to legal advice and assistance, the placing of the burden of proof on the prosecution, and the right not to incriminate oneself, which are usually regarded as appropriate to a civilized legal system. We owe it to ourselves to scrutinize such legislation carefully to ensue that we are not restricting confidentiality rights more severely than absolutely necessary, and that the safeguards are adequate.

Judges, politicians, and commentators must vigilantly scrutinize all proposals for new or extended power of the type introduced in the Drug Trafficking Offences Act 1986, and extended in subsequent legislation. We can too easily become desensitized to the serious civil liberties implications of such creeping extensions of state power. If we do, we may wake one day to find that, by a series of small steps, each of which seemed justifiable at the time, we have fundamentally changed the ethos of our legal system, and produced one in which legal protections for the individual are insignificant, and the legal power of the investigative arms of the state is overwhelming.

11

SEX, SEXUAL ACTIVITY, AND FAMILY LIFE

This chapter deals with a range of privacy interests which are particularly closely related to people's freedom to organize the most intimate details of their lives according to their own preferences. The first matter to be considered is the allocation of individuals to a particular sex, particularly important when a person's legal status, rights, and obligations are affected (s. 11.1). Secondly, the chapter addresses people's sexual orientations, and their freedom (or lack of it) to give expression to their sexual predilections privately or publicly (s. 11.2). The third topic is respect for family life, particularly as it affects rights in respect of child care (s. 11.3). The interests considered in this chapter operate in three different but related ways. At one level, they advance people's freedom to choose a life-style and to give effect to it, so long as it does not interfere unduly with the rights of others. This seems to demand relatively limited state intervention, setting the boundaries between competing claims to freedom, and policing them, but not otherwise intervening in the conduct of citizens. But people's freedom is constrained by their physical attributes and by the social and legal norms which are built on those attributes. It is the duty of the state to ensure that the legal norms are fair, and to protect citizens against discrimination on the basis of factors over which people have no control. The right to protection against discrimination justifies relatively extensive state intervention, although the state will still not be making choices for people, or taking responsibility for their choices.

The role of the state, and the level of interference with individual choice which is justifiable, is more extensive when protecting children within families. Children's interests need special protection, because children are not usually parties to the decision to found a family, which will usually have been taken by adults before the birth or adoption of the child (although children of one union may sometimes have a say in the formation of subsequent unions by their parents). Once born or adopted into the family, children will usually be unable, for a considerable time, to protect their own interests against those of parents or guardians. In this period, the state may take responsibility for monitoring and, if necessary, assuming the care of the children. Nevertheless, in a society which is built on the notion that the family is (in the words of Article 10(1) of the International Covenant on Economic, Social, and Cultural Rights) 'the natural and fundamental group unit of society',[1] to be accorded '[t]he widest possible protection and assistance . . . particularly for its establishment and while it is responsible for the care and education of dependent children', some room must be left to parents to implement their opinions about the best way of bringing up children. Principles must be developed to control the way in which the state intervenes in family life, to try to ensure, as far as possible, that the parents' freedoms and ways of life are not unnecessarily prejudiced by the state's imposition of its notions of proper child-rearing practice. As the Lord Chancellor, Lord Mackay, has said, 'The threat to the poor and to minority groups, whose views of what is good for a child may not coincide closely with that of the majority, is all too apparent.'[2]

Each of the interests on which this chapter touches therefore makes substantial demands on society to adjust its legal system so as to recognize different forms of relationship and to protect those who embark on them. English law has only recently begun to grapple with these problems. The European Convention on Human Rights provides a framework for the discussion. The relevant provisions of the Convention are Article 3, providing that no one is to be subjected to inhuman or degrading treatment; Article 8, guaranteeing respect for private and family life, subject to such limitations as are in accordance with the law and necessary in a democratic society for one of a number of purposes, including the protection of health and morals; Article 12, which guarantees the right of men and women of marriageable age to marry and found a family, according to the national laws governing the exercise of this right; and Article 14, which requires the High Contracting Parties to the Convention (the states) to secure the enjoyment of these and the other rights and freedoms guaranteed in the Convention without discrimination on grounds such as sex, birth, or other status. As the Convention has been interpreted by the Commission and the Court, it can make it illegal in international law for a state to discriminate in certain ways against homosexuals, or to legislate against making available information about birth control.

In addition, the UN Convention on the Rights of the Child, which was concluded in 1989, includes a number of provisions which require States Parties to the Convention to protect families as a whole. The Preamble declares that the States Parties are 'convinced that the family, as the fundamental group of society and the natural environment for the growth and welfare of all its members and particularly children, should be afforded the necessary protection and assistance so that it can fully assume

[1] The European Social Charter (1961), Art. 16, describes the family as 'a fundamental unit of society'.
[2] Lord Mackay, 'Perceptions of the Children Bill and Beyond' (1989) 139 *NLJ* 505–8 at p. 508.

its responsibilities within the community'. Accordingly the Convention imposes on States Parties certain duties in respect of children, including a duty to treat their interests as a primary consideration in all actions concerning them (Article 3), and the duty to undertake measures to implement children's economic, social, and cultural rights to the maximum extent of their available resources (Article 4). The UK is a State Party, having acceded to the Convention in 1991.

11.1 A RIGHT TO A SEXUAL IDENTITY

Sex is one of any person's most significant characteristics. A considerable body of theory has developed exploring the consequences of this. In particular, it has been convincingly argued that the distinction between men and women has formed the basis for discriminatory social structures in nearly all societies, in which '[f]or the most part men occupied the "public" sphere of political and commercial activity, women occupied the "private" sphere of domestic life, and the law respected those boundaries'.[3] However regrettable it may be, a person's sex has both legal and social consequences.[4] Socially, sex is one of the factors which defines one's self-image and the expectations of others. It also affects one's legal status and capacity to enter into legal relationships with others (although its legal significance has diminished where statute has eroded the common-law disabilities affecting women, and particularly married women).[5] For example, possibilities for marriage, with its attendant privileges and responsibilities, are limited by the requirement that the parties must be of different sexes. Criminal liability may attach to homosexual acts which do not attach to similar acts between people of different sexes. Since the ability to enter into close, legally protected personal relationships, and the freedom to express one's sexual orientation, are important and (within certain limits) legitimate aspects of personal autonomy, the assignment of a sex is fundamental to legal personality.

However, sex is not clear cut, and may conflict with gender (the psychological and social experience of being considered a man or woman). People's biological sex may be uncertain or ambiguous, and (rarely) people combine the gonads of both sexes, producing a bisexual individual. More commonly, an individual may feel like a woman but appear to display the physical characteristics of a man (or vice versa). Such a person

[3] Deborah L. Rhode, *Justice and Gender: Sex Discrimination and the Law* (Cambridge, Mass.: Harvard University Press, 1989), 9.

[4] Katherine O'Donovan, *Sexual Divisions in Law* (London: Weidenfeld & Nicolson, 1985), ch. 3.

[5] Married Women's Property Act 1882.

suffers a disjunction between self-image and the expectations of others. This condition, known medically as gender dysphoria syndrome, will always be profoundly uncomfortable and can lead to serious psychological disturbances. Growing understanding on the part of the medical professions has led to increased availability of therapy. Drugs and surgical procedures can bring a person's physiognomy more closely into line with his or her psychology, and counselling can help people to cope with the social, psychological, and sexual difficulties which such treatments (or a decision not to undergo them) may engender. Nevertheless, medical reassignment of sex can lead to legal difficulties.

(1) English law

In view of the personal, legal, and social implications of this type of treatment, which will include surgical removal of external genitalia and may also include reconstructive surgery (for example, in the case of male-to-female transsexuals, surgically fashioning an artificial vagina), one might expect it to be legally regulated. In some countries, laws set an age below which consent to such treatment may not lawfully be given, or limit the circumstances in which it may lawfully be carried out.[6] English law, by contrast, does not regulate this treatment differently from any other. There is no such special regime as there is in respect of reproductive medicine under the Human Fertilisation and Embryology Act 1990. As in the context of other types of medical treatment, legal rules safeguard people against having therapy imposed on them without their consent. Although there is a category of harm, or physical invasion of one's body, to which people are incapable of consenting as a matter of law and which would constitute the crime of maim at common law, it seems to be accepted that one can lawfully make a decision to accept castration and related surgery, with proper medical safeguards, if responsible medical opinion would regard it as appropriate therapy for gender dysphoria syndrome.[7] To put it at its lowest, it should be no less possible to consent to such surgery than to consent to extensive cosmetic surgery.

The fact that treatment is not against the law does not mean, of course, that it is necessarily readily available to all who want or need it. Like other treatment offered by the National Health Service, the needs of those who seek it must compete with the needs of people seeking other treatments in the battle for resources, and must pass through the filter of medical ethics

---

[6] A. Cremona-Barbaro, 'Medicolegal Aspects of Transsexualism in Western Europe' (1986) 5 *Med. Law* 89, cited by J. K. Mason and R. A. McCall Smith, *Law and Medical Ethics*, 3rd edn. (London: Butterworths, 1991), 41: the minimum age is 18 in Sweden and 25 in Germany.

[7] *Corbett* v. *Corbett* [1971] P. 83, [1970] 2 All ER 33.

which denies this radical treatment to those for whom it is not regarded as medically necessary. In the UK, a very small proportion—said to be around 1 per cent—of those who seek treatment are regarded as suitable to receive it.[8] Like other rights related to health care, the right to sex reassignment therapy is thus an example of a qualified legal liberty, or limited freedom from interference with a decision to undergo it, rather than a right to have it giving rise to a claim against the state or medical practitioners. As with many other rights, the practical worth of the liberty allowed by law is restricted by fiscal and moral considerations and by medical ethics.[9]

Although English law does not impose any special impediment to obtaining sex change therapy, neither has it so far been prepared to recognize therapy as changing a patient's legal status. A person who was registered as male at birth is not permitted to have that allocation of sex altered after treatment to replace the physical stigmata of manhood with those of womanhood, and vice versa. This can interfere with the right to marry. Marriage in English common law was defined as the union of one woman and one man, for life, to the exclusion of all others. Although the provision for divorce by statute, and recognition of certain polygamous marriages celebrated abroad, has watered down the absolute nature of this commitment, the law still assumes that people are capable of having only one sex, which they retain throughout life, and which is identified exclusively by reference to the biological characteristics of genitalia, chromosomes, and hormones, at the time of birth. There is a duty to register a birth within forty-two days, and the child's sex must be declared. Thereafter, there is no power to have the register of births altered to reflect the result of sex reassignment therapy; alteration is possible only in the event of a change of name within a year, legitimation, or adoption.[10] Nor is there any means of authorizing the issue of a sex reassignment certificate, recognizing the changed position following therapy, as there is in South Australia.[11] As a result, a small group of people who are psychologically of one sex, and have had the genitalia of the opposite sex surgically removed, are condemned to go through life officially recorded as having been born with the opposite sex.

The once and for all assessment of sex on the register of births reflects the position at common law. In *Corbett* v. *Corbett*,[12] a biological man had undergone sex reassignment therapy, including surgery, to become a woman, April Ashley. She had gone through a marriage ceremony in Gibraltar with a man, who subsequently petitioned in England for nullity.

[8] Mason and McCall Smith, *Medical Ethics*, 41.   [9] See further Ch. 18, below.
[10] Births and Deaths Registration Act 1953, ss. 2, 13, 14; SI 1968/2049, re. 16.
[11] Sexual Reassignment Act 1988 (South Australia), s. 7(8)(*b*).
[12] [1971] P. 83, [1970] 2 All ER 33.

After an extensive review of the authorities and medical opinions, Ormrod J. held that under English law it is of the essence of a marriage that the parties should be a person of the male sex and one of the female sex. He distinguished between sex, which he regarded as determined by physical characteristics, and gender, the psychological and social attributes relating to a person's sex. Surgery might change external genitalia, but could not alter a person's chromosomal structure. A man remained a man, and a woman a woman, regardless of surgery, from their births to their deaths. He was prepared to accept that Miss Ashley might have been female by gender, but, testing sex by reference to genital, chromosomal, and gonadal features at birth, he held that she remained of the male sex. Sex, rather than gender, was held to be essential to capacity to marry because marriage is the basis of the family, and a capacity for heterosexual intercourse is essential to marriage. Adopting physical sex at birth as a determinant of capacity to marry, the judge held that the 'marriage' had been between two men, and was void.

The law as to nullity of marriage is now laid down by statute, but the effect appears to be the same. Section 11 of the Matrimonial Causes Act 1973 provides that a marriage is void if the parties to it are not respectively male and female. In *Franklin* v. *Franklin (otherwise Jones)*,[13] an important first-instance decision, the court rejected arguments that 'male' and 'female', unlike 'man' and 'woman', refer to gender, which cannot be determined exclusively by reference to biological characteristics, rather than to sex. In that case, a man went through a ceremony of marriage in England with someone who had been born with male biological characteristics and was registered as male at birth, but was psychologically a woman, and had undergone sex reassignment therapy. The court, reaffirming the traditional view of marriage and applying the reasoning of *Corbett* v. *Corbett* to the position under the 1973 Act, held that the marriage was void. Sex reassignment therapy will therefore not enable a transsexual who was categorized as male at birth to contract a valid marriage with a man under English law, or someone who was registered as female to marry a woman.

This is unfortunate. The decisions treat the physical distinction between men and women as absolute, whereas in fact individuals are now scientifically regarded as lying on a continuum, with female physical characteristics at one extreme and male ones at the other. The law is thus out of touch with scientific understandings. Furthermore, it is hard to sustain the logic of Ormrod J.'s reasoning in *Corbett*. A marriage which does not produce children is not void, or even voidable, on that account,

---

[13] [1990] *Family Law* 455. See S. M. Cretney, *Elements of Family Law*, 2nd edn. (London: Sweet & Maxwell, 1992), 15–16.

so the function of founding a family, while it might form a social justification for the institution of marriage, does not form the basis for the legitimacy of any individual marriage. Non-consummation makes a marriage voidable but not void, so inability to perform heterosexual intercourse should not in principle make it impossible for two people to contract a valid marriage.[14] The essential basis for the relationship, it might be thought, is love and support, rather than intercourse or child-rearing. To speak as if sexual intercourse is the essential role of a woman in marriage[15] seems to relegate the matrimonial home to a form of legitimized brothel. Nevertheless, there is no sign of the law being changed.

This has implications for criminal liability, because certain offences can be committed only by people of a particular sex. Rape can be committed only by a man against a woman.[16] As regards the offender, this raises no problem, since surgery on a male/female transsexual removes the male genitalia without which rape is impossible, while surgical techniques have not yet succeeded in constructing a functional penis for female/male transsexuals. The transsexual victim of rape is more problematic, however. Assuming that the law treats a person's biological nature as categorized at birth as unchangeable, a man who has penetrative sexual intercourse against that person's wishes with a female/male transsexual (assuming this to be possible in the light of any surgical procedures which have been carried out on the victim) commits rape. On the other hand, a man who commits the same acts against a male/female transsexual with a surgically constructed artificial vagina would not be guilty of rape, because the victim would not be regarded as a woman. At most, the defendant would be guilty of indecency between men[17] or of an indecent assault on a man.[18] Such a result might be considered absurd. There are good reasons for ignoring the victim's chromosomal sex when deciding whether a man is guilty of rape. In particular, the offender is not in any position to know what anyone's chromosomal sex is, and has to go entirely by external appearances. In these circumstances, in order to safeguard the rights of the person who regards herself as a woman, there is much to be said for applying the view of Willmer LJ in SY to the victim of rape. If a man intentionally has non-consensual sexual intercourse with a person who looks like a woman and has a vagina, that should be regarded as rape.

The law need not ignore an artificial vagina in this way. In SY v. SY,[19] a husband applied for a decree of nullity of marriage on the ground that

[14] O'Donovan, *Sexual Divisions*, 67.
[15] *Corbett* v. *Corbett* [1971] P. 83 at p. 106, [1970] 2 All ER 33 at p. 48, *per* Ormrod J. See O'Donovan, *Sexual Divisions*, 65–7.
[16] Sexual Offences Act 1956, s. 1(1).   [17] Ibid., s. 13.   [18] Ibid., s. 15.
[19] [1963] P. 37, [1962] 3 All ER 55, CA.

the wife (who had been registered as female at birth) had a vestigial vagina, which made consummation impossible. The court found that a vagina could have been correctly surgically by forming an artificial passage, and held that the law would then recognize sexual intercourse as constituting consummation. The decree was therefore refused. Willmer LJ, *obiter*, said that if true sexual intercourse were impossible for a woman with an artificial vagina, she could not be raped, and he regarded such a result as 'bordering on the fantastic'.[20] This might be thought to support the claim that a male/female transsexual with an artificial vagina could be raped. The decision in *SY* was distinguished in *Corbett* v. *Corbett*,[21] on the ground that a woman with a vestigial vagina was nevertheless a woman, while a male/female transsexual remained chromosomally a man. However, this merely goes to show that we are on slippery ground when assigning a sex to people in the grey area between the two sexes. The wife in *SY* was regarded in 1962 as a woman, albeit imperfectly formed, while today it has been suggested that she would probably be classified as a chromosomal male with testicular feminization.[22] The law is being left behind scientific developments in understanding sex.

Certain other offences are defined in ways which depend on the offender or victim being a man or a woman, and so create difficulties when either is a transsexual. In *R.* v. *Tan*,[23] the *Corbett* doctrine was followed, so that people were treated as having the biological sex assigned at birth. The charges arose out of acts of prostitution performed by a woman, Moira Tan, and a male/female transsexual, Gloria Greaves, the proceeds being shared with a man, Brian Greaves. Gloria Greaves was convicted of being a man living on the earnings of Tan's prostitution, contrary to section 30 of the Sexual Offences Act 1956; and Brian Greaves was convicted of living on the earnings of prostitution of a man, Gloria Greaves, contrary to section 5 of the Sexual Offences Act 1967. On appeal, although it would have been open to the Court of Appeal to overrule *Corbett*, the defendants did not launch a frontal assault on the the earlier decision, attempting instead to distinguish it. It was argued on their behalf that the *Corbett* doctrine should be restricted to the law of marriage, and Gloria should be regarded (as she regarded herself) as a woman, so that neither conviction could stand. The Court of Appeal rejected this, holding that it would be unacceptable to adopt different approaches to assigning sex for different purposes by treating Gloria as a man for the purpose of capacity to marry but as a woman for the purpose of section 30 of the Sexual Offences Act.

[20] [1963] P. at p. 60, [1962] 3 All ER at pp. 62–3.
[21] [1971] P. 83, [1970] 2 All ER 33.
[22] Mason and McCall Smith, *Medical Ethics*, 43.
[23] [1983] QB 1053, [1983] 2 All ER 12, CA.

Nevertheless, the use of purely biological criteria for assigning sex remains questionable in principle. The defendants in *Tan* had argued that, for the purposes of section 30 of the 1956 Act and section 5 of the 1967 Act, a person should be considered a woman if she had become philosophically or psychologically or socially female. This approach would not have required any steps to be taken by hormone therapy or surgery to change the physical state of the person. It would have allowed people to redefine their sexes at will, and that would have made it too easy to evade liability for offences have a person's sex as an essential part of their definition. Yet if it would be unacceptable that a person should be able to define his or her own sex at all, it might still be justifiable to base assignment of sex on a combination of physical, psychological, philosophical, and social factors, rather than on physical characteristics alone. The need for consistency does not dictate that the law should adopt a one-dimensional criterion.

(2) The European Convention on Human Rights

In a number of cases it has been argued that the refusal of English law to accept sex reassignment therapy as giving rise to a change of sex for legal purposes violates the European Convention on Human Rights. In particular, it has been argued that one's sex is a significant feature of one's private life, so that a refusal to recognize a change of sex constitutes a failure of the respect for private life guaranteed under Article 8 of the Convention. It has also been argued that such a refusal violates a person's right to marry under Article 12, and demeans the person concerned in his or her own eyes and in the eyes of other members of society, so as to amount to degrading treatment contrary to Article 3 of the Convention.

The Commission has interpreted the Convention more dynamically than the Court has in this field. In an early decision, the Commission held admissible a petition alleging that a West German administrative decision to refuse to rectify the petitioner's birth certificate after sex reassignment therapy gave rise indirectly to a breach of Article 5(1) (liberty and security of the person) and Article 6(1) (right to a fair and public hearing by an independent and impartial tribunal established by law to determine civil rights and obligations). Following this, the government reached a friendly settlement in which it agreed to rectify the birth certificate.[24] This appears to be the only case in which those Articles have been invoked by a transsexual petitioner. In another decision, this time concerning the refusal of Belgian law to reassign a person's status on their

---

[24] *X* v. *Federal Republic of Germany*, Application No. 6699/74, Report of 11 Oct. 1979, 17 CD 21.

change of sex, the Commission held that Article 8 and Article 12 had been breached, and Belgian law was amended in consequence.[25] The case was referred to the Court, which however did not examine the merits, holding instead that, contrary to the Commission's initial decision, the petitioner had not exhausted domestic remedies, so the complaint had been inadmissible.[26]

Decisions of the Court have been more cautious. In *Rees* v. *United Kingdom*,[27] a female/male transsexual complained of alleged breaches by the UK of Articles 8 and 12. As regards the right to marry, the Court in *Rees* unanimously rejected the complaint. It noted that Article 12 protects the right to marry 'according to the national laws governing the exercise of this right'. The exercise of the right is therefore subject to national law. A state is free to prefer a traditional view of marriage, as a relationship between people of opposite sex, to a more flexible view, and to embody that preference in its national law governing marriage.[28]

This is, with respect, a weak argument. It cannot mean that there are no limits to a state's freedom to make national law concerning the capacity to marry, as that would make Article 12 entirely vacuous. The Court accepted that the laws could not properly be so drawn as entirely to deprive certain people of marriageable age of the very essence of the right to marry (whatever that may mean). Nevertheless, a person in Rees's position, who regards himself as a man, and so would want to marry a woman, but is regarded by the law as a woman, will be unable to marry any person whom he might want to marry. This is a very substantial restriction on the right to marry, making it entirely worthless to people in the position of the applicant. It is not enough to reply that the state is free to prefer a traditional view of marriage as a union of people of opposite sexes. It fails to explain why the state should be free to define sex purely by reference to biological sex as understood at birth, so as to exclude people whose psychological gender is only understood later from the rights and obligations of marriage. The weakness in the argument is underlined by the consideration that biological sex, at birth and later, is sometimes not easy to establish by reference to the appearance of genitalia. Doctors in such circumstances assign to a baby the sex which they think he or she is most likely to be able to support socially in later life. Chromosomal sex is not evident to the child/adult or to social contacts at any time, and medical and scientific developments in the field have been

[25] *Von Oosterwijck* v. *Belgium*, Application No. 7654/76, Report of 1 Mar. 1979 upholding the complaint on the merits.
[26] *Von Oosterwijck* v. *Belgium*, Eur. Ct. HR, Series A, No. 40, Judgment of 6 Nov. 1980, 3 EHRR 557.
[27] Eur. Ct. HR, Series, A, No. 106, Judgment of 17 Oct. 1986, 9 EHRR 56.
[28] *Rees* at paras. 49 and 50 of the Judgment.

so rapid that the medical view of a person's sex may change within a small part of the person's lifetime.[29] It is hard to see why the state should be free to place such reliance on a doctor's decision, made without foreknowledge of the later development of the child or science, in making law to govern capacity to marry.

In *Cossey* v. *United Kingdom*,[30] the petitioner, Caroline Cossey, a male/female transsexual, had taken a female name in 1972, and had dressed as a woman and adopted a female role since then. She had undergone hormone therapy and breast augmentation implant surgery between 1972 and 1974, and had then undergone gender reassignment surgery. She enjoyed a full life as a woman, psychologically and physically, and was capable of sexual intercourse with a man. She held a passport as a woman, and worked as a successful fashion model. In 1983 she wished to marry a Mr. L., but was told by the Registrar General that such a marriage would be void in English law because she would be classified as a man. The Registrar General also refused to give her a birth certificate showing her sex as female, because the birth certificate merely records details as at the date of birth. Miss Cossey lodged an application to the European Commission of Human Rights, alleging breaches of Articles 8 and 12. Her engagement was broken off. A subsequent marriage to a Mr X was later declared to be void by the High Court.

The Commission decided by ten votes to six, following the *Rees* case, that there had been no violation of Article 8, but found a violation of Article 12 by the same margin.[31] The UK government referred the case to the Court. All the judges accepted that the case was indistinguishable from *Rees*. By fourteen votes to four the Court held that there was no breach of Article 12, reaffirming the decision in *Rees*. The majority observed that Miss Cossey's inability to marry a woman was not the result of any legal impediment, and argued that Article 12, speaking of men and women having the right to marry, gives support to the traditional view of marriage as a union of two people biologically of different sexes. The number of Contracting States which treated marriage between a male/female transsexual and a man as valid was insufficient to suggest that there had been a general abandonment of the traditional concept of marriage. Attachment to that concept was held to provide sufficient reason for allowing national law to maintain exclusively biological criteria for determining sex for the purpose of capacity to marry.[32]

Regarding the right to respect for private life under Article 8, the

[29] Mason and McCall Smith, *Medical Ethics*, 42–3.

[30] Eur. Ct. HR, Series A, No. 184, Judgment of 27 Sept. 1990, 13 EHRR 622.

[31] *Cossey* v. *UK*, Application No. 10843/84, Eur. Commn. HR, Report of 9 May 1989.

[32] Judgment at paras. 45–6.

Court in *Rees*, in a twelve–three majority decision, noted that the guarantee in Article 8 of respect for private life is not always straightforward to interpret. The notion of respect is not clear cut. The Court decided that the obligation to respect private life might in some circumstances carry with it a duty on the state to take positive action to advance the right, but deciding what positive steps are demanded by the respect which is properly due involves balancing the general interests of the community against the interests of the individual concerned. In striking that balance, the state necessarily enjoys a margin of appreciation. The Court in *Rees* held that the diversity of practices between states in relation to recognition of sexual reassignment showed that there was no settled view amongst the parties to the Convention as to the appropriate response. In such a case the margin of appreciation allowed to each state is wide. The Court, in deciding whether the margin has been overstepped, must assess whether the actions of the state interfere with a transsexual's private life more than is justified by any countervailing general public interest.

The Court did not regard the inability to secure rectification of the register of births as a serious matter, since the register was considered to record only historical information (the view taken at the time of birth), and in the absence of special provision for secrecy (such as operates in respect of adoption and legitimation) any change would be visible in the register and might be a cause of continuing embarrassment.[33] Although the applicant was still regarded as a woman for the purposes of marriage, pensions, and some (but not all) employment law matters, for most legal purposes sex makes no difference in English law. People are free to use any name of their choice, and are not required to carry an identity card or any other document displaying their given names or sex. Passports can be issued in a person's new names, and there is an administrative discretion as to whether to describe the person as Mr. or Miss. The applicant had had his new names put on his passport, although the Passport Office had refused to use the prefix 'Mr.' A male–female transsexual has been treated as a woman by agreement with the authorities for national insurance purposes. Because of this, the majority of the Court did not regard refusal of official recognition of the change of sex as interfering sufficiently with the applicant's private life to amount to a failure of the respect due under Article 8.

Yet these are nearly all example of administrative discretion. Whenever the law has to determine these matters in a contested case, the biological sex registered at birth is taken as determinative. The National Insurance Commissioner has applied the test of biological sex at birth when sex was

---

[33] *Rees* at paras. 40 and 43 of Judgment.

contested in respect of retirement ages.[34] The Sex Discrimination Act
1975 demands that people be classified as either men or women for its
purposes, and in *White* v. *British Sugar Corporation*[35] an industrial tribunal
applied *Corbett*. In *White* the applicant, who had been classified as a
woman at birth but wanted to be treated as a man, had not undergone
sex reassignment therapy. It is not clear how a post-operative transsexual
would be regarded for the purposes of the Act, but the likelihood is that
there too the *Corbett* test would be applied.

The resulting position is far from satisfactory. In view of the centrality
of people's sexes to their personalities and aspirations, and to society's
expectations of them, a consistent refusal by law to accept person's commitment to a reassigned sex, involving major surgery and drug therapy
over an extended period, and confirmed by doctors, constitutes a serious
violation of respect for that person's private life. Such a violation can be
justified under Article 8(2) only if it is in accordance with the law, and is
necessary in a democratic society for one of the legitimate purposes[36]
listed in that Article. It is hard to see how an interference of this magnitude can be said to be necessary for any of those purposes, or justified by
any other compelling public interest which can stand against the fundamental violation of the subject's private life and self-esteem. Only if the
interference is shown to be for a legitimate purpose does the margin of
appreciation become relevant. As Judge Martens pointed out, dissenting
in the later case of *Cossey* v. *United Kingdom*,[37] the margin of appreciation
is a doctrine of judicial self–restraint, which comes into play to prevent
judges from substituting their ideas of the correct response to an interference with Article 8 rights for those of the government of the state, so
long as the state is taking some steps to remedy the interference. The
margin cannot be invoked to deflect the Court's criticism from a state
which has refused to take any action to remedy a serious and apparently
unjustifiable violation of rights.[38]

In *Rees*, the Court stated that the matter should be kept under review
in the light of social and scientific developments. Nevertheless, in *Cossey*
the Court refused, by a margin of ten votes to eight, to depart from the
decision. The majority considered whether developments had occurred
which would make it proper to depart from *Rees*. However, they concluded[39] that there had been no relevant scientific developments, and the

---

[34] Decision CP6/76.   [35] [1977] IRLR 121.
[36] They are: the interests of national security, public safety, or the economic well-
being of the country; the prevention of disorder or crime; the protection of health or
morals; or the protection of the rights and freedoms of others.
[37] Eur. Ct. HR, Series A, No. 184, Judgment of 27 Sept. 1990, 13 EHRR 622.
[38] See Terence Walton, 'A Measure of Appreciation' (1992) 142 *NLJ* 1202–4.
[39] At para. 40 of the Judgment.

societal developments—including a resolution of the European Parliament[40] and Recommendation 1117 of the Parliamentary Assembly of the Council of Europe, both adopted in September 1989, encouraging harmonization of the laws and practices of the various member states in the field of recognizing reassignments of sex—demonstrated the same diversity of opinion among states as had been noted in the judgement in *Rees*. They decided that there was no ground for departing from the earlier decision, although they reiterated their consciousness of the seriousness of the problems and distress which transsexuals face, and the need to keep the matter under review in the future in order that the Convention can be interpreted and applied in the light of current circumstances.[41]

The majority judgment is open to the same criticisms as the *Rees* judgment. For this reason, Judge Martens, dissenting from the majority, argued that *Rees* had been wrongly decided, even as the law and social conditions stood in 1986. In addition, he and several other judges argued that, since the *Rees* judgment, societal attitudes had changed sufficiently to justify departing from it. The Parliamentary Assembly of the Council of Europe in its 1989 recommendation had expressly endorsed the growing belief that national laws should recognize the new sex of transsexuals, while the European Parliament had called on member states of the European Community 'to enact provisions on transsexuals' right to change sex by endocrinological, plastic surgery, and cosmetic treatment, on the procedure, and banning discrimination against them'. This increased tolerance had been reflected in legislation and judicial decisions giving legal recognition to people's reassigned sex (sometimes subject to rules imposing medical safeguards) in fourteen member states of the Council of Europe, including Turkey, which in other respects is by no means one of the most liberal European states. In three dissenting opinions, Judges Macdonald and Spielmann, Judge Martens, and Judges Palm, Foighel, and Pekkanen, concluded that this showed a societal development sufficiently important to justify departing from the *Rees* decision. Judge Martens castigated the majority for their caution in the face of moral attitudes which, while changing everywhere in Europe, were changing more slowly in some countries than in others. For the Court to adapt its interpretation of the Convention to relevant societal change only if almost all member states had adopted the new ideas was, he said:

inconsistent with the Court's mission to protect the individual against the collectivity and to do so by elaborating common standards. Caution is indeed called for, but in another direction: if a collectivity oppresses an individual because it does not want to recognize societal changes, the Court should take great care

[40] [1989] *OJ* C256/33.   [41] At para. 42 of the Judgment.

not to yield too readily to arguments based on a country's cultural and historical peculiarities.[42]

This is a compelling argument, up to a point. A human rights court should be slow to allow the views of groups in some of the countries within its jurisdiction to deprive individuals of redress for humiliation resulting from lack of respect for a central element in their private lives. This is a point which the majority of the Court chose not to address. At the same time, there are difficulties which the dissenting judges did not directly address. As in all situations where a judicial body confronts an executive body, important but unstated considerations of institutional politics were in play in *Cossey*. Any international human rights agency ultimately depends for its success on maintaining its moral authority over the states within its jurisdiction. There is always a tension between the agency and the state which is subject to it. By giving too little weight to deeply held cultural or moral beliefs in particular states, an agency can weaken its own authority in respect of those states for all purposes, without benefiting the oppressed individuals in the case immediately before it. It is proper for a court to weigh the seriousness of the alleged violation of the particular rights in issue against the deleterious effects which might follow from going too far, exacerbating the tension to a point where the court's moral authority over the state concerned is overborne by that state's commitment to the moral standards which the court is overriding.

This forces the Court to ask a sociological question: how deeply committed are the states or the peoples of Europe to the values which support the oppression of which the petitioner complains? If, like Judge Martens, one considers that there is a growing public tolerance for unconventional modes of existence, and acceptance of the importance of privacy, it is important to take account of these social developments in interpreting the Convention. Nevertheless, as Judge Martens himself accepted, this is not capable of proof.[43] By using the recommendations of supra-national and international parliamentary institutions as evidence for these social changes, the dissenting judges adopted a mode of sociological interpretation which gives great weight to the views of members of a cosmopolitan élite (which, incidentally, lacks legislative or executive authority in member states, although the members of the European Parliament are at least directly accountable to their electorates back home), but may not reflect the views of ordinary citizens in European states. This leads to a deeper, normative question, which is dividing the Court: whether, in interpreting Convention provisions in a context in which moral views appear to be changing, the Court should give greater weight to the established

---

[42] Dissenting opinion at para. 5.6, 13 EHRR at p. 663. See also pp. 644, 664.
[43] 13 EHRR at pp. 660–1.

(b) that the harm or likelihood of harm is attributable to the care given to the child, or likely to be given if an order is not made, not being what a parent could reasonably be expected to give, or the fact that the child is beyond parental control;[144] and

(c) that it is in the best interests of the child to make the order, and making the order would be better for the child than making no order.[145]

The court must also take account of the arrangements which the authority has made, or proposes to make, for permitting people to have access to the child, in accordance with the presumption that the child in care has a right to parents and certain other people.[146]

This last point is important in the light of the decision of the European Court of Human Rights in *Andersson* v. *Sweden*[147] that restriction of parental access to children in care violates Article 8(1) of the European Convention on Human Rights, and is justifiable under Article 8(2) as being for the protection of health and morals, or the rights of the child, only if the restriction is proportionate to the threat. In that case, the authorities had stopped all letters and telephone contact. This was held to be unnecessary and disproportionate, and deprived the authorities of the benefit of the justification under Article 8(2). Similarly, it has been held in *Eriksson* v. *Sweden*[148] that an indefinite prohibition on a mother removing her daughter from a foster home, when there was no longer any ground for considering that the mother was unable to care for the child, breached the rights of the mother and the child under Article 8.

It seems likely that the present state of English law, including procedures and criteria for child–care decisions contained in the Children Act 1989 and supplementary standards of fairness in administrative decision making laid down by judges in judicial review proceedings, are adequate to meet the requirements of Article 8 and Article 6(1) of the European Convention. If they are applied in practice, it should maintain a reasonable balance between the various interests involved. However, there are signs that the people who have to implement the procedures have not always been as familiar as they might be with the standards expected of them. In 1990, two years after the Butler-Sloss Report, Hollings J. found it necessary to remind local authorities of the safeguards recommended in that report in respect of investigative interviews with children in cases of suspected abuse, and of the importance of fairness to the parents or others concerned.[149] It is to be hoped that the training which has been given to social workers and others since 1990, in preparation for the coming into

[144] Children Act 1989, s. 31(2).   [145] Ibid., s. 1(1), (5).
[146] Ibid., s. 34.
[147] Eur. Ct. HR, Series A, No. 226, Judgment of 25 Feb. 1992, 14 EHRR 615.
[148] Eur. Ct. Hr, Series A, No. 156, Judgment of 22 June 1989, 12 EHRR 183.
[149] *Re A. and others (minors) (wardship: child abuse: guidelines)* (1990) [1992] 1 All ER 153.

hardships which transsexuals face than to speculation about the moral views of a range of European societies.

In view of the deep divisions within the Court, and between the Commission and the Court,[44] together with the promise in both *Rees* and *Cossey* that the matter would continue to be kept under review in the light of social and scientific developments, the law of the Convention on this issue is not settled. Although the wide margin of appreciation allowed to stated by the Court in those cases might suggest that it would be rare for a state's laws to be held to breach the Convention, the most recent decision of the Court on this matter makes it clear that there are circumstances in which even the margin of appreciation will not protect a state which fails to recognize a change of sex for domestic legal purposes. In *B. v. France*,[45] the applicant was a male/female transsexual. She alleged a breach of Article 8 in that the French authorities had refused to alter her birth certificate to show her new sex and forename. The authorities had taken the view that she had intentionally brought about the change of sex by artificial processes, and considered that recognizing the change would allow a person voluntarily to alter his or her civil status. The French *Cour d'appel* accepted that there are cases where irreversible necessity compels an amendment to a person's status, but held that such necessity was not established in B.'s case. She had merely undergone plastic surgery to change her external appearance, rather than undergoing hormone therapy, counselling, and reconstructive surgery. In particular, she had not gone through the procedures approved by the National Council of France's Medical Association, namely treatment by a qualified medical team in the course of which they reach the conclusion that the transsexual's position is genuine and irreversible and that no form of psychological or psychiatric treatment will help.

Despite the weakness of the evidence for saying that Miss B.'s change of sex was simply a recognition of an existing psychological state of affairs, apparently putting her in a less favourable position than the applicants in *Rees* and *Cossey*, the European Court of Human Rights held, by fifteen votes to 6, that the French decision infringed Article 8. The Court again refused to depart from its earlier decisions, holding that the societal changes since *Rees* had not yet established a sufficiently broad consensus on the proper approach to transsexualism. Nevertheless, the Court distinguished those cases because of differences between French and English law concerning the effects of refusal to recognize a change of sex. On the

---

[44] The Commission's Delegate at the hearing in *Cossey* told the Court that the Commission had referred the *Cossey* case to the Court in the hope that the Court would depart from the judgment in *Rees*.

[45] Eur. Ct. HR, Judgment of 25 Mar. 1992, noted by Susan Millns, 'Transsexuality and the European Convention on Human Rights' [1992] *PL* 559–66.

balance between the interests of the community and those of the individual, the Court took account of Miss B.'s determination to change her sex, and of the ease with which an annotation could be inserted on Miss B.'s birth certificate to reflect her current status, as had been allowed in other cases in France. The refusal of some courts in France to allow a change of forenames was also a factor which distinguished the French position from that in England, and was relevant to respect for private life. In view of the legal requirement in France (but not England) for people to carry identity cards identifying their sex, and to show them on demand, the Court held that the discrepancy between B.'s apparent sex and that recorded in official documents had reached a sufficient degree of seriousness to be considered incompatible with her right to respect for her private life, and not to be justified by the state's margin of appreciation. It was for the state to decide how to remedy the breach as a matter of national law.[46] The Court accordingly awarded 100,000 French francs for non-pecuniary damage, and 35,000 French francs in costs, as just satisfaction under Article 50.

This decision shows that an important factor, in deciding whether a refusal to recognize a change of sex amounts to a violation of the right to respect for private life under Article 8, is the impact which the refusal has on the individual in the light of the effects of civil rights and obligations related to legal status. As matters stand, this results in an apparently curious position. Article 8 effectively gives rights to transsexuals in some, but not all, states to recognition of their changed sex. People in countries where few disabilities, obligations, or embarrassments are imposed on transsexuals by operation of law have no right to official recognition of their reassigned sex. However, this seems to miss the point of Article 8. Respect for private life is not simply a matter of protecting people from the embarrassment of external scrutiny of their personal situations. It involves respect for the individual's own dignity, and sense of being valued. This has been recognized independently by the German *Bundesverfassungsgericht* and by the Appellate Division of the Superior Court of New Jersey, in decisions cited in the dissenting opinion of Judge Martens in *Cossey*.[47] In the New Jersey case, the court ruled that recognition would 'promote the individual's quest for inner peace and personal happiness, while in no way disserving any societal interest, precept of public order or precept of morality'.[48] This is an important aspect of the right to respect for, rather than merely avoidance of discrimination resulting

[46] A further complaint that France's treatment of Miss B. had been inhuman and degrading and had violated her rights under Art. 3 was not proceeded with.

[47] 49 *BVerfGE* 286; *M.T.* v. *J.T.* 2 FLR 2247 (1976), respectively. See 13 EHRR at pp. 647–8.

[48] *M.T.* v. *J.T.* 2 FLR 2247 (1976).

from, private life. To the extent that the Court guarantees that right to respect, including self-respect, to some but not all citizens of the High Contracting Parties to the Convention, it is hard to resist the conclusion that the Court, like the government and Parliament of the UK, has so far failed to discharge its responsibilities.

11.2 SEXUAL FREEDOM

If there are circumstances in which the right to be treated by law as being of the sex which best reflects one's psychological make-up is protected by the right to respect for private life under Article 8(1) of the Convention, the same is true of respect for the means whereby a person gives expression to the sexuality which is part of his or her sexual constitution. But there have traditionally been legal limits on sexual freedom. In England and Wales, the law interferes with sexual freedom mainly by imposing criminal liability in respect of disapproved acts. Liability is imposed partly to protect vulnerable people (such as children, those suffering from mental disorder or disability, and people subject to the authority of others) against having sexual activity forced on them when they are not in a position to choose rationally for themselves or to refuse to co-operate. In addition, the law is used to protect sexual morality, an aim which has become more controversial as the principle expounded by John Stuart Mill in his essay *On Liberty*, that the sole ground for restricting a person's freedom should be that it causes harm to others,[49] has grown in popularity. Mill argued that people who are specially likely to have a distorted view of their own interests or who are likely to be at a disadvantage in protecting them—young or mentally handicapped people, or those subject to the orders of others—must be specially protected against harm, but otherwise people should be free to decide for themselves what constitutes a harm for them and what would be a good. Mill's principle has formed the foundation for two important official reports: the *Report of the (Wolfenden) Committee on Homosexual Offences and Prostitution*, which recommended a relaxation of the punishment of homosexual acts;[50] and the *Report of the (Williams) Committee on Obscenity and Film Censorship*,[51] which used it as a basis for recommendation for reform of the law of obscenity.

However, Mill's rationalist view that identifiable harm to identifiable people constitutes the sole justification for imposing criminal liability was contentious. It was opposed by moralists of many persuasions. Lord

[49] See Ch. 1, above. [50] Cmd. 247 (London: HMSO, 1957).
[51] Cmnd. 7772 (London: HMSO, 1979), examined further in Ch. 15, below.

Devlin attacked it in a famous Maccabean Lecture, asserting the proper role of law as protector of established moral standards, rather than an instrument for changing moral views. He argued that there is a core of social morality which binds societies, and which must be maintained, using the criminal law in support if needed, lest civil society collapse. The Law Lords, in 1961, followed the Devlin line, asserting a power to create new criminal offences in order to protect public morality as understood by the judges.[52]

Chief among offences which consist of sexual behaviour considered immoral or socially harmful was buggery.[53] This is constituted at common law by sexual intercourse involving penetration *per anum* by a man with another man or a woman, or *per vaginam* by a man or woman with an animal. Not only is consent not a defence, but the consenting party is guilty of the offence as a principal. Section 12 of the Sexual Offences Act 1956, providing that: 'It is an offence for a person to commit buggery with another person or with an animal', merely incorporated the common-law definition. The moral passions engendered by the issue of homosexual buggery in particular made the issue too hot for government to handle, and it was not until 1967 that the law in England and Wales was liberalized, as a result of a private member's Bill which became the Sexual Offences Act 1967.[54]

In many states of the United States, too, buggery is illegal. Although the federal courts have developed a constitutional right to privacy which includes a right to contraception and some consensual sexual activity, the most recent decision of the Supreme Court has retreated from giving constitutional protection to buggery, at any rate between men. In *Bowers* v. *Hardwick*,[55] the Court upheld by a five–four majority a Georgia statute which criminalized sodomy between consenting adults in private. The majority held that there is no fundamental right to homosexual buggery such as might benefit from due process protection under the Fourteenth Amendment. The minority argued that the case was not about buggery *per se*, but rather about the fundamental right to privacy, but they were outvoted.

The European Court of Human Rights has a rather better record on protecting sexual freedom. In 1981, the Court held in *Dudgeon* v. *United*

[52] *Shaw* v. *DPP* [1962] AC 220, [1961] 2 All ER 446, HL.

[53] See J. C. Smith and Brian Hogan, *Criminal Law*, 7th edn. (London: Butterworths, 1992), 476–9.

[54] In Scotland, a similar change was introduced latter, by Criminal Justice (Scotland) Act 1980, s. 80. The law in Northern Ireland changed in 1982: see below.

[55] 478 US 186 (1986), discussed by Anon., 'The Supreme Court, 1985 Term: Leading Cases: Right to privacy' (1986) 100 *Harv. LR* 200–20 at 210–20; Anthony Lester, 'The Overseas Trade in the American Bill of Rights' (1988) 88 *Columbia LR* 537–61 at 558–61; James Michael, 'Homosexuals and Privacy' (1988) 138 *NLJ* 831.

Kingdom[56] that the blanket criminalization of homosexual acts violated the rights of homosexual men to respect for their private lives. That case concerned the law in Northern Ireland, which was altered as a result to bring it more closely into line with that in mainland Britain.[57] Similarly, in *Norris* v. *Ireland*[58] the Court held that Ireland's total ban on homosexual acts violated the right to respect for private life. At the same time, Article 8(2) permits states to restrict practical expressions of that respect in order to protect health and morality (allowing governments to take account of prevailing moral standards in its territory) or the rights and well-being of others, so long as any interference with the right is in accordance with the law and necessary in a democratic society. This gives scope for argument about the demands of morality, health, and the rights or well-being of others, and the extent to which it necessitates interferences with people's sexual freedom. In *Dudgeon* the Court decided that the state's legitimate interest in protecting the health and morals of its citizens, and particularly of its youth, must be respected by allowing the UK Government a wide margin of appreciation in setting the age at which men could lawfully consent to homosexual activity. A minimum age of 21 was within the margin of appreciation.[59] But the margin of appreciation has limits. In *Norris*, the Court held by a majority of eight votes to six that the total ban on homosexual activity in Ireland went further than could be considered necessary for the protection of the morals of youth, and, being disproportionate to any aim which could legitimately be pursued under Article 8(2), fell outside the margin of appreciation and violated Article 8. In what follows, the English law is evaluated in the light of these Convention standards.

(1) Homosexual acts[60]

It would be wrong to imagine that the criminal law was aimed exclusively at homosexual acts. Buggery may be either a heterosexual or a homosexual act, as will be clear from the definition of the offence given above. Furthermore, homosexual acts between women over the age of 16 have never been criminal, although indecent assault on a woman (whether by a man or another woman) is an offence under the Sexual Offences Act 1956, section 14. Most female homosexual acts, such as cunnilingus, masturbation, and tribadism, are capable of amounting to

[56] Eur. Ct. HR, Series A, No. 45, Judgment of 23 Sept. 1981, 4 EHRR 149.
[57] Homosexual Offences (Northern Ireland) Order 1982.
[58] Eur. Ct. HR, Series A, No. 142, Judgment of 26 Oct. 1988, 13 EHRR 186.
[59] Eur. Ct. HR, Series A, No. 45, Judgment of 23 Sept. 1981, 4 EHRR 149, at para. 62 of the Judgment.
[60] Tony Honoré, *Sex Law* (London: Duckworth, 1978), ch. 4.

indecent assaults, but normally partners in a female homosexual act would be able to give consent, which would prevent the act from being an assault, if it did not produce bodily harm. However, under section 14(2) a girl under the age of 16 cannot give a consent which would prevent an act being an assault for the purposes of the section. This effectively means that the age of consent for homosexual activity by women is the same as for heterosexual activity.[61]

On the other hand, there was a total ban on male homosexual acts, which would all constitute either buggery or acts of gross indecency between men regardless of age or consent. It was left to a private member's Bill to translate into law the more liberal sexual atmosphere of the 1960s. The Sexual Offences Act 1967, section 1(1) provided that 'a homosexual act in private shall not be an offence provided that the parties consent thereto and have attained the age of twenty-one years'. Homosexual acts are defined as buggery and acts of gross indecency.[62] Gross indecency has not been defined either by statute or by the courts, despite being the subject of a separate statutory offence, but acts of gross indecency include fellatio, masturbation, genital apposition, and other forms of contact with other people's genitals.[63] The reform left untouched situations in which homosexual practices were deemed to be prejudicial to good discipline: the Act preserved criminal liability for buggery by members of the armed forces or by members of the crew on board a merchant ship.[64] In order to protect particularly vulnerable groups, people suffering from a severe mental handicap are deemed to be incapable of giving the necessary consent at any age, and staff are criminally liable for homosexual acts committed against patents in mental hospitals.[65] This provision, while removing one source of unfairness to homosexual men, brought with it several curiosities.

(i) *The limited meaning of privacy.* Without attempting a definition of the phrase 'in private', section 1(2) of the 1967 Act specifies two situations which are not to be treated as being in private. One is a public lavatory. This is unexceptionable, if one accepts that part of the purpose of the prohibition is to protect the sensibilities of members of the public who would be shocked or upset by seeing homosexual acts, and would have no warning of what was going on before entering the lavatory. Using

---

[61] Sexual Offences Act 1956, s. 6.   [62] Sexual Offences Act 1967, s. 1(7).

[63] For discussion, see Honoré, *Sex Law*, 90.

[64] Army Act 1955, s. 66; Sexual Offences Act 1967, ss. 1(5), 2. This was held not to give rise to an admissible petition under the European Convention on Human Rights, because of the special need prevent disorder in the army: Eur. Commn. HR, Application No. 9237/81, *B. v. UK*, 34 DR 68 (1983), 6 EHRR 354.

[65] Sexual Offences Act 1967, s. 1(3), (4).

criminal law to safeguard sensibilities is hard to justify within the strict definition of Mill's harm principle, but may be acceptable if (with Feinberg)[66] one regards a serious assault on one's deeply held moral beliefs as so offensive as to amount to a form of personal harm. More controversially, the subsection provides that a homosexual act is not in private when more than two people take part or are present. This is an extraordinary provision. It has no parallel in the law relating to heterosexual acts, and is quite unjustifiable if the acts are taking place on private premises, all the participants and observers are consenting adults, and other people are excluded. Once it is accepted that homosexual acts in private between consenting adults ought not in principle to give rise to criminal sanctions, it is hard to see any justification for imposing the wholly arbitrary limitation that only two people may be present, making it impossible for male homosexual voyeurs to satisfy themselves lawfully unless they are content to watch one other man masturbating alone.

(ii) *Heterosexual buggery.* It remains a crime for adults to participate in heterosexual buggery, even consensually and in private, despite the fact that this evinces as little respect for the private lives of heterosexuals as the law formerly did for homosexuals and heterosexuals alike. It is thus arguable that the current law violates the rights of heterosexuals under Article 8 and Article 14 (the anti-discrimination provision) of the European Convention on Human Rights. The Criminal Law Revision Committee has recommended that the law should be changed to legalize heterosexual anal intercourse between consenting parties each of whom has reached the age of 16, placing it in the same legal position as other forms of sexual intercourse.[67] However, Parliament has not so far acted on this recommendation.

(iii) *Age of consent.* The age of consent to homosexual buggery, set at 21 by the 1967 Act, is five years higher than the age of consent for vaginal intercourse or for female homosexual acts. In *Dudgeon*, it was argued that this represents a failure of respect for male homosexuals' private lives under Article 8. However, the Court held that differential ages for consent fall within a state's margin of appreciation to fix an age at which consent may be effective in law in order to protect health and morality and the rights and well-being of others. The UK Government considered that the social risks of female homosexual activity to young people were not as serious as those attendant on male homosexuality. It is implicit in the Court's decision that, to be within the margin of appreciation, the

---

[66] Joel Feinberg, *Offense to Others* (New York: OUP, 1985), chs. 7 and 9.
[67] CLRC Fifteenth Report, *Sexual Offences*, Cmnd 9213 (London: HMSO, 1984), para. 6.7.

age of consent must be reasonable in the light of the legitimate object of protecting young people and those unable to decide sensibly for themselves. If the state were to set an age so high as to interfere significantly with the exercise of the right by people indisputably old enough to make their own decisions, the interference with respect for their private lives would be disproportionate to the legitimate aim pursued. The Criminal Law Revision recommended in 1984 that the age of consent to homosexual buggery should be reduced to 18, in line with the age at which people are considered to be sufficiently mature to make other significant decisions,[68] but this has not been acted on.

Other legal provisions discriminate in a number of ways against people's wishes to take part in sexual practices which others would regard as unconventional or immoral. This discrimination generally takes to form of criminal offences specifically aimed at certain types of sexual activity, or used to penalize expressions of some selected types of sexual behaviour. However, there are also circumstances in which certain sexual predilections may justify discrimination against a person in the field of employment.

(2) Acts between males in private or in public

There are offences which are committed by acts between males, but not by acts between males and females or between females. Under the Sexual Offences Act 1956, section 13, it is an offence for a man (but not a woman) to commit an act of gross indecency with another man whether in public or in private, or to be a party to or procure the commission of such an act.[69] It is now not an offence, however, for a man to procure the commission of an act of gross indecency between himself and another man, if that act would be lawful by virtue of section 1 of the Sexual Offences Act 1967, being a homosexual act in private between two men who have attained the age of 21 years.[70]

(3) Other acts in private: assault, indecent assault, and sado-masochism

Offences are committed by men or women who commit indecent assaults on any woman or man in public or in private.[71] These aspects of the law of offences against the person effectively outlaw certain types of violent sexual activity even between consenting adults in private, whether homosexual or heterosexual. In particular, sado-masochism,

---

[68] Ibid., para. 6.13.   [69] 'Man' includes 'boy': Sexual Offences Act 1956, s. 46.
[70] Sexual Offences Act 1967, s. 4(2).
[71] Sexual Offences Act 1956, s. 14 (indecent assault on a woman) or 15 (indecent assault on a man).

which is said to form an element in the sexual techniques of many people, is probably always illegal if the judicial decisions to date are correct. However, it is far from clear that they are right in principle.

It is a battery intentionally to inflict on a person violence, or to put someone in fear of immediate violence, which is intended or likely to cause bodily harm, without the consent of the victim. The victim's consent will justify bodily harm in some circumstances if the victim is of an age and mental condition which permits the law to recognize that consent, at least so long as the harm is no more than trifling (on which see below) or is inflicted for a therapeutic purpose (see Chapter 4, above). However, in two cases it has been held that the law will refuse to recognize consent where the purpose inflicting the violent is to secure sexual gratification. In *R. v. Donovan*[72] the defendant had beaten a girl, aged 17, with a cane, with her consent. His purpose was to obtain sexual pleasure. He was convicted on charges of indecent assault and common assault. The Court of Criminal Appeal decided that the girl's consent was irrelevant, because it would be contrary to public policy to take account of consent where the sole purpose was sexual gratification. The conviction was quashed on the technical ground that the jury had not been asked to consider whether the degree of violence used was intended or likely to cause bodily harm. Although Sir James Fitzjames Stephen, in his *Digest of Criminal Law*,[73] suggested that one was entitled to consent to bodily harm so long as it does not amount to a maim (which, as noted above in connection with sex reassignment therapy, is an offence at common law), the Court of Appeal has since held that nobody may give an effective consent to any degree of bodily harm unless some public interest is served thereby. On that ground, it was held that young men who agreed to settle an argument by a fist fight were guilty of assault, and could not use each other's consent to the fight to justify the bodily harm which resulted. The court accepted (*obiter*) that a public interest was served by properly conducted games and sports, lawful punishment of children, reasonable surgical procedures, and dangerous exhibitions,[74] and in a later decision it was held that boys could consent to rough and undisciplined play.[75] However, the judges acknowledge no public interest in sado-masochism between consenting adults, a position recently reaffirmed by a majority of the House of Lords (Lords Templeman, Jauncey, and Lowry, Lords Mustill and Slynn dissenting) in *R. v. Brown*, where convictions under sections 20 and 47 of the Offences Against the Person Act 1861,

---

[72] [1934] 2 KB 498, CCA.
[73] 4th edn., 148–9.
[74] *Attorney-General's Reference (No. 6 of 1980)* [1981] 2 All ER 1057, CA.
[75] *R. v. Jones* [1987] Crim. LR 123, CA.,

arising out of a sado-masochistic encounter, were upheld notwithstanding the participants' consent.[76]

This position is unprincipled and incoherent.[77] An appeal to some public interest served by certain types of consent to bodily harm does not explain what public interest is served by rough and undisciplined play by children, or why no such interest is served by rough, but far from undisciplined, play by adults (for sado-masochistic violence between consenting adults is generally ritualistic and carefully administered). Even if it is possible to explain this apparent discrepancy, the object of respecting consent to medical treatment and the rough and tumble of sport is primarily to protect the individual interests of the participants as they perceive them, rather than to advance any public interest. It is a recognition of individual autonomy, the right of individuals of sufficient understanding to make their own decisions about what is good for them. In principle, this should apply equally to people's sexual preferences. Indeed, it is hard to see how the interest (whether public or private) in allowing people to express their sexuality, which forms a fundamental part of people's personality, could be less important than the interest in allowing people to pursue sports. Sport is fun, but sex, for many people is more than fun: it is a form of self-expression. It is even harder to see how sado-masochistic activity between consenting adults in private could be contrary to public policy.

Finally, the current legal rule as explained by the majority of the House of Lords in *Brown*, making it impossible to consent to any actual bodily harm for sexual purposes, appears to have the effect of outlawing mere love bites or scratches as it does torture and mutilation. This appears to infringe the privacy rights of both homosexuals and heterosexuals, can hardly be a genuine response to a pressing social need such as to make it necessary in a democratic society for the purposes of Article 8(2) of the European Convention on Human Rights, and in any case seems disproportionate to any legitimate object which the law might be pursuing. At one point in the Court of Appeal's decision in *R. v. Brown*[78] Lord Lane CJ appears to have suggested that it might be considered inappropriate to lay charges under the Offences against the Person Act 1861 in respect of mere 'incidents in the course of private activities, whether homosexual or heterosexual', but charges were appropriate where there is wounding or actual bodily harm. This is hard to understand, for three reasons. First, if there were no wounding or bodily harm, there would be no basis for a

---

[76] [1993] 2 WLR 556; [1993] 2 All ER 75, HL, affirming [1992] 2 WLR 441, [1992] 2 All ER 552, CA.

[77] For detailed discussion, see L. H. Leigh, 'Sado-masochism, Consent, and the Reform of the Criminal Law' (1976) 39 *MLR* 130–46.

[78] [1992] 2 All ER at p. 557 *per* Lord Lane CJ.

criminal charge under the Offences against the Person Act 1861 or the Sexual Offences Act 1956. Secondly, private acts and acts which cause bodily harm are not mutually exclusive categories. Thirdly, as the European Court of Human Rights pointed out in cases concerning laws against homosexuality, people are not free to give expression to their sexuality if they are liable to criminal prosecution at the administrative discretion of the prosecuting authorities.[79]

The law at present undervalues people's autonomy, and appears to violate the right to respect for private life under Article 8 of the European Convention on Human Rights. Although, in *R.* v. *Brown*, Lord Lane CJ in the Court of Appeal and Lord Templeman in the House of Lords did not think that the decision of the European Court of Human Rights in *Dudgeon* v. *United Kingdom* applied where wounding or bodily harm was inflicted, there can be little doubt that a law which interferes with sexual activity in private even where no lasting serious bodily harm is caused will be regarded as disproportionate to the legitimate aim of protecting morality and health under Article 8(2) of the Convention. It is to be regretted that the House of Lords was unable to put the law on a more rational and principled footing which distinguishes between those who are capable of consenting and those who are not, and those who indulge in acts in private and those who perform in public. It is doubtful whether the European Commission and Court of Human Rights will consider that the interference with the right to private life which the decision in *Brown* represents can be justified as necessary in a democratic society for the purpose of protecting morality or the rights of others under Article 8(2) of the European Convention on Human Rights. The defendants in that case were not proselytizing for a sado-masochist lifestyle. They were not forcing themselves on an unwilling public, or corrupting youth. They were not inflicting grievous bodily harm. The law is in need of statutory amendment. However, a ruling from the European Court of Human Rights is likely to be needed to stir Parliament into action, since there are probably more votes to be lost than won through legalizing sado-masochism, even when it consists only of the infliction of a carefully controlled amount of harm on one consenting adult by another.

Offences of indecent assault[80] present a further difficulty. Any offence which contains as part of its definition a requirement of indecency is subject, even more than offences founded on immorality, to the whims and fashions of social acceptability. An indecent assault is an assault or battery (i.e. an intentional, non-consensual act putting the victim in fear of

---

[79] *Dudgeon* v. *UK*, Eur. Ct. HR, Series A, No. 5, Judgment of 23 Sept. 1981, 4 EHRR 149; *Norris* v. *Ireland*, Eur. Ct. HR, Series A, No. 142, Judgment of 26 Oct 1988, 13 EHRR 186.

[80] Sexual Offences Act 1956, s. 14(1).

immediate violence, or actually inflicting of violence) which is indecent. But what is needed to establish indecency? If the objective nature of the act is incapable of being regarded as indecent, the assault or battery is not indecent, regardless of the intention of the perpetrator. Thus removing a girl's shoe, or touching the bottom of her skirt, are not indecent assaults (although they may amount to common assaults), even if the perpetrator derives sexual gratification from the act.[81] It seems that there are only two ways in which an assault or battery may be indecent.[82]

First, if the nature of the act is unquestionably indecent in the circumstances, the assault is indecent whatever the defendant intended. As Lord Griffiths has said: 'A man might strip a woman with the motive of obtaining sexual gratification or, alternatively, with the motive of revenge to humiliate her; but whichever his motive he would undoubtedly be guilty of indecent assault because his intentional stripping of her clothing is an indecent affront to her sexual modesty.'[83] This use of criminal law to protect people against forcible affronts to their sexual modesty is a legitimate attempt to prevent harm and safeguard privacy.

Secondly, if the objective nature of the act in its context is equivocal, the assault will be indecent if the perpetrator had an indecent purpose, and evidence of purpose is admissible to establish the offence. This was decided by a majority of the House of Lords in R. v. Court,[84] where the defendant, a shop assistant, had placed a 12-year-old girl customer across his knees and spanked her over her shorts. There was nothing in the nature of the spanking to show that this was anything other than a misguided and unjustified disciplinary chastisement. However, when the police asked the perpetrator why he had done it, he was unwise enough to admit that he was indulging a buttock fetish. This statement was held to be admissible in order to establish the indecency. The reasoning of the majority was the the offence includes as part of its mental element the intention to behave in a way that ordinary people would regard as indecent. Evidence of motive was admissible to prove this element. However, it is inconsistent to assert that the mens rea includes this element of subjective indecency when the objective nature of the act is equivocal, but not when the act is objectively indecent. It is an odd offence in which the mens rea alters from subjective to objective depending on the exterior manifestations of the behaviour which is to be penalized. The indecency should properly be regarded as part of the actus reus of the offence,

---

[81] R. v. George [1956] Crim. LR 52 (Streatfield J., Lincoln Assizes); R. v. Thomas (1985) 81 Cr. App. R. 331, CA.

[82] Smith and Hogan, Criminal Law, 468–71.

[83] R. v. Court [1989] AC 28 at p. 35, [1988] 2 All ER 221 at p. 224 per Lord Griffiths.

[84] [1989] AC 28, [1988] 2 All ER 221 (Lord Keith of Kinkel, Lord Fraser of Tullybelton, Lord Griffiths, and Lord Ackner; Lord Goff of Chieveley dissented).

not the mens rea. It might be desirable to treat the perpetrator's indecent motive as potentially an element of the actus reus of an indecent assault, and evidence of the admission might properly have been admitted for that purpose, but the majority's reasoning in *Court* is not wholly satisfactory even if one regards the result as desirable.

However, it is far from clear that the result is desirable. To include the motive of the defendant as an element in the actus reus of the offence comes close to using the criminal law to penalize immoral thoughts. The effect of *Court* is that more severe penalties may be imposed on a defendant for an assault which affords him sexual satisfaction than for an exactly similar assault which affords him some other sort of satisfaction. For example, a shopkeeper who suspects a child of shop-lifting might derive considerable moral satisfaction from giving the child a disciplinary spanking. This would probably amount to a common assault and battery, with a maximum penalty of one year's imprisonment on conviction on indictment.[85] It seems a little unfair that another shopkeeper whose satisfaction is sexual as well as moral would be liable to up to ten years imprisonment for indecent assault.[86] The objective quality of the two acts, and their impact on the victim, are the same, so the increased liability is entirely attributable to moral disapproval of certain motives or sources of satisfaction. A harm-based, utilitarian justification for imposing criminal liability provides no justification for distinguishing between the two cases.

(4) Paedophilia

An act of indecency on a child which amounts to an assault is always criminal. Children under the age of 16 are unable to consent validly to any act which amounts to an indecent assault, even if it does not cause any bodily harm.[87] This is because of the perceived need to protect children from exploitation, and safeguard them against potentially serious errors of judgement due to lack of experience and understanding. For the same reasons, committing any act of gross indecency, not amounting to an assault, with or towards a child under the age of 14, or inciting a child under that age to commit such an act with oneself or another, is an offence.[88] In addition, it is an offence, without legitimate reason, to take, distribute, show, or advertise indecent photographs of a child,[89] or knowingly to possess such a photograph for one of those purposes[90] or for

---

[85] Offences against the Person Act 1861, s. 47.
[86] Sexual Offences Act 1956, Sch. 2, as amended by the Sexual Offences Act 1985, s. 3.
[87] Sexual Offences Act 1956, ss. 14(2) (girls), 15(2) (boys).
[88] Indecency with Children Act 1960, s. 1.
[89] Protection of Children Act 1978, s. 1(1).   [90] Ibid., s. 1(1)(c).

one's personal use.[91] The effect is to make virtually any sexual activity involving children illegal. The restriction of the right to respect for pae-dophiles' private lives, which this entails, is justifiable under Article 8(2) of the European Convention on Human Rights by reference to the pro-tection of the rights of the children concerned, even without reference to the object of protecting health and morality.

(5) Acts between males in public

It is an offence under section 32 of the Sexual Offences Act 1956 for a man (or boy) 'persistently to solicit or importune in a public place for immoral purposes'. The classic setting for this is a public toilet. The offence presents two problems. First, it discriminates against men, since women cannot be convicted of it. Secondly, people's conceptions of an immoral purpose may differ, so there is a risk that a defendant might be convicted in one part of the country, or by one jury, in relation to a pur-pose which would have led to an acquittal elsewhere or by a differently constituted jury, not because different views are taken as to the evidence but because different moral standards prevail. This risk is only partly reduced by the decision in *Crook* v. *Edmondson*[92] that the immorality must relate to sexual conduct to fall within the section. Sexual mores have changed markedly over the last thirty years, although at different rates and in different directions depending on geographical location, social class, and ethnic or cultural background. In a number of cases since the Sexual Offences Act 1967 legalized certain homosexual acts in private between consenting adults, defendants have argued that homosexual pur-poses should no longer be regarded as immoral within the meaning of the Act. The changes in standards of sexual morality have been acknowl-edged by the Court of Appeal to the extent that it is now for the jury to decide whether a particular purpose is immoral, although the trial judge must not leave a case to the jury unless satisfied that the purpose is at least capable of being properly regarded as immoral.[93] At the same time, the Court of Appeal has accepted that there are serious problems involved in dealing with crimes which rely on immorality as part of their definition. There may be a tendency for jurors to be overly influenced by the offen-siveness of a defendant's conduct when accosting somebody, allowing their attention to be distracted from the immorality or otherwise of the defendant's purpose in soliciting. Judges must carefully direct juries as to what is required of them. When a defective direction leads to a

---

[91] Criminal Justice Act 1988, s. 160.   [92] [1966] 1 All ER 833, DC.
[93] *R.* v. *Ford (Graham)* [1977] 1 WLR 1083, [1978] 1 All ER 1129, CA; *R.* v. *Gray* (1981) 74 Cr. App. R. 324, CA; *R.* v. *Goddard* (1991) 92 Cr. Ap. R. 185, CA; *R.* v. *Kirkup* [1992] NLJ Rep. 1612, CA.

conviction, the Court of Appeal has to quash the conviction unless it can apply the proviso to section 2 of the Criminal Appeal Act 1968 on the basis that, even had the jury been properly directed, it would have been bound to convict. When invited to apply the proviso in these cases, the Court decided in *R. v. Gray*[94] that any jury would inevitably have decided that homosexual activity was immoral, albeit not illegal, and differently constituted courts have since regarded themselves as bound to follow that view until such time as Parliament reviews the law and incorporates a different model of immorality.[95]

With respect, however, this approach seems questionable both in law and in morality. If the morality or otherwise of a purpose is a question for the jury, it must be a question of fact from a legal point of view. If so, it is hard to see how the Court of Appeal in 1992 could be required as a matter of law to follow the factual conclusion of a differently constituted court, eleven turbulent years earlier, that a jury could not have regarded homosexual activity as other than immoral. In *R. v. Kirkup*, Staughton LJ said that there was no evidence before the court to convince it that moral judgements had altered significantly since 1981. This, however, misstates the issue. Under the proviso to section 2 of the Criminal Appeal Act 1968, the judges of the Court of Appeal ought to look to the prosecution to convince them that standards of morality are so clear as a matter of fact that no jury could have taken the view that homosexuality is not immoral. The burden of proof is on the prosecution. By shifting it to the defence, the Court of Appeal misconstrued the section.

This exacerbates a problem which would exist in any case. The judges recognize that it is not satisfactory for them to have to decide questions of morality as a basis for criminal liability. Parliament and the courts should, ideally, refrain from creating offences which are premised on unspecified moral postulates. Merely to refer the matter to popular morality leaves the standards of criminal liability to be determined by jurors, which is scarcely less objectionable than having them decided by judges. One may question whether it is appropriate for anyone to decide that somebody else's purposes deserve punishment by reason of immorality. In the spirit of Mill, Wolfenden, and Hart, some identifiable harm should be required in order to justify criminalizing conduct. Mere immorality of purpose is not enough. The offence under section 32 of the Sexual Offences Act 1956 is objectionable as an attempt to criminalize conduct which may be harmless, merely by reason of the immorality of the ulterior object of the actor. However, the section illustrates one of the weaknesses of the European Convention on Human Rights: although

[94] (1981) 74 Cr. App. R. 324, CA.
[95] *R. v. Goddard* (1991) 92 Cr. App. R. 185, CA; *R. v. Kirkup* [1992] NLJ Rep. 1612, CA.

the law may violate men's right to respect for their private lives under Article 8(1), it seems likely that the violation would be justifiable as an attempt to protect morals under Article 8(2), so long as it is in accordance with the law and not disproportionate to the aim pursued. It is strongly arguable that a human rights convention which permits rights to be interfered with in order to protect morality, without any harm being established, gives too much weight to what Professor Ronald Dworkin has called 'external preferences',[96] people's desire to outlaw behaviour the thought of which offends them even when it does not materially affect them.

Other parts of the law regulating sexual activity display a similarly prurient concern to discover and punish immoral purposes or thoughts, apart from any harm which may be done by their manifestation. Some examples follow.

(6) Other sexual activity in public

Behaviour which is acceptable in private is not necessarily acceptable in public. The sight of sexual intercourse, and acts of gross indecency, is deeply offensive to many people. The outrage to feelings which this sort of offence engenders may be severe enough to constitute a harm against which it is justifiable to seek protection from the criminal law.[97] At the same time, people's susceptibilities to this sort of outrage, and the kinds of behaviour which precipitate it, vary greatly. If the code of public conduct sanctioned by the criminal law were designed to avoid outraging the most susceptible citizens, the range of behaviour and expression to which we could give vent in public might be absurdly restricted. The framers of criminal law have tended to balance the interest in free expression against that in freedom from outrage by treating the problem essentially as one of public order: conduct has been treated as criminal, both formerly under the Public Order Act 1936, section 5, and now under the Public Order Act 1986, section 4, if the outrage which it is intended or likely to occasion makes it likely to precipitate public violence.[98]

However, there are signs that Parliament and the courts are inclined to press criminal liability rather further than this might suggest. Section 5 of the Public Order Act 1986 makes it an offence to use threatening, abusive, or insulting words or behaviour, or disorderly behaviour, within the hearing or sight of a person likely to be caused harassment, alarm, or distress thereby. This has the capacity to allow public displays of physical affection, particularly between homosexuals, to be penalized. Although

---

[96] Ronald Dworkin, *Taking Rights Seriously* (London: Duckworth, 1978), 234–6.
[97] Feinberg, *Offense*, ch. 9.   [98] See further Ch. 17, below.

showing affection for another person could not normally be regarded as insulting (unless that person did not consent to the display, and regarded it as implying a sexual orientation which he or she found insulting),[99] the Divisional Court held in *Masterson* v. *Holden*[100] that magistrates were entitled to decide that heterosexuals might feel insulted at seeing two homosexuals cuddling and kissing each other on the lips in Oxford Street, London, at 1.55 a.m. If this is correct, and the same approach is applied to prosecutions under section 5 of the Public Order Act 1986, the freedom of homosexuals (particularly, perhaps, men) to express their feelings in public will be severely curtailed, since it would seem to follow from the decision that magistrates would often be justified in deciding that the behaviour would be likely to cause harassment or distress to a heterosexual observer.

However, the decision in *Masterson* v. *Holden* is of dubious authority. It gives a more expansive interpretation to 'insulting' than is justified by the decision of the House of Lords in *Brutus* v. *Cozens*[101] that 'insulting' should be given its natural meaning. The approach in *Masterson* is therefore hard to support as a matter of law. It is also objectionable in principle. It extends criminal liability more widely than is authorized by Parliament, and it does so in a manner which is likely, in practice, to discriminate against homosexuals, since it is unlikely that any prosecutor or magistrate would consider a heterosexual couple publicly kissing to be insulting. Even leaving aside the possibility of improper discrimination on the basis of sexual orientation, the use of the criminal law to penalize normal behaviour expressive of affection, whether between heterosexuals or homosexuals, where there is no risk of public disorder or violence being caused, seems insensitive and inappropriate.

(7) Prostitution[102]

The law takes a dim view of prostitution, sometimes said to be the world's oldest profession. While prostitution is not actually unlawful in itself, a range of criminal offences penalize those who manage prostitutes, permit their premises to be used for prostitution, or keep, manage, or let premises which are used as a brothel.[103] A brothel requires the presence

---

[99] *Parkin* v. *Norman* [1983] QB 92 at pp. 100–1, [1982] 2 All ER 583 at pp. 588–9, *per* McCullough J.

[100] [1986] 1 WLR 1017, [1986] 3 all ER 39, DC. The defendants were charged under the Metropolitan Police Act 1839, s. 54(13).

[101] [1973] AC 584, [1972] 2 All ER 1297, HL, a case on s. 5 of the Public Order Act 1936.

[102] Honoré, *Sex Law*, ch. 5.

[103] Sexual Offences Act 1956, ss. 31, 33, 34, 35, 36; Sexual Offences Act 1967, s. 6.

of at least two prostitutes, but a person who provides sexual services for
money to one customer at a time can be charged with keeping a disorderly house at common law if the services are available to the public and
are such as outrage public decency (provision for flagellation, humiliation, bondage, and torture apparently falls into this category) or are
otherwise calculated to harm the public interest to such an extent as to
call for punishment.[104] Women who loiter to solicit in a public place for
the purpose of prostitution commit an offence.[105] Men who persistently
solicit women for the purpose of prostitution commit an offence,[106] and
it is a special offence (because of the harassment to women caused by
kerb-crawlers) to use a car solicit a woman for the purpose of prostitution
in a manner or in circumstances likely to cause annoyance to the woman
or nuisance to other people in the neighbourhood.[107] This form of
annoyance constitutes a harm which may justify criminal sanctions, but it
is hard to see how prostitutes who merely loiter waiting to be picked up
by punters do any harm. Parliament will not attempt the impossible task
of driving prostitution out of society, but seeks instead to make it a marginal, hole-in-the-corner activity which it is difficult to pursue without
falling foul of the law in one way or another. For people who for some
reason depend on prostitutes to satisfy their sexual appetites, this battery
of legal obstacles makes the fulfilment of that part of their private lives
constituted by their sexuality into a difficult and uncomfortable affair.

(8) Sexual orientation as a legitimate ground for discrimination

Generally speaking, a person's sex is not a legitimate ground for discriminating against him or her. In the fields of employment, housing, and provision of goods and services, it is generally unlawful to discriminate on
this ground,[108] although exceptions are made where small groups of
people are living or working together, where sex is a genuine occupational qualification for the job in question, and where clubs with fewer
than 25 members choose new members by screening them for personal
acceptability. However, the legislation does not directly protect people
against discrimination on the ground of their sexual orientation.
Although it would probably be unlawful to discriminate only against
male homosexuals or only against lesbians, since this would treat one sex
less favourably than the other in the same situation, it would apparently

[104] R. v. Tan [1983] QB 1053, [1983] 2 All ER 12, CA.
[105] Street Offences Act 1959, s. 1.   [106] Street Offences Act 1985, s. 2.
[107] Ibid., s. 1.
[108] Sex Discrimination Act 1975. See Evelyn Ellis, Sex Discrimination Law (Aldershot:
Gower, 1988), ch. 3, Catherine O'Donovan and Erika Szyszczak, Equality of Sex
Discrimination Law (Oxford: Basil Blackwell, 1988), chs. 3 and 4.

be lawful for an employer to discriminate equally against all homosexual men and women. This is an important gap at a time when homophobia is tending to increase as a reaction to fear of AIDS. Practising male homosexuals form one of the most prominent 'high risk groups', alongside intravenous drug abusers and haemophiliacs. This fear, besides fanning public prejudice which already exists,[109] has led life insurance companies to increase premiums or restrict cover. Even if discrimination on the ground of sexual orientation proved to be within the remit of the Sex Discrimination Act 1975, differential treatment of high risk groups by insurance companies would be lawful if based on reasonable actuarial or other data.[110]

Discrimination against homosexuals is apparently legal when terminating a person's employment. Industrial tribunals apply the principles of the Sex Discrimination Act 1975 in unfair dismissal cases, when deciding whether it was fair or reasonable in the circumstances to dismiss an employee, and the tests of fairness and reasonableness are to be applied to the circumstances of each case. There may, therefore, be cases in which it is permissible to dismiss a person for rhetorical or physical expressions of their sexuality. An example of dismissal for political rhetoric is *Boychuk* v. *Symons Holdings Ltd.*,[111] in which a lesbian employee was held to have been fairly dismissed for refusing to remove a Gay Liberation badge. Examples of lawful dismissal in respect of the physical expression of homosexuality are cases in which people are dismissed from posts after conviction for acts of gross indecency. However, in these cases the context is all-important. If there is no evidence that customers or other staff mind one way or the other about the person's sexuality, and the expression does not interfere with the employee's ability to do the job, the dismissal will probably be regarded as unfair.[112] But if the expression adversely affects the employee's ability to do the job (for example because of the reaction of customers, as in *Boychuk*), or if the employer is providing a public service such as education or residential child care, in respect of which there is considerable public disquiet at the risk of child abuse, it is likely to be fair to dismiss a teacher or carer who has been convicted of an act of gross indecency, even if it was not connected with the job.[113]

In principle, it is unacceptable to discriminate against homosexuals.

---

[109] It was given legislative expression in the Local Government Act 1986, s. 2A (inserted by the Local Government Act 1988, s. 28), which makes it unlawful for local authorities to promote homosexuality or its teaching.

[110] Sex Discrimination Act 1975, s. 45. See Ellis, *Sex Discrimination Law*, 123–4.

[111] [1977] IRLR 395, EAT.

[112] *Bell* v. *Devon and Cornwall Police Authority* [1978] IRLR 283.

[113] *Nottinghamshire County Council* v. *Bowley* [1978] IRLR 252, EAT.

The reasons go beyond the objection to discrimination in itself. People's homosexuality is not necessarily patent. If a person chooses to dress or behave in ways which make clear their homosexual orientation, they are making a statement about their own personality. Such statements are an emanation of the person's private life, commitments, and beliefs, and as such are entitled to respect. In terms of human rights, to subject people to disadvantage on the ground of their self-expression violates the right to respect for their private lives, contrary to Article 8(1) of the European Convention on Human Rights, because it undermines their self-esteem. But the matter does not end there. By openly associating themselves with a group which is increasingly playing a political role, agitating for respect and fair treatment, the homosexual who declares his or her sexual orientation may be making a political, as well as a personal, statement. The right to freedom of expression is protected by Article 10 of the Convention, considered further in Chapters 12 to 17 below. Article 10 protects people against discrimination on the ground of their expressed views if the discrimination amounts to an interference with their freedom to express the views, although it is a potential weakness of Article 10 that it permits states to justify an interference if it is prescribed by law and necessary in a democratic society for (inter alia) the protection of health or morals. The Commission has even left open the possibility that Article 10 might protect the right to the physical as well as verbal or representational expression of homosexual feelings of love, although this decision has been described in a leading commentary as 'remarkable'.[114]

Discrimination on the ground of sex in respect of the right to freedom of expression is outlawed by Article 14. This Article does not cover sexual orientation, but the Commission has decided that Article 14 might prohibit a state from subjecting male homosexuals to more or less favourable treatment than female homosexuals in the exercise of other rights under the Convention.[115] This is similar to the position under the Sex Discrimination Act 1975. However, the Court, in a number of unsatisfactory decisions which include one on the treatment of homosexuals in Northern Ireland, has held that it is possible for the state to justify discrimination if there are some objective and reasonable grounds for it, despite the absence of any reference in Article 14 itself to any grounds

---

[114] Application No. 7215/75, *X* v. *UK* (1978) 21 *Yearbook of the European Convention on Human Rights* 354, decision on admissibility; P. van Dijk and G. J. H. van Hoof, *Theory and Practice of the European Convention on Human Rights*, 2nd edn. (Deventer: Kluwer, 1990), 411.

[115] Application No. 7215/75, *X* v. *UK* (1978) 21 *Yearbook of the European Convention on Human Rights* 354, decision on admissibility; (1980) 19 DR 66 (Report); Application No. 7525/76, *X.* v. *UK* (1979) 22 *Yearbook of the European Convention on Human Rights* 156.

justifying such discrimination.[116] This permits far more discrimination between classes of homosexuals than does the law in England and Wales.

A weakness of English law relates to the reluctance of the courts to review governmental decisions concerning the treatment of certain homosexual public employees. As noted above, there is a tendency to treat as fair the dismissal of public employees for traits which cause public disquiet in the context of those employees' responsibilities. This is explicable in terms of the special responsibility of education authorities and social services departments to provide services in a way which protects the welfare of clients and is responsive to the demands and concerns of the community. The courts respect assertions of public interests by those who are regarded as being in a particularly good position to judge the public interest. This has a strange effect in relation to the national-security implications of homosexuality. As a result of the social and legal stigma which has historically attached to homosexuals, homosexuals have tended to try to keep their homosexuality private, if not secret. This has exposed them to the risk of blackmail by people who threaten to expose them. People in contact with secret information who are susceptible to blackmail obviously pose a security risk, and on that basis inquiries about people's sexual proclivities and activities have regularly formed part of security vetting procedures. However, the risk of blackmail and the associated security risks are reduced when the person is open about his or her homosexuality. There would appear to be little, if any, rational justification for refusing to employ a person on work which affects sensitive issues of national security merely because that person is a homosexual, if the person openly admits the fact. The courts seem to accept this, but have so far failed to carry the argument through to its logical conclusion. In *R. v. Director, GCHQ, ex parte Hodges*,[117] a man employed at GCHQ in a security-related capacity 'came out', publicly acknowledging his homosexuality. He was told that he was to be moved to other, less sensitive duties. Internal appeal processes having failed, he applied for judicial review of the decision. The Divisional Court, accepting that in all likelihood Mr. Hodges posed less of a security risk after coming out than he had previously, and that the decision to move him therefore seemed hard to justify rationally, nevertheless refused to quash the decision. Displaying the judges' traditional deference to executive assertions as to the demands of national security, the court decided that it would be inappropriate to conclude that the decision was one which no reasonable Director of GCHQ could have reached. Because there was

---

[116] See *Dudgeon v. UK*, Eur. Ct. HR, Series A, No. 45, Judgment of 22 Oct. 1981, 4 EHRR 149; *Abdulaziz, Cabales, and Balkandali v. UK*, Eur. Ct. HR, Series A, No. 94, Judgment of 28 May 1985, 7 EHRR 471, criticized by van Dijk and van Hoof, *Theory and Practice*, 544–5.

[117] [1988] COD 123.

no ground other than irrationality on which the decision could have been impugned, the law provided Mr. Hodges no remedy for a form of discrimination which seems hard to justify on the basis of the facts.[118]

11.3 SOME OTHER ASPECTS OF THE RIGHT TO RESPECT FOR PRIVATE AND FAMILY LIFE

This section notes the impact of certain other aspects of the right to respect for private and family life under Article 8 of the European Convention on Human Rights, and some associated rights, on people's rights in English law. Whereas the earlier parts of the chapter have been concerned mainly with questions of legal status and criminal liability, this section illustrates the interaction of principles of civil liberties and human rights with the technicalities of family law. One aspect of this concerns the right to marry, examined in s. 11.1 above. Another concerns the dissolution of marriages. In England and Wales, there are procedures for dissolving marriages which have irretrievably broken down, but this is not the case in all jurisdictions. In Ireland, for example, the influence of Roman Catholic canon law, with its insistence on the lifelong nature of the marriage vows, has resulted in civil law offering no procedure for divorce to Irish citizens. The European Court of Human Rights has considered the extent to which the right to respect for private and family life demands that people should have a legal channel for ending marriages into which they have entered. In *Johnston* v. *Ireland*[119] it was held that the total absence in the Republic of Ireland of a procedure for dissolving a marriage once it has been validly entered into does not violate Article 8 of the Convention. The absence of any means of obtaining a divorce did not prevent the parties to the marriage from entering into lasting unions with other people, and so did not infringe the right to respect for family life. The law merely prevented the parties to the extra-marital union from solemnizing their union in legal form. On the other hand, where the second, unsolemnized union produces issue, the child of the union is not to be disadvantaged at law by reason of her parents' unmarried state. The Irish law of illegitimacy, which subjected the child of an extra-marital union to legal disadvantages as compared with children of a valid marriage, did evince a lack of respect for the child which was held to breach Article 8.

Article 8 has a greater impact where a marriage or similar relationship is subsisting. The right to respect for family life has restricted the discretion of states to exercise immigration law in such a way as to divide

[118] See Sandra Fredman and Gillian S. Morris, *The State as Employer: Labour Law in the Public Services* (London: Mansell, 1989), 372–3.

[119] Eur. Ct. HR, Series A, No. 112, Judgment of 18 Dec. 1986, 9 EHRR 203.

families, as noted in Chapter 7 above. This affects the position of immigrants who are entitled to remain in a country because they have married a person who is entitled to reside there, but who are then divorced. No family relationship will then subsist between the parties to the dissolved marriage, so Article 8 will not prevent the deportation of the person who has no entitlement to reside there in his or her own right. However, if there are children of the union, each child has a family relationship with each parent, whether or not the children reside with them, which continues after the parents have divorced or separated. The natural parent–child relationship is entitled to respect, and is protected under Article 8(1). It will be an improper interference with the right to respect for family life if a state deports a parent whose children will remain behind, unless the deportation can be justified under Article 8(2).[120] The UN Convention on the Rights of the Child, adopted by the UN General Assembly in 1989 and to which the UK became a party in 1991, goes further. Article 9, paragraph 3 provides: 'States Parties shall respect the right of the child who is separated from one or both parents to maintain personal relations and direct contact with both parents on a regular basis, except if it is contrary to the child's best interests.'

In the field of the legal regulation of relationships between parents and children, English law has moved steadily from the idea of parental rights over their children towards the notion of parental responsibility. This trend was exemplified by the decision of the House of Lord in *Gillick* v. *West Norfolk and Wisbech Area Health Authority*[121] that parental rights derive from the primary responsibilities of parents to care for and maintain their children. The Children Act 1989, sections 2 and 3, reinforced the emphasis on parental responsibility, making it the foundation of the legal relationship between parents and their children;[122] and the emphasis on responsibilities (particularly paternal responsibilities) for maintaining children is fundamental to the scheme of the Child Support Act 1991, which requires fathers to support their children financially, and imposes penalties, in the form of withheld social security benefits, on a parent who refuses to disclose information about the other parent, unless the Secretary of State considers that there are reasonable grounds for believing that it would lead to a risk of harm or undue distress being caused to prevent the parent or any child living with her.[123]

The European Court of Human Rights has been active in using Article

---

[120] *Berrehab* v. *Netherlands*, Eur. Ct. HR, Series A, No. 138, Judgment of 21 June 1988, 11 EHRR 322.

[121] [1986] AC 112, [1985] 3 All ER 402, HL.

[122] See Richard White, Paul Carr, and Nigel Lowe, *A Guide to the Children Act 1989* (London: Butterworths, 1990), ch. 2.

[123] See Cretney, *Elements*, ch. 10.

8 to strike a balance between the interests of parties to family relationships, and establishing principles to govern the proper role of the state in intervening in those relationship when they seem to have gone wrong in ways which endanger the interests of some of the parties. The Court has taken a wide view of the term 'family'. It is not restricted to married couples and their children, nor to parents living together with their children, and includes diverse cultural views of family life, and extended family ties such as grandparent–grandchild relationships.[124] The discussion examines (1) the rights of parents and children in the face of interference with the family relationship by public authorities, and (2) the right of children to know about their family backgrounds and to make contact with their natural families following separation.

(1) Interfering with family relationships

The decision to remove a child from his or her family, and decisions about subsequent the care of the child, are always difficult. In a number of cases, children who were not taken into care have been killed or seriously injured in their families, and the social services departments of the local authorities concerned, which are primarily responsible for deciding whether or not to intervene, have been severely criticized. As public concern grew during the 1970s and 1980s about the prevalence of physical and later sexual abuse of children by those close to them, pressure grew on social workers and doctors to act to remove children from risk in cases of suspected abuse. However, taking children into care is always a shattering event for the children, parents, and their wider families and friends. If the state interferes in families without adequate cause, suspicion is cast on the innocent, and there is a risk that families will be broken up because of child-rearing practices which do no real harm to the children but are not regarded as ideal by the social workers concerned. When large numbers of children were diagnosed as having suffered sexual abuse in Cleveland, and were unceremoniously whisked away from their families, a backlash started, as parents mobilized public opinion in a challenge to the decisions.

As media attention turned towards the parents' and children's plight, concern focused on four issues. First, doubts were expressed about the methods of diagnosis used, about the types of questioning which led children to make (or appear to make) allegations of abuse, and about the tendency to interpret the children's responses to questions uncritically in the

---

[124] Application No. 5302/71, *X and Y* v. *UK*, Eur. Commn. HR, Decision of 11 Oct. 1973, 44 CD 29; *Marckx* v. *Belgium*, Eur. Ct. HR, Series A, No. 31, Judgment of 13 June 1979, 2 EHRR 330; *Berrehab* v. *Netherlands*, Eur. Ct. HR, Series A, No. 138, Judgment of 21 June 1988, 11 EHRR 322; van Dijk and van Hoof, *Theory and Practice*, 378–9.

light of the interviewers' preconceived idea that abuse had taken place. Secondly, it became clear that decisions were taken at case conferences attended only by the police, doctors, and social workers, at which the parents were often given no opportunity to challenge the evidence or to answer the allegations before the children were taken into care. Thirdly, the process of seizing children, usually without warning and often in dawn raids on their homes by police and social workers, was insensitive and unnecessarily cruel to all concerned. Fourthly, the families often had no adequate legal procedure for challenging the decision to remove their children.

The matter was examined, in the light of the Cleveland cases, by a judicial inquiry, conducted by Dame Elizabeth Butler-Sloss. In a full and thorough report,[125] which criticized many aspects of local authority decision-making and implementation, Dame Elizabeth made numerous recommendations concerning safeguards on the conduct of interviews with children, and proper decision-making procedures. At about the same time, the Divisional Court, in a series of cases in which parents applied for judicial review of case conference decisions, held that parents whose conduct is impugned and whose children are liable to be taken into care as a result are usually entitled to be informed of the fact and to be allowed to make representations, in person or in writing, to the case conference which would make decisions about the children. This was held to be required by the principles of procedural fairness in most cases, although there might be situations in which the urgency of the case, or the risk of serious harm to the child, might justify a different course.

Simultaneously, in a string of judgments the European Court of Human Rights upheld complaints from parents that their children had been taken into care without adequate legal or administrative safeguards. First, the Court established that respect for family life entailed the institution of fair procedures when decisions are made by social service officers affecting the integrity of the family unit. In *W., B., and R.* v. *United Kingdom*,[126] the Court held that the right to respect requires that the parents be involved in the decision-making process to a degree sufficient to enable them to protect their interests. The arrangements then in place for involving the parents in decisions to place the children of the applicants in long-term fostering with a view to adoption were found to be insufficient for that purpose. Similarly, it was held that a local authority, when making decisions about access to children in care, must take account of relevant considerations, including the views of the parents. It

---

[125] *Report of the Inquiry into Child Abuse in Cleveland*, Cm. 412 (London: HMSO, 1988).
[126] Eur. Ct. HR, Series A, No. 121, Judgments of 8 July 1987, 10 EHRR at pp. 29, 87, and 74 respectively.

followed that parents should normally be informed of the course which the authority was contemplating and be given an opportunity to make representations. Failure to give that opportunity evinced a lack of respect for family life which would violate Article 8 in the absence of good reasons, based on the legitimate objectives in Article 8(2), for not informing the parents and giving them an opportunity to put their point of view. Furthermore, the right to remain together as a family is a civil right which is protected under Article 6(1), with the effect that adequate opportunities for independent review of the decision must be available to the children and their parents in order to satisfy the right to a fair and impartial hearing by an independent tribunal in determining civil rights and obligations.[127]

Under the Convention, therefore, the obligation on the state to respect family life goes beyond taking steps to prevent harm to children. The risk of harm to children has to be weighed against the interests of the parents and the value of maintaining the family unit, which would be threatened by intervention. Parents or guardians are regarded as having substantive rights, as well as procedural rights, because of the right to respect for their private and family life and their cultural and ethical traditions. As it is put in the UN Convention on the Rights of the Child, Article 3, paragraphs 1 and 2, the best interests of the child are to be a primary consideration, but (because the family is regarded as the fundamental social unit for ensuring the well-being of children) protection and care offered to children is to take into account the rights of duties of parents, legal guardians, or other individuals who are legally responsible for the child, and to this end the state is to 'take all appropriate legislative and administrative measures'.

It is therefore not necessarily sufficient for the authorities simply to conclude that the child would be better off in care. Whenever a child is taken into care, the object should be to reunite the family if possible. The interference with respect for private and family life which might be justified by the need to protect children's health or rights must be accompanied by safeguards adequate to satisfy the criteria laid down under Article 8(2) of the Convention. In particular, decisions to intervene in family life must be supported by reasons adequate to justify both the nature and the extent of the intervention. Failure to meet these requirements will render the interference disproportionate to the aim pursued, failing the 'necessary in a democratic society' test under Article 8(2). Thus in *Olsson* v. *Sweden*[128] the Court found an unjustifiable interference

---

[127] *O.* v. *UK*, Eur. Ct. HR, Series A, No. 120, Judgment of 8 July 1987, 10 EHRR 82.

[128] Eur. Ct. HR, Series A, No. 130, Judgment of 24 Mar. 1988, 11 EHRR 259 at paras. 72–83 of the Judgment.

with respect for family life where the Swedish authorities, having justifiably (as the Court held) taken several children of one family into care, separated them, placed two of them a long way from their parents, and restricted visits, making the eventual reuniting of the family more difficult.

The approach of the English courts has been mixed. Whether or not influenced by the European Convention, judges in judicial review proceedings began to insist on parents being given an opportunity to participate in case conferences where decisions were being made which intimately and adversely affected the parents' lives, despite any inconvenience which this might cause to the health and social workers. Failure to offer an opportunity for parents to put their cases was characterized as a breach of principles of natural justice or fairness, vitiating the decisions reached. This included not only decisions about access, but also a decision to place a child's name on a child abuse register as a suspected victim of abuse.[129]

Although administrative law was introducing procedural rights for the parents, the availability of review of decisions on their merits was cut down. Wardship had been used as a means of testing whether or not a local authority's decision was, in substance, in the best interests of the child. However, in *A. v. Liverpool City Council*[130] the House of Lords had held that it would be inappropriate for the English High Court to allow the wardship jurisdiction to be used to review the merits of child-care decisions taken by local authorities under their statutory powers. Henceforth, the exercise of a local authority's statutory powers was to be reviewable only on ordinary judicial review principles, for illegality, procedural impropriety, or irrationality. In *In re W. (a minor) (wardship: jurisdiction)*[131] the House of Lords, while recognizing the hardship which this caused to parents who were apparently the victims of injustice, reluctantly refused to overrule its earlier ruling.

This did not meet the requirements of the European Convention on Human Rights. The absence of a legal procedure for testing the merits of a decision to terminate access by a parent to a child in care was held to breach Article 6(1) of the Convention in *O. v. United Kingdom*,[132] while undue delay in deciding proceedings relating to access was held to violate the right to respect for family life in *H. v. United Kingdom*.[133] Despite

---

[129] *R. v. Norfolk County Council ex parte M.* [1989] QB 619, [1989] 2 All ER 359; *R. v. Harrow LBC, ex parte D.* [1990] 3 All ER 12, CA.

[130] [1982] AC 363, [1981] 2 All ER 385, HL.

[131] [1985] AC 791, [1985] 2 All ER 301, HL.

[132] Eur. Ct. HR, Series A, No. 120, Judgment of 3 Dec. 1987, 10 EHRR 82.

[133] Eur. Ct. HR, Series A, No. 120, Judgment of 8 July 1987, 10 EHRR 95.

this, in *In re M. and H. (minors) (local authority: parental rights)*[134] the House of Lords refused to depart from its earlier decisions. Instead, they left it to Parliament to reconsider the position, noting that some procedural protection had already been granted by statute in anticipation of the decisions of the European Court of Human Rights.[135]

The legal procedures available to a parents to obtain redress are, nevertheless, still weak. Local authorities must provide a procedure for considering representations in relation to children who are being looked after by them or are in need, and that at least one person who is neither an officer nor a member of the authority must take part in the discussion of the representations and of any action to be taken as a result.[136] But this is hardly likely to satisfy a person who is aggrieved by a decision to dismantle his or her family. Besides having no power to obtain judicial reconsideration of the decision, the aggrieved parent has no right to claim damages for a wrongful interference with family life. In *F. v. Wirral MBC,*[137] the Court of Appeal upheld a decision of Hollings J. to strike out a claim for damages. The plaintiff claimed damages for interference with parental rights, arising of the way in which the local authority had exercised its powers in respect of her two daughters after she had placed them in short-term voluntary council care in 1978. Specifically, she argued that decisions to restrict her access to the children, and to move from short-term to long-term fostering arrangements, had interfered with her parental rights as guaranteed under the European Convention. The Court of Appeal considered that, in the light of *Gillick* v. *Wisbech and West Norfolk Area Health Authority,*[138] parental rights stem from parental duties to care for and protect the child, and do not give a right to damages for interference by a stranger. The court also rejected a claim based on negligence or breach of statutory duty, holding that the authority's functions in relation to children was administrative, and sounded only in public law, not in private law. It was said to be inappropriate to allow parents a right of action in view of the fact that the authority's duties were owed to the child, with a duty to take account of the interests of the parents. In the event of deliberate and wrongful damage to a parent's interests, damages might be available in the tort of misfeasance in a public office, but otherwise there is no private-law liability.

On the other hand, a child who is or has been in care might be able to bring an action against the council, in appropriate circumstances, for

---

[134] [1990] 1 AC 686, [1988] 3 All ER 5, HL.
[135] Child Care Act 1980, Part IA, added by Health and Social Services and Social Security Adjudications Act 1983, s. 6 and Sched. 1.
[136] Children Act 1989, s. 26(3), (4); Representations Procedure (Children) Regulations, SI No. 894 of 1991, reg. 9.
[137] [1991] 2 All ER 648, CA.   [138] [1986] AC 112, [1985] 3 All ER 402, HL.

damages for negligence or breach of statutory duty. The council owes
duties of care to the children in its care, and the only ground for denying
a cause of action to a child would be if it were felt that there was a compelling public interest in protecting local authorities against liability to
those who are or have been in their care, analogous to the protection
which the police have against liability in respect of negligent investigative
behaviour.[139] But the position of a local authority in relation to children
in its care is very different from the relationship between the police and
members of the public. Local authorities adopt specific duties for the
welfare of known children, and there is a special relationship between
the authority and the children in its care. Only if it could be said that the
local authority's responsibilities for children were to monitor and administer their upbringing, rather than to deliver care of an acceptable standard, could the authorities legitimately escape liability for failure to meet
their responsibilities. Under section 23(1) of the Children Act 1989, an
authority looking after a child has duties to provide accommodation for
the child and to maintain the child. The authority has a wide discretion
in making arrangements for matters other than accommodation, subject
to compliance with regulations made by the Secretary of State,[140] but if
an authority failed to make any such arrangements, or made arrangements
which were self-evidently inadequate, there would seem to be no ground
to exclude legal liability for loss or suffering which resulted.

The Children Act 1989, section 1(1), reasserts the primacy of the
child's interests. It provides that the child's welfare is to be the paramount
consideration when a court is deciding any question relating to the
upbringing of the child (the welfare principle). However, despite recommendations by Dame Elizabeth Butler-Sloss in the Cleveland Report that
the House of Lords decisions should be reconsidered,[141] the Act did
nothing to alter the approach of the House of Lords, preferring instead to
restrict the freedom of the local authorities to invoke the wardship jurisdiction.[142] Nevertheless, under the Act a child may enter care only by an
order of the court, acting on a report from the local authority and in
accordance with the welfare principle. Voluntary entry into care, with
the consent or at the request of a parent without review by a court, is
ended.

Before making a care order or a supervision order in respect of a
child,[143] the court must be satisfied:

(a) that the child is suffering or is likely to suffer significant harm, and

[139] *Hill* v. *Chief Constable of West Yorkshire* [1989] AC 53, [1988] 2 All ER 328, HL.
[140] Children Act 1989, s. 23(2)(f).
[141] *Child Abuse in Cleveland*, Cm. 412 (1988).   [142] Children Act 1989, s. 100.
[143] These provisions apply to children under the age of 17 years, or (if married) 16
years.

force of the Children Act 1989, will have increased the awareness of all concerned of the dangers inherent in the exercise of powers to interfere in family life.

(2) Child's knowledge of family background

Knowing about one's family background has been recognized as an important psychological need. For children and adults, knowing where we come from is a significant element in our sense of identity. The significance of knowledge about our history has been acknowledged by the European Court of Human Rights, which decided in *Gaskin* v. *United Kingdom*[150] that people who have been in care have 'a vital interest, protected by the Convention, in receiving the information necessary to know and understand their childhood and early development'. This confers a prima facie right of access to their files, subject however to the need for confidentiality of public records, important for receiving objective and reliable information and for protecting third parties.

Mr. Gaskin alleged that he had been ill-treated while in care, and wished to see his file to find out about his past and come to terms with it. He applied to the High Court for an order of discovery under section 31 of the Administration of Justice Act 1970, permitting the court to order disclosure to a person who is likely to be a party to legal proceedings in respect of personal injury, but this was refused. The Court of Appeal agreed with the judge that the public interest in maintaining confidentiality in such documents clearly outweighed the applicant's interest in obtaining the information.[151] Thereafter the DHSS issued Circular LAC(83)14, setting out the principles which were to govern disclosure of information: access to documents was to be permitted if the contributor of each confidential document consented to its disclosure. On this basis, the council released some documents to Mr. Gaskin, but withheld others, and there was no procedure available for challenging the refusal of contributors to the file to permit access.

The European Court of Human Rights held unanimously that the applicant had had no right to receive the information under Article 10, but held by sixteen votes to one that the withholding of personal files gave rise to an issue under Article 8, and by eleven votes to six that the refusal of access constituted an unjustified interference with the right to respect for private and family life. The majority accepted that the confidentiality of the file served a legitimate aim under Article 8(2), and that, in achieving that aim, the state enjoyed a margin of appreciation which permitted it in principle

---

[150] Eur. Ct. HR, Series A, No. 160, Judgment of 23 June 1989, 12 EHRR 36, at para. 49 of the Judgment.
[151] *Gaskin* v. *Liverpool City Council* [1980] 1 WLR 1459, CA.

to make access dependent on the consent of the contributor. However, in such a system the interests of the individual seeking access had to be protected against lack of consent by a contributor who was unavailable or who improperly refused consent. An independent authority should have been able to decide whether to override the absence of consent in such circumstances. The English system at the relevant date had no independent review body, and so the restriction on access was disproportionate to the aim pursued. However, by the time the decision in *Gaskin* was delivered, the Access to Personal Files Act 1987 had been passed, and regulations had been made under it which gave rights of access to personal files equivalent to those envisaged in the judgment.[152]

In *Gaskin*, the applicant at least knew who had been his genetic parents and who had been responsible for his upbringing. However, in some cases this knowledge may be unavailable, and the individual's sense of identity may be confused. A child might be adopted early in life, or be born to a surrogate mother, or be conceived by means of artificial insemination using sperm, ovum, or both, from a person or people other than those who are to bring up the child.[153] The Warnock Committee considered how easy it should be for children to find out who their genetic or carrying parents are, if they have been brought up as their own children by others.[154] Socially, genetic parenthood is usually not particularly important, and both the social parents and the donors of sperm or ova and surrogate mothers might wish the contributions of outsiders to be confidential, allowing the children to regard themselves exclusively as offspring of the social parents. Yet, psychologically, a child might feel incomplete, forced to make do with only a partial self-image and understanding, if genetic information is withheld.

This is a field in which the English law has so far come only a limited way towards keeping up with the implications of fast-moving social and scientific developments. Different considerations apply to adopted children, to those conceived by artificial means but carried by the woman who later brings up the child as its mother, and to those who are conceived artificially and carried by a surrogate, with a view to being brought up by others.

(i) *Adopted children.* Adoption is a legal procedure for changing the legal parentage of the child.[155] It used to be considered inappropriate to tell

---

[152] The effect of the Act is discussed in Ch. 8, s. 8.4, above.

[153] Gillian Douglas, *Law, Fertility and Reproduction* (London: Sweet & Maxwell, 1991), chs. 6, 7; Gillian Douglas and N. V. Lowe, 'Becoming a Parent in English Law' (1992) 108 *LQR* 414–32.

[154] *Report of the Committee into Human Fertilisation and Embryology* (Chairman: Dame Mary Warnock), Cmnd. 9314 (London: HMSO, 1984), paras. 4.21–4.22, 6.6, 7.7.

[155] See Cretney, *Elements*, ch. 12.

children or adoptive parents anything about the children's biological parents. When most children were adopted as very young babies, this was comprehensible: babies could be brought up in the security of their new family without threatening intimations that another identity and background might be lurking. Now that more than half of all adoptions are of children aged 5 or over, and a very large proportion of adoptive parents are already related to the child concerned,[156] this is less sensible. It is now thought to be good practice to bring children up in the knowledge of their backgrounds as far as possible, and this has been reinforced by two statutory provisions which facilitate the discovery of background information and the establishment of links with a child's natural parents, once the adopted person has reached the age of 18.

Section 51 of the Adoption Act 1976 (as amended by the Children Act 1989, Schedule 10, paragraph 20) provides that a person who has been adopted is entitled to be provided by the Registrar General of Births, after reaching the age of 18, with a copy of the record of the person's birth from the births register. The person must first be informed that counselling is available, but the right appears to be absolute if the person decides to exercise it. However, there is a public policy exception implied in the Act, allowing the Registrar General to refuse to provide counselling or to release the information in certain exceptional circumstances. This was decided by *R. v. Registrar General, ex parte Smith*.[157] The applicant, who had been adopted at the age of nine weeks, had been imprisoned for life for the unprovoked murder of a stranger in a park. While in prison, he killed a cell-mate, apparently in the belief that the man was his adopted mother. He was convicted of manslaughter by reason of diminished responsibility, and sent to Broadmoor. While there, he applied for a copy of the record of his birth from the register of births. The Registrar General obtained medical reports which suggested that the applicant might react emotionally by redirecting some of his hostility from his adopted mother towards his natural mother, and that he might put his natural mother's life in danger if he were ever to escape or be released. The Registrar General refused to release the information sought, and the applicant applied for judicial review of the decision.

The Divisional Court and the Court of Appeal held that public policy exceptions to apparently unqualified statutory rights might be implied in an Act where they appeared to reflect the likely intention of Parliament. In the circumstances of the case, concerning a double killer with an abnormal personality, Sir Stephen Brown P. considered that there was 'a very real and present apprehension for the safety of the . . . natural

---

[156] See Cretney, *Elements*, 230.
[157] [1991] 2 WLR 782, [1991] 2 All ER 88, CA.

mother'; identifying her 'might even be tantamount to signing her death warrant'.[158] Staughton LJ agreed, holding that the exception could not depend on showing that the person had the present intention of attacking his natural mother. He thought that a statutory duty might not be enforced 'if there is a significant risk that to do so would facilitate crime resulting in danger to life'.[159] McCowan LJ thought that a person would not be permitted to enforce his right under section 51 'if there is a current and justified apprehension of a significant risk that he might in the future use the information obtained to commit a serious crime.'[160] With respect, the 'serious crime' formulation might be considered rather too flexible for comfort. A right given by Parliament without express qualification is not lightly to be limited. It is submitted that the formulation by Staughton LJ is to be preferred, as imposing the restriction on the exercise of the right which is most clearly justified by considerations relating to the welfare of third parties.

Section 51A of the Adoption Act 1976 (added by the Children Act 1989, Schedule 10, paragraph 21) provides for the Registrar General to keep an Adoption Contact Register. The register is in two parts. In one part, the name and address is kept of any adopted person over the age of 18 who has exercised, or is in a position to exercise, the right under section 51, and who notifies the Registrar General of a wish to contact a relative. In the other part of the register is kept the name and address of any person who has attained the age of 18, has satisfied the Registrar General that he or she is a relative of the adopted person and has the information necessary to obtain a copy of the adopted person's birth certificate, and has notified the Registrar General of a wish to contact the adopted person. The Registrar General shall then transmit to the adopted person the name and address of any relative listed in the register. The register is not open for public inspection, and the name and address of the adopted person must not be supplied to the relative: only the adopted person can initiate the contact.

(ii) *Children born to surrogate mothers*. Before the passage of the Human Fertilisation and Embryology Act 1990, a woman who bore a child was treated as the mother of the child. If she was married her husband was presumed to be the child's father, although this presumption might be rebutted by evidence that the woman had been inseminated (artificially or otherwise) with sperm from another man, who would then be treated as the father. It made no difference that the mother had carried the baby under an agreement with another woman to act as surrogate for the other. The position remains the same under section 27 of the 1990 Act.

---

[158] [1991] 2 All ER at p. 93.   [159] Ibid. at p. 95.   [160] Ibid. at p. 96.

However, there are two ways in which the parental responsibilities and rights of the surrogate may be terminated. First, the party or parties who commissioned the arrangement may adopt the child. If this happens, the child will in due course be able to obtain information about his or her birth and may be able to contact relatives in the usual way under sections 51 and 51A of the Adoption Act 1976, after reaching the age of 18. Secondly, section 30 of the 1990 Act, drafted hurriedly during the passage of the Bill and subject to a number of serious criticisms, introduced the notion of a 'parental order', which requires the child to be treated in law as the child of the commissioning parties.[161] Such an order requires the free and fully informed consent of the surrogate and the legal father of the child to the making of the order, unless the person in question cannot be found or is incapable of agreeing. An unreasonable refusal to consent cannot be overridden.

(iii) *Other artificial insemination techniques.* Where the conception is brought about by artificial insemination, the legal father is the person whose sperm were used. If the sperm are those of the woman's partner, there is no legal problem. However, if the process involves use of sperm provided by a donor, the name of the donor is unlikely to be known to the mother or her partner. The Human Fertilisation and Embryology Act 1990, section 8, amends the usual legal rules on parenthood in such cases. When a married woman is artificially inseminated with the sperm of a third party, her husband is to be treated as the father unless he can prove that the sperm was not his and that he did not consent to the insemination.[162] If the insemination took place in the course of a treatment provided for the mother and a man, regulated under the licensing regime laid down for such treatment by the 1990 Act, the man is to be treated as the father.[163]

Where these rules apply, there may be good reasons to permit the child to find out about his or her genetic parents. However, the Warnock Committee, while recommending that children should be able, on reaching the age of 18, to find out basic details of the ethnic origin and genetic health of the donors of the sperm, egg, or embryo, considered that the identity of the donors should never be disclosed, in order to protect confidentiality and minimize the extent to which the donors' existence could intrude into the child's family relationships.[164] The statutory scheme follows these general principles. Section 31 of the 1990 Act

---

[161] For discussion, see Douglas, *Law, Fertility and Reproduction*, 158–61.
[162] Human Fertilisation and Embryology Act 1990, s. 28(5), (2).
[163] Ibid., s. 28(3).
[164] *Report of the Committee of Inquiry into Human Fertilisation and Embryology*, Cmnd. 9314, paras. 4.21–4.22, 6.6, 7.7.

requires the Human Fertilisation and Embryology Authority to maintain a register, and permits a person aged 18 or over to demand information from the authority showing whether a person other than his or her legal parents was a biological parent of the applicant. The precise amount of information to be supplied to a person is to be settled by delegated legislation, but section 31(5) provides that the regulations are not to require the authority to identify the biological parent.[165] This is the worst of all possible worlds. Applicants are to be told that they are, or might be, the biological offspring of people other than those who have been regarded as their parents up to that time, thus whetting their curiosity, but are disabled from obtaining information which might assuage the curiosity.

11.4 CONCLUSIONS

English law has a mixed record in relation to rights concerned with sex, sexuality, and family life. In relation to child-care law, parental rights and responsibilities, and the role of social service agencies in maintaining or intervening in the family unit, the UK has done reasonably well in responding to concerns expressed by both the European Court of Human Rights and the various reports on child-care matters which have appeared in the last decade. Legislation has also been generally effective in providing a right for people to find information about their histories, while balancing the right against the needs of good administration and other people's right to confidentiality. On the other hand, the law has failed to respond as effectively where morality, particularly sexual morality, is implicated; but in these areas the European Court of Human Rights has proved as disappointing as Parliament, and less dynamic than the Commission.

It is, perhaps, fair to conclude that the rights of individuals are protected in proportion to the political significance of the groups from which they come. Members of groups which lack wide political support, such as the mental patient in *R. v. Registrar General, ex parte Smith*, homosexuals, or transsexuals, find their rights-claims are not taken as seriously, either by Parliament or courts, as members of populous, popular, and increasingly vocal groups, such as parents. The rights of the underprivileged are liable to be too easily overridden by arguments which, on analysis, appear unconvincing. But this is an inevitable result of the essentially political nature of the present UK Constitution, in which rights depend on political muscle as much as, if not more than, on arguments of principle.

[165] Douglas, *Law, Fertility and Reproduction*, 132–6.

PART IV
EXPRESSION

12

FREEDOM OF EXPRESSION

Part 4 is concerned with expression and its protection. The present chapter examines the reasons why freedom of expression is important, and the limits on its protection under international and English law. Chapter 13 looks at a special aspect of freedom of expression, the freedom of the media. The chapters which follow examine the balance between freedom of expression and other interests, as translated into law in the context of the protection of state interests (Chapter 14), individuals' sensitivities and moral welfare (Chapter 15), the administration of justice (Chapter 16), and public order (Chapter 17).

This chapter begins with a brief account of some of the leading justifications advanced for protecting freedom of expression, and notes the problem of setting limits to the freedom, particularly where the people exercising it do not respect the freedom of others. Next, the formulation of the freedom, and its limits, in international law is examined, with special attention to Article 10 of the European Convention on Human Rights. There follow two sections examining the extent of freedom of expression in English law, and the way in which it is specially protected or particularly restricted in certain situations.

12.1 THE JUSTIFICATIONS FOR, AND LIMITS OF, FREEDOM OF EXPRESSION

(1) The importance of freedom of expression

The liberty to express one's self freely is important for a number of reasons.[1] First, self-expression is a significant instrument of freedom of conscience and self-fulfilment.[2] From the point of view of civil liberties, this is probably the most important of the justifications which can be offered for free speech. In Chapter 1, the commitment to liberty was grounded

---

[1] See Frederick Schauer, *Free Speech: A Philosophical Enquiry* (Cambridge: CUP, 1982); D. F. B. Tucker, *Law, Liberalism and Free Speech* (Totowa, NJ: Rowman & Allanheld, 1985); Eric Barendt, *Freedom of Speech* (Oxford: Clarendon Press, 1987), ch. 1.

[2] John Milton's *Areopagitica* is the most famous of the arguments on this ground. For discussion, see Schauer, *Free Speech*, chs. 5 and 6; Tucker, *Law, Liberalism and Free Speech*, 11–56.

in the idea of individual autonomy, an ability to live a life according to choices consciously made between a reasonable range of options. The freedom to choose between values, and to live one's life according to one's choice, is the essence of liberty. Freedom of expression has an important role to play here. If one takes seriously one's choice of values, it will be important to be able to express them through words and action alike. This has important implications for the types of expression which merit protection by law. It becomes impossible to restrict the freedom to verbal forms of expression. Any act may have expressive content, if it amounts to an expression of one's chosen values. Conversely, there may be verbal or written textual outpourings which do not merit protection, because they do not express any such choice between values. For this reason, Edwin Baker has argued that, while the First Amendment to the US Constitution 'bars certain governmental restrictions on noncoercive, nonviolent, substantively valued conduct, including nonverbal conduct',[3] it does not bar controls on commercial speech, including advertising. The latter are not substantively valuable: they are not expressions of life choices, but are (at best) instrumentally useful ways of exercising commercial freedom, or informing potential purchasers about products.[4] This would be a more powerful argument if the liberty model were the only theoretical framework for justifying protection for freedom of expression, but it is not. There are others, which overlap with it in core areas, but also extend beyond it to justify free speech on other grounds at the peripheries.

The second justification concerns epistemology. Freedom of expression enables people to contribute to debates about social and moral values. It is arguable that the best way to find the best or truest theory or model of anything is to permit the widest possible range of ideas to circulate. The interplay of these ideas, challenging each other and allowing the strengths and weaknesses of each to be exposed, is more likely than any alternative strategy to lead to the best possible conclusion. This treats freedom of expression as an instrumental value, advancing other goods (the development of true or good ideas) with a consequential benefit for the individual and society. This is the basis on which freedom of expression appealed to John Milton, in *Areopagitica*, and to the utilitarian mind of John Stuart Mill, who gave the most famous, and most convincing, justification for freedom of speech in *On Liberty*.

Mill argued on utilitarian grounds that there was a distinction in principle between facts and opinion. When dealing with opinions, all should be freely expressed, subject to any restrictions necessary to protect against

---

[3] C. Edwin Baker, *Human Liberty and Freedom of Speech* (New York and Oxford: OUP, 1989), 5. The main argument is developed in ch. 3.

[4] Baker, *Human Liberty*, ch. 9.

identifiable harm. This wide freedom would benefit individuals by allowing them to choose between the widest possible range of opinions, where
none could be definitively shown to be right or wrong. This would maximize personal autonomy. It would also extend freedom of political
choice, and bolster democratic processes by encouraging rational debate
which, it was confidently expected, would render it more likely that the
best solution would be found for any problem. Assertions of fact, on the
other hand, could by definition be either true or false. There would be
good reason to allow free expression of the truth, as this would lead to
advances in knowledge and material improvements in society, but this
does not justify permitting free expression of falsehoods. However, it is
not always possible to say whether an assertion is true or false, and many
benefits may flow from allowing statements of fact to be asserted so
that they may be tested, even if they are ultimately found to be false.
(This is particularly important in the physical sciences if one accepts Karl
Popper's portrayal of scientific advance as occurring through the testing
and falsification of factual hypotheses.)[5] This cannot in itself justify the
publication of factual claims which are known to be false, but on a rule-
utilitarian analysis the benefits of a general principle permitting freedom
of expression are held to outweigh the disbenefits resulting from particular applications of the rule. It is therefore preferable to permit freedom to
express opinions and facts, even if untrue, rather than to adopt a general
rule which permits censorship and coercion in relation to expression.

This approach is sometimes linked with the notion of a market-place
of ideas, in which the best ideas win through the operation of market
forces. The market-place theory was influential in the USA, where it was
developed by the Supreme Court to justify First Amendment protection
for unpopular speech, such as advocacy of racist theories by the Ku Klux
Klan,[6] but also to deny protection to those forms of expression—such as
obscenity—which were regarded as offering nothing worthwhile to the
market-place of ideas, and so having no redeeming social merit.[7]
Obscenity was considered to be useful, if at all, only as a sex aid.[8]
However, the fact that it adds nothing valuable to the market-place of
ideas does not necessarily mean that obscenity, or any other form of
expression, ought not to be protected. There is a privacy issue which
then arises: even if material is of purely prurient interest, and is resorted
to as an aid to (let us say) masturbation, it is hard to see how the state can

---

[5] Karl Popper, *The Logic of Scientific Discovery* (London: Hutchinson, 1959); Karl
Popper, 'Science: Conjectures and Refutations', in his *Conjectures and Refutations*, 4th edn.
(London: Routledge & Kegan Paul, 1972), 33–65.
[6] *Brandenburg* v. *Ohio*, 395 US 444 (1969).
[7] *Roth* v. *US*, 354 US 476 (1957). See the discussion by Baker, *Human Liberty*, 8–11.
[8] Schauer, *Free Speech*, 182.

have a sufficient interest in its effects to justify making it unavailable for use by consenting adults.[9]

The market-place-of-ideas model has implications for commercial speech. In a market economy, commercial speech, including advertising, may be useful in order to permit information about products and the relative merits of commercial competitors to be promulgated, facilitating informed choices by customers. Thus in a liberal society with a market economy, freedom of expression could be thought to support an important aspect of collective economic life. This depends on the assumption that the information will be presented to the market, through advertising, in a way which enables potential customers to choose between products. That is, of course, highly questionable. Much very successful advertising gives remarkably little information about the product. Magazine and poster advertisements for cigarettes rely almost wholly on image, and purposely give no information (save the health warning required by law) about the qualities of the product. The same applies to most liquor advertisements. The argument does not justify protection for all commercial speech, unless one takes the view that, on a utilitarian analysis, the social costs involved in vetting commercial speech would outweigh the benefits.

A third justification for free expression is that it allows the political discourse which is necessary in any country which aspires to democracy.[10] It reinforces the personal-autonomy justification by mandating protection for the political expression of those who regard participating in politics as an aspect of their self-fulfilment as people and citizens. The power of this justification depends on the view which one adopts about the structural arrangements which democracy entails. A democratic rationale for freedom of expression makes perfect sense if applied to a society in which the operative model of democracy is one in which the people have the right to participate directly in day-to-day governmental decision making, or to have their views considered in the choice of policies by government. It works less well if the prevailing model is one in which the people merely choose a government, which is then free to get on with the job of governing until the time comes for it to account to the people for the way in which it has used power. The representative system, such as we have in the UK, would offer less support to free-expression rights than a participatory system.

[9] Harry Kalven, Jun. (ed. by Jamie Kalven), *A Worthy Tradition: Freedom of Speech in America* (New York: Harper & Row, 1988), 34.
[10] The leading exponent of this democratic justification is Alexander Meiklejohn, *Political Freedom: The Constitutional Powers of the People* (New York: OUP, 1965). For discussion, see Schauer, *Free Speech*, ch. 3.

Nevertheless, a measure of free speech (and more especially freedom of information) remains necessary to any sort of democracy. As the Privy Council observed in *Hector* v. *Attorney-General of Antigua and Barbuda*:[11]

In a free democratic society it is almost too obvious to need stating that those who hold office in government and who are responsible for public administration must always be open to criticism. Any attempt to stifle or fetter such criticism amounts to political censorship of the most insidious and objectionable kind. . . . [I]t is no less obvious that the very purpose of criticism levelled at those who have the conduct of public affairs by their political opponents is to undermine public confidence in their stewardship and to persuade the electorate that the opponents would make a better job of it than those presently holding office. . . . [T]heir Lordships cannot help viewing a statutory provision which criminalises statements likely to undermine public confidence in the conduct of public affairs with the utmost suspicion.[12]

Fourthly, freedom of expression facilitates artistic and scholarly endeavour of all sorts. This is not, perhaps, a separate head of justification. It is a specialized form of the first and second heads, and depends on accepting that art and scholarship are valuable in their own right.

These justifications draw mainly on three values: personal autonomy, which is served by maximizing the range of information and choice of opinions to which people have access; truth, which may be advanced by full information and open debate (at any rate if conducted under conditions of fairness in which no one ideology is permitted to dominate or dictate the terms of the discussion);[13] and democracy, which depends on some choice at least being available in the market-place of ideas, as well as drawing strength from the combination of personal autonomy of electors and legislators in the political sphere and the hope that it will lead to the selection of the 'best', or 'most true', policies. For example, where a government proposes to introduce a law regulating commercial advertising, the autonomy of consumer choice favours free advertising, subject to any controls needed to ensure that people are not misled by false claims which advertisers might make for products. Were there no constraints on freedom of expression, the difficulty would arise that one of the objects of upholding free expression—truth—could be defeated if it were in a person's commercial interests to do so. There is an element, as the Williams Committee noted, of bad expressive coinage driving out the good,[14] and it is important to regulate expression to limit the extent to which this can happen.

---

[11] [1990] 2 AC 312, [1990] 2 All ER 103, PC.   [12] [1990] 2 All ER at p. 106.

[13] See Jurgen Habermas, *Communication and the Evolution of Society*, trans. T. McCarthy (London: Heinemann, 1979).

[14] *Report of the Committee on Obscenity and Film Censorship* (Chairman: Professor Bernard Williams), Cmnd. 7772 (London: HMSO, 1979).

There will inevitably be situations in which these values come into conflict with each other or with other values, but this does not mean that the liberal harm principle is incoherent. It merely means that the principle itself cannot determine the area within which the principle is to operate. For instance, does the democracy interest require respect for the right of political activists to make demonstrably untrue statements in an attempt to curry favour with the electorate? Is there a trade-off between the demands of truth and the demands of democracy? What happens if there is an expression of opinion which is so offensive to right-thinking people that it is likely to provoke public disorder and violence?

(2) Conflicts of values: tolerance and the need to maintain respect for rights

There is a dilemma for liberals. One can be too liberal; free expression may operate in a way which leaves free expression itself weaker. This is an abuse of the right, and must be restrained. It fails to respect the fundamental justifications for free expression, and this may lead to the conclusion that people who abuse the right to free expression sacrifice it to the extent of the abuse. As noted below, the European Convention on Human Rights accepts that the right carries with it responsibilities, and restrictions on the right are necessary in order to give effect to the responsibilities. Being too liberal tends to undermine the freedoms which are valued. This is expressed in the International Covenant on Civil and Political Rights, Article 5, paragraph 1 as follows: 'Nothing in the present Covenant may be interpreted as implying for any State, group or person any right to engage in any activity or perform any act aimed at the destruction of any of the rights and freedoms recognized herein or at their limitation to a greater extent than is provided for in the present Covenant.' The concept of an act which aims at destroying or limiting a right may seem fairly narrow, but an act may be part of a larger programme which has that aim. All such acts may justifiably be restrained by law, or states would awake one morning to find that a series of acts, none of them individually capable of destroying the right, have effectively taken it away incrementally.

However, Article 5(1) refers to acts which are *aimed at* the destruction of rights. This may sometimes unduly restrict a state's duty to control expression. Sometimes it is clear that a person's, or party's, political objectives, if implemented, would infringe rights, but it is not clear that the person or party aims to produce those effects. 'Aim' appears to have a subjective meaning: it is not enough merely that the person or party is intentionally doing something which has, or is objectively likely to have, a destructive effect; the person or party must subjectively intend to produce that effect, or (perhaps) recognize the risk and be prepared to live with it. But it may be very necessary to restrain expression which can objectively be seen to threaten rights, even if that is not the intended consequence. Subjective tests are appropriate when apportioning blame for harms caused to others. They are not so relevant when considering whether restrictions are required to safeguard the rights of others. The latter is not a matter of blame, but concerns the proper steps to respond to a pressing social need and an assault (albeit possibly inadvertent) on the rights of others.

If one accepts that the objective test is appropriate, and that it will sometimes be necessary to restrict the freedom of expression of people who are not morally blameworthy in order to protect the rights of others, it may be hard to decide at what point, or to what extent, it is proper to intervene. The American Nazis who planned to hold a meeting in an area of Skokie, Illinois, which had a very substantial Jewish population raised this problem. The U.S. Federal Court of Appeals held that the right of free speech under the First Amendment of the Constitution overrode other competing values,[15] but it is questionable whether this is a liberal resolution of the problem or merely a legalistic one.[16] Had there been no constitutional provision giving priority to free speech interests over others, the conundrum could not have been resolved within the resources of free speech theory alone. To be helpful in these situations, a free speech principle should, as Dr. Geoffrey Marshall has pointed out, either be multi-tiered, arranging interests in hierarchical order, or incorporate a distinction between the core and periphery of free speech protection 'so as to permit suppression of those [forms of speech] that fall outside the topmost level or privileged core of the area protected by the principle'.[17] In the U.K. the Constitution does not contain anything which compels one type of interest to be given priority over others, and neither Parliament nor the courts have expressly laid down an authoritative basis for deciding these matters. Even the standards contained in the European Convention on Human Rights, as interpreted by the

---

[15] *Collin* v. *Smith*, 578 F.2d 1197 (1978, 7th Circuit), affirming 447 F. Supp. 676 (ND Ill.). The US Supreme Court denied certiorari, over a dissent by Blackmun J.: *Smith* v. *Collin* 439 US 916 (1978). In the event, the Nazis did not march through Skokie, but held a meeting in another nearby area.

[16] See Joel Feinberg, *Offense to Others* (New York: OUP, 1985), 86–96; Laurence H. Tribe, *Constitutional Choices* (Cambridge, Mass.: Harvard University Press, 1985), 219–20; Denis Galligan, 'Preserving Public Protest: The Legal Approach', in Larry Gostin (ed.), *Civil Liberties in Conflict* (London: Routledge, 1988), 39–64; Norman Dorsen, 'Is There a Right to Stop Offensive Speech? The Case of the Nazis at Skokie', and Stephen Sedley, 'The Spider and the Fly: A Question of Principle', in Gostin (ed.), *Civil Liberties*, 122–35 and 136–44, respectively.

[17] Geoffrey Marshall, 'Press Freedom and Free Speech Theory' [1992] *PL* 40–60, at p. 60.

Commission and Court, are not very helpful, for the Court has never been willing to arrange the rights protected by the Convention in hierarchical order. However, as will be seen in Chapter 17 below, there is an implicit ordering in the UK Constitution, and it is not wholly favourable to free expression: the common law and statute actually exhibit a preference for public peacefulness and the avoidance of incitement over freedom of expression, without considering whether the substance of the views expressed threatens liberal democratic values. This is hard to reconcile with any rights-based standards, and leads (as we shall see in the chapters which follow this one) to tension between our law and Article 10 of the European Convention on Human Rights.

This is just one aspect of a wider problem. Sometimes, it seems to the state that it is necessary to abridge people's rights to free speech in order to safeguard or advance some pressing national interest. Liberals may accept that this can be necessary—the state is responsible for fostering and maintaining the conditions which make liberty possible and, perhaps, valuable[18]—but will want to impose fairly stringent tests to be satisfied before such a restriction, which benefits no individual's rights directly and limits the rights of all, is acceptable. Very often, this requires legislatures or courts to conduct a balancing exercise. Where a particular exercise of the right to freedom of expression violates another person's rights, for example the right to reputation or privacy, the legislature or court must decide which takes priority in the circumstances. This can be seen in the way that the US law on defamation accords less protection to the reputations of public figures, who put their reputations on the line by the nature of the life-styles which they have chosen, than to other citizens. English defamation law makes no such distinction.[19]

In context of criminal liability for speech, under the First Amendment to the U.S. Constitution the Supreme Court has developed a number of tests to aid in the balancing exercise. One, the 'bad tendency' test, which asked whether the speech in question had a tendency to undermine society or created a palpable risk of harm, gave relatively weak protection to free speech.[20] It was rapidly supplanted by another, the 'clear and present danger' test. This is simple to state but hard to apply. It asks whether there is a clear and present danger that the speech in question will bring about substantive evils that Congress is constitutionally entitled to outlaw.[21] If there is, the liberty of speech is protected only by the due-process reasonableness and certainty requirements of the Fifth and Fourteenth Amendments. Impressive as the clear-and-present-danger test

[18] See Ch. 1.   [19] This is considered in Ch. 13.
[20] *Frohwerk* v. *US*, 249 US 204 (1919); *Debs* v. *US*, 249 US 211 (1919).
[21] *Schenk* v. *US*, 249 US 47 (1918) at p. 52, *per* Holmes J. See further *Whitney* v. *California*, 274 US 357 (1927) at p. 366 *per* Brandeis J.; *Dennis* v. *US*, 341 US 494 (1951).

sounds, one authority on the U.S. Constitution has noted that the test has sometimes been rather easily satisfied: 'The clear-and-present-danger test supposedly favours free speech more than the bad-tendency test, but these standards are applied unevenly.'[22] As Peter Macmillan suggested, in its day-to-day operation this test 'amounts to little more than a restatement of the bad tendency test: the court will overrule the legislature only when legislative judgement is unreasonable. This in turn may well amount to no more than the protection offered by the due process clause.'[23] The protection for free speech has been to some extent improved by a requirement that advocacy consisting of pure speech (unmixed with non-verbal action) is not to be proscribed unless it is directed to incite unlawful action,[24] but the lesser protection accorded to categories of expression designated as 'speech-plus' (i.e. combined speech and action), and 'fighting words', still leaves the right to free speech somewhat exposed.

This emphasizes the gap between employing the rhetoric of strong protection for civil liberties or human rights and producing results which consistently respect freedoms in practice, even under a constitution which protects free speech as a fundamental right. Ultimately, freedom depends on the good sense and balance of legislatures, governments, and courts. When one of them loses its sense of balance, as arguably happened in the British Government's desperate efforts to stop publication of a book which had already been published round the world—*Spycatcher*, by Peter Wright—in the mid-1980s, it is hard to protect freedoms or to avoid making the law look an ass.[25]

(3) Stifling publication: prior and subsequent restraint[26]

Because of the high value usually placed on freedom of expression, it is thought to require particularly strong grounds to justify using the law to attempt to prevent a person from speaking, as opposed to penalizing them afterwards if their expression justifies it. Grounds which might suffice for penalizing expression after the event, such as the harm or offence which it causes, will not always suffice to justify prior restraint. Indeed, in the U.S.A. it used to be thought that the First Amendment to the Constitution protected the press only against prior restraint. In the market-place of ideas, there is something to be said for allowing people to speak, because what they say might be socially valuable, even if it is

[22] Louis Fisher, *American Constitutional Law* (New York: McGraw Hill, 1990), 535.
[23] P. R. Macmillan, *Censorship and Public Morality* (Aldershot: Gower, 1983), 478.
[24] *Brandenburg* v. *Ohio*, 395 US 444 (1968).
[25] This is considered further in the Chs. 13 and 14.
[26] Barendt, *Freedom of Speech*, 114–25.

punishable. The social utility of the utterance may mitigate the penalty, if indeed there is any prosecution. Even if an utterance is damnable, liberal society usually considers that there is a right to publish first and be damned afterwards, rather than being restrained from publishing at all. Not only does prior restraint interfere with freedom of expression, it takes away society's opportunity to judge for itself whether a publication is worthy of condemnation. The decision is instead left to a judge or censor, who is likely to be unaccountable for his decision, if only because people will be unable to judge whether the censor was right. Even the judge may not have the best evidence available, as prior restraint often occurs at an interim stage in proceedings without full examination of the facts on the merits. Nevertheless, this approach is open to certain counter-arguments.

First, in some ways a person's awareness that he may later be subject to subsequent restraint inhibits publication, and is a disguised form of prior restraint. It is undeniable that a person may be influenced in deciding whether to publish by the knowledge that he may make himself liable to criminal penalties or damages by doing so. Even subsequent condemnation, therefore, has some effect on the freedom of expression of a rational person. However, this can be exaggerated. At least the decision whether or not to publish is left to the publisher, respecting his autonomy. He may decide to run the risk only for matters which he feels to be particularly important, but if there is a serious threat of offence or harm flowing from the publication it is right that the threat should be avoided except where justified by important matters.

Secondly, it might be thought illogical to be prepared to punish somebody for doing something, but not to be prepared to ban it beforehand. On the other hand, this again is a reflection of a liberal attitude in society, which allows people to make decisions about their action beforehand (treating knowledge of likely legal consequences as merely one reason for acting in a particular way, which may be outweighed by other reasons)[27] so long as they are prepared to take responsibility for their actions subsequently when called to account by the community.

Finally, prior restraint may be more objectionable when it restrains publication permanently than for a short time, for example pending trial of an action; it may be more objectionable to restrain merely offensive or embarrassing ones than those which cause actual damage. The degree of the restriction is significant. At its most extreme, prior restraint may be more objectionable if designed to silence any public expression by a person than if it is designed simply to restrain publication of a particular item of information or opinion. This point was ignored by the Privy Council,

[27] Joseph Raz, *Practical Reason and Norms* (London: Hutchinson, 1975).

in considering the impact on freedom of expression of requirements for publishers to pay large licensing fees and lodge sums by way of indemnity against legal liabilities, in *Attorney-General for Antigua* v. *Antigua Times*.[28] However, the U.S. Supreme Court was alive to the threat in *Grosjean* v. *American Press*[29] and *Minneapolis Star and Tribune Co.* v. *Minnesota Commissioner for Revenue*.[30] It is important to be conscious of the fact that prior restraint, like subsequent restraint, has gradations of seriousness, and may be justified in order to deal with a particularly pressing need. What mechanisms are available in English law to effect a prior restraint?

(i) *Criminal matters*. There is no procedure in English criminal law for a court to order the publication of a book, article, or piece of information to be restrained unless publication would prejudice the administration of justice (see Chapter 16, below). The general rule is that injunctions will not issue to restrain a threatened breach of the criminal law. Unless the publication would constitute a civil wrong, for which the civil remedy of injunction might be available, courts must wait for the allegedly criminal publication to take place and then try the publisher or distributor for the offence. However, there are certain circumstances where an injunction might be available. The Attorney-General can always seek an injunction to restrain the commission of a public wrong, either of his own motion or at the relation of a member of the public (a 'relator action'). This is an exercise of a prerogative power, flowing from the Crown's duty to protect the public interest as *parens patriae*. A local authority may also bring an action for an injunction under section 222 of the Local Government Act 1972. Finally, a private citizen may bring an action in respect of a public wrong if it causes him special damage, or if he has a special interest in its suppression. However, this is of limited importance, as the courts regard the the relator procedure as somewhat anomalous, and actions by others are expensive (both private citizens and local authorities may have to undertake to compensate the defendants for loss or damage which they suffer as a result of the injunction if the plaintiffs lose at trial, in addition to the potential liability to indemnify them for their costs).

(ii) *Civil-law principles*. There are three main civil-law grounds on which a person may be liable to sanctions for imparting information or ideas: the tort of defamation, the equitable duty of confidentiality, and contempt of court. As explained above, it is relatively unusual in this country to obtain an injunction restraining publication of allegedly defamatory material before trial, at least where the defendant intends to justify the alleged

---

[28] [1976] AC 16, P.C.   [29] 297 US 233 (1936).
[30] 460 US 575 (1983). See Barendt, *Freedom of Speech*, 123.

libel. In relation to breach of confidence, however, the law is much more willing to grant interlocutory injunctions, because refusing to do so would permit the confidence to be disclosed, and the purpose of the action thwarted. For this reason, the government has in recent years made increasing use of the law of breach of confidence when trying to combat revelations. This is considered below. In relation to contempt of court, the courts have fairly extensive powers to restrain or postpone publications. These are exercised in the public interest, rather than the interest of the state, and are considered in Chapter 16 below.

12.2 FREEDOM OF EXPRESSION IN INTERNATIONAL LAW

The right to freedom of expression is protected by all the major international human rights instruments.[31] Under the U.N. Universal Declaration of Human Rights, the International Covenant on Civil and Political Rights, and the European Convention on Human Rights and Fundamental Freedoms, the right is stated as including rights to hold opinions and to receive and impart information and ideas. On the other hand, the International Covenant and the European Convention also recognize that the exercise of these freedoms carries with it special responsibilities, and so may be subject to restriction for specified purposes. These are most fully worked out in the European Convention, Article 10, which provides:

(1) Everyone has the right to freedom of expression. This right shall include freedom to hold opinions and to receive and impart information and ideas without interference by public authority and regardless of frontiers. This Article shall not prevent States from requiring the licensing of broadcasting, television or cinema enterprises.

(2) The exercise of these freedoms, since it carries with it duties and responsibilities, may be subject to such formalities, conditions, restrictions or penalties as are prescribed by law and are necessary in a democratic society, in the interests of national security, territorial integrity or public safety, for the prevention of disorder or crime, for the protection of health or morals, for the protection of the reputation or rights of others, for preventing the disclosure of information received in confidence, or for maintaining the authority and impartiality of the judiciary.

The general principle in paragraph (1) may be restricted only on grounds which fall within one of the specific exceptions enumerated in paragraph (2), and the exception must by 'prescribed by law' and 'neces-

---

[31] See Paul Sieghart, *The International Law of Human Rights*, 327–36; John P. Humphrey, 'Political and Related Rights', in Theodor Meron (ed.), *Human Rights in International Law: Legal and Policy Issues* (Oxford: Clarendon Press, 1984), 171–88.

sary in a democratic society'. The licensing of broadcasting, television and cinema enterprises under paragraph (1) is considered in Chapter 13, on media freedom. Here it need only be noted that the Convention does not permit licensing regimes to be imposed on the dissemination of printed material, which may be restricted only in accordance with paragraph (2).

The European Court of Human Rights has developed an extensive caselaw on the meaning of 'prescribed by law'. It was originally argued by governments that the term merely meant that there should be some legal basis for the restrictions in positive law, or even that the restriction, though not specifically authorized, should not be unlawful under positive municipal law. This would have meant that the Court and Commission would have been able to inquire whether the restriction was lawful under municipal law, but would have been prevented from requiring that the municipal law met any supranational standards of formal propriety, such as clarity or publicity. This was accepted by the Commmission and was not raised before the Court until the *Sunday Times case*.[32] There, the question arose whether the English common-law offence of contempt of court by prejudging the result of pending proceedings before a judge, was 'prescribed by law' within the meaning of Article 10(2). The *Sunday Times*, which had been the subject of an injunction to restrain a contempt in English proceedings, argued that the law was so vague and uncertain, and the principles on which the House of Lords had upheld the injunction so novel, that they could not be said to have been prescribed by law. The Court held that two of the requirements which flow from the expression were:

(1) the law must be adequately accessible: the citizen must be able to have an indication that is adequate in the circumstances of the legal rules applicable to a given case;

(2) a norm cannot be regarded as law unless it is formulated with sufficient precision to enable the citizen to regulate his conduct: he must be able—if need be with appropriate advice—to foresee, to a degree that is reasonable in the circumstances, the consequences which a given action may entail.[33]

The Court recognized that any law is to a greater or lesser extent vague, and any type of law is subject to interpretation, and so their practical effects may be to some degree uncertain. The need for law to be reasonably flexible was also recognized. The Court therefore accepted that the common law could be regarded as 'law' for the purpose of authorizing a restriction under Article 10(2) (any other conclusion would in any case have been contrary to the intention of the drafters of the Convention: see

[32] Eur. Ct. HR, Judgment of 26 Apr. 1979, Series A, No. 30, 2 EHRR 245.
[33] Para. 49 of the majority judgment.

paragraph 47 of the judgment), and after looking at the leading decisions and the formulation of the principles in *Halsbury's Laws of England*[34] the Court concluded that the applicants had not been without an adequate indication of the existence of the 'prejudgment principle': 'Even if the court does have certain doubts concerning the precision with which that principle was formulated at the relevant time, it considers that the applicants were able to foresee, to a degree that was reasonable in the circumstances, a risk that publication of the draft article might fall foul of the principle.'[35]

On the other hand, the question whether or not a restriction is necessary in a democratic society for one of the purposes specified in paragraph (2) is by its very nature open to controversy, and the Court and Commission have felt that, as long as the restriction is prescribed by law and a plausible case can be made for the need for the restriction for an authorized purpose, a democratic government must be allowed a substantial measure of discretion ('margin of appreciation') as to the form of restriction which it imposes. This has been considered in Chapter 8, section 3(3), above, in relation to privacy rights, and the same principles apply. The main requirements are that the restriction should be directed to meeting a 'pressing social need', and that it should not be disproportionate to that need. The implications of this for laws restricting freedom of expression are among the subjects considered in the remainder of Part IV.

12.3 FREEDOM OF EXPRESSION IN ENGLISH LAW

Free expression is not a legal term of art in England and Wales. It seems that the form which the expression takes is an important determinant of the scope of the freedom which will be allowed to it. It encompasses words, whether spoken, written, or printed, and works of art, but does not appear to include physical manifestations of support for an opinion. This is regarded as a separate matter—freedom of demonstration or protest rather than freedom of expression—and, as noted in Chapter 17 below on protest and public order, is somewhat circumscribed. In similar vein, the European Commission of Human Rights decided in *X* v. *United Kingdom*[36] that the expression of an opinion through the performance of the act of sexual intercourse was not a protected form of expression. However, it is questionable whether the distinction between the form and the content of expression can be maintained. In the USA, the

[34] 3rd edn. (current at the time of the events which gave rise to the application), vol. viii, paras. 11–13.
[35] At para. 52 of the judgment.   [36] (7215/75) 19 DR 66.

Supreme Court accepts that the manner of expression may be an integral part of the communication of ideas itself, giving expression to the strength of feeling as well as the intellectual content of the ideas expressed. Accordingly, the Court has held that the First Amendment to the Constitution, in precluding Congress from making any law which abridges freedom of speech, protects 'symbolic speech', such as burning a flag to protest against conscription into the US army to fight in Vietnam,[37] as well as verbal expression. It also protects an expression of opinion expressed in offensive terms, for example 'Fuck the Draft' emblazoned on a jacket worn in a courthouse.[38] It would be strange if, under the European Convention on Human Rights, which is drafted in terms of expression rather than speech, the range of types of expression protected were to be narrower than under the speech-based US First Amendment. If it were so, under the Convention a mime might not be protected despite carrying the same message as a speech.

English law recognizes that people are generally free to express themselves and to impart information in any way they please, in the same way that they are free to do anything else, except in so far as that freedom is restricted by particular legal constraints. There are three special cases in which a positive right to free expression operates.

(1) Proceedings in Parliament

Members of the House of Commons and the House of Lords are free to say anything in Parliament without being called to account in the courts for what they say.[39] This absolute privilege attaching to parliamentary proceedings was one of the demands made by MPs in the petition presented to the new King William and Queen Mary on their accession in 1688, and was incorporated in the Bill of Rights 1689, which provided 'that the freedom of speech and debate or proceedings in Parliament ought not to be impeached or questioned in any court or place out of Parliament'. It frees members from the fear of prosecution by the government, or civil actions, in respect of expressions of opinion or statements of fact in Parliament. Furthermore, attempts by outside bodies to discipline MPs for views expressed in Parliament, or their voting behaviour, is a breach of privilege. Examples include attempts by trade unions which sponsor Labour MPs to pressurize them or penalize them when they do not toe the union line.[40] (Abuse of the privilege can be dealt with only

---

[37] Texas v. Johnson 109 S. Ct. 2533 (1989).
[38] Cohen v. California, 403 US 15 (1971).
[39] J. A. G. Griffith and Michael Ryle, Parliament: Functions, Practice and Procedures (London: Sweet & Maxwell, 1989), 86–90.
[40] For examples, see Griffith and Ryle, Parliament, pp. 96–8.

by the Committee of Privileges of the House concerned, which may impose and enforce penalties in cases where it considers it to be appropriate.) There is statutory protection for those who publish papers printed by order of the Houses or under their authority.[41] This means that House of Commons and House of Lords papers, and their publishers, are immune from criminal and civil proceedings. Reporters who are making a fair and accurate report of proceedings in Parliament, while not covered by parliamentary privilege, have qualified privilege against actions for defamation; this is lost if the publication is actuated by malice.

An important side effect of freedom-of-speech provisions in Parliament is the protection offered to the views of M.P.s' constituents, expressed through the medium of petitions.[42] These are presented by a Member on behalf of the constituent concerned, either publicly on the floor of the House of Commons (immediately before the adjournment is moved, or at the start of business on a Friday) or privately (being placed in the petition bag situated behind the Speaker's chair). If presented publicly, they may be read out. They are published in full in the daily issue of the 'Votes and Proceedings' of the House of Commons. Petitions were very important in the nineteenth century, particularly those leading up to the electoral reform of 1832. Since 1839, there has been no debate on petitions (save in exceptional circumstances when standing orders are suspended), but they may be used to make political points, such as the existence of widespread support for, or opposition to, a policy or piece of legislation, and they sometimes elicit observations by the responsible Minister. Although petitions no longer carry the force which they once had—Sir Ivor Jennings wrote that 'under the modern procedure the right of petitioning is of no use whatever'[43]—they retain importance as a way in which constituents can make their representatives aware of their views (the figures on petitions show a dramatic leap in the numbers presented during the middle and late 1980s,[44] when the government had a huge parliamentary majority and were embarking on some very unpopular policies), and as one of the symbols reminding MPs that they represent constituents, not merely parties.

[41] Parliamentary Papers Act 1840, reversing the common-law rule in *Stockdale* v. *Hansard* (1837) 9 A. & E. 1. See, on the history, Eric Stockdale, 'The Unnecessary Crisis: The Background to the Parliamentary Papers Act 1840' [1990] *PL* 30–49, and on the modern use of the law, Patricia M. Leopold, 'The Parliamentary Papers Act 1840 and its Application Today' [1990] *PL* 183–206.

[42] See Griffith and Ryle, *Parliament* 267–8, 383–4.

[43] Ivor Jennings, *Parliament*, 2nd edn. (Cambridge: CUP, 1970), 28.

[44] Figures are given in Griffith and Ryle, *Parliament*, p. 268, show a jump from numbers between 20 and 30 per session to 957 in 1984–5, falling to 108 in 1986–7, and rising again to 356 in 1987–8.

(2) Petitioning the monarch

The Bill of Rights 1689 proclaimed: 'That it is the right of the subjects to petition the King and commitments and prosecutions for such petitioning are illegal.' This safeguarded the right to bring grievances before the monarch and, by extension, Ministers of the Crown, seeking redress. The preparation of a petition was sometimes used as an occasion for political agitation, and was regarded by the government with grave suspicion at times when they thought that the state was under threat. For example, during the French Revolution and Napoleonic Wars the government took action to prevent meetings to prepare petitions from being used for revolutionary purposes. In 1795, Pitt's government introduced, and Parliament passed, legislation making a meeting of more than fifty people 'for the purpose or on the pretext of considering of or preparing any petition, complaint, remonstrance, or declaration, or other address to the King, or to both houses, or either house of parliament, for alteration of matters established in church or state', into an unlawful assembly unless notice had been given.[45] Through the nineteenth century, after the last Seditious Meetings Act, that of 1817, lapsed, petitions to the Crown were far less important than petitions to Parliament, and they are now of only historical importance.

(3) Statutory rights to public assistance in expressing views

Certain Acts impose duties on organizations or people to facilitate free expression in certain circumstances. There is the right of parliamentary candidates to use rooms on school or local authority premises for election meetings free of charge at reasonable times between the date of receipt of the election writ and the day preceding polling day. Similar provisions apply to candidates in local government elections.[46] Any person who acts or incites others to act in a disorderly way at such a meeting, for the purpose of preventing the transaction of the business of the meeting, and fails to give his name and address when asked to do so by a constable at the request of the chairman of the meeting, commits an offence.[47]

Before parliamentary and European Assembly elections, candidates are allowed to send one free postal communication to each elector, or to have one unaddressed communication delivered free to each registered delivery point in the constituency.[48] Such communications must, however, comply with the general law, for example that relating to race

[45] Seditious Meetings Act 1795, s. 1.
[46] Representation of the People Act 1983, ss. 95 and 96, as amended by the Representation of the People Act 1985, Sched. 4,
[47] Representation of the People Act 1983, s. 97.   [48] Ibid.

relations and incitement to racial hatred, which puts a constraint on the material which can be sent out by extremist political parties.[49]

By convention, the broadcasting bodies allow parties to use the medium for party political broadcasts.[50] The duty of political impartiality, imposed on independent companies by the Broadcasting Act 1990 and on the B.B.C. by its Charter, is observed by allowing a Committee on Political Broadcasting to allocate air time between the parties. However, in the 1983 and 1987 elections the Committee failed to agree, and the main parties in Parliament have been allocated five 10-minute broadcasting slots. Limiting broadcasting opportunities to those parties which had seats in the previous Parliament, as has long been the practice, has caused some problems and allegations of unfairness. In particular, it disadvantages political parties which have no M.P.s, even if they command a significant amount of support in the country.

In one Scottish case, a Communist candidate responded by arguing that the cost of the broadcasts to the broadcasting organizations should be divided up between the candidates who benefited from them. If this had been done, it would have resulted in the Conservative candidate in one constituency, the former prime minister Sir Alec Douglas Home, having exceeded his permitted election expenditure. An election petition alleging that Sir Alec's election was therefore void failed, however, on the ground that expenditure was attributable to a candidate only if it was the intention of the person or body incurring the expenditure to assist the election chances of that candidate.[51]

This does not deal with the root of the problem, which is the inequality of access to the media of information and persuasion. The current arrangements are intrinsically conservative, making life difficult for new parties. The matter is not free from controls under international law. The European Commission of Human Rights has ruled that, while there is no right to access to the media under Article 10 of the European Convention on Human Rights, the selective barring of one party might amount to a breach of Article 10, either alone or in combination with the anti-discrimination provisions of Article 14.[52] In Scotland, in *Wilson* v. *IBA*,[53] in the run up to the referendum on Scottish devolution under the Scotland Act 1978, an interim interdict was granted to prevent the independent broadcasters from carrying a series of planned party political

[49] See generally H. F. Rawlings, *Law and the Electoral Process* (London: Sweet & Maxwell, 1988), 181–9.

[50] Alan E. Boyle, 'Political Broadcasting, Fairness and Administrative Law' [1986] *PL* 562–96.

[51] *Grieve* v. *Douglas-Home* 1965 SC 313.

[52] *X and Association of Z* v. *UK* (4515/70), 38 CD 86 (Eur. Comm. HR, 1972).

[53] 1979 SC 351.

broadcasts which would have had the effect of giving three times as much air time to one side of the debate as to the other.

This is particularly easy to establish when the debate revolves round a single issue, with a simple yes–no choice. It is more complicated when there is an election with candidates from many parties standing. It is possible that selective allocation of broadcasts here might breach the fairness and impartiality requirements imposed on the BBC by its Licence and Agreement, and on the Independent Television Commission and the independent broadcasters by the Broadcasting Act 1990. But attempts to obtain judicial review of the allocation have so far been unsuccessful in such cases.[54] The courts are understandably unwilling to land themselves with the politically delicate task of allocating air time.[55]

(4) Educational institutions

Another duty to facilitate free speech (though not other forms of expression) is imposed on the governing bodies of (a) universities, and (b) colleges maintained by, or substantially dependent on assistance from, local education authorities or grants under the Education Act 1944, providing further education (including colleges of education). Such bodies are required to take 'such steps as are reasonably practicable to ensure that freedom of speech within the law is secured for members, students and employees of the establishment and for visiting speakers'.[56] This duty was imposed after a number of incidents in the mid-1980s in which visiting speakers at universities and colleges, particularly members of the Conservative Government and other visiting speakers or staff with Conservative sympathies, were heckled or threatened and the governing bodies of the institutions had decided to ban the meetings or suspend the staff in order to prevent violence. The duty is expressed to include, in particular, 'the duty to ensure, so far as is reasonably practicable, that the use of any premises of the establishment is not denied to any individual or body of persons on any ground connected with—(a) the beliefs or views of that individual or of any member of that body; or (b) the policy or objectives of that body'.[57] A code of practice is to be issued and kept up to date by the governing body, setting out the procedures to be followed and standards of conduct to be observed in relation to the organization and conduct of meetings,[58] and every person and body concerned

---

[54] R. v. Broadcasting Complaints Commission, ex parte Owen [1985] QB 1153, [1985] 2 All ER 522, DC.

[55] See generally Rawlings, Law and the Electoral Process, 151–62; Boyle, 'Political Broadcasting' (see n. 50).

[56] Education (No .2) Act 1986, s. 43(1).

[57] Ibid., s. 43(2).

[58] Ibid., s. 43(3).

in the government of the establishment is under a duty to take such steps
as are reasonably practicable to ensure that the code is complied with,
including the institution of disciplinary measures where appropriate.[59]

The statute provides for no specific sanction or remedy supporting the
duty, so it seems to be enforceable only if a person with a sufficient interest in the matter applies for mandamus. In the only case on the provision
to have been reported so far, *R. v. University of Liverpool, ex parte Caesar-
Gordon*,[60] the Divisional Court had to consider the way in which the
interest in freedom of speech which the code is expected to protect
should be balanced against wider public order considerations. The
University of Liverpool Conservative Association applied to the
University Guild of Undergraduates for permission to hold a meeting
which would be addressed by a member of the South African embassy in
London. The Guild granted provisional permission subject to various
conditions, some of which related to the maintenance of order. For
example, the meeting was to be by invitation only, and was not to be
advertised. The police were worried about the effect which the meeting
would have on people in nearby Toxteth, with its large coloured population. After members of the University administration had met members
of the Merseyside Police Force, the University Registrar wrote to the
chairman of the Conservative Association, Mr Caesar-Gordon, withdrawing permission to hold the meeting on the ground that it was no
longer reasonably practicable to ensure that good order would be maintained. On appeal, the decision was upheld by the University Vice-
Chancellor.

The applicant sought judicial review of this decision. He accepted that
it was proper for the University to take account of the risk of disorder on
or affecting its premises, or affecting its property, students, or members
elsewhere. However, he argued that the decision was *ultra vires* because it
took account of other, irrelevant, considerations, and that the conditions
(notably those restricting publicity and restricting entry to holders of valid
student or staff cards) were *ultra vires* because they restricted freedom of
speech contrary to section 43. Watkins LJ, giving the judgment of the
Divisional Court, held that the duty to take 'such steps as are reasonably
practicable to ensure that freedom of speech within the law is assured'
under section 43(1) is a qualified duty. The University must issue a code
of practice to be followed by members of the University in connection
with activities on its premises. The duty on the University under section
43 is therefore local to the University and its premises. It was not thought
to have been Parliament's intention to impose the intolerable burden on
universities of taking into consideration persons and places outside its

---

[59] Ibid., s. 43(4).   [60] [1991] 1 QB 124, [1990] 3 All ER 821, DC.

control.[61] It was therefore ultra vires for the university to take account of the risk of disorder elsewhere, and the court granted a declaration to that effect. Matters relating to public disorder elsewhere were the concern of the police, who could consider whether to exercise their powers under the Public Order Act 1986 or at common law to ban or impose conditions on the meeting.

On the other hand, the court upheld the lawfulness of some quite substantial conditions which the University had imposed when it was thought that the meeting would take place. These included banning publicity until the morning of the meeting, requiring that those attending should be able to produce a valid student or staff card, and reserving the right to charge the Conservative Association for the cost of security at the meeting. The court decided that these conditions could reasonably have been considered 'necessary in the interests of free speech and good order in the event of the meeting taking place'. Accordingly they were not *ultra vires* section 43. Educational institutions therefore have considerable leeway in relation to the conditions which they can impose, as long as the conditions (i) are reasonably considered necessary to uphold free speech and good order against attempts at disruption in the event of the meeting taking place, and (ii) relate to the people and premises under the institution's control, rather than a risk of disorder elsewhere which is not the institution's responsibility. The discretion to charge organisers of meetings for the cost of security is a particularly important protection for educational institutions, which often find their budgets inadequate to meet basic educational needs and are understandably reluctant to sink money into policing operations.

12.4 LIMITATIONS AND CONDITIONS ON FREEDOM OF EXPRESSION

A number of provisions are designed to give effect to the responsibilities which, as the international instruments note, freedom of expression carries with it. These include rules to protect people against unfair pressure to adopt or change opinions, or to prevent people from using a privileged position to peddle their ideas from a more advantageous position than is available to competitors. This involves a restriction on the free exchange of ideas, and a derogation from the general principle in favour of free expression derived from John Stuart Mill. However, it has often been thought to be permissible in order to prevent people who have positions which give them special authority from abusing their position by seeking

---

[61] [1990] 3 All ER at p. 826.

to impose their opinions on others who are vulnerable to suggestion. The resulting limitations on freedom of expression represent a form of paternalism, achieved by imposing obligations (particularly on educators) to present balanced accounts of controversial matters to those under their charge.

(1) Restricting freedom of expression in education

The best example of this type of restriction is contained in the Education (No 2) Act 1986, which attempts to regulate the discussion and teaching of political opinions in schools. Section 44(1)(b) requires local education authorities (LEAs), governing bodies, and head teachers of maintained schools to forbid the promotion of partisan political views in the teaching of any subject in the school. The obligation could be enforced against any recalcitrant LEA, governing body, or head teacher, by mandamus in an application for judicial review. Presumably the effect on a teacher who ignores such a prohibition would be that he would be liable to disciplinary proceedings by the LEA. One worrying feature of the provision is its poor drafting. The phrase 'partisan political views' is of uncertain width. It may be limited to expressions of views concerning matters of party politics, whereby a teacher (or other contributor to class discussion, including a pupil, as the Act applies to the whole process of teaching, not merely to that part of lessons in which the teacher is speaking) expresses a preference for the opinions or policies of one recognized political party. However, if the section is so limited it is very badly expressed. A more natural reading of the phrase would interpret it as covering any partisan view (that is, an expression of a preference for one view rather than another, where opinions are divided) on any political issue (that is, an issue concerning the organisation, constitution, or government of the state).

'Promotion' seems most appropriately to apply to taking steps which actively encourage others to adopt the same views, rather than giving an account of one's own position when asked to do so. If that is correct, this provision does not excessively limit a teacher's freedom of expression within the class. It seems that a teacher who is asked for his political view on a particular matter could properly answer the question, as this would arguably not amount to promoting the views but only to expressing them. Indeed, it would often be counterproductive to prevent a teacher from explaining the political views which underlie his or her account of a topic, as the explanation of a teacher's viewpoint can help students to evaluate it. This is particularly likely to be the case in lessons covering the humanities, civics, or social studies. Naturally, the provision does not prevent teachers from pursuing party politics outside teaching time.

Nevertheless, when explaining his or her political position the teacher may be required by the LEA, governing body, or head teacher, to make sure that students also understand that there are other possible views, and what those are. This requirement may arise because section 45 of the Act requires LEAs, governing bodies, and head teachers, to 'take such steps as are reasonably practicable' to ensure that pupils are offered a balanced presentation of opposing views where political issues are brought to their attention at school or while taking part in extra-curricular activities provided or organised for registered pupils by or on behalf of the school. This means that standing instructions or codes of practice, with possible disciplinary consequences, may demand balance in class, as well as in the school's policy in relation to visiting speakers or visits to outside meetings and discussion groups. At the same time, because the legislation leaves a reasonable amount of discretion in the hands of LEAs, governors, and head teachers as to the manner in which they carry out their obligations, the potentially draconian effects of the Act may turn out to be limited. If problems arose, and a complaint were made to the LEA, the governors would find it difficult to know how to deal with it, as the guide issued to school governors by the Department of Education and Science makes no mention of the governors' responsibilities under these provisions.[62] A briefing booklet does mention the responsibilities, but gives no details.[63]

The silence on this subject may suggest that the problem is less common than one might have supposed from the fact that the government felt that legislation was required. There have so far been no reports of the legislation causing any problems to teachers, and it is more than likely that the vast majority of teachers of all political persuasions have always behaved, and continue to behave, according to the standards of professionalism and integrity of which the legislation is merely a partial codification. The only problems appear to have been caused by the government itself. In 1991, the government produced what it called a *Parent's Charter*, explaining the changes which the government had introduced and intended to introduce to schools, and outlining the rights and obligations of educators and parents in respect of children's education. Mr. Kenneth Clarke, the Secretary of State for Education, encouraged head teachers to distribute copies of this document to parents. A number of authorities, including Richmond upon Thames London Borough (controlled by the Liberal Democrat Party), instructed head teachers not

---

[62] Dept. of Education and Science, *School Governors: A Guide to the Law* (London: HMSO, July 1991 issue).

[63] Central Office of Information, *School Governors: The School Curriculum, Briefing Booklet no. 1* (London: Dept. of Education and Science, 1991), 6–7. This refers governors to DES Circular 7/87 for further details. While head teachers will have received this circular, it is not normally sent to governors.

to distribute copies, on the ground that there was a serious risk that the *Charter* was 'promoting partisan political views', in that it set out the Conservative Party policy on education, which was, in certain respects, a matter of contention between political parties. If this were so, it would have been unlawful for the material to be distributed at school without (at the very least) distributing further material at the same time which balanced it by putting the competing views of other parties, under section 45 of the 1986 Act. Nevertheless, many authorities had already distributed the material, a sign of the way in which provisions such as these are effective only if someone has a special awareness of them and a particular interest (political or otherwise) in implementing them.

It is hard to see how any government which introduces legislation such as sections 44 and 45 of the Education (No. 2) Act 1986, then proceeds to distribute politically contentious material through schools, can avoid standing convicted of double standards. Essentially, the motivation behind the legislation seems to have been to prevent the use of schools for partisan political purposes of which the government disapproved, but not for partisan purposes of which they approved. This approach fails to maintain the neutrality between visions of the good which is a part of the liberal thinking on which, as noted in Chapter 1 above, civil liberties are based.

A further example of double standards is that the requirements of the 1986 Act apply only to maintained schools, and not to independent schools. The ostensible reason for this was that it was part of the efforts of central government to prevent public money, collected from people of a variety of political persuasions, being used to promote narrow, factional, political standpoints.

The fact that the legislation imposes no obligation on the governors and head teachers of independent schools suggests that the government was less concerned to restrict the indoctrination of pupils with the conservative beliefs which predominate in the independent sector of education than to control the socialist views which were thought to dominate certain parts of the teaching profession in the maintained sector. On the other hand, the exclusion of independent schools from the Act may flow from respect for the property rights of owners of independent schools, and for the right of those parents who can afford to do so to buy an education for their children which accords with the parents' political, religious, or other conscientiously held, opinions, rather than from overt political bias on the part of the government.

Whatever the shortcomings of the legislation may be as it applies to teachers, their lot under the Act is better than that of junior pupils. Section 44(1)(*a*) of the Education (No. 2) Act 1986 requires LEAs, governing bodies, and head teachers of maintained schools to forbid registered junior pupils (i.e. those under the age of 12) at the schools to pursue partisan political activities. Despite some slight ambiguity, there can be little serious doubt that the words of the subsection, 'the pursuit of partisan political activities by any of those registered pupils at the school who are junior pupils', were intended to cover pursuit of such activities anywhere by registered pupils *of* the school, rather than merely while they are on school premises. This impression is borne out by comparison with the similar wording in paragraph (*b*) of section 45, which is clearly intended to cover extra-curricular activities whether conducted on school premises or elsewhere.[64] Any attempt to enforce such a prohibition, or to punish a pupil for breaching it, would constitute an extraordinary restriction on pupils' political liberty and freedom of expression. This is particularly serious in view of the potentially wide meaning of 'partisan political activities', similar to that of 'partisan political views' mentioned above in relation to section 44(1)(*b*). It would clearly breach the rights to freedom of thought and expression under Articles 9 and 10 of the European Convention on Human Rights.

Lest it should be thought that these rights are available only to adults, and not to junior pupils, it must be borne in mind that in the United Nations Convention on the Rights of the Child (1989)—which the UK ratified in 1991—Article 13(1) guarantees to children the right of freedom of expression, and Article 13(2) permits such restrictions to be imposed on the right 'as are provided by law and are necessary: (*a*) for respect of the rights or reputations of others; or (*b*) for the protection of national security or of public order (*ordre public*), or of public health or morals.' The restriction represented by section 44(1)(*a*) of the 1986 Act could not by any stretch of the imagination fall within, or be a reasonably proportionate means of achieving, such a justifiable objective. The provision must be repealed. If it is thought necessary to prevent children from being exploited for political purposes, for the sake of their moral welfare, this should be done by a far more restricted provision which takes account of the age and understanding of the child, and the circumstances surrounding the activity.

(2) Freedom of expression and central government civil servants

Apart from the Official Secrets Act 1989 and the equitable doctrine of confidentiality, which are outlined in Chapter 14, sections 1 and 2,

---

[64] Central Office of Information, School Governors: The School Curriculum— Briefing Booklet 1, 6–7, appears to interpret this provision as imposing an obligation on governors to ensure that junior pupils 'are not involved in partisan political activity either on the school premises *or organised elsewhere by any member of staff acting in his or her capacity as such*' (italics added). This would be a sensible way of interpreting the section, but, it is submitted, is not open on the plain words of the statute. If it reflects the effect which the Dept. intended that the section should produce, the section was badly drafted.

below, the rights of civil servants to participate in political activity and to express themselves publicly are not constrained by law. Instead, they are regulated by well-understood conventions, attitudes, and rules, given expression in what used to be called Estacode and is now the Civil Service Pay and Conditions of Service Code. Breach of these rules is a disciplinary offence for civil servants. In relation to their political activities, the Code follows the recommendations in a 1978 report.[65] Certain political activities by some types of civil servants are subject to restriction. For the purposes of these rules, civil servants are divided into three groups.

First, there are politically free civil servants. These are people who are not part of the machinery of policy making and advising government: civil servants who are not of office grade and industrial civil servants. They are permitted to undertake any form of political activity at national or local level. Secondly, most clerical and executive officers below the rank of principal equivalent do not do politically sensitive work in advising ministers or forming policies, or speaking on behalf of government or meeting the public. They are permitted to take part in any political activity at the local or national level, short of becoming a candidate for Parliament or the European Assembly. Candidacy for those bodies is likely to involve overt political partisanship which could compromise the appearance of political neutrality of a civil servant's department, so the candidate must resign from the Civil Service before standing.

Thirdly, there are higher grade civil servants and trainees, who are liable to be involved in advising Ministers, those who speak for the government to the public and outside bodies, and those lower grade clerical and executive officers who deal with the public day to day in tax and social security offices. These are in a 'politically restricted' category. This means that they are not permitted to be candidates for Parliament or the European Assembly; to hold national office in political parties; to speak publicly on matters of national political controversy; to express views on such matters in letters to the press, books, articles, or leaflets; or to canvass on behalf of candidates in national or European Assembly elections, or for political parties. At the same time, those in the politically restricted category who are not speaking for the government in public or facing members of the public as part of their normal work may be permitted to undertake local political activity: candidature for, or co-option to, local authorities; holding local office in political parties; speaking publicly on matters of local political controversy; expressing views on local matters in the press, etc.; and canvassing on behalf of candidates for election to local authorities, or for local political organisations.

[65] *Report of the Committee on the Political Activities of Civil Servants*, Cmnd. 7057 (London: HMSO, 1978).

The freedom of those in the second and third categories is dependent on approval from the civil servant's department; permission is unlikely to be granted to people who are working closely with a Minister in a private office or policy division, or on matters which are acutely politically sensitive or affected by national security considerations. Even if permission to take part in political activities is granted, the civil servant is expected to avoid embarrassing Ministers or departments, and to express themselves with moderation, and in theory (although this is virtually impossible to achieve in practice) they are to avoid committing themselves so strongly to one party 'as to inhibit or appear to inhibit loyal and effective service to Ministers of another party'.[66]

Finally, it should be noted that there are further restrictions, not directly concerned with freedom of expression but rather with the related right to freedom of association, in respect of public-service employees in jobs which are concerned with national security. Apart from the restrictions on party political activity noted above, the government announced in January 1984 that it had given an order which unilaterally altered the conditions of service of employees at the Government Communications Headquarters (GCHQ) in Cheltenham, restricting freedom of association by banning membership of trade unions. This was a move to prevent the work of GCHQ being disrupted by industrial action. It was challenged in an application for judicial review of the order. Glidewell J. held that the government had breached the unions' legitimate expectation that they would be consulted before any changes to the conditions of service were introduced. This decision was reversed by the Court of Appeal. The House of Lords held that the unions had a legitimate expectation of consultation, and that it had been breached, but decided that the national-security implications justified the breach, and upheld the ban.[67] Although it is arguable that the House gave excessive weight to an affidavit filed by Sir Robert Armstrong, the Cabinet Secretary, claiming that consultation would itself have threatened national security, the European Commission of Human Rights subsequently decided that the order was justifiable under the national-security exception to Article 11 of the Convention.[68]

Apart from party political and trade union activity, there are restrictions on the freedom of civil servants to give information about their work to the press or to Members of Parliament. The absence of

[66] *Civil Service Pay and Conditions of Service Code*, paras. 9934. See also paras. 9925–6, 9929, and 9952–4. These provisions are discussed by Peter Hennessy, *Whitehall* (London: Fontana, 1990), 368–71.

[67] *Council of Civil Service Unions* v. *Minister for the Civil Service* [1985] AC 374, [1984] 3 All ER 935, HL.

[68] *Council of Civil Service Unions* v. *UK* 20 DR 228 (1987); 10 EHRR 269. See further K. D. Ewing and C. A. Gearty, *Freedom under Thatcher* (Oxford: Clarendon Press, 1990), 130–6.

freedom-of-information legislation reflects a deeply rooted élitism of those in government, and an obsessive secrecy, which, as Peter Hennessy has written, is 'built into the calcium of a British policy-maker's bones', a carry-over into government of the essential privateness of English life.[69] Apart from the coaching manual on *Talking about the Office*,[70] which is really about how to *avoid* saying anything significant about the office at social gatherings, there are detailed rules restricting information which can be given to Parliamentary Select Committees, in answer to Parliamentary questions, or to individual M.P.s.[71] The restrictions on talking to Select Committees, contained in the 'Osmotherly rules',[72] include an injunction to every official against appearing before any Select Committee without the Minister's approval, unless the Committee issues a formal order for his attendance. When before the Committee, the official must comply with ministerial instructions as to how to answer questions. While being as helpful as possible to the Committee, the official must refuse to divulge information where necessary in the interests of good government and national security, which is said to encompass advice to Ministers, questions concerning politically controversial matters, communications between departments on policy matters, communications between Ministers, and anything which might tend to show the level in the department at which any decision was taken.

This is inconsistent with the purpose of the Select Committees, which were designed in 1979 to make government more accountable to Parliament for its activities. Members of Parliament cannot hope to hold government effectively to account unless they can find out what it is doing. The people best able to give that information are civil servants, and the Osmotherly memorandum, in keeping with the ethos of the civil service, denies to Parliament some of the best evidence concerning the running of government. It also makes it possible for Ministers to mislead the House of Commons, or to deny it the information which is its life blood, with relative impunity, subject only to the risk of the truth being leaked by a rogue civil servant.

In these circumstances, leaks can have a useful 'whistle-blowing' function, putting a stop to abuse of power. They have, on occasion, caught out Ministers. When Mr Michael Heseltine MP, then Secretary of State

[69] Hennessy, *Whitehall*, 346–7.

[70] Classified as 'restricted', this cannot be consulted by the public. It is cited in Hennessy, *Whitehall*, 357–8.

[71] James Michael, *The Politics of Secrecy* (Harmondsworth: Penguin, 1982); Geoffrey Marshall, 'Ministers, Civil Servants, and Open Government', in Carol Harlow (ed.), *Public Law and Politics* (London: Sweet & Maxwell, 1986), 80–90.

[72] *Memorandum of Guidance for Officials Appearing before Select Committees* of 16 May 1980, General Notice GEN80/38, drafted by an assistant secretary in the Civil Service Dept., Mr E. B. C. Osmotherly, and known by his name: Hennessy, *Whitehall*, 361–3.

for Defence, refused in May 1983 to supply information to Mr Tam Dalyell MP about the sinking of the Argentinian cruiser *General Belgrano* during the Falklands campaign, Mr Clive Ponting, then a civil servant in the Ministry of Defence, disclosed the information secretly. He was discovered, and prosecuted unsuccessfully under the Official Secrets Act 1911, section 2 (since repealed). He argued at his trial that the disclosure was in the interest of the state, providing him with a defence under section 2, because he had disclosed the material in pursuit of a duty which the civil service owes to Parliament. This claim was rejected by the trial judge, McCowan J., who held that the civil servant's duty was to the Minister, that the interests of the state were what the government of the day said they were, and that it was not open to a civil servant, a court, or a jury to override the government's view.[73] However, the jury, influenced perhaps by the clever campaign waged by Mr. Ponting and his advisers in and outside the court, and the lack of sensitivity to public opinion which the government had displayed, acquitted despite the judge's ruling.[74]

This did not make the civil service or the government believe in the value of freedom of information. The official reaction, predictably, was to reassert the absolute importance of secrecy. First, a tough statement of the civil servant's responsibilities was promulgated by Sir Robert Armstrong, the Cabinet Secretary.[75] He stressed that the responsibility of the civil service was exclusively to the government of the day, not to the public or Parliament. This went beyond the prevailing orthodoxy, according to which civil servants were servants of the Crown and nation, and not of politicians.[76] Armstrong went on to remind civil servants that the Minister, not the civil service, is responsible to Parliament for the conduct of the department's affairs, and that they have a duty of lifelong obligation to keep the confidences to which they become privy in the course of their duties. Secondly, when the Official Secrets Act 1989 was drafted, the duty of lifelong confidence of Crown servants in respect of matters relating to security and intelligence, defence, international relations, crime, and special investigation powers, was backed up by criminal sanctions in sections 1 to 4. Thirdly, provisions based on the Armstrong memorandum and the 1989 Act were included in the Civil Service Pay and Conditions Code, paragraphs 9910–13, when the Code was revised in the light of the 1989 Act.

[73] *R. v. Ponting* [1985] Crim. LR 318.

[74] Patrick Birkinshaw, *Freedom of Information: The Law, the Practice and the Ideal* (London: Weidenfeld & Nicolson, 1988), p. 81; Clive Ponting, '*R. v. Ponting*' (1987) 14 *J. of Law and Soc.* 366–72; Rosamund M. Thomas, 'The British Official Secrets Acts 1911–1939 and the Ponting Case' [1986] Crim. LR 491–510.

[75] *The Duties and Responsibilities of Civil Servants in Relation to Ministers*, set out in a Written Answer of 26 Feb. 1985, 74 HC Debs., cols. 128–30.

[76] Hennessy, *Whitehall*, p. 346.

This closes the door to unauthorized leaks which reveal improper behaviour in government or the civil or security services, although it is still open to Ministers to leak without much fear of prosecution. It leaves the civil servant with problems, however. What is he to do if asked by a Minister or superior officer to do something which he believes to be unlawful? Armstrong exhorted the civil servant to take the matter to the permanent head of the department. What if the civil servant faces a fundamental issue of conscience? Such crises are to be discussed with a superior officer, or the permanent head of the department (who, presumably, can be relied on to advise against revealing anything publicly). There is now a right to appeal to the head of the Home Civil Service,[77] although a head who follows the Armstrong line is unlikely to sympathize with a civil servant who finds it hard to square secrecy with his conscience.

(3) Political activity by local government employees

Whereas in central government, the code of behaviour for civil servants limits their political activities in well-understood ways on a semi-consensual basis, the political freedom of local-government employees has been a more contentious matter in recent years. In 1989 the government, concerned about political activities undertaken by Mr Derek Hatton, a Labour councillor in Liverpool while on the payroll of another council, introduced legislation to curb what they saw as an abuse. The Local Government and Housing Act 1989 identified certain politically sensitive posts, and effectively excluded their holders from representative political activity. The Act created a category of 'politically restricted posts'. Holders of these posts are disqualified from becoming elected members of local authorities or of the House of Commons.[78] Furthermore, the terms and conditions of their employment are deemed to contain provisions laid down centrally by the Secretary of State for the Environment by regulation.[79] This opens the possibility that government might make it a breach of a person's contract of employment to take part in any political activity, or to support certain parties. This is a dangerous power to leave in the hands of central government, with only limited opportunities for parliamentary oversight.

Politically restricted posts fall broadly into three categories. First, there are the chief officers, such as the chief executive and those in charge of specific areas of the authority's work, their deputies, the monitoring

---

[77] Bailey, Harris, and Jones, *Civil Liberties Cases and Materials*, 429; according to the authors, the appeal procedure has not yet been used.

[78] Local Government and Housing Act 1989, s. 1(1), (2).

[79] Ibid., s. 1(5).

officer,[80] and people appointed to assist elected members of particular political groups with their work as members. Such posts involve advising elected members on policy, and are not thought to be suitable to be held by anyone who has committed political affiliations.[81] Next, there are two groups of posts which the local authority is required to specify. First, there are jobs with salaries above a sum (currently £19,500) fixed by the Secretary of State. These people are, presumably, particularly influential, and it is thought to be important to avoid political bias. Secondly, there are people who, on a regular basis, advise the authority or its committees, sub-committees, and joint committees, or speak on behalf of the authority to journalists and broadcasters (the information or press officers).[82] The advisory and public-representation roles, respectively, of people in these posts are thought to require an appearance of political neutrality. Teachers, who are employed by education authorities but do not regularly advise or represent the authorities, are excluded from the category of politically restricted posts.[83]

These restrictions understandably precipitated an outcry from local-government officers who saw them as a serious infringement of their democratic rights. NALGO, the local-government officers' union, produced a circular, *Will YOU be banned in 1990?*, describing the legislation as 'among the most draconian attempts to remove the civil and political rights of council officers'. A person who is affected may apply for exemption from political restriction to an official appointed by the Secretary of State under section 3 of the 1989 Act, but this is hardly a satisfactory protection for the right to participate in the government of one's country or locality. Even if exemption is granted, the Act limited the amount of paid leave which a person could have from an authority in order to act as an elected member (other than chairman) of another. The professional standards of most local government officers are sufficiently well developed to know how far they can go without compromising their positions as advisors. The legislation looks like a sledgehammer taken to crack a nut of relatively limited significance.

(4) Publicity by local authorities

Another example of the same type is the attempt to stop local authorities from using ratepayers' money to promote political objectives (in the Local Government Act 1986) or homosexuality (in the Local Government Act 1988, section 28, inserting section 2A into the Local

---

[80] This is a person who must be appointed under s. 5 to monitor the legality of the activities of the council, its committees, sub-committees, officers, etc.

[81] Local Government and Housing Act 1989, s. 2(1).

[82] Ibid., s. 2(1), (2), (3).   [83] Ibid., s. 2(10).

Government Act 1986) which many ratepayers might find repulsive.
However, all this legislation was introduced by and passed under the
auspices of the Conservative Government led by Mrs. Thatcher, and it
would be hard to acquit the government of attempting to suppress the
expression of views opposed to their own on political and moral
matters.[84]

(5) Publicity by central government

It has been said that there is a prerogative power, of which central government can take advantage, to publish information to citizens. This was
used to justify the campaign in favour of membership of the European
Communities in the period leading up to the referendum on accession.[85]
In view of the reluctance of government to permit access to information
in this country, noted in section (2) above,[86] one would expect this to be
a little used power. However, a great deal of publicity is produced on
behalf of the government, and its promulgation has recently become
politically contentious. Few would object to public information campaigns designed to encourage people to take up their entitlements to state
benefits, or to educate us about HIV and AIDS. However, there is a grey
area where it becomes hard to distinguish between the public information purpose and the party political purpose behind publications such as
the *Citizen's Charter.*

There is no legal regulation of the nature and content of government
publicity. There is a degree of self-regulation, under the Central
Government Convention on Publicity and Advertising.[87] These conventions are not intended to be legally binding. It is possible that a decision
to publish might be struck down in judicial review proceedings. There is
authority for saying that government publicity can be reviewed by the
courts if the advice which it contains is illegal, or if it is published in bad

---

[84] For thorough analysis of the law relating to local government publicity, see Chris
Willmore, *Letting People Know: Local Government Publicity and the Law*, 2nd edn. (London:
Association of Metropolitan Authorities, 1988). Early experience of the 1986 Act suggested that it was having little impact, because most local authorities assumed that, as the
legislation had been aimed at 'loony left' councils, it did not affect them, while those
councils which might have been worried about it generally either found ways round it or
decided to carry on as before and wait to see whether they would be challenged (few
were). H. F. Rawlings and C. J. Willmore, 'Propaganda on the rates? Local Authority
Publicity and the Local Government Act 1986', paper presented to the Third Bristol
Colloquium on Law and Politics, May 1988.

[85] *Jenkins* v. *A.-G.*, *The Times*, 13 Aug. 1971.

[86] See also Norman S. Marsh, 'Public Access to Government-Held Information in the
UK: Attempts at Reform', in Norman S. Marsh (ed.), *Public Access to Government-Held
Information* (London: Stevens, 1987), 248–91.

[87] C. R. Munro, 'Government Advertising and Publicity' [1990] *PL* 1–9.

faith or for an improper purpose (particularly if it breaches the conventions which set out the extent of the proper purposes).[88] Nevertheless, this is somewhat speculative, as no application for review of government publicity has so far been successful. In any case, the constraints on central government are far less severe than those which central government has seen fit to impose on local government by statute. Presumably this is because central government (or the party in power) is more likely to approve of its own publicity than of local government publicity which may be pushing a message inconsistent with that which central government wishes the public to believe.

12.5 CONCLUSION

Freedom of expression, as a general principle, is well established in English law. However, in order to understand its true scope, and to protect against the gradual restriction of the freedom which can easily result when what appear to be good prudential or utilitarian reasons are offered for limiting the freedoms of a few people in particular situations, we need to look at the areas in which the main battles over freedom of expression are now fought. The main problems in English law concern the position of the media, and certain systematic restrictions which the law places on the exercise of free expression. The multiplicity of ends which are served by maintaining free expression raise questions about the type and extent of restraints which are justifiable. These matters form the subject of the next five chapters.

[88] *R. v. Secretary of State for Social Security, ex parte Greenwich LBC, The Times*, 17 May 1989, D.C., discussed by Munro, 'Government Advertising and Publicity' [1990] *PL* 1–9.

13

MEDIA FREEDOM

This chapter examines the role of, and forms of control over, the media of mass communication, in the context of legal treatment of the freedom to receive and impart information and ideas. Starting with an outline of the background to the subject, the chapter goes on to consider controls over ownership of the media and the content of publications, and the extent of protection for freedom of expression by the media in English law, including the limiting effect of the law of defamation. Section 4 is devoted to certain special legal protections given to journalists in English law, and a conclusion is offered in section 5.

13.1 BACKGROUND

(1) Relationship to freedom of speech

There is an obvious connection between press freedom and freedom of speech. Like speech, the press is a medium for broadcasting information and opinion. It is therefore important on a number of grounds. First, as a tool of self-expression it is a significant instrument of personal autonomy. Secondly, as a channel of communication it helps to allow the political discourse which is necessary in any country which aspires to democracy. Thirdly, it helps to provide one of the essential conditions for scholarship, making possible the exchange and evaluation of theories, explanations, and discoveries. Fourthly, it helps to promulgate a society's cultural values, and, where they are in flux, facilitates the debate about them, advancing the development and survival of civilization.

(2) History: press licensing

The press has developed a special meaning and a particular significance over and above that attaching to freedom of speech. The invention of the printing press, and more particularly its introduction to England by William Caxton in 1477, vastly increased the capacity of books and pamphlets—especially political ones—to reach people of all sorts. This made it a powerful medium for instruction, but also for opposition to the established order. The Roman Catholic Church had quickly responded to the use of the printing-press on mainland Europe by printing its own books and banning others which were deemed to be incompatible with orthodox teaching. In England, the government did the same. Printing presses were too powerful to be unregulated. The regulation took two forms (in addition to the criminal law of sedition which might apply to speech as well as printed matter): presses had to be licensed in order to be used legally, and publications had to be licensed, with the payment of a tax on each. Unlicensed presses or publications might be seized, and the printers and publishers were liable to severe penalties.[1]

This continued into the eighteenth century, when the government accidentally allowed the Licensing Acts to lapse. This caused considerable embarrassment in the litigation surrounding issue 45 of *The North Briton*: the Secretary of State had issued warrants under legislation which turned out to be no longer in force, making the subsequent seizure of persons and property by the King's Messengers unlawful.[2] Governments continued to be rightly wary of the power of mass communication, however. A small but important part of the work of writers and printers was political. The capacity of publishers to scrutinize the workings of government and Parliament, to criticize them, and to suggest alternative policies, could significantly affect the standing of a government. This might lead to public disorder or even, it might be feared, revolution. As the electorate became increasingly large and literate during the nineteenth century, the press might sway voters and influence the results of elections. For good or ill, the press was a powerful instrument for achieving popular political consciousness and operating electoral democracy.

(3) Reactions to threats to press freedom

Reactions to governments' overuse of powers to control the press varied. There was civil disobedience in countries, like England, where constitutional means of protecting press freedom were out of reach. Where upheavals led to new constitutional orders, these would often include special protection for press freedom, as in the First Amendment to the Constitution of the USA in 1789–91, or section 2 of Canada's Constitution Act 1982, declaring it to be one of the fundamental freedoms of everyone. Such provisions may make it necessary for courts to hold a law to be unconstitutional if, for example, it stifles freedom to criticize the government, by imposing criminal penalties on people who

---

[1] Simon J. Lewis, 'An Instrument of the New Constitution: the Origins of the General Warrant' (1986) 7 *J. of Legal Hist.* 256–72.

[2] Simon J. Lewis, 'The Relationship between Bureaucracy and Law: The Fall and Rise of the General Warrant', unpublished LL.M. dissertation, Univ. of Bristol, 1984.

make or publish false statements likely to undermine public confidence in the conduct of public affairs.[3]

In England, there is no constitutional protection for press or media freedom. However, under the influence of the European Convention on Human Rights, the courts and Parliament have slowly come to recognize that there is a special public interest in press freedom, and legislative steps have been taken to protect it. How successful these have been will have to be assessed in due course. But the importance of mass communication can be used to support an argument for regulation of the industry, as well as arguments for freedom from interference. For example, it is important to prevent the channels of communication from being dominated by a narrow range of ideas. Balance is important, and this inevitably entails some external interference with the editorial freedom of publishers. Much press law is concerned with the attempt to permit enough intervention (and the right kind of intervention) to maintain freedom of communication, without permitting so much that it stifles that which is to be protected.

13.2 REGULATION OF THE MEDIA[4]

The right of the printed media to be free of direct government controls was won in the eighteenth century in Britain. When new methods of communication were invented in the twentieth century—radio, television, satellite and cable broadcasting—the balance between regulating the industry to protect quality and independence and threatening that independence by overregulating it became particularly important, and was among the factors which led to regulation of the electronic media in ways no longer contemplated for the printed media. At the same time, concern has built up about the lack of responsibility on the part of some journalists, editors, and newspaper proprietors, and this might eventually lead to increased regulation of newspapers in the future.

(1) Newspapers: ownership and control

Although the printed word has long been substantially protected against governmental control, even in the field of newspaper ownership some regulation is needed to prevent a small group of people gaining a

---

[3] See *Hector* v. *A.-G. of Antigua and Barbuda* [1990] 2 AC 312, [1990] 2 All ER 103, PC.

[4] See generally Geoffrey Robertson and Andrew Nicol, *Media Law: The Rights of Journalists and Broadcasters*, 3rd edn. (London: Penguin, 1992), chs. 13 and 15; Thomas Gibbons, *Regulating the Media* (London: Sweet & Maxwell, 1991).

stranglehold over the communications industry, and using their proprietorial muscle to influence editorial policy. Left to themselves, market
forces might put a few newpaper proprietors in a position to censor the
flow of information (or disinformation) to the public, and deny any out-
let to some legitimate political and social opinions. To assist freedom of
the press and the free flow of information and ideas, state action is needed
to avoid oligopolistic control over the press by commercial magnates
who are, by virtue of their interests, unlikely to be sympathetic to left-of-
centre political and social ideas.

Because the newpaper industry, unlike broadcasting, is no longer
licensed in the UK, the controls over concentration of ownership are no
more (and no less) strong than those which apply in relation to other
industries. The Monopolies and Mergers Commission has a role in preventing anti-competitive concentrations of power, as does the European
Commission. The public interest in the freedom of the press is a consideration which weighs with them, and it is an area of competition law
which is highly contentious.[5] However, the field is only incidentally
related to civil liberties law, and this volume will not deal with it in any
detail.

In principle, subject to the restraint of competition law, all are free to
set up in business as publishers so long as they do not contravene any law.
Printing presses need no longer be officially licensed. Generally speaking,
therefore, the ability to publish printed material depends only on ability
to pay for materials, distribution, and so on. Publishing is, in theory, regulated by market pressures rather than by government. In practice, in this
as in other spheres, the operation of a publishing market in the United
Kingdom has tended to lead to an oligopoly. The costs of establishing a
publishing business are very high; newcomers need to be well capitalized
in order to have a chance of success. Nowhere is this more true than in
relation to mass circulation newpapers, which are controlled by a few
powerful publishers. Of recent attempts by outsiders to break into the
daily newspaper market, only the *Independent* has succeeded in establishing itself.

Proprietors of newspapers tend to exercise editorial control on political
grounds. Two consequences follow from this. First, while the right to
publish is in theory available to all, it is restricted by access to capital. As
in relation to other rights, inequalities of resources make the freedom to
publish a liberty of unequal worth. To some minor degree, the effects of
this are contained by granting public money to candidates in elections to
support their campaigns. However, the amounts of money are small, and

---

[5] Richard Whish, *Competition Law*, 2nd edn. (London: Butterworths, 1988), 701–9,
Robertson and Nicol, *Media Law*, 502–7, and Gibbons, *Regulating the Media*, 97–9, provide surveys of the area.

they do not help parties and commentators between elections or campaigners who are not affiliated to a recognized party. Secondly, the market orientation of the industry leads to inequality of access to publication. Writers with views which are unpopular with those who own and edit mass circulation newspapers have less opportunity to bring their writing before the public than those whose views are in tune with those of the press barons. In political terms, this means that the capitalist right is likely to be advantaged over the socialist left in access to the press, and that the newspaper industry, taken as a whole, is liable to be less effective in scrutinizing a right-wing, capitalist government than a left-wing, socialist one. This can have the effect of skewing the market-place of ideas within which the system of electoral democracy operates.

Whether this is seen as a problem will depend on one's political and economic preferences. From one viewpoint, the practical and symbolic value of a free press is undermined if it is subject to market forces. These admit opinions to be valuable only to the extent to which they can be shown to enjoy *economic* support in the market. On this view, freedom of speech should be no more privileged against unfavourable market conditions than any other consumer preference. However, such a view can be challenged on two grounds.

First, it can be argued that attempting to subject freedom of speech or of the press to free-market liberalism is self-defeating. In order to make liberalism work as a political system, the necessary conditions for its operation must be in place. These include respect for individual autonomy and freedom to publish ideas. By subjecting the latter freedom to market forces, free-market capitalism treats the conditions for liberalism as being of contingent rather than intrinsic importance. This, it might be said, is an incoherent position for market capitalists to adopt, since a measure of individual freedom is a prerequisite for capitalism itself. But this argument is flawed. Free-market capitalism may thrive on individual freedom, but it is not predicated on the observance of the full range of individual rights. It demands respect for economic rights, particularly those needed in order to make trading possible, but it does not necessitate liberal political freedoms or respect for non-economic aspects of personal autonomy. Capitalism can flourish in countries which are far from being politically liberal or respecting individual autonomy as a fundamental value. Japan provides an example of such a country. Indeed, there may be circumstances in which free speech threatens capitalist market freedoms, for example by advocating a move to a more controlled economy.

A second, more promising, defence of freedom of the press is based in values operating at a higher level than those of the market economy. Why, one can ask, is the market economy worth preserving? Utilitarian capitalists would reply that it is the most efficient means of maximising aggregate social wealth. This is a controversial and non-falsifiable claim. Liberal capitalists, by contrast, will argue that markets give the best opportunity for people to explore and exploit their abilities, formulating and giving effect to a plan for life. This makes the market a forum in which people can express their autonomy. There are, however, other spheres of personal autonomy, and it is by no means clear that these are less worthwhile than those which can be realized through the market. Subjecting the availability of all expressions of autonomy to the market fails to remain neutral between socially acceptable types of life plan. It places special value on those which require a market, and undervalues others which demand restrictions on the freedom of the market in order to make it more equal rather than more free. Liberalism requires that different visions of the good should be equally respected as long as they do not undermine society or inflict harm. For liberal capitalists, then, as opposed to utilitarian ones, there should be little difficulty in accepting that it may be necessary to restrain the free operation of the market economy in order to advance non-economic visions of the good.

In short, political liberalism requires a degree of control over the operation of markets in order to protect liberal values against market-expressed preferences. However, the extent to which such control is desirable or acceptable will depend on the view which individuals or society as a whole take of the relative weights attaching to different freedoms. Where newspaper proprietors have bought or built up their newspapers as businesses, limiting their editorial freedom is a potential restriction of their freedom of expression (forcing them to publish expressions with which they disagree or of which they disapprove, for example in order to provide political balance) and is also an interference with their freedom to use their property in the way which seems best to them. In a capitalist economy, it is plausible to expect economic liberals to regard it as improper—a form of disguised taxation—to force a proprietor to fund a publication in order to give publicity to ideas or information which the proprietor would rather not see published. Even those who favour freedom of expression might not be prepared to support it under circumstances in which its exercise conflicts with freedom of property.

The most obvious practical implications of this relate to the vexed question of rights of reply. At present, there is no obligation on newspapers to allow space for people to reply to stories or opinions which have been published about them. The more responsible newspapers will publish corrections where errors have been made, and publish letters from people replying to articles, but other newspapers have in the past been less scrupulous. The industry responded to agitation, in and out of Parliament, for legislation requiring newspapers to give space to members of the public for replies to allegations made in earlier issues, by adopting a Code of Practice in 1991 which includes three significant provisions. Paragraph 1 provides that significant inaccuracies, misleading statements, and distorted reports should be corrected promptly and with due prominence, and an apology should be published whenever appropriate. Paragraph 2 provides: 'A fair opportunity for reply to inaccuracies should be given to individuals or organisations when reasonably called for.' This does not suggest that there should be a right to reply to expressions of opinion or to misleading presentations of accurate facts, and it leaves it to the editor in the first instance to decide whether a request for an opportunity to reply is 'reasonable'. Paragraph 3 provides: 'Newspapers, while free to be partisan, should distinguish clearly between comment, conjecture and fact.'

The Code of Practice was a response to complaints that some newspapers have fabricated news items, misrepresented people's opinions, or behaved improperly while gathering information, and to the suggestion in the Calcutt Report that there might be legislation if the industry failed to behave more responsibly in future. But, as paragraph 3 makes clear, the aim is to secure respect for rights to reputation or privacy, rather than an attempt to enforce access to the media for a range of views, or balanced political reporting. Newspapers are property, and it would be seen as a violation of the proprietors' rights, both of ownership and of free expression, to insist that they pay to support the propagation of views with which they disagree. Proprietors are free to be fair and balanced if they want to be (although among national dailies only the *Independent* has an official editorial policy which is politically non-aligned), but they will not be compelled to behave as if they were a public-service undertaking using state money.

If there is a desire to use newspapers to secure access to means of publication for all points of view, it will be necessary to dilute the proprietorial element in newspaper ownership. This might be managed, for example, by providing a state subsidy to cover the cost of producing a proportion of the news and comment parts of the newspaper (excluding commercial advertising space), and requiring that proportion to be devoted to opposing viewpoints for the sake of balance. However, as yet no government has seen fit to act so as to limit the freedom of newpaper proprietors. Political parties which rely on the press to stir up public support would be taking a major risk if they tried to force such an arrangement on proprietors. It is particularly unlikely that a Conservative Government would ever take such a step: as the Conservative Party has most of the national press on its side (demonstrated once again during the 1992 general election campaign), they have little to gain and much to lose.

(2) Control over content and investigative methods: newspapers

The existing British system of controls over newpapers relies largely on self-regulation, and its effectiveness is questionable. The press has proved resistant to proposals to give people rights of reply when they feel that they have been libelled or misrepresented, and has been very slow to put in place any structures for establishing and enforcing standards of professional integrity, truthfulness, and responsibility among journalists and editors. The free market in newspaper sales has encouraged the less responsible editors and proprietors to allow anything as long as it sells newspapers. Self-regulation by the industry's own appointed watchdogs had little effect on editorial behaviour generally, and in some newspapers abuses abounded.[6] The law has not been able to do much to keep them in check: after one of the grosser abuses of taste, in which a photographer without consent took a picture of a dangerously ill television actor and a newspaper published it, the Court of Appeal lamented the lack of a remedy against the press (represented on this occasion by the *Sunday Sport*) for infringement of privacy.[7] The Press Council, a body for self-regulation by the industry, was largely ineffective in imposing standards. Only recently, after a report by a Committee chaired by Mr (now Sir) David Calcutt QC,[8] did the newspaper industry establish procedures to clean up their practices.[9]

The Newspaper Publishers' Association and the Newspaper Society, representing proprietors of national and local newspapers, put in place a Code of Practice, worked out by a committee of newspaper editors. This sets out professional and ethical standards for journalists and editors. Next, they established a Press Complaints Commission to adjudicate on complaints about breaches of the Code, in place of the largely discredited Press Council. The Commission's powers are similar to those of the Press Council: it can censure newspapers or journalists, and can tell (but not compel) editors to publish adjudications. However, it has no power to require a newspaper to publish a correction or give a right of reply to an aggrieved person, no procedure for acting as mediators to resolve disputes, and no power to award compensation or impose penalties. The main procedural difference between the Commission and the old Press Council, from the complainant's point of view, is that the Press Council would not consider complaints if the complainant was contemplating legal action, whereas the Commission will not require the complainant to

---

[6] Gibbons, *Regulating the Media*, 158–66.

[7] *Kaye v. Robertson* [1991] FSR 62, CA. See Ch. 8 above.

[8] Home Office, *Report of the Committee on Privacy and Related Matters*, Cm. 1102 (London: HMSO, 1990).

[9] C. R. Munro, 'Press Freedom—How the Beast was Tamed' (1991) 54 *MLR* 104–11.

give up the legal right to seek damages or other remedies before it will investigate the complaint.

The Press Complaints Commission has a strong press element in its membership. Apart from Lord McGregor, its chairman, ten of its other fifteen members have links with the media. The predominance of insiders over outsiders on the Commission is intended to achieve two goals: first, to ensure that the Commission understands how newspapers work; secondly, to make its adjudications acceptable to journalists. It is thought that people within the industry will be more likely to accept and adapt to criticisms from a peer group than attacks from an outside body. The Commission started work only as recently as January 1991, and has yet to prove itself. The make-up of the Commission brings to mind the Sellar and Yeatman representation of trial by one's peers under Magna Carta: 'That the Barons should not be tried except by a special jury of other Barons who would understand.'[10] The press claims that the Commission has indeed altered attitudes of editors and journalists towards news coverage.[11] The work of the Commission has been aided by the appointment, by individual newspapers, of readers' complaints ombudsmen. These do not investigate complaints themselves—that is left to the editorial staff—but they keep an eye on standards of behaviour on the paper, watch the process by which complaints are handled, and publish regular reports in the newspaper about their findings.

When the Calcutt Committee reported in June 1990, it accepted that statutory regulation would be less than ideal, but recommended that the performance of the press and its self-regulatory organ, the Press Complaints Commission, should be kept under review to see whether they observed standards which would make statutory regulation unnecessary. By the time Sir David Calcutt reported in January 1993 on his review of the operation of the Commission,[12] there was evidence of further invasion of privacy by the press and of a half-hearted response by the Commission. Personal information, obtained by unlawful entry, secret surveillance, or bugging devices, and amounting to invasions of privacy, had been published concerning the private lives of public figures (including Mr Paddy Ashdown, leader of the Liberal Democrats, Mr David Mellor, the Minister then responsible for the review of press self-regulation, the Duchess of York, and the Prince and Princess of Wales), without effective action by the Commission. Private individuals who had

[10] W. C. Sellar and R. J. Yeatman, *1066 and All That* (Harmondsworth: Penguin, 1960), 34.
[11] Maggie Brown, 'Newspapers Pass First Test of New Self-Regulation', *Independent*, 18 Sept. 1991.
[12] Sir David Calcutt QC, *Review of Press Self-Regulation*, Cm. 2135 (London: HMSO, 1993).

suffered similar invasions of privacy had, in some cases, not complained to the Commission, either through ignorance of its existence or because they feared that further publicity would follow, and a number of those who had complained were dissatisfied with the way in which the complaints were handled.[13]

Sir David concluded that self-regulation had not worked, and recommended that a package of measures, originally examined by the Privacy Committee in 1990, should now be implemented. Chief among these was the establishment of a statutory Press Complaints Tribunal with jurisdiction over all newspapers, journals, and magazines. It would be chaired by a judge or senior lawyer, and would have power to order a publisher to print an apology in a form, edition, and position specified by the tribunal. It would also be empowered to award compensation and impose fines.[14] Alongside this, Sir David recommended the imposition of criminal sanctions and civil liability on anyone who unlawfully entered private property, or placed a surveillance device there, or took a photograph or recorded the voice of anyone, intending to obtain personal information with a view to its publication. There would be a defence if the act was done to prevent, detect, or expose a crime or other seriously anti-social conduct, to protect public health or safety, to prevent the public being misled by a public statement or action of the person concerned, or if it was done under lawful authority. He also recommended that the government should give further consideration to the introduction of a tort of infringement of privacy.[15]

The publication of the recommendations, which had been widely leaked in advance, was greeted with predictable reactions. Representatives of the press, raised the spectre of censorship and feared that a cloak of secrecy would enshroud corruption in high places. Others regarded the review as a timely reminder that the press, like other major industries, needed to show that it could act responsibly towards the public in the course of its pursuit of profit. The government was in a difficult position, not wanting to appear to be shackling press comment or to be acting out of self-protection, particularly as several of its own members (including the Minister originally responsible for the review, who had since resigned, and the Chancellor of the Exchequer) had recently been the subject of press comment on their private lives. A private member's bill, the Freedom and Responsibility of the Press Bill, was introduced by Mr Clive Scoley MP in 1992, and despite not having government support was making progress early in 1993. In the short term, however, it seems unlikely that the main Calcutt proposals will become law.

There can be no doubt that the best solution would be for the press to

---

[13] Ibid., chs. 4 and 5.   [14] Ibid., paras 6.17–6.22.   [15] Ibid., ch. 7.

adopt standards of responsible, professional behaviour, and to police them. Editors and journalists are concerned to be seen by the public as professionals, with a code of ethics and a sense of public responsibility. Unfortunately, they seem to want that public regard without the shackles which normally accompany it. One of the features which distinguishes professions from other groupings is that the former have criteria and procedures for admission to membership, and disciplinary procedures and measures (including the withdrawal of the right to practise), which are designed to impose and uphold standards of ethics and responsibility which protect those with whom the professional has to deal. Until journalism adopts a professional organization of this sort, its claim to be free of regulation in the public interest will always be suspect.

For structural reasons, however, it would be difficult and perhaps impossible to make such a professional body work. Professionals are typically not employed by a single client. Many journalists and all editors, on the other hand, are tied to the proprietor of the newspaper, magazine, or journal on which they work. The proprietor's main aim is profit, and, being the person who pays the piper, will not unnaturally expect to call the tune.[16] The standards and procedures of a professional body of dependent journalists could hardly hope to stand up against such economic power. Regrettable as it is, if society is serious about reining in abuses of press freedom, it might ultimately prove to have no alternative to a Calcutt-style package of measures, at least while the press industry continues to be controlled by an oligopoly of proprietors. If, on the other hand, society wants to protect the press against statutory incursions on its freedom, it will have to accept the inevitable abuses as the price of the benefits.

(3) Reasons for regulating the broadcasting media

The new forms of mass communication were, and are, carefully regulated. There are five interrelated reasons for this. First, governments realized the potential of channels of mass communication for contributing to democracy or undermining it. They hoped to foster a public service ethos in broadcasting, so that it would be a medium for educating and improving the population.[17] This was important to some early broadcasters, notably Lord Reith, the first Director-General of the BBC, as well as to government. Secondly, in order to do this it was necessary to keep the media of mass communications from having programme policy dictated entirely by market forces. A strong public sector and regulation of the

[16] See Thomas Gibbons, 'Freedom of the Press: Ownership and Editorial Values' [1992] PL 279–99.
[17] Gibbons, Regulating the Media, 32–40.

independent sector, when one started to operate, were called for. Initially, the novelty and cost of broadcasting technology helped to discourage press barons from entering the broadcasting arena, and made it easier to ensure that the powerful new means of communication did not fall into the wrong hands. (This was similar to the early history of printing, when presses were expensive and skilled printers scarce.)[18]

Thirdly, when commercial broadcasters appeared on the scene, and a regulatory scheme was being developed for them, it was thought to be important to preserve a diversity of ideas by preventing oligopolistic concentrations of power in the hands of a few, usually rich and conservative, media magnates, and to ensure that licences were granted only to people who could be expected not to abuse the privilege. The need to preserve propriety has been a motivating factor in the regulation of commercial broadcasting over much of the world. In Australia, for example, the Australian Broadcasting Tribunal can refuse a licence to anyone who is shown not to be a fit and proper person to hold one.

Fourthly, government hoped to ensure that civilized standards were maintained, to uphold social values. Accordingly, the Royal Charter of the BBC has always set standards which have to be observed in relation to good taste, decency, protecting children, political impartiality, and so on.[19] The same standards are set for the independent broadcasting services by the Broadcasting Act 1990, section 6. It is the responsibility of the Governors of the BBC, under its Charter, and of the Independent Television Commission under section 7 of the 1990 Act, to produce a code giving guidance to programme-makers on the standards to be observed in order to preserve good taste and decency, especially in relation to children's viewing, to avoid offending the feelings of the public, and to control the portrayal of violence. The independent sector, too, is subject to extensive rules, even if the measures put in place to enforce them do not always have teeth. The ITC published its programme code in 1991.[20] A further code of practice is provided by the Broadcasting Standards Council, which has responsibility under Part VI of the Broadcasting Act 1990 for monitoring programmes, considering complaints about them, and publishing its views on programmes after they have been broadcast.[21] Finally, the Broadcasting Complaints Commission has power under section 143 of the 1990 Act to consider complaints from people about unjust or unfair treatment in radio or television programmes broadcast by either the BBC or independent companies, and about invasions of privacy. The BCC has no power to order the

---

[18] See J. R. Hale, *Renaissance Europe 1480–1520* (London: Collins, 1971), 188–9.
[19] See now *B.B.C. Licence and Agreement*, Cmnd. 8233 (1981).
[20] Gibbons, *Regulating the Media*, 126–38.
[21] Broadcasting Act 1990, ss. 153, 154; Gibbons, *Regulating the Media*, 155–8.

companies to give a right of reply or to broadcast a correction or apology, but can only publicize its findings.[22]

Fifthly, wavelengths for broadcasting were limited. This purely technical consideration sharply distinguishes broadcasting from newspapers, and justifies a higher level of regulation. In theory, if not in practice, there is nothing to prevent any number of newspapers being published simultaneously. The only controlling mechanism needed is that of market forces. This is not true of broadcasting. Some control over the allocation of wavelengths is needed in order to ensure that there are sufficient for all legitimate broadcasters. In the USA, the shortage of broadcasting wavelengths has been held to justify limiting the First Amendment rights of broadcasters, allowing the Federal Communications Commission (FCC) to exercise a rulemaking and regulatory function over broadcasting.[23]

A form of regulation designed to cater for the technical problems of available wavelengths in crowded airwaves, and to enable some control to be imposed over quality and propriety of programmes which can now easily be beamed across frontiers, is the European Convention on Transfrontier Television, which most European states have now signed.

In two recent cases, the European Court of Human Rights has had to consider the relationship between restrictions imposed on trans-border broadcasting and the guarantee of freedom of expression under the European Convention on Human Rights. This is a problem which could simply not have been foreseen when the ECHR was drafted, so some creative interpretation has been necessary in order to make it compatible with technological developments. Article 10(1) of the Convention recognizes the right of states to impose licensing systems on broadcasting, television, and cinema enterprises, and Article 10(2) allows interference with freedom of expression to be justified in certain circumstances. In the first case, *Groppera Radio AG and others* v. *Switzerland*,[24] the Swiss Federal Council adopted an Ordinance in 1983 which prohibited Swiss cable companies, which needed a licence to rebroadcast programmes, from rebroadcasting programmes from transmitters which did not comply with the relevant international agreements on telecommunications and radio. A cable co-operative, which had been receiving and rebroadcasting programmes from an Italian transmitter, was ordered to stop doing so, and was unsuccessful in its attempts to challenge the order in the Swiss Federal Court. When the case reached Strasbourg, the European Commission of Human Rights by a narrow majority held that there had been an interference with the rights of the co-operative and the owners of the Italian transmitter (Groppera Radio AG), and that this could not be

[22] Gibbons, *Regulating the Media*, 149–55.

[23] *National Broadcasting Co.* v. *US*, 319 US 190 (1943).

[24] Eur. Ct. HR, Judgment of 28 Mar. 1990, Series A, vol. 173.

justified under Article 10(2). The case was referred to the Court, which agreed that there had been an interference contrary to Article 10(1). However, by sixteen votes to three the Court decided that the interference was justifiable under Article 10(2). The order had had two aims which were compatible with the Convention: compliance with and enforcement of the international arrangements on telecommunications (the prevention of disorder is an object which extends to disorder in the ether as well as on the ground), and the protection of the rights of others (the licensees who were complying with the order). Furthermore, the order was within the margin of appreciation left to states in deciding whether the order was necessary in a democratic society. Although Groppera argued that it was not a Swiss company, and therefore should not be subject to damage from Swiss law, it was reasonable (having regard to the international nature of broadcasting) for the Swiss authorities to treat Groppera, which had been transmitting into Switzerland from just over the Italian–Swiss border, as being in reality a Swiss station transmitting to Switzerland, which had positioned itself outside Switzerland solely in order to evade the controls imposed, consistently with the Convention, on Swiss enterprises.

This shows a readiness on the part of the Court to take account of the international nature of (particularly) satellite broadcasting, and to interpret the Convention in the light of the purpose of other international covenants designed to enable governments of states to regulate the material reaching their countries for rebroadcasting, so long as the principles applied are in accord with those in Article 10(2).

The second case, however, shows the limits of the margin of appreciation. In *Autronic AG* v. *Switzerland*,[25] the Swiss regulatory authority, the Post and Telecommunications Authority, had in 1982 refused to grant Autronic a licence to show at an exhibition a Soviet television programme received directly from a Soviet telecommunications satellite, on the ground that it could not grant authorization unless the Soviet authorities had given their express agreement to the rebroadcast. The Federal Court refused to entertain an application for a public-law appeal, on the ground that Autronic had no direct economic interest which was worth protecting. In this case, the European Court of Human Rights, in agreement with the Commission, held that there had been a violation of Article 10, which could not be justified under Article 10(2). Although the objects pursued were legitimate (preventing disorder in broadcasting, and preventing the disclosure of confidential information), the refusal of permission was not necessary in a democratic society, because the programme had not contained confidential information, it had been

---

[25] Eur. Ct. HR, Judgment of 22 May 1990, Series A, vol. 178.

intended for public consumption in the Soviet Union, and it had been transmitted by the Soviets via the satellite in uncoded form. Accordingly, the refusal of permission fell outside the margin of appreciation allowed to states. As a result of the ruling, Swiss law was amended to bring it into line with the Convention.[26]

These decisions illustrate four features of the way the European Convention on Human Rights applies to broadcasting. First, the right to freedom of expression under Article 10(1) applies to 'everyone'— companies and other agencies with legal personality as well as natural persons. Secondly, it is legitimate for the state to limit freedom of expression by broadcasters and telecommunicators so far as is necessary to give effect to a licensing system, subject to the manner of the restrictions being compatible with Article 10(2). Thirdly, one of the legitimate objects of a system of control is to give effect to international treaties on broadcasting, in order to preserve the international order relating to this field of activity. Fourthly, in deciding how best to do this, states have a margin of appreciation which, as usual under Article 10, is substantial but not unconfined.

A further legitimate object of national regulation is to protect the intellectual property rights of programme-makers and broadcasters. It is permissible, on this ground, for organizations to prevent people from getting access to programmes without paying appropriate licence fees. One way of preventing this is to encode programme transmissions, and to restrict access to decoders to people who pay the fee. In the UK, this has been held to be a legitimate way of enforcing rights under the Copyright, Designs and Patents Act 1988, section 298.[27]

For these political, cultural, and technical reasons, communication over the airwaves is subject to regulation of a sort which it would have been unthinkable to apply to printed publications at any time after the late eighteenth century, save in time of war. It is, however, important to limit the control which politicians in or out of government can exercise over this important medium of communication. The need to preserve the accessibility of the broadcasting media to a diversity of opinions, and to protect it against totalitarian control, assumed constitutional significance in countries with constitutions which guarantee the right to free expression, and which rely on the courts to prevent the concentration of control and powers of censorship in the hands of politicians. Professor Barendt has pointed out that the controlling role of the courts is evident in countries such as post-war Italy and the Federal Republic of Germany. Under such constitutions, the constitutional courts were able to play a

---

[26] Committee of Ministers, Resolution DH (91) 26, adopted on 18 Oct. 1991, appendix.

[27] *BBC Enterprises Ltd.* v. *Hi-Tech Xtravision Ltd.* [1991] 3 All ER 257, HL.

part in the development of broadcasting regulation, ensuring that central government intervention in broadcasting policy was not excessive, that governmental discretion was cabined, that private broadcasting stations, when permitted, were regulated to ensure freedom of expression, and that free expression on public services was secured.[28] The responsibility placed in the hands of judges in these countries illustrates the relativity of questions of legitimacy. It makes no sense to ask whether it is legitimate in a democracy for judges to exercise such authority over the structure of broadcasting, until one knows more about the circumstances in which the democracy came into being, the resulting constitutional ethos, and the alternative to giving control to the judges. The issue is not simply whether the exercise of power by judges is legitimate, but whether it is more legitimate than the exercise of similar powers by (for example) politicians. The answer to the latter question depends on how much one feels entitled to trust politicians, given the country's recent history.

(4) Regulating control over broadcasting organizations

In the field of television franchises, the current system (much criticized in the light of the first round of franchise allocations in 1991) is for the Independent Television Commission, a body largely independent of government, to allocate licences on a regional basis to the highest bidder in a silent auction, subject to being satisfied that the highest bidder would be capable of maintaining an adequate range and quality of programmes.[29] There are restrictions on the people who are to be allowed to hold franchises: they must satisfy the Commission that they are 'fit and proper' people for the job, and the Commission is to try as far as possible to ensure that the franchise holder is a national of a member state of the European Community, and is not a political or religious body or an advertising agency. In addition, the Commission is to avoid, as far as possible, allowing control of interests in the franchise holders from becoming concentrated in too few hands, or falling into the hands of people who hold controlling interests in newspapers. This anti-monopolistic approach is designed to maintain whatever scope there may be for expression of a variety of views through the media.

The BBC is controlled by its Governors, with cash controls imposed by government by way of its power to set the licence fee from which the

[28] Eric Barendt, 'The Influence of the German and Italian Constitutional Courts on their National Broadcasting Systems' [1991] *PL* 93–115. Privatization of broadcasting in France is among the matters discussed by Tony Prosser, 'Golden Shares: Industrial Policy by Stealth' [1988] *PL* 413–31 at p. 422; see also Decision 88–248 of 17 Jan. 1989 of the *Conseil Constitutionnel*.

[29] Broadcasting Act 1990, s. 2(2)(*b*).

BBC derives the lion's share of its income.[30] As the Governors are appointed by government, this leaves them open to suspicion that they are subject to political pressure and patronage. This was particularly acutely felt when the current Chairman of the Governors, Mr Marmaduke Hussey, was appointed by the Conservative government: he was a well-known supporter of Conservative policies, and this, together with the resignation of the Director-General, Alistair Milne, soon afterwards, led to fears that the independence of the BBC was under threat.[31] It is hard to regulate a service in the public interest (as seen by government) without impinging on its political independence.

(5) Control over content: broadcasting

By comparison with the *laissez-faire* attitude of successive modern governments to newspaper proprietors, the modern media—broadcasting of wireless and television programmes by radio, satellite, and cable, and the distribution of video recordings—are heavily regulated. Many of these matters, including controls in the interests of state security, are examined in the chapters which follow. Here, we should note five matters.

(i) *The requirement of balance*. The BBC, under its Charter and Licence and Agreement, and the independent broadcasters, under section 6(1) (*b*) and (*c*) of the Broadcasting Act 1990, are obliged to ensure that news is purveyed with due accuracy and impartiality, and that matters of political or industrial controversy, or concerned with current public policy, are treated with due impartiality. Independent television companies are bound by rules setting out what is required by the impartiality requirement, promulgated by the Independent Television Commission in its Code of Practice.[32] Expressions of partisan views are permitted, but opposed viewpoints should also be given sufficient prominence for any bias to be balanced out over the whole of the programme or series of programmes. The Commission is to exert itself to ensure that the personal views of licence holders and broadcasters on matters of political or industrial controversy, or which relate to current public policy, are not expressed on the air.[33] This is designed to prevent the proprietors of broadcasting stations from using the airwaves in the partisan way in which newspaper proprietors are allowed to use the columns of their newspapers.

The impartiality requirement imposes restrictions on the right to free

---

[30] Wireless Telegraphy Act 1949, ss. 1 and 2.

[31] See Gibbons, *Regulating the Media*, 50–8, 140–2.

[32] Broadcasting Act 1990, s. 6(3), (5). Similar provisions are made in respect of the Independent Radio Authority under Part III of the Act.

[33] Broadcasting Act 1990, s. 6(5).

expression of proprietors and operators of independent broadcasting services which would not be acceptable if applied to privately owned newspapers. Both here and in the USA, this has in the past been justified by reference to the special features of broadcasting: its pervasiveness and the limited number of broadcasting outlets. The tension between the rights of broadcasters and those of people wanting to be broadcast, and the influence of models of the market in ideas on the solution to it, can be illustrated by looking at the position in the USA, where the argument takes place in the context of First Amendment rights to freedom of speech. Insisting on impartiality and balance within programmes helps to secure access to the media for a wide variety of viewpoints. This was formalized in the USA as a recognized limitation on the First Amendment rights of broadcasters. The regulatory body, the Federal Communications Commission (FCC), developed a principle in 1949 requiring the broadcasters to give fair coverage to each side of the argument on any public issue (the 'fairness doctrine').[34] The Supreme Court later held this restriction to be compatible with the First Amendment, as it served to advance the free speech rights of those who might otherwise be denied access to an important forum for expressing their views: in effect, the regulation bolstered the market-place of ideas in a setting where the market was imperfect, in that opportunities for access to it were artificially limited.[35] However, if market conditions changed, allowing a wider range of broadcasting outlets, the Court accepted that the position might be reconsidered.[36] The doctrine, in its application to private broadcasters, became a contentious political football: the Reagan administration considered that the market had changed its character, with many more broadcasting stations available than in 1949, and agitated for the abolition of the doctrine. Congress failed to respond, so in 1989 the FCC itself reversed the doctrine, holding it now to be a breach of the First Amendment rights of broadcasters. Congress is attempting to reintroduce the doctrine by legislation.[37]

In the UK, the number of channels is still far below that in the USA, and it remains plausible to argue that access to the media is best maintained by way of an impartiality requirement. Although there has never been a mechanical requirement of equal time being allocated to both sides of an argument on television, there was a judicial suggestion that the impartiality requirement might be breached where one side of an argument received three times as much air time as the other. *Wilson* v. *IBA*[38]

---

[34] 13 FCC 1246 (1949).   [35] *Red Lion Broadcasting Co.* v. *FCC*, 395 US 367 (1969).
[36] *FCC* v. *League of Women Voters of California*, 468 US 364 (1984) at pp. 377–8 nn. 11 and 12.
[37] Louis Fisher, *American Constitutional Law* (New York: McGraw-Hill, 1990), 549.
[38] 1979 S.C. 351.

concerned television broadcasts by political parties in the period of campaigning leading to the referendum in Scotland on Scottish devolution under the Scotland Act 1978. Because of the attitudes taken by the various parties, the broadcasts on the issue planned by the independent companies would have given three times as much time to proponents of a 'No' vote as to advocates for a 'Yes' vote. The court granted an interim interdict to restrain the IBA from permitting the broadcasts pending trial of the action, on the ground that there was an arguable case of a breach of the impartiality requirement in the legislation governing independent television broadcasting. As noted in Chapter 12, however, this has not been held to require that equal (or indeed any) time be allotted to competing candidates in elections,[39] unlike the position in the USA, where Congress has legislated to provide that, where one political candidate receives time on the air, others must be allowed equal time.[40]

Fairness and impartiality requirements, while superficially attractive as ways of securing access to a limited market, are both difficult to apply and morally questionable. It is difficult to form an objective view about the presence of bias or partiality in presentation over a period. There are regular complaints that broadcasters are politically biased. All political parties appear to feel that they have been denied a fair crack of the whip in terms of time allocated to them, or attitudes of interviewers and reporters. It is always hard to know how far such claims are justified, and how far they merely represent politicians' hypersensitivity. The government is particularly likely to feel aggrieved about the substance of reporting, since one of the jobs of reporters and interviewers is to probe and challenge official versions of events. The impartiality requirement is not a complete solution to this. Furthermore, insisting on impartiality involves regulation of content of expression which is ideologically questionable, in that it assumes that all expression is in some sense equally valuable. This view was questioned in Chapter 12 above. It sometimes has a moral cost, in terms of truth and free expression. As Baker has written: 'Balance may often be good. But it is not the philosophy of a first amendment that protects liberty and dissent. And sometimes it is misguided. Sometimes, some positions are just wrong.'[41] Nevertheless, it is not necessarily true, as Baker suggests, that the consequence will tend to be bland, with reporters adopting middle-of-the-road positions on divisive issues. It may have the effect of putting the position of each side clearly before the other, with a net gain to the quality of the democratic decision-making process on the issue.

---

[39] *Grieve v. Douglas Home* 1965 SC 315; *R. v. Broadcasting Complaints Commission, ex parte Owen* [1985] QB 1153, [1985] 2 All ER 522, DC.
[40] 47 USC, s. 315(*a*) (1982).
[41] C. Edwin Baker, *Human Liberty and Freedom of Speech* (New York and Oxford: Oxford UP, 1989), 260.

In the UK, the matter of impartiality is not subject to judicial decision. Instead, the Codes of Practice produced by the ITC and the BBC hold sway, and the Broadcasting Complaints Commission can adjudicate on complaints about unfairness.

(ii) *The Broadcasting Complaints Commission*. This was established in 1981, and now has statutory responsibility for considering and adjudicating on complaints of partiality, unjust or unfair treatment of people in programmes, and of unwarranted invasions of privacy. It consists of people who are unconnected with broadcasting, but are appointed by the government. The BCC can entertain complaints about any licensed broadcaster, but has no jurisdiction over matters of taste. It has jurisdiction to consider complaints about unfairness in the treatment of political parties, but has a discretion as to whether to investigate a complaint. It is not required to do so if it would thereby be involved in going beyond an assessment of whether a particular broadcast was fair to the complainant, and into a consideration of the political fairness of broad editorial policies.[42] The Commission has been criticised for being out of touch with some of the needs of programme makers, but has accepted that programmes must not be required to be bland, that interviewers must challenge the assertions and views of those whom they interview in order to make the process useful, and fairness must be judged on the basis of an overview of the entire programme, not by picking out small parts of it. Nevertheless, it has been argued that the Commission is over-tender to the claims of rogues and powerful individuals or organizations to fairness of treatment, demanding standards of natural justice which would never be imposed by a court on judicial review and which effectively undermine public-interest investigative journalism on television.[43] The Commission has no power to force a broadcasting body to alter a programme or policy, or to order an apology or right of reply, but can require broadcasters to announce the results of adjudications, and to make corrections where necessary.[44]

(iii) *The role of the Governors of the BBC, the ITC, and the BSC in matters of taste*. Under the Codes of Practice issued by the BBC and the ITC, there are guidelines on the types of programmes which should not be broadcast (e.g. films rated R18 by the British Board of Film Classification), and times when they should be broadcast so as to avoid an excessive risk of causing offence or harming children who might be

[42] R. v. *Broadcasting Complaints Commission, ex parte Owen* [1985] QB 1153, [1985] 2 All ER 522, DC.

[43] Geoffrey Robertson, *Freedom, the Individual and the Law* 6th edn (Harmondsworth, Penguin, 1989), 247–8.

[44] Broadcasting Act 1990, Part V; Gibbons, *Regulating the Media*, 149–55.

watching. The Governors of the BBC have a potential role as censors of all programmes to be broadcast. Before the Broadcasting Act 1990, the Governors of the IBA exercised a similar role, forced on them against their wills by the decision of the Court of Appeal.[45] This led to accusations that political appointees with no experience of programme making were becoming too closely involved in editorial and programme making decisions.[46] As regards the independent sector, this threat has been partly removed by the Broadcasting Act 1990. Section 11(3) makes it clear that there is never to be an obligation on the ITC to watch programmes in advance of their broadcast, reversing the effect of the earlier Court of Appeal decision; and there has clearly never been a legal obligation on the BBC Governors to act as programme censors. On the other hand, it would probably not be unlawful for them to do so, going beyond a monitoring role.

Matters of portrayal of violence, sexual conduct, and taste and decency, also fall within the jurisdiction of the Broadcasting Standards Council (BSC).[47] This body has no power to force a broadcasting body to alter a programme or to order an apology or right of reply. These matters are essentially left to the good sense and sensitivity of the broadcasters themselves, reflecting the caution which is rightly shown over interfering with editorial freedom.

(iv) *The Home Secretary's 'veto' power.* The Home Secretary has power to issue a notice ordering the holder of a broadcasting licence to broadcast any announcement specified in the notice, or to refrain from broadcasting any matter, or classes of matter, specified in the notice. Before requiring an announcement to be broadcast, he must be satisfied that it is expedient in connection with his functions as Secretary of State. There is no such condition in connection with veto power.[48] These provisions put great power into the hands of a government minister. They could be used to stifle political reporting, and have indeed been used in 1927 and 1955 in short-lived attempts to prevent controversial broadcasts or undermine the role of Parliament as the nation's debating chamber on political matters. Yet the veto power has been used only five times, and has not been employed for party political advantage. It is likely that a notice

[45] *A.-G. ex rel. McWhirter* v. *I.B.A.* [1973] 1 QB 629, CA.

[46] *Report of the Committee on the Future of Broadcasting* (Chairman: Lord Annan) Cmnd. 6753 (1977); Robertson, *Freedom, Individual and Law*, 236–40.

[47] Broadcasting Act 1990, Part VI; Gibbons, *Regulating the Media*, 155–8.

[48] These obligations are imposed on the BBC by its Licence and Agreement, Cmnd. 8233, cl. 13, and on the independent licence holders under the Broadcasting Act 1990, s. 10(1), (3). The licence holders may, but need not, announce that the notice has been issued: s. 10(2), (4).

issued for party advantage would be subject to judicial review on the grounds of irrationality and improper purposes.

At present, only one notice is in force. It was made by the Home Secretary in 1988 to prevent statements by members of the IRA being broadcast in the voice of the spokesmen themselves, as part of the drive to limit the terrorists' access to publicity. It is of limited effect, as statements can be read by a newsreader, or (on television) an actor can dub the words over a film of the spokesman speaking. This has led to criticism, and to challenge in an application for judicial review, on two grounds which seem to be mutually inconsistent: first, that the notice is irrational because it does not go far enough to be effective in its aims; and, secondly, that it interferes with the broadcasters' freedom of expression in a way which is disproportionate to the aim of maintaining national security and preventing crime, and so infringes Article 10 of the European Convention on Human Rights. The challenge in the English courts failed. In *R. v. Secretary of State for the Home Department, ex parte Brind*[49] the House of Lords was not prepared to hold that the Home Secretary had reached a conclusion which no reasonable Home Secretary could have reached in deciding that it was necessary to introduce the ban in order to combat terrorism. Nor were their Lordships willing to hold that the ban was disproportionate to the aim pursued, or that the Secretary of State had failed to take account of a relevant consideration in not applying Article 10 of the European Convention on Human Rights. The decisions of the Secretary of State and the House of Lords are, at least, not incompatible with the Convention: in Ireland, a rather more extensive ban was imposed on the media in relation to reporting on terrorist organizations, and the European Commission of Human Rights held an application to Strasbourg to be inadmissible in *Purcell v. Ireland*.[50]

(v) *Informal pressure.* One reason why it has rarely been necessary for Home Secretaries to invoke their formal veto powers is the ease with which informal pressure can be brought to bear. There has been considerable pressure applied by the Conservatives during the 1980s. This has often happened in respect of the reporting of incidents involving the security forces in Northern Ireland, or carrying out duties elsewhere combating terrorism. The Conservative Party has made it clear that its members consider that the media, or elements within them, are biassed against the armed forces and the security forces. To give but one example, in 1988 Sir Geoffrey Howe, then Foreign Secretary, attempted to persuade the Chairman of the IBA, Lord Thomson of Monifieth, to

[49] *R. v. Secretary of State for the Home Dept., ex parte Brind* [1991] 1 AC 696, [1991] 1 All ER 720, HL.
[50] Application No. 15404/89, Decision of 16 Apr. 1991.

postpone showing *Death on the Rock* (a programme about the killing of three IRA terrorists by British security forces in Gibraltar) until after the conclusion of the inquest on the three in Gibraltar. The Foreign Secretary suggested that the broadcast might prejudice the result of the inquest, or lead to contamination of evidence, causing witnesses to change their stories.[51] This approach was rejected by the IBA, and the programme was broadcast, but an orchestrated campaign followed from the government and the Conservative Party alleging bias by the IBA. An independent report largely exonerated the producers and programme makers, and concluded:[52] 'Whatever view is taken of the state of public opinion and the legitimacy of Government intervention, the making and screening of *Death on the Rock* proved that freedom of expression can prevail in the most extensive, and the most immediate, of all the means of mass communication.'

There has also been a steady pressure applied by the Conservatives to the broadcasting authorities over alleged political bias in reporting the news and making current affairs programmes. Thinly veiled threats that the BBC will suffer when its licence is due for renewal in 1996 were made before the 1992 general election campaign. Happily, they did not appear to have cowed broadcasters; at any rate, the Conservative Party claimed to have noticed evidence of bias against it in the reporting of the campaign.

(5) Self-regulation and the D notice system[53]

One of the ways in which the press displays its sense of responsibility towards the state is its participation in a system of informal regulation of the content of publications in the interests of defence. The Defence Press and Broadcasting Committee (DPBC) is a joint committee of the Ministry of Defence, publishers, and broadcasters, which offers advice on proposed publications and broadcasts.

The Committee is concerned with damage to national security. Specifically, the DPBC reviews whether the publication or broadcast contains information which falls into categories which the government considers it necessary to keep secret. If it concludes that a publication threatens national security within one of its areas of concern, it suggests changes. If the advice is not accepted, it may issue a D notice to the editor, publisher, or broadcasting body. There is one D notice, in a standard

[51] Lord Windlesham and Richard Rampton QC, *The Windlesham/Rampton Report on Death on the Rock* (London: Faber & Faber, 1989), ch. 11.
[52] Ibid., 145.
[53] Douglas Fairley, 'D Notices, Official Secrets and the Law' (1990) 10 *O. J. of Legal Studies* 430–40.

form, for each area of the Committee's responsibility as defined (fairly broadly) by the Ministry of Defence. At present, there are eight categories of D notice: (1) defence plans, operational capability, state of readiness and training; (2) defence equipment; (3) nuclear weapons and equipment; (4) radio and radar transmissions; (5) cyphers and communications; (6) British security and intelligence services; (7) war precautions and civil defence; (8) photography, etc., of defence establishments and installations.

There are two main ways in which the DPBC works. In the first, a publisher or broadcaster approaches the Committee, through its secretary (who is normally a senior officer in the armed forces, currently a rear admiral) and asks whether the Committee feels that any changes are needed in the publication to avoid damaging the national interest. The second method is for contact to be initiated by the secretary to the Committee, who receives information from publishers and others—including reading *The Publisher* magazine—about forthcoming books and programmes. When he hears of a publication or programme which, he thinks, might fall within one of the categories of material with which the committee is concerned, he may write to the publisher or broadcaster, saying that it is possible that the publication may contain information within the scope of one of the categories and offering to advise on whether it does so if the broadcaster or publisher wishes to supply a copy of the book. The tone of the letter is helpful and businesslike. There are no threats. Where the publisher is one who does not normally participate in the D notice system, copies of the relevant D notice and of the *General Introduction to the D Notice System*[54] are enclosed.

Participation in the process is entirely voluntary, as are any changes which are made in the text or programme as a result of the Committee's advice (which is only advice: it has no legal force). The Committee will not give a security clearance; it has no power to do so. If it considers that a programme or publication does not threaten national security, the Secretary writes to inform the publisher, editor, or broadcaster that he does not consider that any change is necessary to avoid potential prejudice to national security.

The fact that the Committee's advice has no legal force has both an up side and a down side from the point of view of a publisher, editor, or broadcaster. The positive aspect is that the editor commits no criminal offence or tort merely by virtue of publishing in defiance of advice from the Committee. As the whole process is voluntary, and the press and broadcasters are strongly represented on the Committee (albeit heavily

[54] This is a very informative document; the text is reproduced in S. H. Bailey, D. J. Harris and B. L. Jones, *Civil Liberties Cases and Materials*, 3rd edn. (London: Butterworths, 1991) 431–32.

dependent on advice from the Ministry of Defence and service members) it is a form of self-regulation. The negative side of this is that a notification that no advice is considered necessary does not assure the editor, broadcaster, or publisher that the publication will not attract civil or criminal sanctions. This is made clear in the Committee's *General Introduction to the D Notice System*, paragraph 8 of which states,

There is no direct relationship between the D Notice system and the Official Secrets Acts. Nothing in the D Notice system relieves an editor of his responsibilities under the Acts, though D Notices have a useful function in reminding editors that publication of the information which they protect could contravene the provisions of the Act.

The D notices therefore have a warning function, but the fact that no D notice has been issued, or advice given, does not exonerate an editor. The Committee does not perform a judicial function, and is a consultative, negotiating body between the Ministry and the press and broadcasting media. Nevertheless, there is a substantial overlap between the Acts and the D notices. For example, D notice No. 6, *British Security and Intelligence Services*, after stating that the security and intelligence services must work as far as possible in conditions of secrecy (a proposition which many would dispute), asserts that the publication of detailed information about their activities or methods, or the disclosure of identities, is likely to prejudice present and past operations, and make day-to-day work more difficult. It goes on to request (this is, after all, a voluntary system) that nothing should be published without reference to the secretary about *inter alia* specific operations, how operational methods are applied, identities of service employees and their families (although the name and personal details concerning the new Director of MI5 were released, in a remarkable moment of openness, in December 1991), the addresses and telephone numbers of the services, organizational structures, numerical strengths, training, and technical advances. The list of matters covered is so extensive that it would be surprising if many matters were excluded which could possibly be caught by the Official Secrets Acts.

Similarly, the D notice system confers no defence on participants against actions by the government for restraint of publication, or account of profits, on the ground of breach of confidence. When in 1987 the BBC was planning to broadcast a radio series, *My Country Right or Wrong*, exploring aspects of national security in the light of the *Spycatcher* litigation, the producer sought advice from the secretary of DPBC, who indicated that no advice was necessary. Despite this, the government sought, and obtained, injunctions restraining the BBC from broadcasting the series on the ground of breach of confidence.[55] Although the injunctions

[55] See Fairley, 'D Notices', above.

were subsequently lifted when the government acknowledged that the programmes were no threat to security, the BBC was subjected to a great deal of expense and trouble, and the programmes were long delayed, some being broadcast only in 1991 by Channel 4, the BBC having apparently got cold feet.

This lack of fit between the advice (or lack of it) given, and D notices issued (or not), by the Secretary and the Committee on the one hand, and the actions of government in pursuing legal remedies to restrain or penalize publication on the other, has brought the D notice system into some disrepute. Editors and publishers wonder what benefit they obtain from seeking and complying with advice from the Committee. The secretary has been reported as saying that his advice concerns a threat to national security, not whether there is a breach of confidence. This is undoubtedly true. If one wanted advice on the latter point, one would be unlikely to seek it from a rear admiral at the Ministry of Defence, or a committee made up of publishers and defence officials. On the other hand, it would be useful if the Committee could speak for the Department, instead of representing a compromise between different interest groups. It would then be able to advise an editor whether the Department intended to take legal proceedings in the event of the broadcast or publication going ahead. What is unhelpful in the present scheme is not that the Committee and its secretary do not give legal advice, but that they cannot give advice about the way in which the Department intends to exercise its discretion to bring proceedings. Without such a power, the advice is likely to be of limited value to the publishing and broadcasting community, and is most useful to the Department in frightening off a certain number of possibly lawful publications behind closed doors, without the need for or benefit of a judicial hearing.[56] The collaborative, consultative nature of the D notice system, intended as its great virtue, is threatening to undermine it because of the limited value of the advice which it can give.

13.3 THE EXTENT OF PROTECTION FOR MEDIA FREEDOMS

Originally, freedom of the press related only to freedom to set up a printing press and to publish without prior restraint by the state. To some

---

[56] In relation to the newspaper publication of extracts from Anthony Cavendish's *Inside Intelligence* (privately printed in 1987), in respect of which the Secretary had given a 'no advice' intimation, the government's action for breach of confidence failed. However, the publishers were taken all the way to the House of Lords, and would probably have lost had the government's claim been based on the contents rather than the class of material into which the publication fell: *Lord Advocate* v. *The Scotsman Publications Ltd*. [1990] 1 AC 812, [1989] 2 All ER 852, HL.

extent, echoes of this minimalist approach continue to resonate in judicial pronouncements in England and Wales. For example, in *British Steel Corporation* v. *Granada Television Ltd.*[57] Lord Wilberforce said: 'Freedom of the press imports, generally, freedom to publish without precensorship, subject always to the laws relating to libel, official secrets, sedition and other recognised inhibitions.' This is an unduly narrow view, which reflects the failure of the UK to provide protection for freedom of expression, and the consequential freedom of judges and Parliament to limit press freedom more or less as they choose.

In the USA, where the First Amendment gives constitutional status to press freedom, and in the law of the European Convention on Human Rights, media freedom has a far wider connotation. It is understood to mean the rights of writers, publishers, and broadcasters to conduct their activities and purvey information and ideas, and to be protected when their scrutiny of government offends it. It means, also, the right of the public to a press which is independent of domination by government and private interests alike. However, it is still essentially a negative rather than positive right. In other words, it limits the range of circumstances and ways in which it is legitimate for public authorities to interfere with free expression. It usually places no obligation on the State to make available the facilities and materials which people need in order to take advantage of the freedom.[58]

There are, then, two distinct aspects to freedom of the press today so far as they bear on civil liberties: first, the extent of rights to obtain and communicate information and publish opinions; secondly, the scope of protections for journalists, publishers, and others against attack by government and others. This is subject to the framework provided in international law by Article 10 of the European Convention for the Protection of Human Rights and Fundamental Freedoms.[59]

[57] [1981] 1 All ER 417 at p. 455.

[58] Marshall points out that Art. 125 of the 1936 USSR Constitution did undertake to provide such materials and facilities, although this provision had limited practical operation: Geoffrey Marshall, 'Press Freedom and Free Speech Theory' [1992] *PL* at p. 40. On positive rights in England and Wales, see Ch. 12, s. 3, above.

[59] Art. 10 provides: '1. Everyone has the right to freedom of expression. This right shall include freedom to hold opinions and to receive and impart information and ideas without interference by public authority and regardless of frontiers. This article shall not prevent States from requiring the licensing of broadcasting, television or cinema enterprises. 2. The exercise of these freedoms, since it carries with it duties and responsibilities, may be subject to such formalities, conditions, restrictions or penalties as are prescribed by law and are necessary in a democratic society, in the interests of national security, territorial integrity or public safety, for the prevention of disorder or crime, for the protection of health or morals, for the protection of the reputation or rights of others, for preventing the disclosure of information received in confidence, or for maintaining the authority and impartiality of the judiciary.'

This section examines the extent to which the right to freedom of expression, as elaborated in Article 10(1), is protected in English law, concentrating on rights to receive and impart information.

(1) Freedom to receive information and ideas without interference by public authority and regardless of frontiers

Obtaining information is an essential part of the job of any investigative journalist, political commentator, or scholar, and is therefore an important incident of freedom of expression whatever rationale for the freedom is adopted. The general rule in English law is that a person is free to receive any information whatsoever, although there may be restrictions (discussed below) on the use which can be made of some types of information. Until the Official Secrets Act 1911, section 2, was repealed by the Official Secrets Act 1989, it was an offence for a person to receive certain types of secret material and information. Now, by contrast, a person who merely receives material commits no offence although, as discussed below, it may be an offence to under section 1(2) of the Official Secrets Act 1920 or under the 1989 Act to disclose or refuse to return the material. (The effects of the 1989 Act are explained in Chapter 14, below.)

Nevertheless, there remain substantial limitations on freedom of access to information. The main one is the ingrained secrecy which afflicts the civil service, and much of the rest of the British establishment, and which works to the advantage of governments by insulating them to some extent against the uncomfortable, albeit democratically important, experience of public scrutiny.[60] This attitude is not easy to reconcile with a functioning democracy. In a democracy, where the electorate is expected to monitor state organs and periodically express a view about their performance, there is no obvious reason why information about government should be treated as confidential unless there is a compelling reason for thinking that it is in the interests of the public that it should not be released. Allowing government departments to claim that information about the way they work is confidential stifles the flow of information to the public which is necessary in order for the behaviour of government to be scrutinized. Governments and other state organs usually have neither competitive, commercial interests nor personal or family interests.

This was partly recognized by the Croham Directive of 1977, in which the head of the home Civil Service recommended that the 'working assumption' should be that all background material to decisions will be published. This might have led to greater openness, but it was a modest

---

[60] Clive Ponting, *Secrecy in Britain* (Oxford: Basil Blackwell, 1990), ch. 4.

move, and the final decision was, inevitably, to lie with the minister responsible for the decision in question. It is ironic, but in keeping with the prevailing commitment to secrecy, that the Croham Directive itself, while recommending greater openness, was confidential, and became public only when leaked to *The Times*.[61] It is not surprising that the Directive has been largely ineffective in increasing the flow of information from the civil service to the public. The present government claims a greater commitment to openness than its predecessors; it will be instructive to watch developments, particularly as the Citizen's Charter[62] contains no commitment to increasing the flow of information from central government such as might permit an informed assessment of its performance.

In representative democracies the electorate needs information about what is being done in their name by their representatives, in order to make sensible choices at elections and make known concerns during the term of a Parliament. The media are the primary channels for such information. The importance of the press is recognized by government, which provides special briefings for lobby correspondents, and selective 'official leaks' from unattributable sources. However, it is not clear that these always provide the full story. Some newspapers now refuse to participate in the lobby system, suspecting that it is used to manipulate the press and ensure that material favourable to the government is published, rather than providing a full information service. More investigative forms of journalism, together with extensive use of the full range of information which is in the public domain, is at least an essential complement to lobby briefings if the press is to do its job of informing the public. In this role, the press is an agency of the public, and there is no reason why it should be allowed special access to information beyond that which would be available to any member of the public.

The news media at their best provide fora for assessing and criticising the work of government, Parliament, and other public bodies. In a system which allows the executive to dominate the House of Commons, an independent forum for public scrutiny of government is a valuable aid to open government. Here, the media perform a constitutional role in their own right. The free and open investigation and discussion of government by journalists helps to encourage proper and responsible government. They are performing functions akin to those of the parliamentary Select Committees, but independently of Parliament, and form a fourth estate of the realm, with real importance in permitting scrutiny of government. In this context it would be possible to justify giving special privileges to the media, in the same way that MPs enjoy privileges in relation to

---

[61] Ponting, *Secrecy in Britain*, 69.   [62] Cm. 1599 (1991).

speech within Parliament and, to some extent, with respect to information gathering.

Yet, apart from the pervasive aura of secrecy surrounding government, there are also numerous legal contraints on access to government-held information. First, anyone who seeks to persuade a person to disclose information or material in circumstances in which disclosure would be a crime, or who knowingly assists the disclosure, is guilty of conspiracy to commit, inciting, or aiding and abetting the offence. Secondly, there are restrictions on the availability of public records. The Public Records Act 1958 restricts the public availability of administrative or departmental records belonging to the monarch in the UK or elsewhere, in right of HM Government, including records of or held by any government department in the UK (other than registers of births, deaths, marriages, and adoptions), offices, commissions, and other bodies or establishments under HM Government in the UK.[63] Such records are preserved only if selected for permanent preservation, and are then not made available until, at the earliest, thirty years after 1 January in the year following the year in which the record was made. When the person making the selection considers that records which have been selected for preservation contain information which was obtained from members of the public under such conditions that it might constitute a breach of good faith to make the records available, the Lord Chancellor has an uncontrolled discretion to attach conditions to public access or to deny public access altogether for a further period. In addition, the government can sometimes make use of the law of breach of confidence to limit disclosure of information.

Despite some claims to the contrary,[64] these are not limited, principled restrictions on a general right to freedom of information. The processes of democratic accountability have been facilitated by legislation requiring that local–authority accounts and papers relating to meetings of authorities and their committees normally be open for public inspection.[65] The central government civil service is exhorted to greater openness by the Croham Directive, but this is not backed by legislation of the sort which applies to local government. The full weight of the law, criminal and civil, has been brought to bear on members of the civil service like Clive Ponting, or of the security services like Kathy Massiter and Peter Wright, who attempt to reveal alleged improprieties in the behaviour of ministers or their services.

[63] Public Record Act 1958, Sched. 1, para. 2(1). The Act does not apply to departments or bodies wholly or mainly concerned with Scottish affairs: ibid., para. 2(2).

[64] See e.g. *A.-G.* v. *Guardian Newspapers (No. 2)* [1988] 3 All ER 545 at pp. 640 *per* Lord Keith of Kinkel and 660 *per* Lord Goff of Chieveley.

[65] Local Government (Access to Information) Act 1985.

Unlike the USA, Canada, Australia, and New Zealand, we have no Freedom of Information (FOI) Act which might have the effect of creating a presumption in favour of openness. The arguments most often advanced against FOI (subject, of course, to restrictions for national security and the preservation of individuals' privacy) are (i) that it would be excessively expensive to operate, (ii) that it would interfere with the free exchange of ideas and information within government, and (iii) that it would undermine the constitutional doctrine of ministerial responsibility to Parliament, under which the minister is accountable for decisions, not the civil servants who give advice. Experience from other countries shows that these are not compelling objections.[66]

1. The cost is substantial when the system is used a great deal, and is only slightly offset by the fees which are charged (usually a basic fee, plus an hourly rate for the time spent on tracking down material requested and reviewing it to see whether any of it falls within categories exempted from disclosure). However, unquantifiable benefits flow from putting a FOI system in place: there are usually thought to be improvements in record-keeping practice and in the quality of service delivered and decisions made, which represent an efficiency improvement for government. It is a matter for judgement whether the gains are worth the cost.

2. The effect of FOI on candid discussions in government is also unquantifiable. Cabinet papers are normally exempt from disclosure under the legislation.

3. Canada, Australia, and New Zealand all have Westminster-style systems of government. To give an example of how this can be made compatible with FOI, Australia excluded from FOI access to material which would reveal the opinions expressed or advice given in the process of deliberation within government, except for purely factual information. With such an arrangement, there is no reason why ministerial responsibility should be compromised or free discussion inhibited.

---

[66] Detailed discussion of this subject falls outside the scope of this book. See Norman S. Marsh (ed.), *Public Access to Government-Held Information: a comparative symposium* (London: Stevens & Sons, 1987); Patrick Birkinshaw, *Freedom of Information: The Law, the Practice and the Ideal* (London: Weidenfeld & Nicolson, 1988), ch. 2. The paragraphs which follow have also benefited from an unpublished paper by Robert Hazell, 'Freedom of Information in Australia, Canada and New Zealand', presented to the 3rd Bristol Colloquium on Law and Politics, 1988; and Rodney Austin, 'Freedom of Information: The Constitutional Impact', in Jeffrey Jowell and Dawn Oliver (eds.), *The Changing Constitution*, 2nd edn. (Oxford: Clarendon Press, 1989), 409–50. On the working of Australia's Freedom of Information Act 1982, see the Australian Senate Standing Committee on Legal and Constitutional Affairs, *Freedom of Information Act 1982: Report on the Operation and Administration of the Freedom of Information Legislation* (Canberra: AGPS, 1987).

The institution of FOI could, therefore, lead to an important advance for the quality of public administration, as well as improving democratic processes by giving the press, and thereby, indirectly, the public, better information about the way in which the nation's government is carried on. It might reduce the need for civil service 'whistle-blowers' to reveal, without authority, excesses and illegalities committed by politicians and public servants. It would also assist in improving the quality of personal information which is held by government.

At the same time, it would be wrong to overestimate the potential effect of FOI. The use to which FOI is most often put is to obtain access to personal files, rather than to reveal the inner workings of government. Australian FOI legislation has not yet gone to the lengths of giving a right to the data subject to have records updated or corrected; as protection for personal information, at least, the limited UK legislation on personal records discussed in Chapter 8, where it applies, is in advance of that in Australia. Legislating for FOI is not a guarantee of open government. The latter relies on a changed ethos in government and public administration, which will not be achieved simply by passing legislation. The aspirations of FOI need to be accepted by the people in government and public administration before real change will occur. It is not coincidental that section 3 of the Australian Commonwealth's Freedom of Information Act 1982 and section 4 of New Zealand's Official Information Act 1982 set out the objectives of the Acts, and exhort all concerned to interpret the Acts purposively. Section 3 of the Australian Commonwealth's Act provides:

(1) The object of this Act is to extend as far as possible the right of the Australian community to access to information in the possession of the Government of the Commonwealth by

(a) making available to the public information about the operations of departments and public authorities and, in particular, ensuring that rules and practices affecting members of the public in their dealings with departments and public authorities are readily made available to persons affected by those rules and practices; and

(b) creating a general right of access to information in documentary form in the possession of Ministers, departments and public authorities, limited only by exceptions and exemptions necessary for the protection of essential public interests and the private and business affairs of persons in respect of whom information is collected and held by departments and public authorities.

(2) It is the intention of the Parliament that the provisions of this Act shall be interpreted so as to further the object set out in sub-section (1) and that any discretions conferred by this Act shall be exercised as far as possible so as to facilitate

and promote, promptly and at the lowest possible cost, the disclosure of information.

This turns on its head the assumption of a governmental right to secrecy. Only if a similar ethos of openness made headway in the UK, encouraged by a real commitment to the kinds of objectives set out in section 3 of the Australian Commonwealth's Act, would FOI legislation in the UK be likely to lead to a real movement towards openness in government. As in Australia, it is probable that, to be effective, a commitment to openness would need to precede the enactment of FOI legislation. If it does not exist, legislation alone probably will not produce it.

(2) Freedom to impart information and ideas without interference by public authority and regardless of frontiers

In principle, this freedom exists so far as it is not limited by law. Like other freedoms, it is residual. The issue, therefore, is the extent of the restrictions on the liberty in English law. A number of the most significant of these restrictions are discussed in Chapters 14 to 16, below. However, here it is appropriate to deal with one which is particularly important to the media, because of its pervasive implications for news reporting and the chilling effect on free expression of the financial consequences: the tort of defamation.[67]

The law of defamation operates to protect reputation, a legitimate ground, recognized under Article 10(2) of the European Convention on Human Rights, for restricting freedom of expression. A publication which lowers a person in the opinion of right-thinking people is defamatory, infringes the right to reputation, and attracts an award of damages. All legal persons, including corporate bodies, have a right to reputation, and so can normally sue in respect of statements which defame the corporation (as opposed to its officers). However, governmental bodies such as local authorities are not entitled to sue for defamation, because there is an overriding public interest in a democracy in uninhibited criticism of the organs of government.[68] Nevertheless, individual politicians and office holders may sue in respect of allegations of corruption or incompetence. This has the potential to stifle public debate and inhibit investigative journalism, and offers well known people a way to make some easy

---

[67] Colin Duncan and Brian Neill, *Defamation*, 2nd edn. (London: Butterworths, 1983); Eric Barendt, *Freedom of Speech*, (Oxford: Clarendon Press, 1987), ch. 6; Robertson and Nicol, *Media Law*, ch. 2.

[68] *Derbyshire County Council* v. *Times Newspapers Ltd*. [1993] 1 All ER 1011, HL.

money (only the well off can usually afford to sue for defamation, as legal aid is not available). To protect the public interest in open debate and freedom of information, therefore, English law provides certain defences against liability.

At common law, a defendant is allowed to 'justify' (that is, assert the truth of) the defamatory statement. If it is shown to be true, the plaintiff cannot obtain damages, because he has no right to a reputation which is better than he deserves. It is a defence to show that the defamatory statement was contained in a fair and accurate report of court or parliamentary proceedings. Such reports attract what is called 'qualified privilege': the publication is privileged against liability, but only so long as those responsible were not actuated by malice. This defence is particularly important for press reporters. Because it allows them to inform the public about what is being done in its name by officials, it fosters public accountability and appears to recognize the position of the press as a fourth estate, having a constitutional role as a channel of information between state officials and citizens. Another defence, conferred by the Defamation Act 1952, arises where the defendant can show that the publication consisted of fair comment, in good faith, on a matter of public interest. This is different from justification, in that it applies to expressions of opinion, not assertions of fact. It therefore finds its rationale, in freedom of speech terms, in the value of fostering public debate, rather than in the advancement of truth. (To some extent, however, these two aims overlap, since one of the reasons for encouraging free debate is the hope that it will maximize the chance of finding the correct or best answer to problems.)

A further factor which partially relieves the potential of the law of defamation to chill comment is the judicial discretion as to interim relief. English courts will not usually grant an interlocutory injunction to restrain publication of an alleged libel if the defendant is asserting qualified privilege for the publication, or intends to argue at trial that the allegation is true, because of the importance of leaving free speech unfettered until it is clear that an allegation is untrue and has infringed the plaintiff's rights.[69] This means that issuing a libel writ does not automatically lead to prior restraint of further discussion of the matter. However, an injunction may be granted in special circumstances. One is where further publication would give rise to a substantial risk of serious prejudice to the trial of the action. In such circumstances, publication would be a contempt of court attracting strict liability,[70] and the court will grant an injunction restraining it. As libel actions are regularly tried before a jury,

[69] *Bonnard* v. *Perryman* [1891] 2 Ch. 269, CA, at pp. 284–5 *per* Lord Coleridge CJ.
[70] Contempt of Court Act 1981, s. 2; see below.

there is likely to be a substantial risk of prejudice if the allegations are repeated in, for example, a mass circulation popular newpaper, but the degree of risk and the seriousness of the prejudice will be affected by the likely time lag between the publication and the expected commencement of the trial of the action.[71] Another situation in which prior restraint may be allowed is where the defendant can be shown to be proposing, dishonestly and maliciously, to publish the material knowing that it is untrue.[72]

In some other jurisdictions, gagging writs are rather more freely available. For example, in some of the Australian states (New South Wales, Queensland, and Tasmania, as well as the Australian Capital Territory) truth is no defence unless, as well as being true, the publication is for the public benefit (in Queensland, Tasmania, and the ACT) or related to a matter of public interest (in New South Wales).[73] Furthermore, courts in Australia, while respecting rights to freedom of speech and publication,[74] tend to be slightly less reluctant than those in England to grant injunctions restraining publication of alleged libels pending trial.[75] There are historical reasons for this: when the country was a penal colony, the law of libel was designed to prevent people raking up a convict's past, perhaps long after he had served his sentence and become a respectable member of society. The defamation action there protects the right to a fresh start, or to protect recent reputation against the past. However, the effect has been that, in law, the right to a fresh start for convicted criminals who have served their sentences, a private interest, outweighs the public interest in freedom of information about public figures. For example, it made it easier for Sir Joh Bjelke-Petersen, the former premier of Queensland, to suppress publication of information concerning corruption and incompetence in the government of Queensland, until it was finally brought into the open by a Royal Commission of Inquiry (the Fitzgerald Inquiry).[76]

[71] *Attorney-General* v. *News Group Newspapers Ltd.* [1987] QB 1, [1986] 2 All ER 833, CA (allegations about Mr Ian Botham's behaviour while on an England cricket tour to New Zealand; eleven-month delay between publication and likely trial made it inappropriate to grant injunction).

[72] *Quartz Hill Consolidated Mining Co.* v. *Beall* (1882) Ch. D. 501, CA; *Harakas* v. *Baltic Mercantile and Shipping Exchange Ltd* [1982] 1 WLR 958, [1982] 2 All ER 701, CA.

[73] See R. P. Balkin and J. L. R. Davis, *Law of Torts* (Sydney: Butterworths, 1991), 580–1, 585–6.

[74] *Church of Scientology of California Inc.* v. *Readers' Digest Services Pty. Ltd.* [1980] 1 NSWLR 344.

[75] See *National Mutual Life Association of Australasia Ltd.* v. *GTV Corporation Pty. Ltd.* [1989] VR 747; *Chappell* v. *TCN Channel Nine Pty. Ltd.* (1988) 14 NSWLR 153; Balkin and Davis, *Law of Torts*, 620–1.

[76] *Report of a Commission of Inquiry Pursuant to Orders in Council* (Brisbane: Queensland Government Printer, 1989).

Despite the various defences and the judges' reluctance to grant interim injunctions restraining publication, which make the tort of defamation less of a scourge of the press in England than in (for example) Queensland, there are objections to it from a civil libertarian standpoint. The main objection is that, despite the various defences, the threat of an action inhibits free comment. Public figures, who depend for their livelihoods on publicity, may obtain substantial damages when the publicity is bad rather than good, unless the newspaper can establish a defence. Juries have recently shown a tendency to award extraordinarily large sums in damages to public figures in libel actions, examples being the recent awards to Jeffrey Archer (£500,000), Mrs Sutcliffe, the former wife of the Yorkshire Ripper (£600,000, reduced by a settlement between the parties to £60,000 following a successful appeal on quantum), and Esther Rantzen, the instigator of Childline (£250,000 for a libel concerning an alleged cover-up in relation to an informant's offences). Even where the newspaper knows or believes that the report is true, or that a comment is fair, it might be unwilling to risk trying to prove it. It can very difficult to establish an allegation on the balance of probabilities. Informants may be unwilling to be identified or testify (a special rule protects newpapers against orders to disclose their sources in defamation actions), and they might not be believed against the word of the public figure in court. Furthermore, if a newspaper tries to establish the truth of its allegations and fails, the attempt is likely to aggravate the damages. In 1972, Tony Weir criticized the rule allowing public authorities to bring actions for defamation,[77] and the Faulks Committee recommended restricting the right of public authorities to sue.[78] Only now have the judges to a limited extent acted on the recommendation in the *Derbyshire County Council* case (above, n. 68).

In the USA, by contrast, the Supreme Court has long held that the First Amendment to the Constitution, which prohibits any abridgement of freedom of the press, restricts liability for defaming public figures to situations in which the defamer can be shown to have acted maliciously.[79] The decision reflected the 'profound national commitment to the principle that debate on public issues should be uninhibited, robust and wide open, and that it may well include vehement, caustic, and sometimes sharply unpleasant attacks on government and national and public officials'.[80]

This difference in approach is instructive, because it shows how complex is the exercise of balancing the rights which conflict when setting

[77] J. A. Weir, 'Local Authority v. Critical Ratepayer—A Suit in Defamation' [1972A] CLJ 238.
[78] *Report of the Committee on Defamation* (Chairman: Mr Justice Faulks), Cmnd. 5909 (1975), paras. 332 ff.
[79] *New York Times* v. *Sullivan* 376 US 254 (1964).
[80] Ibid. at p. 270 *per* Brennan J.

the scope of liability for defamation. It is obvious that freedom of expression is to be balanced against rights to reputation; that is clearly recognized in Article 10(2) of the European Convention on Human Rights. But the special rule in the USA requiring public figures to prove malice appears to show that freedom of expression has greater weight, and the right to a personal reputation lesser weight, when the expression concerns public figures than when it is about private citizens. Two factors contribute to this. There is a significant public interest in the behaviour of those who hold or seek public office. Democracy requires that the electorate should have full information about candidates for office. One might wonder why this should lead to a restriction of defamation liability where it is open to a defendant to justify a publication on the ground that it is true. However, the difficulty of establishing that a statement is true, and the risk that fear of defamation actions might inhibit people from publishing the truth about public figures, could justify a special restriction on liability. The argument is based on rule utilitarian principles: a rule which facilitates the free flow of opinions and information is likely to be less harmful than other rules. But there is another factor which runs parallel with that. Those who hold themselves out as public officials or potential leaders seek publicity, and it can plausibly be thought that they should accept the risk of damage arising from innocently mistaken publicity, though not malicious falsehoods. After all, politicians can benefit from inaccurately complimentary reports, so they should take the rough with the smooth and bear the risk that some reports will be misleadingly, but innocently, derogatory. This, however, is not a view which holds sway in the UK, where politicians are seen by the law (though not by themselves) as merely ordinary citizens going about their everyday business.

13.4 PROTECTIONS FOR THE MEDIA

There are three kinds of protections which English law offers the press against interference with their function of informing people about matters of legitimate public interest. First, there is the common-law exception from restraint of breaches of confidence. Secondly, there is statutory exemption from revealing sources in certain situations under the Contempt of Court Act 1981, section 10. Thirdly, there are special provisions in the Police and Criminal Evidence Act 1984 which purport to offer some protection against the grant of warrants to search for evidence amongst journalists' papers, and impose conditions on the circumstances in which journalists will be required to produce or grant access to material for the purpose of a criminal investigation.

(1) Public-interest exception to duties of confidence[81]

As explained in Chapter 10, a breach of confidence may be justified where there is a public interest in disclosure which outweighs the public interest in maintaining the confidence. This enables the press to publish, in certain circumstances, confidential material which shows that someone has been acting contrary to the public interest. The clearest example of this was provided in *Lion Laboratories Ltd.* v. *Evans*,[82] where the material published showed that a model of the Lion Intoximeter, a machine for measuring the alcohol levels in breath specimens, was unreliable. People were being convicted of drink-drive offences on the basis of evidence provided by these machines. It was held that the fact that the information was confidential to the manufacturer did not prevent publication, because it was in the public interest for it to be widely known in order to prevent unjust convictions. It was not necessary that the evidence should reveal criminality or even wrongdoing on the part of the person to whom the duty of confidence was owed. The issue is whether there is a genuine public interest in publication which is weightier than that in maintaining the confidence. This is an example (perhaps a rare example) of the courts allowing the press to exercise a role as scrutineers, on behalf of the public, over the conduct of business which protects the public.

However, that case has been described as the high-water mark of the public-interest justification for breach,[83] and there are limits to it. The main one is that publication must be the most appropriate way of proceeding. If the material appears to reveal criminal conduct, it will usually be more appropriate to make the material available to the police, so that they may investigate without having the matter prejudiced by publicity, than to spread it across the country in newspapers and broadcasts. For this reason, the publication of recordings of telephone conversations with a leading jockey, which were said to suggest that races were being fixed, was restrained in *Francome* v. *Mirror Group Newspapers Ltd.*[84] However, if the matter raises questions of genuine public interest, as where conversations appear to reveal serious miscarriages of justice and widespread police malpractice, it will not be inappropriate to retail the information to the public at large as well as drawing it to the attention of the authorities.[85] Knowing that such matters are receiving public attention is a powerful

---

[81] Robertson and Nicol, *Media Law*, 142–5.

[82] [1985] QB 526, [1984] 2 All ER 417, CA.

[83] Raymond Wacks, *Personal Information: Privacy and the Law* (Oxford: Clarendon Press, 1989), 111 n. 233.

[84] [1984] 1 WLR 892, [1984] 2 All ER 408, CA.

[85] *Cork* v. *McVicar*, *The Times*, 1 Nov. 1984.

inducement to the authorities to investigate them thoroughly and make the results of the inquiry publicly available.

The duty of confidence protects private information more extensively than public information. However, the distinction between public and private information is not easy to draw. For example, information passed between partners during marriage might seem to be a classic example of private, or personal, information. For this reason, the Duke of Argyll was restrained, after the dissolution of his marriage to the Duchess of Argyll, from publishing, in a daily newspaper, details of the Duchess's behaviour during their marriage.[86] Yet in a very similar case, *Lennon v. News Group Newspapers Ltd.*[87] the Court of Appeal refused to restrain publication by the ex-wife of John Lennon, the former Beatle, of intimate details of their relationship. It was said that Mr. Lennon had forfeited the protection of the courts for the privacy of the marriage relationship because he had himself courted publicity about his married life and had published details of the relationship for gain. One cannot, it seems, publicize some aspects of one's married life and claim that others, which one's partner wants to publicize, are private.

(2) Keeping sources secret: Contempt of Court Act 1981, section 10

Obtaining information is an essential part of the job of journalists. The press, however free of formal constraints it might be, would have nothing to publish if journalists could not obtain information. As noted above, the absence of a general right to freedom of information in the UK makes journalists, like police officers, rely on informants, often from inside the organizations which the journalists are investigating. If it is accepted as being in the public interest to inform the public about certain matters, those who supply information may be acting in the public interest, yet be breaching civil duties of confidence and even the criminal law (particularly where governmental information is concerned, which is likely to be protected by the Official Secrets Acts). If the public-interest role of journalists is to continue, it is important that their informants should not be discouraged from providing information, lest the flow of information to the public should dry up. The press therefore has a long and, on the whole, honourable tradition of refusing to divulge the identity of sources.

However, the common law never recognized any privilege for journalists from the ordinary legal obligations which affect other people. They had no right to refuse to reveal their sources,[88] and could therefore

---

[86] *Duchess of Argyll v. Duke of Argyll* [1967] 1 Ch. 302.   [87] [1978] FSR 573, CA.

[88] There is a limited exception in the form of the 'newspaper rule' in defamation: newspapers which are defendants in defamation actions cannot be forced to reveal the name of the source of the information on which they base the stories of which the

be imprisoned and fined for contempt of court if they refused to comply with an order to reveal sources. The court had a discretion as to whether to make such an order, or to allow questions which might lead to a source being identified, and in exercising the discretion would balance the general public interests which might be served by requiring disclosure against the particular public interest in safeguarding the flow of information by allowing journalists to honour undertakings as to anonymity given to sources.[89] Such orders might be made for a number of reasons. For example, a court, tribunal, or inquiry might want to take evidence from the source instead of hearsay evidence from the journalist on the matter in question. This occurred in *Attorney-General* v. *Mulholland, Attorney-General* v. *Foster*,[90] the leading English authority on the common-law position, which arose during the inquiry conducted in 1963 by Viscount Radcliffe into the circumstances surrounding the operation of the Vassall spy ring. The journalists refused to answer questions which were relevant to the inquiry and, in the chairman's opinion, proper, on the ground that answering would have involved naming their sources. The case was referred to the High Court[91] for the journalists to be dealt with for contempt. The journalists' claim to be entitled to keep their sources secret was rejected by the High Court and the Court of Appeal.[92] The journalists went to prison, and gained a degree of notoriety and a reputation for keeping confidences.

The experience of the U.S.A. shows that adopting a constitutional right to freedom of the press does not necessarily confer any incidental right to protect sources. There, too, constitutional law sets the value of the rule of law against the interests in press freedom and investigative journalism. In *Branzburg* v. *Hayes*[93] the Supreme Court by a majority held that the First Amendment protection for press freedom did not entitle journalists to refuse to testify before a grand jury about their description, used in published articles, of (in one case) how two men had made hashish from marijuana, and (in the other) about the Black Panthers (a militant organization suspected of involvement in crime). The interest in detecting crime overrode the journalist's interest in protecting the anonymity of his news sources: as White J., writing for the majority, put

plaintiffs complain. For doubts about the scope of the rule, see *Georgiou* v. *Delegates of Oxford University Press* [1949] 1 KB 729, [1949] 1 All ER 342. For the position in Australia, see *John Fairfax & Sons Ltd.* v. *Cojuangco* (1988) 165 CLR 364, HC of Australia.

[89] *British Steel Corporation* v. *Granada Television Ltd.* [1981] AC 1096, [1981] 1 All ER 417, HL. See Alan Boyle, 'Freedom of Expression as a Public Interest in English Law' [1982] *PL* 574–612.

[90] [1963] 2 QB 477, CA.   [91] Tribunals of Inquiry (Evidence) Act 1921, s. 1(2).

[92] *A.-G.* v. *Mulholland; A.-G.* v. *Foster* [1963] 2 QB 477, CA. See also *A.-G.* v. *Clough* [1963] 1 QB 773.

[93] 408 US 665 (1972).

it, 'The crimes of news sources are no less reprehensible and threatening to the public interest when witnessed by a reporter than when they are not.' There is a public interest in the ability of the press to gather information, but providing information to the public is not a function of the press alone:

The informative function asserted by representatives of the organised press . . . is also performed by lecturers, political pollsters, novelists, academic researchers and dramatists. Almost any author may quite accurately assert that he is contributing to the flow of information to the public, that he relies on confidential sources of information, and that those sources will be silenced if he is forced to make disclosures before a grand jury.

Accordingly, suggestions that journalists are uniquely in need of a First Amendment privilege against disclosing information were considered to be unfounded. While the argument of the majority is probably exaggerated—journalists remain the most significant and regular purveyor of information to most people—the majority considered that claims that coerced disclosure would discourage people from providing information, or cause the flow of information to the public to dry up, or enable the police to turn journalists into an investigative arm of the state, were too speculative to override the interest in the detection of crime, particularly as grand juries can, and often do, sit in private.

However, public and legislative disquiet about the moral dilemmas which the decisions presented led to legislation to give some protection to journalists. In America, statutory 'shield laws' for journalists existed in some states before *Branzburg* v. *Hayes*, and more were enacted by states and Congress in response to the decision. In this country, it took nearly twenty years after the cases arising from the Vassall inquiry before a statute attempted to deal with the matter.

The opportunity came when the law of contempt fell to be considered by Parliament in the light of the report of the Phillimore Committee on Contempt of Court and the Law Commission's report on offences of interfering with the course of justice. Section 10 of the Contempt of Court Act 1981 provides:

No court may require a person to disclose, nor is any person guilty of contempt for refusing to disclose, the source of information contained in a publication for which he is responsible, unless it be established to the satisfaction of the court that disclosure is necessary in the interests of justice or national security or for the prevention of disorder or crime.

The section attempts to strike a balance between, on the one hand, the public interest in journalists and other authors being able to secure information by assuring their sources of anonymity and freedom from reprisal, and, on the other hand, competing public interests. It provides for the interest in freedom of information to be overridden only in order to secure the public interests in justice, national security, and prevention of disorder or crime, and then only if it is *necessary* to override the source's anonymity in order to secure one of the specified objectives. It has been accepted that the privilege is capable of applying to material obtained for the purposes of publication, even if it has not yet been included in a publication, since to hold otherwise would thwart the purpose of the Act in protecting the anonymity of sources of information.[94] The Act indicates a general policy which is applicable by analogy in cases other than court proceedings.[95] It has also been held that, unless the case falls within one of the exceptions, the section rules out both orders directly requiring naming of a source and orders to do anything which might indirectly enable the source to be identified, even if the effect is to make it impossible for someone to obtain recovery of goods in an action for conversion; the section therefore had to be considered when deciding whether to order a newspaper to return to the Ministry of Defence a leaked document, the property of the Ministry, which had marks on it which would have enabled security staff to identify the person who had passed the document to a journalist of the newspaper.[96] Even if a case falls within one of the exceptions, the court retains a discretion to refuse to order disclosure, although it will rarely be appropriate to exercise that discretion unless (for example) disclosure is necessary for the prevention of crime, but the crime is a very minor one, or disclosure would put the journalist's life at risk.[97]

Unfortunately, section 10 has presented problems relating to the proper interpretation of the terms of the exception to the privilege.[98] In *Re an Inquiry under the Company Securities (Insider Dealing) Act 1985*[99] inspectors were appointed under the Financial Services Act 1986 to investigate suspicions of insider dealing by means of leaks of price-sensitive information from government departments. A journalist, Jeremy

[94] *X Ltd.* v. *Morgan-Grampian (Publishers) Ltd.* [1991] 1 AC 1, [1990] 1 All ER 616, HL.

[95] *Re an inquiry under the Company Securities (Insider Dealing) Act 1985* [1988] AC 660, [1988] 1 All ER 203, HL.

[96] *Secretary of State for Defence* v. *Guardian Newspapers Ltd.* [1985] AC 339 at pp. 349–50, [1984] 3 All ER 601 at pp. 606–7 *per* Lord Diplock, considering the relationship between s. 10 of the 1981 Act and the judge's discretion to order return of goods under s. 3(3) of the Torts (Interference with Goods) Act 1977. The paper was returned. A civil servant, Miss Sarah Tisdall, was subsequently prosecuted for an offence under section 2 of the Official Secrets Act 1911 (now repealed and replaced by the Official Secrets Act 1989).

[97] *Re an inquiry under the Company Security (Insider Dealing) Act 1985* [1988] AC 660 at p. 703, [1988] 1 All ER 203 at p. 208 *per* Lord Griffiths.

[98] See Stephanie Palmer, 'Protecting Journalists' Sources: Section 10, Contempt of Court Act 1981' [1992] *PL* 61–72.

[99] [1988] AC 660, [1988] 1 All ER 203, HL.

Warner, had published two articles, one accurately forecasting the result of a Monopolies and Mergers Commission investigation into the Scottish and Newcastle Breweries bid for Matthew Brown, and the other accurately forecasting the advice which the Director-General of Fair Trading was to give in relation to another takeover bid. It seemed that Mr Warner must have obtained inside information, and the inspectors wished to question him about his sources. He refused to divulge his sources, as to do so would have destroyed the trust on which journalists and sources rely. The inspectors referred the matter to the High Court with a view to having Mr. Warner dealt with for contempt. The question arose whether or not section 10 of the Contempt of Court Act 1981 gave him a 'reasonable excuse' for his refusal.[100]

For the inspectors, it was argued that the case fell within the exception to the privilege under section 10, disclosure being 'necessary . . . for the prevention of . . . crime'. For the journalist, it was argued that disclosure would not be necessary unless the inspectors showed that there was no other way of obtaining the information, and that 'prevention of crime' did not extend to discovering who had committed a crime in the past. The House of Lords rejected Mr. Warner's arguments. 'Necessary' was said to have a meaning somewhere between 'indispensable' (which would be a stronger word than necessary) and 'useful or expedient' (which would be too weak).[101] If the objectives to be achieved were particularly important, something rather closer to the 'useful' end of the scale than the 'indispensable' end might suffice; it was for the judges to decide what it might mean in the context of each case.

This interpretation is somewhat unsatisfactory, as it comes close to saying that the word has no core meaning beyond 'really needed in all the circumstances', and such judgments are liable to make the scope of the privilege vary from case to case in an unpredictable and, perhaps, an unprincipled way. It would not matter unduly, however, if the purposes for which the privilege might be overridden under section 10 were to be strictly construed. Yet this was not done. The House treated the prevention of crime as having a wide meaning, encompassing anything calculated to deter or control crime generally, rather than a narrow meaning, limited to the prevention or detection of a particular suspected crime. The detection of leaks fell into that category, since leaks of price-sensitive information made possible insider dealing, and tracking down sources of leaks was essential in order to stamp out the criminal offence of insider dealing. It followed that the inspectors were not required to identify any particular offence which the information might enable them to bring

[100] Financial Services Act 1986, ss. 177, 178.
[101] In *Secretary of State for Defence* v. *Guardian Newspapers Ltd*. [1985] AC 339, [1984] 3 All ER 601, HL, 'necessary' was interpreted somewhat similarly.

home to an offender, so long as they could point to a type of crime (insider dealing) which, Parliament had decided, there was a pressing social need to control.

The courts have tended to apply the same expansive approach to interpreting the other purposes for which the privilege may be overridden. In *Secretary of State for Defence* v. *Guardian Newspapers Ltd.*[102] the House of Lords had to consider the scope of the national-security exception, in a case where the Secretary of State was seeking to recover a copy of a document, passed by a Civil Servant to a journalist, in order to identify the source. A majority of the House of Lords (Lords Diplock, Roskill, and Bridge) decided that a civil servant remaining in post, having already leaked a secret document, gave rise to a threat to national security, and it was necessary to track that person down in order to prevent possible future threats. Lord Fraser and Lord Scarman dissented, on the ground that there was only sketchy evidence before the court that the source of the leak would be likely to be in a position to repeat the leak or that a threat to national security (as opposed to a breach of confidence) would result in any case. In view of the willingness of the majority to draw inferences favourable to the government from admittedly unsatisfactory evidence, instead of subjecting it to rigorous examination and rejecting it if it did not come up to scratch, it seems that the prevailing tendency is to interpret the exceptions broadly. Indeed, Lord Bridge has said that where a case is shown to concern national security, or the prevention of crime, the court will virtually always decide that disclosure is necessary.[103]

In relation to the exception from the privilege where necessary in the interests of justice, it looked at first as though the judges might take a relatively restricted view. In Mr. Warner's case, Lord Diplock said that 'justice' was to be construed as referring in the technical sense to 'the administration of justice in the course of legal proceedings in a court of law, or, by reason of the extended definition of "court" in section 19 of the Act of 1981 before a tribunal or body exercising the judicial power of the state."[104] In another case, *Maxwell* v. *Pressdram Ltd.*,[105] the late Mr Robert Maxwell was (as so often) suing the magazine *Private Eye* for libel, and wanted defendants to reveal the source of defamatory allegations about the financial relationship between Mr. Maxwell and the Labour Party. This was relevant to the claim, because Mr. Maxwell had claimed aggravated and exemplary damages, and it would be relevant, in deciding

---

[102] [1985] AC 339, [1984] 3 All ER 601, HL.

[103] *X Ltd.* v. *Morgan-Grampian (Publishers) Ltd.* [1991] 1 AC 1 at p. 43, [1990] 2 All ER 1 at 8–9.

[104] *Secretary of State for Defence* v. *Guardian Newspapers Ltd.* [1985] AC 339 at p. 350, [1984] 3 All ER 601 at p. 607.

[105] [1987] 1 WLR 298, [1987] 1 All ER 656, CA.

whether to award such damages, to know whether Mr. Ingrams's assertion that he was relying on a reliable source of high standing was true.
The trial judge (Simon Brown J.) and the Court of Appeal decided not to
make an order that the source be named. 'Necessary', they felt, must
mean more than relevant. It would not be right for a plaintiff to be able
to obtain information normally denied under section 10, by the simple
expedient of including a claim for aggravated or exemplary damages. In
that case, it was reasonable to conclude that the matter could be adequately (though not ideally) dealt with by allowing the jury to see the
witnesses under cross-examination, and giving them a strong direction at
the conclusion of the case. The statutory public interest in not disclosing
sources should not be lightly overridden.

In   However, in   X Ltd.   v.   Morgan-Grampian (Publishers) Ltd.,[106] Lord
Bridge, with whom the other members of the House of Lords agreed, gave
a less restricted meaning to the term 'necessary in the interests of justice'.
He thought that it was apt to cover any situation where disclosure was
necessary to enable a person to exercise a legal right to avert a legal wrong,
whether or not it proved necessary to resort to legal proceedings.

Thus, to take a very obvious example, if an employer of a large staff is suffering
grave damage from the activities of an unidentified disloyal servant, it is
undoubtedly in the interests of justice that he should be able to identify him in
order to terminate his contract of employment, notwithstanding that no legal
proceedings may be necessary to achieve that end.

It may be noted that this example is close to the situation which obtained
in the Guardian case, where the Ministry of Defence was keen to identify
the servant (Miss Tisdall) who had passed the document to the journalist;
yet the House in the Guardian case was quite clear that the only exception under section 10 which could possibly be applicable would be the
national-security exception. The Morgan-Grampian case therefore appears,
on the face of it, to represent a considerable broadening of the judicial
interpretation of the exceptions to the privilege. However, as we shall
see, it is not quite that simple.

In the Morgan-Grampian case, a copy of a draft business plan, drawn up
by the plaintiff companies for the purpose of negotiating a loan, had been
stolen. The next day, an unidentified telephone caller had contacted a
journalist, Mr. Goodwin, and told him details concerning the companies
which, it was reasonable to suppose, were derived from the stolen copy.
Mr. Goodwin had then telephoned one of the companies to verify some
of the information before writing an article based on it for the newspaper
on which he worked, The Engineer. The companies thereupon applied for
an order for discovery against Mr. Goodwin, requiring him to disclose his

[106] [1991] AC 1 at p. 43, [1990] 2 All ER 1 at p. 9.

notes of the telephone conversation in order to help them to identify the source so that they could commence proceedings to recover the copy.[107]

The House of Lords, affirming the courts below, held that the interests of justice made disclosure necessary. However, it became clear that the result under the 'interests of justice' head of disclosure is not as automatic as that under the prevention of crime and protection of national-security heads, considered earlier. The fact that the interests of justice might be served by disclosure will not always lead to an order, because, before disclosure can be said to be *necessary* in the interests of justice, a plaintiff will have to show that the interests are so preponderantly strong as to override the public interest in protecting sources recognized by the section. Whereas this will be readily assumed when the relevant interests in favour of disclosure relate to preventing crime and maintaining national security, the interests of justice head requires the court to undertake a serious balancing exercise. Lord Oliver in the Warner case had said, 'Necessity is a relative concept and the degree of need before an act or measure can be said to be "necessary", although not, clearly, a question which is to be answered without reference to some objective standards, must, in the end, be and remain a matter of judgment.'[108] In Mr. Goodwin's case, he said:[109]

It means 'really needed' and it involves not so much a discretion as a value judgment. But the formation of a value judgment may, and, indeed, nearly always will, involve the consideration of factors which will be equally relevant to the exercise of a discretion. Moreover, there is nothing in the section which dictates that the judgment regarding whether disclosure is 'really needed' is to be conducted without reference to the prohibition which the section has imposed. The true question, in my opinion, is not 'is the information needed in order to serve the interests of justice?' but 'are the interests of justice in this case so pressing as to require the absolute ban on disclosure to be overridden?'

The House thus decided that it would be necessary to consider in the round all the features of cases under the 'interests of justice' head. Relevant factors will include the seriousness of the implications for the plaintiff (is he seeking to protect his very livelihood or merely a minor property interest?), the magnitude of the legitimate public interest in the information which the source has provided, and (perhaps curiously) the manner in which the source obtained the material, since it will require a

---

[107] Such an order is available against anyone who is mixed up in the tortious acts of another, unidentified, person and is able to supply information enabling the tortfeasor to be identified: *Norwich Pharmacal Co.* v. *Customs and Excise Commissioners* [1974] AC 133, [1973] 2 All ER 943, HL.

[108] See *Re an inquiry under the Company Securities (Insider Dealing) Act 1985* [1988] AC 660 at 708–9, [1988] 1 All ER 203 at p. 212.

[109] [1991] 1 AC at p. 53, [1990] 2 All ER at p. 16.

very strong public interest in disclosure to justify protecting a source who has committed an illegitimate act, such as a serious breach of confidence or theft.[110] This list of considerations is somewhat encouraging; indeed, one may be forgiven for wondering why the same degree of scrutiny should not be applied to all the other heads of exception under section 10.

However, the protection for journalists remains precarious, for two reasons. First, the weight given to the way in which the source has acted seems excessive. Any source within an organization is likely to have committed a breach of confidence at least, and if the source had behaved with perfect legality and propriety there would be little reason for him or her to insist on the anonymity which it is the policy of section 10 to allow journalists to protect. Secondly, once the journalist's protection is acknowledged to be subject to an element of judicial discretion, it will be very rare for an appeal court to upset the decision of a first-instance judge that he is satisfied that disclosure is necessary in the interests of justice. In the *Morgan-Grampian* case itself, Lord Oliver was prepared to accept that the trial judge and the Court of Appeal had had material before them on which they could reasonably have come to the conclusion that the interests of justice required disclosure.[111] If that is the test, the chance of an appeal offers little comfort to a journalist. The journalist's right to withhold disclosure under section 10, which Lord Scarman in the *Guardian* case thought might come to be properly regarded as a constitutional right,[112] turns out to be built on the shifting sands of judicial value judgments.

(3) Protection for journalistic material in criminal investigations

Journalists often receive or seek out information, or take photographs or films, which might be useful to police investigating criminal offences. At common law in England and Wales, there has never been a recognized privilege for journalists against being required to surrender their notes, films, etc., in either civil[113] or criminal proceedings. Thus there was no legal bar to a search warrant being issued (usually by a magistrate) to search for evidence in newspaper offices, on an *ex parte* application by the

---

[110] [1991] 1 AC at p. 44, [1990] 2 All ER at 9–10 *per* Lord Bridge.

[111] [1991] 1 AC at p. 54, [1990] 2 All ER at p. 17. Lord Bridge was rather more positive: see 44, 10.

[112] *Secretary of State for Defence* v. *Guardian Newspapers Ltd.* [1985] AC at p. 361, [1984] 3 All ER at p. 615.

[113] *Senior* v. *Holdsworth, ex parte Independent Television News* [1976] 1 QB 23, [1975] 2 All ER 1009, CA: no privilege, but summons set aside on grounds that the order had been drawn in excessively wide terms.

police. Any limitation depended on the good sense of the police and the discretion (rarely if ever exercised) of magistrates. A similar position obtained in Canada, where search warrants were available, although judges have exhorted those issuing warrants to give particularly careful consideration to such applications.[114] The same was true in the United States, where the freedom of the press under the First Amendment to the Constitution did not offer newspapers any higher protection against searches than was available to all under the Fourth Amendment. If the Fourth Amendment's requirement for a warrant was satisfied, the police could constitutionally search for evidence, without prior warning or an *inter partes* hearing, even the premises of third parties who were not suspected of being implicated in the offence. This was settled by the Supreme Court in *Zurcher* v. *Stanford Daily*.[115]

In the USA, the decision in *Zurcher* was greeted with widespread public condemnation. In 1980, Congress passed legislation[116] which replaced the warrant procedure whereby investigators, who wanted access to material as evidence of crime which was held by innocent third parties, were able to apply *ex parte* for a search warrant giving them freedom to enter premises and rummage through records. Instead, investigators now have to apply for a subpoena requiring the production of specified material. There is, if necessary, an *inter partes* hearing in which the third party can adduce arguments against the order, either in principle or as to its scope. The third party is not then at peril of a search of its premises. The federal legislation protects the press against state and federal investigators, to extend the scope of First Amendment rights, and protects other innocent third parties against federal investigators only (although some states have enacted similar legislation).

In England and Wales, too, legislation has given some procedural protection to the interests of the media. Under the Police and Criminal Evidence Act 1984, a partial shield against enforced disclosure in criminal investigations was given to 'journalistic material'. Under sections 11 and 14, all 'journalistic material' became either excluded material (if it is held in confidence and consists of documents or other records)[117] or special procedure material (if it is not held in confidence, or is in any other form).[118] The effect of this was that no search warrant could be granted in respect of such material unless the highly restrictive conditions on the grant of warrants under Schedule 1, paragraph 12, were met.[119] In relation to most investigations, the police now have to apply for an order for access or production rather than a warrant, and the procedure requires notice of the application to be given to the person holding the material,

---

[114] *Re Pacific Press Ltd. and R.* (1977) 37 CCC (2d) 487. [115] 436 US 547 (1978).
[116] 94 Stat. 1879 (1980). [117] PACE 1984, s. 11(1)(*c*).
[118] PACE 1984, s. 14(1)(*b*). [119] PACE 1984, s. 9.

who can argue at an *inter partes* hearing before a circuit judge that the access conditions are not met.[120] The exceptions are: cases where a warrant can properly be issued under Schedule 1, paragraph 12; and investigations into terrorist offences and drug-trafficking offences, where a circuit judge may issue a warrant *ex parte* even in respect of excluded material, without the need to comply with the special conditions under Schedule 1, paragraph 12, of the the 1984 Act.[121]

So far as press freedom is concerned, two questions must be addressed. First, what types of material does 'journalistic material' include? Secondly, when will it not be in the public interest to require disclosure of journalistic material under Schedule 1 to the 1984 Act?

(i) *What is journalistic material?* 'Journalistic material' is defined as material acquired or created for the purposes of journalism which is in the possession of a person who himself acquired or created it for that purpose.[122] Thus a journalist's notes of an interview are journalistic material; so is material gathered from anyone for the purpose of writing a newspaper article, even if the person supplying it did not himself acquire or create it for journalistic purposes; so is a photograph taken with a view to possible publication. In all these cases, it does not matter whether or not the material is, in the end, used in print. The test is whether (*a*) the person who created or acquired it did so for the purposes of journalism, and (*b*) the person now in possession intends to use it for those purposes. A photograph which is taken by a press photographer and passed to the editor of a newspaper with a view to publication is therefore journalistic material in the hands of the editor.

The classification does not depend on the person who created, acquired, or is now in possession of the material being a journalist by profession. It depends only on people having the relevant intention or purpose, not on their status or calling. What, then, are the purposes of journalism?[123] They can be summarized as being the provision for the public, or a section of the public, of reliable, published information on current events, with informed comment where appropriate or desired. It may cover publication in newspapers, magazines, or through the broadcast media. It is not clear whether it includes publication in book form;

---

[120] For discussion of the availability of orders in respect of excluded and special procedure material generally, see above, Ch. 10. This section concentrates on aspects which are special to journalistic material.

[121] Drug Trafficking Offences Act 1986, s. 27; Prevention of Terrorism (Temporary Provisions) Act 1989, Sch. 7, para. 3. Under the latter Act, a warrant may in certain circumstances be granted by a Secretary of State.

[122] PACE 1984, s. 13(1), (2).

[123] For full discussion, see David Feldman, *The Law Relating to Entry, Search and Seizure* (London: Butterworths, 1986), 104–6.

this is not the classical form of journalism, in which material is published within a very short time of the events to which it relates.[124] If the book is to be published reasonably soon after the events, there is no reason why the principle should not apply to material compiled for it. The time element is flexible, in any case, and must be a matter of degree, because although investigative journalism is undoubtedly journalism an investigation may last years before the results are published. There seems to be no reason to exclude publications in the form of dramatized documentaries, as long as they are sufficiently topical. However, it goes too far to say that journalism 'includes any form of publication':[125] it certainly would not apply to most novels, nor to many works of scholarship in the fields of history, law, science, nor to most plays other than (perhaps) dramatized documentaries. All these forms of publication are likely to lack the necessary quality of topicality. They may make news, but will usually not themselves be journalistic.

(ii) *Where does the public interest lie in respect of disclosure?* The effect of material being journalistic is that disclosure will not be ordered, nor a warrant granted, unless one of the sets of access conditions is satisfied.[126] The most important aspect of these for press freedom relates to special procedure material, which is, in this context, journalistic material which does not consist of documents held in confidence. These can be sought under the 'first set of access conditions', i.e. those under Schedule 1, paragraph 2, in cases where before the 1984 Act no search warrant could have been obtained, because there was no provision for granting warrants in respect of the offences. For this purpose, it is necessary to show (*inter alia*) that the public interest would be served by an order requiring access to the material. (This is not necessary under the second set of access conditions, which apply where, before the 1984 Act, a search warrant could have been granted.) When, if ever, will the public interest *not* be served by ordering access?

In the light of the caselaw of the House of Lords on section 10 of the Contempt of Court Act 1981, above, it seems likely that the public interest will nearly always be served by requiring access where it is likely (in the words of paragraph 2 of Schedule 1 to the 1984 Act) to be relevant evidence of, or of substantial value to an investigation relating to, a

---

[124] At common law, it was unclear whether the so-called 'newspaper rule', under which newspapers being sued for libel could not be forced to disclose the sources of the information on which the libel was based, applied to books as well as periodicals: see *Georgius* v. *Delegates of Oxford University Press* [1949] 1 KB 729, [1949] 1 All ER 342.

[125] This is the view expressed by Michael Zander, *The Police and Criminal Evidence Act 1984*, 2nd edn. (London: Sweet & Maxwell, 1990), 35.

[126] For discussion of the access conditions, see above, s. 10.3 (2).

serious arrestable offence. This seems, indeed, to be the way in which the courts have been treating the access provisions. In *Chief Constable of Avon and Somerset* v. *Bristol United Press*,[127] a production order was made in respect of unpublished photographs of the St Paul's riots of 1986, in the possession of Bristol United Press and Bristol Press and Picture Agency Ltd. The application was opposed on the ground that to allow the police to take evidence in this way would compromise the impartiality of the press, who would be seen as agents of the police, and would be subject to increased risk of violence next time they went into an area where rioting was occurring. This argument was rejected by the judge, who pointed out that the press would be protected by the fact that the photographs were being handed over pursuant to a court order rather than volutarily. He also thought that it was unlikely that the press would be more likely to be subjected to violence because of the risk of rioters being identified following an order for production of unpublished photographs, than because of the risk, which always existed, that the photographs would actually be published and the rioters identified from published photographs.[128] Any added risk was outweighed by the weighty public interest in clearing innocent suspects of crime and identifying the guilty. This approach was approved when the order was challenged in an application for judicial review.[129] The message from these cases appears to be that, once it is shown that material is likely to be evidence of a serious arrestable offence, judges will have no hesitation in holding that disclosure is in the public interest. This means that there is, in practice, no room for a balancing of public interests under either set of access conditions in Schedule 1 to PACE.[130]

The importance accorded to the detection of crime should, however, not be treated as being absolute. If it were absolute, the requirement to consider the public interest would be redundant, adding nothing to the other access conditions. To give effect to the evident intention of Parliament, the types of consideration which were identified by Lord Bridge in relation to the Contempt of Court Act 1981, section 10, in *Morgan-Grampian*[131] should properly be equally applicable under the first set of access conditions under Schedule 1 to the 1984 Act. Regrettably,

[127] *Independent*, 4 Nov. 1986, Bristol Crown Court (Stuart-Smith J.).

[128] Stuart-Smith J. applied the dictum of Lord Denning M.R. in *Senior* v. *Holdsworth, ex parte ITN Ltd.* [1976] 1 QB 23, CA, relating to a witness summons in respect of unbroadcast news   [129] *R.* v. *Bristol Crown Court, ex parte Bristol Press & Picture Agency Ltd.* (1986) 85 Cr. AR. 190, DC.

[130] This mirrors the position in relation to other types of excluded material and special procedure material: see *R.* v. *Northampton Crown Court, ex parte DPP*, [1991] 93 Cr App R 376, DC. Protections are procedural only: see *R.* v. *Crown Court at Middlesex Guildhall, ex parte Salinger* [1993] 2 All ER 310, DC.

[131] [1991] 1 AC at p. 44, [1990] 2 All ER at pp. 9–10, considered above.

the approach of the courts to the cases so far reported cannot, on a true reading of paragraph 2 of Schedule 1, be sustained, and it is to be hoped that it will soon be possible for higher courts to examine the matter afresh.

13.5 CONCLUSION

The message of this chapter can be summed up by saying that there is a good deal of rhetoric about the importance of a free press as a channel of information to the public on matters of public interest, and a certain amount of support for the idea that this requires journalists' sources to be protected against being unmasked in at least some circumstances. However, as yet, the practical impact of the ideas has been limited. The judges seem a little afraid of the potential effect of the new public interest in freedom of information, and are determined to cabin it as closely as possible at present, by recognizing it while at the same time subjugating it to other public interests with which they are more familiar, such as the interests in national security and the control of crime. It may be, however, that this is only a temporary phase, and that as time passes and the judges become more at home with the idea of a free press they will gradually release the public-interest shackles. If this is to happen, it is likely that the influence of Article 10 of the European Convention on Human Rights will be decisive. As Lord Scarman said in the *Guardian Newspapers* case in 1984, in relation to the journalist's privilege against disclosure of sources under the Contempt of Court Act 1981, section 10:

Counsel for the Guardian described the section as introducing in the law 'a constitutional right'. There being no written constitution, his words will sound strange to some. But they may more accurately prophesy the direction in which English law has to move under the compulsions to which it is now subject than many are yet prepared to accept. The section, it important to note in this connection, bears a striking resemblance to the way in which many of the articles of the European Convention for the Protection of Fundamental Rights and Freedoms . . . are framed: namely a general rule subject to carefully drawn and limited exceptions which are required to be established, in case of dispute, to the satisfaction of the European Court of Human Rights.[132]

Is this the way in which, in years to come, we will see the English judges moving?

More generally, there is a risk that government intervention to maintain standards will degenerate into political pressure in relation to programme making, using threats or carping criticism. This seems to have happened in 1988, in the furore surrounding the broadcast of *Death on*

[132] [1985] AC at p. 361, [1984] 3 All ER at p. 615.

the Rock. There is a temptation for even the fairest minded government to use pressure against those who have the job of exposing its behaviour to public scrutiny. There is correspondingly a need for all concerned to continue to be vigilant and strong-minded to ensure that this independence is not whittled away by legal assaults, political intimidation, and behind–the-scenes pressure.

14

RESTRICTING EXPRESSION TO PROTECT THE SECURITY OF THE STATE

This chapter examines restraints on freedom of expression which are imposed in the interests of the security of the state: prior restraint through use of the doctrine of breach of confidence, and subsequent restraint through imposing criminal penalties under the Official Secrets Acts, and for seditious libel and related offences. In order to clarify the complex relationship between prior restraint by the civil law and subsequent restraint by the criminal law, the first section sketches some of the background. After that, prior restraint by means of the law of breach of confidence is considered, and the remaining sections look at various criminal offences which penalize certain communications after they have occurred.

14.1 BACKGROUND

(1) Three background elements

Three matters, noted above in Chapter 12, form the backdrop to the discussion of state interest restrictions on free expression.

(i) *The ethos of secrecy.* The day-to-day running of the British government is infected by a virus of secrecy. Compared with the USA or Australia, the government of the UK is a private affair, taking place behind a veil, a corner of which may be lifted to allow limited parliamentary scrutiny but which is otherwise normally kept lowered. The secretive ethos of the civil service is supported by statutes such as the Official Secrets Act 1989, and by the civil services conduct code.[1] It contrasts markedly with the position in the USA, where concern over the potentially anti-social effects of governmental impropriety led Congress to provide statutory protection to whistle-blowers.[2] Secrecy is also to some extent bolstered

---

[1] See Gavin Drewry and Tony Butcher, *The Civil Service Today* (Oxford: Basil Blackwell, 1991), 131–3.

[2] The Civil Service Reform Act of 1978, *PL* 95–454. Similar protection has been extended to other branches of the public service. For discussion of UK and USA developments, see Yvonne Cripps, 'Disclosure in the Public Interest: The Predicament of the

by ingrained judicial attitudes, when issues come before the courts. Judges tend to consider that the government is uniquely well placed to assess where the national interest lies. This is, to some extent, correct: the secrecy which surrounds government ensures that other bodies, which might possibly claim a say in making such choices, are starved of information.

Thus in pre-trial civil proceedings the government can often assert a public interest in maintaining the confidentiality of information, sources, or documents, as a ground for resisting discovery of documents.[3] The common law recognizes that a certain degree of secrecy is inevitably necessary in government and the public service, in order to enable public bodies to do their jobs and to encourage frank discussion within government of issues which arise for decision. The judges therefore allow claims to public-interest immunity from discovery in the course of litigation, based on the class of documents into which the particular documents. For example, the public interest may require the Crown and other public bodies to refuse to disclose the following: Cabinet minutes and any documents brought into existence for the purpose of framing high-level government policy, including papers written by relatively junior officials;[4] minutes of discussions between heads of departments;[5] papers brought into existence for the purpose of preparing submissions to Cabinet;[6] and papers held by other public bodies, such as the police, if production is likely to impede the body in carrying out the purpose for which it was brought into existence.[7]

Nevertheless, the protection offered by public-interest immunity is not absolute. It applies only if, and so long as, the public interest in preventing harm to the nation or the public service outweighs the public interest in making the information available for the purpose of the due adminis-

Public Service Employee' [1983] *PL* 600–33; R. A. Parker, 'Whistleblowing Legislation in the United States: A Preliminary Appraisal' (1988) 41 *Parliamentary Affairs* 149–58; Graham Zellick, 'Whistle-blowing in United States Law' [1987] *PL* 311–13; J. G. Starke, 'New United States Legislation in 1989 for the Protection of Whistle-blowers' (1989) 63 *ALJ* 592–4; Report of the Ontario Law Reform Commission, *Political Activity, Public Comment and Disclosure by Crown Employees* (Ontario: Ministry of the Attorney General, 1986); Note, 'Canadian Law Reform Report on "Whistleblowing" by Public Servants' (1987) 61 *ALJ* 319–22.

[3] *Burmah Oil Co. Ltd.* v. *Bank of England* [1980] AC 1090, [1979] 3 All ER 700, HL; *Air Canada* v. *Secretary of State for Trade* [1983] 2 AC. 394, [1983] 1 All ER 910, HL.
[4] *Conway* v. *Rimmer* [1968] AC 910, HL, at p. 952 *per* Lord Reid; *Sankey* v. *Whitlam* (1978) 142 CLR 1, HC of Australia.
[5] *Australian National Airlines Commission* v. *The Commonwealth* (1975) 132 CLR 582, HC of Australia, at p. 591.
[6] *Lanyon Pty Ltd.* v. *The Commonwealth* (1974) 129 CLR 650, HC of Australia.
[7] *Neilson* v. *Laughame* [1981] QB 736, CA; *Makanjuola* v. *Commissioner of Police of the Metropolis* (1989) [1992] 3 All ER 617, CA; *Halford* v. *Sharples* [1992] 3 All ER 624, CA.

tration of justice.[8] In some cases, some judges have displayed a healthy scepticism when faced by claims that disclosure of documents would inhibit frank advice and exchanges of view amongst Ministers or between Ministers and civil servants,[9] or by assertions that the return of leaked documents was necessary in the interests of national security.[10] In the past, judges were also ready to inspect documents in respect of which a class claim to immunity was made, and exercise their own judgement as to the balance between the competing public interests.[11] Subsequently, British judges have been less critical of expansive claims to privilege.[12] Recent cases have placed a major obstacle in the way of obtaining disclosure in the UK, because the courts will not embark on the balancing exercise, which the limits on public-interest immunity appear to require, unless the party seeking disclosure can at least show 'that the documents are very likely to contain material which would give substantial support to his contention on an issue which arises in the case, and that without them he might be "deprived of the means of . . . proper presentation" of his case'.[13] This is intended to prevent fishing expeditions among public papers, and to take account of the difficulty which our judges feel in assessing the sensitivity of different classes of documents, but it places a considerable burden on the party seeking discovery, who must have a clear idea about what he is likely to find before he has a chance of looking at it, and must convince the court that it will substantially assist him.[14] Judges have refused to order production of material likely to contain information which is already in the public domain, on the ground that the party already has access to it and will not be substantially assisted by discovery in that regard.[15]

[8] *Conway* v. *Rimmer* [1968] AC 910 at p. 940, [1968] 1 All ER 874 at p. 880, *per* Lord Reid.

[9] *Conway* v. *Rimmer* [1968] AC 910, [1968] 1 All ER 874, HL. Similar vigilance was evident in *Williams* v. *Home Office* [1981] 1 All ER 1151.

[10] See Lord Fraser of Tullybelton and Lord Scarman, dissenting, in *Secretary of State for Defence* v. *Guardian Newspapers Ltd.* [1985] AC 339, [1984] 3 All ER 601, HL.

[11] *Campbell* v. *Tameside MBC* [1982] QB 1065, [1982] 2 All ER 781, CA.

[12] See the majority speeches in *Secretary of State for Defence* v. *Guardian Newspapers Ltd.* [1985] AC 339, [1984] 3 All ER 601, HL; Ch. 13, s. 4(2), above.

[13] *Air Canada* v. *Secretary of State for Trade (No. 2)* [1983] 2 AC 394 at p. 435, [1983] 1 All ER 910 at p. 917, *per* Lord Fraser of Tullybelton, quoting Lord Radcliffe in *Glasgow Corporation* v. *Central Land Board* 1956 SC (HL) 1 at p. 18. This formulation represents the view of the majority (Lords Fraser, Wilberforce, and Edmund-Davies). Lords Scarman and Templeman adopted a slightly less restrictive approach, allowing inspection where disclosure might assist either party or the court in dealing with the issues, but they concurred in the result on the facts of the case.

[14] See e.g. *Bookbinder* v. *Tebbit (No. 2)* [1992] 1 WLR 217.

[15] *Air Canada* v. *Secretary of State for Trade (No. 2)* [1983] 2 AC 394, [1983] 1 All ER 910, HL.

The Australian approach is rather different. The High Court of Australia insists that whenever a claim to public interest is raised the court, and nobody else, is responsible for deciding whether, on balance, the public interest favours disclosure of the documents. In order to do this, the court must always privately examine the documents in question, even if the papers relate to Cabinet discussions, national policy, or investigations by the security service, ASIO.[16] If the court decides that parts of a document should be kept secret, it will still order disclosure if the document can be sealed or otherwise packaged in such a way as to allow disclosure of the non-secret parts while maintaining the secrecy of those parts which deserve protection.[17] If the document has been published already, the claim to immunity from disclosure will be rejected,[18] not (as in the UK) strengthened. The greater confidence of the Australian judges in assessing the public interest in secrecy, and their less deferential attitude to government as compared with their English counterparts, are aspects of Australia's open approach to government in general, which contrasts starkly with the ethos in the UK.

The influence of the ethos of secrecy on judges is particularly powerful in the context of national security. For example, in *Council of Civil Service Unions* v *Minister for the Civil Service*,[19] an application for judicial review of an order made without prior consultation banning trade unions from GCHQ, the House of Lords accepted, without demanding evidence, the government's claim that consulting the unions would self-evidently have endangered national security. The government's argument that the security implications of disclosure are either self-evident, and so need no evidence, or have to be taken on trust, is hard to sustain when neither the courts nor the other parties know what the evidence might show. Judges have also been reluctant to review the Home Secretary's discretion to deport aliens when he considers that to be conducive to the public good, often on national-security grounds.[20] The desire to protect the security of the state is laudable, but potential harms need to be carefully balanced against potential benefits from disclosure. It is by no means self-evident that the government is the body best able to evaluate the balance between its own interests and those of others.

(ii) *The special evil of prior restraint.* Libertarians traditionally view prior restraint of expressions of opinion and information as being a more serious infringement of liberties than subsequent imposition of penalties.

---

[16] *Sankey* v. *Whitlam* (1978) 142 CLR 1; *Alister* v. *R.* (1984) 154 CLR 404 (Gibbs CJ, Murphy and Brennan JJ, Wilson and Dawson JJ dissenting).
[17] *Sankey* v. *Whitlam* (1978) 142 CLR 1 was such a case.
[18] Ibid. at p. 45, *per* Gibbs ACJ.
[19] [1985] AC 374, [1984] 3 All ER 935, HL.   [20] See Ch. 7, s. 3, above.

This view is persuasive if one considers that the value of liberty—in this case, freedom of expression and communication—lies in its tendency to advance personal autonomy, in the sense of the freedom to make one's own choices. Where the law imposes a penalty on someone who expresses himself in a certain way, but takes no prior, preventive steps to coerce him to keep quiet, he retains the freedom to make his choice for himself. The risk of suffering the penalty will be one factor which he will take into account in deciding whether or not to speak out, but he may decide that the risk is outweighed by the importance to him or to others of what he wants to say. Forcing him to remain silent removes from him that freedom, and fails to respect his autonomy. On the other hand, if one adopts an instrumental view of the justification for maintaining individual liberty, one can take the view that the end which justifies criminalizing certain types of expression might well be better served by denying people the ability to choose to flout the law. Using criminal law to punish publications can have a chilling effect on freedom of expression and demands substantial justification. If one takes the view that the appropriate criteria for recognizing and restricting liberties are social and teleological—that is, directed to achieving an ulterior purpose, such as a vision of the ideal society—rather than being individual- and autonomy-related,[21] it is far from clear that the liberal preference for any restraints on expression to be subsequent rather than prior restraint is rational. Each type of restraint needs to be justified on similar grounds and to the same standards.

(iii) *Criteria for justifying interferences with freedom of expression under the European Convention on Human Rights.* Under the European Convention of Human Rights, the right to receive and impart ideas and information under Article 10(1) can justifiably be interfered with in the interests of national security under Article 10(2), on condition that (*inter alia*) the interferences are in accordance with a procedure prescribed by law and are necessary in a democratic society for the purpose of protecting national security. To meet these criteria, the steps taken must be intended to answer a pressing social need, must be grounded in domestic law in a form which makes them sufficiently accessible to people who are subject to the laws and sufficiently clear to enable those people to understand their likely effects with reasonable certainty, and must be proportionate to the legitimate objectives pursued. A law imposing criminal sanctions on conduct may be a more effective constraint on behaviour if it is clear and its operation predictable than if the law is unpublished or uncertain. A restrictive law, even if is complies with these requirements, therefore

---

[21] See Ch. 1 above.

has potentially extensive effects on free expression, and needs to be subjected to careful review in the light of the proportionality requirement.
As we shall see, in *Attorney General* v. *Guardian Newspapers Ltd. (No. 2)*[22]
Scott J. at first instance made extensive use of the ECHR criteria when
assessing the weight to be attached to various public interests affecting an
application for an injunction to restrain newspaper reports of and extracts
from Mr. Peter Wright's book, *Spycatcher*. The results of the judge's
analysis were accepted by a majority of the Court of Appeal and the
House of Lords. Although the Court of Appeal and the House of Lords
did not expressly use the Convention in carrying out the balancing exercise, no judge questioned the proposition that it might be relevant.

(2) Using criminal law to protect national security

The approach of successive British governments to the problem of
restraining speech or disclosures which may threaten the security of the
state has traditionally relied primarily on the criminal law. Fear of
German espionage operations in 1911 led to a panic measure, the Official
Secrets Act 1911, which replaced earlier official secrets legislation[23] with
a series of provisions which included some so broad in their scope that
they would have been laughable had they not been so draconian. The
legislation was rushed through Parliament with unseemly haste. Parts of
the Act remain in force today. Section 1 is a straightforward anti-
espionage provision, aimed at people who do things which threaten security even if they have no such intention.[24] Section 7 makes it an offence
to harbour spies or fail to report them when they have met on one's
premises. These measures present few problems from a civil liberties
standpoint, since the threat to the state from such activities would normally be thought to justify the restrictions.

Section 2 of the 1911 Act, however, has been replaced by the Official
Secrets Act 1989. The old section 2 represented a very extensive restriction on open government and press freedom, to the point where, for
several decades, debates about freedom of information and national security in the United Kingdom came to be conducted largely in terms of
competing proposals for its reform. As the 1989 Act was the result of
these debates, we must say something about the old section 2. It was an
extraordinary provision. Headed 'Wrongful communication, etc., of
information', a phrase in which the 'etc.' was more important than the

---

[22] [1990] 1 AC 109, [1988] 3 All ER 545, HL.

[23] The long title of the 1911 Act was: 'An Act to re-enact the Official Secrets Act
1889, with Amendments.'

[24] Geoffrey Robertson and Andrew Nicol, *Media Law*, 3rd edn. (London: Penguin,
1992), 428–30.

'communication', the section made it an offence for anyone who holds or had held office under the Crown, or was a government contractor, or had been employed under such a person, to communicate without authority any sketch, plan, model, article, note, document, or information relating to or used in a prohibited place, or which has been entrusted to the person in confidence or obtained in contravention of the Act, unless communicating it to a person to whom it was his duty in the interest of the state to communicate it. Finally, it was an offence willingly to receive such an article knowing, or having reasonable ground to believe, that it was being communicated in contravention of the Act.

Although in its original form section 2 was by no means narrow in scope, it was subsequently extended by the Official Secrets Acts 1920 and 1939. In its widened form, it covered secret official code words and passwords, and made it an offence for a person in possession of the information, etc., to use it for the benefit of any foreign power (whether or not an enemy), to use it n any way prejudicial to the safety or interests of the state, to communicate it directly or indirectly to a foreign power or in any other manner prejudicial to the safety or interests of the state, or to fail to comply with any direction issued with lawful authority regarding the return or disposal of the item. It was also made an offence to retain it contrary to the person's duty to fail to take reasonable care of it.

The provision was subject to criticism on a number of grounds. First, it was thought to be overinclusive: the detailed descriptions of material or information which was restricted were effectively made redundant by the inclusion of anything held by a person 'which has been entrusted in confidence to him by any person holding office under His Majesty or which he has obtained *or to which he has had access owing to his position as a person* who holds or has held office under His Majesty . . .'.[25] The words in italics covered any information, whether confidential or not, which came into the possession of a civil servant or other person holding office under the Crown in the course of his duties. This included such matters as the number of cups of tea served in a government department. Many prosecutions under section 2 were not concerned with national security at all, but involved people who had misused information about people obtained from police or departmental records.[26] Where information was considered to be confidential, the person receiving it would have his consciousness of his obligations reinforced by being required to sign a piece of paper stating that he had been told the nature of the information and understood that he was subject to the provisions of the Official

[25] Official Secrets Act 1911, s. 2(1), as amended; emphasis added.

[26] David Hooper, *Official Secrets: The Use and Abuse of the Act* (London: Secker & Warburg, 1987), app. 1, pp. 243–73, provides a very useful summary of 73 selected prosecutions brought under s. 2 of the 1911 Act.

Secrets Acts 1911–39, either in relation to that particular piece of information (for example, where the person was neither a person holding office under the Crown nor a government contractor) or in respect of all information coming to him in the course of his duties.[27] Where any information, however innocuous, about government might be subject to the Act, it weakened the moral authority of the Act over all information, including that which was potentially damaging to the state. While it is true that such information might be used by the intelligence service of a foreign power as a way of testing the credibility of informants who claim to have access to the inner reaches of government, it would be an exaggeration to say that divulging such information in itself represents a significant threat to the safety of the state.

Secondly, the criminal provisions in section 2 were anomalous in that the only *mens rea* which the prosecution was required to prove was an intention to communicate or receive the material. It was not necessary to prove that the defendant knew what the material was, or that it was likely to harm the interests of the state. Even the limited defence that the defendant was under an obligation to communicate the material in the interests of the state was restricted severely by the interpretation placed on it by McCowan J. in *R. v. Ponting*.[28] The defendant had been a senior civil servant in the Ministry of Defence. He had sent documents concerning the sinking of the Argentine battle cruiser, the *General Belgrano*, during the Falklands war to Mr Tam Dalyell MP, who had been trying to uncover the circumstances in which the ship had been sunk. Mr. Ponting believed that the government had been misleading Parliament over the affair. He was prosecuted under section 2, despite the fact that nobody suggested that the disclosure had affected national security. For Mr Ponting it was argued that Mr Dalyell was a person to whom it was his duty, in the interest of the state, to communicate the documents, because civil servants had a constitutional duty to Parliament to facilitate the discharge of its functions as well as an obligation to the government of the day. The prosecution asserted, and McCowan J. accepted, that the interests of the state were to be defined by the government of the day, and for practical purposes were identical with the interests of the government of the day. The judge relied on speeches in a House of Lords decision on section 1 of the Act,[29] but those speeches had established a rebuttable presumption that the implementation of government policy was in the interests of the state, rather than an irrebuttable presumption that whatever the government wanted was in the interests of the state.

---

[27] This procedure was popularly but misleadingly known as 'signing the Official Secrets Act'. The text of the declaration is reproduced in Hooper, *Official Secrets*, 276.
[28] [1985] Crim. LR 318.
[29] *Chandler* v. *DPP* [1964] AC 763, [1962] 3 All ER 142, HL.

Thirdly, the width of the section left it open to the government to use it to stifle the flow of information to those, such as MPs, who had a legitimate use for it in performing their constitutional function as scrutineers of government activity. This inhibited both the work of Parliament and the disclosure of iniquity, incompetence, or mendacity, on the part of Ministers, members of the security services, and civil servants. The potential use of section 2 to stifle such 'whistle-blowing' by civil servants was demonstrated in the *Ponting* case. In *R. v. Ponting*, despite McCowan J.'s direction on the meaning of section 2, the jury acquitted Mr Ponting, probably reflecting public contempt for the government's attempt to conflate its own narrow political interest with the state's interest. The government was certainly not beyond criticism. Successive governments have made selective use made of secrecy obligations: when the government, or individual members of the government, wanted information to be made public for political purposes, they would authorize disclosure, usually on a non-attributable basis.[30] If the disclosure disadvantaged the government politically, as in the *Ponting* case, a prosecution might follow. This had been exploited by Mr. Ponting's advisers inside and outside the court in a highly effective public-relations exercise.[31] The jury's decision in *Ponting*'s case sounded the death knell for section 2, notwithstanding the effort by the Cabinet Secretary after the case to restate the principles governing a civil servant's obligations in a way which excluded any constitutional responsibility to Parliament, or indeed to anyone other than the government of the day.[32] In 1985 the Attorney General decided not to prosecute Miss Kathy Massiter, a former MI5 officer who had revealed to a television production company information about the activities of MI5, including surveillance (including telephone taps) on members of the Campaign for Nuclear Disarmament, the National Council for Civil Liberties, and trade unionists. These activities appeared to have had little to do with national security, and in some cases were arguably unlawful: Miss Massiter cast doubt on the propriety of some of the warrants which had been issued for telephone interceptions. Although the revelations were clearly in breach of section 2 of the Act, Miss Massiter had clearly been motivated only by a desire to reassert proper systems of accountability over the security service, and her action commanded considerable

---

[30] Something of this sort happened in the Westland affair: see Hooper, *Official Secrets*, ch. 16, and Rodney Austin, 'The Westland Affair: Open Government by Error' (1986) 39 *Current Legal Problems* 269–82.

[31] Hooper, *Official Secrets*, ch. 12; Clive Ponting, 'R. v. Ponting' (1987) 14 *J. Law and Soc.* 366–72; Rosalind Thomas, 'The British Official Secrets Act 1911–1939 and the Ponting Case' [1986] *Crim. L.R.* 491–510; Gavin Drewry, 'The Ponting Case: Leaking in the Public Interest' [1985] *PL* 203–12.

[32] See Ch. 12, above.

public sympathy. Sir Michael Havers QC, the Attorney General, quickly decided against prosecuting her.[33]

It was by now widely accepted that section 2 had to be replaced, and attention turned to deciding the best approach to drafting a new provision. However, the debate was not taking place in isolation from wider security issues. It reached a climax at a time when the processes for maintaining secrecy and stifling whistle-blowing were under intense media and judicial examination in relation to the proposed serialization of the book *Spycatcher* by Mr. Peter Wright, a former MI5 officer. This focused attention on the legal arrangements available for prior restraint, and the way in which the law balanced the public interest in knowing how the state is run against the interest asserted by state organs in keeping their activities secret.

(3) Civil law and prior restraint of breaches of secrecy

From the government's point of view, it is always preferable to prevent disclosures rather than punish the perpetrators after the damage has been done. If public interests are really under threat, prior restraint is a more efficient way of upholding them than subsequent restraint. It is a feature of the criminal law that it does not normally provide for the prior restraint of communications. Injunctions will normally not issue to prevent breaches of the criminal law, although it is open to the Attorney-General, as guardian of the public interest in maintaining compliance with the criminal law, to commence an action for an injunction, either on the relation of a member of the public or of his own motion, if he deems it to be in the public interest.[34] But when seeking to uphold governmental secrecy by restraining threatened disclosures, it would not always have been sufficient for the Attorney-General to rely on prospective breaches of the Official Secrets Acts 1911–1939, because the courts might not regard the case as falling within the types of situations in which such discretionary remedies could properly be granted, stated by Lord Wilberforce as follows:[35] 'It is an exceptional power confined, in prac-

---

[33] Hooper, *Official Secrets*, 174–81.

[34] J. L. J. Edwards, *The Law Officers of the Crown* (London: Sweet & Maxwell, 1964), 286–93; *Gouriet* v. *Union of Post Office Workers* [1978] AC 435, [1977] 3 All ER 70, HL; David Feldman, 'Injunctions and the Criminal Law' (1979) 42 *MLR* 369–88; J. L. J. Edwards, *The Attorney General, Politics and the Public Interest* (London: Sweet & Maxwell, 1984), 129–45. The similar power of local authorities under Local Government Act 1972, s. 222, extends only to cases in which an authority is acting in the interests of inhabitants of its area, and so is not normally appropriate to protecting the national interest as a whole: Barry Hough, 'Local Authorities as Guardians of the Public Interest' [1992] *PL* 130–49 at pp. 139–43.

[35] *Gouriet* v. *Union of Post Office Workers* [1978] AC 435 at p. 481, [1977] 3 All ER at p. 83 *per* Lord Wilberforce.

tice, to cases where an offence is frequently repeated in disregard of a, usually, inadequate penalty (see *Attorney-General (on the relation of Manchester Corporation* v. *Harris)*[36] or to cases of emergency (see *Attorney-General* v. *Chaudry).'*[37]

In 1975, government lawyers hit on a ground for seeking an injunction restraining publication which did not require them to show that these conditions were satisfied. When the literary executors of Richard Crossman, a former Labour Cabinet Minister, were preparing his diaries for publication, the Attorney-General sought to restrain publication on the ground that the diaries revealed details of discussions within Cabinet which were protected by a duty of confidence owed by every Cabinet Minister to his colleagues.[38] The advantage of an application for an injunction to restrain a breach of confidence is that in governmental matters it is usually relatively easy to establish the existence of a duty of confidence, as the whole system of government is dominated by the idea that almost everything is confidential. The doctrine of breach of confidence had been developed in private-law contexts, protecting business and privacy interests, as noted in Chapter 10, above. If adopted in a public-law setting, it would have had the effect of casting the workings of government into yet deeper shadow. This would have appealed only to members of the government and to civil servants and members of the security services.

In the event, Lord Widgery CJ admitted breach of confidence to the public-law sphere, but subject to a major qualification: before it could be invoked by government, the government would have to demonstrate that a public interest required that the publication in question be restrained. This interest would then be weighed against any favouring publication. This imposed a double burden on the Attorney-General: first, to show that the material in question was held in confidence; secondly, a burden not carried by private plaintiffs in breach of confidence actions, to show a public interest in maintaining the confidence. Lord Widgery adopted this approach from the judgments of the US Supreme Court in *New York Times Co.* v. *United States,*[39] where by a six to three majority the Court had, on a balance-of-interest analysis, rejected an attempt by the US administration to enjoin publication by the *New York Times* of a classified document, *History of US Decision-Making Process on Viet Nam Policy* (the so-called 'Pentagon Papers'). The administration had argued that publication would damage national security, but this claim was not accepted by the majority, partly because of the largely historical significance of the material.

[36] [1961] 1 QB 74.   [37] [1971] 3 All ER 938.
[38] *Attorney-General* v. *Jonathan Cape Ltd*. [1976] QB 752, [1975] 3 All ER 484.
[39] 403 US 713 (1971)

In the case of the Crossman diaries, there was little dispute about the confidential nature of Cabinet discussions. Each member of the Cabinet is bound by the convention of collective Cabinet responsibility, one element in which is an expectation that the course of discussion in Cabinet will not be disclosed.[40] However, the Attorney failed to discharge the burden of showing that there was an indefinitely continuing, overriding public interest in maintaining the secrecy of Cabinet discussions. The governmental interest in maintaining confidence had to be balanced against the public interest in free expression, particularly, in a democracy, freedom to impart information about the way in which government is conducted. Lord Widgery CJ accepted that the balance favoured enforcing the confidence up to a point, but held that the public interest in protecting confidences in public law did not operate indefinitely. In 1975, the events and issues covered by the first volume of the diaries lay ten years or more in the past, so Lord Widgery decided that publication would not interfere with free and frank discussion in the current Cabinet. Against this, Dr. Geoffrey Marshall has argued persuasively that, when laying down a legal principle concerning the publication of details of Cabinet discussions, the question should have been whether knowing that today's discussion might be published in ten years would inhibit today's ministers, not whether publishing a ten-year-old discussion would prejudice today's discussions.[41] This is a criticism of the way in which Lord Widgery weighed the relevant interests. It does not affect the fundamental principle which Lord Widgery laid down, namely that the obligation of secrecy on Cabinet ministers are neither absolute nor of infinite duration, and that the extent of the obligation depends on a balance of public interests which is to be settled by the courts. An attempt to induce ministers voluntarily to accept restrictions on what may be published, based on the *Report of the Radcliffe Committee of Privy Councillors on Ministerial Memoirs*,[42] appears to have been successful. Many Cabinet Ministers have since brought out their own memoirs and diaries, in the process adding greatly to people's understanding of the way in which British Cabinet government works.

Unlike the Pentagon Papers, the Crossman diaries raised no issue of national security. Nevertheless, Lord Widgery said, *obiter*, that 'the court must have power to deal with publication which threatens national security'.[43] The next time the public law of breach of confidence became an

---

[40] Geoffrey Marshall, *Constitutional Conventions* (Oxford: Clarendon Press, 1986), 58–61.

[41] Marshall, *Constitutional Conventions*, at p. 60.

[42] Cmnd. 6386 (1976). The Committee was set up to consider the position in the light of the Crossman diaries case.

[43] *Attorney General* v. *Jonathan Cape Ltd*. [1976] QB 752 at p. 769, [1975] 3 All ER 484 at p. 495.

issue, in the *Spycatcher* case, the government was relying in part on national-security arguments. Initially they succeeded, but at trial the government ultimately failed to show either that the material in question was still secret, or that there was a continuing interest in secrecy which overrode that in publication.[44] This is considered further in the next section.

The decision in the *Spycatcher* case made the prospects for using the civil law of breach of confidence to control leaks of government information look much less rosy, and the government turned its attention back to subsequent restraint and the use of the criminal law. Proposals for reform of the Official Secrets Acts 1911–39, replacing the blanket provisions of section 2 of the 1911 Act with more narrowly drawn and carefully directed categories of secret information and material, had been made regularly—for example, by the Franks Committee[45] in 1972. A Protection of Official Information Bill, introduced in 1979 by the Conservative government, was withdrawn. In the absence of further government-sponsored legislation, there were various attempts by backbenchers to introduce an amending bill. The last of these was a Protection of Official Information Bill, introduced by Mr. Richard Shepherd MP during the 1987–8 session. This was defeated when the government took the highly unusual step of issuing a three-line whip to compel its supporters in the Commons to vote against a private member's bill introduced by one of its own back-benchers. Eventually, the government came forward with its own proposals in a White Paper,[46] translated into legislation as the Official Secrets Act 1989. This at last repealed and replaced the discredited section 2 of the 1911 Act.[47] Instead of a blanket prohibition on disclosure of all types of information, the 1989 Act specific the types of material which are to be protected by the criminal law and the kinds of people subject to criminal sanctions for making disclosures. The main features of the 1989 Act are explained in section 3 below.

This brief survey of the background to the legal treatment of the security interests of the state can best be concluded by drawing attention to brings out three features of the problem of legally restricting freedom to impart and receive information in order to protect national security. First, national security is difficult to define. It used to be given a relatively narrow meaning, if the role of the security service (MI5), as described in 1952 by Sir David Maxwell Fyfe (then Home Secretary) in a memorandum to

---

[44] *Attorney-General v. Guardian Newspapers (No. 2)* [1990] 1 AC 109, [1988] 3 All ER 545, HL.

[45] *Report of the Franks Committee on Section 2 of the Official Secrets Act 1911*, Cmnd. 5104 (1972).

[46] Home Office, *Reform of Section 2 of the Official Secrets Act 1911*, Cm. 408 (1988).

[47] Patrick Birkinshaw, *Reforming the Secret State* (Hull: Hull University Press, 1990).

the Director-General, is any guide: 'the defence of the realm as a whole from external and internal dangers arising from attempts at espionage and sabotage and from the actions of persons and organisations whether directed from within or without the country which may be judged subversive to the state.' This was a wide and politically charged formulation: subversion is a weasel word, and, as experience elsewhere in the world has shown, what is honest political opposition to one person can easily be regarded as subversion by a government or security service. Evidence suggests that the security service exploited the idea of subversion during the 1950s and 1960s to launch operations motivated by right-wing political bias against trade unions, the Labour Party, and liberal or civil liberties groups. The duties of MI5 have now been placed on a statutory footing by the Security Service Act 1989. Section 1(2) defines its functions rather more widely than Maxwell Fyfe did:[48] 'the protection of national security and, in particular, its protection against threats from espionage, terrorism and sabotage, from the activities of agents of foreign powers and *from actions intended to overthrow or undermine parliamentary democracy by political, industrial or violent means*' (italics added). The notion of subversion is happily absent from this formulation. None the less, the suggestion, in the words italicized in this passage, that national security requires that parliamentary democracy (itself a problematic term) should not be undermined by political means, is ominous. It seems to be overinclusive, threatening repression of the non-violent expression of a brand of political thought. It is a throw-back to the eighteenth century, when a non-violent attack on any institution or official of the state was liable to be stigmatized as a seditious libel.[49] It is at least arguable that one of the important principles of modern parliamentary democracy is that it should be permissible to put before the electorate any political creed, including advocating non-parliamentary processes of democracy of even anarchy, so long as it is done peaceably and in a time, place, and manner which is not likely to give rise to public disorder or racial hatred.

Secondly, there is a problematical relationship between the public interest, national security (which is just one aspect of the public interest, but may sometimes be accorded overriding weight), and the interests of the government (which in a system dominated by party politics are largely partisan, rather than being the interests of either the nation or the public). The sensitivity of this relationship is illustrated by cases which gave the appearance that the criminal law was being used in an attempt to prevent political embarrassment to the government.[50] (The attempts

---

[48] For full discussion of this legislation, see Ian Leigh and Laurence Lustgarten, 'The Security Service Act 1989' (1989) 52 *MLR* 801–36.

[49] See s. 4(2), below.

[50] Besides the *Ponting* case, see e.g. the account of the trial in 1971 of Mr. Jonathan

backfired.) It becomes still more sensitive if, as suggested above in relation to the Security Service Act 1989, the protection of national security is held to take on a substantive political content, requiring officials to discriminate against certain types of political belief.

The third characteristic is the complex interaction of civil and criminal law. Governments have used each in turn, or both together, in order to maintain a system in which secrecy is normal practice. It is possible that there may in the future be cross-pollination between the standards in security matters laid down by the two systems. When the *Spycatcher* case was before the courts, Scott J pointed out that it was open to Parliament to provide guidelines for the relative weightings of different public interests in civil proceedings to restrain publication of state secrets, but that, as Parliament had not done so, the judges had to use their own judgement.[51] Later, in *Lord Advocate* v. *The Scotsman Publications Ltd.*,[52] discussed further below, the government was applying unsuccessfully in civil proceedings for an interim interdict preventing a Scottish newspaper from publishing extracts from the memoirs of a former officer of MI6, the secret intelligence service. By this time, the Official Secrets Act 1989 had been passed, but had not yet been brought into effect. In the House of Lords, Lord Templeman based his rejection of the government's claim on his view that the 1989 Act, creating criminal offences, provided guidance as to the circumstances in which restraint of expression is necessary in a democratic society. Noting that third parties who disclose material passed to them in breach of the Act do not commit an offence unless their disclosure is damaging to the state, Lord Templeman said:

In my opinion the civil jurisdiction of the courts of this country to grant an injunction restraining a breach of confidence at the suit of the Crown should not, in principle, be exercised in a manner different from or more severe than any appropriate restriction which Parliament has imposed in the 1989 Act and which, if breached, will create a criminal offence

under that Act.[53] This is a welcome assertion of an important liberal principle in relation to freedom of expression: namely that prior restraint is, at least, no less objectionable than subsequent restraint by criminal sanctions, and should therefore be no more extensive in its operation. A similar approach may be implicit in the speeches of Lord Keith, with whom Lord Griffiths and Lord Goff agreed, and Lord Jauncey. They held that

Aitken, then a journalist, under Official Secrets Act 1911, s. 2: Jonathan Aitken, *Officially Secret* (London: Weidenfeld & Nicolson, 1971). Mr. Aitken is now an MP, and following the May 1992 general election became Minister for Defence Procurement.

[51] [1990] 1 AC 109 at p. 144; [1988] 3 All ER 545 at p. 570.
[52] [1990] 1 AC 812, [1989] 2 All ER 852, HL.
[53] [1990] 1 AC at p. 824, [1989] 2 All ER at p. 859.

the government was not entitled to the interim interdict because disclosure would cause no damage to national security. However, they did not employ or endorse Lord Templeman's explicit linking of the civil-law principles to the criminal law; indeed, Lord Jauncey was the only other Law Lord who even mentioned the 1989 Act. The authority for saying that the link exists, and that prior restraint is not to extend beyond the reach of the criminal law, is therefore by no means unequivocal.

14.2 PRIOR CONSTRAINT AND THE PUBLIC INTEREST: BREACH OF CONFIDENCE, *SPYCATCHER*, AND ITS IMPLICATIONS.[54]

The efficiency, from the government's point of view, of stifling information or opinion before it can do harm falls to be balanced against the public interest in the flow of information and the exchange of opinion necessary to a functioning democracy. The conflict between these interests was seen in stark form in the litigation which surrounded the attempts by a number of newspapers to serialize or report on a book, *Spycatcher*, by Peter Wright, who had been a scientific officer in the counter-espionage branch of the security service, MI5, from 1955 to 1973, and had been on the personal staff of the Director-General of MI5 as adviser on counter-espionage from 1973 until he retired in 1976. The book, completed and in the hands of Australian publishers in 1985, contained an account of Mr. Wright's work for MI5. It included accounts of buggings and burglaries, including an attempt to bug the suit occupied by Mr. Kruschev at Claridges when he was on an official visit to the UK; an allegation that Sir Roger Hollis, a previous Director-General of MI5, had been a double agent employed by the USSR; and various allegations concerning (*inter alia*) a plan to assassinate President Nasser, and a conspiracy by some officers to discredit Mr. Harold Wilson and destabilize his government.

Whether or not these accounts were true (and official inquiries failed to find convincing evidence to support the allegations concerning Sir Roger Hollis and the conspiracy against the Wilson government), the information and allegations were stale. They related to a period preceding Mr Wright's retirement, and had nearly all been published before by other writers without any legal action being taken against them. Nevertheless, the government considered that publication had to be stopped as a matter of principle. The government argued that, because Mr Wright had been a member of the security service, he was under a

---

[54] See generally Francis Gurry, *Breach of Confidence* (Oxford: Clarendon Press, 1985); Raymond Wacks, *Personal Information: Privacy and the Law* (Oxford: Clarendon Press, 1989), ch. 3; Robertson and Nicol, *Media Law*, 3rd edn., pp. 172–96.

lifelong duty of secrecy in respect of matters which came to his attention in the course of his duties. It was said to be in the public interest to prevent disclosures by members and former members of the security and intelligence services, for two main reasons. First (irrespective of the content of any disclosure), the confidence and morale of the services depended on maintaining absolute trust that their discussions, policies, and actions would not be disclosed by colleagues and former colleagues. Secondly, good international relations, and particularly co-operation and sharing of information with the intelligence and security services of friendly powers, depended on being able to ensure that confidences would not be breached by officers. In order to prevent a breach of this trust, the government invoked the law of breach of confidence.[55]

The government's first step was to sue the Australian publishers in New South Wales for an injunction restraining publication, or, failing that, an account of profits.[56] Before the hearing, two English newspapers, the *Observer* and the *Guardian*, obtained details of the allegations made in Mr Wright's manuscript, and published them in June 1986, together with a description of the nature of the pending New South Wales proceedings. The Attorney General obtained injunctions in England restraining those newspapers from further publication of the allegations, and interim injunctions to preserve the confidentiality of the material pending trial of the action. In the form in which the interim injunctions were upheld by a majority of the House of Lords, they restrained not only publication of extracts from the *Spycatcher* manuscript, but also publication of reports on the Australian proceedings.[57] In contempt proceedings, it was subsequently held that the injunctions against the *Observer* and the *Guardian* also bound other newspapers which had notice of them.[58] Nevertheless, news of the allegations continued to leak out in the UK and abroad. The New South Wales application failed.[59]

---

[55] Scott J. was later to point out that the government's claim was not strictly based on a duty of confidence, as it encompassed secret material unearthed by Mr. Wright's own efforts, without being confided to him, and also all information, whether confidential or not, which Mr. Wright acquired in his capacity as a member of MI5: [1990] 1 AC at p. 144, [1988] 3 All ER at p. 571. Nevertheless, it was accepted that the principles of breach of confidence were applicable by analogy, subject to any special extensions or restrictions necessitated by the public-law nature of the case.

[56] For an account of the history of the proceedings and of the allegations published in *Spycatcher*, see the judgment of Scott J in *A.-G. v. Guardian Newspapers (No. 2)* [1990] 1 AC at pp. 120–38, [1988] 3 All ER at pp. 552–66.

[57] *A.-G. v. Guardian Newspapers Ltd.* [1987] 1 WLR 1248, [1987] All ER 316, HL.

[58] *A.-G. v. Newspaper Publishing plc* [1988] Ch. 333, [1987] 3 All ER 276, CA; *A.-G. v. Times Newspapers Ltd.* [1992] 1 AC 191, [1991] 2 All ER 398, HL.

[59] *A.-G. v. Heinemann Publishers Australia Pty Ltd.* (1987) 8 NSWLR 341, affirmed CA of NSW (1987) 10 NSWLR 86, and HC of Australia (1888) 165 CLR 30.

Meanwhile, the editor of the *Sunday Times*, having heard that *Spycatcher* was to be published shortly in the USA, negotiated a serialization with the American publishers, and obtained from them a copy of the manuscript. On 12 July 1987, the day before the book was published in the USA, the *Sunday Times* published extracts from the manuscript in the UK. By now, the government seemed engaged in a futile attempt to stop people from discovering that which they already knew. Sir Nicolas Browne-Wilkinson VC discharged the English interim injunctions, accepting that they could no longer serve their main purpose in preserving the alleged confidentiality of the information in *Spycatcher* pending trial, but his decision was reversed by the Court of Appeal, and on appeal their decision was upheld by a majority of the House of Lords.[60] Finally, at the end of 1987, the government's action came on for its full trial. In the course of this litigation, the courts went a substantial way towards settling the scope and enforceability of duties of confidence in respect of information about, or held by, the state.

The remainder of this section examines the conditions for prior restraint of threatened breaches of confidence. It then looks at two further matters: other remedies available to government, and the implications of the European Convention on Human Rights in this field.

(1) Conditions for prior restraint for breach of confidence

(i) *The nature of breach of confidence in public law.* As noted in Chapter 10, above, breach of confidence is a civil wrong capable of imposing sanctions on publication of information (though not mere opinion). Remedies are available where information is confidential and the defendant obtained it in circumstances which imposed on him a duty to maintain the confidentiality of the information. Duties of confidence may either arise under contracts, or be imposed by equity. In considering the applicability of duties of confidence to government information in *Attorney-General* v. *Jonathan Cape Ltd.*,[61] Lord Widgery CJ had recognized that actions for breach of confidence have the potential to interfere substantially with the capacity of MPs, the press, and the public to scrutinize and evaluate government. Since there is a public interest in a democracy in being able to evaluate and debate government organization and policies, he subjected the duties of confidentiality in respect of information about government to certain limits. The most significant limits are the following.

---

[60] *A.-G.* v. *Guardian Newspapers Ltd.* [1987] 1 WLR 1248, [1987] 3 All ER 316 (Lords Brandon, Templeman, and Ackner; Lords Bridge and Oliver dissented).
[61] [1976] QB 752, [1975] 3 All ER 484.

1. Government cannot assert a duty of confidence in respect of information about its activities unless it can demonstrate a clear public interest in maintaining secrecy, which in practice means showing that damage would flow from disclosure.

2. Disclosure of a confidence will not be restrained if it can be shown that there is a public interest in revealing it which outweighs the public interest in keeping it secret.

3. To justify prior restraint, the material must usually retain its confidential quality at the time of the litigation, although the scope of the duty of confidence depends on the identity of the particular defendant. This means that remedies for breach or threatened breach of confidence are likely to be restricted once the material reaches the public domain.

Condition (1) applies to government over and above the conditions which are normally imposed on a person wishing to restrain a breach of confidence. Once a private plaintiff shows that information is of a confidential type, usually because it concerns trade secrets or intimate details of private life, the court will normally assume that there are legitimate private interest grounds for wanting to protect it (see Chapter 10). By contrast, because the government carries on its activities solely for the public benefit, it is assumed to have no legitimate private interests to protest. The courts therefore demand that public bodies demonstrate that a legitimate public interest justifies using principles of private law to secure the secrecy of information which is held for public purposes. Governmental bodies must therefore satisfy the court both that the material is confidential and that it is in the general public interest to keep it secret.

Condition (2) allows for what is sometimes called the iniquity defence to operate in public law. A person is not bound by a duty of confidence to keep secret iniquitous behaviour or other matters if it is in the public interest that they should be investigated or exposed. However, a person wishing to take advantage of the iniquity defence must show that the allegation appears to be based on substantial grounds, and that any disclosure was made to a person and in a manner appropriate to the matter in question.

Even if the balance comes down in favour of publication, it does not follow that publication should be to the world through the media. In certain circumstances the public interest may be better served by a limited form of publication perhaps to the police or some other authority who can follow up a suspicion that wrongdoing may lurk beneath the cloak of confidence.[62]

---

[62] *A.-G.* v. *Guardian Newspapers Ltd. (No. 2)* [1988] 3 All ER at p. 649 *per* Lord Griffiths. See also *Francome* v. *Mirror Group Newspapers* [1984] 1 WLR 892, [1984] 2 All ER 408, CA.

Condition (3) is partly an aspect of (1). Where material has been widely publicized before trial, as in the *Spycatcher* case, it will be hard to persuade a judge that it remains in the public interest to restrain publication, as generally any damage which could flow from the disclosure will already have occurred.

This set of conditions form the judges' way of accommodating the democratic demand for open government within governmental claims that certain public functions (notably security and international relations) cannot be effectively performed in the glare of publicity. The compromise recognizes that government, as a public agency, has legitimate concerns which are different from those of ordinary citizens. At the same time it seeks to ensure that governmental bodies do not exploit their special constitutional position in circumstances where it is not in the public interest for them to do so.

This approach has gained currency in a number of common-law jurisdictions. In the USA, besides being determinative of the issues in the Pentagon Papers case, it was influential in limiting the scope of 'executive privilege', asserted by President Nixon in the course of the Watergate scandal.[63] In Australia the approach was developed by Mason J., of the High Court of Australia, to deal with an attempt by the federal government to restrain publication of confidential matters. In *Commonwealth of Australia v. John Fairfax & Sons Ltd.*,[64] the Australian Federal government sought to restrain further publication by the defendants of a book, *Documents on Australian Defence and Foreign Policy 1968–75*, which contained previously unpublished communications between the Australian and Indonesian governments and their diplomats. The relationship between Australia and Indonesia was politically sensitive, because of a division of opinion in Australia concerning the appropriate response to Indonesian claims over East Timor. The Australian government sought an interlocutory injunction to restrain publication of the book, on two grounds. First, it was argued that publication would be a breach of the government's copyright in the material. On this point, the government was ultimately successful. However, the government also argued that the material was confidential, as it was not 'public property and public knowledge'.[65] It had probably been leaked by a public servant in breach of his or her duty, and the publishers knew that the documents were classified and that the government had not authorized publication.

Nevertheless, the confidentiality claim failed. Mason J. accepted that ordinary citizens are entitled to protection against unauthorized publica-

---

[63] *US* v. *Nixon*, 418 US 683 (1974).   [64] (1980) 147 CLR 39, HC of Australia.

[65] This generous definition of confidentiality was derived from Lord Greene MR in *Saltman Engineering Co. Ltd.* v. *Campbell Engineering Co. Ltd.* (1948) [1963] 3 All ER 413, CA, at p. 415.

tion, to their detriment, of the secrets of their private or business lives. But when a government seeks to invoke confidentiality protection for governmental information, the court must ask itself what detriment the public interest, rather than the government or the governing party, suffers from an unauthorized disclosure.

The equitable principle has been fashioned to protect the personal, private and proprietary interests of the citizen, not to protect the very different interests of the executive government. It acts, or is supposed to act, not according to standards of private interest, but in the public interest. This is not to say that Equity will not protect information in the hands of the government, but it is to say that when Equity protects government information it will look at the matter through different spectacles. . . . It is unacceptable, in our democratic society, that there should be a restraint on the publication of information relating to government when the only vice of that information is that it enables the public to discuss, review and criticize government action. Accordingly, the court will determine the government's claim to confidentiality by reference to the public interest. Unless disclosure is likely to injure the public interest, it will not be protected.[66]

This places the public interest in open government in a democracy at the centre of any consideration of a governmental claim to confidentiality. It follows that the various public interests which are asserted by the government (in that case, the interest in maintaining trust and a free flow of information between governments when conducting international affairs) must be weighed against others which are proved or of which judicial notice is taken (such as the interest in open government and democratic accountability). On the facts of the *John Fairfax* case, the latter interests were held to outweigh the former, not least because the book had already achieved some currency and the continued circulation of the information which it contained could not be prevented by restraining publication of further copies. In essence, this is a similar form of reasoning to that employed by Lord Widgery CJ in the *Jonathan Cape* case (where however there had been no previous publication) and in the judgments which followed the full hearing of the *Spycatcher* case.

The public interest in national security goes beyond keeping secrets. As developed in the *Spycatcher* case, it takes account of the efficiency of the security and intelligence services, and of other branches of the public service. Indeed, in *Attorney General* v. *Guardian Newspapers Ltd. (No. 2)*[67] Lord Griffiths, noting that Article 10(2) of the European Convention on Human Rights accepts that it may be justifiable to restrict freedom of expression in order to protect national security,[68] treated the national-security implications as quite separate from confidentiality:

---

[66] (1980) 147 CLR 39 at p. 51–2, *per* Mason J.
[67] [1990] 1 AC 109, [1988] 3 All ER 545, HL.
[68] [1990] 1 AC at p. 273, [1988] 3 All ER at p. 652.

The worldwide publication of *Spycatcher* disposes of the Attorney General's claim based on confidential information, but the claim based on national security remains to be examined. If I had thought that further publication would so damage the morale of the security service that they could not operate efficiently I would have been prepared to grant the injunction in the interests of national security. Of course, I think no such thing.[69]

If correct, this would mean that publication of non-confidential information by third parties could be restrained if that were necessary to maintain staff morale at an efficient level. However, maintenance of morale is the responsibility of MI5 managers, not courts of equity. As Lord Goff said:

In our civil law there is, so far as I am aware, no ground for restricting publication of information relating to national security other than breach of confidence. Information relating to national security is, of its very nature, prima facie confidential. . . . [A]ny such publication, if threatened, can therefore be restrained by injunction as a threatened breach of confidence, subject of course to the usual limitations on the duty of confidence. One of these is that information is no longer confidential once it has entered the public domain; once information relating to national security has entered the public domain, I find it difficult to see on what basis further disclosure of such information can be restrained.[70]

On this view, the fact that a disclosure may affect the efficiency of the security service is only one element (though an important one) in the balance of interests which affects the availability of remedies for breach of confidence. It is not an independent head of claim. Lord Goff's approach is to be preferred, on principle, to that of Lord Griffiths, which would have created an entirely new basis for equitable relief.

(ii) *Weighing the interests: the difference between interlocutory and final hearings.* The English courts appear to have established that the weight given to relevant interests will vary, depending on whether the proceedings are interlocutory or final. Where the substance of the government's claim relies on the confidentiality of the material, an interim injunction is likely to be granted to restrain publication pending trial of the action, because publication would often destroy the confidentiality which is the subject-matter of the action. There is a public interest in ensuring that wrongdoers are not able to destroy the plaintiff's cause of action in advance of its enforcement. Restraining a publication pending trial is only a temporary interference with freedom of expression and communication, and is thought to be easier to justify than the permanent ban imposed by a final injunction. The only circumstance in which an interim injunction is

[69] [1990] 1 AC at p. 275, [1988] 3 All ER at p. 654.
[70] [1990] 1 AC at p. 291, [1988] 3 All ER at p. 666.

likely to be refused is where the court decides that the government has failed to meet the requirements laid down in *American Cyanamid Co.* v. *Ethicon*[71] for the grant of an interlocutory injunction. The House of Lords there decided that the court must balance (*a*) the plaintiff's need, if successful at trial, to be protected against injury which could not be adequately compensated by an award of damages at trial, against (*b*) the defendant's need, if successful at trial, to be protected against injury, which could not be adequately compensated under the plaintiff's undertaking in damages, resulting from having been restrained from exercising his rights pending trial. Accordingly, the court must first decide whether there is a serious issue to be tried. (The plaintiff need not show a strong prima-facie case, or a likelihood of succeeding at trial.) If there is, the court must see whether damages would adequately compensate the plaintiff if successful at trial. In cases concerning national security, damages will never adequately compensate the government. On the other hand, nor will it be possible for the defendant to rely on being compensated if successful, as the courts will not require the Crown to give an undertaking in damages when applying for an interim injunction.[72] The court must therefore decide whether the balance of convenience between the parties favours granting an injunction. When the merits are evenly balanced, the court should grant the injunction to preserve the *status quo.*

The effect of these principles in national-security and breach-of-confidence cases is that only where the plaintiff government accepts that there will be no further detriment to the public interest from publication will an interim injunction be refused. Such a case was *Lord Advocate* v. *The Scotsman Publications Ltd.*,[73] where the House of Lords approved a decision of the Court of Session to refuse the Lord Advocate an interim interdict restraining the publishers of a newspaper from publishing a serialization of the memoirs of *Inside Intelligence* by Anthony Cavendish, a former MI6 officer. The book had already been privately distributed, and the newspaper had come by a copy innocently. The government denied that further publication would harm national security, but argued that publication should be restrained to enforce the lifelong duty of confidentiality attaching to officers of the security and intelligence services. The House of Lords decided that, while it would have been appropriate to restrain the initial publication by Mr. Cavendish, no public interest would be served by restraining the further publication by an innocent third party where no damage would result. On the other hand, where government asserts that some damage to security will be done by a

[71] [1975] AC 396, [1975] 1 All ER 504, HL.

[72] *F. Hoffmann-La Roche & Co. AG* v. *Secretary of State for Trade and Industry* [1975] AC 295, [1974] 2 All ER 1128, HL.

[73] [1990] 1 AC 812, [1989] 2 All ER 852, HL (Sc.).

breach of a duty of confidence, and there is a serious issue to be tried, the court will virtually always grant an interim injunction, safeguarding the government's interest pending a full hearing of the case, regardless of the court's view of the likely result of the trial, for on an interlocutory application the court is not well placed to assess the strength of the evidence.

At the hearing of the action, the position is very different. The public interest in the due administration of justice, which justified the interim injunction, will usually cease to be a relevant consideration, and the case for a permanent interference with free expression will stand or fall on its own merits. This means that the grounds for granting an interim injunction are very different from those for granting a final injunction. This is well illustrated by the *Spycatcher* litigation.

(iii) Spycatcher: *the interlocutory proceedings*. In the interlocutory proceedings, the Court of Appeal, in a ruling upheld by a majority of the House of Lords on appeal, did not perform the balancing act demanded under the *John Fairfax* and *Jonathan Cape* cases. They reversed the decision of Sir Nicolas Browne-Wilkinson VC to discharge the interim injunctions, because following *American Cyanamid* they felt that, in interlocutory proceedings, they were more concerned with the public interest in the administration of justice than with the substantive law of breach of confidence. They held that the government had an arguable case for a permanent injunction, notwithstanding the previous widespread publication of the *Spycatcher* allegations by other authors and publishers in this country and by publishers of Mr. Wright's memoirs abroad, and that damages would not adequately compensate the government if they succeeded at trial. In the House of Lords, two members of the majority, Lord Brandon and Lord Ackner, decided that the balance of convenience favoured restraining publication temporarily pending trial, because further publications would have destroyed any remaining confidentiality which the government sought to protect as the subject-matter of the action.[74]

The House granted a very wide injunction, which forbade publication of the contents of *Spycatcher* and even fair and accurate reports of the proceedings concerning *Spycatcher* then in progress in New South Wales. Because of the perceived importance of preserving (so far as possible) the subject-matter of the action, Knox J. later held that a public library authority, with knowledge of the proceedings, which purchased *Spycatcher* would be in contempt of court, notwithstanding the duty to operate an efficient library service under the Public Libraries and Museums Act 1964, section 7, and the public demand for the book.

[74] *A.-G. v. Guardian Newspapers Ltd.* [1987] 1 WLR 1248, [1987] 3 All ER 316, HL.

Nevertheless, the libraries could continue to take newspapers, and would not have sufficient *mens rea* to be held in contempt if they merely failed to check each newspaper to see whether it contained material breaching the injunction against publicizing the *Spycatcher* allegations.[75]

However, granting an injunction of this width was questionable on civil liberties grounds, in the light of the world-wide publicity already given to the allegations in the book. If one takes seriously the public interest in freedom of the press as a means of informing people about matters of public interest, that interest needs to be weighed against the public interest in maintaining confidentiality and protecting the integrity of the legal process. Where, as was admitted by the majority in the *Spycatcher* case, it was already very unlikely that a permanent injunction would be granted at trial, that fact must diminish the weight to be given to the interest in protecting the subject-matter of the action (which was already as good as destroyed) and the maintenance of confidentiality. For this reason Sir Nicolas Browne-Wilkinson decided at first instance, and Lord Bridge and Lord Oliver held in their powerful dissenting speeches in the House of Lords, that it was improper to continue the interim injunctions once publication of the allegations in the United States, and publicity all over the world, had seriously undermined the secrecy of the information contained in Mr. Wright's book. Furthermore, Lord Bridge and Lord Oliver considered that Article 10 of the European Convention on Human Rights would be breached by the continuation of the injunctions, a view subsequently confirmed by a majority of the European Court of Human Rights.

A second ground was advanced, by Lord Templeman and Lord Ackner, for granting an interim injunction, although neither this nor the first ground seems to have commanded the support of more than two of the five Law Lords. (This makes it hard to identify a *ratio decidendi* in the case.) This second ground was that the injunction should be continued to protect the public interest in the proper functioning of the security service, which Sir Robert Armstrong, the Cabinet Secretary, had said to be threatened by the risk that morale would be harmed by allowing disclosures by former officers. While the interest in the proper performance of the functions of the security service deserves substantial weight, it is only one of a number of public-interest factors affecting the duty of confidentiality which should be weighed against each other in deciding what remedies (if any) should be made available for breach of confidence. We will return to this matter when considering the final hearing.

The majority of the House of Lords in the interlocutory appeal treated

[75] *A.-G.* v. *Observer Ltd.; Re an application by Derbyshire County Council* [1988] 1 All ER 385.

the grant of a temporary injunction pending trial principally as a matter to be settled according to the balance of convenience, having strictly limited human rights implications because of the nature of the restraint on free expression. When the newspapers' publishers petitioned under the European Convention on Human Rights, the case was examined principally by reference to the justifiability of the interference with freedom of expression under Article 10(2) of the Convention.[76] The European Court of Human Rights held that the law on interim injunctions had been sufficiently clear to be said to be 'prescribed by law', as the criteria for granting interim injunctions were well established in the common law by the House of Lords decision in *American Cyanamid Co.* v. *Ethicon Ltd.*[77] Is also held that the aim of the injunctions, to maintain the authority of the judiciary by preserving the subject matter of the action, was legitimate within Article 10(2).[78] However, the question remained whether the interference was 'necessary in a democratic society' for those purposes. This required the Court to consider four factors.

1. Freedom of expression constitutes one of the essential foundations of democratic society, and is as applicable to offensive, shocking, or disturbing ideas as to inoffensive ones.[79]

2. This was particularly important in relation to the press, which has the responsibility for imparting information and ideas to a public which has the right to receive them.

3. 'Necessary' implies the existence of a pressing social need, as the Court had earlier held in the *Sunday Times* case.[80]

4. The Court had to apply the principle of proportionality to the measures adopted, to see whether they were proportionate to the aim pursued, and whether the reasons supporting them were relevant and sufficient.

Applying these considerations, the Court held by a majority of fourteen to ten that the injunctions had originally been justified, having regard to the margin of appreciation allowed to the English courts in assessing the exigencies of the case. However, the Court held unanimously that the situation changed radically once the book *Spycatcher* was published in

---

[76] *Observer and Guardian* v. *UK* Eur. Ct. HR, Series A, No. 216, Judgment of 26 Nov. 1991, 14 EHRR 153; *Sunday Times* v. *UK (No. 2)*, Eur. Ct. HR, Series A, No. 217, Judgment of 26 Nov. 1991, 14 EHRR 229. See Ian Leigh, '*Spycatcher* in Europe' [1992] *PL* 200–8.

[77] [1975] AC 396, [1975] 1 All ER 504, HL.

[78] Protecting the position of parties to an action forms a legitimate element in maintaining the authority and impartiality of the judiciary: *Sunday Times* v. *UK* 2 EHRR 245.

[79] *Lingens* v. *Austria*, Eur. Ct. HR, Series A, No. 103, Judgment of 8 July 1986, 8 EHRR 407.

[80] Eur. Ct. HR, Series A, No. 3, Judgment of 26 Apr. 1979; 2 EHRR 245.

the United States in July 1987. At that point, confidentiality was destroyed, and the desire to maintain the authority of the court by preventing further prejudice to the Attorney-General's claim did not constitute a sufficient reason for the purposes of Article 10(2), because the substance of the Attorney-General's interest, the confidentiality of the matters canvassed in *Spycatcher*, had already been destroyed. The majority decision of the House of Lords in *Attorney General* v. *Guardian Newspapers Ltd.* on 30 July 1987 to continue the injunctions had probably served no useful purpose, and had prevented the press from exercising its right and duty to purvey information, which was already available, on a matter of legitimate public concern. Accordingly, the interference with press freedom represented by the injunctions was no longer 'necessary in a democratic society' after 30 July 1987. Lord Bridge's prophecy that the government would 'face inevitable condemnation and humiliation by the European Court of Human Rights' thus proved accurate.[81]

Ten judges, in partly dissenting judgments, held that the interim injunctions had offended against the principle of necessity in the period between their first granting on 11 July 1986 and 30 July 1987. Judge Morenilla argued that the appropriate standard to adopt in a case of prior restraint would be that of the US Supreme Court in cases such as *Nebraska Association* v. *Stuart*,[82] admitting such restraint only where disclosure would be sure to result in direct, immediate, and irreparable damage to the nation or its people.[83] However, such an approach might make it unnecessarily difficult for plaintiffs to protect their legitimate interests in obtaining a fair trial of their actions (in accordance with rights guaranteed under Article 6 of the Convention) in cases where the alleged wrong consists of a threatened, wrongful disclosure. The judgment of the majority of the European Court of Human Rights strikes a reasonable balance between the rights of the press and the interests of the justice system in maintaining confidentiality pending final hearing of the case. Indeed, by the time the *Spycatcher* case came up for final judgment in the House of Lords, it had become clear to everyone that the world-wide publicity given to Peter Wright's allegations made it unreasonable to restrain any newspapers from making use of the material.

The judgment of the European Court of Human Rights may influence future cases at both the final hearing and the interlocutory stages. At interlocutory hearings judges can probably develop the *American Cyanamid* principles in the light of the judgment, taking account of the effect of past publicity when assessing the balance of convenience. It might not be necessary to overrule *Attorney General* v. *Guardian*

[81] *A.-G.* v. *Guardian Newspapers* [1987] 1 WLR at p. 1286, [1987] 3 All ER at p. 347.
[82] 427 US 593 (1976). [83] 14 EHRR at p. 220.

Newspapers Ltd. Since (as pointed out earlier) it is not clear that there is any *ratio* for the decision which could be said to bind lower courts, it could simply be regarded as a decision on the particular facts of that case, having no wider significance. At the final hearing, as we shall see, the balancing of public interests is likely to have to take account of the requirements of proportionality and pressing social need developed under the caselaw of the European Court.

(iv) *The final hearing, and the claim to a permanent injunction.* When the government's claim for a permanent injunction restraining publication came finally to be tried on its merits, the approach adopted by Lord Widgery CJ in the *Jonathan Cape* case and by Mason J. in the *John Fairfax* case came into its own. It formed the basis for the judgment of Scott J. at first instance, and was applied by all three judges in the Court of Appeal and all save Lord Griffiths in the House of Lords.

The House of Lords, upholding the decision of Scott J. at first instance and a majority decision of the Court of Appeal, unanimously held that the publicity given abroad to the publication of Peter Wright's allegations, together with their previous publication by other authors, had effectively undermined the confidentiality of the material. They also held, by a four to one majority, that any damage which the articles published in the *Guardian* and the *Observer* in 1986, reporting the progress of the litigation in New South Wales, might have done to the public interest in national security was outweighed by the public interest in the freedom of the press to report court action. In the House of Lords, Lord Goff said:[84]

. . . the articles were very short: they gave little detail of the allegations; a number of the allegations had been made before; and in so far as the articles went beyond what had previously been published, I do not consider that the judge erred in holding that, in the circumstances, the claim to an injunction was not proportionate to the legitimate aim pursued.

The House refused an injunction permanently restraining the *Guardian* and the *Observer*, or anyone else, from publishing extracts from or reviewing or commenting on the book, because the material in it was by then in the public domain. Furthermore, the House refused an injunction against future publication of material derived from Mr. Wright. Even the *Sunday Times* was to be free to publish. ·

All the judges accepted that Mr. Wright, as a former member of MI5 was prima facie subject to a lifelong duty of confidentiality in respect of matters which came to his attention in the course of his service. Several of them considered, *obiter*, that he or his publishers would have been

[84] [1990] 1 AC at p. 290, [1988] 3 All ER at p. 665.

restrained by injunction from any further publication, had they been within the jurisdiction of the English courts, even after widespread publicity for the allegations. However, they differed as to the reasons for this. Scott J., all the judges in the Court of Appeal, and, in the House of Lords, Lord Griffiths and Lord Jauncey, considered that a person should be unable to relieve himself of an obligation of confidence by his own wrongful act of publication, regardless of any other obligations which might arise therefrom. Lord Brightman and Lord Goff considered that even Mr Wright's obligation of confidence ceased once the information was published and so lost its confidential character (albeit by Mr Wright's own wrongful act). They and Lord Keith thought that the sole reason for preventing a person in Mr Wright's position from further publications of old revelations would be to prevent him or his publishers from profiting by their own wrongs. In other words, any injunction would be punitive rather than protective; it would not advance any legitimate national-security interest, but might be available to prevent unjust enrichment or a breach of copyright. The aim of preventing people from making an illicit profit by breach of duty can legitimately be pursued even after the information has been disclosed by others. The question for a court of equity is not merely whether the information remains secret, but whether the particular defendant is subject to an obligation not to take a benefit from disclosing it. For this reason, the government has a remedy by way of account of profits where anyone has profited by breaching the duty of non-disclosure, and it may be proper to use the two remedies—injunction and account—against different people at different times. How had Mr Wright's publication and the publicity which had attended it affected the obligations of those further down the information chain? The courts dealt separately with the positions of the different defendants: the *Guardian* and the *Observer*, which had never had any dealings with Mr. Wright, his licensees, or agents, and were merely reporting matters which had come into the public domain; and the *Sunday Times*, which had entered into a licensing agreement with Mr. Wright's licensees to publish extracts from *Spycatcher*, and so were affected by the equitable effects of Mr. Wright's breach of duty.

However, the first issue related equally to all the defendants. Applying the test laid down in the *Jonathan Cape* and *John Fairfax* cases, had the government shown that continued restraint would be in the public interest? All the judges reaffirmed that it is the duty of the court to weigh and strike a balance between the competing public interests, that of the government in maintaining the efficiency of the security service and that of the newspapers in maintaining the freedom of the press. The judges rejected the claims, advanced by Sir Robert Armstrong, the Cabinet Secretary, on behalf of the government, that government alone should be the arbiter of the weight to be attached to the public-interest considerations which go into the government's side of the scales, opposed to publication.

Scott J., followed by the higher courts, also rejected the government's claim that the supposed requirements of national security should always override freedom of expression or of the press: 'I found myself unable to escape the reflection that the absolute protection of the security services that Sir Robert was contending for could not be achieved this side of the Iron Curtain.'[85] But the judge also rejected the view of the newspaper editors that no prior restraint on the press could be permitted:

Society must pay a price both for freedom of the press and for national security. The price to be paid for an efficient and secure security service will be some loss in the freedom of the press to publish what it chooses. The price to be paid for free speech and a free press in a democratic society will be the loss of some degree of secrecy about the affairs of government, including the security service. A balance must be struck between the two competing public interests. . . . It is open to Parliament, if it wishes, to impose guidelines. The United States Congress has done so in the form of the First Amendment. Parliament has not. And so it is for the courts to strike the balance.[86]

There are therefore two stages through which the government must go when seeking to restrain an alleged breach of confidence. First, they must be able to indicate a recognized public interest which will be aided by restraining the breach. Secondly, having done so, they must convince the court that, in the circumstances, the need to protect that public interest should be accorded greater weight than the advancement of other interests, public or private, which would be adversely affected by granting an injunction. For the court, public interests have two dimensions: relevance to the issue, which is an absolute; and weight, which is relative to other relevant interests, in the light of the arguments on each side.[87]

This has implications for the extent and duration of the duty of confidence in respect of information. The duty's extent and duration in relation to the same information may be different for different people. Officers and former officers of the security service, such as Mr Wright, bear a lifelong duty not to speak on matters coming to their attention in the course of their service, a duty now reinforced by criminal sanctions under the Official Secrets Act 1989, section 1(1). But third parties might not be subject to the same duties as Mr. Wright, because different private and public interests may act on them.[88] In particular, journalists owe no

[85] A.-G. v. Guardian Newspapers Ltd. (No. 2) [1990] 1 AC at p. 143, [1988] 3 All ER at p. 570.
[86] [1990] 1 AC at pp. 143–4, [1988] 3 All ER at p. 570.
[87] [1990] 1 AC at p. 154, [1988] 3 All ER at p. 578.
[88] [1990] 1 AC at p. 156, [1988] 3 All ER at p. 580.

contractual or fiduciary obligation to the government, and owe duties to the public in the name of press freedom. Scott J. accepted that Article 10 of the European Convention on Human Rights, guaranteeing the right freely to impart information and ideas, was capable of affecting the balance of interests in the case of publication by a newspaper. He held that the courts ought to strike a balance consistent with the government's obligations under the Convention. In doing so, the courts were entitled to have regard to the caselaw of the European Court of Human Rights, holding that interferences with the right to freedom of expression under Article 10 could be justified only where the restriction addressed, and was proportionate to, a pressing social need in respect of a legitimate aim under Article 10(2).[89] Lord Goff, in the House of Lords, expressly approved this approach,[90] and all the judges who heard the case, with the exception of Lord Donaldson M.R. in the Court of Appeal and to a more limited extent Lord Griffiths in the House of Lords, accepted that Scott J. had been entitled to come to the conclusion which he reached on the balance of public interests, implicitly accepting that he was entitled to employ Convention-based reasoning for that purpose. Because everything depends on a balance of interests which bears differently on different people, journalists who come innocently upon information which has been disclosed in breach of confidence are less likely to be restrained by the courts from publishing it than journalists who have induced or assisted the breach of confidence. The law on confidence has other objects, including the moral and commercial from profiting by its breach. It is therefore not absurd to regard people as having different duties in respect of the same information at the same time.

Invoking the European Convention on Human Rights as an aid to evaluating the relative weights of different interests might be thought to infringe the spirit of the decision in *R. v. Secretary of State for the Home Department, ex parte Brind*,[91] where the House of Lords held that it would not be irrational for a Home Secretary to fail to give effect to the terms of the Convention, and that the Convention could not be determinative of issues in the English courts. However, the arguments advanced by the majority in that case (Lords Bridge, Roskill, and Templeman) made it clear that there was room for Convention-based reasoning when developing the common law,[92] and the fear of the Convention being brought into English law by the back door, expressed by Lord Ackner in *Brind*, is unfounded where a judge merely uses the Convention as one of a

---

[89] [1990] 1 AC at pp. 156–9, [1988] 3 All ER at pp. 580–2.
[90] [1990] 1 AC at pp. 283–4, 290; [1988] 3 All ER at pp. 660, 665.
[91] [1991] 1 AC 696, [1991] 1 All ER 720, HL.
[92] For fuller discussion of the effects of *ex parte Brind* on the applicability of the Convention in English law, see above, s. 2.5(2).

number of factors influencing the weight to be attributed to public or private interests, the importance of which was already well recognized in English law quite independently of the Convention.

It is not easy for a court to weigh a public interest in enforcing a duty of confidence against competing interests, including that in developing an informed electorate and providing information on which consumers can make informed decisions. The government may claim that it would be contrary to the public interest to reveal to the court the detailed information which would be needed in order to perform the balancing act with confidence. This problem has in the past encouraged judges to accept fairly sketchy accounts of reasons for thinking that disclosure of material would be injurious to the public interest. The effectiveness of courts' assertion of their constitutional role as arbiters of the balance of interests in these cases depends on judges' willingness to subject governmental claims to careful, critical scrutiny. One of the features of the *Spycatcher* case was the willingness of the judges to examine critically, and to discount, the assertions of the government that further publication of the Wright allegations would damage the efficiency of the security service. Scott J.'s judgment, in an analysis of the public-interest arguments favouring a permanent restraint on publication, concluded that all the damage which the government feared must already have occurred, or was highly speculative. Commenting on the suggestion that further publication would damage morale in MI5, Lord Griffiths, in some ways the member of the House of Lords most sympathetic to the government's case, flatly denied that further publication would have so damaged the morale of the security service that they could not operate efficiently.[93]

This is refreshingly realistic. It is not sensible to accept the word of government without question, because it would be too easy for government to stifle the flow of information in order to protect the convenience and reputation of Ministers or civil servants under the guise of guarding against some unspecified national harm. Admittedly the courts will not always (or perhaps usually) be in a good position to judge the intelligence implications of releasing information. This much was recognized by a majority of the US Supreme Court in *Snepp* v. *United States*,[94] where a former CIA agent had published a book without first submitting it for security clearance as required under an express term in his contract of employment. Although the book contained no classified material, the Supreme Court upheld by a six to three majority the grant of an injunction security clearance. The majority did not consider that the contractual term infringed Snepp's First Amendment rights, and accepted the gov-

[93] [1990] 1 AC at p. 275, [1988] 3 All ER at p. 654. See also Lord Goff at pp. 291, 666.

[94] 444 US 507, 62 L. Ed. 2d 704.

ernment's claim that neither the author nor the court might foresee the way in which a former agent, in publishing non-classified material, would facilitate the identification of other agents and endanger lives or channels of information. This shows how national-security concerns may limit even constitutionally guaranteed rights. On the facts, the English courts would have reached the same conclusion, since an obligation of silence applies to all security-service personnel, regardless of the confidentiality or otherwise of particular information. However, the House of Lords in the *Spycatcher* case refused an injunction which would have imposed a blanket restriction on third parties, the newspapers, publishing stories derived from future allegations which Mr. Wright might make, overriding the government's speculative assertions about the effect which such revelations might have on security. The approach of Australian courts to such assertions by government is as robust as that of the English judges, as shown by Powell J.'s judgment in the Supreme Court of New South Wales in the *Spycatcher* case. He rejected Sir Robert Armstrong's claim that further publication of the *Spycatcher* allegations would damage the UK's security, as distinct from causing embarrassment to the government.[95]

In view of the judges' conclusion that no damage would be caused to the public interests advanced by the government to justify an injunction, because of the widespread publicity already given to Mr. Wright's allegations, it was unnecessary to consider the iniquity defence advanced by the newspapers. Nevertheless, it was considered. Scott J. drew a distinction between matters such as the adequacy of the system for securing accountability of the security service, which were matters of legitimate public debate but could not justify reporting unauthorized disclosures about the operation of the service, and matters such as the attempt to assassinate President Nasser or destabilize the Wilson government, which involved iniquity of a high order such that it was in the pubic interest to inform the public. 'The press has a legitimate role in disclosing scandals in government.'[96] It is the purpose of the duty of confidence in this sphere to facilitate the efficiency of the security service, not to prevent the government of the day from being exposed to embarrassment or pressure.[97] In the House of Lords, it was suggested that it would be in the public interest for their recipient to air allegations only if (in the words of Lord Goff) 'following such investigations as are reasonably open to the recipient, and having regard to all the circumstances of the case, the allegation in question can reasonably be regarded as being a credible allegation from an

[95] *A.-G.* v. *Heinemann Publishers Australia Pty Ltd.* (1987) 8 NSWLR 341 at pp. 377–9.
[96] [1990] 1 AC at p. 167, [1988] 3 All ER at p. 588.
[97] [1990] 1 AC at p. 167, [1988] 3 All ER at p. 589.

apparently reliable source'.[98] This would seem to be satisfied in the case of Mr Wright, a former MI5 officer whose evidence had been accepted by other writers on the security service in the past. The seriousness of the allegations would also probably have justified publishing them in the news media, rather than referring them to the police or a member of Parliament. On the other hand, it could not justify publishing the details of other MI5 operations contained in the remainder of *Spycatcher*, nor could it justify publishing extracts from those other parts of the book which could not claim to be serving a legitimate public interest.

(2) Other remedies available to the government

Although the government failed to obtain a permanent injunction restraining publication of Peter Wright's material in England and Wales by any of the newspapers, they succeeded in another, subsidiary aim: they obtained an order against the publishers of the *Sunday Times* for an account of profits accruing from its publication of extracts from Mr Wright's memoirs on 12 July 1986, the day before *Spycatcher* was published in the USA. The publication had detrimentally affected the government's interest because at that stage there had been no such publication elsewhere as would destroy the confidentiality of the material, and the publishers of the *Sunday Times*, by entering into a licensing agreement with the American publishers, had effectively put themselves in the shoes of Mr Wright and were infected by his breach of trust. This is in line with the subsidiary purpose of the law of breach of confidence, that of ensuring that people do not profit from their wrongful appropriation of confidential information. The action for an account of profits is distinct from an action for an injunction. The former does not chill free expression; it merely makes it unprofitable. Even in the USA, with the tenderness which American courts display for freedom of speech under the First Amendment, in *Snepp* v. *United States*[99] a former CIA agent, who, in contravention of a contractual undertaking not to publish such material without first having the manuscript vetted by the CIA, had published a book on the Vietnam war which contained no classified information, was made to account for his profits to the government. There are good reasons for permitting publication in the public interest, but there are few good reasons for allowing people who make themselves a party to wrongdoing to profit from their actions.

Apart from the right to an account of profits, the government may be able to restrain publication if they hold the copyright in the material.

---

[98] [1990] 1 AC at p. 283, [1988] 3 All ER at p. 660.
[99] 444 US 507 (1980), US Supreme Court.

This was the ground on which the Australian government succeeded in obtaining an interim injunction restraining publication of documents relating to the East Timor crisis in *Commonwealth of Australia* v. *Fairfax & Sons Ltd.*[100] This remedy is useful only where the recipient of the material plans to reproduce it in whole or part, as in the *John Fairfax* case. It is not clear that it would have availed the government in the *Spycatcher* case or in *Lord Advocate* v. *The Scotsman Publications Ltd.*, as the publications in those cases consisted of an original account of events, incorporating confidential information, rather than a reproduction of copyright material. In these cases, Wright and Cavendish respectively held the legal copyright.[101] However, in the final *Spycatcher* hearing several of the judges thought that the legal copyright might be held under a constructive trust for the benefit of the government, giving them an equitable copyright, because of the author's breach of confidence.[102] The government nevertheless disclaimed any reliance on equitable copyright, perhaps, as Lord Donaldson M.R. suggested, because the newspapers could still have relied on a 'fair dealing' defence under section 6 of the Copyright Act 1956 (now the Copyright, Designs and Patents Act 1988, section 30) to justify their reports on the book.[103]

(3) Conclusion

After this long discussion, an attempt at a brief summary of the main principles might be helpful.

(a) A person, X, is subject to a duty of confidence in relation to a piece of governmental information, φ, if and only if the balance of public interests which apply to that person in relation to that information favours maintaining secrecy. This will be the case only if the government can show some damage to the public interest which would flow from disclosure.

(b) Even if X is prima facie subject to a duty of confidence in relation to φ, publication may still be justified by a sufficiently powerful countervailing public interest, such as the need to uncover iniquity. However, broadcasting it through the media will not necessarily be justified: the

---

[100] 147 CLR 39, HC of Australia.

[101] A suggestion that authors guilty of turpitude lose copyright is unsustainable. The better view is that the authors had the legal copyright, but that, because of their behaviour, no court of equity would grant them remedies to enforce it: see Lord Jauncey of Tullichettle [1990] 1 AC at p. 294, [1988] 3 All ER at p. 668; Yvonne Cripps, 'Breaches of Copyright and Confidence: The Spycatcher Effect' [1989] *PL* 13–20.

[102] See [1990] 1 AC, [1988] 3 All ER, at pp. 140, 567, respectively (Scott J.); 194–5, 608–9 (Lord Donaldson MR); 211, 621 (Dillon LJ); 266, 647 (Lord Brightman); 276, 654 (Lord Griffiths); and 288, 664 (Lord Goff).

[103] [1990] 1 AC at p. 288, [1988] 3 All ER at pp. 608–9.

publication must (i) be in a appropriate form and to an appropriate person, having regard to all the circumstances; and (ii) be limited to those matters which serve the public interest in question.

(c) At the interlocutory stage, an injunction is likely to be granted to prevent disclosure pending trial, so long as some harm would result from publication and there is an arguable case to try. At the trial, a permanent injunction will not be granted if the material is in the public domain and further publication will cause no further significant harm (unless to prevent a person implicated in iniquity from profiting by it). An account of profits can be ordered against a person implicated in iniquity.

14.3 NATIONAL SECURITY AND THE CRIME OF IMPARTING INFORMATION: OFFICIAL SECRETS ACT 1989[104]

The failure of the government to obtain a permanent injunction in the *Spycatcher* case made it clear that securing prior restraint of publications concerning government was likely to be less easy than the government would have liked, even if it was not to be as difficult as in the USA. The government realised that it was likely to be forced back on the criminal law, and subsequent restraint, in order to influence editorial decisions about publication of governmental confidences. However, as noted in section 1 above, the main statute providing criminal penalties for unauthorized disclosures and receipts of information, section 2 of the Official Secrets Act 1911 as amended, was by then a discredited instrument. The government's response, eventually, was the Official Secrets Act 1989, which swept away section 2 of the 1911 Act, replacing it with a series of more specific prohibitions on disclosure. In most cases, these related to classes of information in which there is an understandable public interest in confidentiality, concerning the security and intelligence services, defence, international relations, and criminal investigation. It is no longer an offence to be the recipient of unsolicited information from a person who is infringing the Act. There is also a general defence, applying to all offences under the Act, where a person who has made a disclosure proves that at the time of the alleged offence he believed that he had lawful authority to make the disclosure and had no reasonable cause to believe otherwise.[105]

In some ways, therefore, this is a liberalizing measure, and it was introduced by the government on that basis. Nevertheless, there are two illiberal aspects. First, in a reaction to their failure in *Spycatcher*, the

---

[104] Robertson and Nicol, *Media Law*, 3rd edn., pp. 418–28.
[105] Official Secrets Act 1989, s. 7(4). See also s. 8(2).

government drafted section 1(1) of the Act in a way which makes it a criminal offence for members or former members of the security and intelligence services ever to reveal anything which came into their possession by virtue of their position. Thus the person who receives and publishes it may be guilty of a criminal offence even if no injunction would have issued to restrain publication as a civil wrong, for instance because the material is already well publicized. Secondly, while in other cases the prosecution must prove that a defendant's disclosure was damaging, there is such requirement in respect of charges under section 1 of the 1989 Act. Thirdly, no defendant under any section of the 1989 Act can argue that disclosure was in the public interest. Such a defence was, in theory, available under the 1911 Act, although its scope was uncertain: see section 1 above. A public-interest defence is also available in civil proceedings: see section 2 above. It is curious that under all provisions of the 1989 Act criminal liability may be imposed in circumstances when no injunction could have been obtained to restrain publication.

Under section 1 of the 1989 Act, a person who is or has been a member of the security service (MI5) or intelligence service (MI6), or has been notified in writing by a Minister that he is subject to the provisions of the section (this can happen to anyone who, in the Minister's opinion, is undertaking work which is or includes work connected with the security or intelligence services and is of such a nature that the interests of national security require that he should be subject to the provision), is guilty of an offence if, without lawful authority,[106] he discloses any information, document, or other article relating to security or intelligence which is or has been in his possession by virtue of his position or in the course of his work while the notification was in force. There is a defence if the person can show that he did not know, and had no reason to believe, that the information, etc., related to the security or intelligence services.

Section 2 provides that anyone who is or has been a Crown servant or contractor,[107] even if not covered by section 1, commits an offence if without lawful authority he makes a *damaging* disclosure of information, a document, or other article relating to defence[108] which was in his possession by virtue of his position.[109] A damaging disclosure is one which *either*

(*a*) damages the ability of any part of the armed forces to carry out their tasks, or leads to loss of life or injury to members of those forces or serious damage to the equipment or installations of the forces; *or*

---

[106] 'Lawful authority' is defined by s. 7.   [107] These terms are defined by s. 12.
[108] This is widely defined: see Official Secrets Act 1989, s. 2(4).
[109] Ibid., s. 2(1).

(b) otherwise endangers the interests of the UK abroad, seriously obstructs the promotion or protection by the UK of those interests, or endangers the lives of British citizens abroad; or

(c) is of such a nature that it would be likely to have any of those consequences.[10]

It is a defence for the person concerned to prove that he did not know, and had no reasonable cause to believe, that the information, etc., related to defence or that its disclosure would be damaging.[111] This defence is ambiguously worded. It is not clear whether there are actually two defences (*either* that the defendant did not know and had no reasonable cause to believe that the material related to defence, *or* did not know or have reasonable cause to believe that its disclosure would be damaging) or only one, with the accused carrying the burden of a two-part test (the 'or' in the middle being conjunctive rather than disjunctive). In principle, an ambiguity in a criminal statute should be resolved in favour of the defendant, particularly as the purpose of the 1989 Act was avowedly to replace and cut down the very wide criminal liability imposed under section 2 of the Official Secrets Act 1911. However, a court might take the view that it is not unreasonable to penalize behaviour which the accused has reason to believe would be damaging, even if he does not know that it is. It will be interesting to see how the courts interpret this section.

Further penal provisions apply, by virtue of section 3 of the 1989 Act, to Crown servants and government contractors who make damaging disclosures of material relating to international relations, or any confidential material obtained from another state or international organization, which he has by virtue of his position.[112] Here, a 'damaging' disclosure is one which endangers the interests of the UK abroad, which seriously obstructs the promotion or protection of those interests, which endangers the lives of British citizens abroad, or which, if unauthorized, would be likely to have any of those effects.[113] The mere fact that material is confidential and obtained from another state or international organization may (but will not necessarily) be enough to establish that unauthorized disclosure might have those effects.[114] There is a defence if the accused proves that at the time of the alleged offence he did not know, and had no reasonable cause to believe, that the information, etc., was of a type covered by the section, or that its disclosure would be damaging.[115] The interpretation of this subsection raises difficulties similar to those which arise in relation to the defence under section 2.

Section 4 of the 1989 Act goes on to criminalize disclosure without lawful authority, by a person who is or has been a Crown servant or con-

---

[110] Official Secrets Act 1989, s. 2(2).   [111] Ibid., s. 2(3).   [112] Ibid., s. 3(1).
[113] Ibid., s. 3(2).   [114] Ibid., s. 3(3).

tractor, of information concerning criminal intelligence and investigations, which is or has been in his possession by virtue of his position.[116]
The section applies to two types of information, documents, or other
articles. First, there are items disclosure of which has, or is likely to have,
the effect of resulting in the commission of an offence, facilitating an
escape from legal custody or prejudicing the safekeeping of people in custody, or impeding prevention or detection of offences or the apprehension of suspects.[117] Secondly, it applies to information etc. gathered, or
relating to the obtaining of information, by means of, an interception of
communications authorized by a warrant issued under the Interception of
Communications Act 1985, section 2, or action taken under a warrant
issued under the Security Service Act 1989, section 3.[118] There are two
defences under this section. The first, a general defence, is available to
any defendant who can prove that at the time of the alleged offence he
did not know, and had no reasonable cause to believe, that the section
applied to the information etc. in question.[119] The other defence applies
only to a person charged with an offence in respect of a disclosure which
is alleged to have actually resulted in the commission of an offence, the
facilitation of an escape or an act prejudicing the safekeeping of people in
custody, or the impeding of the prevention or detection of offenders or
the apprehension of suspects. This defence is available if the accused can
prove that at the time of the alleged offence he did not know, and had no
reasonable cause to believe, that the disclosure would have any of those
effects.[120]

In section 5, the 1989 Act deals with third parties who come into possession of material which has been disclosed by others. It provides that,
when information, a document, or other article protected by sections 1,
2, 3, or 4 of the Act:

(i) comes into a person's possession as a result of an unauthorised disclosure
(whether to him or to someone else) by a Crown servant or government contractor; or

(ii) is entrusted to a person by a Crown servant or government contractor on
terms requiring it to be held in confidence or in circumstances in which the servant or contractor could reasonably expect it to be so held; or

(iii) is disclosed without lawful authority to any person by a person entrusted
with the information, etc., under (ii) above,[121]

a person is guilty of an offence under section 5 (as long as the disclosure
does not constitute an offence under any of sections 1 to 4) if:

(a) he discloses it without lawful authority; and

---

[115] Ibid., s. 3(4). [116] Ibid., s. 4(1). [117] Ibid., s. 4(2).
[118] Ibid., s. 4(3). [119] Ibid., s. 4(5).
[120] Ibid., s. 4(4). [121] Ibid., s 5(1).

(*b*) he knows or has reasonable cause to believe that it is protected against disclosure by sections 1 to 4, and that it came into his possession in one of the ways mentioned above;[122] *and*

(*c*) the disclosure is damaging within the meaning of section 1, 2 or 3; *and*

(*d*) the person knows or has reasonable cause to believe that it is damaging.[123]

The effect of this section is that a third party who comes into possession of information or material by way of a chain, any part of which consists of an unauthorized disclosure, may be guilty of a section 5 offence if he further discloses it. However, he commits no offence in disclosing the information or material unless the disclosure by him is damaging and he knows or has reasonable cause to believe that it is. This makes the extent of any previous publication relevant, importing considerations similar to those which apply to breach of confidence under *Attorney General* v. *Guardian Newspapers Ltd. (No. 2)*,[124] and adding to them a *mens rea* requirement. On facts similar to those relating to *Spycatcher*, it means that the newspapers would not be liable under section 5 for publishing Mr Wright's allegations once publicity elsewhere for them had inflicted all the possible damage. Before that, the newspapers would have been liable, if they knew or had reasonable cause to believe that the disclosure was damaging, and would have had no public-interest defence.

Other acts which constitute criminal offences under the Act are:

(*a*) disclosure without lawful authority of ay information, document, or other article which the confider knows, or has reasonable cause to believe, came into his possession as a result of an offence of spying contrary to section 1 of the Official Secrets Act 1911;[125] or

(*b*) disclosure without lawful authority of any information, document, or other article which relates to security, intelligence, defence, or international relations, and which was communicated in confidence to another state or an international organization by or on behalf of the UK, and which has been disclosed to any person without the authority of the state or a member of the organization concerned, where the disclosure by the accused was damaging and the accused knew or had reasonable cause to suspect that the disclosure would be damaging;[126]

(*c*) Crown servants, including a person in whose case a notification under section 1(1) is in force, retaining documents or articles contrary to their official duty, or government contractors failing to comply with official directions for their return or disposal, or Crown servants or gov-

---

[122] Official Secrets Act 1989, s. 5(2), (5).
[123] Ibid., s. 5(3).
[124] [1990] 1 AC 109, [1988] 3 All ER 545.
[125] Official Secrets Act 1989, s. 5(6).
[126] Ibid., s 6(1).

ernment contractors failing to take reasonable care to prevent unautho-rized disclosure of documents or other articles which they have in their possession by virtue of their positions and which it would be an offence under the Act to disclose.[127]

Viewed as a liberalizing measure, the 1989 Act is something of a disap-pointment. While more certain and specific than section 2 of the 1911 Act which it superseded, the 1989 Act continues to make it difficult to obtain information about the workings of government and those who are, in name at any rate, our servants. It reflects a governmental ethos which is profoundly suspicious of outsiders, resistant to accountability, and antipathetic to the idea of freedom of information. The defences do not protect the rights of subjects. They do not protect the public interest, save in cases where the government's view of the public interest is the correct one. It is, in this context, extremely worrying to remember that in Sir Robert Armstrong's memorandum to civil servants following the Clive Ponting case, and in the trial judge's direction to the jury in the Ponting case itself, it was said that the interests of the state are synony-mous with its interests as defined by the government for the time being. This meant that there was, in theory, no room for a defendant to argue under the old section 2 that it was in the interests of the state to leak information to the elected representatives of the people, in order to counteract suspected mendacity or incompetence on the part of the gov-ernment or its servants. Under the 1989 Act, the prosecution is not even nominally required to show that the unauthorized disclosure was not in the interests of the state. Nor is there any defence of public good (as under the obscenity legislation) or public interest (as in civil actions for breach of confidence). This produces the curious result that a person may escape prior restraint by injunction, or civil liability, for breach of confidence by taking advantage of the public–interest defence, and then suffer criminal penalties for a disclosure which has been held in the civil courts to be in the public interest. However, while curious, it is perhaps in line with the liberal ethos of freedom to communicate information and express ideas that a person should, in the public interest, be free to decide to take a risk. If so, the protection for that ethos is no better than shaky when people acting, perhaps, in the public interest, providing informa-tion needed for the democratic process to operate (as in the Ponting case), as put *in terrorem* by the threat of severe criminal sanctions.

---

[127] Ibid., s. 8.

14.4 CRIMINAL SPEECH, OPINION, AND DISAFFECTION: SEDITION AND RELATED OFFENCES[128]

This section deals with the criminal law which applies to those who attempt to undermine the state directly.

(1) Treason and treason felony[129]

Since feudal times, actions which constitute a breach of the subject's obligation of allegiance to his lord the monarch have been punishable with death, as treasons. As defined and extended by statute, such actions include compassing or imagining the death of the King, the queen, or their eldest son and heir, within or without the realm; violating the king's companion, the king's eldest daughter before her marriage, or the wife of the king's eldest son and heir; levying war against the king's enemies in the realm, being adherent to them or giving them aid or comfort anywhere,[130] or killing the king's justices when in the performance of their offices.[131] Any person who owes a duty of allegiance by reason of being under the protection of the Crown can be guilty of treason. In *R*. v. *Joyce*, the House of Lords held that an alien who had been in the UK, and so under the protection of the Crown, remained under its protection when he went abroad with a British passport which he had obtained by deception. His broadcasts (as 'Lord Haw-Haw') from Germany during the Second World War, designed to undermine British morale and assist the German war effort, were therefore treasonable.[132] This can be seen as a particularly vindictive extension of the law of treason to permit the execution of an alien for expressions uttered abroad which had been a thorn in the flesh of the government during the war; it is inconceivable that the passport would have been held to give Joyce any enforceable rights against the Crown, yet it was enough to hang him.

Related offences extend criminal liability to words and publications.

---

[128] See Michael Supperstone, *Brownlie's Law of Public Order and National Security*, 2nd edn. (London: Butterworths, 1981), ch. 11.

[129] J. C. Smith and Brian Hogan, *Criminal Law*, 6th edn. (London: Butterworths, 1988), 827–33. This discussion is omitted from the 7th edn.

[130] *R*. v. *Casement* [1917] 1 KB 98, CCA.

[131] Treason Act 1351, 25 Edw. III, stat. 5, c. 2; Treason Act 1795, s. 1. See also Treason Act 1842, s. 2, which introduced a lesser penalty than that for high treason in the case of people who (among other activities) point or shoot firearms at the monarch. This Act was passed following two such incidents while Queen Victoria was driving in public in 1842. An earlier attempt had been made on the Queen's life by an insane youth, Edward Oxford, in 1840.

[132] [1946] AC 347, [1946] 1 All ER 186, HL.

Anyone owing a duty of allegiance to the Crown who anywhere com-
passes, imagines, invents, devises, or intends (a) to deprive or depose the
Queen from her titles, or (b) to levy war against the Queen in the UK in
order to compel her to change her policies (in effect, her government's
policies), or (c) to put force or constraint on, or intimidate or overawe,
Parliament or either House thereof, or (d) to move or stir any foreigner
to invade the UK or any of the Queen's dominions, is guilty of treason
felony, and this offence may be committed either by acts or by words,
writing, or other publication.[133]

The creation of the offence of treason felony reflects a move in political theory away from identifying the state with the monarch: the formulation of the crime recognizes the significance to the state of institutions
other than the monarchy, which by the time of Queen Victoria had
waned in practical importance. Attempts to stir up dissatisfaction with the
policies of the government of the day were, in effect, attempts to undermine the established institutions of the state, in times when there was
little democracy and the forces of public opinion were not regarded with
any respect. The criminal law addressed this objective through the law of
sedition.

(2) Sedition

Words and publications play an important role in stirring up discontent
and violent opposition to the established order, and ever since medieval
times steps have been taken to criminalize attempts to undermine the
state by means of scurrilous publications, particularly in times of unrest
when insurrection has been threatened or feared. By the end of the eighteenth century, the crime of seditious libel at common law was backed
up by statutes which (for example) made meetings of more than fifty
people, to make speeches or raise petitions critical of the established institutions of the state, into unlawful assemblies unless advertised in advance
according to statutory requirements as to notice. These statutes were
most often passed in times of war, and the latest of them, the Seditious
Meetings Act 1817 (passed amid fear of Jacobinism and foreign invasion
in the aftermath of the Napoleonic wars) remained in force, although
long unused, until at last repealed by the Public Order Act 1986, in line
with a recommendation from the Law Commission.[134]

At common law, the main weapon in the government's armoury is the
crime, rarely invoked in this century, of seditious libel. This originally

[133] Treason Felony Act 1848, s. 3.
[134] Law Commission Report No. 123, *Criminal Law: Offences Relating to Public Order*
(London: HMSO, 1983), 86–7, paras. 8.4–8.5, especially n. 7; Public Order Act 1986, s.
40(3) and Sch. 3.

covered any attack on any institution of the state.[135] One commentator
has described the original crime as being committed whenever anyone
published 'a speech or writing with intent to bring into hatred or contempt, or excite hostility towards, the Crown, government, Parliament,
and administration of justice, or with the aim of inducing reform by
unlawful means or of promoting class warfare'.[136] This reflects the historical use of sedition to stifle criticism of government policy,[137] potentially
including all democratic debate and party-political activity, as it encompassed almost any political opposition to the government of the day.[138]
As we shall see, the modern law is a good deal more restricted than this,
and takes account of a more enlightened view of the value of political
opposition to government, which made it less acceptable for governments to use the law to stifle opposition. At the same time, procedural
changes introduced by Fox's Libel Act 1792, which required a jury,
rather than the judge, to decide whether statements were defamatory,
made it easier for defendants to canvass political issues before juries.

This made prosecutions for seditious libel less attractive to government. Instead, attention turned from defamation to public-order concerns.[139] Accordingly, more recent cases have stressed that the speaker or
publisher must intend to provoke violence aimed at disturbing the government by force in order to be liable to conviction.[140] Today, the *actus
reus* consists of publishing or speaking words which have a tendency to
incite public disorder involving physical violence, having regard to the
likely effect of the words on ordinary people and on the audience which
is addressed.[141] According to Professor Sir John Smith and Professor
Brian Hogan: 'words are seditious (i) if they are likely to incite ordinary
men whether likely to incite the audience actually addressed or not; or
(ii) if, though not likely to incite ordinary men, they are likely to incite

---

[135] *R.* v. *Burns* (1886) 16 Cox CC 355.
[136] This formulation is by Eric Barendt, *Freedom of Speech* (Oxford: Clarendon Press,
1987), 153.
[137] Sir James Fitzjames Stephen, *A History of the Criminal Law of England* (London:
Macmillan, 1883, 3 vols.), ii. 299–376.
[138] *Hector* v. *A.-G. of Antigua and Barbuda* [1990] 2 AC 312, [1990] 3 All ER 103, PC.
[139] See Michael Lobban, 'From Seditious Libel to Unlawful Assembly: Peterloo and
the Changing Face of Political Crime *c.*1770–1820' (1990) 10 *Oxf. J. of Legal Studies*
307–52.
[140] Barendt, *Freedom of Speech*, 155, refers to *R.* v. *Aldred* (1909) 22 Cox CC 1 at p. 4
per Coleridge J, and the note by E. C. S. Wade, 'Seditious Libel and the Press' (1948) 74
LQR 203 on *R.* v. *Caunt* (unreported, Birkett J); *Boucher* v. *R.* [1951] 2 DLR 369,
Supreme Court of Canada. See also *Hector* v. *A.-G. of Antigua and Barbuda* [1990] 2 AC
312, [1990] 3 All ER 103, PC.
[141] See *R.* v. *Aldred* (1909) 22 Cox CC 1, especially at pp. 3, 4, *per* Coleridge J; *R.* v.
Burns (1886) 16 Cox CC 355, at p. 365 *per* Cave J.

the audience actually addressed.'[142] This appears to be a fair account of the cases, as long as (i) is read subject to a proviso that if, in the context in which the words are spoken or published, it is highly unlikely that any intemperate people will be present and no disorder results, the words are not to be regarded as seditious. It follows that in England and Wales the crime of seditious libel has a public-order aspect.

The *mens rea* of sedition is in doubt, for two reasons. First, there has been a certain element of uncertainty, now largely laid to rest, as to whether the prosecution must prove specific intent to produce disorder, or whether it suffices to establish basic intent. Sir James Fitzjames Stephen, the nineteenth-century codifier and historian of the criminal law, at different times gave two inconsistent answers to this question. In his *Digest of the Criminal Law of England*, he required only deliberateness in publishing or speaking words which had a seditious tendency. The intention to produce public disorder was inferred from that act.[143] This is inconsistent with general principles of criminal law, but is in line with the approach to *mens rea* taken in other types of criminal libel, such as blasphemous libel.[144] However, Stephen adopted a different view in his *History of the Criminal Law*,[145] where he takes the view that a requirement of specific intent—an intention to produce public disorders—had become part of the *mens rea* by virtue of the Libel Act 1792. It is this later view which appears to have been adopted in more recent English decisions. In *R. v. Burns*,[146] Cave J. told the jury that there must be a distinct intention, going beyond mere recklessness, to produce disturbances, in order to establish the necessary *mens rea*. Similarly n *R. v. Caunt*,[147] where a newspaper editor was prosecuted in respect of an article which was alleged to create a risk of disorder because of its anti-Semitic bias, Birkett J instructed the jury that the prosecution had to prove that the defendant intended to provoke such disorder, and the jury acquitted.

Secondly, there is doubt about the matters as to which the requisite intention must be directed. Classically, seditious libel was concerned with words calculated or intended to stir up violent opposition to the institutions of the state.[148] More recently, however, it has been said to extend to words which are intended, not to obstruct established authority by violence, but to set sections or classes of the community at each other's

---

[142] J. C. Smith and Brian Hogan, *Criminal Law*, 7th edn. (London: Butterworths, 1992), 751.

[143] Sir James Fitzjames Stephen, *A Digest of the Criminal Law*, 4th edn. (London: Sweet & Maxwell, 1887), art. 94. See now Criminal Law Act 1967, s. 8.

[144] See. Ch. 15 below.   [145] ii. 359.   [146] (1886) 16 Cox CC 355 at p. 364.

[147] Unreported, 1947; see Wade, (1948) 64 LQR 203.

[148] See Lord Cockburn, *Examination of Trials for Sedition in Scotland* (Edinburgh: D. Douglas, 1888), i. 8.

throats. This makes safeguarding harmonious relations between sections of Her Majesty's subjects as much the purpose of sedition law as preventing violent insurrection against the state. In *R. v. Caunt*, above, Birkett J. told the jury that words intended to stir up hatred of Jews could be seditious. The essence of this manifestation of the offence was creating division and disaffection between classes of Her Majesty's subjects, creating conditions for violence. The prosecution did not need to show that the speech or publication actually led to violence, or was likely to lead directly to violence.

The need for such an extension is not clear. In recent years, this aspect of the offence has been largely superseded by public-order legislation, including the statutory crime of inciting racial hatred.[149] Seditious libel is now often represented as a sledge-hammer to be used against nuts. However, the statutory crime of inciting racial hatred does not protect purely religious, rather than racial, groups.[150] For this reason, in 1989 Muslims campaigning against Salman Rushdie's book, *The Satanic Verses*, attempted to prosecute the author and publishers for seditious libel, arguing that the book's representation of Islam created hostility between Her Majesty's Muslim and non–Muslim subjects, in that it provoked widespread violence and threats of violence between Muslims and others by vilifying Islam and ridiculing its prophets and adherents. In *R. v. Chief Metropolitan Magistrate, ex parte Choudhury*[151] the applicant applied for summonses accusing the defendants of (among other things) seditious libel by distributing the book. The magistrate refuse to issue the summonses, and the applicant applied for judicial review of the refusal.

The court adopted the formulation of the *mens rea* in *Boucher* v. *R.*,[152] in which the Supreme Court of Canada held that a pamphlet, published in Quebec by a Jehovah's Witness, about the animosity of officials and Roman Catholic clergy towards Jehovah's Witnesses, would not constitute a seditious libel, whether or not it was intended to stir up feelings of ill will and hostility between classes of subjects. The Divisional Court in *ex parte Choudhury* held that seditious libel is founded on: 'an intention to incite to violence or to create public disturbance or disorder against His Majesty or the institutions of government. Proof of an intention to promote feelings of ill will and hostility between different classes of subjects does not alone establish a seditious intention.'[153] The violence, distur-

---

[149] Race Relations Act 1976, s. 70, as substituted by the Public Order Act 1986 (see Ch. 17, below); Public Order Act 1986, ss. 4, 5.
[150] See *Mandla* v. *Dowell Lee* [1983] 2 AC 548, [1983] 1 All ER 1062, HL; below, Ch. 18.
[151] [1991] 1 QB 429, [1991] 1 All ER 306, DC. See Marcus Tregilgas-Davey, '*Ex parte Choudhury*: An Opportunity Missed' (1991) 54 *MLR* 294–9.
[152] [1951] 2 DLR 369.
[153] [1991] 1 QB at p. 453, [1991] 1 All ER 306 at p. 323, *per* Watkins LJ.

bance, or defiance must be 'for the purpose of disturbing constituted authority', which means 'some person or body holding public office or discharging some public function of the state'.[154] The Divisional Court decided that there was no evidence that Mr. Rushdie or his publishers had had the requisite intention, and so held that there was no possibility that a prosecution could succeed. The application for judicial review of the magistrate's decision was therefore dismissed.

If the Divisional Court decision on this point is correct, Birkett J. in *Caunt* was wrong to extend the reach of the crime to catch those inciting racial hatred or class violence. It leaves a lacuna in the law, in that the criminal law offers no protection against those who spawn religious hostility unless they fall within one of the statutory public-order offences under the Public Order Act 1986. At the same time, the formulation in *ex parte Choudhury* potentially gives seditious libel a wider reach than previously thought, in that it may be committed if there is an intention to disturb by violence the operation of a person or body holding no public office if performing public functions. This would compel courts to perform a functional analysis of the activities of the state and of the person or body concerned, perhaps allowing a person to be prosecuted for seditious libel who had incited the overthrow of an organization delivering public services, such as the National Health Service. This overcomes the difficulty which might be caused by the lack of any developed conception of 'the state' in the constitutional law of the UK.

From a civil liberties standpoint, anything which expands the scope of the crime of seditious libel in any way is to be deprecated. It is properly for Parliament, not the courts, to impose restrictions on freedom of expression, whether in the interests of the state or of social harmony. The willingness of Parliament to take steps in the Public Order Act 1986, and the limits to those steps, should make judges hesitate before creating new inroads into freedom of speech which are not authorized by statute. The decision in *ex parte Choudhury* to limit the *mens rea* of the offence to a specific intention to 'incite to violence or to create public disturbance or disorder against His Majesty or the institutions of government'[155] is to be welcomed. Conversely, the extension to protect people performing public state functions but not holding public office, is to be regretted. Even now, the scope of the offence remains uncertain, as in modern times it has so far been the subject of decisions of a fairly low level of authority. It is by no means impossible that those who inspired riots against the government's plans to introduce the Community Charge in 1988 and 1989 might have been guilty of seditious libel, apart from any other public-order offences with which they were charged. The uncertainty surrounding the scope of

[154] Ibid.   [155] Ibid.

the offence makes it particularly objectionable as a restriction on expression, since people potentially held *in terrorem* may be afraid to exercise political rights guaranteed under Articles 9, 10, and 11 of the European Convention on Human Rights. The potential is present, despite the fact that the charge is rarely laid and still more rarely successfully prosecuted: the European Court of Human Rights has held that a person may be a victim of a law which breaches the Convention even if he has never personally been charged or threatened with proceedings under that law, and the state organs have announced an intention of not invoking legal procedures to enforce the law.[156] If democratic freedom depends on people remaining ignorant of, or refusing to be intimidated by, the law, and the good sense of the government in refusing to enforce it, one might regard it as being on insecure foundations.

Nevertheless, the general effect of developments over the last 200 years has been that the potential of the law of seditious libel to stifle criticism of government and political debate, evident in practice and as a matter of legal theory until the nineteenth century, is not great. Even before the nineteenth century, there were always people ready to ignore the law in order to assert rights and contest what the saw as abuse of power. Having citizens who are willing to challenge the law in the interest of a higher value, and being prepared to tolerate such behaviour, are, perhaps, the distinctive characteristics of a free society. In practice, the law of seditious libel has rarely been invoked, and those prosecutions which have taken place have tended to lead to acquittals at the hands of juries.

This pattern is replicated in the USA, where the commitment to free speech and a free press enshrined in the First Amendment to the Constitution in 1791 did not prevent the Congress from passing the Sedition Act of 1798 less than ten years later, amid fears that the USA might be sucked into the war between Britain and France. The Act made it criminal to 'write, print, utter or publish' false, scandalous, and malicious writings against the government, Congress, or President, or 'to bring them, or either of them, into contempt or disrepute; or to excite against them, or either of them, the hatred of the good people of the United States, or to stir up sedition'. The object of the Act was to silence opposition to the government. It was unsuccessful: heated debate continued, despite prosecutions. President John Adams was defeated in the presidential election of 1800, and Thomas Jefferson, the new president, pardoned all who had been convicted under the Act. Although the constitutionality of the Act was never tested, it came to be regarded by Congress as unconstitutional. A leading authority on the First

---

[156] *Johnston* v. *Ireland* Eur. Ct. HR, Series A, No. 122, Judgment of 18 Dec. 1986, 9 EHHR 203.

Amendment, Leonard Levy, has shown that, although in theory the law of sedition as it operated both under British rule and under the Sedition Act 1798 should have significantly constrained free political expression, in practice tough, uncompromising criticism of government normally flourished.[157] The First Amendment reflected the dominant ethos of the society as regards free expression; the law of sedition was, for most people most of the time, an irrelevance.

(3) Incitement to disaffection[158]

Statutory offences have been created by the Incitement to Mutiny Act 1797 and the Incitement to Disaffection Act 1934. The 1797 Act makes it an offence to endeavour, maliciously and advisedly, to seduce any member of the armed forces away from his duty to and allegiance to Her Majesty or induce him to commit an act of mutiny. It was a response to fears that the naval mutinies at the Spithead and the Nore had been incited by supporters of the revolutionary regime in France, and were intended to provoke open rebellion in Britain. In fact, the Spithead mutiny was essentially a limited piece of industrial action, in which sailors maintained their patriotic allegiance to the Crown and their opposition to the enemy while pursuing well-justified improvements in their conditions. They were successful in securing a royal pardon, improved pay and conditions, and shore leave at the end of a voyage. The Nore mutineers were more antagonistic towards the established state institutions: demands included democratization of the fleet, and the Thames was blockaded; but the Nore mutiny was also less well organized, and collapsed.[159] The 1797 Act was allowed to lapse in 1805, but was revived in 1817. The maximum penalty has been reduced from death to imprisonment for life. There has now been no prosecution under the Act for many years,[160] yet, despite a provisional recommendation from the Law Commission that it should be repealed,[161] it remains in force.

The Incitement to Disaffection Act 1934, which largely echoed the terms of the Incitement to Mutiny Act 1797, was specially passed to deter Communist propaganda amongst members of the armed forces. Section 1 makes it an offence for a person maliciously and advisedly to endeavour to seduce 'any member of His Majesty's forces from his duty or allegiance

---

[157] Leonard W. Levy, *Emergence of a Free Press* (New York: Oxford University Press, 1985), especially at p. x.

[158] D. G. T. Williams, *Keeping the Peace—The Police and Public Order* (London: Hutchinson, 1967), 179–92.

[159] The story is told by G. E. Manwaring and Bonamy Dobrée, *The Floating Republic* (London: Geoffrey Bles, 1935).

[160] Supperstone, *Brownlie's Law of Public Order*, 240.

to His Majesty'. This provision is somewhat wider than the equivalent term in the 1797 Act: under the 1934 Act, a defendant can be punished for seducing a member of the forces from his duty, even if he does not also seduce him from his allegiance to the Crown. Under section 2(1), it is an offence to have in one's possession or under one's control 'any document of such a nature that the dissemination of copies thereof among members of His Majesty's forces would constitute' an offence under section 1, with the intention to commit, aid, abet, counsel, or procure, the commission of such an offence. The consent of the D.P.P. is required before anyone may be prosecuted for these offences (section 3(2)), and in truth there have been few prosecutions. The most recent was the trial in 1975 of fourteen pacifists who had distributed leaflets to troops explaining how they could register conscientious objections to serving in Northern Ireland, or, if they were not excused, desert. This ended in an acquittal which led the Attorney-General, Mr Sam Silkin, to express his regret that the prosecution had been brought.[162]

A similar provision in the Police Act 1964 makes it an offence to cause, attempt to cause, or do any act calculated to cause, disaffection amongst members of any police force, or to induce, attempt to induce, or do any act calculated to induce, any member of a police force to withhold his services or commit breaches of discipline.[163] These provisions, which date back to 1919, were originally aimed at people intent on undermining public order and social stability,[164] but, as Robertson has pointed out, are now in disuse, perhaps because the commonest offenders today are probably officials of the Police Federation when advocating industrial action in pursuit of claims for improved wages, resources, and working conditions for police officers.[165]

14.5 CONCLUSIONS

The security of the state and its institutions is an important public interest. Yet the law which buttresses those institutions is inevitably viewed with suspicion by democrats and libertarians, as a threat to state security can too easily be asserted by those in power, as a justification for restricting a wide range of freedoms in ways which protect the interests of the

---

[161] Law Commission Working Paper No. 72, (2nd Programme, Item XVI), *Codification of the Criminal Law: Treason, Sedition and Allied Offences* (London: HMSO, 1977), para. 94.

[162] See Geoffrey Robertson, *Freedom, the Individual and the Law*, 175–6.

[163] Police Act 1964, s. 53.   [164] Williams, *Keeping the Peace*, 192–7.

[165] Geoffrey Robertson, *Freedom, Individual and Law*, 6th edn. (Harmondsworth: Penguin, 1989), 176.

governing party rather than the public. At a time like the present, when the perceived external threat to the state from the activities of the USSR has disintegrated, extremist influences over domestic movements such as the trade unions appear to be in abeyance, and the main danger seems to stem from the random, sometimes deadly, but generally fairly limited activities of Irish republican paramilitaries and international terrorists, it is not surprising that governmental demands for secrecy provoke scepticism. The strict limits to the availability of prior restraint of expression by injunction in English law, and the restriction of the scope of criminal liability for disclosures, seditious libels, and similar offences, are responses to a changing atmosphere in English political life. So far, only relatively small steps have been taken. One of the most interesting is the appointment of Mr William Waldegrave, the Cabinet Minister with special responsibility for implementing the Citizen's Charter, to encourage freedom of information among government departments following the general election in May 1992. However, he gives priority to making available 'well-prepared, usable, readily available comparative information' rather than giving access to information for which people ask.[166] It will be instructive to see, over the coming years, how far the ethos of secrecy gives way to a genuine commitment to open government.

[166] Anthony Bevins, 'Waldegrave Fails Test of Ending "Secrecy Culture"', *Independent*, 10 June 1992, is one of several reports on the efforts by that newspaper to test the government's commitment to open government.

15

RESTRICTING EXPRESSION TO PROTECT MIXED PUBLIC AND PRIVATE INTERESTS: BLASPHEMY, OBSCENITY, AND INDECENCY

This chapter examines a number of criminal offences and regulatory mechanisms which have the effect of abridging freedom of expression and of the press in order to protect individuals, and (on some views) the public in general, against non-material harm to moral and religious integrity, sensibilities, and standards of public behaviour. This group of restrictions on freedom of expression is highly contentious. For adherents to the harm principle as expounded by John Stuart Mill, the harm flowing from permitting free speech, in the form of hurt feelings and injured sensitivities, is outweighed by the benefit which accrues from permitting free intercourse of ideas.

Blasphemous libel is extremely difficult to define.[1] It can be said, as a rough guide, that matter is blasphemous if it denies the truth of Christian doctrine,[2] or of the Bible,[3] or vilifies God or Jesus, in terms of wanton and unnecessary profanity which are likely to shock and outrage the feelings of ordinary Christians.[4] The fact that the prohibition is somewhat uncertain in scope, and protects only Christian sensibilities, makes it highly controversial, despite the fact that prosecutions are very rare. It is far from clear that such a restriction on freedom of expression can be justified within a framework of liberal philosophy. Even if one accepts (as do some liberals, including Joel Feinberg[5] in his work on the moral limits of the criminal law) that offence is a form of harm, and that conduct or expression which provokes sufficiently grave offence can justifiably be criminalized, there is the problem, left over from the days when blasphemy protected state interests, that it protects only the state religion, and so fails to protect adequately other religious, and non-religious, beliefs.

[1] J. C. Smith and Brian Hogan, *Criminal Law*, 7th edn. (London: Butterworths, 1992), 723–5; St. John A Robilliard, *Religion and the Law: Religious Liberty in Modern English Law* (Manchester: Manchester University Press, 1984), ch. 2.

[2] *R. v. Taylor* (1676) 1 Vent. 293.

[3] *R. v. Hetherington* (1841) 9 St. Tr. (NS) 563.

[4] *R. v. Lemon* [1979] AC 617, [1979] 1 All ER 898, HL, especially per Lord Russell of Killowen and Lord Scarman.

[5] Joel Feinburg, *Offense to Others* (New York: Oxford University Press, 1985), 54.

Obscenity, as defined by statute in England and Wales, is criminalized to protect those who come to it willingly against moral harm—depravity and corruption—which the obscene article is held to threaten.[6] This crime therefore does not protect people's right to keep their sensitivities free from outrage, but instead either guards their moral integrity in a wholly paternalistic way, doing what is considered best for them whether or not they want it, or protects some public interest in maintaining moral standards in a way which overrides personal freedoms and desires. For this reason, it presents particular difficulties for those who seek to justify or formulate obscenity law in accordance with a civil libertarian philosophy.

Offences dealing with indecency, by contrast, aim to protect people's sensibilities.[7] The moral justification for regulating or criminalizing indecent expression is therefore essentially the same as the modern moral justification for criminalizing assaults on religious convictions. It is also subject to a similar objection. Although the indecency laws appear to apply to all forms of indecency, and are not, like blasphemy, limited to protecting the feelings of a particular religious or philosophical creed, the definition of indecency is heavily influenced by cultural and ethnic factors. Things may be indecent to a devout Muslim or Orthodox Jew which would not be indecent in the eyes of a communicant of the Church of England. A vicar might have regarded some things as indecent fifty years ago which would not be regarded in that light by a modern vicar. The fact that indecency is a cultural construction means that the law of indecency is likely to protect a limited range of notions of decency. If the law stops short at protecting a common core of sensitivities, it will be attacked by those whose sensitivities, deeply felt but not shared with others, are left unprotected. If it goes further, it will be attacked by those of the dominant culture who feel that their freedom of expression is being abridged unjustifiably.

This chapter examines the way in which English law has sought to come to terms with these problems. Blasphemous libel is examined first; then, the foundations of liability for indecency and obscenity; common-law offences of indecency and obscenity; statutory offences; and, finally, controls by way of licensing and regulation.

15.1 BLASPHEMOUS LIBEL: STATE AND RELIGION

Blasphemous libel was originally an offshoot of the ecclesiastical offence of heresy, and was at first triable only in church courts. The state first

---

[6] Smith and Hogan, *Criminal Law*, 7th edn., 730–42; Geoffrey Robertson and Andrew Nicol, *Media Law*, 3rd edn. (London: Penguin, 1992), 106–38.

[7] Robertson and Nicol, *Media Law*, 3rd edn., 147–60.

took an interest in enforcing sound religious doctrine when uprisings inspired by heretical religious movements threatened the stability of the state. Statutes against heresy were passed under King Henry IV and King Henry V, aimed principally at the Lollards.[8] In the early sixteenth century, the rise of Protestantism and the significance of the link between the position of the secular prince as a protector of the church, and the position of the church as protector and guarantor of the legitimacy of the prince, gave the secular arm a particular interest in stamping out challenges to established religions. In England, the Court of High Commission seems to have treated various forms of expression (sedition and blasphemy among them) as criminal libels,[9] and in 1539 the Act of the Six Articles imposed ordinary criminal liability on people who denied orthodox doctrine, for example by denying transubstantiation.[10] During the seventeenth century the position became very uncertain. Under the Protectorate, section 35 of the Instrument of Government 1653 encouraged sound doctrine, but under section 36 nobody was to be compelled to the public profession of Christianity by penalties or otherwise. Although Jews were readmitted to the country and permitted to worship, savage attacks were launched against Quakers, and their leaders George Fox, James Nayler, Francis Howgill, and William Dewsbury were sentenced for blasphemy by Parliament and suffered horrible punishments.[11]

After the Restoration, greater religious tolerance became normal, but religious affiliation was an important consideration in the choice of William, Prince of Orange and his wife Mary to succeed the Catholic King James II in 1688. (Even today the monarch must be a communicant of the Church of England.)[12] The Court of King's Bench began to treat criminal libels, including blasphemies, which had earlier been dealt with by the Court of High Commission, as misdemeanours at common law.[13] An early example of such a case, containing a classic statement of the elements of the offence as then understood, was *R. v. Taylor*.[14] Hale CJ directed the jury that calling religion a cheat, as the defendant had done in that case, was an attack on Christianity, the constitutionally established religion of the state, and that, since the state religion was one of the but-

---

[8] Stat. 5 Ric. II, c. 5 (1382); Stat. 2 Hen. IV, c. 15 (1401), *De haeretico comburendo*, under which heresy was indictable, but triable in the ecclesiastical courts; Stat. 2 Hen. V, c. 7 (1414); Sir James Fitzjames Stephen, *History of the Criminal Law* (London: Macmillan, 1883), ii 448–57.

[9] On the work of the Council, Court of High Commission, and Star Chamber, see Sir William Holdsworth, *A History of English Law*, (London: Methuen, 1924), v. 208 ff.

[10] Statute 31 Hen. VIII, c. 14.

[11] The history is described by Leonard W. Levy, *Constitutional Opinions: Aspects of the Bill of Rights* (New York: Oxford University Press, 1986), 40–71.

[12] Act of Settlement 1700, Stat. 12 & 13 Will. III, c. 2, ss. 2 and 3.

[13] Stephen, *History of Criminal Law*, ii. 470.   [14] (1676) 1 Vent. 293, 86 ER 189.

tresses of the legitimacy of the state and the law, 'to reproach the Christian religion is to speak in subversion of the law'. For this reason (if it be a reason) it was held to be justifiable for the civil courts to exercise jurisdiction in respect of blasphemy alongside that of the ecclesiastical courts, which had a more obvious interest than the state's in punishing (for example) clergymen who joke about the biblical miracles.[15] Blasphemy as a crime, therefore, was concerned more with the protection of the state than with the protection of religion *per se*, and was an offence more akin to seditious libel than to outraging public decency. Blasphemous libel thus grew up as a means of protecting the state religion against attack at a time when the legitimacy of the state was intimately bound up with respect for the state religion, and the religious beliefs of the monarch were central to the legitimacy of his claim to the throne. The criminal law was protecting state interests rather than the sensibilities of citizens. Religion remains a powerful cultural influence on individuals, officials, legislators, and judges in many countries. This is often reflected in constitutional arrangements.

One difficulty is how to reach a consensus on what constitutes a religion, a matter on which even theologians disagree. In the UK, the predominant constitutional position of the Anglican Church is reflected in a wide range of institutions, notably the monarchy and the role of bishops in the House of Lords. Tax exemptions are also available in the UK for bodies which pursue religious purposes, and so fall within the definition of a charity.[16] However, this presents the Charity Commissioners and the courts with difficult problems in deciding what constitutes a religion. In *R. v. Registrar General, ex parte Segerdal*[17] the Court of Appeal held that a chapel used by the Church of Scientology was not a 'place of meeting for religious worship' entitled to relief from rates, because with a few exceptions (including Buddhism) religious worship involves doing reverence to a deity. The court decided that scientology is a philosophy rather than a religion. It follows that neither Freemasonry[18] nor the South Place Ethical Society[19] are charitable as being for the advancement of religion, because their activities do not sufficiently display the characteristics of 'submission to the object worshipped, veneration of that object, praise, thanksgiving, prayer, or intercession'.[20] However, the distinction

---

[15] *R. v. Woolston* (1729) 1 Barn. KB 162, 94 ER 112.

[16] Robilliard, *Religion and the Law*, ch. 4.

[17] [1970] 2 QB 697, [1970] 3 All ER 886, CA.

[18] *United Grand Lodge of Ancient, Free and Accepted Masons of England* v. *Holborn Borough Council* [1957] 1 WLR 1080, [1957] 3 All ER 281, CA.

[19] *In re South Place Ethical Society; Barralet* v. *A.-G.* [1980] 1 WLR 1565, [1980] 3 All ER 918.

[20] *R. v. Registrar General, ex parte Segerdal* [1970] 2 QB 697 at p. 709, [1970] 3 All ER 886 at p. 892 *per* Buckley LJ.

between religions and other forms of philosophy presents insuperable problems. Buddhism is not theistic, but is commonly regarded as a religion. The English courts treat Buddhism as an exception to the general rule, but this makes it hard to find a principled ground for excluding scientology from the category of religions. By contrast, the High Court of Australia has decided that religions are not necessarily theistic, and that scientology qualifies as a religion for the purposes of tax relief.[21] In the USA, the Supreme Court has also adopted a non-theistic view of religion, allowing exemption from conscription on the ground of religious conviction to one who holds a 'sincere and meaningful belief, which occupies in the life of its possessor a place parallel to that filled by the God of those admittedly qualifying for the exemption on the grounds of religion'.[22]

Instead of attempting a definition, it would be preferable (but perhaps not much easier) to approach the issue from a policy orientation, by asking whether the particular philosophy or creed benefits society morally in a way which merits special legal privileges. One would then have a range of privileges for specifically recognized religious groups, without the need to agree a definition of religion. Article 44.1.2 of the 1937 Constitution of Ireland (repealed in 1972 by the referendum which approved the Fifth Amendment to the Constitution Bill) did this, recognizing 'the special position of the Holy Catholic Apostolic and Roman Church as the guardian of the Faith professed by the great majority of the citizens'. Some other named (and some unnamed) religious denominations were also 'recognized'.[23] This had certain consequences for the law of charities, for the ability of the bodies named to hold property, for privilege between priest and penitent, and for the law of standing in legal proceedings. Interestingly, the repeal of these constitutional provisions has not made the state, or the judges' interpretations of the Constitution, less Catholic. In the Preamble, the people of Eire adopt the Constitution 'In the name of the Most Holy Trinity, from Whom is all authority and to Whom, as our final end, all actions both of men and States must be referred, . . . Humbly acknowledging all our obligations to our Divine Lord, Jesus Christ . . .'. In *Norris* v. *Attorney General*[24] the Supreme Court held that this required the courts to view a claim by a homosexual, that

---

[21] *Church of the New Faith* v. *Commissioner for Pay-Roll Tax* (1983) 154 CLR 120.

[22] *US* v. *Seeger*, 380 US 163 (1965) at p. 176 *per* Clark J., writing for the Court.

[23] Article 44.1.3 of the 1937 Constitution, recognizing the Church of Ireland, the Presbyterian Church in Ireland, the Methodist Church in Ireland, the Religious Society of Friends in Ireland, 'as well as the Jewish Congregations and the other religious denominations existing in Ireland at the date of the coming into operation of this Constitution'. The final clause potentially reopened the debate about the nature of a religious denomination.

[24] 1984 IR 36.

his personal freedom under the Constitution had been improperly abridged by laws against homosexual practices, in the light of Christian teaching which generally disapproved of homosexuality. Similarly in *Attorney General (at the relation of Society for the Protection of the Unborn Child (Ireland) Ltd.) v. Open Door Counselling Ltd.*[25] an appeal to Christian doctrine was made to help to justify an injunction against the provision of advice about contraception and abortion. Under such a Constitution, a crime of blasphemous libel protecting only the Roman Catholic Church could hardly be attacked on constitutional grounds.

In the USA, immigrants over the centuries have often being escaping religious persecution in Europe, not because they thought that religion was unimportant, but because it was fundamental to their lives. Respect for religious pluralism is supported by the First Amendment, which guarantees freedom of religion and forbids Congress to establish any religion. Legislatures and presidents regarded spiritual belief as being sufficiently important as an antidote to the materialist beliefs of the USSR, and more recently for its own sake, to justify promoting religious belief. Since 1956, the national motto has been 'In God we trust'.[26] Although it has been said that this has no theological significance such as to breach the First Amendment,[27] the Supreme Court had earlier held that it is permissible for a public (i.e. state-funded) school to release students for religious education elsewhere during school time at the request of parents, since (according to Douglas J., writing for the majority in a 6–3 majority decision) this allows schools to respect the religious nature of American society.[28] The view that religion is important (even if individuals should have a free choice between religions) has influenced the U.S. Supreme Court in upholding the constitutionality of tax exemptions for religious purposes.[29] Nevertheless, the Court has consistently refused to allow religion to be forced on people, or to give any protected status to religion. Compulsory acts of religious worship by students in public schools have been held to contravene the establishment clause of the First Amendment.[30] A law which imposes a penalty, or requires a licence, for expressing anti-religious views, including virulent criticism of a religion, is unconstitutional.[31] A law which prevents public-school teachers from teaching the theory of evolution, on the ground that it is inconsistent with the Book of Genesis, is unconstitutional, because, as Fortas J. put it,

---

[25] 1988 IR 593.   [26] 36 USC s. 186 (1956).

[27] *Aronow v. US*, 432 F.2d 242 (USCA, 9th Cir., 1970).

[28] *Zorach v. Clauson*, 343 US 306 (1952).

[29] *Walz v. Tax Commission*, 397 US 664 (1970).

[30] *Engel v. Vitale*, 370 US 421 (1962); *Lee v. Weisman*, 112 S. Ct. 2649 (1992).

[31] *Cantwell v. Connecticut*, 310 US 296 (1940).

delivering the judgment of the Supreme Court in *Epperson* v. *Arkansas*:[32] 'The First Amendment mandates governmental neutrality between religion and religion, and between religion and non-religion.' As early as 1872, in *Watson* v. *Jones*,[33] the Supreme Court had affirmed that, in the USA, 'The law knows no heresy, and is committed to the support of no dogma, the establishment of no sect.' Under such a constitution, there is no room for a law criminalizing blasphemy, save on public-order grounds.

The law of blasphemy as it exists today in England is premised on the special status of religious belief over non-religious belief, a position hard to justify in a philosophically plural society, and on the special position of the Anglican Church within the state. However, the legitimacy of the modern British state today relies more on popular consent, based on its record of respect for democracy or freedom, than on the Church of England. This has made it necessary to find another justification for retaining the offence. Blasphemous libel remains a common-law offence, but is now generally regarded as protecting the religious sensibilities of individual believers, rather than the state. Nevertheless, the link with the state and its established religion lives on as a factor limiting the scope of the offence, long after the reason for it has passed away. Even today, only attacks on Christianity, and (as forms of Christianity vary) on the established form (the Church of England), may amount to criminal blasphemy at common law. That, indeed, was what Alderson B. told the jury in *R.* v. *Gathercole*:[34]

. . . a person may, without being liable to prosecution for it, attack Judaism, or Mahomedanism, or even any sect of the Christian Religion (save the established religion of the country); and the only reason why the latter is in a different situation from the others is, because it is the form established by law, and is therefore a part of the constitution of the country.

Thus, but for the historical circumstance of Henry VIII's decision to part company with the Church of Rome, Roman Catholicism might still have been the religion enjoying a special position in the state, and only attacks on that denomination would have constituted blasphemy at common law.

This was comprehensible when English society was substantially homogeneous in its religious beliefs. Yet even in 1815, it has been said,

[32] 393 US 97 (1968) at pp. 103–4. See also *Torcaso* v. *Watkins* 367 US 488 (1961), holding unconstitutional a requirement that public officials should swear an oath affirming belief in God.
[33] 13 Wall. 679 at p. 728, 20 L. Ed. 666 at p. 676 (1872), *per* Miller J. delivering the judgment of the court.
[34] (1838) 2 Lew. CC 237 at p. 254, 168 ER 1140 at p. 1145.

there were more dissenters than communicants of the Church of England in Wales and some parts of England; Presbyterianism was the strongest denomination in Scotland; and there was a growing minority of Roman Catholics.[35] As the rationalist movement grew in strength, and immigration (Roman Catholic, Jewish, and, as the twentieth century progressed, Muslim, among other religions) mushroomed, the idea that the legitimacy of the state's laws rested on the established church might have appeared to make the laws less, rather than more, secure. There would therefore have been good reasons for abolishing the crime of blasphemy altogether, as a field in which the state no longer had the necessary interest to justify criminalizing expression. However, in *Bowman v. Secular Society*,[36] the House of Lords, while holding that a bequest to a society which aimed to propagate atheism was not illegal, felt unable to take the responsibility for overturning the crime of blasphemous libel, which would have involved judicial legislation overruling centuries of precedents. More recently, the Law Commission has unanimously recommended that the offence should be abolished, but could not agree on what, if anything, should replace it.[37]

If the offence is to be retained with the protection of religious sensibilities as its rationale, in a multi-ethnic, multi-cultural society, where there is a need to maintain social harmony between major sections of society, each of which takes its religion seriously, this would naturally tend to lead to a recognition that the law of blasphemy should protect an ever wider range of religious beliefs. But, although in *Bowman v. Secular Society*[38] Lord Sumner described as 'strange' Alderson B.'s direction in *Gathercole* that a statement was blasphemous only if it attacked the established denomination of the Christian religion, no court has felt able to take even that relatively small step away from centuries of authority.

In the most recent case on the subject, *R. v. Chief Metropolitan Magistrate, ex parte Choudhury*,[39] the applicant, a Muslim, had sought a summons charging Salman Rushdie with blasphemous libel in respect of the publication of the book *The Satanic Verses*, on the ground that the book blasphemed against (*inter alia*) God (Allah), the Prophet Abraham and his son Ishmael, Muhammad (Pbuh) the Holy Prophet of Islam, his wives and companions, and the religion of Islam. The magistrate refused

---

[35] Sir Llewellyn Woodward, *The Age of Reform 1815–1870*, 2nd edn. (Oxford: Clarendon Press, 1962), 502. See also E. P. Thompson, *The Making of the English Working Class* (Harmondsworth: Penguin, 1968), 28–58; Christopher Hibbert, *The English: A Social History 1066–1945* (London: Grafton Books, 1987), 640–3,

[36] [1917] AC 406, HL.

[37] Law Commission Report No. 145, *Offences against Religion and Public Worship* (London: HMSO, 1985).

[38] [1917] AC at p. 459.   [39] [1991] QB 429, [1991] 1 All ER 306, DC.

to issue the summons, on the ground that the crime of blasphemy protects only Christian beliefs. The applicant applied for judicial review of this decision. The Divisional Court, after an exhaustive review of the matter, held that the limitation to Christian beliefs was settled law, and that it was outside its powers to extend the offence to religions other than Christianity. Even had it not been so bound, the court considered that it would not have been willing to initiate an extension to other religions. There were three reasons for this. First, the judges did not feel able to delimit the meaning of 'religion' sufficiently clearly to give a clear idea of the scope of the new offence. Secondly, the creation or widening of an offence at common law, although possible in theory, risked contravening the prohibition in the European Convention on Human Rights, Article 7, on retrospectively criminalizing actions or omissions. Thirdly, it would have been inappropriate judicial behaviour where there was no settled agreement (and had been none for over 100 years)[40] on whether it was appropriate to extend or abolish the offence, a lack of consensus illustrated by the powerful division of opinion in the Law Commission's report on the subject. We are therefore left with an offence which protects directly only the religious sensibilities of communicants of the Church of England, although it incidentally protects adherents to other religions so far as their beliefs overlap with central tenets of Anglican belief.

How wide is the protection offered to this select group of religionists? Although *R. v. Taylor*[41] might suggest that any aspersion on the Church of England would be criminally blasphemous, this is not the case. Admittedly, a wide range of material is protected against aspersion. For example, an attack on the Old Testament is impliedly an attack on Christianity, since Christian theology regards the Old and New Testaments as intimately connected, the Old forming the basis for the New, so that an attack on the Old Testament threatens to undermine the New Testament.[42] However, much depends on the manner of the attack and the state of mind of the attacker. There must be an intention to subvert the established church, and, as Watkins LJ has observed, this must be achieved by means of 'scurrilous vilification'.[43] Discussion and differences of opinion are tolerated, so long as they are carried on 'in a sober and temperate and decent style' as opposed to cases where 'the tone and spirit is that of offence, and insult, and ridicule, which leaves the judgment really not free to act, and, therefore, cannot be truly called an appeal to

---

[40] See C. S. Kenny, 'The Evolution of the Law of Blasphemy' (1922) 1 *CLJ* 127–42.

[41] (1676) 1 Vent. 293.

[42] *R. v. Hetherington* (1840) 4 St. Tr. (NS) 563, especially at pp. 596 *per* Lord Denman CJ.

[43] *R. v. Chief Metropolitan Magistrate, ex parte Choudhury* [1991] 1 QB 429 at pp. 442–3, [1991] 1 All ER 306 at p. 314, DC.

the judgment, but an appeal to the wild and improper feelings of the human mind . . .'.[44] For a conviction, there must have been an attack of the latter sort on the established church's religion, scriptures, or sacred persons or objects.

In practice, however, this distinction between appeals to judgement and appeals to raw feelings, based in nineteenth-century rationalism, is difficult to maintain. Literary forms using rhetorical devices such as metaphor rather than reason to deliver their message can cross the boundary from the permissible to the impermissible. In *R. v. Lemon*[45] a jury decided that suggestions that Jesus had contemplated or enjoyed homosexual acts with the apostles, contained in a poem by Professor James Kirkup about a homosexual who had been converted to Christianity and published in *Gay News*, a magazine aimed at homosexuals, amounted to a blasphemous libel. It did not avail the author or publishers to argue that the purpose of the poem was to suggest that God's love is capable of encompassing an infinite range of people and practices. The jury was entitled to look at the medium rather than the message.

In fact, the *actus reus* of the crime of blasphemy has been expressed in so many different ways that it is hard to know what conduct is or is not caught by it. For example, in *R. v. Lemon* Lord Diplock spoke of publications which 'shock and arouse resentment among believing Christians', while Lord Scarman approved a definition of the offence as covering any publication 'which contains any contemptuous, reviling, scurrilous or ludicrous matter relating to God, Jesus Christ, or the Bible, or the formularies of the Church of England as by law established'.[46] It will be immediately evident that these formulations are not identical. The differences between formulations of the *actus reus* resulted from differences of opinion about the proper orientation and objective of the crime of blasphemy. The increasingly pluralistic nature of religious beliefs (or lack of them) in society undermined the idea that attacks on Christianity are more likely than attacks on other religions to 'shake the fabric of society generally' or subvert the law.[47] Another possible approach was to treat

---

[44] *R. v. Hetherington* (1840) 4 St. Tr. (NS) 563 at 590 *per* Lord Denman CJ.

[45] [1979] AC 617, [1979] 1 All ER 898, HL.

[46] [1979] AC 617, [1979] 1 All ER 898, at pp. 632, 900–1, *per* Lord Diplock, and 658–9, 921–2, *per* Lord Scarman, quoting *Stephen's Digest of the Criminal Law*, 9th edn, (London: Macmillan, 1950), art. 214.

[47] *Cp.* Lord Sumner in *Bowman* v. *Secular Society Ltd.* [1917] AC 406 at pp. 459–60. In *R. v. Lemon* [1979] AC 617 at pp. 658–9, [1979] 1 All ER at pp. 921–2, Lord Scarman accepted that the crime of blasphemy 'belongs to a group of criminal offences designed to safeguard the internal tranquillity of the kingdom', and went on to advocate legislative intervention to extend its protection to the religious feelings of all religions as the best means of achieving that objective, in the mean time maintaining the protection given to Christians under common law.

blasphemy as a simple public-order offence, made criminal because intemperate attacks on Christianity are likely to cause a breach of the peace. But the idea that a threat of a breach of the peace was an essential element of blasphemy was rejected in *Bowman* v. *Secular Society Ltd.*, since 'to insult a Jew's religion is not less likely to provoke a fight than to insult an Episcopalian'.[48] Accordingly, blasphemy is now viewed as an offence aimed at saving Anglicans from suffering a sense of outrage at attacks on their religion. This object of protecting religious sensibility enabled the Court of Appeal to uphold a conviction where a publication described Jesus entering Jerusalem 'like a circus clown on the back of two don- keys'.[49] It would seem that either Anglicans are thought to be extremely sensitive, or a very low level of offensiveness will suffice. Similarly, a poem giving a homosexual viewpoint on the spectacle of the crucifixion of Jesus was held to be blasphemous in *R.* v. *Lemon*.[50]

The intention required to constitute the *mens rea* of blasphemy has been expressed as 'an intention to publish material which in the opinion of the jury is likely to shock and arouse resentment among believing Christians'.[51] It is not necessary that the accused should be shown to have intended to shock or arouse resentment, or even to have been indifferent as to whether shock or resentment resulted from his actions.[52] This approach has been followed by analogy in relation to the offence of out- raging public decency, discussed below, in s. 3(2). However, it com- pounds an unsatisfactory state of affairs in which a common-law crime, carrying an unlimited penalty, has an uncertain purpose, an uncertain *actus reus*, and minimal *mens rea* requirements.

The English law of blasphemy, it seems to be generally agreed, is in need of reform. Unfortunately, there is no agreement about the nature of the necessary reform. In essence, there are only two options: the aboli- tion of the offence, and its extension (with, perhaps, modifications) to cover insults to all or most religions. Each of these options has its sup- porters. As noted above, Lord Scarman supported the idea of generalizing the protection of religious susceptibilities, but felt that only Parliament

---

[48] Lord Sumner in *Bowman* v. *Secular Society Ltd.* at pp. 459–60. *Cp.* the mistaken remark by Avory J. when directing the jury in *R.* v. *Gott* (1922) 16 Cr. App. R. 87 at p. 89.

[49] *R.* v. *Gott* (1922) 16 Cr. App. R. 87, CCA.

[50] [1979] AC 617, [1979] 1 All ER 898, HL.

[51] *R.* v. *Lemon* [1979] AC 617 at p. 632, [1979] 1 All ER 898 at pp. 900–1, *per* Lord Diplock.

[52] The *mens rea* requirement is therefore less demanding than that laid down in *R.* v. *Ramsay and Foote* (1883) 15 Cox CC 231, where Lord Coleridge CJ at p. 236 approved a formulation which demanded either malicious or wilful intention to pervert, insult, or mislead, or a state of indifference to the interests of society.

could take that step.[53] The Law Commission, on the other hand, unanimously recommended abolishing the common-law offence, and, although a minority favoured introducing a statutory provision which would protect religious sensibilities, the majority of the Commission recommended that religious beliefs should not have more extensive protection than other types of beliefs.[54] This view treats the matter simply as a public-order issue: insults to any religion would be punishable if (and only if) they threatened to provoke public-order offences, or constituted some other specific criminal offence. Those who advocate creating a wider offence, which would protect adherents of all religions against having their religious sensibilities outraged, treat the sensibilities of those who believe in religion as a special interest, more significant than people's interests in (for example) philosophy, politics, art, music, and football, none of which are specially protected against outrage by the criminal law.

There is some philosophical support for such a weighting of interests. Joseph Raz and John Finnis each give special status to religious beliefs. For Raz, freedom of religion is primarily a social good, because, in addition to the fact that it may form a central tenet of a person's chosen path through life, it is worthy of protection on the ground that it is seen as a socially useful phenomenon.[55] For Finnis, religion is a self-evident good, because people seek an understanding, for its own sake, of their relationship with the forces which created the universe.[56] However, while these theories demand protection for freedom of religious belief and practice, it is by no means clear that they entail laws imposing criminal sanctions on anyone who offends another's religious sensibilities. Indeed, it is possible that such a law might itself threaten the religious freedom of members of religions whose innocent expressions of belief might outrage members of other religions which are fundamentally intolerant of the beliefs of others. The law might also threaten the right of people to express atheist beliefs or agnosticism, both philosophical positions which express a position in relation to the creative forces of the universe no less than, though different from, orthodox religious positions.

As well as offering only questionable support for a law of blasphemy, the Razian argument for the importance of religious freedom might in some circumstances justify a restriction of that freedom. If the value of religious freedom is primarily social, as Raz suggests, then it would seem to follow that society is justified in restricting the freedom to pursue those religions which, so far from upholding social morality, strike at the root of established social values. For example, it is arguable that the

---

[53] R. v. Lemon [1979] AC 617, [1979] 1 All ER 898, HL.

[54] Law Commission, Offences against Religion.

[55] Joseph Raz, The Morality of Freedom (Oxford: Clarendon Press, 1986), 251–2.

[56] John Finnis, Natural Law and Natural Rights (Oxford: Clarendon Press, 1980), 89–90.

Muslim attack on Salman Rushdie, far from deserving the support of an extended law of blasphemy, justifies active legal steps against those Muslims who threaten to commit heinous criminal offences against Rushdie. The *fatwar*, a sentence of death which would not be recognized in any British court, is, as a matter of English law, an incitement to murder. Any religion which supports or requires such action strikes at the root of the ideals of the rule of law and the sanctity of life on which (among other things) liberal Western society is based. A society which is so liberal that it turns a blind eye to such threats has gone beyond liberalism into a form of relativism in which it fails to stand up for the rights and freedoms which it purports to hold as fundamental. It is, indeed, licence rather than liberalism, and represents an open invitation to those who would undermine liberty of conscience and toleration in the name of respect for religion.

It is therefore perhaps not surprising that the European Commission of Human Rights has decided that, while a state has a discretion to penalize scurrilous attacks on religious beliefs which are deeply held among its citizens,[57] the right to freedom of religion under Article 9 of the European Convention does not compel freedom for adherents of any religion to bring legal proceedings in respect of such scurrilous abuse.[58] Although it has sometimes been argued that the existing English law of blasphemy breaches Article 14 of the Convention, as it discriminates against non–Christians,[59] the text of Article 14 outlaws discrimination on the ground of (*inter alia*) religion only in respect of 'the rights and freedoms set forth in this Convention'. Once it has been decided that the right to freedom of religion does not encompass a right to have criminal sanctions imposed for scurrilous attacks on tenets of a religion, it is hard to see how a domestic law which imposes such sanctions differentially can be said to breach Article 14. It is no answer to point out that a restriction, justifiable under another Article, on a right which is, in fact, recognized in the Convention, may contravene Article 14 if imposed in a discriminatory way:[60] there is no warrant for extending such a principle to cases in which an applicant is asserting a right which is not recognized within the Convention. A stronger argument could, however, be made

[57] *Gay News Ltd.* v. *UK*, Eur. Comm. HR, Application No. 8710/79, Decision of 7 May 1982; 28 DR 77, 5 EHRR 123.

[58] *Choudhury* v. *UK* Application No. 17439/90, Decision of 8 Mar. 1991, (1991) 12 *Human Rights LJ* 172.

[59] e.g. by Sebastian Poulter, 'Towards Legislative Reform of the Blasphemy and Racial Hatred Laws' [1991] *PL* 371–85 at p. 375.

[60] This is Poulter's argument, 'Towards Legislative Reform', at p. 372, relying on *Grundrath* v. *Federal Republic of Germany* (1967) *Yearbook of the European Convention of Human Rights* 626 at p. 678; *Belgian Linguistics Case (No. 2)* Eur. Ct. HR, Series A, No. 6, Judgment of 23 July 1968, at paras. 7–9; 1 EHRR 252 at pp. 283–4.

on the basis of the ICCPR, Article 26, which provides that all are entitled to the equal protection of the law, which must provide effective protection against discrimination on the ground of (*inter alia*) religion. The question would appear to turn on the issue of whether the different treatment of groups is based on reasonable and objective criteria, a matter on which opinions might differ.[61] International human rights law is, therefore, unhelpful on the form which any new law should take.

It is clear that any criminal offence which replaces blasphemy would need to cover all religious beliefs if it were to be acceptable in a pluralist society such as modern Britain.[62] At the same time, there is a widespread liberal mistrust of criminal laws which seek to penalize expressions of opinions merely on the ground that some people find the opinions, or the manner in which they are expressed, objectionable.[63] A possible compromise would treat a person's religious beliefs as special interests for the purposes of the criminal law in the same way that a person's membership of a racial group is treated as a special interest. That would lead to legislation which would criminalize attacks on religious beliefs to the same extent as attacks on racial groups. Such a proposal has been advanced by Sebastian Poulter.[64] This would impose sanctions on behaviour which met the same criterion as are set out in Part III of the Public Order Act 1986, namely an intention to stir up hatred against a racial (or, in this case, religious) group. Such hatred affects religious groups in much the same way as it affects racial groups, and should be subjected to the same criminal-law regime. Indeed, some religious groups[65] (though not Christians or, perhaps, Muslims) are also racial groups within the meaning of the current legislation.

On this model, it would be an offence to use threatening, abusive, or insulting words or behaviour, or to display any written material which is threatening, abusive, or insulting, with the intention of stirring up hatred against a racial or religious group, or whereby such hatred is likely to be stirred up. It would be hard to object to such legislation on principled grounds; indeed, it is possible that such behaviour would in the past have constituted seditious libel (though not blasphemy) when directed against a religious group such as Anglo-Jewry.[66] The legislation would not

[61] See *Annual Report of the Human Rights Committee, 1987*, UN Doc. A/42/40, p. 139.

[62] See e.g. *Report of the Bishop of London's Group on Blasphemy* (London, 1988).

[63] Joel Feinberg, *Offense to Others* (New York: Oxford UP, 1985), accepts that offensiveness is an evil, even when not harmful (i.e. against anyone's interests), but argues that criminalization is justified only if the offence is wrongful (i.e. interferes with rights) and profound.

[64] Poulter, 'Towards Legislative Reform', at pp. 377–85.

[65] e.g. Jews and Sikhs are covered by existing legislation, as they constitute ethnic groups as well as religious ones: *Mandla* v. *Dowell Lee* [1983] 2 AC 548, [1983] 1 All ER 1062, HL.   [66] Robilliard, *Religion and the Law*, 8–10.

automatically outlaw outrage to sensibilities. If one feels that the risk of such outrage is necessarily concomitant with having sensibilities, and that it should not attract criminal sanctions, this will not be a serious concern. Those who are not of this view would perhaps see some justification for widening the scope of the offence to make the use of threatening, abusive, or insulting words, behaviour, or written material a criminal offence if it is intended to outrage the feelings of a significant number of members of a racial or religious group.[67] However, many would be likely to see such an extension of the criminal law as an unacceptable infringement of freedom of expression, in the absence of a clear and imminent risk that public disorder would result from the words, behaviour, or display of written material.

Any such legislation would face certain problems. Issues which would have to be addressed include whether the offence should also cover vilification of non-religious philosophies; if not, whether 'religious belief' should be defined in the statute or left to the judges to interpret;[68] and whether 'religious belief' encompasses atheism, agnosticism, devil worship, scientology, and polytheism. The *mens rea* for the offence would also need to be considered: should it require a specific intent, or would recklessness, negligence, or (as under the blasphemy law) strict liability be applied? These problems are likely to make reform of the blasphemy law a contentious subject for some time to come, especially if the combative response of some parts of the Muslim community to the perceived insults to their beliefs in Salman Rushdie's book *The Satanic Verses* becomes common among other religions.

15.2 FOUNDATIONS OF THE LAW OF DECENCY: PUBLIC MORALITY AND PRIVATE SENSIBILITY

Expression of a sort which might contravene accepted standards of social morality is potentially subject to restrictions of three types in English law. First, there are various statutory and common-law offences for which people may be prosecuted. Secondly, there are provisions restricting access to material, and requiring outlets selling the material to be licensed and regulated. Thirdly, there are provisions allowing seizure and forfeiture of immoral goods in certain circumstances, without the need for anyone to be shown to have committed any offence. The law is in a confused state. It has developed over the centuries since the invention of

---

[67] This is Dr Poulter's proposal, 'Towards Legislative Reform', at p. 378; note his proposed redraft of the Public Order Act 1986, s. 18(1).

[68] Dr Poulter's preference is for leaving this to the judges: 'Towards Legislative Reform', 379–80.

printing. Common-law rules and statutory rules, laws controlling indecency and laws controlling obscenity, exist side by side.[69] It is not clear whether the objective of the law is, or should be, to put a stop to pornography, and, if so, why; to prevent pornography from falling into the wrong hands; to maintain standards of morality, and, if so, whose; to stop people from being upset by public displays; or to achieve some combination of those objects. Were it acceptable to criminalize or contain all conduct or expression which the dominant members of society found offensive or immoral, it would seriously restrict the range of discussion of ethical and political issues, since many expressions of opinion will be found offensive by those who disagree either with the opinion or with the way in which it is expressed.

This section examines the foundations for such laws against a background of liberal theory. On this view, tolerating offensive conduct and speech is one of the prices to be paid for a reasonably free and open society. Alternatively, free-speech theory can be regarded as a forum for debate, in which societies develop their intellectual attitudes. A bias in favour of toleration can best be developed and systematized in cases concerning relatively innocuous forms of offensiveness, and, once established, can then be applied and extended in relation to other, potentially more upsetting, offences.[70] In a pluralist society there is unlikely to be agreement about moral standards, and in a liberal society it is a commonplace assumption that choice between moral values is primarily a matter for individuals. There is a widely, but not universally, accepted view in Britain of the limits of the criminal law. The job of the law, and particularly criminal law, is to exclude from the range of individual choice those acts which are incompatible with the maintenance of society and the safety and rights of its members. It is no part of its job to seek to uphold the preferences of one part of society over those of another part, save in limited circumstances: namely, when the preferences of some members of society cause harm, rather than mere inconvenience or offence, to others. Since being articulated by John Stuart Mill in *On Liberty*, published in 1859, the 'harm principle' has been adopted as a basis for philosophical discussion, and for the recommendations of the Home Office Departmental Committee on Obscenity and Film Censorship, chaired by Professor Bernard Williams (the Williams Committee).[71]

---

[69] Geoffrey Robertson, *Obscenity: An Account of Censorship Laws and their Enforcement in England and Wales* (London: Weidenfeld & Nicolson, 1979), chs. 1 and 2.

[70] Lee C. Bollinger, *The Tolerant Society: Freedom of Speech and Extremist Speech in America* (Oxford and New York: Clarendon Press, 1986), esp. 137–40.

[71] Ch. 1 above; *Report of the Committee on Obscenity and Film Censorship* (Chairman: Professor Bernard Williams), Cmnd. 7772 (London: HMSO, 1979), hereafter 'Williams Committee Report'.

However, there is considerable variation between people's views of what constitutes 'harm' for this purpose. Some people, impressed by the wide range of interferences with rights which would become permissible if harm is given an extended meaning, restrict it to harm which is objectively verifiable according to established scientific criteria. They therefore look for physical or psychological harm which constitutes a condition or syndrome recognized by competent medical or social scientific opinion. On this basis, the Williams Committee took the view in 1979 that the burden of establishing harm lay on those who seek to justify interference with liberty of expression, and that those people had failed to discharge the burden of showing a causative link between reading or watching pornography and committing criminal or anti-social acts.[72] Others, instead of concentrating on material harm, are prepared to take account of moral or ideological harm. This is less easy to establish on objective criteria than the former kind of harm.[73] It is more impressionistic, and allows people to propose interferences with liberty on the strength of assertions of social or moral harm which cannot be scientifically tested. The main difference between Professor H. L. A. Hart and Sir Patrick (later Lord) Devlin, in relation to the proper relationship of morals to law, did not concern whether harm should be the basis for legal interference with liberty of expression. They agreed that it should, but disagreed about the type of harm which should be regarded as significant. Hart favoured reliance on personal harm, following the line traceable to John Stuart Mill, while Devlin considered that attacks on any basic moral standards threatened, and so caused harm to, society as a whole, weakening the bonds which hold it together, even if no identifiable individual suffered immediate and identifiable personal harm. Accordingly, Devlin was prepared to contemplate the criminal law enforcing a wider range of moral demands than was Hart.[74]

The moral basis of society is important, but it is probably impossible to

[72] Williams Committee Report, ch. 6, para. 10.8, and (for a summary of the research) app. 5.

[73] This is not to say that assessing psychological harm does not depend on judgement. Clearly it does. The difference, however, lies in the fact that psychiatric diagnosis proceeds on the basis of criteria which are agreed in advance by those who do the job, and which rely on observable symptoms or manifestations of abnormality, so that diagnosis is testable and falsifiable. This is not true of most other forms of harm.

[74] Sir Patrick Devlin, *The Enforcement of Morals* (Oxford: Oxford University Press, 1965), ch. 1; H. L. A. Hart, *Law, Liberty, and Morality* (Oxford: Oxford University Press, 1963). For further discussion, see Joel Feinberg's attempt to distinguish between offensive and harmful conduct, and to explain the justification for putting up with at least some offensive conduct, in *Offense to Others*; P. R. Macmillan, *Censorship and Public Morality* (Aldershot: Gower, 1983), 105–26; H. L. A. Hart, 'Between Utility and Rights' 39 *Columbia LR* 828–46.

establish which moral standards are basic to the survival of any society and which are merely peripheral. It would be unsafe to allow indiscriminate criminalization of all immoral conduct or expression, both because of the uncertain scope of morality in a pluralist society and because the resulting interference with freedom would be likely to cause social and economic stagnation. At the same time, people sometimes suffer offence which is of such a type, and so intense, as to be experienced subjectively as a form of harm which may be as wounding as physical harm. When this happens, it is understandable that there are demands for the cause to be repressed by law. These demands are ultimately political demands, rather than moral or legal ones, and have to be addressed by members of society in the context of a debate about the type of society in which they wish to live.

In 1979, the Williams Committee, adopting a physical or psychological harm test and deciding that the link between pornography and such harm had not been proved, made a number of recommendations which, if implemented, would have gone some way towards clarifying the law, if not making it more socially acceptable than it was before. The Committee recommended that there should be no constraints on the written word, however explicit or offensive, or on written words which were accompanied by inoffensive illustrations. This is a far-reaching proposal. Even the US Supreme Court has not granted First Amendment protection to all written matter. Books can be banned in the United States if they are obscene: that is, appealing to prurient interest as judged by contemporary community standards; depicting or describing, in a patently offensive way, sexual conduct which has been specifically defined by the relevant law; and lacking in serious literary, artistic, political, or scientific value.[75] Child pornography may be banned in the United States,[76] and children and young people under the age of 17 may be denied access to material which would not be regarded as obscene in adult hands.[77] It is perhaps not surprising that the government in the UK was unwilling to make pornography more readily available in the UK than in the USA in order to achieve some kind of principled consistency in the law.

Taking the view that pictures are more harmful than words, the Committee recommended that it should be a criminal offence to trade in or import paedophilic photographic material which portrays indecent activity involving people under the age of 16, or sadistic photographs in

[75] *Miller* v. *California*, 413 US 15 (1973).

[76] *New York* v. *Ferber*, 458 US 747 (1982). Using children under 16 in pornographic films and photographs is a federal crime.

[77] *Ginsberg* v. *New York*, 390 US 629 (1968); *Virginia* v. *Booksellers Association*, 484 US 383 (1988).

which physical harm appears to have been inflicted on people in a sexual context. Other pictorial pornography which portrays, deals with, or relates to violence, cruelty, or horror, faecal or urinary functions, sexual functions, or genitalia, should be restricted if its unrestricted availability is offensive to reasonable people by reason of the manner in which those matters are portrayed or dealt with. The Committee recommended that such material should be available only to people over the age of 18, either by mail order or in shops which admit only those aged 18 and over, exhibit warnings of the type of material sold, and do not display pornographic material in a way which allows it to be visible from the street. The idea was to keep the material out of the way of people who might be offended or harmed by it, such as children and people encountering it unawares.

The restriction of these controls to material dealing with defined matters would have given some objectivity to the notion of offensiveness. However, although the Williams Committee had managed to achieve unanimity among its members, its report was attacked from all directions. The newly elected Conservative government was not prepared to relax restrictions on written matter. In this, they were supported by an odd alliance of the moral conservatives, liberals, and feminists, who are opposed to pornography for different reasons.[78] We will examine some of these in a moment. The Williams Committee's proposals to restrict access to offensive material was more favourably received. Legislation to some extent modelled on the proposals has been passed, and is explained in section 5 below. Generally, however, the notion of restricting sexually offensive material is problematic, for two reasons.

First, the standard of offensiveness can be criticized as being unacceptably indeterminate standard for the law governing the availability of public expression.[79] The implication of this is liberal in a traditional sense: any interference with freedom must be aimed at meeting a pressing social need and should be circumscribed in sufficiently clear terms to enable people to know what the law is, and plan their activities accordingly. This standard is laid down in the caselaw of the European Court of Human Rights as a condition for the justifiability of interferences with freedom of expression under Article 10(2) of the Convention in order to protect morals.

[78] A. W. B. Simpson, *Pornography and Politics: A Look Back to the Williams Committee* (London: Waterlow, 1983), chs. 3 and 5. The book is a re-evaluation of the report and of its political reception by a distinguished legal scholar who was a member of the Committee.

[79] For a critique of the principle of offensiveness, see Barendt, *Freedom of Speech*, 272–9. For a more fully worked out model of the type of offensiveness which might justify a liberal in interfering with free expression, see Feinberg, *Offense to Others*.

Secondly, restricting, but not banning, offensive matter can be seen as based on a misconception about the type and significance of the harm which pornography works. Feminist theorists have argued that, apart from any causal relationship between access to pornography and crime or offence, all pornographic representations of heterosexual activity harm all women. The harm is done by degrading women, presenting them as dominated by men in a context in which such domination is thought to be regarded as natural and even enjoyable. Women may, as Catharine MacKinnon has written, be entirely dehumanized in pornography, becoming merely recipients of treatment by men.[80] MacKinnon, and Andrea Dworkin, argue that sexual explicitness in the representation of this sort of relationship, combined with sexual arousal in the viewer or reader, cause or reinforce attitudes of men towards women, and of women towards themselves (particularly if they find the pornography arousing), which tend to encourage male domination in all areas of life.[81] Pornography is seen as a form of discrimination against women, which merits banning as such.[82] Attempts to ban pornography on the ground that it constitutes a particular representation of the relationship between the sexes have failed in the USA (indeed, in a sense were self-defeating), because they necessarily imply that pornographers are advancing a political perspective, and this will tend to bring them within the protection of the First Amendment.[83]

MacKinnon's and Dworkin's attempts to politicize pornography as violence against women faces a further problem. It assumes that all pornography is the same. In reality, there are many varieties, reflecting many different types of sexual activity. It is only possible to argue convincingly that all pornography is violence against women if one imposes a definition which artificially limits pornography to material which represents sadistic heterosexual or lesbian activity. Other types of pornography may represent violence against entities other than women (dogs, pigs, children, men), but is it objectionable (if one believes it is) because it reflects violent and dominating attitudes in the relationships between the parties, or because it may be in some way harmful, or because it is revolting? To insist on the equation $P = V$ (where P is pornography and V is violence against women) wrongly treats pornography 'as one indivisible

---

[80] Catharine MacKinnon, *Feminism Unmodified: Discourses on Life and Law* (London: Harvard University Press, 1987), 176.

[81] MacKinnon, *Feminism Unmodified*, 147; Andrea Dworkin, *Pornography: Men Possessing Women* (London: The Women's Press, 1981).

[82] The relatively unusual form of pornography which represents women dominating men would presumably be regarded as equally discriminatory and violent, although in a different direction, and so equally merit banning.

[83] *Hudnut* v. *American Booksellers Association, Inc.*, 771 F.2d 323 (US 7th Cir.), affd. 475 US 1001 (1986).

phenomenon', as Professor Simpson observed. One can accept that this is the commonest form of pornography, so it is unfair to suggest, as Simpson does, 'it is hard to believe that some feminist writers have ever seen any'.[84] Yet the feminist analysis, once accepted, leaves open the question as to the appropriate criterion for action against other types of explicit and offensive appeals to prurient sexual interest.

A variant on the radical feminist view, influenced by the post-modernist school of literary and social criticism, argues that nothing is intrinsically pornographic, but that a representation of activities becomes pornographic because of the conventional ways in which the representation is viewed. Material can be defined as pornographic only in terms of the way in which people read or view it, but material which is seen as pornographic may affect the way in which life is viewed if women come to be seen as being, in general and without reference to specific contexts, sexually arousing. This tends to make the social rules which shape attitudes into the centre of attention, and does not attempt to homogenize pornography. It thus avoids some of the problems which face the more radical feminist critique of pornography, but as a corollary places relatively little reliance on the capacity of law to change the social rules which dictate how images are understood, and so tends to discourage legal action against pornography.[85]

In the UK, the Williams Committee's reliance on the harm principle left greater room for control of pornography by treating the rationale for control as being to protect people against harmful material, or material which is so offensive that the offence caused constitutes a harm, rather than suggesting that the reason for controlling pornography might be that it carries an unacceptable political message. But the idea of harm or offensiveness as a root justification for restricting people's freedom is always controversial, and may allow the most sensitive or the most vulnerable to dictate the behaviour of the rest of society, in political matters as well as morality or decency.

If it is arguable that rejecting or modifying Mill's harm principle threatens to open the way to intolerance and more or less arbitrary interference with freedom of expression, it is equally arguable that unqualified adoption of Mill's approach undermines rights. For example, Ronald Dworkin describes the Williams Committee's strategy as combining a free-market approach derived from Mill with a 'slippery slope' argument which evaluates types of expression by reference to the effect they might have, directly or indirectly, on some social goal, rather than by reference to rights. This, he argues, fails to respect people's right to equal moral

[84] Simpson, *Pornography and Politics*, 71.
[85] For discussion, see Carol Smart, *Feminism and the Power of Law* (London: Routledge, 1989), ch. 6.

independence, because it makes people's rights to express themselves in certain ways, or to have access to certain types of expression, subject to other people's mere preferences. It creates the potential for the entire structure of rights to be overwhelmed on utilitarian principles. If one regards the constitution as being based on respect for rights, therefore, the Williams Committee's strategy can be seen as threatening the basic structure of the constitution.[86]

Despite the fact that both Ronald Dworkin and feminist theorists such as Andrea Dworkin and Catharine MacKinnon are opposed to the approach of the Williams Committee, their reasons are very different. Ronald Dworkin's arguments confront the feminist approach as much as that of the Williams Committee. Any attempt to control publications on the basis of offensiveness, either of their content or of the background of rules or power relations which they reflect, to people who are not likely to have to read or view them, will tend to be hard to justify on individual rights grounds. The question is whether rights ought to be restricted to achieve some wider social purpose. The answer to this question is essentially a matter of social and political choice. That the line will be drawn in different places by different societies is recognized by the European Court of Human Rights. In its caselaw under Article 10(2) of the European Convention on Human Rights and Fundamental Freedoms, the Court has accepted that the steps necessary in a democratic society for the protection of morals will depend on the type of morality to which a country is committed. It is not part of the Court's job to lay down moral standards for societies, so the Court will allow a substantial 'margin of appreciation' to states in deciding what moral standards they should enforce.[87] However, once a society has settled on a view of morality, the Court will examine, under Article 10(2), whether the means adopted to give effect to that moral vision are prescribed by law and necessary in a democratic society.

---

[86] Ronald Dworkin, *A Matter of Principle* (Oxford: Clarendon Press, 1986), ch. 17, esp. pp. 336–5.

[87] The *Handyside* case, Eur. Ct. HR, Series A, vol. 24, Judgment of 7 Dec. 1976, 1 EHRR 737; *Müller* v. *Switzerland*, Eur. Ct. HR, Series A, vol. 133, Judgment of 24 May 1988, 13 EHRR 212. An appeal to the freedom to provide services in EC law under Article 59 of the Treaty of Rome, to prevent an Irish court holding that providing information about abortions was unlawful, failed in *The Society for the Protection of Unborn Children Ireland Ltd.* v. *Grogan*, [1991] 3 CMLR 849, ECJ.

15.3 COMMON-LAW OFFENCES OF INDECENCY AND OBSCENITY[88]

At common law, there are several offences of indecency and obscenity.[89] The offence of obscene libel has now fallen into disuse, replaced by the Obscene Publications Acts 1959 and 1964 and other statutory provisions governing broadcasting, theatre, and cinema. Although the common-law offence was not formally abolished, there is now a statutory bar to prosecuting anyone for a common-law offence involving publication of any matter 'where it is of the essence of the offence that the matter is obscene'.[90] However, this does not prevent a person being prosecuted for a common-law offence the essence of which is indecency or immorality not amounting to obscenity. Nor does it preclude prosecution for common-law offences which depend, not on publication, but on an agreement to publish. Accordingly, the offences of outraging public decency, conspiracy to outrage public decency, and conspiracy to corrupt public morals, all remain crimes at common law.[91]

(1) Conspiracy to corrupt public morals

The crime of conspiracy to corrupt public morals consists of an agreement between two or more people to do any act which, if completed, would be likely to have the effect of undermining morality. It is unique among remaining offences of conspiracy, in that the conspiracy is criminal whereas the completed act, carried out by a single person, would not necessarily be criminal: there is no offence of corrupting public morals *per se*, although often the circumstances may give rise to the offence of outraging public decency or an offence under the Obscene Publications Act 1959. However, on the facts of *Shaw* (see below) it was by no means clear that the *Directory* would have satisfied the conditions for the statutory offence. Because the criminality of corrupting morals is held to arise from the conspiracy rather than the corrupting act itself, even the completed act can be charged only as a conspiracy.

---

[88] Law Commission, Working Paper No. 57, *Codification of the Criminal Law: Conspiracies Related to Morals and Decency* (London: HMSO, 1974); Law Commission, Report No. 76, *Criminal Law: Report on Conspiracy and Criminal Law Reform* (London: HMSO, 1976), 72–125.

[89] On the emergence of the concept of obscenity in English law, see Macmillan, *Censorship*, ch. 1.

[90] Obscene Publications Act 1959, s. 2(4).

[91] *Shaw* v. *DPP* [1962] AC 220, [1961] 2 All ER 446, HL; *Knuller* v. *DPP* [1973] AC 435, [1972] 2 All ER 898, HL; *R.* v. *Gibson* [1990] 2 QB 619, [1991] 1 All ER 439, CA.

For example, in the leading case, *Shaw* v. *Director of Public Prosecutions*,[92] the defendants were compilers and publishers of *The Ladies Directory*, a publication in which prostitutes advertised and gave details of the services which they offered. For the prosecution, it was argued that providing, in one place, a directory of that sort would make it easier for people who were so inclined to indulge their lusts. Although prostitution is always present in society, facilitating access to it in that way was said to increase the likelihood that people would resort to prostitutes. This, it was said, threatened to undermine significant moral values concerning sex and family life. Accordingly, the agreement between the defendants to publish the *Directory* amounted to a conspiracy to corrupt public morals. This argument was accepted by the trial judge, the Court of Appeal, and a majority of the House of Lords, which decided that the offence was available at common law by reason of the judges' role in taking steps to protect society against threats to its moral foundations. This is an argument which has much in common with that advanced by Devlin for permitting the criminalization of certain types of immoral conduct.

Lord Reid, who dissented in *Shaw*, thought that the majority was indulging in judicial legislation, and that it was the job of Parliament, not the courts, to alter the law to extend the bounds of criminal liability. This was particularly the case where the allegation against the defendants was of a conspiracy to cause moral harm to society, rather than physical or psychological harm to individuals. This approach, relying on the desirability of extensions to the criminal law in morally contentious fields being carried out by a democratically accountable body, is much closer to being an application of the harm principle of J. S. Mill and H. L. A. Hart than to Devlin.

In so far as the law on the subject before *Shaw* gave little indication to potential publishers of either the crime's existence at common law or its scope, the imposition of criminal liability on the defendants in that case might well have contravened Article 7 of the European Convention on Human Rights: '1. No one shall be held guilty of any criminal offence on account of any act or omission which did not constitute a criminal offence under national or international law at the time when it was committed. . . .' However, after *Shaw*, what was then a novel extension of common-law criminal liability is reasonably well settled law, so much so that Lord Reid felt bound to accept the authority of *Shaw* in a subsequent case.[93] It would therefore not be possible to use Article 7 to impugn any conviction on this charge on facts arising after the decision in *Shaw*. Another issue remains, however: namely, whether or not the imposition

---

[92] [1962] AC 220, [1961] 2 All ER 446, HL.

[93] *Knuller (Publishing Printing and Promotions) Ltd.* v. *DPP* [1973] AC 435, [1972] 2 All ER 898, HL.

of liability for such a publication could breach Article 10's guarantee of protection to freedom of expression. The guarantee covers commercial expression, such as advertising,[94] as well as literary, scholarly, or current-affairs material. It is, therefore, necessary to consider whether the restriction imposed by the offence of conspiring to corrupt public morals is justified by paragraph 2 of Article 10. In view of the wide margin of appreciation allowed to states in deciding what is necessary in order to protect morals, it is likely that the European Court of Human Rights would hold that this common-law offence is justified under Article 10(2).

(2) Outraging public decency and conspiring to outrage public decency

The common-law offence of outraging public decency is committed by anyone who says or does or exhibits in public anything which outrages public decency, whether or not it is obscene.[95]

(i) *What is the difference between indecency and obscenity?* Both indecency and obscenity, as the words are ordinarily used, relate to standards of propriety. They are seen as standing at different points on a continuum of impropriety.[96] Indecency might be described as a breach of propriety which is seriously offensive (otherwise it would not be necessary to criminalize it) but not grossly or outrageously offensive. Obscenity, in its common usage, is a good deal more offensive than indecency. However, as Lord Sands said in *McGowan* v. *Langmuir*:[97]

It is easier to illustrate than define, and I illustrate it thus. For a male bather to enter the water nude in the presence of ladies would be indecent, but it would not necessarily be obscene. But if he directed the attention of a lady to a certain member of his body his conduct would certainly be obscene.

It has been said that 'an indecent article is not necessarily obscene, whereas an obscene article almost certainly must be indecent'.[98]

However, the distinction is somewhat complicated by the statutory

---

[94] *Barthold* v. *Federal Republic of Germany*, Eur. Ct. HR, Series A, vol. 90, Judgment of 25 Mar. 1985, 7 EHRR 383.

[95] *R.* v. *Gibson* [1990] 2 QB 619, [1991] 1 All ER 439, CA, applying *dicta* in *Shaw* v. *DPP* [1962] AC 220 at pp. 281 and 292, [1961] 2 All ER 446 at pp. 460 and 467, *per* Lord Reid and Lord Morris of Borth-y-Gest respectively; *Knuller (Publishing Printing and Promotions) Ltd.* v. *DPP* [1973] AC 435 at p. 493, [1972] 2 All ER 898 at p. 935, *per* Lord Simon of Glaisdale.

[96] *R.* v. *Stanley* [1965] 2 QB 327, [1965] 1 All ER 1035, CCA, especially at pp. 333, 1038 *per* Lord Parker CJ.

[97] 1931 JC 10, at p. 13, a Scottish decision followed by the English Court of Criminal Appeal in *R.* v. *Stanley* (see n. 96).

[98] *R.* v. *Stanley* [1965] 2 QB at p. 333 *per* Lord Parker CJ.

meaning given to 'obscene' by, and for the purposes of, the Obscene Publications Act 1959. This Act was framed to penalize conduct by reference to the harm principle, rather than to impose sanctions on all moral improprieties so as to protect people's sensibilities. By section 1(1), an article is deemed to be obscene if its effect as a whole is such as to tend to deprave and corrupt people likely to read, see, or hear it. The statute thus centres its attention on likely victims, and demands an assessment of the harm which such people would suffer. By contrast, indecency has been held to be a quality of articles or actions, judged objectively and without reference to the intentions of the author or the damage (if any) done to observers.[99] The question, in relation to indecency, is whether a person's sense of decency would be outraged by what occurred, not whether anyone would be depraved, debauched, or corrupted.[100] Accordingly in *R. v. May*[101] it was held that the defendant, a schoolmaster, had been properly convicted after he had asked pupils to order him to perform acts of an explicitly sexual nature, despite there being no evidence that the pupils themselves were offended, depraved, or outraged; they may, indeed, have derived a degree of malicious amusement from the exhibition.

The offence extends to cover all forms of outrage to decency, not merely outrages to sexual decency. For example, in *R. v. Gibson*[102] it was held to encompass displaying for sale, in a gallery open to the public, two ear-rings, each said to have been made out of a freeze-dried human foetus of three or four months gestation, attached to the ear of a model's head by means of a ring fitting tapped into the skull of the foetus. It is not necessary to provide evidence that anyone's feelings were in fact outraged,[103] nor that the defendant did anything to draw anyone's attention particularly to the indecent act or article.[104] However, there must be an act which is objectively indecent. It will not suffice to obtain a conviction merely that the accused did something with an indecent intent, or did something which can reasonably be interpreted as an act preparatory to an act of indecency, such as leaving notes in public places suggesting a time and place for a rendezvous for purposes which might be, but were

---

[99] *R. v. Graham-Kerr* [1988] 1 WLR 1098, 88 Cr. App. R. 302, CA (prosecution under Protection of Children Act 1981, s. 1(1)(*a*)); *Kosmos Publications* v. *DPP*[1975] Crim. LR 345, DC (prosecution under Post Office Act 1953, s. 11).

[100] *Cf. Knuller* v. *DPP* [1973] AC at p. 468, [1972] 2 All ER at p. 913, *per* Lord Morris of Borth-y-Gest.

[101] (1989) 91 Cr. App. R. 157, CA.

[102] [1990] 2 QB 619, [1991] 1 All ER 439, CA, discussed by Mary Childs, 'Outraging Public Decency: The Offence of Offensiveness' [1991] *PL* 20–9.

[103] *R. v. May* (1989) 91 Cr. App. R. 157, CA.

[104] *R. v. Gibson*, [1990] 2 QB 619, [1991] 1 All ER 439, CA; *R. v. Lunderbech* [1991] Crim. LR 784, CA.

not stated to be, indecent.[105] It was held in *Gibson* that the defendants had done enough to meet this requirement: the maker of the ear-rings, Mr Gibson, had actively sought publicity, making it known that the ear-rings were made of human foetuses, while the proprietor of the gallery, Mr Sylveire, had invited the public into the gallery knowing that the ear-rings were there. This was sufficient to show that the act of displaying the foetuses was a public one for the purposes of the common-law offence.

Unlike the statutory obscenity offence under the 1959 Act, there is no defence of public good under the common law. Furthermore, being an offence of indecency rather than obscenity, it is apparently not necessary (or, indeed, relevant) that the defendant should intend to outrage public decency, or even be aware that it might be outraged. All that is needed by way of *mens rea* is for the defendant to have done something deliberately, and for that something to have been of a quality which, objectively, outraged public decency. Any other approach, said the Court of Appeal in *Gibson*, would make it possible for a defendant to escape liability by the very baseness of his own standards.[106] In any case, the Court took the view that intention to outrage decency would virtually always be inferred (even without the legal presumption, abolished by the Criminal Justice Act 1967, section 8, that people intend the natural and probable consequences of their acts) once outrage is established to the satisfaction of the jury.[107] However, there might be situations in which it would be impossible to make the inference, for example where a defendant suffered from a mental disability which, without constituting insanity under the *McNaghten* rules, made it difficult for him to appreciate the way in which his actions would be viewed by others. It would be unfortunate to stigmatize such people as criminals.

It was held in *R. v. Gibson*[108] that offences under section 1 of the 1959 Act are 'factually and morally distinct' from outraging public decency at common law.[109] Two separate reasons have been offered for this. First, the latter do not necessarily involve the former, and so prosecutions for them are not precluded by section 2(4) of the 1959 Act. At first sight it is not easy to see why the Obscene Publications Act 1959 should not be applied to a case such as *Gibson*. Although, in principle, there is a clear distinction between outraging decency and corrupting morals, in particular cases there may be an overlap, especially if, as suggested above, 'an

---

[105] *R. v. Graham-Kerr* [1988] 1 WLR 1098, CA; *R. v. Rowley* [1991] Crim. LR 785, CA.
[106] [1990] 2 QB at p. 627, [1991] 1 All ER at p. 445.
[107] [1990] 2 QB at p. 629, [1991] 1 All ER at p. 447 *per* Lord Lane C.J.
[108] [1990] 2 QB 619, [1991] 1 All ER 439, CA.
[109] [1990] 2 QB at p. 624, [1991] 1 All ER at p. 443 *per* Lord Lane CJ.

obscene article almost certainly must be indecent'.[110] As obscenity is not restricted to sexual matters (as will be seen below), it is hard to see why, on the facts of *Gibson*, it should have been thought to be inappropriate to apply the test for obscenity to the case. This would have enabled the defendants to avail themselves of the defence of public good under section 4 of the 1959 Act.

Secondly, there is a technical legal distinction between the statutory offence, the gravamen of which consists of the completed publication and its consequences, and a common-law conspiracy to corrupt public morals (or outrage public decency), in which the *actus reus* is the agreement to act rather than the act itself and its consequences.[111] This gives rise to the strange position in which a person who is charged with an inchoate crime is denied defences which would have been available had the completed crime been charged. In the wake of *Shaw* v. *Director of Public Prosecutions*[112] a number of MPs sought, and the Solicitor General gave, assurances[113] that the prosecuting authorities would not seek to use the common-law crimes of conspiracy to corrupt public morals and conspiracy to outrage public decency in cases where doing so would effectively deprive defendants of protections for liberty of speech given by the Obscene Publications Acts 1959 and 1964. This was intended to allay a fear that the liberalizing purpose of the 1959 Act would otherwise be frustrated.[114] However, in the light of the decision of the Court of Appeal in *Gibson* this risk seems to have re-emerged.

Lord Lane CJ suggested that 'in this type of case . . . it is unlikely that a defence of public good could possibly arise.'[115] However, this is highly questionable once one accepts that social comment on matters of public concern may be made otherwise than by verbal means. The defendants might, for instance, have wanted to argue that the use of human foetuses was an an ironic technique, attempting to shock observers into realizing the cheapness of human life and the lack of protection offered to unborn children. The display of the ear-rings might have been presented as a political comment on the failure of the legislature to give adequate protection to embryos which are produced by *in vitro* methods of fertilization. It would by no means be inevitable that a jury would have been unimpressed by the public-good defence, and it is unfortunate that a

[110] *R.* v. *Stanley* [1965] 2 QB 327 at p. 333, [1965] 1 All ER 1035 at p. 1038 *per* Lord Parker CJ.

[111] *Shaw* v. *DPP* [1962] AC 220 at pp. 268 *per* Viscount Simonds, 290 *per* Lord Tucker, 291 *per* Lord Morris of Borth-y-Gest.

[112] [1962] AC 220, [1961] 2 All ER 446, HL.

[113] 695 HC Debs. 1212 (3 June 1964); 698 H.C. Debs. 315–16 (7 July 1964).

[114] See *Knuller* v. *DPP* [1973] AC at p. 456, [1972] 2 All ER at pp. 903–4 *per* Lord Reid.

[115] [1990] 2 QB at p. 625, [1991] 1 All ER at p. 444.

defendant with such a potential defence should be prevented from putting it before the jury merely because the prosecution elects to charge an alternative offence. *Gibson* appears to be an example of a case in which the defendants' rights were abridged by an exercise of the prosecutor's discretion.

This sits oddly with the assurances given to the House of Commons in 1964 in relation to the common-law conspiracy offences, and gives rise to serious doubts about the appropriateness of charging any form of writing or representation with the common-law offence unless the defendant agrees in advance that the public-good defence would be inappropriate. It is strange that a defence of public good should be available where the accused is alleged to have published an obscene article which threatens the actual harm of inducing depravity or corruption, but not where it is alleged that he has merely offended against public decency. The strangeness is amplified by the fact that a person convicted on indictment of the common-law indecency offence is subject to an unlimited term of imprisonment, whereas a person convicted on indictment of the supposedly more serious obscenity offence faces a maximum term of three years' imprisonment.[116] The possibility of overlap between the common-law and statutory offences has been long understood by prosecutors, as the assurances given by the law officers in 1964 show. Furthermore, there is an anomaly in prosecuting a display of ear-rings at common law when a film showing the making or display of the ear-rings would have to have been prosecuted, if at all, under the Obscene Publications Act 1959, with the public-good defence being available. This results from the provision, inserted into the 1959 Act, preventing prosecution of film exhibitions for the common-law offence where it is of the essence of the offence that the exhibition was 'obscene, indecent, offensive, disgusting, or injurious to morality'.[117] The accident that wider words were used when this provision was introduced in respect of film exhibitions in 1977 than were used in section 2(4) in 1964 does not provide a principled argument for maintaining the anomaly. There is no reason to treat films differently from other displays, or to treat the completed offence of outraging public decency differently from a conspiracy to commit the offence.

(ii) *Problems with outraging decency.* In 1976, the Law Commission recommended that the common-law offence of outraging public decency should be abolished, because of the vagueness of the definition of the offence.[118] *Gibson's* case illustrates some of this vagueness. There are cer-

---

[116] Obscene Publications Act 1959, s. 2(1). In each case, the defendant is also liable to an unlimited fine.

[117] Ibid. s. 4A, as inserted by the Criminal Law Act 1977 and amended by the Cinemas Act 1985.   [118] Law Commission, *Criminal Law.*

tain questions concerning the *actus reus* of the crime of outraging public decency which are unanswered after *Gibson*. They mainly concern the cause of the outrage. Did it lie in the fact that the ear-rings were made from human foetuses? Would the offence have been made out if the ear-rings had merely looked like human foetuses but been modelled realistically in clay or plastic? Is the source of the outrage to decency one's revulsion at the idea of human beings (albeit at an early stage of development) being treated in that way, or in the spectacle of something in the form of a human child being used for a frivolous purpose? If the former, did the outrage flow from the fact that people were told that they were made from human foetuses? Would the offence have been made out if the ear-rings had really been made from plastic, but people had been told that they were real foetuses as a publicity gimmick? If the essence of the outrage flowed from the use of human foetuses, would Gibson have been properly convicted had the ear-rings been made of animal foetuses, or of human material removed from a live person during surgery? Would the offence be committed by a person who made jewellery from an embryo of (say) one month's gestation, instead of three or four months, if people would not be able to recognize the one month embryo as a distinctively human form?

None of these questions can be answered with confidence. However, if it is correct that the essence of the offence lies in the outraging of people's sense of decency, what people are led to believe about an exhibit would seem to be at least as important as what it really is. That being so, a person may be convicted of the offence for doing something which other people wrongly but reasonably believe to constitute a form of action which, if it happened, would outrage their sense of decency. Such an offence is wider than could conceivably serve a worthwhile social purpose. To take another example, in 1991 a popular outcry followed revulsion when a rather gory colour photograph of a newly born naked baby was plastered over advertising hoardings to promote (with stunning inappropriateness) the wares of a clothing retailer. Could the publishers of the advertisements have been charged with outraging public decency on any of the bases suggested above? Would a prosecution have served any socially useful purpose?

There are other problems with the offence. Many cases which might be charged as the common-law offence will overlap with statutory offences. The latter may include a public-good defence (as in the Obscene Publications Act 1959) which is not available to defendants charged with the common-law offence. Statutory offences will have the maximum penalty limited by the statute; the common law offence exposes defendants to an unlimited penalty. It is anomalous to allow prosecutors and sentencers to evade the limitations imposed by Parliament by electing to charge the common-law offence. For all these reasons, the proper approach would be to enact the 1976 recommendations of the Law Commission and abolish the common-law offence.

(3) The common-law offences and the European Convention on Human Rights

The crime of conspiracy to corrupt public morals, despite being an interference with freedom of expression guaranteed by Article 10(1) of the Convention, seems in principle to be a legitimate exercise of the state's authority to protect morals under Article 10(2). It may, however, be questioned whether the scope of the offence is sufficiently clear to allow those potentially subject to it to understand their legal position. If it is not clear enough, the crime may be held not to be 'prescribed by law' within the meaning of Article 10(2). There may also be a question of whether the offence goes further than is necessary in a democratic society for the protection of morals. If the offence breaches the principle of proportionality, it will fail to come within the justification provided by Article 10(2).

A more substantial problem arises in relation to outraging public decency and conspiring to outrage public decency. Each of these represents an interference with the freedom of expression guaranteed under Article 10(1), and it is by no means clear how they could be justified under Article 10(2). They do not purport to be used for the protection of morals; indeed, one of the planks on which the Court of Appeal's decision in Gibson rested was the submission of counsel for the prosecution 'that the object of the common law offence is to protect the public from suffering feelings of outrage'.[119] It is clear from the caselaw of the European Court of Human Rights that there is a major difference between protecting sensibilities from outrage and protecting morals: the freedom of expression guaranteed by Article 10(1) covers all expression, including that which is provocative, shocking, or disturbing to many people.[120] That being so, it is hard to see how the existence of a crime could be justified when its very essence consists of shocking people without harming morals. One can go further. The effect of an outrage to public decency (unlike a conspiracy to corrupt public morals) is not so much to undermine morality as to reinforce it, since those whose sense of decency is outraged are likely to end up having their values reinforced by the experience.

The crimes of outraging public decency and conspiring to outrage public decency would seem in principle to be incompatible with Article

[119] [1990] 2 QB at p. 627, [1991] 1 All ER at p. 445 per Lord Lane CJ.
[120] e.g. Oberschlick v. Austria, Eur. Ct. HR, Judgment of 23 May 1991.

10 of the Convention. However, this may not be the view of the European Commission of Human Rights, which, in September 1991, ruled inadmissible an application made by the defendants in *Gibson*, and effectively held the common-law offence to be within the permitted purpose of upholding public morality purpose under Article 10(2).[121] That may possibly be true of the way in which the offence was used on the particular facts of that case: there was a plausible argument that moral standards were in issue there. It is a feature of the caselaw under Article 10 of the Convention that states are allowed an extensive margin of appreciation in setting the bounds of public morality as it applies in their territories. Nevertheless, it should not be lightly assumed that the use of the common-law charge is justifiable under Article 10(2) in all the cases to which it potentially applies. If it were used in a way which did not involve considerations of morality, as opposed to mere decency, justification under Article 10(2) would be far more difficult.

15.4 THE STATUTORY OBSCENITY AND INDECENCY OFFENCES

(1) The Obscene Publications Acts 1959 and 1964

Under the Obscene Publications Act 1959, section 2, it is an offence to publish any obscene article, whether or not for gain, or to have possession of an obscene article for publication for gain.[122] The Act catches any obscene article containing or embodying matter to be read or looked at or both, any sound record, and any film or other record of a picture or pictures.[123] The Act thus covers compact discs, video cassettes,[124] television and sound broadcasts,[125] and computerized images, as well as more conventional articles. It also catches any article from which the images, etc., are intended to be reproduced or manufactured,[126] such as

---

[121] Application No. 17634 v. UK.

[122] Obscene Publications Act 1959, s. 2(1), as amended by Obscene Publications Act 1964, s. 1(1). A person is deemed to 'have' an article for publication for gain if, with a view to such publication, he has the article in his ownership, possession, or control: Obscene Publications Act 1964, s. 1(2). The offence may therefore be committed by someone who owns articles which are actually in the possession of another person, or who is in control of articles which are owned by and in the possession of someone else. In Scotland, see Civil Government (Scotland) Act 1982, s. 51.

[123] Obscene Publications Act 1959, s. 1(2).

[124] *Attorney-General's Reference (No. 5 of 1980)* [1980] 3 All ER 816, CA.

[125] Obscene Publications Act 1959, s. 1(4), (5), (6), inserted by Broadcasting Act 1990, s. 162(1)(b). Previously, television and sound broadcasts were exempted by a proviso to s. 1(3) of the 1959 Act, which was repealed by s. 162(1)(a), s. 20,3 and Sch. 21 of the 1990 Act.

[126] Obscene Publications Act 1964, s. 2(1).

photographic negatives or casts; possession of such articles is deemed to be possession of an article for publication for gain if the articles to be produced or manufactured from them are intended for publication for gain.[127] There is, however, a defence for the person in possession if he can prove that he had not examined the article and had no reasonable cause to suspect that it was of a type which might make him liable to be convicted under section 2 of the 1959 Act.[128]

Publication is widely defined: it includes distribution, circulation, selling, letting on hire, offering for sale or for letting on hire, giving, lending, or (where the article contains or embodies matter to be looked at or a record) showing, playing, or projecting. This is sufficiently wide to encompass cable television. Although broadcasting has been brought within the scope of the legislation by the Broadcasting Act 1990, the separate regulatory framework described in Chapter 13 above should normally prevent material which has any chance of infringing the 1959 Act from being broadcast.

The test of obscenity is that the effect of an article, taken as a whole,[129] must be such as to tend to deprave and corrupt persons who are likely, having regard to all relevant circumstances, to read, see, or hear the matter contained or embodied in it.[130] This test is based on the harm principle, although the harm contemplated is of a sort which is peculiarly hard to pin down.[131] What constitutes being depraved and corrupted? The judges have, on the whole, not attempted much in the way of guidance, beyond making it clear that articles which are objectively filthy, lewd, repulsive, or indecent according to community standards are not necessarily obscene within the meaning of the Act.[132] The US Supreme Court's approach to the First Amendment offers far less protection to free speech than is provided by the 1959 Act in England and Wales. It seems that the First Amendment is interpreted as permitting the control of works which in England would be regarded as indecent but not obscene. The test in the USA is whether the material would be found by an average reader, applying contemporary community standards, to appeal to prurient interest, depicting or describing sexual conduct in a patently offensive way, without serious literary, artistic, political, or scientific

---

[127] Obscene Publications Act 1964, s. 2(2).   [128] Ibid., s. 1(3)(a).

[129] If the article is made up of several separate articles, each of these may be examined separately: Ibid., s. 1(1). Thus each item in a magazine containing several articles or short stories, or a collection of essays, falls to be individually assessed: R. v. Anderson [1972] 1 QB 304 at p. 312, [1971] 3 All ER 1152 at p. 1158 per Lord Widgery CJ.

[130] Obscene Publications Act 1959, s. 1(1). See Robert, Obscenity, ch. 3.

[131] The test was adapted from the common–law obscenity test: R. v. Hicklin (1868) LR 3 QB 360; Macmillan, Censorship and Public Morality, 5–12; Robertson, Obscenity, 29–30.

[132] e.g. R. v. Anderson [1972] 1 QB 304, [1971] 3 All ER 1152, CA.

value.[133] The reference to community standards (which are not applied to the assessment of a work's literary, artistic, political, or scientific value, which is regarded as constant)[134] is related to what we would regard as indecency, and assumes that local rather than national community standards are to be applied.[135]

However, the English test for obscenity is more demanding. To tend to deprave and corrupt people, material must degrade the reader or viewer. This need not be manifested in the shape of a change in behaviour; indeed, one may encourage people to commit improper behaviour without corrupting or depraving them. Corruption is an affliction of the mind and emotions, which may but need not be evidenced by behaviour.[136] But what is this affliction, and what should juries look for when deciding whether material has a tendency to induce it? A tendency to arouse erotic feelings, or feelings of sexual arousal, cannot in itself be depraving or corrupting, since such feelings are normal in everyday life and may even be necessary for the propagation of the species. Perhaps the best explanation is that an article depraves and corrupts a person only if it results in a suspension or destruction of the moral standards which that person applies self-critically. In other words, pornography is obscene, within the English definition, if it makes it possible for a person to contemplate doing, seeing, or hearing something with less feeling of guilt than previously would have been engendered. Obscenity blunts one's self-critical moral faculties. This is consistent with the principle that a book which produces in its likely readers an aversion to the behaviour described is not obscene, the so-called 'aversion theory'.[137] It ought to follow that psychological evidence will be admitted as to the likely effect of material on the average reader, but in fact such evidence is admissible only in relation to the effect on special groups, such as children, whose reactions might be outside the experience of the jury.[138]

People may be depraved or corrupted by all sorts of things. Most prosecutions centre on sexual matters, but it seems to be accepted by the courts that violence is capable of depraving and corrupting people,[139] and there is statutory authority for supposing that crime, cruelty, and other

[133] *Miller* v. *California*, 413 US 15 (1973).

[134] *Pope* v. *Illinois*, 481 US 497 (1988).

[135] *Jacobellis* v. *Ohio*, 378 US 184 (1964) at p. 200 *per* Warren CJ (dissenting). In the same case, Stewart J. said that, while he could not define obscenity, he knew it when he saw it (at p. 197).

[136] *DPP* v. *Whyte* [1972] AC 849, [1972] 3 All ER 12, HL.

[137] *R.* v. *Anderson* [1972] 1 QB 304, [1971] 3 All ER 1152, CA.

[138] *DPP* v. *A & BC Chewing Gum Ltd.* [1968] 1 QB 159, [1967] 2 All ER 504, DC.; *R.* v. *Calder & Boyars* [1969] 1 QB 151, [1968] 3 All ER 644, CA.

[139] *DPP* v. *A and BC Chewing Gum Ltd.* [1968] 1 QB 159, [1967] 2 All ER 504, DC (picture cards depicting scenes of violence, distributed free with packets of chewing gum).

'incidents of a repulsive and horrible nature' may be corrupting, at any rate to children.[140] Moral and spiritual corruption, the undermining of moral values, is the evil at which the offence is directed. An article or book which glorifies, or incites people to indulge in, drug abuse can be considered likely to deprave and corrupt, and so is capable of being obscene.[141] The depravity or corruption may, but need not necessarily, be manifested in outward behaviour.[142]

The courts have taken the view that moral depravity and corruption is a matter of degree. People may be more or less depraved or corrupted; a person may therefore be corrupted more than once,[143] so that selling pornographic material to 'dirty old men' is likely to deprave and corrupt them still further, and constitutes an offence under the Acts.[144] The material which may deprave and corrupt people will depend, to some extent, on the age and suggestibility of the audience likely to come in contact with it. Material may be liable to corrupt young children which would not have that effect on adults. The test is whether it is likely to deprave or corrupt 'persons who are likely, having regard to all the relevant circumstances, to read, see or hear the matter contained or embodied in it'.[145] Not all such people need be likely to be depraved or corrupted, nor a majority of them, but it has been held necessary that a substantial proportion be likely to be so affected in order to ground a conviction.[146]

There is therefore the potential for the legislation to restrict freedom of expression considerably. The potential interference with freedom of expression is, however, mitigated in two ways. First, there is the legal defence of public good under the legislation, which allows publication of

---

[140] Children and Young Persons (Harmful Publications) Act 1955, s. 1.

[141] *John Calder (Publications) Ltd.* v. *Powell* [1965] 1 QB 509, [1965] 1 All ER 159, DC; *R.* v. *Skirving* [1985] QB 819, [1985] 2 All ER 705, CA. On the other hand, it has been said that prosecution policy is to use the law mainly against hard-core pornography, especially that which depicts unorthodox sexual activity. 'DPP officials have their lines to draw, and they draw them fairly consistently at the male groin: nudity is now acceptable and even artistic, but to erect a penis is to provoke a prosecution.' Geoffrey Robertson, *Freedom, the Individual and the Law* (Harmondsworth: Penguin, 1989), p. 190.

[142] *DPP* v. *Whyte* [1972] AC 849, [1972] 3 All ER 12, HL. Some judges consider that their experience in criminal and matrimonial cases confirms that obscene articles do, sometimes, provoke changes in patterns of conduct: see e.g. *R.* v. *Holloway* (1982) 4 Cr. App. R. (S.) 128, CA, at p. 131 *per* Lawton LJ. However, the Williams Committee decided that the causal link between pornography and anti-social conduct had not been established on the basis of the scientific evidence.

[143] *R.* v. *Shaw* [1962] AC 220, [1961] 1 All ER 330, CA. (The case went to the House of Lords on another point: [1962] AC 220, [1961] 2 All ER 446, HL.)

[144] *DPP* v. *Whyte* [1972] AC 849, [1979] 3 All ER 12, HL

[145] Obscene Publications Act 1959, s. 1(1).

[146] *R.* v. *Calder & Boyars Ltd.* [1969] 1 QB 151, [1968] 3 All ER 644, CA, esp. at pp. 168, 648 *per* Salmon LJ; *DPP* v. *Whyte* [1972] AC 849, [1972] 3 All ER 12, HL, esp. at pp. 870, 25 *per* Lord Cross of Chelsea.

an article to be justified even though it is obscene. Secondly, there is a bureaucratic safeguard provided in the role of the Director of Public Prosecutions, who has regard to the wider public interest when deciding whether or not to institute or take over forfeiture proceedings or criminal prosecutions.

(i) *The defence of public good.* Unlike the common law and Scottish law,[147] section 4 of the 1959 Act provides that a person is not to be convicted of an offence against section 2, and no forfeiture order is to be made, in respect of any article (other than a moving picture film or soundtrack) if it is proved that the publication 'is justified as being for the public good on the ground that it is in the interests of science, literature, art or learning, or of other objects of general concern'.[148] Obscene moving picture films and soundtracks are allowed a more limited justification. Publication of these is justified if proved to be 'in the public good on the ground that it is in the interests of drama, opera, ballet or any other art, or of literature or learning'.[149] In other words, the interests of science and 'other objects of general concern', such as news journalism on current affairs, do not serve to justify a film unless it also serves the interests of literature, learning, or art.

Since the provision offers justification to articles which are obscene, it is not suprising that the courts have tended to interpret the scope of section 4 fairly narrowly. They have generally limited it to explorations of matters falling within the words of the section on a literal interpretation (so that sex education for children was held not to be within 'learning', a noun signifying the fruits of scholarship rather than the correlative of teaching)[150] or which clearly relate to the public good. For example, in relation to the concluding words of section 4(1), they have recognized that sociological or ethical merit may justify publishing an obscene book, because of the potential benefit for society as a whole in having social and ethical matters canvassed.[151] Similarly, religious merits were considered in

---

[147] There is no statutory defence of public good under Civic Government (Scotland) Act 1982, s. 51, but a defence may exist at common law for literary, scientific, artistic, and philosophical works which are appropriate for study by serious scholars. See *Galletly v. Laird* 1953 SLT 67; K. D. Ewing and W. Finnie, *Civil Liberties in Scotland: Cases and Materials*, 2nd edn. (Edinburgh: W. Green & Son, 1988), 309.

[148] Obscene Publications Act 1959, s. 4(1).

[149] Ibid., s. 4(1A), added by Criminal Law Act 1977, s. 53.

[150] *Attorney-General's Reference (No. 3 of 1977)* [1978] 1 WLR 1123, [1978] 3 All ER 1166, CA. Accordingly, the trial judge had been wrong to admit expert testimony on the educational merits of such material. It might, perhaps, still be arguable that sex education is a matter of 'general concern'.

[151] *R. v. Calder & Boyars Ltd.* [1969] 1 QB 151, [1968] 3 All ER 644, CA, on *Last Exit to Brooklyn*.

the *Lady Chatterley's Lover* trial.[152] On the other hand, although some pornography may serve a therapeutic end, enabling people to relieve their sexual tensions harmlessly who might otherwise suffer psychological illness or indulge in anti-social and, perhaps, criminal acts towards others, the judges have held that the therapeutic value of obscene articles for some members of the public is not 'in the interests of . . . other objects of general concern'.[153]

The ultimate arbiter of the public good under this provision is the jury, but evidence of expert opinion is permitted in order to give guidance on the literary or other merit of a publication, presumably because jurors are not necessarily equipped to make judgements about the artistic, literary or other qualities of publications.[154] Thus the Bishop of Woolwich was among the many eminent people who gave evidence on behalf of *Lady Chatterley's Lover* in 1960, and Professor Ronald Dworkin gave evidence on behalf of the publishers of *Inside Linda Lovelace*, described by a leading authority as '[t]he last, and undoubtedly the worst, "serious" book to be prosecuted',[155] in 1976.

If the jury concludes that the article has some literary, scientific, artistic, or other relevant form of merit, they must then decide whether or not it is for the public good. This requires the jury to perform a balancing exercise. Jurors must ask themselves whether the good flowing from the merits identified by the defendant outweigh the public harm which flows from the risk of people being depraved and corrupted by the article. Of relevance will be the number of those likely to be depraved and corrupted, the strength of the tendency to deprave and corrupt, and the depth of the likely depravity of corruption; these will be balanced against the strength of the relevant merits of the article.[156] As Geoffrey

---

[152] *R. v. Penguin Books*, unreported. See C. H. Rolph, *The Trial of Lady Chatterley* (Harmondsworth: Penguin, 1961); Bernard Levin, *The Pendulum Years: Britain and the Sixties* (London: Pan Books, 1972), 280–92.

[153] *R. v. Metropolitan Police Commissioner, ex parte Blackburn* [1973] QB 241, [1973] 1 All ER 324, CA, at pp. 250, 329 *per* Lord Denning MR; *DPP v. Jordan* [1977] AC 699, [1976] 3 All ER 775, HL.

[154] Obscene Publications Act 1959, s. 4(2). However, the experts must confine their evidence to the merits of the article. They are not normally allowed to guide the jury as to whether the article is obscene or not. The latter issue lies entirely within the jury's commonsense judgement (*R. v. Calder and Boyars Ltd.* [1969] 1 QB 151, CA; *R. v. Anderson* [1972] 1 QB 304, CA) unless the people who are said to be in danger of being depraved or corrupted have special characteristics which might lie outside the experience of members of the jury, such as young children (*R. v. A & BC Chewing Gum Ltd.* [1968] 1 QB 159, CA, as explained in *Anderson* at p. 313 *per* Lord Widgery CJ).

[155] Robertson, *Freedom, Individual and Law*, 189.

[156] *R. v. Calder & Boyars Ltd.* [1969] 1 QB 151 at p. 171, [1968] 3 All ER 644 at pp. 649–50, *per* Salmon LJ.

Robertson points out,[157] there is a certain sense of absurdity in deciding that it is for the public good for an article to be published despite the fact that it will deprave and corrupt a significant number of people. However, to argue that this makes the test meaningless goes too far. Many of the decisions which people have to make in life, and a very high proportion of the decisions which have to be made in government, require apparently incommensurable goods and harms to be weighed against each other. The acquittals of publishers of books such as *Inside Linda Lovelace* and *Last Exit to Brooklyn* shows that the jury, performing for this purpose a function in balancing goods and harms which can properly be regarded as governmental, is not often overwhelmed by the absurdity of what they are asked to do. It is true that, when separate proceedings are brought against each distributor of an article, rather than bringing one prosecution against the producer, different juries may reach inconsistent decisions. But this should not blind us to the fact that the prospect of having to satisfy a jury on a matter such as this provides a useful check on the over-enthusiasm of would-be prosecutors, and may even offer a positive protection to freedom of expression.[158]

(ii) *Bureacratic controls: prosecution policy.* This second means of mitigating the effects of interference with freedom of expression relies on the ability of the Director of Public Prosecutions to impose some reasonableness and consistency on the types of cases in which proceedings are brought. Thus proceedings in respect of commercial (16 mm) films may be instituted only with the consent of the Director of Public Prosecutions.[159] However, other prosecutions may be brought by any citizen, subject to the power of the Director of Public Prosecutions to take over the conduct of the case and offer no evidence, or the power of the Attorney-General to intervene and enter a *nolle prosequi*. Furthermore, any constable may obtain a warrant to seize articles under section 3 of the 1959 Act, bring them before a justice of the peace, and (except in the case of 16 mm films) apply for forfeiture. Another way of evading the control of the Director of Public Prosecutions has been used in the past. This involved the police in visiting booksellers and inviting them to sign disclaimers in respect of allegedly obscene articles, which would then be carried away and destroyed without any court proceedings. From the points of view of both booksellers and police this saved a great deal of trouble and formality. However, it helped to put the booksellers at the

---

[157] *Freedom, Individual and Law*, 191–2.

[158] For a more sceptical view of the role of juries, see Penny Darbishire, 'The Lamp that Shows that Freedom Lives: Is It Worth the Candle?' [1991] *Crim. LR* 740–52.

[159] Obscene Publications Act 1959, s. 2(3A), added by Criminal Law Act 1977, s. 53.

mercy of corrupt police officers,[160] and was criticized by the *Report of the Parliamentary Select Committee on Obscene Publications.*[161] The object of requiring all seized goods to be taken before a justice of the peace, under section 3 of the 1959 Act, was to root out this practice, but it continued, perhaps because the police thought that taking articles which the owner had disclaimed did not constitute a seizure, and attracted further criticism from the Court of Appeal in *R. v. Metropolitan Police Commissioner, ex parte Blackburn (No. 3).*[162] However, even when the Director of Public Prosecutions is involved and the statutory procedures are being followed, there are ways in which the public interest in art, literature, science, and other worthwhile undertakings may be subverted through the use of section 3 itself.

Section 3 of the 1959 Act provides search, seizure, and forfeiture powers. It permits a justice of the peace, on an information laid by the Director of Public Prosecutions or a constable,[163] to issue a warrant authorizing search of any premises, stall, or vehicle if he or she is satisfied that there is reasonable ground for suspecting that obscene articles are kept there for publication for gain, and seizure of any offending articles found, with any documents relating to a trade or business carried on there.[164] If a person is charged with and convicted of having the obscene articles for gain, contrary to section 2, the court which convicts him must order forfeiture of the articles.[165] Where nobody is proceeded against under section 2, or the accused is acquitted, the articles seized, if not returned to the occupier, are to be brought before a justice of the peace, who may summon the occupier to show cause why the articles should not be forfeited. If satisfied, after a hearing (in which the occupier, owner, author, or other person through whose hands the articles passed are to be heard if they appear), that the articles are obscene and were kept for publication for gain, the court must then order forfeiture of the articles.[166]

[160] Sir Robert Mark, *In the Office of Constable* (London: Collins, 1978), 173–4, 263 ff.
[161] HC 123–1 of 1957–8.   [162] [1973] QB 241 at pp. 252–4.
[163] Criminal Justice Act 1967, s. 25. This provision was intended to prevent repetition of the incident when the D.P.P. decided not to prosecute the publishers of *Last Exit to Brooklyn,* but private individuals none the less brought forfeiture proceedings under s. 3 of the 1959 Act without requiring a conviction. The forfeiture proceedings succeeded, and the DPP consequently felt bound to institute a prosecution of the publishers, which ultimately failed: *R. v. Calder & Boyars Ltd.* [1969] 1 QB 151, [1968] 3 All ER 644, CA.
[164] Obscene Publications Act 1959, s. 3(1), (2).
[165] Obscene Publications Act 1964, s. 1(4).
[166] Obscene Publications Act 1959, s. 3(3), as amended by Criminal Law Act 1977; s. 3(4). Where the seized items consist of film of a width of at least 16 mm, in respect of which a prosecution could be instituted only by the D.P.P. (see s. 2(3A)), forfeiture proceedings in the absence of a conviction may be brought only if the warrant was issued on an information laid by or on behalf of the D.P.P.: s. 3(3A), added by Criminal Law Act 1977, s. 53.

The power to order forfeiture without a conviction is objectionable because it deprives the publishers of the opportunity to deploy the public-good defence, which is available only in criminal proceedings. In the summary forfeiture proceedings, forfeiture follows automatically once a book is found to be obscene and to have been kept for publication for gain. In 1964, during the passage of the bill which became the Obscene Publications Act 1964, Mr Roy Jenkins MP proposed an amendment which would have guaranteed to publishers a right to elect for jury trial in respect of any book in relation to which they intended to raise a defence of public good. The amendment was widely supported, following a disgraceful incident in which the publishers of Cleland's *Fanny Hill* had been denied jury trial because, according to the Director of Public Prosecutions, they had behaved so responsibly that a criminal prosecution would have been oppressive.[167] As Robertson comments, 'The DPP's attitude was catch-22: a responsible publisher could never, by definition, obtain a fair trial—this right was reserved for those who acted irresponsibly.'[168] To head off the amendment, the Solicitor General gave an undertaking on behalf of the law officers that the ordinary policy of the DPP would be to prosecute rather than use section 3 proceedings whenever the publisher indicates an intention to continue to publish the work regardless of the result of the forfeiture proceedings, to publish in circumstances which would constitute a criminal offence.[169] However, this turned out not to offer much protection to publishers. Prosecutors have sometimes been unwilling to find out what publishers' intentions are, so the publisher has to be alert and knowledgeable in order to take advantage of the undertaking. There are several examples of abuse of section 3.[170] The law in this area gives excessive discretion to the police, the DPP, and to justices of the peace. It should be changed: (*a*) to allow the public good defence to be available against forfeiture under section 3 as well as against conviction under section 2; (*b*) to require the publisher of articles to be served with notice of proceedings for forfeiture which are taken following seizure of articles from a wholesaler or retailer; and (*c*) to allow the publishers a statutory right to elect for trial by jury where they want to advance a public-good defence.

Although the offences under the Obscene Publications Act 1959 and 1964 are the most significant restrictions on free expression in the name of morality, there are numerous other statutory offences concerning

[167] See Levin, *Pendulum Years*, 297–9, on the proceedings against the bookseller of John Cleland's *Fanny Hill*.

[168] Robertson, *Obscenity*, 106.

[169] HC Deb. 7 July 1964, col. 302, Sir Peter Rawlinson S-G.

[170] Robertson, *Obscenity*, 106–8; Robertson, *Freedom, Individual and Law*, 193; *Olympia Press* v. *Hollis* [1974] 1 All ER 108.

indecency and obscenity, some of which affect freedom of expression. The main ones are briefly outlined here.

(2) The Children and Young Persons (Harmful Publications) Act 1955

This was enacted in reaction to a spate of horror comics. It set out to penalize anyone who prints, publishes, sells, or lets on hire a book, magazine, or similar work, which is of a kind likely to fall into the hands of children or young persons, and which consists wholly or mainly of cartoon stories portraying commission of crimes, acts of violence or cruelty, or incidents of a repulsive or horrible nature, in such a way that the work as a whole would tend to corrupt a child or young person into whose hands it might fall.[171] There is no defence of public good. On the other hand, all prosecutions require the consent of the Attorney-General.[172] In view of the range of comics which would need to be the subject of proceedings if this legislation were taken seriously, it is not surprising that it has rarely if ever been invoked. Legislation such as this might, however, come into its own if the law on obscenity were to be reformed so as to remove restrictions on what might be published to adults. As the Williams Committee recognized, pornography has different effects on people of different ages, and it would be justifiable on grounds of paternalism to protect children and young people from some kinds of publication, even if paternalist arguments were held insufficient to justify criminalizing sale to adults.

(3) The Indecent Displays (Control) Act 1981

This applies to Scotland as well as England and Wales. It is justified by similar, though not identical, arguments to those invoked in support of the offences under the Obscene Publications Acts 1959–64. Section 1(1) makes it an offence to display publicly[173] any indecent matter.[174] This both protects young people from being offended or corrupted (an argu-

---

[171] Children and Young Persons (Harmful Publications) Act 1955, ss. 1, 2(1).

[172] Ibid., s. 2(2).

[173] Under s. 1(2) and 1(3), matter is publicly displayed if it is displayed in, or so as to be visible from, any public place, i.e. any place to which the public have access at the time, except (i) a place for which people have to pay for entry, where the payment includes a payment for the display, and (ii) a shop or part of a shop which cannot be reached without passing an adequate warning notice (the required terms of which are set out in s. 1(6)), and to which people under 18 are not admitted.

[174] This does not apply to theatres or cinemas, or to broadcast or cable programmes, all of which have their own regulatory schemes. Nor does it apply to displays in museums, or to displays by or on the authority of the Crown or a local authority, in buildings occupied by them: Indecent Displays (Control) Act 1981, s. 1(4).

ment from paternalism), and saves adults from being the unwilling observers of things which they would have chosen to avoid (an argument from autonomy).

(4) The Theatres Act 1968

In the case of the theatre, following the ending of the routine censorship of plays which had been one of the responsibilities of the Lord Chamberlain, the Theatres Act 1968, section 2, provides that it is an offence to present or direct a public[175] performance of a play which is obscene,[176] the definition of obscenity being (*mutatis mutandis*) similar to that under the Obscene Publications Act 1959. A public-good defence is provided by section 3. It is also an offence to present or direct a public performance of a play involving the use of threatening, abusive, or insulting words or behaviour, with intent to provoke a breach of the peace or where it is likely, taking the performance as a whole, that a breach of the peace is likely to be occasioned.[177] The Attorney-General's consent is needed for prosecutions under the Theatres Act 1968. Finally, it is an offence to present or direct a public performance of a play intending thereby to stir up racial hatred or where, having regard to all the circumstances, racial hatred is likely to be stirred up.[178]

(5) The Post Office Act 1953, section 11

This makes it an offence to send any obscene or indecent article, whether in the form of writing, pictures, or in any other form, through the post. The important element here is the objective quality of the article, not its effect on the recipient. Thus an article may be indecent, in that it is repulsive, filthy, lewd, or loathsome, even if it would not have been obscene within the meaning of the Obscene Publications Act 1959.[179]

(6) Indecent photographs of children

Taking, or permitting to be taken, an indecent photograph of a child[180] is an offence; so is showing or distributing such a photograph, or having one in one's possession with a view to its distribution or showing,[181] or

---

[175] See Theatres Act 1968, s. 7.   [176] See Robertson, *Media Law*, 3rd edn., 138–47.
[177] Theatres Act 1968, s. 6.   [178] Public Order Act 1986, s. 20.
[179] *R. v. Anderson* [1972] QB 304, [1971] 3 All ER 1152, CA; *Kosmos Publications* v. *DPP* [1975] Crim. LR 345, DC.
[180] For this purpose, 'child' means a person under the age of 16, not the more usual 14.
[181] It is also an offence to have possession of such a photograph without intending to show or distribute it, although there is then a defence if the accused has a legitimate rea-

publishing an advertisement for such a photograph.[182] There are search, seizure, and forfeiture provisions[183] to much the same effect as those in section 3 of the Obscene Publications Act 1959. The impetus for these provisions was provided by the discovery of paedophile pornography rings, which gave rise to concern about the exploitation of children. The provisions are capable of interfering with freedom of expression, but would appear to be justifiable under Article 10(2) of the European Convention on Human Rights by reference to the protection of morals.

(7) Import controls

Customs legislation forbids the importation of indecent or obscene articles.[184] Forbidden articles are liable to forfeiture.[185] This is a potential restriction on the right to to receive and impart information and ideas regardless of frontiers, under Article 10(1) of the European Convention on Human Rights. However, where the effect of the legislation is to subject importers from other member states of the European Community to restrictions which do not apply to UK producers, it conflicts with, and is overridden by, Article 30 of the Treaty of Rome, because it constitutes a quantitative restriction on imports. Under Article 36, it is permissible to control imports on grounds of (*inter alia*) public morality, but only if the prohibition or restriction do not 'constitute a means of arbitrary discrimination or a disguised restriction on trade between Member States'. Banning obscene articles, while a breach of Article 30, is justified under Article 36, because such articles would be liable to lead to forfeiture and criminal prosecutions if marketed by UK nationals,[186] under the Obscene

son for possessing it, or had not seen it and neither knew nor had cause to suspect that it was indecent, or had received it unsolicited and had not kept it for an unreasonable time: Criminal Justice Act 1988, s. 160. However, this provision interferes with privacy interests rather than freedom of expression.

[182] Protection of Children Act 1978, s. 1. 'Photograph' includes the negative of the picture, and also film and video recordings: s. 7.

[183] Ibid., ss. 4, 5.   [184] Customs Consolidation Act 1876, s. 42.

[185] Customs and Excise Management Act 1979, s. 49. In forfeiture proceedings, the public-good defence is not available. It has been suggested that this breaches E.C. law where the importation is from a member state of the E.C., but this has been rejected by the courts: *R. v. Bow Street Metropolitan Stipendiary Magistrate, ex parte Noncyp Ltd.* [1990] 1 QB 123, where Woolf LJ in the Divisional Court suggested at p. 132 that none the less it would be a judicially reviewable abuse of power for a Customs officer to seize and forfeit goods which, in previous criminal proceedings, had been held to be justifiable under the public-good defence in the Obscene Publications Act 1959, s. 4. In the Court of Appeal, however, Glidewell LJ at pp. 145–6 doubted whether an application for judicial review in such circumstances would succeed.

[186] The question is whether there is a legal market in the items in the UK. The answer may vary between different parts of the UK, because of the different legal systems operat-

Publications Act 1959. However, banning imports of articles which are indecent but not obscene will not be justified under Article 36, because such goods are not generally illegal in this country. Accordingly, an importer of obscene books does not have a defence under Article 30 of the Treaty of Rome,[187] but an importer of merely indecent items does.[188] In response to this, instead of changing the law to treat imports from European Community member states differently from imports from elsewhere, there has been an administrative policy of not seizing or prosecuting in respect of imports of merely indecent goods.

(8) Indecent details of legal proceedings

It is an offence to print or publish, or cause or procure to be printed or published, certain matters in relation to any judicial proceedings. In particular, it is unlawful to print, etc., any indecent matter, or indecent medical, surgical, or psychological details, if the publication would be calculated to injure public morals.[189] In context, it is clear that, if the matter is indecent, the issue is the likely effect on public morals, not the intention of the publisher or printer. This criminalizes a type of publication relating to judicial proceedings which would not be punishable as a contempt of court (see Chapter 16, below) because it neither interferes with the administration of justice nor amounts to breach of a court order.

There is also a blanket prohibition on publishing more than the barest information relating to matrimonial matters, although it is not clear whether this is to protect the privacy of the parties, to avoid public morals being harmed by titillating details, or both. In relation to proceedings for the dissolution or annulment of marriage, judicial separation, overseas adoption, or declarations as to parentage or legitimacy, and proceedings concerning maintenance orders,[190] the only details which may be published[191] are: the names, addresses, and occupations of parties and witnesses; a concise statement of charges, defences, and countercharges

ing in Scotland, N. Ireland, and England. The court will take an overall view to see whether the item is, broadly speaking, marketable legally over the country. See Case 34/79, *R.* v. *Henn* [1981] AC 850, [1980] 2 All ER 166, ECJ and HL; *R.* v. *Bow Street Metropolitan Stipendiary Magistrate, ex parte Noncyp Ltd.* [1990] 1 QB 123, CA.

[187] Case 34/79, *R.* v. *Henn* [1980] AC 850, [1980] 2 All ER 166, ECJ and HL.

[188] Case 121/85, *Conegate Ltd.* v. *HM Customs and Excise* [1987] QB 254, [1986] 2 All ER 688, ECJ and Kennedy J. (importation of life-size, inflatable, rubber dolls).

[189] Judicial Proceedings (Regulation of Reports) Act 1926, s. 1(1)(*a*).

[190] Ibid., s. 1(1)(*b*); Family Law Act 1986, s. 56, replacing Matrimonial Causes Act 1973, s. 45; Magistrates' Courts Act 1980, s. 71.

[191] In relation to proceedings in magistrates' courts, similar restrictions apply to reports in newspapers and periodicals of domestic proceedings. They seem not to apply to reports in broadcast and cable programmes. See Magistrates' Courts Act 1980, s. 71. 'Domestic proceedings' are defined in s. 65.

(but not the evidence led in support or rebuttal of them); submissions on points of law, and the court's decisions on them; and the judge's summing up to jury and the jury's findings (if the case is heard before a jury), the judgment of the court, and any observations made by the judge in giving judgment. Even these truncated details are permitted only so far as they do not include indecent matter which would be calculated to injure public morals.[192]

There is no public-good defence, but there is an exception from liability in relation to law reports and publications of a technical character intended for circulation among members of the legal and medical professions.[193] In other cases, an administrative safeguard is provided by the proviso that, in England and Wales, no prosecution for these offences may be commenced without the Attorney-General's sanction.[194]

Although criminal liability is imposed, there is no express provision for a court to make an order restraining publication. Normally, courts will not enjoin the commission of criminal offences, but a party who would suffer special damage from publication of details which would constitute a criminal offence may be able to obtain an injunction restraining reports. Although it will rarely be proper to grant such an injunction, one was granted restraining a party to divorce proceedings from reporting details of allegations made in the proceedings which were not supported by evidence at the hearing.[195] The special damage, in that case, arose from a potential combination of interference with privacy and injury to reputation.

15.5 REGULATION AND LICENSING

The regulation of the broadcasting and cable programme media is considered in Chapter 13, above. This section notes the regulatory schemes for three other conduits of expression: cinema, video recordings, and sex shops.

[192] Judicial Proceedings (Regulation of Reports) Act 1926, s. 1(1)(b); Domestic and Appellate Proceedings (Restrictions of Publicity) Act 1968, s. 2(3), as amended by Matrimonial Causes Act 1973, s. 45, Family Law Act 1986, s. 68, and Family Law Reform Act 1987, s. 33.
[193] Judicial Proceedings (Regulation of Reports Act 1926, s. 1(4); Magistrates' Courts Act 1980, s. 71(5).
[194] Judicial Proceedings (Regulation of Reports) Act 1926, s. 1(3); Magistrates' Courts Act 1980, s. 71(4).
[195] *Duchess of Argyll* v. *Duke of Argyll* [1967] 2 Ch. 302, [1965] 1 All ER 611.

(1) Cinema

Premises require a licence before they can be used for the purpose of film exhibitions.[196] Licensing is the responsibility of the district council (or, in London, the borough council) for the area concerned. The authority has a very wide discretion as to the people to whom, and the terms on which, they grant licences, and may impose special conditions when the exhibition is organized wholly or mainly for children.[197] Pursuant to this, they may, and customarily do, decide which films may and may not be shown, and provide for age limits for admission to particular films. Although authorities usually follow the recommendation of the British Board of Film Classification[198] in respect of individual films, they need not do so, and have sometimes refused licences to show films to which the Board has granted a certificate, or given licences to films refused a certificate by the Board.[199] There is a right of appeal to the Crown Court against a refusal of a licence or against a condition which the authority has imposed.[200]

(2) Video recordings

In the Video Recordings Act 1984, a scheme was introduced to regulate the supply, for reward or in the course or furtherance of a business, of video recordings.[201] The authority designated by the Home Secretary to act as regulator under the legislation is the British Board of Film Classification.[202] The Board has the job of deciding whether to issue classification certificates to video recordings, and, if so, how to classify them.[203] It is an offence to supply a video recording, or to have a video recording in one's possession for the purposes of supply, if it has not been granted a classification certificate, unless it is an exempted work.[204] It is

---

[196] Cinemas Act 1985, s. 1(1). 'Film exhibition' means any moving picture show other than a simultaneous television broadcast: s. 21(1). See generally Robertson and Nicol, *Media Law*, 3rd edn., 564–72; S. H. Bailey, D. J. Harris, and B. L. Jones, *Civil Liberties Cases and Materials*, 3rd edn. (London: Butterworths, 1991), 300–5.

[197] Cinemas Act 1985, ss. 1(2), (3) and 2(2).

[198] On the constitution and work of the Board, a self-regulatory body first established by the film industry in 1912, see Robertson and Nicol, *Media Law*, 3rd edn., 566–9, 583–93.

[199] See *R. v. Greater London Council, ex parte Blackburn* [1976] 1 WLR 550, [1976] 3 All ER 184, CA.

[200] Cinemas Act 1985, s. 16.   [201] Video Recordings Act 1984, s. 3.

[202] On the work of the Board in relation to video recordings, see Robertson and Nicol, *Media Law*, 3rd edn., 575–83.

[203] Video Recordings Act 1984, s. 4.

[204] Ibid., ss. 9 and 10. 'Exempted works' (defined in s. 2) are those which are designed to inform, educate, or instruct; are concerned with sport, religion, or music; or are video games. However, recordings which depict, to any significant extent, human sexual

also an offence to supply a video recording in breach of the terms on which a classification certificate has been issued.[205] The classification certificate may provide that the recording is not to be supplied other than in a licensed sex shop, and it is an offence to supply such a recording in any other place.[206] This legislation was introduced in the wake of concern that 'video nasties' were falling into the hands of children, and being watched by them. It is an aspect of paternalistic concern for children's welfare. Although it is still open to a parent to hire or buy a recording for which a classification certificate has been issued, the adult then has the responsibility for safeguarding his or her children.

(3) Sex shops

Concern that towns and cities were being affected by a proliferation of shops retailing articles and books of an explicitly sexual nature, and a feeling that each locality should be able to decide whether and to what extent it was desirable to control such shops in the light of the character of the area, led to the enactment of section 2 of the Local Government (Miscellaneous Provisions) Act 1982. This enables any district council, or (in London) borough council or the Common Council of the City of London, to resolve that a licensing scheme for sex establishments under Schedule 3 shall come into force in its area. If a licensing scheme is in force, the council decides how many (if any) sex shops there are to be in its area and where they may be situated, and licenses the operators. It is an offence knowingly to operate a sex shop without a licence in an area in which a licensing scheme is in force. The effect of the Act has been to drive sex establishments out of some areas entirely, although the major proprietors have fought a gallant but largely unavailing rearguard action through the courts. In consequence, the outlets for the distribution of sex articles and the showing of sex films are increasingly concentrated in relatively few areas.[207]

activity, associated acts of force, or restraint; mutilation or torture of, or other acts of gross violence towards, humans or animals; or human genital organs or excretory functions, are not exempted works. Nor are recordings exempted works which are designed to any significant extent to stimulate or encourage human sexual activity, associated acts of force or restraint, or mutilation, torture, or other acts of gross violence in relation to humans or animals.

[205] Video Recordings Act 1984, s. 11.
[206] Ibid., s. 12. On the meaning of 'licensed sex shop', see below.
[207] For a full account of the background and the legislation, see Colin Manchester, *Sex Shops and the Law* (Aldershot: Gower, 1986).

15.6 CONCLUSION

Mystery and confusion surrounds the law in the fields covered by this chapter. Difficulties exist on two levels. At the deeper level, there is no agreement about the ends which the law is intended to serve. It is not clear whether it protects social or individual interests; whether it is concerned to prevent offence or to impose a moral standard; whether it is soundly based in any philosophy, and if so whether that philosophy enjoys general agreement and is compatible with liberal values of freedom of choice and action. The only recent attempt in the UK to develop a coherent legal strategy to deal with obscenity and indecency law on the basis of an agreed philosophical position, the Williams Committee Report based on the harm principle, has largely been ignored by legislators, and has been attacked both as justifying a utilitarian interference with rights and as undervaluing intuitively significant values: a gut reaction against certain forms of expression may be right and socially important.

Even liberals committed to personal and political freedom may find their values leading them in several directions at once. In relation to blasphemy, freedom to express religious beliefs may interfere with other people's freedom to hold and express different beliefs, and may offend people even if it does not interfere with their freedom of conscience. Pornographic and indecent expression raises still more acute difficulties. If one believes in a free market in ideas, with values being controlled by the choices of purchasers, people should be free to produce and market most types of material for which there is a market. On the other hand, someone who follows Raz, treating moral autonomy as demanding a combination of a reasonable range of available options and the mental ability to choose between them,[208] may regard material which depraves and corrupts people as interfering significantly with one's ability to exercise free and rational choice (if one accepts the validity of the idea of personal or moral corruption). On this view, it is justifiable to interfere with people's freedom to publish or read obscene works, in order to protect their own or other people's autonomy. One's view of freedom of expression in these fields therefore depends not merely on whether or not one is a liberal, but on what sort of liberal one is.

The result of this in practical terms is that the substance of the law reflects all the oddities and inconsistencies of the conflicting ideals and ideologies which have given rise to it. Blasphemy law is recognized as being consistent with no known philosophy, but there is no political will to change it. The complex relationship between the common law

---

[208] Raz, *Morality of Freedom*, 425.

offences of indecency and corruption of public morality on the one hand and the Obscene Publications Act on the other exemplifies yet further confusion, to some extent made inevitable by the way in which, as in relation to blasphemy, the law is forced to accommodate standards and beliefs left over from an earlier stage in its development. The earlier ideas may be no worse than those current today, but they are likely to be hard to reconcile with them.

At some stage, Parliament will have to decide comprehensively what it wants to ban and why. One powerful incentive to embark on the process, although not a necessary precondition to it, would be the enactment of a domestic bill of rights requiring respect for freedom of expression. Until the attempt is made, and it will be a painful nettle for politicians and judges to grasp, we will have to live with a system of legal control over expression which owes little to notions of civil liberties or human rights.

16

RESTRICTING EXPRESSION TO FURTHER A
PUBLIC INTEREST: CONTEMPT OF COURT

This chapter examines a variety of restrictions, all criminal or quasi-criminal in form, which are directed to securing the integrity of the system of justice as a public (rather than individual or state) interest. Generally speaking, the law recognizes the public interest in open justice,[1] and in permitting fair and accurate contemporaneous reporting of legal proceedings.[2] At times, however, these interests come into conflict with other interests, such as the right of parties to a fair trial of their cases, rights of privacy, and the public interest in maintaining public order and morality. The conflict between these interests is universal, but the constitutional context in which it falls to be resolved varies from place to place, and affects the balance between the opposing interests.

In the USA, there is a constitutional guarantee of a right to a public trial in criminal prosecutions under the Sixth Amendment, but this right belongs only to the accused, and accordingly can sometimes be waived by the accused in respect of pre-trial hearings, in order to avoid adverse publicity which might make a fair trial impossible.[3] On the other hand, the general public has a right, implied in the First Amendment, to attend criminal trials, and this right has been held to promote a number of public interests: in particular, public trials allow an independent check on the fairness of judicial procedure, educate the public in an aspect of civic organization, help to maintain public trust in the judicial system, and satisfy the desire to see justice done. Accordingly, a defendant cannot choose to have the trial itself closed to the public.[4] The same applies to the part of the hearing in which potential jurors are examined before a jury is empanelled.[5] The press is prima facie entitled under the First Amendment to report on offences and on the progress of all stages of investigations and proceedings. An order for prior restraint of such reports is permissible only where publication of details would create a

---

[1] *Scott* v. *Scott* [1913] AC 417, HL.

[2] e.g. Administration of Justice Act 1960, s. 12(1), recognizing the general principle while authorizing certain restrictions; Contempt of Court Act 1981, s. 4.

[3] *Gannett Co.* v. *Pasquale*, 443 US 368 (1979).

[4] *Richmond Newspapers, Inc.* v. *Virginia*, 448 US 555 (1980).

[5] *Press-Enterprise Co.* v. *Superior Court of California*, 464 US 501 (1984).

clear and present danger that publicity would impair the defendant's right to a fair trial by an impartial jury. Even if there is such a danger, a blanket ban on reporting will not be justified unless the court is satisfied that alternative measures would be incapable of protecting the defendant's rights.[6]

In England and Wales, there is no constitutional right equivalent to the First Amendment to the US Constitution. The provisions of the European Convention on Human Rights, to which state institutions are subject, do, however, form part of the background of constitutional principles. As we have seen in earlier chapters, Article 10 of the Convention guarantees freedom of expression subject to certain justifiable restrictions. In addition, Article 6 guarantees a right to a fair and public trial. But the Convention does not go as far as the US Constitution in either guaranteeing to litigants the right to a public trial, or in guaranteeing the right of the press and public to attend trials. Article 6(1) of the Convention provides:

In the determination of his civil rights and obligations or of any criminal charge against him, everyone is entitled to a fair and public hearing within a reasonable time by an independent and impartial tribunal established by law. Judgment shall be pronounced publicly but the press and public may be excluded from all or part of the trial in the interests of morals, public order, or national security in a democratic society, where the interests of juveniles or the protection of the private life of the parties so require, or to the extent strictly necessary in the opinion of the court in special circumstances where publicity would prejudice the interests of justice.

As the *Report of the Committee on Contempt of Court* observed in 1974, although contempt is not a standard criminal charge, and in Scotland is not a criminal offence at all, 'it would be contrary to the spirit of the Convention if contempt procedure, both in England and Wales and in Scotland, did not comply with Article 6'.[7] The Committee went on to argue that most of the law of contempt complied with the requirements of Article 6. This is not surprising, since the exceptions from the right to a public hearing under Article 6, which are mirrored in the International Covenant on Civil and Political Rights, Article 14(1), go beyond anything available in English law, and, as Professor Sir James Fawcett observed, 'are so large and loosely expressed as to cover almost any denial of public hearing'.[8] Broadly speaking, and with limited exceptions, English law allows interference with public trials and with free reporting of and public comment on the judicial system only where they would

[6] *Nebraska Press Association* v. *Stuart*, 427 US 539 (1976).
[7] Cmnd. 5794 (1974) para. 18.
[8] J. E. S. Fawcett, *The Application of the European Convention on Human Rights*, 2nd edn. (Oxford: Clarendon Press, 1987), 160.

interfere with the interests of justice. Such restrictions as are permitted are enforced chiefly through the instrumentality of the law of contempt of court, and the power of the courts in certain circumstances to order restrictions on or postponement of reports of cases or the details of evidence. These form the subject of this chapter. Contempt is considered first, and then orders imposing restrictions on reporting and more general prior restraints are examined.

16.1 THE NATURE OF CONTEMPT OF COURT[9]

The law has always taken steps to enforce respect for its procedures and to protect them against abuse.[10] Punishment for contempt of court is part of the armoury which the courts have deployed for these purposes. Contempt of court has been defined as 'an act or omission calculated to interfere with the due administration of justice'.[11] It restricts freedom of expression in a number of ways. First, the types of criminal contempt[12] known as 'contempt in the face of the court' and 'scandalizing the court' are capable of restricting both the conduct of people before the court, and people's freedom to comment elsewhere on proceedings. Secondly, the head of criminal contempt which consists of prejudicing proceedings, which may attract strict liability (subject to the provisions of the Contempt of Court Act 1981, considered below), can restrict pre-trial comment and reporting of the trial itself. Thirdly, since breach of an undertaking to the court or of an order made by the court is a civil contempt, any such undertaking or order which requires that matters be not published will restrict freedom to publish information or opinions or to receive them, on pain of punishment. The second and third types of contempt are particularly likely to be committed by the press and broadcasting media.

The scope for the law of contempt to restrict the right to freedom of

---

[9] See generally C. J. Miller, *Contempt of Court*, 2nd edn. (Oxford: Clarendon Press, 1989); Nigel Lowe, *Borrie and Lowe's Law of Contempt*, 2nd edn. (London: Butterworth, 1983); Eric Barendt, *Freedom of Speech* (Oxford: Clarendon Press, 1987), ch. 8.

[10] For the background to this, see Ronald L. Goldfarb, *The Contempt Power* (New York: Columbia University Press, 1963), 1–100; R. Dhavan, 'Contempt of Court and the Phillimore Committee Report' (1976) 5 *Anglo-American LR* 186–253.

[11] Anthony Arlidge and David Eady, *The Law of Contempt* (London and Edinburgh: Sweet & Maxwell/W. Green, 1982), 30, citing *Helmore* v. *Smith* (1886) 35 Ch. D. 436 at p. 455 *per* Bowen LJ.

[12] Criminal contempts are regarded as a sufficiently serious attack on the administration of justice to deserve punishment. Civil contempts, such as non-compliance with a court order, are those which the court punishes in order to coerce the contemnor into complying. On the distinction, see Arlidge and Eady, *Law of Contempt*, 46–77.

expression is, therefore, substantial. This section attempts to explain the current state of English law, and to evaluate it in the light of civil liberties considerations. The treatment of freedom of expression and its permissible limitations under international human rights law provides a valuable backdrop. It would be hard to justify the law of contempt under the very general terms of Article 19 of the Universal Declaration of Human Rights, which gives unqualified recognition to the right to freedom of expression. There is more scope for the law of contempt under Article 19(2) and (3) of the International Covenant on Civil and Political Rights, which permits restrictions of freedom of expression only if they are provided by law and necessary (a) for the protection of the rights and reputations of others, or (b) for the protection of national security or of public order (ordre public), or of public health or morals. Protection of the rights of others would justify restricting expression which would prejudice a litigant's right to a fair hearing under Article 14(1), but would not justify restrictions on comments about the behaviour of judges which are imposed solely in order to uphold the dignity of the judiciary.

The European Convention on Human Rights leaves more scope for the law of contempt in all its aspects. This is not surprising, as the UK would have been unlikely to agree to an instrument which required it to abolish a substantial part of contempt law. Article 10(1) guarantees freedom of expression, but Article 10(2) permits that freedom to be interfered with under certain circumstances 'for the protection of the reputation or rights of others, . . . or for maintaining the authority and impartiality of the judiciary'. This has been held to permit restrictions which protect the interests of litigants in having a fair trial of their claims,[13] but it also allows more extensive restrictions to protect judicial dignity and reputation. However, in order to be justifiable within Article 10(2) of the Convention, restrictions of this sort must be:

(a) prescribed by law, a requirement which the law of contempt has so far been held to satisfy; and

(b) necessary in a democratic society for a legitimate purpose under that paragraph, which means that the restriction must be a response to a pressing social need and must be proportionate to its purpose.[14]

The discussion of the law in this section is divided up as follows. First, the meaning of 'court' for contempt purposes is examined and then common-law criminal contempts: contempt in the face of the court; scandal-

---

[13] *Sunday Times* case, Eur. Ct. HR, Series A, No. 30, Judgment of 26 Apr. 1979, 12 EHRR 245; *Observer and Guardian* v. *UK*, Eur. Ct. HR, Series A, No. 216, Judgment of 26 Nov. 1991, 14 EHRR 153.

[14] *Sunday Times* case, Eur. Ct. HR, Series A, No. 30, Judgment of 26 Apr. 1979, 12 EHRR 245.

izing the court; prejudicing or impeding proceedings; contempt by pre-judgment. The rest of the section deals with strict liability for contempts by way of publication, under the Contempt of Court Act 1981: strict lia-bility under the Contempt of Court Act 1981; the time when proceed-ings become active; circumstances in which there is a substantial risk of serious prejudice to proceedings; the section 5 defence, where prejudice is incidental to a discussion in good faith of matters of public interest; the defence of ignorance under section 3.

(1) What is a court?

A preliminary matter which arises is the notion of the 'court', contempt of which is penalized. Judicial activities are today carried on by a wide variety of courts, tribunals, and other bodies, and the public interest in safeguarding the administration of justice extends, more or less com-pellingly, to all of them. However, if penalties are to be imposed for con-tempt of court, it is important, in the interests of certainty, to know what bodies are covered by the rules. In the leading case on the matter, *Attorney-General* v. *British Broadcasting Corporation*,[15] the House of Lords had to consider a programme about the activities of the Exclusive Brethren, a religious sect. The programme criticized the sect, and argued that its meeting rooms were not places of public religious worship within the meaning of the General Rate Act 1967, section 39, and were there-fore ineligible for exemption from liability for rates. The Attorney-General, seeking an injunction to restrain the broadcast, argued that this programme would prejudice the determination of this issue at a pending hearing by a local valuation court. The BBC argued that the local valua-tion court was not an inferior court for the purpose of the contempt jurisdiction. The Divisional Court and Court of Appeal held that it was such a court. However, on appeal to the House of Lords it was held that the nomenclature attached to a body was not decisive, and that a local valuation was not a court of law such as to attract the protection of the law of contempt. Viscount Dilhorne thought that, where Parliament had not called a body a court, it could not be a court, although where Parliament had called a body a court, it might still not be a court of law for contempt purposes. The other Law Lords, however, did not give even that limited overriding power to the name conferred by Parliament on a body. Lords Scarman and Fraser distinguished between bodies dis-charging judicial functions (courts) and those discharging administrative functions (tribunals),[16] and made the substance of the body's activities

[15] [1981] AC 303, [1980] 3 All ER 161, HL.

[16] Note that an administrative body may be under a duty to act judicially, i.e. fairly and without bias, in some of its activities. This is true e.g. of licensing bodies, and of those

central to its classification, as did Viscount Dilhorne in relation to bodies which were called courts. Lord Edmund-Davies accepted the distinction, but held that none of the features of judicial or administrative bodies respectively was decisive as to the correct classification of a particular body.

The Contempt of Court Act 1981 (below) provides that for its purposes the term 'court' 'includes any tribunal or body exercising the judicial power of the state'.[17] This adoption of the judicial power test, however, gives little help to those who had to decide on the classification of various types of body, and it is perhaps fair to conclude that the range of bodies which can be protected by the contempt jurisdiction 'is inextricably bound with the ambit of contempt itself and in the end might better be resolved as a matter of policy rather than upon technical definitions'.[18] This was certainly the approach in *P.* v. *Liverpool Daily Post and Echo Newspapers plc*,[19] where the House of Lords held that a mental health review tribunal was a court for contempt purposes. Among other grounds for reaching this decision, Lord Bridge[20] (with whom the other Law Lords agreed) approved the reasoning of Lord Donaldson MR in the Court of Appeal on this point.[21] Lord Donaldson had pointed out that the tribunal had been set up under the Mental Health Act 1983, enacted in part to bring English law into line with the requirements of Article 5(4) of the European Convention on Human Rights. Article 5(4) requires that people deprived of their liberty by arrest or detention are to be entitled to have the lawfulness of their detention 'decided speedily by a court', and to have their release ordered if the detention is held to be unlawful. Before 1982, English law had not provided such a procedure in relation to mental patients detained pursuant to a restriction order (an order which may be imposed by a criminal court where a person is convicted of an offence and is made the subject of a hospital order). Accordingly, in *X* v. *United Kingdom*[22] the European Court of Human

who have the responsibility for determining applications for warrants to search premises or arrest people. Nevertheless, this does not make those functions judicial. See *Shell Co. of Australia Ltd.* v. *Federal Commissioner of Taxation* [1931] AC 275, PC, at pp. 296–7 *per* Viscount Sankey LC; David Feldman, *The Law Relating to Entry, Search and Seizure* (London: Butterworths, 1986), 73–4; and *Love* v. *A.-G. of New South Wales* (1990) 169 CLR 307, especially at p. 322, HC of Australia.

[17] Contempt of Court Act 1981, s. 19.

[18] Lowe, *Borrie and Lowe*, 2nd edn., p. 317. See generally N. V. Lowe and H. F. Rawlings, 'Tribunals and the Laws Protecting the Administration of Justice' [1982] *PL* 418–50.

[19] [1991] 2 AC 370, reported *sub nom. Pickering* v. *Liverpool Daily Post and Echo Newspapers plc* [1991] 1 All ER 622, HL.

[20] [1991] 2 AC at p. 417, [1991] 1 All ER at p. 630.

[21] [1991] 2 AC 370, [1990] 1 All ER 335, CA.

[22] Eur. Ct. HR, Series A, No. 46, Judgment of 24 Oct. 1981; 4 EHRR 188.

Rights had held that the U.K. was in breach of the Convention in this regard. The Mental Health (Amendment) Act 1982 therefore gave the mental health review tribunals power to determine whether the legal criteria for detention were met in relation to patients detained under restriction orders made by other courts, and to order the release of patients unlawfully detained.[23] Lord Donaldson continued:[24]

If such a tribunal is not a 'court' for all purposes, the Human Rights Convention is not being complied with, since there is no indication that 'court' in the convention has any different meaning from that which it bears in English law. However, I have no doubt that in law a mental health review tribunal is a court. Contrary to what is stated in [*Attorney-General* v. *Associated Newspapers Group plc*],[25] it did not inherit an executive function. It was given a new and quite different function.

Farquharson LJ set out the factors which influenced him to hold that the tribunal was a court:[26]

The tribunals are independent of the state; they do not exercise a purely administrative function; they are required to act judicially and make their findings on the basis of the evidence submitted to them; they can administer an oath to the witnesses called before them; they have, and have had since their introduction in 1959, the power to release, conditionally or otherwise, patients detained under the Mental Health Acts, and since 1982 patients subject to a restriction order under section 65 of the 1959 Act or section 41 of the 1983 Act. Decisions of such consequence affecting the release from detention of patients who are subject to hospital orders made by the criminal courts of the country come within the description of 'any tribunal . . . exercising the judicial power of the State'.

The correct approach, therefore, is to see whether the tribunal in question is making decisions which dispose of claims to or disputes over entitlements on the basis of legal criteria, and to ask whether there are any indications in the circumstances surrounding the establishment of the tribunal that it ought to be regarded as a court rather than an administrative body.

(2) Contempt in the face of the court

Contempt in the face of the court is committed by anyone who, in court, interferes with the proceedings, abuses the process of the court, or

[23] The relevant law has since been consolidated in the Mental Health Act 1983, and in rules made thereunder.
[24] [1991] 2 AC at p. 381, [1990] 1 All ER 335 at p. 341.
[25] [1989] 1 WLR 322, [1989] 1 All ER 604, DC, holding that a mental health review tribunal was not a court for the purpose of contempt proceedings. This decision was not followed by the Court of Appeal in the *Liverpool Daily Post and Echo* case, and was overruled by the House of Lords.
[26] [1991] 2 AC at p. 395, [1990] 1 All ER at p. 352.

threatens, insults, or interferes the judge, any witness, a juror, or a party. It includes refusal by a witness to answer questions, an assault on the judge, or casting aspersions on a juror. It encompasses demonstrations in court.[27] It has also been held, in some Australian cases, to cover demonstrations outside courts, at least where potential jurors are given leaflets which seek to encourage them to be sceptical about the value and accuracy of evidence to be given by some of the witnesses.[28] Accusations by counsel that the judge has acted unjudicially may, if sufficiently scurrilous, amount to contempt. While it may be painful for people in court to have to moderate their language and behaviour, it is essential for the smooth functioning of the justice system that courts should be able to regulate their procedure and protect it by summary action against attempts[29] at disruption. There is a resulting restriction of freedom of expression, but the restriction is insubstantial and is fully justified by the need to maintain the authority of the judicial process.

Potentially a more significant threat to liberty lies in the fact that it is open to the trial judge in the case in respect of which the contempt is committed to institute summary action against the contemnor, summoning him, accusing him, judging him, and sentencing him.[30] Until 1960 there was no right of appeal against the judge's decision, but an appeal to the Court of Appeal was eventually provided by the Administration of Justice Act 1960, section 13. This power of a court to act of its own motion is rarely exercised. The usual course is for the Attorney-General or a party aggrieved by the contempt to bring a motion before the High Court to commit the alleged contemnor to prison for contempt, proving the charge in the usual way before an impartial tribunal.[31] However, the summary procedure remains available, and contravenes both the right to be tried by an independent and impartial tribunal, under Article 6(1) of the European Convention on Human Rights, and the right to have adequate time and facilities for the preparation of a defence and the right to legal assistance, under Article 6(3)(b) and (c). In *Balogh* v. *Crown Court at St. Albans*,[32] the Court of Appeal laid down some guidelines for the use of the summary power. Mr Balogh had stolen a cylinder of laughing gas (nitrous oxide) and had found out which ventilation duct led from the roof of the Crown Court into the courtroom. Balogh had intended to introduce the gas into a courtroom where a pornography trial was in

[27] *Morris* v. *Crown Office* [1970] 2 QB 114, [1970] 1 All ER 1079, CA.

[28] *Registrar, Court of Appeal* v. *Collins* [1982] 1 NSWLR 682, CA of NSW; *Prothonotary* v. *Collins* (1985) 2 NSWLR 549, S.C. of NSW.

[29] On attempts to commit contempt, see *Balogh* v. *Crown Court at St Albans* [1975] QB 73, [1974] 3 All ER 283, CA; Lowe, *Borrie and Lowe*, 2nd edn., 18–19.

[30] *R.* v. *Almon* (1765) Wilm. 243 at p. 254 *per* Wilmot CJ.   [31] RSC Ord. 52.

[32] [1975] QB 73,[1974] 3 All ER 283, CA.

progress, via the ventilation duct, next-door to one presided over by Mr Justice Melford Stephenson, a judge not given to levity in the discharge of his judicial duties. The police found the gas cylinder in his brief-case before he had an opportunity of carrying out the plan. Melford Stephenson J., the senior judge, summarily sentenced him to six months imprisonment for contempt of court. Balogh appealed. He succeeded on the ground that he had not committed contempt, or even attempted to commit it, his acts being merely preparatory to the completed offence. Lord Denning MR (with whom Stephenson and Lawton LJJ agreed) said that summary punishment should be imposed only in cases where there was sufficient urgency to warrant it, for example where the contemnor is interfering with witnesses or jurors. In other cases, such as *Balogh*, where there is no urgent need to protect the administration of justice, the judge should invite counsel to represent the accused, with a remand in custody if necessary. But Lord Denning did not entirely disapprove of the judge's actions. 'The judge acted with a firmness which became him. As it happened, he went too far. That is no reproach to him. It only shows the wisdom of having an appeal.'[33]

Such judicial ambivalence towards the use of a power of summary punishment which infringes the Convention is the best possible reason for abolishing the power. The potential clash with the standards of the Convention was recognized by the Phillimore Committee in 1974. The Committee recommended that legal aid should be made available to people accused of contempt in the face of the court, and that they should be allowed to be legally represented. Subject to that, it recommended that the summary procedure should be retained, on account of the advantages of speed, and the judge's personal knowledge of the circumstances of the contempt which might lead to greater leniency than an independent judge would feel able to permit.[34] The modest change which was recommended, even if it is implemented, arguably would not go far enough to meet the UK's obligations under Article 6. Statutory reform is needed to guarantee the rights of those accused of contempt in the face of the court.

(3) Scandalizing the court

Scandalizing the court potentially represents a far more extensive incursion on freedom of expression. It has been defined as: 'Any act done or writing published calculated to bring a Court or a judge of the Court into contempt, or to lower his authority . . .'.[35] This appears to be a very

[33] [1975] QB at pp. 86–7, [1974] 3 All ER at p. 290.
[34] *Report of the Committee on Contempt of Court*, Cmnd. 5794, paras. 30–1.
[35] *R. v. Gray* [1900] 2 QB 36 at p. 40 *per* Lord Russell CJ. The decision came not long

broad *actus reus*, and taken at face value would threaten a good deal of the critical commentary on judicial decisions which may be found in respectable law journals. However, it is qualified to take account of three matters: (*a*) the fact that the law of contempt protects the administration of justice rather than the feelings of judges; (*b*) the need for open justice to be scrutinized; and (*c*) the right of citizens to comment on matters of public concern. As Lord Atkin said in *Ambard* v. *Attorney-General for Trinidad and Tobago*:[36]

. . . no wrong is committed by any member of the public who exercises the ordinary right of criticising in good faith in private or public the public act done in the seat of justice. The path of criticism is a public way: the wrong headed are permitted to err therein: provided that members of the public abstain from imputing improper motives to those taking part in the administration of justice, and are genuinely exercising a right of criticism and not acting in malice or attempting to impair the administration of justice, they are immune. Justice is not a cloistered virtue: she must be allowed to suffer the scrutiny and respectful even though outspoken comments of ordinary men.

The critic in that case committed no contempt by drawing attention to the human element in sentencing, which can lead to inconsistency between sentences for similar offences. But critics must not impute improper motives to judges or others, nor act in malice, nor attempt to impair the administration of justice (for example, by bringing the judicial system into disrepute).

This ban on imputing improper motives to judges might be thought to be unobjectionable. For example, in a case like *Badry* v. *Director of Public Prosecutions of Mauritius*,[37] where a person asserted that a claim for compensation by an injured worker was dismissed by the Supreme Court because the judge was influenced by the fact that the defendant was an important commercial concern in the area, the assertion could be understood as tending to undermine both the finality and authority of the decision in that particular piece of litigation, and the moral authority of the court generally. The Privy Council decided that it constituted a contempt. Yet it is not clear why there should be a blanket ban on such assertions. The law of contempt should take account of the public interest in the performance of the courts being publicly aired and discussed, and it is unrealistic to suppose, as Lord Atkin apparently assumed in *Ambard*, that it would always be wrong to impute improper motives to a

after Lord Morris, in *McLeod* v. *St. Aubyn* [1899] AC 549 at p. 561, PC, had opined that this head of contempt was obsolete in England. The article which was in issue in Gray (reproduced in part in the report of the case in 82 LT 534) is probably among the most vitriolic attacks on overweening judicial self-importance in English literature.

[36] [1936] AC 322 at p. 335, [1936] 1 All ER 704 at p. 709, PC.
[37] [1983] 2 AC 297, [1982] 3 All ER 973, PC.

judge. In the UK, we are fortunate in the general level of rectitude among our judges. However, there is no guarantee that this will always be the case, or that it is true of all common-law jurisdictions. There is a public interest in people being able to air serious misgivings about the quality of judges, whether these derive from apparent weaknesses in their reasoning abilities or from suspected corruption or bias.

For this reason, the High Court of Australia held early in its existence that it was not necessarily a contempt to impute lack of impartiality to a judge. In *R. v. Nichols*,[38] Mr. Justice Higgins had stopped counsel from criticizing the government. A newspaper commented that the judge was a political judge, who had been appointed to the bench only because he was a servant of a particular political party. The High Court held that this did not constitute a contempt of court. Griffiths CJ, delivering the unanimous judgment of the Court, pointed out that public confidence in the judges depends on their behaviour, and that the press has a role in maintaining judicial standards by way of open and critical public scrutiny of judicial performance, in the public interest. He said:[39]

> . . . I think that, if any judge of this Court or of any other Court were to make a public utterance of such a character as to be likely to impair the confidence of the public, or of suitors or any class of suitors in the impartiality of the court in any matter likely to be brought before it, any public comment on such an utterance, if it were a fair comment, would, so far from being a contempt of court, be for the public benefit, and would be entitled to similar protection to that which comment upon matters of public interest is entitled under the law of libel.

The same approach has subsequently been followed in Australia and New Zealand,[40] and an eminent Australian commentator has described it as a qualification, 'at least as far as Australasian law is concerned', of Lord Atkin's statement in *Ambard*.[41] In New South Wales, the judges seem to have become increasingly relaxed in the face of criticism. When the President of the Builder's Labourers' Federation (then a powerful trade union) gave a television interview outside a court, saying that the verdict in the case which he had just watched (in which protesters against a tour of Australia by the South African rugby union team had been convicted of malicious damage to property for damaging the goalposts at the Sydney Cricket Ground where rugby football is played in winter) was a miscarriage of justice which illustrated the extent of racism in Australian

---

[38] (1911) 12 CLR 280.

[39] Ibid. at p. 286.

[40] See e.g. *R. v. Fletcher; ex parte Kisch* (1935) 52 CLR 248; *A.-G. for New South Wales v. Mundey* [1972] 2 NSWLR 887; *Solicitor-General v. Radio Avon Ltd.* [1978] 1 NZLR 225, at pp. 230–1.

[41] Geoffrey A. Flick, *Civil Liberties in Australia* (Sydney: Law Book Co., 1981), 131.

society, it was held to be no contempt. The judges chose to interpret his words as an attack on society, not on the judges.[42]

It is true that the position in the UK would be rather different if our judges follow the *Ambard* formulation of the contempt rule, but one of the problems is that it is hard to know in advance what will be held to constitute a contempt in any jurisdiction. The effect of criticism on the due administration of justice may vary between societies, and in any society its effects may vary from time to time. For example, in small communities, where everyone knows the judges personally and the authority of the courts may depend more on personal than institutional authority, an attack on the judge may seriously undermine respect for law.[43] In larger societies, the law is more impersonal, its authority is less affected by the idiosyncrasies of its individual personnel, and the approach adopted in the United States seems particularly attractive. There, the First Amendment to the Constitution, protecting freedom of speech and of the press, has been held to permit criticism, even if not altogether in good taste, unless it constitutes a clear and present danger to the administration of justice. '[A]n enforced silence, however limited solely in the name of preserving the dignity of the bench, would probably engender resentment, suspicion, and contempt much more than it would enhance respect . . .'[44]

The political and constitutional structure of a society will also affect the position of the courts. If the constitution demands a separation of power between the executive and an independent judiciary, as one of the pillars of the rule of law, any direct attack on a judge by a member of the executive will threaten to undermine that independence and the associated constitutional principles. Where, as in the Canadian case *Re Borowski*,[45] the alleged contemnor is a government minister who not only accuses a judge of basing a decision on political views (something which has often been said of English judges by the media and legal commentators in sensitive cases) but also threatens to remove the judge from office, the law of contempt is protecting an important constitutional principle which goes beyond safeguarding the dignity or authority of the courts and the adminsitration of justice against vulgar abuse. The public interest in maintaining respect for law may require different forms of contempt

---

[42] *A.-G. for New South Wales* v. *Mundey* [1972] 2 NSWLR 887.

[43] See Keith Patchett, 'Small is Different?', in Geoffrey Hand and Jeremy McBride (eds.), *Droit sans frontières: Essays in honour of L. Neville Brown* (Birmingham: Holdsworth Club, 1991), 43–52. Western legal processes grafted on to a small society may still rely for their authority on charismatic forms of domination.

[44] *Bridges* v. *California, Times-Mirror Co.* v. *California*, 314 US 252 (1941) at pp. 270–1 *per* Black J. Even allegations of judicial bias in pending proceedings have been held not to constitute contempt: *Pennekamp* v. *Florida*, 328 US 331 (1946). See further Barendt, *Freedom of Speech*, 218–23.

[45] (1971) 19 DLR (3d) 537.

law in each type of society. Even in Australia, there is a strange ambivalence to the crime of contempt by scandalizing the court. While the High Court was following a substantial tradition in *Nichols* when it asserted the importance of public criticism in keeping judges up to the mark,[46] and allowed allegations of bias to be made against judges if they amounted to fair comment, it had been held to be a contempt to accuse a judge of behaving in a thoroughly unjudicial way.[47] It seems that, in Australia, the rhetoric of fair comment has turned into practice, superseding the earlier practice of suppressing criticism.

In England, it has been said that 'if reasonable argument or expostulation is offered against any judicial act as contrary to law or public good, no Court could or would treat that as a contempt of Court'.[48] These considerations demand protection for the reasoned opinions of commentators, even if outspoken or even intemperate. It was on this ground that the Court of Appeal held that Mr Quintin Hogg, QC, MP, PC, who later became Lord Hailsham LC, was not guilty of contempt for publishing an article in *Punch* magazine vehemently criticizing a decision of the Court of Appeal (which he wrongly attributed to the Divisional Court). The Court had said that the police might in some circumstances be acting unlawfully if they turned a blind eye to the operation of illegal gambling clubs in Soho.[49] Mr. Hogg argued that the police should not be blamed for the persistence of such clubs when the fault lay with the the legislation and the courts (including the Court of Appeal), which (he wrote) had interpreted the legislation in unrealistic, contradictory, and erroneous decisions, which made it very difficult to obtain convictions and so made it unreasonable to expect the police to prosecute. He suggested that the Court of Appeal should apologize to the police for the trouble and expense to which they were put by the decisions of the courts. Mr. Raymond Blackburn, the applicant in the earlier proceedings against the police, invited the Court of Appeal to commit Mr. Hogg for contempt. The Court decided, however, that it would be wrong to invoke the contempt jurisdiction in order to shelter itself from criticism, even erroneous criticism. It was anyone's right to comment rumbustiously on judicial decisions, so long as it was done in good faith, without intending contempt, and kept within the bounds of reasonable courtesy (although, according to Salmon LJ, it need not necessarily observe the

---

[46] *In re Syme; ex parte The Daily Telegraph Newspaper Co.* (1879) 5 VLR (L) 291, especially at p. 296, SC Victoria; *In the matter of 'The Evening News'* (1880) 1 NSWLR 211 at p. 239, *per* Sir James Martin CJ.

[47] *In the matter of 'The Evening News'* (1880) 1 NSWLR 211. See Flick, *Civil Liberties* , 128; *R. v. Dunbabin, ex parte Williams* (1935) 53 CLR 434.

[48] *R. v. Gray* [1900] 2 QB 36 at p. 40 *per* Lord Russell CJ.

[49] *R. v. Commissioner of Police of the Metropolis, ex parte Blackburn* [1968] 2 QB 118, CA.

canons of good taste). The decisions of the courts must be left to look
after themselves; their judgments must be their own vindication; and the
judges ought not to allow themselves to be deflected from duly administering justice by criticism.[50]

In the light of this, it is hard to know what the bounds of the offence
are. If it is a contempt to cast doubt on the impartiality of a judge, as
Badry accepts, what is the position of people who argue that judges
exhibit traits and preferences in their judgments which are the result of
institutional conditioning over a long period? For example, if one suggests that the judges (or certain judges) are predominantly conservative in
their politics, or lack sympathy with the objectives and methods of collective bargaining and industrial action by trade unions, is this a contempt
of court? There are, perhaps, two possible answers.

The first answer would be that the proposition amounts to a contempt
only if it implies that judges act unjudicially, by ignoring or twisting relevant legal rules or principles to give effect to their personal preferences in
their judgments. It would, therefore, not be a contempt to suggest that
the rules and principles which the judges are required to administer
embody such attitudes, and that these attitudes happen to coincide with
the judges' own; nor would it be a contempt to assert that judges have
political views, unless the further claim were made that the judges' decisions are entirely determined by those views rather than by the law. This
turns on the interpretation of an utterance in the light of a nice distinction between judicial attitudes, legal values, and the causative link
between those attitudes and values and the results of particular cases,
which may well not have been present in the mind of the author.
Although it may be possible for the courts to use the distinction to acquit
rather than convict for contempt in doubtful cases, it may equally be
employed to the opposite end.[51]

Alternatively, it might be said that the answer depends on the stability
and structure of particular societies. If the independence of the judicial
system is firmly established in a given society, its integrity, and the due
administration of justice, will not be undermined (and might well be
enhanced) by allowing robust and vigorous criticism of its decisions. On
the other hand, in societies where the judges' independence of the executive is weak or threatened, or the fair administration of justice is threatened by public unrest or mob rule, there may be stronger grounds for

---

[50] R. v. *Commissioner of Police of the Metropolis, ex parte Blackburn (No. 2)* [1968] 2 QB
150, [1968] 2 All ER 319, CA
[51] Contrast *A.-G. for New South Wales* v. *Mundey* [1972] 2 NSWLR 887 with the
Canadian approach in *Re Borowski* (1971) 19 DLR (3d) 537, or that of the Privy Council
sitting on appeal from Mauritius in *Badry* v. *DPP of Mauritius* [1983] 2 AC 297, [1982] 3
All ER 973.

restricting some types of criticism of the judges, particularly those which encourage the executive or others to disregard court decisions and interfere with proceedings. There may, therefore, be a core of good sense in the apparently patronizing and possibly racist comment by Lord Morris, in *McLeod* v. *St. Aubyn*,[52] that 'in small colonies, consisting principally of coloured populations, the enforcement in proper cases of committal for contempt of Court for attacks on the Court may be absolutely necessary to preserve in such a community the dignity of and respect for the Court'.

Uncertainty about the essential nature of the offence of contempt by scandalizing the court raises the issue of the compatibility of the law with the requirements of Article 10 of the European Convention on Human Rights. Potential liability for the offence undoubtedly interferes with free expression, so the question is whether the interference is justifiable under Article 10(2) as being prescribed by law and necessary in a democratic society for maintaining the authority and impartiality of the judiciary. It is possible that the law is sufficiently accessible, certain, and predictable to be said to be prescribed by law,[53] although this is not free from doubt. There can be no doubt, at least, that the purpose of the law is to maintain the authority of the judiciary, a legitimate objective under Article 10(2). However, the test of necessity in a democratic society is harder to meet. It requires that the law of scandalizing the court should be a response to a pressing social need. Given the conditions in this country at present, where the authority of the courts is not seriously in question (except in relation to criminal miscarriages of justice, where steps are being taken to improve the reputation of the judiciary by remedying some of the errors which have been made in the past), it is hard to see any pressing social need which demands general protection for the judges against public comment. Even given the margin of appreciation which the European Court of Human Rights allows to state authorities to settle the needs of their own societies, it is hard to see how the law on scandalizing could be said to be proportionate to the aim pursued. Not only is it counter-democratic, but it is also highly unlikely to achieve its purpose: the more thoroughly expression is suppressed, the more it is likely to fuel, rather than allay, suspicions about the conduct and attitudes of the judges. It is noteworthy that in Canada it has been held that the law of contempt by scandalizing the court is incompatible with the guarantee of freedom of expression and the press under section 2(*b*) of the Canadian Charter of Rights and Freedoms, and is not a permissible limit of that right under

---

[52] [1899] AC 549, PC, at p. 561.
[53] *Sunday Times* case, Eur. Ct. HR, Series A, No. 30, Judgment of 26 Apr. 1979, 2 EHRR 245.

section 1 of the Charter because the law is disproportionate to any legitimate purpose which it might serve.[54]

The risk that the law offends against the Convention should concentrate minds on reform. The Phillimore Committee wondered whether the offence of scandalizing the court should be entirely abolished, but eventually recommended that it should be narrowed substantially. The Committee thought that the law of contempt is there essentially to protect the integrity of the legal process and to prevent prejudice in particular cases. It should not be used against people who criticize judges, or publish vituperative comments, unless they create a risk of serious prejudice to some particular, identifiable proceedings.[55] This would bring the law back into line with the Convention's requirements, because it would ensure that criminal sanctions could be imposed only in cases where they would be proportionate to the legitimate objective of maintaining the authority of the judiciary in a democratic society, but no action has so far been taken to implement the proposal. On the other hand, a further recommendation would, if implemented, create further difficulties in relation to the Convention. The Committee recommended that there should be a new statutory offence of publishing material which imputes improper or corrupt behaviour to judges, in the performance of their judicial functions, with intent to impair confidence in the administration of justice.[56] They suggested a defence if the allegation is both true and for the public benefit.[57] Such a defence would be needed if the interference with freedom of expression were to be proportionate to a legitimate aim in a democratic society, as required under Article 10(2) of the Convention.

The Law Commission later considered the matter. It thought that the test for intent to impair confidence in the administration of justice would probably be unworkable, and disliked the idea that liability could ever be imposed for making a true allegation of judicial impropriety. It therefore recommended that it should be an offence to publish or distribute false matter, which imputes corrupt judicial conduct to any judge, tribunal, or member of a tribunal, knowing it to be false or being reckless whether it is false, with the intent that it should be taken as true.[58] This would have given adequate protection to the reputation of the judicial service, while allowing robust criticism, investigative journalism, and satire, leaving

---

[54] R. v. Kopyto (1987) 47 DLR (4th) 213, Ontario CA.

[55] Report of the Committee on Contempt of Court, Cmnd. 5794 (London: HMSO, 1974), paras. 161–2.

[56] Ibid., para. 164.   [57] Ibid., paras. 166–7.

[58] Law Commission Report No. 96, Offences Relating to Interference with the Course of Justice (London: HMSO, 1979), para. 3.70.

other attacks on judges to the law of defamation. However, no action has been taken to implement any of these proposals.

(4) Prejudicing or impeding proceedings

The main objects of the contempt power are to guarantee access to judicial decision-making and to safeguard the fairness of legal processes for intending litigants. Interfering with a party, witness, or juror, by any means, is a criminal contempt at common law, and is punished in order to maintain the integrity of the legal system and its ability to determine fairly all cases which come before it. Thus a prison governor was guilty of contempt of court when he stopped an inmate's letter attempting to initiate proceedings to have the governor committed for contempt of court in relation to an earlier interception, and it seems that intercepting a letter to a solicitor giving instructions about pending litigation would also be a contempt if, without legal authority (such as valid Prison Rules), it impeded the prisoner's ability to pursue legal proceedings.[59]

Sometimes a publication can have the effect of impeding access to justice, and when it does so it may constitute a contempt. In *Attorney-General v. Hislop*[60] the editor of the periodical *Private Eye* was being sued for libel by Mrs Sonia Sutcliffe in respect of allegations that she had known that her husband, Peter Sutcliffe, had been the notorious mass murderer, the 'Yorkshire Ripper', and had lied to the police in order to provide him with a false alibi. The defence included a plea of justification. The editor then published further articles, repeating the allegations. After Mrs Sutcliffe had won the libel action, the Attorney-General instituted proceedings against the editor, alleging that he had committed a contempt of court. The judge found that in publishing the articles the editor had intended to deter Mrs Sutcliffe from pursuing her libel action, rather than to prejudice jurors. He went on to decide that there was no real or substantial risk of the trial being impeded or prejudiced, and so no contempt. The Attorney-General appealed to the Court of Appeal, which reversed the decision and fined the editor and the publishers £10,000 each. By publishing libels, intending to deter another party to litigation from pursuing her claim, they had given rise to a substantial risk that the course of justice would be impeded, as it was likely that a litigant might be put off. There is, said the judges, a real difference between bringing home to another party the strength of one's own case, and publishing material which holds that party up to public obloquy and scurrilous abuse. The former is permissible, but the latter is a contempt,

---

[59] *Raymond v. Honey* [1983] 1 AC 1, [1982] 1 All ER 756, HL.
[60] [1991] 1 QB 514, [1991] 1 All ER 911, CA.

because it is likely to impede justice, as had been accepted by all the members of the House of Lords in *Attorney-General* v. *Times Newspapers Ltd.* (the Thalidomide case).

This is a particular problem in relation to actions for defamation. The general rule is that the court will not grant an interlocutory injunction restraining repetition of an alleged libel which the defendant intends to justify, because until it is clear that an allegation is untrue the public interest in free speech outweighs the private interests of the possibly unwronged plaintiff.[61] Yet if publication is likely to be a contempt, an injunction may be granted. It is hard to imagine a case in which republishing the allegations could avoid either prejudicing jurors or impeding justice by deterring the plaintiff from having his day in court, unless (as in *Attorney-General* v. *News Group Newspapers Ltd.*)[62] the action is certain to proceed and the trial is unlikely to take place soon enough for the effect of the republication to be likely to continue until then.

The common law offence of contempt by prejudicing or impeding proceedings was a strict liability offence of wide scope. However, the Contempt of Court Act 1981, section 6(c), while preserving common-law liability under this head of contempt, did so only 'in respect of conduct *intended* to impede or prejudice the administration of justice' (italics added). It is therefore no longer a strict liability offence. Indeed, it has been held that it is now a crime of specific intent, rather than basic or general intent. Following the recommendations of the Phillimore Committee,[63] Lord Donaldson M.R. has said:[64]

I am quite satisfied that . . . what is 'saved' [by section 6(c) of the 1981 Act] is the power of the court to commit for contempt where the conduct complained of is specifically intended to impede or prejudice the administration of justice. Such an intent need not be expressly avowed or admitted, but can be inferred from all the circumstances, including the foreseeability of the the consequences of the conduct.

The surrounding circumstances may include the interest of the alleged contemnor in the case in issue, as where a newspaper's editor published

---

[61] *Bonnard* v. *Perryman* [1891] 2 Ch. 269.

[62] [1987] QB 1, [1986] 2 All ER 833, CA, where the Court of Appeal discharging an injunction which had previously been granted restraining newspaper publishers from repeating allegations concerning the behaviour of Mr Ian Botham, an England cricketer, while on tour in New Zealand. The allegations were the subject of libel actions against those who had originally published them, but the trial was likely to be delayed for at least ten months.

[63] *Report of the Committee on Contempt of Court*, Cmnd. 5794 (1974), discussed by Dhavan, 'Contempt of Court and Phillimore', 186–253.

[64] *A.-G.* v. *Newspaper Publishing plc* [1988] Ch. 333 at pp. 374–5, [1987] 3 All ER 276 at pp. 303–4.

allegations about somebody, intending to sponsor a private prosecution against that person in respect of the allegations contained in the publication.[65] Similarly, where a newpaper editor published extracts from *Spycatcher*, knowing that proceedings were in progress against another newspaper to preserve rights of confidentiality in respect of the material and knowing that publication would help to compromise the duty of confidence owed by the other newspapers' publishers, the court could infer that the publication was intended to prejudice the administration of justice.[66] This aspect of the contempt power enables the court to safeguard the integrity of its procedures, but may (as in the *Spycatcher* case) have the effect of extending the effect of an injunction far beyond the people to whom the injunction is addressed. This is, in principle, a cause for concern, as the third parties who are liable to be punished for contempt for breaching the injunction would not have been able to appear before the court to oppose the grant of the injunction. It is particularly unfortunate in the context of *Spycatcher*, where the interim injunction in question had been granted to preserve any remaining confidentiality attaching to matters dealt with in the book: as the House of Lords later decided that different people, and different newspapers, may be differently affected by the competing public interests, it is conceivable that newspaper *X* may be liable to punishment for contempt for breaching an injunction addressed to another newspaper, *Y*, in circumstances which would not have justified the grant of an injunction had one been sought directly against newspaper *X*. Such an extension of the effect of injunctions beyond their proper limits by the procedural sidewind of contempt proceedings against a third party should not be permitted. If extended protection is required for plaintiffs, it should be achieved through injunctions of express general application, where all know where they stand and will have standing to apply to discharge the injunction.[67]

It is possible that this deliberate contempt of court by publication at common law may, in two respects, cast the net of liability more widely than under the Contempt of Court Act 1981. First, although at common law the publication no longer attracts strict liability, the *actus reus* of the common law offence may be wider than that for statutory contempts. Whereas the 1981 Act applies only where proceedings are active, as we shall see in sections (6) and (7) below, it is possible that common-law contempt by prejudicing or impeding proceedings applies to publications even before any proceedings are active or pending. Secondly, common-law contempt is not limited to the types of publications contemplated by the Contempt of Court Act 1981, which is limited to those which create

---

[65] *A.-G. v. News Group Newspapers plc* [1989] QB 110, [1988] 2 All ER 906, DC.

[66] *A.-G. v. Times Newspapers Ltd.* [1992] 1 AC 191, [1991] 2 All ER 398, HL.

[67] *Cp.* the comments by C. J. Miller in *All ER Rev. 1991*, 65–6.

a substantial risk that active proceedings will be seriously impeded or prejudiced. The common law offence covers other types of conduct as well, such as bringing improper pressure to bear on a party to litigation to discontinue it.[68] This widening, if it is upheld, may impose a significant fetter on the ability of journalists and others to uncover and publicize wrongdoing, and to pursue the alleged wrongdoers. The extra scope of the interference with investigative journalism, and the reasons which prompted the extension, can be seen from the two cases in which it has so far been discussed.

In *Attorney-General* v. *News Group Newspapers plc*,[69] a newspaper, the *Sun*, had launched a campaign seeking the prosecution of a doctor who, it was alleged, had raped an 8-year-old girl who had been staying with his family at the time. The county prosecuting solicitor, acting on counsel's advice, and the Director of Public Prosecutions, both decided that there was insufficient evidence to prosecute. The newspaper decided to try to bring the suspected man to justice, and agreed with the girl's mother to give financial support for a private prosecution. This was widely publicized. In addition, after Geoffrey Dickens MP had named the doctor in the House of Commons under cover of parliamentary privilege, the newspaper published the doctor's name, and also published interviews with the girl's relations accusing the doctor of being 'a beast and a swine', and printing statements from potential witnesses which seemed to incriminate the doctor and prejudge the issues in any forthcoming prosecution. Up to this time, no proceedings were active within the meaning of the Contempt of Court Act 1981. Seven weeks later, a private prosecution was commenced against the doctor when an information was laid. In due course, the doctor was acquitted at trial.

After the acquittal, the Attorney-General brought proceedings for contempt of court against the owners of the *Sun*, News Group Newspapers plc. For the Attorney-General, it was argued that a person could be liable for common-law contempt not only when proceedings were 'pending' (i.e. had already been commenced) but also when they were 'imminent' (i.e. before they had been commenced).[70] This was because '[i]t is possible very effectually to poison the fountain of justice before it begins to flow'.[71] Although at the time of the publications no proceedings were pending, it was argued that they were 'imminent', because the publishers intended that the private prosecution should be commenced as soon as possible, and were actively pursuing that goal. The Divisional Court

[68] *A.-G.* v. *Times Newspapers Ltd*. [1974] AC 273, [1973] 3 All ER 54, HL; *A.-G.* v. *Hislop* [1991] 1 All ER 911, CA.
[69] [1989] QB 110, [1988] 2 All ER 906, DC.
[70] Lowe, *Borrie and Lowe'*, 2nd edn., pp. 162–3.
[71] *R.* v. *Parke* [1903] 2 K.B. 432 at p. 438 *per* Wills J.

accepted this argument.[72] Although 'imminence' is a vague and uncertain term, it applies when there is 'a likelihood or a real risk that they will be instituted in the near future and when there is a real risk that the kind of publication as here would interfere with the course of justice'.[73] On this basis, contempt liability for intentionally prejudicing or impeding the course of justice might apply to publications about a suspect during the progress of a police investigation or a manhunt, unless there was likely to be a long delay before trial to mitigate the risk of prejudice.[74]

But counsel for the Attorney-General went further. He argued, and the Divisional Court accepted,[75] that there was no authority precluding liability for contempt even before proceedings are imminent. The overriding principle is that the administration of justice must be protected. This may require punishment of acts occurring after the conclusion of proceedings, as where someone seeks to penalize a witness for having given evidence,[76] and may equally require sanctions to be imposed in respect of conduct occurring before proceedings are imminent.[77]

The apparent width of this restriction on press freedom is somewhat modified by the meaning given to 'intention' for the purpose of the common law offence: a publisher would not be liable unless he knew that proceedings were likely to follow soon enough to make prejudice likely, and intended that to happen. Nevertheless, the extension of liability was challenged in a subsequent case, *Attorney-General* v. *Sport Newspapers Ltd.*,[78] and divided the judges. Here, the police were trying to trace a 15-year-old girl who had disappeared. They issued to the press a description of a man whom they wanted to contact. The editor of The *Sport* published a front-page story describing the man as a vicious rapist and sex monster, revealing previous convictions for rape and indecent assault. In due course the suspect was arrested, charged, and convicted of murder. Subsequently the Attorney-General brought contempt proceedings against the publishers. The Divisional Court held that the editor and publishers had not had the necessary intention to prejudice or impede the course of justice. However, the judges also expressed views about the period of time affected by the common law of contempt.

Bingham LJ accepted that the *News Group Newspapers* case had marked a novel extension of liability for contempt beyond the time when

---

[72] [1989] QB at p. 135, [1988] 2 All ER at p. 921.

[73] *A.-G.* v. *News Group Newspapers plc* [1989] QB 110 at p. 132, [1988] 2 All ER 906 at p. 919 *per* Watkins LJ.

[74] Lowe, *Borrie and Lowe*', 2nd edn., 167–8.

[75] [1989] QB at pp. 132–5, [1988] 2 All ER at pp. 919–21.

[76] *A.-G.* v. *Butterworth* [1963] 1 QB 696, [1962] 3 All ER 326, CA.

[77] Ibid., at pp. 725, 332 respectively *per* Donovan LJ.

[78] [1991] 1 WLR 1194, [1992] 1 All ER 503, DC.

proceedings were pending or imminent. He recognized that this made the ambit of the contempt power wider in England and Wales than in Scotland or Australia, where it is limited to preventing prejudice following the commencement of proceedings by arrest or charge.[79] However, he felt that it would be wrong to depart from such a clear and recent decision. By contrast, Hodgson J. was impressed by the difficulties which the decision posed for investigative journalists who publish damning information about malefactors, in the hope that legal action will be taken to stop them in the public interest. In such circumstances, legal proceedings would be contemplated, and the journalist, editor, or publisher might well be liable to committal for contempt. This position would tolerable only if the law were regularly not enforced. He felt that prosecutions for perverting the course of justice would suffice to deal with the most serious cases, and the law of contempt ought not to be extended to cases where a charge of perverting the course of justice would be inappropriate. Accordingly, he would have declined to follow the *News Group Newspapers* decision had it been necessary to do so.

It is submitted that the law of contempt ought not to be extended in ways which make its scope more uncertain than it already is, or which subject people to the risk of committal for contempt by prejudicing proceedings when they do not know whether or when those proceedings are likely to follow. However, as long as the offence is one of specific intent, the need for intention rather than recklessness will limit liability to cases where the likelihood of proceedings is known to the alleged contemnor. Where, as in Hodgson J.'s example, an investigative journalist hopes that the revelations in an article or broadcast will precipitate the commencement of proceedings, but does not himself intend to commence them, it is submitted that the requisite *mens rea* would not be present. Alternatively, the prospect of proceedings would be so speculative at the time of publication that the *actus reus*, involving likelihood of prejudice, would not be made out. It will behove journalists to check on whether proceedings are contemplated before they publish, but, if none are contemplated, the journalist need not normally be deterred by worries about contempt liability, even under the extended *News Group Newspapers* test. For the same reasons, it would seem that this extension to the law of contempt, while an interference with freedom of expression under Article 10(1) of the European Convention on Human Rights, would be justifiable as being prescribed by law and necessary in a democratic society for the maintenance of the authority of the judiciary and the protection of the rights of litigants, under Article 10(2).

---

[79] *James* v. *Robinson* (1963) 109 CLR 593, HC of Aust.; *Hall* v. *Associated Newspapers Ltd.* 1979 JC 1, High Ct. of Justiciary.

Reform by statute would be welcome. The Phillimore Committee on Contempt of Court and the Law Commission both recommended that this head of contempt should be replaced by statutory offences to penalize only those interferences which take the form of violence, threats of violence, blackmail, or bribery.[80] This would make it clearer what type of tactical behaviour is impermissible in relation to an opponent in litigation. In doing so, it would remove a certain amount of uncertainty as to the types of behaviour which constitute contempt, and relieve the danger that people might be liable for behaving towards each other in ways which would normally be lawful but which become unlawful because of the circumstance that one of them is a party in active litigation. However, as yet, no action has been taken on the Law Commission's recommendations.

(5) Contempt by prejudgment

One of the major considerations in this area is that people who are parties to litigation of any sort should be entitled both to have the matters in issue decided by the court, and to have the decision of the court accepted as final. Any action which prevents people from having their day in court, or interferes with the fairness of the proceedings by way of pre-trial publicity, or creates widespread public prejudice against a party, may be a contempt of court, and it is important for journalists, broadcasters, and publishers to moderate their reporting to take account of this. The law of contempt thus tempers press freedom to a significant degree.

At common law, a comment which prejudged the result of a trial or hearing, or which created a real risk that the course or result of civil or criminal proceedings would be impeded or prejudiced, was a strict liability form of contempt. It was not necessary to show that the contemnor intended to prejudice the proceedings, nor was it necessary for the comment to be widely disseminated (although, as a matter of fact, it was usually the media which were prosecuted for this offence). The sensitivity of the courts to any attempt to prejudge matters was shown by *Attorney General* v. *Times Newspapers Ltd.*[81] In that case, people who had been born suffering from physical deformities, allegedly as a result of their mothers having consumed a drug, Thalidomide, for morning sickness during pregnancy, sued the manufacturers, Distillers, for compensation. The preparation for the litigation dragged on over many years, and, in an apparent attempt to build up public pressure on Distillers to settle, the *Sunday Times* ran an article which examined the evidence and effectively

[80] *Report on Contempt of Court*; Law Commission, *Interference with the Course of Justice.*
[81] [1974] AC 273, [1973] 3 All ER 54, HL.

concluded that the drug had caused the deformities and that Distillers had been negligent in marketing it. This was held by the House of Lords to amount to contempt by prejudging the issues which the court would have had to deal with. There was no real likelihood of the judges being biased as a result of reading the article, but the prejudgment rule was designed to uphold the authority of the court and prevent trial by media, irrespective of any actual bias.

The prejudgment test was heavily criticized by the Phillimore Committee on Contempt of Court, on the ground that, while it is desirable to prevent trial by media, judicious comment and expressions of opinion are not in a watertight category and shade into prejudgment, especially when the person expressing the opinion is regarded by readers as authoritative or the views (however tentative) are expressed persuasively. The line drawn by the majority of the House of Lords, between balanced comment which is permissible and prejudgment which is not, was therefore hard to draw, and was an unsatisfactory basis for an offence of strict liability which imposed a substantial limitation on freedom of expression and freedom of the press.[82] The matter was the subject of an application to the European Commission of Human Rights, and eventually came before the European Court of Human Rights.[83] The Court held that the law of contempt represented a restriction on freedom of expression guaranteed under Article 10(1) of the European Convention on Human Rights. The Court went on to consider whether the restriction could be justified under Article 10(2). It decided that the restriction was imposed for a legitimate purpose and was 'prescribed by law', because the prejudgment rule applied by the House of Lords had been known about beforehand. While its precise scope had not been entirely clear, any rule of law has a 'penumbra of doubt' surrounding its 'core of certainty',[84] and the prejudgment rule was not unreasonably uncertain for a common-law rule. Nevertheless, the Court decided by a narrow majority (eleven judges to nine) that the restriction was not justified under Article 10(2), because it went further than was 'necessary in a democratic society . . . for maintaining the authority and impartiality of the judiciary'. Although a state has to be allowed some discretion in deciding what is necessary for a given purpose in its form of democratic society,

---

[82] *Report on Contempt of Court*, para. 111. The Committee proposed that strict liability should be imposed only where a publication creates a risk that the course of justice would be seriously impeded or prejudiced. This formed the basis of section 2(2) of the Contempt of Court Act 1981, with the additional requirement that the risk should be 'substantial'.

[83] *Sunday Times* case, Eur. Ct. of HR, Series A, vol. 30, Judgment of 26 Apr. 1979; (1979) 2 EHRR 245.

[84] H. L. A. Hart, *The Concept of Law* (Oxford: Clarendon Press, 1961), 119.

this so-called 'margin of appreciation' is not unlimited. A rule which protects the authority of the judiciary is justifiable, but the prejudgment rule was a disproportionate interference with freedom of expression, because the House of Lords had held that it prohibited publication of an article which, on the facts, was expressed in moderate terms, gave a balanced account of the evidence and arguments, and was on a matter of undisputed public concern. The principle of freedom of expression is subject to exceptions, but these rest, on the whole, on public interests rather than matters of principle, and must be interpreted narrowly. Such an interference could not, in the Court's view, be seen as necessary in a democratic society.

(6) Strict liability for contempt: the Contempt of Court Act 1981

The decision of the European Court of Human Rights in the *Sunday Times case* was one of the important spurs to legislative reform. The Contempt of Court Act 1981 limited the applicability of strict liability for contempt of court to 'publications'[85] addressed to the public or a section of the public.[86] These publications are contempts for the purposes of the strict-liability rule only if proceedings are active at the time of publication,[87] and the publication creates a substantial risk that the course of

---

[85] '. . . for this purpose "publication" includes any speech, writing, broadcast, [cable programme] or other communication in whatever form, which is addressed to the public at large or any section of the public'. Contempt of Court Act 1981, s. 2(1); words in brackets added by Cable and Broadcasting Act 1984, Sch. 5, para. 39(1). Although the word 'includes' makes it possible that this is not an exhaustive definition of 'publication', the context makes it reasonably clear that it is intended to mark the outer limits of the meaning of the term, and is comprehensive and exhaustive: *Secretary of State for Defence* v. *Guardian Newspapers Ltd.* [1985] AC 339 at p. 348, [1984] 3 All ER 601 at p. 606, HL, per Lord Diplock. The intention is, as the Phillimore Committee recommended (*Report*, para. 77), to ensure so far as possible that the strict liability offence is limited to those in the business of publishing, with appropriate safeguards, and that other people are liable in contempt for what they say and do only if their conduct is deliberately prejudicial or obstructive: see C. J. Miller, *Contempt of Court*, 2nd edn. (Oxford: Clarendon Press, 1989), 143–4.

[86] The possibility of contempt by publication to a section of the public was a dilution of the Phillimore Committee's recommendation, but seems justified in the light of the risk of prejudice by press conference. It would, for example, very properly have made possible contempt proceedings for what Miller, *Contempt of Court*, 174, calls 'the extraordinary behaviour of the police in calling a congratulatory news conference' after the arrest of Peter Sutcliffe, the 'Yorkshire Ripper', in 1981. No action was taken, but both the officers concerned and vitually the whole newspaper industry could have been liable for the intense prejudice caused to Sutcliffe's chance of a fair trial. See the Press Council report on the affair, *Conduct in the Sutcliffe Case* (London: Press Council, 1983).

[87] Contempt of Court Act 1981, s. 2(3).

justice in the proceedings in question will be seriously impeded or preju-diced.[88]

(7) When are proceedings active?

The times when proceedings are 'active' are defined in Schedule 1 to the Act. First-instance criminal proceedings are active from the earliest moment when an initial step is taken.[89] The initial steps are: arrest with-out warrant; the issue (grant in Scotland) of a warrant for arrest; the issue of a summons to appear, or, in Scotland, the grant of a warrant to cite; the service of an indictment or other document specifying the charge; and an oral charge (except in Scotland).[90] The proceedings remain active until criminal proceedings are concluded by: acquittal or sentence; any other verdict, finding, order, or decision (such as a finding of no case to answer, or a decision that the prosecution amounts to an abuse of process) which puts an end to them; discontinuance by the prosecution;[91] or operation of law, as where twelve months elapse after the issue of an arrest warrant without an arrest being made,[92] or a time limit for prose-cution expires.[93] One implication of this is that public discussion of a person's involvement in high-profile suspected wrongdoing may be cur-tailed where anyone is arrested for an offence in connection with the matter, even if the arrestee is subsequently released on bail and no crimi-nal proceedings are ever brought.

First-instance civil proceedings become active from the time when arrangements for the hearing are made (in England and Wales, when the case is set down for trial if provision is made for this under Rules of the Supreme Court, or, in other cases, when the date for the trial or hearing is fixed), or (where no previous arrangements have been made) when the hearing begins.[94] They remain active until they are disposed of, discon-tinued, or withdrawn.[95] Appellate proceedings (which include applica-tions for judicial review)[96] are active (where leave is required) from the

---

[88] Contempt of Court Act 1981, s. 2(2).   [89] Ibid., s. 2(4) and Sch. 1, para. 3.

[90] Ibid., Sch. 1, para. 4.

[91] This may be effected by withdrawal of the charge or by entering a *nolle prosequi*; by discontinuance under the Prosecution of Offences Act 1985, s. 23; by express abandon-ment or being deserted *simpliciter* (in Scotland); or (in England, Wales, and Northern Ireland) where proceedings are commenced by arrest without warrant, by releasing the person, without charge, otherwise than on bail. See Contempt of Court Act 1981, Sch. 1, para. 7, as amended by Prosecution of Offences Act 1985, Sch. 1, para. 4.

[92] Contempt of Court Act 1981, Sch. 1, para. 11.   [93] Ibid., Sch. 1, para. 5.

[94] Ibid., Sch. 1, paras. 12, 13. For Scotland, see para. 14.

[95] Ibid., Sch. 1, para. 12, which also provides that each interlocutory hearing and (in the County Court) pre-trial review is to be treated as a separate proceeding for this pur-pose.

[96] Ibid., Sch. 1, para. 2.

time of the application for leave to appeal or apply for review. Where no leave is required, they are active from the moment when notice of appeal or of an application for review is given, or when the originating process is commenced (for example, an originating summons or writ). The proceedings remain active until they are disposed of, abandoned, discontinued, or withdrawn.[97] Where, in criminal proceedings, an appeal results in the case being remitted to the court below, or in a new trial or *venire de novo* being ordered, the further proceedings are treated as active from the moment the appellate proceedings conclude.[98]

(8) When is there a substantial risk that the proceedings in question will be seriously impeded or prejudiced?

The scope of the strict liability offence under section 2 of the Contempt of Court Act 1981 is not self-evident. The terms in which the section is couched are vague, and may be interpreted either expansively or narrowly. The most authoritative guidance was provided when the section was considered by the House of Lords in *Attorney-General* v. *English*.[99] The defendants were the editor and owners of the *Daily Mail*, which had published an article by Mr Malcolm Muggeridge endorsing the position of a handicapped, pro-life parliamentary candidate who opposed action (or inaction) by doctors and nurses to allow certain handicapped babies to die if they judged that the babies' lives would be intolerable in the event of survival. In the course of the article, Mr Muggeridge had asserted that it would be very unlikely that a baby without arms (such as the candidate had been) would have been allowed to survive today: 'Someone would surely have recommended letting her die of starvation, or otherwise disposing of her.' Unfortunately for all concerned, the article was published during the trial of Dr Leonard Arthur, a consultant paediatrician, for the alleged murder of a Down's syndrome baby under just such circumstances.[100] The trial was attracting wide publicity, and the article was widely discussed. Although the article did not refer to Dr Arthur or the trial, the Attorney-General took the view that it might have prejudiced Dr Arthur's chance of a fair trial. When the trial was over (Dr Arthur was acquitted), the Attorney-General brought contempt proceedings against the newspaper's editor and owners. It was accepted that they had not

[97] Ibid., Sch. 1, para. 15.
[98] Ibid., Sch. 1, para. 16. The same applies in Scotland where the appellate court grants authority to bring a new prosecution: *ibid.*
[99] [1983] 1 AC 116, [1982] 2 All ER 903, HL.
[100] For discussion, see Ian Kennedy, *Treat Me Right: Essays in Medical Law and Ethics*, (Oxford: Clarendon Press, 1991), 154–74; above, Ch. 3.

intended to prejudice the trial, but counsel for the Attorney-General relied on the strict liability rule under section 2 of the 1981 Act.

The Divisional Court held that the publication had been a contempt, and the defendants appealed to the House of Lords. Lord Diplock, with whom the other Law Lords concurred, agreed with the Divisional Court that the article fell within the terms of section 2(2), although he went on to hold that the publication was protected under section 5 (see below). The fact that Dr Arthur had subsequently been acquitted was irrelevant, because the risk is to be assessed at the time when the publication occurred, in order to deter any prejudicial publication, rather than with the benefit of hindsight. Nevertheless, the approach taken in by Lord Diplock to the meaning of section 2(2) suggested that it would not have a particularly liberalizing effect on the law of contempt. Lord Diplock held that the adjective 'substantial', when applied (somewhat inappropriately) to the noun 'risk', serves only to exclude remote risks. It does not provide any more demanding measure of the seriousness of the risk involved.[101] Lord Diplock declined to paraphrase serious impediment or prejudice to the course of justice in the proceedings, for the purpose of interpreting section 2(2). The word 'serious', he pointed out, refers to the impediment or prejudice, not to the degree of risk. One has to look at the possible consequences of the publication. If it might lead to the outcome of the trial being influenced, or to the jury being discharged,[102] it would be a serious impediment or prejudice. On this view, the widely quoted statement by the (then) Secretary of State for Northern Ireland, during the trial of three alleged terrorist plotters (the 'Winchester Three') who had exercised the right to remain silent under questioning, that the right to silence was to be restricted in Northern Ireland because only those with no innocent explanation need to make use of the right, might have amounted to a strict-liability contempt under section 2. The three were convicted, but their convictions were later quashed on appeal because of the possible influence of the statement on the jury.[103] However, as the Secretary of State was speaking in the course of his duties, proposing a change in the law in Northern Ireland, the prosecution would probably have failed to discharge the burden imposed by section 5 of the Act of showing that the publication was not a discussion in good faith of public affairs or other matters of public interest, or that the risk of impediment or prejudice to the proceedings was more than merely incidental to such a discussion (see section 9 below).

---

[101] [1983] 1 AC at p. 142, [1982] 2 All ER at pp. 918–19.

[102] It does not matter that the trial actually continued. The question is whether there was a substantial risk of it being retarded, slowed down, delayed or hindered: *A.-G.* v. *BBC*, *Independent*, 3 Jan. 1992, DC.

[103] *R.* v. *McCann* (1990) 92 Cr. App. R. 239, CA.

However, in the light of subsequent decisions it would be wrong to dismiss the 'substantial risk' and 'serious impediment or prejudice' requirements as insignificant hurdles for the prosecution under section 2(2). As early as 1983, there were signs that lower courts were treating the subsection as imposing a stringent test to be satisfied before strict liability could be imposed for contempt.[104] If the court is prepared to credit jurors with reasonable independence of mind and judgment, a prejudicial publication may not create a substantial risk of prejudice. Neither the inaccuracy of a statement in a newpaper, nor the fact that it might be a libel on a party to proceedings, will necessarily give rise to a substantial risk of serious prejudice if one believes that jurors, magistrates, or judges have the sophistication to recognize that much of what is printed in newspapers is unreliable.[105] Furthermore, the longer a time lag there is between the publication and the trial, the less substantial the risk is likely to be.[106] Not only must the risk be substantial; that risk must also relate to serious impediment or prejudice in order to discharge the burden of establishing liability under section 2(2). As Lord Donaldson MR has said:[107]

. . . 'substantial' as a qualification of 'risk' does not have the meaning of 'weighty', but rather means 'not insubstantial' or 'not minimal'. The 'risk' part of the test will usually be of importance in the context of the width of the publication. To declare in a speech at a public meeting in Cornwall that a man about to be tried in Durham is guilty of the offence charged and has many previous convictions for the same offence may well carry no substantial risk of affecting his trial, but, if it occurred, the prejudice would be most serious. By contrast, a nationwide television broadcast at peak viewing time of some far more innocuous statement would certainly involve a substantial risk of having some effect on a trial anywhere in the country and the sole effective question would arise under

[104] See Lowe, Borrie and Lowe, 2nd edn., p. 122.
[105] A.-G. v. Times Newspapers Ltd. and others, The Times, 12 Feb. 1983, DC. See further Lowe, Borrie and Lowe's Law of Contempt, 2nd edn., 121–2; S. H. Bailey, D. J. Harris, and B. L. Jones, Civil Liberties Cases and Materials, 3rd edn. (London: Butterworths, 1991), 353–5. For a similar view before the 1981 Act, see R. v. Kray (1969) 53 Cr. App. R. 412 at p. 414 per Lawton J. However, in A.-G. v. BBC, Independent, 3 Jan. 1992, DC, the fact that a news report concerning a trial was 'literally strewn with error' seems to have disposed the court towards holding it to be a contempt, although technically the accuracy or otherwise of the report is irrelevant to s. 2, being relevant only to the defence under s. 4(1) once it has been decided that the publication is caught by the strict-liability rule under s. 2. Are judges' expectations of the BBC so high that they are disappointed when its reporters prove to have feet of clay? Probably not.
[106] A.-G. v. News Group Newpapers Ltd. [1987] QB 1, [1986] 2 All ER 833, CA (repetition of allegations subject of libel action not within s. 2 of the 1981 Act where there would be a delay of at least ten months between republication and trial).
[107] A.-G. v. News Group Newspapers Ltd. [1987] QB 1 at p. 15, [1986] 2 All ER 833 at p. 841, CA.

the 'seriousness' limb of the test. Proximity in time between the publication and the proceedings would probably have a greater bearing on the risk limb than on the seriousness limb, but could go to both.

This makes it clear the the provisions of section 2(2) limit the scope of the old, common-law, strict liability rule as expounded in the *Times Newspapers* case in a more than cosmetic way: the fact that a publication prejudges or prejudices the merits of a case will not of itself make the publisher liable, unless either the publication gives rise to a substantial risk of serious prejudice or impediment to the course of justice in the proceedings (the statutory strict liability offence), or the publisher was deliberately interfering with the course of justice, for example by threatening witnesses or a party (the common-law offence, demanding *mens rea*).

Furthermore, in the *Times Newspapers* case the Law Lords had differed (*obiter*) as to whether it would be a contempt for a person to hold a litigant up to public obloquy or to exert pressure on a party to litigation to settle or not to insist on enforcing his or her full legal rights. The House of Lords had discussed, *obiter*, an earlier article in the *Sunday Times*, which had not been the subject of proceedings, in which Distillers, the defendant company, had been criticized for the way in which it was contesting the litigation, and which implied that this was a case in which the company should refrain from insisting on its strict legal rights. Two members of the House (Lords Diplock and Simon of Glaisdale) had thought that a person who put a party (in that case, the defendant company) under any pressure, or held it up to public obloquy, to dissuade it from exercising its constitutional right to have the allegations against it decided by a judge, was guilty of contempt. The view that litigation concerns only the parties, and other people should not be permitted to exert their economic or other power in an attempt to support one party, has a long history. It dates back to attempts between the thirteenth and the sixteenth centuries to control the mischief of maintenance, which threatened to undermine the enforcement of the common law.[108]

However, Lord Reid had taken the view that it was perfectly proper for people to use their economic power for moral purposes:[109]

Why would it be contrary to public policy to seek by fair comment to dissuade Shylock from proceeding with his action? Surely it could not be wrong for the officious bystander to draw his attention to the risk that, if he goes on, decent people will cease to trade with him. Or suppose that his best customer ceased to trade with him when he heard of his lawsuit. That could not be contempt of

---

[108] King Henry VII gave his new court, the Court of Star Chamber, jurisdiction over maintenance cases in 1487 (3 H. VII, c. 1), and is usually credited with eradicating maintenance through the Statute of Liveries 1504 (19 H. VII, c. 14), although Henry VIII again found it necessary to prohibit the practice in an Act of 1540 (32 H. VIII, c. 9, s. 3).

[109] [1974] AC 273 at pp. 295–6, [1973] 3 All ER 54 at p. 61.

court. Would it become contempt if, when asked by Shylock why he was sending no more business his way, he told him the reason? Nothing would be more likely to influence Shylock to discontinue his action. It might become widely known that such pressure was being brought to bear. Would that make any difference? And though widely known must the local press keep silent about it?

This series of rhetorical questions highlights the difficulty of finding a principle which prohibits illegitimate use of economic or moral power for personal gain, while excluding from liability those activities which would normally be regarded as permissible if not morally laudable. Lord Reid had taken the view that fair and temperate criticism of a party was permissible, although unfair or intemperate criticism would be a contempt.[110] On this basis, Lords Reid and Cross of Chelsea decided that the article which consisted of a fair and balanced account of the evidence would not have been a contempt.[111] On the other hand, for Lords Diplock and Simon, fair and temperate criticism of a party might have the effect of holding it up to public obloquy, and so constitute a strict-liability contempt.

In this uncertain state of divided opinions the law remained for some time.[112] Under the Contempt of Court Act 1981, however, it is clear that strict liability will attach to such a publication only in limited circumstances. In particular, a comment which is not made to the public or a section of the public will not attract strict liability, and will be a contempt only if intended to impede or prejudice the administration of justice;[113] while, since prejudging the result of a case attracts strict liability only if there is a substantial risk that the course of justice will be seriously impeded or prejudiced, the scope of the prejudgment rule will be far narrower in relation to proceedings before judges than in those before magistrates, juries, or (perhaps) tribunals with lay members.

(9) The 'discussion of public affairs' and 'fair report of legal proceedings' exceptions to the strict liability offence

Section 5 of the Act provides that a discussion in good faith of public affairs or other matters of public interest is not subject to the strict-liability rule if the risk of impediment or prejudice to active legal proceedings is merely incidental to the discussion.[114] As noted above, the House of Lords in *Attorney-General* v. *English* held that the publication of

---

[110] [1974] AC at p. 297-8. [111] See [1974] AC at p. 326 *per* Lord Cross.
[112] Nigel Lowe argues that Lord Morris, though more ambivalent than Lords Reid and Cross, was of their view: *Borrie and Lowe*, 2nd edn., p. 147. For analysis of the differences between their approach and that of Lords Diplock and Simon, see ibid., 146–9.
[113] Contempt of Court Act 1981, s. 6.
[114] Ibid., s. 5.

Mr Malcolm Muggeridge's article on the treatment of handicapped babies fell within section 2(2) of the Act, but exempted the publishers from strict liability because of the effect of section 5. In *English*, it was not disputed that the article had been published in good faith as a contribution to a continuing public debate on a matter of general public interest, namely the morality of mercy killing, and the treatment of hopelessly handicapped neonates in particular. Lord Diplock therefore held that it was for the Attorney-General to show that the risk of prejudice to Dr Arthur's trial which resulted from publication had not been 'merely incidental' to the discussion. The Divisional Court had treated certain parts of the article as unnecessary to the argument, and as casting imputations on doctors generally. However, as Lord Diplock said, the test is whether the risk of prejudice was merely incidental to the discussion, not whether the article could have been written without the potentially prejudicial parts. He contrasted the article with the articles on Thalidomide which had been in issue in the *Times Newspapers* case. The Thalidomide articles had been directed to the litigation against Distillers, but Mr. Muggeridge's article had made no mention of Dr Arthur's trial. Some risk of prejudice to the trial was probably incidental to any meaningful discussion of the pro-life candidate's election programme, and the risk which materialized was, on the facts, properly to be regarded as 'merely incidental' to it.[115] Lord Diplock appears to be balancing a fairly wide interpretation of section 2(2) with a relatively stringent standard which the prosecution must discharge under section 5, but there are clear limits to the scope of the section 5 exception. The main one is that an article or programme which sets out to expose the behaviour of a particular person, who is a party to active proceedings, will constitute a strict-liability contempt, as the prejudice will (as in the *Times Newspapers* case concerning Distillers) be the direct result of the main thrust of the article, rather than an incidental effect of a discussion of some other matter of general public importance.[116]

A similarly liberal interpretation of section 5 is evident in *Attorney-General* v. *Times Newspapers and others*.[117] This was a series of proceedings for contempt against different newspapers for their reporting of and commenting on the case of Michael Fagan, who was arrested for intruding into the Queen's bedroom in Buckingham Palace. In proceedings against The *Mail on Sunday*, which before Mr Fagan's trial had published an article by Lady Falkender casting seriously prejudicial slurs on the defendant's character and alleged a homosexual liaison between Mr Fagan and a member of the Queen's bodyguard, it was held that the article satisfied the test in section 2(2), but was exempted from strict liability by section

---

[115] [1983] 1 AC at pp. 143–4, [1982] 2 All ER at pp. 919–20.
[116] *A.-G.* v. *TVS Television Ltd.*, *The Times*, 7 July 1989, DC.
[117] *The Times*, 12 Feb. 1983, DC.

5. This was said to be because the article formed part of the discussion of the Queen's safety, a matter of legitimate public concern. This sensitivity towards freedom of public discussion on matters of public interest contrasts markedly with the attitude of the courts in certain other cases (notably the *Spycatcher* cases, considered in Chapter 14). It is not easy to resist the suspicion that the press are freer to 'discuss' parties to litigation who do not enjoy the sympathy of the courts than they are to 'discuss' the affairs of those parties who are regarded as more 'respectable' (for want of a better adjective).

The Act provides a further exception in section 4, which exempts from strict liability all fair and accurate reports, in good faith, of legal proceedings held in public, although the court in question may in certain circumstances order that publication be postponed, or that certain details exempt from disclosure in court be not published.[118] The section 4 exception mirrors one which was previously available at common law.

(10) Ignorance as a defence under the 1981 Act

In addition to the above elements which the prosecution must establish in order to bring home strict liability on a publisher, the Act provides for one defence in regard to which the burden of proof lies on the defendant. The publisher or distributor is not strictly liable if, having taken all reasonable care, he or she does not know and has no reason to suspect that proceedings are active, or that the publication contains the sort of material which might give rise to strict liability under section 2.[119]

16.2 ORDERS RESTRICTING OR POSTPONING REPORTING

Generally speaking, in the light of the public interest in open justice,[120] trials are open and anyone may observe them and report on them. Magistrates, judges, and jurors, sitting in public, are not entitled to adopt a practice of keeping their names secret for the purposes of preserving their privacy.[121] They perform a public function, and it is a valuable check on their behaviour that their identities should be known. However, there are limits to the principle of openness where justice cannot be done effectively in public.[122] This leads to a number of restrictions on freedom to report court proceedings, which include:

(a) restrictions on reporting certain cases heard in private;

[118] Contempt of Court Act 1981, ss. 4, 11. See below, s. 2(2)(iii) and (iv).
[119] Contempt of Court Act 1981, s. 3.   [120] *Scott* v. *Scott* [1913] AC 417, HL.
[121] *R.* v. *Felixstowe Justices, ex parte Leigh* [1987] QB 582, [1987] 1 All ER 551, DC.
[122] *Scott* v. *Scott* (see n. 120).

(b) orders postponing the reporting of matter which might prejudice the fairness of proceedings;

(c) restrictions on reporting names in cases involving children, rape trials, and blackmail cases;

(d) restrictions on reporting material disclosed on discovery.

Breaches of these orders or rules constitute criminal contempt of court and are punishable as such. In this section, the various heads will be examined in turn.

(1) Hearings in private

As part of their inherent power to regulate their own proceedings to ensure that justice can be done, all courts have a discretion to sit in private, but it should be exercised only in exceptional cases where justice could not be done while sitting in public.[123] For example, it would be ridiculous to expect the hearing of an application for an injunction to restrain a breach of confidence to be heard in open court where the effect would be to allow publication of the information which it is the purpose of the proceedings to keep confidential.[124] Some statutes expressly provide for matters to be dealt with in private. These include the Official Secrets Act 1920, section 8(4), and a range of family matters under the Matrimonial Causes Act 1973 and (in magistrates' courts' domestic-proceedings jurisdiction) the Magistrates' Courts Act 1980, section 69(4). However, where there is no mandatory, statutory requirement that proceedings be held in private, the discretion should be sparingly exercised. The effect of excluding the public, including journalists, goes beyond a restriction of the public interest in freedom of information and expression on matters of public interest. It represents a move away from the ideal of justice being administered under public scrutiny. Because of this, it is a course of last resort, and normally more restrained steps should be employed, such as allowing people to observe proceedings but making orders restricting publicity.

Generally, the courts are sensible of the importance of justice being seen to be done, and they will not permit privacy to be imposed merely to save witnesses or defendants the embarrassment of giving evidence as to intimate details of their private lives, if these are a necessary element in

---

[123] *Scott v. Scott* [1913] AC 417; *R. v. Chancellor of Chichester Consistory Court, ex parte News Group Newspapers Ltd., Independent,* 10 Sept. 1991, DC.; *R. v. Dover Justices, ex parte Dover District Council and another, Independent,* 21 Oct. 1991, DC.

[124] Law Commission, Report No. 110, *Breach of Confidence,* Cmnd. 8388 (London: HMSO, 1981), para. 4.110.

[125] *R. v. Chancellor of Chichester Consistory Court, ex part News Group Newspapers Ltd., Independent,* 10 Sept. 1991, DC, *per* Mann LJ.

the pursuit of justice.[125] However, a good deal of latitude is allowed to judges and magistrates as long as they direct themselves properly on the relevant principles of law. This, combined with the reluctance of reviewing courts to intervene as long as the first-instance judges or magistrates had some material on which to base their decision, sometimes fosters suspicions that the power is used by magistrates who sympathize with defendants, in order to spare them embarrassment, rather than in the interests of justice.[126] Sometimes it will be hard to distinguish between a desire to avoid embarrassment and the needs of justice. For example, it has been held that a judge is entitled to exclude the press where there is some indication (albeit not very substantial) that witnesses would be so distressed at having to discuss intimate details in public that they would be unable to give full evidence.[127] The question is whether exclusion of the press and public is necessary in the interests of justice.

When it comes to the reporting of cases heard in private, for reasons of justice, national security, or otherwise, the matter is governed by the Administration of Justice Act 1960, section 12. This provides that publishing information relating to proceedings before a court, judge, or tribunal sitting in private (including a hearing in camera or in chambers) is not, in itself, to be a contempt of court save in specified cases.[128] The cases in which it will be a contempt of court to publish any information about the proceedings are:[129]

(a) where proceedings relate to the wardship or adoption of an infant, or relate wholly or mainly to the guardianship, custody, maintenance or upbringing of, or access to, an infant;

(b) where proceedings are brought under what is now Part VII of the Mental Health Act 1983, whereby judges deal with matters which previously came within the judges in lunacy acting on behalf of the Crown as *parens patriae*, or under any provision of the Mental Health Act 1983 authorizing an application or reference to be made to a mental health review tribunal or a county court;

(c) where the court sits in private for reasons of national security during that part of the proceedings about which the information is published;

---

[126] See e.g. *R. v. Reigate Justices, ex parte Argus Newspapers Ltd.* (1983) 147 JP 385, DC; *R. v. Malvern Justice, ex parte Evans* [1988] QB 540, [1988] 1 All ER 371, DC.

[127] *R. v. Chancellor of Chichester Consistory Court, ex parte News Group Newspapers Ltd.*, *Independent*, 10 Sept. 1991, DC.

[128] Administration of Justice Act 1960, s. 12(1), (3). On the meaning of 'court', see *P. v. Liverpool Daily Post and Echo Newspapers plc* [1991] 2 AC 370, [1991] 1 All ER 622, HL, discussed above. [129] Administration of Justice Act 1960, s. 12(1).

[130] *P. v. Liverpool Daily Post and Echo Newspapers plc* [1991] 2 AC 370 at p. 416, [1991] 1 All ER 622 at p. 629, *per* Lord Bridge.

(*d*) where the information relates to a secret process, discovery, or
invention which is in issue in the proceedings;

(*e*) where the court, acting within its powers, expressly prohibits the
publication of all information relating to the proceedings, or of
information of the particular description which is published.

The above provisions apply to information relating to the proceedings,
and make it prima facie a contempt to publish such information in those
circumstances,[130] although the section preserves any defences which a
person accused of contempt would normally have, so a breach of section
12(1) is not automatically and conclusively a contempt.[131] It has been
said, in relation to wardship proceedings, that 'information relating to
proceedings' in section 12 covers 'information which the person giving it
believes to be protected by the cloak of secrecy provided by the court.
"Proceedings" must include such matters as statements of evidence,
reports, accounts of interviews and such like, which are prepared for use
in court once the wardship proceedings have been properly set on
foot.'[132] The existence of the proceedings is therefore not secret.
Furthermore, it is permissible to publish the text of the judgment, or a
summary of the whole or part of it, unless the court, acting within its
powers, expressly prohibits such publication.[133] Thus not all information
about proceedings is information 'relating to' them for the purposes of
section 12. The test, as expressed rather imprecisely in the *Liverpool Daily
Post and Echo* case, is whether the information in question is 'within the
mischief which the cloak of privacy in relation to the substance of the
proceedings is designed to guard against', or 'information about the proceedings which ought to be kept secret'.[134] If the judge thinks that it is
appropriate to prevent publication of information which might not be

---

[131] Administration of Justice Act 1960, s. 12(4), as explained in *Re F. (a minor) (publication of information)* [1977] Fam. 58, [1977] 1 All ER 114, CA, at pp. 99, 130–1 respectively
per Scarman LJ, approved in *P. v. Liverpool Daily Post and Echo Newspapers plc,* [1991] 2
AC at p. 421, [1991] 1 All ER at p. 633, per Lord Bridge. Subs. (4) is not altogether
unambiguous, and an alternative interpretation (rejected in the above cases) would be that
the paragraphs (*a*)-(*e*) of subs. (1) provide an exhaustive list of the cases in which publication of information relating to proceedings is capable of being a contempt of court. See
Miller, *Contempt of Court,* 2nd edn., 349.

[132] *Re F. (a minor) (publication of information),* [1977] Fam. at p. 105, [1977] 1 All ER at
p. 135 *per* Geoffrey Lane LJ.

[133] Administration of Justice Act 1960, s. 12(2). This assumes that there is power in the
court to order that the judgment be not reported. The power may exist at common law,
but is probably limited to cases in which publishing the judgment would interfere with
interests of the sort set out in paragraphs (*a*) to (*d*) of subs (1). Where there is to be publication of the judgment in such cases, the names or other sensitive details may be disguised
to protect the anonymity of the vulnerable parties.

[134] *P. v. Liverpool Daily Post and Echo Newspapers plc* [1991] 2 AC at pp. 422–3, [1991] 1
All ER at p. 634, *per* Lord Bridge.

considered by an outsider to be private or to relate to the substance of the proceedings, the way to do it is to make an express prohibition, if the power to do so exists, so bringing the case within section 12(1)(e). Even where there is an embargo on publication of information, it is not necessarily permanent, as information may lose its confidential quality with the passage of time.[135] The implications of each paragraph (a) to (e) will now be considered.

Under paragraph (a), it follows from the above that publishing the fact that wardship proceedings are taking place, or have taken place, in respect of an identified minor, would not be a contempt. Nor is it a contempt to publish the name and address of a ward unless there has been an express order not to publish.[136] In deciding whether to grant an injunction restraining publication in cases going beyond the strict terms of section 12(1)(a), the High Court is exericising an inherent jurisdiction originating in the Crown's role as *parens patriae*. It has to strike a balance between protecting the ward's privacy and the right of free publication. Where there is such a contest between the interests of the child and the freedom of the press, the courts will hesitate to interfere with press freedom to publish. The courts have to weigh up the competing interests. In this balancing exercise, the guarantee of freedom of expression under Article 10 of the European Convention on Human Rights will be given substantial weight, and it follows that the welfare of the child is not the paramount consideration in this type of case, which concerns freedom of publication rather than matters directly related to the care of the child.[137] The privacy of the child will almost inevitably prevail where the publication relates to matters of the sort which fall within section 12(1)(a) of the 1960 Act, or the publication is merely pandering to the curiosity of the public. On the other hand, the freedom of the press is likely to prevail where the press is acting in the public interest, for example when it is publishing the results of an investigation into a matter affecting the public, or is informing the public about the way in which a local authority exercises its child-care powers. It will normally be possible to satisfy the public interest in favour of publication without identifying the ward to people other than those who already know the facts; any restriction on publication should be no wider than necessary in order to protect the

---

[135] *Re F. (a minor) (publication of information)* [1977] Fam. at p. 107, [1977] 1 All ER at p. 137, *per* Geoffrey Lane LJ.

[136] *Re L. (a minor) (wardship: fredom of publication)* [1988] 1 All ER 418, concerning a newspaper article, with photograph, about a minor, who had been made a ward of court, and the funeral of members of her family who had died in the ferry disaster at Zeebrugge; *Re W. (wardship: publication of information)* [1989] 1 FLR 246, concerning the publication of the names of children affected by the controversy surrounding the diagnosis of children as having suffered sexual abuse in Cleveland.

[137] *Re W. (a minor) (wardship: freedom of publication)* [1992] 1 All ER 794, CA.

ward from the risk of harassment.[138] If the proposed publication is likely to upset the ward but refers to relatives of the ward rather than the ward herself or wardship proceedings, it is unlikely that an injunction will be granted. People will not normally be spared embarrassment unrelated to their children merely because the children have been made wards of court.[139]

Where the balance requires it, an order may be made which allows some information to be published but requires other information to be suppressed where that is necessary for the ward's welfare. For example, it may be desirable to protect the ward against intrusion, as in *Re C. (a minor) (wardship: medical treatment) (No. 2)*,[140] concerning a ward whose medical condition and proposed treatment had been the subject of proceedings which had attracted a good deal of publicity.[141] Because the intrusions of the press could have adversely affected the quality of the care which the ward could be given, and might discourage parents of similarly placed minors from allowing their children to become wards of court, an injunction was granted prohibiting soliciting or publication of information identifying the ward, her parents, the hospital where she was being treated, or anyone concerned in her care, notwithstanding the fact that the ward's condition was such that she would not be personally conscious of any interference with her privacy. In the same way, in *Re M. and N. (minors) (wardship: freedom of publication)*[142] the Court of Appeal granted an injunction which, while allowing publication of information about the way in which the local-authority social services department had allegedly acted in taking two children into care, prohibited publication of information which might enable the children in the case to be identified. But if the court considers that the case raises a matter of genuine public interest, it will not grant an injunction restraining publication. Such a case arose in *Re W. (a minor) (wardship: freedom of publication)*,[143] where a local authority had placed a ward, who had previously suffered homosexual abuse, with a male homosexual couple as foster parents. The council's policy was said to raise public-interest questions which it would be proper for newspapers to ventilate, so long as care was taken as far as possible to avoid details which might identify the ward in question (and it was accepted that it might not be possible entirely to avoid this). On the

---

[138] *Re M. and N. (minors) (wardship: freedom of information)* [1990] Fam. 211, [1990] 1 All ER 205, CA; *Re W. (a minor) (wardship: freedom of publication)* [1992] 1 All ER 794, CA.
[139] *Re X. (a minor) (wardship: restriction of publication)* [1975] Fam. 47, [1975] 1 All ER 697. *Cp. X County Council* v. *A* [1984] 1 WLR 1422, [1985] 1 All ER 53.
[140] [1990] Fam. 39, [1989] 2 All ER 791, CA.
[141] *Re C. (a minor) (wardship: medical treatment)* [1990] Fam. 26, [1989] 2 All ER 782, CA, discussed in Ch. 3 above.
[142] [1991] Fam. 211, [1990] 1 All ER 205, CA.   [143] [1992] 1 All ER 794, CA.

other hand, a newspaper's private interest in contesting a libel action will not entitle it to have access to wardship files, where there is no wider public interest to protect.[144] Where an injunction is granted, it must be done in express terms, which must clearly identify the people who are bound by it,[145] the boundaries of the restraint,[146] and must be no wider than necessary in the circumstances to protect the welfare of the child.[147]

Under paragraph (b) it is permissible to publish the fact that the court or tribunal is sitting to hear an application from a named patient, because (according to the House of Lords in P. v. *Liverpool Daily Post and Echo Newspapers plc*)[148] it was the purpose of the legislation to protect the privacy of medical considerations, and the fact that a particular patient had (as in that case) applied to be released is not within the cloak of privacy protected by the Act. It followed in the *Liverpool Daily Post and Echo* case that the newspaper was also permitted to publish the result of the application, although not the tribunal's reasons, which would fall within the protected area of privacy.

Paragraphs (c) and (d) speak for themselves. Under paragraph (e), it remains a contempt to disobey an express *intra vires* order by the court or tribunal prohibiting the publication of all information relating to the proceedings (this term having the meaning explained above) or information of a particular description. The order must be express, and the description of the matters not to be published must be clear, as seen above in relation to paragraph (a).

(2) Restrictions on reporting information concerning hearings held in public

There are several restrictions which affect reporting of hearings held in public. Besides the provisions of the Judicial Proceedings (Regulation of Reports) Act 1926,[149] there are provisions which allow people to remain anonymous, and provisions permitting details of cases to be suppressed at certain stages in the litigation. The main ones are as follows.

(i) *Rape cases.* From the moment when she makes an allegation or complaint of rape, it is an offence to publish or broadcast matter likely to lead to the identification of the complainant, unless a judge of the Crown

---

[144] *Re X, Y, and Z (minors) (wardship: disclosure of documents)* [1992] 2 All ER 595.

[145] An order in respect of a ward can be made against the world, but will not bind those who have no notice of it: *X County Council* v. *A* [1984] 1 WLR 1422 at p. 1426, [1985] 1 All ER 53 at p. 56 *per* Balcombe J.; *Re L. (a minor) (wardship: freedom of publication)* [1988] 1 All ER 418 at p. 421 *per* Booth J.

[146] *Re L. (a minor) (wardship: freedom of publication)* [1988] 2 All ER at p. 423 *per* Booth J.

[147] *Re M. and another (minors) (wardship: freedom of publication)* [1990] Fam. at p. 225, [1990] 1 All ER 205 at p. 211 *per* Butler-Sloss LJ.

[148] [1991] 2 AC 370, [1991] 1 All ER 622, HL. [149] See Ch. 14, s. 4(8) above.

Court has made a direction expressly permitting such a publication or broadcast in the interests of the administration of justice, for example in order to encourage potential witnesses to come forward.[150] However, there is no similar provision to benefit complainants in cases of alleged indecent assault.

(ii) *Children*. Under the Children and Young Persons Act 1933, section 39(1) as amended, a court may, in any proceedings, direct that no media report of the proceedings 'shall reveal the name, address or school, or include any particulars calculated to lead to the identification, of any child' concerned in the proceedings as a party, witness, or subject of the proceedings. The court may also direct that no picture shall be published 'except in so far (if at all) as may be permitted by the direction of the court'. The order must be made in that form. It is not permissible for the court to identify the particulars which would be calculated to lead to the child's identification, apart from the name, address, or school of the child. They must be left to the good sense and caution of the journalists and editors.[151] Journalists therefore have to be aware of the risks involved in publishing details not covered by the order. If, for example, defendants charged with indecently assaulting a child are members of a small, closely knit community, publishing the names of the the defendants might well make the child identifiable. In such a case, the court often gives advice to the media, which is virtually always respected. But even if no advice is offered, Glidewell LJ has said:

If the inevitable effect of making an order is that it is apparent that some details, including for instance the names of defendants, may not be published because publication would breach the order, that is the practical application of the order: it is not a part of the terms of the order itself.[152]

Reporters and editors therefore need to exercise considerable care and judgement in deciding what features of a case may be reported when a court has made an order under section 39.

---

[150] Sexual Offences (Amendment) Act 1976, s. 4, as amended by Criminal Justice Act 1988, s. 158. The 1976 Act followed in the main the recommendations of the *Report of the Advisory Group on the Law of Rape*, Cmnd. 6352 (London: HMSO, 1975), chaired by Mrs. Justice Heilbron. The Act went further than the Report recommended, in extending anonymity to the accused as well as the complainant. The protection for the accused was withdrawn by the Criminal Justice Act 1988, s. 158. In New Zealand, courts assert a common law discretion to order that a defendant's name be not reported in a wide range of cases. For discussion, see Roderick Munday, 'Name Suppression: An Adjunct to the Presumption of Innocence and to Mitigation of Sentence' [1991] *Crim. LR* 680–8, 753–62.

[151] *R. v. Crown Court at Southwark, ex parte Godwin* [1991] 3 All ER 818, CA.

[152] Ibid. at p. 823.

When an order is made under section 39, it is open to a judge to discharge it. However, where one judge has made an order and another discharges it, the latter must give reasons for doing so, and the reasons are open to review by the High Court on an application for judicial review. Judges should bear in mind the harm to children which may result, so that a heavy responsibility is borne by a judge who withdraws the protection of an order. In *R. v. Crown Court at Leicester, ex parte S (a minor)*[153] the Divisional Court quashed a decision by a judge to revoke a section 39 order in respect of a 12-year-old boy who had pleaded guilty to arson. On the boy's first appearance before the Crown Court, the judge had made an order that he be not identified. A different judge, passing sentence later, decided to revoke the order because of 'exceptional circumstances', without saying what these circumstances were. This convinced the Divisional Court that the second judge had exercised his discretion without taking account of relevant matters, or that the decision to revoke the order was wholly unreasonable within the meaning of *Associated Provincial Picture Houses Ltd. v. Wednesbury Corporation.*[154]

(iii) *Other cases of anonymity for witnesses.* At common law, there is a power to order that witnesses should be given anonymity, being identified only by letter (e.g. 'Mr. Y'). This power is exercisable 'in the interest of furthering justice as a continuing process',[155] i.e. the wider interests of the civil and criminal process, apart from the need to do justice to the parties in the particular case. Examples of the use of the power include cases where it is necessary to protect victims of alleged blackmail, in order, first, to avoid a situation in which the stories which they had been paying to keep private would become public through the prosecution of the alleged blackmailer, and, secondly, to avoid discouraging other blackmail victims from seeking legal relief. In *R. v. Socialist Worker Printers and Publishers Ltd., ex parte Attorney-General*[156] the *Socialist Worker* newspaper published the names of two alleged blackmail victims who had been giving evidence against Miss Janie Jones, despite an order of the trial judge that the witnesses should be known as Mr Y and Mr Z. The editor of the newspaper, Mr Paul Foot, apparently felt that this was an example of tenderness towards members of the establishment rather than a genuine attempt to further the cause of justice. The publication of the names of the witnesses was held to be a contempt, being both an affront to the court's authority and an act likely to interfere with the course of justice by inhibiting balckmail victims from giving evidence in the future.

Another example of a case where a court might exercise the power to

---

[153] [1992] 2 All ER 659, DC.   [154] [1948] 1 KB 223, [1947] 2 All ER 680, CA.
[155] Miller, *Contempt of Court*, 2nd edn., 312, and generally 312–20.
[156] [1975] QB 637, [1975] 1 All ER 142, DC.

permit witnesses to remain anonymous, particularly in cases which involve sensitive security matters, is where the witness is a member of the security or intelligence services, and for reasons of national security or safety it would be contrary to the public interest to allow the name to be given. If anonymity were not ordered in such cases, the prosecution might well not call the witness. This could easily lead to the withdrawal or collapse of that prosecution, and a reluctance to prosecute in future cases where members of the security or intelligence service would have to give evidence.

There are limits to this power. It is fairly clear from the leading House of Lords decision that there must be an order or direction from the judge before publication of the name will be a contempt. A request will not suffice. What is more, even if there has been an order, it will not be a contempt to publish the name if the witness himself, in the course of evidence, gives away his identity or makes it possible to identify him. *Attorney-General* v. *Leveller Magazine Ltd.*[157] concerned committal proceedings in relation to an alleged breach of the Official Secrets Acts. A witness, 'Colonel B.', was granted anonymity for reasons of national security. In the course of his evidence, however, he let the cat out of the bag by mentioning that his promotion had been reported in *Wire*, the magazine of the Royal Corps of Signals. Two magazines, *The Leveller* and *Peace News*, followed up this lead, identified him from the item in the *Wire*, and published details of his name and career. The House of Lords held that this was not a contempt, since Colonel B. had himself given away his identity.

This result does not seem strange at first sight: it would be odd to go to great lengths to protect information which has already passed into the public domain, especially if it was revealed by the person who was intended to benefit from the order, however unfortunate it may be that it should have been disclosed. Nevertheless, on further examination the picture is not quite so clear. Two matters should be considered. First, the damage to prosecution policy in future cases is not alleviated by the fact that the witness himself gave the game away in the present case. Secondly, letting slip a clue to the identity of the witness in court may not cause serious damage to the public interest if people in court do not realize how it may be used to identify the witness, and journalists do not report the connection between the slip and extraneous evidence of identity to people who understand its significance. In a case like *Leveller Magazine*, publishing the results of the researches which were prompted by Colonel B.'s slip in court could easily have done substantial damage to

---

[157] [1979] AC 440, [1979] 1 All ER 745, HL. For discussion of the implications, especially in terrorism trials in Northern Ireland, see Gilbert Marcus, 'Secret Witnesses' [1990] *PL* 207–23.

the public interest beyond anything which the slip in itself caused. This risk would further discourage prosecutors in further cases from calling witnesses such as Colonel B., and injure the interests of justice.

In *Leveller*, therefore, even after the witness let slip the clue to his identity, the continuance of the order might have been in the wider interests of justice. If it is in the interests of justice to make an anonymity order in the first place, the same interests of justice may require that the information should be kept confidential, whatever the witness might accidentally let slip under the pressure of giving evidence. It is strange to allow the long-term interests of justice to be subject to the accidental slip of a witness's tongue.

Viewed from this angle, the result of the *Leveller* case suggests a degree of confusion between two different objectives: the protection of the course of justice, and the protection of privacy and confidentiality. The latter aim is principally a matter for the witness, and it would be understandable to say that it is up to the witness to protect his interests as best he may, or waive his protection. The former aim, by contrast, is a public-interest objective, and the court should be able to restrain publications which could harm that interest, so long as the risk is well established rather than speculative, and the harm would be substantial. Courts must be willing to scrutinize critically claims that anonymity is necessary in the interests of justice.

The confusion between public and private interests contributes to another doubt which survives the *Leveller* decision, concerning the scope of any order. At common law, an order was effective as regards the course of proceedings, but there was doubt in the House of Lords as to whether or not the order could prohibit people, including those not in court to hear the ruling, from using the witness's name outside the court, gagging reporting. Orders as to publication may bind people who are not before the court so long as they know of the order and act with the intention of prejudicing the course of justice in the proceedings in question, as the *Spycatcher* saga demonstrated.[158] However, it is not clear whether an order is similarly binding when made to protect interests which go beyond the integrity of the particular proceedings in which the order is made. In the *Leveller* case, the question did not directly arise. Viscount Dilhorne and Lord Edmund-Davies, *obiter*, took the view that there was no common-law power to make an order with such extended effects, and Lord Diplock expressly left the question open.

The matter was to some extent clarified by the Contempt of Court Act 1981, section 11. This does not grant a power to make an anonymity order during proceedings, but provides that, where a power exists to

---

[158] *A.-G.* v. *Times Newspapers Ltd.* [1992] 1 AC 191, [1991] 2 All ER 398, HL.

allow 'a name or other matter to be withheld from the public in proceedings before the court', the court is to have power to give directions 'prohibiting the publication of that name or matter in connection with the proceedings'. These directions may be 'such . . . as appear to the court to be necessary' to achieve the purpose for which the name or other matter is being withheld in the proceedings. This does not alter the effect of the *Leveller* case, because, being parasitic on a power to order anonymity in court, the power to give directions regarding publication fails once the name is mentioned in court and anonymity is lost.[159] However, it does make it clear that in certain circumstances, having made an order regulating procedure in the court, the court may make a further order to prohibit or delay publication of the interdicted details, and the latter order will be valid if (and only if) the former was. Section 11 provides that the order must be 'in connection with the proceedings', so it could not extend to prohibiting comment on the behaviour of a person apart from his role as a witness.[160] The circumstances justifying an order prohibiting publication under section 11 must be related to the proceedings. It is not enough that the witness fears that an ex-wife will be able to track him down and molest him if publicity draws attention to his whereabouts.[161]

(iv) *Substantial risk of prejudice to the administration of justice.* Under the Contempt of Court Act 1981, section 4(2), there is power to order postponement (rather than permanent prohibition) of any report of proceedings or part of proceedings where it appears to the court to be necessary in order to avoid a substantial risk of prejudice to the administration of justice in those proceedings, or in any other pending or imminent proceedings. The court may order postponement of reports for such period as it thinks necessary for that purpose.[162] It is therefore important that the terms of the order should be clear.[163]

This power applies in a wider range of circumstances than would give rise to strict liability for contempt of court: the latter requires that the substantial risk relate to *serious* prejudice to the administration of justice, whereas a substantial risk of *any* prejudice will justify the court in using its power under section 4(2). Because of this, there is a question over the

---

[159] R. v. *Arundel Justices, ex parte Westminster Press Ltd.* [1986] 1 WLR 676, [1985] 2 All ER 390, DC.

[160] See Miller, *Contempt of Court*, 2nd edn., 317. On the form of orders under s. 11, see *Practice Note*, [1982] 1 All ER 1475, [1983] 1 All ER 64.

[161] R. v. *Evesham Justices, ex parte McDonagh* [1988] QB 553, [1988] 1 All ER 371, DC.

[162] A similar power existed at common law before the 1981 Act. See, generally, Miller, *Contempt of Court*, 2nd edn., 326–38. For a study of the operation of the powers under ss. see 4 and 11, see Clive Walker, Ian Cram, and Debra Brogarth, 'The Reporting of Crown Court Proceedings and the Contempt of Court Act 1981' (1992) 55 *MLR* 647–69.

[163] See *Practice Note*, [1982] 1 WLR 1475, [1983] 1 All ER 64.

effect of breaching an order. Since the subsection does not provide that breach is automatically to be treated as a contempt of court, it is arguable that it is not a contempt unless (under section 2(2) of the Act) it is shown that either (a) the publication gave rise to a substantial risk of serious prejudice, and was not part of a discussion in good faith of public affairs or other matters of public interest, in which the risk of impediment or prejudice to legal proceedings is merely incidental to the discussion, as required by section 5 of the 1981 Act, or (b) it would have amounted to a common-law contempt because of the contemnors intention to prejudice proceedings, as in the *Spycatcher* cases. This restrictive view of contempt liability for breaching a court order was accepted by the Court of Appeal in *Attorney General v. Guardian Newspapers Ltd.*[164]

However, in *R. v. Horsham Justices, ex parte Farquharson*[165] a majority of the Court of Appeal (Shaw and Ackner LJJ, Lord Denning M.R. dissenting) had previously held that section 4(1) impliedly created a new head of strict liability contempt, as the rule protecting fair and accurate reports, made contemporaneously and in good faith, was made subject to the other provisions of section 4, including section 4(2).[166] Curiously, the decision in *ex parte Farquharson* appears not to have been cited to the court in *Guardian Newspapers*, so the next court facing the issue will be free to choose between the conflicting decisions of the Court of Appeal, with the possibility of holding that the later decision, reached without reference to the earlier, was *per incuriam*. In principle, the later decision, and Lord Denning's dissenting judgment in the earlier one, are preferable. It is unsatisfactory for a journalist (or anyone else) to be convicted of contempt for publishing in breach of an order which is ultra vires the judge who made it. Nevertheless, there is authority (albeit unsatisfactory on civil liberties grounds, and arguably inconsistent with other authorities) for saying that a conviction for contempt may be founded on a refusal to comply with a possibly invalid order, unless and until the order has been quashed in judicial review proceedings.[167] This represents a direct assault on the principle of legality, which requires that penalties should not be imposed for an act which was not unlawful according to the law in force at the time when it was committed. It is to be hoped that the matter will speedily be settled by the House of Lords in favour of the *Guardian Newspapers* approach.

In order to give rise to the requisite risk of substantial prejudice, the nature of the proceedings has to be considered. Judges will be expected to be able to avoid being prejudiced by newspaper reports, so the risk of inducing bias in the tribunal will not justify an order where the

---

[164] [1992] 3 All ER 38, CA.   [165] [1982] QB 762, [1982] 2 All ER 269, CA.
[166] See generally Miller, *Contempt of Court*, 2nd edn., 332–8.
[167] *DPP v. Channel 4 Television Co.* [1993] 2 All ER 517, DC.

proceedings which may be prejudiced are trials before judges alone. Even where juries are likely to be involved, the courts give credit to the ability of jurors to be guided by the evidence given in court, rather than what they read in newspapers.[168] It is also proper to give credit to the reporters for having the sense and awareness to avoid prejudice. For example, in the trial of Ernest Saunders on charges arising out of his conduct during the attempt by Guinness plc to take over Distillers, the issues and charges were so complex that the judge ordered the indictment to be severed, so that the accused would be tried separately on different counts which arose out of interconnected facts. The judge, Henry J., refused to make an order under section 4 in respect of the first trial, trusting that the reporting would be fair and accurate and published with a view to preserving the fairness of the second trial. He also expected the media to put in place suitable internal disciplines to secure the standard of reporting and the fairness of the second trial. The Court of Appeal held that the exercise of the discretion raised no issue of law, no wrong principles having been applied.[169] However, in an appropriate case there is power, for example, to postpone reports of evidence given at 'old style' committal proceedings, where evidence is given and cross-examination takes place, because of the risk of prejudice to the trial.[170]

(v) *Committal proceedings.* Apart from section 4(2) of the Contempt of Court Act, and predating it, the Criminal Justice Act 1967, section 3, later replaced by the Magistrates' Courts Act 1980, section 8, provides that the only details or committal proceedings which may be reported are normally: the identity of the court and the names of the examining justices; names, addresses, and occupations of parties and witnesses; ages of the accused and witnesses; the offences with which the accused is charged, or a summary of them; names of counsel and solicitors; any decision disposing of the case or committing the accused for trial; the charges (if any) on which the accused is committed; where proceedings are adjourned, the date and place to which they are adjourned; arrangements for bail; and whether legal aid was granted.[171]

Normally, therefore, the reports of committal proceedings are sketchy, in order not to prejudice any subsequent jury trial. However, the accused

---

[168] *R. v. Kray* (1969) 53 Cr. App. R. 412 at p. 414 *per* Lawton J; *R. v. Horsham Justices, ex parte Farquharson* [1982] QB 762 at pp. 794–5, [1982] 2 All ER 269 at p. 287 *per* Lord Denning MR; *A.-G. v. Times Newspapers, The Times,* 12 Feb. 1983 (concerning reports about Michael Fagan, who had effected an entry to the Queen's bedroom).
[169] *R. v. Saunders,* [1990] Crim. LR 597, CA.
[170] *R. v. Horsham Justices, ex parte Farquharson* [1982] QB 762, [1982] 2 All ER 269, CA; *R. v. Beck, ex parte Daily Telegraph plc* [1993] 2 All ER 177, CA.
[171] Magistrates' Courts Act 1980, s. 8(4).

may want to have details widely reported, perhaps feeling that a fuller report would serve to bring the proceedings to the notice of potential witnesses in his behalf, or would counter adverse publicity preceding charge. The section therefore allows an accused to apply to have reporting restrictions lifted. On such an application, the justices must make an order lifting restrictions, unless the accused has one or more co-accused, one of whom objects. Where there is such an objection, the justices must hear representations from the accused, and may order that restrictions be lifted only if they are satisfied that it is in the interests of justice to do so.[172]

The relationship between section 8 of the Magistrates' Courts Act 1980 and the Contempt of Court Act 1981 is slightly complicated. Breach of the prohibition on reporting under the 1980 Act is a statutory offence, attracting a fine.[173] It is not a contempt of court unless there was an intention to prejudice proceedings (common-law contempt) or the case falls within section 2(2) of the 1981 Act (strict liability). Furthermore, it seems that under the 1980 Act the court cannot take account of the interests of parties in other cases; if justices think it appropriate to restrict reporting in order to protect such interests, they must make an order under section 4 (or, in some cases, section 11) of the Contempt of Court Act 1981. The two powers therefore coexist side by side, dealing with different problems.[174]

(vi) *Serious fraud: transfer of proceedings.* Similar provision to that contained in section 8 of the Magistrates' Courts Act 1980 is made in respect of Crown Court in relation to serious fraud offences. The Criminal Justice Act 1987, section 11, makes it an offence to report applications to the Crown Court for dismissal of charges and preparatory hearings where a serious fraud offence has been transferred from a magistrates' court to the Crown Court.

(vii) *Restrictions on reporting material disclosed on discovery.* A final discretion to prohibit publication of material read or referred to in open court concerns material handed over during the process of discovery of documents. Such material is made available by each side only for the purposes of the

---

[172] Ibid., s. 8(2), (2A), inserted by the Criminal Justice (Amendment) Act 1981, s. 1(2). See *R. v. Horsham Justice, ex parte Farquharson* [1982] QB 762, [1982] 2 All ER 269, CA and *R. v. Leeds Justices, ex parte Sykes* [1983] 1 WLR 132, [1983] 1 All ER 460, DC, on the burden on an accused seeking to have the objections of a co-accused to reporting overridden.

[173] Magistrates' Court Act 1980, s. 8(5). Proceedings in England and Wales for this offence may be commenced only by or with the consent of the A.-G.: *ibid.*, s. 8(6).

[174] *R. v. Horsham Justices, ex parte Farquharson* [1982] QB 762, [1982] 2 All ER 269, CA. See Miller, *Contempt of Court*, 2nd edn., 320–5.

litigation, and is received by the other side subject to an implied under-taking that it will be used only for that litigation. Any other use normally requires the leave of the court. In *Home Office* v. *Harman*,[175] the House of Lords held that it was a contempt for Miss Harman, a solicitor represent-ing a prisoner in an action against the Home Office, to show to a jour-nalist documents which had been handed over by the Home Office pursuant to an order for discovery.[176] The relevant parts had been read aloud in open court; nevertheless, it was a breach of the implied under-taking, and so a contempt, to show them to a journalist for the purposes of journalism. Lord Diplock categorized the issue as narrow and techni-cal, and denied that it gave rise to any human rights issues. Lord Scarman, dissenting, and expressing opinions which he shared with Lord Simon of Glaisdale (who had died after hearing argument but before delivering his speech in the appeal), held that the information was in the public domain, and argued that a restriction on publishing such information was a breach of the principles of open justice, press freedom, and Article 10 of the European Convention on Human Rights. The effect of the majority decision was, as one commentator wrote, that litigants faced 'an obliga-tion uncertain in scope and indefinite in duration'.[177]

Miss Harman petitioned the European Commission on Human Rights, which held her application to be admissible.[178] A friendly settlement fol-lowed, which involved (*inter alia*) a change to the Rules of the Supreme Court.[179] RSC Order 24, rule 14A now provides that an undertaking to use discovered documents only for the purposes of the litigation ceases to have effect when the documents are read or referred to in open court. However, the Rule leaves the court a discretion to order otherwise on an application from any party or from the person to whom the documents belong, for 'special reasons'.[180] It seems that the special reasons need not be very special. It has been held that, if a party objects to disclosure, the public interest in maintaining confidence in the confidentiality of the system of discovery will normally result in an order restraining disclosure being made.[181] Accordingly, despite the efforts of the European Commission of Human Rights, the result of what has been called 'one of

[175] [1983] 1 AC 280, [1982] 1 All ER 532, HL.
[176] See *Williams* v. *Home Office* [1981] 1 All ER 1151.
[177] Ian Eagles, 'Disclosure of Material Obtained on Discovery' (1984) 47 *MLR* 284–302, at p. 297. For comment on the Court of Appeal judgments, see N. V. Lowe, 'Discovering Contempt' (1982) 1 *CJQ* 10–17.
[178] Application No. 10038/82, *Harman* v. *UK*, Eur. Comm. HR, Decision of 11 May 1984, 38 DR 53.
[179] Application No. 10038/82, *Harman* v. *UK*, Eur. Comm. HR Report of 15 May 1986, 46 DR 57.
[180] RSC Ord. 24, r. 14A.
[181] *Bibby Bulk Carriers Ltd.* v. *Cansulex Ltd.* [1989] QB 155, [1988] 2 All ER 820.

the most controversial decisions of recent years'[182] remains substantially untouched, as a standing affront to Article 10 and common sense alike.

16.3 CONCLUSION

The contempt-of-court law can adversely affect rights, particularly rights in respect of free expression, in the interests of the administration of justice, particularly the right of litigants to a fair trial. Care is needed to restrict the contempt law to its proper ambit. Contempt and free expression are not always in opposition to each other. The law of contempt is designed to protect the integrity and fairness of the legal process. Free expression may have the same purpose, and restricting free expression, while perhaps being fair to the parties in individual cases, is liable to weaken the quality of justice as a whole if pressed too far. Like the quality of government, the quality of justice and public confidence in it depend on rigorous public scrutiny and, where necessary, sharply critical commentary, particularly after recent revelations of miscarriages of justice. There is no real justification for the offence of scandalizing the court in the context of a large and developed democratic society where the authority of the judiciary depends on institutional factors rather than matters personal to individual judges. Furthermore, there is a risk that the rules on contempt by prejudicing proceedings may be abused by people who want to silence discussion or revelation which might be in the public interest. There is at least a suspicion that the government was using the law in this way in the *Spycatcher* affair, discussed in Chapter 14 above. Even where no contempt proceedings are brought, the threat that they might be available may put the press and broadcasting media in fear of penalty, and might be a means of bringing pressure to bear illegitimately on editorial judgement.

The prior restraint imposed on publicity in order to maintain the prospects of a fair trial, particularly by way of court orders in criminal cases and those involving juveniles, are generally well policed by the judges. They have the potential to stifle the openness of justice, but that may be considered a necessary price to pay for the protection of other interests. Until the press as a whole is in a position to impose and enforce standards of professional ethics and responsibility, some legal controls will be necessary, and it is important to ensure that neither the legal rules which restrict free expression nor their application should be overinclusive.

---

[182] Miller, *Contempt of Court*, 2nd edn., 338.

17

PROTEST AND PUBLIC ORDER

This chapter examines the extent of protection for rights of protest, which often collide with the desire for peace and good order in public places. The first section outlines the basis for rights to protest and the second looks at the central notion of the Queen's peace and its impact on the policing of public order. Section 3 examines statutory public order offences, and the following sections are concerned with powers to regulate and control public meetings and processions in the interests of order. The sixth section examines the role of bail conditions and binding over in maintaining order and restricting freedom of expression and protest. Some conclusions are drawn in the final section.

17.1 THE BASIS FOR RIGHTS TO PROTEST

The European Convention on Human Rights, Article 11, provides:

1. Everyone has the right to freedom of peaceful assembly and to freedom of association with others, including the right to form and join trade unions for the protection of his interests.

2. No restrictions shall be placed on the exercise of these rights other than such as are prescribed by law and are necessary in a democratic society in the interests of national security or public safety, for the prevention of disorder or crime, for the protection of health or morals or for the protection of the rights and freedoms of others. This Article shall not prevent the imposition of lawful restrictions on the exercise of these rights by members of the armed forces, of the police or of the administration of the state.

In every society there is a tension between the desire of citizens to be free from annoyance and disorder and their wish to be free to bring to the attention of their fellow citizens matters which they consider to be important. The way in which any legal system resolves the tension, and the balance which it strikes between the competing interests, is indicative of the attitude of that society towards the relative value of different sorts of freedom. A society which tolerates a good deal of annoyance or disorder so as to encourage the greatest possible freedom of expression, particularly political expression, is likely to be one in which the public, political activities of citizens are regarded as making a useful contribution to the health of a democratic system. The citizens will enjoy a right, if not an obligation, to participate in political debate, and to try to persuade other people to their point of view. The problem is that this inevitably leads to other people's right to be free of that sort of persuasion, and of its accompanying annoyance and even offence, being circumscribed. The job of the lawmakers is to decide when the interests of society in being free of unwanted persuasion or disorder outweigh the interest in free expression of opinions and persuasion.

This may happen in two types of situation: first, where the manner of the expression or the substance of the message infringes some other interest which is so weighty that no restriction of it should be allowed; secondly, where the infringed interest is not that important, but the manner of expression or the substance of the message impinges on it to an extent which is disproportionate to the benefit which would be gained by allowing the expression. An extreme example of the former would be a person killing another in order to publicize a political programme (the classic form of political terrorism); the latter might (according to one's viewpoint) be thought to be exemplified by the use of a large number of people in an industrial dispute picketing premises to prevent others from going to work.

This chapter examines the problem in the context of public order. In England and Wales, although statutes and judicial decisions have recognized that the expression of views and information is in the public interest, the law tends to operate in terms of freedoms, powers, and duties rather than rights in public–law matters (as already noted in the context of other rights and liberties). The influence of the European Convention on Human Rights in redefining freedoms as rights has as yet borne only limited fruit. The central issues in this field, therefore, are the incidental impact on freedom of protest of rights developed for other purposes (such as the right to pass and repass on the highway), and the direct impact of the powers and duties of police and others to preserve the peace, enforce the criminal law, and safeguard the interests of non–protesters.

This is related to rights of free expression and freedom of association. Protest is a form of expression. In the United States, it has been held that the First Amendment to the Constitution often protects verbal and non-verbal forms of political protest from legal prohibition, even if it causes very considerable offence.[1] Thus burning the national flag, the Stars and Stripes, has been held to be protected as symbolic speech. The Supreme Court has held attempts by states and Congress to legislate for the

---

[1] *Stromberg* v. *California* 283 US 359 (1931), invalidating a California law against displaying red flags; *Thornhill* v. *Alabama* 310 US 88 (1940), invalidating an anti-picketing law which had been interpreted as preventing a single picket from carrying a placard outside a factory.

criminalization of flag burning to be unconstitutional. This has outraged conservatives and patriots, and has led to moves to introduce a constitutional amendment which would except flag burning from the protection of the First Amendment. So far, the legislative proposals have failed to achieve the necessary two-thirds majority support in each House of Congress, showing the substantial impact of which constitutional protection for free expression is capable.[2] In this country, however, there is no special entrenchment of free-speech rights, although Parliament and some of the judges have recognized its importance in a society with democratic aspirations.[3]

In the context of protest (unlike the position in relation to some other freedoms) it would be misleading to assume that the central principle is that people are free to do anything which they have not been lawfully forbidden to do. Protest, like expression, is an activity which makes more demands on others than do rights to privacy, family life, or freedom from arbitrary arrest or detention. The latter types of rights demand only self-restraint from others. Rights to free expression and protest, by contrast, require (if they are to be effectively used) some form of communication with others, and so presuppose that the freedom of other people from annoyance is to be restricted at least so far as necessary to allow the protester to impart the nature of the protest and invite people to join in protest or discussion. It therefore goes beyond pure liberalism, which would permit people and groups to buy or hire a private hall to ventilate their grievances or policies (if they can afford to do so) but would not allow them to force their opinions on non-consenting adults. The European Court of Human Rights has held that the right to freedom of association under Article 11 of the European Convention is infringed when people's freedom to choose when and with whom they do not wish to associate is seriously interfered with, either by imposing severe sanctions on them for refusing to associate (as where people lost their jobs for refusal to join a particular union under a closed-shop agreement) or by restricting people's range of choices so that they have no real choice.[4]

The logic of this applies to rights to protest: the right to protest implies a duty to provide opportunities for people to be protested at, but the right to be free from annoyance and unwanted invasions of privacy suggests that the right to protest must be balanced by a negative right to choose whether or not one wants to be the object of protest. These com-

[2] *Texas* v. *Johnson* 109 S. Ct. 2533 (1989); *Eichman* v. *US* 110 S. Ct. 2404 (1990); Murray Dry, 'Flag Burning and the Constitution' [1990] *Supreme Court Review* 69–103.

[3] See Chs. 12 and 13, above.

[4] *Young, James, and Webster* v. *UK*, Eur. Ct. HR, Series A, No. 44, Judgment of 13 Aug. 1981, 4 EHRR 38. See Barendt, *Freedom of Speech* (Oxford: Clarendon Press, 1987), ch. 10.

peting rights must be balanced, as Lord Scarman pointed out in his report on the Red Lion Square disorders.[5]

Further problems arise over the location of protests. There are few recognized public places for protesting. Most protests occur on public streets, but some happen on private property. Do private-property owners have any duty to allow their property to be used as a forum for protest? In the USA, the public streets have been progressively supplanted by privately owned shopping malls as the main places where the public gather and shop. This has led to a shortage of spaces in which protests can be made so as to reach a large number of members of the public effectively. In such circumstances, there is a natural desire to carry the protest into the private shopping malls, and the right to protest comes into conflict with the private interests of property owners in their property and privacy, which are likely to prevail unless the right to protest on private property is protected by a statute which is compatible with the property owner's rights under the Federal Constitution.[6]

The justification for freedom of protest is a combination of (1) the value of self-expression as a way of developing personality and giving effect to choices as autonomous individuals, (2) the value to the community of having such freedom in order (as J. S. Mill wrote: see Chapter 1 above) to maximise the available choice of opinion and policy, thereby improving the chances of finding the best possible policy or most accurate account of the world; (3) the importance of public dissent in keeping government responsive to public opinion; and (4) discouraging deviance by making clear that government is being continuously watched and evaluated. But these interests, important as they are, have to be weighed in each context against citizens' interests in privacy, freedom of movement, and freedom from physical attack or abuse.[7] It is therefore understandable that the structure of rights to protest should be rather different from that of rights of assembly and association and freedom from arbitrary interference with liberty.

17.2 THE BASIC VALUES: PUBLIC ORDER AND THE QUEEN'S PEACE

The absence of entrenched legal rights to protest in England and Wales means that the central value in this field of law is public order. The

---

[5] Sir Leslie Scarman, *Report on the Red Lion Square Disorders of 15 June 1974*, Cmnd. 5919 (London: HMSO, 1975).

[6] *PruneYard Shopping Centre* v. *Robins* 447 US 74 (1980).

[7] Frederick Schauer, *Free Speech: A Philosophical Enquiry* (Cambridge: Cambridge UP, 1982), 203 ff.; Barendt, *Freedom of Speech*, 193–9.

maintenance of order, or a certain level of order, is essential for the exercise of freedoms, their protection under the rule of law, and the operation of a liberal economy. A desire for order, not as an end in itself but as a means to allowing the fullest possible exercise of freedoms, is not, therefore, inherently repressive. Its importance to liberty can perhaps be fully understood only by those who have lived in societies where it was absent. A certain minimal level of order is a necessary, though not a sufficient, condition for liberty. This is reflected in English law. Liberal critics of the way in which the law approaches the tension between freedom of protest and public order normally object to the degree of order which the law demands, or the indeterminacy of the rules for regulating protest:[8] indeterminacy undermines liberty by making its scope uncertain, expanding the discretionary power of the police, and easing the constraints on state power which the rule of law demands. The critics do not usually say that there should be *no* constraints on rights of protest.

(1) The Queen's Peace

The fundamental concept in public-order law in England has historically been, and to some extent remains, the Queen's (or King's) Peace. This started as a special case of the 'peace' which attached to all dwelling places and churches, and was extended from the environs of the royal court across the country, first when the medieval kings took the main thoroughfares under their protection, later by grants of protection to individual royal servants and traders, and finally (this was common by the fourteenth century) when the royal justices allowed litigants to bring certain matters (such as trespass) within the jurisdiction of royal courts by pleading that wrongs had been done *vi et armis* or *contra pacem domini Regis*.[9] Such pleas were soon treated as being non-traversable, so that the jurisdiction of the royal courts could not be contested in cases of violence. This aided the Crown in its battle for legal authority with manorial and other local courts, and also helped to extend a uniform criminal and land law across the country.[10]

---

[8] See e.g. John Baxter, 'Policing and the Rule of Law', in John Baxter and Laurence Koffman (eds.), *Police: The Constitution and the Community* (Abingdon: Professional Books, 1985), 38–61; Patricia Hewitt, *The Abuse of Power: Civil Liberties in the UK* (Oxford: Martin Robertson, 1982), ch. 5.

[9] S. F. C. Milsom, *Historical Foundations of the Common Law*, 2nd edn. (London: Butterworths, 1981), 286–90.

[10] See Jack K. Weber, 'The King's Peace: A Comparative Study' (1989) 10 *J. of Legal Hist.* 135–60; Sir Carleton Kemp Allen, *The Queen's Peace* (London: Stevens & Son, 1953), 23–66; Frederick Pollock, *Oxford Lectures and Other Discourses* (London: Macmillan, 1890), 65–90; David Feldman, 'The King's Peace, the Royal Prerogative and Public Order: The Roots and Early Development of Binding Over Powers' [1988] *CLJ* 101–28 at 103 ff.

Despite the modern connotation of the term 'peace', in law it has never been concerned with absence of noise. It rather functions in contradistinction to 'war': peace is a freedom from violence or the threat of violence. As the basis of public–order law, the centrality of 'peace' expresses the idea that people should be free to act as they choose so long as they do not cause violence. It has long been the duty of public officials (Keepers of the Peace, then Justices of the Peace, and constables) to preserve the peace, meaning to prevent or end anything which involves or threatens to provoke violence against citizens. But this duty has not been limited to public officials. All citizens have a duty to preserve the peace. As early as the tenth century they were organized for that purpose (among others) in the *frith-borh* under ordinances of King Edgar (AD 959–75) and King Ethelred (978–1016),[11] and it has never since been doubted that officials who perform peace-keeping roles are doing their duty as citizens (albeit with special additional responsibilities) rather than doing something special as agents of the state. Thus in *Albert* v. *Lavin*[12] Mr. Albert had been trying to jump the queue at a bus stop when PC Lavin, off duty and out of uniform, decided that this was likely to lead to a breach of the peace and restrained him. Albert, not believing that Lavin was a constable, punched Lavin and was charged with assaulting a constable in the execution of his duty. The case was argued before magistrates and in the Divisional Court on the footing that the issue was whether Albert would have a defence if, as the magistrates found, he had honestly but unreasonably believed that Lavin was not a constable. In the House of Lords, the Law Lords pointed out that Albert would not have been entitled to resist anyone who was performing the citizen's duty of restraining an actual or reasonably apprehended breach of the peace. It therefore did not matter what Albert had believed or whether the belief had been reasonable: Lavin was in fact a constable, and had been in the execution of his duty as constable and citizen whatever Albert had believed. This is the clearest illustration of the duty of all citizens to preserve the 'peace'.

The 'peace' therefore has great potential for allowing people to contain other people's scope for protest and other sorts of behaviour which affect the public. Because of its elasticity, the Law Commission recommended that the concept 'breach of the peace' should no longer be used as part of the definition of criminal offences,[13] and this was accepted when the Public Order Act 1986 was drafted. However, unlike the criminal

---

[11] See Stubbs, *Select Charters*, 9th edn., ed. H. W. C. Davis (Oxford: Oxford University Press, 1913), 83–5.

[12] [1982] AC 546, [1981] 3 All ER 878, HL.

[13] Law Commission No. 123, *Criminal Law: Offences Relating to Public Order* (London: HMSO, 1983), 7–8.

offences, the peace-keeping powers and duties of citizens and constables have not been regulated or replaced by statute. This makes it important to establish what constitutes a breach of the peace, and the extent of powers to deal with breaches.

(2) What is a breach of the peace?

The meaning of 'breach of the peace' has been the subject of judicial disagreement, but the clear balance of authority favours the view that a breach of the peace consists of violence or the threat of violence. It is clear that not every disturbance, even if in public, constitutes a breach of the peace. In *R. v. Howell*,[14] Watkins LJ said that there must be a positive act which harms a person or damages his messuage[15] in his presence, or which is likely to cause such harm or puts someone in fear of such harm being done. The interest of individuals and the Crown in suppressing violence against the person is self-evident. Attacks on or crimes against property generally do not breach the peace. The extension to attacks on dwellings in the occupiers' presence probably arises from the attendant likelihood that such an attack will be met with violence from the occupiers.[16]

In *R. v. Chief Constable of Devon and Cornwall Constabulary, ex parte Central Electricity Generating Board*,[17] Lord Denning MR suggested that breach of the peace might be considerably wider than this. He said: 'There is a breach of the peace whenever a person who is lawfully carrying out his work is unlawfully and physically prevented by another from doing it.'[18] However, he seems to have been saying not that a breach of the peace is automatic in such circumstances, but rather that, because the workers are entitled to use self-help, including reasonable force, in order to overcome the obstruction to their lawful pursuits,[19] any obstruction could give the police a reasonable apprehension of a breach of the peace, in the sense of violence.[20] The threat of violence against the person, or

[14] [1982] QB 416, [1981] 3 All ER 383, CA, discussed by A. T. H. Smith, 'Breaching the Peace and Disturbing the Quiet' [1982] PL 212–18.

[15] 'Originally, the portion of land intended to be occupied, or actually occupied, as a site for a dwelling-house and its appurtenances. In modern legal language, a dwelling-house with its outbuildings and curtilage and the adjacent land assigned to its use.' OED.

[16] See *Ingle v. Bell* (1836) 1 W. & W. 516; *Cohen v. Huskisson* (1837) 2 M. & W. 477; *R . v. Bright* (1830) 4 C. & P. 387; *R . v. Howell* [1982] QB at p. 426, [1981] 3 All ER at p. 388 *per* Watkins LJ.

[17] [1982] QB 458, [1981] 3 All ER 826, CA.

[18] [1982] QB at p. 471, [1981] 3 All ER at p. 832.

[19] *Holmes v. Bagge* (1853) 1 E. & B. 782 at pp. 786–7, 118 ER 629 at p. 631, *per* Lord Campbell CJ.

[20] See also Lawton LJ, [1982] QB at p. 473, [1981] 3 All ER at p. 834, and Templeman LJ at pp. 478, 839.

messuage in the presence of the occupier, remains essential to constitute a breach of the peace in England and Wales and to trigger the powers and duties which attach to it, so (for example) a person masturbating in a public lavatory where nobody else was likely to see and nobody catching him unawares would be likely to be moved to violence is not conduct likely to cause a breach of the peace.[21]

The violence (actual or threatened) must be unlawful if it is to give rise to a breach of the peace.[22] Reasonable force used to expel a trespasser is not unlawful, and so is not a breach of the peace, although unlawful resistance by the trespasser may amount to a breach of the peace. In the context of the *Central Electricity Generating Board* case, there would have been no breach of the peace had the Board's employees simply carried trespassing protesters away from the Board's land without resistance. This can become complicated, however, where the person trespassing is claiming to be attempting to prevent a breach of the peace. In *McBean v. Parker*, a constable was trespassing on property occupied by the defendant, who used reasonable force in order to remove him. The constable claimed that the use of force against him constituted a breach of the peace, so that at this point he was entitled to remain on the premises and arrest the defendant in order to end the breach. The Divisional Court held that the force, being lawful, could not give rise to a breach of the peace. It would seem that, if excessive force were used in similar circumstances, the force, being unlawful, would give rise to a charge of assault against the defendant, and that would amount to a breach of the peace. However, it would be odd if a constable could assert a power to remain on premises to restrain a breach of the peace constituted by the adoption of unlawful means to achieve his lawful removal from the premises, when the simplest and most effective way of ending the breach would have been for the trespassing constable to depart. One solution to this conundrum would be to apply administrative-law principles to the constable's exercise of discretion: on *Wednesbury*[23] principles, it is arguable that the behaviour of the constable in seeking to remain on the premises, even in the face of excessive force, would be a wholly unreasonable way of trying to achieve his proper purpose of ending the breach of the peace.

---

[21] *Parkin v. Norman, Valentine v. Lilley* [1983] QB 92, [1982] 2 All ER 583, a decision on s. 5 of the Public Order Act 1936 (now repealed).

[22] *McBean v. Parker* [1983] Crim. LR 399, 147 JP 205, DC.

[23] *Associated Provincial Picture Houses Ltd.* v. *Wednesbury Corporation* [1948] 1 K.B. 223, [1947] 2 All ER 680, CA. The principles of irrationality are applicable to the exercise of discretion by police officers: *Holgate-Mohammed* v. *Duke* [1984] AC 437, [1984] 1 All ER 1054, HL.

(3) Can a breach of the peace occur in private?

A breach of the peace can occur on private premises, whether or not it affects anyone outside the premises. The essence of it is violence, not public violence.[24]

(4) What powers exist to prevent or stop breaches of the peace?[25]

The duty to prevent or stop breaches of the peace carries with it a number of powers. These are:

    (*a*) a power to take steps short of arrest to defuse the situation;

    (*b*) a power to arrest and detain;

    (*c*) a power to enter or remain on private premises for the purpose.

This section will concentrate on (*a*) and (*b*); (*c*) is considered in s. 17.5, below.

    A public expression of political or religious beliefs may threaten to give rise to a breach of the peace if the circumstances are such as to raise tempers. Because of this, it has been held that a peace officer (and, presumably, anyone else) may be justified in committing what would otherwise be a trespass to person and property. For example, in *Humphries* v. *Connor*[26] a policeman was held to be justified in removing an orange lily, symbol of the Protestant Unionists in Northern Ireland, from a woman who was wearing it while walking through the Catholic nationalist area of Swanlinbar and thereby provoking the local inhabitants to threaten violence. Similarly in *O'Kelly* v. *Harvey*[27] a magistrate was justified in laying a hand on a man while dispersing a meeting of the Catholic Land League which was being threatened with violent disruption by Fermanagh Orangemen. It does not matter whether the steps are taken against the person threatening violence or those threatened. The main priority is to end the risk of reasonably apprehended violence by whatever means are reasonable and necessary. In the same way, it has been held that a person who has been guilty of no offence and has threatened no violence may be bound over to keep the peace if his behaviour has given rise to a reasonable apprehension that others would be provoked to violence.[28]

    This implies that the authorities can, if they think it appropriate, decide to ban a meeting or march or form of expression, and that some-

---

[24] *McConnell* v. *Chief Constable of Greater Manchester Police* [1990] 1 WLR 364, [1990] 1 All ER 423, CA.

[25] See D. G. T. Williams, *Keeping the Peace: The Police and Public Order* (London: Hutchinson, 1967), ch. 5.

[26] (1864) 17 Ir. CLR 1.   [27] (1883) 15 Cox CC 435.

[28] *Wise* v. *Dunning* [1902] 1 KB 167; *Lansbury* v. *Riley* [1914] 3 KB 229.

one who refuses to desist from any activity or to move a meeting or reroute a procession when there is a reasonable apprehension of a breach of the peace may be arrested and bound over to keep the peace. There are two particular problems. The first concerns the power which it places in the hands of the police to restrict people's freedom to express views (particularly unpopular views), or signify adherence to a set of beliefs, in public. If anybody can stifle the expression of views by threatening violence, freedom of expression and freedom of protest would be worth little. The dictum of O'Brien J. in *R. v. Londonderry Justices*[29] makes a good deal of sense from a libertarian standpoint: 'If danger arises from the exercise of lawful rights resulting in a breach of the peace, the remedy is the presence of sufficient force to prevent the result, not the legal condemnation of those who exercise those rights.' This seems at first sight to gain support from *Beatty v. Gillbanks*,[30] where the Divisional Court quashed binding over orders made against members of a Salvation Army parade when their noisy but peaceable procession through Weston-super-Mare had been disputed by a noisy and belligerent crowd (the Skeleton Army) which disliked the Salvation Army's religious proselytizing and its opposition to alcohol. However, the support is more apparent than real. The magistrates had made the binding over orders on the basis aof finding that the Salvation Army had been guilty of unlawful assembly at common law. The Divisional Court held that this finding was incorrect, and that it would not be right to bind over a person who had committed no offence.

However, later cases have shown that this was mistaken: binding over orders may be made against witnesses, acquitted defendants, or people who happen to be present in court, as a preventive measure without the need to prove that they have committed or threatened any offence.[31] Furthermore, the police have a duty to prevent reasonably apprehended and imminent breaches of the peace, and failure to obey instructions reasonably directed to that end constitutes the offence of obstructing a constable in the execution of his duty.[32] That being so, the decision in *Beatty v. Gillbanks* tells us nothing about how the very wide discretion to act preventively in apprehension of a breach of the peace should be exercised.[33]

---

[29] (1891) 28 LR Ir. 440 at p. 450.   [30] (1882) 9 QBD 308.

[31] For discussion, see Law Commission, Working Paper No. 103, *Criminal Law: Binding Over—The Issues* (London: HMSO, 1987).

[32] *Duncan v. Jones* [1936] 1 KB 218, DC; s. 2(7), below.

[33] For discussion of these problems, see William Birtles, 'The Common Law Power of the Police to Control Public Meetings' (1973) 36 *MLR* 587–99; David G. Barnum, 'Freedom of Assembly and the Hostile Audience in Anglo–American Law' (1981) 29 *Am. J. Comp. Law* 59–96; Smith, *Offences against Public Order* 12–20.

There can be no doubt that there should be a general presumption in favour of protecting the exercise of free lawful expression in public and in private. If it is true, as Lord Denning MR said in *Hubbard* v. *Pitt*,[34] that the law jealously protects the right to free expression and public protest if conducted lawfully, the police must be prepared in normal cases to control the risk of breach of the peace by acting against the person who seeks to disrupt the right of protest and expression, rather than the person who seeks to exericise it. However, this general presumption may be rebuttable. It has to be recognised that protecting a person's right to protest or express opinions against those who seek to disrupt imposes costs on society. It is therefore open to police decision-makers to conclude that the cost of safeguarding the freedom to protest will be disproportionately greater than the cost to public freedom which would result from preventing the protest or public expression from taking place. Although this represents a limitation on freedom of expression and freedom of peaceful assembly, it may not breach the rights guaranteed under Articles 10 and 11 of the European Convention on human rights. The European Court of Human Rights held, in *Plattform 'Ärzte für das Leben' v. Austria*,[35] that there is no absolute obligation on the state under Article 11 to ensure that a demonstration which is lawful is unimpeded by counter-demonstrators. There is an obligation to take reasonable and appropriate steps to allow the peaceful demonstration to proceed, as the right to counter-demonstrate must not be allowed to inhibit the exercise of the right to demonstrate. Nevertheless, the state has a wide discretion as to the measures to be adopted, and if the steps fail because of violence the state will not necessarily have breached the demonstrators' rights. The police would be entitled to restrict the freedom of the demonstrators, so long as the restrictions met the criteria laid down in paragraph 2 of Article 11.

Deciding whether to restrain demonstrators or other people who might be affected involves a discretion which requires consideration of matters going beyond police resource management. Political and moral considerations are influential as well:[36] are there reasons (independent of the balance of costs and freedoms) for wanting to favour the expression of one view over that of another? During the miners' strike in 1984–5, large numbers of striking miners protesting about their grievances confronted police and miners who wanted to go to work. The confrontations between the strikers and the police, and between the strikers and the

---

[34] [1976] QB 142, [1975] 1 All ER 1056, CA. See also Sir Leslie Scarman, *Red Lion Square Disorders*, Cmnd. 5919, 2.

[35] Eur. Ct. HR, Series A, No. 139, Judgment of 21 June 1988, 13 EHRR 204, at paras. 32–4.

[36] Denis Galligan, 'Preserving Public Protest: The Legal Approach', in Larry Gostin (ed.), *Civil Liberties in Conflict* (London: Routledge, 1988), 39–64.

non-strikers, gave rise to a great deal of ill feeling and provoked many breaches of the peace. It would have been simple, cheap, and have required few resources, for the police to have provided a small force to monitor the situation and stop the non-strikers from attempting to go to work. Although there was nothing inherently unlawful in the non-strikers' actions, and it was not unreasonable for them to want to work, restraining them would have been the most efficient way to minimise the chances of a breach of the peace, since the concentration of force required to escort the non-strikers through picket lines, and the high feelings engendered, made it very likely that non-strikers, by attempting to go to work, would provoke a breach of the peace. However, in their discretion, and probably encouraged by the government (which had its own political reasons for wanting to ensure that the strike failed), the police summoned massive reinforcements from forces across the country, through the mutual assistance arrangements co-ordinated by the National Reporting Centre at New Scotland Yard. They then insisted on escorting the non-strikers to work, despite the resulting breaches of the peace. This illustrates the fact that the weighting of the costs and benefits of various courses of action to prevent threatened breaches of the peace is neither a scientific nor an apolitical matter.[37] Professor Denis Galligan has accordingly argued convincingly that a substantial amount of discretion is inevitably needed in public-order policing and policy-making, and that the way forward is to seek ways of making decision-makers publicly accountable for those of their decisions which have political implications.[38]

Furthermore, there may be circumstances in which the views expressed, or the manner of expressing them, is regarded as being so reprehensible that they do not deserve protection. Even in the United States, where freedom of religion, speech, and peaceable assembly are constitutionally guaranteed by the First Amendment, it has been held that, while there are no limits to the forms of opinion which must be tolerated, there

[37] For discussion of policing methods in relation to industrial disputes, see Roger Geary, *Policing Industrial Disputes 1893 to 1985* (London: Methuen, 1985); Richard de Friend and Steve Uglow, 'Policing Industrial Disputes', in John Baxter and Laurence Koffman (eds.), *Police: The Constitution and the Community*, (Abingdon: Professional Books, 1985), 62–71. On tactics and equipment, see P. A. J. Waddington, *The Strong Arm of the Law* (Oxford: Clarendon Press, 1991). For provocative views on aspects of the miners' strike of 1984–5, see Bob Fine and Robert Millar (eds.), *Policing the Miners' Strike* (London: Lawrence and Wishart, 1985), especially the essays by Martin Kettle, 'The National Reporting Centre and the 1984 Miners' Strike', at pp. 23–33, and Nick Blake, 'Picketing, Justice and the Law' at pp. 101–19.

[38] Galligan, 'Preserving Public Protest', at pp. 45–9.

[39] See Louis Fisher, *American Constitutional Law* (New York: McGraw-Hill, 1990), ch. 10.

are limits to the tolerable manner of expression.[39] In this country, where there is no constitutional protection for free expression, there are fewer restrictions on police, courts, or Parliament treating certain opinions as unworthy of protection. However, there is generally a sensitivity to the risk inherent in banning types of opinion. Even the Public Order Act 1936, a panic measure rushed through Parliament in response to violent fascist demonstrations, while permitting orders to be made banning processions, did not allow particular organizations to be singled out. Banning orders could be made only in respect of 'all public processions or . . . any class of public procession so specified'.[40] This avoided discrimination between opinions, but with the incidental result that in the wake of the Brixton riots in 1981 a ban prevented the CND[41] and various groups of Boy Scouts from holding parades. The same position obtains under the Public Order Act 1986, section 13(1), (4), which has replaced section 3 of the 1936 Act. On the other hand, common-law powers to prevent breaches of the peace are exercised in a discretionary way by police officers and others, and are not subject to any parliamentary controls on differential treatment of political groups and opinions. For that, we rely on the good sense and balance of the police.[42]

A second problem, related to the first, concerns the extent of the powers. Do the police have an unfettered discretion as to the steps which they choose to take to combat a breach of the peace? There is no unlimited discretion in English public law. Any exercise of a power which is so unreasonable that no reasonable officer could properly have decided to perform it, or which is directed to an improper purpose, or (perhaps) is disproportionate to the purpose which it is designed to achieve, is unlawful and (as noted above) can be subjected to judicial review on *Wednesbury* principles. There are suggestions in some early cases that the steps taken must be objectively reasonable if they are to be lawful. In *Humphries* v. *Connor*,[43] in relation to dispersing a crowd, O'Brien J. said that the power would not 'protect a constable from any unnecessary, excessive, or improper exercise of such power'.[44] Hayes J., noting that the best way of preventing a breach of the peace will usually be to remove the provocation, continued: 'when a person deliberately refuses to acquiesce in such removal, after warning to do so, I think the constable is authorised to do everything necessary and proper to enforce it. . . . But whether the act which he did was or was not, under all the circumstances, *necessary* to preserve the peace, is for the jury to decide.'[45]

[40] Public Order Act 1936, s. 3(2), (3) (now repealed: see Public Order Act 1986).

[41] *Kent* v. *Metropolitan Police Commissioner*, *The Times*, 15 May 1981, DC.

[42] See Williams, *Keeping the Peace*, ch. 5; S. H. Bailey, D. J. Harris, and B. L. Jones, *Civil Liberties: Cases and Materials*, 3rd edn. (London: Butterworths, 1991), 146–9.

[43] (1864) 17 Ir. CLR 1.   [44] Ibid. at p. 7.   [45] Ibid. at p. 8; emphasis in original.

This objective necessity test has the advantage of being closely in line with the doctrine of proportionality, but it is probably too demanding, as it forces the constable to bear the burden of proving that there was no other practicable way of resolving the problem.[46] A less demanding test is that the constable should reasonably believe it to be necessary. This is a test which is fairer to all parties, and was approved in *O'Kelly* v. *Harvey*.[47] Law LC in the Court of Appeal in Ireland said that he thought that it had been 'substantially decided' in *Humphries* v. *Connor* that: 'if the defendant believed and had just grounds for believing that the peace could only be preserved by withdrawing the plaintiff and his friends from the attack with which they were threatened, it was I think the duty of the defendant to take that course'.

This reinterpretation of *Humphries* v. *Connor* strikes a middle line between subjecting police discretion as to the course of action adopted to a demanding test of necessity, and, on the other hand, leaving it controlled only by a weak test for unreasonableness. In view of the presumption, noted above, in favour of protecting people who are acting lawfully from being prevented from expressing their views, or holding meetings, merely because of violent opposition from other groups, it would be perfectly sensible to adopt the *O'Kelly* v. *Harvey* test (belief on reasonable grounds that it is necessary to interfere with freedom) to justify action against the innocent party, but to leave the police free to act against the troublemaker subject only to a test for unreasonableness. If it is objected that even an innocent person becomes less innocent if he refuses to comply with a request designed to prevent a breach of the peace, it can be conceded that innocence in that context is a relative concept; but the more sinned against, and less sinning, a person is, the more important it is to ensure that his freedom is not interfered with more than is reasonably necessary to prevent a breach of the peace.

(5) Policing methods

The techniques by which the police maintain order, and combat disorder, are complex and controversial. During the late 1970s and early 1980s, fears about public disorder and rising crime rates led to differences of opinion amongst senior police officers and politicians concerning the best way to cope with problems to which, social scientists were revealing, social deprivation, loss of shared values, and a breakdown in social cohesion, all contributed. It became clear that an approach which simply

---

[46] *Cp.* however the House of Lords' less demanding interpretation of 'necessary' in *Re an inquiry under the Company Securities (Insider Dealing) Act 1985* [1988] AC 660, [1988] 1 All ER 203, HL.

[47] (1883) 15 Cox CC 435 at pp. 445–6.

stigmatized law breakers and authorized increasingly forcible police reactions to disturbances would be likely to exacerbate rather than ameliorate the underlying contributory factors.[48] In many cases, the police response to perceived threats of crime and disorder was later perceived as having added fuel to a delicate situation, rather than reduced the risk of violence. For example, the police reaction to a demonstration in Southall in 1979 against South African racism was to make arrests without, as it turned out, adequate controls over the amount of force used or the people against whom it was used. As a result, Blair Peach, a schoolteacher from New Zealand who probably had not been involved in any violence whatsoever, died. The police response to this death led to suspicions of a cover-up, and a non-governmental organization, the National Council for Civil Liberties (now renamed Liberty) was left to provide the fullest report on the incident.[49] In 1981, outbreaks of rioting in Brixton, Southall, Liverpool (Toxteth), Manchester (Moss Side), Birmingham, and Bristol (St Paul's) led the Home Secretary, Mr. (later Lord) Whitelaw, to appoint Lord Scarman to conduct a statutory inquiry into the Brixton riots under section 32 of the Police Act 1964.

Lord Scarman's report established that the conditions favourable to the eruption of the riots were created by social deprivation, lack of involvement of minority ethnic groups in wider community provision (particularly of education), a sense (shown by subsequent studies to have been justified) that the police discriminated against Afro-Caribbean and Asian youths in the frequency with which they stopped and searched them in the street, the failure of the law of street offences to recognize that these young people's culture was a 'street culture', in which the streets were more than a medium for getting from one set of private premises to another, and the relative paucity of social and educational provision by government for areas with large populations of members of ethnic minorities. These conditions, in which young Asians and blacks felt alienated from society and threatened by the police, created an environment in which insensitivity could easily lead to an eruption of violence. This was what happened in Brixton when the police embarked on a massive campaign against what they saw as street crime (notably possession and supply of controlled drugs) in Brixton. Police officers flooded into the area in an operation known as 'Swamp 81'. People were searched in large numbers, and many who were found in possession of drugs (some of

---

[48] Lord Scarman provided the most influential arguments to this effect: *The Brixton Disorders 10–12 April 1981: Report of an Inquiry by the Rt. Hon. the Lord Scarman O.B.E.*, Cmnd. 8427 (London: HMSO, 1981), at pp. 2, 4–16, 100–12.

[49] *Southall, 23 April 1979: Report of the Unofficial Committee of Inquiry* (London: NCCL, 1980; subsequently published by Penguin); *The Death of Blair Peach: The Supplementary Report of the Unofficial Committee of Inquiry* (London: NCCL, 1980).

which form an acceptable part of Afro-Caribbean culture, as tobacco does in some Western cultures) were arrested and charged. People who were simply out in the street were liable to be charged with being a suspected person or reputed thief, loitering or acting suspiciously with intent to commit an arrestable offence;[50] the discretion which this gave to an arresting officer was extraordinary. The attack which this represented to community values and sensitivities sparked off riots which, Lord Scarman found, were anti-police rather than race riots. A similar pattern emerged in Bristol, where the riots were sparked off by one of many police raids on the Black and White Café in the St Paul's district, where many young Afro-Caribbeans spent a good deal of time.

Lord Scarman's inquiry had immediate results. Indeed, the 'sus' offence of being a suspected person was abolished even before Lord Scarman made his final report, by the Criminal Attempts Act 1981, section 9 of which substituted a far more tightly drawn offence of interfering with vehicles with the intention that someone should commit one of the offences of taking and driving away the vehicle without authority, or theft of or from the vehicle. The Police and Criminal Evidence Act 1984 imposed controls on police powers to stop and search people and vehicles (see Chapter 5 above), and backed up those controls with a Code of Practice. Two police disciplinary offences were also created: breach of the Codes, and racially discriminatory behaviour.[51] The Act also institutionalized a system of consultation between the police and local populations about policing matters. Community liaison committees were established, and police forces designated certain officers as community liaison officers with special responsibility for keeping in contact with community leaders.

Police management was also affected. For some time, there had been a debate between senior police managers about the best style of policing for different areas. Chief constables in some rural areas favoured 'community policing', with beat officers getting to know their areas, their problems, and the people who lived there. This idea emerged as a reaction against the increasingly technological reactive policing which developed during the 1960s and 1970s. It was seen by liberals, notably John Alderson, Chief Constable of Devon and Cornwall,[52] as a way of defusing tensions between the police and the community, as well as making for more

---

[50] Vagrancy Act 1824, ss. 4, 6, the much criticized 'sus law'. See for assessments of the working of the sections C. Demuth, *'Sus': A report on the Vagrancy Act 1824* (London: Runnymede Trust, 1978); P. Stevens and C. F. Willis, *Race, Crime and Arrests*, Home Office Research Study No. 58 (London: Home Office Research and Policy Unit, 1979). These provisions were subsequently repealed: see below.

[51] Police and Criminal Evidence Act 1984, ss. 67(8), 101(1)(b).

[52] John Alderson, *Policing Freedom* (London: Macdonald & Evans, 1979).

efficient information gathering and management of disorder. Other, more conservatively inclined, officers saw this as a move from law enforcement to a form of community service, and as being in tension with their ideas of the role of the police service. If too much weight were given to community views, it might lead (it was thought) to the creation of 'no-go areas' where the police would not enter and the law would not run.[53] The 'Swamp 81' operation in Brixton was an attempt to ensure that this would not happen.

Some of the heat was taken out of police–community relations following the Scarman report on the 1981 riots, but the social and economic conditions which Lord Scarman had noted as the background to the riots did not improve—indeed, in many cases they became worse—during the 1980s. Police forces had to give thought to other public-order problems, as in a series of industrial disputes they were given the job of controlling picketing by strikers, and escorting those who wished to work through the picket lines. This caused confrontation between the police and miners during the miners' strike of 1984–5, and later between police and print workers in the Wapping dispute (when Rupert Murdoch moved his newpaper and other print production operations from Fleet Street to the newly redeveloped Docklands area of London, modernized the processes, made many workers redundant, and broke the power of the print unions). There was further confrontation between the police and political protesters, notably at the peace camp at Greenham Common and at a demonstration when Leon Brittan, then Home Secretary, went to speak at the University of Manchester in 1985. The fact that these confrontations took place in front of television cameras tended to present the police with difficult problems. Where violence erupted, claims that it had been caused by demonstrators were sometimes discredited by the evidence of the cameras. Riot-control techniques were kept secret, but when details occasionally emerged it seemed that the police sometimes regarded all protesters as violent even before any violence had occurred, and in such cases the police would start the violence in trying to disperse the crowd. The Police Complaints Authority formed the view that this had happened at Wapping, although criminal charges against the officers suspected were later dismissed because of the time taken to bring them to trial.[54]

On a more positive front, however, attitudes seem to have changed. Although after the miners' strike some police authorities were unsuccessful in trying to prevent their forces being supplied with CS gas and baton

---

[53] See e.g. *R. v. Oxford, ex parte Levey, The Times*, 1 Nov. 1986, CA.

[54] *R. v. Bow Street Stipendiary Magistrate, ex parte DPP; Same v. Same, ex parte Cherry* (1989) 91 Cr. App.R. 283, DC.

rounds ('plastic bullets') for crowd control,[55] CS gas has not been used for riot control since the 1981 Toxteth riot, while water cannon were withdrawn by the Home Office in 1987.[56] The use of horses as weapons against the demonstrators, a potent tactic used by the police at Orgreave during the miners' strike, is uncommon. The need for sensitivity to the context in which threats to public order arise has been recognized by those planning police riot-control techniques.[57] The problem is that the law allows a wide discretion to the police in managing public order without giving much guidance as to the way in which the competing interests should be accommodated. Statutory guidance as to the approved balance of interests has been limited to the creation of new criminal offences in the Public Order Act 1986, which increase rather than limit police and prosecutorial discretion.[58] While it will never be possible to satisfy everybody, there are signs that more careful consideration is now given to the nature of the risk and the attendant dangers when deciding on the amount and type of force which it is reasonable to use in order to prevent crime, as permitted under the Criminal Law Act 1967, section 3.

(6) When and where can powers in respect of breaches of the peace be exercised?

Before a power can be exercised to prevent a breach of the peace, there must be either

(*a*) a breach of the peace in progress, or

(*b*) a reasonable apprehension of an imminent breach of the peace.

Where the power is exercised in an anticipatory way, the court will examine the constable's assessment of the risk to see whether it is honest and reasonable,[59] but will defer to the view of the constable on the spot where there is any doubt about it, taking account of the need for constables to form a view quickly and act on it.[60] This is illustrated by *Duncan* v. *Jones*,[61] where the court held that the magistrates had been entitled to

---

[55] R. v. *Secretary of State for the Home Dept., ex parte Northumbria Police Authority* [1989] QB 26, [1988] 1 All ER 556, CA.

[56] Leonard Jason-Lloyd, 'CS gas: An Indiscriminate Weapon?' (1991) 141 *NLJ* 1043–6.

[57] Waddington, *Strong Arm*, ch. 6, provides a detailed account and discussion of the technicalities of police riot-control equipment, but refuses to discuss tactics in order to preserve the element of surprise which, he says, is important to the success of police operations. Tactics are considered by G. Northam, *Shooting in the Dark: Riot Police in Britain* (London: Faber & Faber, 1988).

[58] See Peter Wallington, '(3) Some Implications for the Policing of Industrial Disputes' [1987] *Crim. LR* 180–91.

[59] *O'Kelly* v. *Harvey*, (1883) 15 Cox CC 435; *Lewis* v. *Chief Constable of Greater Manchester, Independent*, 23 Oct. 1991, CA.

[60] G. v. *Chief Superintendent of Police, Stroud* (1986) 86 Cr. App. R . 92, DC.

[61] [1936] 1 KB 218, DC.

conclude that there was a reasonable apprehension that a breach of the peace would result from a meeting organized in July 1934 to protest against the Incitement to Disaffection Bill, because disturbances had followed a similar meeting organized in May 1933. If this is sufficient to ground a reasonable apprehension of a breach of the peace, it would in effect have allowed the police to impose restrictive conditions on any meeting of any organization (or indeed on any football match) if a previous meeting or match had led to a breach of the peace. This is unsatisfactory, for it gives too much power to the police to stifle public protest and many other sorts of activity without adequate public accountability, legal or political, for their actions. As a matter of law, the reasons for a constable's apprehension of a breach of the peace should be subjected to very much closer scrutiny.

Another issue concerns the spatial and temporal relationship between the breach of the peace and the exercise of police power. The powers operate only when the reasonably and honestly apprehended breach of the peace is 'imminent'.[62] This has been held to mean that the exercise of the power must be sufficiently close both to the time and to the scene of the breach. In *Moss* v. *McLachlan*,[63] the police during the miners' strike stopped miners some miles from a colliery where there had been violent disturbances. The police feared that the miners were on their way to reinforce the pickets at the pit, contributing to a risk of further violence. They instructed the miners to turn back, and arrested those who refused. The Divisional Court held that this was sufficiently proximate in time and place to the disturbances to be a lawful exercise of the power to give instructions and take other steps to prevent a breach of the peace. Although the court's decision was heavily criticized by some commentators and by civil liberties groups, it allows the police a degree of flexibility in the management of an explosive situation. It would make the job of the police unreasonably difficult to insist that the police should have to allow large numbers of people to gather at the expected trouble spot before taking steps to relieve the situation. Nevertheless, such police action in creating an exclusion zone around trouble spots interferes with people's freedom of movement as well as their freedom to protest. The larger the exclusion zone, the greater the level of interference, and the more likely it is that innocent people will be seriously inconvenienced. There were many cases (which were not litigated) in which the police exceeded their powers by stopping people so far away from the scene of trouble that it could not even arguably have been a proper exercise of their power or a reasonable exercise of their discretion. For example, at

---

[62] *R.* v. *Howell* [1982] QB 416, [1981] 3 All ER 383, CA; *Lewis* v. *Chief Constable of Greater Manchester, Independent*, 23 Oct. 1991, CA.

[63] [1984] IRLR 76, DC.

one stage in March 1984 Kent miners (and all who looked like miners) were stopped at the Dartford Tunnel if the police thought that they were heading towards the Nottinghamshire, Durham, or Yorkshire collieries. This had the effect of confining those people to the southernmost counties of England for the duration of the dispute—a disproportionate and, it is submitted, unlawful exercise of state power.

(7) Preserving the peace and the Police Act 1964, section 51

In *Duncan* v. *Jones*,[64] Mrs Duncan had been planning to speak in the street opposite a training centre for unemployed workers. Apparently, there had been a disturbance on a previous occasion when she had addressed a meeting there. The police reasonably anticipated that her speech might precipitate a breach of the peace, and told Mrs Duncan that she was to hold her meeting in another street about 175 yards away. She refused, and began to speak. She was arrested (presumably to prevent a breach of the peace), and was later charged with obstructing a constable in the execution of his duty, under the forerunner to what is now section 51(3) of the Police Act 1964. The magistrates convicted, and their decision was upheld by the Divisional Court, which held that the police had been acting in the execution of their duty in trying to prevent a reasonably apprehended breach of the peace, and had been obstructed by Mrs Duncan's refusal to comply with the steps which the police thought necessary to avert the apprehended breach of the peace. The difficulty with this decision is that the use of the offence of obstruction presents the police with a means of criminalizing non-compliance with instructions about public speech and protest. Not only do the police have preventive powers; they also have the support of penal sanctions on the basis of statutory provisions which had in the past been regarded as aimed against physical obstruction rather than verbal disobedience, and were never intended by their drafters to be used to support public-order powers.[65] The decision made it possible for the police to turn public speech into a potential criminal offence on an *ad hoc* basis, whenever a constable reasonably apprehends a breach of the peace, merely by telling the speaker to stop. This is inconsistent with the notion that limitations on freedom of expression and protest should be prescribed by law, as required under Articles 10 and 11 of the European Convention on Human Rights.

   Duncan v. *Jones* might not be decided in the same way today, for it is

---

[64] [1936] 1 KB 218, DC.

[65] T. C. Daintith, 'Disobeying a Policeman: A Fresh Look at *Duncan* v. *Jones*' [1966] PL 248–61; Supperstone, *Brownlie's Law of Public Order and National Security*, 2nd edn., 111–14; A. T. H. Smith, *Offences against Public Order including the Public Order Act 1986* (London: Sweet & Maxwell, 1987), 174–6; Barendt, *Freedom of Speech*, 208.

now clear that the breach of the peace which is apprehended must be imminent in time and place.[66] Although imminence is a flexible standard, it is not clear that the officers in *Duncan* v. *Jones* did have any reason for apprehending that any breach would be imminent. Nevertheless, this is scarcely a satisfactory basis for a freedom to protest and express oneself in public on controversial issues. The difference between this and the American position is clear: under the First Amendment to the US Constitution, restrictions of freedom of speech and assembly are permissible only if the speaker is inciting people to unlawful action—not merely saying things which other people might react violently against, nor even advocating or promising violence—and the words or behaviour create a clear and present danger of violence.[67]

17.3 CRIMINALIZING PUBLIC DISORDER UNDER STATUTE

(1) Background

Parliament has utilized two means to control public disorder: first, creating criminal offences and attaching powers of arrest to them; secondly, creating statutory regulatory powers to control the routes and other incidents of processions and the terms on which meetings may be held. In doing so, Parliament has had to decide what types of behaviour are absolutely unacceptable, and what behaviour is acceptable if confined within limits. It has also had to settle the limits which are acceptable in the light of the need to maintain the conditions necessary for democracy. Finally, it has had to decide how much of the day-to-day operation of the system of regulation and control, including making decisions which (as noted above in relation to breach of the peace powers) have substantial policy implications, should be within the discretion of police officers and others, and how that discretion should be circumscribed.

Until the passing of the Public Order Act 1986, the criminal offences relating to public order were a mixture of old common-law crimes (riot, rout, affray, unlawful assembly, and public nuisance), and statutory offences to control picketing and the provocative display of uniforms and of armed force. The common-law offences were of considerable antiquity, and they belonged to an age when public gatherings and public

---

[66] *Moss* v. *McLachlan* [1984] IRLR 76, DC.

[67] *Brandenburg* v. *Ohio*, 395 US 444 (1969): quashing conviction of leader of Ku Klux Klan whose speech at a rally had included offensive and derogatory comments about Negroes and Jews; *Hess* v. *Indiana*, 414 US 105 (1973): anti-Vietnam war demonstrators blocking a street were removed by police, and threatened to return later; convictions for disorderly conduct in respect of the threat to return were quashed.

protest were seen as a threat to good government rather than as a part of the democratic activity which today legitimizes government. The essence of common-law riot was a gathering of three or more people (fewer, probably, than would be needed to form a riot in popular or journalistic usage of the word) giving effect to a common purpose, displaying force or violence in such a way as to alarm a person of reasonable firmness and courage, and intending to use force if necessary against anyone who opposes them.[68] Rout was essentially an attempted riot.[69] Unlawful assembly was an offence of uncertain scope,[70] but the Law Commission adopted, as a working definition, an assembly of at least three people with a common purpose either to commit a crime of violence or to achieve any object in such a way as to cause reasonable people to apprehend a breach of the peace.[71] Lord Hailsham LC described it as 'only an inchoate riot'.[72] Affray was unlawful fighting by at least one person (who might be fighting unlawfully even if the other fighter was lawfully trying to restrain him) in a public place, or on private premises where an innocent person was present, in such a way that the bystander was, or might reasonably be expected to have been, terrified.[73]

Alongside these common-law crimes were various statutory offences, of which the most used was section 5 of the Public Order Act 1936 (as amended), forbidding threatening, abusive, or insulting words, behaviour, or visible displays, in a public place or at a public meeting, with intent to provoke a breach of the peace or whereby a breach of the peace was likely to be occasioned. (Some local legislation was to a similar effect.) This section and related local legislation was used by the police as a catch-all provision, taking in any behaviour which did not clearly fall within the common law offences. Section 5 was used very much more broadly than its framers had expected: it had been introduced hurriedly and rushed through Parliament in 1936 as part of a package of measures aimed at quasi-military fascist groups which were terrorizing people with uniforms, military training, and public meetings and marches. Once passed, however, the section was used indiscriminately by police against people making a nuisance of themselves in public toilets, jumping on elasticated ropes from bridges, and doing a variety of other things which the police felt should be unlawful.

[68] *R. v. Caird* (1970) 54 Cr. App. R. 499, CA.

[69] See *Redford* v. *Birley* (1822) 1 St. Tr. (NS) 1071 at cols. 1211, 1214.

[70] For full discussion, see Law Commission Working Paper No. 82 (London: HMSO, 1982), ch. 2.

[71] Law Com. No. 123, *Criminal Law: Offences Relating to Public Order* (London: HMSO, 1983), para. 5.2, adopting the formulation of J. C. Smith and B. Hogan, *Criminal Law*, 4th edn. (London: Sweet & Maxwell, 1978), 750.

[72] *Kamara* v. *DPP* [1974] AC 104 at p. 116.

[73] *Button* v. *DPP* [1966] AC 591. HL; *Taylor* v. *DPP* [1973] AC 964, HL.

The regulatory mechanism in section 3 of the Public Order Act 1936 allowed a chief police officer to seek an order from a local authority with the Home Secretary's consent (in the City of London, from the Home Secretary alone) banning processions or a class of processions for a period not exceeding three months. It also allowed the chief police officer to impose such conditions on the procession as he thought necessary to preserve public order (subject to certain limitations). The power to ban processions, which had generally been used vary sparingly (although there was a spate of banning orders in the wake of the riots in inner-city areas in 1981), left too much discretion in the hands of the police to apply for bans (or, indeed, to impose conditions) where there was no real risk of substantial disorder, and the power to dictate conditions as to a route could make the procession an ineffective way of publicizing a grievance or appealing to the public. At the same time, the police were seeking legislation nationally to impose on the organizers of marches an obligation to give notice of processions so that appropriate measures could be planned to preserve order. Such obligations already applied locally under various local Acts. The greater the risk of major disorder, the stronger grew the acceptance of the need for such notice requirements, and the 1981 riots were influential in this regard. Lord Scarman, generally regarded as a libertarian in civil liberties matters, had opposed the general imposition of notice requirements in his report on the Red Lion Square disorders in 1975, but in his report on the Brixton riots of 1981 he changed his mind, deciding that a need for notice had been shown to exist.[74]

All this prompted a major re-examination of public-order law. The common-law offences were thought to be obscure and outdated; there was disquiet about the operation of the Public Order Act 1936; and the relationship between the common-law and statutory offences was in need of clarification. The statutory offences themselves, and the powers of the police under statute, were thought to need revision. The Law Commission, as part of its programme of codifying the criminal law, took on the responsibility for reviewing the common-law offences. The Home Office, responding to a critical report of the House of Commons Home Affairs Select Committee in the 1979–80 session, published a Green Paper on the 1936 Act in 1980.[75] Eventually, after much debate, proposals for legislative reform were turned into the Public Order Act

---

[74] Compare *Red Lion Square Disorders*, paras. 128–9, with *The Brixton Disorders*, paras. 7.45–9.

[75] Home Affairs Committee, *Fifth Report: The Law Relating to Public Order* HC 756 of 1979–80; *Review of the Public Order Act 1936 and Related Legislation*, Cmnd. 7891 (London: HMSO, 1980); Law Commission Report No. 123, *Criminal Law: Offences Relating to Public Order* (London: HMSO, 1983).

1986. However, one major area which was omitted from both the reviews and the reforms was that of powers to prevent breaches of the peace. This major source of power therefore remains on a common-law footing, as noted above.

(2) The Public Order Act 1986: criminal offences of public disorder[76]

The Public Order Act 1986 abolishes the common law offences of riot, rout, unlawful assembly, and affray,[77] and the offences under section 5 of the 1936 Act. In their place, Part I of the Act introduces five statutory crimes, following the Law Commission's recommendations. In decreasing order of seriousness, these are riot (section 1), violent disorder (section 2), affray (section 3), causing fear of or provoking violence (section 4), and causing harassment, alarm, or distress (section 5). As these offences may be committed either in public or in private places, and offences under sections 1, 2, and 3 may be committed even if nobody else is present.[78] 'Public Order Act' is a misnomer: these offences are aimed at private as well as public disorder.

Riot, the most violent offence, is triable only on indictment and carries a maximum penalty of ten years imprisonment and an unlimited fine.[79] A person commits this offence if:

(a) he is one of twelve or more people present together, who
(b) intends to use violence or is aware that his own conduct may be violent,[80] and
(c) the twelve actually use or threaten unlawful violence[81]
(d) for a common purpose,[82] in such a way as (taken together) would
(e) cause a hypothetical person of reasonable firmness, were one present at the scene, to fear for his personal safety.[83]

This provision increased the number of people required for riot, turning it into a small-crowd offence rather than a small group offence. It also clarified the *mens rea* of the offence.

[76] A. T. H. Smith, 'The Public Order Act 1986 Part I: The New Offences' [1987] *Crim. LR* 156–67; *id.*, *Offences against Public Order*, chs. 3–7.

[77] Public Order Act 1986, s. 9(1). In the remainder of the present section, all s. nos. refer to the Public Order Act 1986 unless otherwise specified.

[78] See ss. 1(4), (5); 2(3), (4); 3(4), (5); 4(2); 5(2).   [79] Section 1(6).

[80] Public Order Act 1986, s. 6(1). Intoxication caused by any means does not negative *mens rea* if a sober person would have realized that his conduct may be violent, unless the defendant shows either (a) that the intoxication was not self-induced, or (b) that it was caused solely by the taking or administration of a substance in the course of medical treatment: s. 6(5), (6).

[81] They need not all satisfy the *mens rea* requirements: s. 6(7).

[82] The common purpose may be inferred from conduct: s. 1(3).   [83] s. 1(1).

Violent disorder is committed by members of a violent small group or crowd who do not (necessarily) have a common purpose. It is triable either summarily (maximum sentence: six months imprisonment and fine not exceeding the statutory maximum) or on indictment (five years imprisonment and unlimited fine).[84] A person is guilty of violent disorder if:

    (*a*) he is one of three or more people present together, who

    (*b*) intends to use or threaten violence or is aware that his conduct may be violent or threaten violence,[85] where

    (*c*) the three actually use or threaten unlawful violence (not necessarily simultaneously)[86] in such a way that (taking their conduct together)

    (*d*) it would cause a hypothetical person of reasonable firmness, were one present at the scene, to fear for his personal safety.[87]

Because of element (*c*), if only three people were present and all are charged with the offence, and one is acquitted on the ground that he did not actually use violence, the other two must also be acquitted. The fact that the third person was aiding and abetting the other two cannot make the three of them, or any of them, guilty of the offence, even if the other two were using violence together.[88] If the evidence is that other people, who have not been charged, were involved in the violence as well, then it will be possible to convict the accused as long as it is proved beyond reasonable doubt that at least three people, including the accused, were using violence unlawfully.[89]

Affray is committed by a person who:

    (*a*) uses or threatens (by conduct, not mere words: see section 3(3))[90] unlawful violence towards another person, and

    (*b*) his conduct, together with that of anyone else who is using or threatening unlawful violence, would cause a hypothetical person of reasonable firmness, if one were present, to fear for his personal safety.

The offence is triable summarily, with the same sentence as for violent disorder, or on indictment, with a maximum prison term of three years.

---

[84] s. 2(7).

[85] s. 6(2). 'Threat' is therefore an objectively, rather than subjectively, judged phenomenon. See also s. 6(5), (6).

[86] They need not all satisfy the *mens rea* requirements: s. 6(7).   [87] s. 2.

[88] *R. v. McGuigan and Cameron* [1991] Crim. LR 719, CA. See also *R. v. Fleming and Robinson* [1989] Crim. LR 658, *R . v. Mahroof* [1989] Crim. LR 72.

[89] *R. v. Worton* [1990] Crim. LR 124, CA. (The appeal was allowed on other grounds.)

[90] As for violent disorder, the test of 'threatening' is objective, not subjective: s. 6(2).

This means that affray, unlike riot and violent disorder, is not an arrestable offence, and so cannot be a serious arrestable offence, within the meaning of the Police and Criminal Evidence Act 1984. A power to arrest without warrant is conferred on a constable by section 3(6), probably unnecessarily, since affray will virtually always give rise to a breach of the peace giving a common-law power of arrest to anyone. The arrest power under the Act is more limited than the common-law power, as it applies only where a constable reasonably suspects that the arrestee is committing the offence, not where he reasonably apprehends that a breach of the peace is about to occur.

Causing fear of, or provoking, violence is an offence committed by a person who behaves in certain ways towards someone else, who must actually be present. A person is guilty if:[91]

(a) he (i) uses threatening, abusive, or insulting words or behaviour, or (ii) distributes or displays to another person any writing, sign or other visible representation which is threatening, abusive or insulting,

(b) in a public place, or in a private place unless the words, behaviour, etc., are used or displayed inside a dwelling and the person to whom they are addressed is within the same or another dwelling,

(c) he intends the words, behaviour, writing, sign, etc., to be threatening, abusive, or insulting, or is aware that they may be threatening, abusive, or insulting,[92] and

(d) he intends, or the conduct is likely, (i) to cause the other person to believe that immediate unlawful violence will be used against him or anyone else by any person, or (ii) to provoke the immediate use of unlawful violence by that person or another.[93]

The offence covers part of the ground previously covered by section 5 of the Public Order Act 1936. Under that section, it was an offence if the words or behaviour were objectively threatening, abusive, or insulting and were either intended or likely to occasion a breach of the peace. Under the new Act, there must be a subjective recognition of the nature of the words or behaviour, and a fear of violence engendered in an identified person. The elements of the old section 5 which are not covered by the offence of causing fear of or provoking violence are incorporated in the less serious offence of causing harassment, alarm, or distress, which is outlined below.

The offence of causing fear of, or provoking, violence is triable

[91] s. 4. [92] s. 6(3). Note also s. 6(5), (6).
[93] Only one offence is created by s. 4, but it may be committed in a number of different ways. See *Wynn v. DPP, Independent*, 4 May 1992, DC.

summarily, with a maximum sentence of six months imprisonment and a fine not exceeding level 5 on the standard scale. It is therefore not an arrestable offence, but a constable is given power to arrest without warrant anyone he reasonably suspects is committing the offence. Again, this is a narrower power than the concurrent common-law power to restrain a reasonably apprehended breach of the peace, which will often be available.

Causing harassment, alarm, or distress is an offence punishable only by a fine not exceeding level 3 on the standard scale. It penalizes anyone who:

(a) (i) uses threatening, abusive, or insulting words or behaviour, or disorderly behaviour, or (ii) displays any writing, sign, or other visible representation which is threatening, abusive, or insulting,[94]

(b) in a public place, or in a private place unless the words, behaviour, etc., are used or displayed inside a dwelling and the person to whom they are addressed is within the same or another dwelling,

(c) within the sight of another person, who must be a real rather than a hypothetical person for this purpose,

(d) who is likely to be caused harassment, alarm, or distress thereby,[95] and

(e) the defendant intends the words, behaviour, writing, etc., to be threatening, abusive, or insulting, or is aware that it may be, or intends or is aware that his behaviour shall or may be disorderly.[96]

The test of awareness and intention is subjective, so the prosecution must show that the accused is aware of the threatening, abusive, or insulting nature of the display etc. If the defendant is not aware of the fact that those seeing a display of, for example, an aborted foetus might think it threatening, abusive, or insulting, he cannot be convicted.[97] This offence covers part of the field previously dealt with by section 5 of the old 1936 Act, but is wider than the old Act, because the new provision does not require that the conduct is likely to occasion a breach of the peace, and it goes beyond the sort of behaviour which is aimed at bystanders, being threatening, abusive, or insulting. Instead, it criminalizes mere horseplay which may be categorized as 'disorderly behaviour'.

However, the rigour of this is slightly modified by giving the accused a defence if he can discharge the burden of proving (on the balance of probabilities) that either:

[94] Note that a person who is part of a crowd of people committing this offence may be guilty as an aider and abettor, even if the person himself was not doing anything specified by the section: see *DPP* v. *Fidler* [1992] 1 WLR 91, DC, and the commentary by Professor J. C. Smith, [1992] *Crim. LR* at p. 63.
[95] Public Order Act 1986, s. 5(1), (2).   [96] Ibid. s. 6(4); note also s. 6(5), (6).
[97] *DPP* v. *Clarke, Lewis, O'Connell and O'Keefe* [1992] Crim. LR 60, DC.

(a) he had no reason to believe that there was anyone within hearing or sight who was likely to be caused harassment, alarm or distress; or

(b) where he was in a dwelling, he had no reason to believe that the words, behaviour, writing, etc., would be heard or seen by anyone outside that or another dwelling; or

(c) that his conduct was reasonable.[98]

Under defence (a), the defendant who can show that he did not believe, subjectively, that a display could have the effect of causing harassment, alarm, or distress to others present would be entitled to be acquitted.[99] This means that people, particularly when demonstrating about emotive issues such as abortion, have some protection against the oversensitivity of others. However, once the effect on observers has been pointed out to a demonstrator, the use of the same display in future is unlikely to attract the defence, since he will no longer be able to say that he had no reason to believe that it was likely to cause harassment, alarm, or distress. Under defence (c), the reasonableness of a display is to be judged objectively. Accordingly, a bench of magistrates was entitled to find that it was not objectively reasonable for anti-abortion campaigners to display a picture of an aborted foetus when demonstrating outside a clinic where abortions were performed.[100]

As there need be no threat of violence or breach of the peace, the power to arrest without warrant for this offence is heavily circumscribed. A constable may arrest without warrant only where the suspect has engaged in 'offensive conduct' (defined as conduct the constable reasonably suspects to be an offence under section 5), the constable has warned him to stop, and the suspect engages in further offensive conduct (which may or may not be of the same type as that which provoked the original warning) immediately or shortly after the warning.[101] The warning need not be given in any set or formal terms. A court will look at the substance of the conversation, and, if it was clear that the constable would arrest the defendant if the behaviour recurred, it will suffice.[102]

This offence, and its related arrest power, have equivalents in other jurisdictions. In Scotland, the common-law offence of breach of the peace is said to encompass any conduct which may reasonably be expected to to cause any person to be alarmed, upset, or annoyed, or to provoke a disturbance, or which is likely to lead to such consequences if

---

[98] s. 5(3).

[99] DPP v. Clarke, Lewis, O'Connell and O'Keefe [1992] Crim. LR 60, DC.

[100] See n. 99.   [101] s. 5(4), (5).

[102] Groom v. DPP [1991] Crim. LR 713, DC.

allowed to continue.[103] In New Zealand there are equivalent statutory provisions. However, any such offence is subject to two objections.

First, it makes criminal a very wide and unpredictable range of types of behaviour. The object of the prohibition on disorderly conduct was to target hooliganism, particularly drunken hooliganism, in public, and it seems to have been assumed that there would be fairly general agreement about what constituted disorderly conduct. However, one may doubt whether this is so. Disorderly conduct is a relative notion, and depends heavily on context. Where one expects high standards of conduct, any non–conforming behaviour may be thought disorderly. Behaviour which would be thought disorderly in a street or a bar, such as abusive shouting, might not be disorderly in a place where expected standards of conduct are lower, such as the floor of the House of Commons or a rugby-club dinner. There is a danger that conduct will be stigmatized as criminal not because of its intrinsic nature, or the expectations of the people in the area where it occurs, but because the police and, at the hearing, the magistrates disapprove of the expected standards of conduct and wish that higher (or different) standards obtained. In terms of civil liberties and the rule of law, it is unacceptable to make the imposition of criminal sanctions depend on uncertain and variable standards.

Secondly, quite apart from the discretion given to the police, Crown Prosecution Service, and magistrates, the arrest power may appear less concerned with preventing harassment, alarm, or distress to citizens than with bolstering the authority of the constable. The event which triggers the arrest is not the original unlawful act but the disobedience to a constable. Generally, there is (probably) no power to arrest for obstructing a constable in the execution of his duty unless the obstruction also amounts to an arrestable offence, another offence carrying a power to arrest without warrant, or a breach of the peace, although conduct which does not amount to any offence may lead to an arrest if a person is reasonably suspected of an earlier offence and the later conduct satisfies the general arrest conditions under section 25 of the Police and Criminal Evidence Act 1984 (see Chapter 5 above). Here, however, the challenge to the authority of the constable, which results where a suspect wants to push his luck or show off to friends by disobeying the constable, may lead to an arrest. Perhaps it is a justification that, because of the definition of 'offensive conduct' in section 5(5), the arrest might avoid further harassment, alarm, or distress to bystanders. Yet this will not necessarily be the case, as it has been held in *Director of Public Prosecutions* v. *Orum*[104] that an offence under section 5(1) may be committed even where the only per-

---

[103] *Wilson* v. *Brown* 1982 SC CR 49; K. D. Ewing and W. Finnie, *Civil Liberties in Scotland: Cases and Materials* 2nd edn. (Edinburgh: W. Green & Son, 1988), 412–14.
[104] [1989] 1 WLR 88, [1988] 3 All ER 449, DC.

son likely to be caused harassment, alarm, or distress is a police officer. Although at trial a court would have to consider whether the conduct, etc. would actually have been likely to cause harassment, alarm, or distress (rather than weariness and boredom) to the constable, given that constables soon become familiar with many impolite forms of behaviour,[105] the constable himself might not be in the best position to make that assessment in the heat of the moment before deciding to make an arrest. In addition, where the 'offensive conduct' relied on is 'disorderly conduct', it raises again all the uncertainties and disagreements which may surround the meaning of the latter term.

Racial hatred. A further public order offence is created in Part III of the 1986 Act, namely the use of words or behaviour, or display of written material, intended or likely to stir up racial hatred contrary to section 18. This is a public-order offence only in the loosest sense, since it can be committed in private premises, and need not lead to any (or any immediate) disorder. A person is guilty of an offence under section 18 if:

(a) he (i) uses threatening, abusive, or insulting words or behaviour, or (ii) displays any written material (but not other types of representation) which is threatening, abusive, or insulting,[106]

(b) in (i) a public place, or (ii) in private unless it is inside a dwelling and the words, etc., are not heard or seen except by people in that or another dwelling, and

(c) he intends thereby to stir up racial hatred or racial hatred is likely to be stirred up thereby.[107]

This replaces a provision which used to form section 70 of the Race Relations Act 1976. It goes beyond being a race relations offence, however, because under section 18 stirring up racial hatred is unlawful only if it is done by means of threatening, abusive, or insulting words, etc. Where this happens in public, it gives rise to a risk of violent reaction which justifies criminal sanctions. However, people may be guilty if they use the words, etc., in private places (other than dwellings) where everyone present agrees with the sentiments expressed. Presumably, the justification for criminalizing this sort of behaviour is that those present may be encouraged to convert their hatred into concrete action later. However,

[105] For discussion of this familiarity in a different context, see *Cheeseman* v. *DPP* [1992] QB 83, [1991] 3 All ER 54, DC.

[106] There is an exception if this is solely for the purpose of being included in a broadcast or cable service programme: s. 18(6). Broadcasts and cable programmes are dealt with under s. 22.

[107] s. 18(1), (2). To establish the necessary *mens rea*, the prosecution must show that the defendant intended to stir up racial hatred, or intended the words, etc. to be, or was aware that they might be, threatening, abusive, or insulting: s. 18(5).

it is unusual for words or behaviour to constitute an offence in the absence of an immediate threat to somebody else. Any attempt to give practical expression to hatred outside is likely to constitute an offence, so it is particularly draconian to impose liability at the pre-attempt stage on words or conduct which might not even amount to an incitement to commit any offence. Fortunately the section has been very rarely invoked. The Attorney General's consent is needed for any prosecution,[108] and everyone concerned with law enforcement is conscious that a prosecution might be counter-productive in terms of public sympathy. Not only does a trial (whether summary or on indictment) give a bigot a privileged platform for his views with plenty of free publicity, but the defendant will be able to claim the moral high ground by concentrating on the inroads which section 18 makes on freedom of expression, freedom of association, and rights of privacy. No less importantly, the sentence (up to two years imprisonment and an unlimited fine after a conviction on indictment, or up to six months and a fine not exceeding the statutory maximum in the magistrates' court)[109] may make the defendant appear to be a martyr.

Part III of the 1986 Act is concerned with racial hatred, not incitement to other sorts of hatred. 'Racial hatred' is defined as: 'hatred against a group of persons in Great Britain defined by reference to colour, race, nationality (including citizenship) or ethnic or national origins.'[110] This uses the same extended definition of 'racial' as was used in the Race Relations Act 1976, and it will be interpreted in the same way as it has been under that Act.[111] As yet, it remains to be seen how courts will interpret 'hatred'. It seems to cover the stirring up of naked ill feeling, but not to encompass messages which affront the dignity or sensitivities of members of the racial groups or their sympathizers. It is also unclear what is meant by 'stir up' hatred. The phrase seems different from 'incite' or 'instigate', as it would include stirring up hatred which already exists. A racist preaching to other racists could be stirring up their hatred, encouraging them to give it free rein, if he expressed their existing shared feelings in a sufficiently provocative way. It seems likely, therefore, that political programmes which advocate forced emigration of certain ethnic groups would not automatically stir up racial hatred, but the manner of their expression might do so.

The harassment, alarm, and distress offence under section 5 of the 1986 Act are capable of applying to racist speech even if it does not stir up racial hatred for the purpose of Part III of the Act. Although this places a restraint on free expression, it is not necessarily an unjustifiable

---

[108] s. 27(1).   [109] s. 27(3).   [110] Public Order Act 1986, s. 17.
[111] See Ch. 18, below.

restraint, as section 5 regulates all threatening, abusive, and insulting speech and behaviour which causes harassment, alarm, or distress, not merely racist speech and behaviour. In terms of the European Convention on Human Rights, there is a question mark over whether there is a pressing social need for such legislation, and whether it is proportionate to the legitimate aim pursued (the prevention of disorder), but it does not on its face discriminate against any one viewpoint more than others. In order to prevent the state from acting as censor of points of view, this is important. As the US Supreme Court has recognized, the protection to free expression given by the First Amendment to the US Constitution does not cover all forms of expression.

The state, then, has a legitimate interest in regulating or banning certain categories of expression, including 'fighting words' which give rise to a clear and present danger of disorder.[112] However, a recent decision of the Court establishes that any restriction must avoid being 'content based': it must be directed against the manner of expression, rather than against the message conveyed. In *R.A.V. v. St. Paul*,[113] the petitioner had allegedly been one of a party which had taped together two chair legs to make a crude cross, and had then burnt it, employing classic Ku Klux Klan symbolism, on a black family's lawn. He had been charged under the Bias-Motivated Crime Ordinance of the City of St Paul, Minnesota, which prohibited the display of a symbol which one 'knows or has reason to know arouses anger, alarm or resentment in others on the basis of race, color, creed, religion or gender'. The Supreme Court accepted the interpretation of the Ordinance by the Supreme Court of Minnesota, which held that it was restricted to 'fighting words', so the Ordinance was not constitutionally overbroad. Nevertheless, the majority held that the Ordinance was facially invalid, because it outlawed expressive behaviour by reference to its content: only fighting words relating to race, colour, creed, religion, or gender were prohibited. People wishing to use fighting words in relation to those subjects were at a disadvantage compared to people wishing to use fighting words against (for example) trades unions or homosexuals. As the minority judges argued, this seems to lead to a potential paradox, in that a limitation on freedom of speech was struck down under the First Amendment for prohibiting, not too much speech, but too little: it appears to create a doctrine under which restrictions on speech can be struck down for 'underbreadth' rather than overbreadth. (In *R.A.V.*, the minority were prepared to strike down the Ordinance on the basis of overbreadth, because it extended to behaviour which merely arouses anger, alarm, or resentment, rather than being

---

[112] *Chaplinsky v. New Hampshire*, 315 US 568 (1942).
[113] 60 USLW 4667, 120 LEd 2d 674 (1992).

limited to conduct which inflicts injury or tends to incite immediate violence, as demanded by *Chaplinsky*. Even the majority relied, as an alternative ground of decision, on the tendency for the Ordinance to be implemented in a discriminatory way, being applied to anti-black advocates rather than advocates against discrimination.) Nevertheless, the significance of the way in which interferences with freedom of expression operate against advocates on particular subjects, or with particular viewpoints, in a discriminatory way emphasizes the importance to civil liberties of political neutrality in the drafting of rules which restrict the liberty.

(3) Watching and besetting[114]

Another criminal offence with public-order implications is that under section 7 of the Conspiracy and Protection of Property Act 1875. This legislation was directed against trades unions, and section 7 deals with intimidation. It makes it an offence for a person, wrongfully and without legal authority, persistently to follow another from place to place, to watch or beset a person's house or place of work, or to follow him, with two or more other persons, in a disorderly manner in or through a street or road, with a view to compelling the person to do or abstain from doing any act which the victim has a legal right to do or refrain from doing. This offence has been deployed against pickets in industrial disputes, but has recently been used against demonstrators in support of political causes such as abortion law reform. In *Director of Public Prosecutions* v. *Fidler*,[115] where demonstrators chanted outside a clinic where lawful abortions were performed, the prosecutor suggested that the offence was committed where people tried to dissuade people from going in to have pregnancies terminated. The Divisional Court held that persuasion, and obtaining or communicating information, did not amount to compulsion within the meaning of section 7, even if verbal abuse was used and shocking pictures of aborted foetuses were displayed. As there was no evidence that anyone had been prevented from performing or undergoing a termination, the charge under section was held to have been rightly dismissed by the justices.

This is an essential limitation on the scope of section 7. Were it not so limited, it could be used to stifle free expression in public on matters of public concern, and to criminalize the behaviour of people exericising their right to protest.

---

[114] Smith, *Offences against Public Order*, 213–18.   [115] [1992] 1 WLR 91, DC.

(4) Obstructing the highway and public nuisance[116]

The control of processions is a very difficult matter, because of the variables which have to be taken into account. These include the number of people processing, which may be unpredictable, the reaction of others to the procession, the traffic implications, and the availability of police resources to ensure that contingencies are provided for. If things go wrong, the police tend to suffer public criticism. This sometimes makes police officers very cautious, particularly where a procession is to take place in support of a cause which is likely to attract a counter-demonstration. The problems facing officers who have to try to keep two rival groups apart are unenviable, and can be seen regularly at soccer matches as well as political demonstrations.

The general principles of law governing processions are relatively straightforward. On the highway, anyone has a *prima facie* right to pass and repass along it, and to make necessary stops for a rest or to make repairs.[117] This applies to people who are part of processions and demonstrations as to anyone else. However, by virtue of statute and common law people have no right to stop on the highway unreasonably. Any wilful obstruction of free passage along a highway without lawful authority or excuse is an offence under the Highways Act 1980, section 137. 'Wilful' here means intentional, in the sense of deliberate.[118] There need not be an intention to obstruct the highway, as long as the deliberate act or omission of the defendant objectively viewed has the effect of obstructing it.[119] A partial obstruction of the highway will suffice, if it is an unreasonable use of the highway.[120]

Obstructing the highway also constitutes a public nuisance at common law if it is unreasonable.[121] The highway authority is responsible for seeing that the highway is kept free for passage. This applies to the police as to other road users:[122] a road block is therefore unlawful unless within

---

[116] Supperstone, *Brownlie's Law of Public Order*, 2nd edn., 42–50; Smith, *Offences Against Public Order*, ch. 11; Ewing and Finnie, *Civil Liberties in Scotland*, 365–8, 388–94.

[117] See e.g. *Harrison* v. *Duke of Rutland* [1893] 1 QB 142; *Hickman* v. *Maisey* [1900] 1 QB 753; for Scotland, *McAra* v. *Edinburgh Magistrates* 1913 SC 1059.

[118] *Arrowsmith* v. *Jenkins* [1963] 2 QB 561, [1963] 2 All ER 210, DC.

[119] *Cooper* v. *Comr. of Police of the Metropolis* (1985) 82 Cr. App. R. 238, DC.

[120] *Homer* v. *Cadman* (1886) 16 Cox CC 51.

[121] *R.* v. *Clark (No. 2)* [1964] 2 QB 315, [1963] 3 All ER 884, CCA: a demonstration by an anti-nuclear-weapons group in London, blocking several streets, not necessarily unreasonable.

[122] The Highways Act 1980 has been held not to bind the Crown, however. It was held that a road may therefore be narrowed in order to facilitate repairs to a Ministry of Defence establishment without the need for any application for permission from the Highways Authority: *Lord Advocate* v. *Dumbarton DC* [1990] 2 AC 580, [1990] 1 All ER

the statutory powers granted by, for example, the Police and Criminal Evidence Act 1984, section 4. This means that, while a moving procession is *prima facie* lawful, sitting down in the road to block the traffic is *prima facie* an unlawful means of protest both at common law and under statute. Where a road user is doing something other than passing along the road, they need lawful authority or excuse.

Lawful authority or excuse takes account of the reasonableness of the activity or inactivity which causes the obstruction. As campaigning depends on bringing matters to the attention of the public, at least where one wants to do more than preach to the converted, streets are cheap and convenient places to make one's views known. With the increasing importance of broadcasting as a means of imparting information and opinions, the public demonstration, leafleting, or picketing might have been expected to decline in importance, but access to broadcasting remains difficult for most people, access to the newspapers depends on editorial and proprietorial discretion (see Chapter 13 above), and special difficulties in obtaining publicity attach to campaigners for local or unpopular causes. Because of this, public demonstrations remain important ways of raising public consciousness of a cause or issue. It is perhaps true, as Sir Robert Mark suggested in the mid-1970s, that: 'Political demonstrations seem to give satisfaction in the main to those taking part. The public as a whole are usually not interested unless affected by inconvenience or aroused by disorder or violence.'[123] However, it is equally true that the satisfaction of participants derives in part from the knowledge that they are taking a rare opportunity to put their views across to others. This is why, as Sir Robert went on to note, 'the right to hold them is much valued and jealously preserved'.[124]

It is therefore not true to say that all unauthorized obstructions to the highway are unlawful. The reasonableness of the obstructer's behaviour, considering the scale of the obstruction and the object in view, must be taken into account, and if the obstruction is reasonable in the circumstances it will provide a lawful excuse under section 137 of the Highways Act 1980.[125] A very minor obstruction may be excused under the *de min-*

1, HL. However, this decision seems to rest on an over-wide view of the bodies which constitute the Crown, and on a contested view of the extent of the 'shield of the Crown' doctrine which has been rejected in Australia and is inconsistent with previous Scottish decisions.

[123] Sir Robert Mark, QPM, 'The Metropolitan Police and political demonstrations', *Report of the Commissioner of Police of the Metropolis for the year 1974*, app. 8, at para. 13. (Quoted in Bailey, Harris, and Jones, Civil Liberties, 3rd edn., 148–9.)

[124] Mark, 'Metropolitan Police', para. 13.

[125] *Nagy v. Weston* [1965] 1 WLR 280, [1965] 1 All ER 78, DC; *Hirst and Agu v. Chief Constable of West Yorkshire* (1986) 85 Cr. App. R. 143, DC.

imis principle.[126] Nevertheless, the reasonableness of the protesters' behaviour provides at best an uncertain defence to a prosecution, as it is dependent on the magistrates' view as to reasonableness. This may vary according to the ethos of particular benches, or perhaps the political or other causes which the protesters espoused.

17.4 POWERS TO REGULATE PROCESSIONS AND ASSEMBLIES IN PUBLIC PLACES[127]

There are various prior restraints on processions and assemblies in public places. Sometimes, private individuals who suffer harm from a procession or assembly in a public place can obtain injunctions to stop the harm. This is particularly common in relation to picketing. Where the picket, was outside an estate agent's office, by people protesting at the effect on the character of Islington of property owners moving in from elsewhere (the so-called gentrification of Islington), an interlocutory injunction was granted to restrain the picket, pending hearing of the estate agent's action for a private nuisance allegedly caused by the protesters in watching and besetting the premises.[128] When picketing forms part of industrial action, the pickets' unions are protected against actions in tort only so long as their members attend only at their own place of work.[129] Injunctions may be granted against the union if pickets attend elsewhere.[130] Major industrial action can cause intimidation of non-striking workers, and produce interference with their right to work which goes beyond peaceful attempts to persuade them to strike.[131] To cater for such cases, there is a Code of Practice on Picketing, which, although not legally binding, represents good practice and may be taken into account by courts when it becomes relevant.[132] Although the relevant statute is not limited by

[126] *Putnam* v. *Colvin* [1984] RTR 150, where, however, the obstruction (more than 30 plant pots containing shrubs) was not thought to be within the *de minimis* principle.

[127] A. L. Goodhart, 'Public Meetings and Processions' (1937) 6 *CLJ* 161–74; D. G. T. Williams, '(2) Processions, Assemblies and the Freedom of the Individual' [1987] Crim. LR 167–79; Smith, *Offences against Public Order*, ch. 8.

[128] *Hubbard* v. *Pitt* [1976] QB 142, [1975] 3 All ER 1, CA.

[129] Trade Union and Labour Relations Act 1974, s. 15, as substituted by Employment Act 1980, s. 16(1); Employment Act 1980, s. 16(2); Employment Act 1982, ss. 14–16.

[130] *Thomas* v. *National Union of Mineworkers (South Wales Area)* [1986] Ch. 20, [1985] 2 All ER 1; *News Group Newspapers Ltd.* v. *Society of Graphical and Allied Trades 1982* [1986] IRLR 337.

[131] This was recognized by NCCL, *Civil Liberties and the Miners' Dispute: First Report of the Independent Inquiry* (London: NCCL, 1984), 6, 10.

[132] Employment Act 1980, s. 3; Employment Code of Practice (Picketing) Order 1980, SI 1980/1757.

statute,[133] the Code describes excessive numbers of pickets as the main cause of violence and disorder on picket lines, which may get out of control, leading to arrests and prosecutions.[134] The Code advises that people demonstrating support for the industrial action should do so well away from the picket line, normally leaving a maximum of six pickets to persuade people not to enter the premises.[135]

It is not the job of the police to enforce industrial relations law, although there were suspicions during the miners' dispute and the action against News International in Wapping that they were doing so. The police are conscious of the importance for their authority and effectiveness of appearing neutral in maintaining public peace and upholding the law when faced by problems arising out of industrial or political action. Nevertheless, as Paul Wiles has written, during the 1980s 'the police's claim to objectivity, as upholders of the rule of law, was undermined because the law in question was seen by many trade unionists as partial'.[136] In relation to both industrial and other demonstrations and meetings, the police have extensive powers, independently of industrial relations law, to prevent obstructions of the highway, including a power to arrest an obstructer whether or not there is any imminent risk of a breach of the peace.[137] The remainder of this section deals with these powers, treating powers in respect of processions and those in respect of other assemblies separately.

(1) Processions on highways

The police have all the usual common-law powers to prevent breaches of the peace. This means that they can give directions as to the route of the procession in order to avoid trouble which emerges during the course of the procession, and arrest people if necessary to prevent the occurrence, continuance, or recurrence of a breach of the peace which is in progress or is reasonably apprehended as being imminent: see section 2, above. However, as the powers can be exercised only when the breach of the peace is imminent in time and place, they cannot be used to ban a procession or to impose conditions on the organizers in advance. This makes them of limited value as aids to planning. The Public Order Act 1986,

---

[133] Trade Union and Labour Relations Act 1974, s. 15 as substituted.

[134] Code of Practice, para. 29.

[135] Ibid., paras. 30, 31. See generally Bryn Perrins, *Harvey on Industrial Relations and Employment Law* (London: Butterworths, 1992), binder 2, division N, s. 18.

[136] Paul Wiles, 'Law, Order and the State', in Cosmo Graham and Tony Prosser (eds.), *Waiving the Rules: The Constitution under Thatcherism* (Milton Keynes: Open University Press, 1988), 153–73 at 163.

[137] Police and Criminal Evidence Act 1984, s. 25; see particularly s. 25(3)(d)(v).

Part II, passed in the wake of the disorders and riots of 1981, has therefore conferred additional powers on the police and imposed certain duties on people who organize public processions. 'Public procession' means any procession in a public place, and 'public place' is defined in turn as meaning any highway (or, in Scotland, a road within the meaning of the Roads (Scotland) Act 1984), and any place to which the public has access at the material time, as of right or by virtue of express or implied permission, on payment or otherwise.[138] It does not include, for this purpose, land to which people can obtain access as trespassers. 'Procession' is not defined in the Act. In a case under the Public Order Act 1936 Lord Denning M.R. defined 'public procession' as 'the act of a body of persons marching along in orderly succession'.[139] It is important that the people be acting in concert. An orderly crowd moving along Oxford Street at sale time is not a procession.

(i) *Notice of processions*. The legislation requires written notice to be given of any proposed public procession which is intended to demonstrate support for or opposition to the views or actions of any person or persons, or to publicize a cause or campaign, or to mark or commemorate any event. This is wide enough to encompass religious and charitable fund-raising processions as well as political ones.[140] The notice must be delivered to a police station in the police area where the procession is to start or (if it starts in Scotland) in the area where it will first enter England.[141] The notice must reach the police station at least six clear days before the date when the procession is intended to be held, either by recorded delivery or by hand.[142] If it is not reasonably practicable for it to be delivered six clear days in advance, it must be delivered by hand as soon as is reasonably practicable.[143] It must specify the intended date, starting time, and route of the procession, and give the name and address of at least one of the people proposing to organize it.[144]

Each organizer of a procession commits an offence, punishable by a fine, if the procession takes place without notice being given, or does not comply with the date, time, or route specified in the notice, unless he can prove either (*a*) that he did not know of, and had no reason suspect, the failure to satisfy the requirements or comply with the specified details in the notice, or (*b*) that any difference in the date, time, or route arose

[138] s. 16.
[139] *Kent v. Metropolitan Police Commissioner, The Times*, 13 May 1981, CA.
[140] s. 11(1).   [141] s. 11(1), (4).
[142] s. 11(5), which excludes the operation of s. 7 of the Interpretation Act 1978, so that notice sent by post is not deemed either to be served when posted or to have been delivered in the ordinary course of the post.
[143] s. 11(6).   [144] s. 11(3).

from circumstances beyond his control or from something done with the agreement, or under the direction, of a police officer.[145] The defence allows an organizer to comply with the request of a constable at the scene to change the route or time, for example in order to avoid a breach of the peace.

The only processions of the kind mentioned above for which notice is not required are (a) those commonly or customarily held in that police area, and (b) funeral processions organized by a funeral director acting in the ordinary course of his business. The latter exception can be important, as (particularly in the case of violent deaths of political activists, or the funerals of people killed in clashes with the police) the funeral procession may be a focus of anger and emotion as well as displaying respect for the dead. However, although written notice of such processions is not required under section 11, the police have power to impose conditions on them under section 12 or, in extreme cases, to make a banning order under section 13.

(ii) *Imposing conditions on processions.* The power to impose conditions on public processions under the Public Order Act 1986, section 12, is bestowed on the chief officer of police beforehand, and on the senior officer at the scene once people have begun to assemble.[146] It can be exercised if the officer reasonably believes, having regard to the time, place and route of the procession, that either (a) it may result in serious public disorder, serious damage to property, or serious disruption to the life of the community, or (b) the organizers' purpose is to intimidate others with a view to compelling them not to do or omit something which they have a right to do or omit.[147] The conditions take the form of directions to the organizers, and may be such as appear to the officer to be necessary to prevent the anticipated disorder, damage, disruption, or intimidation. Section 12(1) provides that they may include, but are not limited to, conditions as to the route of the procession, or prohibiting it from entering any specified public place. Anyone who organizes or takes part in a public procession who knowingly fails to comply with a condition, or who incites another not to comply, is guilty of an offence, but organizers and participants, other than those inciting people not to comply, have a defence if they can prove that the failure to comply arose from circumstances beyond their control.[148]

[145] s. 11(7), (8), (9).
[146] s. 12(2). In Scotland, the power only applies at the scene once people have begun to assemble: s. 12(11).
[147] s. 12(1).
[148] s. 12(4), (5), (6). Organizers and inciters face up to three months imprisonment and a fine; others face a fine: s. 12(8), (9), (10). This is separate from the offence of wilfully

This impliedly presents organizers with further duties: they are responsible, at least in large measure, for ensuring that the procession goes where it is supposed to go. They must exert their persuasiveness and authority to ensure that people not only attend, but that they behave while they are processing. Organisers normally appoint stewards to do this. This should ease the job of the police. In the 1980 Green Paper, the Home Office floated but ultimately rejected the idea that organizers of demonstrations should be made to pay for the policing necessary to prevent disorder at them. It was felt that this would be likely to make it impossible for anyone who lacked very substantial amounts of money to organize a lawful demonstration, removing one of the chief advantages for those who do not have access to the media or money to pay for an advertising campaign. It would also impose a burden on organizers of processions to pay for the policing of counter-demonstrations by people seeking unlawfully to disrupt their lawful procession.[149] The Act, by making the organizers responsible for ensuring that, so far as possible, the details contained in their notice and any conditions imposed by the police are complied with, helps to reduce the burden on the police without making it financially impossible for ordinary people to mount processions. Certain policing operations are paid for by their beneficiaries: for example, soccer clubs can be required to pay for the policing of home matches where substantial numbers of police are needed inside the ground, as this constitutes a 'special police service' for which the police are entitled to charge.[150] However, policing a public demonstration is not such a service, as it is intended to protect the public at large rather than prevent disorder on the private premises of a commercial enterprise.

The discretion which the Act accords to the police, particularly in relation to the nature of any conditions, is staggeringly wide. Even under the power to ban processions under section 3 of the Public Order Act 1936 (now repealed and replaced) it was held that an *intra vires* exercise of the officer's discretion was reviewable by the courts only if the applicant could show that there had been no reasonable ground on which a banning order could have been made.[151] On the wording of section 12 of the 1986 Act, it would seem that the officer would have to be able to show reasonable grounds for believing that disorder, etc., might result from the march, but his judgement about the conditions necessary to prevent such disorder is well nigh unreviewable. Furthermore, the

obstructing a constable in the execution of his duty, contrary to section 51(3) of the Police Act 1964.

[149] Cmnd. 7891, paras. 64–5.

[150] Police Act 1964, s. 15(1); *Harris* v. *Sheffield Utd. Football Club Ltd.* [1988] QB 77, [1987] 2 All ER 838, CA.

[151] *Kent* v. *Comr of Police of the Metropolis, The Times*, 15 May 1981, CA.

discretion is wider than that which used to apply under section 3(1) of the 1936 Act, which prevented conditions being imposed to restrict the display of flags, banners, or emblems unless the restrictions were reasonably necessary to prevent a breach of the peace. This discretion imposes a prior restraint on freedom of expression and protest. Because the statute fails to provide narrowly drawn, reasonable, objective, and definite standards to guide the exercise of the discretion, it would be regarded as facially unconstitutional under the First Amendment to the US Constitution.[152] Furthermore, because the officer exercising the discretion must consider the probably reaction of other groups to the views expressed by the procession, the content of those views is inevitably relevant to the extent of freedom of expression, since those whose views are unpopular with bottle-throwers will have a more restricted freedom than those whose views are popular, or unpopular only with people who are too civilized or apathetic to initiate a fracas over them. Such a content-based prior restraint on freedom of expression in a public forum would, in the USA, be regarded as an unconstitutional interference with First Amendment rights.[153]

The discretion to lay down conditions may be sometimes be partially justified on the ground that conditions are in principle less of a restriction on public expression and democratic activity than a complete ban. However, sometimes a condition as to the route to be taken, or timing, may seriously affect the impact of the procession. For example, as the Green Paper on *The Public Order Act and Related Legislation*[154] pointed out, there may be circumstances in which a march to a foreign embassy is planned to protest a country's policy on, for example, torture or capital punishment. The point of the march would be to make the country's diplomats aware of the strength of public feelings, so that they can inform their government. The point would be partly, if not wholly, lost if the procession had to be routed away from the embassy.

Constables in uniform have power to arrest without warrant anyone whom they reasonably suspect to be committing a section 12 offence.[155] This is apart from the common-law power which they have to arrest in order to restrain conduct likely to provoke a breach of the peace.

(iii) *Prohibiting processions*. If the power to impose conditions is questionable on human rights and civil liberties principles, a power to ban processions entirely is *a fortiori* objectionable. Nevertheless, section 13 of the

---

[152] *Cantwell* v. *Connecticut*, 310 US 296 (1940); *Niemotko* v. *Maryland*, 340 US 286 (1951); *Freedman* v. *Maryland*, 380 US 51 (1965); *Shuttlesworth* v. *Birmingham*, 394 US 147 (1969).

[153] *Forsyth County* v. *Nationalist Movement*, 60 USLW 4597, 120 LEd 2d 101 (1992).

[154] Cmnd. 7891, 1980, para. 68.   [155] s. 12(7).

1986 Act (which replaced section 3(3) and (4) of the 1936 Act) provides a power to prohibit public processions, or a class of public processions, entirely. This comes into operation where the chief officer of police reasonably believes that the powers to impose conditions on a public procession under section 12 will be insufficient to prevent serious public disorder resulting from public processions held in a district or part of a district, because of the particular circumstances existing in that district or part.[156]

Outside London[157] the chief officer cannot make an order himself. He is under a duty (he is not exercising a discretionary power) to apply to the council for an order prohibiting the holding of all public processions, or a specified class of them, in the district or part of the district concerned, for a specified period not exceeding three months. The council may then make an order (though it has a discretion), with the consent of the Home Secretary, either in the terms requested in the chief officer's application or with such amendments to those terms as the Home Secretary is prepared to approve.[158]

In London, the Commissioner of Police of the Metropolis, or (in the City) the Commissioner of Police for the City of London, may make a similar order with the consent of the Home Secretary.[159] This special treatment is the result of several peculiarities in the position of London. First, as the capital city, it attracts far more demonstrations than other places. Traditional gathering places for public assembly, protest, and demonstration, such as Trafalgar Square and Speaker's Corner at Hyde Park, are within its area. This presents special policing problems. Secondly, the Metropolitan Police and City of London Police are responsible for order and security at Westminster and Whitehall, in the environs of Parliament and government, and for foreign embassies. This again presents special problems. Thirdly, the metropolis has no single council or pair of councils covering the entire Metropolitan Police area which could act as a police authority. (Even when there was a Greater London Council, before 1986, it did not operate as a police authority.) The London boroughs are fragmented, and as processions can easily move between boroughs it would be cumbersome to have to obtain orders from large numbers of borough councils, which might make differing political judgements. As the Home Secretary is accountable to Parliament, and as the police authority for London is in a good position to know about the political and policing considerations, the Act bypasses the London borough councils and makes the Commissioner responsible for banning orders, subject to the Home Secretary's approval. In the past,

---

[156] s. 13(1).   [157] s. 13(3).   [158] s. 12(2).

[159] s. 13(4). Orders may be revoked or varied by further orders made in the same way: s. 13(5).

except in the year or so immediately following the Brixton riots in 1981, the power to make orders has been sparingly used, in London as elsewhere.[160]

This three-stage process (chief officer of police, local authority, and Home Secretary)[161] is required because the decision to ban processions combines policing and political considerations. The police must make an assessment of the risks arising from a procession, and to decide on the basis of intelligence and experience, both generally and of local conditions, whether any risk can be avoided by imposing conditions under section 12. If a risk of serious public disorder exists and, in the chief officer's reasonable belief, cannot be avoided by imposing conditions, a further question arises: does the risk outweigh the value of allowing people to express themselves publicly, by any means which are not intrinsically unlawful, in a democracy? This question is essentially one calling for political judgement, and is properly left to the authorities which are democratically accountable: the council, elected locally and knowing local conditions, and the Home Secretary, accountable to Parliament for the maintenance of both order and democracy.

The power to prohibit operates in a much narrower band of circumstances than the power to impose conditions: it does not apply to circumstances giving rise to a risk of serious damage to property, serious disruption to the life of the community, or intimidation, unless the chief officer reasonably believes that they will result in serious public disorder. Of course, this may well be the case, but the chief officer must consider the likelihood and seriousness of the disorder which will result. A minor scuffle, or series of them, will not qualify as serious public disorder; nor, it is submitted, will serious disruption to community life which is not accompanied by violence. Unlike the position under section 12, it is not a sufficient condition for banning processions under section 13 that the chief officer reasonably believes that serious public disorder *may* result. Under section 13, he must reasonably believe that imposing conditions *will* not be sufficient to prevent serious serious public disorder resulting. The more demanding standards under section 13(1) are necessary for two reasons: first, because a ban normally stifles free expression more completely than imposing conditions; secondly, because, in order to avoid discrimination against processions by particular groups or opinions, section 13(1) does not permit the banning of a single procession. Instead, the chief officer of police must apply to the council for an order prohibiting all public processions, or a specified class of processions, in the district or part of a district concerned, for a specified period not exceeding three

[160] Bailey, Harris, and Jones, *Civil Liberties*, 3rd edn., 181–5.

[161] Two-stage process in London—Commissioner of Police of the Metropolis or Commissioner of Police for the City of London, and Home Secretary—s. 13(4).

months. The repercussions of applying for an order may therefore go well beyond the particular procession.

The Act, in section 13(6), provides that the order must, if not made in writing, be recorded in writing as soon as practicable after being made. The Act does not provide for it to be publicized in any way, but it will normally be contained in a press release and publicized widely. Its effectiveness depends on it being known to all who might be planning processions in the area. It is an offence for anyone to organize, take part in, or incite another to take part in a public procession which he knows to be prohibited by a section 13 order,[162] and a constable in uniform may arrest without warrant anyone whom he reasonably suspects to be committing any such offence.[163]

In London, the Commissioners of the Metropolitan Police and City of London Police have a further power, under the Metropolitan Police Act 1839, section 52, to

make regulations . . . for preventing obstruction of the streets and thoroughfares within the metropolitan police district, in all times of public processions, public rejoicings, or illuminations, and also to give directions to constables for keeping order and for preventing any obstruction of the thoroughfares in the immediate neighbourhood of her Majesty's palaces and the public offices, the High Court of Parliament, the courts of law and equity, the police courts, the theatres, and other places of public resort . . .

This authorizes regulations, which have been made by way of Sessional Orders, controlling processions in the vicinity of Westminster. However, the regulations must be concerned with preventing obstructions to the highway or (at common law) breaches of the peace. If they are not directed to those objects, they will be wider than necessary, and (if not severable) will be *ultra vires*. In *Papworth v. Coventry*,[164] a person protesting against the Vietnam war taking part in a well-ordered and peaceable vigil in Downing Street, which did not cause an obstruction of the highway, was charged with failing to comply with a section 52 direction (contrary to section 54(9)) which had purported to ban all assemblies and processions in the Westminster area during the parliamentary session. He was convicted at summary trial, but had his conviction quashed on appeal, because there had been no disorder or obstruction. The scope of the directions, and the manner of their enforcement, must (on ordinary principles of administrative law) be within the objects contemplated by the enabling legislation.

---

[162] s. 13(7), (8), (9).   [163] s. 13(10).
[164] [1967] 1 WLR 663, [1967] 2 All ER 41, DC.

(2) Powers to regulate other assemblies in publicly owned places

Public places are not *res nullius*. They are actually vested in and the property of some body. For example, beaches are vested in the Crown or the local authority;[165] Hyde Park, with its famous Corner, is vested in the Crown;[166] highways, including Trafalgar Square, a traditional venue for meetings, are vested in the Crown or local authorities, subject to a right of members of the public to pass and repass on them.[167]

There have long been regulations covering the use of specific public places.[168] These regulations are subject to judicial review if they are outside the powers conferred by the enabling legislation. For example, in *Director of Public Prosecutions* v. *Hutchinson*[169] a protester at the airbase at Greenham Common had been convicted of entering without permission the area enclosed by the perimeter fence of the base, contrary to By-law 2(*b*) of the RAF Greenham Common Byelaws 1985, made under section 14(1) of the Military Lands Act 1892. This subsection contained a proviso that rights of common were not to be prejudicially affected. By-law 2(*b*) contained no saving for rights of the commoners on Greenham Common, so the House of Lords held that it was *ultra vires*. As the by-law was held not to be severable, the House quashed the defendant's conviction, although she was not herself a commoner. Where an *intra vires* regulation is in force, a local authority may obtain an injunction to restrain threatened breaches. For example, in *Burnley BC* v. *England*[170] the council had passed a by-law banning dogs from certain parks. Protesting dog owners planned a procession with their dogs through one of the parks, as a political statement and act of civil disobedience in support of what they conceived to be their civil liberties. The council obtained interim and final injunctions to restrain the march.

Apart from specific regulations, the use of a highway for an assembly is *prima facie* a public nuisance and a contravention of section 137 of the Highways Act 1980 if passage along the highway is obstructed. Although the police have a discretion as to how to use their powers to remove the

---

[165] *New South Wales* v. *Commonwealth (Seas and Submerged Land Case)* (1975) 135 CLR 337; *Llandudno Urban District Council* v. *Woods* [1899] 2 Ch. 705; *Brighton Corporation* v. *Packham* (1908) 72 JP 318.

[166] *Bailey* v. *Williamson* (1873) LR 8 QB 118, DC. See *Royal and Other Parks and Gardens Regulations 1977*, SI 1977, No. 217.

[167] *R.* v. *Graham and Burns* (1888) 16 Cox CC 420; *Ex parte Lewis* (1888) 21 QBD 191, DC.

[168] See Supperstone, *Brownlie's Law of Public Order*, 35–8; Williams, *Keeping the Peace*, 72–86.

[169] [1990] 2 AC 783, [1990] 2 All ER 836, HL.

[170] (1977) 76 LGR 393 (interlocutory injunction); (1978) 77 LGR 227 (permanent injunction).

obstruction, the fact that other meetings have been held at the same place in the past will not prevent the next one from being prosecuted as an obstruction. Thus in *Arrowsmith v. Jenkins*[171] the Divisional Court upheld the conviction of Pat Arrowsmith for obstructing the highway on a road where she had previously held other meetings to make speeches protesting against nuclear arms. The meeting had largely blocked the road, and had made it difficult for a fire engine to get through. Although Ms Arrowsmith had co-operated with the police by making announcements asking people in the crowd to clear the road, it was held that she had caused the highway to be obstructed and had been rightly convicted.

Alongside the duty to keep the highway clear, the organizers of meetings on highways and elsewhere face two sets of powers. The common law powers to prevent reasonably apprehended breaches of the peace apply to meetings as they do to processions. This was held in *Duncan v. Jones*[172] to entitle the police to direct a speaker to move away to another spot 175 yards away if he is speaking in a place where he is likely to attract a hostile crowd. As noted above, one of the unsatisfactory aspects of the decision itself is the cursory nature of the court's review of the grounds for the constable's asserted belief that an imminent breach of the peace was reasonably to be apprehended. In addition, however, there were dicta which obliquely suggested that the police might possibly be expected to protect the meeting, rather than move it, if the apprehended breach of the peace was likely to result from the acts of people opposed to the views expressed at the meeting, rather than from the behaviour of people supporting the meeting itself. This presents the continuing problem of the duties of the police where a lawful meeting is threatened with disruption by a violent opposition group.

The second set of powers which organizers of public assemblies face is that in the Public Order Act 1986, section 14(1). This permits the chief officer of police or senior officer at the site of the meeting[173] to give directions imposing certain conditions on the assembly. Such directions may be given only if both the following conditions apply.

1. The meeting is a public assembly within the meaning of the Act. A public assembly consists of 20 or more people in a public place (any highway or any place to which the public, or any section of the public, has access as of right or by virtue of any express or implied conditions, on payment or otherwise).[174] This means that most cricket or football

---

[171] [1963] 2 QB 561, [1963] 2 All ER 210, DC.   [172] [1936] 1 KB 218, DC.

[173] Public Order Act 1986, s. 14(2). The chief officer may delegate the power to a deputy or assistant chief constable (in London, an assistant commissioner): s. 15.

[174] s. 16. The place may be indoors or out of doors. These provisions remove doubts which arose under the earlier legislation as to whether or not a railway platform or

matches with two teams of eleven, plus officials, are public assemblies, and the emotions engendered amongst supporters and players regularly give rise to public-order problems. On the other hand, the premises of clubs which have a genuine system for scrutinizing applications for membership are normally excluded, as their members do not constitute a 'section of the public'.[175] People who enter private land as trespassers are not within the definition of a public assembly, and separate powers are provided in section 39 of the 1986 Act to allow the police to direct trespassers to leave land.[176]

2. The officer reasonably believes that, having regard to the place or time of the assembly and the circumstances in which it is to be held (or being held), *either* it may result in serious public disorder, serious damage to property, or serious disruption to the life of the community, *or* the purpose of the organizers is to intimidate others with a view to compelling them to refrain from doing something which they have a right to do, or to do something which they have a right not to do.

These criteria have been considered above in relation to section 12 of the 1986 Act.

The directions may be given to the organizers of or participants in a public assembly. They may include such conditions as appear to the officer to be necessary to prevent the anticipated serious public disorder, damage, disruption, or intimidation, but the conditions may relate only to the place at which the assembly may be held or may continue, its maximum duration, or the maximum number of people who may attend. This gives the officer a very wide discretion which, being couched in subjective language, is likely to be virtually unreviewable in legal proceedings so long as the power has been directed to a proper purpose. When given in advance by the chief officer or his delegate, the directions must be given in writing,[177] which will help to avoid misunderstandings. It is an offence for an organizer or participant knowingly to fail to com-

football-ground terrace, to which access was available on purchase of a ticket or payment of an entrance fee, was a public place.

[175] *Charter* v. *Race Relations Board* [1973] AC 868, [1973] 1 All ER 512, HL. The effect of the case has been restricted for the purposes of race relations law by the Race Relations Act 1976, s. 25, but the case remains good persuasive authority on the meaning of 'section of the public' in statutes. The grounds of football clubs which operate a membership scheme, and admit only members (as Luton Town FC did for some time), may come within this exception.

[176] This was a power aimed mainly at hippy convoys which caused a national stir by ensconcing themselves on farmers' land in Wiltshire and the surrounding areas during the passage of the Public Order Bill, in connection with celebrations of the summer solstice at Stonehenge which were blocked by English Heritage, which controls the site of Stonehenge.

[177] s. 14(3).

ply with a valid direction, unless the accused can show that the failure arose from circumstances beyond his control. This might occur, for example, where a limit on the number of participants is exceeded when the meeting is invaded by a rival group; but in such circumstances it would probably be necessary for the organizer to show that he had taken reasonable steps to prevent gatecrashers, for example by positioning stewards in adequate numbers for normal purposes. A constable in uniform may arrest without warrant anyone whom he reasonably suspects of committing such an offence.[178]

The statutory power to give directions in advance of public assemblies is wider than that available at common law, as it can be exercised well before any breach of the peace is imminent, unlike the power to prevent a breach of the peace upheld in *Duncan* v. *Jones*. It can also be exercised in advance of any obstruction to a highway, unlike the exercise of power which was in question in *Arrowsmith* v. *Jenkins*. It is also exercisable in order to avoid consequences, such as serious disruption to the life of the community, which might not amount to a breach of the peace. Although there is no requirement for organizers of a public assembly (in contrast with a public procession) to give notice of it to the police, in practice the police usually hear in advance about any large assemblies which are being planned, and organizers themselves often consult with police about public-order issues arising from the planned assembly.

On the other hand, once a public assembly is in progress it is hard to see what advantage the statutory powers offer. They go no further than the power in *Duncan* v. *Jones*, except with regard to disruption to community life which does not amount to a breach of the peace (admittedly rather hard to envisage), and are not apt to impose conditions relating to dress or the display of banners or other indications of political or religious adherence, and so are somewhat narrower than the common law power upheld in *Humphries* v. *Connor*.[179] Perhaps the enactment of section 14 reflects a certain concern as to the propriety of relying on heavily criticized common law decisions for a power to interfere in the assemblies of people pursuing lawful purposes in apparently lawful ways.

17.5 REGULATION OF ASSEMBLIES IN PRIVATE PREMISES

(1) Rights to meet in private

State intervention in a private assembly held on private premises potentially interferes with several sets of rights. It may infringe rights to privacy

---

[178] Ibid., s. 14(5), (6), (7).   [179] (1864) 17 Ir. CLR 1.

and property, and (according to the purpose of the assembly) to freedom of expression, religion, or philosophical conviction. Accordingly the powers of state agencies in respect of such assemblies is limited. Where there is a sufficient element of publicity in the surrounding circumstances, Parliament has allowed the police or others a regulatory role, as in relation to public processions and assemblies discussed above, or the powers of the Secretary of State for the Environment under the Trafalgar Square Regulations 1952, SI 1952, No. 776. There is also power to remove trespassers from private land where two or more trespassers have a common purpose of residing on the land for any period, however short, if (a) the occupier has taken reasonable steps to ask them to leave, and (b) the trespassers have either brought twelve or more vehicles on to the land (a provision aimed at hippy convoys prevalent in the spring and summer of 1986), or have damaged property on the land, or have used threatening, abusive or insulting words or behaviour towards the occupier, a member of his family, or one of his employees or agents.[180]

Generally, however, the state has eschewed power to regulate private meetings held in private. This has two sets of implications. First, it means that landowners cannot usually be forced to allow, or prevented from allowing, their property to be used in any particular way. This is similar to the position in the USA, where action taken by a landowner to interfere unreasonably with freedom of speech on his property will not normally be restrained by the courts under the First Amendment to the US Constitution.[181]

Secondly, where the landowner is a public authority or performing a public function, there are few prospects of compelling the authority to allow its property to be used by the public. In the USA, it would be constitutionally improper for a public authority to discriminate in the access which it allowed to different groups for meetings. In the UK, there are certain situations in which people have a right to use public premises for meetings in the course of election campaigns (see Chapter 12, above). There are some signs that courts will constrain the behaviour of public-authority landowners to ensure that their allocation of the property, or use of it, conforms to public-law principles.[182] However, this has never yet been used to impose an obligation on an authority to allow its property to be used for meetings unless there is a statutory requirement, as in the case of election meetings, or a contract, in which case the authority's discretion to change its mind and prevent a meeting

---

[180] Public Order Act 1986, s. 39(1).
[181] *Hudgens* v. *NLRB* 424 US 507 (1976), overruling *Amalgamated Food Employees Union* v. *Logan Valley Plaza* 391 US 308 (1968).
[182] *Wheeler* v. *Leicester City Council* [1985] AC 1054, [1985] 2 All ER 1106, HL.

by an extreme right-wing political party is subject to the ordinary law of contract.[183]

(2) Criminal offences

Certain types of meeting receive special protection from the criminal law. These are meetings which are thought to be for the public benefit in some way. For example, it is an offence to act in a disorderly manner at a lawful public meeting for the purpose of preventing the transaction of business, and a constable who reasonably suspects a person of committing the offence can ask for his name and address.[184] A refusal, or giving a false name or address, constitutes an offence.[185] If the person refuses, or the constable has reason to suspect that a false name or address has been given, the person may be arrested.[186] It is an offence to commit riotous, violent, or indecent behaviour in places of worship,[187] or to use force to prevent a minister from celebrating divine service.[188] However, generally meetings are subject to the ordinary criminal and civil law.

(3) Entry by the police to gatherings on private premises

The only power which has been clearly asserted in relation to private meetings is a common law power to enter, or remain on, private premises in order to stop or prevent a breach of the peace. As noted above, breaches of the peace are regarded as matters in which there is a sufficient public interest to justify an extension of police powers even into private houses. The police may therefore enter or remain on premises to stop a breach of the peace which is in progress, or to conduct a fresh pursuit of a person who has just been causing a breach of the peace. They may also stay for long enough to ensure that the breach is not likely to recur. However, they may not enter premises to arrest a person for a breach of the peace once it has ended and the risk of repetition has abated.[189]

---

[183] *Verrall* v. *Great Yarmouth Borough Council* [1981] QB 202, [1980] 1 All ER 839, CA. See also *Webster* v. *Newham London Borough Council, The Times*, 22 Nov. 1980, CA.

[184] Public Meetings Act 1908, s. 1(1).

[185] Ibid., s. 1(3), added by Public Order Act 1936, s. 6.

[186] Police and Criminal Evidence Act 1984, s. 25; see Ch. 5 above.

[187] Ecclesiastical Courts Jurisdiction Act 1860, s. 2; breach of the Peace of the Church (*círicfrith*) has been a serious offence since the early 7th cent. at latest: Laws of Ethelbert (AD 601–4), c. 1.

[188] Offences against the Person Act 1861, s. 36. See St. John A. Robilliard, *Religion and the Law: Religious Liberty in Modern English Law* (Manchester: Manchester University Press, 1984), 15–19.

[189] *R.* v. *Marsden* (1868) LR 1 CCR 131; *Robson* v. *Hallett* [1967] 2 QB 939, [1967] 2

Less clearly established is an anticipatory power to enter private meetings in order to prevent an apprehended breach of the peace. The scope
of this power is uncertain, having its origin in unreserved judgments in a
decision of the Divisional Court in *Thomas* v. *Sawkins*.[190] That case was
one of several arising from the social and political unrest of the 1930s,
and concerned a meeting at a private hall in Glamorgan in 1934 to
protest against the Incitement to Disaffection Bill, then before
Parliament, and to demand that the Chief Constable of Glamorgan be
dismissed. This was one of several meetings addressed by Alun Thomas,
which the police had attended despite being asked to leave. The magistrates found as a fact that, at previous meetings, seditious speeches had
been made, the Chief Constable had been vilified, and breaches of the
peace had followed. In the instant case, the police again decided to
attend, and the magistrates found that the police had reasonable grounds
for apprehending that there would again be 'seditious speeches . . .
and/or incitements to violence and/or breaches of the peace' at the
meeting. The organizers invited the public to attend the meeting. The
police officers who arrived at the meeting were refused admission, but
entered regardless. They were then twice asked to leave by Alun
Thomas. When they refused to do so, Thomas said that they would be
ejected, but, when he tried to eject Inspector Parry, Sergeant Sawkins
pushed Thomas's arm away. The police stayed, but Thomas later prosecuted Sergeant Sawkins for assault and battery. The matter turned on
whether the officers had had a right to remain. If they had not, Thomas
had been entitled to use reasonable force to remove them after revoking
any implied licence to enter the hall, and the use of force to resist ejection had been unlawful. If the police had a legal right to remain, the
attempt at ejection was unlawful, and the sergeant had been entitled to
use reasonable force to repulse the attempt. The magistrates decided that
the police had been entitled to remain in order to prevent reasonably
apprehended sedition, breach of the peace, or incitement to violence, and
acquitted the sergeant. Thomas appealed by case stated.

Three unreserved judgments dismissing the appeal were delivered in
the Divisional Court. Lord Hewart CJ gave a judgment, which is unsatis-
factorily reported,[191] in which he spoke of a preventive power and duty

All ER 407, DC; *McConnell* v. *Chief Constable of Greater Manchester Police* [1990] 1 WLR
364, [1990] 1 All ER 423, CA. See generally David Feldman, *The Law Relating to Entry,
Search and Seizure* (London: Butterworths, 1986), 321–3.

[190] [1935] 2 KB 249. For discussion and criticism, see A. L. Goodhart, 'Thomas v.
Sawkins: A Constitutional Innovation' (1936) 6 *CLJ* 22–30; D. G. T. Williams, *Keeping
the Peace*, ch. 6, especially at pp. 142–4; Feldman, *Entry, Search and Seizure*, 323–31.

[191] Note the differences between the report at 33 LGR 330, presumably compiled
from the contemporaneous shorthand note, and that at [1935] KB 249, presumably
revised by Lord Hewart subsequently.

of the police to enter premises where a constable has reasonable ground for believing that an offence is imminent or is likely to be committed. This formulation, as it stands, is unsatisfactory in two respects. First, it goes beyond the prevention of breaches of the peace, appearing to encompass any offence. However, the judgment must be read in the context of the findings of the magistrates, which were expressly referred to by Lord Hewart when he spoke of 'such reasonable grounds of apprehension as the justices have found here'. That apprehension related to sedition, breach of the peace, and (which is the same thing) incitement to violence. All the offences consisted of, or entailed, breaches of the peace or the threat of one. That being so, the term 'offence' as used by Lord Hewart must, it is submitted, be understood as applying only to breaches of the peace which, as noted above, infringe a recognized public interest and give rise to special powers and duties of police acting, as Lord Hewart said, *ex virtute officii*. This is particularly important today, after Parliament has established a legislative balance between the competing interests involved in these cases. In the Police and Criminal Evidence Act 1984, sections 17, 18, and 32, Parliament has provided a code of police entry powers in respect of criminal offences, and abolished other powers of entry in respect of offences not involving breaches of the peace in section 17(5). Secondly, Lord Hewart's formulation appears to allow entry before the offence is imminent. However, this cannot stand with later decisions, notably that of the Court of Appeal (Criminal Division) in *R. v. Howell*,[192] to the effect that powers and duties arise only when the breach of the peace is imminent.

Noting that the prosecutor's case depended on the policemen being trespassers, Lord Hewart remarked that it seemed 'somewhat remarkable to speak of trespass when members of the public who happened to be police officers attend, after a public invitation, a public meeting which is to discuss as one part of its business the dismissal of the chief constable of the county'. In other words, the police were to be regarded as members of the public who had been invited to attend, as they had a legitimate interest in the matter under consideration. But this argument fails, because on the facts found by the magistrates any licence issued to the officers had been revoked by the organizers. The question, therefore, was whether the officers had had any independent right to remain, such as might override the withdrawal of their licence. That right could come only from the duty to prevent a reasonably apprehended and imminent breach of the peace.

Avory J. therefore rightly concentrated on the question whether on the facts of the case the organizers could effectively withdraw the invita-

---

[192] [1982] QB 416, [1981] 3 All ER   383, CA.

tion from the officers, and he decided that they could not. He restricted his decision to the prevention of breach of the peace or sedition at widely publicized meetings to which the general public had been invited. Lawrence J. limited his decision firmly to the facts of the case, and so may be thought to have adopted a formulation of the entry power even narrower than that of Avory J. The preventive or anticipatory power of the police to enter should, it is submitted, therefore be seen as restricted to cases where a meeting has been advertised, the public are invited, and the police have reasonable grounds for apprehending that a breach of the peace (or offences involving breaches of the peace, such as sedition and inciting violence) will occur at the meeting if the police are not present. In this form, the power is, as Avory J. pointed out, analogous to the power to bind over to keep the peace when no breach is imminent. It would not allow the police to enter private premises to attend a meeting of a private group against the organizers' wishes.

However, even when so limited the power is controversial. Before the decision in *Thomas* v. *Sawkins*, the official line had been that no such anticipatory power to enter private premises existed at common law.[193] Only ten weeks before the events which gave rise to *Thomas* v. *Sawkins*, the Home Secretary had told the House of Commons that the police had no such power.[194] The presence of the police may be successful in preventing a breach of the peace, but one will never know: as in *Thomas* v. *Sawkins* itself, where there was no violence or disorder an the event, it is impossible to tell whether a breach would have occurred without the police presence. In addition, there is a risk that the presence of the police will stifle debate and free expression. On the facts of *Thomas* v. *Sawkins* itself, this amounted to a probability: the presence of more than thirty officers by the time the meeting started, with batons drawn on entry, looks more like a crude attempt to suppress expressions of public opinion about the Chief Constable. This makes Lord Hewart's comment, 'It goes without saying that the powers and duties of the police are directed, not to the interests of the police, but to the protection and welfare of the public', look disingenuous. However, it is perhaps not unreasonable to allow the police unrestricted access to meetings to which the public has been invited if there is a reasonably apprehended risk of a breach of the peace, as the presence of members of the general public creates a special public interest in maintaining order which, if the meeting were restricted to a private group, could properly be the responsibility of the organizers.

---

[193] See *Report of the Departmental Committee on the Duties of the Police with respect to the Preservation of Order at Public Meetings*, Cd. 4673 (London: HMSO, 1909) at p. 6.

[194] Sir John Gilmour, 14 June 1934, 290 HC Debs. (5th Series) 1968, in connection with the policing of violence at a fascist meeting at Olympia a week earlier.

(4) An entry power in respect of private premises without public meetings?

The question next arises whether the power extends beyond public meetings. There are cases where it has been held that the police have an anticipatory power to enter private premises to prevent reasonably apprehended domestic violence. This was one of the grounds of decision in *McGowan* v. *Chief Constable of Kingston upon Hull*,[195] in which a man had forcibly seized a child from his former cohabitant in order to lure her back. She went to the house with two constables, who entered with her in reliance first on her invitation and secondly on their reasonable apprehension that a breach of the peace might imminently occur. The man assaulted the constables, and was convicted of assaulting them in the execution of their duty. On appeal, it was held that they had been in the execution of their duty, being lawfully on the premises both because of the woman's invitation[196] and because of the reasonable apprehension of a breach of the peace. However, it seems from the report in *The Times* that the defendant might have conceded that the police had a right to enter initially, and *Thomas* v. *Sawkins* was not considered by the court, so the decision is of limited value. Parliament had already created a power to obtain a warrant to enter and search premises where children are reasonably believed to be at risk, and another to make arrests in certain cases.[197] Once an imminent breach of the peace is reasonably apprehended, or is in progress, a constable can enter or remain on land in order to suppress it.[198] This should be a sufficient power. It is anomalous for the courts to invent powers of entry in situations beyond those where Parliament has seen fit to act.

17.6 RESTRICTING PROTEST AND FREE EXPRESSION BY BAIL CONDITIONS AND BINDING OVER

The discussion so far has been about general norms which are used to enable the authorities to regulate public protest in order to prevent disorder, or to criminalize types of behaviour. However, there are certain procedures which allow courts to attempt to control in some detail the behaviour of particular people who are thought to be especially likely to

---

[195] [1968] Crim. LR 34, *The Times*, 21 Oct., 1967, DC. The report in *The Times* is fuller.

[196] For criticism, see Feldman, *Entry, Search and Seizure* at p. 31.

[197] Children and Young Persons Act 1933, s. 40. See now Children Act 1989, ss. 44, 45; Police and Criminal Evidence Act 1984, s. 17; Chs. 5, 9 above.

[198] *Robson* v. *Hallett* [1967] 2 QB 939, [1967] 2 All ER 407, DC; *R.* v. *Lamb* [1990] Crim. LR 58, DC.

break the law or cause breaches of the peace. Sometimes this follows conviction and forms part of the sentence of the court. For example, under the Public Order Act 1986, section 30, a court sentencing someone convicted of a public-order offence connected with football may make an exclusion order which makes it an offence, for a specified period of at least three months, for the defendant to enter premises for the purpose of attending any 'prescribed football match'[199] there. Another sentence which can limit a defendant's freedom short of imprisonment is the conditional discharge. This can affect the ability of convicted people to take part in protests and public assemblies.

That carries the risk that the sentencing power could be used for political rather than penological purposes. However, those subject to the order will at least have been convicted of an offence to which the sentence relates. Far more worrying is the use of coercive powers against people who have not been convicted of any offence, for the purpose of preventing their participation in public protest. There are two procedures which may have this effect: attaching conditions to a grant of bail, and binding over.

(1) Bail conditions

Under the Bail Act 1976 people accused of criminal offences have, *prima facie*, a right to bail pending trial, which may be withheld only if there are 'substantial grounds' for believing that the accused might fail to surrender to custody, commit offences while on bail, or interfere with witnesses.[200] However, when granting bail there is power to attach to a grant of bail

such requirements as appear to the court to be necessary to secure that—
  (a) [the defendant] surrenders to custody,
  (b) he does not commit an offence while on bail,
  (c) he does not interfere with witnesses or otherwise obstruct the course of justice . . . ,
  (d) he makes himself available for the purpose of enabling inquiries or a report to be made to assist the court in dealing with him for the offence . . .[201]

This is often used to require people with no fixed address to reside at a bail hostel, or to observe a curfew, or not to leave the country, pending trial. During the miners' strike of 1984–5, magistrates' courts dealing with striking miners, who had been charged with offences arising out of the strike, commonly attached a more unusual condition to grants of bail,

---

[199] This means an association football match prescribed by order of the Home Secretary, a power exercisable by statutory instrument subject to annulment by negative resolution of either House of Parliament: Public Order Act 1986, s. 36.

[200] Bail Act 1976, Sch. 1, Part I, para. 2.   [201] Ibid., s. 3(6).

namely that the defendants were 'not to visit any premises or place for the purpose of picketing or demonstrating in connection with the current trade dispute . . . other than peacefully to picket or demonstrate at his current place of employment'. The effect was to make the defendants, from pits where the miners had voted to strike, liable to be remanded in custody if they picketed at pits where workers had voted to continue to work. The condition was said to be necessary to prevent the commission of further offences while on bail, but the defendants claimed that it had been routinely imposed on all defendants without regard to the particular circumstances of individual defendants, and without inquiry to discover whether there were substantial grounds for believing that the conditions were necessary for the purposes set out above.

In *R. v. Mansfield Justices, ex parte Sharkey*,[202] the lawfulness of the condition was challenged in conjoined applications for judicial review by nine protesters who had been bailed subject to the condition. It was held that the statutory requirement for substantial grounds when refusing bail could not be implied into the provisions dealing with the less draconian step of imposing conditions on the grant of bail. No formal evidence is required at bail hearings,[203] and the court refused to impose an obligation to look for substantial grounds for believing that offences would be committed without the imposition of a condition. The only basis for reviewing the decisions was that of *Wednesbury* unreasonableness, including failure to take account of relevant considerations. Although the court felt that the procedure adopted in Mansfield Magistrates' Court could easily give the appearance of group rather than individual justice, with eight people in the dock having their applications simultaneously dealt with and the clerk merely attaching stick-on slips, with the condition already typed out, to the bail form, the court was not prepared to find that there were not reasonable grounds for imposing the conditions. It was held that the magistrates were entitled to look beyond the circumstances and record of individual defendants, and take account of the general situation in which large numbers of striking miners were gathering at non–striking pits in Nottinghamshire and conducting picketing by intimidation. Under those circumstances, it was reasonable for the magistrates to accede to police requests for the condition to be imposed, as there was a clear risk of defendants contributing to further offences of intimidation (including assault, which does not necessarily involve a battery, and offences under section 5 of the Public Order Act 1936, now replaced by the Public Order Act 1986, sections 4 and 5) if the conditions were not imposed.

---

[202] [1985] QB 613, [1985] 1 All ER 193, DC.
[203] *Re Moles* [1981] Crim. LR 170, DC.

Indeed, in the case of the only defendant in relation to whom irrelevant considerations appeared to have been taken into account (a Mr
Fellows), the court refused relief because, on a rehearing, any properly
instructed bench of magistrates 'could not fail to impose the same or a
similar condition on any grant of bail'.[204] This amounted to a direction
to magistrates to impose the condition, rather than a decision that it was
not unreasonable for them to have done so, despite the affidavit of the
chairman of the magistrates in that case, stating that in the majority of
cases his bench had granted unconditional bail.

It seems, therefore, to be lawful to use bail conditions to regulate the
behaviour of accused protesters pending trial if there is a risk of further
offences in which they might be tempted to participate, even though the
defendant has not yet been convicted of any offence. In the context of
public protest and industrial action, this represents a major interference
with freedoms of movement, expression, and protest. Where there is no
prospect of a speedy trial, the interference may last for a considerable
length of time. Admittedly the condition imposed in these cases did not
prevent the defendants from protesting, but only prevented them from
doing so at pits other than their own and in ways which were not peaceable. Although at first sight this seems to be a major restriction of the
condition, respecting the defendants' political and industrial right to
protest in support of their side in the dispute, in context the concession is
far less impressive. The dispute was a national one, and was in part a dispute not simply between the National Union of Mineworkers and the
National Coal Board but between striking members of the NUM and
those who had disregarded the union's call for a national strike. (Many of
the non-strikers went on to form a separate union, the Union of
Democratic Mineworkers.) Preventing miners from pits where the strike
was being observed from picketing pits where work was continuing
treated the dispute as a series of local strikes rather than the national strike
which it had in reality become, and interfered with the NUM's attempt
to picket working miners. Nevertheless, perhaps it can be said that the
risk of further participation in potentially unlawful activity by the defendants brought the case within the terms of section 3(6) of the Bail Act
1976. The issue, on this view, is whether or not the magistrates took
proper account of the defendants' political rights when exercising their
discretion to frame and impose the condition.

(2) Binding over[205]

There are procedures whereby a person can be required to undertake to
keep the peace or be of good behaviour, on pain of forfeiting a sum of

---

[204] [1985] QB at pp. 629–30, [1985] 1 All ER at p. 204.
[205] See generally D. G. T. Williams, *Keeping the Peace*, ch. 4; Asher D. Grunis, 'Binding

money (a 'recognizance') in the event that he is proved to have committed anti-social behaviour (which need not be unlawful) or a breach of the peace. This is known as binding over: the person is 'bound over' to keep the peace or be of good behaviour. There are several forms of binding over. It is available as part of the sentence imposed on a convicted offender,[206] or it can be used as a type of deferred sentence[207] or bail condition.[208] More controversially, it can be imposed by magistrates of their own motion on acquitted defendants,[209] witnesses, or anyone who happens to be before the court, if the bench considers that there is a risk of a breach of the peace in the future.[210] It may also be imposed in proceedings brought in order to obtain such an order, commenced by complaint in the magistrates' court, often against people arrested in connection with breaches of the peace.[211] The person to be bound over is required by the court to enter into a recognizance, and may be required to provide sureties. A recognizance is a conditional debt, owed to the Crown, which becomes due if the person breaches the undertaking within a specified time. Although it is a civil obligation, and is in theory undertaken voluntarily (a binding over order cannot be made if the person to be bound over does not agree to it), the court can imprison a person for up to six months for refusing to be bound over.

The undertaking entered into may be in either or both of two forms: an undertaking to keep the peace generally; or an undertaking to be of good behaviour towards a particular person. It forms a convenient way of dealing with certain types of disputes between neighbours or cohabitants, but was developed primarily to provide a way of discouraging public disturbances caused by people who were, and later people who were not, of good repute. The use of the power as a preventive weapon in respect of public disorder thus has a long history, going back well before 1361, and

Over to Keep the Peace and be of Good Behaviour in England and Canada' [1976] *PL* 16–41, arguing for abolition; Law Commission, Working Paper No 103, *Criminal Law: Binding Over—the Issues* (London: HMSO, 1987).

[206] There is some doubt as to whether it can be the only sentence imposed: see the discussion in Law Commission, *Criminal Law: Binding Over*, 16–18.

[207] Binding over to come up for judgment in the Crown Court: *R.* v. *Spratling* [1911] 1 KB 77; Powers of Criminal Courts Act 1973, s. 1(7); Supreme Court Act 1981, s. 79(2).

[208] *R.* v. *Aubrey-Fletcher, ex parte Thompson* [1969] 1 WLR 872.

[209] *Wilson* v. *Skeock* (1949) 65 TLR 418; *R.* v. *South West London Magistrates' Court, ex parte Brown* [1974] Crim. LR 313, DC; *R.* v. *Woking Justices, ex parte Gossage* [1973] QB 448, [1973] 2 All ER 621, DC; *R .* v. *Inner London Crown Court, ex parte Benjamin* [1987] Crim. LR 417, DC.

[210] This power arises from common law and the Justices of the Peace Act 1361. See David Feldman, 'The King's Peace, the Royal Prerogative and Public Order: The Roots and Early Development of Binding Over Powers' [1988] *CLJ* 101–28.

[211] Magistrates' Courts Act 1980, s. 115(1).

in this century has been regularly used in relation to political activists. However, used in this way, the order may have the effect of debarring a person from conducting legitimate political activities, as the standards of behaviour which are applied in deciding whether there has been a breach of the order are unacceptably vague and uncertain. A breach of the peace is a standard which can be tolerably well understood (see above). However, 'good behaviour' seems to put too much power in the hands of magistrates to decide, *ex post facto*, whether a person has behaved in a way which justifies estreating his recognizance. This, as Professor Glanville Williams has argued, threatens an extraordinary breach of rule-of-law standards,[212] and, as Patricia Hewitt notes, allows arbitrary judicial interference with freedom of peaceful assembly and other freedoms.[213] It is somewhat encouraging that the Divisional Court, in *R. v. Central Criminal Court, ex parte Boulding*,[214] held that binding over powers must not be used in such a way as to deter a person, through fear of the consequences, from exercising rights of free speech within the law. In that case, the court quashed an order binding over the defendant, who campaigned on moral grounds against the fur trade, to keep the peace and be of good behaviour for two years in the sum of £500, with the alternative of three months imprisonment, following his conviction for a public-order offence arising out of a demonstration against the Hudson's Bay fur company. The amount of the recognizance was excessive in the light of the defendant's means, and could well have put him *in terrorem*.

This is an important principle, but probably more honoured in the breach than the observance. Too often, binding over occurs where nobody has been threatened with violence, so there has been no breach of the peace. In another recent protest case, *R. v. Morpeth Ward JJ, ex parte Joseland*,[215] the Divisional Court upheld a binding over order against protesters who had invaded a private field to try to interfere with a pheasant shoot. The court held that it was not necessary to show that a breach of the peace had occurred, but only that there be risk that the protesters' behaviour would cause a breach of the peace in the future. Brooke J. considered that, on the facts of the case, 'provocative disorderly behaviour which is likely to have the natural consequence of causing violence, even if only to the persons of the provokers, is capable of being treated as conduct likely to cause a breach of the peace'. There is an evident risk that the bellicose tendencies of one's opponents may be invoked

---

[212] Glanville Williams, 'Preventive Justice and the Rule of Law' (1953) 16 *MLR* 417–27; id., *Criminal Law: The General Part*, 2nd edn. (London: Stevens, 1961), 719.
[213] Patricia Hewitt, *The Abuse of Power*, 125. See also Williams, *Keeping the Peace*, 87 ff; Avrom Sherr, *Freedom of Protest, Public Order and the Law*, (Oxford: Blackwell, 1989), 121–4; Geoffrey Robertson, *Freedom, the Individual and the Law*, 77–8.
[214] [1984] 1 QB 813, [1984] 1 All ER 766, DC.   [215] [1992] *NLJ Rep.* 312, DC.

to justify a prior restraint on one's own freedom to protest and express political ideas. The only difference between this case and the case of the Salvationists in *Beatty* v. *Gillbanks*, presumably, is that the Salvationists, despite behaving in a noisy and provocative way, were not regarded as being disorderly. It is dangerous to allow a judge's or magistrate's perception of disorderliness to become a criterion for rationing freedom of expression and protest.

Even where the importance of freedom of protest is conscientiously respected, the binding over process is subject to three serious objections. First, the uncertainty of the 'good behaviour' standard is likely to put the defendant *in terrorem* regardless of the size of his recognizance. It does not depend on any standards of lawfulness, much less criminality. It is dependent instead on the court's assessment of what constitutes anti-social behaviour. Although, as suggested above, this argument is less compelling in relation to binding over to keep the peace, research conducted on behalf of the Law Commission showed that 79 per cent of orders made were both to keep the peace and be of good behaviour, so the indeterminacy of the 'good behaviour' standard infects a substantial majority of orders to keep the peace.[216] Secondly, it is doubtful whether the power to imprison a person for refusal to be bound over is consistent with Article 5(1)(*b*) of the European Convention on Human Rights, as imprisonment for non-compliance with the lawful order of the court must be 'in accordance with a procedure prescribed by law' to be within Article 5. It is at least possible that the procedure for binding over to keep the peace fails to meet the 'prescribed by law' requirement as this has been interpreted by the European Court in the *Sunday Times* and *Malone* cases:[217] in view of the indeterminacy of the 'good behaviour' standard, the entire process by which the order of the court is made may be flawed, as the defendant has no clear idea of the obligation which he is being required by the court's order to undertake. Thirdly, in proceedings to estreat a recognizance, the person bound over will be unable to predict the standards used to decide whether or not he has been 'of good behaviour'. Altogether this is an unsatisfactory procedure, and, despite its respectable antiquity, the power to bind over to be of good behaviour should be abolished—a course currently under consideration by the Law Commission—and the preventive role be restricted to binding over to keep the peace, or something equivalent, according to readily ascertainable legal standards.[218]

---

[216] Law Commission, *Criminal Law: Binding Over*, 33.

[217] *Sunday Times* v. *UK*, Eur. Ct. HR, Series A, No. 30, Judgment of 26 Apr. 1979, 2 EHRR 245; *Malone* v. *UK*, Eur. Ct. HR, Series A, No. 95, Judgment of 26 Apr. 1985, 7 EHRR 14.

[218] For an account of purposes for which bindovers are used, see Law Commission, *Criminal Law: Binding Over*, 38–43.

17.7 CONCLUSION

At the end of this long chapter, the conclusion can be kept short. English law, while in some areas accepting that there is a legitimate interest in freedom of expression in a liberal democracy, does nothing to establish that freedom systematically in the sphere of public expression and public protest. There are no sites where the right to gather and protest publicly is guaranteed to citizens by law. There are wide-ranging restrictions imposed by the civil and criminal law on the forms of expression which are permissible, and the places where they can take place. Most worryingly, there are wide administrative discretions by which police officers and politicians can impose restrictions or conditions on public processions and assemblies. These may in the short term make it easier and cheaper to maintain order, but democracy and respect for rights are objects which do not always come easy, cheap, or orderly. In weighing up the relative importance of freedom, order, and economy, successive English governments have tended to undervalue the first. This is not to say that there is no freedom of protest: indeed, in practice protest is commendably free most of the time, for most people. However, the rhetoric of freedom is translated into reality by administrative practice and moderation, and those who are not favoured have no rights on which they can rely. This field, perhaps more than any other, makes manifest the consequences of a constitutional and political ethos which values pragmatism above principle, and has little or no room for rights.

PART V
TOWARDS EQUALITY THROUGH RIGHTS?

18

EQUALITY AND SOCIAL AND ECONOMIC
RIGHTS

The purpose of this Chapter is to give an idea of the way in which the pursuit of social and economic objectives, both domestically and by means of international co-operation through treaties, covenants, and international organizations, have influenced the development of rights in English law. The chapter is organized as follows. We begin by examining the idea of equality, and considering measures designed to limit inequalities by restricting the grounds on which people may lawfully be discriminated against. Next, we look at the way in which the notions of restricting inequality and providing a safety net for the worst-off groups in society have been translated into international law by way of treaties. Then we turn to the domestic front, with an introduction to the limitation of inequalities of opportunity by legislation against discrimination on the grounds of race and sex, providing an example of methods of attempting to minimize unevenness in the level playing fields for educational, housing, and employment opportunities, and access to other goods and services. The sections which follow examine other influences affecting tensions between different social entitlements, and between entitlements and the demands of efficiency, in the contexts of education and health care.

18.1 SOCIAL JUSTICE AND THE IDEA OF EQUALITY

'. . . We hold these truths to be self-evident, that all men are created equal, that they are endowed by their Creator with certain unalienable Rights, that among these are Life, Liberty and the pursuit of Happiness . . .' [Unanimous Declaration of Independence by the thirteen United States of America, 4 July 1776.]

The idea of the fundamental equality of all is an important element in the history of ideas. In particular, it has been important in the development of theories of justice. It is arguable that every aspect of the notion of justice is founded on an idea of equality. The notion that like cases should be treated alike and different cases differently is rooted in the belief that equal treatment is morally better than unequal treatment where relevantly similar conditions obtain. Distributive justice theories usually start from the position that equal distributions are presumptively fair, and take the form of arguments justifying inequalities in distribution of social goods by reference to some morally significant criterion in respect of which recipients are not equal. Commutative or corrective justice theories presuppose criteria according to which people can be said to be equal (equality under law presupposes that justice results from the fair application of general legal rules), and then treat breaches of the rule as justifying intervention to redistribute goods to put people as far as possible in the position in which they would have been had the breach of the rule not occurred, thus reinstating a position of equality according to the rules.

Equality is not, however, an easy notion to apply in practice. Unlike some other qualities, such as colour, it is virtually impossible to conceive of equality in the abstract. The only field in which an entirely abstract notion of equality can be maintained is that of mathematics, where the characteristic of equality relates to numbers, which are artificial entities operating in only one dimension. Numbers can be said to be equal or unequal because they are defined artificially so that their numerical value is their only significant feature. In relation to entities which have more than one significant quality, it is not possible to speak of the entities themselves being globally equal or unequal. They might be equal in respect of one characteristic, and unequal in respect of others. In social life, numbers normally have no moral, political, or legal significance in themselves (although they may be morally or politically significant when applied to people, as in the context of majoritarian democracy). People, unlike numbers, have characteristics besides our numerical value which we may consider to be important for different purposes: reliability, kindness, rationality, honesty, status, intelligence, sex, race, ethnicity, and so on. It is our non-numerical characteristics in combination which define our social standing, the way we are seen by others, and (often) the way we see ourselves. Apart from their common status as human beings, people can be said to be equal either by reference to some particular, measurable quality (such as intelligence), or by reference to their standing under some rule prescribing their entitlements or responsibilities. There is no other sense in which two people can be said to be equal.

This has implications for the use of the idea of equality as a criterion of social justice. First, to speak of equality one needs to define the criterion in respect of which equality is sought. For that particular type of equality to be morally relevant to solving a problem, there must be a moral rule or principle establishing that criterion as a morally significant one in relation to the issue in question. Equality has no moral value independently of the moral value of the good, characteristic, or value in respect of which equality falls to be assessed. Secondly, two people may be equal or unequal under a rule in a number of senses. They may be entitled:

(a) to be treated equally by others (regardless of whether that leaves them in similar positions afterwards);

(b) to be placed in a similar position (regardless of whether that involves unequal treatment);

(c) to be equally free to exploit whatever abilities or property they may have without interference (which is very likely to lead to different results for each person); or

(d) to be assisted (unequally) so that they have an equal opportunity to exploit their different talents, etc.

Each of these senses of equality is related to a different political and moral theory. For example, entitlements (a) and (b) are aspects of different models of egalitarianism; (c) is characteristic of classical liberalism, entailing relatively little state intervention; and (d) is related to modified versions of liberalism, such as that of Professor Ronald Dworkin based on the idea of a right to equal concern and respect.[1]

However, none is adequate in itself as a statement of principle, because each leaves open further questions. For example, entitlements (a) and (b) require us to explain what is meant by equal treatment and similar positions respectively, and in what spheres equality is needed (as there may be areas of life where equality is not a requirement, and equality itself might, like justice, signify different values in each field).[2] As Peter Westen has argued,[3] one of the reasons for the enduring appeal of the rhetoric of equality is that it can be accommodated within most moral and political theories, and only on careful analysis does it become clear that it means something different in each of them. Until one has decided in what sense one is seeking to promote equality (in other words, what politico-moral theory one espouses), it is not possible to pursue equality. This leads Westen to regard the idea of equality as empty, in the sense that it does not specify any determinate values of its own independently of the political or moral values on which particular models of equality are founded. We will return to the implications of this for anti-discrimination law in section 18.3, below.

The influence of political theory on notions of equality has made it difficult to achieve consensus within or between states as to the legal rights demanded by the notion of justice. In an effort to maintain the widest possible agreement, social rights have generally been drawn in international instruments so as to limit the impact of economic and social

[1] Ronald Dworkin, *Taking Rights Seriously* (London: Duckworth, 1976), pp. 272–8.

[2] Michael Walzer, *Spheres of Justice: A Defence of Pluralism and Equality* (Oxford: Basil Blackwell, 1983), argues that this is a positive advantage when justifying the criterion of equality as an element in justice.

[3] Peter Westen, *Speaking of Equality: an Analysis of the Rhetorical Force of Equality in Moral and Legal Discourse* (Princeton, N.J.: Princeton University Press, 1991). For debate over Westen's views, see Kent Greenawalt, 'How Empty is the Idea of Equality?', 83 *Columbia Law Review* 1167–85 (1983), a reply to Peter Westen, 'The Empty Idea of Equality', 95 *Harvard Law Review* 537–96 (1982).

inequalities on individuals' capacities to take advantage of liberty, rather than to impose a single notion of what is meant by equality or social justice. Within the United Kingdom, divisions of opinion on the best approach reflect political battle lines. On the whole, socialists have favoured a commitment to equality in the form of common ownership of as much of the economically productive property in society as possible. It is traditionally envisaged that this will be achieved through state ownership of key industries. The socialist state also makes itself responsible for guaranteeing to everyone access to the services which are seen as vital for full personal development and participation in the benefits which society offers. This has been pursued by means of state funding for and provision of services under the banner of the welfare state. Services include health, provided for over forty years by the National Health Service; education, funding for which has since the Education Act 1944 been largely a central government responsibility; and systems of public sector housing and social security benefits to protect the poorest members of society from starvation, homelessness, and the worst forms of degradation.

Few Conservatives would regard it as improper for the state to provide a safety net for the weakest and poorest members of society. However, there is disagreement as to the extent to which provision of the safety net should be regarded as a responsibility of the state rather than private provision. Furthermore, Liberal and Conservative parties in the UK have traditionally rejected socialist plans for state ownership, preferring to rely on the operation of the market to spread ownership of the economic base widely through society. Indeed, the Conservative government since 1979 has embarked on an extensive programme of selling off key strategic industries which previous Labour governments had nationalized. Among those which have been privatized, by making shares available to the public and to investment institutions, are gas, electricity, water, and steel, and (if current plans are implemented) these will soon be followed by the railway network and the coal industry. This is not the place to try to evaluate this programme, but it should be noted that it represents an attempt to achieve a similar goal to that at which socialists aim—namely the widest possible distribution of wealth and control over social assets—but without the intervention of the state.

State intervention in the name of equality, or the limitation of inequality, also occurs in order to combat discrimination on the grounds of race and sex. The object of the United Kingdom's legislation in this area was to minimize the extent to which women and ethnic minorities in this country are disadvantaged in education, housing, employment, and obtaining goods and services. This was not so much an attempt to produce equality of opportunity (which is accepted as being impossible) as to ensure that inequalities could not be imposed on criteria which were impossible to justify on moral grounds. However, there is some ambivalence towards the legislation. As noted in Chapter 7, the history of immigration law runs in parallel with the ups and downs of the labour market. Immigrants are encouraged when needed for economic reasons, but, when unemployment is high and the resources available for housing, health, or education are stretched, racism rears its head, and is liable to be particularly influential in the field of immigration law and practice. Similarly, equal access to employment for men and women, and equal treatment when working, are ideals which can be embraced without too much opposition when the economy is booming and well-remunerated work is plentiful, but which comes under pressure at times of recession.

In the struggle to achieve a society in which everyone has the opportunity to make good use of their freedoms and opportunities, the acknowledgment and pursuit of social and economic rights can be a useful weapon, alongside the individual freedoms which classical liberal theory espouses. Although the idea of rights attaching to groups within society by reason of their distinctive needs is hard to reconcile with individualist theory, some element of concern for people's social positions can be seen to be a possible component of a commitment to individual freedom: as noted in Chapter 1, social arrangements can affect the worth of civil and political rights and freedoms to the individual. The recognition of individual freedom by the state implies that the state should do its best to produce the social and economic conditions in which people can exercise choice and pursue the chosen ends or values. In the United Kingdom, this need for fairness is broadly understood by politicians. For some in the liberal tradition, however, the way of achieving this is a matter for democratic political judgment, which would be improperly constrained if particular interest groups were seen as having special rights, enforceable against the remainder of society, without the need for democratic approval. Others, in a more socialist or collectivist tradition, are happy to accept both that all groups are entitled to expect minimum standards for life, and that these can properly be translated into the language of rights in the form of social or collective rights, of the sort which are contained in international instruments to which we will now turn.

18.2 SOCIAL AND ECONOMIC RIGHTS IN INTERNATIONAL LAW

(1) The United Nations and the International Labour Organization

The field of social and economic rights in international law has grown in recent years as international instruments recognizing such rights have proliferated. The Preamble to the Charter of the United Nations refers to

the determination of the member states to promote social progress and
better standards of life, and for those ends 'to employ international
machinery for the promotion of the economic and social advancement of
all peoples', and Article 55 committed the organization to promoting
(among other objectives) 'higher standards of living, full employment,
and conditions of economic and social progress and development'.
Responsibility for pursuing these objectives was vested by Article 60 in
the Economic and Social Council under the General Assembly, while
Articles 57 to 59 contemplated that some of the work would be done by
specialized agencies, of which the most significant for this purpose has
been the International Labour Organization (ILO).[4]

The ILO originated in 1919, in the aftermath of the First World War,
and its mission is to advance social justice, in the belief (as stated in the
Preamble to its Constitution) that 'universal and lasting peace can be
established only if it is based upon social justice'. To this end, in 1944 the
ILO General Conference adopted a Declaration of Aims and Purposes[5]
which are to inspire the policy of its members. The Declaration contains
a lengthy credo: labour is not to be regarded as a commodity; freedom of
expression and association are essential to sustained progress; poverty anywhere constitutes a danger to prosperity everywhere; and the war against
want must be carried on with unrelenting vigour within each nation and
by means of concerted international efforts. All human beings have the
right to pursue both material well-being and spiritual development in
conditions of freedom and dignity, economic security, and equal opportunity, without discrimination on the ground of race, creed, or sex. To
advance these aims, the ILO has an obligation to further programmes
which will achieve (*inter alia*) full employment, rising standards of living,
worker satisfaction, a minimum living wage, a basic income for all in
need, and a just share in the fruits of progress for all, recognition of rights
to free collective bargaining, adequate protection for the life and health
of all workers, child welfare and maternity protection, and provision of
adequate nutrition, housing, and facilities for recreation and culture. The
list ends with an assurance of equality of educational and vocational
opportunity.

In performing its obligations, the ILO has adopted a number of
Conventions on matters including forced labour (1930); the right of

---

[4] A. H. Robertson and J. G. Merrills, *Human Rights in the World: An Introduction to the
Study of the International Protection of Human Rights* 3rd edn. (Manchester: Manchester
University Press, 1989), pp. 236–41; Francis Wolf, 'Human Rights and the International
Labour Organization', in Theodor Meron (ed.), *Human Rights in International Law: Legal
and Policy Issues* (Oxford: Clarendon Press, 1984), pp. 273–305.

[5] For text, see Ian Brownlie, *Basic Documents on Human Rights* 3rd edn. (Oxford:
Clarendon Press, 1992), pp. 243–5.

workers and employers to establish organizations (1948); collective bargaining (1949); equal remuneration for work of equal value without discrimination on the ground of sex (1951); discrimination in employment
or occupation (1958). The general thrust of these Conventions, and of
the work of the ILO generally, is towards a raising of standards everywhere towards minimum acceptable conditions. The form of social justice which is favoured is not, therefore, the utopian ideal of universal
equality, but a rather more limited notion of justice according to which
needs are catered for, while further benefits of social activity are open to
competition. The competition must, however, be socially just, which
means that it must be accessible to all nationals under conditions of fair
equality of opportunity. In other words, the various Conventions seek to
establish (i) a safety net for all, and (ii) a level playing field on which
competition for the fruits of economic and social progress will be played
out. The rights to organize and bargain collectively, and to be free from
discrimination, are aspects of the arrangements for a level playing field.
Another aspect is the right to equal educational opportunities. This is
advanced by the work of the United Nations Educational, Scientific, and
Cultural Organization (UNESCO), another specialized agency related to
the   United   Nations,   which   adopted   the   Convention   against
Discrimination in Education in 1960.

To put this model of social justice and social rights in perspective, it is
instructive to compare it with the influential model of justice advanced
by John Rawls in *A Theory of Justice*.[6] Rawls's general principle of justice
proposes that an equal distribution of goods is just, unless an unequal distribution works to the advantage of the least favoured group in society.
Similarly, the ILO principles contemplate redistribution of goods, by
means of mechanisms such as taxation and social security payments, without regard to principles of equality save in respect of the equal application
of the criterion of need. However, once a society has advanced to a point
where basic needs are catered for, Rawls contemplates the surplus being
distributed in accordance with a different set of principles (the 'special
conception' of justice). These respect people's individual basic rights,
which (as outlined in Chapter 1 above) are largely concerned with political and personal fulfilment. Distributions of surplus income which are
achieved by means of the exploitation of those rights are just as long as
everyone's basic needs are satisfied, even if the result is substantial
inequality of wealth above the level of basic need. Rawls insists that positions of social, economic and political privilege must be open to all under
conditions of fair equality of opportunity. This, too, is in tune with the
principles in ILO and UNESCO Conventions. However, in two respects

[6] John Rawls, *A Theory of Justice* (Oxford: Clarendon Press, 1972).

Rawls's approach and that of the UN's specialized agencies seem to diverge. First, Rawls gives specially protected status only to basic individual liberties, not to social and economic rights. This difference is partly cancelled out by the second: Rawls expressly insists, unlike the ILO Conventions, that unequal distributions of social and economic goods above the baseline of need are justifiable if and only if the effect is to benefit the least favoured group. The effect is to permit net inequalities of wealth and power to exist, and even to widen, but only if a share of the fruits of them is made available to all. Whether this share of the fruits of progress is fair, as required by the ILO Declaration of Aims and Purposes, is a matter of judgment.

The essential work of the ILO, and other specialist agencies of the UN, such as UNESCO, in the field of human rights, is thus to encourage the universal satisfaction of basic needs, the fair distribution of the fruits of progress both within states and internationally, and to promote equality of opportunity by restraining discrimination in the provision of education, training, employment opportunities, terms and conditions of employment, and social security benefits.

(2) The Council of Europe and the European Community

At a European level, the Council of Europe and the European Community have been moving parallel to the ILO. In 1961, the member states of the Council of Europe signed the European Social Charter,[7] which came into force in 1965. The contracting parties which were signatories to the Charter intended to complement the European Convention on Human Rights by providing for the enjoyment of social rights by nationals of Contracting Parties resident or working regularly within their territory, and refugees.[8] Among the rights contained in the Charter are rights in respect of employment: a right to work, and to do so under fair and safe conditions, for fair remuneration, and with the right to organize and bargain collectively. Alongside these provisions are rights to special protection for women, children, and young people in employment; rights to education, and to vocational training and guidance; rights to provision for health care, social security, welfare services, and care for disabled people; and rights to protection for the family, and particularly for mothers and children. The contracting parties are to secure the rights (in the words of the Preamble) 'without discrimination on grounds of race, colour, sex, religion, political opinion, national

---

[7] For the text of the Charter, see Brownlie, *Basic Documents,* pp. 363–82. For commentary, see D. J. Harris, *The European Social Charter* (Charlottesville, Va.: University of Virginia Press, 1984); Robertson and Merrills, *Human Rights in the World,* pp. 245–55.

[8] Appendix to the European Social Charter, paragraphs 1 and 2.

extraction or social origin', in order to 'make every effort in common to improve the standard of living and to promote the social well-being of both their urban and rural populations by means of appropriate institutions and action'.

There is no enforcement mechanism equivalent to that under the European Convention on Human Rights. Instead, each state is to submit to the Secretary-General of the Council of Europe biennial reports on developments in relation to rights under provisions which that state has accepted, and occasional reports (as requested by the Committee of Ministers) as to the provisions in Part II of the Charter, giving specific rights, which the state concerned has not accepted.[9] Reports are examined by a Committee of Experts appointed by the Committee of Ministers from a list of 'independent experts of the highest integrity and recognized competence in international social questions, nominated by the Contracting Parties.'[10] The Committee of Experts decides whether states have violated rights guaranteed under the Charter. To facilitate consistency between the work of the Council of Europe and that of the ILO, Article 26 of the Charter provides that the ILO is to be invited to nominate a representative to participate in a consultative capacity in the deliberations of the Committee of Experts. The reports from states, and the conclusions of the Committee of Experts, are considered by a Sub-Committee of the Governmental Social Committee of the Council of Europe, on which each of the Contracting Parties is represented. This body presents reports, which often consist largely of opinions as to whether violations of the Charter found by the Committee of Experts have in fact occurred, to the Committee of Ministers. The Committee of Ministers also receives views from the Consultative Assembly of the Council of Europe. The Committee of Ministers may then make necessary recommendations to each Contracting Party, but recommendations require to be approved by a two-thirds majority of the members of the Council of Europe (not all of whom are contracting parties to the Charter).[11]

Until recently, this regime had not been particularly effective in influencing the development of law and policy in the United Kingdom, or (generally) elsewhere in Europe. The Charter, like the various ILO conventions, imposes obligations on the state which take effect in international law, but does not confer enforceable rights on individuals. Individuals, collective groups, and non-governmental organizations (other than the ILO) do not have standing to participate in the regime of regular reports and reviews of progress to which states are subject. The central position of the Governmental Social Committee has meant that

---

[9] European Social Charter, Arts. 21 and 22.
[10] Arts. 24, 25.   [11] Arts. 27, 28, 29.

the operation of the Charter has depended heavily on the political will of the contracting parties to give the Charter a dynamic function. In a geographical area where a fairly high measure of economic prosperity has been achieved by applying predominantly liberal, capitalist politico-economic theories, this political will has predictably been lacking. However, matters changed dramatically with the collapse of the 'Iron Curtain' between eastern and western Europe. When former eastern bloc countries started to apply for membership of the Council of Europe, the Charter was seen as a valuable instrument for evaluating the performance of those countries in protecting and enhancing social and economic rights as they moved from command economies to market economies.

At the same time, the Social Chapter of the treaty establishing the European Community[12] assumed greater importance, being expanded in scope by an Agreement between eleven of the twelve member states (excluding the United Kingdom) as part of the Final Act at the Maastricht summit conference in 1991. This Agreement commits the Community and member states to the objectives of promoting high employment, improved living and working conditions, social protection, equal pay for equal work, dialogue between management and labour, and the development of human resources. The Agreement empowers the EC Council of Ministers to adopt Directives setting minimum standards for gradual implementation, and makes the Commission responsible for promoting the objectives.

The EC Social Chapter does not extend to all the rights encompassed by the Council of Europe's European Social Charter. Nevertheless, the potential for development of social and economic rights in the Community setting, together with the eastern European developments, spurred member states of the Council of Europe to take steps to improve the effectiveness of the Charter. First, the Director-General of the Council of Europe decided to transfer responsibility for the operation of the Charter to the Council's Directorate of Human Rights. This Directorate had always been responsible for the operation of the European Convention on Human Rights, and had been instrumental in raising its profile and encouraging its dynamic development, but the Charter had never been part of its remit. Secondly, the Committee of Ministers established an *ad hoc* committee, consisting of nominated experts, to make proposals for improving the effectiveness of the Charter and its supervisory machinery. The committee's report led to an Amending Protocol to the Charter being opened for signature in 1991. When it enters into force the Protocol will significantly change the supervisory arrangements. The principal changes are as follows.[13]

---

[12] Arts. 117–122 of the Treaty of Rome, as amended.

[13] For authoritative discussion, see D. J. Harris, 'A Fresh Impetus for the European Social Charter' (1992) 41 ICLQ 659–76.

First, responsibility for authoritatively interpreting the Charter will move from the Governmental Social Committee to the Committee of Experts. The main function of the Governmental Committee will become that of advising the Committee of Ministers on the circumstances in which it should exercise its power to make recommendations to contracting parties. This will reduce the direct influence of governments over the interpretation of the rights under the Charter. Secondly, the membership of the Committee of Experts will be increased, to take account of its increased workload, and the Committee will have power to hold oral hearings at which to seek additional information and clarification of reports from contracting parties. Thirdly, the Parliamentary Assembly will change its role, from being consulted by the Committee of Ministers to conducting independent debates on the report of the Committee of Experts. Eliminating the Assembly from the formal supervisory process will speed it up and simplify it.

Further changes are under consideration, including one for a system of collective complaints by employers' and trade union organizations in respect of alleged breaches of the Charter by contracting parties. It remains to be seen whether the political will exists among the parties to subject themselves to a similar type of review to that which the right of individual petition under the European Convention on Human Rights has opened up.

(3) Implementing social and economic rights in domestic law: practice and potential

Because the United Kingdom adopts a dualist view of international law, in which treaty obligations are not automatically incorporated into domestic law, the European Social Charter and the other conventions dealing with economic and social rights do not have direct effect in English law, and are not justiciable in our courts. Indeed, it would often be hard for a court to apply them, since they are in form generally exhortatory rather than prescriptive, and leave a great deal of leeway to states which have to implement them. For instance, judges could not easily fashion remedies which respected the difference between the functions of the judiciary and the executive, or the need for flexibility allowing the pursuit of different political programmes, when addressing provisions such as the following, taken from the ILO Social Policy (Basic Aims and Standards) Convention (1962):

All policies shall be primarily directed to the well-being and development of the population and to the promotion of its desire for social progress. (Article 1, paragraph 1.)

The improvement of standards of living shall be regarded as the principal objective in the planning of economic development. (Article 2.)

All practicable measures shall be taken in the planning of economic development to harmonize such development with the healthy evolution of the communities concerned. (Article 3, paragraph 1.)

The need to regard the obligations on states as variable, to take account of their different economic and social circumstances, is expressly recognized by, for example, Article 2, paragraph 1 of the International Covenant on Economic, Social, and Cultural Rights (1966), as follows:

1. Each State Party to the present Covenant undertakes to take steps, individually and through international assistance and co-operation, especially economic and technical, to the maximum of its available resources, with a view to achieving progressively the full realization of the rights recognized in the present Covenant by all appropriate means, including particularly the adoption of legislative measures.

On the other hand, some obligations would be much more easily justiciable. In relation to the right to safe and healthy working conditions, the parties to Article 3 of the European Social Charter undertake: (1) to issue safety and health regulations; (2) to provide for the enforcement of such regulations by measures of supervision; (3) to consult, as appropriate, employers' and workers' organizations on measures intended to improve industrial safety and health. There is no reason why any of these provisions should be regarded as non-justiciable. Adjudicating on the obligations which they impose would not involve judges in assessing social or economic policy, or in evaluating unusually intractable forms of evidence. Similarly, paragraphs 2 and 3 of Article 2 of the International Covenant on Economic, Social, and Cultural Rights shows how such instruments can set out obligations which are in principle justiciable, while defining the limited field within which states are to enjoy what might be called, as in the case-law of the European Court of Human Rights, a 'margin of appreciation' within which their discretion is largely unfettered:

2. States Parties to the present Covenant undertake to guarantee that the rights enunciated in the present Covenant will be exercised without discrimination of any kind as to race, colour, sex, language, religion, political or other opinion, national or social origin, property, birth or other status. 3. Developing countries, with due regard to human rights and their national economy, may determine to what extent they would guarantee the economic rights recognized in the present Covenant to non-nationals.

Furthermore, the rights which are too vague to be judicially enforceable, or which are necessarily subject to a governmental discretion to act pragmatically in the light of prevailing circumstances, may still not be entirely beyond judicial notice. The Directive Principles of State Policy in Part IV of the Constitution of the Union of India offer a model here. They set out broad policy objectives, requiring the state to direct its policy towards securing social objectives which include an adequate means of livelihood for all citizens, equal pay for equal work for men and women, and the protection and improvement of the environment. The state is said to have a duty to comply with the Directive Principles, which are however not to be enforceable by any court.[14] Nevertheless, the Indian Supreme Court has been prepared exercise judicial review of executive or legislative acts to ensure that the Directive Principles are taken into account as relevant considerations.[15]

The willingness of courts to take such steps depends heavily on local political conditions, particularly on the way in which judges see such obligations and their willingness to risk conflict with government. In Ireland, where Article 45 of the Constitution similarly contains Directive Principles of State Policy, courts have been far less willing to take account of them, perhaps because the opening words of Article 45 provide that the Principles 'shall not be cognisable by any Court', in contrast to the Indian Constitution's 'shall not be enforceable'. Nevertheless, it is conceivable that courts might be prepared to treat those policy objectives which form part of treaty obligations and which are not expressly stated to be non-cognizable as relevant considerations, so that executive decisions taken without considerating them might be subject to judicial review. It would be by no means unreasonable, at a time when international co-operation is of growing importance in all fields, for courts to hold that the international obligations which the United Kingdom government has voluntarily undertaken form at least a relevant consideration to be taken into account by government on ordinary judicial review principles. Unfortunately, there is no clear sign as yet that our courts are prepared to take international law that seriously, and there is at least one expression of judicial opinion to the effect that treating international obligations as relevant considerations in domestic law would lead to the incorporation of international law by the back door.[16]

The principal remaining possibility for making a set of social and economic rights enforceable in English law derives from the Agreement on Social Policy signed at Maastricht (1991). The United Kingdom government did not sign the Agreement, because it believed that implementing

---

[14] Indian Constitution, Art. 37.

[15] *Pandey* v. *State of West Bengal* [1988] LRC (Const) 241; P. P. Craig and S. L. Deshpande, 'Rights, Autonomy and Process: Public Interest Litigation in India' (1989) 9 *Oxford J. of Legal Studies* 356–73.

[16] *Brind* v. *Secretary of State for the Home Department* [1991] 1 AC 696 at pp. 761–2, [1991] 1 All ER 720 at pp. 734–735, *per* Lord Ackner; see also Lord Lowry at pp. 763, 736 respectively. *Cp. R.* v. *Secretary of State for the Home Dept., ex parte Chahal, Times*, 12 Mar. 1993. The matter is discussed further in ch. 2, s. II.5 above.

it would involve an incursion on domestic sovereignty by Community authorities, and would make British industry less competitive. In the short term, ratifying the Social Chapter would make little impact on English law. It would not give rise immediately to enforceable community rights: the Agreement merely permits the Council to adopt Directives laying down 'minimum requirements for gradual implementation, having regard to the conditions and technical rules obtaining in each of the Member States.'[17] In the long term, if the United Kingdom were to ratify the Agreement it would ultimately lead to a set of enforceable social and economic rights. However, these would cover a fairly small field, related principally to employment matters. Although the enforcement measures available would be more effective than those available under the European Social Charter, the rights under the Agreement are nowhere near as comprehensive as those guaranteed, if the government has the commitment to them, under the Charter. There will therefore continue to be a role for the Charter even if the government ultimately signs the Agreement.

18.3 EQUALITY AND DISCRIMINATION

(1) Theory of anti-discrimination law[18]

Discrimination, when it consists of an ability to differentiate right from wrong and good from bad, is an essential part of everyday life. Much of education, and arguably the whole of culture, is directed to establishing acceptable criteria for preferring one work of art, objective, technique, or person to another, end encouraging people to develop their critical faculties to enable them to discriminate effectively according to those criteria. Discrimination becomes morally unacceptable only when it takes a particular form, namely treating a person less favourably than others on account of a consideration which is morally irrelevant. The criterion in question may be the person's colour, nationality, religion, ethnic origin, sex, political beliefs, or one of an infinite number of other factors. This unacceptable form of discrimination is often an emanation of prejudice (in its pure form of a prejudgment in the absence of evidence) against a person on account of that person's inherent characteristics over which he

[17] Agreement on Social Policy Concluded between the Member States of the European Community with the Exception of the United Kingdom of Great Britain and Northern Ireland, Art. 2.

[18] Christopher McCrudden (ed.), *Anti–Discrimination Law* (Aldershot: Dartmouth, 1991) is a useful collection of essays; McCrudden's helpful Introduction, pp. xi–xxxi, includes a valuable bibliography. See also Jeanne Gregory, *Sex, Race and the Law: Legislating for Equality* (London: Sage, 1987).

or she has no control, but (depending on one's moral and political philosophy and the circumstances in which a dispute arises) any criterion may be regarded as either relevant or irrelevant.

The outlawing of certain types of discrimination is justified on the basis of the simple premise that there are certain criteria for treating people differently which should never be regarded as morally relevant, or which are relevant in an admissible way only in a restricted range of situations which can be defined by law. There is usually no objection to discriminating in favour of or against a person on the basis of their voluntary actions, since those are the result of a choice for which it is reasonable to expect the person to accept the consequences (whether good or bad) in accordance with the liberal notions of individual will and individual responsibility. If one has a choice between two acts, either morally reprehensible A or morally admirable B, and one chooses to do the morally reprehensible A, there is no reason why one should not be judged and treated accordingly, although, if the choice is constrained by factors beyond one's control (for example, social and economic circumstances might constrain the range of options available to people in certain social classes or settings), the choice is more apparent than real, and it might reduce the moral force of the action.

If the reason for discriminating is unrelated to one's voluntary acts, and is based instead on matters which are entirely beyond one's control (skin colour, status, family background, nationality, etc.), there is a danger that one will be systematically discriminated against in all situations, losing out all or most of the time on that account. This is socially divisive, because it produces an underclass of systematically disadvantaged people who are unable to improve their position by lawful means. If the differential treatment is based on decisions or actions over which one has some control, but that control is limited by psychological commitments (religion, political beliefs) or the conventions of one's social group (dress, hairstyle), the morality of differential treatment is at best questionable. In such cases, the person seeking to justify differential treatment bears the burden of establishing its moral propriety in the circumstances in question.

The conclusion to which this points is that differentiating between people is not wrong as long as the criteria applied are morally acceptable. What grounds are morally acceptable, and by what principles can one decide whether criteria for differentiating are acceptable? It is usual to start from a presumption in favour of equality. This has two elements. First, people are presumed to be morally equal in the sense of being equally entitled to respect for their moral status by virtue of being human beings. As noted in Chapter 1, this idea forms one of the foundations of the notion of human rights. The principle of moral equality does not always require that all actions be judged in the same way, since standards common to all may require that we distinguish between people with different levels of responsibility for their actions, by reason of mental or physical impairment or exigent circumstances.

Equality as an idea is relevant mainly when there is conflict as to the proper distribution of resources of some sort. Treating people as moral equals does not necessarily entail equal treatment, in the sense of distributing identical benefits and burdens to all. It will do so only when the claimants are in morally identical positions. Our voluntary actions, including the way in which we use our rights in the different situations in which we find ourselves, mean that we may cease to be in identical moral positions as soon as we start acting voluntarily. The principle of moral equality merely requires that we judge and treat people as moral equals: we are to be regarded as equally responsible for our actions, which fall to be judged according to common standards. (This is one of the principles underpinning the rule of law doctrine.) It involves taking account of inequalities in respect of particular characteristics, in order to give effect to the principle of treating people as equals at a higher level of abstraction. Since people who are entitled to be treated as moral equals do not necessarily have equal incomes, wealth, or needs, the principle of moral equality may lead to unequal treatment, with burdens being placed disproportionately on those best able to bear them in order to supply benefits to those in need. This is the basis for the system of 'transfer payments' through progressive taxation and social security payments, and the provision of public services, such as health care and education for all, paid for by means of a system of national insurance contributions and taxes levied on those in remunerated work or with accumulated wealth. Questions of practical equality are related to the resource being distributed and the benefit which it confers: people may be equally wealthy and equally morally good, but when treatment for sickness is being distributed there is no good reason to provide it equally to people who are ill and those who are well: people's different needs, and the extent to which they can be met by the resource under consideration, are morally relevant grounds for differentiating between people in distributing the resource.

This raises problems when it is proposed to legislate against discrimination on particular grounds. To what characteristics is the law to insist that people should be blind, and in which contexts? This problem has a reverse side, in the form of two related issues which any system of social rights and anti-discrimination law must address. First, to what extent does the ideal of equality demand that, as well as being treated on common principles in the distribution of resources and burdens, people should be put in positions where they are equally able to formulate and achieve their goals for life? In other words, does equality imply equality of opportunity, which may be impossible unless people have a right to specially favourable treatment, on the basis of criteria to which we would normally want people to be blind, in order to compensate for the pervasive social effects of past discrimination? Classically, liberal rights theory provides for a limited degree of equality of opportunity. People have equal opportunity in so far as they have equal freedoms. The job of the state is to protect those freedoms, but not to put people into a position where they can make the most of them. But this leads to a problem, noted in Chapter 1: the freedoms turn out to be of unequal value to different people, because some are unable (for financial, social, or family reasons) to exploit them. Secondly, to use freedoms effectively people rely on a reasonable range of choices being available, and those are determined by factors, such as the economic structure of society and the extent to which different activities and products are valued, which are largely outside the control of any individual. The state may have a role, even under some forms of liberal theory, in ensuring that a decent range of choices is practicably open to all.[19]

The connection between these problems makes their solution particularly complex. The provision of choices by state action is a political matter, and the resources and opportunities which are made available are likely to reflect the system of values which is politically dominant. Those values might be incompatible with the principle of moral equality, in that they systematically undervalue the aspirations of certain groups in society and lead to inadequate choice being available. It is a common feature of discrimination on the grounds of sex and race that it produces (or perhaps is produced by) a dominant system of political values in which the opportunities of the subordinated sex or race are restricted. In such a system, an underclass is created, so that, even if members are not formally denied the rights and freedoms guaranteed to others, they are normally unable to make much use of them. The inequality of opportunity which results cannot be broken down simply by removing the formal inequalities of rights. Positive steps are likely to be needed in order to improve the lot of entire underprivileged sections of society, to place them in a position from which they can start to take real benefits from exercising rights and freedoms. In such circumstances, treating people as equals, or treating them with equal concern and respect, is likely to entail unequal treatment which discriminates in their favour, through programmes which are aptly described as positive discrimination or affirmative action. Social rights are useful adjuncts of such programmes, but are not essential. The vital factor is the political will, which may be hard to establish, because favourable treatment for some will mean unfavourable treatment for at least some members of the previously favoured group.

[19] Joseph Raz, *The Morality of Freedom* (Oxford: Clarendon Press, 1986).

To make the problem still more intractable, the opportunities which the systematically disadvantaged group seek might not be those which are traditionally favoured by the dominant set of values. Although there are women who have always wanted to be free from the restrictive paternalism which prevented them from doing the same work and adopting the same working practices as men, it is a recurrent theme of writings on issues of sex and race equality that what at least some members of the underprivileged group (women or ethnic minorities) really desire is not the opportunity to be like the previously dominant group (men, whites, Christians, etc.) but rather the freedom to pursue their own values in their own ways. Treatment of people as moral equals is seen as demanding respect for (even celebration of) difference, rather than its elimination. There has been a growing move away from concern to eradicate sex- or race-based differences towards a concern to minimize sex- or race-based disadvantage.[20] Willingness to treat someone as an equal only if he or she adopts one's own system of beliefs and values is a denial of moral equality rather than an expression of it, and is a deeply patronizing attitude. Nevertheless, it is an attitude which has shaped much of the English approach to racial equality, from Lord Tebbit's suggestion that one might judge the claims of immigrants and their descendants to be treated as British citizens by asking which team they support when England's cricket team plays against other countries, to the views of those who consider it to be a duty of immigrants to assimilate to, rather than just integrate with, the British way of life.[21]

A useful way of approaching these issues in the field of sex and race discrimination law is through the framework of international law, discussed above.[22] The European Commission on Human Rights has decided that discriminating against people on the grounds of race, at least in respect of important matters such as immigration, offends against the prohibition on degrading treatment in Article 3 of the European Convention on Human Rights.[23] A failure to provide legal remedies also breaches the obligations of the state under the International Convention on the Elimination of All Forms of Racial Discrimination (1966) and the

---

[20] See e.g., in the context of sex discrimination, Catharine MacKinnon, 'Toward Feminist Jurisprudence', 34 *Stanford Law Review* 703–37 (1982); Deborah L. Rhode, *Justice and Gender: Sex Discrimination and the Law* (Cambridge, Mass.: Harvard University Press, 1989), *passim*; Katherine O'Donovan and Erika Szyszczak, *Equality and Sex Discrimination Law* (Oxford: Basil Blackwell, 1988), ch. 1.

[21] See Vaughan Bevan, *The Development of British Immigration Law* (London: Croom Helm, 1986), pp. 10–12, 27–8.

[22] See Jack Greenberg, 'Race, Sex, and Religious Discrimination in International Law', in Meron (ed.), *Human Rights in International Law*, pp. 307–43.

[23] See ch. 4, above.

ILO Conventions referred in section 18.2(1). The discussion which follows is concerned with the manner in which domestic law deals with the problems of discrimination.

(2) Grounds of discrimination, and objectives of anti-discrimination law

Of common grounds for discriminating, colour, race, and sex are matters which are virtually always outside the control of the person concerned (save in the rare case where a person has the opportunity to undergo sex reassignment therapy, which presents its own problems, considered in Chapter 11). Nationality is usually outside the control of the individual, except in somewhat unusual situations where people have an opportunity to adopt a new nationality. Yet these personal characteristics do not normally adversely affect one's ability to discharge one's obligations as a citizen towards the state or one's fellow citizens. Sex, race, and nationality therefore have primacy among the characteristics on the basis of which it is thought to be wrong to discriminate.

Religious beliefs and affiliations are usually things which arise involuntarily. Although sometimes people change their religious beliefs, there may be social or political factors which make it difficult or even dangerous to manifest that change. In Northern Ireland, for example, the main social and political divisions around which society is organized are religious in origin, and tension between the main Protestant and Roman Catholic religious–political communities is rife. For this reason, the law in Northern Ireland treats religious discrimination as a principal target for its anti-discrimination rules, in order to make possible some sort of economic and social life encompassing the two communities.

There are other grounds for holding political beliefs and religious beliefs to be morally irrelevant grounds for differential treatment of citizens. In countries which espouse some form of democratic political theory, freedom to choose and express a set of political beliefs, and to join other like-minded people in a political party or interest group, is central to the efficient operation of the democratic process. To discriminate against people on the basis of their choice would tend to undermine the democratic nature of the state. A similar, but not identical, argument applies to religious beliefs. In a society which regards religion as a social good, providing a basis (although not necessarily the only one) for social morality, there are good reasons for permitting people the widest possible choice of religious beliefs in the hope that as many people as possible will find a religion with which they can identify. Like the English law of charities, such societies may take the view that any religion is better than none. Having done so, it would be counter-productive to discriminate against people on the basis of their choices.

The values advanced by anti-discrimination legislation of all types, therefore, are the following. First, it attempts to ensure that distributions of opportunities are made on morally relevant grounds. Secondly, it attempts to uphold the dignity of individuals and groups in their own eyes and in the eyes of others. Thirdly, it seeks to produce a more level playing field than would otherwise be available for competition for resources, by limiting the grounds on which inequalities can lawfully be introduced. Fourthly, it aims to minimize the social friction which may result from an under-privileged underclass being systematically excluded from a fair share of the fruits of social and economic development.

However, there are limits to the restraints which can legitimately be placed on people's or societies' freedom to adopt principles for differential treatment. One type of limit arises from what might be called a right to self-defence. Societies must be free to protect themselves against fundamental attack, so they may discriminate against a religious or political belief if its adherents are necessarily committed, by virtue of their adherence, to acts which undermine the state or the moral and political values on which the state is founded. To defend itself in that way, a society might be forced to discriminate against the implementation of the beliefs concerned, but that discrimination is an indirect result of the legitimate exercise of society's right of self-defence.

Another type of limit on anti-discrimination legislation arises from the fact that a criterion for differential treatment might be morally irrelevant nine times out of ten, but relevant on the tenth occasion. While there may be a strong presumption against differential treatment on the ground of (for example) a person's religion, the presumption is not irrebuttable. There might be circumstances in which people's religious beliefs, if sincerely held, may legitimately be held to bar them from certain opportunities or offices. For example, if the authorities of a religion were to bar its adherents on religious grounds from participating in the dissolution of marriages, it would be unreasonable to insist on its adherents being appointed as judges in a state where divorce is socially and morally acceptable, and where any judge may be called on to adjudicate on divorce petitions. Such a situation almost gave rise to a clash between the United Kingdom government and the Vatican in the 1950s.[24]

(3) The legal meaning of and settings for discrimination in English law

(i) *The meaning of discrimination.* The need to protect people against discrimination on irrelevant grounds, while allowing differential treatment

---

[24] Robert B. Stevens, 'The Independence of the Judiciary: the View from the Lord Chancellor's Office' (1988) 8 *Oxford J. of Legal Studies* 222–48 at 227–9.

on grounds which are morally justifiable, is one of the factors underlying the entire structure of British race relations law and British and European sex discrimination law. Another fundamental element is the need, in order to tackle discrimination effectively, to attack it not only at the level of individual acts of discrimination directed against individuals on improper grounds (known as 'direct discrimination'), but also where discrimination results from the operation of a practice or application of criteria for selection which are not in themselves obviously related to the morally illegitimate criteria of sex or race, but which can be more easily satisfied by people of some races or one sex than another race or sex (known as 'indirect discrimination'). In the United States, under Title VII of the Civil Rights Act of 1964, both direct and indirect discrimination have been held to be unlawful, and the courts have been engaged in combatting apparently neutral practices which have a discriminatory impact,[25] although recent case-law suggests that the conservative majority on the Supreme Court, out of sympathy with the ethos of social equality rights, is making it harder for complainants to prove that criteria for establishing disparate treatment are satisfied.[26]

In the domestic legislation, both direct and indirect forms of discrimination are unlawful. In section 1 of both the Sex Discrimination Act 1975 ('the 1975 Act') and the Race Relations Act 1976 ('the 1976 Act') discrimination may be committed in either of two ways: (a) by treating a person, on grounds of race or sex, less favourably than one treats or would treat others; or (b) by applying to that person a requirement or condition such that the proportion of that person's racial group or sex which can comply with it is considerably smaller than the proportion of people of another race or sex. In the case of discrimination under (b), a plaintiff must also show that the requirement or condition cannot be justified otherwise than by reference to the person's race or sex, and is to the detriment of that person because he cannot comply with it. Thus direct discrimination cannot be justified, while indirect discrimination is capable of justification by reference to criteria other than race or sex, and is actionable only on proof of detriment. Indirect discrimination is justified only if, objectively balancing the discriminatory effect of the requirement or condition against the reasonable needs of the employer, the latter outweigh the former.[27] A belief that it is undesirable to allow

[25] *Griggs* v. *Duke Power Co.*, 401 US 424 (1971).

[26] *Wards Cove Packing Co.* v. *Antonio*, 490 US 642, 104 L. Ed. 2d 733 (1989), discussed by Richard Townshend–Smith, 'American Civil Rights in Retreat' (1992) 12 *Oxford Journal of Legal Studies* 129–34.

[27] *Hampson* v. *Department of Education and Science* [1990] 2 All ER 25, CA, at p. 34 *per* Balcombe LJ (reversed on different grounds [1991] 1 AC 171, [1990] 2 All E 513, HL); *Webb* v. *EMO Air Cargo (UK) Ltd.* [1992] 4 All ER 929, HL.

people to display their membership of a racial group, for example by wearing a turban in school, cannot constitute a justification for rules on school uniform which amount to indirect discrimination, since that would allow discriminators to use as a justification the very attitudes which Parliament intended to combat.[28]

The provisions concerning indirect discrimination are particularly significant, because they emphasize the role of anti-discrimination law as a protector of group rights rather than purely a provider of remedies for individuals. This is reflected in the arrangements for enforcing the legislation, which combine means of individual redress with proactive monitoring and enforcement by public agencies.

There need be no intention to discriminate, either directly or indirectly. If the person doing the act complained of has no intention to discriminate, but is treating someone less favourably than others because of fear of industrial unrest motivated by prejudice on the part of other people, the act is none the less unlawful direct discrimination.[29] Similarly, a condition for the enjoyment of a benefit is directly discriminatory if it relics on a criterion, set by an independent body, which is itself directly discriminatory. The test, as laid down by a three-two majority in the House of Lords in *James* v. *Eastleigh Borough Council*,[30] is whether the condition or disadvantage would have applied to the person but for his or her sex or (as the case may be) race. The test is objective, not subjective. In *James*, the majority (Lords Bridge, Ackner, and Goff, Lords Griffiths and Lowry dissenting) held that there was direct discrimination where a local authority permitted people of pensionable age to swim free in the authority's public swimming baths. Because the age at which pensions could be claimed differentiated between men and women purely on the ground of sex (the age being 60 for women and 65 for men), the condition was discriminatory. Similarly, a council was held to have discriminated directly on the ground of sex when it made more places available for boys than for girls at its single-sex grammar schools.[31]

This 'but for' test involves comparing the way in which the victim was treated with the way in which other people of different sex or race from the victim were or would have been treated in that situation. A question immediately arises as to the relevant group with whose treatment that of a victim should be compared. For example, if a woman is dismissed

---

[28] *Mandla (Sewa Singh)* v. *Dowell Lee* [1983] 2 AC 548, [1983] 1 All ER 1062, HL.

[29] *R.* v. *Commission for Racial Equality, ex parte Westminster City Council* [1984] ICR 770, DC, [1985] ICR 827, CA; *James* v. *Eastleigh Borough Council* [1990] 2 AC 751, [1990] 2 All ER 607, HL.

[30] [1990] 2 AC 751, [1990] 2 All ER 607, HL.

[31] *R.* v. *Birmingham City Council, ex parte Equal Opportunities Commission* [1989] AC 1155, [1989] 1 All ER 769, HL.

because of inability to do the job through a pregnancy-related disability, should one compare her treatment with that of men generally who are unable to do the job for which they are hired, pregnant men (a physical impossibility), men suffering from a physical disability, or some other group? The effect can be seen in a recent decision of the House of Lords under the 1975 Act. In *Webb* v. *EMO Air Cargo (UK) Ltd.*,[32] Ms Webb had been appointed by the company in July 1987 to cover for another employee who was due to go on maternity leave in February 1988. The appointment began almost at once, because six months' training was required for the job. Soon after starting the training, Ms Webb discovered that she, too, was pregnant, and would be unavailable for work during the period when the other employee was due to be on maternity leave. The company dismissed her, as she would have been unable to do the job at the time for which they had specifically appointed her. Ms Webb alleged direct and indirect discrimination on the ground of her sex. The House of Lords decided, on the basis of the 1975 Act, that Ms Webb was not a victim of direct discrimination, because the crucial factor in her dismissal was not her pregnancy but her unavailability for work during the relevant period. Although a male employee could not have been pregnant, a man who was unavailable for work (for whatever reason) at the precise time for which he had been appointed to do the job would have been dismissed. The woman had therefore not been treated less favourably than a man by reason of her sex. In relation to the indirect discrimination claim, the House held that men were more likely than women to be able to satisfy the condition that they be available for work during the specified period, because they could not become pregnant. However, the condition was justified by the reasonable needs of the company's business, which were weightier in the circumstances than the discriminatory effect of the condition.

There are difficulties in reconciling this with the approach of the European Court of Justice to sex discrimination[33] in cases under Council Directive (EEC) 76/207, the Equal Treatment Directive,[34] article 2(1) of which states that 'there shall be no discrimination whatsoever on grounds of sex either directly or indirectly by reference in particular to marital or family status.' This was held by the Court in Case C-177/88 *Dekker* v.

[32] [1992] 4 All ER 929, HL.

[33] The European Community has no general race relations legislation in place, although there are measures protecting the freedom of nationals of one Member State to move to and establish business interests in other Member States: see ch. 7. On the principle of equality in EC law, see Anthony Arnull, *The General Principles of EEC Law and the Individual* (London: Leicester Univ. Press, 1990), esp. ch. 13.

[34] See Evelyn Ellis, *European Community Sex Equality Law* (Oxford: Clarendon Press, 1991), ch. 4.

Stichting Vormingscentrum voor Jong Volwassenen (VJV-Centrum) Plus[35] that it was unlawful to refuse to appoint a woman who was pregnant on the ground of the financial consequences to the employer of doing so. The consequences of appointing a pregnant person, so far as they follow from the fact of pregnancy, are to be regarded as based on the fact of pregnancy, a ground of discrimination which offends against the Directive. This absolutist approach appears at first sight to be inconsistent with the comparison required under the 1975 Act: according to *Dekker*, if unfavourable treatment results from pregnancy it seems to be automatically unlawful. However, this is not necessarily the case. In a decision delivered on the same day as *Dekker*, the Court introduced the possibility of a comparative element in some circumstances. In Case C-179/88 *Handels- og Kontorfunctionoererernes Forbund i Danmark* v. *Dansk Arbejdsgiverforening*[36] (the *Hertz* case) Mrs Hertz returned from maternity leave, but thereafter took considerable periods of sick leave because of complications resulting from her pregnancy. Her employer dismissed her. The Court held that it is within the discretion of Member States to fix periods of maternity leave which allow pregnant women to be absent during the period in which disorders which are inherent in pregnancy and childbirth occur. If disorders occur or continue after that period, they are to be treated in the same way as any other illness. It does not constitute unlawful discrimination to dismiss a woman who is persistently ill over a long period following the end of her maternity leave, whatever the cause of the illnesses, unless a man who was ill for a similar period would not have been dismissed.

Domestic courts, as authorities of the state, are required to take all appropriate measures to give effect to obligations on the state arising under Directives, and this includes interpreting domestic law so as to be consistent with Community law whenever possible.[37] However, the combined effect of *Dekker* and *Hertz* in circumstances such as those in *Webb* is not clear. Does Community law permit a comparative approach so as to allow an employer to rely on a person's unavailability for work through pregnancy as a ground of dismissal when the person was taken on to cover that very period and a man would have been dismissed for unavailability at that time? Faced by this problem, the House of Lords in *Webb* decided to adjourn the case to await the response of the Court to a question which the House referred under Article 177 of the Treaty. The difficulty illustrates the complexity of the notion of discrimination when one tries to protect groups who are likely to be victims of discrimination

[35] [1990] ECR I–3941, CJEC.
[36] [1990] ECR I–3979, CJEC.
[37] Case 14/83 *Von Colson and Kamann* v. *Land Nordrhein–Westfalen* [1984] ECR 1891, CJEC; Case C–106–89 *Marleasing SA* v. *La Comercial Internacional de Alimentaciòn SA* [1990] ECR I–4135.

without making it unduly burdensome for employers to organize their work-places or for people who provide educational and other services to carry on their activities.

Under section 2 of the 1975 and 1976 Acts, it is also unlawful to discriminate against a person by reason that the person in question has alleged that the discriminator has contravened the Acts, or has brought proceedings against the discriminator under the Acts, or given evidence or information in connection with such proceedings, or has done anything at all under or by reference to the Acts, whether in relation to the discriminator or any other person, unless the allegations were made falsely and not in good faith. Discrimination on the ground of suspected past or intended future actions of those types by the person discriminated against are also unlawful under section 2.

As noted above, equal treatment will not always provide equal opportunity. Inequality of opportunity is particularly likely to result where one group suffers from the effects of a history of systematic discrimination which has limited the educational and economic opportunities open to them. In such cases, affirmative action, or positive discrimination, is required to redress the balance by favouring members of that group over members of other groups in order to make up for unavoidable disadvantages. Such action involves the use of race- or sex-conscious selection criteria in order to remove or compensate for, rather than to create, inequality of opportunity. In the USA the decision of the Supreme Court in *Brown* v. *Board of Education of Topeka*[38] that separate schooling for different racial groups could not be 'equal' within the meaning of the Equal Protection Clause of the Fourteenth Amendment to the Constitution led to court-ordered programmes of bussing children between schools and areas in circumstances which gave rise to considerable unhappiness, and incidentally involved courts in taking an active role in controlling school policy. In a follow-up decision, the Supreme Court felt forced to soften its stance somewhat, giving more weight to the opinions of the local school districts as to the speed at which desegregated schooling could be achieved.[39]

Such action to break down segregation is highly contentious, because it will be seen by the disadvantaged members of previously advantaged groups as a straightforward form of discrimination. If the beneficiary of affirmative action has personally suffered from discrimination in the past, and the victim has in the past been a discriminator, there are good compensatory reasons for giving special treatment to make good the lost

[38] 347 US 483 (1954).
[39] *Brown* v. *Board of Education*, 349 US 294 (1955); see also *Swann* v. *Charlotte–Mecklenburg Board of Education*, 402 US 1 (1971) and *Milliken* v. *Bradley*, 418 US 717 (1974).

advantage. However, it is less clear that generally preferential treatment can be justified in order to benefit the disadvantaged group as a whole at the expense of people who have never personally discriminated. There are possible justifications. It might be argued that ethnic diversity in education, housing, professions, etc., benefits the whole of society, and also helps to strengthen the institutions concerned. Another argument is that special action is helpful in producing substantial numbers of (for example) black or women doctors in order to give members of that racial group or sex a role model which will encourage them to take up opportunities which are available. But these arguments have not, on the whole, attracted widespread support in the UK or the USA, being inconsistent with the individualist view of rights on which those legal systems are, by and large, based.

In the USA, some affirmative action programmes have been upheld under the Equal Protection clause of the Fourteenth Amendment and Title VII of the Civil Rights Act of 1964. Although crude affirmative action through quotas has been held to be an unlawful form of state action, less rigid, more judgmental favouring of underprivileged groups in educational settings has been upheld (especially if carried on in order to achieve an appropriately broad educational experience for all).[40] Affirmative action programmes have been treated as appropriate in order to correct direct discrimination against the person whom the affirmative action is designed to benefit, and to remedy 'persistent or egregious discrimination'.[41] The philosophical basis for the latter ground is unclear, but it seems to be taken to justify state grants in aid of business enterprises controlled by members of ethnic minorities.[42] Even affirmative action by means of quotas has been upheld where the action is a temporary measure which has been undertaken voluntarily by a private employer or individual, rather than imposed by a state agency.[43] The American courts and Congress are finding it hard to decide whether (and, if so, when) the Constitution permits them to adopt race- and sex-conscious criteria to benefit certain groups in order to correct past negative discrimination, or whether it requires them to be entirely blind to race and sex.[44]

---

[40] *Regents of the University of California* v. *Bakke,* 438 US 265 (1978); Drew S. Days III, 'Affirmative action', in Larry Gostin (ed.), *Civil Liberties in Conflict* (London: Routledge, 1988), pp. 85–101.

[41] *Local 28 of the Sheet Metal Workers' International Association* v. *EEOC,* 106 S. Ct. 3019 (1986); *United States* v. *Paradise,* 107 S. Ct. 1053 (1987).

[42] *Fullilove* v. *Klutznick,* 448 US 448 (1980).

[43] *United Steelworkers of America* v. *Weber,* 443 US 193 (1979); *Metro Broadcasting* v. *FCC,* 111 L. Ed. 2d 854 (1990).

[44] For full discussion see Henry J. Abraham, *Freedom and the Court: Civil Rights and Liberties in the United States* 5th edn. (New York: Oxford University Press, 1988), pp. 473–534.

In the British legislation, this dilemma is on the whole resolved in favour of race- and sex-blindness. Positive discrimination is generally no less unlawful than other forms of discrimination.[45] There are general obligations placed on authorities responsible for public programmes to ensure that education is provided without discrimination.[46] Local authorities also have a duty to have regard, in the performance of their functions, to the need to eliminate unlawful racial discrimination and promote equality of opportunity and good relations between members of different racial groups, although this has been interpreted by the courts as giving only a limited freedom to authorities.[47] However, there are particular settings in which statute provides that specially advantageous treatment for certain purposes is not to be regarded as unlawful discrimination. For example, vocational training can be offered preferentially to members of one racial group or sex where that group or sex is seriously under-represented in the work-force.[48] In deference to the religious significance of turbans to Sikhs, they are exempted from the requirement to wear protective headgear when riding motorcycles and when working on sites where helmets would normally be mandatory, and it is unlawful to discriminate against Sikhs in respect of employment on account of their lawful refusal to wear protective headgear.[49] The influence of European Community law has led to legislation which permits discrimination in favour of women in employment, vocational training, and in respect of discriminatory practices, where the discrimination is carried out for the protection of women as required by statute,[50] and the Secretary of State has power to exempt from the scope of the Sex Discrimination Act 1989 certain arrangements authorized by statute to make it easier for single parents to take employment.[51] But these provisions do not amount to a general acceptance of affirmative action to remedy the social effects of past discrimination.

(ii) *Contexts in which discrimination is unlawful.* The settings in which discrimination is unlawful are broadly similar in relation to sex and race discrimination, although there are detailed rules dealing with sexually discriminatory terms in contracts of employment under the Equal Pay

[45] *Lambeth LBC* v. *Commission for Racial Equality* [1990] IRLR 231, CA, at p. 234 *per* Balcombe LJ.

[46] Sex Discrimination Act 1975, s. 25; Race Relations Act 1976, s. 19.

[47] *Wheeler* v. *Leicester City Council* [1985] AC 1054, [1985] 2 All ER 1106, HL; *R.* v. *Lewisham LBC, ex parte Shell UK Ltd.* [1988] 1 All ER 938, DC.

[48] Sex Discrimination Act 1975, ss. 47, 48; Race Relations Act 1976, ss. 37, 38.

[49] Road Traffic Act 1988, s. 16(2); Employment Act 1989, ss. 11, 12.

[50] Sex Discrimination Act 1985, ss. 51 (as substituted by Employment Act 1989, s. 3(1), (3)), 51A and 52A (inserted by Employment Act 1989, s. 3(1), (3), (4)).

[51] Employment Act 1989, s. 8.

Act 1970, Article 119 of the Treaty of Rome, and the Equal Treatment Directive and the Equal Pay Directive[52] of the Council of Ministers of the European Community, explained below, which have no parallel in respect of racial discrimination.

Where the special provisions in respect of sex discrimination do not apply, the provisions of the 1976 Act parallel those in the 1975 Act. Both Acts apply generally to employment,[53] education,[54] and the provision of goods, facilities, services, and premises to the public or a section of the public.[55] Private clubs do not constitute a section of the public for this purpose,[56] although those with 25 or more members are now subject to the race relations legislation,[57] but not the sex discrimination legislation (enabling single-sex clubs, including the gentlemen's clubs in London and elsewhere, to continue to operate). Goods, facilities, and services constitute a broad category which has enabled some governmental acts to be scrutinized. For example, the Court of Appeal held in *Savjani* v. *IRC*[58] that tax inspectors were forbidden to discriminate when adopting methods of testing taxpayers' entitlements to tax relief, because the provision of the reliefs allowed by statute was a service within the meaning of the legislation. In that case, the Revenue had unlawfully adopted a practice of imposing requirements of proof on immigrants from the Indian subcontinent claiming child relief for the first time which were not demanded of claimants from elsewhere. On the other hand, the House of Lords has held by a majority of three to two, in *R.* v. *Entry Clearance Officer, Bombay, ex parte Amin*,[59] that the provisions do not cover the work of agencies whose job is to control or police people's activities, rather than to facilitate them. An officer whose job it was to vet potential immigrants was thus not subject to the sex discrimination legislation, and the same would be true of the race relations legislation. This is not a surprising decision on the facts of the case, given that the very nature of immigration law and procedure is inherently discriminatory,[60] but the general way in which Lord Fraser, speaking for the majority in *Amin*'s case, developed his argument raises problems about the applicability of

[52] See Ellis, *European Community Sex Equality Law*, ch. 3.
[53] Sex Discrimination Act 1975, s. 6; Race Relations Act 1976, s. 4.
[54] Sex Discrimination Act 1975, s. 22; Race Relations Act 1976, s. 17.
[55] Sex Discrimination Act 1975, ss. 29–32; Race Relations Act 1976, ss. 20–24.
[56] *Charter* v. *Race Relations Board* [1973] AC 868, [1973] 1 All ER 512, HL; *Dockers' Labour Club and Institute Ltd.* v. *Race Relations Board* [1976] AC 285, [1974] 3 All ER 592, HL.
[57] Race Relations Act 1976, s. 25.
[58] [1981] QB 458, [1981] 1 All ER 1121, CA.
[59] [1983] 2 AC 818, [1983] 2 All ER 864, HL.
[60] Ian Martin, 'Racism in Immigration Law and Practice', in Peter Wallington (ed.), *Civil Liberties 1984* (Oxford: Martin Robertson, 1984), pp. 245–57.

the legislation to such regulatory fields as land use planning and policing (although for a constable to act in a racially discriminatory way is a disciplinary offence).[61]

Barristers are the subject of special provisions. There is evidence that discrimination against female barristers and those from ethnic minorities has been occurring in relation the allocation of tenancies in sets of chambers, the allocation of briefs, and also perhaps (although this is denied by the examining authority) the assessment of practical exercises in the Bar Final Examination. However, because of the anomalous, non-contractual relationship between barristers and their clients, and the special training and working practices of the Bar in respect of pupillages and seats in chambers, there was difficulty in bringing the discriminatory treatment of aspiring ethnic minority and women barristers under the existing legislation. Accordingly special provision was made in the Courts and Legal Services Act 1990 outlawing discrimination against barristers on the grounds of race and sex.[62]

There are some general exceptions from the reach of both sex and race discrimination law. The regime of the legislation does not apply to matters affecting national security,[63] or to charities established before the legislation came into operation.[64] Nor does it apply to certain intimate settings in which small groups of people have to live, work, or play closely together. Partnerships with fewer than six partners are allowed to discriminate when appointing new partners,[65] as are people providing accommodation in small premises where the lessor or vendor is to continue to live in close proximity to the tenant or purchaser.[66] In employment, it is not unlawful to discriminate on the ground of sex or race where the sex or race of the person to be appointed is a genuine occupational qualification.[67]

[61] Police and Criminal Evidence Act 1984, s. 101(1) (racially discriminatory behaviour to be made a disciplinary offence); S. H. Bailey, D. J. Harris, and B. L. Jones, *Civil Liberties Cases and Materials* 3rd edn. (London: Butterworths, 1991), pp. 596–600.

[62] Sex Discrimination Act 1975, s. 35A, and Race Relations Act 1976, s. 26A, as inserted by the Courts and Legal Services Act 1990, s. 64(1).

[63] Sex Discrimination Act 1975, s. 52; Race Relations Act 1976, s. 42.

[64] Sex Discrimination Act 1975, s. 43; Race Relations Act 1976, s. 34.

[65] Sex Discrimination Act 1975, s. 11; Race Relations Act 1976, s. 10.

[66] Sex Discrimination Act 1975, s. 32; Race Relations Act 1976, s. 22; and note ss. 34, 35 of the 1975 Act and ss. 23–26 of the 1976 Act. See further Bailey, Harris, and Jones, *Civil Liberties Cases and Materials*, pp. 604–10; Evelyn Ellis, *Sex Discrimination Law* (Aldershot: Gower, 1988), pp. 114–26.

[67] Sex Discrimination Act 1975, s. 7, as amended by Sex Discrimination Act 1986; Race Relations Act 1976, s. 5. See Richard Townshend–Smith, *Sex Discrimination in Employment* (London: Sweet & Maxwell, 1989), ch. 8.

(4) Race relations legislation

In this section, attention is drawn to some features of the Race Relations Act 1976 and the regime which it establishes. Several of the salient features which concern the Sex Discrimination Act 1975 and the 1976 Act equally have been mentioned above. In the account which follows, a number of matters relating particularly to the 1976 Act are considered: the groups against which discrimination is unlawful, and the work of the Commission for Racial Equality (CRE) established under the 1976 Act.

(i) *Racial grounds and racial groups.* Direct discrimination is unlawful if carried out on racial grounds, and indirect discrimination against racial groups is unlawful. The meanings of these terms are related. Racial grounds are defined as colour, race, nationality, or ethnic or national origins; a racial group is a group of people defined by reference to colour, race, nationality, or ethnic or national origin. A person' racial group is any racial group into which he or she falls, so a person may be a member of a number of different racial groups simultaneously, and one racial group may comprise a number of different racial groups.[68]

The problems which have arisen in relation to this definition mainly concern the idea of ethnic origins. Whereas racial groups are identified primarily by biological and geographical factors, an ethnic group has been held to be defined primarily by social and cultural factors, such as language, religion, history, or culture, which are commonly associated with racial groups. The 1976 Act does not provide a remedy for discrimination on religious or linguistic grounds, but the availability of a remedy for discrimination on the ground of nationality or ethnic or national origin may have the effect of mitigating the effects of that omission. For example, a social group with a distinct culture (which may include use of a distinctive language or commitment to a particular religion) may constitute an ethnic group even if members of the group come from such diverse racial and geographical backgrounds that they do not constitute a group defined by race or national origins.

For this reason, the House of Lords held in *Mandla (Sewa Singh)* v. *Dowell Lee*[69] that a head teacher of a school who refused to allow pupils to wear turbans, thus discriminating against Sikhs, was committing an act of unlawful discrimination under the 1976 Act, because the Sikh community was an ethnic group for the purposes of the Act. Lord Fraser identified two essential conditions for the existence of an ethnic group: a long shared history as a separate group; and a cultural tradition of its own,

[68] See Race Relations Act 1976, s. 3.
[69] [1983] 2 AC 548, [1983] 1 All ER 1062, HL.

including family and social customs. In addition, Lord Fraser noted five relevant, though not essential, factors: either common geographical origin or descent from a small number of common ancestors; a common language; a common literature special to the group; a common and distinctive religion; and being a separate group within a larger community. Lord Templeman thought that an ethnic group must have some of the characteristics of a race: group descent, common geographical origin, and a common history. These were not regarded as essential by Lord Fraser, and Lord Templeman does not mention several of Lord Fraser's essential or relevant considerations. The fact that Lords Edmund-Davies, Roskill, and Brandon agreed with both speeches means that there can be no definitive test, or set of tests, for the existence of an ethnic group. We can only say that some elements are probably essential (although we cannot say which), and that several are important.

It follows from *Mandla* that, alongside Sikhs, Jews form an ethnic group.[70] Gipsies also form an ethnic group, so that a 'No Travellers' sign outside a public house potentially constituted indirect discrimination in the provision of goods and services. (It was not direct discrimination, because it did not treat gipsies less favourably on racial grounds than travellers who were not gipsies.)[71]

(ii) *The Commission for Racial Equality.* The CRE was established under Part VII of the 1976 Act, replacing the Race Relations Board which had operated under the Race Relations Act 1965. The CRE was given a general brief to work towards the elimination of discrimination, to promote equality of opportunity and good relations between members of racial groups, and to keep the working of the Act under review and make recommendations to the Secretary of State for amending it.[72] To further these ends, the CRE is permitted to give assistance (including financial assistance) to organisations, to undertake or assist research and educational activities, and to issue Codes of Practice giving practical guidance for the elimination of discrimination, and promotion of equality of opportunity between racial groups, in the field of employment.[73]

[70] In *Mandla*, Lord Fraser adopted the approach to this matter of Richardson J. in the New Zealand Court of Appeal in *King–Ansell* v. *Police* [1979] 2 NZLR 531.

[71] *Commission for Racial Equality* v. *Dutton* [1989] 1 All ER 306, CA.

[72] Race Relations Act 1976, s. 43. See Bailey, Harris, and Jones, *Civil Liberties Cases and Materials* pp. 614–24; Gregory, *Sex, Race and the Law* chs. 6 and 7; Laurence Lustgarten, *Legal Control of Racial Discrimination* (London: Macmillan, 1980); *id.*, 'Racial Inequality and the Limits of Law' (1986) 49 MLR 68–85; Christopher McCrudden, 'The Commission for Racial Equality: Formal Investigations in the Shadow of Judicial Review', in Robert Baldwin and Christopher McCrudden, *Regulation and Public Law* (London: Weidenfeld & Nicolson, 1987), pp. 227–66.

[73] Race Relations Act 1976, ss. 44, 45, 46.

The CRE has a number of powers in relation to the investigation of suspected discrimination and the enforcement of the law. This exemplifies the twin-track approach to the enforcement of anti-discrimination law, which operates equally under the Sex Discrimination Act 1975, whereby individuals have legal remedies for discrimination which they suffer, while a public agency is responsible for safeguarding wider interests. The two may come together: the CRE is empowered to give assistance to an individual complainant in legal proceedings where the case raises a question of principle or it is unreasonable, in view of considerations including the complexity of the case and the position of the complainant, to expect the complainant to deal with the case alone.[74]

When acting in its own right as an investigator and enforcer, the CRE has power to conduct a formal investigation.[75] Launching a formal investigation, as opposed to conducting general research or informal investigations, has two significant consequences. First, for the purposes of a formal investigation the CRE has power to serve notice on any person requiring that specified information be provided, and may require any person to attend to give oral information and produce documents. Non-compliance with the requirements of a notice is a criminal offence.[76] Secondly, if in the course of a formal investigation the CRE becomes satisfied that a person is committing or has committed an unlawful discriminatory act, or a breach of section 28 (discriminatory practice), 29 (discriminatory advertising), 30 (giving instructions to discriminate), or 31 (putting pressure on another person to discriminate) of the 1976 Act, it can issue a 'non-discrimination notice'. This requires the person not to commit such an act, and where necessary to inform the CRE of steps taken to effect changes to practices or other arrangements and to give information to other people if required. The notice may also require the person to provide such other information as may reasonably be required.[77] At first sight, the formal investigation would seem to be a powerful weapon in the hands of the CRE. However, in practice its potential is limited.

There are two broad types of formal investigation. In the first type of investigation, the terms of reference for the investigation confine it to the activities of named people. These must be informed that the CRE believe that the people have committed an act made unlawful by the Act and

[74] Race Relations Act 1976, s. 66.
[75] Race Relations Act 1976, s. 48. See George Applebey and Evelyn Ellis, 'Formal Investigations: the Commission for Racial Equality and the Equal Opportunities Commission as Law Enforcement Agencies' [1984] PL 236–76.
[76] Race Relations Act 1976, s. 50.
[77] Race Relations Act 1976, s. 58. The person to whom a notice is addressed has a right of appeal on the merits to a court or tribunal: s. 59; *CRE* v. *Amari Plastics Ltd.* [1982] QB 1194, [1982] 2 All ER 499, CA.

that the CRE propose to investigate it, and they must be offered an opportunity to make oral or written representations with regard to it.[78] It follows that the decision to embark on a 'named person' investigation must be reactive, responding to a belief that the person has committed an unlawful act. As a public agency, the CRE is subject to the ordinary principles of judicial review. A decision to launch a 'named person' investigation may therefore be quashed if, before taking the decision, the CRE does not have such a belief,[79] or (perhaps) if it has insufficient evidence to make such a belief reasonable. The usefulness of the power to launch a formal 'named person' investigation has been substantially restricted by this tendency on the part of the courts to interpret restrictively the powers of the CRE to initiate formal investigations proactively. It seems that this is the result of a drafting error in the legislation, which was intended to apply to the course of an investigation, not its inception.[80] In 1985, the CRE proposed an amendment to the 1976 Act to allow them to commence 'named person' investigations without a belief that a named person had committed an unlawful act, but this proposal has not been acted on.

The second type of formal investigation, a general investigation, is less restricted. General notice must be given that the investigation is to take place, but the CRE need not have any prior belief that discrimination is occurring, although there will normally be at least a suspicion. These investigations tend, therefore, to be proactive rather than reactive. Such investigations may be undertaken even where there is no suspicion that anyone has committed an unlawful act, in order to enable the CRE to write a report which will highlight factors putting a strain on good relations between racial groups. For example, the CRE investigated suspected racist practices in the implementation of immigration policy, despite such practices not being capable of being unlawful discrimination within the meaning of the Act. This investigation was permitted because it was directed to promoting good relations between people of different racial groups,[81] and led to a report on *Immigration Control and Procedures* in 1985. However, a general investigation is not as effective as a 'named person' investigation, because general reports flowing from general investigations do not have legal consequences (although there is

---

[78] Race Relations Act 1976, s. 49.

[79] *R. v. CRE, ex parte London Borough of Hillingdon* [1982] AC 779, HL; *In re Prestige Group plc, Commission for Racial Equality v. Prestige Group plc* [1984] ICR 473, [1984] 1 WLR 335, HL; Maurice Monroe, 'The *Prestige* Case: Putting the Lid on the Commission for Racial Equality' (1985) 14 *Anglo–American L. Rev.* 187–203.

[80] Bailey, Harris, and Jones, *Civil Liberties Cases and Materials*, p. 618.

[81] *Home Office v. Commission for Racial Equality* [1982] QB 385, [1981] 1 All ER 1042, Woolf J.

no reason why a non-discrimination notice could not be issued alongside, or before, the report).

The drafting of the Act is a serious drawback to the CRE's effective operation. Its extensive inquisitorial powers operate only in respect of formal investigations, which are hedged about by what Lord Denning has described as 'elaborate and cumbersome' machinery, catching the CRE in 'a spider's web spun by Parliament, from which there is little hope of their escaping.'[82] But there are other barriers to the effectiveness of the CRE besides the defective drafting of its power-conferring statutory provisions. The CRE was criticized by the House of Commons Home Affairs Select Committee in 1981 for the ineffectiveness of its promotional work, and for its lack of achievement in obtaining alterations in the law and in administrative practice from government.[83] It now uses the material gleaned in the course of its investigations to bolster its promotional work, but has still not stimulated substantial responses from government. In part, this is the result of the structure of the CRE: despite (or because of) being a 'quango', theoretically independent of government, it lacks power to enforce its recommendations or even to secure any constructive response to them. The membership of the CRE, including as it does two nominees of each of the CBI and the TUC, contains an element strongly resistant to any change in the existing structures of industry. In short, the dynamism and commitment which a body such as the CRE would need in order to be fully effective is neutralized.[84]

Yet, even if the CRE were given free rein, there might be a still more fundamental problem to be overcome before the drive for equality of opportunity through anti-discrimination law could become truly effective. As Laurence Lustgarten has persuasively argued, the structure of the existing law, stressing negative legal sanctions for infringements of individual's legal rights, makes it unlikely to be able to address the more pervasive social causes of racial discrimination. On this view, to make the legislation effective it would require a real governmental commitment to the idea of equality, leading to amendment of the 1976 Act to permit, and indeed encourage, affirmative action programmes. But even this would provide only part of the strategy necessary to combat such a deeply-rooted social phenomenon as racial discrimination: Lustgarten suggests that it would also be necessary for government to utilize its economic power, and employers and others would need to seek and use information about the ethnic make-up of their workforces, change

---

[82] *CRE* v. *Amari Plastics Ltd.* [1982] QB 1194 at p. 1203, [1982] 2 All ER 499 at p. 502, *per* Lord Denning MR.

[83] *Report on the Commission for Racial Equality*, HC No. 46 of 1981–2 (London: HMSO, 1981).

[84] Gregory, *Sex, Race and the Law*, pp. 133–42.

recruiting procedures, dismantle racial barriers, and change training policies, with the active encouragement and financial support of
government.[85] Without that, equality of opportunity between racial
groups is unlikely to come much closer.

(5) Sex discrimination legislation[86]

The legislation on sex discrimination which is in force in the United
Kingdom comes from two distinct sources. First, Parliament has passed a
number of measures to restrict the unequal treatment of men and
women. Most prominent among these statutes are the Equal Pay Act
1970, which introduced to English law the principle that men and
women doing comparable work should be comparably treated under
their contracts, and the Sex Discrimination Act 1975. Secondly,
European Community law has significantly affected the rights of employees by means of Article 119 of the Treaty of Rome and the Equal Pay
and Equal Treatment Directives of the Council of Ministers, which have
been held to be directly effective and give rise to enforceable
Community rights to which our courts are, in appropriate circumstances,
bound to give effect regardless of inconsistent domestic legislation.[87]

As in relation to race relations legislation, there are two ways in which
discrimination may operate: it may be either direct or indirect. The Sex
Discrimination Act 1975 attempts to deal with both types of discrimination. The Equal Pay Act 1970 was at first thought to deal only with
direct discrimination, but, as will be explained below, as a result of
Community law its protection has been held to extend to indirect discrimination as well. The types of discrimination to which the legislation
applies should therefore be the same.

(i) *The Equal Pay Act 1970*, despite its title, seeks to give a right to
women to be treated equally to men[88] in respect of all terms of the contract of employment.[89] It achieves this by implying an equality clause

---

[85] Lustgarten, 'Racial Inequality' at pp. 78–84.

[86] On European Community law, see Ellis, *European Community Sex Discrimination
Law*, passim. On domestic law, see Ellis, *Sex Discrimination Law*; Gregory, *Sex, Race and the
Law*; O'Donovan and Szyszczak, *Equality and Sex Discrimination Law*; and (in relation to
employment) Townshend–Smith, *Sex Discrimination in Employment*.

[87] See generally Ellis, *European Community Sex Equality Law*, ch. 1; Arnull, *General
Principles*, 238–50.

[88] The legislation applies equally to women and to men, but men cannot complain
under the 1970 Act in respect of terms in women's contracts which give special protection or maternity rights to women: Equal Pay Act 1970, s. 6(1), as interpreted in *Coyne* v.
Export Credits Guarantee Department [1981] IRLR 51.

[89] See Ellis, *Sex Discrimination Law*, ch. 2.

into contracts of service, apprenticeship, or for the personal execution of
any work of labour, under which women are employed at any establishment in Great Britain.[90] This implied clause modifies any other term of
the contract which is or becomes less favourable to the woman than is a
similar term in contract of a man employed to do comparable work.[91]
Because the Act covers more than traditional master-servant employment
relationships, it can be relied on by people who are self-employed contractors taken on for limited periods on a commission basis, as long as the
dominant purpose of the contract is to secure the performance of the
work by the contractor in person.[92] However, in order to take advantage
of the equality clause the woman must establish comparability with a
male colleague, and there are only three grounds under section 1(2) of
the Act on which this can be done.

The first is where she is 'employed on the like work with a man in
the same employment.' For this to apply, their work must be of the
same or a broadly similar nature, any differences being of no practical
importance (as regards the nature of the differences and the frequency
with which they arise in practice)[93] in relation to terms and conditions
of employment.[94] The second is where the woman's work is 'rated as
equivalent with that of a man in the same employment' in the course of
a job evaluation based on factors such as the effort, skill, and decision-
making responsibility which the jobs entail.[95] The third ground of comparability is where, apart from any job evaluation, the woman's work
and the man's work are of equal value, even if dissimilar in nature. This
was not originally in the 1970 Act, but was essential because the Act
would otherwise have been of no use to women working in traditionally segregated occupations, because of stereotyping of gender roles,
where there would be no direct male comparator. Because of this gap in
the provision for equal pay for work of equal value, the Act was held by
the European Court to fall short of the requirements of Article 1 of the
EEC Equal Pay Directive,[96] made under the Article 119 of the Treaty
of Rome.[97] To comply with the ruling, the government introduced

---

[90] Equal Pay Act 1970, s. 1(1), (6).
[91] Ibid., s. 1(2).
[92] *Quinnen* v. *Hovells* [1984] IRLR 227, EAT; *Mirror Group Newspapers Ltd.* v. *Gunning*
[1986] 1 WLR 546, [1986] 1 All ER 385, CA.
[93] *Shields* v. *Coomes (Holdings) Ltd.* [1978] ICR 1159, CA.
[94] Equal Pay Act 1970, s. 1(4).
[95] Ibid., s. 1(5).
[96] EEC Directive 75/117, OJ No. L 45/19.
[97] On the equal pay for equal work principle in Art. 119, see Case 61/81, *Commission*
v. *UK* [1982] 3 CMLR 284; Ellis, *European Community Sex Equality Law*, ch. 2.

the third ground of comparability to the Act by means of delegated legislation.[98]

The Act excepts from its reach provisions relating to death and retirement, but these exceptions have been to some extent undermined by decisions of the European Court of Justice applying the EEC Equal Pay Directive 75/117 and the Equal Treatment Directive 76/207. In particular, it has been held that differential retirement ages and ages for entitlement to occupational pensions, fixed by reference to the ages at which people became eligible for state pensions (men at 65, women at 60) violated the Equal Treatment Directive.[99] Normally, Community rights under directly effective EEC Council Directives are enforceable only against state agencies, and not against citizens or companies, but in Case C-188/89, *Foster* v. *British Gas plc*[100] the Court held that the rights could also be enforced against any person or body which had been given responsibility by law for providing a public service, which was under the control of the state, and which had been given special powers, beyond those given by the rules governing relationships between ordinary individuals, to facilitate performance of that function. Moreover, in Joined Cases C-6/90 and C-9/90, *Francovich and Bonifaci* v. *Italy*[101] the Court held that an individual whose grievance lies against a body which does not fall within the scope of the *Foster* doctrine nevertheless has a cause of action against the state for loss caused by the state's failure to implement a Directive in domestic law in such a way as to enable the plaintiff to pursue a remedy against the person or body which actually caused the loss.[102] These developments are manifestations of the Court's determination to ensure that people are not left without adequate remedies for injuries suffered through non-compliance with Community law, whether by the state or private undertakings.[103]

It is therefore a potentially important guarantee of the right to be free of discriminatory provisions in respect of retirement and pensions that the Court has held that the Equal Treatment Directive makes it unlawful to

---

[98] Equal Pay (Amendment) Regulations, SI 1983/1794, made under the power conferred by the European Communities Act 1972, s. 2(2), (4).

[99] Case 19/81 *Burton* v. *British Railways Board* [1982] ECR 555, CJEC; Case 152/84 *Marshall* v. *Southampton and South–West Hampshire Area Health Authority* [1986] ECR 723, CJEC; Case C–262/88 *Barber* v. *Guardian Royal Exchange Assurance Group* [1991] 1 QB 344, [1990] 2 All ER 660, CJEC.

[100] [1990] ECR I–3133, [1990] 3 All ER 897, CJEC.

[101] [1992] IRLR 84, CJEC.

[102] Erika Szyszczak, 'European Community Law: New Remedies, New Directions? Joined Cases C6/90 and C9/90, *Francovich and Bonifaci* v. *Italy*' (1992) 55 MLR 690–7; Malcolm Ross, 'Beyond *Francovich*' (1993) 56 MLR 55–73.

[103] See Case C–213/89, *R.* v. *Secretary of State for Transport, ex parte Factortame Ltd.* [1990] ECR I–2433, [1991] 1 All ER 70, CJEC and HL.

adopt discriminatory retirement ages as between men and women.[104]
This is particularly significant in view of the weakness, by and large, of
the domestic statutory protection against discrimination in relation to
retirement arrangements. Excluded from the Equal Pay Act 1970, differential retirement ages for employees doing different kinds of work have
been upheld under the Sex Discrimination Act 1975, without the need
to show that the difference is justified by objective criteria relating to the
nature of the work. In *Bullock* v. *Alice Ottley School*,[105] the employers
adopted retirement ages of 65 for maintenance workers and gardeners
(who were men) and 60 for kitchen workers (who were women). The
Court of Appeal, reversing the Employment Appeal Tribunal, held that
employers are free to impose different retirement ages for different classes
of jobs between which there is no comparability, as long as the ages are
not based on direct or indirect gender discrimination. This leaves domestic protection in a weak state for those who are in occupations which are
predominantly staffed by people of one sex, and makes recourse to rights
under Community law increasingly important.

The Equal Pay Act 1970 permits a person who is aggrieved by unequal
contractual terms to bring proceedings against the employer in an industrial tribunal. The employee left to take individual action faces a hurdle in
the form of the employer's defence where the variation between the
woman's contract and the man's contract is proved to be 'genuinely due
to a material factor which is not the difference of sex'.[106] The difference
in question must be significant and relevant in all the circumstances surrounding the employment in question.[107] The European Court of Justice
has ruled that the fact that the woman worker is part-time where the
man is full-time does not justify a differential wage rate where the effect
is indirectly to discriminate against women because women are more
likely than men to be employed part-time.[108]

The onus under the 1970 Act is on individuals to enforce the law
(although employees are likely often to be supported and advised by their
trade unions). This leaves something of a gap, in that discriminatory contractual terms may be imposed not by individual employers but by larger

---

[104] Case 149/77, *Defrenne* v. *Sabena* [1978] ECR 1365, CJEC; Case 152/84, *Marshall* v.
South West Hampshire Area Health Authority (Teaching) [1986] QB 401, [1986] 2 All ER
584, CJEC; Case C–188/89, *Foster* v. *British Gas plc* [1990] ECR I–3133, [1990] 3 All ER
897, CJEC.

[105] [1992] IRLR 564, CA.

[106] Equal Pay Act 1970, s. 1(3).

[107] *Rainey* v. *Greater Glasgow Health Board* [1987] 1 All ER 65, HL, especially at p. 70
per Lord Keith of Kinkel.

[108] Case 96/80, *Jenkins* v. *Kingsgate (Clothing Productions) Ltd.* [1981] ECR 911, [1981]
1 WLR 972, CJEC.

scale collective agreements (to which the trades unions would usually be parties), pay structures, and legal structures for regulating wages. Originally, these were the subject of an alternative arrangement, under which a Central Arbitration Committee determined the lawfulness of the agreements or other structures. However, the Divisional Court restricted the scope for decision-making by the CAC,[109] which was in due course abolished by the Sex Discrimination Act 1986. In its place, the 1986 Act nullifies sexually discriminatory provisions in collective agreements, employers' and professional organizations and qualifying bodies, and trades unions' and employers' rules,[110] but there is no procedure for adjudicating on the legality of provisions at the instigation of a collective plaintiff or applicant. As Dr. Ellis comments, 'The lack of a collective remedy amounts to a serious gap in the legislative framework in relation to this far-reaching form of discrimination.'[111]

(ii) *The Sex Discrimination Act 1975* was drafted to complement the Equal Pay Act 1970, and to extend protection to fields which are not related to the terms of a contract of employment.[112] Most sections of both Acts came into force on the same day, 29 December 1975. The 1975 Act covers discrimination in the provision of housing, education, and good, facilities, and services, as well as access to employment and non-contractual aspects of employment conditions, including non-contractual benefits. As far as employment is concerned, therefore, the anti-discrimination legislation is a sort of jigsaw puzzle, containing pieces derived from the 1970 Act, the 1975 Act, and Community law. There is also scope for the position to be affected by delegated legislation, since section 2 of the Employment Act 1989 permits the Secretary of State to make statutory instruments repealing any other instrument, or a provision in an Act passed before the 1989 Act, which appears to the Secretary of State to require anyone to do an act which is inconsistent with the Sex Discrimination Act 1975.

The field of operation of the 1975 Act, and the meaning of discrimination which forms the basis of its reach, are both similar to the Race Relations Act 1976, save that, for the 1975 Act to bite, the discrimination must be by reference to sex rather than race. Like the 1976 Act, the 1975 Act excludes acts done on national security grounds, and provides a defence in employment cases where sex is a genuine occupational qualification. As noted in Chapter 11, discrimination against homosexuals on the basis of their sexual orientation does not appear to be covered by

---

[109] *R. v. Central Arbitration Committee, ex parte Hy–Mac Ltd.* [1979] IRLR 461, DC.
[110] Sex Discrimination Act 1986, s. 6.
[111] Ellis, *Sex Discrimination Law*, p. 18.
[112] See Ellis, *Sex Discrimination Law*, ch. 3.

the legislation, and for the purposes of the Act a transsexual is probably to be regarded as having the sex assigned at birth, although the post-operative position of those who have undergone sex reassignment therapy has yet to be finally determined. The Sex Discrimination Act 1986, section 4, clarified the position of rules which protect women in the workplace: such rules are now expressly stated not to contravene the anti-discrimination legislation.

Because the 1975 Act has much in common with the Race Relations Act 1976, here only the main outline of the legislation will be explained, together with some points which relate specially to the 1975 Act. Like the 1976 Act, but unlike the Equal Pay Act 1970 since the abolition of the Central Arbitration Committee, the Sex Discrimination Act 1975 operates on two levels. First, there is the personal level, at which individuals who suffer discrimination in a field covered by the Act can bring civil proceedings for damages or other remedies. This is a compensatory and protective procedure. Secondly, there is a public authority, the Equal Opportunities Commission, with the role of monitoring and encouraging the progress of anti-discrimination initiatives on a broader plane. As the government said when announcing the plans for the Commission, 'Although it will be able to represent individuals in suitable and significant cases, its main task will be wider policy: to identify and deal with discriminatory practices by industries, firms or institutions.'[113]

The EOC has had some notable successes. It has taken legal proceedings against the government in order to establish the applicability of principles of Community law where these are more powerfully anti-discriminatory than the domestic law. This is a valuable function, allowing the EOC to perform a function as a representative plaintiff on behalf of women's collective interests, achieving authoritative statements of law earlier than would be possible relying on the uncertainties of litigation by individual plaintiffs. For example, in Case C-9/91, *R. v. Secretary of State for Social Services, ex parte Equal Opportunities Commission*[114] the EOC brought an application for judicial review of the UK's state pension arrangements, under which men had a retirement age of 65 as compared with 60 for women. The EOC argued that the differential ages resulted in the Secretary of State being in breach of the obligation under EEC Council Directive 79/7, Article 5, to take measures necessary to abolish discriminatory provisions which fell within the scope of the Directive. By applying for declarations in an application for judicial review, the EOC was able to test the legality of the provisions of the National Insurance

---

[113] *Equality for Women*, Cmnd. 5724 (London: HMSO, 1974), para. 28. For discussion of the role of the Equal Opportunities Commission, see Ellis, *Sex Discrimination Law*, ch. 5.

[114] [1992] 3 All ER 577, CJEC.

Act 1946 and the Social Security Act 1965. The Divisional Court facilitated the process by making a reference to the European Court of Justice under Article 177 of the Treaty of Rome, allowing an authoritative interpretation of the Directive's requirements to be obtained.

However, the EOC's capacity to take legal action against the government to establish the law suffered a setback only four months after the Court's decision in that case. In *R. v. Secretary of State for Employment, ex parte Equal Opportunities Commission*,[115] the EOC applied for judicial review of a statement by the Secretary of State that the conditions for receiving redundancy pay under the Employment Protection (Consolidation) Act 1978, under which part–time workers have to work for five years before being eligible as compared with only two years for full-time workers, were not inconsistent with Community law on equal pay and equal treatment of men and women. In a retrograde step, a majority of the Court of Appeal, reversing the Divisional Court, held that the EOC had no power to bring an application for judicial review of the Employment Secretary's statement. Kennedy and Hirst LJJ decided the case at least partly on the basis that the Employment Secretary's opinion on the law, expressed in a letter to the EOC, was not susceptible to judicial review, since it affected nobody's rights or obligations and subjected nobody to any detriment or advantage. Dillon LJ dissented, considering that the statement was reviewable. This dissenting view has considerable merit, on both principled and pragmatic grounds. There is probably no absolute requirement that litigation should concern a decision or order affecting rights or obligations; the prevalence of circulars and letters of guidance as instruments of government policy, and the weight attached to them by administrators and others, makes it important that the legality of the opinions expressed should be reviewable. In a field of law which affects many people, certainty is desirable, and it is at least as convenient for the matter to be clarified by legal action by the EOC as for it to wait on the possibility of litigation by individuals, perhaps supported by the EOC. The majority decision closes off a way of clarifying the relationship between UK law and Community law.

But the impact of the decision on the EOC's enforcement role could have been still more extensive. Kennedy LJ considered that the EOC had no power under the Sex Discrimination Act 1975 to bring proceedings against the Employment Secretary. It had power to support proceedings by individual applicants in industrial tribunals, but in relation to the government the role of the EOC was, thought Kennedy LJ, that of adviser, not opponent. Fortunately, Dillon and Hirst LJJ disagreed with Kennedy LJ. The issue relating to the acceptability of parties to judicial review

[115] [1993] 1 All ER 1022, CA.

proceedings is whether the applicant has a sufficient interest in the matter to which the application relates.[116] There can be little serious doubt that a body established by statute to monitor and encourage the progress of the campaign against sex discrimination should be regarded as having a sufficient interest in allegedly discriminatory redundancy conditions to allow it to test their legality by reference to Community law. Kennedy LJ considered that the right of individuals to bring proceedings, coupled with the power of the European Commission to bring proceedings against the United Kingdom in the Court of Justice under Articles 169 and 170 of the Treaty of Rome, was sufficient. But those processes are unpredictable and may be long drawn out. Had Kennedy LJ's view on this point prevailed, the EOC would have been seriously emasculated in its enforcement role.

Even as matters now stand, the EOC's record as an upholder of equality of opportunity is mixed. In 1986 a valuable study by Vera Sacks concluded that the EOC's management practices led to a failure to plan or evaluate its work effectively.[117] This has not been helped by some notable legal reverses. Although the Commission has substantial powers to obtain information and documents in the course of investigating suspected discriminatory practices, as long as they could be obtained in civil proceedings,[118] legal limitations on the Commission's formal investigative powers, which mirror those of the Commission for Racial Equality, have much reduced their effectiveness. It is not clear how committed the government is to combating discrimination, and the result is that there is a limit to what the Commission, or any other official body, can achieve.

(6) Conclusion

The field of anti-discrimination legislation in the United Kingdom is limited. Outside Northern Ireland, there is no legislation against religious discrimination. In relation to race, there is doubt over the groups which are protected by the legislation, although the legislation and its enforcement machinery are probably stronger than any legislation on racial discrimination elsewhere in Europe. As regards sex, there is a plethora of interlinked provisions of domestic and Community law. This adds to the complexity which inevitably afflicts any scheme built on ideas of comparability of treatment. In the case of both sex and race discrimination, the emphasis is on eradicating unjustifiable inequalities of treatment in like

---

[116] Supreme Court Act 1981, s. 31(5); RSC Ord. 53, r. 3(7).

[117] Vera Sacks, 'The Equal Opportunities Commission—Ten Years On' (1986) 49 MLR 560–92.

[118] Sex Discrimination Act 1975, s. 59.

cases, and the criterion of likeness has been narrowly drawn (as shown by *Bullock* v. *Alice Ottley School*).[119]

Although favourable treatment for disadvantaged groups is not unlawful under the legislation, neither the government nor the two Commissions currently have any systematic programme for affirmative action.[120] Indeed, such a programme, whether aimed at channelling resources preferentially towards disadvantaged racial groups or at giving them advantages in education, housing, or employment by means of quotas and differential entry or access conditions, would be inconsistent with the government's general philosophy, which is based on individual rights and individual action in a substantially free market rather than special assistance by the state to raise needy groups above a subsistence level. The role of law, and of the Commissions, in combating discrimination is of symbolic significance, and is materially important to those who benefit directly from them. But the law is not the answer, and perhaps can never be expected to do more than set limits beyond which discrimination will not be allowed to go. As in the case of race relations, to improve the position of disadvantaged groups, and to secure the improvements in society which will flow from that, political and moral will is required on the part of all members of the advantaged majority to change practices, starting with the practices of government itself. This will not be achieved by law alone.

18.4 RIGHTS IN AND TO EDUCATION

(1) The right to education in international law

In view of the importance of education to the fulfilment of individual potential, the satisfaction of personal aspirations, the development of social and cultural values, and the enhancement of economic prosperity, it is scarcely surprising that the right to education is prominent in international human rights instruments. Article 13 of the International Covenant on Economic, Social and Cultural Rights recognizes the right of everyone to education directed to the full development of the personality and its sense of dignity, and the strengthening of respect for human rights and fundamental freedoms. In particular, primary education is to be compulsory and available free to all; secondary education, while not necessarily compulsory or free, is to be equally accessible to all and

---

[119] [1992] IRLR 564, CA.

[120] On the steps taken by government to instigate equality of opportunity in public sector employment, see Sandra Fredman and Gillian S. Morris, *The State as Employer: Labour Law in the Public Services* (London: Mansell, 1989), ch. 9.

progressively free; and higher education is to be made equally accessible to all, on the basis of capacity, by every appropriate means, including the progressive introduction of its free provision. In Article 13, the states parties also covenant to respect the liberty of parents and guardians to choose private schools for their children so far as they conform to minimum educational standards laid down by the state, and also to respect their rights to secure their children's religious and moral education in conformity with the parents' or guardians' own convictions. Similar provisions are contained in the UN Convention on the Rights of the Child, Articles 22–24.

Except so far as is necessary to provide education which respects any parental or moral requirement for the sexes to be separately educated, or for special education on the part of particular religious or linguistic groups, the right to education is to be met without any distinction, exclusion, limitation, or preference, on the basis of race, colour, sex, language, religion, political or other opinion, national or social origin, economic condition, or birth.[121] In the United Kingdom, this is achieved partly by making the Sex Discrimination Act 1975 and the Race Relations Act 1976 applicable to the provision of education, and partly by providing for free education for all under the Education Act 1944 while permitting the teaching of minority languages and religion within the National Curriculum under the Education Reform Act 1988.

It is noteworthy that the international treaty provisions go beyond recognizing a right to education. In so far as they affect children of primary school age, they impose a duty on parents and guardians to ensure that children receive appropriate education, and a duty on the state to impose such a duty on parents and guardians. Other instruments adopt a similar approach. In Latin America, for example, while Article XII of the American Declaration of the Rights and Duties of Man (1948) provides that 'Every person has the right to an education', Article XXXI provides: 'It is the duty of every person to acquire at least an elementary education.' The duty-based approach to acquiring an education is, as we shall see, reflected in English law. It should also be noted that the international human rights instruments, while imposing no educational curriculum, impose a duty on states to ensure that educational arrangements respect human dignity and parents' or guardians' moral and religious convictions. The right to engage in religious teaching is also protected by Article 9 of the European Convention on Human Rights. In addition, Article 2 of the First Protocol to the Convention provides:

No person shall be denied the right to education. In the exercise of the functions which it assumes in relation to education and to teaching, the State shall respect

---

[121] UNESCO Convention Against Discrimination in Education, 1960, Art. 1.

the right of parents to ensure such education and teaching in conformity with their own religious and philosophical convictions.

As noted in Chapter 4, the European Court of Human Rights has interpreted 'philosophical convictions' broadly to include views on methods of discipline, and this has precipitated changes in the domestic law on the subject.

(2) Access to education in English law

The Education Act 1944 places an obligation on parents[122] to ensure that their children are educated. Under section 36 of the 1944 Act, parents and guardians have a duty to cause their children of compulsory school age (at present, up to the child's sixteenth birthday) to receive suitable, efficient, full-time education. This is normally to be achieved by registering the child at a school, whether provided by a local education authority, or grant maintained by government and run by its school governors, or operated independently by a private individual or body. Under section 39(1), the parent commits an offence where a child of compulsory school age fails to attend regularly at the school where he or she is registered. There is provision for permitting a child to be educated at home, but the local education authority will require to be satisfied that the education offered is suitable, efficient, and full-time.

To be effective, this duty needs to be balanced by an obligation on public authorities to ensure that adequate schools are available. Section 8 of the Education Act 1944 imposes an obligation on local education authorities to provide schools for primary and secondary education in its area. These schools are to be sufficient in number, character, and equipment to cater for all ages and abilities up to the end of compulsory school age. In principle, the education provided at these schools is to be free. It need scarcely be emphasized that a failure to provide such schools is capable of undermining both the right of the child to education and the duty of the parent to ensure that the child takes advantage of it.

The right to education in English law is, therefore, combined with a duty, imposed principally on the parents of the children concerned, to take advantage of the education which is offered, up to the end of compulsory school age. Because the rights and duties in respect of education extend beyond elementary school age, they more than meet the obligations adopted by the United Kingdom under the International Covenant on Economic, Social, and Cultural Rights, and under the UN

---

[122] 'Parent' includes those with parental responsibilities under the Children Act 1989, whether or not they are natural or adoptive parents.

Convention on the Rights of the Child. This is only to be expected of a nation in one of the more prosperous regions of the world.

The delivery of education is subject to a number of general principles imposed by statute. Some of these are designed to secure respect for parental choice as to the philosophical, moral, and religious values which are to inform children's educational experiences. For example, section 76 of the Education Act 1944 provides that children are to be educated in accordance with the wishes of their parents, so far as that is compatible with the provision of efficient instruction and training and the avoidance of unreasonable public expenditure. The freedom of parents to choose an education for their children within the publicly funded sector of schooling has been extended, in form if not generally in substance, by a number of reforms introduced by the Education Act 1980. Under this Act, each local education authority is to make arrangements for enabling parents to express a preference as to the school which their child will attend. It is the authority's duty to comply with the parents' preference, except in three circumstances: (a) where giving effect to the preference would prejudice the provision of efficient education or the efficient use of resources; (b) where the school is an aided or special arrangement school and compliance would be incompatible with the agreement entered into between the school and the authority; or (c) where selection to the school is based wholly or partly on aptitude or achievement (as in the case of the remaining selective grammar schools), and the child does not meet the selection criteria.[123] Where a parent's preference is not complied with, the parent has a right to appeal to a special committee, the decision of which is binding on authorities[124] and is, in turn, subject to review both by courts on ordinary judicial review principles and by the Local Government Commissioners (the local ombudsmen).[125]

The primacy to be accorded to a parent's preference has been used to allow parents to remove their children from schools at which a substantial proportion of pupils are members of a different ethnic or religious group. Where the Christian parents of a child whose first language is English object the child receiving an education in an environment where many of the children are not native English-speakers and where education includes a full treatment of non-Christian religious beliefs and festivals, it has been held that the local education authority is entitled to place the child in a different school which more closely reflects the parents' wishes. Although this has the capacity for allowing parental preference to pro-

---

[123] Education Act 1980, s. 6.

[124] Ibid., s. 7; Trevor Buck, 'Schools Admission Appeals' [1985] JSWL 227–51.

[125] David Bull, 'Monitoring Education Appeals: Local Ombudsmen Lead the Way' [1985] JSWL 189–226; Jack Tweedie, 'Rights in Social Programmes: the Case of Parental Choice of School' [1986] PL 407–36.

duce segregated schooling for different ethnic or religious groups, it has been held that reallocating a child to a new school on such a basis does not contravene the Race Relations Act 1976, as the authority is not discriminating on racial grounds where it merely gives effect to the preferences of the parents as demanded by the 1980 Act.[126] Religious, as opposed to racial, discrimination is permitted, however, in order to preserve the character of a school which is established to provide a particular type of education. For example, in *Choudhury* v. *Governors of Bishop Challoner Roman Catholic Comprehensive School*[127] a voluntary aided school founded to provide education on Christian, and specifically Roman Catholic, principles was held to be entitled to discriminate in favour of Christians, and particularly Roman Catholics, in its admission policy when selecting pupils if the number of parental preferences for having children educated there exceeded the number of places available. This policy was reasonable, in view of the ethos which the school had been established to maintain, and it was not unlawful to have regard to it as a reason for refusing to give effect to the expressed parental preferences of Hindu and Muslim parents under section 6 of the Education Act 1980. Although this did not figure in the reasoning of the House of Lords, the importance of making available specialist schools for religious groups, as one way of fulfilling the obligations of the state under Article 13 of the International Covenant on Economic, Social, and Cultural Rights, justifies an approach which will enable the schools to safeguard their ability to deliver the type of religious and moral education which they are designed to deliver.

Nevertheless, the outcome of these cases illustrates a tension which exists within education, and in respect of many if not all social rights, between the social commitment to making a benefit available to all and the desire of individuals to ensure that they benefit from it fully according to their lights, without consideration for the wider goals (such as social integration and understanding between ethnic groups) which might be legitimate, if subsidiary, objectives of a policy in relation to a benefit such as education. Taking social goals and converting them into rights which may be claimed by individuals tends to elevate the idea that society has a role in advancing individuals at the expense of the good of society as a whole, and ignores the notion that individuals have a reciprocal responsibility towards society to make choices or accept decisions which help to make social programmes work effectively. The extent to which individuals, when taking advantage of a publicly provided social facility

---

[126] *R.* v. *Cleveland County Council, ex parte Commission for Racial Equality*, *Times*, 25 August 1992.
[127] [1992] 3 All ER 277, HL.

such as free schooling, can legitimately claim a right to have that provision moulded to their own objectives, regardless of any inconsistency between their objectives and those of society, is one of the most significant problems for the idea of social rights. It should perhaps be remembered that advancing the ability of individuals to fulfil their own potentials and plans for life is only one, albeit an important one, of the social benefits which social rights are designed to offer. If governments make social rights no more than handmaidens of individual choice, the rights themselves may come to lack the social dimension which is one of their foundations. The competing claims of the individual and the collectivity in relation to social rights is one of the recurring problems for social rights theories.

The extent to which individualism dominates the right to education is, in reality, limited. The provisions of the 1944 and 1980 Education Acts do not automatically entitle parents to the education of their choice for their child. Instead, they have process rights, which may result in their preferences being accorded a higher priority than local authority admissions policy, but which can have this effect only within the limits imposed by the need for the authority to provide efficient education for all.[128] Nor does the legislation entitle parents who are members of particular ethnic or religious groups to insist on schools being provided at public expense for their children in which they can be educated in the traditions and teachings of that group or religion. Two factors combine to restrict this: first, the need for the education to be accepted as efficient; secondly, the qualified nature of a local education authority's duty to provide adequate schools, or to respect parental preferences in respect of those which are available.

(i) *The need for efficient education.* Parental choice in education has been restricted by provisions in the Education Reform Act 1988, Part I, Chapter I, enabling the government to lay down the essential elements of educational syllabuses through the National Curriculum and regular testing of children at the ages of seven, eleven, and fourteen. The implication is that delivery of that curriculum is one of the benchmarks of the efficiency in education, in which case it seems that variety in education is likely to be reduced. The Parent's Charter lays down standards which it will be legitimate to expect schools to achieve in delivering the National Curriculum, and provides for systems of complaint where those expectations are not met, but provides no redress for parents who would prefer

---

[128] Tweedie, 'Rights in Social Programmes' at pp. 414–24. Tweedie points out that in Scotland some courts have treated the equivalent rights under the Education (Scotland) Act 1981 as entirely overriding local authority policies, an approach which could ultimately undermine the programme as a whole.

their children not to be taught the National Curriculum. Such children would have to be educated privately. Even if parents are happy with the National Curriculum and its associated regime of testing, the importance of efficient use of resources is paramount when dealing with public funds, and this provides a constraint on the range of options which can be made available. This is a theme which is developed in the following paragraphs.

(ii) *The qualified duty to provide schools.* The local education authority's obligation to provide schools has been held not to be absolute. In *R. v. Inner London Education Authority, ex parte Ali*,[129] the applicant's child had initially been one of 400 to 500 children in the Tower Hamlets area who had not been provided with a school place. The applicant sought judicial review of the Inner London Education Authority's failure to provide sufficient places, and damages. The Divisional Court (Woolf LJ and Pill J.) decided that the duty of the education authority under section 8 could be described as a 'target duty'. It allowed a degree of tolerance within which the authority was to set its own standards. The standards set by the authority could be reviewed by the Secretary of State under a procedure laid down in section 99 of the Act, but even once standards were set it did not follow that failure to meet them would breach section 8, if the failure were due to unforeseeable changing circumstances rather than fault on the authority's part. Furthermore, even if the section 8 duty had been broken it would have been inappropriate for the court to grant relief. Merely to order the authority to comply with its duty would be unhelpful, as the court would not be able to supply any substance to the duty.[130] Nor would breach give rise to a right to damages for breach of statutory duty, as the duty under section 8 was intended to benefit the public in general rather than to give the individual litigant a cause of action. This provides an example of a situation in which the court, by classifying a right in effect as a social or group right rather than an individual right, excludes individual rights, and moves processes of enforcement from the legal to the political sphere. The message which is sent is that social rights are weaker than individual rights, because they are more reliant on political will.

Sometimes other legislation provides enough substance to enable a court to hold that a local authority is in breach of a duty in respect of the provision of schools of a particular type. For example, the House of Lords held that an education authority was in breach of its obligations under the Sex Discrimination Act 1975 in providing fewer selective secondary

[129] [1990] COD 317, DC.

[130] See also *Meade v. London Borough of Haringey* [1979] 2 All ER 1016, CA, concerning the truncated nature of an authority's duty to provide education during a period of industrial action by school caretakers.

school places for girls than for boys, so that girls faced tougher competition than boys and had to obtain higher marks to secure entry. While the authority was under no obligation to provide selective places at all, if it was providing any it had to ensure that they were equally available to boys and girls.[131] Similarly, while neither the authority nor the Secretary of State was under any obligation to provide single sex schools, it has been held to be a breach of their duties to authorise closure of the only single sex school for boys in an area when single sex schools for girls would remain.[132] This did not call for the court to provide substance for the education authorities' duty under section 8 of the 1944 Act. It was not necessary to make a judgment about the academic viability of the schools, nor to show that single sex or selective schools were better than co-educational or comprehensive schools. It was enough to show that a choice in relation to educational facilities was being offered to parents by the authorities, but was being organised in a way which made the choice more accessible to parents of children of one sex than the other. A court can properly make this type of judgment.[133]

This attention to discrimination in the availability of choice is consistent with the ethos of the Education Act 1980, much of which was designed to increase parental choice in relation to schools for their children, and with the idea that civil liberties are valuable primarily because of their role in advancing freedom of choice, and thereby promoting autonomy, for citizens, without going to the extent of permitting judges to dictate to authorities the type of facilities which are to be available. However, the courts are able to give effect to values of this sort only if they appear to be spelt out in the legislation. There are areas in which the courts confront apparently conflicting values in the legislation. For example, legislation outlaws discrimination on the ground of race, defined as including ethnic origin, but the provision of schools to cater for the religious beliefs of parents may automatically lead to direct or indirect discrimination, which was held in *Choudhury* v. *Governors of Bishop Challoner Roman Catholic Comprehensive School*[134] to be lawful. Where values conflict, the resolution must be found in the light of the educational purposes which underlie the Education Acts.

---

[131] *R.* v. *Birmingham City Council, ex parte Equal Opportunities Commission* [1989] AC 1155, [1989] 1 All ER 769, HL.
[132] *R.* v. *Secretary of State for Education and Science, ex parte Keating* (1985) 84 LGR 469, DC (Taylor J.).
[133] See *R.* v. *Secretary of State for Education, ex parte Keating* (1985) 84 LGR 469, especially at p. 475 *per* Taylor J.; *R.* v. *Birmingham City Council, ex parte Equal Opportunities Commission* [1989] AC at p. 1194, [1989] 1 All ER at p. 774 *per* Lord Goff.
[134] [1992] 3 All ER 277, HL.

This, however, starkly raises two issues. First, it makes it particularly important that there should be publicly-funded schools provided for all religious groups. It becomes necessary to accept a potentially controversial proposition: that the goal of efficient education does not necessarily demand an education designed to facilitate people's assimilation to western, Judaeo-Christian values.[135] Secondly, it points up one of the problems which would arise if legislation against religious discrimination were to be introduced on similar lines to the Race Relations Act 1976. If religion is regarded by some adults as an important element in their children's education, it would be impossible to provide such education on a specialized basis in separate establishments without risking liability. Perhaps any such legislation would need to exclude the provision of education from its scope. There would be little difficulty in doing this in such a way as to comply with the United Kingdom's obligations under international law. Even under the Convention Against Discrimination in Education, adopted by the United Nations Educational, Scientific, and Cultural Organization (UNESCO) in 1960 and to which the UK is a party, the duty on states to eliminate religious discrimination in education does not extend to the 'establishment and maintenance, for religious or linguistic reasons, of separate educational systems or institutions offering an education which is in keeping with the wishes of the pupil's parents or legal guardians . . . .'[136] By using the word 'separate' the Convention seems to accept the inevitable necessity of allowing the groups running such schools to limit the availability of that education to children from other groups, in order to safeguarding the freedom to maintain the educational ethos of the group for which separate education is allowed.

Another problem for the providers of educational facilities concerns the recent moves towards encouraging schools to become self-governing, under the control of the governors and head and funded directly from central government, rather than being controlled by local education authorities. This has presented courts with impossible dilemmas when faced by a local authority claiming that the Minister's decision to allow a school to adopt this new status is making it unreasonably difficult for the authority to plan its allocation of resources between those schools which remain under its control in such a way as to provide education of appropriate nature and quality for all the children who need it within its catchment area. Where the statutory discretion given to the Minister is sufficiently broad, the courts can insist that the effects of the decision on other schools in the area must be taken into account as a relevant consideration, but cannot require

---

[135] See R. v. *Secretary of State for Education and Science, ex parte Yusuf Islam, Times,* 22 May 1992.

[136] Convention Against Discrimination in Education, Art. 2(b).

the Minister to treat it as the primary or paramount consideration.[137] Such decisions can undermine the capacity of the authority to provide efficient educational facilities, and so reduce the effectiveness both of education in the area and of any remaining choice which parents in that area may enjoy. When social rights clash with individualism or with governmental discretion (or both), their value is much reduced, because so much of their effectiveness depends ultimately on the political will of those funding and running the programmes in which implement the rights.

(3) Exclusion from education in English law

The right of children to be educated is subject to one major limitation. Under the disciplinary system laid down in the Education (No. 2) Act 1986, the head teacher has the responsibility for formulating and promulgating principles and procedures for encouraging self-discipline and controlling misbehaviour. Where these measures include the power to exclude children from school, indefinitely or for a set period, the power may be exercised only by the head teacher.[138] It is implicit in this arrangement that it is not unlawful for the head teacher to exclude a child. This disrupts the child's education, and, where the child is excluded for a substantial period or indefinitely, it makes it difficult for the child's parents to comply with their legal obligation to ensure that the child receives full-time education. Other schools may be unwilling to take a child who has been permanently excluded from a school, particularly at a time when schools are being subjected to scrutiny of pupils' behaviour as one of a number of performance indicators on which funding decisions and parental choices of schools may be made.[139]

Excluding a child from school is an extreme step for a head teacher to take, and (as Department of Education guidance makes clear) is properly to be regarded as a last resort; but it may be necessary where a pupil is behaving in so disruptive a way that the efficient education of other pupils is being disrupted, and other steps to persuade the disruptive child to behave better have been tried unsuccessfully. The obligation of the school is to provide education for all its pupils, and it would be wrong to allow this aim to be thwarted by the behaviour of a few. As already noted, the right to education is accompanied by a duty to receive it, and the right to a free education at public expense carries with it reciprocal responsibilities, on the part of the pupil and his or her parents, to the

[137] See eg R. v. Secretary of State for Education and Science, ex parte Avon County Council [1991] 1 All ER 282, CA.

[138] Education (No. 2) Act 1986, s. 22.

[139] On the duty to publish information about schools, see Education Act 1980, s. 8.

whole school community. Where a head teacher finds that a child's behaviour interferes unacceptably with the work of the class or the ethos or running of the school, there may come a time when the school's responsibilities towards other pupils, and the disruptive pupil's failure to recognize or discharge responsibilities to the community, make it desirable to exclude the pupil.

However, Parliament has recognized that the temptation to be rid of a troublesome pupil may sometimes lead to children being unnecessarily excluded for the sake of convenience, rather than to maintain the viability of the school and its educational ethos. It seems that an increasing trend is developing in which head teachers, under pressure to achieve outstanding examination results and low truancy rates in order to attract more pupils, and thereby more funds, exclude poorly performing pupils as well as disruptive ones. Protections for children who have been excluded from publicly funded schools, and for their parents, are therefore needed, and to some extent are provided by statute.[140] A school which has excluded a pupil must inform his or her parents. If the total period or periods of exclusion in a term exceeds five days, or will result in the child being deprived of the opportunity to sit a public examination, the local education authority and governing body must be told of the exclusion and the reasons for it.[141] The authority must then consider whether to reinstate the pupil.[142] In the case of a grant-maintained school, over which the local education authority has no control, the school's articles of association must make provision for an appeal against a decision to exclude a pupil permanently,[143] and it will be good practice to arrange for an appeal procedure in other cases on the same model as applies in respect of schools controlled by local education authorities.

If the authority or the governors decide not to reinstate the pupil, the parents have a right to appeal against the decision. (The pupil has no independent right of appeal unless over eighteen years of age.) The authority, or (in the case of grant aided schools) the governors, must establish an appeal committee to determine the matter. The committee's decision is binding.[144] Administrative law principles, including that of natural justice or fairness, apply to such hearings, so care needs to be taken in choosing the membership of the committee. In a case where a

---

[140] These do not apply to independent schools. Where such a school does not include a disciplinary procedure in its contract with parents, the parent probably has no legal remedy if the child is summarily expelled or suspended: *R. v. Headmaster of Fernhill Manor School, ex parte Brown, Times*, 5 June 1992, DC.

[141] Education (No. 2) Act 1986, s. 23.

[142] Ibid., ss. 24, 25.

[143] Education Reform Act 1988, s. 58(5)(f).

[144] Education (No. 2) Act 1986, s. 26.

teacher from the school was a member of the committee, the Divisional Court held that there was such a real likelihood of bias as to vitiate the proceedings.[145] It is, however, perhaps permissible for a teacher—even the head teacher—to be present in an administrative capacity, as long as it can be shown that that person exerted no influence over the final decision and the parents did not object.[146]

These provisions represent a compromise between the need to protect people against interferences with the right and obligation to receive an education, and the need to ensure that the education can be provided efficiently. That there is any legal regulation of the procedure is a welcome development: for too long decisions about school discipline, including exclusions, were made behind closed doors, and were not judicially reviewable. However, there are weaknesses in the system of control over this type of interference with the right to an education. First, it is unfortunate that the child has no statutory right of appeal independent of his or her parent. If a *Gillick*-competent child is able to accept medical treatment without parental intervention, it is curious that a parent's decision not to appeal against an authority's decision not to reinstate the child should prevent the child from appealing. No doubt the child could apply for judicial review of the decision, but that is hardly a convenient or (usually) a speedy remedy. Secondly, there are ways of avoiding the operation of the system at all: parents can be persuaded that it would be in their best interests to remove their child before the school has to expel him or her, and the parent's decision to take that advice negates the reporting and appeal mechanisms.

Thirdly, although section 8 of the Education Act 1944 imposes on local authorities a duty to provide schools which are sufficient to cater for all abilities and aptitudes, it is proving increasingly difficult to provide for those children who have been excluded from school because of their disruptive behaviour or truancy records. In the era of parental choice and a market in education, schools are tending to reject troublesome children who could damage a school's reputation or adversely affect the examination and behaviour records on which its funding depends. This provides another example of the tension between two objectives in the field of maximizing social goods through social rights: the liberal objective of increasing parents' control over the education offered to their parents, and the social objective of ensuring that everyone, however troublesome or intractable, receives a decent education.

---

[145] R. v. *Board of Governors of Stoke Newington School, ex parte M*, unreported, 21 January 1992.
[146] R. v. *Governors of the London Oratory School, ex parte Regis* (1989) 19 *Family Law* 67, DC.

18.5 RIGHTS TO HEALTH CARE

(1) Health care rights in international law

It is helpful to distinguish between the rights of people who are enjoying health care to particular standards of treatment, or respect for their privacy and autonomy during treatment (which can be described as 'rights in health care' and are discussed in chapters 3, 4, and 6 above), and rights to receive health care ('rights to health care') which form the subject of this section. The former are pre-eminently matters of individual entitlement, while disputes concerning the latter cannot be resolved without a political decision about the allocation of resources between competing claims and programmes. The provision of modern health care is very expensive, and where the state makes itself responsible for securing a certain level of health care for its citizens the nature and proper extent of that care, and the level at which it should be resourced, are likely to be matters of controversy. We start by looking at the way in which rights to health care are provided in international law, and then look at the position in the United Kingdom.

In the light of the importance of preventive medicine and holistic medicine in improving or maintaining the standards of health in the community, international human rights treaties recognize that rights to health care should cover all forms of care. Political decision-making should take account of the interests of people who are not patients in the sense of being ill at present. Decision-makers are entitled, indeed bound, to allocate resources to programmes in the light of the costs and beneficial effects of programmes of public health, including health education. 'Public health' here can be taken to include provision of drainage, sewers, and maintaining a standard of living which will enable people to provide for basic needs.[147]

The breadth of the right to health care can be illustrated by reference to some relevant international instruments. Article 25 of the United Nations Universal Declaration of Human Rights (1948), for example, provides:

1. Everyone has the right to a standard of living adequate for the health and well-being of himself and of his family, including . . . medical care . . .
2. Motherhood and childhood are entitled to special care and assistance. . . .

This confers an extensive right on individuals against their governments, but it is only indirectly a right to health care. The government of a state

---

[147] For a valuable discussion, see Jonathan Montgomery, 'Recognising a Right to Health', in R. Beddard and D. Hill (eds.), *Economic, Social and Cultural Rights: Progress and Achievement* (London: Macmillan, 1992), pp. 184–203.

must provide for an adequate standard of living for its citizens, but is not required to be the primary health care provider: if the standard of living is high enough to allow citizens to provide for their own health care, that seems to suffice. Art. 11 of the European Social Charter makes it clear that the individual has primary responsibility for his own health:

With a view to ensuring the effective exercise of the right to protection of health, the Contracting Parties undertake, either directly or in co-operation with public or private organizations, to take appropriate measures designed inter alia:
    (1) to remove as far as possible the causes of ill-health;
    (2) to provide advisory and educational facilities for the promotion of health and the encouragement of individual responsibility in matters of health;
    (3) to prevent as far as possible epidemic, endemic and other diseases.

Furthermore, the provision of services which it does fall to government to supply may be provided in association or by arrangement with private organisations if that seems best. There is no right to specific types of health care directly from government, though government has a duty to review health care provision to ensure that private organisations are fulfilling their side of any bargain and adequately satisfying demand for care.

There are, however, three ways in which Article 25 seems to envisage positive obligations on government. First, the government will, in practice, have to provide the infrastructure of drains, sewers and similar preventive community health measures necessary to secure an adequate standard of living for health. Standards of living are not purely a matter of individual wealth. Secondly, complementing the individual's duty to take care for his or her own health is a responsibility lying on government to educate citizens to keep themselves healthy: there is, in short, a right to health education. Thirdly, if there are people who are unable to provide themselves with medical care, either because they are not financially independent or because the private market in health care cannot or will not cater for their needs, the state must provide the service, and must ensure that the quality of the service is 'adequate for the health' of the citizens concerned. It will almost always be necessary for the state to act to provide care for chronically sick and disabled people, both because private health insurance schemes find it unprofitable to cater for these groups and because of the shortage of resources for home visits, post-operative therapy, and geriatric and in-patient psychiatric care, in the private sector. Fourthly, Article 25(2) of the Universal Declaration treats mothers (including pregnant women) and children as entitled to special care. Although this would not require the provision of special treatment facilities to enable women to overcome obstacles to becoming mothers, it does seem to impose an obligation on the state to treat the interests and needs of these groups as of special importance when allocating resources between programmes.

The Universal Declaration is not a treaty, and so does not directly impose obligations on states in international law. However, relevant provisions in instruments which do give rise to binding obligations, such as Article 1(11) of the European Social Charter, are relevant. Article 1(11) provides:

Everyone has the right to benefit from any measures enabling him to enjoy the highest possible standard of health.

In itself, this does not confer a right to any particular level of health care or to the provision of any specific services. It is a non-discrimination provision, requiring the signatories to ensure that everyone has an equal opportunity to benefit from whatever services are available. However, the requirements are amplified by Art. 11, quoted above. Necessarily, international instruments such as this leave room for the standards which they set to be interpreted and implemented by each state in the light of local conditions: the states enjoy a margin of appreciation. They do not purport to confer enforceable rights on individuals to any particular level of government action or protection; instead, they impose general obligations, but leave it up to the states to decide how best to give effect to them. Phrases like 'as far as possible' show that the kinds and levels of services must depend crucially on economic and social conditions within each state. It is significant that the UN International Covenant on Economic, Social and Cultural Rights, 1966, refers in Art. 11(1) to the 'right to an adequate standard of living for himself and his family, including adequate food, clothing and housing, and to the continuous improvement of living conditions,' just before it goes on in Art. 12 to recognise the 'right to the enjoyment of the highest attainable standard of physical and mental health', and to require governments to take steps to create conditions 'which would assure to all medical service and medical attention in the event of sickness'.

The link between standards of living and standards of care is expressly stated in the American Declaration of the Rights of Man (Latin American States, 1948), Art. 11:

Every person has the right to the preservation of his health through sanitary and social measures relating to food, clothing, housing and medical care, to the extent permitted by public and community resources.

Just as it would be unrealistic to expect governments to provide higher standards of care than the socio-economic infrastructure can support, it would be unrealistic to expect government to shoulder the whole burden of health care for individuals. Responsibilities are shared, and the allocation of social resources between health and other programmes, and between different types of health care programme, are pre-eminently matters of political judgment, reached in the light of theories of social justice.

So far as possible, it is sensible for politicians and health administrators to allocate resources so as to cater for the predicted needs of the population, but those resources are restricted by government's ability to raise revenue, its overall spending targets, and its assessment of the priorities between health and other government responsibilities such as social security benefits, education and defence. The total volume of resource available to health administrators may therefore be insufficient to meet the demands placed on the service, and this has proved to be an increasing problem as medical science has developed technologically complex and massively expensive forms of treatment and drugs. Indeed, these aggravate demand as well as making it more expensive to meet it, since conditions can now be treated which would have been irremediable a short time ago. The amount which should be raised from the taxpayers, and the proportion of that which should be devoted to health care, are thus ultimately matters of political judgment. It is unlikely to be satisfactory to make them the object of legal rights, whether in the international or domestic legal fields. Within the resource constraints, citizens' rights are political and procedural: to have their needs weighed fairly against other people's needs, and their preferences balanced against other people's preferences, without irrelevant considerations being taken into account by the decision-maker.

(2) The position in the United Kingdom

The United Kingdom has a publicly-funded National Health Service. In England and Wales, section 1 of the National Health Service Act 1977 places a duty on the Secretary of State for Health 'to continue the promotion of a comprehensive health service designed to secure improvement—(a) in the physical and mental health of the people of those countries, and (b) in the prevention, diagnosis and treatment of illness'. To this end, the Secretary of State is under a duty to provide such health services as he thinks necessary in order to meet all reasonable requirements.[148] But the NHS is currently under pressure from a number of directions.[149] Financial restraint has been a feature of public sector economic policy since 1979. Resources for the service are growing less fast than the costs of treatment, and new funding arrangements are making

---

[148] National Health Service Act 1977, s. 3.

[149] J. K. Mason and R. A. McCall Smith, *Law and Medical Ethics*, 3rd edn. (London: Butterworths, 1991), pp. 253–61.

the provision of services more than ever subject to accounting controls. Furthermore, the introduction of performance indicators for hospitals, shortly to be converted into published league tables, directs attention to the efficiency of a hospital's work rather than to the clinical quality of the service provided. The rights of patients which the government recognizes are related to efficiency, comfort, and speed: the Patient's Charter sets out goals on waiting lists, timeliness of appointments, and so on, because these are more easily measurable and less costly than other standards which might be measured.

Alongside the public sector, there operates a private health care sector: private health insurance schemes, private general practitioners, consultants doing paying client work, hospitals devoted wholly or mainly to private patients, and private services offered in health service hospitals. The gap between the private and public health care systems is being narrowed by the institution of self-governing hospital trusts, fund-holding general practitioners, and the changed role of health authorities from providers of health care to purchasers of health care from increasingly independent providers.

This tends to substitute the market for the political process as the primary mediator of tensions between the desirability of providing treatments of different types and the economics of health care. Where people are unable to obtain necessary treatment for themselves or members of their families, they may resort to litigation in an attempt to force the health authority to provide it by law, or as a means of raising the public profile of their grievance in order to bring pressure to bear on the authority to capitulate. Where this happens, the courts are generally unwilling to force authorities to expend money and other resources in ways different from those indicated by the authorities' professional or political judgment.

The right to receive treatment, or any particular standard of health service provision, is not a legal right under English or Scottish law. Health service managers have certain duties under the legislation which established the National Health Service, including a duty on health authorities to balance their budgets,[150] but such provisions do not confer legally enforceable rights on patients. As discussed above, in relation to the right to life, the provision of public service health care is at present a matter of considerable political controversy. Although this has not always been the case (until the mid-1980s politicians and managers regarded a commitment to continuously raising the range and standard of provision as being politically non-contentious), spiralling costs have produced serious

---

[150] National Health Service Act 1977, s. 97A, as inserted by Health Services Act 1980, s. 6.

disagreements as to the ways in which health care should be distributed, administered, and (where necessary) rationed. This has affected the balance between health care in the community—including matters of health education and sanitation—and the treatment of individuals for disease.

Health care resourcing decisions are of a type which is sometimes called 'polycentric': that is, they involve a number of different interests, which compete and have to be weighed against each other. Because of the adversarial nature of legal procedure, which is based on the assumption that a single plaintiff will normally face a single defendant, it would be difficult to ensure that all these interests were adequately represented before the court. As a result, judges have understandably taken the view that it would be inappropriate to grant remedies for failure to provide particular services or therapies, as this would in effect put the courts in the position of specifying to health providers and managers, health authorities, and indirectly central government, what services should be provided for whom, where they should be based, and how much money should be made available for them. There would be a risk that the courts would have to take over policy making for the health service. Courts in the United Kingdom lack developed public interest litigation processes, or even Brandeis brief procedures, which would enable them to hear a wide range of parties on issues of social and medical policy, so the exercise would be doomed to ignominious failure. It is therefore unsurprising that attempts to use applications for judicial review to compel the Secretary of State to fund additional hospital buildings, in order to reduce surgical waiting times and enable people to be treated more quickly, have failed in the light of financial constraints.[151]

Similarly, attempts to compel health authorities to provide treatment denied on the basis of shortage of resources are almost always doomed to failure. In *Re Walker's Application*,[152] a baby in need of heart surgery had had his operation postponed five times because of a shortage of pediatric intensive care nurses. There was no immediate urgency in the case, and Macpherson J. and the Court of Appeal refused to second guess the Health Authority's allocation of resources. Even where there has been greater urgency for the individual patient, courts have been unwilling to

[151] *R. v. Secretary of State for Social Services, ex parte Hincks* (1979) 123 Sol Jo 436, Wien J, affirmed CA: J D Finch, *Health Services Law* (London: Sweet and Maxwell, 1981), pp. 38–39. However, the CA left open the possibility of judicial review on the ground of irrationality in the *Padfield* sense of a decision so unreasonable that no reasonable decision-maker, properly understanding the facts and the law, could have taken it.

[152] *Times*, 26 November 1987, CA.

intervene,[153] although the publicity may elicit a change of policy on the part of the health authority or doctors concerned.[154]

Courts are similarly reluctant to review the decisions of health authorities and doctors as to the relative priority to be given to various treatments, and how to allocate places on NHS programmes of (for example) renal dialysis treatment for patients suffering from kidney failure, intensive care cots for premature babies in need of specialised surgery and nursing, or *in vitro* fertilisation facilities for couples wanting children. In *R. v. Ethical Committee of St. Mary's Hospital (Manchester), ex parte H.*,[155] Schiemann J. refused judicial review of a decision by a hospital ethical committee and a consultant that the applicant, who wished to have children but was infertile. She had previous convictions which had led the local Social Services department to refuse her application to become a foster parent or to adopt a child. The Ethical Committee had a policy of excluding from the IVF programme women who were unacceptable as foster or adoptive parents. This was held not to be an unreasonable policy. However, Schiemann J. said:

if the committee had advised, for instance, that the IVF unit should in principle refuse all such treatment to anyone who was a Jew or coloured then I think the courts might well grant a declaration that such a policy was illegal. . .[156]

Such matters are seen as calling for clinical, managerial, and political judgment in roughly equal measure, and such matters are not seen as being justiciable. This means that NHS patients cannot obtain orders that particular treatment or services be provided. It might be possible, however, for them to obtain compensation for failure to provide it. So far, no case has decided whether a person whose treatment is delayed or denied by the NHS by reason of lack of resources can recover damages for breach of statutory duty. However, for the reasons outlined above, it is likely that courts would regard resource issues as non-justiciable, and would therefore decide that it would be wrong to interpret the statute as conferring rights on patients.

Patients' rights to compensation for non-treatment are limited to those at common law to recover damages for negligence. If resources to treat a patient are available but medical staff fail to treat a patient in circumstances in which no responsible body of medical opinion would regard that failure as medically appropriate, damages will be available. However, where the necessary resources are not available the plaintiff is unlikely to

---

[153] *R. v. Central Birmingham Health Authority, ex parte Collier*, 6 January 1988, unreported, CA. The patient in this case was later operated on, but died soon afterwards.
[154] See Mason and McCall Smith, *Law and Medical Ethics*, pp. 260–61.
[155] [1988] 1 FLR 512, [1987] N.L.J. Rep. 1038, DC.
[156] [1987] N.L.J. Rep. at p. 1039.

succeed in an action against the health authority for negligence in failing
to provide the resources. In the light of recent decisions of the House of
Lords on the scope of the duty of care owed by public authorities, it
seems likely that the relationship between a health authority (a fortiori a
central government department) and a particular patient or potential
patient is insufficiently proximate to give rise to a duty to provide
resources for that patient. In the field of housing, decisions relating to the
allocation of the resources of a public agency between competing claims
are regarded as essentially political and non-justiciable in the absence of
an express statutory requirement to the contrary.[157] The same is probably
true of decisions concerning the funding of different sorts of treatment or
care. Any duty owed by planners and decision-makers would seem to lie
in the field of public law, and is satisfied if the decision is intra vires, is
reached in good faith taking account of relevant considerations, and is
not wholly unreasonable. This is consistent with the nature of rights to
health care: they are essentially social rather than individual rights, given
effect through governmental action which, domestically as in international law, properly depends on economic and political judgment.

This can be illustrated in relation to the provision of treatment for
infertility.[158] It would be possible to derive a right to such treatment for
all infertile citizens from the right, under Articles 8 (respect for family
life) and 12 of the European Convention on Human Rights. Article 12
provides:

Men and women of marriageable age shall have the right to marry and to found
a family, according to the national laws governing the exercise of this right.

However, the European Court of Human Rights has so far treated
Articles 8 and 12 as subject to a considerable margin of appreciation for
states, as seen in Chapter 11, and it is unlikely that any positive obligations arising under Article 12 could require the state to provide particular
treatments on demand. The right to found a family is thus principally a
negative right—a right to be free of state interference—and to the extent
that it gives a right to state assistance it is an example of a social right,
rather than an individual one: in setting bounds to the right, the state has
to take account of the wider social implications of its implementation.

In the United Kingdom, there are programmes of treatment for infertility at several units, but candidates for treatment are carefully selected,

---

[157] R. v. Hillingdon LBC, ex parte Puhlhofer [1986] AC 484, [1986] 1 All ER 467, HL.
The effect of the decision in the housing field was later reversed by the Housing and
Planning Act 1986, s. 14.
[158] Gillian Douglas, Law, Fertility and Reproduction (London: Sweet & Maxwell, 1991),
ch. 6; Margaret Brazier, Medicine, Patients and the Law 2nd edn. (Harmondsworth:
Penguin, 1992), ch. 12; Mason and McCall Smith, Law and Medical Ethics, ch. 3.

both because of the excess of demand for treatment over the available supply, and because (as the Warnock Committee accepted) the moral implications of fertility treatments seem to require that it should not be provided where it would be morally or socially inappropriate to do so.[159] This is a controversial claim, because the factors which are examined tend to stress the 'normality' of patients, as seen from the doctors' perspectives. Criteria used by adoption agencies when vetting potential adoptive parents tend to be carried over into decisions about treatment for infertility, and this has been formalized by the Human Fertilisation and Embryology Authority in its Code of Practice, issued in 1991 under the Human Fertilisation and Embryology Act 1990, section 25. Paragraph 3.21 of the Code of Practice, for example, refers to the need for a treatment centre to make such inquiries of 'any relevant individual, authority or agency as it can'. These might include inquiries designed to show that the patient would be unsuitable as a parent because of a criminal record, social problems, employment record, or for a variety of reasons which relate to choice of lifestyle rather than failure to measure up to the ideal (about which there is, in any case, no consensus) of an ideal parent. While it might be thought important that social resources should not be expended on providing people with children who are likely to become long-term burdens on society because of the inadequacy of their parents, there is a risk that the process will result in systemic discrimination against disfavoured social groups.[160] As shown by *R. v. Ethical Committee of St. Mary's Hospital (Manchester), ex parte H.*,[161] described above, the law offers little protection against such risks.

The conclusion which seems to flow from this is that rights to health care are principally political, subject to politico-economic and moral considerations, and this is consistent with the approach to health rights in the major international instruments. At times of public expenditure cuts, or limitations on growth, health care takes its share of the burden. This is inevitable. Individual rights tend to relate to process rather than substance, even under the Patient's Charter. To give a right to particular types or levels of health care through the NHS would reduce both the government's control over the provision of public programmes and public expenditure, and, to some extent, also the health professionals' power. The law can offer little substantive assistance to individuals. If this is true of the delivery of health care to individual patients, it is even more marked in relation to the provision of community health initiatives,

---

[159] *Report of the Committee of Inquiry into Human Fertilisation and Embryology*, Cmnd. 9314 (London: HMSO, 1984).

[160] The Code of Practice is discussed by Gillian Douglas, Bill Hebenton, and Terry Thomas, 'The Right to Found a Family' (1992) 142 NLJ 488–90, 537–8.

[161] [1988] 1 FLR 512, [1987] NLJ Rep 1038, DC.

including health education campaigns, provision of sanitation facilities, and work of environmental health officers.

18.6 CONCLUSION

The current status of social and economic rights in international law is that they are well established, but they are indirect: instead of conferring enforceable entitlements to benefits on groups or societies, they impose obligations on governments, subject to a substantial element of discretion to take account of economic and social circumstances when balancing competing goals and claims. Where governments feel free to pursue social or economic benefits for their citizens, and are not ideologically opposed to treating them as social rights, the citizens may benefit. However, there are problems in treating these benefits as rights. They are on the whole unsuitable for judicial enforcement. Where legislation is founded on individualist principles, permitting victims of infringements of rights to obtain remedies, the attachment to individual rights may either undermine the policies and efficient operation of the authorities which have to deliver the service (as in the case of education) or provide at best only a partial remedy for a social evil to which law is an inadequate response (as in the case of anti-discrimination law). The refusal to address social problems is endemic to liberal individualist societies. If society and state were committed to tackling social problems, particularly in relation to establishing equality of opportunity by providing a basic minimum level of education and health care opportunities for all and combating discrimination on the ground of membership of a group or groups, discussing possible courses of action in terms of social or economic rights might be helpful at the level of symbolism, and persuasive as a matter of rhetoric. But the commitment must precede the symbolism if the rhetoric is to represent anything substantial, and the problem of accommodating social and economic rights within a system based on individual liberty and political control over public programmes is one which is unsolved, if indeed it is soluble.

19

LIBERTY AND POLITICAL WILL

This Chapter is not a conclusion, either in name or in substance. It would be impossible to have a true conclusion for a book on civil liberties and human rights, because the subject is in a state of constant, dynamic development, although it is not always easy to see the direction in which it is moving. The range of rights is elastic, and the circumstances in which they can come into play are infinite; any worthwhile conclusion would be no more than the beginning of a new exploration in different directions, and a conclusion which seeks to close off the subject is worse than useless. Nevertheless, it is perhaps worthwhile, at the end of a book which has ranged over a wide variety of matters, to bring together some of the main themes which have emerged from the previous eighteen chapters. Accordingly, the Chapter aims to draw attention to some persistent themes and factors which have run through earlier chapters and which affect the way in which civil liberties and human rights are (or are not) conceptualized and protected under English law.

(1) The primacy of negative rights

The rights which we have are on the whole negative, based on the classic liberal doctrine that it is the main job of government to establish the conditions for freedom and to refrain from interfering with people further than necessary to achieve that end. Although in Chapter 1 it was argued that the distribution of liberty to all would be useless to some unless steps were taken to ensure that all beneficiaries of rights were in a position to use their freedoms constructively, the state action required for the implementation of public programmes for this purpose is subject to political control. As pointed out in Chapter 18, the extent to which it is helpful or realistic to express aspirations for such state action in terms of social, economic, or any other variety of rights is questionable. The implementation of such rights, like the advancement of any social interest which requires positive action or expenditure on the part of the state, is mediated through the political system, is subject to considerable executive discretion, and is likely to be a less weighty consideration than budgetary constraints and the need to maintain international competitiveness, particularly in times of recession. The move from recognizing the

importance of rights to ensuring that everyone has an equal opportunity
to benefit from them is only just beginning. The drive to secure the
equal worth of individual rights, by way of rights in social programmes
and anti-discrimination legislation, is barely under way yet, but is likely
to be encouraged by the growing influence of the European Social
Charter. This, ultimately, is a matter of political commitment; it will be
interesting to observe its progress.

(2) The substantial but limited significance of entrenched bills of rights

Examination of the role of the European Court and the European
Commission, and sidelong glances at the work of the US Supreme Court
and judges elsewhere, show that the enactment of a justiciable and constitutionally entrenched Bill of Rights can be a powerful political and legal
weapon in the hands of those who are in danger of having their rights
systematically infringed or abrogated. Nevertheless, useful as it may be,
such legislation has been seen to be an incomplete answer to the demands
of individuals and groups. Bills of Rights are only as extensive as the
rights which they identify and protect, and only as powerful as the politicians who draft them and are bound by them and the judges who enforce
them wish them to be. Any failure of will on the part of any of these
people will leave the citizens unprotected.

The entrenchment of a Bill of Rights, besides being only a partial
answer, may not be strictly necessary. Entrenched or not, the values of a
Bill of Rights must be imbibed, preferably at an early age, by everyone,
and must exercise a practical as well as a symbolic influence over the
work of politicians, judges, ombudsmen, and those responsible for internal complaints and review procedures in public agencies. There is evidence from abroad that, if judges have the appropriate determination,
they can make something of very unpromising statutory material. The
New Zealand judges are currently struggling to give some weight to the
New Zealand Bill of Rights Act 1990, an unpromising piece of legislation
but one which may prove to have more impact on the law than its
drafters probably expected or hoped.

Other people besides judges must take responsibility for protecting
rights, whether under a Bill of Rights or without one. Special parliamentary procedures for scrutinizing legislation, and freedom of information
legislation to open up government to the public gaze, will also be important elements in developing the system in a rights-conscious way. Legal
approaches to achieving this are increasingly receiving attention,[1] and this

---

[1] See Patrick Birkinshaw, *Government and Information: the Law Relating to Access,
Disclosure and Regulation* (London: Butterworths, 1990).

encourages the hope that the conditions for the political, as well as legal, protection of rights may be improving. Parliamentarians have a particularly heavy responsibility, because they carry the burden of scrutinizing legislation which, in our system, can so easily violate rights. But the ethos of rights must be accepted more generally. It must influence private or privatized bodies supplying goods and services to the public: gas and electricity supply companies, for example, control people's happiness and their abilities to achieve goals and advance plans at least as effectively as government departments or agencies.

(3) The need for politicians and others to believe in rights, and to recognize the responsibilities which go with them

In order to protect rights, politicians must think them important. This is true both of rights which would impose positive obligations on the state, as in the case of social and economic-equality-related rights, and of classical, liberal individualist rights to freedom from state interference. If the political will to respect rights is absent or in abeyance, the rights will not long flourish. This is no less true in democratic countries than others. Indeed, there is a particular danger that governments which are subject to electoral accountability will be too ready to restrict the rights of unpopular groups in order to be seen to be active in relation to some perceived problem which is exercising the electorate. Chapters 5, 9, and 10 showed the results of a clash between commitment to rights and a government's determination to be seen to be tackling crime: there is a risk of either a gradual erosion of rights, or of a wholesale restriction (as in relation to the right to silence in the criminal process in Northern Ireland, or the detention provisions of the Prevention of Terrorism (Temporary Provisions) Act 1989, or access to confidential information under the Drug Trafficking Offences Act 1986). In such cases, rights cease to enjoy primacy, and are liable to be traded off against more pragmatic, albeit often important, considerations.

The political will is particularly important where, as in the United Kingdom at present, there is no entrenched constitutional protection for rights. Although there are signs of a changing judicial attitude to rights, the English judicial approach has traditionally been one which gave relatively little weight to them, whether in domestic or international law.[2] While this remains the case, the attitudes of politicians and administrators to the protection of rights assume prime importance. As a means of shap-

---

[2] See ch. 2, above. For a comparison with the position in the Caribbean, led by the availability of constitutional Bills of Rights, see Albert K. Fiadjoe, 'Judicial Attitudes to Commonwealth Caribbean Constitutions' (1991) 20 *Anglo-American L. Rev.* 116–30 at 120–6.

ing those attitudes consistently with internationally accepted standards, recourse to the European Commission and Court of Human Rights, and other international human rights agencies, is likely to be increasingly important: left to itself, the domestic political process is likely to tend towards devaluing rights and over–emphasizing order. This was illustrated in relation to the position of disadvantaged groups in prisons and mental hospitals in Chapter 6, in relation to immigration in Chapter 7, and with reference to public order law in Chapter 17.

Ordinary citizens too must internalize the values of individual and group rights, because democracy can be reconciled with respect for rights only if the people who participate in political decision-making, however remotely, exercise their powers in the light of people's rights. For this, education is essential, and the state needs to facilitate it by making available the resources and opportunities for all students to receive a grounding in civil liberties and rights and their personal, constitutional, and political importance.[3] Rights which are essential to the democratic process are particularly in need of protection against erosion, as noted for example in Chapters 13, 14, and 17. It will be interesting to follow the Australian High Court's attempt to develop fundamental common law democratic rights which have constitutional status, noted in Chapter 2, and to speculate about the feasibility or desirability of the judges in this country taking a similar step.

However, if liberties are to retain the support of politicians and others, and if rights are to be regarded as politically respectable and morally compelling values, those who claim them must exercise them responsibly. Claims to freedom lie ill in the mouths of those who refuse to formulate or comply with standards protecting people against abuse. To reject accountability not only undermines the reputation of the people who abuse freedoms, but may also be held to justify curtailing the freedoms themselves, with a consequential loss to all. This risk seems to be particularly acute in relation to press freedom in the light of Sir David Calcutt's review of the arrangements for press self-regulation, examined in Chapter 13. The desire to exercise freedom unaccompanied by the trammels of self-critical social responsibility is a tendency from which adults, as well as young children, have to be weaned. If those of us who enjoy freedom of the press do not appear to treat it seriously and responsibly, it should come as no surprise if politicians and others regard our actions as devaluing the freedom, and come to consider that it is legitimate to restrict it. Whilst one may consider that the Calcutt proposals go further than necessary to secure press responsibility, the representatives of the press undermine the strength of their own case by indulging in a form of

---

[3] See Claire Palley, *The United Kingdom and Human Rights* (London: Sweet & Maxwell, 1991), especially ch. 4.

brinkmanship with government which makes it look as if they are prepared to put press freedom substantially at risk.

This is a topical example of a responsibility which attaches to all rights.
Those who exercise rights enjoy them by the consent of others, and must
be careful not to abuse their liberty by using the freedom in ways which
deny others their rights or threaten the society by whose authority the
rights are granted. Rights will inevitably sometimes conflict, and the
bounds of each will have to be established by political or legal decision.
At other times it may be permissible to flout other people's rights as part
of a campaign of civil disobedience in order to achieve some greater
social good. But in all such cases, a liberal citizen will respect freedom,
and will permit its restriction or infringement only to achieve a goal
which can be justified within a framework of liberal theory, and then
only to the smallest extent necessary to achieve the goal.

(4) The importance of remedies

Lastly, the range and type of remedies is important. We saw how constraints in legal remedies may restrict the value of legal rights. For example, in relation to the police many rights are protected by administrative
review, disciplinary proceedings, or a court's duty or discretion to
exclude evidence at trial. Where substantial remedies are not provided,
rights are not likely to be taken seriously. Increased attention to remedies
in public law generally[4] has led to a number of more specialist studies,
and, in relation to the police, an influential text, devoted entirely to
remedies for police misbehaviour, has gone into a second edition.[5] The
signs are that ingenious attempts to develop the law into new fields to
provide remedies for prisoners and patients have been less successful, as
explained in Chapters 4 and 6. Provision of remedies is central to commitment to rights, and, if judicial remedies are to be restricted, other
remedies must be provided and made to work effectively if rights are not
to be compromised.

The attempt by government to lay down standards and give effect to
them by way of a Citizen's Charter, with a range of Charters dealing
with specialized areas of administration and service delivery, has some
potential as an alternative to giving real rights, but has yet to prove itself.
The work of partially independent bodies such as the Equal
Opportunities Commission and Commission for Racial Equality has been
shown to face structural problems which make it hard for them to function

[4] Patrick Birkinshaw, *Grievances, Remedies and the State* (London: Sweet & Maxwell,
1985).
[5] Richard Clayton and Hugh Tomlinson, *Civil Actions Against the Police* 2nd edn.
(London: Sweet & Maxwell, 1992).

as effectively as would be desirable. Nevertheless, they offer a way of merging a collective approach to remedying injustice with an individualist one, and provide a model which could be developed usefully in the future. The debate over the types of remedies which should be available in respect of different kinds of rights is important, and will no doubt continue alongside the growing pressure for a Bill of Rights.

(5) The continuing challenge

If this book has a concluding message, it is that the future of civil liberties and human rights is at least as important as the present, and more important than the past. The United Kingdom has, on the whole, a respectable (although not unblemished) record for maintaining and exporting respect for rights and liberties. However, the continuation of that record is not guaranteed. As experience elsewhere in the world shows, the belief in the importance of equal liberties, and of achieving equal value of liberty for all, is hard to maintain, particularly in adverse social and economic circumstances. The danger that standards will be allowed to slip, or that our achievements in the field of rights will be outstripped by developments elsewhere, is always present. A constitutional resettlement is not, perhaps, a necessary condition for meeting the danger successfully, but without one the task which we face will be even more demanding, politically and socially, than the task of formulating a new constitution and a Bill of Rights, and working out the proper role of the judiciary in relation to it, would be. The weaknesses of the present system for protecting rights against ill-judged legislative action are well known; this book alone offers numerous examples of the resulting law. If some other way of proceeding is wanted, the onus is on those who oppose the idea of a Bill of Rights to put appropriate machinery in place, and to display the determination needed to make it work. But any method of safeguarding our rights, let alone improving them, will require us to review them constantly, to debate them rigorously, and to protect them forcefully when they are challenged. The words of John Philpott Curran are as true now as on 10 July 1790, when he first uttered them in connection with the right of election of the Lord Mayor of Dublin: 'The condition upon which God hath given liberty to man is eternal vigilance; which condition if he break, servitude is at once the consequence of his crime, and the punishment of his guilt.' The challenge is to plan for the future with ideals but without complacency, and to have faith in democratic processes without ignoring the capacity of any political system to subvert the liberty on which it is founded.

INDEX

sedition (*cont.*):
  inciting class hatred as 678–9
  inciting racial hatred as 678
  inciting religious hatred as 697
  police entry to seditious meetings
    832–3
  as public order offence 677
seizure of property:
  after arrest 220–1, 258
  during search of premises 422–9
  retention of seized goods 427–9
  by trespassing constable 425–7
  see also Anton Piller orders; search of the
    person; stop and search
self-determination, right of national 19–20
serious arrestable offences 228–9
Serious Fraud Office 442–3
sex:
  allocation of, at birth 497
  administrative discretion and 504–5
  civil rights and obligations 509
  criteria for assessing 497–501
  gender distinguished from 495–6
  legal implications of 495
  personal status 508
  reassignment therapy 496–7
  sexual activity as self-expression 507
  see also sex discrimination; transsexuals
sex discrimination:
  Central Arbitration Committee, abolition of
    883
  in collective agreements 883
  contexts in which unlawful 871–3, 883
  direct and indirect 865–6, 879
  in education 866, 893–4
  in employment 866–9, 870–1, 879–80
  meaning of 'discrimination' 865–71, 883–4
  pornography, effect on attitudes to women
    and 703–4
  pregnancy 867–8
  remedies for 879–80, 881, 884
  retirement and pension provision 881
  state's obligations concerning, in EC law
    867–8, 880–2
  see also anti-discrimination legislation;
    discrimination; Equal Opportunities
    Commission
sex shop licensing 730
sexual orientation 493
  autonomy and 495
  discrimination on ground of 525–9, 883
  morality and 515, 520
  see also gender; homosexuality; sado-
    masochism; sex
silence, right of 247
  duties to provide information and 248–9
  impact of legal advice 250 n., 251

inferences from refusal to answer questions
  249–51
rate of exercise of 250
slavery 36–7
social and economic rights 11–12, 17–18, 31,
  64
  education, tension with individual rights in
    891–6
  fair distribution of goods as 851–2
  freedom from discrimination 848, 852,
    871–3
  health 899–908
  housing 848, 873
  justiciability of 855–8, 903–5
  liberalism and 847–8
  necessary to make freedom valuable 849
  political commitment required for 908, 910
  resource limitations affecting 901–2
  satisfaction of need 851–3
  Social Fund, controls over 75
  social security 75, 848
  socialism and 17–18, 31, 847–9
  standard of living and 899–901
  status of 908
  see also health, right to; education
socialism and rights 17–18, 31, 847–8
special procedure material:
  access to 451, 456–62
  drug trafficking, terrorism, and 469–72
  meaning of 455–6
  procedures relating to 462–6
  responsibilities of judges 461–2, 471–2
  search warrants for 466–9, 474
speech:
  fighting words 813–14
  form and content 560–1, 793–4, 813
  freedom of, theory 699
  inciting unlawful acts 802
  symbolic 561, 783
  see also expression, freedom of; protest,
    freedom of
stop and search 172–84
  consent to searches 183–4
  differential impact of use of powers 176–8,
    182–3, 796–7
  effectiveness of powers 183
  extent of searches 178–9
  grounds for searches 177–8, 181–3
  procedures 173–6
  records of searches 175–6
  'Swamp 81' 796–7
surveillance:
  electronic 376
  of prisoners 383–4

tattooing 159
terrorism 225, 249